The Children's
Encyclopedia

VOLUME EIGHT

Printed in Great Britain by
The Amalgamated Press, Ltd., London

IT WAS SAID OF DRAKE THAT HE NEVER HARMED THE HAIR OF A WOMAN'S HEAD   HERE SIR FRANCIS IS
PAYING A HURRIED CALL ON THE SPANISH LADIES OF PANAMA

THE CHILDREN'S ENCYCLOPEDIA

FOUNDED
by
ARTHUR MEE

VOLUME EIGHT

THE EDUCATIONAL BOOK COMPANY LIMITED
LONDON

CONTENTS OF THIS VOLUME

FISHES IN BRITISH RIVERS AND LAKES

1. BROWN TROUT   2 RAINBOW TROUT   3 MILLER'S THUMB, OR BULLHEAD   4. BLEAK   5. THREE-SPINED
STICKLEBACK   6. TWAITE SHAD   7 SEA TROUT   8 PERCH   9. POPE OR RUFFE   10. LAMPREY   11. BURBOT
12. SALMON   13. EEL   14. STURGEON

See pages 4975, 5095, and 5227 for the story of Fishes

A GROUP OF FAMILIAR BRITISH FISHES

1. MIRROR CARP   2. GRAYLING   3. MINNOW   4. CHUB   5. ROACH   6. RUDD   7. LOACH   8. BARBEL
9. BREAM   10. COMMON CARP   11. GUDGEON   12. DACE   13. TENCH   14. PIKE

The Story of the Boundless Universe and All Its Wondrous Worlds

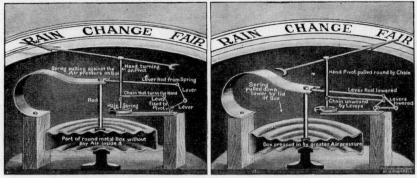

The most familiar barometer is the aneroid barometer. The first picture shows its various parts and the second shows how these work. The air presses down with greater or less force on the metal box, from which all the air has been exhausted, and this moves the hand, or indicator.

THE PRESSURE OF THE AIR

WE speak of matter as being solid or liquid or gaseous; but of these three states two are much more like each other than they are like the third. Water is very different from the air above it; but there is one important respect in which water and air are far more like each other than either is like the solid ground, and that is that they will both run or flow.

In the solid ground there are forces of cohesion and of symmetry holding together the molecules, so that the shape of the whole is maintained; but the shape of the air or water—if we can speak of such a thing—changes from moment to moment if it is allowed to, because both air and water flow. So liquids and gases are known as fluids in the language of science.

Now, in any fluid, at any time, and at any place, there is a pressure which is called fluid pressure, and there is at least one instance of fluid pressure which we have all measured many times, though perhaps we did not know we were doing so. That is the pressure of the air. This atmospheric pressure is by far the most important kind of fluid pressure in our lives; and we must spend a little time in studying it.

We know that we really live at the bottom of a great ocean of air. On the floor of this ocean we live and crawl about, and if we can swim in it for a little while at a small height—as we do in aircraft— we are very proud of ourselves.

Everywhere in this immense ocean there is fluid pressure. Perhaps the first and most important consequence of this fluid pressure is that it enables us to breathe. What happens when we breathe is that we make a movement which tends to empty the space in our lungs of everything; but as that space is in communication with the outer air, the atmospheric pressure drives some of the outer air into the space we make. Thus, without the atmospheric pressure we could not breathe, and therefore could not live.

Now, only about three centuries have passed since, in studying a case like this, men said that the reason why air or anything else would rush into an empty space, if it could, was that Nature objected to anything being empty. The phrase which they used, and which they accepted as an explanation, was *Nature abhors a vacuum;* vacuum being Latin for an empty place. But about three centuries ago it was discovered *why* Nature abhors a vacuum, and also to what extent Nature abhors a vacuum. It was found that what really happens is always the consequence of

ASTRONOMY · GEOLOGY · GEOGRAPHY · CHEMISTRY · PHYSICS · LIFE

fluid pressure. We owe this discovery to an Italian named Evangelista Torricelli, the most famous of Galileo's pupils.

We all know that it is possible by means of a pump to pull up water, and it was found that there was a certain height to which water would rise in a pump—about thirty feet.

But in no pump will water rise, say, fifty feet. Thus it was observed that there was a limit to Nature's dislike of a vacuum. Torricelli thought that other fluids would behave as water does. He thought also that the water rises in a pump because of the pressure of the atmosphere, and that if he took a much heavier fluid than water it also would rise, but, being heavier, would rise so much less. He took the heaviest of all fluids, which is mercury, and proved that the mercury does rise in the same way as water does, but to a much lower height.

THE PRESSURE OF AIR THAT WILL BALANCE A COLUMN OF MERCURY

It is easy to understand the famous experiment of Torricelli which proved for the first time the existence of atmospheric pressure, and explained why it is that Nature abhors a vacuum. If we fill a glass tube (closed at one end) with mercury, and turn it upside down in a cup that already contains mercury, what will happen to the mercury inside the tube ? We might expect that all the mercury would run out of the tube into the cup, but it does not. Something holds up the column of mercury in the tube. The Earth, we know, is pulling by gravitation on the mercury; what is the opposing force that holds it up? The answer is that it is the atmosphere pressing down on the surface of the mercury in the cup, and pressing some of it up into the tube.

Now, if the tube is short, the mercury will fill it; but if we use a tube three feet long, and, having filled it with mercury, turn it upside down in a cup of mercury, the whole of the mercury will not be held up. On the average, the mercury will drop about six inches. In other words, the pressure of the atmosphere is about equal to supporting a column of mercury thirty inches high.

It is interesting to ask what fills the space in the tube above the level of the mercury when the mercury drops. There cannot be any air there; and we might suppose that there must be nothing

there—that it must really be a genuine vacuum. In fact it is as nearly a complete vacuum as we can obtain, and it is known as a Torricellian vacuum. It is not perfectly empty, for liquid mercury easily turns itself into a gas, or vapour, and so, though there is no air in a Torricellian vacuum, it contains a certain amount of the vapour of mercury. It is in some degree possible, by various means, to prevent the mercury from evaporating much; and so we can get in such a tube the nearest approach to empty space that is possible for us.

HOW WE CAN MEASURE THE PRESSURE OF THE ATMOSPHERE

We have noticed that it is possible to measure the length of a column of mercury in one of these tubes, and so, if atmospheric pressure were greater or less one day than the next we ought to notice that the column of mercury in the tube is of a different length on the two days. If atmospheric pressure is high, strong, and pressing down more firmly on the surface of the mercury in the vessel, it ought to be able to hold up a longer column of mercury; and if the atmospheric pressure is low, it will not hold up such a long column of mercury.

When we think of a man pressing down with his fist on a table, or of the game people sometimes play at fairs when a man strikes with a hammer on a knob, making a weight run up a pole, we realise what happens in the column of mercury. This experiment of Torricelli's not only proves the existence of atmospheric pressure, but also enables us to measure it.

WHAT HAPPENED TO A TUBE OF MERCURY ON A MOUNTAIN

But, apart from such changes as may occur owing to something happening in the atmosphere, we ought to be able to show that if we rise high up in the atmosphere the mercury in the tube falls, because the higher we rise the less is the weight of air above us, and the less must be the atmospheric pressure. In the same way the pressure of water increases as we go down in the sea, as every diver knows.

A still more famous man than Torricelli, the great French thinker Blaise Pascal, made this experiment soon after Torricelli's work was begun. Acting on his instructions, his brother-in-law carried one of Torricelli's tubes up the Puy de Dôme, and found, as Pascal anticipated, that the mercury in the tube fell as he ascended the mountain, and rose as he descended, because the weight of the atmosphere overhead diminished as he went up and increased as he came down.

The variation of the atmospheric pressure at different heights has many interesting results. For instance, when men go up in the air they feel the consequences of the steady lessening of the pressure on which breathing depends, and they may suffer very severely; there is a thing called mountain sickness, which depends on this lessening of atmospheric pressure. A good many people sleep badly at low pressures of the atmosphere —that is to say, when they go among mountains—and do better at sea, where, of course, the pressure of the atmosphere is as high as it can be.

When people have lived for a few days at some great height, the body produces a greatly increased number of red blood cells—those which carry oxygen from the lungs to the various tissues.

On a mountain-top the air is so rare, as we say (or the atmospheric pressure so low), that the body must make arrangements accordingly. It is very wonderful that it can adapt itself in this fashion to the altered conditions of the atmosphere.

MEASURING A MOUNTAIN WITH AIR

The height of a mountain can be measured with a barometer. In the left-hand picture we see a barometer on a mountain about a mile above the valley. The pressure of the atmosphere on the cistern X causes the mercury to rise to a certain height in the tube V. Down in the valley the greater weight of the air on the cistern makes the mercury rise higher in the tube, and by comparing the two readings of the barometer the height of the mountain is discovered.

In a Torricelli tube for measuring the pressure of the atmosphere we have what we may call a barometer, which really means a weight measurer. Every time we look at the barometer we are measuring the pressure of the atmosphere, for that is all the barometer does.

The pointer is so made as to indicate the height in inches of the column of mercury which the atmosphere is holding up, then and there.

The relation of the barometer to the weather lies in the fact that, on the whole, the most important thing in deciding the weather is the atmospheric pressure. If the atmospheric pressure is very high there will be no disturbance; if it is very low the air will be rushing in from places where the pressure is higher. That means wind, and wind in turn may mean rain.

So we see where the connection between the barometer and the weather comes in; and when we find that the barometer cannot quite be trusted as a weather-glass we must remember that the causes of weather are complicated, and that atmospheric pressure is only one of them.

The barometer also gives us a way of discovering how high a mountain is, or at what height above the earth an aeroplane is flying. We merely have to find out how much the mercury falls for every thousand feet we go up. There is however, one serious condition attached to this method, which is—first climb your mountain ! That is often impossible; and in any case there are more accurate ways of measuring heights than by observing a barometer.

The ordinary barometer that we see everywhere is really Torricelli's instrument; but the end of the tube is usually turned up so as to make it U-shaped.

HOW THE MERCURY IN THE TUBE MOVES THE POINTER OF THE BAROMETER

If we float an iron ball on the top of the mercury, where the tube is open, we can easily attach to the ball some arrangement with a pointer which can tell us what the height of the mercury is in the tube, or it can be made to point to words like *fair* or *rain*.

There is another kind of barometer which has no mercury or any other liquid in it, which is called an aneroid barometer. This literally means the barometer that has no fluid in it. It is simply a round, flat metal box which has been emptied of air as far as possible. The top and the bottom of the box are pressed towards each other by the atmosphere, and it is not difficult to make arrangements by which we can easily read off the extent to which the box is being pressed.

If we took an ordinary mercury barometer and made it warm the mercury would expand and the same weight of it would take up more space in the tube, as most things do when they are warmed. Therefore we should always be able to allow for the temperature when using a barometer.

So a good barometer always has a thermometer, or heat measurer, with it. In making a barometer we should first boil the mercury, so as to get out of it all the air and water-vapour that we can. If we omit to do this the air and water-vapour will pass out of the mercury into the vacuum at the top of the tube, and will prevent the mercury from rising as high as it should do.

THE AIR PRESSURE ON OUR BODIES WHICH IS EQUAL FROM ALL DIRECTIONS

If we take our reckoning at Greenwich we find that the pressure of the atmosphere is equal to the pressure of rather more than fourteen pounds on every square inch of surface. Our own bodies are, of course, exposed to this great pressure on every square inch of their surface; and if the pressure were wholly a downward one we could not stand it. But a great law about fluid pressure is that at any place it is the same in all directions. Therefore, though we are pressed down upon, we are also pressed in upon from the side, and thus we are equally supported from all directions, and the atmospheric pressure does us no harm. If it should happen that at any part of our bodies we were not equally pressed upon, we should soon notice a startling result. If we take a little glass tube, and burn something in it so that it becomes filled with hot air, and then quickly press the mouth of it against the skin, it is interesting to see what follows. The air inside the tube is very hot, and air, like most things, expands when it is hot. But in a little while the air becomes cooled, and as it cools it shrinks. This means that the pressure inside the tube is lower than outside it. Another way of putting this is that the pressure on the piece of skin covered by the tube is less than the atmospheric pressure on the rest of the body.

A BOY'S GAME THAT PROVES A SCIENTIFIC LAW

The laws of force are bound to have their way; the pressure on the skin outside the tube squeezes some of the fluids of the body up into the tube, and the skin inside the tube—which is not being pressed upon as the rest of the skin is—is forced up into the tube by the pressure of the fluid underneath it, sometimes quite a long distance, forming a sort of little finger of skin.

If a medical student has nothing better to do, and puts three or four such tubes on his forehead, and walks about with them sticking there, he looks absurd, but he teaches those who see him that the pressure of the atmosphere on the surface of our bodies is something very real.

The game boys play with a sucker and a stone also depends on atmospheric pressure. We know that a piece of soft leather, when moistened, will hold a stone and lift it up; but the instant the corner of the leather is raised, and the air is allowed to rush in, the stone will drop.

We have seen that it is atmospheric pressure by which we breathe. Sometimes, however, instead of wishing to draw air into our lungs, we wish to draw water into our mouths. Take the case of drinking through a straw, or of filling a syringe when spraying fruit trees. It is atmospheric pressure that we use in these cases. When we suck through the straw all we do is to lower the pressure at the end of the straw in our mouths, and then the pressure on the surface of the fluid in the tumbler pushes some of it up the straw.

If we keep the tip of our tongue over the end of the straw, we can hold the column of fluid in the straw in spite of the attraction of gravity. But when we take our tongue away, and allow the pressure at both ends of the straw to be equal, gravity has no force to oppose it, and the column of fluid falls.

Such use of a straw is just the same as the way in which a syringe is filled; and an ordinary pump is just the same as a syringe. Inside the pump is a thing called a piston, which fits it closely, and when the piston is raised it lowers the pressure inside the pump and liquid is sucked up—that is to say, it is pushed into the pump-cylinder from outside by atmospheric pressure.

Atmospheric pressure is the most important, and perhaps the easiest to understand, of all kinds of fluid pressure. When we go more closely into the laws of fluids we find them exceedingly difficult, yet one or two results are easy to understand.

THE EXTRAORDINARY MAN WHO FOUND THE LAW OF EQUAL PRESSURE

The law that the pressure of a fluid at any point is equal in all directions has already been mentioned, but if we are to state this law quite correctly we must add one word. We must say not "a fluid," but "a motionless fluid."

Of course, directly we introduce a new condition—for example, the motion of the fluid—then the whole case is changed. For instance, we hardly feel the atmospheric pressure, but we *do* feel the wind.

This law of the equality of fluid pressure in all directions stands to the credit of that extraordinary Frenchman Pascal. He is to be called extraordinary because his mind was so complete. People who study religion and duty, and good and evil, read the works of Pascal because he thought so deeply on those subjects; people who study pure mathematics have to make acquaintance with Pascal; and people who study what happens in a tumbler of water have to study Pascal, too.

Now, it is interesting to invent an experiment to prove the truth of Pascal's law. It we take an empty bottle and cork it, and push it down into deep water, or sink it by attaching a weight to it, the fluid pressure will force the cork into the bottle. It does not matter whether the bottle is right side up or upside down, or at any angle—the result is the same. Therefore, to take the example of a fish swimming in the water, it is subjected to a pressure upwards as well as downwards and sideways. The point is that the fluid has no greater tendency to press in one direction more than in another.

Here we find the great difference between fluid pressure and the pressure of this book on the table. Pressure exerted by one solid thing on another is in one direction only.

GASES THAT CAN BE COMPRESSED AND LIQUIDS THAT CANNOT

The great laws of fluid pressure are the same for both kinds of fluids; but it is plain to everyone that, however true this may be, there must be some great difference between the kind of fluid we call a gas and the kind we call a liquid. If we take any gas, or any mixture of gases, and squeeze it, we find that it can be squeezed. When we cease to apply force it expands again. The proper way of saying this is that a gas is compressible; but the other kind of fluid which we call a liquid is practically not compressible.

It has been proved that it is possible, with very great pressure indeed, to compress water a very little, and we should understand this; but still there remains the great difference that a gas is readily compressible and that a liquid is *for all practical purposes* incompressible. Now, as gases can be compressed by pressure, we should know whether there is any law governing the results. There is such a law.

THE DISCOVERY OF ROBERT BOYLE WHICH EXPLAINS A GAS EXPLOSION

It was discovered by, and is named after, a celebrated Irishman named Robert Boyle, who lived in the seventeenth century. Boyle's law says that if the temperature of a gas remains the same, the greater its pressure the less space it fills. If this pressure is to rise the volume must fall; and if the pressure is to fall the volume must rise. This means that a certain proportion of gas will exert more pressure as it occupies a smaller space, and perhaps cause an explosion.

(Next chapter in this group, page 5317)

THE FOUNDER OF THE BRITISH EMPIRE

SIR WALTER RALEIGH HEARS THE SAD NEWS OF THE
DISAPPEARANCE OF HIS BRITISH COLONY

RALEIGH LAYS DOWN HIS CLOAK FOR
QUEEN ELIZABETH TO WALK ON

THE FOUNDER OF THE BRITISH EMPIRE IS TAKEN
TO THE TOWER TO LANGUISH AND DIE

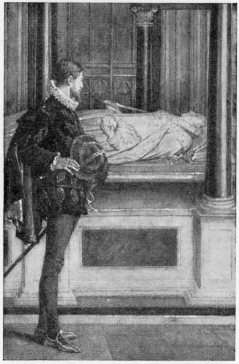

RALEIGH, RELEASED FOR A TIME FROM THE
TOWER, AT THE TOMB OF QUEEN ELIZABETH

The Story of Immortal Folk Whose Work Will Never Die

Sir Walter Raleigh writing while a captive in the Tower

FOUNDERS OF THE EMPIRE

MANY enthralling wonders have been revealed to us in these pages, wonders of human life, of science, of literature, of Nature, but there is no wonder more profound than that of the British Empire or Commonwealth to which we all belong.

There is nothing more novel and incredible in the records of science and discovery than this Empire which has given birth to so many of them, for there has never been another commonwealth of nations like this. We have never had an Alexander or a Caesar, but lesser men of English blood have given us realms which those great figures never knew, though they deemed themselves masters of the entire world.

Alexander and Caesar were familiar with much of Asia, with Europe, and with the northern coastal fringe of Africa, no more. Our flag flies over four and a half million square miles of Africa, into which neither Greek nor Roman ever dared to venture; we have over three million square miles in Australasia and Oceania, realms undreamed of by the ancients, and nearly four million square miles in America, which was a second continent unguessed at by the legions of Greece and Rome.

The deeds of a few incredible men founded this wide empire, an empire of more than a quarter of the land surface of the world, centred on a group of islands in a misty sea, themselves but a four-hundredth part of the land surface of the globe.

Our British Commonwealth, which a few immortal hands first moulded, embraces about 14 million square miles of territory, with more than 600 million men and women and children.

We have every kind of climate—summer in the south when winter chills the north, summer in the north when the south puts on its winter cloak; Arctic climate, tropical climate, temperate climate; every known race of animals, every kind of gems and metals; every fruit and vegetable.

All nations are represented within our boundaries, all the hues and religions of mankind. We have white men, red men, brown men, yellow men, black men. We have Christians, Jews, Parsees, Hindus, Mohammedans; we have millions who have not yet forsaken their idols, all fellow-citizens with ourselves.

How came our little nation possessed of such unexampled treasure of life and territory, of splendour and riches, the wonder and envy of the rest of the world?

May we say, without arrogance, that unique qualities have combined to make the British race the great conquering,

EXPLORERS · INVENTORS · WRITERS · ARTISTS · SCIENTISTS

civilising, and humanising power that it has been? We have been formed, as a nation, after the fashion of some marvellous compound blended by a master scientist in a laboratory.

Our Little Treasure Island was as a crucible, in which through long centuries were combined race elements blending into a matchless nation. We received Roman blood into our British blood; there followed the vitalising strain of Saxons, Angles, Vikings, and Normans. All came in as virile conquerors and were absorbed, mingled with the parent stock. We ceased at last to receive and to be invaded: an amalgam of the greatest military and intellectual forces of the age. We ourselves went forth as conquerors. We gained more of France than the French kings owned; Brittany, Maine, Touraine, Poitou, Guienne, and Gascony were ours; their taxation paid for our pleasures and luxuries at home. Our armies won renown in Spain and were feared in Northern Italy as the ancient Gauls had been.

THE GREAT LOSSES WHICH PROVED A BLESSING IN DISGUISE

Fortunately this great wave of conquest passed. We were cut off at last from our gains in Europe in time to prevent our becoming a second Rome. That would have been disastrous to us in England. Our French-speaking kings would have reigned in Europe and made us a petty province; our glorious language would never have developed, nor would the institutions which have made British rule a pattern to the world.

We lost the Empire in Europe won by the men who fought at Crécy, Poitiers, and Agincourt, and founded an Empire more romantic out in the strange uncharted seaways of the world. We were to lose the greater part of that second Empire, too, in time; for, though we do not always recollect, the present is the third Empire which has called our land Mother.

It was an Imperial estate which we surrendered in North America in 1783. Very rightly it was yielded up, with its immense possibilities that have now assumed the form of the most energetic and powerful aggregation of white men in any single area of the world. With it were restored to Spain and France scattered possessions we had won from them by war. It is in the last century and a half that we have added new realms that constitute our third and largest Empire.

But to return to the era which found us a tiny people shut up, without outside possessions, in our own islands. The reverse of fortune was the best thing that could have happened for us, for our blood no longer flowed in torrents on foreign fields, our national safety was never endangered by international wars. We had our own wars at home, for the fighting instinct remained rank and fiery, but we got over that in time.

AN IMMORTAL COMPANY OF SCHOLARS, SAINTS, AND MEN OF ACTION

It was during this period of seclusion, as it were, that the nation seemed really to find itself; then that it flowered into an intellectual and gallant intensity such as it had never known before.

It reformed its Church, gave the people the Bible in English, cultivated a noble literature, and time bred a strain of men whose deeds read now like dazzling fables.

The new spirit in religion gave us saints; the new spirit of ecstasy in literature gave us Ben Jonson, Marlowe, Spenser, Shakespeare, and Milton. And on a tide of religion, romance, and hardy adventure rose, in one superb rush of life, those master men of the age, Frobisher, Hawkins, Gilbert, Raleigh, Grenville, and the peerless Drake. Where in all history is to be found the equal of this immortal company of saints, scholars, and men of action?

It was this noble company of adventurers that founded our first Empire. We have crossed and recrossed their tracks already, for they have come into the drama of events which succeeded the discovery of America and the opening of the route to India by sea. We have seen how the Pope divided between Spain and Portugal the lands newly discovered and to be discovered, and how all the rest of mankind were forbidden by these two nations to approach the new realms.

THE PROUD SPIRIT OF THE PEOPLE OF ELIZABETH'S ENGLAND

We were a nation of not more than five millions, without an army, without a navy of account. Spain had a matchless army, and her vessels dotted both the Atlantic and the Pacific, and bullied us off the seas.

But it was impossible to dictate ignoble submission to a people of the spirit of Elizabeth's England. The land was volcanic, throbbing with energy of brain and

DARK DAYS FOR SIR WALTER RALEIGH

RALEIGH BEFORE HIS JUDGES

SIR WALTER RALEIGH ON HIS WAY TO THE TOWER

heart, fired with zeal for its religion, for revenge against those who affronted and wounded the sons of its creed, and humanly envious of the enormous riches which Spain was daily culling from her possessions in the New World.

Then, as ever, the population of our islands was thought too great for its space, and men in court and in camp dreamed of that fabled Cathay where gold and spices were. Never did fond illusion furnish forth nobler and more gallant deeds of knight errantry than the dream of those wondrous lands which were never to be found.

With whom the dream dawned it is difficult to say. Raleigh, Sir Humphrey Gilbert, Sir Philip Sidney, all the great men about Elizabeth's court, talked of it, wrote of it, and planned to find it true. It was a document drawn up by Gilbert, which he himself was unable to put into effect, that sent Sir Martin Frobisher off North-West in his little cockleboats, bound for China through the icefields.

We need not follow him again, for we know already what he did—the tale of his island of fabulous gold, the Arctic bay to which he gave his splendid name, his forays into far and frigid Labrador.

WHAT THE OLD FOLK THOUGHT OF THE NARWHAL'S TUSK

We must remember that the only thing he brought back which was ultimately deemed of positive value was the tusk of a dead narwhal. Everybody regarded this as the veritable horn of a unicorn, and it was thought to possess such magic qualities that it was accepted as a talisman by Queen Elizabeth. It was a text around which was preached many a discourse of terror in those great whimsical days.

These heroes of ours did not fear the terrible Spaniards; they did not fear the sea and its storms and icebergs, they did not fear enterprises in lands where the people were strange and savage and all the conditions appalling. But they did fear the unreal, they were afraid of the perils which never, never were. All these grand fellows doing such marvels in their tiny rotten ships were convinced of the existence of demons, witches, and supernatural monsters. A navy of Spanish war galleons could not have stayed the course of Francis Drake, but an army of saints could not have made him disbelieve in witchcraft on the seas and on the land.

It is not cowardly to acknowledge fears; it is heroic to overcome them, and that is what all these wonder men did. The witches of which Shakespeare writes in Macbeth, the enchantments of Prospero in The Tempest:

> . . . the Cannibals that each other eat,
> The Anthropophagi, and men whose heads
> Do grow beneath their shoulders

of whom Othello discourses, were as real to Elizabethan scholars and men of action as wireless and electrons are to us.

THE SIMPLE MIND OF A SCHOLAR WHO WAS ALSO A GREAT SAILOR

When Sir Humphrey Gilbert set sail from Newfoundland on the voyage that was to end his life, he saw, we are told, a great sea monster. Probably it was a seal or a walrus, but to this scholar sailor it appeared " a lion in the ocean sea, or a fish in the shape of a lion "; and he interpreted it as a good omen, for, he said, he " rejoiced that he was to war against such an enemy, if it were Satan himself." We shall see presently how ardent was the imagination of Drake under the same sort of stimulus.

But how came Gilbert at Newfoundland: courtier, man of law, warrior, admirable legal administrator ? He and Raleigh were sons of the same mother, who had been twice married. Gilbert was the elder by 13 years, having been born in 1539, while Raleigh entered the world in 1552. Poor Devonshire gentry of decayed fortunes, they both had an admirable university education, and Gilbert, forsaking law for arms, rendered notable service in many directions before fulfilling his heart's desire to found an English colony " in Cathay."

THE DEATH OF THE DISCOVERER OF NEWFOUNDLAND

Raleigh was with his brother in the company, but ill fortune, dissensions, and a disastrous encounter with a strong force of Spanish off Cape Verde sent the expedition home in ruin. Gilbert spent six years in poverty, and complained that he had to sell the clothes off his wife's back.

His tide served afresh in 1583, when, with four little craft, he steered West again, and at the end of seven weeks entered the harbour of St. John's, Newfoundland. With an enthusiasm matching Balboa's when he took possession of the Pacific for Spain, Gilbert claimed the new land for England. On August 5,

1583, the British Empire was founded in the island for whose discovery Henry the Seventh had paid Cabot ten pounds.

We all know the sequel. Gilbert turned homewards on August 20, in his ten-ton ship, the Squirrel. A great gale arose in the afternoon of September 9. A companion ship passed near the Squirrel, and the crew saw Gilbert calmly seated on the heaving deck, one of his beloved books in his hands. He looked up from his reading to say, "We are as near to Heaven by sea as by land." In that serene faith he went to his doom, for the ship soon foundered.

The sublimity of these Elizabethans in face of death was a solemn and wondrous thing. Philip Sidney's conduct through his days of agony was like a lovely poem; Grenville, the unmatched fighter, was a noble Christian as his life ebbed through a score of wounds; Drake was a placid lion; Raleigh was grace, sweetness, and resignation. They could fight like giants, but they died with the dignity of saints.

THE SPLENDID KNIGHT WHO WAS THE FATHER OF U.S.A.

Raleigh's fate was sadder, far, than Gilbert's. He was one of the truly universal men of the age. We think Michael Angelo and Da Vinci incomparable, with their manifold and varied accomplishments, until we come to our own seamen. Here was a paragon of men in this soldier, sailor, scholar, poet, historian, writer of the noblest prose; a patriot who was a seer, a scientist who was a true adventurer of the most exalted type.

The father of the United States, as he is called, Raleigh was the friend of Spenser, and made him give the world his immortal Faerie Queen; he was the darling and victim of Queen Elizabeth, and ultimately fell, his noble head beneath the axe, at the instance of the meanest king this land has ever had—the slobbering James the First, as Macaulay calls him.

Barrister and soldier, this son of Devon was fighting at 17 for the Huguenots in France, was with Gilbert at 26 on the first abortive voyage, fought in Ireland and in the Netherlands, and was called to Court to receive heaped favours and riches from the Queen. The best thing she did for him was to make him a vice-admiral, for there was sea blood in his veins, and the sea and beyond were ever calling him.

So, in 1584, he sent out a fleet to the American mainland, and there, in that memorable year, Virginia, so called in honour of Elizabeth, was founded in hope and expectation. Hopes and expectations alike were at first falsified, as was many another dream of the age. But in the next three years Raleigh fitted out two more expeditions for the same goal. Neither succeeded. The people wandered away and were lost, and their fate is one of the pathetic mysteries of history, though it is believed that they are still represented in certain Red Indian Tribes.

EUROPE'S DEBT TO RALEIGH FOR FINDING THE POTATO

All that Raleigh derived from his land of golden dreams were tobacco and potatoes. He could not dream what enormous results were to flow from those two substances, though he planted and cultivated both in Ireland. Europe has doubled and trebled its population on the potato, and tobacco has produced fortunes greater than the mines which Spain once worked in South America.

Only the merest summary of Raleigh's career is possible: his voyage to Trinidad and exploration of the Orinoco; his valour and skill against the Armada, his wonderful feat in destroying a second Armada at Cadiz, his capture of Fayal in the Azores; his imprisonment by James the First on a sham charge of conspiracy; his release and hopeless quest of gold in Guiana; his shameful death by the headsman's axe on October 29, 1618, in Palace Yard, Westminster, near where his body now lies in St. Margaret's Church.

His colony of Virginia did flourish in the end, our first Imperial foothold on the American mainland, the cradle of George Washington and of seven of the first 21 Presidents of the United States. However, we owe the development of Virginia not to Raleigh, who vainly spent £40,000 on the project, but to Captain John Smith, a son of Lincolnshire, who was born at Willoughby in 1580, and at 16 was a soldier of fortune in the French army, then in the Low Countries.

CAPTAIN JOHN SMITH AND HIS ASTOUNDING ADVENTURES

With manhood, and after serious study at home, he returned to Europe and underwent adventures which seemed fitter in fiction and poetry than in actual history. He was thrown overboard from a pilgrim ship, rescued and sold into slavery by a pirate, and then became a soldier against the Turks, three of whose champions he defeated singlehanded in sight of their army. He was a prisoner of war and was again sold into slavery, to escape once more, reach Morocco and an English ship, and so at last to come home, aged 25!

All this is wondrous strange, but the importance of John Smith to the world is that he went out in 1606 to Virginia, expecting to find gold, and found only poverty, discontent, and incompetence. How he gradually enforced his splendid will, diverted the colonists from begging and stealing to habits of industry and thrift, how he was saved from assassination by Princess Pocahontas and became the official head and guiding spirit of the Colony—all this and more are part of the history of Virginia.

THE SPLENDID WORK WHICH MADE A PROSPEROUS COLONY OF VIRGINIA

Smith explored more than 3000 miles of coast-line, by sea and river; he prepared the first authentic maps of New England; he housed his followers and gave them their first church and their first fortress; and, returning to England, he sent out other colonists, aided them from home, developed fisheries, and generally acted as a fairy godfather to the New England in the Wild West. A very great and exemplary man was Captain John Smith, and Virginia does well to honour his memory.

But we must come to Drake, for, after all, such men as he and Sir Richard Grenville, who with one little ship fought a whole fleet of Spain, were mainly responsible for the success of those who landed and set up the first English homes in the New World.

Much that they did was piracy, viewed from our standpoint now; but it was an age of piracy. There was no such thing as international law. Might was right. Protestants believed it holy to despoil Roman Catholics; Roman Catholics believed they pleased God if they robbed and tortured Protestants.

HOW SIR RICHARD GRENVILLE TURNED THE TABLES ON HIS FOES

A Cornishman of the year 1541 or thereabouts, Grenville was the son of a man who sailed and sank for England, and himself followed suit, in perhaps the most dramatic fight ever seen on the ocean. A proud fierce man, he was of the sort necessary for an age when one English

ship had to multiply itself by the skill and valour of its captain and crew into the might of a dozen.

Grenville played a part in the pioneer voyages, as his charter said, " for the discovery of sundry rich and unknown lands "; he was associated with Gilbert and Raleigh; and he sought, without finding, the lost colony sent by Raleigh. On the way home he showed his exceptional mettle, his astonishing audacity.

A Spanish ship tried to capture him. Grenville liked nothing better than such an enterprise. He captured his would-be captor! Having fought her to a standstill, he set out to take possession. He had no boats with which to board her, so he and his men made use of a raft of old sea-chests, which fell to pieces just as they reached the enemy. They brought the Spaniard home!

The fight of fights, however, was that which followed a swoop by 53 Spanish ships upon a little English fleet of 16 ships which were taking in water at Flores in the Azores, and had a tragic toll of sick men aboard. Lord Howard, the admiral, rightly decided to retire while he might, and gave orders to Grenville to follow him.

THE FIERCE FIGHT OF THE REVENGE AGAINST OVERWHELMING ODDS

Either he could not or he would not. At any rate, he left his departure too late, and in the little Revenge, in which Drake had helped to defeat the Armada, he passed out into the enemy midst, and was becalmed, the wind taken from his sails by the towering ships of Spain.

No matter how the figures be minimised, 20 of those 53 Spaniards were warships and 15 of them fought against the little Revenge. The pulse leaps even to-day as we read the narrative. All the evening and all the night this one small ship fought till she had but 20 men left, most of them wounded; all her powder exhausted, her pikes bent and broken, and Grenville dying.

He desired the master gunner to sink the ship, and the master gunner said " Aye, aye." But there were some who had wives and children, and they pleaded that after such a fight as the world had never seen before they might now yield and live to battle another day. The dying Grenville mournfully consented, and he died upon a hostile deck while the little

JOHN SMITH GOES DOWN THE STRAND

CAPTAIN JOHN SMITH MEETS A RED INDIAN FRIEND FROM VIRGINIA WHILE TAKING A WALK DOWN
THE STRAND IN LONDON

Revenge went down to be lost evermore in the sea. The story of that fearful engagement is recorded for all time in the grandest ballad Tennyson wrote, but the poem, which will be found on page 4437, is taken from Raleigh's writing, and merely turns to rhyme the noble prose of that great master of our tongue.

It was a famous victory, but what was it all about? asks the poet of another occasion. What were all these battles about?

THE BATTLES AGAINST THE SPANIARDS FOR THE FREEDOM OF THE SEAS

On our side they were for freedom, for the right to sail the seas and plant our flag and people on lands yet unclaimed. It was this mission that made Drake supreme above all our heroes. To sap the tyrannical Spaniard's strength, to sink his ships, to seize his wealth, to make the ocean safe for English craft upon their lawful occasions, this was the mission to which he consecrated himself.

Crowndale, near Tavistock, in Devon, gave Drake birth in the year 1540, but Kent was his nursery, for it was to Chatham that his father took him. The father had a sort of minor chaplaincy in the Navy, and his home, when not at sea, was an old hulk in the dock. There young Francis drank deep of the traditions of the sea, and as a mere stripling himself went forth into the unknown, apprenticed to the owner of a trading craft, who, at his death, left his beloved assistant the little ship.

In this Drake traded into strange waters on his own account, till the threat of Spain to seize all English ships in the Channel caused him to sell out and join his uncle, the future Sir John Hawkins, in an expedition to a port on the Spanish main. The English, storm-beaten and in distress, were promised friendship by outnumbering Spaniards in port, then treacherously attacked and forced to flee with only two of their five ships saved.

THE LOST SHIPS WHICH WERE ENGAGED IN A SHAMEFUL TRADE

We can the more readily reconcile ourselves to that loss from the fact that the English cargo was flesh and blood, a consignment of Negro slaves brought from Africa for sale to the Spaniards. Hawkins was the first English sailor to engage in this unholy traffic. He thought it no wrong. Nobody thought it wrong. There was precedent for it in the Bible, in Greece, in Rome, in every empire and nation that ever existed, and John Hawkins, one of the most formidable fighting sailors who ever lived, was a slave-trader unashamed.

We hear no more of Drake in this hideous traffic in human lives. He was a merciful and God-fearing man. His father had taught him to regard the Creator as a personal God, ever present with him, to whom to turn in time of trouble.

But Drake, though so cheery and gay-hearted, had all the gloomy and terrible superstitions of his times. He believed strange lands and strange seas to be the abode of demons. He thought fogs and mists to be the direct work of Satan against him. He believed that demons and holy spirits were ever about him, contending for his soul. He believed in sorcery and enchantments, as did all the brightest minds of that age of genius and credulity.

But these beliefs never deterred this man of stout heart and great courage; he fought down the imaginary demons and he ever prayed God to enable him to frustrate the designs of Satan.

DRAKE'S AUDACIOUS ATTACK ON A WEALTHY SPANISH TOWN

No fears of the unearthly deflected him from his pursuit of the Spaniards who were making the seas impossible for freedom. He had a practical way of repaying them in full for injuries done to himself and his race. Such a method we see in his amazing adventure, with two small vessels and 75 young men, on what we now call the Isthmus of Panama.

There he attacked the great Spanish town of Nombre de Dios, the port into which the Spaniards poured their treasure of gold and silver and precious stones from the New World mines for transport to Spain. One fine night in the summer of 1572 Drake and two boatloads of men suddenly fell on the town, threw its guns into the sands, dashed into the citadel, and burst open a store of silver bars which reached to the roof. Drake himself led the way towards another repository, where gold untold was guarded.

The alarm was general now, and the English were heavily outnumbered. A great storm broke, ruining their armament, and Drake fell, weak from a wound in the thigh. Still he urged on his men. " I have brought you to the mouth of the Treasure-House of the World ; blame nobody but yourselves if you go away empty."

The seamen replied that his life was dearer to them than all the wealth of the Indies—for they still thought America to be India, we see. They bore him away to safety, and in a few weeks he was up and doing, planning to waylay the mule train which crossed the isthmus with treasure for the city he had nearly looted.

Here we have two examples of the pious nature of this extraordinary man.

Native Indians, who hated the Spaniards, were to be his guides, but before he would let them serve him he made them " adopt the Protestant faith," burn their idols, and learn the Lord's Prayer by heart. Then forth he went in the name of England!

It was on this march that, baulked by tropical vegetation, he ascended a high tree to look out. It was a moment of magic in his life. There he saw the Atlantic at his back, and before him the wide Pacific Ocean; and there, in that spirit of devotional exaltation which was part of his nature, he " besought Almighty God of His goodness to grant him life and leave to

SIR FRANCIS DRAKE IN A TREE-TOP SEES THE PACIFIC OCEAN FOR THE FIRST TIME

SIR FRANCIS DRAKE PURSUES THE ARMADA

sail once in an English ship in that sea." Then he took from the caravan what gold and silver and precious stones he could, in such quantity that two tons, which it was impossible to carry away, had to be buried on the spot. We have read elsewhere of Drake's magnificent voyage round the world. It began in a foray against the Spaniards, with a view to injuring their shipping and decreasing their treasure ; and what was intended to be an out-and-home cruise became a world voyage by accident.

After beating his way through the Magellan Strait, a voyage only some 370 miles long, but occupying three weeks of constant anxiety and terror, he emerged into that ocean which he had prayed he might sail. He was now caught by a storm which blew him over 600 miles to the south-east of Cape Horn, the southernmost point of South America.

Drake's reply was to return thanks to God for the storm as a gracious sign from Heaven to lead him to the great discovery that America did not extend to the South Pole, but that there was a seaway from the Atlantic into the Pacific without the necessity of facing the terrors of the Strait, "the haunt of demons."

He fought and pillaged ships so astonishingly along the Pacific seaboard that he felt it unwise to return by the way he had come, lest he should meet inconveniently powerful Spanish ships on the way back, so he light-heartedly attempted to find and sail that North-West Passage which other gallant men had been trying to reach from England.

THE FIRST SEA CAPTAIN TO
SAIL ROUND THE WORLD

That failing, he cheerfully faced a voyage home across the Pacific, a trip of 20,000 miles, in a sort of glorified fishing smack well gunned and manned. And he did the voyage without mishap, by way of China and the Cape of Good Hope, the first English keel in those waters, and himself the first captain to sail round the world.

He brought home treasure enough to ransom kings, he lived to play the foremost part in the defeat of the Armada, and to " singe the King of Spain's beard," as he used to call his desperate operations, wherever a hostile fighting ship could be found to face him.

Drake's career ended on the scene of one of his greatest exploits, in the sea off Nombre de Dios, where he was seized with fever, sickened, and on January 28, 1596, as one of his contemporaries said, "Quietly in his cabin he yielded up his spirit to his Creator."

HOW ENGLAND WAS ENRICHED BY
KNOWLEDGE OF WEST AND EAST

He had been mainly instrumental in saving us from Spain, in making the seas safe for our ships to sail. He had enriched us with treasure and knowledge of West and East. A single capture of his from the East Indies opened English eyes to the value of the East, and prompted the formation of that company which led to our mastery of India itself.

In one respect Drake was more fortunate than some of his great contemporaries. He was in high honour with Queen Elizabeth, as indeed was only right, and his countrymen followed the royal example. On his return home from his epoch-making voyage round the world the Queen thought fit to order his ship, the Golden Hind, to be preserved as a " monument of his own and his country's glory."

One other hero of those spacious days can be noted (we have referred to him elsewhere), the most mysterious of all. We do not know who Henry Hudson was. That he was born in London is assumed, that he may have been the grandson of a London alderman is possible, that he was a gifted mariner by 1607 is certain, for in that year, accompanied by his little son John, he began the first of his four famous voyages in quest of Eldorado, the golden land of dreams.

We cannot trace his origin owing to the many different ways in which people of his title spelled their names in those times: Hudson, Herdson, Hoddesdon, Hogeson, and so forth, but he becomes a historical character with the 1607 voyage, which was none other than a cool proposal to sail " to the Pole."

He failed, as he was bound to fail. He failed again when he sought the North-East Passage, and a third time when, deserted by Dutch companions, he was unable to force a way by the north and west; but he did explore Nova Scotia and the Chesapeake and Delaware bays and the great river which bears his name.

HENRY HUDSON GOES OUT TO DIE
IN A LITTLE OPEN BOAT

But his most tragic failure of all was in 1607 when, after wintering amid frightful privation and misery in frozen Hudson Bay, he was turned adrift, with his son and a few men, in a little open boat, by a cowardly and mutinous crew, and drifted away to a miserable death.

In a sense all his voyages were failures, yet they were signally productive, for they each carried knowledge a little farther than before, and they inspired high-hearted emulation in many a follower. His name lives in a river, in a bay, and in a territory of immense size which has become a source of great natural wealth. He did not live in vain, and in his death he kindled a great beacon-light.

Such, then, were the men, such the means, by which our British Empire was founded. These heroic souls cleared the seas and carried our first colonists to lands that were wild and terrible, to become the beginnings of homes for millions of people and property without parallel. They were the beginners and the founders of the Empire, which in the end never has betrayed, and never will betray, the cause of human liberty.

TWO GENTLEMEN OF THE EMPIRE

SIR RICHARD GRENVILLE ORDERS THE MASTER GUNNER TO SINK THEIR STAUNCH LITTLE SHIP
THE REVENGE

SIR HUMPHREY GILBERT TAKES POSSESSION OF NEWFOUNDLAND IN 1583

BRAVE LITTLE GRIZEL TAKES HER FATHER'S MESSAGE TO ROBERT BAILLIE. See story on page 5217

The Great Stories of the World That Will Be Told for Ever

THE TRICKS OF SCAPIN

This story of the tricks of a valet is told by Molière, often called the Shakespeare of France. It is from his play Les Fourberies de Scapin.

LÉANDRE was in great trouble. His father intended to marry him to the daughter of a wealthy friend.

Old Géronte was rich, but he wished his son to be richer than himself, and he had settled everything accordingly. And old Géronte was stubborn: it was no use saying no to him.

Now, not only did Léandre not care for his father's choice, but he loved the penniless Zerbinette. A tragic story was that of young Zerbinette; she was the only one saved from a wreck, and had been carried off by gipsies, to remain their property till she could find enough money to buy her freedom. Léandre had worked hard to deliver her, but he had not yet got the whole sum, and, alas, the gipsies were moving far away. Once the gipsies were gone who would care enough to save poor Zerbinette?

Such was Léandre's state of mind when his valet, Scapin, entered the room.

Scapin knew everything; and he loved to have a finger in every pie.

"Never mind, sir," he exclaimed; "trust to me and I will find the money."

Scapin flew to old Géronte: "Oh, poor, poor Mr. Géronte! O unfortunate day! Your son, sir, your son!" he cried out.

"Well, what about him?"

"Your son has fallen into disgrace!"

"What disgrace!"

"I found him very sad this morning and suggested a promenade by the harbour. There a nice-looking young Turk offered to take us for a little sail on his boat, and, once a few miles out, he claimed my master as his prisoner, and will take him to Algiers unless £100 is sent at once."

"Ah, mischief take the Turk! Tell the rogue I'll send the police after him!"

"The police? Out at sea! You are joking, sir!"

"Well, then, serve your master like a true friend. Promise the Turk that if he sends my son back you will take his place till I find the money to set you free."

"You don't know the man, sir. He wouldn't have a wretch like me. For pity's sake, think of your son!"

"Then here are the keys. Take them, and bring back all the rags you can find to be sold to the broker."

"But, sir, how much shall I get for your rubbish? Five pounds at the utmost, and time flies. In an hour the boat will be off to Algiers. My poor master! Heaven knows I did my best to save you!"

"Ah, Scapin, it occurs to my mind that I received some gold yesterday. Here it is. Take it, sirrah!" The old miser brought a fat purse out of his pocket. "Now run away," he cried.

"Run with what, sir? You put the purse back into your pocket."

"Ah! So I did! Take it!"

So Zerbinette was saved.

But, if Scapin sometimes succeeded in his tricks, he also sometimes failed, for everyone knew him; and when anything shocking occurred who could be suspected but the cunning valet? Thus, when he met with Léandre a day or two later, his young master called out as soon as he caught sight of him.

"Ah! Ah! Here you are! I am delighted to see you, Master Rogue!"

"What have I been doing, sir?"

"What? How dare you ask! But I will hear the truth from yourself, or I will turn you out."

"Ah, sir, would you be heartless enough to send me away?"

"Speak, then; out with your crime!"

"Well, sir, as I must, I shall confess that some time ago I drank that little keg of Spanish wine."

"Ah, then it was you, rascal!"

"Yes, sir, and I beg your pardon!"

"I am very glad you do, but there is something else you must tell me."

"But indeed, sir, there is really nothing more that I can say."

"Hurry on, rogue, or you leave this house at once."

"Well, sir, three weeks ago you sent me with a gold watch to Mademoiselle Zerbinette? I came back saying that the watch had been stolen from me. It was I who had stolen it."

"Ah! Was it so? Good news indeed! Yet that is not the thing I am wanting you to confess."

"Is it not?"

"No, sirrah! There is something else. Be quick."

Scapin was a rogue indeed, for he seemed to have so many crimes to confess that he did not know which to choose next. But for once Scapin was not to blame. Somebody had told Géronte of Léandre's plans to marry a moneyless girl, and Géronte had banished him from his sight. But this time Scapin had not been the guilty party, and so he was forgiven.

The valet and his master were planning the wedding of Léandre and Zerbinette, whom they had set free with Géronte's £100, when old Argan called with stirring news to tell. Zerbinette, released from the gipsies, was no other than Argan's own daughter, lost in a wreck long ago.

Argan was a bosom friend of Géronte, and as he was very rich nothing now stood in the way of the marriage, and the two lived happily ever after.

THE LAD WHO SLEPT AT HIS POST

THE American Republic has been greatest when she has acted according to the spirit of her greatest President, Abraham Lincoln.

Yet they used to say he was not strong enough for war because he could not bear to sign a death sentence. To a friend he once said, "You do not know how hard it is to let a human being die when a stroke of your pen will save him."

Here is a story which shows Lincoln as he really was.

Exhausted by a long march, a farmer's boy had to do double guard to spare a comrade who was ill, and, overcome by fatigue, he slept at his post.

The sentence on him for sleeping on guard in the presence of the enemy was death. When Lincoln, who had the power to pardon, heard of this, he went to see the lad. First he talked to him about the farm and his work on it. Then he said, "My boy, you are not going to be shot. I believe you when you tell me that you could not keep awake, and I am going to trust you. I shall send you back to your regiment. But I have been put to a great deal of trouble on your account, and I want to know whether you will pay the bill."

The lad said his friends might if it were not more than five hundred dollars.

"No," said the President; "my bill is a very large one. Your friends cannot pay it. Only one man can pay it. His name is William Scott. I want you, William Scott, so to do your duty that when you die you will feel you have done your duty as a soldier. Then my bill will have been paid."

William Scott promised; and he kept his word. He was badly wounded, and before he died he sent a message to Lincoln that he had paid the bill as far as he was able, and he wished he could have lived longer to pay more.

BRAVE GRIZEL HUME

TWELVE o'clock strikes. Clouds are flying across the Moon, but sometimes she shines clear on the castle. Presently a short figure leaves the shadow of the walls and hurries into the cover of some bushes.

Who is it skulking along in the gloom? A dwarf? A spy? What is happening?

That pile of stones is Redbraes Castle, and this is Scotland in 1678. The land is full of fugitives, of plots, of traitors. Have you forgotten how, at the Reformation, Scotsmen bound themselves by a Covenant to resist Popery and foster the Protestant faith? When Charles the Second was allowed to return from exile he signed the Covenant, and signed it again on his coronation. But now that he is secure in power he has denounced the Covenanters, and sends soldiers to hunt them to their death like wild beasts.

And that little slinking figure? It is a girl of thirteen called Grizel Hume. That great castle is her father's but she goes in mortal terror. Suppose she met a soldier, a tinker, a poacher, who would spy on her, and take blood-money for betraying her secret? The little girl's knees tremble, and her heart beats so loudly that she thinks it can be heard a mile off. She carries a little bundle of cold, greasy food, smuggled from her plate during meals. It was terrible today when one of the little ones cried: " Oh, greedy Grizel! She has eaten *all* her meat already! "

She and her mother exchanged horror-stricken glances; some word of reproof was said. Did the servants notice?

What was that? She stands stock still, unable to breathe. Again the noise behind the hedge. Then a cat slips through and runs across the road, a wing dangling from her mouth. Grizel wants to laugh out loud in her relief, but she steals on in silence. How long and open the way seems each night! But she must not think of that. Why, she did something far more difficult a year ago.

Robert Baillie lay in Edinburgh prison, innocent but doomed. Sir Patrick Hume had an important message for him, yet to go to Edinburgh was to fall into the soldier's hands. So twelve-year-old Grizel was sent, for who would suspect her? Who would guess that she had taken part in the struggle for free conscience since she was ten years old, or think her capable of taking part in a perilous plot?

She was frightened then as she was now, but did she not slip into the cell behind the warder and crouch in the dark corner safely after all? Once more she saw the astonished faces of Baillie and the little boy who shared his father's imprisonment. Ah! where were they now? The soldiers had dragged Baillie, dying, and in his night clothes, to the scaffold, where he was hanged and quartered. If they caught her father—but no, they should not.

Now a spire rises out of the trees, and gravestones shine in the moonlight. Everything is very still except for a little whimpering wind. Grizel stops, checks her panting, and waits for a cloud. As soon as the Moon is veiled she darts across the churchyard, picking her way neatly among the graves, and then, cowering against the church door, slowly, cautiously, opens it. She is safely inside. A glance about the empty place, and she tiptoes across the aisle.

She is hidden in a shadow; now she has vanished. Where has she gone?

Grizel has crept into the family vault. Something stirs in the darkness, and a voice whispers her name. Fumbling hands find her, and her arms are clasped round someone's neck.

" Father," she breathes, " how are you? Not chilled too much? You must be famished. Look, here is your poor food."

As he eats Grizel sits in the cold darkness and whispers cheerfully. The soldiers are still here. Again today they searched every nook and cranny of Redbraes. But they will go, and the evil times will pass, and right will triumph! She tells him of the children's quaint sayings, gives him news of the estate, and discusses various plans for his escape.

At last she kisses him good-bye till to-morrow night; then, leaving him with the ancestors whose honour he keeps untarnished at so dreadful a price, she begins her return journey.

.   .   .   .   .

Some years have passed; we are in the parlour of a small Dutch house. A very beautiful girl is patching a coat while she hears her brother's lessons. Her own faded dress is darned at the elbows, but she rises with the air of a great lady when a visitor comes in.

The stranger is a tall, handsome youth

who wears the cavalier-like finery of the Prince of Orange's Guards.

As he salutes her the girl says:

" My father and mother are out walking, sir. I am sorry. Can I in some way serve you? "

To her surprise the youth answers with a Scottish accent: " I am heartily sorry, too, mistress. I came to pay my humble duty to Sir Patrick, who was my father's friend. Will you tell him? My name is George Baillie."

The girl starts, glows, and exclaims: " Sir, this is not our first meeting! "

Then the youth cries: " I remember! The dungeon in Edinburgh! "

They sit and talk of their fathers. Sometimes they are sad and wrathful, but they never regret all they have lost in a great cause. She tells him how, after Baillie's death, his executioners hunted down Sir Patrick; how he hid in the family vault; how afterwards she and one other with their finger-nails scraped a hole in the earthen cellar floor at Redbraes, and he lay there; how at last he escaped to Holland; how his possessions were all seized; how she and her mother went to London, begging for enough of their own to live on, and got a hundred and fifty pounds; how the family succeeded in getting to Holland, all but one girl, and

how Grizel returned to Scotland to rescue her. Now they were bitterly poor, but they were all united and all free.

In the midst of such talk Sir Patrick returns, and when he knows the guardsman's name cries out: " No one could be more welcome to me! "

The years of poverty and exile go peacefully by. Grizel and George love one another and, even if they have little hope of marriage, they are content not to ask too much good fortune of life. Her father is safe, they are betrothed—that is enough.

Her heroism and beauty make Grizel's story read like a romance ; nevertheless it is true, even to the happy ending.

Let us return to Scotland. It is fourteen years since we saw Grizel steal out in the moonlight. Now the Sun shines on banners and flowers, scarves and feathers, sleek horses and painted harness, as a procession sets out for the church, where the bells are pealing loud enough to crack themselves. Charles and James have gone; the Prince of Orange is King of England, and Sir Patrick Hume is Earl of Marchmont, Lord Chancellor of Scotland. At his side rides Lady Grizel, the most courted beauty in two countries. But her bridal white today is for no brilliant wedding; in the church it is only George Baillie who waits for her.

THE BLUE JACKAL

A JACKAL, prowling round a town one night, fell into an indigo tank and came out dyed blue.

" No one will know me now that I am this splendid colour," said he to himself, " so I will pretend that I am king of all the beasts."

He began by ruling over the jackals, and then the lions and the tigers submitted to him. This made him proud and insolent, and he no longer took any

notice of his jackal friends. They therefore determined to expose him to the other beasts and end his reign.

One night they gathered round the self-make king and began to howl, and as soon as the blue jackal heard the others yelling his natural instinct led him to do the same. At once all the other creatures in the jungle knew him to be nothing better than a jackal, and he lost for ever his crown and his authority.

THE BRAHMIN AND THE POTS

A BRAHMIN went to rest in a potter's workshop, taking with him his staff and a little dish containing some meal that had been given to him. As he lay on the ground he began to meditate on what was best for him to do.

" If I sell this meal," he said, " I can buy some of these pots with the proceeds. Then I can sell those and make a profit, and with the money I can buy clothes to

sell. And so, in time, I shall be worth many thousands of rupees. Then I shall buy a house and marry, and if my wives quarrel I shall take my stick—like this— and punish them—thus."

As he thought these things he waved his staff, smashed his own dish, upset the meal in the dirt and dust, and broke many of the potter's vessels. So ended his wonderful castles in the air.

THE ADVENTURES OF REYNARD THE FOX

Nobody knows who wrote the Adventures of Reynard the Fox. They are about a thousand years old, and are found in the literature of many countries. Reynard is an artful knave who deserves to be punished, but somehow escapes every time. The stories were written as parables, and were meant to point out the evils of rulers and priests when men dared not write openly of such things.

REYNARD IS SUMMONED TO COURT

Sir Tibert the Cat was sent by King Lion to summon Reynard the Fox to appear at Court, to answer for his offences.

When he arrived at Reynard's castle the fox promised to return with him to the court. " But," said the fox, " you must remain for the night, and tomorrow we will travel together." Sir Tibert agreed to this. Then the fox began to lay a meal, but all he could provide was honey.

" That is food I care nothing about," said the cat. " Have you not a mouse ? "

" Oh," replied Reynard, " come with me to the priest's barn; it is full of mice! "

So the two set out for the barn.

" There is the entrance," said the fox, pointing to the hole by which he had entered the night before and stolen a hen.

Now, the priest had set a trap near the hole inside the barn, and when Sir Tibert crept in he was caught in the trap. His mewing soon brought out the priest, who, supposing him to be Reynard, began striking out with a stick. Thereupon Sir Tibert seized the priest's leg with his teeth, and while the worthy man and his wife were attending to the wound Sir Tibert bit through the cord that held him and made off as fast as he could.

REYNARD TELLS OF A TREASURE

When at last Reynard the Fox was brought to the court so many witnesses appeared against him that he was found guilty and sentenced to death. He asked that he might make a confession of all his misdeeds, and in the course of this confession he said something that made the king listen very carefully.

" My lord the king," he declared, " in Flanders there is a dense wood by a river, and in it I have hidden a great treasure. I want you to get this treasure ; then perhaps you will remember your devoted servant Reynard."

The animals who had accused the fox now began to feel very nervous, for King Lion, having learned exactly where the treasure was supposed to be hidden, forgave the fox and made him a nobleman.

" Hear, all you knights and gentlemen," said the king. " Sir Reynard is now one of the chief officers of my court, and I do charge you, upon pain of death, to show him the greatest reverence." Reynard now asked permission to make a pilgrimage to Rome, and he set out, accompanied by the hare and the ram.

Soon the party arrived at Reynard's house, and the fox asked Bellin the Ram to keep guard outside while Kayward the Hare went into the house to see Reynard's meeting with his family. Once inside it was not long before the hare was killed and eaten. Then the fox came out, and, giving a bag to the ram, asked him to take it to the king.

" Where is Kayward ? " asked Bellin.

" Oh, he is talking with his aunt, and wants you to go on; he will overtake you."

The ram carried the bag to the king.

" Sire," said he, " this is a present from Sir Reynard, who rested at his castle."

" Open the bag! " said the king.

The bag was opened, and out fell the head of poor Kayward the Hare.

" Alas! " said the king, " unhappy monarch that I am ever to have given credit to a sly and traitorous fox."

REYNARD ESCAPES

The day after Bellin the Ram had brought the head of Kayward the Hare to the king Laprel the Coney came into the court weeping and crying:

" O king! deliver your subjects from the wicked attacks of Reynard the Fox. I was passing his castle yesterday, and he came out telling his beads so devoutly that, instead of hastening away, I saluted him, and immediately he gave me such a blow that I was nearly killed."

At this moment in came Corbant the Rook in a great state of excitement.

" Oh, my lord, hear me! " he cried. " I was on the common this morning when I saw Reynard the Fox lying apparently dead and stiff on his back. My wife went and put her head to his mouth to see whether he was breathing when suddenly the wicked creature snapped at her and bit her head off."

The king was furious. Reynard was brought to trial a second time, sentenced to death once more, but again he escaped by talking of the treasure and by promising to go in search of it himself for the king.

THE STORY OF THE DAYS

SUNDAY · MONDAY · TUESDAY · WEDNESDAY · THURSDAY · FRIDAY · SATURDAY

Have you ever met Mr. and Mrs. Day? A more useful family you will never meet. They are, in fact, the best servants of the human race, and do as much work in their time as anything or anybody on the face of the Earth. We must make their acquaintance.

The seven-roomed house in which they live is called The Week, and it stands in Month Street, which is one of the twelve roads running through Year Town in the wonderful country of Time. We will enter this house and go through the

" Hullo, Mr. Sun Day! How are you? Glad to see you. But everybody's that, eh? There is no member of your family quite so popular as you are! Come! I hope you are glad to see me, too. I've brought a little friend with me who wants to know how you got your name, and to hear something of your history."

" How I got my name? Well, that's an old story, that is. How I got my bad name isn't nearly so old, and how I am getting my good name is quite a new story. Nevertheless, just to oblige your

AGES AGO MEN WORSHIPPED THE SUN AND CALLED THE FIRST DAY OF THE WEEK AFTER HIM

seven rooms together. Mr. Day lives in one room, Mrs. Day in another, and their five children have each a room to themselves. But they are only separated from each other by walls of Sleep, and they talk to each other through the telephone of Dreams.

Now, this is the first room, occupied by Mr. Day, who does less work than the rest of the family, but who is very far from being idle. He puts on a surplice and holds church services, and he also has to provide millions of human beings with amusement and recreation. He is known by the name of Sun Day.

young friend, I'll run the whole three stories into one, and begin with the old one.

" Far back in the history of the world people could see nothing so wonderful, nothing so beautiful, and nothing so useful as the Sun. They had in them what is called the *instinct of worship*—that is to say, they had a feeling that there was Something greater, stronger, and more glorious than themselves—Something that they ought to fear, reverence, and worship. The Sun seemed to these first people the token or sign of that Something, and they worshipped it. The Sun, in fact, became the visible expression of God.

" Now, when the world got wiser and men knew more about the true God they still kept the old idea of the heathen in their heads, and called the Christian Sabbath, which means the day of rest, Sunday. They no longer worshipped the Sun, but they called the first day of the week after him, and that is how I got my name.

" People loved me then, and I gave rest, and pleasure, and festivity to hundreds of generations. Well, as time passed on, people began to make me anything but a sun-day ; they made me a black day. Children were not allowed to play, books and games were put away

" Well, let us pass to the next room and see what Mrs. Day will tell us."

" I've no time to stay to gossip. I'm a busy woman. Everybody knows that I'm the busiest Day in the week. It's coming after Sunday that does it. Ah, he's a lazy fellow, my husband is! The mess I have to clear up after him! I don't believe in holidays, except Easter Mondays. Let everyone do his work! "

" We mustn't interrupt her," said Mr. Day. " Her name of Mon is short for Moon. She is really Moon Day, the day sacred to the wife of the Sun. In ancient times people called the goddess of the moon

MONDAY WAS SACRED TO THE MOON, THE WIFE OF THE SUN, WHO WALKED IN THE WOODS

and locked up in cupboards as something wicked, and all my precious hours were spent in gloom and solemnity.

" Then it was that I got a thoroughly bad name. People said Sunday was the gloomiest day in the week ; they ate too much, and sat about yawning and grumbling. Just lately I've reminded them that the Founder of Religion once said: The Sabbath was made for Man, not Man for the Sabbath. They don't quite understand just yet what that means. Some of them are noisy and wild and foolish on the Sabbath. But it will come right soon. People will use me for rest of body and mind in a proper way."

Diana, and temples were built for her. They used to think that Phoebus Apollo, the Sun god, drove his flaming chariot across the sky by day, and that Diana drove her silver chariot through the sky by night. They loved Diana because she was gentle and beautiful. Woods were sacred to her because she could be seen walking through them. Round cakes were made on her feast day, with candles stuck round them. Boys and girls considered Diana their own particular goddess and loved her."

And now we must peep into the room of Mr. and Mrs. Day's eldest son, Master Tues Day. You observe that he has only

TIW, GOD OF BATTLES, CAPTURED THE WOLF-SPIRIT, AND TUESDAY IS NAMED AFTER HIM

one hand, and the story of how he lost the other is the story of how he got his name.

Our Saxon forefathers had a god of battles named Tiw (called by the Norsemen Tyr), and when a terrible wolf-spirit named Fenris had to be captured, because he was troubling the whole Earth, it was Tiw who undertook the dangerous venture. The spirits of the mountains had made a chain out of the hardest things in the world to find—the sound of a cat's footstep, the beard of a woman, the roots of a mountain, the voice of fishes, the longings of a bear, the spittle of birds. With this strange chain Fenris was to be bound.

But Fenris would not allow even this soft-looking chain to be put round his neck, and said he would only suffer it if the gods would promise to take it off again, and would send a god to put his hand in the wolf's mouth. Tiw was the only god brave enough to volunteer. He put his hand in the mouth of Fenris, and Fenris was bound; then, in his rage at being captured, he bit off the hand of the god. It is curious that the French name for Tuesday is Mardi—that is, the day of Mars, who was also a war god like the Saxon Tiw, who gives us Tiw's Day, or Tuesday.

The second son of Mr. and Mrs. Day is named after Woden (the Norse Odin), the greatest of the Teutonic gods. Woden lived in a palace built entirely of gold

WEDNESDAY IS CALLED AFTER WODEN, WHO SENT RAVENS ROUND THE WORLD FOR NEWS

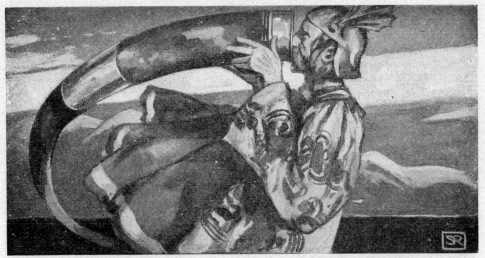

THE MORE THOR, THE GOD OF THURSDAY, TRIED TO DRAIN THE HORN, THE MORE IT FILLED

and silver, which was called Valhalla. Two ravens stood on his shoulders, and when he wanted news of the world he sent these ravens to fly round the Earth and bring him reports of everything they saw and heard.

Round about him stood maidens with helmets, and spears, and shields, and these maidens, named Valkyries, were sent down to Earth to bring the souls of heroes slain in battle to feast with Woden in Valhalla. While they feasted Woden listened to their stories and drank mead. He never ate anything himself. Our friend Wednes Day is rather odd and capricious in his habits. He sends his Valkyries to bring boys and girls into Valhalla for a half-holiday, leaving the rest of the world hard at work. But he is a good fellow, and everybody likes him. He lives in the middle of the house, and seems to be saying all day long : "Work away ; work away ! Sunday will soon be here again."

And now here we are at the fifth room, occupied by Master Thurs Day. Is not he a big, strong, vigorous fellow ? If ever you have a hard bit of work to do start at it on Thursday—the day of strength and power. Thurs Day gets his name from Thor, the strongest of all the Teutonic gods. Thor had a hammer which no man could lift, a pair of iron gloves, and a belt which, when it was

FRIDAY WAS NAMED AFTER FRIGG, THE WIFE OF WODEN, SO THAT SHE MIGHT NOT BE JEALOUS

fastened round him, doubled his great strength. But once the mighty hammer was lost, and a giant named Thrym hid it. He said he would only give it up if the goddess Frigg would marry him. Thor disguised himself in Frigg's dress and went to visit the giant. Imagine the giant's surprise when he saw the lovely goddess eat a whole ox and eight salmon at a single sitting! The companion of Thor explained that the journey had made the goddess hungry.

refused to marry Thrym. How this female Day got her name is rather sad. Woden was Frigg's husband, Thor her son; and it was only in case she might be jealous that our ancestors named a day after her when they had given one to Woden and one to Thor. However, Friday is a very sacred day, though some people are superstitious enough to think it is a day of ill-luck.

And now here is another half-holiday room, Satur Day, who gets his name

SATURDAY IS THE DAY OF SATURN, IN WHOSE HONOUR THE ROMANS USED TO FEAST AND DRINK

Thor was given back the hammer, and slew Thrym and all the other giants. But there were some things beyond even his power. He tried to lift a cat, and could not; it was the serpent Midgard, which holds the Earth in its embrace. He tried to drain a horn dry, but the more he drank the more it filled, for the other end of the horn was fastened to the sea.

The sixth room belongs to Mr. and Mrs. Day's only daughter, Fri Day, named after the goddess Frigg, who

from the Roman god Saturn. Saturn was a god who ate his own children and behaved in a very barbarous fashion. We will not say much about him. For us Saturday is one of the pleasantest days in the week, though some of the games and behaviour of our Saturday crowds are unworthy of us as British men and women. It is a very good thing for us that the Day family are now, practically speaking, Christians. The more Christian they become the better we shall like them.

NOUREDDIN AND THE WONDERFUL PERSIAN

WHEN the good Haroun al Raschid became Caliph of Baghdad he made his cousin Zenebi King of Balsora, and Zenebi then sought for a woman worthy to be his queen. He ordered his minister to find him a maiden perfect in charm and beauty and excellent in wit and intelligence.

For a long time the minister tried in vain to discover this maiden; but one morning a merchant brought to his house a Persian slave-girl of great loveliness and marvellous gifts. The minister gave the maid a set of rooms in his house, and resolved to introduce her to the king. But in the course of the day the minister's son Noureddin saw her, and fell deeply in love with her, and she fell deeply in love with him, so that when the minister came to conduct her to the royal palace he found her sitting with Noureddin.

"Oh, unhappy boy," he cried, "you have ruined me! The king will be certain to find this out."

But, after struggling between his affection for his son and his duty to the king, the minister gave way, and allowed Noureddin to marry the beautiful Persian. He then tried to keep the king quiet by pointing out how hard it was to discover a maiden in whom great beauty and great wisdom were joined. But the king found out about the Persian maid, and sent his men to bring Noureddin and the maid to him.

Fortunately, a friend of Noureddin's heard the order, and hurried out and warned him, and Noureddin and the beautiful Persian at once fled from Balsora, and got on a ship sailing to Baghdad. When they arrived at Baghdad they did not know where to stay. After wandering about the streets till they were tired they entered a gate leading to a splendid garden, and sat down by a fountain and fell asleep. In the evening an old man came to the spot and woke them up.

"Pardon us, pray, for falling asleep here," said Noureddin. "We are strangers in Baghdad, and we walked about the city until we were tired. This garden is really the most delicious spot I have ever seen. Oh, what a happy man you are to possess such a place!"

Now, the garden was really one of the pleasure-grounds of the great caliph, and the old man was only one of the keepers. But he was so flattered at being taken for the owner of the place that he offered to show Noureddin and the beautiful Persian over the lordly pleasure-house which stood in the middle of the garden opposite the royal palace. He led them up the golden staircase, into the great hall built of jasper and adorned with the richest treasures of the kingdom.

At the sight of all the splendour Noureddin was filled with joy, and he gave the old man a handful of gold, saying: "Do please, allow me to provide a banquet this evening. Give this gold to one of your slaves, and get him to buy a supply of meats and fruits and wine."

The old man ran out into the streets and bought a rich repast, and returned with it to the pleasure-house, and Noureddin and the beautiful Persian lighted all the costly lamps by the eighty windows of the great hall, and then they sat down to the feast.

Now, the Caliph of Baghdad had a good view of the pleasure-house from his palace, and he was much surprised to see lights shining in all the windows of the great hall. Any other ruler would have sent some courtier to inquire into the matter, but Haroun al Raschid liked to see into things himself. Disguising himself as a beggar, he went into the garden just as the beautiful Persian was singing to the sound of a lute.

"What a sweet voice!" he said to himself. "I must certainly find a way to see this charming singer without making myself known."

As he was wondering what to do he saw a man poaching fish in the river that ran through the garden.

"Have you managed to catch any fish?" he inquired.

"Two," replied the poacher.

The caliph bought them, and, entering the pleasure-house, said to Noureddin: "I see you are holding a feast here, and as I have just caught two fine fish I thought I would bring them to you."

"Very well," said Noureddin. "Go and fry them in the kitchen."

The caliph did so, and returned with the fried fish, and served the three merrymakers with it.

When Noureddin had eaten his portion he gave Haroun al Raschid a handful of gold saying: " Pray accept this small gift. I have never tasted a better cooked fish in my life."

The caliph took the gold, and thanked Noureddin, and said: "And now may I ask a great favour ? I should very much like to hear your lovely wife sing one or two songs."

The beautiful Persian at once took up her lute and sang song after song, and the caliph listened to her with exceeding delight. And in between the songs Noureddin related to him the story of his marriage and his flight.

Haroun al Raschid then told Noureddin that he was really the caliph, and he sent a letter to King Zenebi commanding him to retire from the throne, and made Noureddin and the beautiful Persian King and Queen of Balsora.

OISIN RETURNS FROM FAIRYLAND

Finn, his warriors, and his son Oisin once sat by the side of Loch Lena.

They were a goodly company, for this was in the old days, when Ireland was ruled by a race of men far taller and more beautiful than any to be seen on Earth at the present time.

Presently they saw a maiden riding toward them alone. Her mantle was sewn with golden stars, and her horse was shod with silver. She was very lovely, and she spoke as one accustomed to be obeyed.

" I have come from very far, O Finn," she said, " even from the Land of Undying Youth. The king of the fairies is my father."

" What do you want from me, damsel ?" replied Finn, trembling.

" The love of Oisin," replied the beautiful stranger. " Will you come with me, Oisin ? "

None of the warriors could stir or speak after she said these words. As in a dream they saw Oisin rise and go to her side and mount the fairy horse. She shook the bridle, and they rode away.

They rode over ocean and forest until they entered a golden haze. Sometimes they saw towers, sometimes riders passed them. At length they reached the Land of Undying Youth.

In this beautiful country Oisin loved the damsel, and had many knightly adventures. But after some weeks he began to long to see his kinsmen again.

The damsel lent him her enchanted horse, and bade him return on its back nor ever dismount, for if his foot touched the Earth he could never again find his way to the Land of Undying Youth.

Oisin rode back through the haze till he came to Ireland. Then he sought out his father's stronghold on the Hill of Allen. He drew rein at the place, and looked about him as one dazed or mad, for the stout walls and the strong beams had vanished. Nothing stood on the hill but thistles and docks.

He shouted the names of Finn, of his servants, of the good hounds Bran and Skolawn. But there was no answer except the whimpering of the wind.

Oisin, stricken with terror, rode on, and presently he saw some men at work trying to raise a boulder. He had never seen even slaves so small and feeble-looking. They had never beheld any man so tall and magnificent as this strange horseman coming toward them.

"I will help you," said Oisin, and, leaning from the saddle, he heaved up the boulder for them with one hand.

But the strain of it burst the girths; he fell to the ground. The men screamed and ran away. For the horse vanished into mist, and the glorious youth lay moaning on the ground, a feeble old man.

By and by they took courage, and, returning, questioned him.

"I am Oisin, son of Finn," he said. "I pray you tell me where is my father ? "

" Do you mock us, or are you mad ? " cried the people. " Those names are three hundred years old. Those evil, pagan days are over. The good Patrick has come to teach us better ways."

But Oisin could not believe that his kin had all perished long ago. He spoke on, and the people grew enraged.

Then the overseer of the work spoke: " Let us take the man to Patrick. Let Patrick say how the blasphemous dog shall die."

Therefore they spared Oisin. As for St. Patrick, he received the old man gently, gave him shelter, and bade his scribes write down all Oisin told them of the Ireland that was past. But very soon Oisin went away to a land where he found his father at last.

Nature's Wonderful Living Family in Earth and Air and Sea

The Blue Shark

FISHES OF THE DEEP SEA

WE have tracked life all over the Earth, limbed life, winged life; up the mountains, down the valleys, from tree-tops to the silent cavern and the mountain's hollow heart; and, in company with life that draws its breath in fluid form, we have floated with the current, down streams of ease to the ocean's margin, and peeped at existence in the shallows which lap and fret the steeped toes of our land.

And now the story must be renewed in appalling deeps. Down in the deep sea is life abounding, strange and even loathsome, a complex of terrible perfection, with here and there such radiant beauty as is not to be explained by human intelligence.

Only a selection of this vast sea assembly could be discussed, if a whole volume were at our disposal; as it is we can only look rapidly at some of the things which, if they did not exist, a nightmare alone could suggest. First then, the sharks, whose near kindred, the rays, have already swum into our ken.

To say that they are the tigers of the deep will not quite serve, for the sharks number in the family giants which, like those mammalian monsters, the baleen whales, are guiltless of offence against Man unless themselves attacked by him. The whale-shark and the basking shark are content with a simple, if extensive, diet of small fish, far out at sea.

The dog-fish nearer home are sharks also, but they are harmless to us because they are too small to be deadly. They used to be a plague to our fishermen, preying on fish wanted as human food, breaking the fishermen's lines and cutting the nets with their sharp teeth. Because they had so unattractive a name they were not regarded as of service at our tables.

Then someone thought of calling them rock-salmon, and now the dog-fish, as well as yielding up their spiny skins for the shagreen of commerce, come to land as fish of excellent quality for frying.

There respect for the shark tribe ends, for many of the species are man-eaters, find them where we may. The whale-shark, sometimes 60 feet long, is the second largest animal in the world, so we may be thankful it is a peaceful beast, living as it does on creatures much smaller than Man.

But the terrible white sharks run to as much as 40 feet, with great teeth, not in one row to the jaw as ours are, but row behind row, so that as one set wears down, the one behind moves forward, rendering the shark always fully equipped for battle and murder.

PREHISTORIC LIFE · MAMMALS · BIRDS · REPTILES · FISHES · INSECTS

Very ancient are the sharks. Their huge frames are mounted, not on a skeleton of bone, as is the case with most fish, but on a skeleton of exceedingly tough cartilage, so that when they die little but their teeth remains to attest their past. Taking teeth as a guide, it has been ascertained by deep-sea dredging that the sharks of old time were monsters in comparison with which present-day types are insignificant. So they, like the reptiles and the former mammals, had their giant age.

SOME EXCEPTIONS TO THE RULE THAT THE SHARKS ATTACK MAN

The white shark is entirely carnivorous, as, indeed, all sharks are. But with the great species that term has a special significance, for it means that the big ones all attack human beings if afforded the opportunity. From the list of offenders we may rule out several varieties. There is the Port Jackson shark, claimed by our Australian cousins, but really common to the seas of that continent, to Japan, and away to California.

This is an innocent one from the fact that its teeth, arranged in series, are adapted to crushing up the shells of molluscs, and on the contents of these it feeds. The zebra shark of the Indian Ocean, 10 to 15 feet in length, keeps well out at sea, so has a clean sheet as far as humanity is concerned. The fringed-gilled shark of Japan is too small to be hurtful to us, as are the three known species of Crossorhinus from the same latitudes, sharks which have extraordinary, leaf-like filaments about their heads, living bait to lure fish to the shark's jaws. They, too, pass without unfriendly comment.

HOW THE THRESHER SHARK MAKES SURE OF A BIG MEAL

The porbeagle shark, so named from its supposed resemblance to the porpoises, is a 10-footer, a fish-eater with an appetite, but known to assail men. The fox-shark, or thresher, well-known in British waters, is a fisherman bold, but, thanks to its small mouth, it escapes condemnation in respect of its attitude towards ourselves. Its name of thresher it derives from its habit of threshing the water when the shoal which it is pursuing tends to scatter.

A thwack of the long, high-lobed tail on the surface of the water, and the fish scurry together—safety in numbers, as the herd instinct teaches—and are then taken in mouthfuls.

We are left then with such demons as the white shark, the Greenland shark, the blue shark, and the hammerheads; and the greatest foe of these is the first. As we all know, the mouth of the familiar shark is placed on the underside of the head. It would be profitable to discuss this curious design if we knew its meaning, but we do not. It has one blessed result, that the shark must turn over to bite a big object, and to that fact many a bold human swimmer has owed his life.

Sharks do not always turn in this way to bite, because it may not be necessary to do so. The hammerhead never does, for the reason that its mouth is placed far in advance of the ordinary shark mouth. Indeed, the structure of this creature is unique. The head is broadened out and flattened, expanding on each side into a singular process, each bearing one of the eyes. But freakish though he seems, the hammerhead is one of the fiercest of all sharks, and the dread of every man who is compelled to enter deep water in the Indian Ocean.

BEASTS OF PREY THAT PROWL THE SEAS LIKE HYENAS IN THE JUNGLE

Still, this one is not as terrible as the great white shark, which can bite off a man's leg or sever his body at one snap of its terrible jaws. The Greenland shark is another ferocious foe to man, but it hunts the whale, as a rule, tearing out the giant's tongue or ripping its live flesh from its body. Ordinarily alert and wary, it is so gross and ravenous a feeder that when thus riving the flesh from a struggling whale it may be approached quite close in a boat and harpooned as though it were drugged.

The blue shark is a frequent visitor to British waters, though happily it does not, as a rule, swim inshore. Small by comparison with the white shark, this one ranges between 15 and 25 feet, and a man would be but part of a meal for it.

The records of all these sharks are very horrifying, but it would serve no purpose to draw on details so unnerving. Considering the sea as a jungle, we must regard the sharks as among the beasts of prey, brutes with hyena-like instincts, cowardly, or let us say discreet, in that they will not attack a man who valiantly kicks out at them in the water, but will have him with fatal sureness if he slackens.

The thought of their habits is hateful,

CREATURES OF THE OCEAN DEEPS

FILE-FISH

COFFER-FISH

DOG-FISH

SQUID

BASKING SHARK

THE CUTTLE-FISH

THREE MEMBERS OF THE OCTOPUS FAMILY

but a shark's opinion of a shark-harpooning man, if the fish had thought and reason, would be as salutary to us as our opinion of him, if he but knew it.

They are scavengers. They eat the foulest organic matter cast into the sea; they have been known to swallow bags, tins, sacks of coke. One, in pursuit of a whale's tongue, made a mistake in its intended victim. The whale was one of the sperm species. It opened its mouth as wide as a shark could desire, but took the shark in bodily and swallowed it.

A little later the whale was pursued and captured. Then came a horrible discovery, for inside the whale was the shark, 15 feet in length and as lively and vicious as when at large in the sea.

THE TERRIBLE SAW-FISH THAT CAN CUT A MAN IN HALVES

After all, a shark gives a clean, terrific bite which is swift death. We may go farther and fare worse; and not so very far either, for next-door to the sharks in relationship are things still more horrible.

These are the saw-fishes. Here we have huge brutes in which the upper jaw is continued into a long, flattened beak, both edges of which are set with dreadful teeth, Nature's own attempt at a saw fashioned out of bone built up out of living particles from the blood.

This saw is used by the fish to gash open the soft under parts of a whale and to feed on the product of the attack. But there is another purpose. As the giraffe delivers an amazing sidelong blow with his horns, so the saw-fish, with a corresponding movement of his saw, can cut a man in halves.

We often see these implements of saw-fishes in museums and antiquarian shops, and little dream of the story behind them. In 1923 an English party out in Panama Bay, which Drake once knew so well, had an adventure with saw-fishes which would have sent the old-time seamen frantic with superstitious alarm.

THE FIERCE GIANT WHICH DRAGGED A YACHT FROM ITS ANCHORS

One saw-fish which was taken on a baited 14-pound steel hook bolted with it like a harpooned whale. It dragged a fishing boat at a great pace for a quarter of a mile. In so doing it approached the steam yacht owned by the party. Frank Mitchell Hedges, the proprietor of the yacht, cast a rope on to the vessel, where it was attached to a capstan to prevent the saw-fish from pulling away.

But the fish was by no means mastered. It hauled at the rope, dragged the yacht from its anchors, and towed it hither and thither for three hours. Eventually it was conquered, drawn inshore, and landed, when, instead of the little thing that the sight of these saws in shop windows suggests, it proved to be 29 feet long, 19 feet round, and weighed two and a quarter tons.

Later a female saw-fish 31 feet long, 21 feet round, and weighing 5700 pounds, was caught in the same waters. In other amazing hauls from those same tropical waters came a shark weighing 1760 pounds, with jaws in which two men were able to stand upright, back to back, and a hammerhead weighing three-quarters of a ton.

Similarity of sound causes confusion between the saw-fish and the sword-fish, though the two genera are far apart in the scheme of classification. The sword-fish is, in name at any rate, a playmate in our nurseries, for, as his scientific title is one of the few beginning with X, he is in the alphabet books of rhymes, where X stands for Xiphias.

THE FURIOUS FISH THAT WILL TILT AT A SHIP WITH ITS SWORD

Our nurseries, then, are entertaining ruffians unawares. The Xiphias, common to deep, hot seas, sometimes swimming down sea lanes of warm current as far as England and Ireland, and known to thrust far up certain rivers in the tropics, is one of the things most to be feared by man in the waters.

The bodily length of the adult fish is some 15 feet, and the sword, which is a sort of very dense bone spear, is upward of a yard long. In practice the sword-fish's methods are quite unlike the stealthy horrors of the saw-fish. Here it is an appalling charge, like a rhinoceros at a thorn bush. All the impetus of a little island of furiously darting bone and muscle is behind the blow of the sword, which is driven right through an inoffensive human bather, or deep into the vitals of a whale or lesser creature.

The sword-fish tilts at a ship with as genial a ferocity as at a man. Many a tough little craft in the old days of unsheathed wood came never again to port from far journeys to the tropics, and a

NATURE'S CHILDREN OF THE SEA

ARCHER-FISH

LESSER SPOTTED GLOBE-FISH

THE FOX-SHARK OR THRESHER

JAPANESE SAW-FISH

HAMMER-HEADED SHARK

THE TOPE

PORBEAGLE SHARK

The pictures on these pages are reproduced by courtesy of Messrs. Berridge, Warne, and others

sword-fish may have known why. For these savage brutes will charge a ship as soon as look at it.

There is in London evidence of their prowess in this direction. There is the broken sword of a fish which drove its implement through the hull and 13 inches of solid timber of a ship which was sailing between Bombay and Calcutta. A second trophy is a broken sword which went through 22 inches of ship's timber.

These deadly living swords were five inches and more in circumference. Had they not snapped off and remained in the openings which they caused, those two ships would have been added to the long roll of tragedies unexplained at sea.

CREATURES WITH MANY LIMBS AND A GREAT BEAK LIKE A PARROT'S

Next in this unpleasant gallery we must rank sea creatures which are not fishes but a lower order, the Cephalopods, in which occur the octopus, cuttlefish, and the squids. One cannot resist the thought that some of the strange old legends of classical times may have arisen from a contemplation of the habits of these dreadful creatures—Prometheus chained to his rock, ever in course of destruction by the beak of a rapacious bird, for instance.

Carrying eight arms, every inch of them studded with sucker discs, the octopus devotes all its ingenuity and strength to clutching a victim, man or fish, and drawing him or it with irresistible force to a cruel mouth like the horny beak of a huge parrot. The rest is a rending and ripping, piecemeal. The lesser sorts are to be found in British waters; but though their clinging tenacity may so seriously impede a swimmer's actions as to cause him to drown, they are not often to be feared.

THE FEARFUL THING THAT HAPPENS WHEN A SQUID MEETS A WHALE

In warmer waters, however, they are an abiding terror to bathers, and the creatures of which the diver goes most in fear. His only chance of escape is to strike at the enemy's eyes. Often that is impossible, and it frequently happens that man and octopus are drawn together to the deck, the brute writhing and gripping till it is hacked in fragments from the terrified diver.

But if we had squids in our seas! We have not; they are creatures of the wide ocean, which would hardly find a living in less spacious surroundings. Here are nightmares in real life, with bodies weighing perhaps half a ton, with eight huge arms, with tentacles 30 feet long, and armed with discs as big as saucers, each disc carrying a ring of horny hooks like the claws of tigers. The talons hook and hold, the discs cling by suction, and the victim is drawn irresistibly to that awful central beak.

What forms their food we do not know. When seen they are commonly in conflict with a great sperm whale, their arms writhing like ship masts, clutching, gripping, tearing at the whale, while the whale bites and snaps at its living bonds.

It is from the contents of the stomachs of whales which have been caught that we obtain our knowledge of these great squids. The body of one was said to match a ship's barrel which held 350 gallons; pieces of its tentacles were found to be eight feet long and eight feet high. What a picture of immensity these figures suggest—and what a swallow for a whale!

All the Cephalopods have the habit of swimming backward. They propel themselves by squirting water in a forward direction, so producing a rearward motion of their bodies, the retreat being aided by the discharge of a fluid which darkens the water and acts as a smoke screen.

HOW AN ENEMY FROM THE SEA HAS HELPED THE LAWS OF ENGLAND

This fluid is the sepia which was the first of pigments used by the ancients other than that obtained from vegetable substances. The chalky shell-like internal framework of the cuttle-fish is also put into good purpose. As cuttlefish bone it is a treasured addition to the diet of aviary birds, but ground fine it serves as " pounce " to powder the parchment on which lawyers write their deeds. The laws of England, so far as they have been committed to parchment, have needed the aid of pounce ground from the dried skeleton of an enemy from the sea.

Having now glanced at the giants and ogres which swim the surface, let us spend a moment in the deeps. Their range begins beyond the sunlight which penetrates faintly in clear water to a depth of 1200 feet. Deeper than that the fishes are what we call abyssal types.

It would seem that all the fish here are highly specialised developments of types which swim in more generalised conditions. They are not unique of themselves, but unique only in the life to which they have taken, and in the manner in which they have evolved equipment and habits to fit their dismal circumstances. We do not know as much about them as we desire to do, from the fact that no implement has yet been devised which can bring up great fish, which we are sure must be there, from the deeps of the sea.

Small things can be captured in ingeniously contrived trawls, but not monsters, if monsters exist. The greatest depth at which fish have been taken is just under 18,000 feet, in the western Atlantic, but there are places more than 34,000 feet

seas have life in its most astonishing forms. In some cases the eyes are enormously developed; in others there are no eyes at all. Some have phosphorescent lamps which they light, lamps like electric bulbs at the head, lamps like glow-worms scattered along the sides of the body.

All have huge teeth, and for the most part they are able to eat prey larger than themselves. Some of the eyeless fish have these powers to light the waters. The presumption is that the light is not for themselves but to lure other fishes, and that the lamp-bearers, having a highly organised sense of smell or touch, are able

THE ELFIN SHARK AND THE FRILLED SHARK

deep, and life is there if we could reach and capture it intact.

One difficulty in bringing such life to the surface is that fish hauled from the abysses are accustomed to sustain enormous pressure from the water overlying them. That pressure amounts to four and a half pounds to the square inch for every ten feet we descend; but, as the fish's body is charged with fluid, the pressure is from within as well as from without, so equalising the stress and rendering life possible. Remove the external pressure, however, and the effect is disastrous. The fish bursts.

Still, venturesome students have made their hauls, and we know that the deep

to take advantage of the near approach of inquisitive inquirers to snap them up. The species of creatures in the abysses are many in number, and all are among the most hideous and formidably armed creatures known to science.

The scabbard-fish, known to Australians as the frost-fish, from its extraordinary habit of wriggling to shore when frost puts a nip in the water, is nevertheless essentially a deep-sea creature, but as we see, it makes its way even to the land.

Such a habit reversed was possibly responsible for the gradual retreat of all the mystery fish from the shores to the open ocean, and from the strife and competition of the surface, deeper and deeper to the very bottom of the ocean, to an existence suitable to them, it seems, yet as joyless, as dark and colourless as that of the proteus in its gloomy home in the subterranean depths of a mountain.

But defence and weapons of aggression are not peculiar to these fish. The globe-fishes are as prickly as hedgehogs for defence; they have such formidable beaks that one has been known to eat its way out of the shark which swallowed it, and the sac-fish branch of the family has the power to inflate a membrane covering its abdomen, turn upside down, and float with such wind or current as cares to propel it. The sunfishes, some of which are 15 feet long and weigh half a ton, have only a roughened skin, not spines.

THE HIGHLY-COLOURED FISH THAT HAS HORNS LIKE A COW

Nearly allied to these are the Balistides, a singular group, the file-fish, or trigger-fish, and the coffer-fish. The last-named fishes are brilliantly coloured, their hue being a danger signal. But there is armament of a more material nature about the coffer-fishes, for they have bony horns which give them the name of cow-fishes. File-fishes, often beautifully tinted, are even more interesting. They have jaws of incredible strength. They not only bite off knobs of solid coral, but they crack the great shells of the pearl oysters, and devour the contents. And thereby hangs a tale of sheer wonder.

The file-fish preys on the oyster, the ray preys on the file-fish. Now, a certain worm-like parasite undergoes an early stage of its existence in the body of the file-fish, and completes its course in the body of the ray, which devours its first host.

Here it lays eggs, and the young hatch out and escape from the body of ray into the water over the oyster bed. The parasites enter the open shells of the oyster, and there begin their career. The ticklish oyster, unable to bear the irritation, pours out a fluid which we call nacre, and in that imprisons and kills the parasite intruder.

THE FATE OF THE TINY WORM THAT LIVES IN THE HEART OF A PEARL

More and more nacre is distilled about the intruder. It hardens, glossy and lovely, and in course of time is the true pearl which divers risk their lives to seek. The finest pearls that adorn the throats of lovely women are simply the sepulchres of little worms, buried alive for their audacity in penetrating the sanctuary of an offended oyster.

Having mentioned the file-fish, we had better guard ourselves against the danger of confounding this with the tile-fish. This is one with a history serving to remind us that great catastrophes occur in Nature as in the midst of life in civilised lands.

First discovered in the warm waters of the Gulf Stream off the coast of Massachusetts in 1879, the tile-fishes swarmed and constituted a highly prized food for customers of American fishing fleets. In the spring of 1882, however, there came an unwanted succession of great gales. The effect of these was as if they pushed aside the stream of warm water in which the tile-fishes lived, and seas of frigid water replaced the warm.

The result was amazing. The tile-fish caught cold and died, just as swarms of fish gathered about the lock gates of the Thames died of chill when a deluge of freezing flood water poured in during the summer of 1911.

HOW NATURE PROTECTS HER CHILDREN FROM THE EFFECTS OF CALAMITY

After the American storms died down, fishermen went again to catch tile-fish. Not one was alive. They covered the surface of the water, floating dead for a distance of 300 miles. A careful computation showed that 1400 million tile-fish were dead on that sea. Years elapsed, and then tile-fish returned in small numbers, multiplied, and slowly re-stocked the scene of that great disaster. How they returned we can only guess.

Some few may have fled in fright, while there was yet time, to warmer waters out of reach of the invading currents of cold, and ancestral memory of the old hunting grounds may eventually have brought them back. Or others, not originally of that area, may gradually have drifted in to colonise the delectable province.

But we can see, from this clean-cut example, how local species have died out in the past. It is to guard against such wholesale extinctions that Nature charges her children with an energy which makes them disperse themselves as widely as possible, and so minimise the risk of total obliteration.

We leave a thousand aspects of our subject untouched. For truly the sea is inexhaustible, and so is the life within it.

PICTURE-STORY OF IRRIGATION

This huge water-wheel at Hama, in northern Syria, 75 feet in diameter (nearly three feet bigger than the Laxey wheel in the Isle of Man) is the largest in the world. The wheel runs without stopping, day and night all the year round, and raises water in buckets to the aqueduct for irrigation purposes.

THE OLDEST WAYS OF IRRIGATION

Here is a peasant in northern India raising water for irrigation by a lever device known as a shadoof.

In the Japanese rice-fields some irrigation is carried on by means of treadmill water-raisers like this.

Here is another way of raising water by treadmill which is often practised in India.

Sometimes animal power is used bullocks being driven down an incline to haul up water for irrigation.

THREE GREAT DAMS IN INDIA

In scientific irrigation on a big scale a great dam is built across a river to hold up the waters and prevent them from running to waste. They are released as required. This dam is at Tajewala in India.

Here is another Indian dam, at Dhanauri, which enables people to cross the Upper Ganges Canal and at the same time regulates the flow of water from the reservoir in which it is stored.

This mile-long dam at Sukkur, in India, holds up the waters of the River Indus and enables them to be diverted, as needed, into canals which irrigate six million acres of former unproductive land in Sind.

DAMS IN AUSTRALIA AND SOUTH AFRICA

This barrage on the River Murray at Blanchetown was the first of a series built on the South Australian reaches of the river to provide water for irrigating new settlements. The lock seen in the foreground is for navigation purposes. Mildura, in Victoria, is the centre of the Murray irrigation scheme.

This aerial view shows Hartebeestpoort Dam, west of Pretoria. It is one of the largest irrigation schemes in South Africa, the water stored in the lake serving the farming area of Brits and Rustenburg in Transvaal.

THE WATER IS CARRIED TO THE FARMS

This electrically-controlled irrigation system is in use in some parts of Australia. It requires no supervision, for the pump which sprays the crops is turned on and off according to the requirements of the soil.

Here is an irrigating channel in Canada, where the water is used not only for feeding the growing crop, but also as drink for the flocks or herds on the farm.

In Australia the precious water is often stored in big concrete dams, with sluice-gates and conduits to drain it to the fields when required, as shown here.

Where the water is at a high level it will run to the farms by gravitation, but in flat country it has to be pumped. Here is a pumping station in Australia.

TAPPING THE UNDERGROUND WATERS

Nearly everywhere in Australia there are adequate supplies of water underground, but these must be tapped by artesian wells, as we see in this picture.

In the larger trenches on the farms there are sluice-gates, like this one in California, for regulating the flow of water into the network of smaller trenches.

Sometimes the water is carried to the trenches through wooden troughs, as shown here. This walnut orchard in California was once a stretch of barren land on which nothing useful would grow, but irrigation has wrought a wonderful transformation, creating prosperity out of poverty.

THE GIANT RESERVOIRS OF AMERICA

Some of the biggest irrigation dams in the world are found in America, where so much arid and desert land has been reclaimed. This is the great Roosevelt Dam, completed in 1911, which holds up hundreds of mil'ions of gallons of water of the Salt River in Arizona.

The Hoover Dam, shown in this aerial view, was built in the Boulder Canyon of the Colorado River. It is 726 feet high, causing the waters to pile up to form a reservoir over a hundred miles long, the largest artificial lake in the world, for irrigation and power purposes.

IRRIGATION WORKS OF THREE CONTINENTS

This great dam across the Blue Nile at the village of Makwar, near Senna, in the Anglo-Egyptian Sudan, was built as part of a scheme for irrigating a thousand square miles of land in the Gezira province.

Here is the Burrinjuck Dam in New South Wales, which holds up the waters of the Murrumbidgee River to form a reservoir 40 miles long, which supplies an agricultural area of a million acres.

The Aswan Dam holds up the flood waters of the Nile in Egypt, which can be released as required for irrigation of a large area. The level of the dam has been twice raised since it was built in 1902.

He⁻e are the headgates of the main canal at the Bassano Dam, a vast irrigation project on the Bow River in Alberta. The controlled waters irrigate more than 600,000 acres.

WHERE THE DESERT BLOSSOMS AS THE ROSE

The desert of the Rio Grande, in New Mexico, U.S.A., as it appeared before any irrigation works were begun. The soil is fertile, but the climate is arid, and nothing but useless scrub and cactuses could grow there.

Here is the same place after the great Rio Grande irrigation works had been carried out. The whole of a vast area is watered, and huge quantities of vegetables, fruit, and other products are grown every year.

This is another example of how the desert has been made to blossom as the rose by means of irrigation. It shows a fruitful almond orchard flourishing in Colorado where formerly was nothing but arid wilderness.

THE IRRIGATION OF THE RICE FIELDS

IN JAVA RICE IS GROWN IN TERRACED FIELDS, WHICH ARE ABUNDANTLY IRRIGATED

The picture of the Aswan Dam on page 5242 is reproduced by courtesy of Sir Murdoch MacDonald and Partners

Plain Answers to the Questions of the Children of the World

Peterhouse, Cambridge, where Henry Cavendish studied science

HAS THE EARTH EVER BEEN WEIGHED ?

STRICTLY speaking the Earth cannot be weighed, for it has no weight. Weight is the amount of pull the Earth exerts on any object, and so it cannot pull itself. When we speak of weighing the Earth, we really mean finding out its mass, or the amount of matter in it.

There are various ways of doing this. The earliest plan was to suspend a plumb-line first on one side of a mountain, and then on the other side, to discover how much the plumb-line was attracted out of the straight by the mountain. If the mountain was of the same density as the Earth as a whole, its attraction of the plumb-line could be calculated. The scientists first proceeded to find the density of the mountain, by reckoning its size, and examining the density of its material. In this way the mountain known as Schiehallion, in Perthshire, was found to be two and a half times as dense as water. The action of the plumb-line showed that the Earth was one and four-fifth times as dense as the mountain, and therefore the Earth's density must be two and a half times one and four-fifths—or four and a half. Later experiments showed that the density of the Earth was 5·527 times (a little more than five and a half times) that of water, which always counted as one, or the unit of measurement.

The size of the Earth was worked out from its diameter, and found to be about 260,000 million cubic miles, and from this the mass, or amount of material in the globe, was found to be approximately 6000 *million million million tons*.

The Earth was weighed as far back as 1798, by the famous chemist Henry Cavendish, who did it in a room! Instead of using a mountain to deflect a plumb-line, he used two large and two small balls of lead and a torsion balance—a very delicate apparatus for measuring horizontal forces. An arm is hung by its centre of gravity by a thin wire or fibre of silk, and the force to be measured is applied at one end of the arm, which moves horizontally, the angle through which the arm turns being in proportion to the force.

Cavendish attached to each end of his balance a small leaden ball, two inches in diameter, and weighing just over a pound and a half. Then two large balls of lead, each twelve inches in diameter, and weighing about 350 pounds, were hung from another arm, which could also twist round horizontally. The big balls were placed at right angles to the torsion rod, on which hung the little balls, and were gradually brought round till they were near the little balls. The attraction exerted by the big balls on the small ones turned the

FIRE · WIND · WATER · LIFE · MIND · SLEEP · HOW · WHY · WHERE

delicate torsion arm slightly, and the angle through which it moved was measured. Then the two large balls were turned round the other way, and the twist again measured.

With great patience Cavendish was able to calculate the density of the Earth as 5·448, or nearly five and a half, which has since been proved to be almost exactly correct. From the density he was at last able to reckon the mass, or weight.

Sometimes a pendulum is used in weighing the Earth. A pendulum of given length swings more slowly at a great height than at sea-level, but it does not swing quite so slowly at the top of a mountain, as it would do if the mountain were not there, and the pendulum were suspended in space. The attraction of the mountain can therefore be compared with the pull of the Earth when we calculate the amount of matter in the mountain.

At Munich, in 1879, Professor Von Jolly arranged two pairs of scale pans on a tower, one pair being 69 feet below the other. Two glass globes loaded with quicksilver were put in the upper pans, and two empty glass globes in the lower. The balance remained horizontal. Then the loaded and empty globes were transposed, on one side only, and that side at once showed an increase of weight due to the extra attraction of the Earth when the heavy globe was nearer to its centre. Next a large leaden sphere was placed under the lower pan with the heavy globe, and now that side of the balance showed a still greater weight. With these figures the density of the Earth could be calculated and its mass worked out.

A still more elaborate method was carried out at Birmingham University early this century by John Henry Poynting, when Professor of Physics there, but it is too difficult to describe here. But the accuracy of the apparatus used was such that variations were never out more than a 5000-millionth of the total mass.

What Was the Garden of the Hesperides ?

The Hesperides were three famous nymphs respected as demi-gods by the ancient Greeks. Daughters of Hesperus, gifted with the power of vanishing at will, the Hesperides had been chosen by Juno to look after a garden very dear to the Queen of Olympus. It was an extra-ordinary garden, where grew golden apples that possessed a powerful charm.

The sacred precincts were fabled to stand close to Mount Atlas in Africa. To preserve the entrance to the sacred place, Juno had set a dragon, a terrible monster with a hundred heads, and wonderful eyes that never closed, so that nobody ever ventured to approach the gate lest they should be devoured. Hercules, compelled by Fortune, was the first who ventured to get some golden apples.

After Hercules had successfully accomplished one of his twelve famous labours, killing the dragon and getting some of the golden apples, wise Minerva soon took them back to their native ground, for they could not be preserved anywhere else.

It has often been thought that the golden apples were the oranges of Spain. That country always very much impressed the ancients as a mysterious land, probably because it lay so far from Greece.

What Are The Chiltern Hundreds ?

A member of the House of Commons cannot resign his seat, but by accepting an office under the Crown his seat legally becomes vacant. Therefore, when an M.P. wishes to resign he is appointed Steward of the Chiltern Hundreds—a range of hills in Buckinghamshire—an old office with no duties, and is thus set free.

What Makes a Kite Fly ?

The case of the kite proves to us that the air has a great power of holding things up, as the kite has no wings, and yet does not fall. The air supports it. If we took all the stuff of which a kite is made and rolled it into a tight ball, it would drop like a stone. So it is not that the kite is made of something lighter than air. The reason why it flies is that it is spread out as wide as can possibly be, so that it has a large surface for the air to support it. But, of course, if there were no air at all the kite would drop at once, as the bird would, whether it were flying or not. Neither the kite nor the bird could rise or swim in nothing. The Latin word meaning empty is *vacuus*, and a place that is quite empty is called a *vacuum*. Nothing can soar in a vacuum.

But the kite flies not only because it presents a large surface to the air, but also because it is slanted to the wind in such a way that the wind pressure forces it to rise.

HENRY CAVENDISH WEIGHS THE EARTH

This **is** how Cavendish weighed the Earth in a room in **1798**. To each end of a delicate, suspended arm he attached a tiny leaden ball, and to each end of another arm a leaden ball weighing **350 pounds**. The big balls attracted the little ones, first on one side and then on the other, and by measuring this attraction through a spy-glass from outside, Cavendish worked out the pull of the big balls. Then, knowing the pull of the Earth and the weight of the balls, he compared them and was able to calculate the Earth's mass, or weight.

How Does the Snail Get Its Shell ?

The snail makes its shell from its own skin. Our own skins, we know, can make things which are fairly hard, such as our nails; and it is also true that the hardest things in our bodies, our teeth, are really made from our skin. There are really few things more wonderful than the way in which soft, living creatures, mostly made of water, are able to make the hardest things, like teeth and shells and pearl, and so on. If we look carefully at the skin of creatures like the snail we can see how its outside cells are specially made so that they gradually get harder and harder, until they cannot be called skin at all, but are really nothing else than shell. We can watch very much the same thing if we look at the cells at the base of our nails, or the cells that make the horns of animals, and see how the soft skin is gradually changed.

Why Does the Moon Look so Big When Low Down over the Sea ?

Because we look straight ahead at it, instead of raising the eye to see it, and so see it generally at an angle. This was the answer given a few years ago by an American psychologist. He made experiments to show that this will always happen for physiological reasons, whether the object viewed is the Moon, the setting Sun, or group of stars like the Plough, which appears larger when lower down than when high in the sky. When we look at the Moon through our thumb and finger respectively just above and below it, the Moon appears to shrink, but at once becomes large when we widen the gap through which we are inspecting the Moon. This simple explanation, which excludes all others, shows that this is an example of optical illusions.

Why am I Giddy When Looking Down From a Height ?

Everyone does not become giddy when looking down, and anyone who is in good health can learn in time by practice how to look down from a height without turning giddy. There are two explanations of this giddiness. One is the general explanation that the fear of falling disturbs the working of the brain. Now, our sense of being balanced, and our feeling that we are able to balance ourselves, depend on the proper working of the brain; and so the fear of falling may make us giddy, just as giddiness may be caused at times by other kinds of fear. But people who are not in the least afraid, or who do not at all expect to be afraid, may turn giddy when they look down from a height, and there is a very interesting explanation of this. Part of our power of balancing ourselves depends on vision. We know how we are apt to bump against a companion when walking at night, for instance. And even though we can balance ourselves without the aid of sight, we are apt to feel giddy if our eyes play us tricks, as they do sometimes at a height.

Is There a Rule in the Colour of Flags ?

Yes; both the proportion of one colour to another, and the size of the material used for national flags, are officially fixed. Flags are mostly made of bunting because it is light, tough, and durable. It is made in 40-yard lengths, nine inches wide; and when a flag is a yard in height it is technically called a four-breadth flag.

In the Middle Ages the size of a banner denoted the rank of its owner. A banner was usually square; a king's was five feet square, a baron's three feet. A standard flag was long and tapered towards its fly, the fly being the portion farthest from the mast. The part near the mast is the hoist.

The Union Flag must be either square or a rectangle with the length twice the width. The Union flag was once made up from the crosses of St. George and St. Andrew only; but when, in 1801, the cross of St. Patrick was added, it was found difficult to give equal prominence to all the crosses. That is why the arms of the red cross do not meet each other if taken across the centre of the flag. In the hoist half of the flag the arm of St. Andrew's white cross, with its blue background, is above the red arm of St. Patrick's cross. The thin strip of white below this red arm is a portion of the white background of the St. Patrick's flag, and not part of St. Andrew's cross. In the fly half of the flag these positions are reversed.

The following are the proportions of the colours. St. George's Cross has red one-fifth of the width of the flag, and white one-third of the red. St. Patrick's Cross has red one-third of the red of St. George and white one-sixth the red of St. George. St. Andrew's Cross has white one-half the red of St. George.

When we see the French flag we probably think the three colours are equal in width, but this is not so.

When the present French flag was first flown in 1794 the colours were equal in width, but owing to their different degrees of visibility at a distance the blue looked larger than either the white or the red, and the red looked smaller than the white. Scientific experiments were made, and now the proportion of each colour is fixed so that in every 100 parts the blue is 30, the white 33, and the red 37.

The flags of the International Code of Signals are known all over the world. There is a flag for every letter and numeral and many of them can be used singly to convey a message. For instance, the code flag for the letter B is red, and if flown alone by a ship indicates that the ship is carrying explosives. Although not a code flag, a white flag usually means truce or surrender.

Is the Body Wearing Away?

Almost every part of your body, except bone and the enamel of your teeth, is wearing away, but no part disappears, because it is being unceasingly renewed. Through all the years of youth the inside of a bone is ever busy building up. It is packed with specks of living matter, working for ever in the dark to make your foot firm, your arm strong, your backbone amazingly supple and also strong. Here they make a ridge, here a curve; here they chisel a groove for a nerve or a hole for a blood-vessel to pass through. This work that goes on always is wonderful enough, but what shall we say of the cells for making new bone that are held in reserve in every bone in our body? They have nothing to do as long as things go well, but let a bone be broken, and the bone-builders, who have never made a bone before, set to work to make one now. The doctor puts the broken ends together and leaves them, and these cells, working in darkness, which have never seen a bone but have lain there doing nothing from the beginning, waiting for this very day, design and make and shape a bone to fit the break exactly, and they do their work so well that your doctor will tell you he has never known a bone break where it has once been set. " I dressed his wounds; God healed him," a great doctor said, and he spoke the truth.

What is the America's Cup?

The America's Cup was once known as the Queen's Cup, and was originally offered by the Royal Yacht Squadron in 1851 for the winner of an international yacht race. It was first won by an American yacht over a course round the Isle of Wight, and has ever since been the property of the New York Yacht Club, though British and Canadian yachts have made repeated attempts to win it back. Challengers have now to compete for the Cup in American waters, where the race is usually held over a 30-mile course near Sandy Hook lightship in New York Bay.

Why Does a Hen Not Crow?

When we study birds we find it a general rule that the male birds are the most brightly coloured, and it is the male birds that sing. The feathers of the female birds are usually less bright, and their voices are not so melodious. It is probable that both the bright colouring of so many male birds and their singing, are things that have been evolved to make them prominent and pleasing in the eyes of the females. Among animals it is usually the females that choose the males they like best, and these are usually the finest specimens of their kind.

We may say that the crowing of a cock is not to be called singing, and certainly it is a very ugly noise compared with the singing of the lark, or the thrush, or the nightingale; but it is really the cock's way of singing, and probably it gives pleasure to the hens. Even among ourselves the notion of what is good singing varies very much with different people. Their father, for instance, does not sing as well as their uncle, according to some young people; and the hen has as good a right to her opinion of the cock's singing as human beings have.

Why Does a Railway Platform Slope at the End?

The chief reason why railway platforms always end in a slope is that a Board of Trade regulation insists on a slope instead of steps or an abrupt drop. This rule was made in order to prevent railway officials or passengers falling from the platform-end in the dark or in a fog, and it is probable that thousands of accidents have been prevented in this way, the slope giving fair warning to a man when he has come to the end of the platform.

Could a Man Ever Walk From France to England?

Yes, for in past ages England and France were joined by land, and it was only the invasion of the sea, due to some disturbance, that made Britain an island cut off from the mainland of Europe. The Straits of Dover are so shallow, even today, that if St. Paul's Cathedral were sunk in them the dome would be seen above the water in the deepest part. The North Sea and the English Channel are not very deep, and, as can be seen by the map on this page, Europe once jutted out much farther into the Atlantic than it does now.

Scotland and Norway were also joined together at one time, the estuary of a big

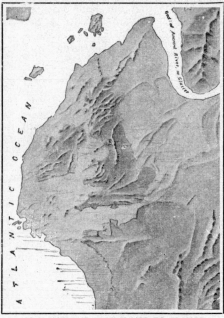

HOW ENGLAND WAS JOINED TO FRANCE

river or a massive glacier being where the Cattegat now is. The seas immediately round Britain are so shallow that a very slight fall in the sea level would suffice to join Britain once more to the Continent, and, on the other hand, a slight rise of the sea could flood south-eastern England and the Flemish plain, and put a wide sea between Britain and the mainland. Geologists tell us that at different times in the past both these conditions have occurred.

There is no doubt that when the British Islands were joined to Europe men and animals passed freely over them from other parts of the Continent. But Britain has far fewer animal species than the Continent, and this was explained by Alfred Russel Wallace, who believed that the greater part of the British Isles was submerged during the Glacial period. He explains it as follows:

" We know," he says, " that just before and during the Glacial period we possessed a fauna almost or quite identical with that of the adjacent parts of the Continent, and equally rich in species. The submergence destroyed this fauna, and the permanent change of climate, or the passing away of the glacial conditions, probably led to the extinction or migration of many species in the adjacent Continental areas, where they were succeeded by the assemblage of animals now occupying Central Europe. When England became Continental these entered our country, but sufficient time does not seem to have elapsed for the migration to have been completed before a subsidence again occurred, cutting off the further invasion of land animals, and leaving us without the number of species which our favourable climate and varied surface entitled us to."

How Many Worlds Are There?

A world like ours stands alone. If by that is meant that it alone supports life as we know it, we may safely say that we know no other, for such life exists only within a narrow range of temperatures of some 400 degrees Centigrade (about 750 degrees Fahrenheit). Such conditions do not appear to exist on any other planet of our solar system, and could not exist in the thousands of degrees on stars. But among the uncounted millions of stars in all the spiral nebulae, galaxies of stars like our own, which even before the great 200-inch reflecting telescope on Mount Palomar in California could be brought to bear on them, numbered about 100,000, there should be some 1000 million dark bodies that we shall never see. Some of these should be worlds like our own ; though Sir James Jeans was of the opinion that the number of stars or suns which supported a family of planets was very small in comparison with those that could not. However much the Palomar 200-inch may increase the number of these island universes, many of them brighter, bigger, and younger than our own galaxy, the problem of worlds will remain substantially the same.

Are Pictures of the Things we See Printed on the Eye?

The word photograph means a light-picture, and that is exactly what photographs are—pictures printed by the light on a film or a plate. This film is covered with chemical substances which light affects, according to its power, and the place where it strikes. The back part of the eye is in these respects the same as the photographic plate. It also contains chemical substances which are changed by light and therefore it is true that pictures of what we see are printed on the retina of the eye.

But there is a tremendous difference between the retina of the eye and the plate of a camera. If the picture printed on the eye stayed for any length of time we could not see anything moving. If our eyes are to be useful it is necessary that the pictures printed on them should rapidly pass and be replaced by another picture. This is where the wonder comes in—that it should be possible, in a tiny fraction of a second, for the back of the eye continually to remake, from the materials supplied it by the blood, the chemical substances which light affects when we see.

What Makes a Current in the Sea?

A current is not the same thing as a *wave*, which, though it seems to move onwards, is really due to the water moving up and down. After the wave has passed the water is in the same place as it was before. But in the case of a current the water is actually moving from one place to another. There is a lake in Switzerland through which a river runs, and by the difference in the colour of the water you can see where the river is. In that case it is easy to understand what makes it. The water of the river is falling to the sea, which is lower down than the place where the river started, and it is really the Earth's attraction which is pulling the water of the river through the lake, so making the current.

Now, in the sea, currents are due to something which is pulling or pushing part of the water through the rest of the water. These currents may be due to many causes; sometimes it may be a steady wind blowing for some time in one direction, driving some of the water before it. More often, perhaps, currents are due to differences in the heat of the water. Warm water in cold water will keep to itself, so to speak, and will move through the sea. If the sun shines brightly on a particular part of the sea it makes the water there hotter, and so may start a current. Indeed, the currents of water in the sea are often due to very much the same causes as the currents in the air.

Why Does Hot Water take up More Room than Cold?

It is not true that in all cases water expands when heated, because if we take water at the freezing temperature, and then slowly heat it, we find that it shrinks until it reaches 4 degrees on the Centigrade scale of temperature. That, however, is a special exception, and it is perfectly true that if we go on heating the water after 4 degrees Centigrade it does expand, and take up more room. This is true of almost anything, whether a solid or a liquid or a gas.

We can find some kind of explanation for this if we think of heat as a to-and-fro motion of the tiny parts of which all matter is made. The hotter the thing, we suppose, the wider is this to-and-fro motion of its tiny atoms.

Suppose we have a crowd of children, and all the to-and-fro motion each of them makes is just so much as is required for breathing. Fifty such children could be packed into a very small space; but if, instead of making only this little movement, each of them wanted all the time to be making little runs of five yards backwards and forwards, we should plainly not be able to pack these fifty children into as small a space as before.

If, instead of children, we think of the atoms of matter, and if we think of heat as sending these atoms of matter running to and fro, we shall see why water and other things swell when they are heated.

The behaviour of water at the temperature of zero Centigrade (freezing point) when heated to 4 degrees Centigrade is certainly contradictory. At 4 degrees Centigrade water is at its greatest density. If cooled below 4 degrees it *expands* in volume and its specific density decreases. Some answer to this problem comes through experiments in subjecting water to pressure of thousands of pounds to the square inch: when even boiling ice can appear.

Why Does a Piece of Hot Iron Turn Red ?

When iron turns red this means that it is producing light of the particular kind that impresses our eyes as red, and we see the iron by this light. When it is cold, we see the iron only by light reflected from its surface. If the cold iron be put in the dark we cannot see it, but red-hot iron glows in the dark. The point is, then, that the red-hot iron shines by its own light ; it makes light of its own. The character of the light given out by the iron will depend on how hot it is, for we know that if red-hot iron is heated still more it turns white.

This fact about iron is common to most substances. When they are heated to a certain point they become luminous. Heat and light are both forms of energy and when enough heat is applied some of it will appear as light. This may be taken to supersede the older explanation that as the iron or other substance becomes heated the molecules of matter are incited to jostle one another and so to produce heat and subsequently light.

Why Do The Swiss Speak Three Languages ?

During the first four centuries of the Christian era, all Europe south of the Danube and west of the Rhine was civilised by the Roman legions, and these two rivers were lined with fortresses to keep back the uncivilised tribes that lived in Central Europe. But when the Romans lost their power great hordes from Central Europe poured over the two rivers, flooding the countries to the south and west, and destroying nearly all the good work done by the Romans.

One tribe, the Allemanni, crossed the Danube, and settled in the mountains of what is now Switzerland ; another, the Franks, crossed the Rhine, and entered the mountain region from the west. The languages of these two tribes were German and French, and they have been used by their descendants ever since. Italian became a third language much later, when the Swiss invaded and annexed land on the south of the mountains where it was the tongue of the people. There is even a fourth language, used by a few, called Romansch, a relic of the early Roman occupation.

Why do we Walk more Slowly Uphill than Down ?

When we walk on the level we have only to work against such things as the resistance of the air, and the weight of our legs as we lift them up and down. When we walk downhill less effort is required because we are to a certain extent being pulled nearer the centre of the Earth. When we walk uphill the work is very hard, because then we have, by sheer muscular effort, to lift our whole bodies away from the centre of the Earth in defiance of gravitation.

It is said that to walk up a steep hill at a given pace costs us twenty times as much effort as to walk at the same pace along the level. The reason is exactly the same as the reason why we lift a heavy weight in our hand more slowly than we let it down. In one case we are pulling against gravitation, and exerting a greater force than gravitation; in the other case we are exerting only a comparatively little force against gravitation so that the weight shall not fall to the ground too quickly.

Will the Earth Ever Stop Spinning ?

All celestial bodies, of which the Earth is one, spin. One cause appears to be operating to stop the spin, or rotation, and it is the tides, which are themselves caused by the Moon. (A much smaller tide is that caused by the Sun.) On the side under the Moon the Moon's attraction on the Earth's surface water is greater than its actions on the Earth's centre; and its attraction on the Earth's centre is greater than its attraction on the water on the opposite side of the Earth. There are, therefore, always two tides on the Earth's surface : and it is suggested that their combined effect acts as a brake on the Earth's rotation. But it only shortens the Earth's day by one-sixty-sixth part of a second in 2500 years. There is no saying if this action will eventually stop the spin, for other unforeseen conditions may arise.

What is Adam's Apple ?

Adam's apple is the name given to the lump in the front of the neck where the throat is. It began with the old nonsense which said that a piece of the apple which Adam ate stuck in his throat, and made this curious lump.

SCULPTURES ANCIENT AND MODERN

JOHN THE BAPTIST AS A BOY, BY PAUL DUBOIS

FATIGUE, BY EMIL RENKER

MUSIC, BY JOHN BÖRJESON

FATHER'S CONSOLER, BY ERNST HERTER

THE BROKEN DREAM, BY MARIUS REMONDOT

TEARS, BY ERNST SEGER

SYMPATHY, BY ADDA BONFILS

THE FAREWELL, BY ROBERT CAUER

THE YOUNG JOHN THE BAPTIST
BY DONATELLO

SAINT CECILIA, ATTRIBUTED
TO DONATELLO

CUPID, STUNG BY A BEE, SEEKS SYMPATHY FROM VENUS, BY BERTEL THORWALDSEN

CHARITY, BY BERTEL
THORWALDSEN

AN ANCIENT SCULPTURE OF ANDROMEDA
RESCUED BY PERSEUS

THE BROTHER'S KISS
BY MADRASSI

VIOLETS, BY RAOUL
LARCHE

THE GIRL SKITTLE
PLAYER

MERCURY, THE MESSENGER OF THE GODS, ADOPTS HIS FAMILIAR WAND, BY ANTONIN IDRAC

CUPID AND PSYCHE, BY BERTEL
THORWALDSEN

HAMLET, BY SANDOR
JARAY

THE SHEPHERD'S RETURN
BY JEAN DANNHÄUSER

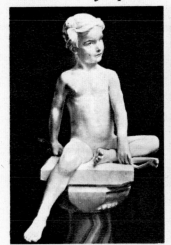

LOVE TRIUMPHANT, BY MAX
BLONDAT

MIGNON, BY EUGENE
AIZELIN

AFTER THE BATH, BY FRITZ
HEINEMANN

A DAINTY GROUP OF DANCING GIRLS

ARION RIDING ON THE DOLPHIN
BY ERNEST EUGENE HIOLLE

THE SPRINGTIME OF LIFE, BY
F. BRAHMSTAEDT

A CHILD'S KISSES, BY MARIUS
SAIN

THE ECHO, BY JULIUS W. FRICK

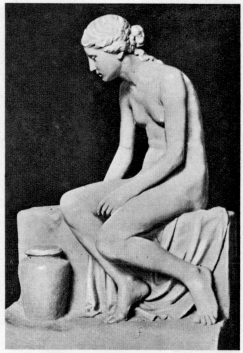

THE NYMPH AT THE WELL, BY BURKHARD EBE

HEINRICH HEINE, BY ERNST HERTER

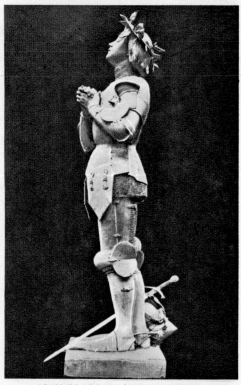

JOAN OF ARC, BY ANTONIN MERCIE

The pictures in these pages are reproduced by courtesy of Messrs. Alinari, Anderson, Bonnaire, Braun, Brogi, the Muchmore Gallery, Stender, and others

The Wonderful House We Live In, and Our Place in the World

Shipping in the West India Docks, London

TRADE BETWEEN NATIONS

WHEN we were speaking of the meaning of wealth, we noticed how large a part is played in human affairs by the division of labour, people devoting themselves entirely to particular jobs, so that one man does nothing else but make boots or parts of boots, and another does nothing else but make bicycles or parts of bicycles.

Trade is a natural result of this division of labour. Robinson Crusoe on his island did everything for himself—at least until he discovered Friday—and, therefore, trade for him did not exist. If, however, we imagine a hundred people living on an island, we see that as soon as they began to divide themselves up between different occupations the need for exchanges between them would spring up. One man would make a weapon and exchange it, perhaps, for a hat made by another. That would be a simple exchange of goods which we call Barter; and in the early days of mankind trade was all done in that way. Afterwards, as we shall presently see, Money was invented to help exchange.

It is impossible to exaggerate the importance of trade to mankind, for it takes a thing from where it is made to where it is needed, and until a thing becomes available to a person who needs it, it has not really become useful. It may be said

with truth that wealth is matter in the right place, and the matter can only be got into the right place by inventing some means of exchanging the many different things which are made at home and abroad.

We can remind ourselves how important it is to transfer things from places where they are not wanted to places where they are wanted, by taking the case of common gravel. Often it appears to be valueless where it lies. In a place where building is done, however, gravel is a very important raw material, used with cement in making concrete. Therefore great trouble is taken to dig the gravel in the place where it is not needed and to transport it by road or rail to where building is going on. This trade in gravel changes a useless thing into a very valuable thing.

So, every working day, men are busy all over the world producing things which are rapidly transported, by land or by sea, to places where they are needed. Where once a few barbarians doing little or no trade gained a meagre living, great populations exist because of the trade which has been built up during centuries of development.

The need for trade or exchange is so great, indeed, that *if we were all making things, we should make them in vain.* People

BODY, MIND, AND SOUL · CITIZENSHIP · ECONOMICS · GOVERNMENT

would simply be piling up heaps of goods which would not serve any useful purpose. That is why a large proportion of working people is needed, not to make things, but to carry them, or to deal in them, or to work in some other way, as in a bank, to help trade by providing it with facilities.

THE WORK OF MANY PEOPLE THAT GIVES A THING ITS VALUE

Millions of people have to be employed in making or repairing roads, docks, harbours, and railways used in the transportation of goods, and in building, repairing, or working in warehouses, stores, shops, and offices concerned with the storage and sale of goods. A man working on a railway and helping to take coal from Derbyshire, where they have plenty of it, to London, where they have none, is just as much a producer of coal as if he were a miner. If the railwayman did not transport the coal it would be useless for the miner to hew it.

To go a step farther, it would be useless either for the railwayman to carry coal or for the miner to hew it, if offices and stores were not set up to enable people to buy coal when they need it. And, as with coal, so with other things. They have not only to be produced, and carried by sea and land, but they must be stored and sold in convenient markets or shops. The more simple we can make the exchanging of goods the better it is for everyone. If a commodity has to pass through many hands before reaching its final destination, the cost to the consumer will be proportionately high.

THE MILLIONS OF WORKERS IN BRITAIN AND HOW THEY EARN THEIR LIVING

In a little country like Britain, with its population of about 50 million people, there are more than 24 million men, women, and young people earning their living. About half of them are engaged in producing things. Some of them are farmers and fishermen, producing food; some are miners and quarrymen, getting coal, ores, and stone out of the ground. About ten million work in factories, making motor-cars, clothing, furniture, saucepans, machinery, and all the other varied products of our industries; others build houses, factories, roads, and bridges; and some work to provide us with electricity, gas, and water.

The other half of the working population produces not goods but services. That is to say, instead of making things for people to use, they do useful things for them. A large number are engaged in transport by land, sea, and air, and others are busy in trade, buying and selling goods, wholesale or retail. They work in order to get the goods from the factory to the people who want to use them. It would be useless to produce wireless sets if there were no trains to carry them to all parts of the country, and no shops in which the consumers could make their choice. Another large group of people work for the central government, maintaining law and order, administering the country, and serving in the armed forces, while others work for local councils. All this work is necessary, for there must be a system of government before production can be carried on. Other services are those of the people who teach in schools, or care for our health, or amuse us in theatres.

THOSE WHO HELP PRODUCTION WITHOUT ACTUALLY MAKING THINGS

Sometimes people who deal are called *middlemen*, as if it were a reproach to deal rather than to make. The reproach is not deserved if the middleman's business is well organised, and if he deals fairly. The work of merchants, retail shopkeepers, agents, brokers, bankers, insurance men, and other commercial workers is indispensable under present conditions, because it provides goods at the points where they are needed, and gives us the *useful distribution of articles after they are made.*

The banker helps buyers and sellers, and so takes a real part in production. The lawyer who interprets the law, or who settles a dispute, either by private negotiation or by conducting a lawsuit, is equally indispensable in the present state of society.

Insurance companies make it easier for firms to produce, for they need to worry less about possible disasters such as fire or shipwrecks.

No small part of the wealth of Britain arises from successful trading in commodities which we do not produce ourselves at all.

Before the Second World War, indeed, Britain was the greatest market in the world for the products of many foreign countries, such as wool, tea, cocoa, spices, tobacco, cotton, hides, india-rubber, and ivory. People came from all lands to buy these goods from our merchants. The trade gave employment to many of our people, and brought in money from abroad. Our ships, too, did much work for foreigners, carrying merchandise from one country to another, and our banks and insurance companies did much foreign business. The money which foreigners paid for the various services done for them helped to pay for imports of all the things which we need from abroad. The more of this trade we can recover year by year the better off we shall become.

Doing things for foreigners can be just as useful as making things for them. When we send them the produce of our factories, in the form of goods, they are known as *visible exports*. When we sell them our services, they are *invisible exports*, because they cannot be seen in the same way as manufactures can be. One important type of invisible export before the Second World War was the interest which many people obtained on money they had invested abroad. These interest payments meant that this country was able to buy more imports. Most of our foreign investments were sold during the war, so that the interest no longer comes in. Thus, an important source of foreign money disappeared.

HOW THE POPULATION GREW AS THE TRADE OF BRITAIN EXPANDED

Some people think home trade is very much more important than the foreign trade we carry on by means of our thousands of ships; but no one can make this mistake who understands how small the wealth of Britain would be if we depended on home trade only.

If we look at a map of the world we quickly see what a tiny place our country is, although it is the home of so many hard-working people. How is it, then, that our tiny country is able to support fifty million people ?

There was a time when Britain had a very small population indeed. When the Battle of Waterloo was fought in 1815, England, Scotland, Wales, and Ireland had between them about sixteen million people, so that in those days there was only one person in the country for three who exist in our time.

At the beginning of the nineteenth century our trade was very small, and the population lived chiefly on the nation's produce. It was only by building up a great oversea trade that we were able to support an increasing population.

We are sometimes apt to forget this, and to fancy that because we are now able to maintain so many people, we do it as a matter of course. Unfortunately, it is not the case that our living can be secured without an enormous foreign trade. If we did not earn plenty of imports by shipping enormous quantities of manufactures, and by dealing in foreign and colonial produce, *our population would shrink as quickly as it has grown.* Our working people would be driven to emigrate.

EVERYDAY COMFORTS WHICH WERE UNDREAMED OF A HUNDRED YEARS AGO

It is not only that we have now three times as many people as in the time of our great-great-grandfathers but that we enjoy, even after two World Wars, a much better standard of living than was dreamed of as possible a hundred years ago. In those old days men often despaired of good wheat bread being eaten regularly by common people, and all the comforts now considered commonplace—such as tea and chocolate, cheap mutton from New Zealand, coffee from tropical America—were things almost unheard of. When things happen commonly and regularly we get so used to them that we cease to wonder at their appearance, but the British people of 1815 would have been lost in wonder if they had suddenly seen in the shops, at prices at which they could buy, the thousand and one comforts which now exist.

THE HOME INDUSTRIES WHICH DEPEND ON MATERIALS FROM ABROAD

Let us think for a moment of the great trades of our country, which employ millions of people, and notice what are the foundations on which those trades have been built up.

There is the great staple trade of Lancashire, the cotton industry. It depends on a raw material which can only be grown in semi-tropical countries. If we did not earn that cotton by sending out other goods to pay for it, there would be starvation in Lancashire and in many other places which trade with Lancashire.

Or take the great woollen and worsted industries, which are so important to Yorkshire. The fleeces of our home sheep would not keep our wool trades going for more than a very small part of the year. Over a century ago we did actually work on our own wool almost entirely, and we used about a hundred million pounds of wool in a year. In a typical pre-war year we not only used up a hundred million pounds of home-grown wool, but also over 500 million pounds of imported wool. So that, if our oversea trade was cut off, *five out of six of our workers in wool would have nothing to do.*

THE WOOD FROM OTHER COUNTRIES WHICH HELPS TO BUILD OUR HOMES

Or let us turn to the building and furniture industries, which use very large quantities of hard and soft woods, such as fir, pine, oak, mahogany, walnut, rosewood, and so on.

Some of these timbers we have in very small quantities; others we have not at all. So great is our need for timber that we import millions of pounds' worth in a normal year ! If we could not get timber from other countries we should soon have to stop building, because our own forests are so small and it takes many years for newly-planted trees to mature to the age at which they may be expected to yield useful timber.

Not a few trades, like the cotton industry, are entirely dependent on oversea supplies.

The rubber manufacturing industry, for instance, which has been growing bigger in recent years, depends mainly on rubber obtained from tropical trees. All our road transport vehicles, buses, lorries, and cars, depend on imported petrol and oil to keep them running, as well as needing rubber tyres.

THE FORESTS OF OTHER LANDS WHICH PROVIDE US WITH PAPERS AND BOOKS

Then there are those very important materials, aluminium, gutta-percha, sulphur, and asbestos, which between them afford a livelihood to tens of thousands of manufacturing workers.

Another important example is the paper trade. The making of paper, dealing in it, printing on it, bookbinding, and dealing in books, journals, and newspapers, means the livelihood of some 400,000 people, and nearly the whole of this tremendous complexity of industries is based on materials which have to be imported.

Some paper is imported ready-made, but the rest is manufactured in this country out of wood pulp, esparto grass, and other materials. It is true that old paper can be pulped and used again to some extent, thus saving some imports, but without foreign supplies of paper or raw materials the living of a multitude of people would vanish.

The only way in which we can get all the food which our population needs, and the raw materials essential for keeping our industries busy, is to earn enough foreign money to pay for them by selling our manufactures, and our services, to foreigners. We must pay for our imports with exports. *The secret of maintaining a big population in our small islands is to get into the country, by outside trade, mountains of food and raw materials. This can only be done if there is a large volume of trade between nations.*

THE PEACE WHICH IS ESSENTIAL TO THE PROSPERITY OF THE WORLD

The natural wealth of the British Isles is limited. We have some things, such as coal, which other people are willing to buy, but we could pay for very few imports if we depended on what we can produce from materials of our own. Our greatest natural resources are the skill and training of our people. We reached a high standard of living as the workshop of the world, working for all nations and being well paid for doing it. When we export goods which have been made out of imported materials, we are really selling work, the work which has turned the materials into something different. In the same way, when our ships carry other people's cargo, or our insurance companies insure an American building against fire, it is British work which is being sold.

If we were selling a commodity which other people must have to keep their industries going, such as aluminium, then we would be certain of being able to earn foreign money, with which to pay for imports. As we can only sell our work, in competition with the work of other people all over the world, we are not so fortunately placed. The more trade there is between nations, the more opportunities we shall find of working for the world. Without peace, trade between nations is unlikely to grow. We have, therefore, to strive all the more earnestly to bring about that state of peace in the world without which good trade is impossible.

The Story of the Marvellous Plants that Cover the Earth

Fly-Orchis   Ground Pine   Dwarf Orchis

FLOWERS OF THE DOWNLAND

PERHAPS the most striking flower of the downland is the deadly nightshade, whose handsome but deadly black berries seem to have a fatal fascination for children, and sometimes even for older people, and have been responsible for not a few deaths and many illnesses.

At one time the plant was much more common than now, but on account of its deadly character it has been rooted out in many places. We read more about it on page 4289.

The black nightshade, a near relation, is also found growing on the downlands. It may be anything from a few inches to a foot high, and bears small white flowers very much like those of the woody nightshade, or bittersweet. These give place to round green berries which turn black when ripe, but the plant continues flowering all through the summer and autumn. It possesses narcotic properties, and is used for medicinal purposes.

The greater number of plants growing on the downlands are members of the composite family. Perhaps the commonest of these, though not the most beautiful, is the groundsel, a favourite food of many small birds. It is a smooth plant from six inches to a foot high, with deeply-toothed leaves and flower-heads in close clusters, and is generally self-pollinated.

Another closely allied plant is the hoary rag-wort. It grows about two feet high, has angular, cottony stems, and yellow flowers growing in a dense, flat head. Its leaves are cottony on the underside. A sister plant is the field flea-wort, which has a short, thick rootstock, its larger leaves springing on stalks from the root, while the upper ones are fewer and narrower. The flowers, with yellow florets, grow in small clusters, and the whole plant is shaggy and cottony.

A much more attractive flower than either of these is the great knapweed, called in some parts of the country by its old French name of matfelon. It is bigger than the black knapweed, or hardheads, and can easily be distinguished from that by its feather-like leaves. The large flower-heads are very conspicuous on account of their bright crimson florets.

The common saw-wort, another composite of the downland, is the only species of its order growing wild in Britain. In appearance it is something like a very slender knapweed, and it has small flower-heads with crimson florets.

The nipple-wort is another member of the composite family, the only species of its order growing in Britain. It is two or three feet high, has leaves something like those of the dandelion, and

BOTANY & ITS WONDERS · FLOWERS · TREES · HOW THINGS GROW

small but numerous flower-heads with from eight to twelve yellow florets. The hawkweed picris is also a slender plant with yellow flower-heads, but its stems are rough, with hooked bristles. Its sister plant, the bristly ox-tongue, is a stout, much-branched plant two or three feet high, also with yellow flowers, and with many prickles.

THE YELLOW FLOWERS AND TOOTHED LEAVES OF THE HAWK'S-BEARD

There are many hawk's-beards growing wild in Britain, but the one most commonly found on the downlands of the south is the fetid hawk's-beard, a very bristly plant with toothed leaves and heads of bright yellow flowers about three-quarters of an inch across.

Many of the composite flowers of the downland are very much alike in appearance, though belonging to different orders of the family. Another of them is the long-rooted cat's-ear, a hairy plant a foot high, with yellow-rayed flowers, looking very much like the dandelion; and still another is the hairy hawk-bit, or thrincia, half the height, but similar in appearance.

Quite a number of thistles, which also are members of the composite family, are found on the downlands. One of these, the milk-thistle, is not a native of the British Isles, but is now found growing in many parts. It is a stout, smooth plant that sometimes reaches a height of five feet, and its deep, glossy leaves, divided feather fashion, have milk-white veins and are often eaten when young as a salad. The stalks, also, may be eaten, and are very nutritious.

THE THISTLE WHICH IS SOMETIMES BOILED AND EATEN AS A VEGETABLE

As a matter of fact, the plant was formerly cultivated for culinary purposes, and in an old botanical work we are told that " the young shoots in the spring, cut close to the root with part of the stalk on, is one of the best boiling salads that is eaten, and surpasses the finest cabbage." The milk-thistle has spread over large areas of Australia, having been introduced there accidentally by the early settlers, and it forms a very troublesome weed.

It must be remembered that when beaten up or crushed in a mill to destroy the spines, all thistles form excellent food for cattle and horses, and in earlier days thistles were used to a great extent in Scotland for this purpose. The seeds of all of them, too, yield a good oil, and twelve pounds of the seed of cotton-thistle are said to produce by pressure three pounds of oil.

The woolly-headed plume-thistle is the stoutest of all our native thistles, but it is not so high as some of the others, rarely reaching more than five feet. The leaves are green and hairy on top and white and cottony underneath, and are deeply divided, the lobes ending in sharp, stout prickles. The flower-heads, which are clustered two or three together, are dull purple, and are often three inches across, being globular in shape, with thick, white wool and long spines.

The musk-thistle, though growing only two or three feet high, is a very handsome plant of the downland, having large, handsome flower-heads of crimson. The leaves are deeply lobed, and both they and the stems are woolly, the leaves having many protecting spines.

THE COMMON THISTLE THAT THE RABBITS LOVE TO EAT

One other thistle of the downland may be mentioned, the common sow-thistle, sometimes called the milk-thistle, though that name is better given to the plant mentioned above, and known to botanists as Mariana lactea. The sow-thistle is two or three feet high, and generally has smooth stems, the leaves being divided into lobes and bordered with prickly teeth. The flower-heads are rather small, and the florets are pale yellow. This plant is very common in Britain, and is widely distributed over the world. It is a favourite food of wild rabbits.

All the thistles are very succulent, and their stems contain a milky juice; but it must be remembered that they are very near relations of the lettuce, which we cultivate and eat for this very reason.

One other composite plant of the downland is very common, the goat's-beard, or, as it is called by country folk, Jack-go-to bed-at-noon. This curious name was given on account of the flower's habit of closing up at noon. The plant is smooth and erect, reaching a height of about two feet from the ground, and its leaves are long, narrow, and tapering like grass leaves. The solitary flower-heads are yellow, very much like those of the dandelion, and the fruits form in a feathery head like the dandelion's.

Of the rose family, several members grow on the downlands, chief among them being the sweet briar, a name that arouses poetic memories, for it is the eglantine of Shakespeare and other poets, though Milton, when he speaks of the "twisted eglantine," means the honeysuckle. It is a very close relation of the dog-rose, and is an erect, compact bush with many curved or hooked prickles. The leaflets are small and double-toothed, and the flowers pink and smaller than dog-roses.

The plant is equally distinguished from the other roses by the pleasant odour given out by the leaves when they are rubbed between the hands. This is due to an aromatic substance contained in small glands, scattered freely over the leaf stalks and underside and edges of the leaves.

Another member of the rose family, the salad burnet, forms a great deal of the turf on some of the dry chalk downs in the south of England. It is very nutritious for sheep and cattle, and was formerly much cultivated as a fodder plant. Burnet is another spelling of brunette, meaning brown, and the name was given because of the reddish-brown colour of the flower-heads, while the adjective salad was added on account of the use to which the leaves were formerly much put. They are still used in country places for salad purposes.

The drop-wort, another of the rose family, is a spiraea, and has very elegantly cut leaves and

DROP-WORT

YELLOW-WORT

BITING STONECROP
5267

crowded clusters of white, scentless flowers that are pink when they are in bud.

Many British orchids are found on the downlands, and the most attractive and ornamental of these is the bee-orchis, so called from the resemblance of the flower to a bee. It is abundant on some parts of the chalk downs in the south of England, and in many other parts of the country, though it is not found in Scotland. It was of this flower that the poet wrote:

> I sought the living bee to
> find, [bee.
> And found the picture of a

The plant is about a foot high, and the flowers grow from three to six together in a loose spike. No one can mistake this orchis for any other, for its appearance and its name are well linked. A close relation is the spider-orchis, a somewhat similar plant though rarer, with the sepals green instead of pink; and another relation is the fly-orchis, a slender species a foot high, with blossoms closely resembling the fly in appearance, even to the antennae.

A very common orchid of the downland is the sweet-scented orchis, so called because of the delicious fragrance of the flowers, greatly intensified in the evening and particularly after a shower of rain, when the odour can be detected at a considerable distance. A near relation, the butterfly-orchis of the heaths and woods, is also delightfully fragrant. The sweet-scented orchis grows a foot high, and its flower buds are red or deep lilac in colour.

The dark-winged, or dwarf, orchis rarely grows more than four or five inches high, and the stem is surmounted by a dense head of thirty or forty dark purple flowers. After a time the flowers get lighter and become almost white.

Autumn lady's tresses is another of the British orchids found growing on the downland. The root consists of two or three brownish, oblong, downy tubers, and from these spring a number of greyish-green oval leaves. The flower stem, usually six inches high, grows from the side of the tuft of leaves, and the small white flowers are arranged in a half spiral and are very fragrant in the evening.

HOW THE SAINFOIN CAME INTO ENGLAND IN THE SEVENTEENTH CENTURY

The pea family has several representatives on the downland. The common sainfoin, or cock's-head, is a handsome plant about two feet high, with leaves divided into from 17 to 25 leaflets, and the flowers, which grow in compact clusters, are rosy-red with darker veins, sometimes variegated with white. On the Continent of Europe it has been cultivated for hundreds of years, and was introduced as a fodder crop into England in the seventeenth century. It is now a crop of great importance in England. Crimson, or grass, vetchling is another member of the pea family found wild on woodlands, though less frequently than sainfoin. It is a beautiful plant and has small flowers, deep crimson in colour.

Of the ranunculus, or buttercup, family we have the beautiful Pasque flower, that blossoms about Eastertide, hence the name, and the equally beautiful Christmas rose. Though found growing wild, this is not really a native British plant, but comes from the south-east of Europe, and has escaped from cultivation. It is really a hellebore, a close relative of the green hellebore and the bear's-foot.

THE SWEET MARJORAM WHICH ESCAPES FROM THE GARDEN AND RUNS WILD

The sweet marjoram, one of the labiates, is another instance of an introduced plant escaping in many parts and running wild, though not a native. It really comes from the Mediterranean regions, but has its near relation in Britain in the wild marjoram, formerly cultivated as a pot-herb. Another labiate is the ground pine, or yellow bugle, a hairy, tufted plant from four to six inches high, with spreading, reddish-brown stem that smells strongly of turpentine. The leaves are much divided, and the flowers are yellow with red spots.

The biting stonecrop, or wall-pepper, a member of the stonecrop family, is a small plant with prostrate stems and golden-yellow flowers which stud the higher and drier parts of the downs with patches of gold a yard or more across. Like the other members of its family, its leaves are thick, this being a useful provision of Nature, enabling plants growing in dry situations to store up plenty of moisture.

The clustered bellflower is a good representative of the campanula, or bell-flower family, and is quite common on the downland. It is a stiff, erect plant, with a hairy stem a foot or more high, crowned with a cluster of funnel-shaped flowers, deep violet-purple in colour. The plant is, of course, a near relation of the harebell. Another campanula of the downland is the round-headed rampion, with deep blue flowers in globular heads, developing later into oblong fruits.

THE MEMBERS OF THE GENTIAN FAMILY WHOSE FLOWERS EXPAND BY DAY

Several gentians are found on the downlands, among them yellow-wort, with large, handsome yellow flowers that expand only between nine o'clock in the morning and four in the afternoon; tufted centaury, a tiny plant about three inches high; and common autumn gentian, an erect plant generally less than a foot high, often acquiring a livid green or purplish tinge. The pale purplish flowers only expand when the sun is shining brightly.

The representative of the teasel family on the downland is the small scabious, easily distinguished from the devil's-bit scabious by its more or less divided leaves of a lighter green, and by its lighter coloured flowers, which are lilac rather than purple. Of the mallow family we have the dwarf mallow, a smaller species than the common mallow. It has pale pink or pale blue flowers less than an inch across.

Among the figworts on the downland we find the great snapdragon, an antirrhinum, and the pale blue toadflax. The first of these is a handsome plant, with spikes of large pouched crimson, pink, or white flowers. The pale blue toadflax is a slender, erect plant a foot high, with pale lavender flowers, veined with purple.

Four pages of coloured pictures of Flowers of the Downland are given on 5393-96

The Story of the Peoples of All Nations and Their Homelands

The old town of Algeciras on the south coast of Spain

SPAIN AND HER STORY

THERE was a time when the Spanish nation was the most powerful in the world.

" In the sixteenth and seventeenth centuries," writes Mr. V. S. Pritchett in his masterly study The Spanish Temper, " the Spaniards were the master-race of the world, the founders of the first great empire to succeed the Roman Empire, more permanent in their conquests and administration than the French, who followed them, successful where the Germans have never yet succeeded, the true predecessors of the British Empire-makers of the eighteenth and nineteenth centuries."

In those days of glory her fleets commanded the newly-explored seas ; her adventurers explored and took possession of continents ; the riches of Spain were envied by all nations; her rulers regarded themselves as arbiters of the fate of Europe.

And before that period of her greatness, when Spain went out into the wide world to call nearly half of it her own, she had been at home a bulwark for Europe against the fierce Mohammedan aggression of Africa and Asia; she was, as she has always remained, a champion of Christendom.

In brief, the story of Spain is one of centuries of glory, succeeded by a long twilight of tragedy, which culminated in one of the most dreadful Civil Wars that ever tore a nation apart. But throughout that bitter struggle her people displayed the same pride and courage and virility that once built them an empire. Those same qualities are sustaining them in the building of a new and better Spain.

Spain, the biggest country in Europe after Russia and France, occupies four-fifths of the Iberian peninsula, with the mountain range of the Pyrenees separating her from the rest of the continent.

Its central part is high, a tableland averaging 2500 feet above sea level, isolated from the coasts by great mountain chains and itself split up by other ranges with saw-like peaks (sierras) soaring from 7000 to nearly 9000 feet.

These are not the loftiest peaks of Spain, which, indeed, is Europe's most mountainous country after Switzerland. The Pyrenees rise over 11,000 feet within the Spanish frontier line, and the most southerly range in Granada, the Sierra Nevada, parallel with the Mediterranean coast, also overtops 11,000 feet. But the central tableland is of such commanding importance in the history and the life of Spain that it must preface any notice of the country.

Through long periods Spain was divided

THE FIVE CONTINENTS & 100 NATIONS & RACES THAT INHABIT THEM

by its mountain ranges into separate kingdoms. Within these mountain enclosures, with differences of soil, climate, and human occupations, we also find differences of race and language. It was only slowly through the ages that Spain came to be regarded as a single country.

It is not unnatural, if we judge historically, that the peninsula is still divided between two countries—Spain and Portugal. It has been half a dozen countries, and deep differences continue in Spain itself, in human character, in race, language, habits, pursuits, and even in the food in common use. Spain has always been, and, indeed, is today, moulded humanly by the configuration of the land. That is the foundation of its chequered story, past and present.

THE SQUARE PENINSULA MORE THAN TWICE AS BIG AS THE UNITED KINGDOM

Spain, with Portugal, is an approximately square peninsula, over 550 miles from north to south, and 650 miles from east to west. Spain alone is of rather more than twice the extent of the United Kingdom, and Portugal is a little bigger than Ireland. Upwards of 28 million people inhabit Spain and the Canary and Balearic Islands.

The coast-line of Spain is generally bold; but from the mouth of the River Guadiana nearly to Gibraltar, and again past Alicante and Valencia on the Mediterranean side, it runs low. Nearly the whole of the coast of Portugal is low, and the slope of the great mass of the peninsula, except the north-east, is from east to west with a deflection towards the south-west. That is the general lie of most of the mountain ranges, and of all the chief rivers except the Ebro in the north-east.

Across the north of Spain the Pyrenees extend westward through the ancient kingdom of Navarre, the Basque country, Asturias, and Galicia to the open Atlantic. This range takes the general name of the Cantabrian Mountains.

The eastern end of the Pyrenees spreads broadly into Spain, and almost covers the rugged province of Catalonia. Between Navarre and Catalonia the Pyrenees sink southward by gradual slopes down into the eastward-sloping valley of the Ebro, in which lay the old kingdom of Aragon. This whole Pyrenean mountain land, with its extension westward to the

Atlantic seaboard, is a northern region quite different from any other in Spain. Rain falls plentifully in the mountains north and north-west ; indeed, there is too much rather than too little rain, and the mountains of Portugal, Galicia, and Asturias rob inland Spain of the treasure brought by the Atlantic clouds. The climate of northern Spain is mild. It is a land of grass and flowers and forests.

MOUNTAINS THAT FORM THE WATERSHED OF A TREELESS VALLEY

Southward of the Ebro valley, from the neighbourhood of the town of Burgos to the province of Valencia, runs to the south-east a mass of mountains forming on one side the watershed of the bare, treeless valley of the Ebro, and on the other side the lofty eastern edge of the great central tableland down whose westward tilt the long rivers Douro, Tagus, and Guadiana flow to the Atlantic.

This tableland, lofty, wind-swept, deficient in moisture, is crossed from east to west by two ranges of mountains. Southward of the River Douro, which has the Cantabrian Range as its northern watershed, is the principal central mountain range of Spain, passing under various names through the middle of the tableland. The best-known part, north of Madrid, is the Sierra de Guadarrama. The range extends into central Portugal as the Serra da Estrella.

THE OLD KINGDOM IN WHICH THE SPAIN OF TODAY BEGAN

On this tableland, north of the range, were the ancient kingdom of Leon, which also extends into the northern mountains and the basin of the River Minho, and the kingdom of Old Castile, around which Spain finally gathered into a more or less united Christian nation.

South of the Sierra de Guadarrama, and extending to the Sierra Morena, was New Castile, stretching south-eastward to Murcia by the plain of La Mancha, and westward to Portugal across the impoverished sheep-walks of Estremadura. Midway through New Castile run from east to west the Mountains of Toledo, forming the watershed between the basins of the River Tagus and the River Guadiana.

South of the Sierra Morena was the great Moorish province of Andalusia, crossed by mountain ranges, of which the chief is the lofty Sierra Nevada, and drained by the

HOW THE ORANGES COME TO US

PICKING ORANGES IN VALENCIA

GRADING THE ORANGES

WRAPPING UP THE ORANGES IN TISSUE PAPER

PACKING ORANGES IN CASES FOR EXPORT

LOADING SHIPS IN THE DOCKS AT VALENCIA

Guadalquiver, the Great River of the Moors, or Wady-el-Kebir.

Here we are in a quite different Spain, the Spain of Seville, Cordova, Malaga, and Granada, of hot summers, warm winters, sub-tropical growths, rich and beautiful, a land of finely ornamental architecture, coming from a past civilisation of rare taste alien to the central and northern parts of the country. It is a region which could be the natural home of a people reared on the neighbouring African continent, and here for centuries ruled the Moors at the time when they had reached the highest stage of their civilisation.

THE PORT FOUNDED BY THE PHOENICIANS OF THIRTY CENTURIES AGO

The first accounts we have of the people living in the peninsula came from the Greeks, Phoenicians, and Romans, who visited the country and described its people as a small, dark-skinned race called Iberians. There is doubt as to what finally happened to these Iberians from whom the peninsula takes its name, but it is widely held that the Basques of the south-western Pyrenean slopes are the remnant of these ancient inhabitants, who have elsewhere been absorbed by other races.

The earliest Greek and Phoenician seafarers came to trade and not to stay, except that as early as 1100 B.C. the Phoenicians are credited with the founding of the port of Cadiz. Much later, when the Phoenicians had founded Carthage as their chief commercial centre and were repelled from trade with Italy by the Romans, they developed a trade in Spain and founded there a New Carthage, which is now the seaport Cartagena. Later still, in their wars with Rome, they advanced overland through Spain, where they gathered recruits, and passed through France to attack Italy. The Romans, returning the attack, cleared the Carthaginians out of Spain, and eventually conquered the whole country, which they held for over 400 years.

HOW SPAIN HELPED ROME IN THE DAYS OF HER DECLINE

Whom did they find there? By the time of the Roman conquest, and perhaps long before, Celtic tribes had entered the country and had apparently mixed with the Iberian tribes already there.

That the Roman influence thoroughly dominated Spain is proved in several ways. Signs of their works, in aqueducts and irrigation, remain to this day. From Spain came some of their most famous rulers and writers—the great emperors Trajan and Hadrian; and notable authors like Seneca the Younger, Lucan, Martial, and Quintilian, the famous expert in education. Spain, in fact, imparted vigour to declining Rome, and Latin became so firmly the foundation of the common speech in the peninsula that it was never challenged.

After the withdrawal of the Roman garrisons, early in the fifth century, various German or Gothic tribes poured across the Pyrenees and overran the country, but were soon absorbed by Roman and Christian influences. They played a very important part in Spain for nearly 300 years, and added new elements to the Iberian and Celtic strains of population.

In 711 came the most sensational of all the invasions of Spain. In that year a Moslem Berber chief named Tarik, helped by the enemies of the Gothic King of Spain, Roderic, crossed the Strait of Gibraltar, and in eight years overran nearly the whole peninsula. The Moslems then passed on into France, but were defeated by the Frankish general Charles the Hammer and flung back into Spain, where they ruled absolutely for over 400 years, and ruled as vassals to Spanish kings for 350 years more.

THE MEN OF THE NORTH WHO HELD THEIR OWN AGAINST THE ARABS

The history of Spain through the earlier centuries of Mohammedan occupation was one of the emergence of Christian kingdoms in the north, and the slow recovery of the country State by State. The mountaineers of the Cantabrian Range never were subdued by the Arab invaders. The Basques, and the men of Navarre, Asturias, and Galicia rallied at once when the enemy had passed by, and in these districts and in Leon, Castile, Aragon, and Catalonia Christianity rose again, while a lingering warfare went on for centuries with the Moslem power in southern Spain.

The weakness of Moorish government in Spain was that it was as divided as the Christian kingdoms of the north. The invaders had been Arabs and Berbers. The Arabs were the ruling caste and despised the Berbers from the Algerian hills. To the Berbers the Arabs, or Moors, gave the bleak and inhospitable central Spanish plateau, and reserved for themselves the warm, rich valleys of the south.

WORKS AND WORKERS OF SPAIN

A GREAT STEELWORKS AT BILBAO

GIRLS AT WORK IN A POTTERY
FACTORY IN HUELVA

MAKING MATS AND BASKETS OF
ESPARTO GRASS IN ALMERIA

A SCENE IN A
CORK YARD

A PYRAMID OF SALT
IN CADIZ

WOMEN OF MURCIA GATHER-
ING MULBERRY LEAVES

The strength of the Arab rulers of Andalusia was that they were tolerant in religion and easy-going in taxation. So the Christians of the south found it quite possible to live in comfort there, and the Jews, who formed an appreciable and valuable part of the population, had a pleasanter life than they had known under the Gothic kings. The conquered people of the south therefore were by no means eager to change from a not uncomfortable toleration to the unknown rule of men from over the northern mountains, who were certainly less advanced in taste and culture than the Moors who were beautifying the cities of southern Spain.

A YEAR FAMOUS IN THE HISTORY OF SPAIN AND THE WORLD

The beginning of comparatively modern history in Spain came with the marriage of King Ferdinand of Aragon with Queen Isabella of Leon and Castile. It brought all Spain, except Granada, under a single crown, and Granada, the last Moorish stronghold, was captured in 1492, the year when Columbus left Spain to cross the Atlantic. Before that great event the joint sovereigns had established the frightful Spanish Inquisition with the object of bringing all the people of Spain under one religion as well as one monarchy.

After Ferdinand's death Spain had the additional misfortune of falling under the government of Charles the Fifth, who dragged her into European wars with which she had no real concern, and Charles's successor, Philip the Second, the man whose portraits are so familiar to us, and who married our English Queen Mary, carried religious persecution into the Low Countries, which he inherited from his father.

THE GREAT DISCOVERY THAT BROUGHT WEALTH AND POWER TO SPAIN

Philip's belief that he had a religious mission of conquest led him to attempt the invasion and defeat of England, and for that purpose he gathered his Great Armada, the most formidable fleet which up to that time had ever sailed the seas.

Spain was now at the height of her power, and unquestionably the leading nation of the world. She had secured enormous riches in gold and silver from the newly-found Western World, which the Pope, regarding it as his gift, had committed to Spain's guardianship. Her ships commanded the open seas by sheer power of numbers. The Hapsburg Emperor Charles the Fifth had trained her armies for war, and they were renowned for discipline and bravery. The unlimited scope for discovery and conquest in America aroused the love of adventure in her sons. She had to a large extent cast out the Moors and the Jews who had brought prosperity to southern Spain. The riches and industries of the Low Countries were at her mercy, and there her army, under the greatest and sternest of her generals, waited to cross over to conquer England.

No nation was ever nearer being master of the world than Spain at that moment; and the Spaniards knew it. They were as proud at heart as ever ancient Rome was in its days of almost universal conquest. The whole Iberian peninsula was theirs, for Portugal had been mastered and annexed. She also had large possessions in North Africa and Italy.

WHEN SPAIN WAS A NATION OUTWARDLY STRONG BUT INWARDLY WEAK

But even at that time a really thoughtful survey of the condition of Spain would have told a different tale, for Spain's ambitious claims, and her methods of stamping out all opposition by force, had in them the seeds of disaster.

The wealth she seized had had a demoralising effect on herself, for it led to gross extravagance, forced up prices, and did not stimulate the productive industry at home which lays firmly the foundations of prosperity. The many kinds of people in the different regions of the peninsula, who had little communication with each other over her rugged mountains, and were harassed by taxation to support her ambitious schemes abroad, were uneasy under the despotic rule which roughly clamped them together as one nation. Outwardly Spain looked magnificently strong; inwardly she was badly prepared to withstand the sudden shock that was to come.

That shock fell on her with startling effect when her mighty Armada, shattered by battle and tempest, defeated and dispersed, failed to make the least impression on England. It was a united England that faced the Spanish foe. Her fleet put out into the Channel to defy the might of Philip, once the husband of an English queen, and now bent on the religious conquest of England. But England was

LIFE AMONG THE PEOPLE OF SPAIN

SELLING GOAT'S MILK
IN BARCELONA

A CATTLEMAN OF
ANDALUSIA

GOING TO MARKET
NEAR CARTAGENA

REAPERS AT WORK IN THE FIELDS OF CASTILE

A DONKEY CART IN THE STREETS
OF BARCELONA

A MAN OF
ALICANTE

A WATER SELLER IN
VALENCIA

A QUAINT MOUNTAIN
CART

A PEASANT WOMAN
OF ALICANTE

OXEN HAULING SEAWEED FOR
USE AS MANURE

sound at heart. Not so the Spain of those days ; under the impact of defeat she crumbled from within.

After the Armada's defeat, the decline of Spanish power was swift. She was impoverished by foreign wars and torn by internal disturbances, and Portugal regained her independence. When England had plainly taken from Spain the command of the seas in the eighteenth century she allied herself with France only to meet with defeat after defeat, and at last to find herself betrayed by Napoleon, and obliged to submit temporarily to the weakest of his brothers as her king. Then it was to England that she looked for help, and for years English, Spanish, and Portuguese armies fought the French to and fro among the mountains of the Peninsula all the way between Lisbon, the Pyrenees, and to the gates of Toulouse beyond.

THE SPANISH COLONIES BREAK AWAY FROM THE HOMELAND

Early in the 19th century Spain lost her colonies across the seas. Those immense regions of the American continent owned by Spain by right of discovery and conquest, speaking the Spanish tongue, and occupied considerably by men of Spanish race, took early opportunities of breaking away from the colonising Mother country. Mexico, Central America, and South America (except small parts owned by Britain, Holland, and France), all became independent countries and republics.

Before the nineteenth century closed, the last of the Spanish Indies, West and East, had reached such a state of confusion, through incessant war with Spain, that the United States of America took up their cause, and forcibly gave them representative government. Thus Spain lost Cuba, Puerto Rico, and the Philippine Islands, the final fragments of her once vast dominions overseas. Now, counting the Balearic and Canary Islands, which are now provinces of Spain itself, little of her colonial empire remains besides a part of Morocco. Of this we read on another page (see Index).

THE UNHAPPY YEARS OF THE TWENTIETH CENTURY

Almost throughout the whole of the 19th century Spain had been a sorely troubled land, torn with dissension, weakened by long years of war, and lacking rulers wise and strong enough to meet drastically changed circumstances. And the early years of the 20th century proved no better. Disorder followed disorder ; riots succeeded riots, with Barcelona the great storm centre ; government succeeded government.

Despite German attempts to induce her to fight the Allies, Spain remained neutral during the First World War ; but internally her condition grew steadily worse. A military defeat in Morocco in 1921 led to further unrest and in 1923, after an army revolt against the Government, constitutional rule was abolished and a dictatorship was set up under the crown.

General Primo de Rivera held sway as dictator for nearly seven years. He restored public order, suppressed rival factions with a firm hand, and did much to improve communications, public works, and the general standard of living. But the economic crisis of 1929, felt by almost every nation in the world, led to his downfall and he had to flee the country.

A weak emergency government took over, and then came the end of the monarchy. The claim of Catalonia for independence and a growing will for political freedom among the more educated Spaniards led to one of the most surprising revolutions Europe has seen.

DICTATORSHIP FOLLOWED BY THE DECLARATION OF A REPUBLIC

It really began with a monster demonstration in a bullring at Madrid where representatives of all the progressive parties met peaceably and warned the king of the coming change. In the April of 1931 a Republic was proclaimed.

King Alphonso left the country, and a Chamber of Deputies was elected, and a democratic Constitution was framed.

At first the Government, or Cortes, did well, especially in education, a vital need for a land in which half the population could neither read nor write. Primary education was made free but compulsory, while over 50 secondary schools were established to prepare pupils for the university. (Despite all the difficulties, educational progress has been maintained. Spain now has nearly 60,000 State elementary schools, including upwards of 120 secondary schools.)

The Communists and Anarchists whose chief centre was at Barcelona, the capital of Catalonia, were regarded with suspicion by the Dictators of Italy and Germany and real hatred by the parties of the Right in Spain. When, therefore, an able army chief, General Franco, revolted against the Republican Government in 1936, he was supported by troops from Italy, skilled technicians from Germany, and tanks and aeroplanes from both countries. For nearly three years a desperate civil conflict raged, the great majority of the Spanish people displaying a heroism and disregard of suffering which astonished the world.

The civil war ended in April 1939, when the Republicans in Madrid surrendered

Wonderful strides have been taken to provide new homes for citizens, for farmworkers, for fishermen.

Projects for soil improvement, drainage, irrigation, and electric power are all under way as part of a vast Land Settlement scheme which seeks to re-create the agriculture of this great country. On these developments Spain's standard of living must be largely dependent, for she is predominantly an agricultural country. She has wheat and wine and oil and one of the world's best climates for sub-tropical fruits throughout her southern and eastern

WATER-CARRIERS
OF CACERES

OLD PEASANTS OF THE
BASQUE COUNTRY

A PEASANT AND HIS
WIFE TAKE A RIDE

to the Nationalists. Then the British and French Governments recognised the authoritarian Government of General Franco.

He has continued to keep a strong hold on affairs, and under his rule the Spanish people are tackling the immense task of restoring their ancient homeland.

An immense task indeed, for Spain is not a rich country. She has appreciable mineral wealth, much of it as yet undeveloped ; but her iron deposits in the north, and those of lead and copper are approaching exhaustion. She also has industries capable of expansion, though they lack an adequate home market.

But despite all the difficulties, the task is being tackled with a will. Since the civil war, which led to terrible havoc, new roads, new bridges, new schools, and new health centres have been built.

provinces, but is in sore need of fertilisers. Alicante gives a name to the world for grapes, Valencia for raisins, and Barcelona for nuts, and the Spanish cork forests bottle the wines of the world.

Spain has extensive hilly tracts suitable for sheep-rearing and cattle-breeding, and the aggregate of her pastoral products is very considerable. In short, Spain is richly endowed with a wide variety of gifts, though her climate is tantalisingly bleak or baking on her lofty central tableland, and spreads reminders of African deserts about her southern provinces.

But the idea of energetic development for many years was almost restricted to the north-eastern province of Catalonia. In recent years the Falangist Party, working through national syndicates, have been trying to invigorate industry—shipbuilding, for example. There is a system of

Old Age Pensions, Family Allowances, and Health Insurance, about eighty-five million pounds being paid out in 1950. To encourage the increase of the population, too, every baby born receives a Post Office Savings Bank book with one peseta to start it.

For the visitor the country is extraordinarily attractive, because of the varied character of its scenery, the life of the people, and the interest of the survivals from a time when cultured Mohammedanism made its incursion into Europe.

SAN SEBASTIAN AND THE RICH DISTRICT OF THE MOUNTAINOUS NORTH

Spain has about 11,000 miles of railway, two-thirds being owned by the State. The railway entrances to Spain are west and east of the Pyrenees, the western line leading to the mineral-bearing northern province, and onward to Madrid in the middle of the central tableland; and the eastern line from Toulouse to the vigorous manufacturing district of Catalonia, with its dominating city of Barcelona, which has over one-and-a-quarter million people.

Following the northern line, the beautiful seaside resort of San Sebastian is soon reached. Farther westward are the mineral exporting port of Bilbao in the Basque country, the port of Santander, the mineral town of Oviedo in Asturias, and in Galicia the ports of Corunna and Vigo. This is the rich district of the mountainous north between the Cantabrian Range and the sea. Railways from the prosperous north meet at the inland junction of Palencia. Not far away is Burgos, once the capital of Old Castile and famed for its Gothic cathedral.

THE CENTRAL TOWN WHERE ALL THE RAILWAYS MEET

Before reaching Madrid, the southward line passes through Valladolid, a university town. The famous university town of Salamanca lies more to the westward. Segovia, north of the central mountain chain, has some magnificent Roman remains. South of Madrid is the city of Toledo, once famous for its sword blades, long the stronghold of Moslem power on the Castilian plateau, and later capital of Castile.

Madrid, built as a central capital, has increased its population to over a million-and-a-half largely as the railway junction for the middle of Spain. Its climate, changing from great heat to great cold, and its situation on a bare and unproductive country, are disadvantages, but round it official Spain revolves. Its picture galleries are among the most famous in Europe, the homes of masterpieces by Velasquez, Murillo, and Goya, as well as works by a modern school of outstanding brilliance in colouring.

The eastern railway system of Spain passes through Barcelona, by far the most prosperous and up-to-date of Spanish cities, a crowded manufacturing centre for cotton, lace, woollen, and linen goods, as well as a much frequented port. The towns farther south in the great fruit-growing districts are Valencia, Alicante, Murcia, and the ancient seaport Cartagena. Murcia is a mineral producing district, especially rich in lead. The chief town in the Ebro Valley is Saragossa. It has a university, and lives in history for its heroic defence against the French in the Peninsular War.

THE FINE BUILDINGS THAT OUTSHONE THE GLORIES OF BAGHDAD

Southern Spain has iron, copper, coal, and lead. To the visitor its attractions are the fine scenery and the amazing wealth of architecture left by the Moors in the cities they beautified—Seville, Granada, and Cordova. Other Southern cities are Malaga, Cadiz, renowned in British history, and Jerez.

The Alcazar, the Cathedral with its Giralda Tower, and Pilate's House at Seville; the Alhambra at Granada; and the Mezquita, or Mosque, at Cordova, built to outshine the glories of Damascus and Baghdad, are among the architectural wonders of the world.

There can be no denying that for a visitor Spain is one of the most rewarding and fascinating countries in Europe. Spaniards have always taken great pride in showing visitors these venerable monuments. But Spaniards nowadays take even greater pride in the new developments that have taken shape in recent years, in the face of incredible hardships and difficulties.

The noble buildings of the past reflect glories of a bygone age. The vast modern developments reflect the spirit of a new Spain—a Spain determined to forge ahead and take her rightful place among the more progressive nations of the world.

The maps of Spain will be found with the maps of Portugal in the section beginning on page 5403

THE WONDER LAND OF SPAIN

A QUIET COURT IN THE ALHAMBRA, THE OLD MOORISH PALACE AT GRANADA

MODERN DWELLINGS FOR WORKERS NEAR THE TOWN OF VIGO

THE BEAUTIFUL FAÇADE OF THE CHURCH
OF SAN PABLO, VALLADOLID

THE ALCAZAR AT SEGOVIA, BUILT IN THE
FOURTEENTH CENTURY

A MODERN DAM AT CÁRCERES

BLAST FURNACES AT SAGUNTO IN VALENCIA

THE CATHEDRAL AND THE OLD STONE BRIDGE ACROSS THE EBRO AT SARAGOSSA

THE ALCAZAR AT SEVILLE

THE GATE OF SANTA MARIA, BURGOS

TOLEDO BRIDGE ACROSS THE MANZANARES, MADRID

A MARKET PLACE IN SEGOVIA

ALICANTE, THE GREAT SEAPORT
OF VALENCIA

PUERTA DEL PUENTE, CORDOVA, A TRIUMPHAL
ARCH ERECTED IN THE TIME OF PHILIP II

THE PORT OF SAN SEBASTIAN ON THE BAY OF BISCAY

A STREET MARKET BY THE RIVER SEGURA
IN MURCIA

THE RAMBLA, THE MAIN STREET OF OLD
BARCELONA

THE PROVINCIAL MUSEUM, VALLADOLID

THE UNIVERSITY AT VALLADOLID

THE ROAD LEADING TO THE OASIS AT ELCHE, AN OLD MOORISH TOWN A FEW MILES FROM ALICANTE

THE HOUSE IN VALLADOLID WHERE
COLUMBUS DIED

THE ALHAMBRA AT
GRANADA

THE OLD CITY OF SALAMANCA ON THE RIVER TORMES

THE WONDERFUL ROMAN AQUEDUCT
NEAR TARRAGONA

THE HILL CITY OF
TOLEDO

THE CATHEDRAL AND ARCHBISHOP'S PALACE
AT VALENCIA

THE WALLED CITY OF
AVILA

THE RIVER GUADALQUIVIR AT SEVILLE

THE SPLENDID BRIDGE ACROSS THE GUADALQUIVIR, AT CORDOVA, BUILT BY THE ARABS IN
THE EIGHTH CENTURY

A CORNER OF THE TOWN OF BILBAO

THE SEAPORT OF MALAGA

THE ANCIENT PORT OF CARTAGENA

THE CARRERA DE DARRO, GRANADA

A BRIDGE ACROSS THE PISUERGA AT VALLADOLID

THE MEDICAL BUILDING IN THE UNIVERSITY OF MADRID

ON THE ROAD TO MADRID, WITH ITS MODERN BUILDINGS AND ROYAL PALACE

INSTITUTES OF GEOLOGY, GEOGRAPHY, AND FHARMACOLOGY, UNIVERSITY OF MADRID

BLOCKS OF MODERN FLATS ON THE OUTSKIRTS OF MADRID

The pictures in these pages are by courtesy of the Spanish Embassy in London, The Exclusive News Agency, Messrs. Underwood and Underwood, and others

One Thousand Poems of All Times and All Countries

HENRY HUDSON'S LAST VOYAGE

Is anything in all the history of the sea sadder than the story of Henry Hudson, turned adrift by his cruel crew with his little boy and two faithful men? Here an American, Dr. Henry Van Dyke (1852–1933) imagines Hudson talking in his boat on Hudson Bay on the last day that history heard of him, June 22, 1611. We seem to catch the throb in Henry Hudson's voice as he says, "My little shipmate, come and lean your head against my knee." Hudson's name is written on the map of the world—in Hudson Bay, Hudson River, Hudson Island, and Hudson Bay Territories.

ONE sail in sight upon the lonely sea,
    And only one! For never ship but
mine
Has dared these waters. We were first,
My men, to battle in between the bergs
And floes to these wide waves. This gulf
    is mine;
I name it! and that flying sail is mine!
And there, hull-down below that flying sail,
The ship that staggers home is mine, mine,
    mine!
My ship Discoverie!

                The sullen dogs
Of mutineers, the bitches' whelps that
    snatched
Their food and bit the hand that nourished
    them,
Have stolen her. You ingrate Henry
    Greene,
I picked you from the gutter of Hounds-
    ditch,
And paid your debts, and kept you in my
    house,
And brought you here to make a man of
    you!
You, Robert Juet, ancient, crafty man,
Toothless and tremulous, how many times
Have I employed you as a master's mate
To give you bread? And you, Abacuck
    Prickett,
You sailor-clerk, you salted Puritan,
You knew the plot and silently agreed,
Salving your conscience with a pious lie!

Yes, all of you—hounds, rebels, thieves!
    Bring back
My ship!

          Too late—I rave—they cannot hear
My voice: and, if they heard, a drunken
    laugh
Would be their answer; for their minds
    have caught
The fatal firmness of the fool's resolve,
That looks like courage, but is only fear.
They'll blunder on, and lose my ship, and
    drown,
Or blunder home to England and be
    hanged.
Their skeletons will rattle in the chains
Of some tall gibbet on the Channel cliffs,
While passing mariners look up and say:
"Those are the rotten bones of Hudson's
    men
Who left their captain in the frozen
    North!"

O God of justice, why hast Thou ordained
Plans of the wise and actions of the
    brave
Dependent on the aid of fools and cowards?

Look—there she goes—her topsails in
    the sun
Gleam from the ragged ocean edge, and
    drop
Clean out of sight! So let the traitors go
Clean out of mind! We'll think of braver
    things!

POEMS · SONGS · BALLADS · VERSES AND RHYMES WITH MUSIC

Come closer in the boat, my friends. John
King,
You take the tiller, keep her head nor'-
west.
You, Philip Staffe, the only one who chose
Freely to share our little shallop's fate
Rather than travel in the hell-bound ship—
Too good an English sailor to desert
Your crippled comrades—try to make
them rest
More easy on the thwarts. And John,
my son,
My little shipmate, come and lean your
head
Against my knee. Do you remember still
The April morn in Ethelburga's Church,
Five years ago, when side by side we
kneeled
To take the Sacrament with all our men
Before the Hopewell left St. Catherine's
Docks
On our first voyage? It was then I vowed
My sailor-soul and yours to search the sea
Until we found the water-path that leads
From Europe into Asia.

                I believe
That God has poured the ocean round His
world,
Not to divide, but to unite the lands.
And all the English captains that have
dared
In little ships to plough uncharted waves—
Davis and Drake, Hawkins and Frobisher,
Raleigh and Gilbert—all the other names—
Are written in the chivalry of God
As men who served His purpose. I would
claim
A place among that knighthood of the sea;
And I have earned it, though my quest
should fail,
For, mark me well, the honour of our life
Derives from this: to have a certain aim
Before us always, which our will must
seek
Amid the peril of uncertain ways.
Then, though we miss the goal, our search
is crowned
With courage, and we find along our path
A rich reward of unexpected things.
Press towards the aim; take fortune as it
fares!

I know not why, but something in my heart
Has always whispered: " Westward seek
your goal! "
Three times they sent me east, but still
I turned
The bowsprit west, and felt along the floes

Of ruttling ice along the Greenland coast,
And down the rugged shore of Newfound-
land,
And past the rocky capes and wooded bays
Where Gosnold sailed—like one who feels
his way
With outstretched hands across a darkened
room,
I groped among the inlets and the isles
To find the passage to the Land of Spice.
I have not found it yet—but I have found
Things worth the finding!

              Son, have you forgot
Those mellow autumn days, two years ago,
When first we sent our little ship Half
Moon—
The flag of Holland floating at her peak—
Across a sandy bar, and sounded in
Among the channels to a goodly bay
Where all the navies of the world could
ride?
A fertile island that the red man called
Manhattan lay above the bay: the land
Around was beautiful and friendly fair,
But never land was fair enough to hold
The seaman from the calling of the sea.
And so we bore to westward of the isle,
Along a mighty inlet, where the tide
Was troubled by a downward-flowing
flood
That seemed to come from far away—
perhaps
From some mysterious gulf of Tartary?
Inland we held our course; by palisades
Of naked rock; by rolling hills adorned
With forests rich in timber for great ships;
Through narrows where the mountains
shut us in
With frowning cliffs that seemed to bar the
stream;
And then through open reaches where the
banks
Sloped to the water gently, with their fields
Of corn and lentils smiling in the sun.
Ten days we voyaged through that placid
land,
Until we came to shoals, and sent a boat
Upstream to find—what I already knew—
We travelled on a river, not a strait.

But what a river! God has never poured
A stream more royal through a land more
rich.
Even now I see it flowing in my dream,
While coming ages people it with men
Of manhood equal to the river's pride.
I see the wigwams of the red men changed
To ample houses, and the tiny plots

Of maize and green tobacco broadened out
To prosperous farms, that spread o'er hill
    and dale
The many-coloured mantle of their crops.
I see the terraced vineyard on the slope
Where now the fox-grape loops its tangled
    vine,
And cattle feeding where the red deer roam,
And wild bees gathered into busy hives
To store the silver comb with golden sweet:
And all the promised land begins to flow
With milk and honey. Stately manors rise
Along the banks, and castles top the hills,
And little villages grow populous with
    trade,
Until the river runs as proudly as the Rhine,
The thread that links a hundred towns
    and towers!

Now, looking deeper in my dreams, I see
A mighty city covering the isle
They call Manhattan, equal in her state
To all the older capitals of earth—
The gateway city of a golden world—
A city girt with masts, and crowned with
    spires,
And swarming with a million busy men,
While to her open door across the bay
The ships of all the nations flock like doves.
My name will be remembered there, the
    world
Will say, " This river and this isle were
    found
By Henry Hudson, on his way to seek
The North-West Passage."

                Yes, I seek it still—
My great adventure and my guiding star!
For look ye, friends, our voyage is not
    done;
We hold by hope as long as life endures!
Somewhere among these floating fields of
    ice,
Somewhere along this westward widening
    bay,
Somewhere beneath this luminous northern
    night,
The channel opens to the Farthest East—
I know it—and some day a little ship
Will push her bowsprit in, and battle
    through!
And why not ours—tomorrow—who can
    tell ?
The lucky chance awaits the fearless
    heart!
These are the longest days of all the year;
The world is round and God is everywhere,
And while our shallop floats we still can
    steer.

So point her up, John King, nor'-west by
    north,
We'll keep the honour of a certain aim
Amid the peril of uncertain ways,
And sail ahead, and leave the rest to God.

DIRGE FOR A SOLDIER

This poem from an American pen, as the third verse indicates, was written by George H. Boker, who died in 1890, and whose chief writing was in the form of drama.

CLOSE his eyes; his work is done.
    What to him is friend or foeman,
Rise of moon or set of sun,
    Hand of man or kiss of woman?

    Lay him low, lay him low,
In the clover or the snow!
What cares he ? He cannot know.
    Lay him low!

As man may he fought his fight,
    Proved his truth by his endeavour;
Let him sleep in solemn night,
    Sleep for ever and for ever.

Fold him in his country's stars,
    Roll the drum and fire the volley !
What to him are all our wars?
    What but death bemocking folly?

Leave him to God's watching eye;
    Trust him to the hand that made
        him.
Mortal love sweeps idly by;
    God alone has power to aid him.

    Lay him low, lay him low,
In the clover or the snow!
What cares he ? He cannot know.
    Lay him low !

SONG

The English language has no more exquisite little love song than this by Hartley Coleridge, the fanciful-minded son of his more famous father. It shows how true love can endow with beauty the friend who is admired above all others.

SHE is not fair to outward view
    As many maidens be;
Her loveliness I never knew
    Until she smiled on me.
Oh, then I saw her eye was bright,
A well of love, a spring of light.

But now her looks are coy and cold,
    To mine they ne'er reply,
And yet I cease not to behold
    The love-light in her eye:
Her very frowns are fairer far
Than smiles of other maidens are.

THE NORMAN BARON

In this fine poem by Longfellow the poet has taken a subject from the history of England in the Middle Ages. He prefixes to his poem a passage from a French history of the Conquest of England which may be translated thus : " In those moments of life when the thoughts of man become more calm, and the voice of selfishness speaks less strongly than the voice of reason, when overcome by domestic sorrow, by illness, or under the shadow of death, the barons sometimes repented of having enslaved the people, and felt they had done a thing displeasing to God, Who had created all men in His image." The poet perhaps overpraises the baron's death-bed repentance.

In his chamber, weak and dying,
　Was the Norman baron lying;
Loud without the tempest thundered,
　And the castle turret shook.

In this fight was Death the gainer,
Spite of vassal and retainer,
And the lands his sires had plundered,
　Written in the Domesday Book.

By his bed a monk was seated,
Who in a humble voice repeated
Many a prayer and paternoster
　From the missal on his knee;

And, amid the tempest pealing,
Sounds of bells came faintly stealing,
Bells that from the neighbouring kloster
　Rang for the Nativity.

In the hall the serf and vassal
Held that night their Christmas wassail;
Many a carol, old and saintly,
　Sang the minstrels and the waits.

And so loud these Saxon gleemen
Sang to slaves the songs of freemen
That the storm was heard but faintly,
　Knocking at the castle gates

Till at length the lays they chanted
Reached the chamber terror-haunted,
Where the monk, with accents holy,
　Whispered at the baron's ear.

Tears upon his eyelids glistened
As he paused awhile and listened,
And the dying baron slowly
　Turned his weary head to hear.

Wassail for the kingly stranger
Born and cradled in a manger !
King, like David, priest like Aaron,
　Christ is born to set us free !

And the lightning showed the sainted
Figures on the casement painted,
And exclaimed the shuddering baron,
　Miserere, Domine !

In that hour of deep contrition
He beheld, with clearer vision,
Through all outward show and fashion,
　Justice, the Avenger, rise.

All the pomp of earth had vanished,
Falsehood and deceit were banished,
Reason spoke more loud than passion,
　And the truth wore no disguise.

Every vassal of his banner,
Every serf born to his manor,
All those wronged and wretched creatures,
　By his hand were freed again.

And, as on the sacred missal
He recorded their dismissal,
Death relaxed his iron features,
　And the monk replied, *Amen !*

Many centuries have been numbered
Since in death the baron slumbered
By the convent's sculptured portal,
　Mingling with the common dust;

But the good deed, through the ages
Living in historic pages,
Brighter grows and gleams immortal,
　Unconsumed by moth or rust.

THE MAN OF THE NORTH COUNTRIE

The writer of these lines, pleading for a better understanding between people, had a sad history. He, Thomas D'Arcy McGee (1825-68), was an Irishman who went first to America and then to Canada, after resenting strongly British rule in Ireland. But over the water he changed his opinions, and was murdered by the Irish party known as Fenians.

He came from the North, and his words
　were few,
But his voice was kind and his heart was
　true;
And I knew by his eyes no guile had he,
So I married the man of the North
　Countrie.

Oh ! Garryowen may be more gay
Than this quiet street of Ballibay;
And I know the sun shines softly down
On the river that passes my native town;

But there's not—I say it with joy and
　pride—
Better man than mine in Munster wide;
And Limerick town has no happier hearth
Than mine has been with my man of
　the North.

I wish that in Munster they only knew
The kind, kind neighbours I came unto;
Small hate or scorn would ever be
Between the South and the North
　Countrie.

THE GIFT

Canadian-born Bliss Carman (1861–1929) here expresses the great truth that to gain all we can from life by unceasing activity is good provided that we spend what we gain on a wise love of our fellow-men, and not in selfish pursuits

I SAID to Life, ' How comes it,
   With all this wealth in store
Of beauty, joy, and knowledge,
   Thy cry is still for more?

' Count all the years of striving
   To make thy burden less,
The things designed and fashioned
   To gladden thy success!

' The treasures sought and gathered
   Thy lightest whim to please;
The loot of all the ages,
   The spoil of all the seas!

' Is there no end of labour,
   No limit to thy need?
Must man go bowed for ever
   In bondage to thy greed?'

With tears of pride and passion,
   She answered, ' God above!
I only want the asking
   To spend it all for love!'

THE WORLD'S AGE

The world wants manly men, with faith in God and the world's future in their hearts. Such a man was Charles Kingsley, and here is a poetical example of the vigour with which he expressed his faith and rejected whining unbelief.

WHO will say the world is dying?
   Who will say our prime is past?
Sparks from heaven, within us lying,
   Flash, and will flash till the last.
Fools! who fancy Christ mistaken,
   Man a tool to buy and sell,
Earth a failure, God-forsaken,
   Ante-room of hell.

Still the race of hero-spirits
   Pass the lamp from hand to hand;
Age from age the words inherits
   " Wife, and child, and fatherland."
Still the youthful hunter gathers
   Fiery joy from wold and wood;
He will dare as dared his fathers,
   Give him cause as good.

While a slave bewails his fetters;
   While an orphan pleads in vain;
While an infant lisps his letters,
   Heir of all the ages' gain;
While a lip grows ripe for kissing;
   While a moan from man is wrung;
Know, by every want and blessing,
   That the world is young.

A BIRTHDAY THOUGHT

This birthday aspiration, by an unnamed poet, is true as it is expressed in the last verse, but it is overdone in the two lines that come immediately before for the contentment that has no further ambition lacks imagination.

I LIVE once more to see the day
   That brought me first to light;
Oh! teach my willing heart the way
   To take Thy mercies right!

Though dazzling splendour, pomp, and show
   My fortune has denied,
Yet more than grandeur can bestow
   Content hath well supplied.

I envy no one's birth or fame,
   Their titles, train, or dress,
Nor has my pride e'er stretched its aim
   Beyond what I possess.

I ask and wish not to appear
   More beauteous, rich, or gay;
Lord, make me wiser every year,
   And better every day.

ONE OF US TWO

In these verses Ella Wheeler Wilcox seeks to express the pathos of married life broken by death. Shakespeare has pointed the moral in the line in which he says that we should " love that well which we must leave ere long."

THE day will dawn when one of us shall hearken
   In vain to hear a voice that has grown dumb;
And morns will fade, noons pale, and shadows darken
   While sad eyes watch for feet that never come.

One of us two must some time face existence
   Alone with memories that but sharpen pain,
And these sweet days shall shine back in the distance,
   Like dreams of summer dawns in nights of rain.

One of us two, with tortured heart half broken,
   Shall read long-treasured letters through salt tears,
Shall kiss with anguished lips each cherished token
   That speaks of these love-crowned, delicious years.

One of us two shall find all light, all beauty,
   All joy on earth, a tale for ever done;
Shall know henceforth that life means only duty.
   O God! O God! have pity on that one!

POETRY

THE DAY IS COMING

Here is one of the poems by William Morris written in his character of reformer, a character that also produced several prose sketches of a bettered world. It is taken from The Pilgrims of Hope and Chants for Socialists, in Longmans Pocket Library, by permission of the author's Trustees.

Come hither, lads, and hearken, for a
    tale there is to tell
Of the wonderful days a-coming, when all
    shall be better than well.

And the tale shall be told of a country, a
    land in the midst of the sea,
And the folk shall call it England in the
    days that are going to be.

There more than one in a thousand in the
    days that are yet to come
Shall have some hope of the morrow,
    some joy of the ancient home.

Then a man shall work and bethink him,
    and rejoice in the deeds of his hand,
Nor yet come home in the even too faint
    and weary to stand.

Men in that time a-coming shall work
    and have no fear
For tomorrow's lack of earning and the
    hunger-wolf anear.

I tell you this for a wonder, that no man
    shall then be glad
Of his fellow's fall and mishap to snatch
    at the work he had.

For that which the worker winneth shall
    then be his indeed,
Nor shall half be reaped for nothing by
    him that sowed no seed.

O strange new wonderful justice! But
    for whom shall we gather the gain?
For ourselves and for each of our fellows,
    and no hand shall labour in vain.

Then all Mine and all Thine shall be Ours,
    and no more shall any man crave
For riches that serve for nothing but to
    fetter a friend for a slave.

And what wealth then shall be left us
    when none shall gather gold
To buy his friend in the market, and
    pinch and pine the sold?

Nay, what save the lovely city and the
    little house on the hill,
And the wastes and the woodland beauty,
    and the happy fields we till;

And the homes of ancient stories, the
    tombs of the mighty dead;
And the wise men seeking out marvels,
    and the poet's teeming head;

And the painter's hand of wonder; and
    the marvellous fiddle-bow,
And the banded choirs of music; all those
    that do and know.

For all these shall be ours and all men's,
    nor shall any lack a share
Of the toil and the gain of living in the
    days when the world grows fair.

JOY PASSING BY

There is always an undertone of sadness in the verse of William Barnes, though he was a robust man who lived long. He knew life well, and had an ear for its pathos. But one can hardly feel that he is quite sincere in this poem. He was too healthy for all his joys to pass him by. There is no more concentrated expression of a husband's loss than " my wife to my hands left her few bright keys."

When ice all melted to the sun,
    And left the wavy streams to run,
We longed, as summer came, to roll
In river foam, o'er depth and shoal;
And if we lost our loose-bowed swing
We had a kite to pull our string;
    Or, if no ball
    Would rise or fall
With us, another joy was nigh
Before our joy all passed us by.

If leaves of trees, that wind stripped bare
At morning, fly on evening air,
We still look on for summer boughs
To shade again our sunburnt brows;
Where orchard blooms' white scales may
    fall
May hang the apple's blushing ball;
    New hopes come on
    For old ones gone,
As day on day may shine on high
Until our joys all pass us by.

My childhood yearned to reach the span
Of boyhood's life, and be a man;
And then I looked, in manhood's pride,
For manhood's sweetest choice, a bride,
And then to lovely children, come
To make my home a dearer home.
    But now my mind
    Can look behind
For joy, and wonder, with a sigh,
When all my joys have passed me by!

Was it when once I missed a call
To rise, and thenceforth seemed to fall;
Or when my wife to my hands left
Her few bright keys a doleful heft;
Or when before the door I stood
To watch a child away for good;
    Or where some crowd
    In mirth was loud;
Or where I saw a mourner sigh;
Where did my joy all pass me by?

COUNTRY AND CITY

This quaint defence of the country life of the olden times compared with the more polished ways of the town was written by Thomas Campion, who lived in the same period as Shakespeare. He worked into his verses true humour and condensed description. Old words that may need explanation are nappy, strong or heady; tutties, nosegays ; silly, which once meant simple, but not foolish. The flail was used for threshing corn from the ear when that work was done by hand. The word break was pronounced to rhyme with speak, and is still spoken so in some rural districts.

Jack and Joan, they think no ill,
  But loving live, and merry still;
Do their week-days' work, and pray
Devoutly on the holy day;
Skip and trip it on the green,
And help to choose the Summer Queen;
Lash out at a country feast
Their silver penny with the best.

Well can they judge of nappy ale,
And tell at large a winter tale;
Climb up to the apple loft,
And turn the crabs till they be soft.
Tib is all the father's joy,
And little Tom the mother's boy;
All their pleasure is content,
And care, to pay their yearly rent.

Joan can call by name her cows
And deck her windows with green boughs;
She can wreaths and tutties make,
And trim with plums a bridal cake.
Jack knows what brings gain or loss;
And his long flail can stoutly toss:
Makes the hedge which others break,
And ever thinks what he doth speak.

Now, you courtly dames and knights,
That study only strange delights,
Though you scorn the homespun gray,
And revel in your rich array;
Though your tongues dissemble deep,
And can your heads from danger keep;
Yet, for all your pomp and train,
Securer lives the silly swain.

YE MARINERS OF ENGLAND

Thomas Campbell, the Scottish poet, who lived from 1777 to 1844, chiefly in England, had the gift of writing patriotic verses with a clear, ringing fervour. These embody finely British pride in the national sea story and its heroes.

Ye mariners of England
  That guard our native seas,
Whose flag has braved a thousand years
  The battle and the breeze,
Your glorious standard launch again
  To match another foe,
And sweep through the deep,
  While the stormy winds do blow;
While the battle rages loud and long,
  And the stormy winds do blow.

The spirits of your fathers
  Shall start from every wave—
For the deck it was their field of fame,
  And ocean was their grave;
Where Blake and mighty Nelson fell
  Your manly hearts shall glow,
As ye sweep through the deep,
  While the stormy winds do blow;
While the battle rages loud and long,
  And the stormy winds do blow.

Britannia needs no bulwarks,
  No towers along the steep;
Her march is o'er the mountain-waves,
  Her home is on the deep.
With thunders from her native oak
  She quells the floods below—
As they roar on the shore,
  When the stormy winds do blow;
When the battle rages loud and long,
  And the stormy winds do blow.

The meteor flag of England
  Shall yet terrific burn;
Till danger's troubled night depart
  And the star of peace return.
Then, then, ye ocean-warriors,
  Our song and feast shall flow
To the fame of your name
  When the storm has ceased to blow;
When the fiery fight is heard no more,
  And the storm has ceased to blow.

THE POETRY OF EARTH IS NEVER DEAD

No poet ever lived more constantly in the atmosphere of poetry than John Keats. He felt it everywhere and it was his dearest delight to express it in words. To some people the chirping of grasshoppers and crickets is an irritating intrusion, but to Keats it was a form of Nature's song.

The poetry of earth is never dead:
  When all the birds are faint with
    the hot sun,
  And hide in cooling trees, a voice will run
From hedge to hedge about the new-mown
    mead;
That is the grasshopper's—he takes the
    lead
  In summer luxury; he has never done
  With his delights, for when tired out
    with fun
He rests at ease beneath some pleasant
    weed.
The poetry of earth is ceasing never:
  On a lone winter evening, when the frost
  Has wrought a silence, from the stove
    there shrills
The cricket's song, in warmth increasing
    ever,
  And seems to one in drowsiness half lost
  The grasshopper's among some grassy
    hills.

HIGHLAND MARY

Highland Mary was one of the many sweethearts Robert Burns loved and lost, but her he lost by death so that she remained in his mind with special tenderness. A statue to Highland Mary has been erected on the banks of the River Clyde at Dunoon. Drumlie means muddy, or turbid.

YE banks and braes and streams around
    The castle o' Montgomery,
Green be your woods, and fair your flowers,
    Your waters never drumlie!
There simmer first unfauld her robes,
    And there the langest tarry;
For there I took the last fareweel
    O' my sweet Highland Mary.

How sweetly bloomed the gay green birk,
    How rich the hawthorn's blossom,
As underneath their fragrant shade
    I clasped her to my bosom!
The golden hours on angel wings
    Flew o'er me and my dearie;
For dear to me as light and life
    Was my sweet Highland Mary.

Wi' mony a vow and locked embrace
    Our parting was fu' tender.
And, pledging aft to meet again,
    We tore oursels asunder;
But, oh! fell Death's untimely frost,
    That nipt my flower sae early!
Now green's the sod and cauld's the clay
    That wraps my Highland Mary!

O pale, pale now, those rosy lips
    I aft hae kissed sae fondly;
And closed for aye the sparkling glance
    That dwelt on me sae kindly;
And mouldering now in silent dust
    That heart that lo'ed me dearly!
But still within my bosom's core
    Shall live my Highland Mary.

O CAPTAIN! MY CAPTAIN!

Here is one of the most pathetic and heart-stirring poems in the English language. It is Walt Whitman's farewell to Abraham Lincoln after the assassination of the President in the hour of victory which closed the civil war in the United States and brought freedom to the slaves.

O CAPTAIN! my Captain! our fearful
    trip is done.
The ship has weathered every rack, the
    prize we sought is won,
The port is near, the bells I hear, the
    people all exulting,
While follow eyes the steady keel, the
    vessel grim and daring;
    But O heart! heart! heart!
      O the bleeding drops of red!
        Where on the deck my Captain
          lies,
          Fallen cold and dead.

O Captain! my Captain! rise up and hear
    the bells;
Rise up—for you the flag is flung, for you
    the bugle trills,
For you bouquets and ribboned wreaths,
    for you the shores a-crowding,
For you they call, the swaying mass, their
    eager faces turning;
    Here, Captain! dear father!
      This arm beneath your head!
        It is some dream that on the deck
          You've fallen cold and dead.

My Captain does not answer, his lips are
    pale and still;
My father does not feel my arm, he has no
    pulse nor will;
The ship is anchored safe and sound, its
    voyage closed and done,
From fearful trip the victor ship comes in
    with object won;
    Exult, O shores, and ring, O bells!
    But I, with mournful tread,
      Walk the deck my Captain lies,
      Fallen cold and dead.

THOU ART, O GOD!

These melodious verses are a hymn of gratitude for the beauty and glory of the world, which is one of the revelations of the Divinity that surrounds us. The writer is Tom Moore, the Irish poet. Smoothness in style and delicacy of sentiment are always present in his verses.

THOU art, O God, the life and light
    Of all this wondrous world we see;
Its glow by day, its smile by night,
    Are but reflections caught from Thee.
Where'er we turn Thy glories shine,
And all things fair and bright are Thine.

When day, with farewell beam, delays,
    Among the opening clouds of even,
And we can almost think we gaze
    Through golden vistas into heaven,
Those hues that mark the sun's decline
So soft, so radiant, Lord, are Thine.

When night, with wings of starry gloom,
    O'ershadows all the earth and skies,
Like some dark, beauteous bird, whose
    plume
Is sparkling with unnumbered eyes—
That sacred gloom, those fires divine,
So grand, so countless, Lord, are Thine.

When youthful spring around us breathes
    Thy spirit warms her fragrant sigh;
And every flower the summer wreathes
    Is born beneath that kindling eye.
Where'er we turn Thy glories shine,
And all things fair and bright are Thine.

LITTLE VERSES FOR VERY LITTLE PEOPLE

PLAYGROUNDS

IN summer I am very glad
  We children are so small,
For we can see a thousand things
  That men can't see at all.

They don't know much about the moss
  And all the stones they pass,
They never lie and play among
  The forests in the grass.

They walk about a long way off;
  And, when we're at the sea,
Let father stoop as best he can
  He can't find things like me.

But when the snow is on the ground,
  And all the puddles freeze,
I wish that I were very tall,
  High up above the trees.

Laurence Alma-Tadema

MY MOTHER

WHO fed me from her gentle breast,
  And hushed me in her arms to rest,
And on my cheeks sweet kisses prest?
  My Mother.

When sleep forsook my open eye
Who was it sang sweet hushaby,
And rocked me that I should not cry?
  My Mother.

Who sat and watched my infant head
When sleeping on my cradle bed,
And tears of sweet affection shed?
  My Mother.

When pain and sickness made me cry
Who gazed upon my heavy eye,
And wept for fear that I should die?
  My Mother.

Who dressed my doll in clothes so gay,
And taught me pretty how to play,
And minded all I had to say?
  My Mother.

Who ran to help me when I fell,
And would some pretty story tell,
Or kiss the place to make it well?
  My Mother.

Who taught my infant lips to pray
And love God's holy book and day,
And walk in wisdom's pleasant way?
  My Mother.

And can I ever cease to be
Affectionate and kind to thee,
Who wast so very kind to me,
  My Mother?

Ah, no! the thought I cannot bear,
And if God please my life to spare
I hope I shall reward thy care,
  My Mother.

When thou art feeble, old, and grey
My healthy arm shall be thy stay,
And I will soothe thy pains away,
  My Mother.

And when I see thee hang thy head
'Twill be my turn to watch thy bed,
And tears of sweet affection shed,
  My Mother.

Ann Taylor

THE FAIRY FOLK

COME, cuddle close in Daddy's coat
  Beside the fire so bright,
And hear about the fairy folk
  That wander in the night.
For when the stars are shining clear
  And all the world is still
They float across the silver moon
  From hill to cloudy hill.

Their caps of red, their cloaks of green,
  Are hung with silver bells,
And when they're shaken with the wind
  Their merry ringing swells.
And, riding on the crimson moth
  With black spots on her wings,
They guide them down the purple sky
  With golden bridle rings.

They love to visit girls and boys
  To see how sweet they sleep,
To stand beside their cosy cots
  And at their faces peep.
For in the whole of fairyland
  They have no finer sight
Than little children sleeping sound
  With faces rosy bright.

On tip-toe crowding round their heads
  When bright the moonlight beams,
They whisper little tender words
  That fill their minds with dreams;
And when they see a sunny smile
  With lightest finger tips
They lay a hundred kisses sweet
  Upon the ruddy lips.

And then the little spotted moths
  Spread out their crimson wings,
And bear away the fairy crowd
  With shaking bridle rings.
Come, bairnies, hide in Daddy's coat
  Beside the fire so bright—
Perhaps the little fairy folk
  Will visit you tonight.

Robert Bird

The south wind brings wet weather;
   The north wind wet and cold together;
The west wind always brings us rain;
The east wind blows it back again.

A cat came fiddling out of a barn
   With a pair of bagpipes under her arm.
She could sing nothing but fiddle-cumfee,
The mouse has married the bumblebee.
Pipe, cat; dance, mouse;
We'll have a wedding at our good house.

Ladybird, ladybird, fly away home;
   Thy house is on fire, thy children all gone,
All but one that lies under a stone;
Fly thee home, ladybird, ere it be gone.

The fair maid who the First of May
   Goes to the fields at break of day,
And washes in dew from the hawthorn tree,
Will ever after handsome be.

If I had as much money as I could spend
   I never would cry " Old chairs to mend !
Old chairs to mend, old chairs to mend; "
I never would cry " Old chairs to mend!"

If I had as much money as I could tell
I never would cry " Old clothes to sell;
Old clothes to sell, old clothes to sell; "
I never would cry " Old clothes to sell ! "

Oh, who is so merry, so merry, heigh ho!
   As the light-hearted fairy, heigh ho, heigh ho?
He dances and sings
To the sound of his wings,
With a hey, and a heigh, and a ho!

Oh, who is so merry, so merry, heigh ho!
As the light-hearted fairy, heigh ho, heigh ho ?
   His nectar he sips
   From a primrose's lips,
With a hey, and a heigh, and a ho!

Taffy was a Welshman, Taffy was a thief,
   Taffy came to my house and stole a piece of beef;
I went to Taffy's house, Taffy was not at home;
Taffy came to my house and stole a marrow-bone;
I went to Taffy's house, Taffy was not in;
Taffy came to my house and stole a silver pin;
I went to Taffy's house, Taffy was in bed;
I took up a poker and flung it at his head.

Rock-a-by, baby, thy cradle is green;
  Father's a nobleman, mother's a queen;
And Betty's a lady, and wears a gold ring;
And Johnny's a drummer, and drums for the king.

⊡   ⊡

Robin and Richard were two pretty men;
  They lay in bed till the clock struck ten;
Then up starts Robin, and looks at the sky:
" Oh, brother Richard, the sun's very high!
You go on with the bottle and bag,
And I'll follow after on jolly Jack Nag."

The King of Clubs he often drubs
  His loving queen and wife.
The Queen of Clubs returns his snubs,
  And all is noise and strife.
The Knave of Clubs gives winks and rubs,
  And swears he'll take her part!
For when our kings will do such things
  They should be made to smart.

The Diamond King I fain would sing,
  And likewise his fair queen,
But that the knave, a haughty slave,
  Must needs step in between.
" Good Diamond King, with hempen string
  This haughty knave destroy!
Then may your queen, with mind serene,
  Your royal love enjoy."

The King of Spades he kissed the maids,
  Which grieved the queen full sore;
The Queen of Spades she beat those maids
  And turned them out of door.
The Knave of Spades grieved for those jades,
  And did for them implore;
The queen so gent, she did relent,
  And vowed she'd strike no more.

Pussy-cat Mole jumped over a coal,
  And in her best petticoat burnt a great hole.
Poor pussy's weeping—she'll have no more milk
Until her best petticoat's mended with silk.

⊡   ⊡

Brian O'Lin had no breeches to wear,
  So he bought him a sheepskin and made him a pair
With the skinny side out and the woolly side in;
" Ah, ha, that is warm! " said Brian O'Lin.

Brian O'Lin and his wife and wife's mother
They all went over a bridge together;
The bridge was broken and they all fell in.
" Mischief take all! " quoth Brian O'Lin.

BABY GOES TO TOWN

EVERY evening Baby goes
    Trot, trot, to town,
Across the river, through the fields,
    Up hill and down.

Trot, trot, the Baby goes,
    Up hill and down,
To buy a feather for her hat,
    To buy a woollen gown.

Trot, trot, the Baby goes;
    The birds fly down, alack!
" You cannot have our feathers, dear,"
They say, " so please trot back."

Trot, trot, the Baby goes;
    The lambs come bleating near.
" You cannot have our wool," they say,
    " But we are sorry, dear."

Trot, trot, the Baby goes,
    Trot, trot, to town;
She buys a red rose for her hat,
    She buys a cotton gown.

                Mary F. Butts

PRINCE TATTERS

LITTLE Prince Tatters has lost his cap!
    Over the hedge he threw it;
Into the river it fell " kerslap! "
    Stupid old thing to do it!
Now Mother may sigh and Nurse may fume
For the gay little cap with its eagle plume.
" One cannot be thinking all day of such
    matters!
Trifles are trifles! " says little Prince
    Tatters.

Little Prince Tatters has lost his coat!
    Playing, he did not need it;
" Left it right there, by the nanny-goat,
    And nobody never seed it! "
Now Mother and Nurse may search till
    night
For the little new coat with its buttons
    bright;
But—" Coat-sleeves or shirt-sleeves, how
    little it matters!
Trifles are trifles! " says little Prince
    Tatters.

Little Prince Tatters has lost his ball!
    Rolled away down the street!
Somebody'll have to find it, that's all,
    Before he can sleep or eat.
Now raise the neighbourhood quickly do,
And send for the crier and constable too!
" Trifles are trifles, but serious matters,
They must be seen to," says little Prince
    Tatters.

              Laura E. Richards

LITTLE TROTTY WAGTAIL

LITTLE trotty wagtail, he went in the
    rain,
And twittering, tottering sideways, he ne'er
    got straight again.
He stooped to get a worm, and looked up
    to get a fly,
And then he flew away ere his feathers
    they were dry.

Little trotty wagtail, he waddled in the
    mud,
And left his little footmarks, trample
    where he would.
He waddled in the water-pudge, and
    waggle went his tail,
And chirrupt up his wings to dry upon the
    garden rail.

Little trotty wagtail, you nimble all about,
And in the dimpling water-pudge you
    waddle in and out;
Your home is nigh at hand, and in the
    warm pig-sty,
So, little Master Wagtail, I'll bid you a
    good-bye.

              John Clare

THE CAPTAIN'S DAUGHTER

WE were crowded in the cabin—
    Not a soul would dare to sleep—
It was midnight on the waters,
    And a storm was on the deep.

'Tis a fearful thing in winter
    To be shattered by the blast,
And to hear the rattling trumpet
    Thunder " Cut away the mast! "

So we shuddered there in silence—
    For the stoutest held his breath—
While the hungry sea was roaring
    And the breakers talked with death.

As thus we sat in darkness,
    Each one busy with his prayers,
" We are lost! " the captain shouted,
    As he staggered down the stairs.

But his little daughter whispered,
    As she took his icy hand,
" Isn't God upon the ocean,
    Just the same as on the land? "

Then we kissed the little maiden,
    And we spake in better cheer,
And we anchored safe in harbour
    When the morn was shining clear.

            James Thomas Fields

POETRY IN THE THEATRE

(FOR OLDER CHILDREN)

THE great majority of the poems you have already read in these volumes were written to be *read*. But some of the greatest poetry ever written was composed with the prime purpose of its being *spoken* on the stage. This is, of course, the case with the poetic passages in the plays of Shakespeare and some of the world's other great dramatists.

Here is an extract from one of the soliloquies in Shakespeare's " Hamlet." The word soliloquy means " speaking alone," and is most commonly used in connection with a character in a play who speaks his innermost thoughts when alone or regardless of the presence of others. Often the speech helps the audience to appreciate some detail of the plot or some facet of the character. Here Hamlet has met the band of travelling players; he ponders on how well the chief player spoke some lines, and reproaches himself for his delay in bringing his wicked uncle to justice. This passage is from Act II of the play.

> About, my brain! I have heard
> That guilty creatures sitting at a play
> Have by the very cunning of the scene
> Been struck so to the soul that presently
> They have proclaim'd their malefactions;
> For murder, though it have no tongue, will speak
> With most miraculous organ. I'll have these players
> Play something like the murder of my father
> Before mine uncle: I'll observe his looks;
> I'll tent him to the quick: if he but blench,
> I know my course. The spirit that I have seen
> May be the devil; and the devil hath power
> T'assume a pleasing shape; yea, and perhaps
> Out of my weakness and my melancholy,
> As he is very potent with such spirits,
> Abuses me to damn me. I'll have grounds
> More relative than this. The play's the thing
> Wherein I'll catch the conscience of the king.

Read the above extract over carefully; then practise saying it aloud. It is a very famous soliloquy, and, as with a great deal that Shakespeare wrote, some of its phrases have passed into everyday speech. Learning wonderful poetry such as this, and learning how it should be delivered, will help you to cultivate an appreciation of the spoken word and the power and majesty of which it is capable. Now here is a free rendering, in simple language, of what the above lines mean:

Now, let me think! I have heard that people who have done wrong have sometimes been forced to confess it when, watching a play, their consciences are pricked by something the players happen to say or do. I will ask these players to put on a play about a man who murders his brother, just as my uncle, as I believe, murdered my father. When my uncle is watching the play, I will watch him. Perhaps he will go white with rage or fear, and then I will know what to do. The spirit of my dead father has appeared to me and told me how he met his end. I think it was my father's spirit, but perhaps I only imagined it; or perhaps the devil, who is very cunning, is playing me a trick. But this play will prove to me whether the king, my uncle, is guilty or not.

(Now turn the page for a picture of Hamlet delivering this famous speech)

(*Photograph by Angus McBean*)

John Neville, of the Old Vic Theatre Company, as Hamlet, Prince of Denmark.

POETRY IN THE THEATRE

(*Photograph by Angus McBean*)

John Neville and Claire Bloom, of the Old Vic Theatre Company, as Romeo and Juliet in Shakespeare's play of that name. Now turn the page for an explanation of this scene and some of the lines spoken by Juliet.

5301

POETRY IN THE THEATRE
(FOR OLDER CHILDREN)

ON the previous page you see the famous balcony scene from Shakespeare's "Romeo and Juliet." Romeo's family, the Montagues, and Juliet's family, the Capulets, hate each other, but Romeo and Juliet themselves have fallen in love with each other. Romeo, at great risk to them both, steals into the grounds of the Capulets' house, to talk to Juliet, who appears on her balcony. Here are some of the lovely lines spoken by Juliet on this occasion. The scene is from Act II of the play.

Thou know'st the mask of night is on my face,
Else would a maiden blush bepaint my cheek
For that which thou hast heard me speak tonight.
Fain would I dwell on form, fain, fain deny
What I have spoke: but farewell compliment!
Dost thou love me? I know thou wilt say ' Ay ';
And I will take thy word; yet, if thou swear'st,
Thou mayst prove false; at lovers' perjuries,
They say, Jove laughs. O gentle Romeo!
If thou dost love, pronounce it faithfully:
Or if thou think'st I am too quickly won,
I'll frown and be perverse and say thee nay,
So thou wilt woo; but else, not for the world.
In truth, fair Montague, I am too fond,
And therefore thou mayst think my haviour light:
But trust me, gentleman, I'll prove more true
Than those that have more cunning to be strange.
I should have been more strange, I must confess,
But that thou over-heard'st, ere I was 'ware,
My true love's passion: therefore pardon me,
And not impute this yielding to light love,
Which the dark night hath so discovered.

As with Hamlet's soliloquy given on page 5299, you should try saying this speech aloud, with perhaps members of your family, or friends, as your " audience." This scene from " Romeo and Juliet " contains verse which must be counted among the loveliest and most famous ever written by any poet. Now here is a free rendering, in simple language, of what the above passage means:

If it were daylight, instead of night, I might blush at the thought of how I spoke my thoughts aloud just now, when I did not know that you were there to overhear me. Perhaps I should deny that I ever spoke such words, or meant them. But I will not! I know you love me, Romeo, and I might tease you into saying so. I am not ashamed to return that love. I speak truly when I say this. I am not pretending, as others might. Forgive me for speaking like this. I hope you will think no less of me because of my behaviour in confessing so openly that I love you. The dark night has discovered our secret.

Imperishable Thoughts of Men Enshrined in the Books of the World

The Oldest Books in the World

IN our last chapter on Literature, the great literature of ancient Greece, we saw how it began with the poems of Homer. They were perhaps the oldest books that are still being universally read. We say perhaps because there is some doubt as to whether, when Homer was composing his immortal verse, the earliest narratives in the Bible, telling the stories of the fathers of the Jewish race, such as Joseph and his brethren in Egypt, had or had not been actually written. Probably these earliest surviving writings, in Asia and in Europe, were written about the same time. But in any case, if we except the Bible as not a book in the ordinary sense, the books of Homer, the Iliad and the Odyssey, remain as the oldest of all the volumes on the world's bookshelf. Everyone knows the lovely Bible stories from Asia. Here we trace in outline the first great stories of Europe, Homer's Iliad and Odyssey.

THE STORY OF HOMER'S ILIAD

WE should know the meaning of the word Iliad before we can listen to the story. It is the English form of a Greek word meaning " about Ilium," and Ilium was the name of a town that stood on the coast of Asia Minor.

It is usually referred to in English as Troy, and it was the capital city of Troja; but it was known to the Greeks as Ilium. Its inhabitants were called Trojans.

The Iliad, which was composed by Homer, a Greek poet, nearly three thousand years ago, tells of a great war carried on by the Greeks against the Trojans, but what is true in it and what is the fancy of the poet we cannot very well say, as fact and fiction are mingled together.

The King of Troy was named Priam, and the name of his wife was Hecuba. Of their many sons, Hector was famed for his bravery, and Paris for his good looks. It happened that Paris was sent on an embassy to Menelaus, King of Sparta, in Greece. The king was married to Helen, a woman so fair that she was thought to be the most beautiful woman in all Greece. When Paris arrived in Sparta the king was away, and Paris was false to him. He made Helen a captive and carried her off to Troy. Greece, which is a land of many islands, was not then united under one king, but had many independent rulers and princes. So when the King of Sparta found that his queen had been

stolen away, he called together a great meeting of the princes, and his own brother Agamemnon was elected " sovereign lord of all the Greeks " to lead them in a war against the Trojans for the recovery of Helen. At the marriage of Helen and Menelaus the Greek princes had promised to take up the cause of the beautiful Helen if any need arose.

The story then goes on to tell us how the Greeks made preparations for the war, how the army was reviewed, and how the boats for carrying the soldiers were got ready for sea.

It tells also of the many famous warriors who were to take part in the war. Chief among these was Achilles, the bravest of the Greeks; then there was Ulysses, the wisest; while Nestor was the eldest and most experienced of them all. When all was ready the mighty army set sail for Troy, and, landing on the shore, soon laid siege to the city. For ten long years the siege continued, battle after battle was fought, and also single combats between the leaders, but no decisive victory was won by either side.

Thus, nine of the years had worn away when trouble began among the Greeks themselves. A great quarrel arose between Agamemnon and Achilles over a very little matter—a slave who had been given to Achilles having been taken away by Agamemnon. As a result of this quarrel,

ROMANCE · HISTORIES · DRAMAS · ESSAYS · WORLD CLASSICS

Achilles withdrew to his tent, and would not support Agamemnon in any of the next skirmishes that took place between the Trojans and the Greeks. Growing bold, because the mighty Achilles fought no more, the Trojans now began to press the besiegers. Fearing that the Trojans might even score a victory, the noble Greek Patroclus, the dearest friend of Achilles, dressed himself in the armour of that powerful warrior, and led the Greeks once more against the Trojans. He drove them back into their city, but himself fell, mortally wounded.

Achilles had now more reason than before to make war against the enemy that had killed his well-loved friend. Arrayed in new armour made for him by Vulcan, he goes forth to avenge Patroclus, and is met by Hector, the finest fighter of all Troy. Now takes place the greatest battle of the long war. Hector soon falls before Achilles in his wrath, and the body of the Trojan prince is dragged three times around the city by the chariot of his conqueror before it is given to Hector's father, Priam, who bears it back within the walls of Troy, where the dead hero is mourned by Hecuba, his mother; by Andromache, his wife; by the captive Helen, and by all the Trojans. A great funeral is given to the hero of Troy:

Perform, ye Trojans ! what the rites require,
And fell the forests for a funeral pyre;
Twelve days, nor foes nor secret ambush dread;
Achilles grants these honours to the dead.

Thus commands Priam, the king, and with a short description of the final honours paid to the dead hero the story ends. But this, of course, was not the end of the war. The chief purpose of Homer's great and lengthy poem is to show what Achilles did during the siege of Troy, and not to give a complete account of the war.

THE STORY OF HOMER'S ODYSSEY

AFTER the Trojan War the Greeks returned home, but Ulysses was fated to wander for many years before he regained his native land, and the Odyssey contains the stories of his adventures during those years. The Greek name for Ulysses was Odysseus, and so the word Odyssey means " about Odysseus."

When the Greeks set sail from the coast of Asia Minor to return to their own beautiful homes, none of the princes was more anxious to regain his native land than the wise and brave Ulysses. But, in spite of all that his sailors could do, adverse winds drove his ships far from the Isles of Greece. At home his wife Penelope, and his son Telemachus, were waiting for him, but they had to wait for ten long years, during which the wanderer had many adventures. We can only mention a few.

Instead of being carried towards Greece, the ships of Ulysses were blown along the coast of Asia Minor, and, being sore pressed by hunger, he and his men at length were forced to land and attack the inhabitants of a small town, who fled before them. The Greeks, with plenty to eat and drink, gave themselves up to merry-making. Meanwhile, the inhabitants came back and attacked them, slaying more than half of the sailors who had landed. The others had a narrow escape from like fate when returning to their ships.

Ulysses and his men who thus escaped landed afterwards on the island which we now call Sicily, and here they wandered about until they came to a great cave. In this cave were placed huge pans of milk, and the place showed other signs of being inhabited. It was, indeed the home of one of the fabulous giants who, like all the gods and goddesses of these ancient stories, existed only in the imagination of the people of that time. The giant was named Polyphemus, and an uglier or more cruel giant it would be difficult to imagine. He had only one eye, and it was set in the middle of his forehead. He was chief of a race of fierce and terrible one-eyed giants called Cyclopes, who were skilled herdsmen but despisers of Zeus.

Ulysses and his men were waiting in the cave that evening when the giant came home, driving before him into the cave a flock of giant sheep, and rolling before the entrance a stone which twenty ordinary men could not have moved. To him Ulysses came forward and, offering a skin of wine, pleaded for mercy to himself and his men. The giant drank the wine and was delighted with it. He promised a boon to Ulysses for his gift; but as he immediately proceeded to eat up two of the Greeks, it was clear they could not hope for any mercy from this monster of savagery.

HELEN, THE BEAUTIFUL WIFE OF THE KING OF SPARTA, WALKING ON THE WALLS OF TROY.
FROM THE PAINTING BY LORD LEIGHTON
This picture is reproduced by courtesy of Messrs. Henry Graves

Polyphemus then asks Ulysses to tell him his name, but the prince is too wise to let him know who he is, so he replies:

"No-man is my name.
By that distinguished from my tender years,
'Tis what my parents call me, and my peers."
The giant then: "Our promised grace receive,
The hospitable boon we mean to give:
When all thy wretched crew have felt my power,
No-man shall be the last I will devour."

HOW ULYSSES AND HIS MEN ESCAPED FROM THE GIANT POLYPHEMUS

Six days of terror pass by, and the giant each evening reduces the followers of Ulysses by two before the wise prince hits upon a way of escape. On the seventh night, while Polyphemus lies stretched on the floor asleep, Ulysses sharpens a great stake of wood, and, assisted by his men, rams it hard into the eye of the giant. Savage roars of pain awaken others of the fabulous inhabitants of the island, but they cannot enter owing to the stone that blocks the cave. So they call to their great chief to know who hurts him, and from his den he answers:

Friends, No-man kills me; No-man in the hour
Of sleep, oppresses me with fraudful power.

To this they call back:

If no man hurt thee, but the Hand Divine
Inflict disease, it fits thee to resign.

Then they go away and leave him. But all the Greeks together are unable to move the stone, and so they have to wait till dawn, when the giant himself, now blinded, pushes the stone away to let his flock of enormous sheep go forth. He himself sits by the entrance, meaning to prevent the Greeks from escaping. But Ulysses has been wise enough to expect this, and has had one of his men bound under each of the sheep, so that as the animals pass through the door they carry all the Greeks with them. Ulysses and his crew succeed in escaping to the ships, and thus ends the third of his wonderful adventures by land and sea.

THE LESSONS TO BE LEARNED FROM THE ADVENTURES OF ULYSSES

A stranger adventure still befalls the Greeks when, in their wanderings, they come into the hands of a witch named Circe, who gives them wine to drink that turns them into beasts. Here, again, Ulysses is too wise to be caught by any snare, and refuses to drink the wine. It is well for him that he does, as his wisdom makes the witch admire him, and for his sake she restores all his companions to their natural shapes.

Many of the adventures of Ulysses are full of meaning for us, and teach us valuable lessons if we care to take them. One of the most interesting is the adventure of the Sirens, who are beautiful singing maidens that sit along the shore and sing so sweetly that the sailors are tempted to come to land. But these Sirens are really furies, who kill the men that land, and strew their bones along the shore. Here, again, the crafty wisdom of Ulysses secures the safety of his crew. He puts wax in the ears of his sailors so that they may not hear the singing of the Sirens, and thus they row safely past the place of danger.

Their next adventure is the sailing between a rock called Scylla and a terrible whirlpool called Charybdis, which Ulysses succeeds in doing. But we must now come to the end of these extraordinary adventures and see Ulysses landed safely on the barren shores of Ithaca, the Greek island of which he was the king.

THE BEAUTIFUL PENELOPE, WHO WAITED FOR HER LORD'S RETURN

Twenty years had passed since he first sailed away to take part in the great war against the Trojans, and all this time his wife Penelope, who is famed for her goodness, her beauty, and her wisdom, has been patiently awaiting his return. Many other men have been anxious to marry her, and have come to the palace, saying, "Ulysses is dead, or he would have returned ere now." But she has refused them all, telling them she would never wed again until she had woven a shroud, and as she undid each night what she had woven during the day, the shroud was never made.

When Ulysses reached his palace some of the princes who wished to marry Penelope were there. Nobody but his old nurse and his dog knew the king, who was so changed in his twenty years of wandering. But Ulysses told his son Telemachus who he was, and together they killed the princes who had been pestering Penelope. Then Ulysses sought his wife, who at first could hardly believe it was her husband back again, but at length was overjoyed to think her wise and noble king was safe at last and all his wanderings done.

The Story of the Most Beautiful Book in the World

Jesus talking to the boys and girls who gathered about him in Galilee

LITTLE TALKS OF JESUS

As we go about the world doing the will of God we are to have no fear. We are to go our ways trusting that He without whose notice not a sparrow falls will watch over His own.

THE harvest truly is great, but the labourers are few. Pray ye therefore the Lord of the harvest that He would send forth labourers into His harvest.

Go your ways: behold I send you forth as lambs among wolves. Carry neither purse nor scrip nor shoes, and salute no man by the way.

And into whatsoever house ye enter, first say, " Peace be to this house."

And if the Son of Peace be there, your peace shall rest upon it; if not, it shall turn to you again.

And in the same house remain, eating and drinking such things as they give, for the labourer is worthy of his hire. Go not from house to house.

And into whatsoever city ye enter and they receive you, eat such things as are set before you; and heal the sick that are therein, and say unto them, " The kingdom of God is come nigh unto you."

But into whatsoever city ye enter and they receive you not, go your ways out into the streets of the same, and say, " Even the very dust of your city, which cleaveth on us, we do wipe off against you; notwithstanding, be ye sure of this, that the kingdom of God is come nigh unto you."

He that heareth you heareth me; and he that despiseth you despiseth me; and he that despiseth me despiseth Him that sent me.

Beware ye of the leaven of the Pharisees, which is hypocrisy. For there is nothing covered that shall not be revealed; neither hid, that shall not be known. Therefore whatsoever ye have spoken in darkness shall be heard in the light; and that which ye have spoken in the ear in closets shall be proclaimed upon the house-tops.

And I say unto you, my friends, Be not afraid of them that kill the body and after that have no more that they can do; but I will forewarn you whom ye shall fear.

Are not five sparrows sold for two farthings? and not one of them is forgotten before God. But even the very hairs of your head are all numbered. Fear not, therefore; ye are of more value than many sparrows.

GREAT FIGURES OF THE OLD TESTAMENT · THE LIFE OF JESUS

I AM THE GOOD SHEPHERD

There are no more familiar sayings of Jesus than these. He is the Good Shepherd whose sheep we are and we must follow him. We must learn to know his voice; we must not be deceived by those who come to us as wolves in sheep's clothing, speaking and teaching falsely in his name.

THE LOST PIECE OF SILVER

VERILY, verily, I say unto you, He that entereth not by the door into the sheepfold, but climbeth up some other way, the same is a thief and a robber.

But he that entereth in by the door is the shepherd of the sheep. To him the porter openeth, and the sheep hear his voice; and he calleth his own sheep by name, and leadeth them out.

And when he putteth forth his own sheep, he goeth before them, and the sheep follow him, for they know his voice. And a stranger will they not follow, but will flee from him, for they know not the voice of strangers.

Verily, verily, I say unto you, I am the door of the sheep. All that ever came before me are thieves and robbers, but the sheep did not hear them. I am the door; by me if any man enter in he shall be saved, and shall go in and out, and find pasture The thief cometh not but for to steal, and to kill, and to destroy: I am come that they might have life, and that they might have it more abundantly.

I am the Good Shepherd: the good shepherd giveth his life for the sheep. But he that is an hireling, and not the shepherd, whose own the sheep are not, seeth the wolf coming, and leaveth the sheep, and fleeth; and the wolf catcheth them, and scattereth the sheep. The hireling fleeth, because he is an hireling, and careth not for the sheep.

I am the Good Shepherd, and know my sheep, and am known of mine. As the Father knoweth me, even so know I the Father; and I lay down my life for the sheep. And other sheep I have, which are not of this fold; them also I must bring, and they shall hear my voice; and there shall be one fold, and one shepherd.

My sheep hear my voice, and I know them, and they follow me; and I give unto them eternal life; and they shall never perish, neither shall any pluck them out of my hand. My Father, which gave them me, is greater than all, and none is able to pluck them out of my Father's hand. I and my Father are one.

THE DOOR OF THE FOLD

Therefore doth my Father love me, because I lay down my life, that I might take it again. No man taketh it from me, but I lay it down of myself. I have power to lay it down, and I have power to take it again. This commandment have I received of my Father.

BE YE AS LITTLE CHILDREN

VERILY I say unto you, except ye be converted and become as little children ye shall not enter into the kingdom of heaven.

Whosoever therefore shall humble himself as this little child, the same is greatest in the kingdom of heaven; and whoso shall receive one such little child in my name receiveth me.

But whoso shall offend one of these little ones which believe in me, it were better for him that a millstone were hanged about his neck, and that he were drowned in the depth of the sea.

Woe unto the world because of offences! It must needs be that offences come, but woe to that man by whom the offence cometh!

What man of you, having an hundred sheep, if he lose one of them, doth not leave the ninety and nine in the wilderness, and go after that which is lost, until he find it? And when he hath found it, he layeth it on his shoulders, rejoicing; and when he cometh home, he calleth together his friends and neighbours, saying unto them, " Rejoice with me; for I have found my sheep which was lost." I say unto you that likewise joy shall be in heaven over one sinner that repenteth more than over ninety and nine just persons which need no repentance.

Either what woman, having ten pieces of silver, if she lose one piece, doth not light a candle, and sweep the house, and seek diligently till she find it ? And when she hath found it, she calleth her friends and her neighbours together, saying, " Rejoice with me, for I have found the piece which I had lost."

Likewise, I say unto you, there is joy in the presence of the angels of God over one sinner that repenteth.

Even so it is not the will of your Father which is in heaven that one of these little ones shall perish.

(Next chapter in this group, page 5433)

" GO YOUR WAYS "

" ARE NOT FIVE SPARROWS SOLD FOR TWO FARTHINGS ? "

WHAT IS WRONG WITH THIS RAILWAY STATION?

Every one of us enjoys watching the comings and goings of people and trains at a busy railway terminus. But in a station like the one shown here, there would be a great deal more than this to interest us, for the artist in his drawing has purposely made many mistakes. It will be an excellent test of our powers of observation if we can find them all. A list is given on page 5438.

The Interests and Pleasures of Life for All Indoors and Out

A rock garden in a pleasant setting against a background of shrubs

BUILDING A ROCK GARDEN

THE cultivation of alpine plants is a comparatively modern form of gardening, and is a most fascinating hobby, for in a properly constructed rock garden covering only a few square yards a surprisingly large number of beautiful and interesting plants from the high mountain ranges can be grown in any average country or suburban garden.

Interest at first centred in the cultivation of plants from our own mountains, from the Swiss Alps and the other high ranges of Europe, and many of these plants still rank among the most satisfactory for the main planting of the rock garden—aubrietias and golden alyssum, dwarf alpine pinks and harebells in great variety, mossy and lime-encrusted rosette saxifrages, vivid blue vernal gentian and creeping phloxes, and alpine primroses, or Primulas as serious gardeners call them, of bewildering form and beauty.

But as interest in rock gardening increased, it was natural that intrepid plant collectors should carry the search further afield. From the Rockies of North America to the Andes of the South, from the Himalayas and the vast mountainous regions of Burma, China, and Tibet, aptly named the " roof of the world " and hitherto in large part unexplored by Europeans, collectors have enriched our knowledge of the flora of the world, and our gardens with plants of rare and entrancing beauty.

Yes, plant treasures from all the mountain ranges of the earth are at your disposal, and in the majority of cases their cultivation is not difficult, provided you study their needs. Their homes are on the windswept mountain ranges, and so, in choosing the position for the rockery, you must select a site as open to the sun and air as possible. Especially should it be clear of large spreading trees, whose roots would rob the alpine plants of food and moisture, while the drip from the leaves, and shade, would soon complete their destruction.

Having selected the site, you must decide on the size and shape that the rock garden is to take, and this will, of course, depend largely on the kind of rock available. Fortunate are those who live in districts where rock occurs naturally, for then the problem is easily solved.

The loveliest rock of all is waterworn Westmorland or Yorkshire limestone, but the cost of this is beyond the means of the average gardener. The porous Tufa limestone from Derbyshire is excellent, and so are any of the harder, and less expensive, sandstones.

Even if you can only obtain a few pieces of natural rock, do not despair of making an attractive rock garden, for by placing these in prominent positions, and building up with rough pieces of concrete from road or house demolition, you can provide homes

CRAFTS · GAMES · NEEDLEWORK · PUZZLES · SCIENCE EXPERIMENTS

for many plants that will soon hide any ugliness in the concrete. For the important thing to remember, in building a rock garden, is that it is intended primarily to provide homes for alpine plants, not merely to display the rock.

If a sunny bank is available, it will be quite easy to convert this into a cliffed rock garden by building irregular terraces, with wide ledges of deep soil broken here and there with rocky drifts. Otherwise, perhaps the simplest form of construction is what is generally termed a hill and valley garden.

This is built on both sides of a gently-winding path, which is excavated a foot or so deep to provide soil for building up into mounds of irregular form on either side. If subsidiary paths are desired, these are dug in the same way. The paths will look most attractive if provided with flat stepping stones and surfaced with an inch or two of limestone or granite chippings, in which all kinds of dwarf creeping and mat-forming plants can be grown—creeping thymes, the dwarfest alpine pinks, campanulas, and so on.

Before starting to build the rock mounds, it is well to make sure that the soil is suitable for growing alpine plants: a most important factor. It must be well drained and so, unless it is naturally very light, plenty of stones and limestone chippings, and possibly a little sand, should be mixed with it. If the soil is poor, it can be enriched by adding turf soil (loam), leafmould, and peat as planting proceeds.

Building of the mounds should start at the margin of the paths, and the aim should always be to arrange the rocks as naturally as possible. By setting some of the lower rocks back into the bank, little pockets will be made and any appearance of formality avoided. As building proceeds, cliffs and promontories can be created by placing two or three pieces of rock together, and ramming soil firmly between them, to provide homes for the encrusted saxifrages, houseleeks or sempervivums, sedums, and other crevice-loving plants.

For ramming the soil firmly between and about the rocks, a hammer handle, or short length of broomstick pointed at one end, is very useful, and so is a small brush of birch twigs for cleaning soil from the rocks. Take care to bury the rocks to half their depth, and let them slope downwards at the back so that they will drain surface water into the soil: nothing looks less attractive than a heap of soil with rocks lying on the surface, or sticking out in all directions in " plum-pudding " fashion.

Arrange the rocks with their strata running continuously as they occur in Nature, setting some at angles to form pockets for special plants; always make the ledges wide enough for the plants to root deeply into the soil, and when making sloping drifts between cliffs of rock, bury plenty of stones for drainage, and break the surface here and there with an outcropping rock.

After the rock garden has been built, it should be left for a few weeks for the soil and rocks to settle before putting in the plants, which can be ordered in the meantime from one of the many nurseries that specialise in alpine plants.

For the crevices between the rocks, where they must be planted very firmly and wedged with pieces of turf soil and stones, some of the most useful to begin with are: Androsace sarmentosa, a very lovely little pink-flowered cushion plant; the trailing cream Snap-dragon called Antirrhinum Asarina; the tiny white flowered Sandwort or Arenaria montana; the smallest of all Thrifts, soft-pink Armeria caespitosa; the Cheddar Pink (Dianthus caesius) and many others; and encrusted Saxifrages, Houseleeks (Semper-vivums), Stonecrops (Sedums) and alpine Auriculas (Primulas) in great variety.

On the ledges, to drape the rocks with glorious masses of flowers, you can plant Aubrietias, golden Alyssum, and shrubby Sun Roses (Helianthemums), with perennial white Candytuft (Iberis),trailing Gypsophila repens; pink-flowered, grey-leaved Grecian candytuft, Aethionema grandiflorum; and the little pink-flowered Erigeron mucronatus, which flowers the summer through.

A few of the very dwarf alpine shrubs and conifers—slow-growing Pines and Cypresses—will add character and interest to the rock garden, and to complete the picture the drifts and pockets can be planted freely with blue Harebells or Campanulas in variety, especially those called muralis, garganica, and pusilla; Anemones and dwarf Aquilegias; spring-flowering Gentiana verna and autumn-flowering G. sino-ornata; rose-red Geranium sanguinium, mat-forming Phloxes, purple and red Thymes, mossy Saxifrages, alpine Veronicas, and Violas. These represent but a very small proportion of the many lovely little plants available, but if you start with some of them you will soon want to grow more once your rock garden has become established.

Miniature rock gardens made in old unglazed stone sinks, or shallow concrete troughs, and mounted on brick supports, make delightful garden ornaments if planted with dwarf, free-flowering alpine plants. They are very easy to make and manage. You cover the outlet hole with wire gauze, put a few broken stones over it, then fill the sink with a mixture of equal parts of good soil and granite chips, pressing it firm. Small rocks are arranged to produce a miniature alpine effect, and the plants then set among them.

AN ATTRACTIVE BELT IN POKER-WORK

POKER-WORK is a method of making patterns on wood by burning, so changing the surface to brown in colour.

Electric needles can be used, but the work is simply and easily done with the little machine, not always easy to get, shown in our first picture.

It consists of a delicate little point made of platinum fixed into a metal tube, with a covered handle, which is a non-conductor of heat, so that it prevents the hand from getting hurt. This point is attached to a bottle of benzoline by an india-rubber tube. Also connected to the bottle by

A POKER-WORK MACHINE

another tube is a bulb, which takes the place of bellows. After the point has once been heated in the flame of a candle, it can be kept red-hot as long as required by pressing the bulb—that is, blowing the bellows. This is because benzoline is very inflammable and gives off a sort of vapour, which rises through a hole in the bottle-cork, gets up into the indiarubber tubes, and so passes along to the point where it is burned. As it burns, it keeps the point red-hot. There is absolutely no danger in using this machine, though, of course, it is not meant for little fingers, but only for bigger boys and girls.

THREE KINDS OF POINTS

The three points shown here are large, flat, and pointed. The large one is for deep work and rough wood, the flat one for shading and filling in, and the fine one for outlining a delicate pattern and for fine work generally.

Wood is not the only material which can be used for poker-work. Leather lends itself well to this form of decoration, so we will make a belt.

Before we begin, though, we must practise a little on a piece of plain white wood, with a smooth surface. It will help us to learn how to manage the machine.

We shall find out by experiment how hard to blow, because, of course, the harder we blow the hotter becomes the point. Leather, for instance, needs less heat than wood. If we are using too much heat, a small flame will flicker at the end of our point as it touches the wood. This must be avoided, because it makes the surface black instead of brown, by burning it too deeply.

The chief effects are got by contrast of colour—that is, light and dark

TWO WAYS OF FILLING IN

THE BELT

browns—and difference in the depth and the thickness of the lines.

The tones of brown vary from a pale yellowish tint to a brown which is almost black. And the lines can be merely faint marks, just indicating the vein of a leaf, or quite deep cuttings in the wood.

Then there are different ways of filling in backgrounds. Two are shown here, and we shall be able to invent others for ourselves. In the first one, the flat point is used. It is pressed along the surface of the wood in rows more or less straight, and the pattern so formed suggests fine leather. The other pattern is more like the grain of wood, and is done by passing the fine point rapidly over the surface, backwards and forwards, keeping it steadily at the same heat, and holding it so that it lies as flat as possible.

Sometimes colour may be added to a pattern. Ordinary wood-stain may be used, or water-colour, afterwards varnished for protection.

Designs composed of flower leaves and simple shapes are the best for this work, and the belt in the picture is pokered in a design of small leaves, though its chief charm is that the leaves themselves are burned right away, and fastened behind is a strip of ribbon, cloth, or felt, which shows through the holes.

The sort of belt to use is a plain, light fawn leather, of the most ordinary kind, with a smooth surface and a plain buckle. We pencil in the leaf-shapes at intervals all along the strip, taking care that the design does not interfere with the buckle-holes when we come to that end, and then fill in the connecting lines.

We use the fine, thin point to pierce the leather round the outline of the leaves, going over the line several times with a fair amount of heat, and the piece will drop out; then we carefully darken the edges with the point, and smooth away any little bits which destroy the leaf-shape.

The border at the edge is the darkest part. We make that fairly solid with one of the " filling in " patterns. The space between the border and the lines which connect the leaves is dotted with the sharp point. We should hold the poker in an upright position for this, and press gently, taking care to make the dots of equal depth.

FLOWERS AROUND THE HOUSE

ALMOST anyone can arrange a lot of flowers successfully, but an artist can obtain a picturesque result with a very few. Most of us, however, would get a better effect with some ideas to guide us.

The centre flowers in a bowl which has in it a glass, china, or wire support for the stalks, should be in height about one and a half times the width of the bowl. This is the conventional way to fill a bowl with flowers.

But in small rooms, especially of the cottage type, nothing looks prettier than shallow bowls and little glass dishes of various shapes, filled with short-stalked flowers arranged like a Victorian posy, with an edging of feathery green—carrot tops do well for this.

It is saving where there is a small garden, for there can be a good show indoors without leaving gaps in the borders. Instead of several spikes, say, of delphiniums or campanulas, a few single flowers are taken from where they will not be missed. Sometimes petals only can be used to give a touch of colour, and fallen blossoms of fruit trees can be brought into this scheme, which is an idea that can be worked out all the year round.

These simple arrangements would look insignificant in lofty rooms. There something strikingly tall is needed, and the tallest flower or leaf should be three or four times the height of the vase or the width of the bowl. The tallest flower need not be the centre one. A group at one side of a bowl looks artistic.

A basket makes a very attractive flower vase, and jam pots or anything old can be put inside to hold the water, for they will be hidden. Nasturtiums massed in it as if they are growing, with a long runner twined up one side of the handle, will brighten a dull corner or act as a firescreen in summer.

When flowers are scarce, have sprigs of evergreen in the basket, and up one side leaning above the handle, sprays of winter jasmine or garden broom. The flowers of the winter jasmine may come out, but the broom will have neither flowers nor leaves. All the same, it looks effective and can always be used to add height.

A top-heavy vase can be steadied with a layer of sand in the bottom, and if we are short of flower holders, a small piece of crumpled wire netting serves splendidly. Florist's baskets and bowls are often arranged with the help of wire, and even the humble rubber band does duty as a flower prop at times. We can remember this when a heavy flower head will not stay where we put it.

THE PUZZLE OF THE SIAMESE FLAG

WILFRID and his sister Phyllis had been making various kinds of flags, so as to have a good string of them to hang up on special occasions. The Union Jack and Stars and Stripes were rather difficult, but they managed these between them, and a lot of the European flags were comparatively easy.

"Now," said Phyllis, "let us make the flags of some of the countries in Asia."

"A good idea!" replied Wilfrid. "We will make the Chinese and Siamese, to begin with."

"I know the Chinese flag," said Phyllis, "but I don't remember the Siamese. What is it like?"

PHYLLIS HAD PUT THE ELEPHANT IN THE CORNER

"I'm not quite sure," answered Wilfrid, "but I know one of their flags has a white elephant on it."

"Can you draw me a picture of the elephant so that I shall know just how to make it?" asked Phyllis, and Wilfrid did so. Then he went off to play in a cricket match.

When he returned he asked Phyllis how she had got on with the Siamese flag.

"Oh," she answered, "I've done it. Here it is." And, unfolding it, she held the flag up for him to see. Wilfrid roared with laughter at the sight.

"Just like a girl!" he said. "Why, you've put the elephant in the corner, and it should be in the middle."

"Well, I can easily alter that," replied Phyllis.

"Don't be silly," said her brother; "you will have to make an entirely new flag."

"Oh, no!" said Phyllis. "I shall cut this one up and rejoin the pieces."

And she did so with great success. The elephant was right in the middle of the flag. How many pieces did she cut the flag into, and how did she fit the pieces together? The solution is given on page 5438.

ANSWER TO THE PUZZLE OF THE DOG'S KENNEL ON PAGE 5194— These diagrams show how George cut up the old broken table to make a door for the dog's kennel.

HOW TO PLAY RACKETS AND SQUASH

RACKETS, popular in England (chiefly at certain public schools), India, and the United States, is not thought to be an ancient game, as little seems to have been heard of it before the early nineteenth century. The game of Squash Rackets, said to have developed from it at Harrow School towards the end of that century, is steadily growing in popularity. Many clubs, hotels, and blocks of modern flats have squash courts, a comparative few have provision for playing rackets.

The two games are in the same family as fives, a description of which game appears on page 5564. The main difference is that a fives player strikes the ball with his hand. In rackets, of course, a racket is used. It is similar to the lawn tennis variety, but the frame is smaller and the handle longer.

As the diagrams of the two courts show, they also are different from a fives court. The rackets court is larger and has a back wall in addition to the front and side walls. The white ball, about the size of a large walnut, is leather-covered.

For the single game with one player on each side, the court should be about sixty feet by thirty. For the double game with two players on each side, it should be about eighty feet by forty. The walls and floor are coloured black.

Across the front wall, seven feet nine inches from the ground, is painted a white line, known as the service line or cut line. The lower part of this wall, to a height of two feet three inches from the ground, is covered with wood, and is known as the board. The object of this is to enable the players to know by the sound whether a ball strikes above or below the play line, as the top of the board is called. The back part of the court is divided into two equal oblong sections, into one of

SQUASH RACKETS IN PLAY

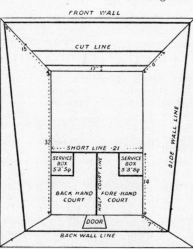

FRONT WALL
CUT LINE
SHORT LINE ·21
SERVICE BOX 5'3"·5'9"
SERVICE BOX 5'3"·5'9"
BACK HAND COURT
FORE HAND COURT
HALF COURT LINE
SIDE WALL LINE
DOOR
BACK WALL LINE

PLAN OF A SQUASH COURT

which the ball must be served. The service boxes are spaces, eight feet eight inches long by six feet seven inches wide, marked on the floor, from which the server strikes the ball.

When it has been determined, by the spin of the racket, who shall serve first, the server stands in the left section box, and throws the ball up and strikes it so that it will hit the front wall above the service line, and rebound into the right-hand section of the back of the court marked B in the diagram on the next page. The opposite player then strikes the ball, either volleying it or hitting it after it has bounced on the ground once. In doing so he must see that he hits the front wall above the board.

If when being served the ball should first strike a side wall, or the roof or floor before hitting the front wall, the striker loses his innings. The ball must hit the front wall above the white line first, and then fall into the back right court B if served from the left service box, or into the back left court A if served from the right service box. Anything else is called a fault, and the other player need not take it. If, however, he attempts to take it, the game goes on as if the service had been correct.

If the server wins his point he crosses to the right service box and serves. If the opponent fails to return the ball the server scores an ace or point. The server becomes hand-out; that is he gives place to his opponent, who becomes the server, if he makes a fault twice in succession, if the ball in returning strikes his person, if he serves the ball on the board or out of the court, if the ball served touches any other part of the court before striking the front wall, if he fails to return the ball in play so that it goes out of the court, or if the ball in play touches him in the act of striking. In any of these cases the server-in is out, and the previous hand-out takes his place as server.

A let is when either player undesignedly prevents his opponent from returning the ball served or in play, or when the ball in play touches the striker's opponent on, or above, the knee, and is thereby prevented from reaching the front wall above the board. In case of a let, the service counts for nothing and the server serves again. The ball served or in play may be struck either before it reaches the ground or after it has bounced once. The player who first scores fifteen wins the game.

In the double game play is very similar, but there are one or two additional regulations.

If the server loses his point his partner takes his place, each pair of players having to be put out before the next pair goes in. The game is fifteen, but at thirteen all the out-players may set to five, and at fourteen all, to three. Should the ball after being served touch the server or his partner before bouncing on the ground, the server is out. If a player in returning the ball strikes the body or racket of his opponent, he is out, or has one point counted against him, according to whether he is in or out. If a player intentionally impedes a striker, or takes a ball out of his proper turn, a point is counted against him. For the best game, the floor and walls of the court cannot be too hard. A really strong service is of vital importance, and may possibly result in winning a game outright.

SERVICE BOXES

60'

24'

A   B

←------- 30' -------→

SIMPLE PLAN OF
RACKETS COURT

Few games give better exercise or need a quicker eye and a stronger wrist. A player to succeed at rackets must have considerable endurance.

Squash rackets, played in a similar manner but with a soft ball, gives equally good exercise. It is, however, not so strenuous, and therefore is within the ability of women players. It brings every muscle into play, and for both men and women is a good and easy way of keeping fit for summer games during the winter months.

As can be seen by the measurements given in the diagrams, the court is much smaller than that of rackets, which limits the game to singles, though there are double courts in America where the "team" game has a certain degree of popularity.

The rules governing the game of squash are not dissimilar from those of rackets already given, except that each game is nine points only. Originally it was fifteen points as in rackets, but was altered in 1926.

Squash is unlike most other games played with a racket in that good service is not often an ace-winning stroke. It counts, of course, but more depends upon the accurate placing of the ball, on developing the forehand and backhand drives, and neat and nimble footwork. Correct footwork and balance should be learned from the beginning. Steps should be short and, at the ready position, the feet should be a little apart with the weight equally distributed between them.

IMPOSSIBLE FEAT THAT APPEARS SIMPLE

HERE is what seems a very simple feat, yet nobody can do it. It makes a good game for a party, and is interesting as well as entertaining, for it teaches an important scientific lesson.

We place a low stool close up against the wall. Standing with our feet together, twice the width of the stool from the wall, we stoop down and grasp the stool as shown in the picture, with one hand on each side, at the same time resting our head against the wall.

Then we have to rise steadily erect without moving our feet and without jerking our body. It seems so simple, yet directly we try to do it we find ourselves helpless.

The explanation is, of course, that by standing in this position and holding the stool, we have thrown our centre of gravity far to the front and beyond our control. If

the wall were not there we should fall over forward, as we can guess by the pressure on our heads, for we are in what science calls a state of unstable equilibrium.

It is the kind of feat that those of us who are boys like to try among ourselves. But as it is a quiet game, it might be followed by something more exciting, like Over the Line.

Two boys stand facing each other across a line marked on the floor or ground, with arms raised sideways nearly level with the shoulders. Then they clasp hands, and lean forward until their chests touch. At a word they both push, and the one who succeeds in pushing until he himself has passed completely over the line is the winner.

Winner takes on winner until the strongest of the party comes through invincible.

The Story of the Boundless Universe and All its Wondrous Worlds

Boiling a kettle of liquid air on a block of ice   An egg boiled in liquid air, that cannot be broken

HOT THINGS AND COLD THINGS

WE know that matter may exist in a solid, liquid, or gaseous state, and we know, too, that, as a general rule, what we call heat makes a great difference in this respect.

We take water and we make it cold, and if we go on making it cold long enough, it becomes solid. If we begin with this solid water, or ice, and add heat to it, it becomes liquid. We might say, then, that liquid water is ice plus heat, that is to say, ice with heat added. If now we add more heat to this liquid water, or, in short, if we boil it, it all disappears, and we know that it has gone into the air as water-vapour, or gaseous water.

So we can go further and say that water-vapour is liquid water plus heat, just as liquid water is ice plus heat. If that sounds reasonable, we are already on the way to understanding what heat is, and as it is heat that we now have to study, we cannot do better than get this notion of heat as something added to matter, something that, as a rule, when added, makes the difference between the different physical states of matter.

Now, the all-important question about which men have argued for ages is the question as to what this something is.

We are fortunate enough nowadays to be able to come in at the end of the argument and get the result without the trouble of working it out. There is in heat a something that is undoubtedly real. We know there is nothing unreal about the heat of a red-hot poker. But is it a kind of matter? Is it a thing that we can weigh?

Now, though Einstein's theory of relativity and experiments with the atom have shown that all matter is energy and all energy matter, the disappearance of mass equivalent to the energy, or heat, set free is so minute as to be, for practical purposes, unweighable. It has been calculated, for example, that the energy supplied by Niagara Falls to power stations every 33 hours is only equivalent to one gram of matter.

Heat is a form of energy, it is, in effect, motion.

We know, too, that there are many kinds of motion, and, of course, it does not do to say that heat is motion unless we add that it is a very special and particular kind of motion, quite distinct from any other. Heat is a special to-and-fro motion, which we have learned to call a vibration, of very tiny particles of the atoms or molecules of which matter is made.

ASTRONOMY · GEOLOGY · GEOGRAPHY · CHEMISTRY · PHYSICS · LIFE

Now, this idea, simple enough in itself, has very startling consequences.

Let us consider a simple case like that of water. Let us imagine that we have a little liquid water before us; it may be cold or hot water, but, in any case, it has a certain amount of heat in it; in other words, its molecules are vibrating at a certain rate and, as we may suppose, with a particular length of swing to each vibration.

THE SWINGING OF THE MOLECULES THAT MAKES WATER HOT

Now, if we add heat to this water, we are adding to it—on our notion of what heat really is—more motion of this particular kind. Well, when the molecules of the water get this extra motion added to them, perhaps taking the form of a quicker motion, or perhaps taking the form of a longer swing, or perhaps both, the time comes when it is simply impossible for the molecules to swing so freely or so quickly, and yet to hold together in the way that makes liquid water. With so much heat in it, the water has to become gas, other things being equal, and it does so. It boils. This water-vapour, as it now is, may have still more heat added to it, nor can we say what limits there are in this direction.

But now let us travel in the other direction. Instead of adding heat, which is a special kind of motion, to the water, let us begin to take from it the heat that it already has. We know that, when we cool the water, in course of time it turns solid. Other things being equal—and we have to say this because the question of the pressure of the atmosphere really comes into this too—the molecules of the water can no longer be related in the way that makes the water liquid, if we take away from them too much of that particular kind of motion which we call heat. Deprived of much of this motion, the molecules have to arrange themselves in a different way, so that we have ice.

ICE THAT CAN BE COOLED AND ICE THAT CAN BE HEATED

Now, though we all agree that liquid water may be hotter or colder, because we notice this every day, perhaps we are not all quite sure that ice may be hotter or colder; yet it certainly may. We can cool the ice as we cooled the water, and all the time we are taking away from it this particular kind of motion called heat;

and so we may go on and on steadily lessening its heat up to a certain point.

Now, if a man has a certain amount of money, it may be added to, and there is no particular point at which no more can be added, and so it is with the addition of heat to anything. But if we start taking away a man's money, say, at the rate of one farthing after another, the time is bound to come—and bound to come whether he started with a penny or with a million pounds—when he has no more money, and, whatever we do to him, we cannot make him lose any more.

Now, what is true of money must be true of anything else, such as the kind of motion we call heat. As we cool the ice, we are taking this motion away from it, but the amount of it that the ice has is not infinite, and in course of time, if we go on steadily—though this may be tremendously difficult or impossible—we shall take away all the heat that was in the ice, and when that happens we shall have something which is absolutely cold.

There is now no heat in the ice; the utmost part of the kind of motion we call heat has left it. So far as that kind of motion is concerned, its molecules and atoms are still; they cannot be colder. If heat is such as we suppose, this must be a possibility for matter of all kinds, whether ice or anything else.

THE LOWEST TEMPERATURE TO WHICH MATTER CAN BE REDUCED

Further, it is possible to find out how cold a thing would have to be so that it could be no colder, and we do indeed know what that point is compared with our ordinary scales of temperature, about which we have already learned something. In various ways it has been shown that 273 degrees below the zero on the Centigrade scale is absolute cold. Matter reduced to that point would have no heat in it. Nothing can be colder than this. This discovery is one of the greatest that has ever been made in this part of science, and it has many interesting consequences, as we shall soon see.

First, let us consider the matter of measurement, always so important. We now have something better to go by even than the freezing-point and the boiling-point of water; we have something even better than the freezing-point of mercury or, indeed, of any substance that we know. We have discovered the existence of a point at which the motion that we call heat has ceased to exist.

Plainly, that point must be nothing, or zero, on the best possible scale of temperature. So, while there is a zero on the Centigrade scale, and on various other scales, we now have discovered the *real zero*, where heat and temperature really begin; and this we call the *absolute zero*, All over the world, men of science think and write in terms of this real scale of temperature.

HOW THE SIZE OF A THING IS AFFECTED BY ITS HEAT

Any student of heat, going to lectures or reading text-books, will find such phrases as *10 degrees absolute*. The ordinary clumsy way of expressing that point on the scale would be *minus 263 degrees Centigrade*, and, of course, we can see at once what a great advantage it is to reckon on the new scale. It is a great find for science to have discovered Nature's zero of temperature instead of having to fix on some point far above that real zero, and then to call that point the zero because we know no better.

The next question which must occur to everyone who thinks about this is: What is matter like at absolute zero? Let us imagine what this means. We have taken a gas, such as water-vapour or hydrogen, the molecules of which are moving about in a particular way, which we call heat. We have steadily taken away that motion; the gas has steadily become colder, first liquid and then solid. When we have taken away all the motion of this kind, what will be left? We must remember that the substance we are dealing with has steadily shrunk all the time; indeed, not merely part of its size, but by far the greater part of its size to begin with, was due to the heat in it. If, now, as we cool it, its size begins to lessen, is it not quite possible that when we have made it absolutely cold there may be nothing left of it?

WHY WE BELIEVE THAT MATTER DOES NOT DISAPPEAR AT ABSOLUTE ZERO

It has been found that when a gas is cooled, for every degree Centigrade that the temperature is lowered it loses one 273rd of its volume at o degrees Centigrade. Therefore at —273 degrees, that is, at absolute zero, the gas would theoretically have lost 273 273rds, or the whole of its volume, and cease to exist at all. It

was at one time believed that this would happen, but now all known gases have been changed into the liquid form at low temperatures and, of course, when they do so the law referred to, which is known as Gay-Lussac's law, after its author's name, does not hold good, as it is a law for gases only. We now believe that, even at absolute zero, matter would not disappear; in other words, heat is something added to matter, but heat is not matter.

It is believed by astronomers that in the mighty tracts of space between the stars and planets there are quantities, by no means small, of matter, such as is often called *cosmic dust*. Now, students of heat are convinced that in these great spaces the temperature must be practically that of the absolute zero, the coldest possible cold. Therefore, the existence of this temperature does not mean that matter disappears altogether. We have also the evidence provided by our own little attempts on the Earth to reach the absolute zero. Let us now see how far down the scale Man has been able to go, and what results he has obtained.

THE GREAT MARVEL OF LIQUID AIR THAT CAN BE POURED OUT LIKE WATER

It is by no means difficult to make the gas carbon dioxide solid, and then it looks like a sort of snow. After all, snow itself is only solid water-vapour, and the two cases are quite parallel. It is very much more difficult, but still it is possible, to take the mixture of gases which we call air, and first of all to make it liquid by cooling it very much, and then by cooling that liquid still more to make it become quite solid.

Much of the work on this subject was done by Sir James Dewar at the Royal Institution, and by Dr. Kamerlingh Onnes at the University of Leyden in Holland. Liquid air is vastly colder than ice, and it looks like water. It can be stored quite easily in vessels, and poured about just like water. A few drops running over our fingers would do them no harm, because the round drops would bound off and not actually *touch* the skin; but we should not put our fingers in it.

The use of liquid air is one of the most convenient ways of making low temperatures—that is to say, for making other things cold—and it is very largely used in chemistry for this purpose.

It has besides been made up into cartridges with charcoal for use as an explosive, a great volume of air being liberated when the liquid air is made suddenly to evaporate.

No one could tell by looking at it that liquid air was not water, and when it is frozen no one could tell it from ice by looking at it. Solid air is, of course, very much colder than liquid air, but it is very far from reaching the lowest temperatures.

TEMPERATURE WITHIN A FRACTION OF A DEGREE OF ABSOLUTE ZERO

Everyone has heard that water on the top of a mountain boils at a lower temperature than at the base because there is less atmospheric pressure on the water's surface. In a similar way, if pressure is taken from the surface of liquid air by placing it, for example, in a vacuum, the temperature of the liquid air will fall, or, in other words, the liquid air will boil at a lower degree. This is the cascade principle by which successively lower temperatures can be reached; and by its adoption Sir James Dewar was able to produce a low enough temperature to liquefy hydrogen and to show it to a meeting of the Royal Society. From liquid hydrogen, by a similar lowering of the pressure, solid hydrogen can be obtained, and in this, his greatest triumph, Sir James Dewar reached a temperature of 13 degrees above absolute zero.

Afterwards Dr. Kamerlingh Onnes succeeded in liquefying helium and got still farther down the scale. Before he died he succeeded in lowering the temperature to within four-fifths of a degree of absolute zero and declared that he did not think it at all likely that we should ever get down to zero itself. That goal may be, as he thought, unattainable, but since his death one of his assistants at Leyden has got several fractions of a degree lower. Why is it so difficult to abolish the last fractions?

THE GREAT DIFFICULTY OF GETTING ALL THE HEAT OUT OF A THING

In the first place, though one-hundredth of a degree is not much in our ordinary way of thinking, yet that partly depends on the way in which our minds are deceived by figures. If we chose a much finer reckoning, and divided every degree into a thousand degrees, then the interval between solid helium or hydrogen and the absolute zero would seem much larger.

Then, again, it is the fact, and one which applies in many instances in science, that the farther we go the slower we go. We might suppose that to travel from 12 degrees absolute to 8 degrees would be just the same as to travel from 8 to 4 or from 4 to zero; but that is not so. Every degree lower is much harder to conquer than the one reached before.

When we take the temperature of a hot bath we use a thermometer in which the mercury rises up a very narrow glass tube. But as mercury freezes at a temperature far above the very low degrees near the absolute zero it obviously cannot be used. Dr. Kamerlingh Onnes once explained that the task of *measuring* these very low temperatures was almost as big a problem as attaining the low temperatures themselves, and the nearer we approached absolute zero the greater would this difficulty become.

It is believed that at the temperature of the Sun things are too *hot* for most chemical processes to occur, and when we descend instead of ascending, the same result is, in general, true. Just as chemical processes cease at high temperatures, so most of them cease at very low temperatures. Elements which ordinarily combine with each other with great force and perhaps explosive violence, do nothing at all with each other when put together at very low temperatures. Nevertheless, there is also a low-temperature chemistry.

THE WAYS IN WHICH HEAT TRAVELS FROM PLACE TO PLACE

Let us now pass on to another interesting question : how heat travels or spreads from place to place.

It travels by means of radiations, which, agitating in empty space, can be thrown into waves of different shapes and sizes, but all of the same speed—186,000 miles a second. Some of the waves convey light, some heat. The heat from the sun and from incandescent and hot, dark bodies travels in such waves, and heat so conveyed is called radiant heat.

Heat also travels by what we call *convection*, from the Latin word for carrying. Let us take the case of the water in a kettle which is being heated.

We can imagine the special kind of motion called heat being imparted to the molecules of water that lie nearest the bottom of the kettle. It may then be, as indeed it is, that these molecules rise to the surface of the water, and as they rise, of course, they carry with them their heat. Now, the heat which was applied to the under surface of the water has reached its upper surface. It has been bodily carried, so to speak, through the water; and when heat is carried from place to place in this way, we say that this is a case of *convection*.

We may think of this, perhaps, if we care to, as like the case of a buzzing insect. The buzzing and humming are due to the vibration of its wings, and as it flies about it carries the buzzing and humming with it. So we may think of the molecules of matter as buzzing. That buzzing is their heat, and when they travel they carry it with them.

HOW THE WATER IN THE KETTLE BECOMES HEATED ALL THROUGH

In the case of the water in the kettle the heated water rises. It does this because heated water is lighter than cold water. Therefore, by heating one part of the body of the water, we can set the whole body of the water moving, and this applies not only to the kettle, but also to the oceans. It applies equally to other fluids, such as the atmosphere. In all the water of the Earth, and in the Earth's great coat of air, different parts are at different times heated more or less than other parts, and so convection currents are started.

The results are very important, not only because heat is carried about from place to place, but because the matter carrying the heat is also moving about. In this way great ocean currents, and also great air currents, which we call winds, are started. There are constantly going on, for instance, what are called the Trade Winds, so called because in the old days when ships were driven by the wind the ocean trade of the world largely depended on them.

HOW A ROW OF BOYS CAN SHOW THE WAYS IN WHICH HEAT TRAVELS

Heat travels also by what we call *conduction*. The conduction of heat occurs in all circumstances, in solids, liquids, and gases, from solids to liquids, from gases to solids, and so on.

It is the constant law, true everywhere and always, that whenever one thing is hotter than another, heat will flow from the hotter to the colder. Just as we say that water must find its own level, because

of the constant action of the Earth's gravitation, so we may compare heat with water, and say that it must find its own level. The constant tendency of heat everywhere is to make its level equal. Every portion of matter everywhere which is hotter than its surroundings must lose heat to them, just as a river must run downhill.

Now, we must first understand what conduction actually is, and how it differs from convection. In conduction the heat is passed on, or conducted, but the matter which contained it stays where it was. It is like a row of boys in which each one is slapping the next; whereas, in convection, the boys would change places and take their slaps with them. If we remember what heat is, we can begin to imagine how the buzzing, or vibration, of the atoms at one end of a poker might start the atoms farther along vibrating also in the same way, and so the buzzing, or heat, would be conducted along the poker. It is not possible to go more deeply into the nature of conduction than this, because we really do not understand how the atoms or molecules of matter are held together in a poker, or in anything else.

But we can, at any rate, study conduction in many ways, and the first thing we find is that different kinds of matter vary enormously in their power of conducting heat.

THE LIVING TISSUES WHICH ARE BAD CONDUCTORS OF HEAT

Everyone knows that one end of the poker becomes hot when the other end is held to the fire. Yet one end of a piece of firewood may be so hot as to be actually burning, and the other end quite cool, though the stick is far shorter than the poker. The metals in general are very good conductors of heat, as the iron of the poker suggests. On the other hand, tissues made by living things are very bad conductors of heat. Wood is such a tissue, though we do not always think of it as if it were, and we have noticed how badly it conducts heat. Bone, also, and wool and silk, and even linen and cotton tissues always conduct heat very badly indeed.

Though we have to rank the group of the metals as good conductors, yet even among themselves they vary a good deal in their efficiency in this respect.

(Next chapter in this group, page 5441)

BENJAMIN FRANKLIN FLIES HIS KITE IN A THUNDERSTORM AND PROVES THAT LIGHTNING AND ELECTRICITY
ARE ONE AND THE SAME

The Story of Immortal Folk Whose Work Will Never Die

Alessandro Volta

Luigi Galvani

Sir Joseph Swan

John Canton

Michael Faraday

Sir William Watson

Otto von Guericke

Robert Boyle

Hans Oersted

Sir Humphry Davy

THE ELECTRICITY PIONEERS

ELECTRICITY is one of the most wonderful forces placed ready for the service of mankind, yet it is one of the things which hid its secret longest from us.

Men discovered how to turn the strength of animals to account; to make the winds drive our ships across the seas; to apply the power stored up in coal; to raise steam and with it change the face of the world. Yet electricity is greater than these. It can do almost anything. It can light a city, supply power for lifting the heaviest weights, drive trains and trams, cook a dinner, heal a sick child, and kill us if we are not careful. It is in almost everything, though it does not move. All we have to do is to excite it, bring it out, and catch it so that we may use it as we need it. It is so valuable, and does such marvellous things that it is hard to believe that it existed for thousands of years quite unknown to men.

We have already seen on page 233 how, 2000 years ago, men had noticed the peculiar properties of amber and other substances, but it was not until the sixteenth century was well advanced that the world began to take a real interest in electricity. Then William Gilbert, a thoughtful scholar who was one of Queen Elizabeth's doctors, experimented with a number of substances to see whether they, like amber, would, when warmed by friction, attract other bodies. He found that many, including sulphur, sealing-wax, gems, solid resin, rock-salt, and many other things, had the same power. They would attract metals, stones, earths, fluid, and even heavy smoke.

As the first man to examine the question he had to find a name to describe the condition which he excited in these objects, and, as amber was the first substance known to have this power of attraction, and as the Greek name for amber is *elektron*, Gilbert gave the name *electricity* to the condition which heat and friction excited in the things he tried. He is called the father of electrical science. Gilbert lived 63 years, dying in 1603; and his life was very valuable to the world, for every year since he began his discoveries our store of learning concerning electricity has gone on increasing.

Gilbert was a Colchester man. He was followed by a famous Irishman, Robert Boyle, a son of the Earl of Cork. Boyle was born in Munster in 1627. He was a wonderful scholar as a boy, and at ten learned algebra simply because he loved to exercise his mind. He invented a famous air pump, and taught the

EXPLORERS · INVENTORS · WRITERS · ARTISTS · SCIENTISTS

world all about the condition and qualities of air. His work for electricity was to show that electricity remained for some time in a substance after rubbing had ceased, the importance of which discovery we have read about on page 234; and to add new substances which could be electrified. The mere fact that he was noticing electricity was sufficient to set other men thinking about it, for his reputation was very high, especially with the great men on the Continent of Europe.

THE MAN WHO FASTENED TWO THINGS TOGETHER WITH A VACUUM

Boyle died in 1691, five years after the death of Otto von Guericke, a clever man (born at Magdeburg, Prussia, in 1602) who, after an excellent education, visited England and became acquainted with the English scientists of that day. He invented the first air-pump, but that of Boyle's was so much better that the Prussian invention was soon forgotten. Guericke was the first man to show the immense power of a vacuum. He made two hemispheres of metal—that is, two large metal cups, the edges of which fitted together. There was a tap to each through which the air could be drawn out by the air pump. When this was done, so tightly did the two hemispheres cling together that not until the united strength of thirty horses had been employed could they be pulled apart.

Guericke lived far too early. As we read on page 234, he discovered a way of making electric light, but nobody knew what it meant. Electric lighting did not become general until the close of the nineteenth century. Guericke discovered also that bodies which have not been electrified by friction become electrified when brought into contact with other bodies which have been electrified.

Sir Isaac Newton did one notable thing for electricity by showing that a disc of glass, when placed in a brass cylinder and electrified, would attract paper so strongly as to make it leap about inside.

THE GLASS CYLINDER WITH WHICH HAWKSBEE MADE ELECTRICITY

Next came the experiments of Francis Hawksbee. It is not known when he was born, though the year of his death is given as about 1713. He made important experiments with air and mercury, and with a machine for producing electricity by rubbing a glass cylinder with the hand. He, for the first time, drew attention to the fact that the electric sparks which he was able to produce, and the crackling noise they made, resembled lightning.

His son, also Francis Hawksbee, who was born in 1687 and died in 1763, was a gifted maker of scientific instruments. The elder Hawksbee wrote much about his discoveries, and his books, translated into French and Italian, were of great assistance to scientists on the Continent.

All this may seem unimportant, but each little discovery led to others more important. A tree in a forest may not seem of much use as a dwelling to a man, but when the tree-feller and the carpenter and the builder have done their share, the tree becomes an essential part of a house. Now we come to the first step which brings us nearer to the practical uses of electricity.

Stephen Gray was a Bluecoat boy in London at the beginning of the eighteenth century, and by some happy chance gave up his life to the study of electricity. He made a grand discovery.

THE BLUECOAT BOY WHO SENT ELECTRICITY ALONG A THREAD

He found that we can divide matter into two classes—that which can be electrified by friction, and that which cannot be electrified by friction. Then he went a step farther and found that the non-electrics could be made electric by being placed in contact with those which were already electrified. This means, as we should say now, that he had discovered that some substances are conductors of electricity and some are non-conductors of electricity.

An ivory ball did not seem a promising thing with which to work, but Gray got a glass tube, and into its ends he fitted two corks. Into one cork he fixed his ivory ball, and, to his delight, he found that when the glass was rubbed it passed on its electricity through the cork to the ivory ball, and the ivory ball would now attract little things as the glass itself would. This led Gray to many splendid experiments—small in themselves, but dazzling by their results considering he was working in the dark. He tried to make silk conduct electricity, and found it would not; so he tried pack-thread, which did. He put up a line of pack-thread, and supported it by loops of silk, which

THE EXTRAORDINARY WAY IN WHICH OTTO VON GUERICKE PROVED THE AMAZING
POWER OF A VACUUM

28 F 8

would not conduct the current away from the cotton. He was able to send a current of electricity along his line of thread for a distance of 886 feet.

An industrious Frenchman was at work on similar lines at this time. This was a man named Dufay, who, born in 1699, died when only forty years of age, in 1739, three years after Gray. Dufay went over Gray's experiments, and went beyond them. He found that glass tubes could be used to hold up the pack-thread, and he found, too, that by connecting himself with the electrified thread he himself became electrified, and that when another person touched him there was a crackling sound, accompanied by a spark. But the great thing Dufay did was to discover the law of attraction and repulsion in connection with electricity.

HOW MEN'S KNOWLEDGE OF ELECTRICITY BEGAN TO GROW

Positive and negative electricity exist in a substance, and are at rest until that body is rubbed. Thus two electrified silks will not come together, but silk and worsted will, though two electrified woollen threads will keep as far apart as possible. This is like the loadstone or magnet. That part of the loadstone which points to the north will drive away the north pole of another magnet, but will attract the other magnet's south pole, as if it loved it. North and south go together in the magnet, and opposite kinds go together in electricity.

Inventions now went forward rapidly. Machines were made for rubbing glass cylinders with cushions and other things, and they produced so much electricity that sparks could be formed which would set light to spirits, to wax, to pitch, and other things which were thoroughly heated by friction. The increase of knowledge was now turned to account in a new way. Several men saw that, if electricity could be so easily produced in the open air, it ought to be still stronger if produced in a vessel, away from the free air, where it could be kept and tapped as required, instead of being allowed to escape. This advance took place near the middle of the eighteenth century.

A monk living abroad, a foreign inventor, and Professor Pieter van Musschenbroek, of Leyden, in Holland, seem to have had the same idea about the same time, and the outcome was what is called the Leyden jar. We read on page 236 how the first Leyden jar was charged with electricity and discharged again by an assistant who received an electric shock on touching a wire.

THE WONDERFUL THINGS SIR WILLIAM WATSON DID WITH TWO LEYDEN JARS

The Leyden jar, though first made in Holland, was made perfect in England by Sir William Watson (1715–87), another genius of those early days. Watson, a poor tradesman's son, was born in London. Apprenticed to a chemist, he loved science, and when he had made enough money to live on he gave himself wholly to science. He improved the Leyden jar by covering it inside and out with tinfoil. This had important results. He used wires for carrying the current from one Leyden jar to another Leyden jar. Sending the current along the wire, he found that it gave a shock to the person holding the far end of the wire, two miles away, practically at the very instant at which it was released from the Leyden jar. This proved that the action of electricity is almost instantaneous—a most important thing in telegraphy.

More wonders Sir William did with the mysterious force. He electrified a piece of ice, and with that set fire to spirits. He did the same with a drop of water which had been electrified. He fired the gunpowder in a gun with an electric spark, and showed many powers of electricity which had never before been suspected.

By this time the world was getting to know many things electricity could do, but they still knew nothing of its nature.

THE MAN WHO HELPED TO FREE AMERICA AND TO FIND ELECTRIC POWER

There was living in America one of the greatest men the world has seen, Benjamin Franklin, the man who first captured fire from the sky and brought it to the ground.

He was born at Boston in 1706, and began his career, with very little schooling, in a small printing office of one of his brothers. He was very poor, but he had a splendid brain, and never troubled about being short of money. He educated himself entirely by his own efforts. He was first a printer, coming to England to learn what he could here, then setting up in business for himself in Philadelphia.

So famous did he become that he was chosen by his countrymen to come to England as their ambassador. War was about to break out between this country and our American colonies, and he did all he could to prevent it. Seeing that his efforts were hopeless, he returned to America, where he found the war had already begun. He became a leading member of the Government which helped to give America her freedom from British control, and then was sent to France as Ambassador to gain the support of that country against England. After all, he had the delight of opening the arrangements which led to peace between England and America.

The last thing he did in public life was to make a prayer to the American Government against slavery in the United States. That prayer of his was not to be answered until he had been in the grave many years.

So much for his public life. The more important thing for us here is what he did with electricity.

HOW BENJAMIN FRANKLIN SENT UP A KITE TO BRING LIGHTNING DOWN

In the midst of all his work he had time to study and make experiments, so that he was honoured all over the world for his knowledge about the tides and the weather, about colours, and, most of all, about electricity. He was one of the men who suspected that lightning and electricity are one and the same thing. But Franklin was not content to remain guessing, he put his belief to the proof. He made a kite of silk, and on the top of it he fixed a thin wire. He tied a string to the kite, but near his hand he attached a silk ribbon to the string, and where the string and ribbon joined he fixed a metal key. One day in a thunderstorm he sent up his kite into a thundercloud, and waited in a doorway to watch the result.

He had printed a statement expressing the belief that everything that had been done with electricity was no more than was to be observed in lightning. Now had come the hour when he was to make his reputation secure, or be laughed at by the whole world.

The first thundercloud passed without any sign at all, and Franklin feared. A second came over the kite, and he now saw that little loose strands of the string stood out stiff and bristling. He put his finger towards them, and they were attracted towards it. He placed his finger on the key, and instantly he felt a shock and saw an electric spark. Rain fell now and wetted the string of the kite, and electricity ran down the moistened string, and was so abundant that he was able to fill his Leyden jar from the key.

HOW FRANKLIN'S EXPERIMENT GAVE US THE LIGHTNING CONDUCTOR

He had proved that lightning is electricity. He made other trials, and found that some clouds are charged with positive electricity and some with negative electricity, exactly in the same way as in the electricity produced by different bodies on earth. No sooner had he made sure of his facts than he set to work and built lightning conductors. If lightning could be drawn from the skies, as his kite had shown that it could, then it should be possible to guide into the ground the lightning, which, if left to strike freely, might destroy the house. It was in 1752 that Franklin made his great discovery. He lived 38 years afterwards, and when he died, in 1790, not only the whole of America, but the whole of France went into public mourning for him.

Discovery was now well on the way to practical success, and every year added surprises. John Canton (1718–72), who was born at Stroud, became a schoolmaster, and invented valuable electrical instruments. He was the first man to manufacture powerful artificial magnets, and discovered that the air of a room can be electrified just like so many other things.

Giovanni Beccaria, an Italian scientist, found that air surrounding an electrified body itself becomes electrified. Then Robert Symmer made the discovery that silk and worsted stockings, when warmed and rubbed together, become so electrified that a Leyden jar can be filled with the current from them.

A LONDON HERMIT AND HIS GREAT WORK FOR SCIENCE

More important was the work of Henry Cavendish, the brilliant grandson of the second Duke of Devonshire. Born at Nice, in 1731, Cavendish was very rich, and very strange in his manner. He lived the life of a hermit in a beautiful London house. He hated the sight of strangers, not because he was an unkind man, but because he was so shy and modest. His female servants were never allowed to see him. If he had any orders for them he would write them down and leave a note on the hall table.

Science was the great joy of his life. The chief thing he did for electricity was to show that iron wire conducts electricity 400 million times as well as water does. By the aid of electricity he exploded oxygen and hydrogen, and got pure water as the result.

Cavendish lived until 1810, and in his time two Italians arose who quite changed the method of producing electricity. One was Luigi Galvani, who was born at Bologna in 1737, and died there in 1798; the other was Alessandro Volta, born in 1745, at Como, where he died in 1827. We read of their work elsewhere.

THE DISCOVERY THAT PAVED THE WAY FOR ELECTRIC LIGHTING

The discovery of Volta, from which the battery came, caused much excitement and set men working still harder. They found now that they could produce electricity in this way as they liked, and cause it to flow in a steady current over wires, not letting it fly away immediately it was created, as it did from amber and other things. They found also that the current would heat wires, and this was the beginning of electric light.

We owe the most substantial advance ever made in electrical science, its real foundation as a practical agency in life, to the association of two of the rarest men who ever lived—Humphry Davy and Michael Faraday. There have been few more fortunate alliances.

Sir Humphry Davy was born at Penzance in December 1778, the son of a wood carver who had small means but was of good old Cornish stock. Humphry was given the best education the local schools afforded, but it was his native talent which turned his learning to account. He could master a book with ease and speed, and remember what he read. In some ways his youth reminds us of Scott, whom he resembled in his love of poetry, and in his gifts as a weaver of attractive romances.

HOW SIR HUMPHRY DAVY PROVED THAT FRICTION WILL MELT ICE

Two staunch friends of his youth were Dr. Tonkin, who was as a second father to Humphry's mother, and a delightful old Quaker saddler named Robert Dunkin, who was as enthusiastically devoted to science as young Humphry. Dunkin had his friction machine for electricity, his voltaic piles, his Leyden jars, his mechanical models; and of all these he made the boy master before very long.

In Tonkin's attic Humphry carried out the experiments which Dunkin's apparatus suggested, and the good old doctor would say, "That lad will blow us all into the air." Rare disputes were waged between the boy and the Quaker over the researches they both loved.

"Humphry," said Quaker Dunkin, one day, "thou art the most quibbling hand at a dispute I ever met in my life."

"Well, come with me, then," answered the lad, leading his beloved critic to the frozen river to experiment with ice over whose properties they had been battling; and Humphry would pick up two pieces of the ice and rub them together till they melted a little by the heat of friction, and then, left to rest, became united by the influence of a warmer atmosphere.

Davy's rich and original conversation brought him the friendship of a man with an excellent scientific library and apparatus, and here he met Gregory Watt, the son of James Watt, who gave him a definite grounding in chemistry. Charming all men by his blithe spirit and his natural gifts, Humphry, at 20, was taken to Bristol and made assistant in what was called a "pneumatic laboratory for the cure of invalids." Delighted with his investigations of gases, he now turned definitely from his dream of becoming a surgeon, and gave himself wholly to science, to the lasting regret of his old friend Dr. Tonkin, who thought all callings ignoble in comparison with his own.

THE CLEVER YOUNG LECTURER WHO AMAZED INTELLECTUAL LONDON

Davy now made most important experiments with what was called "laughing gas," intoxicating himself in daring tests, and predicting its use as a means of lessening pain in surgical operations. He nearly destroyed himself by inhaling sulphuretted hydrogen and other deadly gases, in quite the approved manner of the knight-errant of science; but he survived and published his results, gaining a reputation which at 23 won him the assistant lectureship at the Royal Institution, London, with £100 a year, lodging, coal, and light.

His lectures created a sensation. He expounded the new science of Galvanism, with his own experiments added, and the most distinguished of London's intellectual society flocked to hear the

THE BOYHOOD OF SIR HUMPHRY DAVY

YOUNG HUMPHRY DAVY MAKING HIS FIRST EXPERIMENTS

inspired stripling. Very soon the Royal Institution made him Professor of Chemistry, and fitted up for him what was then considered a great battery of Voltaic cells. With this force Davy repeated and extended experiments which he had already begun in the breaking down of compounds into their parts and revealing new and unsuspected elements.

HOW THE ELECTRIC ARC LAMP LED TO THE WIRELESS TELEPHONE

Finding that when electricity is passing through two wires the points of the wires, when separated, are burned up by the current, he employed sticks of carbon in place of the wire terminals, saw their ends leap into radiant flame, and so gave us the electric arc lamp, the forerunner of electric lamps, of the Crookes tube which gave us X-rays and radium, and of the thermionic valve which gives us the wireless telephone.

Davy married a rich widow and withdrew from active work, but he rendered enormous assistance to agriculture and wrote many fine papers on scientific subjects, and when he died at Geneva, on March 29, 1829, he was world famous.

He made brilliant contributions to scientific truth, but as he once very charmingly said, his greatest discovery was Michael Faraday.

Faraday, thanks to Davy, proved even greater than his master. He was a blacksmith's son, born in London on September 22, 1791. At 12 years old little Michael became errand boy to a bookseller named Riebau, whose habit it was to buy up job lots of printed matter in sheets, to bind and sell them as books.

Riebau liked his studious boy, so took him as apprentice without fee. The run of other people's libraries made Davy, Scott, and Lamb; access to the printed sheets on which he was working as a boy made Faraday. As Livingstone studied books at his weaving machine, so Faraday read the pages of encyclopedias while binding them, thus setting up a sound scaffolding on which to build his fame.

THE BOOKBINDER'S BOY WHO BECAME A GREAT GENIUS

Michael was 20 when a customer, entering the bookbinder's shop, saw him poring over a treatise on electricity which he was putting into covers. The good man inquired into his habits, and, like the fairy godfather of the stories, gave him something more precious than gold to him, tickets for the last four of Davy's lectures for the season.

The whole career of Faraday was changed by what he heard, and he felt that he must give himself to science. The lectures decided his career, and he himself followed Davy in the lecture room. In time another young man went to hear Faraday lecture on the chemistry of a candle, and wrote the lecture down in shorthand, so that we still have it, from those notes, as a delightful little book. The man who wrote the notes was William Crookes, from whom came the famous vacuum tube which bears his name.

But to return to Michael Faraday. Entranced by Davy's learning and powers of exposition, he was still only an ugly duckling, craving what seemed an impossible change. He made careful summaries and observations on the lectures, wrote them out neatly, and sent them to Davy, accompanied by a petition that he might serve the lecturer.

THE KNOCK AT THE DOOR THAT FARADAY HEARD IN BED

Would that timid knock at the portals of fame be heard? Yes, said Hope. No, said Probability. But late one night, as Michael was getting into his garret bed, a loud knock at the street door was heard, and in came a liveried servant of Humphry Davy, bidding the youth wait upon Sir Humphry in the morning.

The end of it was that Davy, remembering his own early days, and correctly analysing the character of his visitor, warned him of the hardships of the career he aspired to follow, and ended by engaging him. He engaged him as his assistant at twenty-five shillings a week, our greatest genius since Newton.

The cooperation of the two men was perfect. Faraday soon came to assist his senior in his experiments and lectures, and he carried Davy's work farther than it would have gone without his assistance.

Sometimes Sir Humphry Davy would take the industrious apprentice abroad with him, and Lady Davy, not seeing the genius in the awkward youngster, behaved meanly to him, emphasising the fact that he was to act as valet as well as secretary to her distinguished husband, and even making him take his meals with the grooms. But Faraday bore all this with patient and uncomplaining dignity, and

THREE FAMOUS ELECTRICITY MEN

MICHAEL FARADAY IN THE STREETS OF LONDON

THOMAS ALVA EDISON IN HIS LABORATORY

WILLIAM GILBERT SHOWS QUEEN ELIZABETH AN EXPERIMENT IN ELECTRICITY

at the Royal Institution, where he eventually succeeded Sir Humphry, he immortalised himself with discoveries which made him the equal of the mightiest.

We have seen that Oersted found a magnet to be affected by a current of electricity passing through a wire, but Faraday made a greater discovery. He found that wire, moved quickly in the neighbourhood of a magnet, becomes electrified by the magnet; that the current is stronger at the moment of the wire's entering and leaving the field of magnetic force; and that the current flows alternately from one end of the wire and then from the opposite end.

" What is the use of such knowledge? " a lady asked him as she saw him performing his experiment. " Madam," he said, " what is the use of a newborn child? "

**THE NEW AGE MADE POSSIBLE
BY FARADAY'S INVENTION**

The revelation thus simply made was that of Faraday's newborn child of science. Fix the coil of wire between the two poles of a magnet, make it revolve, lead away the current thus generated and we have the electric dynamo. By the dynamo we have the current for the telegraph and the telephone, the ship, the submarine, the aeroplane, the motor-car, the tram, the train, the lighting of our streets and houses; for the waves on which wireless speech is borne around the world, and for the motive power by which the machinery of the world is driven. Was ever there a greater material gift by a single man to the fortunes of the world?

But that was only one thing he did, the others numbered scores. As the founder of electro-dynamics Faraday was a pioneer in the creation of metal alloys, a sort of uncle of our great steel industries. He improved the manufacture of glass and the illumination of lighthouses. He paved the way for photography by his investigation of the vaporisation of mercury at an even temperature. He founded our knowledge of the liquefaction of gases. He advanced the science of sound, applied electricity to the firing of mines, and worked out laws of science in such numbers that we have ever since built on his teachings. He first prophesied the radiant properties of matter which Madame Curie finally proved with radium.

Never was there a more fruitful life, never one more beautiful. Faraday was marvellously delicate and accurate in his experiments, all with home-made apparatus. We may be sure he was the sort of man who sings in his bath, for when some desperate and dangerous experiment began to turn as he wished, he would rock from foot to foot in his joy, rubbing his hands and humming a tune.

**THE FAME THAT CAME TO ENGLAND
IN THE REALMS OF SCIENCE**

A great school of enthusiasts, fired by his example and teaching, grew up in England and made us as famous in science as Shakespeare and Milton had made us in literature. Every honour the learned world could offer was at his disposal, but he refused practically all of them.

He brought new fame and fortune to his native land, and we honour him as one of our noblest sons. " Faraday," said Dr. J. H. Gladstone, a great Victorian scientist who was the author of the Life of Michael Faraday, " was one of that long line of scientific men, beginning with the scholars of the East, who brought to the Redeemer the gold, frankincense, and myrrh of their adoration." It was true, and we are glad that at the end he lived as the guest of the nation in the apartments pressed upon him by the State. There, at Hampton Court, on August 25, 1867, this noble giant of our race passed out.

Many other names come into the story of electricity, but they will be found treated in other parts of this book. It was, for example, the great Lord Kelvin whose work made possible the first Atlantic cable; it may be said that he laid the foundations of submarine communication.

**THE MEN WHO GAVE US ELECTRIC
LIGHT IN OUR HOMES**

The famous name of Edison has also a great place in this story, but he, too, is dealt with elsewhere. Associated with Edison in the invention of the incandescent electric lamp was Joseph Wilson Swan, to whom we owe also many of the inventions which have made photography almost an art. He was a man when he travelled by the stage-coach; he used to lie in his bed hearing the watchman calling the hours of the night; he was an inventor before Darwin published his Origin of Species; and on the banks of the River Wear he would watch men hammering nails into the wooden ships of Old England. Yet he lived on until 1917 to see many of the marvels of our time.

The Great Stories of the World That Will Be Told for Ever

ARION AND HIS GOLDEN HARP

This story, first told in ancient Greece, has been echoing round the world for more than 2000 years.

ONCE upon a time there lived in the town of Corinth a musician called Arion, who played so sweetly on his golden harp that everybody would stop to listen.

Arion lived at the Court of Periander, King of Corinth, who loved to have him there; but after some years the young musician thought he would like to travel and see more of the world. So one day he started off to Sicily.

The natural splendour of the island and its superb buildings delighted the traveller, and he stayed there several years, making new melodies, which he played for lovers of music. Also he made a fortune, for gold was lavished upon him.

However, the day came when Arion longed to see Corinth once again, and his own people, and his friend King Periander. He felt that he did not care so much for wealth after all; and, in any case, had he not already more money than he wanted?

So Arion found a ship sailing to Corinth, and prepared to leave for home.

His chests of gold were put on board, and the next day the crew saw the young man joyously hastening to their vessel holding an instrument they did not know. "How rich he must be with all this gold!" they thought. "How would it be to share this fortune among us?"

All went well at first. There was fine weather, a smooth sea, a breeze just strong enough to swell the sails and carry them gently towards home. Everything seemed to be there for the traveller's enjoyment. Several days passed by, with Arion sitting at the prow and watching the galley ploughing the sea.

But the sailors were wicked men, and the idea of robbing Arion grew stronger among them till they all meant to do it. So one day they decided to get rid of their passenger and steal his gold.

Arion was dreaming in the stern as usual when a seaman approached him. "What do you want?" he asked. "I was just making up a song for my friend King Periander."

"Periander will never hear it," said the sailor, "for we are about to kill you."

"If it is my gold you want," said Arion, "take it all, but spare my life."

"No, no, we must kill you," the men replied, "for how can we be sure you would not betray us at Corinth?"

"Then let me at least enjoy my harp for the last time, and allow me to leave the world as I like," said Arion.

The men consulted together and at last agreed to his request.

Arion, having arrayed himself in his best apparel, took up his harp, struck a few chords, and began to sing.

IMAGINATION · CHIVALRY · LEGENDS · GOLDEN DEEDS · FAIRY TALES

His strains were so heavenly that his enemies gazed on him with wonder, and almost regretted their cruelty; but one more eager than the rest, put in:

" Are you forgetting all the gold locked up in his chests? "

" He is right, he is right! " the rest agreed unanimously.

When Arion had ended his song he cast a last look at the shining sun and then threw himself overboard, the galley sailing smoothly on.

But Arion was not drowned. Attracted by the alluring music, the inmates of the sea had gathered round the ship, and when the hero plunged in, a dolphin proudly offered to carry him ashore.

A lovely journey it was, for the dolphin greatly respected the mysterious gift of his unknown guest, and wished to take him safely home.

However, Arion was exhausted, starving, spent, when he entered the palace of his friend the king.

" What does this mean? " asked the anxious Periander; and the traveller then related his tragic adventure.

Two days later the ship arrived.

" What a treat we shall have! " the sailors were saying joyfully to each other.

The king had them brought before him, and said to them:

" I heard you were coming back from Sicily; can you tell me anything of my dear friend Arion? He must be well known over there."

" We are glad we can reassure your highness about the great musician," one of the men answered boldly. " He is in good health, but he will not come back before he has made a fortune."

At that moment Arion appeared.

" Look! " cried the king. " Look! "

Scared and distracted, the sailors knelt trembling. Surely the gods were in league against them, or how could such things come to pass?

" Have pity on us! " they implored.

" Be silent! " commanded Arion. " I will not be hard on you; but you must give me my fortune back."

Thus Arion remained famous for his kindness as much as for his art, and his story was told all over the world.

THE GIRL WHO WALKED TO LONDON

HELEN WALKER was born early in the eighteenth century. She was the daughter of quite poor people, who were living in Scotland.

There was a law made at that time which was very unjust, and the punishment for breaking this law was death. Helen had a younger sister whom she loved, and this sister was charged with breaking this cruel law. Though she was innocent, it was almost certain she would be condemned.

But it happened that if Helen had been willing to tell the judges a lie she could have saved her sister, and no one would have known.

But Helen had been taught that there is nothing in the world which can make it right to tell a lie. She would have given her own life gladly to save her sister; but she could not tell a lie.

The sister was not like that, and she pleaded passionately, begging her to tell the lie, and reproaching her for her cruelty in refusing to do so easy a thing. But Helen would not do it.

Yet, if she would not lie, there was still one way in which she might, perhaps, save her sister. The judges would condemn her to death; but if Helen could win the king's pardon she would be set free. But the king lived in London, hundreds of miles away. How could a poor girl in Edinburgh get to the king in London? There were no trains. Great people could go in their carriages, or gentlemen might go on horseback; people who could afford it might take the coach. But there was nothing for Helen but to tramp the whole journey on foot, day after day, with the chance of a friendly lift from a cart now and then. Helen started; she walked all the way to London.

In London was a great Scottish lord, the Duke of Argyll, to whom Helen's father had once done some service. Helen sent a letter to the duke to entreat him to help her to see the queen, for the king was away. The duke did help her, and when she came before the queen she pleaded so movingly, showing that her sister was really innocent of breaking the law, that the pardon was granted.

This is a true story, and out of it Sir Walter Scott made up his historical novel The Heart of Midlothian.

THE STORY OF THE MONTHS

JANUARY · FEBRUARY · MARCH · APRIL · MAY · JUNE · JULY
AUGUST · SEPTEMBER · OCTOBER · NOVEMBER · DECEMBER

ALL the gods are dead. Centuries have rolled away since men believed in them. And yet the memory of these old gods and goddesses is enshrined in many forms, and will endure to the end of time.

So deep was the faith of the Romans in their gods that throughout the world the names and characters of these mythical persons are associated with some of the most sacred and some of the most practical affairs of modern life. Ghosts of the dead gods even haunt the months that make up

regarded him as the protector of their gates and doorways. His temple had twelve doors in it, just as the year has twelve months.

It was a clever idea of the Romans to name the first month of the year after Janus, because he suggests looking forward and looking back. Everyone who thinks at all feels at the beginning of a year that it is a time for looking back on the past, and also a time for looking forward to the future. It is a month of beginning as well as a month of ending.

THE ROMANS NAMED THE FIRST MONTH JANUARY, AFTER THE TWO-FACED GOD JANUS

the total of the Christian calendar. Let us imagine that we are witnessing a pageant of the months.

First would come a strange figure, a god with two faces, a god who looks forward and who looks back, and who carries in his left hand a key. This is Janus. The Romans worshipped Janus in a temple that was kept open during war, but was closed in times of peace. He was the god of Beginnings and Ends. The pious Roman who wanted to begin a matter well, or to make a good end of something, implored the assistance of Janus. This god was also the doorkeeper of heaven, and the Romans

The second figure in our pageant is February, a month set apart. At one time February was the last month in the year, but 450 years before Christ it was placed after January instead of before, and became the second month. Later on March was reckoned as the beginning of a year, and February once again became the last month. Now it has settled down to its second place. But every four years February has one day added to its twenty-eight, and so it remains the most restless and unsettled month in the calendar. This extra day is added because a full year consists of 365 days, 6 hours, and at the end

THE NAME OF FEBRUARY COMES FROM A ROMAN FESTIVAL CALLED FEBRUA

of four years these odd six hours have mounted up to a whole day of twenty-four hours; it is given to February to make up for its short allowance of twenty-eight days.

The name February comes from a Roman festival of purification named Februa, in honour of the god Lupercus. The figure that passes before us in the pageant suggests cleansing and purifying. In our own time it is towards the end of February that the housewife thinks about her spring cleaning. The Romans regarded Februa as a festival for spiritual cleansing, but they celebrated the occasion by over-eating.

The third figure in our pageant clatters by in a chariot drawn by two horses, Terror and Flight. It is a threatening figure, brandishing a long spear, lifting a gleaming shield to heaven, and raising its head on high, so that the lightnings play about the great helmet. This is Mars, the god of war.

To the Romans Mars was more than a mere fighter; they regarded him as a god who could do almost anything because he was so strong. They prayed to him for rain, and consulted him in their private affairs, offering on his altar a horse, sheep, wolf, magpie, or vulture. When soldiers went to war they carried with them a cage of chickens sacred to Mars, and before battle they would offer corn to these sacred birds, eagerly watching to see if the food were greedily eaten or rejected; if it was eaten it meant that Mars was on their side,

MARCH, THE NOISY, BLUSTERING MONTH, WAS NAMED AFTER MARS, THE ROMAN GOD OF WAR

THE FOURTH MONTH, WHICH OPENS THE GATES OF SPRING, WAS CALLED APRIL, "THE OPENER"

if it was left that the day would go ill with them. Mars was associated in their minds with thunder and lightning, and yet the Romans believed that the woodpecker tapping the trunk of a tree was the answer of this blustering, noisy god to their prayers. March is very often a blustering month.

How different is the fourth figure in our pageant! It is not a god and not a goddess. It is the Angel of Spring. Gracious, exquisite, tender, and kind, April follows behind the dust of the bloodstained chariot of Mars, sprinkling the Earth with soft showers, and calling up in the ruts and gashes made by the fiery wheels flowers so slight and pretty and delicate that one almost weeps to see them. April is The Opener. The Romans saw that this month opened the gates of birth and restored to life all those lovely and gentle things which had hidden in terror from the blasts of winter. *Omnia aperit!* they exclaimed in admiration; which means " It opens all things." And so this month of beauty and new birth, when the Earth wakes from its winter sleep, when the buds appear on the branches, and the woods are full of song, is called April, The Opener.

MAY IS CALLED AFTER THE GODDESS MAIA, THE DAUGHTER OF ATLAS, WHO UPHELD THE WORLD

JUNO, WHO RODE IN A CHARIOT DRAWN BY PEACOCKS, GAVE HER NAME TO JUNE

Behind April comes the goddess Maia. Her father was named Atlas, and it was supposed that the weight of this vast round world on which we live, with all its mountains and oceans and deep mines, rested upon the shoulders of Atlas. He had seven daughters who lived in a mountain, and Maia was the most famous of all these seven daughters because of her son Mercury, who ran swiftly from Heaven to Earth on errands for the gods and goddesses. Jupiter, the father of all the gods, took Maia and her sisters and placed them near together as stars in the sky. The cluster of six stars called the Pleiades is supposed to be Maia and her sisters. The seventh star of the cluster is invisible. It represents one of the sisters who married a man named Sisyphus, and ever after, because poor Sisyphus had been condemned to roll a stone up a hill eternally, she has hidden her face with sorrow.

Two figures come next, disputing the sixth place in the pageant. One is the goddess Juno, and the other is a man, Junius. Some people think the month belongs to Juno, and others to the great Roman family of Junius.

We will let the two figures fight it out. Neither of them interests us very much. Juno was the beautiful but jealous wife of Jupiter, who drove about in a chariot drawn by strutting peacocks, and Junius was a proud and haughty man, without

JULY WAS AT ONE TIME CALLED QUINTILIS, BUT WAS RENAMED IN HONOUR OF JULIUS CAESAR

AUGUST WAS NAMED AFTER AUGUSTUS, THE FIRST OF THE ROMAN EMPERORS

modesty, humility, or sweetness. These two contend for the brightest and grandest place in the calendar, the month of roses and garden glory. Whichever wins in this contention we shall call June the month of God. We feel no admiration for the goddess or for the man; our hearts are rejoiced by the splendour of summer, and we give the glory of June to the Giver of all beauty and all joy, the mighty God who is also our Father.

The seventh figure in the pageant is one of the greatest men who ever lived, a soldier and an emperor, Julius Caesar. When the year began with March this month was the fifth, and the Romans called it Quintilis, which means the fifth month. Julius Caesar not only conquered nation after nation, and not only made wise laws and wrote immortal books, he also set himself to reform the calendar. He himself made the fifth month the seventh, and because the old name of Quintilis would not suit, and because he himself was born in this month, he said that the seventh month should be named July.

We can read all about Julius Caesar on pages 1535–38 (volume 3) and 2873–76 (volume 4), but in passing we should remember that it was Caesar who conquered part of Britain and first taught the inhabitants to respect civilised laws.

After Julius Caesar follows his grandnephew Augustus. At first he was called Octavius, and ruled the Roman Empire with Mark Antony and Lepidus. Finally he became sole emperor, and did much that added to the glory and power of his magnificent empire. The people, anxious to flatter him, changed his name to

THE NAME OF SEPTEMBER MEANS SEVEN, AND IT WAS AT ONE TIME THE SEVENTH MONTH

OCTOBER IS THE TENTH MONTH ; AT ONE TIME IT WAS THE EIGHTH, AS ITS NAME SUGGESTS

Augustus, meaning noble. Then they called the eighth month August.

But July had thirty-one days, and August only thirty. The Romans thought Augustus would be jealous of Caesar's extra day, and so they took a day from September and tacked it on to the end of August. The eighth month was chosen for the reason that Augustus celebrated the chief events of his life during that time. It was in August that he was made consul, ended his wars, and conquered Egypt. His reign was called the Golden Age, for not only did he bring peace to the war-tired world, but under his patronage literature and art flourished exceedingly.

The immortal poets Horace and Virgil lived at this time, libraries were built, agriculture developed, and temples and buildings rose up on every side in all the magnificence of marble. And it was in the reign of this mighty emperor that far away in Syria the Holy Child was born, whose birth has divided time. Little did the proud emperor imagine, as he boasted in his palace of how he had found Rome made of brick and had left it of marble, that a Child was then living who would divide all the ages of the Earth, and set a Cross between the reign of Augustus and the march of a new religion that was to grow and spread until it reached all lands.

NOVEMBER THE MONTH OF GUY FAWKES, WAS FORMERLY THE NINTH MONTH

Behind the mighty Augustus in our pageant follows only a shamefaced figure VII. It is shamefaced because it knows that it has no right to be where it is.

September is the ninth month of the year, and to call it Septem, which means seven, is quite wrong. But our friend VII raises a glance of appeal, and seems to say to us: "Do not turn me out. I at least serve one useful purpose: I remind you of the distant past, when the year began with March, and when the month following August was in very truth the seventh month of the year."

After VII comes neither god, goddess, nor emperor, but another figure, VIII. Here again is the same shamefaced look

Again comes a figure—IX, meaning ninth month, or, as we say, November, though it is the eleventh. Perhaps we see this figure passing before us disguised under a heavy cloak and a wide-spreading hat, with a barrel of gunpowder tucked under its arm, for November is the month of Guy Fawkes and Gunpowder Plot.

Our Saxon ancestors called it Blood Month because it was at this time they slaughtered many cattle to last them through the dreary months of winter.

Last of all comes another shamefaced figure—X. How strange that December, which is Latin for ten, should be the name for our twelfth month! But, of course, we know now that at one time this was not the

DECEMBER, THE MONTH OF FATHER CHRISTMAS, IS THE TWELFTH, BUT ITS NAME MEANS TEN

and the same appeal to antiquity. Many things as false as the name October are allowed to pass in the world on this same score of antiquity. People dislike altering things; they are too tired or too careless to touch the monuments of the past. The Romans, when they had given the name of their great emperor Augustus to what was then the sixth month, felt that no one would be worthy to have a month named after him, and so let the old simple titles stand—September for the seventh, and October for the eighth month.

Even when the calendar was changed long years after the birth of Christ, and January became the first month, these old names were allowed to remain.

last, but the tenth month, in the calendar. December, which seems to us to mean the end, or the last, means simply the tenth.

However, we do not bother our heads about the origin of the name when December arrives: we can see coming towards us another and more cheerful figure. Big, happy, genial, and generous, comes Father Christmas, through the snow, riding over the hills, with his inexhaustible sack of toys. The gods and goddesses have departed, the Roman emperors have strutted out of sight, and the scene is filled by this jovial English figure, the good and affectionate Father Christmas, who ends up the pageant with a royal cheerfulness and a divine humanity.

LE CHEVALIER ET LA PIERRE MERVEILLEUSE

This is a French translation of the story told in English on page 784

Un brave chevalier anglais fut fait prisonnier en Terre Sainte par les Sarrasins et jeté dans un donjon pour y mourir. Mais un rossignol vint se percher sur la fenêtre du donjon et égaya le chevalier par ses chansons; le chevalier de son côté le nourrit de miettes et en fit son favori. Il prit l'habitude de lui parler comme à un être humain, et lui dit un jour: "Ah, charmant oiseau, si seulement tu pouvais m'aider à m'échapper!"

Le rossignol s'envola aussitôt, et, comme il n'était pas rentré depuis trois jours, le chevalier pensa qu'il avait été tué par quelque faucon. Mais le soir du troisième jour il revint au sombre donjon portant un caillou dans son bec.

Le chevalier prit le caillou et, par hasard, l'approcha de fers; à son étonnement et à sa joie, les entraves se rompirent. Alors il s'approcha de la porte du donjon, la toucha aussi avec la pierre magique, et la porte s'ouvrir.

Le chevalier ne perdit pas de temps pour quitter sa prison, et il s'arrangea à s'échapper en Angleterre, où le rossignol le suivit. Là le chevalier témoigna sa gratitude à son petit ami à plumes, en lui construisant une cage en or avec une porte ouverte sur le jardin de son château.

COMMENT LE ROITELET DEVINT ROI

This is a French translation of the story told in English on page 1890

Quand tous les oiseaux se réunirent pour choisir un roi il y eut beaucoup de disputes pour savoir qui serait l'élu.

"La beauté est ce qu'il nous faut dans un roi," dit le paon.

"Non, nous avons besoin de dignité," dit le hibou. "Voyons qui a l'air le plus sage."

"Ou bien qui parle le mieux," dit le perroquet.

Mais l'aigle s'exclama: "Qu'est-ce qui nous élève au-dessus des autres créatures? Le pouvoir de voler. Il nous faut choisir pour roi l'oiseau qui vole le plus haut." Et comme l'aigle était fort et féroce il obligea l'assemblée à se conformer à l'épreuve de son choix.

A un signal donné, les oiseaux s'élevèrent et essayèrent de se survoler l'un l'autre, mais bientôt l'aigle les dépassa tous et monta à une surprenante hauteur jusqu'à ce que ses forces furent épuisées.

Alors un roitelet, qui s'était perché sur son dos, vola un peu plus haut que l'aigle. Ainsi, au grand dégout de l'aigle, le petit roitelet devint roi.

THE MEN OF THE BIRKENHEAD

On a February night in 1852 the troopship Birkenhead was steaming along on her way to South Africa.

On board her were a number of soldiers, with their wives and children.

As the great ship steamed along the coast of Africa, no one dreaming of danger, her side crashed against a sunken rock, hidden from view.

Everyone hurried on deck, for all knew from the shock that some disaster had happened. But there was no panic. The officers gave their orders, and the men obeyed them as steadily and calmly as if they were on parade.

The soldiers were set to help the sailors, working at the pumps to keep the ship from sinking. But the water came in, and everyone knew there was no hope.

Then they launched the boats. One big boat and two small ones were filled with women and children and pushed off safely; another was swamped by a falling spar; and two were swamped before anyone could be got into them. Then the ship herself broke in two, and slowly began to sink.

The soldiers were already drawn up in ranks. The captain called to them to swim for the boats; but the colonel saw that if they did the boats would be swamped. The men stood firm, awaiting their officer's order. He told them that if they swam for the boats the women and children would be drowned.

So they stood in their lines, waiting for the ship to go down. Then the angry waves dashed over the decks, and the brave soldiers were plunged into the sea. All they could hope for was to keep afloat till the boats reached the shore and could return to pick them up. A few managed to swim ashore by themselves; a few held on to the wreck and were picked up by a passing vessel. But the greater number of those gallant men perished.

Nature's Wonderful Living Family in Earth and Air and Sea

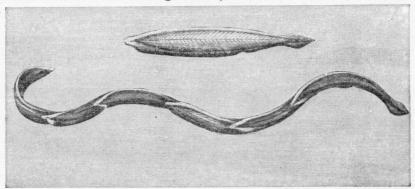

The Common Lancelet, singly and in a chain

MYSTERIES OF THE BORDER LINE

IN Shakespeare's Merchant of Venice part of the plot turns on a plan with which every reader of children's stories is quite familiar.

Three caskets are set up in a palace: one is of gold, one of silver, and one of lead. In one of them lies a deed entitling its chooser to wed the witty Portia.

We all remember how suitors from many lands went to the palace and failed to gain the prize, until Bassanio appeared, chose the leaden casket, and won Portia.

Life itself may be said to resemble that scheme of sealed treasure, though the choice is not left to chance, for that is fixed by steadfast laws. The natural caskets take the form of eggs and seeds, and to determine their contents would prove as puzzling as were the vessels in Portia's palace.

Who but an expert could say what creature will come from an egg picked haphazard from a heap? It might be some bird glorious in song, plumage, and achievement in flight. It might be a bird unable to rise from the ground. It might even be a crocodile or a lizard.

Who but one long trained could predict the future of a seed, foretell the plant, the tree, the vegetable, to which it must give rise? It might be a rose fair as Portia, it might be a weed rank as the heart of

Shylock, or a cabbage, lowly as Gobbo, Shylock's chuckling clown.

But life has its treasure caskets higher than those from which bird, reptile, and plant originate. The great and important animals proceed from eggs, though these in most cases are retained, until hatched, within the parent body. The elephant and the whale, the buffalo and the shark, the gorilla and the grampus, all begin the career which precedes their birth, simply as eggs.

If it were possible for us to examine those eggs, we could not state with certainty what form of life they harbour. One of them might pass for a perfect adult animal consisting simply of a single cell; another might be the cradle of a giant beast or some majestic human genius.

In the old first days of animal life on the Earth, all living forms were as small and humble as the present-day amoeba, which never grows to more than a single cell, but transacts the entire business of existence as a tiny, self-contained unit of pulsing animate matter.

But out of similar simple cells what incredible marvels spring! Each is a child of the past, in each is the unseen marvel of millions of years of history and development. From two such eggs, alike to the eye of the unlearned, two entirely different

PREHISTORIC LIFE · MAMMALS · BIRDS · REPTILES · FISHES · INSECTS

types will proceed, the one to share the mastery of the Earth, the other to become its drudge, or at best to seem an unprofitable servant, the purpose of whose existence remains a mystery.

Every such ovum comes into existence stored with energy and direction, with the power of becoming the thing of wonder it is designed to be: an oak to last a thousand years, a fly whose life in the air will be but a matter of minutes; an unarmed man, a turtle in a fortress of bone, a porcupine speary with spines and prickles, a monkey to climb trees, a worm which can barely raise its head above the ground.

THE WONDERFUL CHANGES TAKING PLACE IN NATURE'S CRUCIBLES

What chemist's crucible can work such wondrous transformations as take place in these crucibles of Nature, the cradle in which the life principle of plant and animal flowers into existence? In one such cradle of future life is a speck of incalculable force from which a giant pine will issue, from a second a ravening lion, from a third a hyena which will grow to such power that it will be able to bite through a steel cable. Every element is there, of endurance, size, power, ferocity; of instinct to hunger, love, battle; all the forces are latent there, in that minute capsule of mystery, like the fortune hidden in the casket of Portia.

It is a wondrous story, slowly unravelled, little by little, through ages of research by wise and patient men. But do we know the whole? Not nearly. We have obtained so much information that we are able to say that before birth and during the early stages which follow birth, life climbs its own ancestral tree, passing swiftly through nearly all the stages which the species has passed during millions of years since each class of life assumed a definite independent career.

DEVELOPMENT THAT IS NOT ALWAYS AN IMPROVEMENT

But we are entering realms of mystery made more mysterious by problems which it has hitherto been impossible to solve; which perhaps never may be solved.

If the present is the child of the past, and life has been progressive, as in a general way we know it has been, then in the species of the past we should expect to trace improvement and development in all.

As we have seen, however, development is not always for the betterment of life. The old reptiles and mammals, in comparison with which present-day elephants are small, developed themselves off the face of the Earth; grew to dimensions so gigantic that they ceased to reproduce healthy offspring, and went down in ruin beyond repair. We have seen it in the case of the sloths, the ostriches, the penguins, in certain wild hideous little dogs that have lost their hair, in the axolotl, which forgets to grow up, and, instead of turning into a perfect land-roving salamander, remains a tadpole, restricted to the water.

Now we are come to another of these perplexing border lines, where one form of life fades, like the colours of a rainbow, into another. Hitherto we have dealt with animals which have a backbone, a spinal column like our own. The spinal column is, of course, that wonderful series of hollow bones through which runs the immense band of nerves called the spinal cord, and it exists in every mammal, bird, reptile, amphibian, and fish.

THE CREATURES ON THE BORDER OF NATURE'S GREAT DIVISION

The presence or absence of a backbone seems to mark off one part of living creatures from the other as clearly as anything can. Yet, on this border line at which we have arrived, once more we find that these clean-cut divisions do not exist in Nature. The backboned animals are called Vertebrates; the backboneless animals are the Invertebrates. But we are face to face with a group of Vertebrates which have not a backbone among them !

It is the old story of relationships again repeated; as with fishlike attributes in the amphibia; amphibian qualities in their descendants, the reptiles; reptilian features in the birds and in the camels, and birdlike habits among the lowest mammals, the egg-laying platypus and echidna.

With a backbone all things seem possible to a species. A large, fine brain may be continued into the spinal cord; without such an outlet the brain cannot become great and complex. It must remain, at best, as in the ants, which seem to have the highest mental attributes in the lower scale, merely ganglions, or nerve bulbs.

Having acquired a backbone, and the associated growth of brain, we must expect that its fortunate owner would progress mightily and go from strength to strength in development of intelligence and physical force. We are to study a type where immense promise of this kind is falsified, a birthright is thrown away, and its heir descends to the lowest form of adult life of which we have any record.

A LITTLE SEA TADPOLE AND WHAT IT BECOMES

Most of us know the name of the tribe, the ascidians, which is a Greek word meaning simply a little skin bag. When we are exploring, during holidays, by the sea, we often find these creatures and call them sea squirts. What can they have to do with such princely gifts as backbones?

If we could make a sea squirt speak, as animals do in tales and fables, and asked him what he had done with his backbone, he would deny that he had ever possessed one, or that he knew such things existed. There resides his tragedy, if tragedy it be.

The ascidian begins life like a little sea tadpole. It has a brain, it has a nerve cord running along the upper side of the back, and it has a notochord. Now the notochord is the forerunner of the bony spinal column. Every vertebrate has it in the earliest stages of formation. It is a gristly rod placed beneath the spinal cord to support it till bones form to enclose the vital substance.

Anyone unversed in the history of these amazing creatures would say, on examining the larval sea squirt and seeing its notochord: Here is a young animal which is developing a true spine and will be a successful vertebrate. At that stage of its career the baby ascidian is as much a vertebrate as the larva of a frog or toad, a thing of infinite promise.

But in a few days the lusty little fellow, dashing about in the waters, ardent for food and adventure, wearies of well-doing. It no longer desires the freedom of the seas, but sinks down to the bottom of the water, attaches itself by muscles about its head to rock, weed, or to timber, and performs an almost incredible change.

THE LITTLE CREATURE WHICH COMPLETELY CHANGES ITS FORM

The agile little body is twisted through an angle of 90 degrees. All the organs undergo a transformation. The busy, thrusting tail, stiff with its notochord of hope, is absorbed as is the tail of a tadpole when changing into a frog. The fine nervous system degenerates into a petty knot or ganglion; the single eye actually withers

and drops out; the nose vanishes into the tail, the muscles of the valiant little swimmer break up into jelly or slime.

Degeneration is rapid, but it is impressively wonderful none the less. For out of the ruin of the first form a new outline arises. The animal becomes shaped like a little sack, or two-mouthed leathern bottle, such as Eastern people employ for the storage and carriage of water.

The simple mouth expands and develops a throat such as it is believed all vertebrates once had. Gill slits multiply about the throat and become richly supplied with blood vessels. Henceforth the sea squirt is fast chained, like Prometheus, to his rock; he will go no more a-roving.

Food is taken in, with water, through one opening, passed through the body, and expelled by the other opening. And through the gill slits such water as is needed for the extraction of oxygen, and is not necessary for food-straining purposes, is passed in order that the life-sustaining gas may be sluiced over the gills.

There is now no more helpless creature in all the seven seas, so far as active pursuit of food and adventure is concerned. But even to the least ambitious, Nature is not unmerciful. She provides a jacket of many wonders for the sea squirt.

THE WONDERFUL COAT WORN BY A LITTLE ANIMAL OF THE SEA

The most famous coat in the world was Joseph's; the most famous in the ocean is the sea squirt's. It is a tunic covering the body, and gives the sea squirt yet another name, that of the tunicate.

The tunic is tough, leathery, membranous, and sometimes embodies grains of sand, or other gritty matter in its make-up, in order, we may suppose, to make it unpalatable to the hungry enemies of the sea squirt. It may be that, and yet not sufficiently forbidding to prevent industrious and ingenious crabs from stripping off the tunic, by a nimble feat of surgery, and using it themselves as a covering disguise.

The most puzzling thing about this tunic, however, is the fact that in some species it consists in part of pure vegetable matter—cellulose. Now, cellulose is the material forming the cell-walls of plants, and is the substance which science has learned to treat with chemicals and convert into artificial silk and into celluloid, paper, and a thousand other things indispensable to commerce.

How comes this framework of the vegetable world into the composition of the tunic in which a sea animal that took the wrong turning invests its degenerate body? We can no more tell than we can tell why it surrenders its pledge of spine, nerve tract, brain, and locomotion.

High as a fish at the outset, the sea squirt sinks lower than the sea anemone. And the great problem is this—did the whole family once possess backbones, or has the whole family risen to the hope of a backbone in infancy, and been unable in maturity to achieve the goal of life?

One opinion has it that the inglorious maturity of the sea squirt results from the lazy existence to which it sinks. Another opinion is that the too great exertion of the larval form exhausts all the energy of the body and brings about a decline, not in the ability to live, but in the ability to live a life of progress conducted at a gallop.

It is not possible that we have in these strange things primitive Life in search of a backbone? May it not be that failures are here repeating themselves, and that some day, in some sea, something better than a notochord will be born into the sea squirt's house, and a new vertebrate added to the catalogue of our families?

THE MILLIONS OF SEA-SQUIRTS ROUND OUR COASTS

In most departments of life we can read the whole history of a species, because its bones lie fossilised in the rocks. We cannot with the tunicates, because, having no bones, they have nothing to leave us; their soft flesh is gone in a twinkling when they die, food for other animals, or dissolved by the action of the water.

There seems to be hope for the family from the fact that some species remain free swimmers all their days, and do not yield up the little rod-supported tail and nerve cord. But in general the position is as stated. The millions of sea squirts round our coasts, and their kindred elsewhere, run through this cycle of degeneration.

The kinds that remain free swimmers are known as the appendicularia. They are quite small active creatures, resembling the larval form of the sea squirts already described. They never settled down to a sedentary existence, nor do they attain the size of those we have considered. The belief is, indeed, that, either they have got the better of the inert stage, or else they have become a race of larvae which

never grow up like the axolotls. But for all their activity and merit, they retain the notochord, and have never yet developed a backbone.

Then there are the primitive free-swimming salpa ascidians, quaint, transparent animals, whose form may be kept in mind from their description as little living barrels with the two ends knocked out.

THE SALPAS THAT JOIN TOGETHER LIKE A LITTLE BRIDGE OF BOATS

But the salpas are not free swimmers in the individual sense; they unite together in the form of a chain, scores of them, and look like a tiny bridge of boats afloat.

Some of the salpas are born by budding off from the parent; others come from eggs. And there is this wonder about these creatures: the adult proceeds to give birth to a child by budding, and in that bud is an egg from which another salpa will emerge. Thus in a single creature we have three generations in sight at the same time, grandchild, mother, grandmother, all growing simultaneously, and grandmother voluntarily forming part of one of these extraordinary chains of linked salpas. But no backbone is there.

Among the commoner forms of our waters we find this communal life as well as isolated existence. Several sea squirts may unite their bodies, joined together as completely as the leaves of a cabbage. But while all use one common outlet for the expulsion of water, they remain proudly individual as to intake, for each retains its own channel for the drawing-in of the water which feeds and supplies it with the needed oxygen.

THE ANIMAL THAT GROWS LIKE A FLOWER ON THE END OF A STALK

Notable forms are the phallusia, in which the coat is raised into many little tubercles or prominences like those of a cactus; the hypobithius, a deep-sea specimen found nearly 1800 feet down; the microcosmus, in which, where mud or sand is prevalent, the animal raises itself on a fleshy stalk, like a flower, to keep itself free from danger of suffocation; the clavelina, which creeps like a vegetable growth along the position to which it is anchored; the botryllidae, which mass together, on rocks or seaweed, into crusts or fleshy carpets.

Most interesting of the many others are the pyrosomas, which grow together in such masses as to render identity almost impossible. The colonies arise from a normal larva, which buds; its successors also bud until huge joint assemblages are established.

One of the group of pyrosomas (called the Amaroucium elegans) is a sheer wonder of the sea. From the usual tunic it produces a crop of sharp and formidable spines. Nor is that all its claim to remembrance, for within it resides the power to light the sea with a lovely radiance. It is phosphorescent. At a hostile touch, or at some unusual commotion of the waves, out flashes this lovely signal, be it warning, S.O.S., or whatever Nature intended it to be. There is nothing lovelier in all the tropics' magic seas than this radiance, which lasts until the occasion prompting it is forgotten; then the living ball of wonder

No true fish is so primitive as the lancelet. It has the desired notochord, running from snout to tail, and a little spinal cord leading to a minute brain in the insignificant head. But it has no ears, it has no eyes, it has no fins such as fish have, but one long primitive fin running the whole distance of the upper part of the body, none at the sides.

It is another of the wonders of the border line. Very ancient, we suppose it to be, but something in the evolutionary process must have ceased to function, for, if the lancelet is really today as it was of old time, it must have begun the course towards the true fishes' goal, have reached a dead-end and have stayed there. But we can only guess; we do not know. The very earliest thing with a backbone dis-

  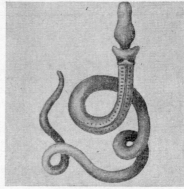

MICROCOSMUS   HYPOBITHIUS   BALANOGLOSSUS

These pictures are reproduced by courtesy of Frederick Warne & Company

sinks to quieter depths, puts out its lamps, and is only a dreamy memory.

All this about an animal which gets its common name from the fact that if we take it up it squirts out water from its body in the way that sea squirts have! But in a quite different order, nearer the fishes yet not of them, we have, in the lancelet, a fish-like little creature which has engaged the brains and pens of generations of men skilled in the mysteries of lowly border-line life.

The lancelet, teeming in our own and neighbouring seas, is a swiftly writhing midget, sharpened at both ends, as it seems, with its muscles much segmented, so affording it the power to wriggle with surprising speed, not only through the water, but into the depths of the sand underlying its native sea. The reason for its importance to science is that it is so imperfect in the tale of progress.

covered by science is a fish in the rocks, but that, with its backbone and its external armour, was as far in advance of the lancelet as an aeroplane is in advance of a boy's paper kite.

With only a notochord for a spinal column, sightless, but suggesting the possibility of a single eye in the middle of its head, without a particle of bone in its body, and only one tiny ring of cartilage round its mouth, the lancelet is a priceless might-have-been; perhaps, in the fulness of time, a may-be. At present it gulps in water, strains out of it little diatoms and things as minute, burrows like an eel in the sand, flops helpless on its side if it seeks to rest level-keeled on the ground, and remains a challenge and a marvel to the wisest natural historian.

Lower still and more repulsive is the marine, worm-like balanoglossus. A rare visitor to British waters, and when found there measuring but a few inches, but in warmer seas attaining a length of two to three feet, this animal seems to represent a stage at which various ancient families branched off on independent lines.

Protruding from the head is a lengthy organ called the proboscis or snout, a sort of little trunk, whose purpose is to tunnel. Behind that is a tough muscular collar in which the mouth is seated, and behind that a muscular worm-like body, charged with glands for the secretion of slime.

Now, arising over the fore part of the mouth and extending into that strange proboscis, is the notochord, the supporting rod of the great nerve channel of the vertebrate. And in the body is a primitive spinal cord, with branches of nerves running to various parts of the frame.

A WORM-LIKE CREATURE THAT BURROWS IN THE SAND BENEATH THE SEA

The gills are those of a vertebrate, and the organs just described are those of a vertebrate in the embryo stage. Yet the balanoglossus is a worm to all external seeming. It lives in the sand of the sea, tunnelling a channel which it coats with slime. As it worms its way through the sand the animal eats it, after the manner of a true worm, digesting the vegetable and animal matter contained in it, and ejecting the indigestible sand, like an earth-worm at work on our lawns.

These hideous creatures are brilliantly coloured: white, yellow, orange-red, green, yet in places they are almost transparent. Though common to shallow waters, these gay living pictures have been dredged from depths of as much as 15,000 feet.

With this colouration is associated a powerful and unpleasant odour, varying in intensity and character with different species. And, as if to show that, while the presence of the notochord and the absence of the vertebrae are common to all, specialisation has provided a favoured few species with a phosphorescent lighting system of exceptional power and beauty.

HOW THE BALANOGLOSSUS REPAIRS ITS DAMAGED BODY

Perhaps the colour and the light are in the nature of warnings to enemies, like the high colours of poisonous insects and of evil-tasting frogs. But that seems insufficient, for the balanoglossus has learned to repair his body with the skill of a shoemaker engaged on a pair of old boots.

Destroy the hinder part of his body and he will renew it; cut off his proboscis and rip away his muscular collar, and he will repair the damage with new material.

Of such are the animals peopling the frontiers between the backboned and the backboneless domains. Science has not exhausted the list. There must be hundreds of life-forms in the deep seas that we have never drawn to the surface. We dredge with a small net with a wide mesh in an unlimited medium. There may exist creatures linking us still more closely, the present with the past, the improved with the undeveloped.

We have here, however, matter enough to summon thinking caps to many reflecting heads. These petty creatures, common objects of sea shores, are the very lowest forms in the scale of vertebrates yet revealed to us. They are the primitives. In point of age, they are great aristocrats, ancient, yet not venerable, as is often the case with decadent aristocracies higher in the scale of life.

We must suppose that they received the offer of a nobler form and more exalted physical conditions, that they began an upward career, wearied of the conditions essential to progress, and got no farther than to preserve in their bodies the beginnings of a story which, carried to completion, might have led to peaks of dazzling brilliance in the scheme of Nature.

LIVING MILESTONES WHICH MARK THE WAY BY WHICH LIFE HAS ADVANCED

The insects lost the world by keeping to cold blood. The humble little friends of this chapter lost their way through failing to make perfect use of the chance which came to them when backbones were in Nature's gift.

They are lowly and ignoble creatures, but they occupy a great space in the literature of science because, with their humility are combined the possibilities of greatness. We treasure them as living milestones marking the way by which all higher life has advanced.

If we could find alive a survivor of human types as much below contemporary savages as these creatures are below fishes, we should devote whole books to him. He would be a missing link in our chain of life. These modest animals are links. Many such links are missing, but these do help to join up our chain and make the gaps less impossible and discouraging.

The Story of the Things We See About us Every Day

A trainload of logs cut from a redwood tree

A TREE AND WHAT IT BECOMES

WHEN we enter a great building like Westminster Abbey we are so surrounded by the magnificence of masonry that we are apt to forget the wooden doors which let us in. Those wooden doors close at night; the lock is turned; they guard the Abbey; they shut out the world; the mighty dead rest safely in their graves because of them. The forest guards the rock.

How the brain works, looking at those old carved and nail-studded doors, and thinking of the day when they grew in some English forest, their roots hidden underground, their branches swaying in the wind, their leaves making a pleasant rustle in the summer air! Birds built their nests in them long before the Wars of the Roses. The woodpecker tapped at their bark long before Shakespeare walked from Stratford across the fields to Shottery St. Mary. Squirrels ran along their boughs while the Normans marched through the land. The doors will be hanging there when you and I, and our children's children, have passed away for ever!

Someone has nobly said that it is good to look on oaks that are kin to those immortal trees that died to live for ever as the Victory and the fighting Téméraire. Have we ever thought of that? The woodman's axe rang in our English forests.

The carter came with his team of willing horses. A sound like tearing thunder rent the air. Down fell a king of the forest. Dead? No; immortal. The carter called to his horses; they slipped and stumbled and strained in the traces; the wheels turned; the whip cracked; off went the forest king to become the Nemesis of a tyrant, a victorious ship of Trafalgar.

Oaks from English fields, under which children had played for many a generation, at whose spreading base primroses grew all wet with April rains, formed the wooden walls of Nelson. Were they ever more beautiful in the forest than on that immortal morning when, with crowding sail, they swept towards Napoleon's challenge, and Nelson stood there in his admiral's frock-coat with the four stars of honour on his left breast, the empty sleeve pinned near them, asking Captain Blackwood if another signal were not needed?

Captain Blackwood made answer that he thought the whole fleet seemed very clearly to understand what they were about. These words were scarcely spoken before that signal was made which will be remembered as long as the language of England shall endure—Nelson's last signal: "England expects that every man will do his duty!"

INDUSTRIES · HOW THINGS ARE MADE · WHERE THEY COME FROM

Dead trees? The beautiful lichen and the glorious bark stripped off; trees no longer, but daubed with paint, clamped with iron, a ship, a fighting ship of England! No, not dead trees; immortal trees; the oaks of England, our forests torn up from the soil of England and hurled at her enemies, woods in movement like the trees in the prophecy to Macbeth; yes, still trees, and trees that will live for ever.

One likes to think, too, of a blind Milton groping his way with a stick cut from an English forest. He saw in his darkness a beam of light, which was freedom, and he fumbled his way to it, tapping the invisible ground with his stick. Drake fought for England, Nelson fought for England, and Milton fought, too. He was one of the greatest minds that ever realised the full dignity of man, and ever hated those who would bind the human race in chains. He fought to set us free. Is it not one of the greatest pictures in England's gallery of heroes, that of the blind Milton groping his way with a stick?

WHAT MILTON WROTE OF ENGLAND ON A TABLE OF ENGLISH OAK

It was on a table of English oak that Milton wrote of England: " Why else was this nation chosen before any other, that out of her, as out of Sion, should be proclaimed and sounded forth the first tidings and trumpet of Reformation to all Europe?"

And from that day forward the march has been continued throughout all fields of our national life. Across the historic predecessor of the table in the House of Commons has been waged the war of Reformation, the war between tyranny and freedom, between truth and falseness.

The architect learned from the forest to build his stately aisles and arch them in with graceful roof of stone. No building of grandeur but has its roots in the forest. Man has gone there to learn how to build. He has gone there for his spears, his bows, and his ships. Our long history is inseparably bound up with the forest.

May we not say, indeed, that history is an arm-in-arm march of Man and Forest? Not only would man never have been able to advance from savagery without trees, but without trees he could not have even been a savage. He could not have been at all.

There is not a traffic of the human race, not an art, not a science, not a comfort, and not a beauty which does not issue from the heart of a tree. Strange, too, is it that the centuries of man's existence are divided by a tree, on one side the centuries before, and on the other the centuries after, the Cross of Christ. If we cross the desert of Sahara we find ourselves ploughing through an ocean of sand. Nothing will grow there. It is a dead land, profitless, empty, appalling. Now, the whole Earth would be one hideous Sahara but for trees. And the Sahara would not be a desert if it were covered by trees.

THE FORESTS THAT FORM AN UMBRELLA TO SHADE THE EARTH FROM THE SUN

Forests present to the Sun an immense umbrella. They shield the soil from rays which would otherwise burn up into smoke-like dust the rich pastures of the earth's surface. Herbage, which grows under the shelter of this great umbrella, is itself a form of sunshade, as it were, a doll's sunshade; it seeks to imitate the mighty forest by protecting the soil from the rays of the sun. Without trees the richest soil would soon become desert land.

Once the mountain slopes of India were covered by magnificent forests; they were cut down and sold for money. The people did not realise that God makes a thing useful as well as beautiful. The beautiful trees, hewn down as a revolution hews down the gilded idlers of society, were in reality the most useful servants of India. It was those idle-looking trees which, in the blessed season of rain, drank up at a million mouths the precious drops of moisture, and stored them up for that dread of India—the sunny day. Now, when the rain falls, there are few forests to catch it; the drops strike the Earth, sink in, or slide to the rivers, and away they go to sea—water running away from a parched and arid land.

THE THOUSAND AND ONE USES OF THE TREES FOR MANKIND

From trees we get coal and materials for buildings; we get valuable drugs, gums, dyes, and articles of food. But, above all these things, it is important to remember that trees influence the air and the soil of the country; that they oppose their quiet strength to the great enemies of our race—extreme heat and extreme cold; and that they have an all-important bearing on the hidden springs of the Earth.

We should cultivate in ourselves a love for trees, and look on them with something more than admiration.

PICTURE-STORY OF TIMBER

The vast forests of Soviet Russia, occupying more than 2,700,000 square miles of its territory, make up one-fourth of the entire forest area of the world. These magnificent pines are in the Moloma Forest in the Kirov Region of the U.S.S.R.

A GIANT OF THE FOREST HAS A GREAT FALL

This picture shows a fallen giant, a Kauri pine, that has just been felled in a New Zealand forest. The Kauri pine, which often grows to a height of a hundred feet, is the king of New Zealand trees. It grows in the northern portion of North Island, and nowhere else in the world. The timber is strong and not difficult to work.

Small trees are felled with the axe, but the giants of the forest are sawn down, sometimes mechanically and at others by hand, as seen in this picture of men felling a tree in Auckland. Having sawn through the great tree in such a way that it will fall in the direction required, the men step aside while the tree crashes to earth.

THE BIG SAWS IN THE FOREST

The big saws that are used for felling trees are not like the small saws used by the carpenter. Handsaws have two handles, and the teeth are generally arranged at intervals in groups of three.

In America mechanical saws worked by small portable engines are used in many parts, and here we see one felling a tree. The backward and forward movement is very rapid.

In Russia, a country of almost unlimited timber resources, lumbering is to a great extent mechanised. Here we see lumberjacks using an electric saw, driven by a mobile generator, to cut down a tree.

GIANT MACHINES THAT HANDLE THE LOGS

When the trees have been felled the logs must be transported to the sawmills to be cut up into planks and beams. Here logs are being mechanically loaded on to a huge trailer in Canada.

Horses, oxen, and elephants are still used in many places to move timber, but they are being fast replaced by machines, such as this powerful haulage apparatus seen at work in a British forest.

GREAT TRACTORS THAT HAUL THE TIMBER

In the thick forests of New Zealand the great trunks have to be hauled sometimes for miles, and tractors of great power, like the one seen in the picture, have to be used.

Tractors, with their caterpillar tracks, can operate over practically any ground, and are the most efficient method of haulage. Here a train of sledges is being dragged along a snow-covered road in Russia by a powerful motor-tractor.

STARTING THE LOGS DOWN THE RIVER

Where a river is available, as in many parts of the United States and Canada, the logs are simply drawn or rolled to the river, placed in the water, and started down stream toward the sawmill, which may be many miles away.

Here we see a great mass of logs that have become jammed during their journey down the St. John River, in New Brunswick. These jams occur suddenly, and men have to go to the place and with long poles ease the logs so that they can resume their journey down the river. Clearing a jam is a difficult and dangerous business.

THE MEN WHO GUIDE THE LOGS

Sometimes the log jams are too big to be untangled with pike poles, and dynamite has to be used. Here one of the drivers, as the men who guide the logs are called, prepares to set a charge.

One of the important industries almost wholly dependent on the great forests is paper-making. This picture shows logs being sorted for distribution to a pulp-mill at Ocean Falls, British Columbia.

THE LOGS ARRIVE AT THE SAWMILL

A jam having been relieved, the procession of logs again begins to move down the river, with the stream, toward the mill. This photograph was taken on the St. Maries River, in Idaho.

Arrived at the mill, the logs are dragged to shore, and an endless chain fitted with hooks, or some similar device, drags them up a slanting way to the mill.

Not only small trees, but large ones, reach the mill in this way, and here we see some bigger timber being drawn from the river up into the mill.

A TORRENT OF TIMBER IN CANADA

This wonderful photograph shows hundreds of thousands of logs of timber being whirled down a swiftly-flowing river in British Columbia. To see such a mass of timber flowing by is a very striking sight.

BUILDING A GREAT RAFT OF LOGS

Sometimes millions of feet of lumber from the vast forests of North America or Scandinavia are made up into giant rafts in a cradle, such as this seen in an Oregon forest.

These rafts are sent vast distances by river and sea, and here we see the lumbermen beginning to build the lumber into a giant raft inside the cradle.

Here the raft has been completed, the logs being held in position by great chains that pass right round the raft, which has just left the cradle and is in the river, about to start on its voyage.

This raft, which is nearly 800 feet long and contains five million feet of timber, is travelling by sea down the Pacific coast of America. It was towed into San Diego harbour, in California, after an ocean journey of two thousand miles.

A RAFT AS BIG AS AN ATLANTIC LINER

Here the great pine raft is seen during its long ocean journey down the Pacific coast from the Oregon forests to California.
It is nearly 800 feet long, 52 feet wide, and draws 34 feet of water, and stands 12 feet out of the water. It is as big as an
ocean liner, and the men who travel with it and live on it during the journey build little timber houses in which to sleep.

THE LOGS ARE SAWN UP READY FOR USE

Logs at the timber yard are sometimes cut up by men using a double-handed saw but more generally mechanical means are used. Here we see small logs being cut up on a modern type of circular saw.

Here is an ingenious machine for cutting up timber. A row of circular saws is so arranged that the saws, electrically controlled by one man, can be raised or dropped at will, thus cutting the planks to the best advantage.

In this picture we see a gang-saw on which logs can be cut into a series of planks of any thickness.

Here is a horizontal bandsaw, an endless band with teeth on one edge, which is carried round two wheels.

Many of the pictures in these pages are by courtesy of the New Zealand Government and the Timber Development Association

Plain Answers to the Questions of the Children of the World

Noonday Rest, by John Linnell

WHAT HAPPENS WHEN WE GET TIRED?

TIREDNESS or fatigue is really due to the poisoning of the brain and the nerves by all sorts of things which are produced in our bodies as the result of work; or perhaps sometimes as the result of too much exposure to sun and heat. Every day's work, if it is at all hard, produces rather more of these poisonous things than we can get rid of as we go on working; and these things really help us, at night, to go to sleep. During good sleep they are all got rid of, and we wake refreshed.

It is easy to show that this is true. We can take a small quantity of blood from a tired animal, such as a dog, without hurting it, and can give this to another dog that is not tired. The second dog at once shows all the signs of a dog that has run a long way and is tired out. The poisons produced in the body of the first dog have got into the blood of the second dog, and it also feels tired.

It used to be thought that the cause of fatigue was the need for more food. The tired person, people thought, had used up his food and needed more; just as a railway engine might be said to get tired if the stoker forgot to supply it with plenty of coal. If this were true, the more utterly exhausted a man was, the bigger the meal that he should take.

But we have learned that this old idea was utterly wrong. The body always contains so large a supply of food material, or fuel, that a man gets tired for some other reason long before he has nearly used it up. Also we have learned that in a state of fatigue it is not possible to digest food properly, and therefore to give a big meal to an exhausted person is very bad for him. He is not fit to use it, and it only upsets him. We should eat only a little, if at all, when we are very tired. The best thing for tiredness is sleep.

We may take water when we are tired, or lemonade, or oranges; because these things, in passing through the body, carry all sorts of poisons away and help us to get rid of them; but above all we must rest and sleep. Generally the people who sleep best are those who work hard. The man who works all day in the fields usually has the best sleep in the world, far better than some unfortunate people who do very little or nothing, and who may even take medicine to help them to sleep. Nature, the best of all doctors, has her own medicine to procure good sleep for every healthy person who works; and natural tiredness produces in our blood the very thing that gives us perfect and natural sleep.

FIRE · WIND · WATER · LIFE · MIND · SLEEP · HOW · WHY · WHERE

Why Does Hot Water Crack Thick Glass More Easily Than Thin?

Hot water cracks a thick glass more easily than a thin one because the heat causes the expansion of the inner layer of the glass, while the outer layer is still cool and unexpanded. The result of this is that the expansion of the inner layer tears the outer layer, which will not stretch and therefore must break. When the glass is thin there is no such unequal expansion. The thin layer of glass expands at the same time, and so there is no undue strain.

What is Artificial Silk?

Artificial silk is an imitation made chemically from wood pulp, or the cellulose of cotton fibre. For over a hundred years men tried to find some substitute for silk. The credit both of the discovery and of the name, artificial silk, belongs to Sir Joseph Swan, who took out the first patent in 1883 and showed his results at the Inventions Exhibition of 1885. In the Science Museum at South Kensington we can see the first d'oyleys crocheted in the new material by the inventor's wife. Sir Joseph had invented the carbon filament lamp in 1877, and he next made experiments to improve these filaments.

His aim was to make a continuous, even thread of indefinite length. Just as the silkworm or spider ejects a fluid through spinnerets into the air which instantaneously makes it solid, so Sir Joseph squirted an emulsion of cellulose nitrate in acetic acid through minute holes into alcohol. The alcohol coagulated the emulsion into a thread. This thread, however, was inflammable, so that it had to be treated with ammonium sulphide to make it safe. The new filament was very lustrous, and Sir Joseph realised that if only he could make it thin enough it would be the basis of a new textile industry. He succeeded in making very fine filaments which could be twisted into threads. A year after Swan had taken out his patent a Frenchman, Comte Hilaire de Chardonnet, took out a patent and seven years later formed a company to make and sell artificial silk.

Other investigators, including a scientist named Stern who had worked with Swan, improved the processes of manufacture, and today artificial silks can be spun as fine as the silk of the silkworm itself.

What is a Rainbow?

A rainbow appears in the sky when rain is falling opposite the sun shining at less than 42 degrees above the horizon. The eye of the observer of the rainbow is on a straight line between the sun and the centre of the bow, and so his eye is the apex of a cone of which the rainbow is the circumference of the base. The seven colours of the solar spectrum form the surface of this cone in successive rings from red outside to violet inside.

As each white ray of sunlight enters the round drop of rain it is refracted and split up into seven coloured rays, some of which pass through the drop while others are reflected, being refracted once again in passing out. Now, as different colours are not equally refrangible, these rays emerge at different angles, with the result that only one colour from each raindrop will travel straight to the observer's eye. He therefore sees the red rays from the raindrops in the outer ring and the violet rays from those in the inner ring, while the colours reaching his eye from the raindrops between them graduate as in the spectrum.

Why Are Names Not Used in Parliament?

If we go to the House of Commons and listen to a debate we notice that when a Member refers to any other member except the chairman of committees he does not say Mr Smith or Mr Brown, but " the honourable Member for Sevenoaks."

This custom has its origin in the fact that Members of Parliament are representatives of the people, and, in referring to each other not by their own names but by the place they represent, it is recognised that the speaker is actually the voice of the people of a certain place.

There is usually only one exception to the rule of not using names in the House of Commons, and that is when Mr Speaker calls on a member to address the House.

There is, however, an extraordinary occasion for naming a member, and that is when he misbehaves himself. Then, Mr Speaker formally names the offender, and a motion is made suspending his right to attend Parliament.

We see, therefore, that while the idea is that a member represents a constituency as long as he conducts himself with dignity, it is never the member for the constituency who loses his dignity, but Mr So-and-so.

THE LIFE-STORY OF AN ORCHARD PEST

 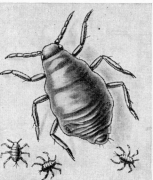 

1. In spring and summer we often see on the bark and leaves of apple trees tufts like cotton wool. Inside these are tiny insects, which are the wingless females of the woolly aphis, commonly known as American blight.

2. The aphides rapidly grow to maturity, producing young at the rate of as many as twenty a day. These also grow and breed, so that there are many generations in a summer. Some of the wool, with its insects, is blown to other trees.

3. Late in the summer winged females are hatched, but why these have wings no one knows. All these creatures injure the tree by penetrating the tissue with their trunks and drawing away much of the life-giving sap.

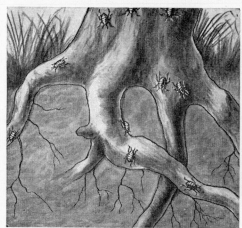 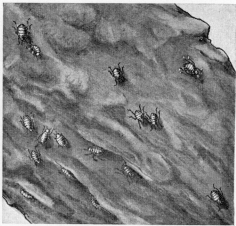

4. As winter approaches many wingless female aphides migrate from the upper part of the tree to the roots, and cause canker wounds which at last kill the roots. The insects hibernate (or pass the winter) there.

5. Other wingless females which do not travel as far as the roots hibernate in cracks and crevices of the diseased bark of the apple tree, the disease being caused by the attacks of many generations of aphides.

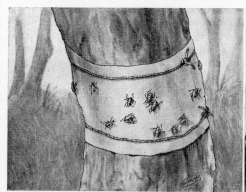 

6. When spring comes the aphides wake up, and those that have slept among the roots crawl up the trunk to the branches. If, however, the tree has a grease band the insects are caught on it by the mucilage which prevents them going farther up the trees.

7. If the tree has no band they reach the upper parts and produce young, and these, when they reach maturity, exude from their pores silky threads that form the woolly tufts shown in the first picture, and among these they hide and multiply with amazing rapidity.

What is a Charter ?

Charter comes from a Latin word meaning paper, and the word is applied to ancient books or papers relating to history, to titles, to privileges, or the like; but it specially means the act by which certain liberties are granted to the people.

Charters are written in formal language, always beginning with an invocation to God. We now use parchment as the material on which they are written, but in earlier times they were engraved on stone, or written on papyrus.

It was the custom in the Middle Ages that kings should take the State archives with them wherever they went. Having done so as usual, it happened once that a French king lost them in a battle. After so great a loss he decided henceforth to have the Charters preserved in a safe place, and this was the origin of what are called State Archives (or Records), which now comprise papers concerning a country's internal or foreign relations.

A charter that has remained famous is the Magna Carta of England, won from King John early in the thirteenth century. It assured the rights of the several social classes and forms the foundation of the British Constitution.

What is the Koran ?

The Koran is the Arabic name for the Muslim Bible, or a collection of messages delivered by Mohammed in his capacity as an inspired Prophet, messages which he gave to the world as being transmitted by the Angel Gabriel and directly revealed to him in visions or in dreams.

The verses of the Koran (scattered in all directions and recorded on parchments, leaves, stones, bones, and other rude materials, or those that were preserved in the memory of his contemporaries) all were collected together and divided into chapters.

Abu Baker was the first to collect the Koran, but his collection was not a complete official version, for there were other fragments still in circulation which led to disputes as to the correct reading of particular passages. To put an end to this position of affairs, fatal alike to the laws and the unity of the Faith, the Caliph Osman ordered a fresh revision of the Koran, its basis being the collection under Abu Baker. The division of the Koran into 114 chapters dates from the time of the Caliph Osman.

As to its contents, it includes not only the whole of his teachings and his legislation, but also a considerable portion of his life, an account of his temporal and spiritual warfare, as also the history and the sayings of the earlier prophets.

Why was Delphi Famous ?

In all times, and with all peoples, man has been eager to know the future and has tried to discover means of foreseeing it.

Thus the Greeks consecrated special temples where they could communicate with the gods through maidens called sibyls. In the ancient world, Delphi was the most famous temple for consulting oracles. It had been dedicated to Apollo, and the Greeks would never start on any great enterprise without inquiring from Apollo whether it was his will that they should do so, and ask what would be the result of their undertaking.

The Pythia was the special priestess of the temple of Delphi. Seated on a tripod above a yawning chasm, from which prophetic exhalations were supposed to escape, the soothsayer at first only gave out her oracles once a year, unless something quite unusual was about to occur. So many people were eager to question Apollo that other virgins had later to give their services.

It was the custom that those who consulted oracles should make great presents to the temples. Thus Delphi became extremely rich in golden statues, brass vessels, ivory seats, and precious works of art. For these, Roman Emperors fought when they were discovered later.

Are There Dogs which Cannot Bark ?

Several do not, such as the sledge dogs, the " huskies " of the Arctic circle, which are descendants of the wolves, and which neither bark, nor snore, but only whine. But there are also dogs in Africa which are not so closely related to the wolf—the Basenji dogs used for hunting in the time of the Pharaohs, and so employed still in some localities. They appear on fourth-century B.C. tombs. Their modern representatives are like wire-haired fox terriers with curly tails. They do not bark but give tongue with something like a Swiss yodel.

Where are the Clouds When the Sky is quite Clear ?

Clouds, as we know, are made of water, and water can exist in the air in many different forms. When it forms a cloud, it is really in the form of liquid drops, like the collection of drops that forms a cloud from our breath on a frosty day. The water that formed the clouds is still in the sky when it is cloudless. What has happened is that, partly owing to the warmth of the sun, and partly, no doubt, to electrical conditions in the upper air, the air is capable of holding all the water in it in gaseous form. This water-vapour is as transparent as air itself; indeed, it is much better for us to regard water-vapour as one of the things that make up the air, just as much as oxygen or nitrogen. It is difficult for us to realise, perhaps, when we look up at the sky on a cloudless day, that we are looking through water, but we are certainly doing so just as if we had our eyes open under water and were looking up. If it were not for the water that forms part of the air, we should be utterly scorched by the heat of the Sun. As it is, however, most of the Sun's heat is caught by the water-vapour, which is very opaque to heat, though it is transparent to light.

When Water is Boiling, Why Can it Not be Made Hotter ?

When water is boiling it can be made hotter, but not as liquid water. Water, like other things, has a certain temperature above which it cannot be a liquid, but must be a gas. That point we call the boiling point. We cannot make water hotter than boiling point, because then it ceases to be what we usually call water, and turns into gaseous water, or water-vapour; but water-vapour may be made hotter than the temperature of boiling water.

If we go on boiling water we are certainly putting heat into it; and we must not fancy that because the liquid water gets no hotter, the heat is being lost, or wasted, or turned into nothing. Nothing is ever lost, or turned into nothing. What the heat does is to put itself into the liquid water, so that that liquid water takes the form of a gas, and the heat still remains, though rather changed, in the energy of movement of the parts of the gas. We can easily prove that the heat is doing something, though it is not making the water hotter, when we find that if we go on boil-ing we boil all the water away; that is, we turn the whole of it into water-vapour.

But, on the other hand, it must be clearly understood that the boiling point of water varies with atmospheric pressure. At ordinary atmospheric pressure it boils, as we know, at 212 degrees Fahrenheit; but on the top of a high mountain, where the atmospheric pressure is less, it will boil at a lower temperature, and at the Dead Sea, which is more than 2000 feet below sea level, and where the atmospheric pressure is therefore greater, its boiling point will be over 212 degrees Fahrenheit. In the early world where the atmosphere was very heavy, the boiling point of water must have been very high.

What Happens When a Leaf Falls ?

We have seen the changes that take place in the leaf as the summer goes away. When the leaf falls to the ground, there are waiting for it many tiny living creatures called microbes, which, as we say, make it decay. But this really means that the stuff of the leaf is changed in such a way that it can be taken up by the plant from the soil and built up again into the plant when the spring comes. This is one of the most beautiful and wonderful things in Nature, and there is no greater lesson we can learn than that what looks like useless death and decay and waste is really nothing of the sort, but a living process that makes for more life. Some may say, Why should not the leaves and flowers live on all the year round, as they do in some plants for special reasons? But the leaf is made in order to use the sunlight, and in the winter there is not enough sunlight, and so the leaf would be wasting its time. So the plant takes what it can use from the leaf and the rest of the leaf is changed, so that the plant can use that, too, when the summer is coming, and there is a use for new leaves.

What Does the Law Mean by an Act of God ?

The law describes this as an accident due to natural causes, directly and exclusively without human intervention, which could not have been avoided by any kind of pains or foresight and care reasonably to be expected. It is an Act of God, for example, if a house is struck by lightning, and damaged, though reasonable precautions have been taken.

Why Do we See Lights When we Get a Blow on the Eye?

This depends on a wonderful law about the nerves of the senses, which was discovered by a German called Müller about the middle of last century. It is that special nerves which belong to the various senses are bound to give us a sensation if they give us anything. As a rule, the particular nerve is only affected by the special thing it is meant for—the eye-nerve by light or the ear-nerve by sound; but if something else has the power of affecting the nerve, then we shall seem to see or hear, whatever the thing that excites the nerves really is. Thus a blow on the eye may affect the eye-nerve, and if the eye-nerve is affected we are bound to get a sensation of light.

The best proof of this great law is furnished by electricity. We have no special sense for electricity, as we have the ear for sound or the eye for light; but electricity is capable of stimulating any nerve in the body. With the electric current we may affect the nose, and the person smells; the eye, and he sees; the ear, and he hears; the tongue, and he tastes; the skin, and he has the sense of touch. We now know how to explain this law. It is not that the nerve of the eye is different from the nerve of the ear, but that it goes to a special part of the brain. Each part of the brain that is concerned in the sensation is *specialised*, that is, can only do one thing.

Can the Foundations of a Building be Relaid?

Many old buildings have had their foundations rebuilt, but the most remarkable example of renewal was that of Winchester Cathedral. Early in the present century it was found that there had been a serious subsidence of the cathedral. A pit was sunk, and it was found that beech trees had been used in the foundation, and while some of them remained sound after 700 years, many had decayed. But more serious than this knowledge was the fact that when the excavation was made to examine the foundations, water rushed in from the River Itchen, and in some parts was soon 14 feet deep. This made the work of repair far more urgent, and it was decided that an immense bed of concrete must be laid right under the cathedral, thus providing a solid foundation capable of sustaining the weight of the old masonry. The water which had rushed in could not be pumped out, for fear of drawing gravel from other parts of the foundation; and as all the work would have to be performed under water an experienced diver, W. R. Walker, was engaged, and to him, working with the architect and the contractors, the ultimate success of this great feat was due. Owing to the peat in the soil the water became black, and everything had to be carried out in pitch darkness. As the diver removed the peat and old timber from under the cathedral, he placed bags of concrete in position, and on top of these great blocks of masonry. In this way the foundations were renewed, piece by piece, and after six years Winchester Cathedral was safe again.

Is It True That we Cannot Bleed Unless a Hole is Made in Our Veins?

It is true that our blood is shut in a set of closed tubes called arteries, veins, and capillaries, and we never can bleed unless a hole has been made in the wall of one of these tubes. A little scratch anywhere in the skin is certainly not likely to strike an artery, for these usually lie deep; nor yet a vein, for, though many veins lie just under the skin, and their walls are much thinner than those of an artery, they are too thick for a slight scratch to pierce.

Between the arteries carrying the blood from the heart and the veins which return it to the heart, the blood runs in tubes as slight as hairs, and therefore called capillaries, which is the Latin name for a hair. Everywhere else the slightest scratch is likely to tear or cut a few capillaries, and then, of course, we bleed. There is no pulse in the capillaries, and so the blood oozes out; but if an artery is cut, like the artery we feel at the wrist, the blood leaps out in pulses.

There would be no use in the blood at all if it simply went round and round in these closed tubes. But all sorts of things are always passing in and out through the walls of capillaries, and that is why we have blood at all.

What is French Leave?

To take French leave means to do a thing without asking permission. It arose from the fact that the French soldiers used to take what they liked from a conquered city, without asking leave or paying.

THE MACHINE THAT SELLS A TICKET

Here is the ingenious machine that accepts coppers or silver and presents a newly-printed ticket, together with the correct change. When coppers are used, they are dropped all together into the chute and, on the way down, trip a delicate lever which sets the motor and other mechanism in motion. Arriving on the coin hopper, a circular plate being revolved by the motor, they are carried round one by one by the small studs and move a lever on the coin check disc four times before they fall out of the hopper and go down a sloping chute into the copper stack tube. When the coin check disc has travelled its proper distance, governed by the value of the fare—in this case fourpence—a tooth on the disc rim moves

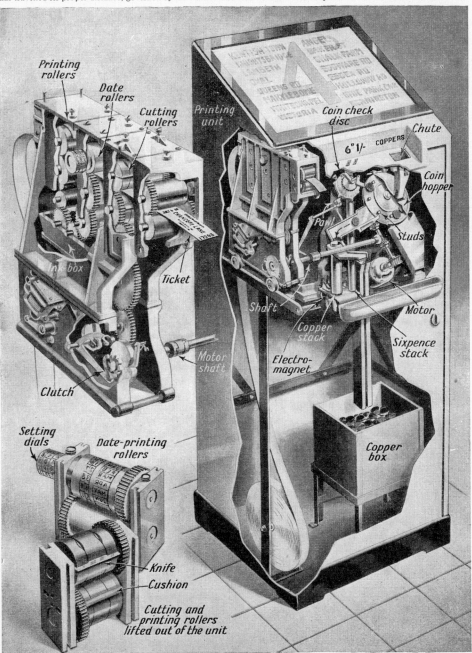

Printing rollers · Date rollers · Cutting rollers · Printing unit · Coin check disc · Chute · 6" 1/- COPPERS · Coin hopper · Pawl · Studs · Ink box · Ticket · Shaft · Motor · Copper stack · Sixpence stack · Motor shaft · Electro-magnet · Clutch · Copper box · Setting dials · Date-printing rollers · Knife · Cushion · Cutting and printing rollers lifted out of the unit

a pawl attached to a connecting-rod, the lower end of which is attached to the clutch of the printing unit. This puts into operation a set of gear wheels, being driven by the horizontal shaft from the running motor. The strip of plain paper is drawn into the back of the unit, where one pair of rollers print the station names, another the date and number, while a third set of rollers cut it. The ticket is then pulled through a pair of pressure rollers and held lightly outside the machine for the passenger to take. Felt rollers take the ink from the box and pass it on to the printing rollers. When a shilling is put into the machine, electro-magnets operate powerful slides which push two pennies and a sixpence from the bottom of the copper and silver stack. A sixpence will operate the mechanism to free only two pennies.

Why Does a Tuning-Fork Sound Louder when it Touches Wood ?

The fact that the sound is louder must mean that more power, in the shape of sound-waves, is reaching our ears; so first we have to ask ourselves whether the thing on which the tuning-fork rests is making the additional sound, and the answer is: Certainly not. We have to explain what happens without for a moment suggesting that any new sound is being made anywhere, even though a greater volume of sound does certainly reach our ears.

We are right when we say that the thing on which the tuning-fork rests actually does resound, meaning that it throws the sound which reaches it back towards our ears. The proper name for it, because it resounds, is a *resonator*. The sound from a tuning-fork, like the light from a candle, flows out in all directions. We, of course, only hear what comes in one direction, and that is really only a very small part of the whole. The resonator increases the amount of sound that reaches our ears, but it makes nothing; and just as much as it increases the sound in our direction, so it diminishes the sound in the direction beyond the resonator.

Why Cannot we See very Small Things with our Naked Eyes ?

If the retina, the curtain at the back of the eye, were a perfectly smooth and continuous thing like a piece of glass, we should be able to see much smaller things than we do. But it is a living thing made of living cells, and each of these can only see one thing at a time. They are a certain size, and take up a certain amount of room, and there is a certain amount of space between them. Thus, the rays of light from a thing must be spread out enough to cover at least two of these cells—perhaps more—before we can expect to see two things separately. Of course, much depends on brightness. If a thing is very bright indeed, it will be seen by one cell of the retina, perhaps. Thus, a star may be seen, though the pencil of light from it is very narrow, while a tiny speck of something under our eyes, which sends a pencil of light just as big, will not be seen until we use a microscope. A large number of the stars we see are really double stars. The telescope shows us this by throwing the light on to more cells than one of the retina of the eye.

What is it that Makes Wrinkles ?

The wrinkles of elderly people are due to a slow process of wasting in the skin. It is a curious thing that we can, by good sense and cheerful minds, control the process of going old in everything that matters, and especially in our brains, but we cannot in the case of our skin—just where old age shows most, and just where it matters least. The skin gets shrivelled and puckered, and especially do we notice wrinkles in people who have got rather thin, for this means that a good deal of fat has disappeared from under the skin, so that it is too loose for the body, and falls into wrinkles. In extremely old people the skin gets so thin, and so much of it wastes away, that all the wrinkles disappear, and their faces get quite smooth.

What is Grass Made of ?

There are hundreds of plants which are all called grasses. What we call grass in the garden or in the fields is the leaf of this plant—green leaves which play exactly the same part in its life as the green leaves of an oak tree play in the life of the oak. The oak and the grass, like a rose-bush, are both true flowering plants, and if we take a little trouble we can soon find the flowers of the grass for ourselves. Like other green plants, the grass is made by the power of sunlight out of certain materials in the air and in the earth.

The elements we find in grass are the same as those that we find in all other living creatures without exception—carbon, oxygen, hydrogen, nitrogen, phosphorus, and a few more. But while we remember that these elements exist in the grass and make it, we must also remember that there is another thing there which is as real as real can be, though we cannot see or handle it. That thing is energy. Grass could not exist if it did not contain energy, which is really the transformed rays of sunlight. This is true of all green plants and of all animals, too. Our bodies actually contain, and could not exist without, some of the sunlight of the past which is stored up in them.

What is a Millibar ?

A millibar is the thousandth part of a bar, which is the unit of atmospheric pressure now used by meteorologists. The bar is equal to the pressure of 29·531 inches of atmosphere at 32 degrees Fahrenheit in latitude 45 degrees.

What is Gretna Green ?

Gretna Green is a village in Dumfries-shire, near the little River Sark that divides England from Scotland. In 1770 an Act was passed in England making hasty marriages more difficult, and it soon became the custom for runaway couples who wished to get married quickly to cross the border to Gretna, where they could be married under Scottish law. Many runaway marriages took place in the smithy there up to 1856, when the Scottish marriage laws were altered.

Who were the Medici ?

Medici is the name of an illustrious family originally from Tuscany. If we are to trust old legends, Charlemagne counted a Medici among his companions. First enriched through trade, the Medici became powerful, thanks to the services their amazing wealth could render the princes of Italy and other countries. In the thirteenth century they became masters in Florence, the capital of Tuscany. A hundred years later Cosimo Medici gathered all his family's wealth into his own hands and governed Florence as an actual dictator. His grandson Lorenzo, called the Magnificent, was one of the greatest figures in Italian history. The Medici gave Italy two popes and France two queens. This great family became extinct in the eighteenth century.

As enlightened patrons of letters and arts, the Medici largely contributed to the development of the Italian Renaissance. They were perhaps the greatest patrons of art the world has ever known.

What is a Panegyric ?

A panegyric is a formal speech of high praise. The origin of panegyrics dates back to the Greeks and may be older. One of the most famous is by Pericles in praise of the young heroes fallen in the Peloponnesian war, and another is about Athens on which Isocrates worked for fifteen years. This sort of speech had a national character for a long time, but it degenerated with the fall of Greece till at last it only served for eulogies of princes and came down to the Romans in that form. The panegyric of the Emperor Trajan by Pliny the Younger has remained a typical model of this form of discourse. Great panegyrics have been famous in the course of history, but they are seldom heard nowadays.

Why is Gold Not Found in England ?

This is a particular way of asking a general question. Why do we find the various elements where we do, and not elsewhere? Until lately most people thought that the elements had always existed as they are now, and so there was no use in asking where they came from. But now we are beginning to learn that the elements have a history. In a few years we may learn how gold came into existence —what other element or elements it was formed from; and so in time we may hope to learn how to explain the present distribution of gold and the other elements in the Earth's crust. We must always remember that gold, like most elements, is much more widely distributed than most people suppose. We usually only hear about the presence of a precious element anywhere when there is enough of it to pay for getting it out. But gold occurs in traces almost everywhere, just as the far rarer element, radium, does. It is found in sea water everywhere, and even in some kinds of earth in parts of England; but there is not enough to be found to pay for the trouble of getting it out.

Who were the Barbary Pirates ?

Formerly the Berber States, along the north coast of Africa, were known collectively as Barbary, so that the corsairs of Tunis, Algiers, and Sallee were called the Barbary pirates. At first the corsairs were manned mainly by Berbers, but later they were joined by European adventurers and Moors, and from the end of the fifteenth century they were the terror of the Mediterranean. Men and women taken by them were held to ransom or sold as slaves. Though many expeditions were conducted against the Barbary ports by European powers, the trouble did not finally come to an end until the French captured Algiers in 1830.

What is the Table-Cloth at Cape Town ?

The most striking feature of the landscape at Cape Town is the huge flat-topped mountain that rises above the city. It is 3600 feet high and a mile long, and is called Table Mountain from its shape. The bay beneath it is called Table Bay, while the dense white clouds that often hang about its summit during the summer months have become known locally as the " table-cloth."

Why are the Doors of Rooms Generally in a Corner ?

Centuries of experience have gone to make the building of the inside of a house, but the reason why doors are usually in the corners is really simple. They are put there because, except in very large rooms, it is desirable to give as great a width of wall as possible for furniture. An interesting thing to notice, however, is that doors are always hinged on the side where the greatest length of wall is, so that any draught that comes in is broken by the wall at right angles.

What is the Stratosphere ?

One of the most surprising discoveries in the whole history of meteorology was that of the stratosphere. Our knowledge of its existence resulted from the use of small sounding balloons by Teisserenc de Bort and Rotch, sent up carrying a case containing an instrument to record pressure, temperature, and humidity. When the balloon burst, as it was designed to do, instrument and records fell.

They showed that the heat (or thermal) structure of the atmosphere in its upper regions was such that the lowest temperatures of the air were at very high levels above the Equator, whereas below the level where this strange occurrence began the temperature fell lower and lower with increasing height. In other words the temperature of the lower regions of the atmosphere was arranged in horizontal layers, and that of the upper regions in what are called isothermal columns. The lower regions were named by Teisserenc de Bort the troposphere, the higher regions the stratosphere, and the level at which the troposphere ends, the tropopause.

The tropopause is a very light, very airy, quite invisible boundary, but as effective for the purpose of arresting rising air as if it were a sheet of flexible steel. It is, in fact, flexible because, though it is the ceiling of the lower atmosphere, and the floor of the atmospheric upper deck, the stratosphere, the tropopause is not always or everywhere at the same height. Above England it is about 35,000 feet, over the Arctic Ocean it sinks to 26,000 feet, and above the Equator it is highest. But it is an absolute stopper to vertical *motion* of the air. Clouds may reach it in a few hours or days, but will take weeks or months to get down again. Consequently, while below the tropopause, and therefore the stratosphere, the air is always stirring and the composition well mixed, we cannot expect these circumstances to repeat themselves in the heights above.

The opinion has been expressed that, while it was more or less certain that the air was getting thinner there, it was possible that at increasing heights there might be less oxygen or more helium. Nothing more can be said about that ; but another supposition that the air might be much stiller in the stratosphere can no longer be maintained.

There are winds in the stratosphere, and much continues to be learned of them by the help of the aeroplanes that penetrate its recesses. But what we do know and learn increasingly is that at greater and greater heights there are electric barriers as invisible but as powerful as the tropopause and our wireless waves can locate them: so that Radar is now taking a hand in dissecting the stratosphere.

Who Were the Spartans ?

The town of Sparta in ancient Greece is said to have been founded by Lacedaemon, and named after his wife, the daughter of Eurotas.

Its inhabitants, the Spartans, stand to us for courage, intrepidity, liberty, love of honour. Trained only for war, it was their trade and they had no other; they fought all the time, either for their own sake or because they were paid by other countries. Should a child be born crippled, he was snatched from his mother as no good for fighting, and thrown into an abyss. The women were as intrepid as the men, and many of them feasted the memory of a son who had been killed by the enemy, or they themselves would kill sons who came home defeated. In military power Sparta kept the lead for five hundred years in Greece, yet the powerful town never conquered its jealousy of Athens, which was the centre of art and letters, the beloved city of all succeeding ages. The most famous Spartan was, of course, Leonidas, the king who was sent by his countrymen to check the advance of Xerxes, King of Persia. With his gallant 300 he stood at bay at Thermopylae. The one man who returned home was treated with scorn.

Paleo Chori is now the place where Sparta stood, but the new Sparta is really Mistra, built a few miles away.

Why are Old Windows Often Bricked Up?

In the bad old days windows were taxed, so that it was made expensive to enjoy fresh air and light. The darker and more badly ventilated a house was the less tax its owner or tenant paid, for there was a tax on every window exceeding six. Many people, when they built a house, put in it as few windows as possible so as to save the taxes. In some cases, however, they left places where windows could be inserted if, at some later date, they became better off and could afford more light and air. On the other hand, there were some people who became poorer, and these would have some of their windows bricked up in order to reduce their taxes. Only in 1851 was this bad tax abolished.

Who Invented the Water-Tube Boiler?

The principle of the great water-tube boilers used in liners, warships, and electric light and power stations was discovered about the year 1827 by a Frenchman, Marc Séguin, of Annonay, near Lyons. The use of steam was then just beginning to become general, but the first boilers were very clumsy and inefficient, consisting usually of a large vessel of water placed over a furnace. Nathan Read, an American, first thought of boiling water in tubes; but Séguin discovered that by using a large number of small tubes instead of a few large ones steam could be produced far more quickly; and to him chiefly we owe the water-tube boiler.

Who was Faust?

At the end of the fifteenth century there lived in Germany a doctor named John Faust, a scholar, who had studied all the sciences of his time, but his pride was such that he wished to have " more than mortal knowledge." So he began to practise magic. The legend says that his inexhaustible passion for learning, and his eagerness to enjoy life, led him to close a bargain with Satan by which he should be granted all pleasures in exchange for his soul. Satan sent Doctor Faust a companion, Mephistopheles, chosen from among the most perverse spirits of the underworld, and for more than twenty years both travelled all over the Earth, and made themselves conspicuous for their wonderful prodigies and excesses of all sorts. At last Doctor Faust was killed by Mephistopheles at midnight in a village of Wurtemberg. The story of Faust, at once so realistic and fanciful, has often been made use of by dramatic authors. In 1588 Christopher Marlowe wrote " The Tragical History of the Life and Death of Doctor Faust." Goethe, the greatest of German poets, devoted several years of his life to the composition of his famous drama, which has been set to music by Gounod and by Berlioz.

What is the Red Indian's Pipe of Peace?

The Red Indian pipe of peace, called the calumet, after the reed from which it is made, is a long pipe in which is smoked the dried leaf of tobacco or other aromatic plants by passing it round. The greatest veneration is attached to the calumet, which the Illinois pretend originated from the Sun itself. It is about two feet long, made of varnished earth, and adorned with plaited hair and showy feathers most artistically worked.

The calumet is a symbol of peace, but sometimes of war. The exchange of the famous pipe between two camps means an eager desire for friendliness. On the contrary, any chief refusing to smoke a calumet offered to him is considered as an enemy ready to wage war.

Will the Earth Ever be Cool Right Through?

A hot liquid will cool quicker in a shallow pan than in a deep vessel, partly because the cold pan takes some of the heat, but especially because it spreads the liquid out, and so exposes it.

In the same way, when we go bathing on a sunny day, we find the shallow pools on the way to the water much warmer than the deeper water. Heat can get in and get out when things are exposed. But if we take a thing like a hot bottle, and wrap it up in a thick layer of blankets, it will be hot for many hours. Now, there never were better blankets than those which the fire inside the Earth is packed in. The air is a blanket many miles thick. The crust of the Earth, too, is a blanket. Also these blankets are being warmed from outside by means of the Sun, and, what with these facts and the fact that new heat is being made by radium, we can understand that it will be long ages before the Earth is cooled through. Yet so it must be.

WONDERFUL BUILDINGS OF ANCIENT DAYS

RELIEFS ON THE WALL OF THE
TEMPLE OF DENDERA

A COLUMN IN THE
TEMPLE OF DENDERA

THE HYPOSTYLE HALL OF XERXES
AT PERSEPOLIS AS IT PROBABLY WAS

THE HALL OF A HUNDRED COLUMNS AT PERSEPOLIS AS IT MAY HAVE APPEARED

A RECONSTRUCTION OF THE GROUP OF PALACES AT PERSEPOLIS

The Story of the Beautiful Things in the Treasure-House of the World

A reconstruction of the Assyrian Palace of Sennacherib at Nineveh

THE BUILDINGS OF THE OLD WORLD

WE have been reading and thinking of the art of the world, its sculpture and painting. We have been trying to understand something of the spirit of beauty that has lived through the ages, free and uncaptured, and is now just as mysterious and powerful as when the first Cave Man made his first drawing on the rocky wall of his cave.

And now we turn to another kind of inspired work, Architecture. At once we know that here is something more than art, though art is near the root of its workings.

The architecture of the world has been created by religion, and the need of temples and churches; by tribal life, ruled over by kings, and the need for palaces; by the growth of organised society, and the need of public speaking places; by the development of domestic life, and the need for homes. Under one or other of these headings most of the great buildings of the world can be grouped.

More than the instinct of beauty and the need for some building has raised the piles of ancient Egypt, of Greece and Rome, of medieval Europe. Into them went something of the mysterious force that makes a country and its native people different from another. This is the reason why architecture can be truly called history in stone.

Architecture as an art is different in this way from sculpture as an art. Statuary is statuary all the world over, whether of Parian marble, or Purbeck marble, or bronze, or stone. For the human form, with which statuary most deals is, broadly speaking, the same all the world over. No such limitations apply to the art of building. A temple, hall, or palace may be in any style, in any form. Architecture varies from one continent to another. It is affected by soil and climate, by the sun's dominance, by the material at hand, and, above all, by the shape of thought, as one might say, of the people producing it, their religion, their beauty instinct, and the work of those who have gone before.

If we think for a few minutes we shall see that the subject of architecture has many approaches, many points of attack; and we shall begin to understand why the sight or picture of a great building has always moved us profoundly. A mass of stones, big or little, put together by men's hands; why should anything so apparently simple be so wonderful?

We shall never know till we understand the secret of life itself, and the working of the human mind, and what the Bible calls the travail of the soul. But we go on trying to know. The power of beauty over us is happily so great that we shall take every

PICTURES · STATUES · CARVINGS · BUILDINGS · IVORIES · CRAFTS

chance of looking at lovely things; great buildings, great statuary, great pictures, and find them an increasing joy. And in so doing we shall build palaces for ourselves wherein our peace may dwell secure.

The magnificent architecture of the world had its beginning in the first rude dwellings made by prehistoric men when they abandoned their caves. They were formed of masses of stones, crudely put together, with stone slabs on the top for a roof. The first builders of the world were pleased and proud when they had made something adequate on the lines of Nature's houses—caves. And they were content, for an indefinite period, with these dwellings. So that when we hear of the great buildings of any powerful empire of the remote past we must remember that countless generations had passed before the art of construction had grown to such an extent as to make temple-building possible.

PRIMITIVE BUILDINGS WHICH SERVE AS LINKS WITH THE PAST

There are remains of these early rude huts in various parts of Europe; some very interesting ones are in Brittany. Curious beehive-shaped huts can still be seen on Lewis in the Hebrides, in Wales, and Cornwall; and at Stonehenge are fragments of one of the earliest temples in Europe. It consisted of a huge circle of massive pillars, placed equally apart, with heavy horizontal stones, set in an unbroken round, roofing the space between the pillars. Other sets of enormous masses of stone lay inside the circle, flanking the slab on which sacrifices were placed.

All the races of the world, developing at different times, passed through this stage of primitive building. The first peoples to produce anything that might be called architecture were the Egyptians and the Chaldeans. It has generally been understood that the most ancient buildings of all were made by the early Egyptians. But we today are living in a marvellous age, when the past is being reconstructed before our eyes. Only a few years have passed since loads of rubbish were daily dug out of the oldest temple on Earth, which was discovered near Ur of the Chaldees, in Mesopotamia. This was the birthplace of Abraham, and was already an ancient city when he set out across the Syrian desert to find a home.

The temple was built some five thousand years before Christ. Until another, still more ancient, is dug out of the mounds of buried cities like Ur, it has the honour of being the oldest in the world, and it is the forerunner of the famous temples of Chaldean history.

THE ANCIENT STORY LYING BURIED IN THE EARTH

We are indebted to archaeologists and excavators for nearly all our information about the buildings of Chaldea, or early Babylon, or Assyria. Little was known about them, for they were buried for many centuries under accumulations of earth until excavations began about the middle of the nineteenth century. From the ruins and fragments unearthed the shape and plan of actual buildings have been reconstructed, helping us to form a good idea of their size and shape.

The " land between the two rivers," the plain of the Tigris and Euphrates, was soft and marshy, and that was why palaces and temples were built on huge platforms and terraces, and rose to several storeys. There was little or no stone, no timber; consequently brick and masses of sun-dried clay were used.

Most of the buildings unearthed belong to one or another of three great periods. First there was the Babylonian or Chaldean time—from about 4000 B.C. to 1300 B.C. Then came the conquest of Babylonia by the Assyrians, and that era lasted from 1300 till in turn Assyria was conquered by the Persians, in 538 B.C. The style of architecture that ran through these eras was almost unchanged; the Persians merely added a richness of their own to the power of their predecessors.

The chief buildings of ancient Babylonia were temples, palaces, and curious pyramidal towers called ziggurats, or holy mountains, which Chaldean priest-astronomers used to make observations. One of them, which, according to Babylonian records, was rebuilt by Nebuchadnezzar, has been excavated. It was a huge erection, built in stages, and surmounted by a temple to Nebo.

THE CITY WALL WITH A HUNDRED GATES OF BRONZE

Towers of all kinds were a favourite feature of Babylonian architecture, and in that flat land must have rewarded the kings who caused them to be built. In the city of Babylon, girdled by its enormous wall that was broken by one hundred bronze gates, there were two hundred and fifty towers. It must have been a very wonderful city, with its palaces and temples and towers—one of them doubtless the Tower of Babel so richly described in the Bible. The crowning glory was Nebuchadnezzar's palace whose famous Hanging Gardens were raised on a series of arches some seventy feet high.

It is interesting to know that these early peoples, being dependent for building on small things like bricks, soon evolved the formation of the curved arch; while in the not very distant land of Egypt, where great masses of stone were found, big enough to go across wide openings, arches were unnecessary, and therefore almost unknown.

THE GRANDEUR OF BABYLON FOUR THOUSAND YEARS AGO

For this same reason, lack of material, the columns which give great natural dignity and beauty to a building were absent from Babylonian architecture. But another kind of dignity was attained by means of the great mass formation of the temples and palaces, the enormous stepped platforms wherefrom, by narrowing stages, the buildings climbed up.

This architecture was more imposing than beautiful, and gave an idea of strength, of lion-like power. Somewhere about 2000 years before Christ lived Babylon was at the height of her grandeur. But a city built only of baked mud and bricks, with just a little stone here and there, could not in the nature of things endure many centuries. " And Babylon shall become heaps," said the prophet. Fortunately for us, enough has been dug out of these heaps to help us, with a little imagination, to reconstruct the marvellous past of this queen of ancient cities.

A PLATFORM THAT TOOK TEN THOUSAND MEN TWELVE YEARS TO BUILD

Nineveh usurped the place of Babylon in importance when the Assyrian dominance came, and her kings seemed to take a delight in building new palaces, leaving the old temples to suffice for themselves. The excavated palace of Sargon, the most important, gives some idea of the monarch's sense of grandeur. It covered about twenty-five acres, and stood on a great platform fifty feet high, made of bricks faced with stone. We know that these buildings of the old world were raised by forced labour. The thousands of prisoners-of-war who formed part of

the booty of any eastern campaign were flung into the builder's service. It has been estimated that one of these Assyrian palace platforms took ten thousand men twelve years to construct.

We think of this palace of Sargon in amazement, with its system of corridors and quadrangles, its seven hundred rooms, its principal court with three entrances guarded by great towers, where man-headed, winged animals twelve feet high were set in pairs as sentries. These monstrous creatures—lions or bulls—now stand in the Assyrian Hall of the British Museum. They are awe-inspiring there, but they must have been terror-inspiring when set in place by the palace portals, high above the plain. So did the blood-thirsty, fighting Assyrian kings try to tell their grandeur in their buildings; the reconstruction of their architecture forms a perfect social history of their period. We know of the kings' tyranny because of the labour necessary to build these palaces; we know of their vainglory from the subjects of the frescoes on the walls; we know the people were of no account because of the humble dwellings of ordinary citizens.

THE WONDERFUL PALACE OF PERSEPOLIS AND ITS HUNDRED COLUMNS

The greatest skill of the Persians centred in the palaces and tombs of Susa and Persepolis. Some of the tombs were cut out of the rock, like that of Darius, others set on pyramidal, stepped platforms, like that of Cyrus. Although Persepolis was by nature set on a platform, they still kept to the idea of the Assyrian royal builders. The platform of the famous palace or group of palaces at Persepolis, about a thousand feet square, was partly hewed out of the rock and partly built. Stone was handy, and another kind of architecture was the result.

Here is something else of the old world for us to ponder—a palace that had an approach of shallow steps some twenty feet wide, which horsemen could ascend, and a great entrance with piers of shining, glazed brick, and the Assyrian man-headed bulls as guard. Within this palace at Persepolis was the famous Hall of the Hundred Columns, a wonderful place with its cedar roof upheld by the hundred columns, thirty-seven feet high, of whose ranks one solitary shaft now stands. Alexander the Great burned the Hall of the Hundred Columns, along with other places, when he conquered Persia.

The Persians made everything glorious in colour and grouping. The palaces of Susa and Persepolis were like kings in their glory, set with glazed bricks that shone in blue and green and yellow. On page 3902 we read of their decorative art applied to their architecture, of the frieze of archers which the Louvre treasures on behalf of the whole world.

The influence of this architecture cradled on the Chaldean plain found its way northward, eastward, and westward. The temple of Solomon and David's palace at Jerusalem, were partly Assyrian in character, and partly Egyptian.

THE MASSIVE TOMBS OF EGYPT THAT WERE BUILT FOR ETERNITY

Fortunately for the world, Egyptian architecture, by its nature, by the material used, and the climate of the country, has proved more enduring than that of the eastern empires.

We have seen that the whole spirit of the Egyptians' art and architecture was deathlessness, duration. Their skill centred in the tombs which they built not for time, but eternity. It was an architecture of religion, very different from that of Assyria and Persia. Kingship and godhead and priesthood were very much mixed up in the character of the monarchs of early Egypt. Palaces were of little interest to them; their temples, and their tombs—where their bodies would be preserved through long ages until the spirit came to life again—were of an absorbing interest; and on them this strange nation, almost unchanged in its four thousand years of life, spent its austere beauty, its solemnity, and its ponderous architecture.

THE SECRET OF THE STRENGTH OF THE OLD EGYPTIAN BUILDINGS

The Nile, the life-giving river of Egypt, was the centre of the people's national existence, and on its banks were built their great temples and tombs. Stone and granite were plentiful; they were quarried in huge blocks. The Egyptian builders were single-minded in their productions. They were not trying to be clever. They wanted their buildings to last for ever; every line, every detail was magnetised to this idea. In this way they were greater artists, greater architects, than they knew.

The chief characteristics of their architecture can be traced to three causes; this

same passion for duration, their climate, and the material they worked with.

The buildings were conceived on a simple plan. The outer surface of the outer wall in almost every case inclined inward a little. The inner surface made a perpendicular line, so that a wall cut through would seem, looking at its thickness, something like a buttress. Thus the Egyptians contrived to build a wall that no ordinary earthquake, and no ordinary enemy attacks, could shake down. In no two temples or pyramids was the angle of inclination the same. The builders had no rule; they had an absorbing idea.

The Egyptian climate was partly the cause of the unbroken lines of their massive walls. In that land of eternal sunshine there was no need to set windows in a temple. A sufficient amount of light came in through the door, or through slits high up on the wall near the roof, or sometimes through a kind of clerestory, as in one of the halls at Karnak. The blind appearance of the walls has a good deal to do with the severity and secrecy peculiar to these buildings. The sense of rhythm necessary to keep a wall from looking "' dead " was supplied by the repetitive lines of the frescoes and sculptures adorning it.

THE GREAT COLUMNS WHICH SUPPORT THE HEAVY ROOFS OF STONE

The material used dictated the dominant style of Egyptian buildings, a style marked by columns and square-headed openings, which were roofed—trabeated is the technical word—with unbroken slabs of stone or granite. The habit of roofing their halls with slabs of stone led to the necessity of placing columns at intervals.

The columns evolved by the Egyptians are of a very interesting nature, and they develop as the architecture develops, with little change, during the long course of its life. And by these columns the interiors of massive buildings were kept alive, so to speak. For a building that has good columns, or good repetitive lines, has got the peculiar quality that we have spoken of before—a rhythmic quality, akin to the steady break of waves on the shore, to the throbbing pulse of great poetry, something that shares the life of the universe.

The earliest columns were in obvious imitation of flower forms, grooved to imitate bunches of stems, with something like a lotus flower for the capital. This design—combined with a great sturdiness of size, as we should imagine—became simplified and amplified at the same time. Before the architecture of Egypt ceased, her builders had produced some of the most beautiful columns the world possesses. Some of them remind us of the Doric column, which the Greeks carried to such perfection.

As their skill in architecture grew and their temples rose, their immense architectural statuary likewise grew. They seemed to know something was needed to connect their gaunt temples with the footways of men. It became a habit with them to form approaches of long avenues of the mysterious creatures to whom the family name of sphinx has been given. The bodies were always bodies of lions, and the heads were, according to some inscrutable decree, either those of human beings, or birds, or rams. We all know about the Great Sphinx, the chief of these, huge beyond thought, which was partly chiselled out of the rock, and partly put together, like a building. The desert, perhaps alone knowing why this monstrous thing was set there, had kept its secret in its own fashion, driving sand over it for centuries. In 1816 the sand was cleared away, and the inscription revealed that the Sphinx had been built about four thousand years before Christ.

THE AMAZING PYRAMID BUILT TO HIDE THE BODY OF A KING

Near the Great Sphinx, at Gizeh, are the equally famous three great Pyramids, the oldest Egyptian tombs, so far as we know. The chief of these, known as the Great Pyramid of Cheops, a king of the Fourth Dynasty, has, like the Sphinx, passed into the world's everyday speech, as a symbol of unreasonable size and mystery, and eternal duration. It seems strange that a building, a solid mass of granite and stone, 481 feet high, with an area of about $12\frac{1}{2}$ acres, should have been constructed solely to hide the body of one king.

Poor little king! so grand, so great, and so tiny! To make his body secure for immortality hundreds of men had to toil for blocks of stone, some of them 20 feet long, to be put together with such genius that not a sheet of paper could be slipped between them.

Tombs of varying sizes and forms mark, like time's sentinels, the slow passage of the Thirty Dynasties of Egyptian monarchs down the four thousand years of the nation's life. Some of them took the form of pyramids like those at Gizeh; some were rock-hewn, like the group at Beni-Hasan, and show by their columns and general plan that a sense of art was developing along the lines of architecture. A later group of royal tombs, near ancient Thebes, were constructed in another manner, corridors being burrowed into the rock, leading to a succession of chambers, in the innermost of which the sarcophagus was placed. One of these was the tomb of Tutankhamen, and we know from that sepulchre what a wealth of art was spent on the burial of an ordinary king, whom history has not greatly distinguished.

THE SPLENDID TOMB OF AN ARCHITECT OF THE PYRAMIDS

The tombs of important private persons were of another character, and generally known as mastabas. They were peculiar, rectangular mounds of masonry, the outer walls sloping inward in characteristic fashion. Three chambers were generally arranged for in the interior; in the innermost the sarcophagus was placed. A very famous mastaba, beautifully decorated in relief, was built at Sakkâra, near Gizeh, for the body of a great personage called Thi, the architect of some of the pyramids.

Generally speaking, Egyptian temples belong to the later half of the country's history. They appear more like huge royal chapels than public places of worship, and were marked by something of the same secrecy that was part of the scheme of the tomb. Only the king and his priests might penetrate into the sanctuary. A considerable number of temples were built along the Nile banks, the most important ones at Thebes, one of the capitals, on whose site the villages of Luxor and Karnak now stand.

ONE OF THE CHIEF GLORIES OF EGYPTIAN ARCHITECTURE

They were all built, with variations, on the same plan. To enter, one passed down the sphinx avenue, and in between the entrance pylons—huge towers with sloping walls and a giant obelisk in front of each. From the entrance one passed into the outer court, with double columns on three sides, open to the sky. Then into the Hypostyle Hall.

This part of the temple has been called the chief glory of Egyptian architecture. It was roofed in, and set thickly with columns of varying beauty according to the period of the temple, and most beautifully decorated. The centre rows of these columns ran up higher than the rest, and thus formed a kind of clerestory as light came through barred stone windows set between the upper parts of the high centre columns, and lighted the hall below just as a clerestory gives light to a church or cathedral. Beyond the Hypostyle Hall lay the sanctuary and other chambers connected with priestly offices. Round the temple building ran a monstrous projecting wall, as high as the highest hall; with the sphinx avenues, the pylons at the entrance, and the sentinel obelisks, the structure must have been an awe-inspiring sight.

THE GREAT OBELISKS THE ROMANS CARRIED AWAY FROM EGYPT

On these obelisks—immense monoliths, square at the base and tapering to the top --the Egyptians spent a great deal of time and labour. The Roman emperors carried a great many away when they conquered Egypt, and there are about a dozen still to be seen in Rome. Cleopatra's Needle, on the Thames Embankment, was one of two obelisks set in front of a temple at Heliopolis, built about 1500 B.C.

The most wonderful of all the Egyptian buildings is the Great Temple of Ammon, the chief of the group at Karnak and Luxor. It was begun by a king about 2466 B.C., and after a long lapse added to by first one Pharaoh and then another. Thus the erection covered many hundred years. Upon it the greatest architectural and sculptural art of Egypt was spent. The Hypostyle Hall alone might stand for a monument of grandeur of this extraordinary nation. The light comes in from the clerestory of the upper central arches and drifts in and out of the immense, ranked columns, so immense that a man standing by them looks like a squirrel at the foot of a high forest tree.

THE ANCIENT TEMPLES THAT STAND ON THE BANKS OF THE NILE

Another temple to Ammon was built in the side of the rock at Dêr-el-Bahari, by the great Queen Hatshepset, who lived about fifteen hundred years before Christ. She had a wonderful sense of beauty, and the columns of her temple, standing in tiers on terraces, apparently clinging to the hillside, and decorated in coloured relief, must have been very arresting.

Temples of all periods, with bewildering names, still stand on the Nile banks at Abydos, Edfu, Abu-Simbel, and other places. One of the greater ones, at Philae, built about 300 B.C., is submerged by the river part of the year, so that only the upper portion can be seen.

It would seem that the architecture of the old world was passing through great stages. Babylon and Assyria made it lion-like, fierce and strong; Egypt made it above all things colossal and enduring. To Greece it was left to make architecture supremely beautiful, of such unquestionable proportions as to be a standard for all succeeding peoples.

Greek architecture stands out now in the world's history as a rounded, complete beauty, a finished development, its principles carried in practice as near perfection as human beings could achieve. But this grand architecture was not entirely the work of the Greeks as we know them; it did not spring up complete, evolved on its own shores out of nothing. An earlier people began it—the people of the Aegean civilisation; and when it began to develop in the hands of the Greeks, two influences were brought to bear upon it. The effect of Egypt is traceable in the kind of architecture called Doric, because of the style of column used, and that of Assyria in the kind of architecture, called, for the same reason, Ionic.

THE BEAUTY-LOVING PEOPLE OF OLD WHO LIVED IN THE AEGEAN ISLANDS

We know from our chapters on painting and sculpture how, long before what we know as the empire of the Greeks arose, a happy, beauty-loving people were living in Greece and the islands of the Aegean Sea. The architecture they evolved, a simple, rude style, is known as Pelasgic, or Primitive. Its most interesting examples are shown in the remains of what is called the Tomb or Treasury of Atreus, a curious, beehive-shaped erection—at Mycenae, the Palace, the Gate of the Lions, and the Town walls, also at Mycenae. Then there is the palace at Tiryns, and the Minoan palace at Knossos, Crete, lately excavated. This home of King Minos is the oldest of the Pelasgic buildings, dating from about 3000 B.C., with additions at later times.

When the Greeks became masters of the Aegean, from this rude beginning, with Egypt and Assyria to give hints, their architecture began to grow.

THE CENTRAL COLUMNS OF THE HYPOSTYLE HALL AT KARNAK AS THEY PROBABLY
APPEARED IN THE DAYS OF THE PHARAOHS

THE GREAT TEMPLE OF LUXOR

A CLOSE VIEW OF THE GREAT PYRAMID
SHOWING ITS HUGE BLOCKS OF STONE

THE STEP PYRAMID AT SAKKĀRA, BELIEVED
TO BE THE OLDEST OF ALL

THE FAMOUS ROCK TEMPLE AT
ABU-SIMBEL

THE SPLENDID COLUMNS OF THE
TEMPLE OF LUXOR

THE DOUBLE PYLON OF THE TEMPLE OF ISIS AT PHILAE

THE STATUES OF RAMESES AT THE ENTRANCE
TO THE ROCK TEMPLE AT ABU-SIMBEL

THE FORECOURT OF THE TEMPLE OF
ISIS AT PHILAE

THE THRONE ROOM IN THE MINOAN
PALACE AT KNOSSOS IN CRETE

THE TOMB OR TREASURY OF ATREUS AT
MYCENAE IN GREECE

THE TEMPLE AT PHILAE, NOW DROWNED FOR PART OF THE YEAR BY THE WATERS OF THE NILE

THE IMPRESSIVE WONDER OF THE SANDS—THE SPHINX NEAR THE PYRAMIDS AT GIZEH

THE GREAT PYLON AT THE END OF THE AVENUE OF SPHINXES AT KARNAK

THE COURT OF THE TEMPLE OF AMMON AT KARNAK AS IT WAS

THE ROCK TEMPLE OF AMMON AT DÊR-EL-BAHARI ON THE NILE

COLUMNS OF THE HYPOSTYLE HALL
AT KARNAK

THE GREAT PYLON OF THE
TEMPLE OF EDFU

THE AVENUE OF SPHINXES LEADING TO THE TEMPLE OF KARNAK

THE SECOND PYRAMID OF GIZEH, WITH
ITS ORIGINAL LIMESTONE TOP

THE GREAT COLONNADE OF THE
TEMPLE OF LUXOR

THE TEMPLE OF KARNAK, WITH ITS OBELISKS STANDING LIKE SENTINELS ABOVE THE NILE

THE TEMPLE OF RAMESES AT KARNAK

The pictures in these pages are reproduced by courtesy of Messrs. Chapman & Hall, Mansell, McLeish, and others

The Wonderful House We Live In, and Our Place in the World

The Phoenicians of old bartering clothes and pottery

MONEY AND WHY WE USE IT

Hᴇʀᴇ is a shilling. It is a piece of silver, stamped on the front with the sovereign's head and on the back with a lion and a crown.

Think what we can do with this shilling. We can transform it into a great variety of things. It will buy some of our food— bread, butter, milk, tea, vegetables, choco- lates—or a ride on the railway, or a pocket handkerchief, or many other things. When we spend our shilling we command the whole world, to the extent of one shillingsworth !

The use of money has been one of the most powerful instruments in building up civilised life. It enables us to exchange our own work, or the products of our own work, for the work of others. It enables us to obtain things made afar off in foreign countries we have never seen.

Let us try to imagine what life would be without money. Suppose we made boots for a living. If money had not been invented we should have to find people willing to change other things for the boots we made. We should have to go into the market and cry: " Who will offer me food, hats, or other useful things in exchange for my boots? " How awkward that would be! We should have to find a hatmaker who thought one of his hats

was as good value as a pair of our boots. We should have to bargain another pair of boots with someone willing to give us a supply of bread.

Barter is clumsy and difficult, because in exchanging goods for goods we have to find the person who happens to want just the thing we wish to exchange. Another difficulty is that many things cannot be cut up into readily exchangeable portions. For example, suppose we have a horse, or a big table, which we desire to barter. We cannot cut up the horse or the table, and therefore we can only exchange them with somebody who can offer a quantity of things equal in value to the whole of our horse, or the whole of our table. This is obviously no easy matter. Barter is so inefficient that, if it was the only means of exchange, there would be little trade. We could not specialise, each on his own particular job, except to a very limited extent, and this would mean we should all be very poor.

There was a time, before the invention of money, when this was the case. That was thousands of years ago, but there are still parts of the world whose people live under primitive conditions, where trade is done in this way, and traders take with them manufactured goods to exchange

BODY, MIND, AND SOUL · CITIZENSHIP · ECONOMICS · GOVERNMENT

for native produce. Indeed, owing to the dislocations of war, international trade even between modern nations has been carried out by barter between their governments, one government promising to exchange, say, machinery, for supplies of food or raw materials.

THE GROWTH OF THE USE OF MONEY

In many different countries, the desire to exchange led long ago to the use of money. This began when people came to look upon some particular article as a general standard by which to measure the value of everything else.

Many different things have been used as money from time to time. At first, they were always things that were an important form of wealth at the time of use. Thus, cattle were among the earliest standards of value, when a man's wealth consisted mainly of his flocks and herds. Corn has also been used, and it was a better form of money than cattle, because it could easily be divided into small amounts.

As civilisation advanced, and metals came into use, they were used as money more and more. This was especially true of gold and silver, which were rare, and very valuable because of their beauty. They could easily be divided into pieces of any size, so that a small enough piece could be exchanged for any article, however cheap. Because they were so valuable, large sums of money could be easily handled. Enough gold to buy a cow, for instance, could be easily carried in the pocket, but enough corn to buy one would need a cart to carry it. Gold eventually became the main sort of money in Great Britain, with other metals used for small change.

WHY GOOD MONEY IS ACCEPTED BY EVERYBODY

Nothing will serve as money unless people have confidence in its use. They will only give up goods in exchange for money if they are sure that other people will be willing to accept this money in exchange for other goods later on. The necessary confidence in money takes two forms.

There must be confidence that money is generally recognised as a medium of exchange.

There must be confidence that money is a safe store of value.

The first rule is easy to understand. People will only accept money if they are confident that other people will be equally willing to accept it from them. The second rule is more difficult. People do not desire money for its own sake, but for the sake of the things they can buy with it later. They want to be sure that, however long they keep their money, it can be exchanged for the same amount of goods as when they first earned it.

When gold was used as money, people had confidence in it, because they knew from long experience that it remained rare and valuable. When they earned a gold coin, they knew that it would keep its value until it was spent, because other people would still want it just as much, and so be willing to give just as many goods in exchange for it. In effect, by using the gold, they could exchange *goods now* for *goods later on*, storing up the value of the goods sold now in the coin until it was later spent on other goods.

WHY POUND NOTES ARE REGARDED AS GOOD MONEY

The English standard money is the Pound Sterling, and this meant legally, at the beginning of this century, a definite coin of gold, called a sovereign. The weight of a sovereign was determined by Act of Parliament, and it was settled by making 1869 sovereigns out of 40 pounds weight of gold at the Royal Mint.

Other coins were used (and are still used) made of silver and bronze. This silver and bronze coinage can only be legally used in making small payments; anybody can refuse to accept payment for more than a shilling in bronze, or two pounds in silver.

Since the First World War a change in our money has been made. Gold is no longer coined into money, and gold is no longer our Standard of Value.

The Bank of England has been authorised to issue Paper Money, which takes the form of £1 and 10s. notes. These notes cannot be changed into gold at the Bank of England, and they have *no intrinsic value*. They are merely scraps of paper. Yet they serve the purpose of money, and they are in effect good money, always accepted by sellers when offered by buyers.

There are two main reasons why pound notes are regarded by everybody as good

SOME OF THE EARLIEST KNOWN COINS

Roman denarius
1st century B.C.

A Syracusan decadrachm

A coin of
Titus

Tigranes, King of
Armenia

Early Roman bar money of
the 4th century B.C.

Demetrius Poliorcetes,
King of Macedonia

Gold coin of Philip
of Macedon

An early British
coin

Coin of Alexander
the Great

An early British
coin

Greek coin of the
5th century B.C.

An early British coin

A coin of the 6th century B.C.

Coin of Apollo of Amphipolis
4th century B.C.

Denarius of Augustus Octavianus
1st century B.C.

money. The first is that they are generally acceptable as a medium of exchange. Apart from the convenience of using notes, this acceptability is laid down by law, for an Act of Parliament has made the notes *legal tender*, which means that people must accept them in payment of debts. The second reason is that people have confidence in our paper money as a store of value, because they know that it is strictly limited in amount. If unlimited supplies of notes were printed, people would cease to have confidence in money, and would be reluctant to accept it in exchange for goods.

**BUYING AND SELLING WITHOUT
THE USE OF MONEY**

So great is the part played by confidence in human affairs ! Before the First World War no one would have believed that anything but a Gold Pound would be accepted as good money. It has been proved in experience, however, that paper tokens, carefully managed, can form a good money, though an imperfect one.

Now we come to an extraordinary thing. When a nation has good money, and when, as a consequence, there is perfect confidence in the national money, *we are able to do most of our business without using money at all*. That, fortunately, is the position we have in our own country.

It is only in small transactions, such as paying wages, or buying retail in shops, that coin is actually used in Britain. In all big transactions connected with wholesale buying and selling, and finance, and in a great deal of retail buying, we do not use coins or banknotes, but just *pieces of paper on which we have written promises to pay*.

**HOW THE CHEQUE SYSTEM HELPS
THE BUSINESS OF THE WORLD**

Such a paper promise to pay is called a Cheque, and is as good as money itself if it complies with the following conditions:

1. The cheque orders a certain bank to pay money, and the bank must be known to be a sound and good one which will always meet its liabilities.

2. The money must be good, sound money, as fortunately we have in our country, so that the amount mentioned on the cheque is a definite known value.

3. The firm drawing the cheque must be known to be honest people who would not make a written promise to pay unless they had the money to meet it.

Every day tens of thousands of business firms are sending cheques, or paper promises to pay, to each other. These cheques are paid into the banks, and the banks on whom the cheques are drawn have a central office, called a Clearing House, which enables them to set off against each other the multitude of cheques drawn on them. Thus, between one bank and another, comparatively little money has to pass, and the cheque system resolves itself into one in which the actual use of money is almost entirely avoided. But let us observe that it is only avoided because of the very nature and conditions of its existence. If we had bad paper money we could not use cheques, but should have to keep in our houses or offices, and carry about with us, great piles of paper notes which had a value tending to fluctuate from day to day.

**THE USE OF MONEY BETWEEN THE
NATIONS OF THE WORLD**

By the early years of this century gold had come to be adopted by nearly all civilised countries as a standard money. This meant that it was easy to change the money of one country into that of another, and if necessary gold could be sent instead of money. This system, when money was based on gold, was known as the Gold Standard.

When each country has its own paper money, the problem is much more complicated, for paper notes are of no use except in the country which issues them. They cannot be spent in other countries. If a man wants to buy foreign goods, he must first exchange his paper money for the money of the other country, which he can spend there. When the paper money of one country is exchanged for that of another, the rate of exchange is determined by bargaining, sometimes between private traders, but mainly between governments. It is difficult to fix steady rates at which one money can be changed for another, and so trade becomes less stable.

Not until people in different countries trust each other, and have confidence in each other's money in the same way that they have confidence in their own, can paper money be a satisfactory means of financing trade between the different nations of the world.

FLOWERS OF THE DOWNLAND

1. BRISTLY OX-TONGUE　　　2. SWEET-SCENTED ORCHIS　　　3. SWEETBRIAR　　　4. GREAT SNAPDRAGON
5. MILK-THISTLE　　6. ROUND-HEADED RAMPION　　　7. TUFTED CENTAURY　　8. BIENNIAL HAWK'S-BEARD

1. CLUSTERED BELLFLOWER   2. BLACK NIGHTSHADE   3. HOARY RAG-WORT   4. NIPPLE-WORT   5. MUSK
THISTLE   6. BEE-ORCHIS   7. PASQUE FLOWER   8. PALE BLUE TOADFLAX   9. LONG-ROOTED CAT'S EAR

1. HAWKWEED PICRIS   2. QUINSYWORT   3. FETID HAWK'S-BEARD   4. SALAD BURNET
5. COMMON SAW-WORT   6. SAINFOIN   7. DWARF PLUME-THISTLE   8. SPIDER-ORCHIS   9. COMMON
AUTUMN GENTIAN

1 MARJORAM   2. GRASS VETCHLING   3. GOAT'S-BEARD   4. FIELD LEAF-WORT   5. WOOLLY-HEADED
PLUME-THISTLE   6. AUTUMN LADY'S TRESSES   7. CHALK MILK-WORT   8. DWARF MALLOW
9. GREAT KNAPWEED

The Story of the Peoples of All Nations and Their Homelands

Lisbon, capital of Portugal, on the River Tagus

PORTUGAL AND HER STORY

FOUR hundred years ago Portugal was one of the world's great Powers. She is still a country of considerable importance and influence. Although her once vast Empire has shrunk, she still has a population of about 21 million, made up of nine million in Europe and 12 million in Africa and the Far East. And they form one national community, divided into provinces at home and overseas, for Portugal has no "colonies," only "territories," or provinces overseas.

Though the power of Portugal at her greatest never quite equalled that of neighbouring Spain—indeed for a time the crowns of Portugal and Spain were jointly held by the king of Spain—she has been able to preserve more overseas territory than her neighbour.

In this country Portugal is often referred to as " our oldest ally " ; and it is true that, from the Middle Ages to the present day, Britain and Portugal have constantly been brought together in friendly co-operation. That is so despite the wide differences in their ways of government and national characteristics, and one reason for this co-operation has been Britain's sympathy with the Portuguese determination to be independent of Spain.

Again and again this country helped Portugal in her resistance. In the days of acute rivalry, with Spain as an overbearing Power, England then being a rising Power, it was an advantage to this country that the greater part of the Atlantic coastline of the Iberian Peninsula should not be a Spanish coastline. Then, too, the trade relations between Britain and Portugal have long been of mutual benefit.

We see in Portugal, then, a friendly country, which has preserved its independence with tenacity, and with only limited resources has kept together into modern times considerable dominions beyond the seas. Where Portugal has relinquished lands, she has done it with a good grace. Such a nation calls for a kindly survey, past and present.

The people who first inhabited Portugal were of the same races as those which occupied Spain. That is, they were of the stock known as Iberians, followed by Celtic tribes, and closely resembled the Asturians and Galicians of northern Spain. Later they were conquered by the Romans, and adopted the Roman language which, as time went on, was changed by local usage into the Portuguese development of the Latin tongue.

THE FIVE CONTINENTS & 100 NATIONS & RACES THAT INHABIT THEM

As in Spain, invasions from the north brought Alans, Suevi, and Visigoths, but did not alter the foundations of language laid by the Romans. Then, in A.D. 711, the Arab invasion from Africa placed the land under Mohammedan rule.

Portugal was under Moorish government for over 300 years, and its southern parts for more than 400 years. To this day the Portuguese people of the south bear visible traces of a partly Moorish origin, though the artistic culture of the palmy days of the Moorish civilisation is not as prominent there as in southern Spain. When Lisbon was finally freed from the Moors in 1147, a band of English crusaders helped Alphonso Henriques the First in its capture.

This Alphonso was the founder of the Portuguese kingship in a line that ruled for 400 years. He was reputed to be a giant of seven feet, and he changed the countship into a kingship, and gained such a repute for bravery that his fame was preserved in Moorish legends as widely as in Portuguese history.

THE FARMER KING WHO MADE A TRADE TREATY WITH ENGLAND

The Burgundian line of kings proved to be a vigorous ruling race. Besides Alphonso the First, conspicuous members of the family were Sancho the First, who developed the town life of the country; Alphonso the Third, who entirely freed Portugal from all claims of suzerainty by the northern Spanish State of Leon; and Diniz, the farmer king who wisely developed agriculture, which had suffered from the expulsion of the Moors, and who made a commercial treaty with England. Diniz also founded (in 1290) the university of Coimbra, the chief seat of higher learning in Portugal; but there are modern universities in Lisbon and Oporto.

Pedro the First also signed mutual trade covenants with the English, and his son John the First, whose succession to the throne was challenged by the Spanish Kingdom of Castile, was aided by 500 English archers in a victorious battle which firmly established Portugal against the rivalry of Spain. Later, John of Gaunt, son of Edward the Third of England, supported John the First with 5000 English soldiers, and the Portuguese King married a daughter of the English Prince. John, who had been elected King by the Portuguese

parliament, reigned 48 years, and it was his son Henry, born of an English mother, who inspired and planned the splendid series of Portuguese voyages which discovered the islands in the South Atlantic Ocean, made known the west coast of Africa, rounded the Cape of Good Hope, and enabled the Portuguese King, Emanuel, to declare himself, in the year 1500, "Lord of the conquest, navigation, and commerce of India, Ethiopia, Arabia, and Persia."

HOW ENGLAND HELPED PORTUGAL TO EXPAND ACROSS THE SEAS

John the First of Portugal has been well-named the Father of his Country, for in his reign, and largely by his sagacity, she rose to greatness. Five English kings in succession ratified the treaty of alliance made between him and Edward the Third at Windsor, and repeated English expeditions supported the Portuguese in their enterprises. When Portugal established her first outpost on the coast of Africa by the capture of Ceuta in Morocco, opposite Gibraltar, her army was strengthened by a body of English men-at-arms sent out by Henry the Fifth, the victor at Agincourt. John realised that Portugal, with her favourable seaboard, but hemmed in on her landward side by Spain, must find expansion across the seas, and through a firm league with England he supported that expansion.

In her wars with the Moors, which enlisted the sympathy of the nations of Christendom, and in her resistance to Spain, which ensured her independence, Portugal had welded herself firmly into a united nation with cause for pride, and she had established a knightly Order of Christ, of which Prince Henry the Navigator was the Grand Master. Her outlet to the world was entirely on the sea, and religion, commerce, and adventure were all enlisted to make her a pioneer country.

THE WONDERFUL DISCOVERIES OF THE DARING SEAMEN OF OLD TIMES

Thus the Portuguese became seafaring discoverers—far more so than Spain. Columbus and Amerigo were Italians, and Magellan was a Portuguese, though they served Spain. The Spanish heroes were conquerors ashore in America; they were not voyagers into the unknown. It was the Portuguese who colonised the Azores and Madeira; found St. Helena and Ascension in the wide Atlantic; took

PEOPLE WE MEET IN PORTUGAL

A COUNTRY DANCE BY PEOPLE OF MINHO PROVINCE

SMILING FLOWER GIRLS
OF FUNCHAL, MADEIRA

A SHEPHERD BOY OF
ALENTEJO

EMBROIDERY WORKERS OF
VIANA DE CASTELO

IN A PRIMARY SCHOOL AT LISBON

possession of Brazil; touched at the lonely island of Tristan da Cunha; explored the west coast of Africa to Guinea, to the Congo, to Angola; doubled the Cape of Good Hope with Bartholomew Diaz in command; established settlements on the East African coast; reached India under Vasco da Gama, and made Goa the centre of their influence in the East; gained the trade of the Persian Gulf; discovered Madagascar and Mauritius; communicated with Abyssinia from the Red Sea; touched at Malacca and established themselves at Timor in the Eastern Archipelago; came into touch with Siam and China; and arrived in Japan.

All this, of course, was not done in the time of Henry the Navigator, but his were the foresight and energy and enthusiasm that started his country on the way to being a World Power, till she almost rivalled Spain as a nation finding wealth beyond the seas. Throughout a whole century of expansion a strong current of friendliness united England and Portugal against Spain as the common enemy.

PORTUGAL, NARROW AND INTOLERANT, CRUMBLES FROM WITHIN

In 1520 Portugal was at the height of her expansion. Then came her fall, swifter by far than her rise. In 1580 she was annexed to Spain and became an unwilling participator in the wars which were to break down the might of Spain itself.

How did that fall come about ? Like Spain, Portugal crumbled from within. She became narrow and intolerant in religion and in business. She tried to make all her people of one religion, and so destroyed the freedom of the mind. She drove out the Jews who had been the mainstays of her trade. Her population was too small to provide manhood for her enterprises far away, and she recruited it by starting a great slave trade, and importing captive Negroes to cultivate some of her southern provinces. She had wealth, but had become weakened in manhood, and in the love of freedom that trebles the power of manhood.

So, eight years before Philip the Second sent forth his ill-fated Armada to conquer England, he was able to increase his dominions nearer home by annexing Portugal.

For 60 years Portugal was under the Spanish yoke, with the monarchy striving to suppress all her people's rights. Then, at last, the weakening power of Spain gave Portugal a chance of regaining her freedom, and she successfully rebelled.

England renewed her friendship and gave her help, and that spirit has been sustained until the present day. Its most active manifestation was during the Peninsular War, when Portuguese troops were brigaded with Wellington's men long after Portugal was cleared of the French invaders.

WHEN AN ENGLISHMAN ADMINISTERED THE LAW OF PORTUGAL

During the advance of the French into Portugal the Portuguese royal family, as the only means of avoiding capture, retired to the great colony Brazil, and remained there until the end of the war, and indeed for some time afterwards, while an Englishman administered the law of the rescued nation. When the Portuguese king returned to reign, his son remained in Brazil and became its emperor when that country finally asserted and was granted its independence.

For the next 100 years Portuguese political life was one of unrest, ending in the flight of the last king, Manuel II, after the murder of his father, and the proclamation, in 1910, of a Republic that for some years had no stability.

Another period of unrest followed during and after the First World War, in which Portugal fought on the side of Britain. Revolution succeeded revolution and not until March 1928 did the country become entirely free of disturbance.

THE PRESIDENT IS HOLDER OF SUPREME AUTHORITY

In 1926 Portugal found the strong rule she needed in the person of General Carmona, and he was still in power in 1933 when a new Constitution was adopted. Under this Constitution the President of the Republic is elected by the people every seven years. On him the nation confers absolute power over the whole political organisation.

It is the President who chooses the President of the Council (the Prime Minister) and approves the other Ministers proposed by him. It is the President who approves the laws. He is the holder of supreme authority, although in practice he leaves the business of government to the Prime Minister and the Council of State, consisting of 15 members.

A SUNNY DAY IN PORTUGAL'S CAPITAL

THE STATUE TO PEDRO IV TOWERS ABOVE THE LISBON SQUARE WHICH BEARS HIS NAME

This new Constitution owed much to a University professor, Dr. Antonio de Olivera Salazar, who had brought order in the nation's finances and had become Prime Minister in 1932. It was Dr. Salazar who raised Portugal and her provinces overseas to a higher state of efficiency than had been known for many years.

INSPIRING LEADERSHIP BRINGS VAST IMPROVEMENTS IN PUBLIC SERVICES

When the Second World War broke out Portugal remained neutral, but in 1943 permitted Britain and the U.S. to set up air and naval bases on the Azores. In the years following the defeat of Germany Dr. Salazar again successfully tackled a serious economic situation in Portugal. His Government began an eight-year plan of industrialisation, including the building of three large dams to secure hydro-electric power.

Under the inspiring leadership of Dr. Salazar vast improvements were made in the public services. Towns and villages formerly accessible only by mule or ox-cart were linked by a network of good motor roads. The railways were placed under a single company.

New houses for the people and new schools for their children have been a main concern of the Government. The mercantile marine has been transformed and ports modernised. At Lisbon there is a magnificent airport.

Continental Portugal, including the Azores and Madeira, has an area of 35,500 square miles. Her overseas territories have an area of over 800,000 square miles, chiefly in Angola in West Africa and Mozambique in East Africa. Portuguese Guinea is bordered by French Senegambia. The islands of S. Thomé and Principe in the Gulf of Guinea have an extraordinarily rich soil, and are famous for their cocoa. The Cape Verde Islands in the Atlantic produce coffee.

THE MOUNTAINS AND RIVERS OF SPAIN THAT RUN INTO PORTUGAL

In the eastern part of the East Indian island of Timor nearly half a million people are under Portuguese administration, the rest, formerly under Dutch rule, now being independent. Macao is a small Chinese settlement near Canton, in Portuguese possession since 1557.

Throughout its whole length Portugal is the continuation of the features of Spain to the westward, the Spanish mountain ranges and rivers being merely prolonged. Portugal has only one considerable river of her own, the Mondego.

The Minho is a frontier stream of the north; the Guadiana, also, to a considerable extent, in the south-east; but the Douro and the Tagus cross the whole country. They are not, however, navigable far inland. Oporto, with over 285,000 people, three miles from the mouth of the Douro, is the centre of the wine trade, which is Portugal's largest business. Lisbon, the capital, on the estuary of the Tagus, has over 790,000 people. Both Lisbon and Oporto are finely situated, and both are great manufacturing centres for clothing fabrics for use in Portugal and her colonies. There are no other large cities. Most of the people are Roman Catholics but there is complete freedom of worship everywhere.

THE IMPORTANCE OF AGRICULTURE IN THE LIFE OF THE PORTUGUESE

Portugal is essentially an agricultural country. Though it has mineral wealth its minerals are little worked except copper, partly through the scarcity of coal and the lack hitherto of hydro-electric power. The climate is healthy, except in the marshy parts of the low-lying southern coast. There is an abundance of rain, especially in the centre and the north, and one effect is a profuse growth of flowers.

The vine and the olive flourish on the hillsides. Maize is grown in the north. There the breeding of oxen and sheep is the leading agricultural interest. Oxen are still used for agricultural work and transport.

Wheat is grown in the central regions. About one-fifth of the country is forest, the most valuable product being cork, which exceeds that of the rest of the world. Fruits are abundant—oranges, lemons, figs, grapes, olives, almonds, and tomatoes. The fisheries are important, particularly the sardine fishery centring on Setubal. The exports are wine, cork, fruits, potatoes, onions, cattle, wool, olive oil, salt, copper, and sardines. Most of Portugal's trade is with Britain and the United States.

Thanks to sound government, and to her strategic position on the eastern shores of the Atlantic—and thus on the route to Africa and the Americas—Portugal's future is bright.

PORTUGAL AND SPAIN

THE CASTLE OF PENA, ON A HILLTOP AT CINTRA IN PORTUGAL

THE WEST FRONT OF LISBON
CATHEDRAL

A STREET LIFT TO THE UPPER
PART OF LISBON

THE ARCH OF THE PRACA DO
COMMERCIO LISBON

THE FINE MODERN BUILDINGS OF PORTELA AIRPORT AT LISBON, CAPITAL OF PORTUGAL

THE GREAT MONASTERY AT MAFRA, 800 FEET LONG AND 700 FEET WIDE

THE CASTLE-LIKE ERMIDA DE SAO BRAZ AT EVORA

THE CHURCH OF THE GOOD JESUS AT BRAGA

OPORTO, THE SECOND CITY IN PORTUGAL, SEEN FROM ACROSS THE RIVER DOURO

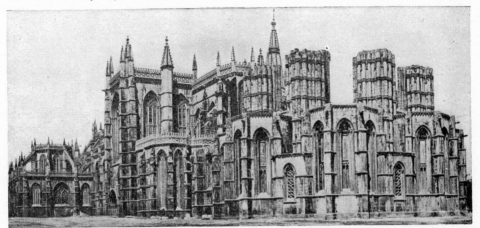

THE UNFINISHED CHAPEL OF THE DOMINICAN MONASTERY AT BATALHA

THE ROMAN AQUEDUCT AT EVORA

THE OLD WALLED TOWN OF BRAGANZA

THE RIVER DOURO WINDS ITS WAY PAST THE TERRACED HILLS

THE OLD UNIVERSITY TOWN OF COIMBRA

A STREET IN SETUBAL

THE RIVER DOURO AT OPORTO

THE AQUEDUCT WHICH CARRIES WATER TO LISBON

THE ROMAN TEMPLE OF DIANA AT EVORA

Many of the pictures in these pages are reproduced by courtesy of the Portuguese Embassy in London

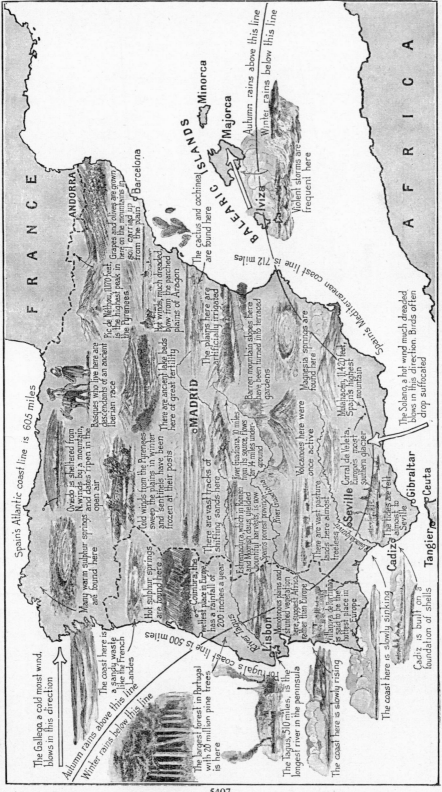

THE SPANISH PENINSULA FORMS A LAND OF STRANGE PHYSICAL CONTRASTS, GLACIERS AND HOT WINDS, VOLCANOES AND SAND DUNES, RISING AND SINKING COASTS, ALL BEING FOUND THERE

THE INTERESTING ANIMAL LIFE OF PORTUGAL AND SPAIN

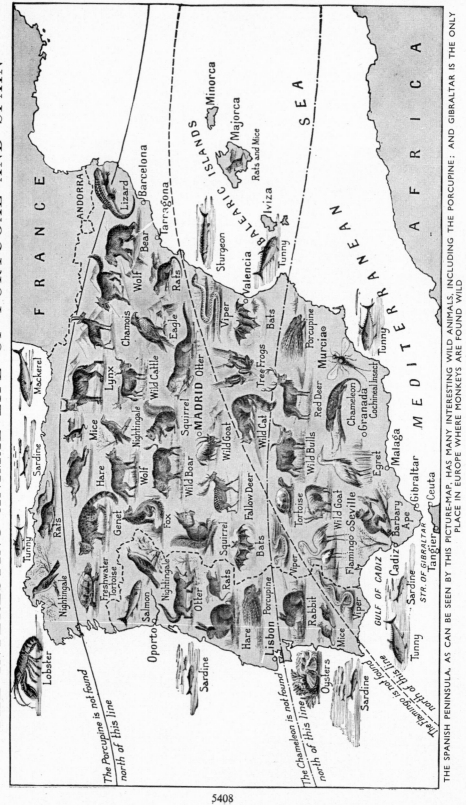

THE SPANISH PENINSULA, AS CAN BE SEEN BY THIS PICTURE-MAP, HAS MANY INTERESTING WILD ANIMALS, INCLUDING THE PORCUPINE; AND GIBRALTAR IS THE ONLY PLACE IN EUROPE WHERE MONKEYS ARE FOUND WILD

THE VARIED PLANT LIFE OF THE SPANISH PENINSULA

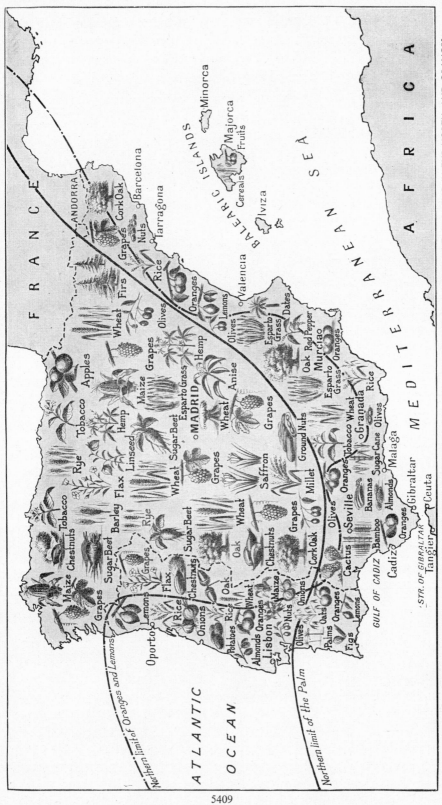

PORTUGAL AND SPAIN, AS CAN BE SEEN HERE, HAVE A VERY VARIED PLANT LIFE, RYE, WHEAT, AND SUGAR-BEET GROWING IN THE NORTH, AND ORANGES, BANANAS, AND SUGAR-CANE IN THE SOUTH

5409

PORTUGAL AND SPAIN AS A WORKSHOP

PORTUGAL AND SPAIN, AS CAN BE SEEN BY THIS MAP, HAVE A VARIETY OF INDUSTRIES. BOTH ARE PRE

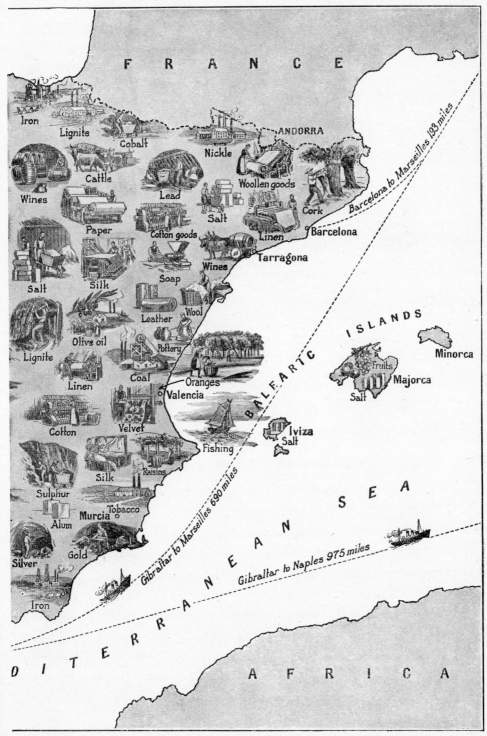

DOMINANTLY AGRICULTURAL COUNTRIES, BUT SPAIN HAS APPRECIABLE, YET UNDEVELOPED MINERAL WEALTH

A HISTORY MAP OF PORTUGAL AND SPAIN

In 1588 the remnants of the Invincible Armada made their way into Gijon harbour

After being damaged by a gale, the Spanish Armada refitted at Corunna and Ferrol and then sailed for England in 1588

In 1386 John of Gaunt landed in Galicia to claim the crown of Castile and Leon by right of his wife, daughter of Pedro the Cruel. He was proclaimed King at Santiago, but when plague ravaged his army he resigned his claim for certain rights

Leon, once the proud capital of a kingdom stretching from the Atlantic to the Rhone, derived its name from the fact that it was once the fortified camp of the 7th Roman Legion

On September 21, 1588, boats went out from Santander and towed the battered flagship of the Duke of Medina Sidonia, commander of the beaten Armada, into the harbour to save it from running on the rocks

Here at Corunna, in 1809, 14,000 troops under Sir John Moore, who were retreating, beat 20,000 French troops. Sir John Moore was killed

Salamanca, whose ancient University with 7000 students once ranked with Oxford and Cambridge, was occupied by Hannibal in 222 B.C. Its convent of San Esteban sheltered Columbus from 1484 to 1486

Columbus died at Valladolid in 1506

The Cid, the great Spanish hero in the war against the Moors, was born at Bivar Castle, near Burgos, about 1040

At Saborosa, about 1480, was born Ferdinand Magellan, whose ship first sailed round the world. Magellan himself, was killed in the Philippines, 1521

Cervantes, the author of Don Quixote, was born at Alcalá de Henares in 1547

MADRID

Oporto has always been antagonistic to Lisbon, just as Barcelona is to Madrid, and the restless character of the citizens is shown by their many risings during the past three or four centuries. There the revolution of 1820 began

In 1556 the Emperor Charles V abdicated his throne and retired to the lovely monastery of Yuste where he died in 1558

The University of Coimbra was founded at Lisbon in 1290, and was permanently transferred to Coimbra in 1537

Here at Alcántara, in 105, Trajan built a fine stone bridge over the Tagus 616 feet long and 190 feet high, and this exists today practically as the Romans left it

Here between 1563 and 1584 Philip II erected the Escorial, a combined palace, monastery, church, and mausoleum. It originated in a vow to St. Lawrence at the battle of St. Quentin and has the plan of a gridiron, in memory of the martyrdom of that saint

Pizarro, the conqueror of Peru, was born at Trujillo about 1471

Lisbon was almost completely destroyed by a great earthquake and tidal wave in 1755 and about 40,000 people lost their lives

Route of the Spanish Armada in 1588

At Sines, about 1469, was born Vasco da Gama, the first modern navigator to double the Cape of Good Hope

The fortified lines of Torres Vedras, where in 1810 and 1811 Wellington held out against the French till ready to drive them out of the Peninsula

Cortes, the conqueror of Mexico, was born at Medellin in 1485

On Aug. 3, 1492, Columbus set sail with three ships from Palos on his great voyage of discovery to America

Velasquez

Murillo

In 1808 Napoleon entered Madrid, abolished feudalism and the Inquisition, and placed his brother Joseph on the throne. Four years later Wellington, who had defeated the French, entered Madrid

Velasquez, the great artist, was born at Seville in 1599 and Murillo in 1618

Here on the banks of the River Guadalete, Roderick, the last Gothic king, lost his army, and for 800 years the Moslems ruled in Spain

Granada, the last stronghold of the Moors in Spain, was taken by the Spaniards under Ferdinand and Isabella in 1492

Admiral Rodney defeated the Spanish fleet off Cape St. Vincent in 1780, and Admiral Jervis (Lord St. Vincent) gained another great victory here in 1797

In 1587 Drake burned many ships at Cadiz intended for the Spanish Armada, and in 1596 the city was sacked by the Earl of Essex. Here at Cadiz (Gadir), the Phoenicians founded their first colony in Spain five or six centuries B.C. It was captured by the Carthaginians in 480 B.C.

Gibraltar, one of the ancient Pillars of Hercules, was captured by the English under Sir George Rooke in 1704 and has been British ever since, although several times besieged and assaulted

Route of the Vandals in 409

Nelson gained his great victory over the French and Spanish fleets off Cape Trafalgar in 1805

PORTUGAL AND SPAIN HAVE HAD A STIRRING HISTORY, AS THIS PICTURE-MAP SHOWS.

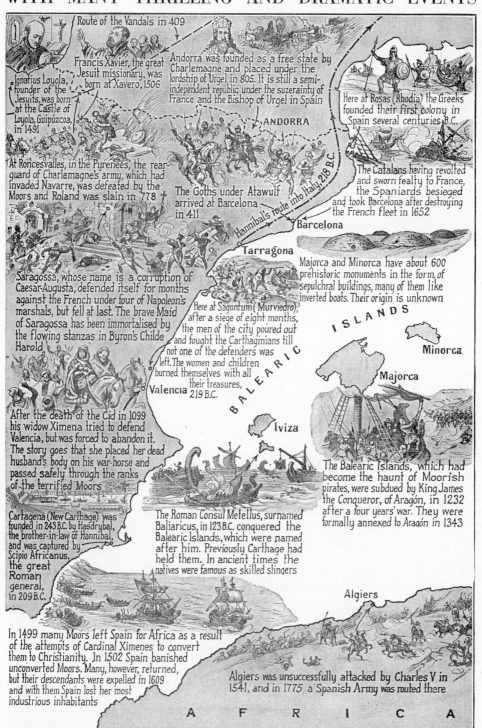

Route of the Vandals in 409

Francis Xavier, the great Jesuit missionary, was born at Xavero, 1506

Ignatius Loyola, founder of the Jesuits, was born at the Castle of Loyola, Guipúzcoa, in 1491

Andorra was founded as a free state by Charlemagne and placed under the lordship of Urgel in 805. It is still a semi-independent republic under the suzerainty of France and the Bishop of Urgel in Spain

ANDORRA

Here at Rosas (Rhodia) the Greeks founded their first colony in Spain several centuries B.C.

At Roncesvalles, in the Pyrenees, the rear-guard of Charlemagne's army, which had invaded Navarre, was defeated by the Moors and Roland was slain in 778

The Goths under Atawulf arrived at Barcelona in 411

Hannibal's route into Italy 218 B.C.

Barcelona

The Catalans having revolted and sworn fealty to France, the Spaniards besieged and took Barcelona after destroying the French fleet in 1652

Tarragona

Saragossa, whose name is a corruption of Caesar-Augusta, defended itself for months against the French under four of Napoleon's marshals, but fell at last. The brave Maid of Saragossa has been immortalised by the flowing stanzas in Byron's Childe Harold

Here at Saguntum (Murviedro), after a siege of eight months, the men of the city poured out and fought the Carthaginians till not one of the defenders was left. The women and children burned themselves with all their treasures, 219 B.C.

Valencia

Majorca and Minorca have about 600 prehistoric monuments in the form of sepulchral buildings, many of them like inverted boats. Their origin is unknown

BALEARIC ISLANDS

Minorca

Majorca

After the death of the Cid in 1099 his widow Ximena tried to defend Valencia, but was forced to abandon it. The story goes that she placed her dead husband's body on his war-horse and passed safely through the ranks of the terrified Moors

Iviza

The Balearic Islands, which had become the haunt of Moorish pirates, were subdued by King James the Conqueror, of Aragón, in 1232 after a four years' war. They were formally annexed to Aragón in 1343

Cartagena (New Carthage) was founded in 243 B.C. by Hasdrubal, the brother-in-law of Hannibal, and was captured by Scipio Africanus, the great Roman general, in 209 B.C.

The Roman Consul Metellus, surnamed Baliaricus, in 123 B.C. conquered the Balearic Islands, which were named after him. Previously Carthage had held them. In ancient times the natives were famous as skilled slingers

Algiers

In 1499 many Moors left Spain for Africa as a result of the attempts of Cardinal Ximenes to convert them to Christianity. In 1502 Spain banished unconverted Moors. Many, however, returned, but their descendants were expelled in 1609 and with them Spain lost her most industrious inhabitants

Algiers was unsuccessfully attacked by Charles V in 1541, and in 1775 a Spanish Army was routed there

A F R I C A

EUROPE'S FARTHEST WEST—A BIRD'S-EYE VIEW OF PORTUGAL AND SPAIN

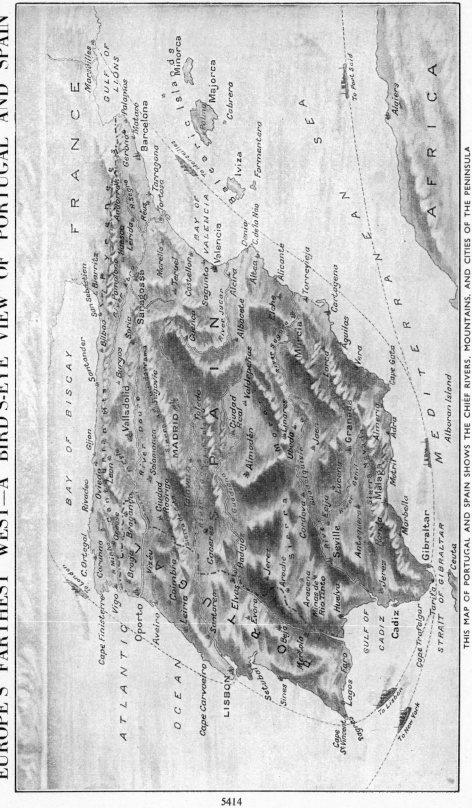

THIS MAP OF PORTUGAL AND SPAIN SHOWS THE CHIEF RIVERS, MOUNTAINS, AND CITIES OF THE PENINSULA

One Thousand Poems of All Times and All Countries

THE RIDE ON A WILD HORSE

Mazeppa was a page-boy in the house of a Polish noble-man, who, angry with him for something he had done, called for a wild Tartar horse he had caught the day before, lashed Mazeppa to its back, and set it free. The horse sped furiously away until it fell dead in the country o Ukraine. There a Cossack set Mazeppa free and brought him back to life. Lord Byron makes Mazeppa tell his story to a king after a great battle, and ends by making him reign on the throne of Ukraine. Here we give the parts of the poem that describe the great ride of Mazeppa.

Away, away, my steed and I,
　Upon the pinions of the wind,
All human dwellings left behind;
We sped like meteors through the sky,
When with its crackling sound the night
Is chequered with the northern light;
Town, village, none were on our track,
　But a wild plain of far extent,
And bounded by a forest black;
　And, save the scarce-seen battlement
On distant heights of some stronghold,
Against the Tartars built of old,
No trace of man.
The sky was dull, and dim, and grey,
　And a low breeze crept moaning by:
　I could have answered with a sigh,
But fast we fled, away, away,
And I could neither sigh nor pray.

We neared the wild wood: 'twas so wide
　I saw no bounds on either side:
'Twas studded with old sturdy trees,
That bent not to the roughest breeze
Which howls down from Siberia's waste,
And strips the forest in its haste;
But these were few and far between,
Set thick with shrubs more young and
　green.

'Twas a wild waste of underwood,
　And here and there a chestnut stood,
The strong oak, and the hardy pine;

But far apart—and well it were,
Or else a different lot were mine:
　The boughs gave way, and did not tear
My limbs; and I found strength to bear
My wounds, already scarred with cold;
My bonds forbade to loose my hold.
We rustled through the leaves like wind,
Left shrubs, and trees, and wolves behind;
By night I heard them on the track,
Their troop came hard upon our back
With their long gallop, which can tire
The hound's deep hate, and hunter's fire;
Where'er we flew they followed on,
Nor left us with the morning sun;
Behind I saw them, scarce a rood,
At daybreak winding through the wood,
And through the night had heard their feet—
Their stealing, rustling step repeat.
Oh, how I wished for spear or sword,
At least to die amidst the horde,
And perish—if it must be so—
At bay, destroying many a foe!

The wood was passed; 'twas more than
　noon,
But chill the air, although in June;
Or it might be my veins ran cold—
Prolonged endurance tames the bold.

The earth gave way, the skies rolled
　round,
　I seemed to sink upon the ground;

POEMS · SONGS · BALLADS · VERSES AND RHYMES WITH MUSIC

But erred, for I was fastly bound.
My heart turned sick, my brain grew sore,
And throbbed awhile, then beat no more:
The skies spun like a mighty wheel;
I saw the trees like drunkards reel,
And a slight flash sprang o'er my eyes,
Which saw no farther: he who dies
Can die no more than then I died,
O'er-tortured by that ghastly ride.
I felt the blackness come and go,
 And strove to wake; but could not make
My sense climb up from below,
My undulating life was as
The fancied lights that flitting pass
Our shut eyes in deep midnight, when
Fever begins upon the brain.
My thoughts came back. Where was I?
 Cold,
And numb, and giddy: pulse by pulse
Life reassumed its lingering hold,
And throb by throb—till grown a pang
 Which for a moment would convulse—
 My blood reflowed, though thick and
  chill;
My ear with uncouth noises rang,
 My heart began once more to thrill;
My sight returned, though dim, alas!
And thickened, as it were with glass.

Methought the dash of waves was nigh;
There was a gleam, too, of the sky
Studded with stars—it is no dream;
The wild horse swims the wilder stream!
The bright, broad river's gushing tide
Sweeps, winding onward, far and wide,
And we are half-way, struggling o'er
To yon unknown and silent shore.
The waters broke my hollow trance,
And with a temporary strength
 My stiffened limbs were re-baptised.
My courser's broad breast proudly braves,
And dashes off the ascending waves,
And onward we advance!
We reach the slippery shore at length,
 A haven I but little prized,
For all behind was dark and drear,
And all before was night and fear.
How many hours of night or day
In those suspended pangs I lay
I could not tell; I scarcely knew
If this were human breath I drew.

With glossy skin, and dripping mane,
 And reeling limbs, and reeking flank,
The wild steed's sinewy nerves still strain
 Up the repelling bank.
We gain the top; a boundless plain
Spreads through the shadow of the night,

And onward, onward, onward, seems,
 Like precipices in our dreams,
To stretch beyond the sight;
And here and there a speck of white,
 Or scattered spot of dusky green,
In masses broke into the light,
As rose the moon upon my right:
 But nought distinctly seen
In the dim waste would indicate
The omen of a cottage gate;
No twinkling taper from afar
Stood like a hospitable star;
Not even an ignis-fatuus rose
To make him merry with my woes:
 That very cheat had cheered me then!
Although detected, welcome still,
Reminding me, through every ill,
 Of the abodes of men.

Onward we went, but slack and slow;
 His savage force at length o'erspent,
The drooping courser, faint and low,
 Or feebly foaming went.
A sickly infant had had power
To guide him forward in that hour;
 But useless all to me;
His new-born tameness nought availed:
My limbs were bound; my force had failed,
 Perchance, had they been free.
The dizzy race seemed almost done,
Although no goal was nearly won:
Some streaks announced the coming sun—
 How slow, alas, he came!
Methought that mist of dawning grey
Would never dapple into day;
How heavily it rolled away—
 Before the eastern flame
Rose crimson, and deposed the stars,
And called the radiance from their cars,
And filled the earth, from his deep throne,
With lonely lustre, all his own.

Up rose the sun: the mists were curled
Back from the solitary world
Which lay around, behind, before:
What booted it to traverse o'er
Plain, forest, river? Man nor brute,
Nor dint of hoof, nor print of foot,
Lay in the wild, luxuriant soil;
No sign of travel—none of toil;
The very air was mute;
And not an insect's shrill, small horn,
Nor matin bird's new voice, was borne
From herb nor thicket. Many a werst,
Panting as if his heart would burst,
The weary brute still staggered on;
And still we were—or seemed—alone.
At length, while reeling on our way,

Methought I heard a courser neigh
From out yon tuft of blackening firs.
Is it the wind those branches stirs?
No, no! from out the forest prance
　A trampling troop; I see them come!
In one vast squadron they advance!
　I strove to cry—my lips were dumb.

The steeds rush on in plunging pride;
But where are they the reins to guide?
A thousand horse—and none to ride!
With flowing tail, and flying mane,
Wide nostrils, never stretched by pain,
Mouths bloodless to the bit or rein,
And feet that iron never shod,
And flanks unscarred by spur or rod,
A thousand horse, the wild, the free,
Like waves that follow o'er the sea,
　Came thickly thundering on,
As if our faint approach to meet;
The sight re-nerved my courser's feet,
A moment staggering, feebly fleet,
A moment, with a faint, low neigh,
　He answered, and then fell.
With gasps and glazing eyes he lay,
　And reeking limbs immovable;
　His first and last career is done!
On came the troop: they saw him stoop,
　They saw me strangely bound along
　His back with many a cruel thong;
They stop, they start, they snuff the air,
Gallop a moment here and there,
Approach, retire, wheel round and round,
Then plunging back with sudden bound,
Headed by one black mighty steed,
Who seemed the patriarch of his breed,
　Without a single speck or hair
Of white upon his shaggy hide,
They snort, they foam, neigh, swerve
　aside,
And backward to the forest fly,
By instinct, from a human eye.
　They left me there to my despair,
Linked to the dead and stiffening wretch,
Whose lifeless limbs beneath me stretch,
Relieved from that unwonted weight,
From whence I could not extricate
Nor him, nor me; and there we lay,
　The dying on the dead!
I little deemed another day
　Would see my houseless, helpless head.

And there from morn to twilight
　bound,
I felt the heavy hours toil round,
With just enough of life to see
My last of suns go down on me.
The sun was sinking—still I lay

Chained to the chill and stiffening
　steed;
I thought to mingle there our clay,
　And my dim eyes of death had need—
　No hope arose of being freed;
I cast my last looks up the sky;
　And there between me and the sun
I saw the expecting raven fly,
Who scarce would wait till both should die
　Ere his repast begun.

I know no more—my latest dream
　Is something of a lovely star
　Which fixed my dull eyes from afar,
And went and came with wandering beam,
And of the cold, dull, swimming, dense
Sensation of recurring sense,
And then subsiding back to death
And then again a little breath.
A little thrill, a short suspense,
An icy sickness curdling o'er
My heart, and sparks that crossed my
　brain—
A gasp, a throb, a start of pain,
A sigh, and nothing more.

I woke.　Where was I?　Do I see
A human face look down on me?
And doth a roof above me close?
Do these limbs on a couch repose?
Is this a chamber where I lie?
And is it mortal, yon bright eye
That watches me with gentle glance?
　I closed my own again once more,
As doubtful that the former trance
　Could not as yet be o'er.
A slender girl, long-haired and tall,
Sat watching by the cottage wall;
The sparkle of her eye I caught,
Even with my first return of thought;
For ever and anon she threw
　A prying, pitying glance on me
　With her black eyes so wild and free.
I gazed, and gazed, until I knew
　No vision it could be—
But that I lived, and was released
From adding to the vulture's feast:
And when the Cossack maid beheld
My heavy eyes at length unsealed,
She smiled, and I essayed to speak,
　But failed—and she approached, and
　made
　With lip and finger signs that said
I must not strive as yet to break
The silence, till my strength should be
Enough to leave my accents free;
And then her hand on mine she laid,
And smoothed the pillow for my head,

And stole along on tiptoe tread,
  And gently oped the door.

She came with mother and with sire—
What need of more!—I will not tire
With long recital of the rest
Since I became the Cossack's guest.
They found me senseless on the plain,
  They bore me to the nearest hut,
They brought me into life again,
Me—one day o'er their realm to reign!

MY PLAYMATE

A subdued note of melancholy tunes this poem by J. G. Whittier. It is the reverie of one who, in later life, revisits a scene made dear to him by memories of a little playmate of his early years. Time has worked great changes and taken the playmates far apart, but the old place they knew in youth is still hallowed to the one who lingers there and has power to touch his memory with tender thoughts.

THE pines were dark on Ramoth hill,
  Their song was soft and low;
The blossoms in the sweet May wind
  Were falling like the snow.

The blossoms drifted at our feet,
  The orchard birds sang clear;
The sweetest and the saddest day
  It seemed of all the year.

For, more to me than birds or flowers,
  My playmate left her home,
And took with her the laughing spring,
  The music, and the bloom.

She kissed the lips of kith and kin,
  She laid her hand in mine;
What more could ask the bashful boy
  Who fed her father's kine?

She left us in the bloom of May:
  The constant years told o'er
Their season with as sweet May morns,
  But she came back no more.

I walk with noiseless feet the round
  Of uneventful years;
Still o'er and o'er I sow the spring
  And reap the autumn ears.

She lives where all the golden year
  Her summer roses blow;
The dusky children of the sun
  Before her come and go.

There haply with her jewelled hands
  She smooths her silken gown;
No more the homespun lap wherein
  I shook the walnuts down.

The wild grapes wait us by the brook,
  The brown nuts on the hill;
And still the May-day flowers make sweet
  The woods of Follymill.

The lilies blossom in the pond,
  The bird builds in the tree,
The dark pines sing on Ramoth hill
  The slow song of the sea.

I wonder if she thinks of them,
  And how the old time seems;
If ever the pines of Ramoth wood
  Are sounding in her dreams.

I see her face, I hear her voice:
  Does she remember mine?
And what to her is now the boy
  Who fed her father's kine?

What cares she that the orioles build
  For other eyes than ours,
That other hands with nuts are filled,
  And other laps with flowers?

O playmate in the golden time!
  Our mossy seat is green,
Its fringing violets blossom yet,
  The old trees o'er it lean.

The winds so sweet with birch and fern
  A sweeter memory blow;
And there in spring the veeries sing
  The song of long ago.

And still the pines of Ramoth wood
  Are moaning like the sea:
The moaning of the sea of change
  Between myself and thee!

WHEN I HAVE FEARS

This sonnet by John Keats is one of the saddest in all our literature. Keats was ill, and felt he might not recover. He knew he had the power to write great poetry. He also was in love. But he feared that life was slipping from him with his dreams of fame and love unrealised. His fears proved true, except that he wrote enough before he died to keep his name alive as long as the English language lasts.

WHEN I have fears that I may cease
    to be
  Before my pen has gleaned my teeming
    brain,
Before high-piléd books, in charactery,
  Hold like rich garners the full-ripened
    grain,
When I behold, upon the night's starred
    face,
  Huge cloudy symbols of a high romance,
And think that I may never live to trace
  Their shadows, with the magic hand of
    chance;
And when I feel, fair creature of an hour,
  That I shall never look upon thee more,
Never have relish in the faery power
  Of unreflecting love—then on the shore
Of the wide world I stand alone, and think
Till love and fame to nothingness do sink.

GOD MOVES IN A MYSTERIOUS WAY

William Cowper, the writer of this noble hymn of faith, was a dear and good man who throughout his life suffered at intervals from the pitiful calamity of a disordered mind. Here we see his triumphant trust in God when his mind was clear. He lived in an age when religion was too often made gloomy by men who did not read God's love aright, but his faith has brought comfort to tens of thousands.

God moves in a mysterious way
   His wonders to perform:
He plants His footsteps in the sea,
   And rides upon the storm.

Deep in unfathomable mines
   Of never-failing skill
He treasures up His bright designs,
   And works His sovereign will.

Ye fearful saints, fresh courage take;
   The clouds ye so much dread
Are big with mercy, and shall break
   In blessings on your head.

Judge not the Lord by feeble sense,
   But trust Him for His grace;
Behind a frowning providence
   He hides a smiling face.

His purposes will ripen fast,
   Unfolding every hour;
The bud may have a bitter taste,
   But sweet will be the flower.

Blind unbelief is sure to err
   And scan His work in vain:
God is His own interpreter,
   And He will make it plain.

DEATH THE VICTOR

James Shirley was a seventeenth-century poet and dramatist who wrote many plays popular in his day. Some of his plays had poems here and there that were deeply impressive. This is an example on the power of Death, which, in one way or another, conquers all of us, though we know that in the end Death itself is conquered.

Victorious men of earth, no more
   Proclaim how wide your empires
     are;
Though you bind-in every shore
   And your triumphs reach as far
     As night or day,
   Yet you, proud monarchs, must obey
And mingle with forgotten ashes when
Death calls ye to the crowd of common men.

Devouring Famine, Plague, and War,
   Each able to undo mankind,
Death's servile emissaries are;
   Nor to these alone confined,
     He hath at will
   More quaint and subtle ways to kill;
A smile or kiss, as he will use the art,
Shall have the cunning skill to break a
     heart.

EARTHLY GLORY

The most justly famous of all the poems scattered in James Shirley's plays is this on the brevity of earthly glory. The best, perhaps, we know of Charles the Second is that this was his favourite poem. The graceful flow of the verse, its apt contrasts, dignity, and perfect ending, make it a classic.

The glories of our blood and state
   Are shadows, not substantial things;
There is no armour against fate;
   Death lays his icy hand on kings:
     Sceptre and crown
     Must tumble down,
And in the dust be equal made
With the poor crooked scythe and spade.

Some men with swords may reap the field,
   And plant fresh laurels where they kill;
But their strong nerves at last must yield;
   They tame but one another still:
     Early or late
     They stoop to fate,
And must give up their murmuring breath
When they, pale captives, creep to death.

The garlands wither on your brow;
   Then boast no more your mighty deeds!
Upon Death's purple altar now
   See where the victor-victim bleeds!
     Your heads must come
     To the cold tomb:
Only the actions of the just
Smell sweet, and blossom in their dust.

VIRTUE

George Herbert, a seventeenth-century parson-poet, wrote much thoughtful verse, often with dainty fancies turned to a good purpose, but mixed with a homely quaintness that is sometimes out of place. For instance, the idea that the redness of the rose may make one's eyes water is quite unwarranted, and the earth turning to coal is a clumsy expression. But Herbert had enough poetry in him to make us forgive his oddity, and the moral he draws is sound.

Sweet day, so cool, so calm, so bright,
   The bridal of the earth and sky,
The dew shall weep thy fall tonight;
   For thou must die.

Sweet rose, whose hue, angry and brave,
Bids the rash gazer wipe his eye,
Thy root is ever in its grave,
   And thou must die.

Sweet spring, full of sweet days and roses,
A box where sweets compacted lie,
My music shows ye have your closes,
   And all must die.

Only a sweet and virtuous soul,
Like seasoned timber, never gives;
But though the whole world turn to coal,
   Then chiefly lives.

SWEDEN

All British people will respond to a man's love of his native land, for they know the feeling well. Here is that same love expressed for his own land by the most popular Swedish poet, Johan Ludvig Runeberg who lived from 1804 to 1877. Though Runeberg wrote in Swedish, he was born and lived in Finland, and his description of forest, lake, and river scenery is quite as true of Finland as it is of Sweden.

Our land, our land, our native land,
  Ring high, O word of cheer!
No hills by heaven's rim that stand,
No gentle dales or foaming strand,
  Are loved more than our northland here,
  The earth our sires held dear.

Our land is poor, or seems to be
  To him who covets gold;
A stranger might not deign to see
The land we love so faithfully,
  But gold to us its mountains bold,
  Its wealth of moor and wold.

We love our brooks that gaily bound,
  Our rushing rivers fleet,
The gloomy forest's mournful sound,
The summer glow, the nights profound,
  All, all that eye or ear can greet,
  Or make our glad hearts beat.

To us there is no fairer spot,
  We suffer here no dearth;
However fate may cast our lot,
A land, a native land, we've got.
  What better could men ask on earth
  To love and hold of worth?

O land of myriad lakes, thou land
  Where song and truth may be,
Where life's rude ocean spares a strand,
Our father's land, our children's land,
  Be not ashamed of poverty,
  Be glad, secure, and free!

THE UNFADING BEAUTY

Thomas Carew was a graceful writer in the period immediately following Shakespeare, and he had in his songs the lingering Elizabethan glamour. Here he charmingly expresses the superiority of inward to outward beauty.

He that loves a rosy cheek,
  Or a coral lip admires,
Or from star-like eyes doth seek
  Fuel to maintain his fires:
As old Time makes these decay,
So his flames must waste away.

But a smooth and steadfast mind,
  Gentle thoughts and calm desires,
Hearts with equal love combined,
  Kindle never-dying fires.
Where these are not I despise
Lovely cheeks or lips or eyes.

VENICE

This fine poem remains true of Venice still, except that the city is now reached by rail, and also by means of a new road bridge. The writer, Samuel Rogers (1763-1855), was a wealthy London banker who wrote poetry, was generous to poorer writers, and was a famous figure in society. His kindness was lessened by the sharpness of his tongue.

There is a glorious city in the sea.
  The sea is in the broad, the narrow streets,
Ebbing and flowing, and the salt seaweed
Clings to the marble of her palaces.
No track of men, no footsteps to and fro,
Lead to her gates. The path lies o'er the sea,
Invisible; and from the land we went
As to a floating city, steering in,
And gliding up her streets as in a dream,
So smoothly, silently—by many a dome
Mosque-like, and many a stately portico,
The statues ranged along an azure sky;
By many a pile in more than eastern pride,
Of old the residence of merchant-kings;
The fronts of some, though time had shattered them,
Still glowing with the richest hues of art,
As though the wealth within them had run o'er.

MISERERE DOMINE

Miserere Domine means Pity us, Lord. The writer, John Godfrey Saxe (1816-1887), was an American poet, whose many poems were usually bright and humorous, but here he shows how grave and tender and humble he was at heart.

Have pity, Lord! we humbly cry,
  With trembling voice and tearful eye;
Thou knowest our ignorance and sin,
And what by grace we might have been;
All—all is known, O Lord, to thee;
  Miserere Domine!

Our public walks and private ways:
The follies of our youthful days;
Our manhood's errors—every stain
Of lust and pride to thee are plain;
For who, O Lord, can hide from thee?
  Miserere Domine!

Too late we mourn our wasted hours,
Neglected gifts, perverted powers;
Affections warm, of heavenly birth,
Lavished, alas! on toys of earth:
How far estranged, O Lord, from thee!
  Miserere Domine!

Our Father! ever-blessèd name!
To thee we bring our sin and shame;
Weak though we be, perverse of will,
Thou art our gracious Father still,
Who knowest well how frail we be.
  Miserere Domine!

HECTOR IN THE GARDEN

Elizabeth Barrett Browning was a Greek scholar when she was quite a child, and so she fed her child-like imagination on the heroic deeds of the heroes in Homer's poems. When, at nine years old, she had a flower-man made in her garden she called him Hector, a warrior at the siege of Troy; and she almost trembled at the thought that the spirit of the bold Hector might perhaps return to Earth and live again in her flower-man. In this poem (from which we omit one verse) she revives her girlish fancies.

NINE years old! The first of any
    Seem the happiest years that come:
      Yet when I was nine I said
      No such word! I thought, instead,
That the Greeks had used as many
    In besieging Ilium.

Nine green years had scarcely brought me
    To my childhood's haunted spring:
      I had life, like flowers and bees,
      In betwixt the country trees;
And the sun the pleasure taught me
    Which he teacheth every thing.

If the rain fell there was sorrow;
    Little head leant on the pane,
      Little finger drawing down it
      The long trailing drops upon it,
And the " Rain, rain, come tomorrow,"
    Said for charm against the rain.

And the sun and I together
    Went a-rushing out-of-doors:
      We our tender spirits drew
      Over hill and dale in view,
Glimmering hither, glimmering thither,
    In the footsteps of the showers.

Underneath the chestnuts dripping,
    Through the grasses wet and fair,
      Straight I sought my garden-ground,
      With the laurel on the mound,
And the pear tree oversweeping
    A side-shadow of green air.

In the garden lay supinely
    A huge giant, wrought of spade!
      Arms and legs were stretched at length
      In a passive giant strength,
And the meadow turf, cut finely,
    Round them laid and interlaid.

Call him Hector, son of Priam!
    Such his title and degree.
      With my rake I smoothed his brow;
      Both his cheeks I weeded through:
But a rhymer such as I am
    Scarce can sing his dignity.

Eyes of gentianellas azure,
    Staring, winking at the skies;
      Nose of gillyflowers and box;
      Scented grasses put for locks,
Which a little breeze, at pleasure,
    Set a-waving round his eyes.

Brazen helm of daffodillies,
    With a glitter toward the light;
      Purple violets for the mouth,
      Breathing perfumes west and south;
And a sword of flashing lilies,
    Holden ready for the fight.

And a breastplate made of daisies,
    Closely fitting, leaf by leaf;
      Periwinkles interlaced
      Drawn for belt about the waist;
While the brown bees, humming praises,
    Shot their arrows round the chief.

And who knows, I sometimes wondered,
    If the disembodied soul
      Of old Hector, once of Troy,
      Might not take a dreary joy
Here to enter—if it thundered,
    Rolling up the thunder-roll?

Rolling this way from Troy ruin,
    In this body, rude and rife,
      He might enter, and take rest
      'Neath the daisies of the breast,
They, with tender roots, renewing
    His heroic heart to life.

Who could know? I sometimes started
    At a motion or a sound!
      Did his mouth speak—naming Troy,
      With an otototoi?
Did the pulse of the Strong-hearted
    Make the daisies tremble round?

It was hard to answer often:
    But the birds sang in the tree,
      But the little birds sang bold
      In the pear tree green and old;
And my terror seemed to soften
    Through the courage of their glee.

Oh, the birds, the tree, the ruddy
    And white blossoms, sleek with rain!
      Oh, my garden, rich with pansies!
      Oh, my childhood's bright romances!
All revive, like Hector's body,
    And I see them stir again!

And despite life's changes—chances,
    And despite the death-bell's toll,
      They press on me in full seeming!
      Help, some angel! stay this dreaming!
As the birds sang in the branches,
    Sing God's patience through my soul!

That no dreamer, no neglecter,
    Of the present's work unsped,
      I may wake up and be doing,
      Life's heroic ends pursuing,
Though my past is dead as Hector,
    And though Hector is twice dead.

A MEMORY

Memory is very capricious in the choice of the tender scenes it holds, as William Allingham reminds us in these gracefully simple lines. He lived from 1824 to 1889.

Four ducks on a pond,
    A grass bank beyond,
A blue sky of spring,
White clouds on the wing:
What a little thing
To remember for years,
To remember with tears!

MY DEAR AND ONLY LOVE

There is some doubt whether this poem, by the Scottish soldier James Graham, Marquess of Montrose (1612–50), is really the love poem it seems to be or a partly concealed political appeal, in which Charles the First is pictured as the lover and the country he ruled as the woman he woos.

My dear and only love, I pray
    That little world of thee
Be governed by no other sway
    Than purest monarchy;
For if confusion have a part,
    Which virtuous souls abhor,
And hold a *synod* in thine heart,
    I'll never love thee more.

As Alexander I will reign,
    And I will reign alone;
My thoughts did evermore disdain
    A rival on my throne.
He either fears his fate too much,
    Or his deserts are small,
That dares not put it to the touch,
    To gain or lose it all.

But I will reign and govern still,
    And always give the law,
And have each subject at my will,
    And all to stand in awe;
But 'gainst my batteries if I find
    Thou kick, or vex me sore,
As that thou sett'st me up a blind.
    I'll never love thee more.

And in the empire of thine heart,
    Where I should solely be,
If others do pretend a part,
    Or dare to vie with me,
Or if *committees* thou erect,
    And go on such a score,
I'll laugh and sing at thy neglect,
    And never love thee more.

But if thou wilt prove faithful then,
    And constant of thy word,
I'll make thee glorious by my pen
    And famous by my sword;
I'll serve thee in such noble ways
    Was never heard before;
I'll crown and deck thee all with bays,
    And love thee more and more.

MY OWN SHALL COME TO ME

This very haunting poem is by John Burroughs (1837–1921), an American, best known for his charming descriptions of Nature, especially of bird life. The central idea of the poem is that our lives are ordained for us, and we fulfil a destiny, which we should accept calmly. Though we cannot know what it is, we can have the will to make it noble.

Serene, I fold my hands and wait,
    Nor care for wind, nor tide, nor sea;
I rave no more 'gainst time or fate,
    For lo! my own shall come to me.

I stay my haste, I make delays,
    For what avails this eager pace?
I stand amid the eternal ways,
    And what is mine shall know my face.

Asleep, awake, by night or day,
    The friends I seek are seeking me;
No wind can drive my bark astray,
    Nor change the tide of destiny.

What matter if I stand alone?
    I wait with joy the coming years;
My heart shall reap when it has sown,
    And gather up its fruit of tears.

The stars come nightly to the sky;
    The tidal wave comes to the sea;
Nor time, nor space, nor deep, nor high,
    Can keep my own away from me.

THE FLOWERS

From 1823 to 1882 lived William Brighty Rands, an essayist and a very charming poet, many of his pieces being written for children. His poems always have a thought or a feeling in them that is very wise and good. The thought in this poem is that Greed and Love cannot exist together, and all the beauty of the world is linked with love.

When Love arose in heart and deed
    To wake the world to greater joy,
" What can she give me now? " said Greed,
    Who thought to win some costly toy.

He rose, he ran, he stooped, he clutched;
    And soon the flowers that Love let fall
In Greed's hot grasp were frayed and smutched,
    And Greed said, " Flowers! Can this be all? "

He flung them down and went his way,
    He cared no jot for thyme or rose;
But boys and girls came out to play,
    And some took these and some took those—

Red, blue, and white, and green and gold;
    And at their touch the dew returned,
And all the bloom a thousandfold;
    So red, so ripe, the roses burned!

LITTLE BO-PEEP HAS LOST HER SHEEP

Lit-tle Bo-peep, she lost her sheep, And did-n't know where to find them,

Leave them a-lone, and they'll come home, And car-ry their tails be - hind them.

Little Bo-peep fell fast asleep,
  And dreamt she heard them bleating;
When she awoke, 'twas all a joke,
  For they were still a-fleeting.

Then up she took her little crook,
  Determined for to find them;
She found them indeed, but it made her heart
    bleed,
  For they'd left their tails behind them.

It happened one day, as Bo-peep did stray
  Into a meadow hard by,
There she espied their tails side by side,
  All hung on a tree to dry.

She heaved a sigh and wiped her eye,
  Then went o'er hill and dale,
And tried what she could, as a shepherdess
    should,
  To tack to each sheep its tail.

LITTLE VERSES FOR VERY LITTLE PEOPLE

M. N. O.

M. N. O. Our Pussy's in the snow!
When she comes back the way
she's gone
She'll have such queer white stockings on.
O Jeremy, Jeremy, Jo, Jo, Jo!

A. B. C. Our Pussy's up the tree!
And now begins with sneeze and cough
To lick her long white stockings off.
No more she'll go into the snow.
Not she, not she, not she!

A WILD FLOWER ALPHABET

A for the Aconite, first of the year,
With its pretty green ruff and its
message of cheer.

B for the Buttercup, able to hold
Dewdrop and rain in its chalice of
gold.

C for the Cowslip, sweet joy of the
spring;
When cowslips are blooming the
nightingales sing.

D for the Daisy, white star of the grass,
Lifting its bright eye to us as we pass.

E for the Eglantine, lovely wild rose,
Sheds fragrance of sweetbriar wherever it grows.

F for the Foxglove, the sentinel tall,
Guarding the forest from summer to
fall.

G for the Gorse of rich golden delight;
Linnaeus went down on his knees
at the sight.

H for the Harebell, so fragile, yet
strong,
The dear little Blue Bells of Scotland
in song.

I for the Iris which grows by the stream,
The Flower of the Rainbow, how
golden its gleam!

J for St. John's Wort, of medical fame,
Balm of the Warrior's Wound was its
name.

K for the Kingcup that loves marshy
fields,
And glorious the harvest of gold that
it yields!

L for the Ling, the dear flower of the
heath,
How tender its colour, how fragrant
its breath!

M for the Meadowsweet, pleasant and
rare
Is the perfume with which it en-
chanteth the air!

N for the Nightshade, or Bittersweet,
flower,
With its berries and blossoms of
poisonous power.

O for the Oxlip, a flower that you'll
find
When cowslips and orchids in posies
you bind.

P for the Primrose, recalling to sight
Paths in the woodlands a-shimmer
with light.

Q for the Quaking grass, name that it
takes
From the way it unceasingly shivers
and shakes.

R for the Rest-harrow, staying the
plough,
Food for the gentle-eyed, ruminant
cow.

S for the Speedwell, of tenderest blue;
From the skies it has taken its exquisite hue.

T for the Traveller's Joy that you'll
find
Where sweet, sheltering hedgerows
wander and wind.

U for the Upright Sea-lavender flower ;
The sand-swallows claim it for
sheltering bower.

V for the Violet, flower of the soul,
Heart's-ease of Paradise, making us
whole.

W for Windflower, so fair to the sight,
That throws o'er the woodlands her
mantle of light.

X forms a cross in the Passion-flower
wild
In Southern America, balmy and
mild.

Y for the Yarrow, all wayfarers know,
As it grows by the wayside wherever
you go.

Z is the ribbon this posy to bind,
With the thoughts and the fragrance
it brings to your mind.

Imperishable Thoughts of Men Enshrined in the Books of the World

Tacitus   Pliny the Elder   Terence   Cicero   Horace

Livy   Sallust   Ovid   Cato   Virgil

THE LITERATURE OF ROME

THE poetry and the tales of the Roman people have a much more romantic beginning than a Latin Primer would lead a schoolboy to suspect.

Before there was any such bothering thing as Grammar, and before there was any such wonderful invention as Writing, the dark-haired and olive-skinned people of Italy worshipped their gods with song and dance, and celebrated their festivals with literary compositions offered to the nymphs and fauns whom they believed to haunt their streams and woods.

Little is known of these primitive utterances of the Latin race. The lullabies sung by the mother to her child, the charms uttered by the wise man for the preservation of the flock or the prosperity of the harvest, the homely maxims of the husbandman, the old proverbs handed down by the patriarchal grandfather to his children's children, the dirges wailed at funerals by hired mourning women, and the songs sung by the leaping priests of Mars as they thrashed the shields of the god with a sort of drumstick—of these interesting things only a few scraps are now to be traced even by the most industrious scholars; but these things are the roots of Latin literature.

We know that one of the proverbs ran, " Be first to be silent, last to speak ";

that the deity was addressed in the form, " Lord of Light, when thou thunderest, all men hear and tremble because of thee "; that a Saturnian verse declared every man to be the architect of his own fortunes; and that the comedies performed with masks had always four characters, a Fool, a Braggart, a Dotard, and a Rogue.

Why is the traditional literature of the Romans so scanty? The answer is that Italy lay for centuries under the terrible scourge of civil war, and that when, after five centuries of tremendous struggle, the city of Rome acquired the mastery of the country, the childish utterances of the Latin soul had long since been stifled. Greek culture had its origin six hundred years before the birth of Jesus. It was not until the beginning of the third century B.C. that an almost barbarous Rome was able to give peace to an almost savage Italy.

The Greeks had long ago established colonies in the south of Italy, and they had given their alphabet to the Romans. When Pythagoras established his monastery in Italy, over 500 years B.C., the city of his choice, Crotona, " far surpassed any city in the mother country in literature, opulence, and refinement." We may easily imagine, then, how the shabby, little, barbarous Rome of those days would

ROMANCE · HISTORIES · DRAMAS · ESSAYS · WORLD CLASSICS

be conscious of intellectual shortcomings directly she came into full contact with the literature of Greece—the poems of Homer, the philosophy of Plato and Aristotle, the history of Thucydides, and the immortal tragedies of Aeschylus.

So we find that the historical beginnings of Roman literature are Greek, and nothing but Greek. At the capture of Tarentum in 272 B.C. a Greek named Andronicus was captured and brought to Rome, where he was sold as a slave to a nobleman named Livius. In the household of this powerful Roman, Latin literature had its true beginning.

Andronicus acted as a tutor to the children of Livius. He needed a text-book for his lessons, and so translated a part of Homer's Odyssey into Latin. On gaining his freedom he called himself Livius Andronicus and became first a schoolmaster, and then, like Shakespeare, an actor, a stage manager, and a play-wright. His plays were rough translations of Greek tragedies and comedies.

THE TROUBLED LIFE OF THE FIRST TRUE LATIN AUTHOR

The first of true Latin authors was a Roman citizen who had fought in the wars against Carthage; his name was Naevius. His tragedies and comedies were translations from the Greek. They were better than the work of Andronicus, and were chiefly comedies. But the life of Naevius, like that of most pioneers, was one of trouble and even of tragedy. By one of his gibes he aroused the wrath of a powerful family in Rome, and was flung into prison; and for indulging too freely in satire on his release he was sent into exile. He deserved a statue in every Roman city, for he turned for inspiration from Greek literature to the deeds of his own countrymen, and gave to the Romans their first epic poem, *Bellum Punicum*. His subject was the great war with Carthage, and in this epic he goes back to the traditional origin of Rome. His picture of Aeneas inspired Virgil to write the greatest work in the Latin tongue.

After Naevius came Ennius, who said he had three hearts, because he could speak Greek, Oscan, and Latin. He, too, was a soldier, and fought in the second Punic war. In 204 B.C. Cato found him soldiering in Sardinia, and persuaded him to come to Rome, where he set up as a schoolmaster and playwright. From this time till his death in 169 B.C. Ennius was one of the most industrious of writers. He said " I never write poetry unless I have got the gout " ; yet he wrote a great deal of verse, as well as translations, epigrams, satires, and Roman historic dramas. The greatest of all his works is his *Annals*, an epic on the history of Rome from the fabulous days of Aeneas down to his own times.

THE WRITER WHO WAS EVER AT THE SERVICE OF THE MANLY VIRTUES

Something of the Roman spirit may be seen in his words:

Broad-based upon her ancient ways and men
Standeth the Roman State.

The reference to *men* in these lines is characteristic of Ennius, who dearly loved a hero and ever held his three hearts at the service of manly virtues. He described Curius as one " whom none with steel might overcome, nor gold "; and of Fabius, the crafty general whose wise tactics made him hateful to nervous and impatient politicians, he says:

One man for us by waiting saved the State.
Nought for men's talk he cared, for safety much.

Alive at the same time as Ennius, T. Maccius Plautus was no less industrious as an author, but as an author of comedy. A famous Latin scholar, Marcus Dimsdale, thus summarises his life:

Born about 254 B.C. at Sarsina, in Umbria, he came to Rome, where he occupied himself as an actor or a stage carpenter. With the savings thus acquired he engaged in foreign trade, lost them again, and returned to Rome in poverty.

To such straits was he reduced that he was obliged to take service with a baker and work in a flour-mill. While in this position he began to write plays, encouraged, perhaps, thereto, by his former connection with the stage.

By these means he seems to have recovered his position, and continued to write till his death in 184 B.C.

A ROMAN WITH SOMETHING LIKE THE GENIUS OF CHARLES DICKENS

Such was the life of the great comic writer whose book lay under the pillow of St. Jerome and was often in the hands of Martin Luther. He wrote in the Greek spirit, he cheerfully speaks of his countrymen as barbarians, and the scene is almost always in the Athens of long ago. But not for these things is Plautus famous. His charm lies in a genial attitude towards the stupidities of mankind, a keen eye for its absurdities, and a mind which has something of Charles Dickens's genius for hitting off character in a few strokes.

He was the first of Romans to produce a compact comedy with an exciting plot, and, although Horace afterwards said of him that he hurries across the stage in slippers down at heel, most scholars agree that Plautus is one of the greatest creators of Latin literature.

Next to Plautus comes Terence (195–159 B.C.), one of Julius Caesar's favourite authors. Some of his phrases have passed into the language of every nation. *Homo sum: humani nihil a me alienum puto* is a philanthropic ejaculation often to be found even in the modern newspaper; it means: " I am a man, and nothing human is beneath my notice." We often see the words, *Quot homines, tot sententiae*, meaning, " So many men, so many opinions." They occur in a play of Terence. One of the characters asks for advice. Advance, says one; Retire, says another; Deliberate, says a third; and *Quot homines, tot sententiae!* exclaims the baffled inquirer.

THE AFRICAN SLAVE WHO WAS RECEIVED INTO THE BEST ROMAN SOCIETY

Terence was not a Roman. He hailed from Africa as a slave, and became the property of a Roman senator who gave him a good education and introduced him into the best Roman society. He was handsome, scholarly, charming. He felt that Plautus was a little vulgar, and disdained to write, as Plautus did, in the language of the street. He dealt with the same rather coarse themes as Plautus, but his manner was altogether different: less boisterous, less rollicking, less slipshod. It was his boast that his plays were " pure discourse." He complains that the Romans preferred a tight-rope acrobat or a gladiator to fine literature; and he often produced plays which were a failure. On one occasion a play of his had scarcely begun when nearly the whole audience rose and made vigorously for the exits: a rumour had spread that there was a boxing match, or something of the kind, across the way.

Such an artist was Terence that success never satisfied him, and in 160 B.C. he went to Athens to study the Greeks in their own land. But for him, the end was at hand. In 159 he died, either by shipwreck on his way home, or of disease in a Greek city—nobody knows which.

From the Romans comes to us the pantomime, with columbine, harlequin, and pantaloon. The Romans called it the *mime*. Laberius is one of its chief authors. He was a knight, and scorned acting, but Julius Caesar in a vulgar mood once forced the old warrior to act with Syrus, a Syrian slave, in one of his own mimes. The proud Laberius came on the stage and in a pathetic prologue explained his humiliating position:

I, who for years past count have kept my name
Unblemished, left my house a Roman knight,
And shall return a mime! I' faith, today
I've lived a day more than I should have lived.

THE PROUD KNIGHT WHO PROPHESIED THE DOWNFALL OF CAESAR

He hit back at Caesar more than once, and in one famous line prophesied the end of that incomparable Roman:

He whom the world fears needs must fear the world.

Marcus Dimsdale, in his History of Latin Literature, gives some examples of the wit of the mime, as learned by schoolboys in the days of St. Jerome; some of them being attributed to Seneca:

Fortune's like glass, most brittle when most bright.
A remedy for all your wrongs: forget them.
I tumbled into love like a cockchafer into a basin.

Something new in Roman literature came to birth with the appearance of Lucilius in 180 B.C. A cavalry soldier under his friend, Scipio Africanus the Younger, Lucilius returned to Rome at a time of political intrigue, saw everything with a cool brain and a mind rooted in the ancient virtues, and proceeded to satirise the evils of his days. It was said of him that he " lashed the city "; but also that he

Assailed the lords and those of humbler birth,
Kind to worth only, and the friends of worth.

LUCILIUS AND HIS GOOD-HUMOURED ANSWER TO HIS FOES

He was a bachelor, a lover of horses, and on the best of terms with his slaves. When attacked, he replied that he didn't in the least mind being soundly drubbed, tossed in a blanket, plucked and singed, or even laughed at; " loss of temper," he explained, " is a crime." Later, in greater hands, satire was to be a distinguished achievement of Roman civilisation.

But a nobler thing than satire was the aristocratic mark of the Roman on the world's literature. History had been always deemed by them a matter to which gentlemen might fitly turn their hands. To write for the mob in a theatre was unworthy of a Roman, and to write poetry was beneath the dignity of a soldier. But history would be read only by the educated, and therefore a cultured Roman citizen might venture to compose historical works.

Thus we find the splendid old Cato (234–149 B.C.) taking up his pen as a part of his patriotism. He loved the old Roman virtues, and hated with all his stubborn soul the slippery character of the average Greek. Therefore, he set himself the task of keeping Greek influences at bay. " Whenever that nation gives us its literature," he said to his son, " the Roman State will be ruined."

Before he turned to history—and he is the father of Roman history—Cato had written on farming, health, and politics for the benefit of his son. Something of his mind and character may be seen in such utterances as these:

Buy not what you want, but what you must have: what you don't want is dear at a penny.

It is better to wear out than rust out.

If nothing is being done, expenditure is going on all the same.

An orator is a good man speaking.

Stick to the matter and the words will come.

HOW CATO SHOWED HIS CONTEMPT FOR THE ARROGANT ROMAN ARISTOCRATS

But the finest of his strokes was the omission of all the names of the generals from his account of the Punic wars, a stroke marked with a sly hit at the self-glorifying Roman families by his particular mention of the name and doings of the bravest elephant on the Carthaginian side. If the old man hated the Greeks, he hated the vanity and swash-buckling arrogance of the Roman aristocracy. He loved Nature, he loved the land, he loved Roman virtue. To prove his contempt for the Greeks he wrote his history in Latin, and from his days onward Roman history was composed in the language of the Romans.

An influence was now at work on Roman character more powerful than that of Greek poetry. It was the influence of Greek philosophy. All the rough eloquence of old Cato could not check the flooding in of Plato's thoughts, Aristotle's investigations, and the semi-scientific philosophy of Epicurus. Greek specula-

tion became the rage in fashionable circles, and once more the Greek school-master was abroad.

Of Lucretius, the great Roman poet-philosopher, we have read elsewhere. The British scholar John Mackail is right in saying, in his volume of Latin Literature, that Lucretius was drunk only with the majesty and glory of Nature. That was his single crime, and scholars have long since forgiven him for it.

THE CHANGE THAT CAME OVER THE POETRY OF ROME

His passion for science enabled him to compose a work which is one of the most splendid and beautiful monuments of poetic genius. Some of his phrases, such as " the serene strongholds of the wise," have comforted lonely thinkers in all ages since his day; while such lines as " the flaming ramparts of the world," and " the solemn fires of night," will never die.

But the Roman mind was beginning to tire of noble and serious poetry. " A great book," said a writer of the time, " is a great bore." The change is marked by Catullus, who was born in 84 B.C., and began by writing love lyrics. He turned away from the great religious problems of man's soul to pour out his heart in love for a Roman lady. At the end of his romance he exclaims " women's promises are writ in water," and speaks of his love as a disease ; and when the lady, repenting of her falseness, sues for his favour, he replies:

Let her not look for love of mine hereafter.

Love that once was is perished—hers the doing—

Drooping like hedgerow blossom by the plough-share touched in its passing.

ONE OF THE GREATEST MASTERS OF STYLE WHO EVER LIVED

He turned to politics, and the same " passionate simplicity " which marked his love poems mark his satires. He was one of the greatest masters of style and managers of metre who have ever lived, and Swinburne says truly that, when an English poet attempts to follow him in these fields, Catullus " makes mouths at our speech." To him it was all so easy, to others an agony of effort.

We now come to the man who " created a language which remained for sixteen centuries that of the civilised world, and used that language to create a style which nineteen centuries have not replaced, and in some respects have scarcely altered."

THE TWO POETS VIRGIL AND HORACE AT THE HOUSE OF THE ROMAN STATESMAN MAECENAS

Cicero, who lived from 106 to 43 B.C., strikes us in many ways as a disagreeable person. He loved power, and would sacrifice his principles to attain it. His brain was now at the disposal of Pompey and now of Caesar. He could thunder, but he could cringe. In some respects he was a coward, and we might almost say of him that he was a man " whom treachery could not trust." Yet he took the simple Latin prose of his day and made it the universal language of man.

THE NEW WEAPON OF THE ROMANS FOR THE CONQUEST OF THE WORLD

He thrust the Greek language out of his path as a superstition and a barbarism. So majestic was the sweep of his prose, so ordered and rounded its sonorous periods, that it filled the heavens with a new music and gave the Romans a newer and greater weapon for their conquest of the world. His favourite quotation was the Greek line that *knowledge of all that is, is the supreme delight*, and his restless soul ranged over the whole field of human inquiry, adding little or nothing to the knowledge of mankind, but giving to all knowledge a prouder expression.

The 19th-century German historian Theodor Mommsen could say of him " Only an advocate, and not a good one "; and Landor that he " sometimes wore at the bottom of his rhetorician's robe a flounce too many "; but no such sneers can do away with Cicero's triumph.

Caesar and Sallust are interesting writers, particularly Sallust, but they contributed little new to literature and need not detain us in this brief summary. We must hasten to speak of Virgil, who was living in Rome from 40 B.C. to 20 B.C. and was a trusted friend of Augustus Caesar. Latin literature was in his time at its highest glory, and in the midst of that glory he shone out as its brightest sun.

THE SHY PEASANT BOY WHO BECAME A GREAT ROMAN POET

Virgil was the child of a peasant, and was born near Mantua. His mother was a daughter of the man who employed Virgil's father, and with her money the father was able to give his son a good education. The boy went to Verona, Milan, and Rome. He was shy and delicate and spoke with a curious slowness. Public life did not attract him. He shrank from noise, crowds, and pushful ambition. With gratitude he returned to the country and wrote poetry about peasants and sweet fields. He conceived the notable idea that something in Nature resists man, and that the chief glory in human life lies in opposing the soul to Nature. The Divine in him had decided that man must rouse the slumbering globe to greater life, thereby " whetting the minds of men with care on care, suffering no realm of His in drowsy sloth to stagnate." Lucretius was a fatalist: Virgil was an evolutionist. Lucretius taught that man was helpless in the hands of Nature; Virgil that man is Nature's master. With pride he hails Italy as " the mighty motherland of harvests and of men." Man made the harvests, and the harvests made man.

When he came to write his immortal epic, The Aeneid, Virgil made his hero Aeneas no superman, no godlike hero of a saga, but the instrument of a higher power. Rome's place in the world is a part of the Divine plan. Aeneas is not merely the father of a nation but the servant of a Destiny which regards all peoples as materials for the Divine plan. And with these high thoughts goes an exquisite passion for simple human pity.

Something I know of trouble, and therefrom
Learn how to help the suffering.

HOW VIRGIL RAISED ROMAN POETRY TO THE LEVEL OF THE GREEK

He elevated poetry and he elevated mankind. In the most beautiful language, and with a strange power of making his words convey the very sounds of that which he is describing (for instance, the galloping of a horse), this shy and solitary man raised Roman poetry to the level of the Greek, and endeared himself to all the generations of mankind.

Of a wholly different temperament was his contemporary Horace, who was born in 65 B.C. and died in A.D. 8. Son of an auctioneer's clerk, who every day in childhood took him to school, he became a man of the world, the friend of the great, and one of the most popular figures in the Roman world. He was an altogether delightful man. He faithfully and gratefully loved the rich patron Maecenas, who gave him a farm and enabled him to live as a poet. He described Virgil, who had introduced him to Maecenas, as " half of my soul." He said of travellers overseas that they change their skies but not their minds; and reminded cranks that " Dame Nature, pitchforked out, will e'er return."

In one respect this easy-going, tolerant, pleasure-loving, and witty Roman was a great man. He saw, as Goethe saw long after, and Carlyle after Goethe, that self-culture is the romance of human existence, that the mind is its own heaven or hell, and that the El Dorado of every man is not across the water, but Here and Now.

'Tis here that what you want you'll find,
Here at Ulubrae, *given an even mind.*

Unlike Cicero and Virgil, Horace deliberately chose the simplest of words, the forms of the commonest speech, and addressed himself modestly and genially to the average human intelligence. Thus he could say of himself that he had " reared a monument more enduring than brass." Simple, true-hearted, and kindly people will always love him.

In this same Augustan age lived Ovid, from 43 B.C. to A.D. 17. An aristocratic and witty observer of the human comedy, he offended Augustus, and died in exile. Some of his verse was considered to have an immoral tendency, and his banishment is said to have been due to this fact. But much of his work was of solid value : he had a serious turn, and could say with truth:

A god within our bosom dwells
And when he stirs we burn.

THE FAMOUS POEM OF OVID THAT INSPIRED WILLIAM SHAKESPEARE

But his chief interest for us is his influence on art. Everybody read and loved his fabulous tales of ancient days. " The gods whose figures sprawl across the ceilings of Italian palaces, or whose merry adventures have been stitched into the tapestries of Gobelins and Arras, are Ovid's gods," says Marcus Dimsdale; and in saying it he reminds us that Ovid's famous mythological poem Metamorphoses inspired Boccaccio and Ariosto, Chaucer and Gower, and the great Shakespeare himself, with many ideas. " The sweet, witty soul of Ovid," says Francis Meres, " lives in mellifluous and honey-tongued Shakespeare."

Of Livy, who flourished between 59 B.C. and A.D. 17, we may say with Dr. Arnold that " the use of him is almost that of the drunken helot: it shows what history should not be." He wrote history with a moral purpose, took what suited that purpose, made no researches, and sought to be eloquent. Nevertheless, so great is his subject, and so keen his instinct for picturesque or dramatic situations, that many will read him in all ages.

But the man himself is profoundly interesting. He wrote history, he said, to escape the sights of evil and folly which everywhere confronted him. To him the Roman Commonwealth was the greatest thing in the world, and he wrote of its order, its discipline, its strength, its simple piety, and its quiet fortitude with the passion of a poet. This history was published in parts, and had something of the success which attended Macaulay's History of England. A Spaniard travelled all the way from Cadiz merely to look on Livy, and returned without bestowing a glance on the palaces and temples of Rome. Marvellous popularity never turned his head. He believed Rome was dying, and his heart was sad.

THE WISE SAYINGS OF SENECA AND HIS REMARKABLE RISE TO POWER

In turning from Livy to Seneca we turn from the full moon of the glory of Rome to the falling twilight. Seneca was born at Cordova, but he was taken to Rome as an infant. He lived from A.D. 3 to 65, and was always a strange character. At one time a vegetarian, slovenly in his dress, and an ascetic, he rose to great power, amassed three millions of money, became Nero's tutor, crawled before emperors, and was sentenced to death for conspiracy. Some of his sayings are admirable:

He most of all possesses riches who least needs them.

Contemplation is a kind of action.

We ought to choose some good man, and always fix him before our gaze, and live as if he were always beholding us.

I am wont to pass into the camps of other folk, not as a deserter, but as an explorer.

HOW PLINY THE ELDER WENT OUT IN A BOAT TO HIS DOOM

The Elder Pliny, who was one of the victims of the destruction of Pompeii, was a historian and a voluminous writer on natural history. His early writings on the wars between the Romans and the Germans were used by Tacitus, whose works, more trenchant in style, superseded those of Pliny. Pliny's 37 books of natural history were a survey of both Nature and Art as they appealed to the Romans.

The Younger Pliny was with the historian when the eruption occurred, and both were in safety; but the historian's intense curiosity led him to cross in a boat to the neighbourhood of Castellamare, to study the eruption from a nearer point of view, and he was overwhelmed in the rain of débris from the crater. The nephew stayed behind, making extracts from a book of Livy. These details are given as part of a letter to the historian Tacitus, graphically describing the eruption.

THE BOOKS OF PLINY THE YOUNGER THAT TELL US OF OLD ROME

The Younger Pliny is now known to us through his nine books of charming Letters, describing in detail the life of a cultured Roman gentleman, and by his Correspondence with Trajan, in which he discusses the persecution of the early Christians. Pliny the Younger served in public offices under Domitian, Nerva, and Trajan, and towards the close of his life was the Governor of Bithynia. After his death a marble tablet was placed in the public baths of his birthplace, Como. Afterwards it was broken into six square pieces, and four of them were built into a tomb in Milan. Only one of these fragments still exists, but the full inscription is known through ancient transcripts. The Younger Pliny's Letters are among the most readable of the books that have come to us from the eighty years that followed the rise of Christianity.

At Martial we can only glance by quoting one or two of his sayings:

There is only one way to replenish my coffers,
I must e'en sell the presents you gave me. What offers?

You honour, Vacerra, the ancients alone,
And never praise poets unless dead and gone;
Your pardon, if unceremonious I seem,
But it is not worth dying to gain your esteem.

With all thy heart embrace thy lot,
Wish not for death, and fear it not.

Most beautiful of all his utterances is the epitaph on a child who died at six years old:

> Rest on her lightly, O Earth;
> Lightly she rested on thee.

FAMILIAR PHRASES THAT HAVE COME DOWN TO US FROM TACITUS

Tacitus, born in A.D. 55 or 56, is one of the great historians. He cared little for form. With him thought was always the first and overwhelming consideration. He sought brevity only that the thought might strike more quickly home. " Wrong a man and you will hate him " is a typical specimen of his thought and his style. Our paradoxical phrase " conspicuous by his absence " may be traced to Tacitus, who also gave us another familiar phrase in " the sinews of war."

This summary must end with Juvenal. It is a suitable end, for Rome is now visibly perishing. Wealth and ostentation, gluttony and drunkenness, superstition and depravity, were preying on the Roman body, which was now almost a corpse, and would not be recognised by Cato any longer as Roman. It was a terrible Rome, in which the poisoning of husbands by their wives was a matter of everyday occurrence. All the old aristocratic notions of duty and simplicity were dead. All the principles of manful self-reliance in the people were trodden underfoot.

Juvenal was no saint, and no great patriot. He was a middle-class man with strong feelings and a contempt for weakness, as well as for vice. But he saw that the change which had come over the population of Rome was perilous and contemptible. He raised no finger to alter this state of things, but wrote fierce and acrid satires to relieve his feelings and amuse his hours. " True are the tears for loss of money shed " is an example of his cynical wit. " No man ever became a villain suddenly " is an example of his clear-sighted moral power.

THE ROMAN SPIRIT AS A BRIDGE FOR THE GREAT SOUL OF PLATO

Most people know of his phrase *Mens sana in corpore sano*, or A sound mind in a sound body. He was not a great man, but he used his skill with terrific energy " to lash the city," and to make wealth look as ridiculous as poverty always makes the poor man look in the eyes of the rich.

When Vespasian died he uttered a jest. " Alack! " he exclaimed. " I fancy I am turning into a god." The truth is, perhaps, that old Cato was right, and that Greek culture was too fine and exquisite a thing to find a resting-place in the tough and rather coarse Roman body. The last days of Rome witnessed unbelievable cruelties and horrors, and to be witty was the chief end of those whose duty it was to guard the soul of civilisation.

Striking is it for us to reflect on the fact that Marcus Aurelius wrote his pretty thoughts and his engaging moralisings, not in the manful Latin language of Cato and Tacitus, but in Greek. The Roman spirit was dead. It had served its purpose as a bridge over which the soul of Plato could pass westward across the world with the sublime ethics of Jesus, to create a new civilisation among the barbarians.

The Story of the Most Beautiful Book in the World

I am the true vine and my Father is the husbandman

CHRIST'S FAREWELL TO HIS DISCIPLES

These words are from the farewell of Jesus to his disciples. They were spoken a little while before Judas betrayed him and the soldiers took him. He leaves in the keeping of his little band of followers his last commandment to the world, that they shall love one another. They are to seek the Spirit of Truth, and to love all men. Though the world will persecute them and hate them, they are to have peace and be of good cheer, for they will overcome, as he did.

I AM the true vine, and my Father is the husbandman. Every branch in me that beareth not fruit He taketh away, and every branch that beareth fruit He purgeth it, that it may bring forth more fruit.

Abide in me, and I in you. As the branch cannot bear fruit of itself, except it abide in the vine, no more can ye, except ye abide in me. I am the vine; ye are the branches. He that abideth in me, and I in him, the same bringeth forth much fruit, for without me ye can do nothing.

If a man abide not in me, he is cast forth as a branch, and is withered; and men gather them, and cast them into the fire, and they are burned. If ye abide in me, and my words abide in you, ye shall ask what ye will, and it shall be done unto you. Herein is my Father glorified, that ye bear much fruit; so shall ye be my disciples.

As the Father hath loved me, so have I loved you; continue ye in my love. If ye keep my commandments, ye shall abide in my love, even as I have kept my Father's commandments, and abide in His love. These things have I spoken unto you that my joy might remain in you, and that your joy might be full. This is my commandment: that ye love one another, as I have loved you.

Greater love hath no man than this, that a man lay down his life for his friends.

Ye are my friends if ye do whatsoever I command you. Henceforth I call you not servants, for the servant knoweth not what his lord doeth; but I have called you friends, for all things that I have heard of my Father I have made known unto you. Ye have not chosen me, but I have chosen you, and ordained you, that ye should go and bring forth fruit, and that your fruit should remain, that whatsoever ye shall ask of the Father in my name He may give it you.

These things I command you, that ye love one another.

If the world hate you, ye know that it hated me before it hated you. If ye were of the world, the world would love his own; but because ye are not of the world, but I have chosen you out of the world, therefore the world hateth you.

GREAT FIGURES OF THE OLD TESTAMENT · THE LIFE OF JESUS

Remember the word that I said unto you: The servant is not greater than his lord. If they have persecuted me, they will also persecute you; if they have kept my saying, they will keep yours also.

But all these things will they do unto you for my name's sake, because they know not Him that sent me.

But when the Comforter is come, whom I will send unto you from the Father, even the Spirit of Truth, which proceedeth from the Father, he shall testify of me. And ye also shall bear witness, because ye have been with me from the beginning.

These things have I spoken unto you that ye should not be offended. They shall put you out of the synagogues; yea, the time cometh that whosoever killeth you will think that he doeth God service. And these things will they do unto you, because they have not known the Father, nor me.

But these things have I told you that, when the time shall come, ye may remember that I told you of them; and these things I said not unto you at the beginning because I was with you. But now I go my way to Him that sent me, and none of you asketh me, Whither goest thou?

But because I have said these things unto you, sorrow hath filled your heart.

Nevertheless, I tell you the truth. It is expedient for you that I go away, for if I go not away, the Comforter will not come unto you; but if I depart, I will send him unto you. And when he is come, he will reprove the world of sin, and of righteousness, and of judgment: of sin, because they believe not on me; of righteousness, because I go to my Father and ye see me no more; of judgment, because the Prince of this world is judged.

I have yet many things to say unto you, but ye cannot bear them now. Howbeit, when he, the Spirit of Truth, is come, he will guide you unto all truth, for he shall not speak of himself; but whatsoever he shall hear, that shall he speak, and he will show you things to come. A little while, and ye shall not see me; and again a little while and ye shall see me, because I go to the Father.

Your sorrow shall be turned into joy.

Your heart shall rejoice, and your joy no man taketh from you.

Behold, the hour cometh, yea, is now come, that ye shall be scattered, every man to his own, and shall leave me alone; and yet I am not alone, because the Father is with me. These things I have spoken unto you that in me ye might have peace.

In the world ye shall have tribulation, but be of good cheer: I have overcome the world.

THE LAST SAYINGS OF JESUS

LITTLE children, yet a little while I am with you.

A new commandment I give unto you, That ye love one another; as I have loved you, that ye also love one another.

Whither I go thou canst not follow me now, but thou shalt follow me afterwards.

Let not your heart be troubled: ye believe in God, believe also in me. In my Father's house are many mansions; if it were not so I would have told you. I go to prepare a place for you.

And if I go and prepare a place for you, I will come again and receive you unto myself, that where I am, there ye may be also. And whither I go ye know, and the way ye know. I am the way, the truth, and the life: no man cometh unto the Father but by me.

If ye shall ask any thing in my name, I will do it.

If ye love me, keep my commandments;

and I will pray the Father, and He shall give you another Comforter, that he may abide with you for ever—even the Spirit of Truth, whom the world cannot receive because it seeth him not, neither knoweth him: but ye know him, for he dwelleth with you, and shall be in you.

I will not leave you comfortless: I will come to you. Yet a little while and the world seeth me no more; but ye see me; because I live, ye shall live also.

Take heed that no man deceive you, for many shall come in my name, saying, I am Christ, and shall deceive many. And ye shall hear of wars and rumours of wars.

See that ye be not troubled, for all these things must come to pass, but the end is not yet. For nation shall rise against nation, and kingdom against kingdom; and there shall be famines and pestilences and earthquakes in divers places: all these are the beginning of sorrows.

COME UNTO ME ALL YE WEARY

THIS BEAUTIFUL PICTURE BY ERNST ZIMMERMANN IS FROM A PHOTOGRAPH BY HANFSTAENGL

Then they shall deliver you up to be afflicted, and shall kill you, and ye shall be hated of all nations for my name's sake.

Settle it therefore in your hearts, not to meditate before what ye shall answer; for I will give you a mouth and wisdom, which all your adversaries shall not be able to gainsay nor resist.

And there shall be signs in the sun, and in the moon, and in the stars; and upon the earth distress of nations, with perplexity; the sea and the waves roaring, men's hearts failing them for fear, and for looking after those things which are coming on the earth, for the powers of

"SUFFER THE LITTLE CHILDREN TO COME UNTO ME" BY PAUL FLANDRIN

And ye shall be betrayed both by parents and brethren, and kinsfolk and friends; and some of you shall they cause to be put to death; and ye shall be hated of all men for my name's sake.

But there shall not a hair of your head perish. In your patience possess ye your souls.

heaven shall be shaken. And then shall they see the Son of Man coming in a cloud, with power and great glory.

And when these things begin to come to pass, then look up, and lift up your heads, for your redemption draweth nigh. Heaven and earth shall pass away, but my words shall not pass away.

(Next chapter in this group, page 5557)

The Interests and Pleasures of Life for All Indoors and Out

IDEAS FOR FANCY DRESS

ALL boys and girls enjoy dressing up and living the part of someone they admire in fact or fiction. Good costume patterns can be bought, but the real fun of fancy dress lies in improvising it ourselves from whatever we can get. Here are some ideas to help us. Except Red Riding Hood they can all be adapted for any age, and can be simple or elaborate, just as our materials allow.

The kind of things we should collect are old net or lace curtains for frocks and trains like those for the Little Princess ; old table-cloths and sheets which will dye well—Red Riding Hood's cape could be made in this way; odd lengths of ribbon, feathers, and flowers for trimming; beads and fancy buttons for jewels; and old hats.

Mother would lend all the clothes for the Old Balloon Woman, who might easily be converted into a Flower Seller by substituting for the balloons a basket of flowers—real if plentiful in the garden, or made from paper (see page 5813). The boy's counterpart is a Street Trader. He would wear an old suit with a scarf and cap, and slung around his neck a cardboard or wooden tray of toys.

Another easy idea for a boy is the Scare-crow, for which any old garments will do. Realistic touches are given by the wisps of straw fastened inside the brim of the hat and the stick through the sleeves for arms, the real arms being inside the coat—this only being necessary while taking part in a fancy dress parade. A pipe could be put in his mouth.

Pyjamas trimmed with fancy braid make a Red Indian suit for a small boy. An older one should also have slung across his shoulders an old blanket decorated with wool em-broidery, or strange signs cut out in coloured felts and stuck on.

For the headdress, a canvas band, two to two and a half inches wide, is cut to fit the head, allowing an overlap, and the feathers are fastened to this, if sufficient, in three graduated rows. Dull feathers should be painted with brightly coloured inks. Braid streamers are fastened each side, and the quills of the feathers and the canvas band are then covered with a strip of bead-embroidered soft leather or braid before being joined at the back. Crêpe-paper—three semicircles (with a slight bulge at the peak of the circle to get the effect of the centre feathers), each of a different colour and size—can be used instead. The curved edges could be fluted between finger and thumb to represent feather tips, the straight edges are stuck to the band.

The Princess's crown is even simpler to make. The shape should be cut out in pliable cardboard covered in gold paper and decorated with pearls and beads. But simplest of all is the Pirate's cap—a bright handkerchief or scarf with two large curtain rings sewn either side for earrings.

Swords and daggers can be cut from cardboard and covered with silver paper or painted. Gold paint can be used with effect, too, and cake frills and d'oyleys of gold and silver paper make excellent lace.

CRAFTS · GAMES · NEEDLEWORK · PUZZLES · SCIENCE EXPERIMENTS

THE COIN IN THE HANDKERCHIEF

THIS is an easy, completely deceptive trick, which may be exhibited offhand, with any penny, and with any handkerchief. Its only drawback is that the necessary movements are difficult to explain in writing.

The performer begins by borrowing a penny and a handkerchief. He may also ask for the loan of a short piece of string, though he should have a piece handy in case none is forthcoming.

Taking the penny in his left hand, and holding it upright between the forefinger and thumb, he throws the handkerchief over it, letting the four corners hang down around it. "Let us settle it comfortably," he remarks. So saying, he nips the coin through the handkerchief, between the first and second fingers of the right hand, held *palm upward* as shown in the picture, and tilts it over toward the left.

The finger and thumb of the left hand release the coin for a moment, and nip it again by its opposite edge, through the handkerchief. The upright hand is then removed.

"Now," says the performer, "you would hardly suppose that this simple movement has already caused the coin to vanish? You wouldn't? You are quite right, for here it is still." To prove it he lifts with the right hand the hanging portion of the handkerchief and shows the coin. "Once more we will cover it over."

HOW TO HOLD THE PENNY

He lets the handkerchief fall around it on all sides. "To make the coin still safer," he says, "I will ask somebody to tie this piece of string round the handkerchief." This is done at a distance of about six inches from the coin. "And now," he continues, "I want the assistance of a strong man."

Someone having volunteered, he says: "Now, sir, I want you to take hold of this handkerchief"—he gives him the hanging portion—"and hold it as tightly as you can. Now you and I will have a little tug-of-war, but in a new way. I am going to try whether I can pull the penny right through the handkerchief. It is not gone yet, you see." He shows the shape of the penny through the handkerchief. "Now pull as hard as you like! One, two, three!" He himself pretends to pull with all his might, and finally lets go the handkerchief with a sudden jerk, the penny remaining in his hand.

The secret lies in the fact that by exactly following the instructions which, if followed closely, will be found in practice perfectly simple, complicated as they may look in print, the coin is left, after it has been shown for the second time and the handkerchief let fall around it, in an outside fold, whence, under the pretence of pulling, it is worked out into the palm of the hand.

Proficiency in this and similar simple coin tricks is a great asset to the young wizard.

ANSWERS TO THE RAILWAY PUZZLE ON PAGE 5310

HERE is a list of the mistakes the artist made in his drawing of a railway terminus:

1. Behind the engine is a tube train coach, while the rest of the train is one long coach.

2. The engine has no coal tender and no windows.

3. The engine has four wheels, but only two wheel cases.

4. The stationary coach has a funnel with steam clouds coming from it.

5. The ticket collector is in military uniform.

6. The numerals on the clock are only 1 to 8, and are reversed on the two faces; the two sets of hands are reversed, and the clock is hanging in mid-air.

7. The Dover-Calais poster shows the famous Forth Bridge, Scotland, while the local services poster shows world routes.

8. The buffet is a sham.

9. The waiting passenger is sitting on an ordinary chair.

10. There are no safety buffers to the railway lines on the left of the platform.

11. The stairs to the Underground go up.

12. The porter's trolley has flanged wheels.

13. The nurse is wheeling the baby in a shopping basket.

14. The Booking Office sign reads Parcels Office, and is too low; it would knock people's hats off.

15. The Information Bureau is a restaurant, and has a brick roof.

16. The sign, To the Trains, is pointing in the wrong direction.

17. Heavy masonry should not be over an open shop front.

18. The bookstall is marked Pastrycooks.

19. The suitcase in the foreground has no lid.

ANSWER TO THE PUZZLE OF THE SIAMESE FLAG ON PAGE 5314—Phyllis cut out one four-sided piece and sewed it in again upside down, as the picture shows.

TELLING THE TIME BY THE CLOCK

THE face of a clock is divided into 12 clear wide spaces and 60 narrow ones. It takes the long hand 5 minutes to cross one wide space, and the short hand one hour to cross the same space.

A minute is 60 seconds, and an hour is 60 minutes. The clock begins with the minutes, and the face of the clock is marked off with tiny lines into 60 narrow spaces. The large hand marks the minutes, and takes exactly one minute to cross one of these narrow

| One o'clock | Five minutes past One | Ten minutes past One | Quarter past One | Twenty minutes past One | Twenty-five minutes past One |

| Half-past One | Twenty-five minutes to Two | Twenty minutes to Two | Quarter to Two | Ten minutes to Two | Five minutes to Two |

spaces. So that this hand takes exactly one hour, or 60 minutes, to pass all the narrow spaces round the clock,

But it would never do to have 60 small spaces leaving us to guess the exact space which the long hand touched. So the wise clockmakers mark off 60 narrow spaces into 12 divisions, each division having 5 narrow spaces. It takes the long hand 5 minutes to cross one of these divisions, 10 minutes to cross two of them, and 60 minutes, or 12 times 5, to cross them all. When the long hand has crossed all these divisions, therefore, we know that 60 minutes, or one hour, has gone.

If we had only to think of minutes, that would be quite enough; but as we reckon time in hours and days, and as there are 24 hours in a day, we must have some means of counting hours, as well as minutes, by the clock.

We do not count 24 hours, but only 12, because twice 12 are 24, and it is simple to count 12 hours before the middle of the day, and 12 after. The clock, therefore, has 12 hours marked, and goes round from 1 to 12, when it begins again. We call the first part of the day A.M., which means *before noon*, and the second part P.M., which means *after noon*.

As the clock needs 12 signs to mark the hours, the figures from 1 to 12 are used to mark off the 12 divisions, and also to mark the 12 hours. While the long hand marks the minutes at the narrow spaces, the short hand marks the hours at the 12 big figures between the spaces.

Let us see how this works. We set the clock, let us say, at 1 o'clock, with the long hand at 12 and the short hand at 1. In 5 minutes the long hand has crossed the first space, and is opposite the big figure 1. That is 5 minutes past 1. In 10 minutes the long hand has crossed the second space, and is opposite the second big figure, which is 2. That is 10 minutes past 1. So the long hand creeps round, in the way shown in the first group of clock faces here.

All this time, of course, the short hand of the clock is moving also, very slowly, and by the time the long hand has gone right round to 12 again, the short hand has travelled to the big figure 2, and it is therefore 2 o'clock. When the long hand has gone right round twice, the short hand has crossed 2 divisions, and points to the big figure 3; and it is therefore 3 o'clock.

Remember that the big figures mark the hours only, not the minutes, so that when the long hand points to the big figure 2 we must not think it is 2 minutes past something. It is *two spaces past*—that is, 2 times 5 minutes. We only count the big 2 as 2 when the short hand points to it.

An exact hour is marked when the long hand is at the beginning of its round, on 12, and the short hand points to a big figure, as shown in the second group of clock faces.

When the long hand is on the right side of the circle, we say that it is so many minutes *past* the hour. But when the long hand begins to go up the left side, we say it is so many minutes *to* the next hour. We can say that it is 40 minutes past 2; but it is much

| Twelve o'clock | One o'clock | Two o'clock | Three o'clock | Four o'clock | Five o'clock |

| Six o'clock | Seven o'clock | Eight o'clock | Nine o'clock | Ten o'clock | Eleven o'clock |

easier to say that it is 20 minutes to 3, and both these mean quite the same.

For the first half-hour we read forward, for the second half-hour we read backward.

The clocks shown have ordinary (Arabic) figures, but many clocks are marked with Roman numerals. Here is a table of these from 1 to 12 : I = 1, II = 2, III = 3, IIII (or IV) = 4, V = 5, VI = 6, VII = 7, VIII = 8, IX = 9, X = 10, XI = 11, XII = 12.

DARTS—THE GAME OF MILLIONS

DARTS, traditionally the game for plough-man and shepherd, and probably regarded at one time as a form of indoor archery, has now captured the imagination of millions. Every social club, every works or Service canteen, has its dart board, and the game requires so little equipment that it has found its place in a host of homes.

Yet it is not an easy game to play. A keen eye is a first requirement. You should also have a faculty for figures, as will be shown when the method of scoring is explained. And you should master the art of the throw. A dart should not be jerked from the hand. The forearm should be rocked in an easy pendulum movement from the elbow to give grace and direction to your effort.

Most of you are familiar with a dart board. It is circular and divided into twenty numbered segments, radiating from a double bullseye, as shown in the illustration. If you place your dart in the inner bull you score 50 ; in the outer bull 25. Moving from the centre, you will see what is known as the treble ring. If you place your dart in this you score three times the value of the number of the segment concerned. Finally, there is the outer ring, known as the double ring, where your darts are awarded twice the value of the particular number.

The board is 18 inches in diameter. The diameter of the outer double circle is 13¼ inches and of the treble circle 8¼ inches. The width of the double and treble rings is three-eighths of an inch. The outer bull is 1¼ inches across and the inner bull half an inch. The board should be placed on the wall at a height of 5 ft. 8 ins. from bullseye to ground, and players make their throws from a distance which varies in different places between eight and nine feet.

Games can be played in straight competition between two opponents; in foursomes, where two partners engage with another two; or between teams of four. To decide who goes first it is usual for each player to throw a single dart, the honour going to the one whose dart strikes the board nearest the bull. For the game itself, each player throws three darts in turn. It is as well to have a black board on which the score can be marked in white chalk.

We will imagine that A is playing B and that they have arranged to play 301 up. The players' names or initials are chalked on the board, with the figure 301 underneath. Whatever is scored is deducted, which means that the number required to win is always

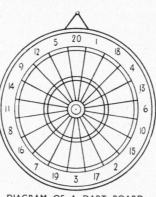

DIAGRAM OF A DART BOARD

shown. You cannot start, however, except by scoring a double. In other words, you must place your dart in any of the sections of the outer ring, or else in the centre bull (double 25).

Supposing A has now the right to first throw, we will assume that his first dart registers a single 20. This does not count. His second, however, is a double 20, which sends him away with 40. His third dart is a 5, so he is now 45. That number is subtracted from the original 301, leaving 256. B then plays and at once scores a double 1. He follows with a treble 19 and misses altogether with his third dart. B, therefore, has scored 59 and now requires 242.

So the game goes on and the exact number must be scored. The original 301 must be reduced to zero and the final throw (like the first) must be a double. This is where a faculty for figures plays its part. Foremost in your mind must be the need for an even figure. For example, you require 15 to get out. If you throw a 6 and a 4 you are left with 5 for the last dart and this cannot be obtained by a double. If you throw, say, a 7, you next require 8, which can be obtained by a double 4. You cannot get out by scoring two single fours. Nor can you get out on a treble.

If you score too many in attempting to get out, your figure remains as it was before you began the throw. Seasoned players will tell you that you cannot do better than leave yourself with 32 (double 16) to obtain. This is the only number on the board that can be split right down to 2 (double 1).

If A is first to succeed, he wins what is known as the first leg of the game. It is usual to play for the best of three when the match is between two players. When teams are engaged a leg is 1001, and the number of legs is decided beforehand, according to the length of time at the players' disposal.

There are many games you can play on a dart board; they are far too numerous to describe here. One, however, that is popular is " Round the Clock," in which the players have to score each number in its proper turn, starting with 1.

There are also many kinds of dart boards, and here it will pay you to buy one of good quality; it will last much longer than a cheap one. The bristle board, made of compressed pig bristles, is particularly durable, since the points of the darts do not destroy the surface.

The darts are of many types and weights, and are a matter of personal choice.

The Story of the Boundless Universe and All Its Wondrous Worlds

This picture illustrates the effect of heat on solid bodies. When a railway line is laid down, space is always left between the rails, as can be plainly seen, to allow for their expansion through heat.

HOW HEAT WORKS FOR US

We know that when things are hot they have power which can be used.

The most famous case of this, which set the clever boy James Watt thinking, is the case of the lid of the kettle of boiling water. The heat put into the water has the power of making the lid move. Now, if heat in the form of steam can make the lid of a kettle move, why should it not start motion in something attached to a wheel? The answer to this question is supplied by every engine driven by heat all the world over today.

On the other hand, just as heat can do work, so work can make heat. One of the old ways of lighting a fire was to rub together two pieces of dry stick, which produced heat enough to make a spark. Anyone can prove that heat is produced by work if he rubs his hand on a coat.

The work of rubbing or striking a match puts heat in it, and when it is hot enough it catches fire. In a word, the kind of motion we call heat can be turned into ordinary kinds of motion, like that of a wheel or the lid of a kettle; and ordinary mechanical motion, as it is often called, can be turned into the special motion which is called heat.

It is worth while to know the simple way in which this may be stated in scientific language. The Latin word for a mass is *moles*, and from that we get the word *molecule*, which means a little mass. Now, when a visible thing is in motion we may call it a case of *molar motion*—the motion of a mass. But heat, which is a case of the motion of the molecules of things, may be called *molecular motion*. So we may say that molar motion may be turned into molecular motion, or molecular motion into molar motion; in other words, work may be turned into heat, or heat may be turned into work.

The importance of understanding this rightly is very great. Heat and work sound very different things.

But if we think of heat as molecular motion, and of work as molar motion, it seems reasonable that one kind of motion should be turned into the other, and also that there must be an absolutely fixed amount of either kind of motion that can possibly be got from the other kind. If that be not so, some motion is being got out of nothing, or some motion is being made into nothing; and we are sure that neither of those things can happen.

What we have just been saying makes the basis of a great and important science called *thermo-dynamics*. We might translate that into " heat-force "; and this

ASTRONOMY · GEOLOGY · GEOGRAPHY · CHEMISTRY · PHYSICS · LIFE

great science deals with all the relations existing between heat and power. This science bears not only on the making and working of all machines made by men, but on the history and the future of the living and eternal machine which we call the universe, made from everlasting to everlasting by God.

A LAW THAT WAS PROVED AFTER TWO THOUSAND YEARS

The great law of the conservation of energy has been established in modern times by the study of heat and work. Before the birth of Jesus great thinkers guessed that what we now call the law of the conservation of energy must be true; but the proof of its truth had to wait until the nineteenth century, and it depends on whether the amount of work we can get from a certain amount of heat, or the amount of heat we can get from a certain amount of work, is absolutely fixed. We have begun to see why this must be as it is, because we see that, after all, what seemed to be such a mystery is only a case of changing one kind of motion into another kind, and that is the thing we see and do for ourselves every day.

There was a famous Manchester man named James Prescott Joule, who proved, about a hundred years ago, that there is a certain amount of work which can be got out of a certain amount of heat; and nowadays we use J, the first letter of his name, to mean the amount of work which can be got out of a certain known or measured amount of heat.

HOW HEAT CAN BE CHANGED INTO WORK, AND WORK INTO HEAT

Thus, we take the amount of heat which can raise the temperature of one pound of water at 60 degrees Fahrenheit up to 61 degrees Fahrenheit, and we find that that amount of heat is equal in power to raising 778 pounds through a height of one foot, or one pound through a height of 778 feet. But what the exact figure is matters nothing at all compared with the all-important fact that this relation actually does exist.

The first law of this part of science is, therefore, that between heat and work there is a constant relation; that either can be transformed into the other. But there follows a second great law which says that, though the first law is true, heat will only travel from a body that is higher in temperature to one that is lower.

The first law is another form of putting the law of the conservation of energy, but the second law says that, though energy is never lost, there are only certain conditions under which we can use it so as to get work done. The energy may be there, but it may not be available, and that is true of all heat wherever it is found, except where it can flow to something that is less hot. For practical use for doing work it is not sufficient that energy be not lost; we must be able to get at it.

Every machine that is run gets warm, and the warmth is given away to the air around it. Our bodies, which are living machines, though they are also more, are always losing heat to their surroundings, and, indeed, it is a general rule that other forms of energy, such as the chemical energy in our food or the chemical energy in the food or fuel of an engine, tend to be turned into heat, and the point is that this heat gets scattered, and cannot be used over again.

THE MACHINE THAT GIVES HEAT WHEN WE WANT IT TO GIVE WORK

Let us see how this affects the engineer. It means that when he makes and uses a machine from which he wants to get work, only part of the energy he puts in comes out as work, and much of it comes out as heat. This heat is not only useless, as a rule, but worse than useless, and much trouble is taken to ensure that the engine does not become too hot to work.

The world, as we know it, is at present living on its supply of coal, and doing so at a tremendous rate, but far less than one-tenth part of the energy contained in the coal is really used by mankind. The rest is frittered away into the air as heat, and wasted.

An ordinary fire is, perhaps, the most wasteful of all ways of transforming energy, but, at any rate, the heat produced is of some use for the time. If we look at any of the engines which are at work all over the world we find that they can all be studied from this point of view. How much of the energy put into them comes out as work, and how much is wasted as heat? We are not far wrong if we say that in many cases one-tenth of the energy is used, and nine-tenths wasted.

Anyone who could invent a machine that would turn into work all the energy put into it, or half, or one-third, or one-quarter, would soon be the richest man in the world. So important is this question, that there are, of course, everywhere men working at it. The word they use is the famous word Efficiency, and their business is to try to increase, if by only one per cent., the efficiency of the engines they are working at—that is to say, the proportion of work they do compared with the amount of useless heat they produce.

THE SECRET OF POWER IN OUR MUSCLES WHICH NO MAN CAN DISCOVER

The most efficient engine in the world is a living muscle, but the secret of its efficiency has yet to be discovered. Even a muscle, however, does not turn into work all, or even half, of the energy supplied to it; the rest is turned into heat, though this heat has to be looked at very differently from the heat produced, say, in the engine of a motor-car, for it keeps our bodies warm, and maintains them at the temperature at which we can best live. A muscle is vastly superior to any machine ever made.

But this question of the production of heat by machines, though of deep practical importance, is of vastly greater importance in another way. It is not only machines that tend to turn useful energy into heat that cannot be used *again*. All the changes of energy that we can discover seem to follow the same course.

Nearly all chemical changes produce heat, and that heat is scattered and lost. Every kind of motion, besides the motion of machines, is in some degree turned into heat by friction, and that heat is scattered and lost. And so we have to learn a new idea which goes along with the great truth of the conservation of energy, and must always be remembered together with it—that, though no energy is ever lost to the world, it may very easily be lost to us.

THE HEAT FLOWING FROM THE SUN AND FOR EVER PRODUCING WORK

We may classify energy in all its forms according to its usefulness for us, and then we discover that it is the general tendency for energy to be *degraded*—to fall in the course of its changes from a more useful to a less useful class. The general end of these changes tends to be that the energy is degraded to the lowest class of all—that of scattered heat, which we cannot use at all. An instance of energy in the highest class is furnished by the energy of the Sun—a body which is far hotter than its

surroundings. The flow of heat from this hot body to less hot bodies produces work, as the downward flow of water from a height may do work.

We have only to consider for a moment what happens to the Sun's radiations to see that, in the course of every change which the power of them undergoes in our bodies or elsewhere, a certain amount is frittered away as heat, and so this energy of the highest class is degraded to the lowest. We do not suffer, and we are not alarmed, and the reason is that there is always a fresh supply of energy coming from the Sun. But that supply, though it will last a long time, cannot be endless.

Now that we know what *the degradation of energy* means, we must learn the use of another word, first used by Lord Kelvin. He spoke of what has ever since been known as *the dissipation of energy*. When we speak of a foolish man who dissipates his fortune we mean that all his money is spent and scattered, and that is what is meant by the dissipation of energy.

WHY WE CAN NEVER GET A REALLY PERFECT MACHINE

We know that if gravitation were unopposed the whole of the matter in the universe would all be gathered together into one mighty heap. In the same way, if all the energy in the universe is steadily degraded and dissipated, taking the form of scattered heat, it will become useless.

If we had a perfect machine we should be able to work it backwards as well as forwards, turning heat into work and work into heat, and never losing anything. There is no such machine, and, according to Lord Kelvin, not even the universe itself is a perfect machine in this sense of the word, for it has a bias towards working in one direction, which is the dissipation and degradation of energy.

If the idea of the dissipation of energy is really true, and the whole truth, it means that the universe must be travelling towards a state of things in which nothing happens—a state which we might describe as the death of the universe. Its matter and energy would still be there, but they would have lost their power of doing anything. Nothing would happen, there would be no life and no motion of any kind. This idea makes us think of the universe as a great clock, made, wound up, and set going. It may run for a very long time, but it must run down at last.

Here we are faced again with the idea of a beginning and an end to the history of the universe. Thus, if we take our Solar System as a case in point, we see that, just because the heat-level is higher in the Sun than in the planets, heat flows from the Sun to the planets, and so life is possible on the Earth.

THE WINDING UP OF THE CLOCK OF THE UNIVERSE

But the spreading out and levelling of the heat in the Solar System must some day come to an end, and with it must end, not only life, but all the other processes in the Solar System which depend on this difference of heat level.

The prospect of the theory of the dissipation of energy is that the Solar System and the whole universe must at last reach a stage in which all the other forms of energy have been degraded and dissipated into heat, and that heat will be spread equally through all the matter of the universe. That would be the end of its history.

We may slightly change the words of a great student who summed up the case, as it was then thought, at the end of the nineteenth century, and who spoke as follows of the doctrine of the dissipation of energy: This remarkable property of all natural processes seems to lead us to the idea of a definite beginning and to shadow forth a possible end; the interval which contains the life or history of Nature being ccupied with the slow but inevitable running down or degradation of the great store of energy from an active to an inactive or unavailable condition.

HOW THE THOUGHTS OF HERBERT SPENCER ARE BEING JUSTIFIED TODAY

Herbert Spencer stood alone among the great thinkers of the nineteenth century in declining to accept the doctrine of the dissipation of energy. He saw too deeply into the nature of things to believe in the old ideas of beginning and ending, and he saw that the argument for the disssipation of energy was not complete. He declared that there must be other processes going on, none the less real, though not so easy to see, which were, so to speak, winding up the clock while other processes, which we could see, were tending to run it down.

Steadily, during the present century, this idea of the dissipation of energy as *completely* true has been losing credit

among those who study these matters, and the deep insight of Herbert Spencer is beginning to be justified by the discovery of processes and possibilities in the universe which lead us to believe that it is indeed a perfect and eternal machine, besides being very much more.

The more deeply we study, the more convinced we are that the real answer to this question is the same as the answer lately discovered to the question about the results of gravitation. There we find that what seems to be a process all in one direction, which must have a beginning and an end, is only half the truth; and when we learn the other half we see reason to believe that the universe can go on from everlasting to everlasting.

In the same way we are beginning to discover the processes which act in the other direction, and which will lead us to the belief, the belief of the wise of all ages, that the universe is from everlasting to everlasting.

WHY TEMPERATURE IS NOT THE AMOUNT OF HEAT IN A THING

We have now learned enough to show us how extremely important is the question of temperature, and by temperature we understand heat-level. It is difference of temperature that gives heat the power of doing work. That difference of temperature means that the heat will flow, and in flowing can be made to do things. Now, what exactly is difference of temperature? Indeed, what is temperature at all?

Our first inclination will be to answer that the temperature of a thing is the amount of heat in it, but we shall find that that is not true. It is true that if we take a given amount of a given thing, and add heat to it, it will get hotter; its temperature will rise, and the rise of temperature means in that case that there is more heat in the thing.

But even if we take a given thing, such as water, we find that to raise a given quantity of it one degree in temperature at some level in the temperature scale requires rather more or rather less heat than to raise its temperature one degree when it is much colder or much hotter to start with. Then, again, there is much more heat in a lot of cool water than there is in a very little water that is hotter, so that again we cannot say that temperature is the amount of heat in a thing. We must think of temperature as if it were like the level of water. Even a little water at a great height, falling into a large lake, has something about it which the lake has not. For instance, it will turn a wheel. Now, temperature is like the level of water, and has no more to do with the amount of heat, as such, than the mere bulk of water has to do with its power. There is something in the slender water-fall that there is not in the lake below, and that something corresponds to the height from which it falls, and enables it to do work. So the temperature of a thing may be compared to the height from which the water falls in the other case; and, other things being equal, the higher the temperature the greater is the work the thing can be made to do as it cools.

The word *thermometer* really means heat-measurer, but we are now ready to learn that, though the thermometer is called a heat-measurer, it is not a heat-measurer, but a measurer of heat-level. Think of the water falling into the lake, and we see the difference. The thermometer corresponds to an instrument telling us what height the water fell from, but nothing about the quantity of water falling. The thermometer tells us nothing about the amount of heat, but only about the heat-level.

The first thermometer was made by Galileo rather more than three hundred years ago. It was an air thermometer, a glass tube ending in a bulb. This tube was heated and then turned upside down in a vessel of water. As the air inside the bulb, which had been heated, began to cool, the water ran up the tube.

The air inside the bulb would occupy more space if it were hot and less if it were cold, and the water would run up the tube accordingly. So, by the height of the water something could be told as to

In these two pictures we see how heat affects a gas. If a balloon be half filled with air, as in the first picture, and placed in front of a fire, the air, as it gets hot, expands and fills the balloon, which will at last burst.

the temperature of the air. Now, directly we consider this we shall see, from what we have already learned, that this instrument was a barometer as well as a thermometer, for the water would partly be pushed up by the pressure of the air.

In this form the instrument was not, therefore, very useful, for no one could tell to what extent it was measuring the pressure and to what extent it was measuring the temperature of the air. What was required was to close the tube altogether after heating it, so that the atmospheric pressure should have no effect on what happened inside it. This was not done until half a century after Galileo's first great invention.

If we wish to make an ordinary thermometer we take a fine tube with a bulb at one end, and fill the bulb and part of the tube with mercury. Then we boil the mercury. This means that part of it forms a vapour, which travels up the tube and pushes away the air in front of it. While this is going on we close the end of the tube and allow the mercury to cool. A practically empty space is then left above the level of the mercury in the tube, and, if the mercury has any reason to expand or contract, it will be able to do so without difficulty in either direction.

The hotter mercury is, the more it swells and the more space it takes up; the colder it is, the smaller the space it takes up. Therefore the level of the mercury in the tube tells us how hot it is. The higher it is, the hotter it is; and the lower it is, the colder it is. This is just the opposite of Galileo's thermometer, for what happened there was that the colder the air inside the higher stood the column of water. Today's clinical thermometers record temperature exactly.

(Next chapter in this group, page 5565)

HOMES AND HAUNTS OF GOOD JOHN WESLEY

THE MARKET-PLACE AT EPWORTH
IN LINCOLNSHIRE

THE RECTORY WHERE
WESLEY WAS BORN

EPWORTH CHURCH, WHERE WESLEY'S FATHER WAS RECTOR.

WESLEY'S FIRST MEETING-HOUSE
GAINSBOROUGH

WESLEY CHAPEL
LONDON

The Story of Immortal Folk Whose Work Will Never Die

Richard Cobden speaking at the Council of the Anti-Corn Law League

GREAT CRUSADERS

Two of the most amazing impulses which have caused masses of men to move on together to do great deeds were the conquering advance of the followers of Mohammed into Christian lands and the response to the knighthood of Christendom to repel the attack, particularly the attack on the Holy Land.

Men flung themselves with a sublime enthusiasm into these wars of the Cross, which we call the Crusades. To be a Crusader meant to be absorbed, heart and soul, in a purpose that was felt to be entirely good, and to pursue it to the end. It is a spirit that always lives in the world just as truly as when East and West clashed in war for possession of the Holy Land.

That spirit of intense devotion to a cause shows itself in innumerable ways, and it accounts for the uprooting, one by one, of many of the most cruel evils which have afflicted mankind. Almost invariably it is one man who, like Peter the Hermit in starting the Crusades, sets forth to remove some obstacle to the good of mankind, and, first convincing and leaguing with a few, goes on to change the minds of many, and to achieve a notable victory.

This is how almost every good cause has been carried to a triumph, in all times and lands. It has stirred the minds of a few

and they have rallied round a crusading leader whose enthusiasm no opposition could quench.

In this chapter we give a number of widely varied instances of crusaders for fine purposes, whose doings remain as examples of how wrongs may be righted, rights may be won, and righteous causes be firmly established.

As a first example we choose a crusader whose name and fame seem to be in danger of falling out of human memory. This is Sir Samuel Romilly, the man who made it his life purpose to clear brutality out of English law.

In his day, the early part of the nineteenth century, there were more than three hundred " crimes," most of them of a trifling character, for which anyone might be hanged. If a man kept company with gypsies his punishment might be hanging. The stealing of five shillings-worth of goods from a shop would forfeit the thief's life, if the judge so decided. A soldier or sailor who begged, as he passed through the country, was liable to execution unless he had on him a pass from a magistrate or his commanding officer. Theft on a navigable river was a hanging matter. These are specimens of the offences that made the laws so brutal that they could not be

EXPLORERS · INVENTORS · WRITERS · ARTISTS · SCIENTISTS

enforced, and brought so-called justice into contempt. Against this appalling and quite ineffective system of threats of death, which often was changed into many years transportation from the country, Romilly crusaded by his writings and by speeches and Bills in Parliament.

SAMUEL ROMILLY'S GREAT SPEECH ON THE ABOLITION OF SLAVERY

He was descended from a French Protestant stock which came into England near the close of the seventeenth century. The first Romilly in England was a waxbleacher; his son a jeweller in Soho; and Samuel (1757–1818), the lawcrusader, was a grandson. After studying the law he became a barrister, and rose to eminence and fortune. As a leader at the Bar he reached an income of £10,000 a year, entered Parliament, and was made Solicitor-General in a Cabinet nicknamed All the Talents because it included so many clever men. In the House of Commons he was as successful as in the law courts. At the end of a speech on the abolition of the slave trade the House of Commons was so moved by his eloquence that it rose and gave him round after round of applause.

This brilliant man, instead of enjoying his wealth selfishly, devoted his energies to the sacred causes of justice and humanity. He succeeded in abolishing the death penalty for some of the offences we have mentioned, and he so impressed the conscience of the nation that after his death, as a result largely of the pity he aroused by his eloquent exposures, the offences for which death could be made the punishment were reduced to one—the crime of murder.

THE TRAGIC END OF A LIFE CROWDED WITH NOBLE DEEDS

Romilly did not, however, live to see his work completed. The death, in 1818, of his wife, to whom he was intensely devoted, so disordered his mind that he took his own life in a fit of despair. Romilly had a sweet and tender nature and a truly manly heart. He used his eloquence for noble purposes, and his name deserves to be held in honoured remembrance.

Many of the world's great crusaders have found their inspiration in religion, the religion that does not mean a selfish saving of a man's soul, but the making of men better men, for the sake of others as well as themselves. This making of men

better, which was the glorious mission of Jesus, when He revealed the Fatherhood of God, is the supreme work of the world, and one of its greatest crusaders was John Wesley. On the page of history he shines as a star of the first magnitude.

He made hundreds of thousands of men better in an age which was apparently dead to religion, dead to seriousness, dead to everything that was not frivolous, empty, and vain.

How did John Wesley do this great work? How was it that he saved the soul of England in the eighteenth century? He mounted a horse and rode to all the parts of England where the working classes lived, and preached to them the religion of Jesus. He avoided the rich; he made his appeal to the magnificent forces of England's working classes.

John Wesley, born in 1703, was a clergyman's son. His father had nineteen children. His mother whipped her children in order to teach them to cry softly. He was strictly trained, but the harshness of his childhood could not destroy in him the glowing light which illumined his noble spirit—the light of God's love. He believed implicity that God *loves* every man, woman, and child; loves them, and desires them to be good that they may be capable of appreciating the joys which await those who love what is right and hate everything that is evil.

HOW A POOR MAN GAVE AWAY THIRTY THOUSAND POUNDS

When he went to Oxford Wesley had £30 a year, lived on £28, and gave £2 away. Next year he had £60, lived on £28, and gave £32 away. Next year he still lived on £28 a year, and gave the rest away. It is said that during his life he gave away £30,000.

There were some very foolish men in the Church of England at that period, who so ill-treated Wesley that, though he was a Churchman, he worked on his own lines. He built chapels wherever he went, organised a great society of worshippers, and preached in the fields and in the streets to anybody who would listen. Sometimes he was roughly used by the mob, but he never lost heart. He used to travel some 5000 miles every year, generally on horseback. He lived to be 88, and almost his last word was the joyful exclamation: " The best of all is, God is with us! " That was the secret of

JOHN WESLEY ON HIS WAY THROUGH ENGLAND

his life. He felt that God was with Man, helping, in His own wise way, the work of improving the human race. Among our English heroes we should always be proud of John Wesley.

John Howard was a queer, quaint, delicate and studious man. He fell ill as a young man, when he was living in lodgings and, not knowing how to express his gratitude to his landlady for all her kindness to him, insisted on marrying her. He was just over twenty, and she was just over fifty. He used to get up at two o'clock in the morning, in the bitterest winter weather, to examine a thermometer at the bottom of his garden. He did not eat animal food. He had usually left his bed and said his prayers before three o'clock in the morning. He studied astronomy, meteorology, and medicine, and spent much time in foreign travel.

THE GREAT EVILS JOHN HOWARD FOUND IN THE PRISONS OF THE WORLD

He might have gone on living this good but rather eccentric life to the end of his days, if he had not been elected the sheriff of Bedford. John Howard was a man who did thoroughly what he had to do, and his business as sheriff lay with the prisons of the county. Most sheriffs ignored this part of their work, but John Howard was of a different character. He inspected the prisons and found them horrible. Not only were the cells reeking with damp, and absolutely soul-killing in their darkness and wretchedness, but the gaolers and turnkeys were allowed to do practically what they liked with their prisoners. A rich prisoner could buy luxuries and bribe the gaolers to procure him comforts; a poor prisoner was neglected, starved, bullied, and treated cruelly in every possible way.

Horrified by what he found, John Howard passed into other counties. The same thing happened there. He visited foreign countries, and saw the same barbarity and wretchedness.

HOW A GREAT ORATOR PRAISED JOHN HOWARD'S WORK FOR HUMANITY

He comforted poor prisoners, and did all he could to better their condition; he addressed kings and governments in the name of humanity, and said that this evil thing must end. His revelations shocked the world. Men stood aghast at the cruelties perpetrated in the name of justice. An immense shame took hold of the human

heart that such things could be done by men to men. Instead of making bad men good, prisons hardened them and made them worse. As for the innocent, the prisons broke their hearts and drove them mad.

Edmund Burke, the great orator, said of John Howard these eloquent words:

He has invited all Europe, not to survey the sumptuousness of palaces, or the stateliness of temples; not to make accurate measurements of the remains of ancient grandeur, nor to form a scale of the curiosities of modern art; not to collect medals or to collate manuscripts; but to dive into the depths of dungeons, to plunge into the infection of hospitals, to survey the mansions of sorrow and pain; to take the gauge and dimensions of misery, depression, and contempt; to remember the forgotten, to attend to the neglected, to visit the forsaken, and to compare and collate the distresses of all men in all countries.

His plan is original; it is as full of genius as of humanity. It was a voyage of discovery; a circumnavigation of charity.

John Howard was 63 when he died in 1790, at Kherson, in Russia, while giving medicines to the poor wretches in hospitals. He was buried there, and the emperor, Alexander, raised a monument to his memory. England has few heroes of whom she may justly feel more proud than John Howard. His life belongs to all the world, and his memory is preserved by every nation.

GEORGE WHITEFIELD, THE TAVERN BOY WHO BECAME A GREAT PREACHER

Among the most romantic stories of crusaders is that of George Whitefield (1714-70). In some ways it is one of the most telling stories in the chronicles of religion. For Whitefield, who was destined to waken the religious sense in thousands of human beings, and who had for his admirers such sceptical men as Hume, such triflers as Lord Chesterfield, such conceited philosophers as Bolingbroke, and such original thinkers as Benjamin Franklin, was born in an inn, spent his boyhood among low characters, and for many years served ale and washed mugs in this tavern kept by his mother at Gloucester.

While forced to do this work, his education was not altogether neglected, and at the grammar school he was so praised for the beauty of his voice that he felt tempted to try his fortune on the stage. But, mysteriously enough, there was a deep religious impulse in the boy. He was conscious of God. He felt the horror of sin. He realised that life is something more than an idle show. Therefore, when he discovered that it was possible for a poor lad to go to Oxford as a servitor, receiving part of his education in return for waiting at table, he embraced this opportunity, and entered the university at the age of eighteen. The Methodists—so called because they lived by rule and method—were beginning to attract attention, and Whitefield joined their fellowship. He was ordained deacon in 1736, and two years later set out for Georgia, in America, at the invitation of Wesley. The effect of his preaching is told by Franklin, who once heard Whitefield appealing for funds towards a scheme of which Franklin did not approve.

HOW FRANKLIN'S MIND WAS CHANGED BY HEARING WHITEFIELD PREACH

I silently resolved he should get nothing from me. I had in my pocket a handful of copper money, three or four silver dollars, and five pistoles in gold.

As he proceeded I began to soften, and concluded to give the copper; another stroke of his oratory made me ashamed of that, and determined me to give the silver; and he finished so admirably that I emptied my pocket wholly into the collector's dish, gold and all.

Whitefield spent his life in preaching. He journeyed all over the British Empire, and everywhere he went people flocked to hear him, and by his wonderful preaching were converted to live better lives. The historian Hume has told us one of Whitefield's appeals:

After a solemn pause, Mr. Whitefield thus addressed his audience: "The attendant angel is just about to leave the threshold and ascend to heaven; and shall he ascend, and not bear with him the news of one sinner, among all the multitude, reclaimed from the error of his ways? Stop, Gabriel! Gabriel, stop ere you enter the sacred portals and yet carry with you the news of one sinner converted to God!"

When he preached in London early in winter mornings, the streets near the chapel would be bright with lanterns carried by the crowds that flocked to hear him. When we think of his origin, and the terrible atmosphere in which the impressionable years of his boyhood were spent, are we not amazed that by speaking of God this man should have drawn hundreds and thousands of people to forsake idle, evil, and useless lives for the pure,

unselfish, and helpful life commanded by Jesus? George Whitefield teaches us that more can be done by speaking of God than by Acts of Parliament. He did not change the conditions of men's lives, but he changed the lives themselves.

THE GOOD THAT IS QUIETLY DONE BY THE SOCIETY OF FRIENDS

The power of intense faith and earnestness in religion is very strangely illustrated in the life and influence of another great crusader, George Fox, the founder of the Society of Friends. Of all the religious sections of Christian people the Friends, whom we generally call Quakers, are perhaps the quietest. They make no outward show. Theirs is an inward religion. It is chiefly seen in good deeds that avoid all sensation. But George Fox, the first Quaker, wandered about the world for more than forty years, a centre for excitement and persecution as he preached a faith which he believed had been given to him by a Divine inward light.

He was born in Leicestershire in 1624, the son of a weaver, and he became a shoemaker by trade, with experience in wool dealing and farming. His education was slight, but he wrote a good deal on religious questions, and his Journal is one of the world's most sincere autobiographies.

George Fox demanded from all men, and most of all from preachers, a personal religion of purity, exaltation, and intensity akin to inspiration. But he lived in days when many of the clergy were slack in their beliefs, and took their services in an easy routine way which did not suggest any deep personal devotion. Such men were described by Fox as professors, and were denounced by him with a lively freedom.

THE GOOD GEORGE FOX WHO WOULD NOT BE BEATEN DOWN

The rougher elements in the crowds that gathered around Fox, as he preached his gospel of exalted conviction and inward purity, felt they had behind them some support from the local clergy and proceeded to bait and ill-treat the lonely preacher. Magistrates regarded his preaching as tending to brawling and disorder, and so he was prosecuted and repeatedly imprisoned as a disturber of the peace, although he believed in the patient endurance of other men's violence.

This treatment in no way daunted the wandering preacher. No ill-treatment, by mobs or by the law, could silence him.

He visited all parts of Britain, the American Colonies, the West Indies, Holland, and Germany, simple in his sincerity and absolutely fearless. Wherever he went he deeply impressed many thoughtful and earnest people, who formed themselves into the Society of Friends, and bore persecutions like his own. At one time during George Fox's life no less than a thousand of his followers were in prison at the same moment.

George Fox, who was 66 when he died in 1691, spent much of his life being driven from village to village, pelted, beaten, unprotected, denounced to the law and punished by it; but his work remains in the existing Society of Friends, which throughout its whole history has a noble record of public service in every good cause, the outcome of a personal faith like his, but which now does not cause its voice to be heard in the street.

Perhaps the most wonderful of all the crusaders of our time, having the most wonderfully varied and far-reaching influence, was William Booth, known everywhere as General Booth, the founder and organiser of the Salvation Army.

THE WORLD-WIDE CRUSADE THAT BEGAN IN THE STREETS OF NOTTINGHAM

He began his work as a Methodist local preacher in Nottingham, and there, on the kerbstone of Hockley, he laid the foundations of the remarkable organisation which is now known throughout civilisation. But when he was twenty he went to London, and after much experience as an open-air preacher he was ordained a Methodist minister. In 1855, when he was 26, he married Catherine Mumford, whose influence as a preacher was hardly second to his own. Hampered in their freedom by the organisation of the Church, in 1861 the Booths struck out a course of Gospel preaching for themselves, known in its early stages as the Christian Mission.

The idea of the Booths was that they should go direct to the mass of the people by means of street services, using bands and songs, and joining care for souls with care for the bodies of the poor. Their services became sensational. Though there was some persecution at first, and vulgar attacks were made on the street gatherings, the Army soon won universal admiration.

General Booth was not only a man with a burning enthusiasm that flamed into eloquence, but he was a genius in organisation. His work for social welfare as well as spiritual regeneration was extended from England on every hand, and when he died in 1912, after he had completed his eighty-third year, his good name was on every tongue, from king to beggar.

The work he had so arduously begun and so skilfully extended, proved to be soundly based. Though some of the more ambitious of his schemes for rescuing " the submerged tenth " from poverty were not carried out on the scale originally contemplated, an enormous volume of redemptive work was done by the Salvation Army, which was an embodiment of General Booth's dauntless spirit.

THE WONDERFUL FRUITS OF THE WORK OF WILLIAM BOOTH

About 20 years after its founder's death the Army had 26,000 officers and cadets working at 16,000 stations, with 107,000 local officers. It had been established in over seventy countries, where it was using over fifty languages. It supported 318 industrial homes, 92 maternity homes, 104 children's homes, 172 slum posts, 16 prison-gate homes, 381 shelters and cheap food depots for the homeless, 224 workshops and factories, and 139 labour bureaus. This enormous amount of practical work, reaching the poorest of the poor, was universally regarded with goodwill, and its influence in the world largely depended on the confidence established by the character and personal magnetism of the great crusader William Booth.

Among moral and political crusaders, the life of Richard Cobden (1804–65) is one of the finest to study. He was born without the influence of title, the power of wealth, or the advantage of opportunity. He would have been ill-educated had he not spent his leisure on self-education. He would have been poor had he not devoted himself with conscientious seriousness to earn his wages in a house of business. He would have died without glory or fame had he not laboured to make goodwill prevail among the nations of the world.

RICHARD COBDEN'S FIGHT IN PARLIAMENT FOR CHEAP FOOD FOR THE POOR

We cannot tell here about the great struggle over the Corn Laws, in which Cobden was the triumphant hero. All we need to know is that Cobden entered the House of Commons convinced that the tax on foreign corn was a bad tax;

FOUR CRUSADERS FOR THE PEOPLE

GEORGE FOX PREACHING IN A TAVERN

JOHN HOWARD AMONG THE PRISONERS

GEORGE WHITEFIELD PREACHING—FROM THE
PAINTING IN THE NATIONAL GALLERY

EDWIN CHADWICK WATCHES THE CHILDREN
GOING TO THE FACTORIES TO WORK

that the members of the House of Commons would hardly listen to him when he first rose to speak; and that in the end food became cheap for the poor; Cobden was acclaimed as a hero, and all the nation acknowledged his great victory.

But Cobden did what some think was a still greater work, and it is this work to which we will pay attention. Let us try to see in our mind a picture of the various nations of the world. See the Frenchman making his silks, the German his dyes, the Englishman his steel, and other nations cultivating the earth with the various produce suited to their lands. Beside each worker stand a soldier and a sailor. The workers sell their goods to each other, and they would be well off if it were not for the soldier and sailor. They have to feed, clothe, and arm those fighting men. So the poor worker pays to keep these protectors at his side.

THE MAN WHO HATED WAR AND TRIED TO TEACH THE NATIONS PEACE

Suppose now that the Frenchman, the German, and the Englishman said to each other: " We will not hurt each other. We will do our own work and trade together. Let us agree to do this, and we shall not have to pay for these fighting men, who keep us poor." What a difference that would make! All the many millions of pounds spent every year on arming for war would be saved.

This was Cobden's great dream. This was the work he started. Richard Cobden *hated* war. He set his life to try to prevent it. He did not go about raging against soldiers and sailors, who are brave men, and very often noble men. But he went to the various nations and tried to spread among them the common-sense of a common friendship.

Side by side in history with Cobden stands the noble Quaker John Bright (1811–89). He was in business when the call to become a public man came to him. Death was, in some measure, the summoner. His young wife, whom he loved devotedly, died of tuberculosis, and the soul of John Bright was bowed to the dust. But, while he was in mourning, Richard Cobden came to him.

" There are thousands of homes in England at this moment," he said, " where wives, mothers, children, are dying of hunger. Now, when the first paroxysm of your grief is past, I would advise you to come with me, and we will never rest till the Corn Laws are repealed."

That was the call. It roused the mourner from contemplating his own tragedy to contemplate the larger tragedy of mankind. Instead of thinking of himself, he thought of others. Instead of bowing himself before the grave of his own sorrow, he went forward to ease the sorrows of the world. This simple, self-educated Quaker had nothing in his soul but devotion to God and love towards his fellow-men.

THE GREAT APPEAL OF JOHN BRIGHT THAT MOVED THE NATION

What would have happened to England if this man had not forsaken his private grief, and laboured for the repeal of the Corn Laws, it is difficult to think. Want and starvation had brought the people to a dangerous and reckless mood—a mood when reason is thrown away and, like famished wolves, the multitude becomes a pack, urged forward by the impulse of hunger. It was to John Bright that the nation listened. Cobden argued; Bright appealed. His appeal was made to righteousness, to justice, to God. The nation listened, was moved, and was converted.

Bright made some mistakes, but, on the whole, his record is a splendid one. Like Cobden, he hated war. He did great work for peace. Most of the heroic work in the House of Commons has been carried forward by deeply religious men. John Bright was one of the great forces in the House of Commons because he did not think of his party, did not seek popularity, but guided his conduct always by the voice of conscience.

THE HAPPY LAD WHO LOVED FLOWERS AND FIELDS AND BIRDS

William Morris (1834–96), as a crusader, was different from those we have read about. His life shows us how various are the ways in which one can work for the improvement of the world. When he was a little boy he would dress up in toy armour, mount a pony, and ride into Epping Forest, dreaming of old romances. He loved flowers. He knew all the animals of the forest. He could recognise any bird by its flight. The little boy was in love with Nature.

When he went to Oxford he wanted to be a clergyman; and there he met another scholar, whose name was Burne-Jones, who had also come to Oxford with the same purpose. These two young men became friends, and in their conversations they talked about making the world a happier place. Gradually it came to them that they could do more work for the world as artists than as clergymen. In those days people cared very little for beauty. Furniture was chosen for its strength, curtains and carpets for their wearing qualities; houses were built without any respect for beauty.

William Morris saw that houses and furniture form what we call a man's environment, and that a person is affected by his surroundings. If we live in a dingy room we find it hard to be cheerful. If we are always looking at ugly things our minds will sooner or later become either ugly or bitter.

HOW MEN'S LIVES ARE MADE UGLY BY UGLY SURROUNDINGS

Long before Morris lived men had seen that evil surroundings were bad, and the Church had always striven to rescue people from living with wicked persons in bad places. Morris did exactly the same work for beauty. He saw that ugly surroundings had a bad effect on people, made them coarse, vulgar, stupid, even wicked. He set himself to teach the great lesson that beauty is something for which men should strive.

If we look in the windows of furniture shops we see that many of the chairs, sideboards, and wardrobes aim at being grand. Many people mistake grandeur for beauty. Morris set himself to fight this idea. He succeeded largely; but the mass of men to this day remain dead to beauty. Morris not only made furniture, but he also designed wallpapers. He printed books on beautiful paper in a beautiful way. Everything in life, he felt, must be beautiful. This was a great work. Beauty is part of human life. In seeking beauty we seek God, for all that is of God is beautiful. A portrait of Morris appears on page 4077.

THE TERRIBLE WAY IN WHICH UNHAPPY PEOPLE WERE TREATED

A subject of great interest that should appeal to every sensitive nature is the humane treatment of those who suffer from a disordered mind and cease to be responsible for their actions. It is strange that, though these sad cases seem to have had special treatment from the great Healer who founded Christianity, they were grossly neglected for nearly 1800 years of the Christian Era.

The insane were treated all through that period, it is to be feared, with habitual cruelty. The ancient superstition that they were possessed by a devil was accepted as a satisfactory explanation, and was made an excuse for barbarous methods of confinement and torture. They were bound with chains, drugged, and bled into weakness, and the places where these and other cruelties were practised seldom came under independent observation.

A change in these methods throughout the civilised world was begun not by medical reform, but through the active humanity of a York tea and coffee merchant, a kindly Quaker named William Tuke. A Quaker known to Tuke died in York Asylum in conditions that strongly suggested he had suffered from gross ill-treatment. This aroused Tuke to investigate the methods of controlling the insane in confinement, and he brought the subject before his fellow-worshippers in the city. The result was that they built an asylum which they called the Retreat, and in it used quiet and kindly methods without violent forms of restraint or terrorism such as had disgraced the asylums of the past.

ROBERT OWEN AND HIS GREAT EFFORTS FOR FACTORY WORKERS

The results which followed were so excellent that attention was drawn to the institution from all parts of the world, and it was seen that the cultivation of cheerfulness and joy, and the provision of suitable occupations, would bring a new hope to large numbers of those who were suffering temporarily from mental affliction. William Tuke began his work in 1796, and continued it until his death at 90, in 1822.

Another man who strove all his days to improve the conditions of his fellows was Robert Owen (1771–1858), founder of the co-operative movement. He did one very great thing; he impressed the world with the truth that factory workers are not mere pieces of machinery ; that their prosperity, health, education, and happiness are of immense importance in making business successful.

Born in Newtown, Montgomeryshire, the son of a saddler and ironmonger, Robert Owen was teaching other children at school by the time he was seven, became manager of a cotton mill at 19, and was partner in a mill employing 2000 people at New Lanark at the age of 30.

It was there, between 1800 and 1828, that he put into practice his ideas on factory reform. He arranged that five per cent of all profits should go to the owners and the remainder be spent on improving the conditions of the workers. He made his factories sanitary ; he introduced unemployment pay ; established a system of schools (Owen claimed to be the founder of infant schools) ; reduced working hours ; and abolished the employment of very young children.

It was largely through the agitation of Robert Owen that Parliament passed the Factory Act of 1819, which, among other things, ruled that no child under *ten* should be employed in factories.

Sir Edwin Chadwick (1800–90), who was born at Longsight, near Manchester, was one of our staunchest crusaders. It is questionable whether any other man has done as much genuine work as he did for the general health of the British people.

SIR EDWIN CHADWICK'S FIGHT FOR THE HEALTH OF THE PEOPLE

In 1832 the condition of the working class in England was appalling. A large proportion of them were paupers, and the Poor Law was working in such a way that it was felt to be a curse. A Royal Commission was appointed to make a national inquiry and report. At this time Chadwick was a writer for the reviews, and his central idea was that a large part of the work of government, local or national, should be to *prevent* evils arising, especially the evil of ill-health, which was so terrible in England that on an average an Englishman lived a shorter life by thirteen years than an inhabitant of Sweden.

Chadwick was made an assistant commissioner, and his energy and clearness of mind in making inquiries were so conspicuous that presently he became a full commissioner, and drafted a famous Report that led to a reform of the Poor Law. When a Poor Law Commission was formed to deal with the whole question he became its secretary.

He held firmly the view that such evils as poverty and ill-health should be grappled with on a national scale. Hitherto the country had clung to parish management. He contended that the parish was too small an area for such work. A parish had neither the knowledge nor independence of mind needed to meet difficulties which were universal. Control of these great questions should be national, or, if local, a wide area should be covered by each authority. In any case a central authority should have power of close inspection to see that the local authority did its duty.

THE GREAT IDEA BEHIND THE WORK OF EDWIN CHADWICK

It was this idea that the wisdom and justice of the country as a whole should be brought to bear on every part of the country that gave Chadwick's labours their high value; and also that raised a big crop of difficulties, for the more ignorant, backward, and deplorable the condition of a benighted parish or district was, the less it wanted to be interfered with from outside, though it might be spreading disease around. Chadwick's first victory was to get the Poor Law administered by a union of parishes instead of individually.

He was also on the Commission for inquiring into the fearful hours and conditions of work of children in factories, which led to the appointment of factory inspectors. It also recommended employers' liability for accidents, though that was only made legal long afterwards. It was Chadwick who secured the appointment of the first Sanitary Commission, and introduced the official registration of the causes of all deaths, which laid the foundation for national care for the health of the public. His inquiries and reports led to the passing of the Public Health Act of 1848, and he was one of the Commissioners of the first National Board of Health, which was finally superseded in 1871 by the Local Government Board.

THE NAME WE MUST ALWAYS HOLD IN HIGH HONOUR

The story of Edwin Chadwick's life is one of thoughtful care for the health of the whole community, a care that was hampered at every turn by ignorance, superstition, and selfish personal interests. Even when his best schemes were made legal by Parliament, they were often not made compulsory, but only permissive, so that those who objected to them locally could decline to adopt them, and they became a dead letter in the districts that most needed them. But, slowly yet surely, Chadwick's plans have triumphed.

One of the most amazing signs of an improving world is the better health of the British public, and the lengthening of human life. If we trace these blessings to their sources we shall find they are very

THE SIGHT THAT MOVED LORD SHAFTESBURY

MOVED BY THE PATHETIC SIGHT OF A PAUPER'S FUNERAL, THE YOUNG LORD SHAFTESBURY, THEN A BOY
AT HARROW, RESOLVES ON HIS LIFE-WORK FOR HUMANITY.

largely due to preventive care, based on an understanding of the Divine laws of health ; and the man who gave our country its start in the right direction, in many ways, was Sir Edwin Chadwick, who was thrust out of official life at an early age for doing, too earnestly, the very things for which those who know the early story of his work now honour his name.

Sometimes a very fine crusader will lose, as his life goes on, some of the fire and inspiration of his earlier years, but if he does that we shall not value the less the work he accomplished when he was fresh and bold, and open to new impulses. Such a man was the good Lord Shaftesbury. To the end of his days he was a kind-hearted humanitarian, deeply interested in many good causes. But in the earlier part of his public life he was a positive crusader.

A RICH MAN'S SPLENDID WORK FOR THE POOR OF HIS COUNTRY

His family name was Ashley, and his ancestors were distinguished. He himself was so placed, by his birth, upbringing, and social surroundings, that it might be expected of him that he would not be naturally concerned very deeply for the masses of the people. He was an aristocrat by descent and disposition, and in politics a Tory. Yet for many years he did fine humane work, in alliance with people with whom he disagreed on most questions, except those which appealed specially to his feelings of humanity and justice.

We can hardly conceive now what England was like in the thirties and forties of the nineteenth century, when the factory system ate up, like a greedy giant, all the joy of life from myriads of children, and even life itself. There was a time when the law of England allowed boys and girls of seven years of age to work in factories from five o'clock in the morning till seven o'clock at night, with only half an hour's rest at noon. There was a time when little boys and girls sat for twelve hours every day in darkness in a coal-mine to pull a string which opened a wooden door in the mine tunnel; when children and women crawled on hands and knees through tunnels too low for them to stand upright, and dragged wagons to which they were harnessed; when girls and women carried heavy baskets of coal up high ladders. There was a time when little boys had to climb up chimneys to sweep them, and sometimes sweep them from the top as they descended

head downwards. Not seldom they were suffocated by the soot and heat, and died in the chimney.

These terrible doings were defended on the ground that if the cheap labour of children was not used England would be ruined by the competition of other nations.

THE LONG FIGHT OF LORD SHAFTESBURY FOR THE CHILDREN OF BRITAIN

It was only after years of argument in Parliament, and repeated defeats, that such enormities as these were made illegal. And even then some of them continued, because effective inspection to see that they were stopped was denied. All through the struggle to abolish these cruelties, from the days when, as a boy at Harrow, he was moved by the sight of a pauper's funeral, Lord Shaftesbury was a crusading leader in the cause of humanity.

It is true that, after having helped to abolish the worst of these brutalities, he did not go so far forward as he might have gone in lessening the hardship of labour, but he fought the battle when the fight was hardest. Then he spent the rest of his life in kindly labours among the poor in London through such institutions as the Ragged Schools, which came before national education. His name lives on, and his spirit too, in the work of the Shaftesbury Society.

A crusader who, against heavy odds, brought a great benefit to the country was Rowland Hill, the man to whom we owe the penny post.

His father was a schoolmaster, and as a young man he took up his father's work with originality and success. Then he became the secretary for a colonising scheme in Australia. It was in 1835, when he was 40, that Rowland Hill made public a postage scheme which had been fermenting in his mind for ten years.

SIR ROWLAND HILL AND HIS CRUSADE FOR THE PENNY POST

We can hardly conceive now the state of England when letters were paid for by the persons who received them, and the charge depended on the distance they had travelled. It was calculated that if an Irish labourer in London sent a letter to his mother in Ireland and received an answer back, the cost would be more than one-fifth of his wages for a week's work. There were areas as big as a good-sized county, in nineteenth-century England, where postmen were unknown, and towns of 10,000 people without a post office. Indeed, posting letters was so complicated, slow, and costly, that nobody used the post if he could find any other way of sending a letter to its destination.

The great enemy of reform was the Post Office itself. It was a secret service, made expensive by innumerable inside processes which nobody outside understood, but which it regarded as sacred. When Rowland Hill set himself the task of studying the letter business he was refused admission to the Post Office, and he had to gather his information from a close examination of reports and accounts. From them he discovered that the cost of carrying a letter from London to Edinburgh was only a thirty-sixth of a penny, though the charge was 1s. 4d.

WILLIAM TUKE

Clearly, if the essential cost was so small, there was gross muddling and bad business to make the charge so high. This started him, as a clear-headed business man, on a business crusade.

His conclusions were put into a pamphlet, in which he advocated prepayment of the cost through a little adhesive stamp, at a uniform rate, regardless of distance. The public was at once convinced he was right ; Parliament was presently convinced, but the Post Office never gave in. It was only when Rowland Hill himself was asked to bring his own scheme into operation that anything was done; and even then the chief secretary of the Post Office was left as his superior officer to hamper his work. It was only when Rowland Hill was made Postmaster-General, after seven years' delay, that the penny post at once bounded into an amazing success. When Rowland Hill retired from the management of the Post Office more than fifty times as many letters were being carried as when he started his single-handed crusade.

His persistent work for this most practical purpose, against intense official resistance, was enthusiastically rewarded.

WILLIAM BOOTH

The public subscribed a present of over £13,000. Parliament made him a public grant of £20,000.

When Rowland Hill died, in August 1879, leaving behind a strong feeling that he was a great national benefactor, he was buried among the great dead in Westminster Abbey.

The penny post conferred vast benefits on the nation; it helped in the development of commerce; it built many friendships by enabling people to correspond quickly and cheaply; it encouraged the simplest people to write and send letters. But postal charges subsequently increased so much that nowadays it is hard to believe the penny post was ever a reality!

If we suppose that crusaders, reformers, and inventors are only to be found among civilised and educated people we make a great mistake. " The wind bloweth where it listeth and thou canst not tell whence it cometh—so is every one who is born of the Spirit," said Jesus; and so it is with genius. It comes everywhere, and has always visited men to their great gain. For some of the most helpful changes made by human inquiry and enthusiasm we are indebted to a time far beyond the reach of history. Writing our thought and talk is one example. No one knows who began it. But within the last 250 years men have seen it begun afresh, from the very beginning, by a wholly uneducated man—a Red Indian half-breed, bent on yet another fine crusade.

In the Hall of Fame of the American Capitol, in Washington, stands, in companionship with Washington and Lincoln, the statue of the Cherokee Indian, Sequoya, and how well he deserves a place there may be judged when his story has been told.

According to the most trustworthy account, Sequoya was the son of an Indian mother whose uncle was the chief of the Cherokee tribe; and his father was George Gist, an American scout, who was taken prisoner by the tribe while he was serving on the British side in the early wars between the English and the French for the possession of Northern America. Gist was a prisoner for six years. When he escaped he left behind his son Sequoya.

The boy lived, in his youth, in the town of Tuskegee, where, in later years, Booker Washington, the most famous American of Negro blood, taught in a college for his own race. But when Sequoya was there he had no education; he could not read, and he knew only vaguely the use of a book. But as he grew up he wandered from place to place as a hunter and fur-trader, and finally became by practice a clever blacksmith. Evidently he was a man with great natural gifts.

THE CHEROKEE WHO DID NOT KNOW THE ALPHABET

By an accident when hunting he became crippled, and then had time for quiet thought. It then struck him how greatly the white man had the advantage in being able to write down his thoughts and pass them on to men at a distance away. Why should not the Indians have the same advantage? He determined that they should have it.

He had no books, and did not know a letter of the alphabet. It struck him that if he could make a separate sign for every Indian word and if all the signs were learned by heart, that would be like the white man's writing. But there were thousands of words and he needed thousands of signs. How could he invent them all, and others learn them all? He tried to do it by scratching and carving his signs on pieces of bark. But the task mastered him, and men laughed at him.

Then he began to study the talk of the tribe more closely, and discovered that the thousands of words were made up of a far fewer number of sounds and syllables in different combinations, and after long study he counted—all in his head, for he could not write anything down—that there were only 85 syllables, or separate complete sounds, in the language of his tribe.

HOW SEQUOYA INVENTED AN ALPHABET AND TAUGHT HIS TRIBE TO READ

Now his task was to invent 85 signs for these 85 syllables. At this point he managed to get hold of an English spelling-book, and from the capital letters, small letters, and figures he made the larger part of the signs he needed. He imitated them roughly, and made some of them upside down, but they served his purpose. To them he added some signs of his own invention till he had the whole of the 85, and to each sign he apportioned a sound in the Cherokee language. He now had only to put down the signs in the order they came in any talk, and the signs talked as they were pronounced.

Then he brought his writing before the tribe and asked them to learn the sign for each sound. A clever Indian with a good memory could connect all the signs with all the sounds in a few hours, and any child could learn them all in a month. In a few months the whole of the Cherokee nation could read and write their own language through Sequoya's signs.

Soon books were printed in this sign-language, and foreign books translated into it, and, as far as the Cherokee words admitted it to be done, the tribe had not only a written language, but a rapidly growing literature.

Sequoya then travelled about to find scattered groups of tribes and teach them to read their language. For this entirely original work — which afterwards was imitated by other tribes—the American Government gave Sequoya a gift of £100, and, later, a pension of £60 a year, which was then (1828) a comfortable living for an Indian whose habits were those of his tribe.

THE GREAT TREES THAT KEEP ALIVE THE NAME OF A GREAT RED INDIAN

Sequoya was fifty when he began to puzzle out his system of writing, he was sixty-two when he brought it fully into use.

In his old age he became possessed by the idea that a large part of his tribe had wandered away far into the west, and that he ought to follow them, find them, and teach them to read and write their native speech. At last he set forth on his search; but he never found his lost people—indeed, they did not exist—but he wore himself out with travel, and died, in 1843, in Mexico.

Could we have a better example of a plain man with no learning who made a written language under the eyes of the modern world, just as other men in the far distant past invented other systems of writing, including our own?

Sequoya's name is not only preserved in the language he recorded in written signs, but his name has been given to one of the giant trees in California—the Sequoia—and so it will live for ever.

SEQUOYA WORKS OUT HIS ALPHABET

THEY LAUGHED AT SEQUOYA AS HE SAT BY HIS WIGWAM WORKING OUT THE CHEROKEE ALPHABET, BUT HE TRIUMPHED AT LAST, AND WAS HONOURED BY THE SCOFFERS AND BY ALL THE WORLD.

THE GEESE WARN THE ROMANS OF THE APPROACH OF THEIR ENEMIES. See story on page 5468

The Great Stories of the World That Will Be Told for Ever

TINY THUMBELINE

ONCE upon a time there lived a young wife who longed to possess a little child, so she went to a fairy and said to her: " I wish very much to have a child, a tiny child. Will you give me one? "

" With all my heart," said the fairy. " Sow this barleycorn in a flowerpot, and then see what will happen."

The woman went home and planted the barleycorn, and immediately there shot up a large flower like a tulip, but with the petals tightly closed.

" What a lovely flower! " said she, and kissed it.

The bud opened at once, and in the centre sat a tiny little girl about an inch high, scarcely bigger than her thumb. So she called her Thumbeline, and put her to bed in a walnut-shell, with violet leaves for a mattress and a rose-leaf for a quilt. During the day she told Thumbeline stories, and taught her to sing, as she played on the table beside her.

But one night a great, wet, ugly toad came and stole away the cradle with little Thumbeline asleep in it, and carried it off to her home in the muddy bank of the brook that flowed past the garden.

" This is just the wife for my son," thought she. But when her ugly son saw Thumbeline all he could say was " Croak, croak, croak! "

" Don't make so much noise or you'll wake her," said old Mother Toad. " She may easily escape, for she is as light as a feather. We must take her out and place her on one of the large water-lily leaves in the middle of the brook, while I prepare the house for you both."

This they did, and when poor little Thumbeline awoke and found herself in the stream she cried most bitterly.

As soon as old Mother Toad had decorated her home with bulrushes and yellow buttercups she and her hideous son swam out to the leaf to fetch the cradle.

Old Mother Toad bowed low in the water and said, " Here is my son, who is going to be your husband. I will come to fetch you soon, and you will be very happy together."

Then they swam off with the cradle, and poor, terrified Thumbeline wept more bitterly than ever.

Now, some little fishes had overheard old Mother Toad, and when they saw the little maid so sad they gnawed away the stem of the leaf, and away it floated down the stream.

Thumbeline became happy again, for everything she passed was so lovely in the sunshine, and the birds on the branches sang to her as she floated by. A pretty little butterfly hovered round her, and at

IMAGINATION · CHIVALRY · LEGENDS · GOLDEN DEEDS · FAIRY TALES

last settled for a moment on the leaf, for he loved her very much.

But presently a great ugly cockchafer came buzzing past. He caught sight of her, and, snatching her off the leaf, flew up with her into a tree. He gave her some honey to eat, and praised her beauty; but when the lady cockchafers saw her they said she was just like a human being.

"How very, very ugly she is!" they all cried; and at last the cockchafer disowned her, and flew down with her and set her on a daisy. Then she wept because she was so ugly that the lady cockchafers would have nothing to do with her.

All the summer Thumbeline lived alone in a wood, dining off the honey from the flowers, and drinking the dew that every morning spangled the leaves around her. But then came the cold, long winter; the flowers all died, the birds flew away, and the snow began to fall. Poor hungry Thumbeline wandered through the stubble of a cornfield hard by until she came to the hole of a field-mouse, who lived snugly down in the ground.

Thumbeline stood at the door and begged for food.

"Poor little thing!" said the good-natured field-mouse. "Come into my warm room and dine with me." And she soon became so fond of the tiny maid that she said: "You may dwell with me all the winter if you will only keep my room clean and neat and tell me stories, for I love stories dearly." And Thumbeline agreed.

In a few days' time the field-mouse said: "We shall have my next-door neighbour, the mole, in to visit us tomorrow. He is richer than I am, has large rooms in his house, and wears a beautiful black velvet coat. It would be capital if you married him; but he is blind and cannot see you, so you must tell him your prettiest stories."

When he came Thumbeline sang to him, and he soon fell in love with her. He invited them to walk down a long dark passage that he had just burrowed from their house to his, lighting them with a piece of tinder.

But when they had gone a short distance they found a swallow lying stretched on the floor; the poor bird had evidently died of cold. Thumbeline felt very sorry, as she loved all the birds, but the mole kicked it with his short legs, saying, "Here's a fine end to all its whistling! How miserable it must be to be born a bird!"

But Thumbeline could not sleep that night, so she got up and wove a carpet out of hay, and spread it round the bird.

"Farewell, dear bird," said she; "farewell, and thank you for your beautiful song in the summer, when all the trees were green and the sun shone so warmly upon us." And she pressed her head against his big body.

To her great surprise she felt something beating within it. It was the bird's heart, and he was not really dead. She quickly laid the hay more closely round him, and he gradually revived.

He remained underground all the winter, and Thumbeline was kind to him and brought him water and food.

When the spring came and the swallow flew away Thumbeline was sad indeed.

Every evening the mole came and talked about how the summer was coming to an end, and he abused the sun and pretty flowers so much that Thumbeline disliked him more and more, and said she would not marry him.

"Fiddlestick!" cried the field-mouse. "Don't be obstinate, child, or I will bite you with my white teeth."

At last the day fixed had arrived, and Thumbeline went to bid a last farewell to the beautiful sun before going to dwell with the mole deep down in the earth.

"Farewell, thou glorious sun!" she cried, as she walked a little way.

"Tweet, tweet!" And she heard a fluttering of wings, and there was the little swallow. She told him her sad fate and how she longed to be free.

"The cold winter will soon be here," said the swallow; "I shall fly far away to the warm countries. Come with me, sweet little Thumbeline, who saved my life when I lay frozen in the dark earth."

"Yes, I will go with thee," said she, and she seated herself on the bird's back. Then the swallow soared high into the air and flew away over forest, lake, and mountain till they reached the warm countries. There the sky seemed twice as high and twice as blue, and there grew the loveliest grapes and citrons and melons.

Near a calm, blue lake stood a half-ruined palace of white marble, and here the swallow had built his nest.

"This is my house," said the swallow, "but I will take you to one of the splendid flowers growing beneath us, and you shall dwell in one of them."

But what was her surprise when she saw sitting on the flower a little manikin, wearing a gold crown on his head and the brightest, most delicate wings on his shoulders, scarcely any bigger than herself. He was the spirit of the flower, and in every flower there dwelled one such fairy, and he was their king.

When he saw Thumbeline he was delighted, for he had never seen so lovely a maiden. So he put his gold crown on her head and asked her to be his queen; and Thumbeline said Yes. And then all the fairies came out from their flowers and brought her presents, and the best of all was a pair of transparent wings, which enabled her to fly from flower to flower.

"You shall no longer be called Thumbeline," said the king to her, "for it is not a pretty name, and you are so lovely. We will call you Maia."

And she dwelled with him ever after.

LITTLE RICHARD'S RIDE

THERE lived in Normandy nearly a thousand years ago a boy named Richard, grandson of the famous Rollo who came with the Vikings of the North to conquer the fair land about the Seine.

Richard had a lonely childhood. His stepmother disliked him, and he rarely saw his father, William Longsword. But when the boy was eight his father became very ill, and, thinking he was about to die, he took Richard to Bayeux and made the barons swear loyalty to the little heir.

Soon after the father was treacherously murdered, and for Richard there began a long series of troubled days. King Louis of France was his enemy, and thought he would have no difficulty in depriving so small a boy of his dukedom.

But there were loyal barons and chieftains who loved and stood by the little fellow; and when the boy was taken prisoner they rescued him. But not long did he remain free, for Louis, under some pretence of kindness, again got possession of the boy, who was then eleven, and shut him up in a tower at Laon in charge of Osmond, a Norman noble.

Now, Osmond was clever, and he taught Richard all he knew during the lonely hours they spent in the tower. Moreover, he loved his little charge, and it pained him to see the boy growing pale and feeble for want of fresh air. Once he dared the King's anger and took Richard out for a gallop across country. Seeing the good this did him, Osmond determined he would find a way to escape with the boy.

It was a wet season, and the damp and confinement in the tower made Richard so ill that the King thought the boy's days were numbered. Osmond wished them to think Richard was really worse than he was, for he had made a plan of escape, and was just waiting a favourable opportunity for carrying it out.

Before long the opportunity came. A great banquet was to be given in the castle, and preparations went merrily forward. According to Osmond's instructions, when the officer paid his usual visit of inspection Richard remained lying on his bed, apparently able to answer questions in only a feeble voice. When the officer had gone Osmond told his little friend that he meant to escape with him that very night, but when Richard eagerly asked "How?" he would not tell him, and only said:

"Eat up your food; you will want all the strength you can get."

The day wore on, and as the hour of the banquet came, and the guests had entered through the gateway, the courtyard and the entrance and passages inside seemed quite deserted. Osmond opened the door of the room, looked down the winding stairway, and listened. Then, beckoning to Richard to follow him, they stole down the steps and across the courtyard.

Fortunately, Osmond knew his way to the barn even in darkness, and with the boy close at his heels he entered it, tore down a truss of hay, snatched up a cord, and bound the hay round the boy's body so that no one would have dreamed there was a small boy in the middle of it. Then he set the bundle against a wall and hoisted it on his back.

"Be quiet. Don't make a sound," he whispered into the bundle.

Now came the dangerous part of the venture, for he had to cross the courtyard in the moonlight to reach the stables.

When he arrived at the stables he put his bundle down, saddled a horse, set Richard free from the hay, and led the horse out through a side door. Then, keeping the boy in front of him, he galloped away with his precious charge.

So little Richard rode to freedom, and lived to rule his dukedom.

LA CHANCE DE JACQUES LE SIMPLE

This is a French translation of the story told in English on page 1146

JACQUES LE SIMPLE était le meilleur tisserand de soie de Spitalfields, mais il n'avait pas la moindre idée de la valeur de la monnaie. S'il sortait avec beaucoup d'argent dans la poche il était sûr de le dépenser, soit pour ses amis, qui avaient l'habitude de l'assiéger, soit pour des choses absolument inutiles.

Jacques le Simple n'en n'était pas seulement là, mais il payait tout ce que les marchands lui demandaient pour n'importe quel article, et, comme tout le monde connaissait ses points faibles, Jacques le Simple était volé quand il allait faire des achats. Il était tout aussi bête en cas de vente, car il acceptait n'importe quel prix en échange de ses marchandises, peu soucieux des sommes plus ou moins absurdement insignifiantes qu'on lui offrait. Aussi sa femme avait-elle l'habitude de faire les achats et les ventes dont ils avaient besoin.

Un jour, cependant, Jacques le Simple résolut de faire une vente par lui-même. Il prit un paquet de belles soieries et les vendit à un négociant pour mille francs. Mais, voyant un homme avec un âne, il l'interpela : " Cet âne me serait bien utile, en voudriez-vous mille francs ? "

L'homme fut naturellement tout prêt à le vendre pour un si bon prix. Bientôt Jacques le Simple découvrit que l'âne était très entêté et qu'il ne voulait pas se laisser diriger.

" Combien donneriez-vous de cette bête ? " dit-il à un marchand de quatre saisons.

" Elle serait chère à douze francs," répondit le rusé marchand.

Jacques le Simple prit les douze francs et les échangea contre un sac de pommes de terre nouvelles. Mais le sac était lourd et Jacques fut bientôt fatigué de son nouveau marché. Aussi le laissa-t-il à une poissonnerie pour un maquereau.

Sa femme se fâcha en apprenant comment il avait dépensé les mille francs, mais, en ouvrant le poisson, elle y trouva une perle d'une remarquable beauté.

" Tiens ! ceci doit bien valoir des milliers de francs ! " s'écria-t-elle.

" Vous voyez bien, ma chère," dit gaîment Jacques le Simple, " j'ai dépensé un misérable billet de mille francs pour acheter un poisson contenant un riche bijou, et cependant vous dites que je n'ai aucune idée de la valeur de l'argent ! "

ANTONIO'S WONDERFUL LION

ON a summer's day in the year 1768 a small peasant lad was flying along the white, dusty road which led from Venice to the little village of Possagno. In both hands he clasped a big lump of clay, which old Pietro the potter had given him that morning.

As the boy, whose name was Antonio, came into the village street several of his playfellows shouted to him to join their games, but Antonio only fled the faster to his own home.

" Just see, Mother ! " he cried, holding up his clay. " See what old Pietro has given me ! What fine castles and birds and flowers I shall be able to make now ! "

Sitting down on the floor, the ten-year-old sculptor set to work. He was too intent on moulding the clay to notice the arrival of a visitor.

The visitor was his mother's cousin, a very grand person in his own and the villagers' eyes, for he was head cook at the castle, where the senator Giovanni Falier, the lord of Possagno, lived in great state. As a rule Thomasso would bring delightful scraps of broken meat, but today he was empty-handed, for he was feeling much too worried to think of anyone but himself.

" What's the matter, Cousin ? " asked Antonio's mother.

" Matter enough, I can tell you," was the tart reply. " Just think ! The master is giving a great banquet tomorrow night, and has ordered me to invent some decoration for the table that has never been seen before."

" But you're so clever that you're sure to think of something," said his cousin.

" I can't ! " said Thomasso irritably. " That's what is worrying me, and the time is getting so short ! The master is tired of my castles and dragons in pastry, and of my sugar birds and trees and flowers; even the lifelike chariot that I carved out of a turnip doesn't please him now, nor yet the upright clock made in sweetmeats. No; nor the almond-paste crown set with jewels of candied gooseberries and cherries. Oh, what ever am I to do? "

" Go on thinking, and you'll get an idea at last," urged Antonio's mother, while Antonio himself was much too busy working at his modelling to look or even to speak.

" Go on thinking! " cried Thomasso. " Well, if that's all the help you can give me I'll be off." And he moved toward the door, brushing past Antonio so roughly that he jerked a beautiful little swan which the boy had just modelled out of his hand.

" Oh, my poor swan; you've quite spoiled it! " cried Antonio sorrowfully. For the swan had struck against the wall and fallen on the floor in a shapeless heap. " Oh, how I detest you! " added the boy, shaking his fist at Thomasso's back.

" Poor man ! He's dreadfully worried today," said his mother. " You ought to be sorry that you can't help him, for think how often he brings you cakes and tarts and other good things! "

" So he does! " said Antonio. And from that moment he became very silent

FROM THAT LUMP OF BUTTER A LION HAD ARISEN

and appeared to be lost in deep thought. Next morning, at sunrise, he was knocking at the kitchen door of the castle.

" Cousin Thomasso," he said, " I've thought of something that I will make for your master's table, something that no one else has ever seen before. Only give me a big block of butter and a little room all to myself, where no one can watch me."

" All right," said the cook. " Of course you'll only waste the butter; still, you may see what you can do."

For twelve hours Antonio toiled at the task he had undertaken, Thomasso calling through the door occasionally for news of his wonderful work. Antonio paid no heed

to his jeers; but just as the sun began to sink, and the hour for the banquet drew near, he flung open the door and displayed his handiwork to the anxious, but now delighted, Thomasso.

From that shapeless lump of butter a lion had arisen, and a truly magnificent animal it was. Every detail, from the finely-moulded muzzle to the tip of its tail, was in faultless proportion.

If Thomasso was struck dumb with delight and surprise, still more so were the host and guests when this masterpiece appeared on the table as its crowning ornament.

Filled with admiration for his cook's performance, the senator sent for him, and loaded him with praise. To the astonishment of all, however, Thomasso, who surely could have cause only for rejoicing, burst into tears.

" Alas ! " he said. " It was not I, but someone else, who moulded that lion."

" Then fetch him here at once," commanded the senator, filled with curiosity as to who the artist could be.

Thereupon, to the further bewilderment of that gay company, Thomasso presently reappeared, pushing a very frightened, ragged little peasant boy in front of him.

Antonio was too frightened to lift up his eyes, but from that moment his fortune was made. The senator apprenticed him to one of the greatest sculptors of the day, and under his care Antonio made such rapid progress that two years later the young sculptor presented his patron with two baskets in marble filled with exquisitely moulded fruits.

These may still be seen in the Falier Palace at Venice. For the little ragged barefoot lad became world famous as Antonio Canova.

THE CLIMB UP THE CAPITOL HILL

WHEN Rome was besieged one of her ablest generals was away from the city, for he had been falsely accused of taking more than his share of plunder at the capture of Veii, a neighbouring city.

Angry with the treatment he had received, Camillus had taken up his abode at Ardea, and by his ability he saved this city from destruction by the Gauls.

When the Romans heard of this exploit they repented, saying: " If only our brave Camillus were here he might save our city also." So they sent a message, begging Camillus to return and help them; but Camillus refused, saying that he was only an exile, and would need some definite authority before he could return to Rome.

Now, the surviving Romans were in the Capitol, which stands high up on the Capitol Hill, and could not be reached without passing through the Gallic lines; but a young Roman, Pontius Cominius, offered to undertake the mission.

Dressed as a peasant, with corks about his neck to keep his head above water, he plunged one dark night into the Tiber, and drifted down to the base of the Hill.

Now came the dangerous part of the venture, for Cominius had to climb up to the Capitol. He clung to grass, vinestem, or point of rock as he dragged his body up the steep ascent, using his bare feet to aid him. On reaching the rampart he was immediately surounded by his countrymen, and told them that Camillus only waited the Senate's decree to come to their help. Camillus was quickly voted Dictator by the few senators who were left, and Cominius returned down the hill.

Though he got safely away, the Gauls noticed that someone had disturbed the creepers, and so they planned a night attack on the Capitol. When they carried this out they found the sentinel asleep, but it was then that the cackling of the sacred geese in the Capitol warned the citizens, and they repulsed the attack. However, the besieged were starving, and were driven to treat with the enemy; but while the ransom was being discussed Camillus appeared on the scene, and exclaimed: " It is with iron, not gold, that Romans guard their country."

Soon after this the Gauls were driven away, and the Romans acknowledged that they owed their rescue to the brave Cominius, who, at the risk of his own life, had brought Camillus back to save them.

THE BOY WHO WROTE TO THE POPE

POPE PIUS THE NINTH once received a letter quite unlike the many he received every day.

It was written on ordinary foolscap paper. There were ink spots on it, crossed-out words, and spelling mistakes. A very young boy living in a suburb of Rome had sent it.

The boy's mother was ill; he had no money to assist her, and he appealed to the Pope for the thirty-seven lire he wanted for medicine.

Pius had an answer sent to the boy, saying that he was ready to receive him the next morning.

On the following day the happy child went to the Vatican, presented his letter of audience, and simply asked that he might speak to the Pope.

The guards, much surprised, turned the letter over and over, but finally let the little Italian in.

His straightforward and determined look immediately appealed to the Pope, who, after a little talk, gave him a golden coin. The boy thanked him, and then innocently called the attention of the Pope to the fact that it was only twenty lire he had received, and he wanted thirty-seven.

" Of course," answered Pius the Ninth, " you are right. Excuse me; I did not remember your letter." Then he took a second coin from his purse.

" But this is too much now," the boy pointed out, "and I have no change. But I will bring it tomorrow."

" That's right; come and see me again tomorrow," replied the Pope.

The boy was prompt at his appointment next morning, and brought the change.

The Pope, meanwhile, had gathered information about him, and had received a most favourable report, so that when the boy entered the room again great news awaited him. The Pope declared that he would provide for his education and see that his mother was cared for in her illness.

And so it was done. The boy was carefully brought up, and became a learned and clever man, worthy of his benefactor.

THE HOUND AT THE GATE

CHULAIN was a mighty warrior who lived in Ireland in the days of long ago.

So great a hero was he that from his boyhood upwards all the country rang with the news of his deeds; and one of the stories the people still love to tell of him was of the time when Chulain was nine years old, and performed the wonderful deed by which he got his name. For until then he was known by another name—Setanta.

The first few years of his life he spent with his mother, who was a princess; but one day, when he was only about eight years old, some travellers came to the house, and the boy heard them talking of the number of kings' sons who lived at the Court of his uncle, the King of Ulster.

"Is it east or west?" begged the boy, and at last the Princess told him how the way there lay far beyond the blue mountains. The next day, without saying a word to anyone, Setanta set out for the King's Court, taking only his hurling stick and ball, and his child's spear and dart.

Now, in those days every boy in Ireland spent a great deal of time playing games, and when little Setanta at last came in sight of the King's palace he saw a great number of boys on the lawn playing ball games and hurling—a game little known in England. Without any more ado Setanta flung himself among them, and played with such skill and vigour that the boys could do nothing against him.

"WILT THOU COME WITH US TO A FEAST?" ASKED THE KING

The tales of these boys, and the games they played, fired the imagination of the little Setanta, and when the visitors were gone he went to his mother and implored her to let him go to his uncle.

"Oh, no, my little son!" said the Princess. "It is too far for a little child like you. You are not yet old enough."

"But how far is it?" asked the child.

"Much too far for you, my little son."

The boy said nothing more, but a few days after he came again to the Princess with the same persistent plea:

"Tell me, I pray you, the way to the Court of my uncle, King of Ulster."

And again she said, "It is too far for you, my little son. Wait till you are older."

Then a great outcry arose among them, and they turned against the newcomer with hard blows and cruelty to drive him away. But little Setanta stood his ground nobly, and fought them as they approached. Meanwhile, this uproar came to the ears of the King and he sent for the newcomer.

"Who art thou?" he asked sternly.

"I am Setanta, the son of the Princess, thy sister, O King!" replied the child.

Then Setanta was taken in with a great welcome, and he took his place in the boy troops, and played with them every day, and learned how to fight with the spear and sword; and thus a year passed away.

Now, at the end of that time a great smith in Ulster prepared a feast for the

King and his court, and invited them thither—in those days in Ireland smiths were accounted great men. The King and his retinue accordingly set out for the smith's house, and their way lay past the lawns where the boy troops were playing. Always interested in boys' play, the King stopped his chariot to watch the games. Awhile he sat there, and then he saw how nobly the little Setanta was playing.

" Seest thou yonder boy Setanta, my sister's son?" said he, turning to the smith. " Without a doubt he will be the champion of Ulster when he is grown. Even now he performs great deeds."

Then the smith also watched the little Setanta, and his heart warmed to the child. " Let him come with us to the feast, O King!" he said. And the King had Setanta summoned to the side of his chariot.

" Wilt thou come with us to a feast in the smith's house?" asked the King, kindly.

" Gladly, O King! " replied Setanta. " But our game is not yet finished. I cannot leave my companions with the play half done. I will follow, if thou wilt? "

Off he ran to his play, where his companions awaited him, and the King's chariot went swiftly on to the smith's house. Arrived there, the King found a gracious welcome, and the smith and the King quite forgot the little Setanta who was to follow. As the afternoon drew dark the smith approached the King.

" All your men are safely housed, are they not, O King? "

" They are all here, every one," replied the King, not thinking of his sister's son.

" In that case," said the smith, " I will let loose my great hound that watches the house for me, and does duty for fifty men."

Then the smith gave orders that all his gates be shut and barred, and his great hound turned out on the plain.

In the meantime the little Setanta had finished his game with his companions, and set out for the smith's house. Many miles lay between that house and the King's palace, but he beguiled the way by hurling his ball far along the road, and running swiftly after it to catch it. Thus he made great progress, and arrived near the smith's house as the dusk came on.

But, as he approached, the hound who was on guard came at him with glaring eyes and gaping mouth, and his roar might have been heard all over Ulster. · But the child stood calmly awaiting the furious animal,

and in his hand he had only the ball and stick with which he played. And when the hound, roaring the while, leaped at him with gaping fangs, he drove his ball straight down his throat, and the dog rolled on the plain. Then Setanta seized him by the legs and dashed him against a rock.

Meanwhile in the hall the feast was going gaily. Never a thought gave the King or his men to the child who was abroad on the plain. But suddenly the music and laughter were shattered by a terrible roar without, and the smith started to his feet.

" Some enemy at the gate! " cried he, seizing his sword.

Then, like a flash, the King remembered. " O evil day," he cried, " when I have come here and forgotten my sister's little son, who was to follow us! Surely he is dead now because of thy hound! "

At that the warriors, led by the King and the smith, started up in the feasting-hall. They did not wait for the doors to be opened, but through windows and over walls they leaped into the plain beyond; and there stood the child unharmed, and beside him the great hound lay dead.

" Evil day for me! " the smith said then. " The child has killed the great hound that was my pride and guard! "

Tears of anger and sorrow stood in his eyes, and he turned to Setanta in wrath. " There will be no welcome for you to-night, boy! " he said. " That hound was the protector of all my goods, my house, and my flocks. Now enemies will enter the gate, and my house will be ruined! "

Then the King interposed. " Canst thou not get another hound? " asked he. But before the smith could reply the brave child went up to him.

" I had to kill thy hound, O smith, or be killed myself. See now. We will procure another hound of the same breed, and until he is grown and trained I myself will be thy hound, and will guard thy house."

So it came to be that the King's nephew lived in the smith's house and kept guard in the place of the smith's great hound. And there he received the name by which he was known all over Ireland and throughout the world. No one ever again spoke of him as Setanta, and he was called Chulain, which means " the little hound of the smith." And when he was a grown man and made his great cry in battle men would hear him coming and would say: " It is the hound! Let us flee! "

Nature's Wonderful Living Family in Earth and Air and Sea

The Shore Crab

CRABS, LOBSTERS, AND THEIR KIN

ONE of the little tragedies of everyday experience is that which comes to us all, when, with zest and satisfaction, we begin to tell a tale which we hope will create surprise, and are brought up short by the remark, "Thank you, I know it all."

In any average company the story of the crabs, lobsters, and the strange little folk to which they are nearly allied in sea and on land, is proof against such disappointment. The facts are so bewilderingly strange that, were they not established truth, they would be received as the gay fictions of a jester, or the morbid fancies of a mind given to the invention of grimly fantastic terrors.

How amusing it would sound, for example, if a comedian appeared on the stage with his hand bound up, declaring that he had been bitten by a crab while up a tree bird-nesting!

And what an adventurer we should think the man who assured us he had been gnawed and maimed by crabs when exploring a mountain height; or that his house had been damaged by myriads of crabs marching right through and over it!

Such things may happen, have happened. The old animal fables on which the minds of our ancestors were fed for centuries seem ludicrous to us now, but

the simplest fact about crabs and their kindred is, in its own way, as startling, almost as unbelievable, as anything the old legends said.

We have no backbones here, no spinal cords; but we have brain, we have highly-organised nervous tissue, we have decided evidence of intelligence, of affection, of passions as ardent as those of angry hornets, of the courage and ferocity we wrongly impute to the modern bulldog.

Moreover, there is a history behind the group which inspires a touch of awe in the imaginative; its members are so immensely ancient. No man with power to think can view a giant sequoia tree for the first time without some sense of gravity. He is in the presence of a living thing over which time and storm have streamed for perhaps thousands of years. Antiquity is always impressive.

But what is the lifetime of a single tree to the lifetime of an Order of Nature? What is the lifetime of any existing species of animals compared with the age represented by animals which are now integral parts of many of the rocks forming the Earth's surface?

Everything changes, everything but eternity passes. Yet here, in the king crabs, we have capable, energetic, living

PREHISTORIC LIFE · MAMMALS · BIRDS · REPTILES · FISHES · INSECTS

fortresses which were lords of the ancient oceans before a single ancestor of the greater, nobler types of today was called into existence. They were monarchs then; they outlived their nearest kindred, they witnessed the rise of all the higher life, they have kept their place in warm seas; kings no longer, but still sufficiently general for us to have them in our grand aquarium at the London Zoo.

Two great allies of the king crabs, the merostomata and the trilobites, are gone; we know not why. The trilobites swarmed the seas like pollen blown from trees into an English stream, yet they are every one now as safely embedded in the rocks as ancient ants in fossil amber. Their contemporaries and cousins, the king crabs, lacking the fine gift of the trilobite to curl up its three-lobed shell, like a common woodlouse, have kept safe within their horseshoe-shaped shells, and are still here, antiquity's living emblem.

The king crabs and their associates seem to have arisen from the creatures which gave rise to bristleworms, and to have developed midway between the spiders and the scorpions. The spider and the scorpion poison us with a bite; the land crab eats us if he can, while we eat his edible shore brother and his cousins the lobster, the crayfish, the prawn, and the shrimp.

HOW THE KING CRAB BURROWS INTO THE SAND OF THE SEA BED

Worms and molluscs are the food of the ancient king crabs, and a sandy or muddy sea bed from 12 to 30 feet deep is their home. They burrow into the sand, by thrusting the fore part of the shell sideways and downwards, the strong tail helping. All the necessary conditions are present at the Zoo, but one has seen an artificial home for king crabs suggesting how a species might become extinct.

The king crab is apt to be capsized. That being so, he uses his tail as a lever, tilts himself forward and sideways so that he falls over and regains his proper position. But in the famous aquarium at Monte Carlo these crabs have a large sea den which has a concrete bottom, so that when one of the animals overturns there its tail cannot grip and dig, and is useless; the crab cannot right itself, but must await the aid of a man.

Now, supposing storms swept the sea bottom clear of sand and mud, as happens off our own coasts. The crabs would be stranded on a rocky bed, where, if they overturned, they could not recover any more than they can in the unnatural conditions at Monte Carlo. They would die, like stranded tortoises or cast sheep. A localised species might disappear by a succession of such disasters—but that does not explain away the outgoing of the once multitudinous trilobites.

THE HISTORY THAT STRETCHES OVER TEN MILLION YEARS

Science, endeavouring to fix some sort of time-table for king crab history, holds that, as an Order, these animals must be at least ten million years old. There is a star whose distance is so tremendous that its light, travelling toward us at the rate of 186,000 miles a second, takes a million years to reach the Earth. What was the animal world like, we wonder, when the light of that star, at this moment reaching us, left its source? At any rate, when the leap across the void began, the king crabs were already nine million years old.

The king crabs were not of the kind with which we are familiar at table. These, with the lobsters and crayfish, are brigaded with the crustacea, which have representatives in many planes of life, in sea and fresh water, in freedom and as parasites. The body of a crustacean is made up of a number of segments, and to these segments are attached the legs, the parts which compose the mouth, and the appendages which resemble short claws rather than legs.

In many of the species the eyes are raised on stalks, and can be moved about like lamps on a flexible arm, but there are others where the eyes are not raised, or if stalked, are not movable. The mouth is, of course, different from that of a mammal or of any other backboned animal, for in the crabs we have an organ made up of three pairs of jaws, or maxillae, which are simply modified limbs.

QUAINT LITTLE LIMBS WHICH HELP THE CRAB TO BREATHE

Such a mouth cannot seize, tear, and rip, as can an animal's, but it must be fed and stuffed by the powerful pincers. But for all that, it is formidably efficient for the work it has to do.

Breathing is by gills, not as with insects, by spiracles; but there are wonderful modifications in species which live mainly ashore. Small appendages near the mouth are kept in constant motion in order to secure a regular current of fresh water for the gills. There are other senses, too, in these quaint-looking little limbs.

With these the crab hears, it feels, it smells. Wonderful that all these offices should be discharged by limbs enclosed in a hard shell. That shell, by the way, is not like the shell of a periwinkle or an oyster, nor does it match the horn of a bison or the bone of a deer's antlers. It is really a sort of half-way house between our skin and true horn or bone, a development, in its highest power, of that wonderful substance, chitin, which affords a covering of mail to insects, and even lines their interior.

The crab is not born with this armament. It begins its career in an egg attached to the limbs of its mother, and when hatched is a speck of life enclosed in a tough little membrane. A mother crab knows her offspring, but we should never dream, until instructed, that the baby crab is a crab at all, so completely unlike the adult form is it, with a streaming long " beak," a sort of cap over its back, and an eye out of all proportion to the diminutive body.

If it escapes the peril of other crabs and the fishes and sea birds, our little crab slowly comes into possession of its first shell. That has to be changed repeatedly, much more often than the skin of a caterpillar is changed.

HOW THE CRAB WITHDRAWS FROM ITS COAT OF MAIL

For, like the caterpillar, the crab cannot grow without exchanging its external covering for a new one. When the shell is fully filled, the body within it turns watery or jelly-like, and the little crab finds its mail split down the back. Tightly fitted in as he is at every joint, he withdraws each leg in turn from the shell, like a boy taking off his boots. Then he liberates the body, one half at a time, and is a helpless little fellow, disarmed, terribly afraid lest some hungry enemy should find him a tender, tempting mouthful.

As the wild duck goes into hiding till his new flight feathers have grown, so the crab must lurk in secret places till he is newly mailed, and fit to face the world and its dangers. Very poorly he must feel at such times, for not only does his entire shell come off, he even moults the coats of his stomach. "A dog's life," we say disparagingly of human conditions, but who would have a crab's?

We must suppose the crab's sense of smell to be acute, for, unlike the lobster, which likes its food " high," the crab will take nothing but fresh meat, unless sorely pressed. Therefore, as it shuns the light for hunting when under observation, and must feed mainly by night, and as at the best its watery home must be rather gloomy, we may take it that its " nose " must be very sensitive to guide it to the bait to which it scurries. It will eat fresh meat; it will catch and eat fish.

THE CRAB THAT WALKED LIKE A FLY DOWN THE SIDE OF A WALL

The crab commonest to our shores is the green shore crab, but many of us know rocky pools which hold little edible crabs. One remembers testing the appetite of an anemone; the creature swallowed eleven little edible crabs, as big as halfpennies, at a single meal!

Our British edible crabs, like some of their foreign kinsmen, are nothing in the way of swimmers; they walk and crawl, and few of us realise how wonderfully agile they are. Like little marine life guardsmen with their cuirasses on, they seem incapable of anything but the stiffest motion. But this is the sort of thing that happens when they are cornered.

On the parapet of a jetty a crab appeared and seemed prepared by destiny for the daring hand of a traveller who reached to snatch it. The crab sidled like lightning along the sharp parapet, then over it round the arched projection jutting from it, and straight down the sea-wall, flat as the wall of a room, precisely as an insect or a gecko would have done in similar circumstances.

We must not expect feats of this sort from our hermit crabs, for they have to carry with them a burden not their own. They are born with the nether part of their bodies quite defenceless, though the fore part has its carapace of mail, and the claws are as potent nippers as any other crab's. They fear to be pinched in halves, so they have to hunt for homes.

HOW A LITTLE HERMIT SOLVES ITS HOUSING PROBLEM

Whelk shells are generally the desired haven. They prefer an empty one, but, driven to an extremity, they will attack the owner, tear it to pieces, and then take possession of the liberated shell. Hermit crabs have their housing problems as permanent and perplexing as our own.

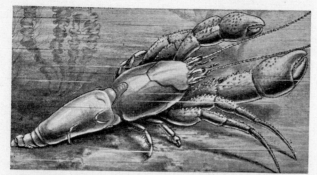

THE HERMIT CRAB SETS OUT TO FIND A HOME

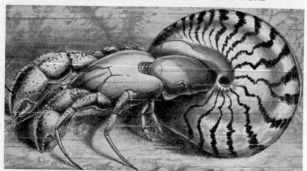

HE DISCOVERS AN EMPTY SHELL AND
CRAWLS INTO IT—BACKWARDS

GROWING TOO BIG FOR HIS HOUSE, THE CRAB FIGHTS ANOTHER
CRAB FOR THE POSSESSION OF A LARGER SHELL

Once in possession of the borrowed home they insert their tails, which are specially modified to enable them to curl round and fit into the whorls of the fortress, while some of their foot-like appendages fasten like suckers to the walls.

The sense of insecurity is not wholly abolished when this sanctuary is gained. The hermit in his shell must have an anemone on it, and the anemone is willing. With the hermit half in and half out, and an anemone mounted on top, together they go roaming in search of food.

The anemone stings the enemy of the hermit; the hermit is as a pack-horse carrying the anemone to food. It is one of the most marvellous partnerships in the wilds. An anemone is an animal only just above the level of a vegetable, yet it has this extraordinary understanding with the hermit crab. We, if we wish to dislodge an anemone from a shell, must tear the lovely little monster to pieces; but when the crab feels his growing pains upon him, and must turn out and find a larger shell, he dismounts the anemone, takes it with him, and mounts it on the new one. How can we account for such agreements between creatures so low in the scale of existence?

Crabs are possibly the greatest of all camouflage artists. Some of them take sponges for partners, instead of anemones; some rob the sea squirt of his tunic and wrap up in that; some, like the spider crabs of our deeper waters, bedeck themselves with seaweed, so that they cannot be suspected to be crabs at all.

They scissor off cuttings of the weed or of sponge, plant them on their shells, and the cuttings grow where they have been placed, and a moving garden of weed masks the crab within. Having noted that our common crabs are crawlers rather than swimmers, we must remember that there are crabs which swim powerfully. The so-called fiddler crabs are of this group, and derive their name from their oar-like feet, with which they make the waters their chariot. We have swimmers in British deeper waters, members of the Portunus group.

Our waters contain some notable species in the spiderlike slender-beaked crab; the great thornback spider crab, a crab so curiously marked as to be called the masked crab; and minute pea crabs which, instead of carrying about anemones or sponges or seaweed, take up their residence within the shells of our common bivalves, living safely in an animate fortress, whose food they share.

But let us go farther afield and take a look at the land crabs. Here the realm of wonder widens its boundaries, for we come to creatures which, while they must still go down to the sea to lay their eggs, as frogs must go back to pond and ditch for the like purpose, yet they themselves, like those amphibians, drown if confined to the water.

One which lives on the verge of the sea burrows into the sand, then, having roughly made its hole, ejects a strong stream of water from its gills, so clearing a passage for breathing, and is content.

Not so the more advanced crabs. They go miles away from the sea.

Some of them are best known to us by the famous calling crab, a title coming from the fact that the crab has one of its foremost claws

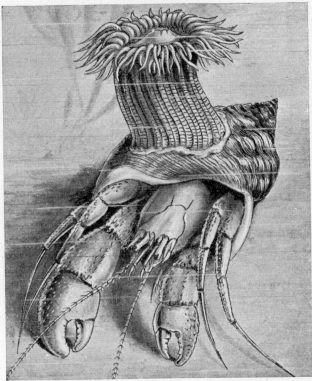

A SEA ANEMONE SETTLES DOWN TO SHARE THE
LIFE OF THE CRAB IN HIS SHELL

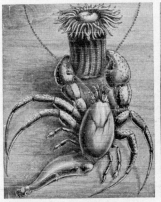

CHANGING HIS HOME, THE CRAB
TAKES HIS LODGER WITH HIM

THE CRAB ESTABLISHES THE
ANEMONE ON THE NEW HOUSE

A CROWD OF SHELLS AND SPONGES OUT FOR
A WALK ON THE SEASHORE

hugely developed, and carries it high and forward when running in such a manner as to suggest to onlookers that it is beckoning someone.

These are crabs which have come ashore for good, save for the egg-laying period. Congregating in swarms, they make great burrows in the sand, like rabbits, combining their efforts with intelligence and art. Darwin thought these the best of the whole group, in point of sense, from a little test made by a well-known naturalist. The man threw several shells towards the crab's burrow, and one entered the hole. Out came the crab in great excitement, bringing the shell with it, and carrying it to a place of safety a foot away. As it returned it noted three other shells, realised that they also were in danger of rolling down the slope into the burrow, and thereupon carried those off to a place of safety as well.

CRABS WHICH PICK UP A HOME AND CARRY IT FAR INLAND

Experience teaches us not to look for our crabs far from sea, but in the tropics there are hermit crabs which take up their homes and walk far inland. They carry with them large, heavy turbo shells. Travellers have found these shells, some empty, some containing the hermits which transported them, a thousand feet up a mountain-side, and one severely bit a naturalist who sought to gather something high up in a tree.

Then there are land crabs which crawl about dry rocks and do not go to sea, the Grapsus strigosus, a little horror, first given its due place in scientific annals by the naturalists of the Challenger expedition. While the party were fishing and bird-hunting on St. Paul's rocks they found themselves surrounded by swarms of crabs, which stole the bait laid out in readiness for the lines, and carried off the fish as they lay new-drawn from the waters.

That was not the worst. Nesting terns had been driven from their young in order that these might be examined, so a big old crab waddled into a nest and seized and carried off a plump young tern to devour it alive at leisure.

That, it may be objected, was an exceptional case, rendered easy by the intervention of man; but let the mind rove to Pitti Island in the Indian Ocean, and there, the traveller tells us, the ground is thick with the remains of young terns, some reduced to clean-picked skeletons, all murdered by crabs.

After that we are prepared for the fact that other crabs regularly raid rabbit warrens, and that others banquet on coconuts. The palm-hunters are usually known as robber crabs.

THE ROBBER THAT CLIMBS UP A TREE IN SEARCH OF FOOD

It had long been recognised that the robber crabs fed on coconuts, but that they climbed the tall palms in pursuit of their booty was deemed a traveller's tale. It is quite true. Apart from the testimony of eye witnesses, a photograph of a robber crab at his work high up in a tree is exhibited at our Natural History Museum.

But how are the crabs to obtain the meat of the nut, which is enclosed in a very hard shell, and that in a dense husk of fibre? Having climbed his tree and brought down his prize, the crab tears off the fibre, strip by strip, then hammers out the " eyes " of the nut with his great claws, and, an entry having been gained, inserts his thin hinder claws, and with these drags out the contents of the nut.

But now we come to land crabs which make us shudder. The robber crabs, big blue fellows, more like lobsters than crabs, can bite a man's finger off, as members of an eclipse expedition in 1922 found out at Christmas Island, in the Indian Ocean. There are others.

There are land crabs which, when they make their annual migration to the sea, go as straight as lemmings on the march. They swarm over houses; they swarm through them. The Christmas Islanders found themselves bitten in their beds as the swarming crabs made their pilgrimage to the distant ocean nursery. The whole land is covered with them as they swarm.

THE FEARFUL CREATURES WHICH NIBBLED THE CLOTHES OF SLEEPING MEN

Then there are the land crabs of South Trinidad, unforgettable from a memorable picture drawn for us by Mr. Cherry-Garrard in his account of the Antarctic voyage which led Scott and his comrades to death. They rested for a while on this little island off Brazil, and were filled with amazement and loathing at the swarms of yellow-and-pink crabs, with dead yellow staring eyes, peeping at them from behind every nook and boulder, as if to say, " You drop down among us and we will do the rest."

A GROUP OF LITTLE ARMOURED CREATURES

COMMON LOBSTER

CRAYFISH

NORWAY LOBSTER

LONG-BEAKED SPIDER CRAB

COMMON SHRIMP

LAND CRAB

A GIANT SPIDER CRAB

COCONUT CRAB

HERMIT CRAB

VELVET FIDDLER CRAB

THORNBACK CRAB

THREE LITTLE PEA CRABS

The pictures on these pages are by Messrs. S. C. Johnson, E. Step, and others

They even nibbled at our boots as we stood, he tells us; to have lain down to sleep would have been suicidal. These crabs, coupled with the hideous giant man-eating grampuses of the sea, left a deeper sense of horror on the minds of those hardy explorers than anything else they encountered, short of the tragic agony of starvation to death in the great white silence.

Mr. Cherry-Garrard had been anticipated by E. F. Knight, who saw those same crabs of Trinidad, and with two comrades, as they lay in their tents that night, was the victim of a massed assault by the little wretches. They began to gnaw the sleepers as they lay. " They would have devoured us had we not awoke; as it was they nibbled holes in our clothes."

Nothing more grim has ever come out of Trinidad than E. F. Knight's picture of these crabs, which, as the three adventurers landed and cooked their evening meal of fish, swarmed in multitudes down the mountain side.

THE GIANT CRAB WHICH USED ITS CLAWS AS A FORK

The crabs, he said, looked like goblin guardians of the approaches to a wicked magician's fortress. They were fearful as the firelight fell on their yellow cynical faces, fixed as that of a sphinx in a horrid grin. We threw them lumps of fish, which they devoured with crab-like slowness, yet perseverance.

A huge beast (continued E. F. Knight) was standing a yard from me; I gave him a portion of fish and watched him. He looked me straight in the face with his outstarting eyes, and proceeded with his two front claws to tear up his food, bringing it to his mouth as with a fork. But all the while he never looked at what he was doing; his face was fixed in one position, staring at me. And when I looked round, lo, there were half a dozen others all steadily feeding, but with immovable heads turned to me with that fixed basilisk stare. It was indeed horrible, the effect nightmarish in the extreme.

After all their feed of fish, it was these same monsters which attacked the sleepers as they lay in their tent that night. The thought of that scene was recalled when, some years ago, a naval officer told something of the fate of the survivors of the German cruiser Emden, which the Royal Navy sank during the First World War, off one of the Cocos Islands.

When H.M.A.S. Sydney drove the beaten raider ashore she could not go to the assistance of the wounded, but had to steam away in chase of the Emden's consort, so 15 hours elapsed before our men could get back to the survivors.

THE WORLD OF MEANING IN THE SAILOR'S SIMPLE WORDS

When at last they came back to the island, they found that " many of the wounded survivors had managed to get ashore, but lay in the hot sun in a pitiful plight, *as the land crabs are very ferocious there*." So says the British sailor. What a world of terrible meaning is compressed into the last half dozen words in that grim sentence!

We may hold the lobster guiltless of all such charges as these, for, though his claws are prodigious in size and power, he has no members of his tribe to outrage his record by deeds so malevolent as those associated with the records of the crabs.

All the ingenious men, says Charles Kingsley, all the scientific men, and all the fanciful men in the world could not invent anything so curious and so ridiculous as a lobster. Of course, that was only Kingsley's fun, or we should have to bring up against his charming memory the testimony of a naturalist of greater repute, Huxley, who immortalised the fame of the lobster in a lecture which is as noteworthy in literature today as Faraday's memorable lecture on the chemistry of a candle.

There are many structural differences between the lobster and the crab, though their relationship is as obvious as their differences. The lobster is long-tailed; the crab short-tailed. In the lobster the tail is a powerful organ of propulsion. The lobster is commonly supposed to use the tail only to project itself backward, but the organ drives the creature forward as swiftly as to rearward.

HOW THE FOND MOTHER LOBSTER LOOKS AFTER HER BABIES

To that broad tail the eggs are attached, the berries, as they are called. From these the little ones emerge, and are for a time attached to the parent, who has affection and skill in their guarding and guidance. Until they are well grown and able to fend for themselves, she mothers them most charmingly.

They gather about her like chicks about a hen, sporting and hunting. At a sign of danger she rattles her big claws, and they scutter for dear life beneath her, when she herself, the last to move, steadily shoots into her rocky retreat.

In life the lobster is a greenish blue; boiled, its coat of mail turns a brilliant scarlet. One of the crimes of the table used to be the boiling alive of lobsters and crabs. It is essential that they should be fresh and so they have to be kept alive till the last moment. But nowadays it is the practice to plunge a thin-pointed knife through the creature at the final moment before dropping it into the hissing cauldron, thus giving it a merciful end.

Lobsters are caught in wicker baskets called pots, attracted by a bait of fish or strong-smelling flesh. They fight among themselves in the pots and bite each other's claws off, so that, if storms delay the visit of the fisherman to his pots, he is certain to find his captures badly maimed when he hauls them up. To prevent such battles en route to market he ties their great pincers together, and that is the secret of the pieces of string we see round lobsters' claws in the shops.

But lobsters and crabs do not always wait for battle to lose their claws. The lobster, in a state of panic, casts his claws, as a slow worm casts the end of its tail. The crab is the more specialised in the matter, for he can discard an entire leg, several legs, in fact, whereas the lobster's renunciation is limited to the great pincers. But pincers or legs, they can be renewed in the same way as the limbs of an injured starfish.

Crayfish are the freshwater representatives of the family. They resemble the lobster in outline, though not in colour, and lack the huge fore claws. They are in many a canal and river which we do not suspect of housing such treasure, for they come out to feed only at night, lurking by day under stones or banks.

WATER FLEA   SAND-HOPPER   WOODLOUSE

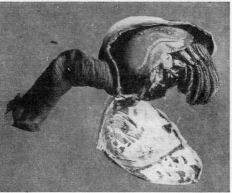

A SHIP'S BARNACLE INSIDE ITS SHELL

When the sun is down, forth comes the crayfish, in quest of worms, insects, small frogs, fish, and vegetation. They obviously hunt by scent, for when men go out to catch them, they bait their hooped nets with a bloater which is decidedly strong. The net is a rough and ready contrivance modelled after the shape of an eel trap.

Even with a contrivance so simple, one has heard of 800 crayfish being caught in a single night in an unfrequented mill stream. That was too big a haul for one stretch of water, for the crayfish is not prolific like the lobster, which lays as many as 100,000 eggs a season.

The crayfish's eggs may number 200, but there may be only a single one, and it takes five years at least for one of the creatures to reach maturity, though after that they may live another fifteen years or so.

In winter they are sluggish, hidden in some recess in the bank, with claws outstretched to seize unsuspecting prey. But the dead season is a busy one for the mother, as it is then that she lays her eggs, so that they may mature and be ready for hatching as spring leads in warmth and new access of life and food to the waters of the crayfish's home.

Next in the order come the shrimps and prawns, active swimmers, whose powerful tails impart a sort of leaping motion through the water. Both admirably match their surroundings, either by resembling the ground over which they swim, or being almost transparent, or again, even changing colours to suit environment. Shrimps are common in fresh water, but we draw our supplies from the seas, supplies so great as completely to defeat all attempt at a calculation in numbers.

The prawns, which are larger and marked by certain well known distinctions, keep farther out from the shore than the shrimps, but both have representatives down in the oozy, unlighted abysses, and there, 3000 feet deep in the Indian Ocean, two species of prawns have been discovered endowed with the art of light-making by means of lovely phosphorescent lamps, fashioned from certain glands in their antennae.

Shrimps are snappers-up of unconsidered trifles, of herbage and flesh, converting garbage into wholesome food. Extraordinary forms are found in their family, some like skeletons, some with preposterously long necks with huge eyes mounted on far-reaching stalks, some with great lobster-like pincers, some fashioned like the praying insect and catching prey with claws of the true mantis type.

We pass on to woodlice, the earthly modern representatives, perhaps, of the defunct trilobite. Although they are true land creatures, their nature seems to remember their origin, for they must have moisture, whether they are doing good work by eating up rotting wood, or behaving as little rascals in devouring our maidenhead ferns or tomato plants in the greenhouse. To speak of their eating tomato plants is not an exaggeration. When the tender seedlings are first planted out it is no uncommon thing for a woodlouse to cut down the entire plant as neatly as a woodman cuts down a tree, and so perishes a growth which, given time, would have borne a peck of tomatoes.

THE WOODLOUSE WHICH CURLS ITSELF UP IN A BALL

As we all know, there are woodlice which do not curl up, and woodlice which do. The abler species, rolling itself into the neatest little ball, is called the pill woodlouse. All woodlice must be precious assets in the wilds turning rubbish and decay to the support of life; but in well tended gardens and conservatories they are an unredeemed scourge to the cultivator, and most difficult to eradicate.

A stride and we are down to the sea again, to make mention of near allies in the sand-hoppers, which science calls the Talitrus locusta. Down in the sand, under seaweed and other gifts of the sea, these little scavengers swarm.

Practically anything organic is food to them. They do not invade our homes and gardens, but eat and eat day and night under cover of their sandy, weedy, sanctuaries, all that would tend to make the shore unsavory and evil to health. Great

leapers, they are themselves food for crabs and shore birds, good friends to us, though very alarming to nervous people, whose timid excavations for sand castles send the little creatures bounding through the air in search of safety.

THE TINY CREATURES WHICH KEEP THE WATER PURE

They are numerous enough to satisfy the calculating faculties of a mathematician, but their freshwater allies, the water fleas, are by comparison like the sands of the shore contrasted with the number of the rocks. There are many species of them enclosed in double-shelled defences, and their life history is full of interest. Here we can give them but a passing certificate for purifying the water from decaying animal matter and for devouring masses of minute vegetable growths.

Omitting many other forms, we must note the barnacles as belonging to our present company. We owe the first revelation of the truth as to the barnacle's crustacean character to Darwin. His discovery and memorable publication on the subject marked a grand triumph of research over guesswork and fable. The barnacle, which is a member of the group of animals technically known as stalked Cirripedia, undergoes many changes in the course of its career, but ends as a true crustacean, anchoring itself by its head to ship, floating timber, or other point of vantage, and gaining a living by kicking its food into its mouth with its curious curved legs.

The creature is of interest to us all from its habit of clinging to ships in such numbers as to slow down their pace through the water and making it necessary to send them into dry dock to be cleaned.

WISE MEN WHO BELIEVED THAT A BARNACLE BECAME A GOOSE

We know the whole story of their strange career now, but the way to it forms one of the strangest chapters in the history of knowledge. Grave scholars believed for ages that the barnacle was the early stage of a goose. The memory of the myth lives to this day in the existing title of the barnacle goose. That fine bird was supposed to arise from the barnacle, and its foolish name was given to it in that belief.

The whole of this family of creatures is crammed with material for thought and wonder, pleasure and interest, and not a little that is frankly terrible. It takes all sorts of life to make up the world.

PICTURE-STORY OF A PAIR OF SHOES

1. Before a pair of shoes can be made, standard patterns for the uppers, varying according to the style, size, and shape of the last, must be made in fibre board, as we see here.

2. In the Clicking Department, where the pictures on this page were taken, the patterns are placed on the skins and the component parts of the uppers are cut out by hand.

3. The workers in this picture are marking the edges of the cut uppers with paint of various colours. This is done so that the different sizes can be quickly and easily identified.

STITCHING THE UPPERS TOGETHER

4. In the Closing Department we see an operation known as skiving, in which the edges are shaved by a machine. The fine edge of the skived upper is then folded over and held in position by adhesive.

5. Various types of sewing machines are used to stitch the component parts of the uppers together; then, the eyelets having been punched and clenched by machine, stitches are inserted in the throat of the shoe, acting as a stay to take strain. This operation is known as barring.

6. While the uppers are being prepared, in another part of the works the soles, insoles, middles, and lifts, or pieces of leather for the heels, are stamped out by presses, using cutting dies ; after which a grading machine levels the cut pieces and registers the substance by stamping.

7. The insoles are rounded to the required size by this machine, which cuts away the excess leather.

8. A channel is cut into the insole to form a foundation for the welt and uppers.

PREPARING THE SHOES FOR THE SOLES

9. Five sets of automatic pincers hold the fore-part of the upper to the last, and insert seven tacks to hold it in position.

10. In this picture a narrow strip of leather, called a welt, is being sewn in, securing it to the upper and insole channel.

11. When the outer sole, after mellowing by water, has been placed in position on the bottom of the shoe, the excess material at the edge of the sole and welt is trimmed away, as this picture shows. A stitching machine then attaches the sole to the welt.

12. In this picture the heel is being attached to the shoe with 15 strong nails, driven under great pressure through the heel lifts, piece sole, seat lift, and insole. Then a machine making rivets from wire fastens on the top-piece, thereby completing the heel.

13. The heel having been attached and trimmed, the edge is scoured by revolving emery wheels to a very fine finish, as we see here.

14. Rapidly revolving rollers covered with abrasive paper scour away the top surface of the leather to give a smooth surface for polishing.

FINISHING THE SHOES FOR THE SHOPS

15. A brushing machine with revolving brushes of different widths cleans the uppers and welts.

16. By means of a current of hot air this machine removes any small creases remaining in the shoe.

17. Before the shoes are examined a coat of polish is sprayed over the uppers, as we see here.

18. From the Packing Department the shoes will go to shops all over the United Kingdom.

These photographs are by courtesy of the True-Form Boot Company; the General Electric Company; and the Electrical Equipment Company.

Plain Answers to the Questions of the Children of the World

The Siloam Inscription, a Jewish newspaper of twenty-six centuries ago

WHEN DID NEWSPAPERS BEGIN ?

THE newspaper in its modern form is usually regarded as beginning in 1566, when the Venetian Government issued written news-sheets and exhibited them in the streets, anyone being allowed to read them on payment of a small coin called a *gazetta*. On this account the news-sheets were called Gazettes, and they became so popular that they were printed. Soon after the date mentioned gazettes were issued in most of the big cities of Europe. The first English newspaper was the Weekly News, published in London in 1622, but in this paper and its successors down to 1641 only foreign news was printed.

But, while newspapers in the modern sense are thus less than four centuries old, something corresponding to the newspaper was found in the ancient world. Accounts of the doings of the imperial armies of Rome were sent to generals in command in all parts of the empire, and these Acta Diurna, or Daily Doings, as they were called, were communicated by the generals to their officers.

Farther back still, items of news, generally about kings or battles, were carved in stone in prominent places in Babylonian and Assyrian cities, and may almost be regarded as the origin of the

newspaper as a record of events. One of the oldest newspapers in this sense is the Siloam Inscription, discovered in 1880 in the rocky aqueduct of the Pool of Siloam at the south-east end of Jerusalem. The characters are one of the early forms of the alphabet used by the Phoenicians, Hebrews, and Moabites, and the language is Biblical Hebrew. The inscription is a very large one.

It dates back to at least 700 B.C., and is one of the oldest Hebrew inscriptions known ; it is a Jewish newspaper of Isaiah's time, and perhaps even of Solomon's time. Freely translated it reads thus :

Finished is the boring. And this was the manner of the boring. The hewers were plying the pickaxe, each toward his fellow, and there were still three cubits to finish, when there was heard the voice of one calling to his fellow; for there was a crack in the rock on the right. And on the day of the boring the hewers struck each to meet his fellow, pickaxe to pickaxe, and the water ran from the source to the pool, two hundred and a thousand cubits. And a hundred cubits was the height of the rock above the heads of the hewers.

It sounds very modern—just such a paragraph as might announce the completion of the cutting of a new tunnel through the Alps, or the boring for a new underground railway, for instance.

FIRE · WIND · WATER · LIFE · MIND · SLEEP · HOW · WHY · WHERE

What is Paper Made of ?

Paper can be made of almost any fibrous vegetable material, and has been made at some time or other of wood, cotton, linen, papyrus, clover, beanstalks, heather, moss, nettles, grass, peat, sawdust, ferns and bracken, seaweed, thistles, tobacco stalks, and even gutta-percha and asbestos. But for practical purposes only a few of these substances are useful. Cotton and linen rags are ideal, but the supply is limited and the cost high. Esparto grass is largely used, but the principal material is wood-pulp, obtained from the pine tree. The supply of wood-pulp, however, has proved quite inadequate of recent years, and experiments are constantly being made to find a new raw material for the papermaker. Probably bamboo will be used some day. The Children's Encyclopedia paper is made from wood-pulp.

What do we Mean by the Length of a Sound Wave ?

When we throw a stone into a calm pond we notice that waves run out across the pond from the point where the stone entered, and that the crests of the waves are a regular distance apart. The distance from the crest of one wave to the crest of the other is the length of the wave. So it is with sound waves. When a bell vibrates it causes waves in the air, which beat against the drum of the ear and produce in our consciousness the sensation we call sound. These air waves, which produce sound, are called sound waves, and their length—as in the case of water waves—is the distance from the crest of one wave to the crest of the adjoining wave. The shorter the wave the higher is the pitch of the sound; but when the wave becomes shorter than a quarter of an inch, its sound is no longer audible to human ears.

What is the Sudd on the Nile ?

The sudd, named after an Arabic word meaning obstacle or barrier, is a strange feature of the Upper Nile. The waters become covered with a mass of floating plants, and these, when mixed with trunks of trees, form floating islands, which press together, and finally grow into an impenetrable barrier, stopping river traffic.

We can therefore imagine the condition of a river like the Nile when it is completely blocked by a vast mass of semi-tropical vegetation; but fortunately a use has now been found for the sudd, and a factory at Khartoum dries it, reduces the material to powder, and presses it into blocks for fuel for the Nile steamers. Efforts have also been made to employ it for thin boarding and for paper-making, but these have not been successful commercially.

What was the Appian Way?

The Appian Way, of which we see a picture on pages 1780 and 5499, was a famous Roman road made in 312 B.C. by Appius Claudius. It first ran from Rome to Capua, then down to Brindisi, over 340 miles away.

It was by this road that Paul entered Rome, being escorted from Appii Forum, a town forty miles away from the city, by the brethren.

A part of that splendid avenue was bordered for 12 miles with marble tombs of great men, like the philosopher Seneca, the triumvir Pompeius, the Scipios, and the three famous men named Horatius. Rich dwellings stood on each side of the road inside the walls.

From Rome to Capua the road was paved with blocks of lava closely set, like all the masonry of the time, and smoothed on the surface.

The beautiful Appian Way, known all over the ancient world, was often embellished by Roman Emperors. Unhappily it fell into ruins in the Middle Ages. Digging has now brought to light a part of the road and many marble tombs. The tomb of Cecilia Metella is one of the best known. It is shown on page 1781.

What is the Secret of Luminous Paint?

Certain chemical substances, such as the sulphides of calcium and barium, have the peculiar property of absorbing light when exposed to it, and giving out this light in darkness. The amount of light is not very great, and gradually diminishes, though on being again exposed to light the material recovers its light-giving power.

Luminous paint contains one of these substances, and, in the case of calcium fluoride, the fluorescence arises from the electric reactions between the positively-charged calcium atoms and the negatively-charged fluorine atoms. Luminous paint is used for clock-dials, numbers on street doors, and other purposes.

THE STORY OF A GNAT BORN IN A BUBBLE

1. The buffalo gnat, so called because its head is something like a buffalo's, is a hump-backed insect, which in some countries causes disease fatal to animals and birds, especially in the neighbourhood of streams.

2. As the mosquito is the creature of stagnant waters so this gnat is the insect of swiftly-flowing streams. The female holds on to a rock above water and, vibrating her wings and abdomen, lays her eggs in patches.

3. The eggs stick to a leaf, or some other object, by means of a gummy covering, and after a week a club-shaped larva hatches out. The head has two fan-like attachments which open and shut continually, drawing tiny water plants into the mouth for sustenance.

4. This larva lives in swift-running streams, and saves itself from being washed away by holding on to the rock by means of suckers below the head and at the rear. It also strengthens its hold by spinning a silken thread by means of which to anchor itself.

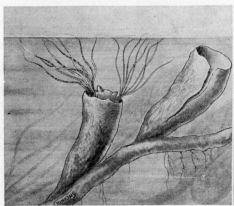

5. After several weeks the larva spins a silken pocket, open at the top, and in this it changes into a pupa, clinging to the sides by means of little spines. The head juts out of the pocket, and breathing tubes reach just above the surface of the flowing water.

6. Two or three weeks later a bubble of air collects in the pocket, the pocket splits, and the gnat rises in the bubble to the surface, where it immediately flies away in search of blood, the wings having dried inside the bubble. Then the story is continued over again.

What do the Three Balls over a Pawnbroker's Shop Mean?

The three golden balls were originally the arms of the famous Lombard family of the Medici, and were probably intended to represent gilded pills, either as a pun on the name Medici or in honour of the profession of medicine in which some members of the family had excelled. When representatives of the Medici family came to London and set up as merchants and moneylenders in what is now Lombard Street, they displayed the three balls over their places of business as their sign. Other moneylenders copied this, and the three golden balls came to be the recognised symbol of those who lent money on receiving the property of borrowers as a pledge.

Why does Black Rod Knock Three Times?

The Gentleman Usher of the Black Rod, so called because he carries an ebony stick surmounted by a golden lion, is by tradition a personal attendant on the Queen. But he is, in addition, an official of the House of Lords, and when the Queen goes to that House to open or close Parliament, or when her consent to Bills is given there by Royal Commission, it is Black Rod's duty to summon the members of the House of Commons to attend her. From the January day in 1642 when Charles the First tried to arrest the five members while the House was in session, the doors of the House of Commons have been closed on Black Rod's approach.

Further, to mark the right of the Commons to undisturbed debate, he is only admitted on knocking for the third time. Twice he knocks and the Commons takes no notice, and at the third knock somebody calls out, "Who is there?" Black Rod answers, and then advances to the bar of the House, bows three times, and says, " Mr. Speaker, the Queen commands this honourable House to attend Her Majesty immediately in the House of Lords." By these picturesque means are the ancient privileges of the People's House remembered and maintained.

Why have Bellows a Round Hole on One Side?

Through this hole enters the air which we blow out of the nozzle. When we part the handles, thereby opening the bellows, the air rushes in through the hole, and when we bring the handles together, and so close the sides of the bellows, the air is forced out. Just inside the hole is a little flap. This is a valve which opens to let the air enter, but when we are closing the bellows it is forced against the hole by the pressure of air inside, and so prevents the air from escaping that way.

Who was Gargantua ?

The giant Gargantua is the hero of a book written by the French philosopher Rabelais (1495-1553). Rabelais introduces this prodigious child to us as feeding on the milk of 17,913 cows every day, and as requiring 405 yards of velvet for his boots, and twice as much for his garment. Until he is five, Gargantua is brought up without any special attention, and then his father entrusts him to the care of Ponocrates. This gives Rabelais an opportunity to show us how complete was the education of a boy of good birth at that time. Later, Gargantua, his tutor, and the page Endemon start off to Paris. The young man rides a huge mare which is known for having swept down by one lash of her tail a whole forest on the way. Passing Notre Dame, the cathedral of Paris, Gargantua steals its chimes because he wants them as bells on the collar of his mount. However, his father soon calls the traveller back. He has waged a war with a neighbouring lord and needs the help of the powerful boy. Thanks to the witty co-operation of a monk, Father Jean, Gargantua is victorious and, as an act of gratitude, he founds the famous Abbey of Theleme, of which the chief rule was: " Do as you please." Married to Badebec, Gargantua becomes the father of Pantagruel, whose adventures follow throughout the book. Allusions to the Abbey of Theleme, Gargantua, and Pantagruel are often met with.

What are the World's Biggest Lakes ?

More than half the fresh water on the surface of the Earth lies in the Great Lakes of North America, one of which, Lake Superior, is easily the largest lake in the world. It is nearly 32,000 square miles in extent, and it is 1000 feet deep. Next after Lake Superior comes Africa's great Lake Victoria, 27,000 square miles, with Lake Huron and Lake Michigan not far behind. Lake Ladoga, about 7000 square miles, in north-west Russia, is the biggest lake in Europe.

What are Hieroglyphics ?

The word hieroglyphic is made of two Greek words meaning sacred carving, and a hieroglyphic is the figure of a familiar object like a tree or animal or weapon drawn to represent a word or syllable or sound. The name was first given to the marks found on the temples and palaces of Egypt, and when we speak of the hieroglyphics we usually mean those of Egypt. Together they form a system of written language, and their interpretation was discovered by deciphering the Rosetta stone of which we read in another part of this book. Some hieroglyphics represent directly the objects drawn; others stand for ideas suggested by those objects; others for ideas whose names are similar to the names of the objects; and others parts of the sounds of those names. The writing of the ancient Peruvians and Mexicans was in hieroglyphics.

Why are There so Many Yew Trees in Churchyards ?

The frequency with which yew trees are found growing in old churchyards has led to a legend that in olden times these were planted by command so that their wood might be available for making longbows, the chief English weapon of those days. But this is not so, as all the best bows were made of foreign yew imported for the purpose. The yews were formerly planted in churchyards for several reasons. In the first place, being evergreen and very long lived, they were regarded as suitable symbols of immortality in the place where the faithful were buried; then the yews were planted round the church, because the branches were often carried in procession on Palm Sunday to represent palms; and finally, being strong and of thick foliage, the yew was planted to protect the church from gales and winds.

Why is a Cone Often Hoisted at the Seaside ?

On the British coasts it is customary to display a storm-signal to indicate the expected prevalence of a high wind or storm, and this takes the form of a cone by day and a triangle of three red lights by night to represent the cone. When the point is downward the storm is expected from the south-east veering through the south, and when the cone or triangle is shown upright, a north-westerly gale veering through the north may be looked for.

Why has a Hop Kiln a Movable Top ?

The curious funnel-shaped top of a hop kiln, or oast-house, is made to move round so that it can always be turned away from the wind. When the hops are drying inside the kiln the vapour rises and passes out through the hole in the top of the roof, but if the wind were blowing down this hole the vapour would be driven back into the kiln and the hops would not dry properly. This possibility is overcome by having a funnel-shaped top to the roof that can be turned in any direction.

Why is the Bottom of a Tin Ridged ?

This is to add strength to the tin. Usually tins which contain powders and other dry substances have flat bottoms, as there is little pressure and therefore no particular need for strength. But in tins which contain meats, salmon, preserved fruits, syrup, and so on, the ends of the tins are very much ridged. This adds strength in a double way. First of all the ridges embody the principle of the arch, one of the strongest devices in architecture, and secondly these ridges provide a certain amount of give in the ends of the tin when the pressure of the interior gases is increased by heat in the process of cooking in retorts. With no " give " in the ends, the pressure might burst the tin.

Why is New Bread More Indigestible than Old ?

The digestion of bread takes place very largely in the mouth itself, by the conversion of the starch into what is called dextrins and maltose, under the action of the saliva. The more thoroughly the bread is chewed and ground into fragments, the more thorough will be the transformation of the starch. It is because of the greater ease with which toast and biscuits can be ground up by the teeth that they are more digestible than bread, and for the same reason old bread is more easily digested than new bread. The indigestibility of new bread is due to the large amount of moisture it contains, which makes it difficult to chew and at the same time prevents it from soaking up the saliva.

What are the Doldrums ?

Parts of the ocean near the Equator where calms prevail. The origin of the name is not certain, but it is believed to be a word made up from dull, similar in form to the word tantrums.

What is Meant by Immunisation ?

When the body is infected with disease germs, it can be likened to a city attacked by invaders. It mobilises, or gathers together, a " garrison" to resist and repel the attack. The feverishness which accompanies a disease is a sign of this resistance ; it is an indication of the fierce struggle which is going on between the defending " garrison" and the attacking germs.

If the germs are powerful enough and multiply fast enough, they may overwhelm the " garrison " and destroy life in the body, but if the attack is repelled then the " garrison " remains on the alert and with strength enough to repel any further attacks. Then a person can be regarded as having " immunity " from the particular disease.

In certain diseases, like those common to childhood—measles, mumps, chicken-pox, scarlet-fever, and diphtheria—a person who recovers is unlikely to suffer from it again ; they have become immunised. In other diseases (for example, the common cold and influenza) the immunity may not last long.

The " garrison " of the body is composed of what are called " antibodies," and they can be mobilised either by natural infection, by injections of mild living forms of the disease germs, or by germs which have been killed but whose presence is sufficient to mobilise the resistance.

The body is then immunised, but as the duration of the immunity varies, people likely to be exposed to disease—such as travellers going into—or passing through—countries where smallpox, typhus, and yellow-fever exist in violent forms—find it necessary to have a number of inoculations.

Is Our Blood Cold when We Feel Cold ?

Our feelings of cold or heat come, as a rule, from the very surface of our bodies. What we judge by is what happens to the skin. If the skin is losing heat quickly we say we feel cold; if it is losing heat slowly, or gaining heat, we say we feel hot. The blood is the most important thing which decides how the skin feels, as a rule; but, of course, in special cases the skin is more affected from outside than from inside, as when we are in a cold draught or exposed to a fire. When we feel cold, our blood is not cold. It is as warm as usual. A very little of it, however, is passing through the skin, and that is why the skin feels cold. Perhaps we are in cold surroundings, and the body is keeping most of the blood to warm the great organs like the brain and the heart.

In certain illnesses the case is very striking. In malaria there is usually a shivering stage, when the patient feels very cold. His skin is pale, and there is very little blood in it; that is why he feels cold. But if we take the pains to find out the temperature of his blood we shall find it much hotter than it ought to be. The patient is, indeed, in the first stage of a fever. In the second stage this hot blood will flood the blood-vessels of the skin, and the quantity and the heat of it will make the patient feel as hot as he previously felt cold.

Why are All Our Fingers Not the Same Length ?

Our hands were originally used for standing and for walking. If we put our hand on a table, as if we meant to walk on the tips of the fingers, we shall see at once what a well-balanced support it makes, just because the fingers are unequal in length—the middle finger the longest, and the short thumb and little finger falling behind and balancing the whole. We see the same thing in the case of animals that have three fingers—as the toes of the forefeet might rightly be called.

What is the Isle of Wight Disease ?

About the end of the nineteenth century a mysterious disease began to carry off the stocks of British bee-keepers, and as the plague is supposed to have originated in the Isle of Wight, or was first noticed there, it has been called Isle of Wight disease. For twenty years the cause of the disease was a mystery, and then it was traced by Professor Rennie, of Aberdeen University, to a microscopic parasite in the body of the bee, interfering with its breathing system, cutting off the supply of oxygen from certain muscles and nerve-centres, and eventually causing death.

How Many Colours has the Rainbow ?

Seven: red, orange, yellow, green, blue, indigo, violet. As we look at the rainbow these glide into one another, so that at the edges the hues seem to be blended into a mixture of the two colours.

Why has a Farm Tractor Deeply-Grooved Tyres?

The purpose of a tractor is to pull heavy loads or farm implements over earth that is frequently soft, so it is necessary to have tyres that are deeply-grooved, which can grip the field surface. Without these deep grooves it would be almost impossible for the wheels to grip the surface and give the tractor sufficient leverage to move forward. Wheels with smooth-surfaced tyres would tend to slip round without gripping.

Who is Tommy Atkins and Who is Jack Tar?

The name of Thomas Atkins was the one once adopted by the War Office as an example of how to fill up the forms in a little pocket manual at one time served out to all soldiers. The name was transferred as a nickname to the soldiers. Jack Tar originated long ago as a nickname for sailors, whose hands and clothes were generally soiled by tar. Some think that Tar stands for tarpaulin or oil-skins. Jack was used because it is the most familiar of all English names.

What is a Billion?

Multiples of a million are counted in tens, hundreds, thousands, and hundreds of thousands of millions, but a million millions is called a billion. A million billions is a trillion, a million trillions is a quadrillion, and a million quadrillions a quintillion, the highest number reached in English reckoning. The French and Americans call a thousand millions a billion, a billion a trillion, and so on up to a decillion, which equals a thousand English quintillions.

Why does Hair Grow after the Body has Stopped Growing?

Certain parts of the body are capable of growing into certain definite shapes and sizes and no farther, whereas other parts of the body have the capacity to keep on growing as long as the body itself is alive. Thus a bone in the leg grows to a certain size and then stops, and nothing we can do to it can make it grow any bigger. On the other hand, structures which are meant to protect the body, such as the skin and hair, are constantly being worn away, and are reproduced as quickly as they are lost.

What are the Horse Latitudes?

Regions of calm in the Atlantic, so called, it is said, because in the old days of sailing-ships vessels were often becalmed here, and had to throw overboard any horses they were carrying because the fresh water on board was almost finished.

What do we mean by " As the Crow Flies "?

" As the crow flies " means as straight as possible, for the crow flies straight to its destination. So to say that two places are twenty miles apart as the crow flies means that, though it may be a much longer distance by road or rail or river, it is only twenty miles in a straight line. " In a bee-line " means the same thing, for a bee, when laden with honey, goes straight home to the hive.

What is the Little Box at the Bottom of a Signal Post?

Usually the cupboards we see at the bottom of railway signal posts are on those signals which cannot be seen from the signal-box, and the object of the cupboard is to tell the signalman that the signals are working properly. Each cupboard contains one electric battery, connected with a small signal in the signal-box; and when the signalman pulls the lever an indicator worked by the battery shows him that the signal has responded.

Why has a Telegraph Pole a Little Roof on the Top?

These little roofs, shaped like a V turned upside down, are known as pole-roofs, and their object is to lengthen the life of the pole. Without them, the rain would collect on the top of the pole, and in course of time the wood would begin to split and decay. The roofs serve a very useful purpose, therefore, and save much trouble and expense by helping to deflect the rain from the top of the pole.

What does "Called to the Bar" Mean?

Qualified students are appointed barristers by the Benchers, or Governors, of the four Inns of Court, who on Call Night sit at a table which was formerly separated from the other part of the hall by a bar. Formerly students, as they were appointed, were called up to this bar, and the expression Called to the Bar still survives. It means appointment to act as a barrister.

Who said Veni, Vidi, Vici ?

Pharnaces, the son of Mithridates, King of Pontus, in Asia Minor, wished to take advantage of the growing rivalry between Caesar and Pompey, who both struggled for power in Rome. This, he thought, was the opportunity for recovering his father's possessions, which had been conquered by the Romans.

Julius Caesar was then in Egypt where he lingered at Cleopatra's luxurious court. At the news of the Asiatic prince's design he hastened to encounter him at Zela in Pontus. There he crushed Pharnaces' army and brought the campaign to such a rapid end that he could sum it up in a letter to the Roman Senate in these simple words: *Veni, vidi, vici*—" I came, I saw, I conquered." The three Latin verbs, with their equal number of syllables, and the recurrence of their consonants, make still more striking the promptitude displayed by Caesar, and the words: *Veni, vidi, vici,* have come down to us as an expression of swift and dramatic success.

What does the Conductor do With His Stick ?

He collects on the tip of his baton the musical powers of the singers and instrumentalists who have placed themselves under his command. Watch the first raising of the little wand by a good conductor as he is about to launch the performance of some great work, and try to imagine his thrill as he realises the musical force he is privileged to wield. For the time being every one of those trained musicians has submitted his will to the conductor's; each is waiting to translate into musical sound his slightest gesture, and the conductor has to realise the work as a whole to produce a beautiful and coherent interpretation of the composition to be performed.

The conductor's part, then, is much more than that of a human metronome (the instrument for measuring musical time). The composer sets down the notes to be played or sung, the musicians produce the corresponding musical sounds, and the conductor takes these scattered letters of the alphabet and with them weaves the enthralling story which holds his audience spellbound. Yet there is an important mechanical side to his work. Notice that kettle-drum player standing at the back. See how keenly he watches the conductor. He is not playing, but is busy counting the 74 bars' rest allotted to him. Now watch the conductor. He gives a quick glance at the player, to be sure he is prepared for his entry. Then the baton gathers in the brass. The excitement is growing. Suddenly the conductor's left hand shoots out, and the kettle-drums crash in confidently just at the climax of this long crescendo.

So the conductor shepherds the members of his flock, the soprano, alto, tenor, and bass singers, and the strings, woodwind, brass, percussion in his orchestra, showing them when and how to sing or play.

Who is Harlequin ?

Harlequin was a character in the Italian comedy of the sixteenth century.

A slender young man, he wore a motley, tight garment, a black mask, and a leather girdle wound about his waist. He held a long, flat wand, a sort of wooden sabre. There is a romantic legend about Harlequin's costume. It is said that some young students of Bergamo, stirred at the distress of a school-fellow and, too poor themselves to buy him a new suit, had settled that each would search for all sorts of bits of stuff he might find and bring them in to their friend. This led to a collection of many colours and the boy was at last clothed in a garment reminding one of a parrot. The costume grew famous at Bergamo, whence it reached the stage, and it has represented ever since the type of the player who first wore it. Alert and hopping about, sharp and witty, always ready to play bad tricks, Harlequin on the stage opposes his mischievous liveliness and humour to the timorous attitude of Pierrot who is his ordinary dupe.

Why must a Big Chimney have Such a Broad Base ?

Factory chimneys are usually built tall in order to provide sufficient draught, or to prevent unpleasant fumes from becoming a nuisance. To give them stability it is necessary to provide for a batter, that is to say, they should be built slightly out of the vertical, so that the weight of the sides should be directed towards the centre. It is generally accepted that all chimneys should have a base at least one-tenth as wide as the chimney is high, and so the taller the chimney the wider it is at the bottom.

The Story of the Beautiful Things in the Treasure-House of the World

The old Roman amphitheatre at Verona

THE GREEK AND ROMAN BUILDERS

WE know from our chapters on sculpture how this small people, the Greeks, in an insignificant country, and within the short span of a few hundred years, stamped the world unalterably with their forms of beauty. And in architecture, as in sculpture and letters, they were destined to a unique place. It would seem as if some god had shaped them, as King Arthur modelled his Order of the Round Table:

A glorious company, the flower of men,
To serve as model for the mighty world
And be the fair beginning of a time.

It is over two thousand years since these masters of art set up their buildings, and they are still the model for a world which has passed through changes and developments inconceivable to them.

Now, we can all judge paintings and we can all judge statuary; judgment of architecture is not so easy, because, to use a homely phrase, there is more in it than meets the eye. And a great many people are uncertain about Greek architecture. They want to know why it is so wonderful.

It is wonderful because it is not only inspired by a sense of beauty, but it is reasonable, logical, and sane.

A building, large or small, is put up in order to roof in a certain space. If it is a good building it must give the impression of having been thought out as a whole, and not just put together, hall on hall, chamber on chamber, and a back entrance and front entrance added.

In speaking of the architecture of the Greeks we are bound to speak of their temples and occasional monuments only; their private dwellings and such palaces as they had have not survived the tragedies of their later history. We can only surmise what they were like from the houses of Pompeii and Herculaneum, which were built under Greek influence. The keynote of their temple architecture is its simplicity. The building was a rectangle, plain and severe, with a gable at each end. Except for sculptural decorations—which were kept within the enclosing rectangular shape—the only " trimmings " were rows of columns. And the genius of this restrained classic architecture lies in its perfection of proportion. Its proportion is so perfect to the minutest detail, that if a man studies and memorises the construction of a temple front, it is as if he had learned the grammar of a language.

Proportion in architecture is a technical and very wide subject. It means, among a great many other things, that the mass of a building must not be too long for its width, too tall for its breadth; it means that vertical and horizontal lines must not

PICTURES · STATUES · CARVINGS · BUILDINGS · IVORIES · CRAFTS

make too broad a shape or too narrow; that a line must be stopped properly and not just end; that a column must not look too thin to carry the superimposed weight, or so thick that it appears clumsy and out of place: " a column with a building added."

THE BEAUTY OF A BUILDING WITH ITS PERFECT PROPORTIONS

We may never have time to study properly the laws of proportion, but we can remember this: perfect proportion reaches out to that mysterious place where calculated skill ends and beauty begins. Or, to put it another way, a building perfectly proportioned is in itself beautiful, no matter of what material or colour, or how plain it is; it delights the eye.

Greek architecture was from the first characterised by the use of columns and by its square, not arched, openings. The genius of its builders was spent in carrying this style to its utmost finish. In so doing, as we suggested in our last chapter, they took what seemed to them good of other countries' work, and refined it to their own use. They left behind the gorgeous splendour of the Assyrians and the secretiveness of the Egyptians. Their ideas of suitability were reasonable, sane. They did not want to build temples like those on the banks of the Nile, enclosed in a mighty, blank wall, with all their beauty concentrated in the dim, mysterious pillared hall where only the privileged might enter. The Greek temples were for the Greek people; they were open to the sun and air, and looked happiest when men and women were passing to and fro.

THE FINE MARBLE THE GREEKS USED FOR THEIR BUILDINGS

The Greeks were fortunate in possessing an unlimited supply of the finest marble. Nearly all their buildings, and all their most important buildings, were constructed of this very delicate and exacting material. It was partly because they worked in marble that their construction was so perfect in detail, and had such a smooth and fine effect. There is a natural clumsiness in stone that hides small defects in treatment; but marble hides nothing. So that the beauty of the Greek work was the beauty of accuracy.

These people lived in a land of clear air, brilliant suns, and sudden, short rains. It was essentially an out-of-door life, and it is probably because of this that no great municipal buildings were erected. Politics and philosophy were discussed out in the town, dramas played in the open air, poetry recited, tales told. It has been suggested that this is one of the reasons why all the temples have open, pillared porticoes where people could take refuge from the shower. In any case, they loved the effect of drifting sun and shadow falling rhythmically across the columns of their temples. The greater buildings had columns all round; all of them had columns front and rear. Inside the ranks of this beautiful guard stood the sacred building, enshrining the chamber where stood the statue of the god or goddess.

The temples were set in a kind of sacred enclosure, in the most effective place, generally the acropolis—the hill of the town or upper city. Sometimes when we see a drawing showing a reconstruction of the Parthenon as it was in Pericles' time, it seems to us rather a severe building, standing alone on its three-stepped platform, or stylobate. We should try to see it in the mind's eye—a dazzling mass of marble, crowning a hill above a sapphire sea, with flying clouds, and movement and life about it.

THE THREE KINDS OF COLUMNS ON WHICH GREEK TEMPLES WERE BASED

Just before the time of Jesus Christ, a learned Roman architect called Vitruvius wrote a book on Greek architecture, and he classified it according to the different kinds of columns and the entablature, or the horizontal portion supported by the columns. This fragment of architectural design he called an Order, because its parts were framed according to a strict rule and order, and not haphazardly put together.

The " label " has been used ever since, and so we have the Doric Order, the Ionic Order, the Corinthian Order, so named from the three columnar designs, on one of which all Greek temples were based. The Romans added two more, the Tuscan and the Composite.

These five Orders have been for almost two thousand years a kind of Bible to students of architecture. By far the most important is the Doric; then comes the Ionic; the Corinthian was evolved when Greece was under Roman dominance, and can therefore scarcely be classed with the other two, which are pure Greek.

The Doric column is said to be the most perfect detail of architecture ever evolved, and depends for its beauty on its extreme simplicity, and the genius of its proportions. It might sound rather childish to say that the chief thing about a column is that it must stop somewhere and somehow; but it is nevertheless true. There are millions of columns in the world, and we can scarcely pass through a city without seeing many kinds. And as we are busy with our own work it has probably never occurred to us that a column is ugly or beautiful according to the proportion of thickness to length, to its base, and the manner in which it is connected with the part of the building resting on it.

The Doric column has no base; it stands directly on the steps of the temple, as we can see in the photographs of the Parthenon and the Theseum, at Athens. As it has no base it cannot have too elaborate a capital. The shaft of the column is in a definite proportion to its height, and it tapers as it rises. We can easily see it grow in imagination, or for that matter we can carve one for ourselves. A square column has its corners shaved off; it is now eight sided; again its corners are shaved off; it is now sixteen sided. These sixteen planes are hollowed out—fluted—and there is the Doric shaft. Sometimes it had sixteen flutes, but usually twenty.

Although the base of the column stands directly on the ground, the top cannot rest directly under the architrave—the plain, horizontal block of marble that comes next to the column—because it looks ugly. And anything that looks ugly is wrong. The fluted shaft needs to be connected in some way with the architrave.

First, near the neck of the shaft, comes a single horizontal line, a warning that the long vertical lines of the flutes are about to end. Then the neck itself is grooved by a number of horizontal lines. Over it the *echidnus* broadens out as a support for the *abacus*, which in turn supports the archi-

Doric   Ionic   Corinthian
THE COLUMNS USED IN GREEK ARCHITECTURE

trave. One of the chief beauties of this famous Order lies in the skilful way in which the horizontal and vertical lines play against each other.

When we look at the photograph of the Parthenon we notice that the architrave is a long line of plain marble, but we do not always see that this undecorated, ungrooved stretch is one of the beauties of the Parthenon. It has a double value. It is a horizontal mass occurring immediately above the vertical mass of the columns and immediately below the vertical lines of the *triglyphs* that form part of the frieze. Also, as we have said, it is a plain mass set between two decorated masses—the grooved columns and triglyphs, and the sculpture of the *metopes*. Triglyphs and metopes alternating make the frieze—an endless repeat of three vertical bands and a square relief. On these triglyphs rests the weight of the roof.

There are no traces of windows in the Greek temples with which we are familiar. It is supposed that enough light came in through the open doorway. And this we can understand, as the light in that sunny land has such a brilliant quality.

The Doric Order was the earliest evolved in Greece, and most of the temples of her great years are built in this style. The Theseum, the temple of Theseus, is in the best state of preservation, but its columns are not so beautiful as those of the Parthenon. At Olympia there was the temple of Zeus, and at Aegina the temple of Aphaia. All these were built in the fifth century. The Parthenon is the greatest. We have already told its story on page 4143.

The Ionic Order was built up on the same principle as the Doric, but its proportions were different; it was less massive, less severe, more ornamental. The length of the Doric shaft was about five times the diameter of its base, that of the Ionic was about nine times the diameter of its base. The Ionic shaft was fluted, like the Doric, but the sharp edges between the flutings were planed down. The Doric shaft rested on the stylobate or uppermost step; the Ionic had a moulded base generally of three layers. Instead of the plain, massive capital of the Doric, the Ionic had a scroll-shaped capital, its lines not unlike the spiral curls of the nautilus shell. It is this capital which is the chief distinguishing mark of the Ionic Order.

In all their work the Greeks were careful to leave the architrave plain; or, if a line were inserted, it was a horizontal line, thus strengthening the unbroken horizontal effect. In the Ionic Order the frieze ran continuously above the architrave, and was not broken up into tryglyphs and metopes like the Doric frieze.

THE LITTLE IONIC TEMPLE NO BIGGER THAN A HOUSE

One of the most exquisite little temples in the world—that of the Wingless Victory on the Acropolis at Athens—was built in the Ionic style. For some reason it pleased the architect, Callicrates, to make this temple just about as big as a house. The lovely little frieze which ran round it, above the Ionic columns, is in the British Museum. The temple, as it stands, was reconstructed from the ruins left by the Turks about the middle of the last century.

A much larger Ionic temple was the Erechtheum, also on the Acropolis, and it shares with the Temple of Diana at Ephesus the honour of being the greatest Ionic buildings set up by Greek architects. In planning the Erechtheum the architect Mnesicles departed from the usual Greek idea of a severe rectangular edifice, and threw the shrines of three different temples together, each abutting on the other, with no symmetry in the whole. At the south side is the famous Caryatid portico. At the north is another portico of very elaborate Ionic columns. A great deal of extra carving was done on them. Among other things on the abacus was the "egg and tongue" ornament so familiar to students in art schools.

In a great many of their temples the Greeks applied gold and colour to throw up the figures on the friezes. This effect was gained in the Erechtheum by the use of black marble as the groundwork of the frieze. The sculptured figures in white marble were attached to the black background by metal clamps. We can imagine how gorgeously beautiful was the finished building.

HOW THE TURKS SPOILED THE BEAUTIFUL TEMPLES OF ATHENS

It is one of the world's tragedies that most of this Greek architecture should be in partial ruin, or in a state of reconstruction. Lovers of art find it difficult to forgive the Turks their barbaric treatment of Athenian temples during the time of their overlordship. They turned the Erechtheum into the women's quarters of a great household. Other troubles came on the temple, and at last Nature herself brought ruin in the shape of a storm, in 1852, which threw down a good part of the re-erected building.

A similar tale attends that marvellous pile so rightly called by the ancients one of the wonders of the world—the Temple of Diana at Ephesus in Asia Minor. It stood on the site of an archaic building—fragments of whose columns are in the British Museum—which was burned down the night Alexander the Great was born, in 356 B.C. The "new" temple was built during Alexander's reign by Democrates the architect, with Scopas as master sculptor, supervising the work of a large number of artists.

This Temple of Diana was the centre of a great part of the national life of that province of Asia. It was more than a building; it was a living institution. Like the medieval monasteries of England, it owned land, and had a large income. All the festivals of the district were held there, and a great army of priests, and what the Bible calls soothsayers, were attached to the temple. Public funds were housed in the precincts. In fact, to have uprooted the Temple of Diana, for about three hundred years after its erection, would have been to tear out the heart of Ephesus.

DEMETRIUS THE SILVERSMITH CRIES OUT AGAINST PAUL

A very rich trade of making silver images and shrines of Diana—much like that of the Christian craftsmen of early Europe—was carried on, as we know from the Acts of the Apostles. These images, together with the temple itself, were denounced by Paul and his followers, and this was the occasion of a great outcry.

BUILDINGS OF OLD GREECE AND ROME

A RECONSTRUCTION OF THE APPIAN WAY BY WHICH PAUL WALKED TO ROME

POSEIDON'S TEMPLE AT PAESTUM AS IT WAS

THE TEMPLE OF JUPITER AT POMPEII

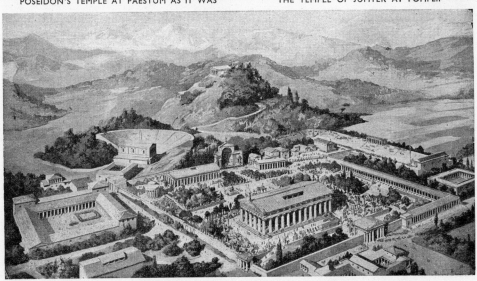

THE BUILDINGS AT OLYMPIA AS THEY APPEARED IN THE GREAT DAYS OF GREECE

"Sirs," cried out Demetrius the silversmith, "ye know that by this craft we have our wealth . . . . Not alone at Ephesus, but almost throughout all Asia this Paul hath persuaded and turned away much people saying that they be no gods which are made with hands . . . . so that the temple of the great goddess Diana should be despised, and her magnificence should be destroyed, whom all Asia and the world worshippeth." And when they heard these sayings they were full of wrath and cried out, "Great is Diana of the Ephesians!" And the whole city was filled with confusion. . . . All with one voice for about the space of two hours cried out "Great is Diana of the Ephesians!"

Pliny, the Roman historian, wrote a description of the temple, and from that information architects have been able to make a reconstruction. There is no doubt that on the temple a great wealth of art was spent. The ranked Ionic columns had wonderful sculpture running round their bases and the lower parts of the shafts. The pediment—the triangular piece of wall between the cornice and the roof of the temple front—was a mass of magnificent carving, showing Diana on her throne, with princes and horses, lions and rams, on either hand, in a procession of honour.

THE BREAKING-UP OF THE GREAT TEMPLE OF DIANA

Toward the middle of the third century after Christ the temple was mutilated by the Goths, and about a hundred years later it was denounced and closed altogether at the order of the Christian Church. It then became a kind of quarry, whence the best marbles were hewed out to help to build the churches of the "new" religion. A great deal of it went into the Cathedral of St. John; eight of its dark green marble columns are in the Church of St. Sophia at Istanbul. The rest of the temple ruins became slowly buried under the dust and debris of succeeding centuries, and lay at peace there, forgotten by spoilers. In 1869 an English architect, Wood, began a course of excavations, and brought fragments home. These are now with the fragments of the earlier archaic temple in the British Museum.

There is a pretty story told by Vitruvius about a Corinthian bronze-worker called Callimachus. This man saw one day, on a girl's grave, a basket with acanthus leaves curling up round it. A square, flat stone, or tile, lay on the basket. The general shape took his fancy, and from the idea, he fashioned in bronze the capital of a small column, in shape like an inverted bell, sheathed with acanthus leaves.

This was the origin of the Corinthian Order, with which we are probably more familiar than either Ionic or Doric, because it has so often been used and is used today in design, and in ornaments—like candlesticks—and in monumental stones for graves, and in woodwork, and in so-called classical architecture.

THE TOWER BUILT FOR WATCHING THE PASSAGE OF THE SUN

The Corinthian Order, as we have said, was less used by the Greeks than the other two Orders. The shafts have a moulded base, much like the Ionic, and the Corinthian also largely resembles the Ionic Order in the way the columns support the roof.

Not many large buildings were planned in this Order, but there are several smaller temples, buildings, and monuments, like the Temple of Apollo at Miletus, the famous Choragic Monument of Lysicrates, at Athens, and the Tower of the Winds, built for observing the passage of the sun and for recording time, also at Athens.

The Choragic Monument, which was typical of a great many in the Street of the Tripods, was a circular structure built on a deep square base, and measuring in all a height of some 34 feet. Six Corinthian columns, 11 feet high, stood round the body of the monument. Above them was a marble dome crowned by an ornament framed to hold the tripod. This was a prize given to the winner in certain games, and was fashioned on the original Tripod, a peculiar seat where the Delphic priestesses sat when they pronounced their oracles and "inspired" sayings.

THE OLD GREEK TOMB WHICH IS NOW IN THE BRITISH MUSEUM

The Greeks, no less than the Egyptians, honoured their dead and made tombs for them, though not by any means on a stupendous scale. One of the earliest, built at Xanthos about 550 B.C., the Harpy Tomb, is now in the British Museum; and there, also, is a model of the Nereid Monument. This was a little building surrounded by Ionic columns, built about two hundred years later than the Harpy Tomb.

We read of the Mausoleum on page 4277. On page 4402 are pictures of the lovely Tomb of the Weepers and the Alexander

ROME IN HER ANCIENT DAYS

A PROCESSION PASSING THE TEMPLE OF CASTOR AND POLLUX IN THE FORUM IN THE GREAT
DAYS OF ROME

INSIDE THE PANTHEON

TRAJAN'S FORUM

Sarcophagus, both being in the Istanbul Museum. These are the most important, and are monuments of beauty. But on all their tombs, whereof numerous fragments remain, the Greek architects and sculptors expended a very fine and finished art.

THE OPEN-AIR THEATRE WHICH HELD THIRTY THOUSAND PEOPLE

Their most important erections, next to the temples, were the huge, open-air theatres, many of which still exist, though in a ruined state. They were built outside the town, in a hollowed space or a natural rocky basin. The germ or kernel of the theatre was the circular orchestra; two-thirds of the way round, it rose tier upon tier of seats, generally cut out of the solid rock in blocks. Behind the orchestra, on a kind of platform, stood the stage, built of stone, forming a permanent background to the play.

The principle theatre of Greece, the Theatre of Dionysus, Athens, was an enormous place, capable of holding thirty thousand people. That at Epidaurus is not so big, but more beautifully planned; it was built by Polyclitus about 350 B.C., and is in a wonderful state of preservation.

We know now something of the principles underlying the work of the Greeks, and if we look at the pictures of their buildings we shall be able to understand what is called their intellectual beauty. We shall see how this architecture was perfect inside its distinct limitations.

THE GREAT SIMPLICITY OF THE BUILDINGS OF OLD GREECE

It was a one-storeyed architecture, had no towers, no arches, no upward fling from the body of the building; it had no mystery, no thrill of the high lights of Egyptian temples ; it was not a stupendous, awe-inspiring architecture; there are many ordinary churches in England bigger than the Parthenon. Its beauty was the beauty of logical thought which showed in its simplicity and its severely held proportions, and the beauty of an exquisite finish and perfection of detail.

The Romans were the inheritors of Greek civilisation abroad and Etruscan at home, and they took what seemed to them best from both styles of architecture. From the Etruscans they took the art of massive wall building, the construction of the arch and the dome—which the Etruscans in turn had inherited from the East—and developed them in their characteristically powerful fashion. From the Greeks they took their columns and square openings.

The Greek style suffered at the hands of the Romans. It would seem that the barbaric strength of the Etruscan work secretly pleased them, but they had a great admiration for Greek art, and, in many cases, when they had planned a building on the Etruscan style, they proceeded to decorate it with the Greek style.

They made strong arches, and then on the piers of the arches put a surface column which supported the entablature—the horizontal portion—above the rounded shape of the arch. So that inside was the arch of the Etruscans, the real strength of the structure, and outside, adorning it, lay the vertical and horizontal decoration of the Greek columnar openings.

We can see this in the Colosseum, Rome. As the Greek columns had been designed for strength to support the roof, and always ran the height of the building, it was perhaps bad art and quite unnecessary to use them as facings for one storey only. But the idea grew and became a distinct style, reappearing in European architecture centuries later.

THE ENDURING STRENGTH OF THE AQUEDUCTS THE ROMANS BUILT

When the Romans were simply building for strength and enduring qualities, and not trying to be artistic, as in their famous aqueducts, they did not trouble to add the Greek columns and architraves, and they built something extremely beautiful and dignified, and never to be forgotten. The aqueduct known as the Pont du Gard at Nîmes in France, is one of the finest things in the world, infinitely more beautiful than the Colosseum. We cannot understand how they could look at it, or the Aqua Claudia, Rome, and not see that they had achieved a singular greatness. Whereas it would seem that they said to themselves: We must have aqueducts, because a town without a good water supply is no town. We must have bridges, because an empire without unbroken high roads is no empire. Let these be made plain and unadorned; we merely ask that they shall last for ever. And *then*—we will have some really beautiful buildings.

But not all their buildings were planned in a combination of arch and square, columnar openings. Some of their temples and basilicas or public halls had many columns supporting the roof or portico openings, and might be described as Roman-Greek, a style wherein the Greek was curiously spoiled and vulgarised by a people who lacked the exquisite Grecian taste. Generally speaking, the Romans were more showy, more ornate. Only one thing did they simplify, and that was the Doric column. To their variation of this Order has been given the name of Tuscan. The other of the two Orders evolved by them was the Composite, whose capital was a mixture of the Corinthian and the Ionic without the pure grace of either.

WHY THE ROMAN ARCHITECTURE DIFFERED FROM THE GREEK

There were two chief reasons for the distinctive style which Roman architecture developed as the empire grew. One was the material to hand, and the other the fullness and complication of their life; and in this it was inevitable that their work should fall away in an ever-widening tangent from the Greek style they admired. Greek architecture, produced by a company of artists, was an architecture of religion; that of the Romans, produced by a race of builders, was the architecture of a great and ever-widening empire. The one was centred on the Acropolis, the other in the Forum or market place, where men gathered to buy and sell, to discuss politics, to learn news. Round the Forum the chief buildings of Rome were grouped, and when the mighty city was in her glory must have been an imposing sight.

Roman architecture included enormous walls, bridges, aqueducts—engineering feats ; it covered a great diversity of buildings—temples, tombs, basilicas or public halls, palaces, baths, circuses, theatres, and amphitheatres.

THE PILLARS AND ARCHES THE ROMANS BUILT FOR GLORY'S SAKE

There were smaller architectural works, like triumphal arches, pillars of victory, and fountains. The arches and pillars they built for glory's sake, to commemorate the greatness of their emperors and generals. In Rome there were the Arches of Titus, Constantine, Septimius Severus; at Ancona the Arch of Trajan, and another at Beneventum in Southern Italy. The arches were either single or triple, adorned with sculptured reliefs, their piers faced with Corinthian or Composite columns.

Of the Pillars of Victory, Trajan's column at Rome, a Roman Doric pillar

115 feet high, freely sculptured, is the most famous. Around the shaft, like a spiral band, runs a winding relief, telling the tale of some of Trajan's exploits. A statue of St. Peter now stands on the top of the pillar, in place of that of the Roman emperor. In the Victoria and Albert Museum, South Kensington, is a full-size plaster reproduction of the Trajan column. Another famous pillar was the Marcus Aurelius column, similarly decorated.

The Romans built fountains in great numbers; there were hundreds of them, public and private, in their cities. They erected them partly out of their love for running water from the fountain's jet, and partly in memory of municipal events and distinguished persons.

There was only a certain amount of marble to be had by the Roman builders. But they had plenty of terracotta, stone, and brick. And early in their development they invented a new material, concrete, whose appearance is a landmark in the history of building construction.

THE MANY USES THE ROMANS MADE OF CONCRETE

We know from existing portions of the Roman Wall in London how enduring their concrete was. It consisted of a mixture of lime and a peculiar sandy earth called pozzolana. Once they had discovered its granite-like qualities, the Romans used their concrete freely, not only as a strengthening substance, but as a building material itself. They made walls, domes, vaulted roofs of solid concrete, or concrete with brick ribs, and faced the structure with marble, brick, or mosaic. This use of concrete has served as a model to builders down through the centuries to the nineteenth, when steel came into use.

As masters of the new medium, the Romans became independent of local conditions in any new, conquered country. Concrete and bricks could be made anywhere ; in nearly all lands there was native stone. Thus it happened that their construction was practically the same all over the empire.

The Romans are of intense interest as builders, even if they were not great artists in architecture. Their construction was what one would expect from so strong a people. Whether it be fragments of walls or patches of mosaic—wherever anything Roman is delved out of the earth it becomes an object of envy to the modern builder. The watchword of the Imperial architects was *To Endure*. Hence that saying, " when falls the Colosseum, Rome shall fall."

After the lapse of time these great people are most remembered for their engineering works, and their domed and vaulted temples. It was natural to them to erect huge buildings. They must have been conscious of the greatness of Rome when they flung up the great dome of the Pantheon. It is interesting to note that stupendousness in architecture like that of the East came into Europe by way of the Romans.

The Pantheon, which is now a Christian church, is the most wonderful temple Rome produced. It is the earliest domed building of which any trace remains, and, being in a good state of preservation, is a guide to Roman architecture of this kind.

THE WONDERFUL OPEN DOME THAT CROWNS THE PANTHEON IN ROME

The entrance, a magnificent portico of Corinthian columns, with a sculptured pediment, must have reminded the Romans of the Greek temples they so admired. But behind these ranked columns, over the rotunda, or circular hall, rose something Greek architects never thought of: a huge round dome where light is spilled through one great centre hole in the roof. When the Pantheon was in its glory of colour and gold and all the enrichments of its artists, the effect of this " eye of heaven " shining down aslant the dome must have been glorious and awe-inspiring.

Among the other sacred buildings which enclosed a polygonal or a circular dome were the Temple of Vesta at Rome, the earliest and most sacred of them all, built about 715 B.C., another to the same goddess at Tivoli, the Temple of Jupiter at Spalato, and that of Venus at Baalbek, in Syria. Of their many rectangular temples, resembling the Greek, the best preserved and finest example is a building now called the Maison Carrée at Nimes. Another fine one, which has suffered at the hands of time and enemy peoples, was the Great Temple at Baalbek. Within all the public buildings, sacred and secular, stood a great array of Greek statues, pillaged from their home.

Of their palaces, basilicas, and public baths, only ruins remain, and we cannot but deplore the loss of such characteristic buildings of a great people. The baths were colossal; a writer has described them as towns in themselves, with their corridors and halls for exercise and rest, and their gardens, all grouped round the chambers of the bath. Here the luxuriousness and grandeur of the Roman displayed itself. We can best visualise them by imagining the apartments of ordinary " Turkish Baths" built like a palace for grandeur.

THE TOWN THE ROMANS BUILT WITHIN THE WALLS OF A PALACE

This same sense of largeness strikes us when we think of their palaces—of the group on Palatine Hill, Rome, imposing even in ruin, and the palace at Spalato, in Dalmatia, within whose walls a town was afterwards built.

The basilicas were large halls where commerce was carried on and courts of justice held. They are interesting to us now as forming a link between Pagan and Christian architecture; on their model were built the first imposing churches of the early Christians.

Of the Roman theatres there are interesting remains at Orange in Southern France, in Rome, and in Athens. They were built somewhat on the lines of the Greek theatres; one of the differences lay in apportioning the central part which had been assigned to the Greek chorus, to Roman dignitaries.

Amphitheatres were a Roman invention—very characteristic of a martial, active people, who gloried in physical exploits. Hence their gladiator shows, whose tradition remains in the Spanish bull fights of today.

THE HUNDREDS OF ARCHES OF THE MIGHTY COLOSSEUM

The Colosseum, built the first century after Christ, was the greatest of these amphitheatres. The Romans gloried in its size and its hundreds of arches which ran in three tiers round the building. Mercifully they left unbroken the long, horizontal lines of the Greek entablatures, and thus gave the circular sweeping walls a distinction they perhaps did not realise.

Another fine amphitheatre is in partial ruin at Verona. These stupendous buildings, like the baths, were erected wherever the Roman civilisation took root, in all their large towns. A faint memory of them exists today in England, in the mounds known as the Maumbury Rings at Dorchester, in Dorset.

BUILDINGS OF GREECE AND ROME

THE PARTHENON AS IT STANDS TODAY ON THE ACROPOLIS OF ATHENS

THE PROPYLAEA—THE APPROACH TO THE ACROPOLIS OF ATHENS

THE NORTH PORCH OF THE
ERECHTHEUM ON THE ACROPOLIS

THE CHORAGIC MONUMENT
OF LYSICRATES AT ATHENS

THE TEMPLE OF THE WINGLESS
VICTORY ON THE ACROPOLIS

THE TEMPLE OF THE OLYMPIAN ZEUS AT ATHENS

THE GREEK BASILICA AND TEMPLE OF POSEIDON AT PAESTUM IN SOUTH ITALY

COLUMNS OF THE TEMPLE OF
CASTOR AND POLLUX IN ROME

THE COLUMN OF MARCUS
AURELIUS IN ROME

A LITTLE TEMPLE AT TIVOLI
A FEW MILES OUTSIDE ROME

THE BEAUTIFUL MAISON CARRÉE AT NIMES

THE PONT DU GARD, THE MARVELLOUSLY PRESERVED ROMAN AQUEDUCT AT NIMES IN PROVENCE

THE GREEK TEMPLE OF CONCORD AT GIRGENTI IN SICILY

THE DORIC COLUMNS OF THE PARTHENON

THE ROMAN COLOSSEUM AT EL DJEM IN TUNIS

THE INTERIOR OF THE GREAT COLOSSEUM IN ROME

COLUMNS OF THE TEMPLE OF APOLLO AT CORINTH

THE TOWER OF THE WINDS AT ATHENS

THE TEMPLE OF NEPTUNE AT SUNIUM

THE THESEUM AT ATHENS, THE BEST PRESERVED BUILDING OF ANCIENT GREECE

THE TEMPLE OF APHAIA AT AEGINA

THE OLD GREEK TEMPLE AT SEGESTA IN SICILY

THE COLUMN OF PHOCAS
IN ROME

THE ROMAN CORINTHIAN
TEMPLE OF BAAL IN SYRIA

COLUMNS OF THE TEMPLE
OF VESPASIAN, ROME

THE GREAT ROMAN ARENA AT ARLES IN PROVENCE

A ROMAN BRIDGE AT PERGAMUM IN ASIA MINOR

THE ROMAN THEATRE AT ARLES

THE TEMPLE OF BACCHUS AT BAALBEK IN SYRIA

THE INTERIOR OF THE ROMAN ARENA AT ARLES

THE COURTYARD OF THE HOUSE OF THE VETTII AT POMPEII

THE ARCH OF SEPTIMIUS SEVERUS IN ROME

THE AMPHITHEATRE AT POLA

The pictures in these pages are reproduced by courtesy of Messrs. Alinari, Anderson, Boissonas, Brogi,
E.N.A., Neurdein, and others

The Wonderful House We Live In, and Our Place in the World

SMALL SUPPLY—BIG DEMAND
From the painting "The Fish Queue," by Evelyn Dunbar, in the Imperial War Museum

VALUE, SUPPLY, AND DEMAND

WE should all understand clearly what we mean by Value.

In common language value means worth. We have already noticed, however, that the same thing may be valuable at one place and worthless in another. Sand, for example, is valuable to the builder who wants to mix it with lime to make mortar, but worse than useless in the desert, where the traveller finds a good deal too much of it. Most things have value in use at some time or place. Water has value in use when we drink it, or when we cook with it, or when we bathe in it, or when, falling as rain on the soil, it gives life to plants. On the other hand, water in the wrong place may be worse than useless to us, as when it leaks through a roof, or comes as a disastrous flood.

When we speak of value in economics, however, we refer not to value in use, but to value in Exchange. A thing which is valuable in use often, but not always, has value in exchange. That we saw when we talked about Wealth. For example, sunlight is so valuable in use that it is the first necessity of existence, but it has no value in exchange because it is unlimited in supply.

The invention and use of money enabled us to measure the exchange value of all things by the measure of value we call Price, and when people commonly talk of value they mean price.

Price is the amount of money we give for a thing, and by the use of prices we are able to compare the value in exchange of one thing with that of another. Thus, if a saucepan costs three shillings, a broom six shillings, and an electric iron thirty shillings, we know that an electric iron is ten times as valuable as a saucepan and five times as valuable as a broom, while a saucepan is only worth half as much as a broom. Before spending our money, we can look at the prices of different things to see how much of each it will buy. Prices are a very good guide to us, in deciding how best to spend what we earn.

The price of a thing is decided by the forces of Demand and Supply, which work on each other in ways which it is very important to understand.

By demand we mean the desire to possess a thing combined with the ability to buy it and the willingness to buy it.

Tom Brown, on his way home from school, looking into the window of the toyshop and seeing some very nice marbles, may desire to have them, but that desire is not " demand " unless he has the money to buy, and unless, also, he is willing to buy at not more than a certain price. We see that demand in the economic sense has no meaning apart from the question of price.

Suppose that Tom had a shilling to spend, and that the marbles he would like

BODY, MIND, AND SOUL · CITIZENSHIP · ECONOMICS · GOVERNMENT

to buy were sixpence each. Much as he wanted marbles, Tom would not give his shilling for only two of them. Therefore, at such a price his desire to buy would not be a demand. If, however, the price was reduced to a penny each, his shilling would buy twelve marbles, and that might turn his desire into demand, and he would go in and buy them.

HOW THE DEMAND FOR A THING VARIES WITH ITS PRICE

So we see how *demand varies with price*. When the price is high the demand is less than when the price is low. We often make up our minds as to whether we will buy this thing or that because of the question of price. Thus, if fish becomes very high in price, people will buy less of it, although they like eating it, and will buy more potatoes because these are cheaper than fish. Our friend Tom, with a shilling to spend, may have a number of desires to satisfy. Perhaps if he had enough money to buy them all, he would buy a penknife, a top, and a ball as well as some marbles. Looking at the prices will help him to make up his mind which of the four things he will buy. If the penknife cost a shilling, he might buy it instead of some marbles. If he could not get a knife at that price, he might spend the money on a top. If a good top could not be obtained for a shilling, he might buy a ball, and so on. Tom, as a buyer, would be guided in the exercise of his demand by price.

No one has an unlimited amount of money to spend on any particular thing. In practice people want many things, but have only money enough to buy some things. Their desire to buy, their ability to buy, and their willingness to buy, vary according to their needs and to the price. If a thing gets dearer they buy less of it. If a thing gets cheaper they buy more of it until they have quite satisfied their need for it.

WHY THE DEMAND FOR A THING CHANGES FROM TIME TO TIME

Also we may note that the quantity of a thing which will be bought varies with the need as well as with the price. For example, in the summer people buy less coal than in the winter, while on the other hand, they will buy more ice cream. Umbrellas and mackintoshes have a ready sale in the winter months, while sun glasses

and bathing costumes are in demand in the summer. Changes in demand also occur through sheer fancy, as when it is the fashion for ladies to change their style of dress.

Another interesting thing about demand is that a fall in the supply of one thing may be, and often is, accompanied by an increased demand for something else which can be used in its place.

For instance, it is easy to see that if a disease killed nearly all the potatoes in the country, so that they became scarce and dear, people would demand more of other sorts of vegetables, such as cabbage, or parsnips. Again, the high price of one thing may reduce the demand for another thing as well as for itself. Suppose coal-gas became exceedingly dear. In that case not only would there be less demand for gas but also less demand for gas heating-stoves and gas cooking-stoves.

THE LUXURIES THAT PEOPLE BUY WHEN THEIR WAGES ARE HIGH

Demand varies greatly with spending power. If Tom has his pocket-money raised from one to two shillings a week he is able to satisfy more of his wants, and in addition to buying more sweets he may form a collection of postage-stamps. When wages rise, wage-earners, in addition to buying food and necessaries, may become buyers of luxuries, such as musical instruments, hair-dryers, or washing machines.

Now let us turn to Supply. *Supply means the quantity of things that can be sold at a certain price.* The man who has things to sell, whether he be manufacturer or merchant, cannot go on supplying goods at a certain price unless it is profitable for him to do so.

If he makes the goods in his workshop or factory he has to meet all the expenses of keeping up the building and the machinery, of paying the workmen and managers their wages, and, in addition, he has to make a margin of profit to form his own income.

Then again, if a man is a merchant or dealer he has to buy the goods, pay for the expenses of stocking them in a warehouse or shop, and the wages of the people who help him to sell, and include in his price a margin of profit for himself. In either case we see that the maker or merchant could not go on supplying at less than a certain figure, which is the lowest he can afford to take. The lower he can make his price by using better machinery, or by better organisation, or by himself buying cheaply, the more customers he can get.

WHY A DAILY NEWSPAPER CAN BE SOLD SO CHEAPLY

Perhaps, by producing on a larger scale, he may be able to lower this price and make a profit. For example, suppose he is a printer making a book. The cost of setting up the type of a book is heavy, and if only ten copies of the book were printed each of the ten copies would have to bear in its price a tenth of the cost of the type-setting. Suppose the cost of setting was £100, then each of the ten books for type-setting alone would cost £10, and probably no one would be willing to buy the book at £10 in addition to the cost of paper and binding and the printer's profit. But suppose ten thousand copies of the book were printed, then the type-setting would only amount to a few coppers instead of £10, for each book. The book could then be sold at a low price and yet yield a profit. The reason that the daily newspaper can be sold at such a low price is because so many people buy it.

It is, of course, very difficult in actual business for anybody to decide at what price a certain supply can be sold. In practice business men judge by experience. It sometimes needs great courage and enterprise to induce a man to make a big quantity of a certain kind of article, in the hope that the price at which he can offer it can be met by the demand of enough persons willing and able to buy at that price.

HOW THE LAWS OF SUPPLY AND DEMAND CONTROL THE PRICE OF THINGS

Price is affected by Demand and Supply in opposite ways. Rising prices lead to a greater supply and a smaller demand. Falling prices, on the other hand, lead to a smaller supply and a greater demand.

It is equally true that a bigger supply, or a smaller demand, leads to lower prices, and a smaller supply, or a bigger demand, to higher prices.

In any market, whether it is in rubber, or in wool, or in pig-iron, or in shares of companies, price is arrived at at any moment by the action and re-action of supply and demand. If there are more buyers than sellers, up goes the price. If there are more sellers than buyers, down goes the price. These rises and falls of price, we see, do not depend on the value in use of the article. Tea of the same quality is just as nice to drink whether it is cheap or whether it is dear; its price on the market depends on the relation of supply to demand. No matter how valuable a thing may be in use, if a large quantity of it comes on the market at one time its price will fall. It is none the worse because it is cheaper; it is simply that it has come on offer in larger supply.

For example, suppose someone discovered how to make artificial diamonds as good as real ones at a low cost, and were to make thousands of them and to bring them all to market. He would not be able to sell them at the present high price of diamonds, which depends on their scarcity. If he wanted to sell them all, he would have to bring down his price, and the price of the natural diamonds, though these were as beautiful and as valuable in use as ever, would also fall.

MASS PRODUCTION WHICH HAS BROUGHT WATCHES WITHIN THE REACH OF ALL

Time was when very few watches were made, and then only at a very great cost. The supply was very small at a price which few could pay. The equality of supply and demand was reached, therefore, at a very high level, and only rich men could possess watches. Nowadays very good watches are made in great factories where each tiny part is turned out by the thousand, so that when the parts are put together the factory-made watch can be offered profitably to the public at a very low figure. At this low price the demand is great, and so the big supply will be bought. If there was not a great demand for cheap watches, it would not pay to produce them on a large scale. Mass production is only possible in the case of things which can be sold in large numbers.

Even if we make an article which has some value in exchange, we must not expect the price it will fetch to be in any way dependent on the trouble or time we have spent in producing it. Somebody else may have discovered how to produce ten such articles while we produce one, and, if so, we must expect the price to be governed, not by our one article, which took us so long to make, but by the offer of ten articles which were made with more skill and less labour. That is why it is so important to learn how to make things well and quickly.

Imagine there are two coal-mines, and that in the one coal can be hewn easily, while in the other, because the seams of coal are thin, it is more costly to get out the mineral. No one will offer a higher price for the coal got out of the poor coal-mine; the coal will only fetch the same price for the same quality on the same day, whether it came out of a good mine or a bad mine, or whether it cost much or little to get. That is why, when coal-mines become very dear to work, they have to be abandoned.

It is also very interesting to notice that the demand at any price, however low, for an article, is limited by human needs, and that, therefore, there is a point for every article at which demand will cease. For example, our capacity to eat bread is limited by our bodily needs. If, therefore, ten times as much wheat came to market as needed, it could not be bought, no matter how cheaply it was offered.

THE CENTRAL MARKETS WHICH KEEP PRICES STEADY

In our modern civilised communities there are recognised markets in which different goods are bought and sold. In ordinary times these big recognised markets help to keep prices steady. We can easily understand this by looking at the pre-war market for tea. If there had been little dealings in every town in the country in the chests of tea imported from India, Ceylon, and China, the price of tea in each town would have been always going wildly up and down because sometimes there would have been more tea than buyers, and sometimes more buyers than tea. Also, the price of tea on any day would have been quite different in two towns. When, however, there was one big whole-sale tea market in London, where all the country's tea was dealt in, the supply and demand of the entire country became expressed and focused, as light is focused by a magnifying glass in one place, and so the whole price of tea became steady. Of course it underwent variations, up and down, but these variations were small as compared with what the local variations

would have been if the wholesale dealing had been widely distributed.

Here are the laws of Supply and Demand in a nutshell. When supply is greater than demand, the price falls; when supply is smaller, the price rises.

Even a small shortage of supply or a small increase in demand often causes a considerable difference in price. When supplies run very short the rise in prices may be very serious indeed and cause suffering to many people.

WHY IT IS SOMETIMES NECESSARY FOR THE GOVERNMENT TO CONTROL PRICES

During the two World Wars, supplies of many goods were short. The war needs used up goods and services in many new ways, and so less were left over for private people to consume. Also, we could import much less than before, because we had not enough ships. German submarines sank many of them, and the rest had to travel in convoys, which meant that they could make fewer journeys. So the Government therefore began to ration some goods. It limited the amount which people could buy. In the case of sugar, for instance, people were not allowed to buy more than a certain number of ounces per week, the amount depending on the supply of sugar in the country. In this way, the demand for the rationed goods was kept down to equal the supply available, and big price rises were avoided.

Many foodstuffs were subsidised as well as rationed, that is to say, the Government arranged for them to be sold for less than they cost, and the loss was made up with money taken from people in taxes. Thus, at one time, eggs were being sold at twopence each, less than they cost and this cost the Government about £27,000,000 a year.

WHY PRICES WERE CONTROLLED FOR SOME TIME AFTER THE WAR

In addition to rationing and subsidies, many prices were controlled. The Government set a limit above which they must not rise. Price control applied to nearly everything which was sold in the shops, and so covered a great number of things which were not rationed.

After the war, there was still a shortage of goods, because it took time to change factories back from production for war to production for peace. But as production increased so controls were removed.

The Story of the Marvellous Plants that Cover the Earth

The Yellow Pansy

FLOWERS OF THE MOUNTAIN

ONE of the most interesting and useful of our mountain plants is the bilberry, or whortleberry. It is a near relation of the cranberry, whose red berries gathered on the moors in the north of England are sold in large quantities for fruit tarts, though most cranberries sold in London come from the Baltic countries.

There are about 350 members of the cranberry family, most of them natives of moist mountain woods in temperate and cold regions; but some are found in tropical Asia and America, and a few in the Pacific islands. Bilberries, cranberries, blueberries, cowberries, and huckleberries are all members of this family, and their fruits are delicious.

The bilberry, sometimes called the whinberry, or wine-berry, because wine is made from the fruits, and the blaeberry, or blue berry, because of the bluish-purple colour of the fruits, is a small branched shrub, from six to eighteen inches high, with many angular stems that creep underground, and throw up erect branching shoots, bearing numerous egg-shaped leaves with saw-like edges, light green in tint.

The drooping flowers, which grow singly, are urn-shaped, almost globular, and are pinkish or flesh-coloured, with a wax-like appearance. They come out about April, and the plant flowers till June. The blossoms are succeeded by berries that are green at first, and then, as they ripen, become a deep purple with a bluish bloom. When the plant grows in an exposed situation the fruits form abundantly. They are sweet and slightly acid, and, though they possess little flavour when eaten raw, are delicious in tarts or when stewed and eaten with cream. At one time the purple juice was used as a dye for paper and linen. Where black grouse abound there is always a great contest between these birds and the human gatherers for the ripe bilberries, for the birds are very fond of this fruit.

It is interesting to examine a bilberry flower and see how Nature protects the pollen from dropping out, although the flower is drooping. The pores of the anthers, or pollen-cases, are pressed against the style, and the pollen cannot escape unless a bee pushes against the inner part of the blossom and shakes the anthers. The bee clings to the mouth of the flower, and, in pushing its tongue in to get at the nectar, strikes against one of the anther tails, which presses away the anther tips from the pistil and allows a shower of pollen to fall on the bee's face.

Another berried plant growing abundantly on mountain heaths in the north is

BOTANY & ITS WONDERS · FLOWERS · TREES · HOW THINGS GROW

the red bear-berry, a member of the heath family. It is a small, low, trailing evergreen shrub, with dark green leathery leaves that turn red in autumn and are slightly curled, or rolled, outwards. These leaves contain a great deal of tannic acid, with a considerable quantity of gallic acid, the acid obtained from oak-galls. On this account the plant has long been valued for medicinal purposes, the leaves being used either in a powdered state or as an infusion. An extract is also prepared from them, and in Sweden they are used in the tanning of leather, and serve the purpose excellently.

The flowers of the red bear-berry appear in small clusters at the ends of the branches and are of a pale-rose colour. They open in May, and are succeeded by bright red berries, which are mealy in texture and form a welcome food for moor-fowl.

Another bear-berry, known as the black bear-berry, is found only in dry, barren mountain spots in the Scottish Highlands. Its leaves have a saw-like edge, its flowers are white, and the berries are black.

THE TRAILING AZALEA OF THE HIGHLANDS WHICH IS NOT REALLY AN AZALEA

The heath family is also represented by the trailing azalea, the original and only azalea of Linnaeus. Found in Britain only in the Scottish Highlands, it is very different in habit from most of the showy plants cultivated in gardens under the name of azaleas, and is called by botanists Loiseleuria, after M. Loiseleur Deslongchamps, a famous French botanist. The trailing azalea is not, therefore, really an azalea as we understand that name. It is a low, tangled shrub, with small evergreen leaves, shiny on their upper surfaces, and with edges rolled back. The flowers, which occur in clusters at the ends of the branches, are small and rose-coloured.

The thrift, or sea-pink, is a relation of the sea lavender. It occurs abundantly on our British coasts, but grows also on the tops of many of the Scottish mountains. The leaves are fleshy and narrow, and grow in tufts, and the rose-coloured or white flowers form in roundish heads on leafless flower-stalks from three to six inches high. They open in April and the plant often goes on flowering till October.

The bird's-eye primrose is so called from the yellow eye on the dainty lilac-coloured corolla of the flower. The leaves are smaller than those of the common primrose, sometimes not an inch long, and underneath they are covered with a white mealy down, hence the plant's botanical name of Primula farinosa, from the Latin word *farina*, meaning flour. Some specimens of this primrose found in northern Scotland have a broader leaf than that of the ordinary bird's-eye primrose.

THE MOUNTAIN FORGET-ME-NOT WHICH IS FRAGRANT IN THE EVENING

The mountain forget-me-not is a member of the borage family and a close relation of the common forget-me-not. It is a short, erect plant with long, spreading hairs, and the deep bright blue flowers, which grow in clusters, give out a very sweet odour in the evening.

One of the handsomest of our mountain flowers is a member of the rose family and has large white flowers, an inch or more across. It is known as the white dryas, or mountain avens, though it does not belong to the same genus as the common avens, or herb benet. It is found in the limestone districts of northern England and Ireland, and is abundant in the north of Scotland. The stems are short and much branched, and form, with their crowded foliage, dense spreading tufts on the ground. The small leaves are shiny above and downy underneath, and the seed cases end in a long, feathery beard.

Another member of the rose family found on mountain pastures is the common lady's mantle, a herbaceous plant about a foot high, with large kidney-shaped leaves, sometimes smooth and sometimes hairy, divided into lobes, and toothed. The small flowers are yellowish-green and grow clustered in a loose, branching head. Another species, the Alpine lady's mantle, with small palm-like leaves, and with inconspicuous flowers, is less common.

THE BEAUTIFUL WOOD VETCH THAT CLIMBS OVER SHRUBS AND SMALL TREES

A member of the pea family found here and there in mountain woods is the large and beautiful wood vetch. It grows as high as six or eight feet, climbing by means of branched tendrils over the shrubs and small trees, and its smooth leaves are divided into about sixteen elliptical leaflets. The flowers, growing in long racemes, are white or cream-coloured, with bluish streaks, and the broad pod contains from four to six seeds.

The yellow mountain violet, or mountain pansy, has a creeping, underground stem branched with runners, and foliage much like that of the garden pansy. The flowers are large and richly coloured, being generally, as the name implies, yellow.

One of the most handsome of all our native mountain flowers is the globe-flower, or witches' gowan, which grows one or two feet high, with palm-shaped leaves, lobed and cut, much like those of the meadow buttercup, of which it is a relation. The flowers are large and pale yellow, and, as the name implies, more or less globular, owing to the fact that from ten to fifteen broad concave sepals converge into a kind of globe, concealing the petals and stamens. The name is a relic of the bad old days of superstition when witches were supposed to use the poisonous properties of the globe-flower for malign purposes. The botanical name is trollius, derived from the Scandinavian word *troll*, meaning a witch.

ALPINE PLANTS THAT GROW IN THE HIGHLANDS OF SCOTLAND

The Alpine meadow-rue is abundant in the Scottish Highlands, but less common in the mountainous parts of England, Ireland, and Wales. The stem is un-branched and the flowers grow in a drooping raceme at the top. Altogether, though not very showy, the little plant is very graceful. It is rarely more than nine inches high, and is often only half that size.

The red Alpine campion is a small tufted plant, rarely more than four or five inches high, with pink or red flowers in compact heads, and is confined to the summits of mountains in the north. The moss campion, sometimes called the dwarf silene, from its botanical name, is a beautiful little plant, growing in dense moss-like tufts often a foot or more round. The stem is much branched, and the short branches are covered with the remains of old leaves and crowned by dense clusters of bright green, narrow leaves. The pink or white flowers, in shape much like those of the other campions, grow singly on short stalks, and sometimes they are reddish purple in colour. Like the red Alpine campion, the moss campion is also confined to the summits of mountains, where it forms a closely matted turf gaily decorated with blossoms. These plants are members of the pink family.

Among the mountain composites are three plants that deserve mention. One is the flax-leaved goldilocks, a near relation of the sea starwort, or aster, but no connection of the common goldilocks, which is a buttercup. It is a smooth, erect plant, from six inches to a foot or a foot and a half high, with a leafy stem dotted closely with very narrow leaves. The bright yellow flowers grow in compact heads, but in Britain they do not have the typical rays of the asters.

THE PRETTY MOUNTAIN EVERLASTING WITH ITS MANY QUEER NAMES

Another of the composites is the cat's-foot, cat's-ear, or mountain everlasting, sometimes called the cudweed, though that name is generally given to other members of the family. It is a pretty little plant, four or five inches high, with a tufted or creeping leafy stalk, and white flowers growing in heads and having the texture generally called everlasting. The male flowers grow on one plant and the female blossoms on another.

A third composite is the Highland cudweed, found on the mountains of the north of Scotland. It is much like the wood cudweed, a white cottony plant, about a foot high, with an unbranched stem, but having broader leaves. The yellow flowers grow in a spike of heads.

Of the saxifrages several are found only at high altitudes. The starry saxifrage, a little plant with its leaves in a rosette, has small, white, star-like flowers growing in a branched raceme or head; the yellow mountain saxifrage, also a small plant, has narrow, fleshy leaves and little yellow flowers spotted with scarlet; the purple mountain saxifrage has larger solitary flowers of bright purple; and the mossy, or cut-leaved, saxifrage, often grown in gardens, has large white flowers.

NONE-SO-PRETTY THRIVING IN THE SMOKY STREETS OF LONDON

But the best known of all the mountain saxifrages is the London Pride, or None-so-pretty, also called in some parts, St. Patrick's cabbage. It is a favourite garden plant, and thrives in the smokiest parts of London, where its dense tufts of leaves often attain a diameter of a foot or more. Though sometimes found growing wild in the lowlands, it is there only an escape from gardens. It is rare even in the mountainous regions of Great Britain, but is more common in south-west Ireland. The leaves are thick and leathery, bordered with coarse teeth, and the small pink flowers, dotted with a darker colour, grow in a loose head on a leafless stalk six inches to a foot high.

Of the crane's-bill, or geranium, family, we find on the mountains the yellow balsam, or touch-me-not, an interesting and elegant plant closely related to the large group of East Indian balsams, including the garden balsams, whose flowers become double with great readiness. The yellow balsam, like the garden balsams, has a thick, juicy stem, swollen where the oblong leaves occur, and grows a foot or two high. The pale green leaves are pointed and toothed, and are very flaccid, or relaxed, and the flower-stalks bear one or two flowers, large and showy, yellow spotted with orange. In Britain they seldom set their seeds, hence the plant is rare. The pods are generally produced by minute imperfect flowers, of which there are sometimes several, on the same stalk as the perfect flowers.

MEMBERS OF THE CABBAGE FAMILY FOUND GROWING ON THE MOUNTAINS

The cabbage family has its representatives in the common scurvy grass, with its heart-shaped leaves and small white flowers, and the Alpine rock-cress, looking like a small-flowered specimen of the lady's-smock of lowland meadows to which it is related. A close examination, however, shows it to be quite different. Its root-leaves are lyre-shaped and cut into wedge-shaped lobes, while those on the flower stem are lance-shaped and not divided. The four-petalled flowers, which form in a corymb, or flat head, are white and sometimes tinted with purple. The leaves and stem are hairy, and the plant is a near relation of the hairy-leaved arabis that flowers so abundantly in our gardens in spring. The scurvy grass is so called because of its value as a medicine in counteracting that complaint.

The persicaria family, to which belong the rhubarb used for tarts and puddings and as a medicine, and the buckwheat, greatly prized in America for making cakes, has one of its members growing fairly abundantly in damp places near the summits of high mountains. This is the mountain sorrel, or kidney oxyria, a plant closely resembling the common sorrel of the meadow. It reaches a height of about ten inches, though generally it is less, and has kidney-shaped leaves varying from half-an-inch to an inch across. The slender stem, almost leafless, ends in a clustered spike of green flowers, and the fruit which develops is a flat nut with a broad, membraneous wing. The whole plant has an acid flavour. Another persicaria is the viviparous bistort, or Alpine bistort, a slender plant six inches high, with a creeping rootstock and spike of pink flowers.

THE MOUNTAIN PLANT NAMED AFTER THE APOLLO OF THE NORTH

Two of the parsleys are found on the mountains, the sweet cicely and the spignel, spicknel, or mew, also called baldmoney, after Balder, the Apollo of the North, to whom the plant was dedicated.

Sweet cicely is a plant two or three feet high, with the much-cut leaf typical of the parsleys, and a head of white flowers which develop into a large dark brown fruit an inch long. The leaves and fruit are remarkable for their highly aromatic and sweet flavour. The spignel, with similarly much-cut leaves, is also highly aromatic, and is eaten by the Highlanders. The flavour is like that of melilot, and when the cows feed on it in spring their milk and butter have the same taste.

Two bedstraws that grow on the mountain are the wild madder and the mountain bedstraw. The wild madder is a close relative of the Indian madder, from whose roots we obtain a valuable reddish-brown dye. It is a straggling plant many feet in length, with nearly evergreen leaves, yellowish flowers, and black berries as large as currants.

The mountain bedstraw is like the heath bedstraw, only more erect, and has white flowers. It occurs only on limestone hills.

THE THYME THAT SHAKESPEARE SAW GROWING ON A BANK

Mountain thyme is one of the labiates, a relation of the common marjoram and the mints. It is a well-known plant, a creeping evergreen, with slender, woody stems thickly covered with small egg-shaped leaves, and bearing at their extremities rounded heads of small purple flowers. It forms thick, dense tufts when growing alone, but when mixed with other herbage on downs and pastures it runs among the grass and other plants, throwing out long trailing stems which take root at intervals. This is the plant Shakespeare wrote of: " I know a bank where the wild thyme blows."

The whole plant is aromatic, the leaves and flowers especially containing a great deal of essential oil, which is sometimes used as a remedy for toothache. This causes the plant to diffuse a fragrant perfume which is very pleasing and which is especially perceptible in hot weather, being then noticeable at quite a distance. It is said that the flesh of sheep which feed on mountain thyme and other aromatic herbs has a very superior flavour. Bees are fond of the flowers of thyme. The lemon thyme of our gardens is only a cultivated variety of the wild thyme of the mountain.

stem, six or seven inches high, the dull purple-blue blossoms being borne on a short, leafy spike. It flowers all the summer. In the Alps this is quite a common flower and is indeed found all over the higher mountain chains of central and northern Europe, and as far north as the Arctic regions. It flourishes a mile

MOUNTAIN SORREL

MOSS CAMPION

YELLOW MOUNTAIN SAXIFRAGE

LADY'S MANTLE

STAR SAXIFRAGE

ALPINE MEADOW-RUE

ROSE ROOT

COMMON SCURVY GRASS

MOSSY SAXIFRAGE

LONDON PRIDE

tic herbs has a very superior flavour. Bees are fond of the flowers of thyme. The lemon thyme of our gardens is only a cultivated variety of the wild thyme of the mountain.

One other mountain plant may be mentioned here, the Alpine bartsia, a member of the figwort family, and a relation of the foxglove and snapdragon. This is a low plant, with a short rootstock and an erect

and a half above sea level, and is particularly abundant in the vast grassy stretches of Siberia. In Britain it is rare, even in Scotland and northern England, being only found in places few and far between, and in Ireland it is unknown. The bartsias were given their name in honour of John Bartsch, an eminent Prussian botanist.

Two pages of coloured pictures of Flowers of the Mountain are given on 5641-42

THE HALL OF THE KNIGHTS

THE STATE OPENING OF PARLIAMENT AT THE HALL OF THE KNIGHTS, THE HAGUE MEETING
PLACE OF THE NETHERLANDS PARLIAMENT

The Story of the Peoples of all Nations and their Homelands

HOLLAND AND ITS PEOPLE

THE highest and lowest lands in Europe are linked together by the River Rhine. Far away amid the mountains of Switzerland it starts on its long journey, leaping like a merry child, till it passes into the quiet waters of Lake Constance. Then, with growing strength, it dashes and roars as it tumbles over the rocks at Schaffhausen, and flows, in staid middle life, rapidly and steadily north, useful and beautiful, for many, many miles through Germany. After passing the grand gate of the Seven Mountains near Cologne it goes slower, as if age had come upon it ; and at last, stretching out weary arms, it seems to be blindly searching for the sea, in which to end its winding course in peace.

The triangle of low land on the shores of the North Sea between France and Germany lies in the grasp of these arms of the Rhine and about the lower courses of the Meuse (called Maas by the Dutch) and the Scheldt, where the great north plain of Europe is narrowest ; it has been known through history as the Low Countries.

Though occasionally united under one rule, this small area has become two distinct countries. The northern and larger part, lying chiefly in the Rhine delta, is the Netherlands ; the southern part is Belgium.

Holland is the name we generally give to the Netherlands, but it is a misleading name, because Holland proper is only an old province of the country, in which today not more than one-third of the Dutch population live.

The land area of the whole of the Netherlands is 12,600 square miles, about twice the size of Yorkshire, and as the home of 10,500,000 people it is one of the most densely populated countries in Europe.

The most astonishing thing about their flat little country is that two-fifths of it lie below sea-level—a rich countryside that has been won from the ocean by the ingenuity and toil of generations of dauntless Dutchmen.

Let us imagine we are visiting the Netherlands and standing on top of one of their great dykes, as they call their sea walls. It is broad enough for a road with trees and buildings beside it. Below us on one side the waves of the sea are breaking on the beach, while on the other side a bank slopes down to green meadows, and we can look into the chimneys of houses down there. The fish in the water on one side are actually higher than the birds in the trees on the other.

Massive indeed are these dykes, built

THE FIVE CONTINENTS & 100 NATIONS & RACES THAT INHABIT THEM

of stones, cement, and willow boughs. Constant care is needed to see that there is no leak in these defences, and that the various gates and sluices are in perfect order.

But water threatens from the inland direction as well, and strong walls along the rivers prevent them from overflowing when the snow in the distant Alps melts. Everywhere are canals and ditches regulating the flow, and electrically operated pumps are continuously at work.

All this unending effort to keep Holland's head above water, so to speak, is in charge of a special Government department called the Waterstaat, which is not content merely to defend the homeland against the invading waters, but has driven them back as well. One of the Waterstaat's greatest feats in modern times has been the draining of the Zuyder Zee, the vast stretch of water, 1200 square miles in extent, which was formed about 600 years ago when the sea burst over the land.

GREAT FERTILE AREA WHICH WAS ONCE THE SEA-BED

The engineers of the Waterstaat began this formidable task by building a gigantic dam wall, over $18\frac{1}{2}$ miles long, which cut off the great bight of the Zuyder Zee from the ocean outside. Then they pumped out the inland sea, leaving two wide expanses of dry fertile soil called " polders," with an area of 175,000 acres. Soon crops were growing and cattle grazing on fields which had long been a sea-bed.

The Dutch engineers have carried on their good work with the intention of creating two even larger polders of 390,000 acres between them. When this work is completed, the former Zuyder Zee will be reduced to a freshwater lake of 300,000 acres which will be a valuable reservoir and a recreation place for holiday-makers.

Another ambitious project now being considered is to reclaim from the ocean its two great arms that reach inland on the southern part of the coastline, which would mean still more land for the Hollanders to live on and cultivate. Yet another plan has the object of reclaiming land on a grand scale between the Frisian Islands and Holland's northern coast. There can be no other nation in the world which, confronted with the problem of a growing population, calmly proceeds to obtain more land by pushing back the sea!

In 700 years the Dutch have added an area of no less than 1,500,000 acres to their small land !

What a triumph of human energy is here, and as if to pay tribute to it, the reclaimed land is crowned in the early summer, with a lovely display of the bulb flowers for which Holland is famous.

THE CAPITAL CITY BUILT ON ISLANDS AND WITH 300 BRIDGES

When we turn from admiring the newly-won land and enter the towns, we are surprised at the number of canals. Amsterdam, the capital, is an outstanding example ; it is built on as many islands as Venice, and its canals are crossed by some 300 bridges.

Most of the Netherlands is as flat as a pancake, yet the visitors can enjoy fine views by mounting the towers of any of the old churches. On a fine day water can be seen gleaming everywhere, with steel railway lines glinting here and there in the sun. And there are still plenty of windmills, which everyone associates with Holland, and which once did the pumping work of the drainage system. The whole pleasant panorama is arrayed in that tender, delicate light which the old Dutch artists knew so well how to capture in their pictures.

Behind all this peaceful scene, however, lies one of the most stirring stories in European history : the rise of poor marsh-dwellers into a wealthy, powerful, and important nation.

THE BRAVE PEOPLES WHO SETTLED IN HOLLAND BEFORE THE ROMANS CAME

These Low Countries were a dull, damp, gloomy region when the early Celtic settlers came to live like beavers among the tangled brushwood on the islands at the mouth of the Rhine.

The bravest of them were the Belgae, who have left their name in Belgium ; but when the Romans came several German tribes, of much the same stock as our own forefathers, had pushed out the Celts. Among them the Batavians and the Frisians were celebrated for bravery and love of freedom, and their determination to protect the land on which they dwelled. The Batavians proved of great use in the Roman armies.

In the fourth century the Frankish

tribes came swarming over the Rhine, and by degrees they absorbed the Frisians and the Batavians, and the rest of the tribes living in the morasses and low plains, till, in the eighth century, all the country fell under the rule of the Emperor Charlemagne. He left the people their native customs, and put chiefs over them as his delegates, whom they had to obey.

Part of Charlemagne's plan was to give wealth and power to the bishops of the newly Christianised tribes, and for nearly a thousand years these prince-bishops were very important. After Charlemagne's death, the empire broke up, and,

We know how the rise of important towns has always helped on the cause of freedom, and, though the towns in the Netherlands are not quite so old as some in France, Italy, and Germany, most of them date from early times. When trade was set moving by the impulse of the Crusades, the towns of the great north and south route began to rise from small beginnings to wealth and power. From the thirteenth to the fifteenth century the towns of the Netherlands did much business with the towns of the famous Hanseatic League of traders. In the fourteenth century there were over 3000

DUTCH PEOPLE IN NATIONAL DRESS IN A STIRRING FOLK DANCE ON THE ICE AT MARKEN

under the weak rulers who followed, the independent nobles became ever stronger.

An old law of one of the small States (Friesland) declares that " the race shall be free as long as the wind blows out of the clouds and the world stands," and this principle has always been kept in view.

But in the bad old feudal days, when the nobles were for ever quarrelling among themselves, and, according to their opportunities, doing their best to take away the liberties of the people, the prince-bishops gained more and more power over men's minds, till no one dared to think for himself.

woollen factories around Malines (now Mechelen, centre of the Belgian railways); Ghent had 40,000 weavers, and the goldsmiths of Bruges were numerous enough to form a regiment by themselves in time of war. The towns of Delft, Haarlem, Rotterdam, and Amsterdam, were all growing, though often devastated by the quarrels of landowners and townsmen.

It was at this time that England grew so much wool for Flemish looms. Linen, too, of various kinds was added to the manufactures.

But all the time when the trade and industry were growing, amid constant scenes of violence and fighting in the streets of the flourishing towns, the struggle against the elements for possession of the country was ever going on. When the fierce winds heaped up the sand in hills on the shore, the Netherlanders planted coarse grass to bind it together to make a rampart. When the river overflowed, the banks were strengthened and heightened; and so by degrees, by patient trial and endeavour, that wonderful skill was attained in building dykes to withstand even the onward rush of the stormy tide, and in making canals and draining lakes. Sometimes, as we have seen, the giant ocean had his way. It was in the thirteenth century that he rushed inland and formed the Zuyder Zee, and it is here that we can see how efficiently the Dutch can act, for in the Weiringenmeer Polder, the first section of the Zuyder Zee to be reclaimed, crops of all kinds were cultivated forthwith.

THE DARK CLOUD WHICH BEGAN TO GROW OVER THE NETHERLANDS

All this effort for generations produced a wise and determined race, few in numbers, living in a small country, yet able to resist in the fifteenth and sixteenth centuries the fierce tyranny of the most powerful of the sovereigns of Europe.

For a dark cloud began to grow over the Netherlands when by seizure, purchase, succession, marriage of heiresses, the most considerable of its states passed under the sway of the Dukes of Burgundy. These dukes wished to annex Switzerland as well as the Netherlands and make one long independent kingdom between France and Germany. The crafty Louis the Eleventh had very much to say about this, and was at constant warfare with Duke Charles the Bold. From the daughter of this bad and bold man was wrested the Great Charter, which led to the first regular assembly of the States-General, the members of which were sent from the provinces and great cities of the Netherlands.

THE SPANISH TYRANT WHO PERSECUTED THE PEOPLE OF THE NETHERLANDS

This young duchess married Maximilian of the Hapsburg family, and their son Philip succeeded to his mother's dominions and married the daughter of Ferdinand and Isabella of Spain. Their son was the famous Charles the Fifth, who gathered into his hand the rule of the Netherlands with that of Spain and Austria. All these countries hated each other, and the liberties of the Netherlands were in terrible danger from a prince who firmly believed that he had the sole right of disposing of the persons and lives of his subjects as well as settling their faith and religion.

Charles, in spite of his wide empire, was always in want of money, and he required the rich cities of the Netherlands, especially of Ghent, to furnish it whenever he chose to ask for it. If it were denied, he took away the charters and rights of those who opposed him, and fined and executed the citizens. Hard as this was, especially when trade from different causes did not bring in so much wealth as formerly, it was not to be compared with the suffering inflicted on the country through Charles's tyranny in matters of religion.

We know how the teaching of Luther raised a storm in Germany and in England. Calvin, another reformer, powerfully affected France and the Netherlands, and in these countries the rulers hated and feared the Protestants not only because their beliefs were contrary to established doctrine, but also because they denied the absolute power of the rulers themselves; and so, as the Netherlanders became more and more convinced that the Reformation was right, and bent all the strength of their determined natures to uphold it, the more bitter became the persecution of those in power, in order to stamp it out. Charles established the terrible Inquisition in the Netherlands, and thousands of people were burned under his stern orders.

THE NATIONAL HERO WHO FOLLOWED A WORN-OUT OLD EMPEROR

His son, Philip the Second, carried out his father's plan only too well, and when the unhappy people prepared to rise in revolt against his cruelties, he sent the Duke of Alva, a man absolutely without pity, to suppress them.

A national hero rose up at this time in William the Silent, Prince of Orange. William was brought up under the eyes of Charles the Fifth. When the worn-out emperor laid down all his crowns to go into a monastery, it was on William's arm that he entered the great hall at Brussels, where the ceremony of renunciation took place.

William very soon ceased to be friends with Philip of Spain, though for years he was called his lieutenant; and after he openly became a Protestant he was leader of the opposition to the bloodthirsty Duke of Alva. The patriots called themselves at first the Beggars. Sometimes they won, especially at sea, sometimes the Spaniards had the best of it, and the struggle went on for many years.

WHEN THE DYKES WERE CUT TO FLOOD THE LAND AND HARASS THE INVADERS

Stories of the heroism shown in this war of independence are told of every town of the Low Countries, the sieges of Haarlem and of Leyden being among the most memorable. Leyden held out a whole year, except for a brief respite, and the heroic defenders were reduced to starvation, but would not give in. There were fights on the slippery ice in the bitter winter. As a last resource, the dykes were cut, and the water flowed over the hardly-won fields, forcing the Spaniards away in haste lest they should be drowned, and enabling the ships that had been waiting, to come right up to the walls of the town, bearing their precious cargoes of food to the starving inhabitants.

After a while the provinces of Holland and Zealand united; and when they felt strong enough, they took the important step of renouncing the authority of Philip. England helped them cautiously, and one of the bravest of the English volunteers who pressed across the North Sea to help the Netherlanders was our Sir Philip Sidney, who, when dying, handed a precious cup of water to another wounded man, saying : " Thy need is greater than mine."

HOW FATHER WILLIAM BECAME HEAD OF THE NEW REPUBLIC

But scenes of war, of sacking fine cities, of senseless cruelty in persecution, could not last for ever, and after several unsuccessful attempts at union and at making peace with Spain, Dutch independence was declared in 1581. William the Silent, affectionately called Father William, was the head of the new Republic. It was nearly seventy years before Spain gave up all her claims and titles, and acknowledged the political independence of the Dutch people.

The victory was followed, as has so often been the case in history, by a tragic act. Three years after the Declaration of Independence the wisest man in Holland was murdered by a ruffian hired by Spain.

No man in the history of the world has deserved more truly the name of Great than this silent Dutchman. To understand him we must realise what he left to take his stand on the side of right. A friend of the great Catholic kings of Spain and France, he gave up his wealth and ease to face danger, calumny, poverty, and outlawry. William was honest enough in feeling, and bold enough in thought, to see that the torture and murder of people for believing what they hold to be true is utterly wrong.

War still went on under his son, Maurice, and the southern States, now Belgium, with their great towns of Antwerp and Ghent, and many others, were reduced to obedience to Spain for many years after the northern States became free. Protestantism had been stamped out, the brave and clever Flemish workers had been driven away to Holland or to England, to the great and lasting benefit of these lands.

HOLLAND SENDS HER FLEETS AND HARDY SEAMEN TO SECURE POSSESSIONS OVERSEAS

It was in 1600 that Queen Elizabeth formed an East India Company to trade abroad, as all commerce had been so hindered by the ambitious plans of Spain. Holland followed suit two years later. Much money was spent on fleets and ports and factories; and from these days the sailors of Holland—trained in the wild fishing-grounds of the North Sea—were to be found all over the world taking possession of the Spanish and Portuguese colonies, and often hotly contesting with the English. New Amsterdam (afterwards New York) was founded across the Atlantic, and to this day both city and people bear witness to the Dutch founders. Dutch navigators discovered Australia and New Zealand, and Dutch pioneers established colonies in South America, South Africa, and the East. The city of Batavia was founded in Java, called after the old province, the kernel of the Mother Country. (Batavia is now Djakarta, capital of the Republic of Indonesia, of which we can read on page 5532.)

Amsterdam and Rotterdam and all the old cities now revived, with the arrival of ships laden with " sugar and spice and all that's nice," at the busy quays.

As soon as peace gave leisure, pumping

works were established to drain lakes and marshes, and the rich meadow land thus gained fed the finest cattle in Europe. Another use to which the land gained from the sea was put was to grow roots for food and various kinds of beautiful flowers like tulips. The Dutch taught all Europe how to garden and farm. At this time, also, Holland became the printing-house of Europe, sending out thousands of books on history and travel, law and medicine. Trades such as diamond-cutting—still carried on at Amsterdam—gave employment to large numbers of skilled workmen.

It was in the seventeenth century that the rivalry between the Dutch and English on the high seas came to a crisis. There were many famous admirals, many brave seamen on both sides. Tromp and De Ruyter are names as well known to us as Blake and Monk, and for years they tried to sweep each other off the narrow seas. London was in a panic when De Ruyter sailed up the Thames in the days of Charles the Second, and sometimes the obstinate sea battles lasted three or four days, for both sides belonged to a stock never knowing when it was beaten.

THE SUDDEN THAW THAT SAVED THE COUNTRY FROM ITS ENEMIES

In the age of Louis the Fourteenth, France made several conquests in the Netherlands, and to save the country the dykes were opened. Later the waters froze, and when the French troops were marching over the ice to attack The Hague a sudden thaw saved the country from destruction. The head of the Republic at this time was the great-grandson of William the Silent. His name was also William, and he married the daughter of our James the Second. When England could no longer bear the tyranny of the Stuarts, William was invited over to be king in James's place. He helped to restore old laws and liberties, and to strengthen the position of the reformed religion.

In the eighteenth century the importance of the united provinces of the Dutch Republic became less than it had been in the seventeenth, and there were many disturbances in the country, which led to the interference of the King of Prussia. But the French Revolution was at hand, and before long the map of Europe was completely changed, and bewildering changes came to the Low Countries, both north and south. The seven united provinces were turned into the Batavian Republic, and a few years later Napoleon turned it into a kingdom for his brother Louis. But that did not last long. He soon took his brother away, and joined Holland and all the other provinces, to France. " They are but the sediments of French rivers," said he, " and therefore clearly belong to me."

WHY BELGIUM AND HOLLAND BECAME TWO KINGDOMS

When the Congress of Vienna remade the map of Europe after Waterloo, the whole of the Netherlands was joined into one kingdom under another William, Prince of Orange. But the northern and southern provinces did not agree about religion—the south being chiefly Roman Catholic—and they differed on many other matters, too ; so, in 1830, the South revolted. The old Spanish Netherlands, which were afterwards Austrian, became the Kingdom of Belgium, and the northern provinces went on as the Kingdom of the Netherlands.

When the First World War broke out Holland and Belgium were in a perilous position. Both countries barred Germany from a stretch of sea-coast which she coveted, and which would have increased immensely her opportunities of attack. Germany, however, had too many enemies in that war to make another one in Holland.

But in the Second World War Holland was occupied by the German Nazis, Queen Wilhelmina and the Dutch Government taking refuge in England. However, the victory of the Allies in 1945 liberated the land from the invaders and in a few years those regions which had been devastated in the war were restored by the industrious Dutch people.

THE TREASURES WHICH CAME WITH THE GOLDEN AGE

In the cities of Belgium (of which we read in the chapter beginning on page 5645) and Holland the story of the past is perpetually before our eyes. Fine cathedrals and churches, grand town halls and buildings of all kinds are like speaking witnesses which link the past with the present.

In many museums are national heirlooms from what the Dutch call their Golden Age—roughly, the 17th century, when the merchant princes of the Nether-

DUTCH CHILDREN AT HOME AND AT SCHOOL

IN THE PLAY-GARDENS OF NEW BUILDINGS AT THE HAGUE

LESSONS IN THE OPEN AIR AT A SCHOOL IN AMSTERDAM

lands encouraged artists to create those masterpieces which have ever since been the admiration of the world.

In other ways this small nation has enriched the world. Names that will be remembered for ever are those of Erasmus, the scholar who did much to prepare the way for the Reformation, Grotius, the famous writer on law, Spinoza, the Jewish philosopher, and Antony van Leeuwenhoek, inventor of the microscope.

THE GREAT STRESS ON EDUCATION AND THE VALUE OF OTHER LANGUAGES

With such cultural traditions the modern Dutch, as we should expect, are enthusiastic about education. They have six universities, the oldest being Leyden, founded by William the Silent in 1574. In addition there are four university colleges.

All Dutch boys and girls must go to school from the age of six to 15, and practically all of them acquire some knowledge of a foreign language—English, French, or German—for they do not expect foreigners to learn Dutch. Visitors are often surprised to find their own language spoken well by everyday folk—taximen, clerks, workers.

The Dutch are a devout people. About 43 per cent of them are Protestants and some 38 per cent Catholics, but they all live and work in harmony, for their nation has a grand tradition of religious tolerance ; the Pilgrim Fathers fled to Holland for that reason before sailing to America.

THE FAMOUS CANAL WHICH LINKS AMSTERDAM WITH THE SEA

Their spirit of independence, their age-old resolve to work out their own salvation, has made the Dutch a prosperous people.

They have the eighth largest merchant fleet in the world, and their port of Rotterdam is third largest after New York and London. Enormous quantities of goods destined for all parts of western Europe are brought to Rotterdam.

Amsterdam is connected with the sea by the great North Sea Canal, in which are the Ijmuiden Locks, claimed to be the largest in the world. From Amsterdam vessels go up the Rhine as far as Switzerland, and more than half the shipping on the Rhine is Dutch, while on the canals and rivers at home barges and light draught ships carry one-third of all the goods distributed throughout the Netherlands.

The little country has over 20,000 miles of railways, and many excellent, straight roads. She claims the world's oldest airline in the celebrated K.L.M. (Koninklijke Luchtvaart Maatschappij), which was launched in 1919, and won the London-Christchurch air race in 1953.

While nature has endowed Holland with a fertile soil, she has been niggardly in her gifts of minerals. Only coal, salt, and a certain amount of oil are found there, which means that the Dutch must import raw materials to make things to sell to other countries. In this business, nevertheless, they have succeeded surprisingly, and have become big exporters of pig iron and chemicals, and more recently they have developed a textile industry.

But when we talk of Dutch exports we at once think of cheese and tulips. Every year Holland sends abroad millions of guilders' worth of flower bulbs, and she is second among the world's exporters of cheese.

THE RICH PRODUCE FROM THE FARMS AND THE MARKET GARDENS

It is indeed amazing how many good things these ten-and-a-half million people produce from the rich soil of their tiny country. Wheat, sugar, vegetables, fruit, meat, eggs, and milk are exported, often in the form of processed foods. Holland's condensed milk, butter, and cheese, potato-flour, and other preserves are found in shops all over the world.

Some parts of the country are just one vast market garden. The Westland district, between The Hague and the Hook of Holland, might be called " Glassland," for it is the region of the hot-houses in which are grown out-of-season tomatoes, grapes, cucumbers, lettuces, and cauliflowers which are flown to Britain, Belgium, and Western Germany.

All these busy commercial activities give us some idea of how the sturdy Hollander keeps the wolf—as well as the sea—from his door !

When the day's work is done most Dutch citizens or townsmen go home to a flat or maisonette. But there are probably not more than three or four flats in the one building ; for they like to have their own front door, and their own staircase to it. On the other hand, they seldom draw curtains at the large windows after dark to shut the family off from the gaze of passers-by, as do most of the neighbouring nations. At night the interior of Dutch homes imparts a friendly, welcoming appearance to a district that otherwise might seem dead and dull to the visitor.

In the country the people live in detached or semi-detached houses, or in terraces. Everywhere there are examples of typical Dutch architecture that so enchants the visitor—the bell-shaped gables, and the bricks of a warm red colour which are made from the clay from the big rivers, and are as characteristic of Holland as its windmills.

THE INDUSTRIOUS AND CLEAN PEOPLE WHO ARE PROUD OF THEIR HOMES

The people love their homes and they are house-proud, too, scrubbing everything that can be scrubbed. But they are proud, also, and with excellent reason, of their many fine public buildings and spick-and-span railway stations.

The Dutch are great builders, and they tackled the job of the Second World War devastation with a will. One of their most spectacular rebuilding feats was the re-creation of the centre of Rotterdam, which had been laid completely flat by the cruel, unexpected bombing at the beginning of the war in May 1940. They have achieved a novel lay-out in a new City centre, concentrating business interests of the same kind in their own separate sections, which is a great help in the intense commercial activities which go on in the largest port on the continent of Europe.

THE DEMOCRATICALLY-ELECTED CHAMBERS OF THE DUTCH PARLIAMENT

A busy people need a sound kind of government and the Dutch, as we should expect from their long struggle for independence, are stoutly attached to democratic ways. They have a constitutional monarchy like ours, and like us they are devoted to their Royal Family, who are descended from William the Silent, the country's first Liberator.

Their well-loved Queen, Juliana, came to the throne in 1948 when her mother, Queen Wilhelmina, voluntarily abdicated after 50 years of rule.

The Dutch Parliament, which is called the States General, sits at The Hague and consists of two Chambers. The 100 members of the Lower Chamber, which resembles our House of Commons, are elected by the people, every person of 23 and over having a vote. The 50 members of the Upper Chamber are chosen by the governing bodies of the eleven provinces into which the Netherlands is divided.

The Netherlands territory is not limited to her little corner of Europe; there are lands across the sea which look to her as the Mother Country. Important among these is Surinam, formerly known as Dutch Guiana, in the north-east of South America. This tropical land first came into the Netherlands' possession at the Peace of Breda in 1667, when it was exchanged with Britain for New Amsterdam.

Surinam, with an area of about 54,000 square miles, is much bigger than the Mother Country, but its population is only some 220,000, consisting of Creoles, Hindus, Indonesians, Chinese, Aboriginal Indians, and Europeans. They have their own government, and their country is in voluntary association with the Netherlands. Surinam's most valuable product is bauxite, the raw material of aluminium.

THE ISLANDS OVERSEAS WHICH HELP FORM A COMMONWEALTH OF NATIONS

Some 500 miles west of Paramaribo, the capital of Surinam, lie the three Dutch islands of Aruba, Curaçao, and Bonaire. They are less than 50 miles from the coast of Venezuela, and Curaçao and Aruba have busy refineries for the crude oil brought to them from Venezuela and Colombia.

Aruba, Curaçao and Bonaire are part of the Netherlands Antilles, of which the three other members are St. Eustace, Saba, and part of St. Martin in the Leeward Islands. The combined population of the Dutch Antilles is 164,000, and the most important of the six islands is Curaçao, whose capital, Willemstad, is the seat of the government. This, like that of Surinam, is independent, the State of the Netherlands Antilles being an equal partner with the Homeland.

Yet another part of Holland's overseas territory is the western part of the great island of New Guinea (see map page 7121, volume ten).

The Netherlands, like Britain, is thus the centre of a commonwealth of nations. Though a small country, her people have contributed a major share to the development of civilisation.

THE REPUBLIC OF INDONESIA

HISTORICALLY linked with the Netherlands is the Republic of Indonesia, one of the new countries that achieved independent life after the Second World War. Previously it had been the Netherlands East Indies, Holland's richest overseas possession.

Indonesia is a State consisting of many islands lying between the south-east of the Asiatic mainland on the one side, and New Guinea and Australia on the other. Between them these islands comprise the immense area of some 692,000 square miles, which supports a population of about 82,000,000 people of different races.

The four largest islands of Indonesia are Java (with Madura) Sumatra, Celebes, and part of Borneo. Thousands of smaller islands are included in the Republic, whose capital is Djakarta, which the Dutch founded in the island of Java, and which was for long known to the world as Batavia. Dutch traders came to Java at the end of the 16th century and expelled the Portuguese colonists. Subsequently the Dutch extended their rule over all these islands, creating an empire which contributed in large measure towards the wealth and power of the home country.

In the Second World War the Japanese captured the Dutch East Indies, but after the defeat of the invaders, Indonesian Nationalists seized power and proclaimed their republic, which was afterwards recognised by the Netherlands at The Hague Round Table Conference in 1949.

Java, cradle of the Dutch influence, is about the size of England, and has a population of about 50,000,000. Its people belong to the Malay race, and like the majority of Indonesians are Mohammedan in religion. They grow rice, sugar, cinchona (for quinine), coffee, tobacco, tea, and indigo; but petroleum is Java's most valuable product, and rubber is also important. The island has the natural disability of being liable to earthquakes.

Across the narrow Sunda Strait from Java lies the bigger island of Sumatra, more than three times the size of England.

The people of Sumatra, fewer in numbers than their neighbours in Java, are also of the great Malayan race. Here, as in Java, the early Dutch pioneers drove out the Portuguese who had settled there earlier in the 16th century. Sumatra is notable for its exports of pepper, nutmegs, and mace (spice).

On the northern side of the Java Sea lies the huge island of Borneo, home of the Dyaks, most of which belongs to Indonesia. This part of Borneo is called Kalimantan, and has an area of 208,285 square miles. It. has a thriving oil industry, with busy oil ports at Balikpapan and Tarakans.

Indonesia's other great island, Celebes, is a picturesque forest-clad land with many deep gorges, 73,000 square miles in extent. Its capital, the seaport of Macassar, takes its name from the Macassars, a Malayan tribe who were the rulers of the island when the Dutch first arrived there in the 17th century.

Today the peoples of the Celebes, of Malayan origin, produce rice and maize, tropical fruits, spices, and coffee. The mineral wealth of their island includes gold, coal, copper, zinc, and salt.

The Moluccas, which the old-time mariners called the Spice Islands, lie between Celebes and New Guinea.

The Republic of Indonesia is ruled by a President and a House of Representatives, and during the years that have passed since this new nation won its independence, it has been making its first, often difficult, efforts in the art of self-government. One of the big problems confronting the State is education. There are six universities, the best-known being at Djakarta, but scattered through the islands are millions of people who are still illiterate. Indonesian educational authorities are well aware of this, and have plans in hand which will eventually make elementary education compulsory throughout the whole of the Republic.

Their country has a bright future, for it has oil, one of the natural resources that can be relied on to make a nation wealthy. There are also tin mines, and factories for making of everyday articles are being speedily developed. Most of the islands have good roads, and railways cover wide regions in Java and Sumatra.

The whole world is watching with sympathy the self-development of the Indonesian people, who are old in their traditional Eastern culture, but as yet young in the ways of Western democratic nationhood.

PICTURES OF HOLLAND

A RACE ON THE ICE AT FRIESLAND

THE LOW COUNTRIES OF HOLLAND & BELGIUM

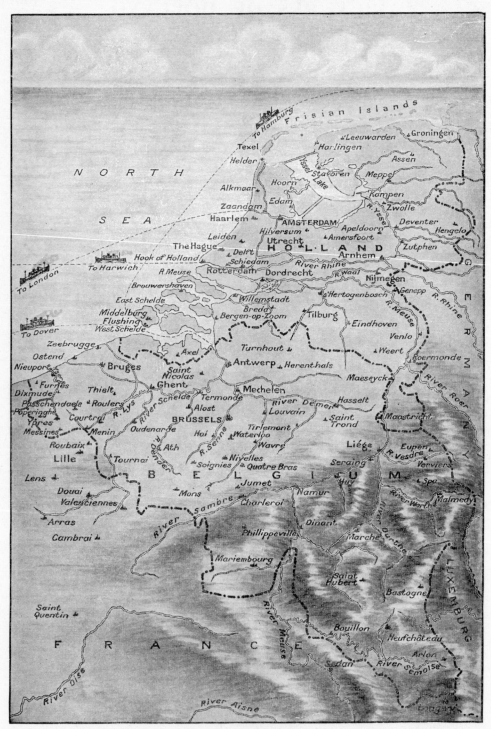

HOLLAND AND BELGIUM WERE FOR CENTURIES LINKED TOGETHER AS ONE LAND, AND MUCH OF
HOLLAND LIES CONSIDERABLY BELOW SEA-LEVEL

THE STIRRING PAST OF THE LOW COUNTRIES

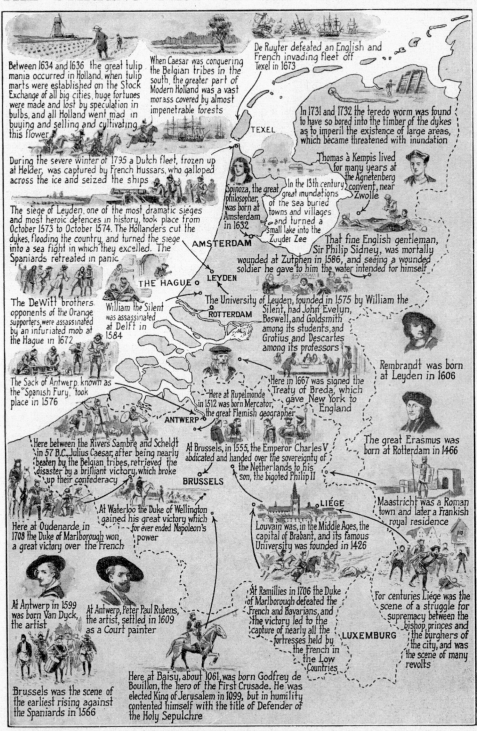

Between 1634 and 1636 the great tulip mania occurred in Holland, when tulip marts were established on the Stock Exchange of all big cities, huge fortunes were made and lost by speculation in bulbs, and all Holland went mad in buying and selling and cultivating this flower

When Caesar was conquering the Belgian tribes in the south, the greater part of Modern Holland was a vast morass covered by almost impenetrable forests

De Ruyter defeated an English and French invading fleet off Texel in 1673

TEXEL

In 1731 and 1732 the teredo worm was found to have so bored into the timber of the dykes as to imperil the existence of large areas, which became threatened with inundation

During the severe winter of 1795 a Dutch fleet, frozen up at Helder, was captured by French hussars, who galloped across the ice and seized the ships

Thomas à Kempis lived for many years at the Agnetenberg convent, near Zwolle

Spinoza, the great philosopher, was born at Amsterdam in 1632

In the 13th century great inundations of the sea buried towns and villages and turned a small lake into the Zuyder Zee

The siege of Leyden, one of the most dramatic sieges and most heroic defences in history, took place from October 1573 to October 1574. The Hollanders cut the dykes, flooding the country, and turned the siege into a sea fight in which they excelled. The Spaniards retreated in panic

AMSTERDAM

That fine English gentleman, Sir Philip Sidney, was mortally wounded at Zutphen in 1586, and seeing a wounded soldier he gave to him the water intended for himself

THE HAGUE

LEYDEN

The DeWitt brothers, opponents of the Orange supporters, were assassinated by an infuriated mob at the Hague in 1672

William the Silent was assassinated at Delft in 1584

The University of Leyden, founded in 1575 by William the Silent, had John Evelyn, Boswell, and Goldsmith among its students, and Grotius and Descartes among its professors

ROTTERDAM

Rembrandt was born at Leyden in 1606

The Sack of Antwerp, known as the "Spanish Fury," took place in 1576

Here at Rupelmonde in 1512 was born Mercator, the great Flemish geographer

Here in 1667 was signed the Treaty of Breda, which gave New York to England

ANTWERP

The great Erasmus was born at Rotterdam in 1466

Here between the Rivers Sambre and Scheldt in 57 B.C. Julius Caesar, after being nearly beaten by the Belgian tribes, retrieved the disaster by a brilliant victory, which broke up their confederacy

At Brussels, in 1555, the Emperor Charles V abdicated and handed over the sovereignty of the Netherlands to his son, the bigoted Philip II

BRUSSELS

LIÉGE

Maastricht was a Roman town and later a Frankish royal residence

At Waterloo the Duke of Wellington gained his great victory which for ever ended Napoleon's power

Louvain was, in the Middle Ages, the capital of Brabant, and its famous University was founded in 1426

Here at Oudenarde in 1708 the Duke of Marlborough won a great victory over the French

For centuries Liége was the scene of a struggle for supremacy between the bishop princes and the burghers of the city, and the scene of many revolts

At Antwerp in 1599 was born Van Dyck, the artist

At Antwerp, Peter Paul Rubens, the artist, settled in 1609 as a Court painter

At Ramillies in 1706 the Duke of Marlborough defeated the French and Bavarians, and the victory led to the capture of nearly all the fortresses held by the French in the Low Countries

LUXEMBURG

Brussels was the scene of the earliest rising against the Spaniards in 1566

Here at Baisy, about 1061, was born Godfrey de Bouillon, the hero of the First Crusade. He was elected King of Jerusalem in 1099, but in humility contented himself with the title of Defender of the Holy Sepulchre

HOLLAND AND BELGIUM, KNOWN COLLECTIVELY AS THE LOW COUNTRIES, HAVE HAD A STIRRING HISTORY, AS THIS PICTURE-MAP SHOWS

THE SEVENTEENTH-CENTURY ROYAL PALACE AT AMSTERDAM

IN QUAINT DORDRECHT

THE LITTLE COAST VILLAGE OF ZOUTELANDE

MILKING TIME ON A DAIRY FARM IN FRIESLAND

OUDE SCHANS, A BUSY WATERWAY IN AMSTERDAM

IN AN AMSTERDAM STREET

BY AN AMSTERDAM CANAL

THE RIJKS, OR NATIONAL MUSEUM, AT AMSTERDAM

THE CATHEDRAL TOWER AND
TOWN HALL, UTRECHT

THE NEW CHURCH
AT DELFT

THE TOWN HALL AT
MIDDELBURG

THE OLD HANSEATIC TOWN OF DEVENTER ON THE RIVER YSSEL

THE INSTITUTE OF SOCIAL STUDIES AT THE HAGUE

THE MARKET SQUARE OF MIDDELBURG

A BRIDGE AT DORDRECHT

AN ANCIENT GATEWAY AT MAASTRICHT

THE MONUMENT TO ADMIRAL
DE RUYTER AT FLUSHING

MEMORIAL TO SIR PHILIP
SIDNEY AT ZUTPHEN

WILLIAM THE SILENT, HOLLAND'S
NATIONAL HERO, AT THE HAGUE

A GENERAL VIEW OF THE HAGUE, CAPITAL OF THE PROVINCE OF SOUTH HOLLAND

THE GREAT CHURCH AT HAARLEM

THE TOWN HALL OF HILVERSUM

THE PALACE OF PEACE
AT THE HAGUE

THE CHEESE MARKET
AT ALKMAAR

THE HALL OF THE KNIGHTS
AT THE HAGUE

THE GREAT MODERN K.L.M. AIRPORT AT SCHIPOL

ROAD AND FARM ON LAND RECLAIMED FROM THE ZUYDER ZEE

A FAMILIAR SCENE ON MANY OF HOLLAND'S LAKES

A LAUNCHING AT ONE OF ROTTERDAM'S SHIPBUILDING YARDS

BULB-FIELDS AT LISSE, IRRIGATED BY CANALS

THE HISTORIC TOWN OF BREDA, WITH ITS 13TH CENTURY GOTHIC CHURCH

POETRY

One Thousand Poems of All Times and All Countries

Signing the Mayflower Covenant—From the sculpture by Cyrus Dallin, by courtesy of Curtis & Cameron

THE CRISIS

James Russell Lowell, poet, critic, ambassador, reaches his highest flight as an inspiring singer in this appeal to his American countrymen to choose the side of goodness and humanity in the great war against slavery.   This exalted poem will send for ever a thrill of joyful self-surrender through all true lovers of liberty. Five verses are omitted here.

WHEN a deed is done for Freedom,
    through the broad Earth's aching
breast
Runs a thrill of joy prophetic, trembling on
    from east to west,
And the slave, where'er he cowers, feels
    the soul within him climb
To the awful verge of manhood, as the
    energy sublime
Of a century bursts full-blossomed on the
    thorny stem of Time.

THROUGH the walls of hut and palace
    shoots the instantaneous throe
When the travail of the Ages wrings Earth's
    systems to and fro ;
At the birth of each new Era, with a recog-
    nising start,
Nation wildly looks at nation, standing
    with mute lips apart,
And glad Truth's yet mightier man-child
    leaps beneath the Future's heart.

FOR mankind are one in spirit, and an
    instinct bears along,
Round the Earth's electric circle, the swift
    flash of right or wrong ;
Whether conscious or unconscious, yet
    Humanity's vast frame
Through its ocean-sundered fibres feels the
    gush of joy or shame ;
In the gain or loss of one race all the rest
    have equal claim.

ONCE to every man and nation comes
    the moment to decide,
In the strife of Truth with Falsehood, for
    the good or evil side ;
Some great cause, God's new Messiah,
    offering each the bloom or blight,
Parts the goats upon the left hand and the
    sheep upon the right,
And the choice goes by for ever 'twixt
    that darkness and that light.

HAST thou chosen, O my people, on
    whose party thou shalt stand
Ere the Doom from its worn sandals shakes
    the dust against our land ?
Though the cause of Evil prosper, yet 'tis
    Truth alone is strong,
And, albeit she wander outcast now, I see
    around her throng
Troops of beautiful tall angels, to enshield
    her from all wrong.

CARELESS seems the great Avenger ;
    history's pages but record
One death-grapple in the darkness 'twixt
    old systems and the Word ;
Truth for ever on the scaffold, Wrong for
    ever on the throne—
Yet that scaffold sways the future, and
    behind the dim unknown
Standeth God within the shadow, keeping
    watch above His own.

POEMS · SONGS · BALLADS · VERSES AND RHYMES WITH MUSIC

Then to side with Truth is noble, when we
share her wretched crust,
Ere her cause bring fame and profit, and
'tis prosperous to be just ;
Then it is the brave man chooses, while the
coward stands aside,
Doubting in his abject spirit, till his Lord
is crucified,
And the multitude make virtue of the
faith they had denied.

Count me o'er earth's chosen heroes—they
were souls that stood alone
While the men they agonised for hurled
the contumelious stone,
Stood serene, and down the future saw the
golden beam incline
To the side of perfect justice, mastered by
their faith divine,
By one man's plain truth to manhood and
to God's supreme design.

For Humanity sweeps onward ; where
today the martyr stands
On the morrow crouches Judas with the
silver in his hands ;
Far in front the cross stands ready and the
crackling faggots burn,
While the hooting mob of yesterday in
silent awe return
To glean up the scattered ashes into
History's golden urn.

'Tis as easy to be heroes as to sit the idle
slaves
Of a legendary virtue carved upon our
fathers' graves,
Worshippers of light ancestral make the
present light a crime ;
Was the Mayflower launched by cowards,
steered by men behind their time ?
Turn those tracks toward Past or Future
that make Plymouth Rock sublime ?

They were men of present valour, stalwart
old iconoclasts,
Unconvinced by axe or gibbet that all
virtue was the Past's ;
But we make their truth our falsehood,
thinking that hath made us free,
Hoarding it in mouldy parchments, while
our tender spirits flee
The rude grasp of that great Impulse which
drove them across the sea.

They have rights who dare maintain them ;
we are traitors to our sires,
Smothering in their holy ashes Freedom's
new-lit altar-fires ;
Shall we make their creed our gaoler ?
Shall we, in our haste to slay,

From the tombs of the old prophets steal
the funeral lamps away
To light up the martyr-faggots round the
prophets of today ?

New occasions teach new duties ; Time
makes ancient good uncouth ;
They must upward still, and onward, who
would keep abreast of Truth ;
Lo, before us gleam her camp-fires ! we
ourselves must pilgrims be,
Launch our Mayflower, and steer boldly
through the desperate winter sea,
Nor attempt the Future's portal with the
Past's blood-rusted key.

THE LOVE OF GOD

Science tells the same story that is here quoted from the
Bible. In incredibly far-off time there will be an end to the
world as we know it, as it comes to us from an incredibly
far-off past. The only thing that makes the Earth's great
drama of progress lovely is the belief that it is planned and
sustained by an eternal purpose of Love. This setting of the
thought is a translation by William Cullen Bryant from a
poem in the Provençal dialect by Bernard Rascas.

ALL things that are on earth shall
wholly pass away
Except the love of God, which shall live
and last for aye.
The forms of men shall be as they had
never been ;
The blasted groves shall lose their fresh
and tender green ;
The birds of the thicket shall end their
pleasant song,
And the nightingale shall cease to chant
the evening long ;
The kine of the pasture shall feel the dart
that kills,
And all the fair white flocks shall perish
from the hills.
The goat and antlered stag, the wolf and
the fox,
The wild boar of the wood, and the
chamois of the rocks,
And the strong and fearless bear, in the
trodden dust shall lie ;
And the dolphin of the sea and the mighty
whale shall die.
And realms shall be dissolved, and
empires be no more,
And they shall bow to death who ruled
from shore to shore ;
And the great globe itself, so the holy
writings tell,
With the rolling firmament, where the
starry armies dwell,
Shall melt with fervent heat—they shall
all pass away
Except the love of God, which shall live
and last for aye.

LITTLE VERSES FOR VERY LITTLE PEOPLE

They that wash on Friday wash in
    need;
And they that wash on Saturday,
    oh ! they're sluts indeed.

Sleep, baby, sleep,
    Our cottage vale is deep;
The little lamb is on the green,
With woolly fleece so soft and clean—
    Sleep, baby, sleep.

Sleep, baby, sleep,
Down where the woodbines creep;
Be always like the lamb so mild,
A kind and sweet and gentle child,
    Sleep, baby, sleep!

Buttons a farthing a pair !
    Come, who will buy them of me?
They're round and sound and pretty,
And fit for the girls of the city.

The grave old clock on the mantel-
    piece
Is ticking the hours away;
There's never a smile on his solemn
    face
    Throughout all the merry day.
      Tick-tock, tick-tock,
    Whatever we do or say.

When his hands are showing a quarter
    to nine
    We must hurry to school away;
The clock never scolds or gives us
    a frown
    If we stop a minute to play.
      Tick-tock, tick-tock,
    Whether we go or stay.

Dribble, dribble, trickle, trickle,
    What a lot of rawdust!
My dolly's had an accident,
    And lost a lot of sawdust!

Robin-a-Bobin
    Bent his bow,
Shot at a pigeon
    And killed a crow.

OLD KING COLE WAS A MERRY OLD SOUL

Old King Cole was a mer-ry old soul, And a mer-ry old soul was he. He called for his pipe, and he called for his bowl, And he called for his fid - dlers three. Now ev - 'ry fid - dler

had a fine fid-dle, and a ver-y fine fid-dle had he. Twee-dle dee, twee-dle dee, twee-dle dee, twee-dle dee, Twee-dle dee, twee-dle dee went the fid-lers three. O there's none so fair as can com-pare with King Cole and his fid-dler s three.

THREE JOVIAL WELSHMEN

THERE were three jovial Welshmen,
  As I have heard them say,
And they would go a-hunting
  Upon St. David's Day.

All the day they hunted,
  But nothing could they find;
But a ship a-sailing,
  A-sailing with the wind.

One said it was a ship,
  The other he said nay;
The third said it was a house,
  With the chimney blown away.

And all the night they hunted,
  And nothing could they find
But the moon a-gliding,
  A-gliding with the wind.

One said it was the moon,
  The other he said nay;
The other said it was a cheese,
  The half o' it cut away.

A PARABLE

This is a parable by Sir Arthur Conan Doyle for people who find themselves too busy to make room for the best.

HIGH-BROW House was furnished well,
  With many a goblet fair;
So when they brought the Holy Grail
  There was never a space to spare.
Simple Cottage was clear and clean,
  With room to store at will ;
So there they laid the Holy Grail,
  And there you'll find it still.

THE RED THREAD OF HONOUR

This is one of the finest stories of military heroism. It was told to the poet by Sir Charles Napier, who commanded in the attack on the fortress of Truckee, away in the Indian hills. The small party of ten British soldiers under a sergeant who fought their way into the fortress, where all were killed, had acted with such bravery that the Mohammedan defenders, before leaving the fort, tied red threads of honour round both the wrists of each dead English hero. This was how they expressed their admiration for their enemies. Sir Francis Hastings Doyle, who wrote the poem, was born in 1810 and died in 1888. He succeeded Matthew Arnold as Professor of Poetry at Oxford in 1867.

ELEVEN men of England
  A breastwork charged in vain;
Eleven men of England
  Lie stripped, and gashed, and slain.
Slain ; but of foes that guarded
  Their rock-built fortress well
Some twenty had been mastered
  When the last soldier fell.

Whilst Napier piloted his wondrous way
  Across the sand-waves of the desert sea,
Then flashed at once, on each fierce clan,
    dismay,
  Lord of their wild Truckee.

These missed the glen to which their steps
    were bent,
  Mistook a mandate, from afar half heard,
And, in that glorious error, calmly went
  To death, without a word.

The robber-chief mused deeply
  Above those daring dead.
' Bring here,' at length he shouted,
  ' Bring quick, the battle thread.
Let Eblis blast for ever
  Their souls, if Allah will :
But we must keep unbroken
  The old rules of the Hill.

' Before the Ghiznee tiger
  Leapt forth to burn and slay,
Before the holy Prophet
  Taught our grim tribes to pray,
Before Secunder's lances
  Pierced through each Indian glen,
The mountain laws of honour
  Were framed for fearless men.

' Still when a chief dies bravely
  We bind with green one wrist:
Green for the brave, for heroes
  One crimson thread we twist.
Say ye, O gallant Hillmen,
  For these, whose life has fled,
Which is the fitting colour,
  The green one or the red ? '

' Our brethren, laid in honoured graves,
    may wear
  Their green reward,' each noble savage
    said :
' To these, whom hawks and hungry
    wolves shall tear,
  Who dares deny the red ? '

Thus, conquering hate, and steadfast to
    the right,
  Fresh from the heart that haughty
    verdict came;
Beneath a waning moon each spectral
    height
  Rolled back its loud acclaim.

Once more the chief gazed keenly
  Down on those daring dead ;
From his good sword their hearts' blood
  Crept to that crimson thread.
Once more he cried : ' The judgment,
  Good friends, is wise and true,
But, though the red be given,
  Have we not more to do ?

' These were not stirred by anger,
  Nor yet by lust made bold ;
Renown they thought above them,
  Nor did they look for gold.
To them their leader's signal
  Was as the voice of God ;
Unmoved and uncomplaining,
  The path it showed they trod.

' As, without sound or struggle,
  The stars unhurrying march,
Where Allah's finger guides them,
  Through yonder purple arch,
These Franks, sublimely silent,
  Without a quickened breath,
Went, in the strength of duty,
  Straight to their goal of death.

' If I were now to ask you
  To name our bravest man,
Ye all at once would answer,
  They called him Mehrab Khan.
He sleeps among his fathers,
  Dear to our native land,
With the bright mark he bled for
  Firm round his faithful hand.

' The songs they sing of Rustum
  Fill all the past with light ;
If truth be in their music
  He was a noble knight.
But were those heroes living,
  And strong for battle still,
Would Mehrab Khan or Rustum
  Have climbed, like these, the Hill? '

And they replied: ' Though Mehrab Khan
    was brave,
  As chief he chose himself what risks
    to run :
Prince Rustum lied his forfeit life to save,
  Which these had never done.'

' Enough ! ' he shouted fiercely ;
  ' Doomed though they be to hell.
Bind fast the crimson trophy
  Round both wrists—bind it well.
Who knows but that great Allah
  May grudge such matchless men,
With one so decked in Heaven,
  To the Fiend's flaming den.'

Then all those gallant robbers
  Shouted a stern Amen ;
They raised the slaughtered sergeant,
  They raised his mangled ten.
And when we found their bodies,
  Left bleaching in the wind,
Around both wrists in glory
  That crimson thread was twined.

Then Napier's knightly heart, touched to
  the core,
  Rung, like an echo, to that knightly
  deed:
He bade its memory live for evermore,
  That those who run may read.

AUTUMN

In this poem of John Keats, one of the most perfect he ever
wrote, autumn is personified as if the season were visible
as a goddess, or in a woman's form. Three stages of the
passing autumn are pictured in the three verses. First the
ripening of the Earth's fruits ; then their gathering and
garnering ; and last, the latter signs of the season's waning.

Season of mists and mellow fruitfulness !
  Close bosom-friend of the maturing sun;
Conspiring with him how to load and bless
  With fruit the vines that round the
    thatch-eaves run ;
To bend with apples the mossed cottage
    trees,
  And fill all fruit with ripeness to the
    core ;
    To swell the gourd, and plump the
    hazel shells
With a sweet kernel ; to set budding
  more,

And still more, later flowers for the bees,
Until they think warm days will never
    cease,
    For Summer has o'erbrimmed their
    clammy cells.

Who hath not seen thee oft amid thy store ?
  Sometimes whoever seeks abroad may
    find
Thee sitting careless on a granary floor,
  Thy hair soft-lifted by the winnowing
    wind ;
Or on a half-reaped furrow sound asleep,
  Drowsed with the fume of poppies, while
    thy hook
    Spares the next swath and all its
    twinèd flowers ;
And sometimes like a gleaner thou dost
    keep
  Steady thy laden head across a brook ;
Or by a cider-press, with patient look,
    Thou watchest the last oozings hours
    by hours.

Where are the songs of Spring ? Ay,
    where are they ?
  Think not of them, thou hast thy music
    too,
While barrèd clouds bloom the soft-dying
    day,
  And touch the stubble-plains with rosy
    hue ;
Then in a wailful choir the small gnats
    mourn
  Among the river sallows, borne aloft
    Or sinking as the light wind lives
    or dies ;
And full-grown lambs loud bleat from
    hilly bourn ;
    Hedge-crickets sing ; and now with
    treble soft
The redbreast whistles from a garden-
    croft,
    And gathering swallows twitter in the
    skies.

BLAKE

Into these eight lines Sir Edmund Gosse, an excellent poet
and wise critic of books, has compressed a splendid tribute
to the eccentric painter and poet William Blake.

They win who never near the goal ;
  They run who halt on wounded feet;
Art hath its martyrs like the soul,
  Its victors in defeat.

This seer's ambition soared too far ;
  He sank, on pinions backward blown ;
But, though he touched nor sun nor star,
  He made a world his own.

IN PRAISE OF A COUNTRYMAN'S LIFE

Very little is known about John Chalkhill, who wrote, about the year 1600, this call to enjoy country life. It was Izaak Walton, the fisherman author, who made these verses public. He had known the poet, who was a friend of Edmund Spenser. It is probable that Chalkhill was a relative of Walton, who, in addition to his own writings preserved poems that would otherwise have perished. The quiet tone of mind of the two men was very similar.

OH, the sweet contentment
　　The countryman doth find!
That quiet contemplation
　　Possesseth all my mind;
　　　　Then care away,
　　　　And wend along with me.

For Courts are full of flattery,
　　As hath too oft been tried;
The city full of wantonness,
　　And both are full of pride;
　　　　Then care away,
　　　　And wend along with me.

But, oh! the honest countryman
　　Speaks truly from his heart:
His pride is in his tillage,
　　His horses, and his cart;
　　　　Then care away,
　　　　And wend along with me.

Our clothing is good sheepskins,
　　Grey russet for our wives;
'Tis warmth, and not gay clothing,
　　That doth prolong our lives;
　　　　Then care away,
　　　　And wend along with me.

The ploughman, though he labour hard,
　　Yet on the holiday
No emperor so merrily
　　Does pass his time away;
　　　　Then care away,
　　　　And wend along with me.

To recompense our tillage
　　The heavens afford us showers;
And for our sweet refreshments
　　The earth affords us bowers;
　　　　Then care away,
　　　　And wend along with me.

The cuckoo and the nightingale
　　Full merrily do sing,
And with their pleasant roundelays
　　Bid welcome to the spring.
　　　　Then care away,
　　　　And wend along with me.

This is not half the happiness
　　The countryman enjoys;
Though others think they have as much,
　　Yet he that says so lies;
　　　　Then come away,
　　　　Turn countryman with me.

ON THE TOMBS IN WESTMINSTER ABBEY

This pointing of one of the most obvious morals of Westminster Abbey, is from the pen of Francis Beaumont, who was one of the most popular of the dramatists of the time of Shakespeare. He lived from 1584 to 1616.

MORTALITY, behold and fear!
　　What a change of flesh is here!
Think how many royal bones
Sleep within this heap of stones:
Here they lie had realms and lands
Who now want strength to stir their
　　hands:
Where from their pulpits sealed with
　　dust
They preach " In greatness is no trust."
Here's an acre sown indeed
With the richest, royalest seed
That the earth did e'er suck in
Since the first man died for sin:
Here the bones of birth have cried
" Though gods they were, as men they
　　died!"
Here are sands, ignoble things,
Dropt from the ruined sides of kings;
Here's a world of pomp and state
Buried in dust, once dead by fate.

WHEN YOU ARE OLD

This beautiful setting of the thought that long after we are dead our love may sustain and comfort and cheer those whom we have loved and lost is from the pen of William Ernest Henley, one of the most vigorous and fearless poets of the last generation.

WHEN you are old, and I am passed
　　away,
Passed, and your face, your golden face,
　　is gray,
I think, whate'er the end, this dream of
　　mine,
Comforting you, a friendly star will shine
Down the dim slope where still you
　　stumble and stray.

So may it be: that so dead Yesterday,
No sad-eyed ghost but generous and
　　gay,
May serve you memories like almighty
　　wine,
　　　　When you are old.

Dear Heart, it shall be so. Under the
　　sway
Of death the past's enormous disarray
Lies hushed and dark. Yet, though there
　　come no sign,
Live on well pleased : immortal and
　　divine
Love shall still tend you, as God's angels
　　may,
　　　　When you are old.

AT EVEN, ERE THE SUN WAS SET

This hymn was written in 1868 by Canon Twells, who, some years later, said he had been asked that it might be included in 127 different hymn-books, and many more had taken it without asking him. It is not strange that it should be so popular, for it probes deeply the failings of men, and offers them a help that many have found unfailing.

At even, ere the sun was set,
 The sick, O Lord, around Thee lay;
O in what divers pains they met!
 O with what joy they went away!

Once more, 'tis eventide, and we,
 Oppressed with various ills, draw near.
What if Thy form we cannot see?
 We know and feel that Thou art here.

O Saviour Christ, our woes dispel;
 For some are sick and some are sad;
And some have never loved Thee well,
 And some have lost the love they had.

And some are pressed with worldly care,
 And some are tried with sinful doubt;
And some such grievous passions bear
 That only Thou canst cast them out.

And some have found the world is vain,
 Yet from the world they break not free;
And some have friends who give them pain,
 Yet have not sought a friend in Thee.

And none, O Lord, have perfect rest,
 For none are wholly free from sin;
And they who fain would serve Thee best
 Are conscious most of wrong within.

O Saviour Christ, Thou, too, art man;
 Thou hast been troubled, tempted, tried;
Thy kind but searching glance can scan
 The very wounds that shame would hide.

Thy touch has still its ancient power;
 No word from Thee can fruitless fall;
Hear in this solemn evening hour,
 And in Thy mercy heal us all.

AULD ROBIN GRAY

This saddest of all tales of true love thwarted was written by an earl's daughter, Lady Anne Lindsay, at the age of 21. The story was imagined, not real. It was composed in 1771, and at once went round the world. More than fifty years passed before Lady Anne, who was then Lady Anne Barnard, admitted to Sir Walter Scott that she wrote these lines on the sorrows of Jennie Gray. The name Robin Gray was that of a herdsman employed by Lady Anne's father. The story is so poignant that it is a relief to know it was only invented.

When the sheep are in the fauld, and the kye at hame,
And a' the warld to rest are gane,
The waes o' my heart fa' in showers frae my e'e,
While my gudeman lies sound by me.

Young Jamie lo'ed me weel, and sought me for his bride;
But saving a croun he had naething else beside :
To make a croun a pund young Jamie gaed to sea;
And the croun and the pund were baith for me.

He hadna been awa' a week but only twa,
When my father brak his arm, and the cow was stown awa';
My mother she fell sick—and my Jamie at the sea—
And auld Robin Gray came a-courtin' me.

My father couldna work and my mother couldna spin;
I toiled day and night, but their bread I couldna win;
Auld Rob maintained them baith, and wi' tears in his e'e,
Said, " Jennie, for their sakes, O, marry me! "

My heart it said nay; I looked for Jamie back;
But the wind it blew high, and the ship it was a wrack;
His ship it was a wrack—Why didna Jamie dee?
Or why do I live to cry Wae's me!

My father urged me sair; my mother didna speak;
But she looked in my face till my heart was like to break;
They gi'ed him my hand, tho' my heart was in the sea;
Sae auld Robin Gray he was gudeman to me.

I hadna been a wife a week but only four,
When mournfu' as I sat on the stane at the door,
I saw my Jamie's wraith—for I couldna think it he
Till he said, " I'm come hame to marry thee."

O sair, sair did we greet, and muckle did we say;
We took but ae kiss and we tore ourselves away:
I wish that I were dead, but I'm no like to dee;
And why was I born to say Wae's me!

I gang like a ghaist, and I carena to spin;
I daurna think on Jamie, for that wad be a sin;
But I'll do my best a gude wife aye to be,
For auld Robin Gray he is kind unto me.

Imperishable Thoughts of Men Enshrined in the Books of the World

Aeneas telling Queen Dido of the misfortunes of Troy

THE MOST FAMOUS ROMAN BOOK

IN our survey of the poetry of Greece we have outlined Homer's great poems The Iliad and The Odyssey, and here we sketch the contents of the great epic from the literature of Rome, the Aeneid of Virgil, the Roman poet who has won the widest fame throughout the ages.

The aim of Virgil was to add historical or legendary dignity to the new imperial house of Augustus Caesar. To do this he followed the style of Homer, who had written nearly eight hundred years before, and traced the origin of the Roman people, before the foundation of Rome, to a band of Trojans who safely withdrew from Troy after its capture by the Greeks.

The hero of the poem is Aeneas, the Trojan prince next in importance to Hector. He is son of Anchises, his fabled mother being the goddess Venus, and the celestial part of the poem is a continued contest between the jealous and vengeful goddess Juno, who pursues and persecutes the hero, and Venus, who interposes to protect him whenever the dangers around him reach the stage of desperation.

Any illustrative translations from Virgil which we give in tracing the story of Aeneas are from the blank verse version of the epic by the British scholar, John Wight Duff. Virgil indicates his subject at once.

Arms and the man I sing, who first from Troy,
Fate exiled, reached the shores of Italy.
On land and deep much tossed, the hero felt
Heaven's lash, for cruel Juno's mindful wrath.
Much, too, his pain in war ere he might found
His city, and bring into Latium
His gods. Hence sprang the Latin race, our sires
In Alba, and the walls of lofty Rome.

Virgil takes his readers at once to Carthage, a city supposed to be under the special guardianship of the goddess Juno. There, according to the plan of the poem, Aeneas is to relate, eventually, the story of the fall of Troy and his wanderings after his escape, much against the wishes of the goddess, for she foresees the future rivalry between Carthage and the Roman descendants of the fugitive Trojan, and so desires to prevent his reaching Italy. This is how Carthage is introduced :

Carthage, an ancient State which settlers he'd
From Tyre, faced Italy and Tiber's mouth
Far o'er the main. This city, rich in wealth,
And valiant in the rugged ways of war,
Did Juno cherish more than other lands;
She harboured the design, if fate allowed,
That this should be the empress of the world.
But she had learned a race of Trojan seed
Would yet o'erturn these Tyrian citadels;
A people ruling wide, in pomp of war,
Would ruin Libya; 'twas destiny!
In fear whereof, recalling battles old
Once waged in war for Greece, her favourite,

ROMANCE · HISTORIES · DRAMAS · ESSAYS · WORLD CLASSICS

The goddess sought to fend from Latium
Afar, imperilled everywhere at sea,
Those Trojans who had 'scaped from Grecian
  sword
Or fell Achilles: so for many a year
Fate driven over every main they roamed—
Such task it was to found the Roman race!

NEPTUNE SAVES AENEAS FROM THE FURY OF THE STORM

Aeneas and his followers have just sailed from Sicily, and Juno induces Aeolus, King of the Winds, to raise a storm against them. Some are lost, but Neptune rebukes the Winds because the storm was raised without his permission, and Aeneas lands safely on the shore of Libya, the part of northern Africa where Carthage is built.

Venus now supports the cause of Aeneas, and complains to her father Jupiter that Juno is persecuting the long-suffering Trojan and his men. This is her plea :

O thou, whose everlasting sway controls
Both man and god with direful thunderbolt,
Wherein hath mine Aeneas angered thee,
Or how have Trojans sinned that, after woes
So great endured, the whole round world for them
Is shut, to bar the way to Italy?
Sure thou didst promise that in lapse of years
From them should spring the Roman leader who,
Of Teucrian blood revived, should rule the waves
And land in absolute supremacy.

Jupiter comforts her by giving her a glimpse of the future. Aeneas, he tells her, will reach Italy, establish himself in Latium, and be followed by his son Ascanius, who will reign as a great prince in Alba Longa, and three centuries afterwards his Trojan descendant Romulus will found Rome.

THE COMING OF THE ROMAN EMPIRE FORETOLD BY JUPITER

And he shall call the Romans by his name.
I set nor check nor period to their power;
I give them boundless empire. Juno dread,
Who now o'eraweth land and earth and sky,
In altered mood shall join with Jove to guard
The Romans, lords of all the toga'd race.

Further, Jupiter foretells that Rome will revenge the fall of Troy by conquering Greece, and the deified Caesars will inaugurate a reign of peace in a world-wide empire. While this conference is proceeding in the celestial regions Aeneas is wandering on the Libyan coast, with his faithful friend Achates, and there Venus

appears to them in the guise of a huntress-maid, and informs them that they are in the realms of Dido, queen of Tyre, who is building herself a new capital at Carthage. She tells Aeneas also that other ships of his have reached the coast safely, and directs him to the queen's palace. It is only as she turns to leave him that he recognises her as his goddess mother. As a parting gift she wraps him in a mist of invisibility. Overlooking Carthage, he and Achates watch the busy building of the city. When they reach a temple within a grove they are touched to see that the decorations on the walls represent the wars of Troy, and Aeneas exclaims :

What spot, Achates, or what land on earth
Teems not with our sad Trojan history?
There's Priam—look! Here, too, hath fame its
  meeds.
Tears haunt the world: man's fortunes touch
  man's heart.

HOW AENEAS WATCHED HIS COMRADES WELCOMED BY QUEEN DIDO

While the wanderers stand in wonderment Queen Dido and her courtly train arrive, and she seats herself on a throne of state in the temple to transact the business of her kingdom. As Aeneas stands by invisible with Achates, some of his shipwrecked comrades approach and appeal to the queen, telling her they are Aeneas's men, and in need of succour. She receives them graciously, saying:

Oh, clear your hearts of dread, and banish care!
Who should not know Aeneas' folk and Troy,
Men, manly deeds, and flames of such a war?
Nay, not so dull are our Phoenician souls.
The city which I found is yours: so beach
Your ships: the Trojan and the Tyrian
Shall find in Dido an impartial queen.
Ah! would that, wafted by the self-same wind,
Your prince Aeneas also graced my court!

When Dido is about to send messengers forth to search for Aeneas in the hope that he, too, may have escaped, the mist of invisibility clears away, and he makes himself known.

Then doth he thus address the queen, and speaks
Sudden to their surprise: 'Lo, I, the man
Ye seek, am here—Aeneas, Trojan born,
Late rescued from the waves of Libya!
Lady, that hast alone felt ruth for Troy
And Troy's unutterable woe, who now
Dost share thy town and home with us, whom
  Greeks

Have spared for weary round on sea and land
Of endless hazards and for beggary:
Queen Dido, to repay thee worthy thanks
Is not within our reach, nor in the reach
Of all the Dardan race throughout the world.
If deities there are who mark the good,
If justice is, and consciousness of right,
Then may the gods reward thee fittingly!
What happy age did yield thee? Say, what line
Owned thee for its fair scion? While the streams
Shall seaward run, while mountain shadows
   course
Athwart the vale, while heaven feeds its stars,
Ever shall Dido's honour, name. and praise
Bide in my heart, whate'er the lands that call.'

Hospitality is offered freely to all by Dido, and at the close of a great banquet she invites Aeneas to tell the story of the final overthrow of Troy, and of the wanderings for seven years of himself and his companions.

Accordingly he tells how, by the counsels of Ulysses, the Greeks erected outside Troy an enormous wooden horse, in which they concealed a number of Greek soldiers, and, having wheeled it near to the gates of the city, they left it

THE WOODEN HORSE BEFORE THE GATES OF TROY

there, and then pretended to withdraw to their ships and give up the siege. When they were gone the Trojans, with great rejoicing, dragged the wooden horse into the city. But at night the Greeks returned, and their comrades, descending from the horse, fired the city and opened the gates, and before the Trojans could rally everything was lost, and their king, Priam, was slain. Then Venus appeared to Aeneas and commanded him to escape.

So he carried off his father Anchises on his shoulders, and, his son Ascanius following him, he left the city. His wife had already perished in the fighting.

Aeneas then tells the story of his wanderings, similar to the Homeric story of the adventures of Ulysses. It is only gradually that the Trojan realises that the land of his quest is Italy. He visits Thrace, passes the Aegean Isles, reaches Crete, passes on to the western shores of Greece, and at last learns from the seer Helenus that Italy must be his destination. On reaching Sicily his father Anchises dies; and the next stage of the journeying is through the tempest to Carthage.

The part of the epic which follows develops the tragedy of Queen Dido. She falls in love with Aeneas. Juno favours the attachment, as it may tend to keep Aeneas away from Italy. A Libyan prince who has been rejected by Dido supplicates Jupiter, who responds by sending Mercury to order Aeneas to continue his journey to Italy. Knowing how deeply Dido is in love with him, Aeneas shrinks from telling her of his intention to leave Carthage; but she discovers his preparations, upbraids him, and appeals to him to stay in Carthage as her husband. But he is acting under the compulsion of the Gods, and he replies:

Brief words shall fit the case.
Imagine not I hoped by stealth to hide
My flight: I never held the marriage torch
Before thine eyes, or entered such a bond.
But now Apollo points to Italy:
So Italy is love and fatherland.

If towers of Carthage and a Libyan town
Can glamour, lady, thy Phoenician eyes,
Why grudge to Trojans the Ausonian soil?
Cease, then, to tire thyself and me with plaints:
'Tis not unbid I follow Italy.

Dido now regards herself as a woman scorned, and fiercely answers:

I was mad
To welcome him, a shipwrecked mariner,
To give a beggar share of sovranty!
I hold thee not; nor yet refute thy words.
Go, follow ' Italy ' before the breeze;
And seek for kingdoms o'er the waves.   I hope
Midway, if powers of goodness can avail,
Thou wilt drain punishment on rocks,
And often call on Dido's name.   Far off
With murky fires I will pursue, and when
Chill death hath severed soul and frame, my ghost
Shall haunt thee everywhere.   Wretch, thou shalt rue
Thy guilt, and I shall hear; the bruit thereof
Shall reach me in the lowest depths of hell.

Then, in a frenzy of despair, she builds a funeral pyre, which, she says, is to burn all tokens and memorials that can remind her of the Trojan sojourner whom she regards as unfaithful to love; but on it she takes her own life as Aeneas sails away toward Sicily, and its flames light his passage from the coast of Libya.

THE GOLDEN BOUGH WHICH KEPT AENEAS FROM HARM IN THE UNDERWORLD

After a stay in Sicily, where he honours his father's memory by a series of games, Aeneas passes on at last to Italy, landing at Cumae, in Campania.   There lives in a cave a far-famed Sibyl, and her he consults as to the dangers ahead of him, and a visit which he wishes to make to his father in the netherworld.   He is told he will be safe in the shades so long as he carries a magical Golden Bough, and this he manages to secure by aid from Venus.

The Sibyl accompanies him where

Before the door—the opening jaws of hell—
Grief and the Venging Cares have set their couch;
There wan Diseases dwell and dolorous Eld,
Fear, ill-advising Famine, loathly Want,
Dread shapes to look upon—and Death and Toil,
Then Death's own brother Sleep, and Evil Joys
Of mind, and on the threshold full in view
Death-dealing Warfare.

Past the tree of Empty Dreams, and appalling but unsubstantial monsters of Shadowland, the prophetess and hero make their way to the eerie waters over which the boatman Charon ferries the spirits of the dead.   The dead crowded the banks, but only those were allowed to cross whose bodies had found a grave.   At the sight of the Golden Bough, Charon ferries the Sibyl and Aeneas across the Styx.   There the wanderer has a fleeting glimpse of Dido, " and knew her dimly through the mirk."   After meeting hero spirits and passing the terrible prison-house of Tartarus, he left the Golden Bough at Pluto's palace and finally reached the Elysian fields.

THROUGH THE IVORY GATE OF SLEEP INTO THE WORLD OF LIFE

Here he found his father's spirit contemplating the fates and fortunes of his descendants, and Aeneas shares in the vision leading up to the glories of Imperial Rome, when Augustus Caesar is enthroned.

This, this is that same hero whom so oft
Thou hast heard promised thee, of birth divine,
Augustus Caesar, who shall found again
The Age of Gold in Latium.

Thus, in vision, the story of Rome is brought up to date in flattery of the reigning emperor.   Aeneas is then instructed respecting the wars in which he will have to fight in Italy; wars that provide the remainder of the poem.   His vision of the future ended, Aeneas, with the Sibyl, returns from the Shades to ordinary life through the Ivory Gate of Sleep.

Aeneas, having reached the Tiber, secures the promise in marriage of the hand of the Princess Lavinia, daughter of King Latinus.   This leads to war in accordance with prophecies of the Sibyl that a foreign bride would again imperil Trojan success.   In the end, after desperate warfare, Turnus, the chief opponent of Aeneas, insists on encountering him in single combat, but when they meet he finds his strength paralysed by the interposition of the goddess who is the guardian of Aeneas, and Turnus is slain.

WHAT THE BOOKS OF VIRGIL TELL US OF OLD ROME

With Aeneas thus safely settled in Italy Virgil's epic closes, and the continuance of the further legendary story of Rome is left for other narrators.   Into his own twelve books, however, Virgil, though we knew he did not fully satisfy himself, has brought an immense amount of Roman legend and belief which throw much light on the national thought and religion.

The Story of the Most Beautiful Book in the World

In this picture by Fra Angelico we see Peter preaching to the people, and Mark writing down his words. It is supposed that Mark learned the facts about the life of Jesus from Peter

THE BIRTH OF CHRISTIANITY

WITH the death of Jesus, nay, even with his arrest in the Garden of Gethsemane, the little flock he had gathered about him to spread his teaching scattered in fear and panic. The disciples of Jesus all forsook him and fled. The devout women, who loved him tenderly, witnessed his tragic death from afar. *Jesus died in utter loneliness.*

These followers of Jesus had expected he would perform some extraordinary miracle, and subdue not only Rome but perhaps the whole Earth. Perhaps they did not believe in this miraculous triumph with any enthusiasm, or with any certainty of its occurrence; but it was a hope struggling in their minds. His meekness under arrest was a terrible blow to their faith. The victory of the priests was a terrible blow to their courage. The death of Jesus was the death of their hope.

Let us make ourselves sure of this state of things. Unless we realise in all its truth the desertion of Jesus, and the panic and despair of his disciples, we shall not be able to feel all that the resurrection meant to these simple men.

It is impossible for us to think that the panic-stricken disciples, *after the igno-minious death of their Master,* would suddenly stand boldly before men and preach the message that had brought him to the Cross, unless they had received some convincing proof that he was more than man.

Christianity could not have been born in the shadow of the Cross unless Jesus had triumphed over death.

We find these poor, frightened disciples transformed suddenly into burning missionaries. We find them forming themselves into an assembly or brotherhood, making rules for the membership of this society, and sending men across the world with the message of the crucified Jesus. Instead of fleeing in despair from Jerusalem, it was in that very priest-ridden city that they formed their society, and taught that Jesus had risen from the dead. The Peter who denied that he knew Jesus in the courtyard of the high priest's palace was foremost after the Crucifixion in establishing Christianity. In fact, all the disciples, except Judas Iscariot, who had destroyed himself, became, after the death of their Master, far more sure of the truth of his teaching, far more courageous in their preaching of it,

GREAT FIGURES OF THE OLD TESTAMENT · THE LIFE OF JESUS

than they had been during his lifetime. It was not while they half hoped and half believed that Jesus would triumph over his enemies and reign in glory that these disciples were earnest and enthusiastic teachers of his gospel. No; it was after his death, after his defeat, after what they thought to be *his* failure and their own bitter disappointment.

THE BIRTH OF CHRISTIANITY IN THE SHADOW OF THE CROSS

This birth of Christianity in the shadow of the Cross is the miracle of history. We can only understand it if we realise how profoundly convinced the disciples were of the resurrection of the Master. Nothing in the Bible is set down more earnestly than the appearance of Jesus after his death on the cross.

And now, before we proceed to read the wonderful story of Christianity's first battles with the world—a story which is still the Life of Jesus, for that Life goes on from age to age, unending and undying—let us carefully consider what Jesus represented to his disciples, what he meant to them, what they understood him to be.

Remember that these plain and rustic men lived in days when language was simple. They knew very few of the words which people use now when they discuss with each other the exact nature of Jesus. We notice that most of those words are very long, and that even when their meanings are explained to us they leave us more or less in darkness. We may learn them by heart. We may recite them. We may say: "This is what I believe." But, if we do not understand them, how can we be sure that we know what we believe concerning Jesus? It is better for us to go back to the disciples, and see what it was that they believed as to the character of their Master.

THINGS THE DISCIPLES KNEW FOR CERTAIN ABOUT THEIR MASTER

An English scholar has drawn up a number of statements concerning Jesus which are all to be proved out of St. Mark's Gospel, the earliest written record, which we will set down here in as simple language as we can. As we grow older we must read these interesting statements for ourselves in their own language. We shall find them in a book called Ecce Homo, one of the most beautiful and lasting books ever written concerning the

life of Jesus. It was written by Sir John Robert Seeley.

The facts in these numbered paragraphs are what the disciples knew for certain about Jesus.

1. He assumed a position of authority. Although he was a carpenter, he set himself above the professional teachers of religion; he made himself a greater teacher than the doctors of divinity.

2. He claimed again and again that he was the king of whom the prophets had long prophesied. This claim was definite. It was not a figure of speech, such as " I am the vine." He died for the fact of it. He did not die for a metaphor.

3. As the promised king, he claimed some mystic and special dignity for himself.

4. He would not accept the teaching of the priests. He read and interpreted the Scriptures for himself. When he was rebuked for not obeying the law of Moses concerning the Sabbath, he replied with a sublime sentence that the Sabbath was made for man, and not man for the Sabbath.

5. He claimed power to forgive sins.

THE TEACHING OF JESUS ABOUT KINGSHIP AND GOODNESS

6. He called a number of men to attach themselves to him. He said: " Come unto me." He gave certain plain and simple rules to this society. His name was their bond of union. He made it clear to them that this society would continue after his death. He foresaw his death, and planned for the continuance of his society afterwards.

7. His disciples believed that he worked miracles. They tell of a certain occasion when he failed to work miracles. If they had been attempting to prove that he was a wonder-worker, they certainly would not have set down this occasion of failure.

8. His miracles were chiefly miracles of healing.

9. Although he gathered the first members of his society from the Jews, he told them that it was to embrace the Gentiles, that is, the foreign nations, as well.

10. Although he declared himself emphatically to be the expected king, he refused to undertake any of the ordinary duties discharged by kings. He gave his disciples a new idea of kingship, something that was inward and spiritual.

11. He required from his disciples personal devotion; he taught them to follow his example in ruling their lives.

12. He spoke to them of a Holy Spirit as directing his life, and said that this same Holy Spirit, if they followed his example, would direct their lives also.

13. He taught them earnestly that good feelings are more important than good deeds. He made his disciples see that a bad man may do a good deed, or that a good man may do a good deed and yet lack something. He made them see that a good deed, to be perfectly beautiful, must flow from a heart filled with good feelings.

14. He also demanded that his followers should do acts of extraordinary virtue. They were not to stop at doing what they had to do, but they must do more than they had to do. It must be a delight to them to love those they were not obliged to love, to give to those they were not obliged to give to, and to help those they were not obliged to help.

15. He condemned all morality and all goodness which was not inward and spiritual. A man who gave alms as a duty, or worshipped in the temple because it was the custom, or said his prayers to be seen and praised by others was condemned by Jesus as a hypocrite. He had great scorn for people who were *mechanically* good.

16. By these teachings, and by claiming to be the King, he incurred the deadly hatred of the Scribes and Pharisees.

17. He required his disciples to desire the welfare of their fellow-men, and declared in beautiful language that this was his own desire, his own purpose in the world. " The Son of Man came not to be ministered unto, but to minister."

18. He went much among sick people, healing them, sometimes with strong signs of emotion.

19. He commanded his disciples to follow this example of healing the sick.

20. He spent much of his time curing moral disease. He was the Good Physician of the worst people, the dregs, the scum, the outcasts of society. He went to those the religious leaders ignored, and the rest of the world despised.

21. He taught the forgiveness of injuries.

If we read these twenty-one statements with understanding, we shall have a workable idea of what Jesus was to his disciples who first preached his gospel. But there is one thing we lack in this, and that is the charm, the compelling sweetness of the

THE HOPE OF THE WORLD—BY HAROLD COPPING
Reproduced by courtesy of the London Missionary Society

Master. No statement can give us that. We begin to have some twilight glimmering of that charm when we consider how he attracted men, men of a rough kind, such as fishermen accustomed to the most dangerous kind of work; how he attracted them, drew them to him, so that they forsook their homes, and followed him in his strange and wandering life. And we gradually acquire, by reading about him, thinking about him, and trying to live as he asks us to live, a love for Christ revealing to us what no words can reveal: his inexpressible sweetness and charm.

We must not leave out of count the charm of Christ's personality in considering the birth of Christianity. If we might add one more to the twenty-one statements, this should be the twenty-second:

" The disciples loved their Master."

Now we may go on with the story of what happened after the Crucifixion.

The disciples, assured now that he was indeed the promised Christ, began to preach his gospel. They had no time then to write down their stories about him, their reminiscences of Jesus; and, unfortunately, they laboured under one terrible and disastrous misapprehension. In one thing they had not realised the truth of what Jesus had tried to teach them. They believed he would come speedily to Earth again, and sit upon his eternal throne.

THE BELIEF OF THE DISCIPLES THAT THE END OF THE WORLD HAD COME

This mistake on the part of the disciples is responsible for the lateness of the written Gospels; they felt there was no need to write, because, before that generation had passed away, he would come again. They had little enough time to preach and convert the world.

But this mistake, which we must ever deplore, was perhaps responsible for the magnificent courage with which those men—that little band of humble, simple provincials—created the Christian religion in the shadow of the Cross. They knew no fear. Nothing the world could do frightened their souls. Everything appeared paltry, except Christ.

The boast of Rome, the power of the Jewish priests, the activity of commerce, the enthusiasm of art, the gossip and tattle of the streets—these things were as dust to them. They had seen and spoken with a man risen from the dead. A risen Spirit had assured them that prophecy was at last fulfilled. The end of the world had come upon them. Christ had risen from the dead. The King had come. Soon, very soon, the power of God would be made manifest to all nations, and to all peoples, throughout the world.

Is it not interesting to notice that these faithful and devout disciples misinterpreted the Master precisely as the priests misinterpreted the prophets. The priests expected the promised Christ to be a conquering and a trampling king. The disciples expected the Master to establish an immediate dominion over all the Earth. They had forgotten his repeated lesson that the Kingdom of Heaven was of slow growth. They had forgotten the parable of the mustard seed.

THE NEW THING THAT WAS BORN INTO THE WORLD

So our first view of Christianity is the spectacle of these earnest and loving disciples preaching Christ's gospel with the assurance that the end of the world had come.

On the day of Pentecost they were all assembled together in one house, when they were conscious of a cold wind in their midst, and they saw what looked to them like a dazzle of flame on the heads of each other. This experience transformed the disciples into the burning and eager missionaries of whom we have spoken.

So enthusiastic were they, so carried away by the force and reality of their experience, that even devout men in Jerusalem took them to be drunken. But when they performed acts of healing, when they preached with extraordinary power of conviction, when they stood up boldly before priests and governors, the inhabitants of Jerusalem perceived that a new thing had been born into the world.

THE MULTITUDES THAT FLOCKED TO HEAR THE PREACHERS

The multitudes listened to the disciples of Jesus. The apostles did wonderful works of healing. They spoke like inspired men. Vast crowds flocked to hear them; many sought entrance into the assembly. They became a power.

But this amazing influence which the humble followers of the Carpenter of Nazareth exercised over the minds of the people did not please their rulers. They were jealous of that usurper of their authority, and took steps to put an end to it.

Then came persecution, and many of the apostles suffered. To the despair of many faithful Christians who were eagerly looking for him, Christ did not come.

Of how the religion of Christ was spread by Paul we have yet to read.

(*Next chapter in this group, page 5679*)

The Interests and Pleasures of Life for All Indoors and Out

Final touches to home-made costumes for a Shakespeare play

ACTING PLAYS AT HOME

IT is grand fun to join with our friends in " putting on " a play at home. Many of us who belong to youth organisations and clubs probably have chances of acting in plays on a real stage in a hall, and many of us also have opportunities of acting in plays at school. But there is not quite the same thrill in such acting as there is in doing a play all on our own without any help from grown-ups.

To put on a successful play at home we really need in our house, or at a friend's, a suitable room to use as a theatre. This should be a fair-sized room with a door at both ends, so that one end can be screened or curtained off for the stage, and the door behind the curtain used for entrances and exits. There should be two lights in the room working independently, so that the one over the audience can be switched off during scenes.

Screens, if we have them, may be used instead of curtains, but to give dramatic effect, smoothly-working curtains are best. To fix up a curtain, get permission to run a wire or curtain rail across the end of the room. Fix the curtains to this with rings on expanding wires which can be bought. If we have curtains that can be drawn along a rail on runners, so much the better. The person who stands behind the curtains to work them on the evening of the play can also be the prompter.

Scenery can be made with brown paper, large rolls of which can be bought quite cheaply, and lengths of it stuck together to the required size. A scene can then be painted on it or drawn with coloured chalks. The finished scene should be hung from near the ceiling at the back of the stage.

" Properties," such as crowns, helmets, hats, and so on, can be made of cardboard or papier mâché. Costumes, too, of course, are home made. However, it is best not to spend too much time and energy on the stage setting and properties for, as Shakespeare said, " The play's the thing."

The best fun is to be had by writing our own play. If we cannot think of an interesting plot, we should try turning one of our favourite stories into a play, something from Hans Andersen's fairy tales, or perhaps the Arabian Nights.

Having decided on a play and the parts to be taken by each actor, the next most important thing, on which the success of the play absolutely depends, is to have an efficient producer. He must be like the captain of a team, and all the actors must agree to do as the producer says. They must speak their lines, make gestures, change their facial expression, and move about the stage as he or she orders—but it is equally important that the producer has a clear idea of how he wants the play to go. If he keeps altering his mind during rehearsals and constantly giving different directions, the cast will become very confused and discouraged.

CRAFTS · GAMES · NEEDLEWORK · PUZZLES · SCIENCE EXPERIMENTS

To be a good producer one must be able to see beforehand in one's imagination the whole play being acted. At the same time if the producer sees one of his cast acting a passage better than he had imagined it being done, he will wisely not interfere. For a good actor is not only one who has learned his lines and does as he is told, but one who tries, all the time he is acting, to *feel* that he is the character he is impersonating.

If possible, have some music in the play—piano, or recorder, or gramophone music, or some other instrument. Give young brothers and sisters a chance to appear. For example, if a queen is to enter, let her train be carried by the younger ones, and let her make a stately procession right round the stage before she stops to speak. Such movements require careful rehearsing. Have plenty of rehearsals, but take care that a rehearsal does not go on too long and become wearisome.

The "make-up" of the actors' and actresses' faces is an important item, and one in which amateurs so often make a mess of the job in every sense of the word ! Too much, and that in the wrong place, is likely to make the audience laugh where they are not intended to.

Professionals and grown-up amateurs, of course, use grease-paint, but applying grease-paint properly is an art in itself, and if we do not understand how to use it, the result will be ludicrous. Burnt cork will help as a substitute, and perhaps a generous elder sister will lend us some lipstick.

False beards and moustaches can be bought fairly cheaply, but there is one thing to remember in using them—make sure they are stuck on securely ! The effect of a dramatic scene is quite spoiled if the hero's moustache falls off in the middle of it ! For make-up, wigs, masks, moustaches, and so on, young home actors and actresses must use their own ingenuity in making use of whatever materials they have to hand—and that is part of the fun. For example, a false horse's or cow's head can be made with a wire frame and painted sacking stretched over it.

If there is not a room in the house suitable to be used as a theatre, a room with a bay window can be used, though a play on a bay window stage must be on a rather modest scale. Screens must be arranged beside the bay window for a "dressing-room," and additional screens are required across the bay window space for a curtain.

GAMES TO PLAY WITH MARBLES

PYRAMIDS

THE pyramid is made by one of the players placing several of his marbles close together in a group and others on the top of them. Round this pyramid a little circle is drawn. He then agrees that any of the other players may "shoot" at it by paying him one marble for every shot. If the aim is successful, the marbles that roll out of the ring belong to the boy who knocked down the pyramid. It has to be built up again for the next "customer." Of course, the owner makes his profit out of those who aim without hitting.

RING-TAW

A CIRCLE of about a foot wide is drawn on a piece of smooth ground, and in it is placed a number of marbles, one or two from each player. Outside and around this, some six feet away, another circle is drawn. The beginner then kneels, with his hand against this outer line, and shoots his playing marble, or "taw," at the group placed in the central ring.

This is done by pinching the taw between the knuckle of the bent thumb and the curve of the forefinger, and suddenly straightening the thumb. If he knocks any out they are his, and he may aim again from the spot at which his taw has stopped. If, however, he misses, and his taw remains within either of the rings, he must leave it there, in case

the next player wishes to shoot at it. If hit, the owner of the taw must hand over one marble, but no taw can be taken, and it can be aimed at only once. The game continues in this way till all the marbles are knocked out of the ring.

PICKING PLUMS

AFTER drawing a long, straight line, each player places upon it one or more marbles, all separated from each other by an inch or two. Then another line is drawn at a distance of eight feet, and each player takes his turn to shoot once at the "plums." Those he knocks out he is supposed to keep as his own; if he misses he gives up a marble.

STAND-UP MEGS

CHALK out a two-foot ring about eight inches from a fence or wall. A line is drawn about seven feet long from the centre of the ring, and another line is drawn across the end of this, at which the players take their stand. Any number may play, but from three to six players provide the best game. A large alley is placed in the centre of the circle, and the players take it in turn, in a standing position, to shy at the alley with a taw. If the player misses, he pays a marble to each of the other players, and if he hits the alley, he receives a marble from each and goes on shooting until he misses, when it is the next player's turn.

THE PROBLEM OF THE CHEQUERED SQUARE

I^N the middle of a provincial town there is a public square of which the inhabitants are very proud. It is paved with granite, and is divided into 64 equal squares like a chessboard. The variations in colour were obtained by using red and grey granite for the alternate squares, with striking effect.

When the local regiment came home, the men were given a great reception. There was a luncheon in the town hall, and afterwards games and sports. The proceedings were brought to a close with a very curious march.

With the band playing at their head, the soldiers marched into the square through one gate, passed under the triumphal arch in the middle of the square, and out at the other gate, after having passed across every one of the 64 small squares into which the whole square was divided. They passed over no square more than once, and made the fewest possible turns.

Of course, the officers worked out the route before by studying the problem with a chessboard; then, when the actual march took place, there was not a single hitch.

Take a chessboard, or rule up for yourself a piece of paper with 64 squares, mark the two gates and the arch, and see if you can draw a line to represent the route taken.

The solution is given on page 5686.

THE OLD WOMAN AND HER PIG

H^{AVE} you ever tried to make toys out of potatoes? It is quite easy to do, as our two pictures clearly show. We are going to make an old countrywoman and her pig.

Many country people keep pigs, and the pigs are fed largely on potatoes, which are an important part of the diet of many country folk. So that there is something appropriate in making an old countrywoman and her pig out of potatoes.

For the woman we shall want a rather long potato with a little round nob on the top for her head. If we cannot get a potato shaped like this, we can manage in another way. We can take a long potato with a rather sharp end; then fasten a tiny round potato on this end with a used match, or a small stick.

First, though, we must wash the potato thoroughly without breaking the skin; then scrape two little round holes for the eyes, cut a curved slit for the mouth and a short slit just above for the nose. Two tiny pins with black heads can be pushed in to make the pupils of the eyes.

If we are clever with paint, we can take some of the red out of our colour-box and paint the woman's lips a bright red. Then add more water to the paint to make it paler, and tint her cheeks a little. A few brown shavings, the kind used as packing in a box of chocolates, or darning wool, can be stuck on for hair.

The rest of the potato will form the body of the woman, and this we must dress in a frock made from green crêpe or tissue paper. If we put over this a white apron—also of paper—it will look better.

The arms and legs can be made of pipe-cleaners or long, used matches. Next we make a bonnet just as we would for an ordinary doll, and tie it on with strings.

The pig is easier still to make, as we see by the lower picture. We must look for a potato with a kind of point at one end which is like the pig's snout. Then we stick four matches in it to make the legs, and put in two large black-headed pins for the eyes. A curly bit of dandelion stem or a thin shaving will do well for the tail, and ears cut out of paper and stuck on, will make our pig look more complete.

We can make other animals, too. For a horse, a donkey, or a dog, we take two oval potatoes, one for the body and a smaller one for the head. A match forms the neck and string makes the tail.

Very tiny new potatoes in a nest of straw represent bird's eggs, and if we search, we shall probably find a small potato shaped like a bird to sit on the nest.

THE GAME OF FIVES

Although an ancient and once exceedingly popular game, Fives today is confined almost entirely to Britain's public schools. It is played in a court which has three sides. There are two kinds of courts, one known as the Eton and the other as the Rugby, after the two famous schools where they originated.

The Eton court consists of three walls coated with concrete, with a stone floor sloping downward from the front wall, and divided into an inner and an outer court by a 3-inch step. On the left wall is a curious buttress called the pepper-box, which has a sloping top, and at the bottom forms a recess with the step known as the pepper-pot.

The Rugby court has front and side walls but no pepper-pot, and its floor has neither slope nor step. Sometimes the Rugby court has buttresses, and in any case a board runs round the court at a height of 34 inches from the ground.

Fives is a game played with the hands and these, therefore, are protected by special gloves. The ball has a cork centre, surrounded by felt and yarn, and weighs 1¼ ounces.

As the Rugby game is the simpler, it is the one described here.

In a single there is one player on each side, and in a double two on each side. In the single, one player takes up his position on the left of the court, which is known as "up," and the other player on the right, which is known as "down."

A DOUBLE IN PROGRESS ON THE ETON COURT

The game starts with the up player throwing the ball against the front wall above the board so that it will rebound on to the right-hand side wall, and then on to the floor. The down player now has to strike the ball so that it will hit the right-hand wall, and then the front wall. As it comes down the up player takes the ball. He can volley it before it strikes the floor, or after it has struck the floor once.

The game being started in this way, each player takes it in turn to strike the ball as it comes back from the wall, and he must at every stroke strike the front wall, either directly or by making the ball bounce on to it from one of the side walls.

Play goes on in this way until one player fails in returning the ball to strike the front wall. If this happens to be the down player, one is scored to the up player. If the one who fails is the up player, there is no score, but the down player now takes the up player's place.

It is only the up player who can score, and that by the failure of his opponent to hit the front wall in returning the ball. A score of fifteen is the usual game, but sometimes this takes a long time to attain.

Skilled players do not, as a rule, get into one another's way, but if by chance one player prevents the other from striking the ball, this is called a let, and is not reckoned against either side.

In the double game the player A takes up his position on the left, or up side of the inner half of the court, and his partner B on the right, or down side of the outer court. His opponent C takes up his position on the right, or down side of the inner court, and C's partner D on the left, or up side of the outer court. Play begins as before, with A throwing the ball at the front wall, so that it will rebound on to the right wall and then come down. C returns it and then, if A misses it, there is no score, but B takes the place of A, and A goes to B's place.

If in the course of play B loses, then that side goes down, and C and D go up, C taking the left-hand inner court where A started. The side which has a player in the left-hand inner court is always the up side, and any miss by the down side counts one to the up side. If the down player who is operating in the right-hand inner court misses three times in succession, he changes places with his partner.

If any player hits the ball so that after striking the wall it bounds out of the court, or if he knocks it directly out of the court, this counts as a miss. The ball must be hit with one blow of the hand or wrist; if touched by any other part of the striker, he loses a stroke. The game is played at a great pace and is exhilarating both for performers and spectators.

The Story of the Boundless Universe and All Its Wondrous Worlds

These pictures show us the outside and the inside of a simple calorimeter, an instrument that measures the quantity of heat in a thing, as a thermometer measures its level of heat, or its temperature. The amount of heat is shown by the quantity of ice melted. The middle picture explains how the instrument works.

HEAT AND TEMPERATURE

THERE are many important facts for us to learn about heat in addition to those we have already considered.

The general rule is that when heat is given to a certain quantity of anything, or taken from it, its temperature changes. We might expect that this would always happen—that we could not add heat to a thing without making it hotter, or take heat from a thing without making it colder. Yet it is easy to prove that this is possible, and also that it does not contradict in the least the law that no kind of energy can be lost, and that all must be accounted for. If we take ice at the melting-point, and add heat to it, we do not raise its temperature; or if we take water at the freezing-point, with a very small piece of ice in it, we can take heat from it, yet its temperature does not fall; or if we take a mixture of ice and water, we can add heat to it or take heat from it without altering its temperature. Lastly, if we take liquid water at the boiling-point in the open air, and add any amount of heat to it, not too rapidly, we make it no hotter. The liquid water disappears, and takes the form of water-vapour, which is itself no hotter than the liquid water was. All these are illustrations of what is called

latent heat. What is true of water is true of other things.

Now, what we notice in every one of these illustrations is that, though the temperature of the water is not changed, its state is. In one case we have ice turning into liquid water; in another we have liquid water turning into ice; in yet another case we have liquid water turning into water-vapour.

Here is the proper definition of latent heat; though it is rather long, it is perfectly clear:

Latent heat is the quantity of heat which must be communicated to a body in a given state in order to convert it into another state without changing its temperature.

That is exactly what these examples illustrate. The heat seems to have disappeared as heat when we put it into ice and turn the ice into liquid water no hotter than the ice was, and so we say that it has become *latent*, using the Latin word meaning " lying hid."

The opposite term to latent heat is *sensible heat*. Here the word sensible is used in its proper meaning, and a thing is called sensible because it can be sensed, or felt. So, when we give heat to a thing and make it warmer, we call it sensible;

ASTRONOMY · GEOLOGY · GEOGRAPHY · CHEMISTRY · PHYSICS · LIFE

but if we give heat to a thing and make it no warmer we say that the heat becomes latent. We must understand that if the heat does not make the thing warmer it must *change the state of the thing*; the heat has to be accounted for in any case. We may quote the simple language in which Lord Kelvin, the great master of this subject, explains the right meaning of the words sensible and latent heat.

THE HEAT WHICH BECOMES HIDDEN IN A BASIN OF ICE AND WATER

When heat given to a quantity of water warms it, the heat becomes sensible to a hand held in the water. When a basin of warm water and a basin of water and ice are placed side by side, a hand dipped first in one and then in the other perceives the heat.

If now the warm water be poured into the basin of ice and water, and stirred for a few seconds of time—unless there is enough of warm water to melt all the ice—the hand perceives no warmth; on the contrary, it perceives that the temperature is the same as it was in the basin of ice and water at the beginning.

Thus the heat which was sensible in the basin of warm water has ceased to be sensible in the water that was in that basin, and has not become sensible in the other. It is therefore well said to have become latent.

The facts of latent heat give us a means of measuring heat itself, for we can measure the amount of ice that can be melted into water without change of temperature, and the more ice that is so melted, the more the heat that is employed. It does not matter in what form the heat is applied; we can measure it equally well. A given quantity of ice may be melted into water of the same temperature, either by being exposed to a great deal of warm water or to a little very hot water. We know that in each case the amount of heat there must have been the same, because it does the same work, turning the same amount of ice into ice-cold water.

THE AMOUNT OF HEAT IN A THING IS NOT THE SAME AS ITS TEMPERATURE

The old name for heat when it was supposed to be a fluid was *caloric*, and the name for the instrument that measures heat is *calorimeter*. We must never mistake the absolute difference between a calorimeter and a thermometer; the one measures the *quantity* of heat, and the other measures its *level*. We, nowadays, call a fixed quantity of heat a calorie, and that will help us to remember the word calori-

meter. When we say latent heat we mean heat itself; when we talk of summer heat we do not really mean heat itself, but the temperature, or heat-level.

Two famous Frenchmen, Laplace the astronomer, and Lavoisier the chemist, invented the first calorimeter, which measured the amount of heat by the amount of ice melted. Another method might be employed. When ice is turned into ice-cold water, heat becomes latent; but heat becomes latent also when boiling water is turned into water-vapour, and so it is possible to make a calorimeter depending on measuring the amount of water evaporated by heat.

We can also measure the amount of heat, without any reference to latent heat at all, by taking water or some other substance at a fixed temperature, and noticing how much a given quantity of it has its temperature raised.

WHAT HAPPENS TO THE HEAT WHEN ICE TURNS INTO WATER

When we come to consider the doctrine of latent heat in the light of our modern knowledge of matter, we see that, though the term is worth keeping, it is rather misleading. The truth is that, when ice is turned into ice-cold water by putting heat into it, the heat which disappears is really turned into something else—something else that makes the difference between liquid water and ice. This something else is the motion of the molecules of the liquid water; and what has really happened is that the heat motion has been turned into that motion on which the liquidness of the liquid water depends.

In the same way, when boiling water is turned into water-vapour of the same temperature by having heat added to it, and when we say the heat has become latent, what we really mean is that the heat motion has been turned into another kind of motion—the motion of the molecules making up water-vapour. We know that all gases, including water-vapour, consist of molecules in very rapid movement. Part of this we know to be the special kind of movement called heat, and of this there may be less or more, because a gas may be hotter or colder.

There is another very important phrase, *specific heat*, which we must study. If we take a given quantity of water and a given quantity of something else, both at the same temperature, and put a certain amount of heat into them, we find that the something else, whatever it is, becomes hotter than the water does. The only exception to this rule is hydrogen gas. Apart from hydrogen gas it is true that in order to make water hotter we require to put into it more heat than into any other substance. For convenience we call the specific heat of water 1, and then the specific heat of all other substances, except hydrogen gas, is less than 1.

WHY THE SAME AMOUNT OF HEAT MAKES ONE THING HOTTER THAN ANOTHER

The chemists have discovered certain remarkable laws about the specific heat of different things. It is not a matter of chance that the same amount of heat given to the same amount of copper and iron, at the same temperature, will not raise the temperature of each in equal degree.

We find that there is a law in this matter, and the specific heat of a substance depends to a great extent on the size and weight of the atoms of the substance. If an element has big and heavy atoms, there will be fewer of them required to make up the given weight of that thing, say, an ounce, than will be required to make up the same weight of another element which has smaller and lighter atoms.

In other words, the bigger the atoms are, the less heat will be required to raise the temperature to a given degree. The scientific way of saying this is that, as a rule, the specific heat of a thing is *inversely proportional to its atomic weight.*

THE REASON WHY THE TEAPOT KEEPS HOT SO LONG

The very high specific heat of water has important consequences in practical life, and this is one of the most valuable properties of this wonderful compound. If we made tea with any other liquid than water, we should find that the tea got cold far more quickly than usual. The fact that water has such a high specific heat means that it will hold a lot of heat. The amount of heat in a given quantity of boiling water is greater than in the same quantity of anything else at the same temperature, because the specific heat is higher. This means that if we wish to boil cold water we have to put more heat into it than we should have to put into anything else, and it also means that, when we have got the water boiled, there is a great deal of heat in it, and so it takes a long time for the hot water to cool.

All this means that water is a great storer of heat, and this fact is equally true of a full teapot, or of the ocean round our shores. We now see more clearly than before the key to the great virtues of an island climate such as ours. The water surrounding us could not do what it does if it were not for this high specific heat of water combined with its low conducting power.

This means that, in the summer, water will swallow up enormous quantities of heat, and these enormous stores of heat collected in summer can be given back to moderate the climate in the winter.

This must conclude our study of heat. It is a subject about which too much cannot be known, because of its immense practical importance in relation to all kinds of machinery, and the using of power for the purposes of human life; and also because of its great bearings on our ideas of the universe, and the history and destiny of things in general.

THE IMPORTANCE OF THE LAWS OF HEAT TO ALL KINDS OF MEN

There is perhaps no other subject in the world which so directly concerns the man who wishes to save a penny in the pound in the working of his factory or his motor-car, or the pure philosopher who wants to know the laws and course of Nature. That is why one of the greatest of all the achievements of the nineteenth century was the discovery of the nature and laws of heat, unknown to all preceding ages.

The discovery of these laws is of enormous daily importance to every one of us now, and it furnishes the proof of that greatest of all scientific ideas, the truth that while all things can be changed into other things, while all forms of power can be changed into other forms of power, *nothing is made out of nothing,* nor is anything ever destroyed.

This greatest of all scientific truths, the law of the conservation of energy, was seen, as by the eye of the prophet, by the earliest thinker of whom we have any record, and has played a part in the history of the human mind for 2500 years. But the proof of it was not obtained until the nineteenth century, and we owe that proof to the great men in Germany, and to the famous Lord Kelvin, the British scientist and inventor.

(Next chapter in this group, page 5689)

DARWIN, WHOSE NAME WILL NEVER DIE

DARWIN STANDING AT THE DOOR OF HIS HOME IN THE VILLAGE OF DOWNE IN KENT

This picture is from a photograph by Elliott & Fry; and the picture on page 5577 is by Messrs. Oliver and Boyd

MEN AND WOMEN

The Story of Immortal Folk Whose Work Will Never Die

Baron Liebig

Count Buffon

John Ray

Von Humboldt

Luther Burbank

Richard Owen

EXPLORERS OF LIFE

IN the world's history there have been many men who have examined the wonder of living things, some consciously seeking the secret of life, others patiently and humbly examining dark corners of the kingdom of life in animals and plants.

Their work is interwoven, as the essence of life in plants and animals is the same; for, as the old botanist Nehemiah Grew used to say in the seventeenth century, both plants and animals came at first out of the same hand, and were therefore the contrivance of the same Wisdom.

Aristotle was the leader of them all, for he it was who first perceived that knowledge of life was not to be gained by speculating about it, but by examination of living things; and it was he who first put forward the unassailable idea that only life can beget life, and that one form of life must beget that form and no other, each, in the Bible's simple words, bringing forth the living creature after his kind. Aristotle is one of those greatest of original thinkers, not perhaps more than fifty in number, without whom—if they had never lived to give their thoughts to others to work on—the world would be as backward as it was in the Stone Age.

Who are the others? A man must be a very great thinker to be counted in that august company. But among them we ought to include Vesalius, who died in a remote Mediterranean island in the year Shakespeare was born; and Harvey, who discovered the circulation of the blood three years after Shakespeare died.

Vesalius was the first biologist to abandon the traditions handed down without examination for centuries, and to examine things for himself. He was the first to dissect the human body scientifically, and he taught only what he himself could see and make others see. He was the founder of anatomy and physiology as we know it, and his work on the structure of the human body, published in 1543, was a new gospel in science. He had pupils from all over Europe, and one of them who came from England, John Caius, founded the college in Cambridge which bears his name, and is the doctor's college to this day.

Indeed, it was at Caius that William Harvey was educated. He studied also at Padua, then a great Italian university. When he was an old man and physician to Charles the First, he sat reading a book while not far away the battle of Edgehill was going on, with the young princes in his care. A picture of this incident is on page 2505. But he was almost a young man, only 38, when he expounded to the College of Physicians his doctrine of the

EXPLORERS · INVENTORS · WRITERS · ARTISTS · SCIENTISTS

circulation of the blood. Most discoveries in science are founded on work which others have done, or may be compared to steps on a ladder; but Harvey's discovery stood almost alone on his own foundations. He was happy in that the merit and truth of his discovery was perceived and acknowledged in his lifetime, and he stands next to Sir Isaac Newton in that century, and perhaps in English science, as the single discoverer of a principle on which all that followed in the same province of thought was founded.

THE MAN WHO FOUND THAT THE BLOOD RUNS THROUGH THE BODY

Harvey's discovery was the first introduction into biology of the laws of mechanical motion, with the teaching of which Galileo was then shaking the world. This great gift to scientific truth brought Harvey into acute disfavour among professional rivals, and his income as a doctor seriously declined. But he was triumphantly justified before he died, and while the storm raged he continued his labours and proofs with the same detachment which he showed at Edgehill.

He had something of Newton's power of rising to childish rapture over what seem little things that grow to greatness in scientific minds. Newton could lose himself in the study of soap bubbles; Harvey would hurry from Court or camp to a bedroom at Oxford where a professor kept hens sitting on eggs for him, so that Harvey might crack one of the eggs and study the great problem of the development of life within it.

One thing, nay two, Harvey could not cure—his excessive vigour of thought, and his gout. In order to meditate in peace he had caves dug at his brother's Croydon house, for, said he, " I love darkness as I can then best contemplate." And often his active brain would fetch him out of bed at night and he would pace his chamber in his nightshirt till calm returned.

THE PHILOSOPHER WHO SAT OUT ON THE ROOF AT MIDNIGHT

When gout plagued him in the silent watches, he would sally forth in the same scanty raiment to the leaded roof of his London home, and sit there with his legs in a pail of freezing water, " till he was almost dead with cold, then betake himself to his stove and so 'twas gone." That was at Cockaine House, in London, on which the Moon often looked down at the Spartan philosopher with his shirt tails flapping in the frosty midnight breeze.

Harvey was a little man of quick and ardent temper, but of boundless charity and affection, a childless husband, a devoted brother, and, in proportion to his means, a princely benefactor to the Royal College of Physicians, which still preserves as its richest treasure the little note-books from which he quietly and modestly delivered the lectures embodying the greatest of revelations ever made up to his own day concerning the human body.

After Harvey, England was never lacking in physiologists. It seemed as if the impulse he gave to the science went on and on. It is true that other countries have made great contributions to it, and it was reserved for the Italian doctor Malpighi, who had in the compound microscope an implement denied to Harvey, to complete Harvey's theory by the discovery of the capillaries, those tiny blood vessels of which every man carries so many that end to end they would reach about 62,000 miles. But England has had many who carried the torch onward, and brought knowledge on from the nineteenth century to the twentieth.

COUNT BUFFON AND HIS THIRTY-SIX VOLUMES ABOUT ANIMALS

At the same time a new spirit had entered into botany and zoology. These were slower in starting, for ancient ways greatly hampered them; and when, in seventeenth-century England, John Ray began to classify plants and animals, and was followed by Nehemiah Grew, zoology had not long emerged from the medieval Bestiaries, and botany, better served, was the science of the Herbalists. It was in the eighteenth century that Count Buffon the Frenchman gave a new impulse to zoology. Buffon's great work, which occupied fifty years of his life, was a description of the world's animals in 36 volumes. It is out of date now, as well it may be, for the last volume was published in 1789; but it gave a tremendous impulse to the study of animal life, and Buffon becomes more than an encyclopedic writer by reason of the fact that he was one of the first to uphold that idea of evolution in living things which was the hall-mark of nineteenth-century science.

By the side of him in fame may be said to stand Carl von Linné, better known by the Latin form of his name as Linnaeus,

FAMOUS EXPLORERS OF LIFE'S MYSTERIES

LINNAEUS KISSES THE ENGLISH EARTH AND THANKS GOD FOR HAVING CREATED THE
BEAUTIFUL GORSE

CUVIER, THE FIRST STUDENT OF FOSSIL REMAINS, AT WORK IN HIS LABORATORY

who was the first great botanist who classified things. Classified botany has moved far since his day; plants long ago ceased to be classed in the orders he laid down which we call the Linnean Orders.

But he was the pioneer, and the work of pioneers must necessarily be only a beginning, on which successors will build and improve. Linnaeus ranged throughout the wild realms of Nature and reduced its parts to a system. He grouped like with like, and pointed to unsuspected kinships.

Thus he classified animals into a series of sub-kingdoms—mammals, birds, amphibia, fishes, insects and worms ; and sub-divided the mammals into five orders. The scheme was primitive and incomplete, but it was a foundation and a framework on which all his successors have built.

His arrangement of the vegetable world was more difficult and imperfect. He grouped plants according to the characters of sex, but in doing so he made it clear that his system was only provisional, a hint and an incitement to men to do better. He urged the necessity of a scheme based, not on a single character, but on the sum total of real affinities, but he himself had not time for the task.

THE COBBLER'S APPRENTICE WHO BECAME A GREAT NATURALIST

" Linnaeus and Cuvier have been to me as gods," said Darwin, in his later days. The Swedish hero, who was born in Smaland in 1707, had a grim struggle throughout his early years. He felt unable to enter the Church in which his father was a clergyman, so the father felt the lad could not be safe unless he had a trade, and apprenticed him to a cobbler.

Happily a discerning parson perceived the boy's genius and had him sent to a university. The young naturalist was so poor on his £8 a year, however, that he could not afford new boots, and had to mend his old ones with the bark of trees.

Nothing daunted him. He was a passionate observer of natural wonders, and, fortunate chance giving him access to good private libraries, he combined reading with first-hand observation. Being entrusted at 24 with an exploring mission to Lapland, he made a magnificent summer march of 3800 miles on foot, and came back with material for books which profoundly affected scientific opinion of the age. Appointed professor of physic and anatomy at Upsala Univer-

sity, he practised as a doctor, bore almost unaided the burden of teaching at the university, toiled unceasingly at his studies and writings, and gradually won the foremost position in the world as the grand simplifier of the cardinal mysteries of Nature.

Travelling, teaching, learning, collecting, he reached England in 1736, and, to the lasting regret of all who cherish the memory of this noble-hearted man, he was coldly received here. That is the common fate of men in whose brain great new truths for the world are born.

THE GREAT MAN WHO KNELT DOWN AND KISSED THE BEAUTIFUL ENGLISH EARTH

But official coolness towards him did not chill the glowing ardour of this gentle soul, for when he first saw English gorse in all its golden glory he burst into tears of ecstasy, and, kneeling down, kissed the ground on which it grew. An attempt is made in a new biography of Linnaeus to discredit this pretty story, on the plea that Linnaeus was here in the late summer, and that gorse is a spring flowering plant; but every country child knows that gorse is always blooming, and is only " out of bloom when kissing is out of favour."

The greatness of Linnaeus was recognised in England long before he died in 1778. After his death a sum of £1000 was raised in London to purchase his collection—2000 books, 14,000 plants, 7000 shells, insects, birds, and mineral specimens. The securing of it had the excitement of a miniature expedition of war, for the King of Sweden sent swift envoys to arrest the collection before it could reach our shores. However, the little ship conveying the treasure came safely through. Around the collection grew up a new institution for the study of Natural History. Founded in 1788, it was called the Linnean Society, and it has been one of the foremost influences in the furthering of science throughout the world. Darwin presented his great theory to the Linnean Society.

THE TEACHINGS OF LINNAEUS THAT LED TO DARWIN'S FAMOUS THEORY

The work that Linnaeus had started, the bringing of order out of confusion, the comparison of species with species of plants and animals from all parts of the world, all contained in that collection of his, had an abiding influence on future botanists and students of animal life.

From the teachings of Linnaeus sprang that tide of study and speculation leading in the nineteenth century to Darwin's theory of the Origin of Species.

But the naturalist who first directly pointed the way towards Evolution was the famous Frenchman Jean Lamarck, who was born in 1744. For unlike Linnaeus and Cuvier, who believed in the sudden creation of the different species, Lamarck upheld the doctrine, as Darwin said of him, " that all species, including Man, are descended from other species."

Lamarck, however, was ahead of his times—his masterpiece, Philosophie Zoologique, in which he developed his views on Evolution, was published in 1809, the year of Darwin's birth. The world was not ready for this startling theory and Lamarck's views were not accepted in his own day.

He began his career as a botanist; then, when he was nearly 50, he turned to the study of animal life and became one of the greatest zoologists of his time. He was the first to distinguish between vertebrate and invertebrate animals by the presence of the vertebral column, and he also gave us the term " Biology."

Lamarck eventually became blind as a result of his labours for science, and it is sad to think that in his latter years he was also very poor. But he went on working, helped by his eldest daughter, at his book on the natural history of invertebrates. He died in 1829.

GEORGE CUVIER, THE FATHER OF THE SCIENCE OF FOSSILS

Another Frenchman who was influenced by Linnaeus was George Cuvier (1769–1832), so diligent a student even when a boy, that the Duke of Wurtemberg sent him to Stuttgart University, where he read the works of the great Swede, and thenceforward devoted himself to natural history. But Cuvier was by nature a discoverer, not a follower. Near where he lived as a private tutor in Normandy some fossils were dug up. Till that time fossils had been regarded as a freak of Nature in no way connected with anything living in the world. Cuvier saw in them the ancestors of living things, and he was the father of the science of fossils (called Palaeontology), which today affords the clues to the age of the inhabited world, and of the beginnings of all that live therein.

Cuvier probed the anatomy of living things in order to compare them with one another. He was what is called a comparative anatomist ; and by discovering in what important structures animals resemble one another, or differ from one another, he classified them anew.

THE WONDERFUL JOURNEY THAT LASTED FIVE YEARS

Cuvier's classes were founded not on mere outward resemblances, though these might help, but on the structure of animals ; and he traced the connection between the form of an animal's feet, or hoofs, or horns, or its stomach and internal organs, with what these things were to do. He showed the relation between form and function. We may note in passing that he, like Linnaeus, thought that species could not change.

Very different was the outlook of Friedrich Humboldt, who was born in Berlin in the same year as Cuvier ; for he was one of the master collectors. While a student at Frankfort-on-Oder he met Forster, who had sailed with Captain Cook, and he became bitten with the idea of travelling and exploring and collecting. But he had to wait till he was 30 before he could make a beginning, for the French wars did not encourage peaceful scientific men to put to sea in search of knowledge. At last he sailed in a Spanish ship to South America, which at that time was, with the exception of Brazil, the western empire of Spain in name, if not in fact. His journey lasted five years.

What a journey it was ! One can imagine this earnest young German braving all the perils of disease and sickness, of unfriendly peoples, of poisonous reptiles, of hunger and thirst, as he explored the unknown waters of the Orinoco and the Amazon, and trod the strange ways, the deserts and mountains and swamps of Ecuador, Venezuela, Colombia, Peru, Mexico, and Cuba.

LIKE A NEW COLUMBUS FINDING A NEW AMERICA

Other travellers followed him, but he was the first to see and reveal to the world the dead-and-gone civilisations of these old countries and peoples, to make known the customs of their living inhabitants, to observe, examine, and collect the birds and animals and fishes that Europe had never seen.

He collected as a naturalist, but his

work did not end there, for other of his observations led nations to follow him and make magnetic surveys. He was the new Columbus who discovered a new America, whose peoples and animals and plants were one with the natural history of the whole world. For five years he had sought his material; when he came back with it it required many years more to classify it and describe it. Humboldt's Cosmos, as he called it, was many volumes long; it aimed at being the natural history of all living things. With what a sigh of regret he must have finished it ! But in a way it was never finished, for when he was 60 away he went again, this time to Northern and Central Asia. He was too old, however, for the hardships of his young manhood, and the journey was shorter, though not unfruitful. He came back to spend the last thirty years of his life writing and re-writing and classifying. When he died, an old man of 90, he was still happy in his unfinished tasks.

THE MOST MAGNIFICENT MONUMENT THAT ART HAS RAISED TO NATURE

Another great pioneer of natural history, who lived in Humboldt's day, was John James Audubon, who described the bird life of America. He was born in the United States, probably in 1780. He was a painter of rare distinction and his greatest work, called The Birds of America, contained coloured pictures, life size, of 1055 species of birds. It was described by Cuvier as " the most magnificent monument that art has ever raised to nature." Audubon died in 1851.

An Englishman who also led the way in the study of bird life was John Gould (1804–81), the son of a gardener, born at Lyme Regis in Dorset. He published the first account of bird life in the Himalaya Mountains. It was to his wife that he owed much of his success, for she painted the pictures of birds and animals for his books. He gave the world 41 big volumes with 2999 plates of illustrations, and also made a collection of 5000 skins of Australian animals which, with his fine collection of humming birds, was sold to the Natural History Museum for £3000.

From Audubon and Gould we must turn to Sir Charles Lyell (1797–1875), a Scotsman. He was influenced by both Humboldt and Cuvier, perhaps more by Cuvier, for Lyell's work was akin to the Frenchman's study of fossils. Lyell was born when Humboldt was still on the Amazon, and he was to have practised as a barrister. But while he was an undergraduate at Oxford he went to the geology lectures of Dean Buckland, and Buckland turned him from the study of the law to the study of the rocks.

THE MAN WHO ROAMED ABOUT AND READ THE STORY OF THE ROCKS

The two went to Scotland to study strata, and from that holiday journey Lyell never turned back. Through Buckland he met Cuvier and Humboldt and he became one of the company of those wise old men. He gave up his profession as a barrister to travel over England and Scotland, in Europe and America, reading with a new vision and an inspired insight the story of the Earth's foundations.

The result of his search is embodied in his volume of Principles of Geology, published in 1830. It won him the title of father of modern geology, and it is still a text book to which the most modern geologist will bow. Before Lyell wrote, geologists declared that the mountains, the rift valleys, the ocean beds as well as the continental plateaus, had all been moulded by mighty convulsions of the Earth when the Earth was young.

HOW LYELL CHANGED OUR IDEAS OF THE PAST

Lyell showed that the causes which altered the Earth's surface now were the same that always had been: that by slow processes, the wearing down by rain and rivers, the erosion of the unfailing winds, the fret of the sea on the coast, continents were shredded of their soil till they sank beneath the ocean, and the oceans by accumulation through millions of years of deposits were slowly lifted up till they became land. Earthquakes and volcanoes there were and always had been; but they were the products of the irresistible slow movements of the changing Earth, not the cause of the changes that are to be seen.

Often it is said that discoveries in science are like a flight of steps, one step built on another. In the lives of the men of science of the eighteenth and nineteenth centuries the men can be seen lifting one another on their shoulders. In 1803 the man who is known to the world as Baron Liebig was born, the son of a poor drysalter of Darmstadt, and he was one of that rare race of people who are born with a divine curiosity and the power to see clearly where it leads them. He was also one of those in whom genius will out, however narrow the surroundings. He was apprenticed to an apothecary, but could not earn the money to pay for a real training in the chemistry to which his mind was bent. Humboldt came to the rescue, liked the poor young man, and found a rich one to send him to the University of Bonn.

Never was money better invested. Liebig's work in chemistry has paid Germany a millionfold since. He was the parent, one might say the originator, of modern organic chemistry, the chemistry of the compounds containing carbon, of which the most important are those belonging to living things.

Many pages might be filled with the names of the chemical problems he investigated, though it is a little odd that the one which everyone remembers, Liebig's extract, was the least important. But the two outstanding achievements of his life were to teach a new way of investigating and analysing organic substances and to teach it to young chemists who came from all over Europe to learn. So sound was his method that it is hardly altered today; so far-reaching was his influence that there has hardly been a chemist since who does not owe something to him; and the study of the chemistry of living things, which he founded, has always had Germany as its chief home. He died in 1873.

THE OLD MONK MENDEL AT WORK IN HIS MONASTERY GARDEN AT BRUNN

If Humboldt set Liebig on his path, Cuvier performed the same service for Richard Owen. Owen was stirred by Cuvier's work on fossils, and was an even greater anatomist. His science was that of showing how one portion of the skeleton or the body was related to another, so that, for example, an animal with horns and hoofs must have one kind of teeth, and an animal with claws must have another. That is a very simple illustration of a very profound kind of knowledge, the knowledge of comparative anatomy. It is the knowledge which made Richard Owen able to reconstruct from the appearance of a leg-bone of an extinct bird, sent to him from New Zealand, the whole skeleton. More bones of this extinct bird, the Dinornis, were found later, and when put together they exactly confirmed Owen's prediction.

It is the same kind of knowledge which enables the Natural History Museum today to put together accurately the fossil bones that have been found, or to say from the mere shape of fossil teeth what their extinct owner was like.

Owen was indebted for the chance of fame to John Hunter, who was a sheer freak of genius. John had a famous brother William, who was a surgeon, but John wasted his youth in careless fun, and never made good his lost time, always going in terror of grammar and spelling. Yet he himself became a marvellous surgeon and the father of modern scientific surgery.

Though possessing a brilliant mind, he was confounded by books, and so studied the living subject instead.

All his money and energy he devoted to getting together an incomparable collection of anatomical and natural history specimens. Hunter died in 1793, eleven years before the birth of Owen, who, when on the point of taking up a sea career in early manhood, was providentially appointed curator of the Royal College of Surgeons, to which Hunter's collection had come, a medley of fine confused ore of learning, all pell-mell, unassorted.

For years Owen worked on this store of virgin riches and minted it into the pure gold of imperishable knowledge. Never had the world seen such a dazzling series of works as he poured forth, year after year, authoritative, inspired, flaming with the pure light of unerring perception.

THE KIND THING THAT LORD MACAULAY DID FOR RICHARD OWEN

Many ill-paid lectureships and unpaid trusts in service of the public fell to Owen, who attained world-wide celebrity on a very few pounds a year. He acquired knowledge laboriously, he spent it royally without price for the good of others, and so for long there was continually the shadow of poverty over this great and lovable man. We must always be grateful to Lord Macaulay for his kindness to Owen, whose appointment as Superintendent of the Natural History Museum he secured in 1856.

I hardly know him to speak to (wrote Macaulay), but his fame is spread over Europe. He is an honour to our country, and it is painful to me that a man of his merit should be approaching old age amid anxieties and distresses. He told me that £800 a year, without a house in the Museum, would be opulence to him. He did not, he said, even wish for more . . . The greatest philosopher may starve while his countrymen are boasting of his discoveries, and while foreign academies are begging for the honour of being allowed to add his name to their list.

Owen got the appointment, and the £800 a year, and so was safe for life. His work in anatomy and palaeontology is included in over 400 publications, and some of his discoveries were, each by itself, sufficient to immortalise an ordinary man, though he, in his modesty, made light of them. He was a delightful character, artistic, merry, a great boy at heart to his dying day, and a prince of good comrades.

Sir Richard Owen lived till 1892, and so overlapped the lifetime of Charles Darwin, whose great work on the Origin of Species was published in 1859, when Owen was in the prime of his scientific life. He outlived Darwin, but it is doubtful if ever he was reconciled to the great innovation Darwin introduced into natural history. Owen, like Cuvier and Linnaeus, believed that species of plants or animals never changed; varieties there might be, but the species remained as it was from the time of its unknown first appearance in the world.

DARWIN'S THEORY THAT A SPECIES CAN CHANGE INTO A NEW SPECIES

Darwin not only believed that species could change, but suggested a way in which the change came about. One pigeon is not like another, nor is a jungle-fowl like a Black Orpington, or a Michaelmas daisy like a yellow chrysanthemum. They are different varieties of the same species. Darwin suggested that now and then a different variety would arise, and would find itself so favoured by its surroundings that it would thrive and propagate where other varieties died. Then it might take on to itself another characteristic which helped it to live on; and then another, and another, and another. Gradually, by the accumulation of these tiny differences, the species would become a new species.

It may be imagined with what a storm of criticism Darwin's new idea, upsetting all the old ideas, was received. He had many great supporters, who fought for his theories side by side with him; and of these the foremost was Alfred Russel Wallace, who independently had come to the same belief as Darwin and whose paper was read at the same time to the Linnean Society.

THE GREAT GIFT OF DARWIN TO ALL THE YEARS TO COME

The battle of the zoologists and botanists was long and loud, though Darwin, who had been many years reaching his conclusions before he published them, went on quietly working on the same lines, accumulating invaluable collections of facts, welcoming honest criticism, examining everything that seemed to be against his theory as well as all the things that seemed to be in its favour.

The great gift of Darwin to his time, and to the science of the years which followed, was not his theory in itself but its power in stimulating students to study living things from a new angle and with a new enthusiasm. He lifted zoology and botany out of the rut into which they had fallen. Side by side with the answer he gave to the great problem of how new species arise, and must arise, he put on a sound foundation, in language that all could understand, the doctrine of the gradual evolution of living things, as they responded to the greater calls life made on them and the greater opportunities it afforded.

And what manner of man was this Charles Robert Darwin, who dared to upset all accepted opinion as to the story of the Earth's living things? He was the simplest, shyest genius who ever lived to find himself famous against all personal expectation, a giant in stature, practically an invalid for the greater part of his life, who, having travelled the world over in five years, settled at the village of Downe, in Kent, and found a short journey to London a feat of endurance.

He was a slow beginner; his mind was strong, tenacious, swift to observe natural detail, and the relation of cause to effect; but ordinary lessons at school and from books were very difficult to him. "You will never be good for anything but shooting and rat-catching," said his father, Dr. Darwin of Shrewsbury. In his rooms at Cambridge University, Charles would practise with his gun, firing caps, not bullets, and extinguishing lighted candles with the puff of air from the barrel.

A mushroom is up in a night and gone in a day; an oak is slow, but lasts for a thousand years. Darwin was an intellectual oak; slowly and with toil his great brain ripened. He got his B.A., but not brilliantly; he was far happier in the fields amid flowers and beetles than in a library. Yet his character, and a mysterious suggestion of latent power in the youngster, attracted grave and older men at the University, and their influence was important. Yet it was not so vital as that of Uncle Wedgwood. Darwin's mother was a Wedgwood, and her elder brother was devoted to young Charles. One day the British Government having planned a round-the-world scientific trip, surveying and observing, Charles yearned to go as naturalist. He had failed as a medical student because his heart was too tender; he had not glittered as a scholar, yet here he was pining for this world adventure.

How his father puffed and fumed! " If you can find one single person of sense who advises your going, I will consent," said the confident parent; and Charles rushed 20 miles across country to Uncle Wedgwood. Uncle Wedgwood was a student of noses, and Charles had an unusually prominent one. " With such a nose as that you ought to do something," said Uncle, who forthwith backed the young man's plan.

Down to his ship went Charles, to Captain Fitzroy, commander of the cruise, Now the captain was a student of noses too, and when he saw Charles's he grumbled, " With a nose like that *you'll* never, never do anything." Luckily he accepted him, and we remember Fitzroy today because Charles Darwin was of his company.

SIR RICHARD OWEN WITH HIS SKELETON OF THE DINORNIS

If any boy, girl, man, or woman, desires a delightful record of travel, adventure, strange sights, strange experiences, strange habits of peoples, animals, birds, and the rest of living creation, let them read Darwin's Voyage of the Beagle, telling of this five-years' cruise to lands in all parts of the world.

The experience formed the groundwork of Darwin's dazzling work in science, but it had the tragic result of ruining his health. He was as bad a sailor as Nelson, and suffered the full agonies of seasickness. This malady, he said, permanently injured his stomach, and thereafter he never passed a day without illness, severe or slight. But he married a Wedgwood cousin, lived at Downe, and became the father of an admirable family, who, with their mother, made his life a paradise, despite his pangs and paroxysms.

The rule was that Darwin was not to be disturbed while at work in his study, but a petticoated little son would steal in from the garden and say to the toiling giant, " Daddy, if you'll tum and play with me I'll give you *sispence!* " and Darwin would go, and return to work a happier man.

THE HAPPY CHILDREN WHO HELPED DARWIN IN HIS FAMOUS WORK

What comrades they were, father and children! Together they examined wild life, bird, animal, reptile, plant. The boys found new grasses, and he thought it wonderful. They helped him in his study of worms; they played musical instruments to enable him to see the effect of air-vibrations on sensitive plants, and they were such good, silent woodmen that they could watch a squirrel climb their father in mistake for a tree!

Worldwide fame came to Darwin, but he could not understand it. He was too humble to believe that he deserved such renown, and he actually believed it all to be the outcome of the charm and goodness of the people who wrote to him and visited him. A truly wonderful man, he died in 1882 at the age of 73.

The science of life would have shrunk without Darwin. It has expanded in other directions than those to which he pointed. Science is still seeking other ways in which new species might arise and the most absorbing study among zoologists and botanists today is that of heredity. While Darwin was still alive, and the whole world was examining his theories, there lived, in a monastery at Brunn, an abbot named Gregor Mendel, who for many years studied almost without notice or recognition the way in which plants handed on their qualities to their descendants. Mendel died a little-known man, but his theories were revived.

The whole mystery of heredity was worked out by this patient and wonderful monk in his monastery garden at Brunn, in what is now Czechoslovakia. He knew the importance of his discoveries, wrote an account of his experiments, and in 1869 sent copies to all the learned bodies in Europe, including the Royal Society.

THE FAME WHICH CAME TO THE MONK MENDEL LONG AFTER HE HAD GONE

The document passed unnoted, and was lost till 1900, when two naturalists, working through the old literature of their subject, found this tremendous document of Mendel's. Then the significance of the work was apparent. The subject was worked out and the name Mendelism was given to this new code of laws revealing a hidden wonder of the natural world.

But Mendel had by then been sixteen years in his grave. If he and Darwin could have met for half an hour, or if Darwin could have read the monk's paper, what a difference it would have made! Mendel died sad and soured, knowing he had opened a new chapter in the history of learning, but doubtful whether the world would ever read that chapter and know him for its author.

But, at last his teachings were known. They live and inspire the work of men in every country, men who, like Luther Burbank in the United States, succeeded in producing new varieties of fruits and plants; or, like Sir Rowland Biffen in England, sought new varieties of wheat with which to enrich the staple food of mankind

THE PERILOUS ADVENTURES OF A MAN IN SEARCH OF RARE PLANTS

The exploration of the life on our planet is not yet complete, and one of the notable explorers of this century was F. Kingdon-Ward (1885–1958) who travelled over many lands, particularly in Asia, in search of rare plants. He had many adventures in his plant-hunting, some of them as perilous as those of men who have gone into the jungle to shoot tigers.

By such men as these is the fund of human knowledge increased.

The Great Stories of the World That Will Be Told for Ever

Psyche and Zephyr—From the sculpture by Harry Bates, by courtesy of Frederick Hollyer

THE LOVE STORY OF THE WORLD

This is one of the best of the beautiful Greek fables, and it is the love story of all ages and all peoples. The name of the heroine, Psyche, means butterfly, and all the words for soul come from this Greek word, because the Greeks saw in the butterfly the suggestion of the soul's resurrection.

THERE lived in the days long ago a king and queen who had three daughters. The youngest was wonderfully lovely; there was no loveliness of the fields that could compare with her.

People made songs to her; foreigners from distant countries visited her father's kingdom to look at her; whenever she appeared in the streets the people threw sweet-smelling flowers in her way.

At last the fame of her beauty reached even to Venus, and the heart of the goddess of beauty became filled with jealousy.

So Venus sent her son Cupid to punish Psyche for being so fair. Cupid found the princess fast asleep, and touched her side to wound her with his arrow. At this touch Psyche woke up, and opened her eyes. Cupid was invisible to her, but now, as she gazed about her, Cupid saw the loveliness of her eyes, and, bitterly repenting that he had wounded so beautiful a creature, he pierced himself with the arrow that had wounded her, scattered healing drops upon Psyche, and flew away.

A strange fate now overtook the beautiful princess. She remained as lovely as ever, but she awakened no love in the hearts of those who beheld her.

The king and queen, fearing that they had sinned against the gods, sought counsel from the Oracle of Apollo.

" This maiden," answered he, " shall never mate with mortal man. Her lord abides her coming on the mountain top. A monster is he, and none can withstand his power."

This decree of the Oracle plunged the kingdom into mourning. Everybody wept and made lamentations for poor Psyche. But Psyche said, " Do not weep for me, my dearest parents; but let me go to my punishment as it has been ordained by Heaven."

So a procession was made, and Psyche was escorted by a vast multitude, who wept and lamented as they went to the mountain where the monster awaited her.

When they reached the summit the parents embraced their child for the last time, the air resounded with the wailing of the people, and Psyche was left alone.

She was standing there, tears in her eyes and terror in her heart, surely the loveliest thing that ever stood on a bleak mountain,

IMAGINATION · CHIVALRY · LEGENDS · GOLDEN DEEDS · FAIRY TALES

when a gentle Wind called Zephyr lifted her and bore her pleasantly to a smiling valley. Here the gentle Wind laid her on a green bank, and Psyche slept.

When she opened her eyes she found herself near a beautiful grove of trees leading to a wonderful and majestic palace, unlike anything she had ever seen on Earth. The doors stood open. No sounds issued from the interior. Pysche approached, ascended the stairs, and entered.

Never had she seen such splendour and delight. The pillars that supported the glittering roof were of gold, the windows blazed like precious stones.

While the wondering and bewildered Psyche gazed about her, a voice said: " Sovereign lady, all that you see is for your own delight. This is your palace, and an invisible host waits on you to do what you command. Our voices you shall hear, but we ourselves you must not see. Enter your chamber, sleep, and eat."

Psyche, having slept, sat down at a table loaded with fruits and dainties pleasant to the senses. While she thus refreshed herself voices sang, and an invisible host waited on her.

Then, invisible to her eyes, entered her immortal husband. He spoke loving words in her ears, and tenderly embraced her, and she was like one in a dream. But she begged that he would reveal himself to her.

"You must not behold me," he answered. " Why should you wish to do so? Do you doubt me? Is there anything for your happiness that I have not done? If you saw me you would cease to love me as your husband; you would fear, tremble, and adore me as a god. I want you to love me as you love me now."

Psyche obeyed these words, and for a long time she was happy. But presently her human heart turned in thought to her parents and her sisters, and she wished to see them and tell them of her happiness. This wish she told to the gentle Wind that had carried her from the mountain-top, and the gentle Wind brought her sisters.

Instead of being pleased at Psyche's happiness, these two sisters felt jealous of her great good fortune. They questioned her concerning her husband, and when they learned that he was invisible they both exclaimed, " He is the monster of whom the Oracle spoke! Psyche, beware! Secretly provide yourself with a lamp and

a dagger, and when next he comes to you, and while he lies asleep, light your lamp and destroy him."

So skilfully did these jealous sisters fill the heart of Psyche with fear that she forgot her faith in her husband, and did as they told her. But when she lighted her lamp she saw, not a monster sleeping at her side, but the most beautiful winged god of whom it was possible to dream. It was Cupid himself. As she watched him a drop of burning oil fell on his face.

He started up, and, seeing her, exclaimed: " O foolish Psyche! You have ended our dream. Love cannot dwell where suspicion lurks. Go back to your sisters, as you believe in them rather than in me."

Psyche fell weeping on the ground, and Cupid spread his wings and flew away.

Unable to live without love, Psyche wandered far, seeking for her husband.

One day she came to a high and lonely mountain, and entered a temple there. The temple belonged to Ceres, the goddess of agriculture, and it was filled with corn and sheaves, all flung down in disorder. Psyche thought it right to make the temple of a goddess more seemly, and set herself to put everything in reverent order. So pleased was Ceres by this pious act that she said to Psyche, " I cannot protect you from the anger of Venus, but I will give you my advice. Rise, then. Go to Venus, submit yourself to her punishment, and try by obedience to win her favour."

Psyche did what Ceres counselled. She travelled to the temple of Venus, and, bowing herself down, prayed for mercy. Venus was cold to her, and addressed her in haughty words. But finally she declared that she would test Psyche.

So Psyche was led to a storehouse filled with grains, so tiny that they were like the sands of the seashore. " Separate these grains," commanded Venus, " and place each kind together."

Poor Psyche gazed with horror at the impossible task which Venus had set her; but just when she was overwhelmed with despair an army of ants entered from the fields, and soon did what Venus had commanded. When Venus saw the task was done she was angered, and set Psyche another task.

She gave her a box and bade her descend to the regions of Night and ask

Proserpine to fill the box with beauty for her mistress Venus. This seemed to Psyche a task from which she could not escape alive, but she set out to obey the goddess, and invisible agencies aided her, so that even from the dreadful regions of Night she returned safely, her box filled.

She had been warned not to open the box; but on her way back to Venus, feeling worn and tired and ill, she began to think: " If my husband saw me now surely he would hate me; but if I opened this box and painted myself with a little beauty I should appear fair in his eyes."

So Psyche opened the fatal box. It contained—nothing! Yes, it contained something, something that man cannot touch or see or know. It contained the Sleep that is Death. This Sleep entered the body of Psyche, and she fell.

It happened that Cupid, who had been longing all this time for his wife, took advantage of his mother's absence to escape from the place where he lay, and set out to discover his Psyche. He found her sleeping on the earth, with the box open at her side. Swiftly he closed the lid, and then, touching Psyche with one of his quickening arrows, he called her back to life.

" Oh, my sweet love," he cried, " for a second time your curiosity has almost destroyed you! But be of good courage. Go and do what my mother has commanded you while I fly away to secure our everlasting happiness."

Then Cupid spread his wings for Heaven, and told Jupiter the story of poor Psyche. So moved was the heart of the King of Heaven that he sent for Psyche and gave her the cup of ambrosia, saying, " Drink, beautiful Psyche, and become immortal; for ever shalt thou be the bride of Cupid."

So Psyche was changed into a goddess, and became for ever the wife of Cupid.

THE BOY WHO SAVED THE HAMLET

DURING the North American Indian War of 1855 one of the most daring acts was that of a boy named Goodman, fifteen years old, so young and yet so brave that his name is honoured by whites and even by the Indians themselves.

He belonged to a family who, when the eastern States became over-populated, decided to move west, and, enchanted by the beauty of Paget Sound, settled on its shores. Our hero was but nine years old at that time, but he could use his bow and arrow and his rifle as well as many older than himself, and could manage the paddle as well as any Indian.

As time passed many families from other States flocked to this part of the country, and the coming of the people so alarmed the Indians that they determined to kill or drive out all the white folk. The white folk knew nothing of this until men, women, and children were suddenly massacred, and the Indian tribe rose in a body against the whites.

Warned of the coming danger, Goodman sent his wife and his two little girls to a village some miles away, and remained with his son to guard the home.

The people set to work speedily to build a fort and provision it, and all who could handle a rifle or a gun prepared for the defence, knowing that a cruel death would befall them if captured by the enemy.

At noon the next day a fleet of war canoes appeared, and a fierce battle began; but, though numbering twenty times those in the fort, the Indians were beaten off.

They, however, had no idea of giving up the attempt. They retreated half a mile away, beached their canoes, lit the campfires, and began their war-dance. Young Goodman then formed a daring plan. He resolved to go alone and seize the enemy's canoes, knowing that the Indians could then do no further harm.

Leaving the fort after dark, he stole through the woods to the camp. The savages were so intent upon their dancing, and became so tired and sleepy, that they did not see the boy as he approached, and Goodman set to work to cut all the canoe ropes. Then, as the tide rose, he pulled the canoes afloat.

Having cut the canoes adrift, he got into one of them, tied another large one to it, and began to paddle to the fort.

As daybreak dawned the Indians awoke to find their canoes drifting away. With a wild shout they sprang into the waves to seize them, but Goodman opened fire upon them and drove them back.

Making his way to the fort, he told his people what he had done. The men went out and secured the large canoes, and the Indians, finding their fleet gone, beat a rapid retreat through the woods.

THE WOMEN OF STANLEY HARBOUR

THE First World War began on the seas with a sad British defeat. A weak British squadron of three ships in the Pacific Ocean was attacked by a more powerful German fleet, and two ships went down with all hands. The Glasgow escaped and, joining a slow old battleship, the Canopus, rounded Cape Horn and entered the harbour at Stanley, the capital of the Falkland Islands.

There they were joined by a powerful British cruiser squadron under Admiral Sturdee, sent out from England to find the triumphant German fleet. Round the Horn came that doomed fleet, the Gneisenau, Scharnhorst, Leipzig, Dresden, and Nürnberg, steering confidently for the Falkland harbour. And then it was that three women played their part in a victory that again gave their country the command of the southern seas.

Many years before, Frederick Durose had gone out from the fen country of Lincolnshire to be the schoolmaster of the Falkland Islands, and, in due course, his sharp-witted little daughter had become Mrs. Arthur Felton, the wife of a sheep-farmer at Fitzroy on the islands.

Pleased indeed were the islanders to have the British fleet lying snugly in their harbour, a safeguard against the prowling Germans; but only Mrs. Felton thought of practically aiding the welcome helpers from the dear Motherland. She sent her two maids to the top of the highest neighbouring headland to watch the distant seas, and presently they came back with the news that three ships were coming in sight on the horizon.

Instantly Mrs. Felton telephoned to the British fleet in the harbour, and sent back her maids to the headland with notebook and pencil, one to observe and jot down the progress of the incoming vessels, and the other to run back with the messages as they were written, so that no time should be lost.

And so these three sharp women became a link between the oncoming, unconscious German fleet and the British fleet lying in wait for them. Presently the whole German fleet was plainly seen approaching on the South Atlantic, and Admiral Sturdee, issuing forth from the harbour, dealt out to them, in a fierce running fight, the same fate that had befallen gallant Admiral Cradock and his two ships.

Only one of the German ships, the Dresden, escaped by flight. The others found their last resting-place on the bed of the Atlantic.

And what of the three women who kept watch and gave the warning? Their part was not forgotten. The British Admiralty sent to Mrs. Felton a cordial letter of thanks and a massive silver salver as a memento of her splendid helpfulness; while to each of the energetic maid-servants they gave a silver teapot, that will, no doubt, be a proudly-shown heirloom for generations to come.

LE ROI QUI ARRIVA À CACHEMIRE

This is a French translation of the story told in English on page 904

IL y a bien des années un prince et une princesse de l'Inde tombèrent amoureux l'un de l'autre; mais leurs pères étaient à la guerre et ne voulaient pas qu'ils s'épousent. Alors les amoureux s'enfuirent et se cachèrent dans une grande forêt.

Mais un soir que le prince cherchait quelque nourriture un voleur enleva la princesse, l'enferma dans une cave, et s'endormit; la princesse alors se leva et l'attacha, puis, s'habillant de ses vêtements, elle monta sur son cheval et partit à la recherche du prince.

Au lieu de le trouver elle arriva le matin suivant à Cachemire. Toutes les rues de la ville étaient encombrées de monde guettant un éléphant avec anxiété. Le roi et toute sa famille étaient morts et le peuple cherchait un nouveau roi. Or tout le monde aux Indes croit qu'un éléphant peut reconnaître qui est de sang royal, aussi avait-on lâché un éléphant et attendait-on pour voir qui il indiquerait comme souverain maître.

À la grande surprise de la foule, l'animal courut à la princesse déguisée et s'agenouilla devant elle. Le peuple, criant de joie, porta la princesse en triomphe au palais, et la couronna roi. Elle se para de vêtements royaux masculins, et personne ne devina qu'elle n'était pas un homme.

Mais quand le prince revint enfin à la ville à sa recherche, elle déclara au peuple qu'elle était une princesse; alors le prince fut nommé roi; elle l'épousa et devint reine.

THE TALES OF UNCLE REMUS

Folk-stories are the tales told among the peoples of the world, tales which have been told as long ago as men can remember. Most of these old, old stories have grown gradually by being told over and over again for generations. It was left to an American writer, Joel Chandler Harris, who died in 1908, to prove that the Negro people of America have as quaint and interesting folk-stories as any other race. Their stories are chiefly about the doings of animals, such as the fox, the rabbit, and the wolf. Uncle Remus, who is supposed to tell these stories, is an old Negro slave. Mr. Harris wrote many books full of these delightful tales in the quaint broken English spoken by the Negroes, and here we give some of his stories in words that are easier to read. Brer means brother.

BRER RABBIT AND BRER FOX

BRER RABBIT was a naughty, cunning little creature. He was always playing tricks on his neighbours, and they were always trying to catch him. One day Brer Wolf says to Brer Fox:

"If we don't get that little varmint for supper tonight," says he, "I'll give up being a wolf, and eat grass. You just run along home and get into bed, and make out you're dead," says he. "And don't you say anything till Brer Rabbit comes and puts his hands on you. Then we'll get him right enough."

So Brer Fox went home and got into bed, and Brer Wolf he marched off to Brer Rabbit's house, and knocked.

"Bad news, Brer Rabbit," says Brer Wolf. "Poor Brer Fox died this morning, and I'm off to arrange the funeral."

Brer Wolf trotted away, and Brer Rabbit went round to Brer Fox's house to see what he could see. He peeped in, and there was Brer Fox looking just as if he was dead. But Brer Rabbit was always too wide-awake to be easily deceived, and he says out loud, as if talking to himself:

"Poor old Brer Fox! I hope he isn't dead; but I expect he is. I'd better sit here till the neighbours come round. But I wonder if he's really dead," says Brer Rabbit in a kind of doubtful way. "Doesn't look like it," says he. "You can always tell when a fox is dead by the way he keeps shaking his hind leg," says he.

When Brer Fox heard this he thought he'd show he was really dead, and began shaking his hind leg; and as soon as Brer Rabbit saw it he ran off, and did not stop till he was safely in his own home.

THE GREAT RACE

BRER RABBIT came to reckon himself just about the cunningest creature alive. But he did not get the better of Brer Tortoise. Brer Rabbit said to him:

"You're a mighty old crawler. If we had a race I'd be able to sow barley as I trotted along, and it would be ripe enough to cut by the time you came by."

"Not if you ran on land and I swam in water," says Brer Tortoise.

Brer Rabbit knew Brer Tortoise was as slow a goer in water as he was on land, and he agreed to race him. They measured five miles along a river-path, and put up a post at every mile.

Now, Brer Tortoise had a wife and four children, and you couldn't tell one from another, they were so much alike.

Early in the morning Brer Tortoise put his wife by the starting-post, a son at each of the first four mile-posts, and he crouched down at the winning-post.

By and by Brer Rabbit arrived, and, seeing Mrs. Tortoise in the water, he cried: "Ready? Go!"

And Mrs. Tortoise did go. She went home. At the first mile-post Brer Rabbit saw the young Tortoise.

"Golly!" says Brer Rabbit. "Old Brer Tortoise swims pretty fast."

When he found the Tortoise at the second post, and then at the third and fourth, he began to feel very faint.

"I must get up more speed," says he. He put his ears back, and did the last mile like a flash of lightning. As he came puffing up toward the winning-post out popped old Brer Tortoise from behind it.

"I thought you weren't coming, Brer Rabbit," says Brer Tortoise. "Been having a rest on the way, have you?" says he, laughing.

Poor Brer Rabbit limped off home, humble and cast down for once in his life.

BRER RABBIT AND MR. BEAR

BRER Fox used to grow peas in his garden, and Brer Rabbit used to creep through a hole in the hedge and steal the peas. So Brer Fox made a mighty cunning trap. A young tree was growing just above the hole. Brer Fox bent this down and tied a rope to the top of it. Then he made a loop-knot at the end of the rope, and fixed this over the hole by means of a stick.

The next morning Brer Rabbit popped through the hole, and knocked the stick away. The loop-knot caught him by the hind legs, the tree flew up, and there was Brer Rabbit dangling high up in the air. By and by Mr. Bear came along.

"What ever are you doing up there?" says Mr. Bear.

"Making a dollar a minute—a dollar a minute!" says old Brer Rabbit.

"How?" says Mr. Bear, very interested.

"A dollar a minute!" says Brer Rabbit. "That is what Brer Fox is paying me to hang up here and keep the crows away from his peas," says he. "But I've plenty of work of my own to do, and you can have this job if you like."

Mr. Bear said that he'd like the job, and Brer Rabbit showed him how to bend down the tree; and it wasn't long before Mr. Bear was swinging up in Brer Rabbit's place. Soon afterwards out comes Brer Fox with a great big stick.

"So it's you, Mr. Bear, that comes stealing my peas, is it?" says Brer Fox. "You old thief, I'll teach you to break into my garden!" says he.

And he gave poor Mr. Bear the thrashing that Brer Rabbit ought to have had.

MR. HORSE AND BRER FOX

ONE morning, after Brer Rabbit had been playing his pranks, Brer Fox set out in search of him.

"Blessed if I don't pay that little varmint back," says Brer Fox.

But Brer Rabbit guessed what Brer Fox was about, and Brer Rabbit had also got up early that morning. He saw a great big horse lying down in a meadow, stiff as a poker, and he watched that horse. By and by he saw the tail move, and so he knew the horse was not dead, but only asleep. Brer Rabbit stepped out into the road, and there he saw Brer Fox.

"Come on, Brer Fox," he says, "and let bygones be bygones. Here's enough

fresh meat lying in the field to last you right through summer."

And he took and showed him the horse.

"Now just you fasten Mr. Horse down so that he can't get away," says Brer Rabbit, "and he's yours."

"But how am I going to do it?" says Brer Fox.

"Well," says Brer Rabbit, "if I was a great big creature like you, I'd get the better of Mr. Horse in no time. I'd just tie myself to his tail, and when he tried to get up—kerblinkety!—I'd hold him down as easily as anything."

Brer Fox wasn't altogether taken with the idea, but he wanted Brer Rabbit to think he was as big and strong as a horse, so he let himself be tied to Mr. Horse's tail. This roused Mr. Horse, and he jumped up and switched his tail to shake Brer Fox off, and Brer Fox was swung about just like a rag in a gale of wind.

"Hold him down, Brer Fox," says wicked old Brer Rabbit. "You're fixed on him right enough."

But Brer Fox was beginning to wish he wasn't fixed on. For Mr. Horse was

getting very angry. After he had bumped Brer Fox on the ground several times he let out with his hind legs, and sent him head over heels into a bramble-bush.

"Looks to me," says poor Brer Fox, as he limped off home, "as if I shall never get the better of old Brer Rabbit."

HOW CHULAIN CROSSED THE BRIDGE

THERE once lived in Ireland a beautiful and gracious woman called Emer. She was not only good, she had a lovely face and a low, sweet voice; and though half the men in Ireland wanted to marry her she would listen to none of them.

It happened that one day Emer was sitting in her sunny parlour with her maidens, working with gold and silver thread on a great piece of embroidery, and suddenly, above the quiet voices of the women and the singing birds in the trees outside, there arose the thud and clamour of a chariot of war going at a great pace.

Emer sent one of her women to the high tower above her parlour to see who was coming. In a few minutes the girl returned with the news that a great chariot was indeed tearing over the plain, drawn by powerful and swift horses; but because of the way the horses tore up the earth, and the sods and dust they raised, she could not see who sat in the chariot.

So Emer went on sewing with her silver thread till the great chariot stopped at the house and the rider descended. Then she lifted her lovely head and looked at him, and she saw that the man who stood before her was no other than Chulain, the hero of Ireland. At that moment Emer fell deeply in love with him, and she knew that she would either marry Chulain or live her life alone.

Now, Chulain had come a great way in order to ask Emer to marry him, but, unhappily, her father had made other plans for her. Accordingly, he sent Chulain away on a great journey into another country, knowing that the house to which he was sending him was guarded by an enchanted bridge, over which very few men succeeded in passing. In this way he hoped Chulain would meet his death.

Chulain set out on his journey, and Emer was left with her sewing maidens in the sunny parlour.

At first the journey was pleasant and gay, and Chulain went on his way eagerly; but the night came on dark and stormy, and the way lay through a treacherous plain, so that the traveller knew not which way to take. He did not dare to sleep, not knowing the country, and was at a loss as to which was his path. As he stood pondering, sword in hand, a great lion came out of the darkness and advanced toward him.

The beast came on with a fierce and terrifying air, but, to the amazement of the hero, made not the slightest attempt to harm him. Whichever way Chulain turned to go the lion went before him, half turned to him; and after this had been repeated a few times Chulain suddenly realised that the beast was there as his friend to help him in his journey.

He accordingly went straight up to him, and the lion offered his side as if to carry him. Joyfully Chulain sprang on his back, and this strange steed bore him through the savage unknown country in four days and four nights; and when at length he set him down he was in a beautiful shaded valley, where a house stood full of friendly people.

The beast disappeared, and Chulain went into the house and rested awhile. And before he set out again the man of the house gave him some wise advice.

" A great danger awaits you outside the house you are seeking," said he in conclusion. " You must beware of the enchanted bridge."

" What is this enchanted bridge ? " asked Chulain then.

" It is a great danger which has swallowed some of Ireland's greatest heroes," replied the other. " But if you succeed in crossing it you will be acclaimed the champion of the country."

Then Chulain went on still more carefully, wishing that he might face an armed host rather than the unseen dangers which lurked on every hand and the enchantment which lay ahead. But always the thought of Emer was with him.

In this way he climbed a great and dangerous mountain and passed through a perilous forest, and at last, many days later, found himself at the house he sought; and there before him lay the enchanted bridge. It spanned the flowing river like many another bridge, and, as Chulain stood pondering as to how he might cross it, many people came out of the house and across the river by another way. They embraced him, and gave him the welcome of a great hero.

" We have heard of your deeds, Chulain, from the time you killed the smith's hound," said they. " But you have a still greater feat to perform. There lies the enchanted bridge, which has been the death of many, many heroes and kings. Only a great champion can cross it. Beware!"

Then all the men and women of the district waited to see Chulain, who was well beloved, attempt the great feat.

There never was such a bridge as that enchanted bridge. Chulain made one step upon it, and at once it seemed to narrow to the width of an inch, and no mortal man could stand upon it. So Chulain sprang back and tried again. This time the bridge became as slippery as a trout in a stream, and he could obtain no footing whatever.

"Try again, Chulain!" cried the waiting crowd. "Surely thou, of all the men in Ireland, must cross the bridge."

Thus cheered by the cries of the men, the hero tried again to perform this extraordinary feat. But this time the middle of the bridge rose before his face, as high as a ship's mast; and again Chulain was obliged to spring back.

Then Chulain was in despair. He had never before been so defeated. Fifty men had he met at a time single-handed; countless high deeds had he performed; but all the dangers of his life seemed as nothing before this present trial.

At last he was seized by a passionate and transforming anger. He went back a pace to gather strength, and the waiting men held their breath. Then he came on again with a furious rush, and before the bridge had time to rise he had leaped high in the air, clean over it, and landed safely on the other side.

There the shouts for the victor greeted him, and the skies rang with cries of joy because Chulain had crossed the bridge that only great heroes could cross.

Chulain rested awhile with the people in the great house, and performed the mission with which the father of Emer had charged him; and soon after he returned home and won the lovely Emer for his bride.

THE BRAVE APPRENTICE

SOMEWHERE about the year 1680 a small boy sat working at a tailor's bench at Bonchurch, in the Isle of Wight.

His master being out of the way, the boy had dropped his needle and was gazing out to sea, wishing he was anywhere but in that shop. He was a poor orphan, and had been apprenticed to the tailoring trade.

As he looked out to sea a squadron of British warships came in sight round a bend of the coast, and in a moment the boy threw down his work, and, running out of the shop, was soon on the beach, where he jumped into a boat and rowed as hard as he could to the admiral's ship.

Life on our warships was then very hard, and recruits were wanted badly, for men were not anxious to join the Navy; so the apprentice was readily accepted.

It was not long before he saw active service, for on the next morning the British ships fell in with a French squadron and fighting began. The boy did his duty well, and when the fighting had been going on for some time, and there seemed no sign of a definite result, he asked a sailor: "How shall we know when the enemy has given in to us?"

"Oh," replied the man, pointing to the flag flying at the masthead of the French admiral's ship, "as soon as that flag is hauled down the victory will be ours."

"Is that all?" said the boy, and hurried away.

In those days vessels did not fight as they do now, with miles of sea between them and almost out of sight of one another. They ran up side by side, and the crew of each tried to board the other.

The tailor's boy sprang upon the deck of the French admiral's ship, which was alongside his own, and, unnoticed in the excitement, climbed up a rope-ladder and seized the French flag. Wrapping it round his body, he descended with it safely to the deck.

No one had seen his daring act, but presently the British sailors noticed that the French flag was gone, and, supposing the enemy had given in, they rushed the deck of the French ship with such force that the enemy was filled with consternation and dismay. The gunners fled from their guns, and in a moment or two the ship was in the hands of the English. Just as victory was assured the apprentice sprang forward and showed the captured flag to his comrades, who received it with the greatest astonishment.

The news soon spread, and the boy was led with his prize into the presence of the admiral, who promoted him on the spot to the rank of midshipman. He reached almost the highest rank in the British Navy, and became Admiral Hopsonn.

GODWIN THE PEASANT BOY

A THOUSAND years ago in England the woods were thicker and gloomier than they are today, and girls and boys never dreamed of going alone into the forest. One bright evening a young Danish warrior named Ulf was wandering about in the woods near the River Severn, vainly trying to find his way to the Danish camp. There had been a battle between the English and the Danes, who were trying to gain England for themselves, and the Danes had been very badly defeated. So Ulf, in trying to save himself from the English, had run into the

of the trees, fearing that he might have come upon an Englishman. Looking cautiously out from his hiding-place, he beheld a yoke of oxen, driven by one of the fairest young boys he had ever seen. Of course he was an Englishman's son, but as he was unarmed and only a lad the Dane ventured to speak to him.

" Good-morrow," he said, stepping out. " What is thy name ? "

The boy looked at him carefully from head to food, and answered, rather timidly: " My name is Godwin, the son of Wulfnoth. And thou—thou art surely a

"THOU ART FOOLISH," SAID GODWIN, "TO EXPECT HELP FROM ONE OF THINE ENEMIES"

woods, and now the night was drawing on and he was very much alarmed. But the more he wandered about the more muddled he became, and he kept going backward and forward without getting any nearer to the edge of the forest.

On the battlefield Ulf's courage never flinched; but as the wind sighed in the trees, and he heard the sound of an unfamiliar voice in the distance and realised that he was far away from his friends, he really did grow afraid.

Suddenly, and quite by chance, he wandered into an open portion of the woods, and crouched down behind one

Dane ? " In those days everyone, even the youngest child, knew a Danish soldier.

" Yes, my lad," said the soldier, " and I have lost my way. Wilt thou not show me how to get back to my camp ? Surely thou knowest the way to the River Severn."

" Yes, that I do most surely," answered the boy, " but not to tell a Dane."

" I beg thee to help me," said the young soldier.

" Thou art foolish," replied the boy, to expect help from one of thine enemies."

" Only leave thy cattle here a while and show me the way, and I will reward thee freely. I have a gold piece in camp I could give thee."

"No, I will not," persisted the boy. "The way is not long, and as for leading thee I would be willing enough, for we are but poor peasants and have fared very ill under the English nobles; but to lead a Dane after yesterday's victory would be dangerous. The peasants along the way are armed, and should they see us they would show no mercy either to thee or to thy guide."

While the boy was talking the soldier had taken from his finger a heavy gold ring which had more gold in it than the boy had ever hoped to possess in his life. This he held out to Godwin.

"Here," said the Dane, "this is for thee if thou wilt lead me. I am very hungry, and if I stay here who knows what may become of me ? The wolves, if they found me, would devour me, and the English would slay me should I fall into their hands; and if neither gets me I shall surely starve to death. Hast thou no pity, my boy ? Here—the ring will be thine."

For a minute the boy looked at the soldier, and finally he said : "I will take nothing from thee, but I will try to lead thee safely to thy camp. But first thou must stop at my father's cottage and eat."

Accordingly, the boy, driving his oxen before him, led the young soldier to the little hut that was his home. There, under the low, damp ceiling in the only room that the hut possessed, the tired warrior passed the day in much-needed rest. Never before had he eaten anything so gladly as the simple fare the peasant set before him, for after the battle and his wanderings he was almost exhausted.

That night, after dark, the boy Godwin started out to lead his soldier friend to the Danish camp, for had they attempted the journey during the day they might had been captured by the English.

As they were leaving the little hut Wulfnoth took the soldier's hand, and said : "Know that it is my only son who trusts himself to thy honour. For my own part I fight neither with English nor with Danes. My only wish is that there might be an end of fighting, and that we poor peasants might be allowed to tend our little crops in quiet and peace. I am letting my son go with thee because thou hast need of him, and there is no chance

for him among the poor peasants of this oppressed land. Having served as the guide of a Dane, there will be no safety for him hereafter among his countrymen. My only request is that thou shouldst present him to thy great king, and that he may receive him into his service. This is all the reward I ask for him."

Ulf promised to do as the father requested, and he and the boy started for the Danish camp. Of course Godwin was sorry to leave his father, but the idea of being admitted into the service of the King of Denmark, and of seeing something of the great world of which he had heard, filled him with indescribable delight.

After several hours' journeying on foot they reached the River Severn and the camp of the Danes. Once inside the camp the warrior Ulf showed Godwin into his own tent, where everything was so splendid that he at once realised that Ulf was a person of great rank. There were two raised seats at the end of the tent, and on the sides were hangings of rich colour.

"Here, my boy," said Ulf to Godwin, who stood looking about him in astonishment. "It is my pleasure that thou shouldst sit beside me. Though thou art a peasant born, thy good deed hath made thee worthy of sitting in the seats of the Danish nobles."

Then, that very night, Ulf led him into the king's tent, which was so much bigger and more gorgeous than that of Ulf that Godwin thought at first he was having a wonderful dream. It was the famous King Canute who welcomed him, and he greeted him warmly.

"Thou art the deliverer of one of my bravest chiefs," said Canute, "and in return for what thou hast done thou, also, shalt become a great chief."

So the little peasant boy worked his way up in the Danish army, and after Denmark had conquered England he was made governor of a province in England, and you may be sure that he did his best to rule the peasants under him better than his father had been ruled.

In every way he was treated like a noble, and it is said he married a very beautiful lady, the sister of Earl Ulf, and had a daughter whom he named Editha. And when this daughter was grown up she married the good King Edward the Confessor, who ruled all England.

LEGENDS OF THE STARS

In the early ages shepherds tending their sheep and goats, huntsmen pursuing the hare, the bear, the wolf, and the lion, sailors on the wide sea meeting whales and sea monsters or seeking fish, fancied that they could make out pictures in the groups of stars. They invented stories about them and about wonderful beings, gods and goddesses, who were more than human, living up there in the sky. Here are a few of the legends dealing with the star-pictures beginning on page 2991.

AN INDIAN LEGEND

ACCORDING to an Indian legend from California, the Sun, Moon, and stars are one big family. The Sun is the great chief and ruler of the heavens, the Moon is his wife, and the stars are his children, whom he has to eat, when he can catch them, to keep himself alive. But when he is up in the morning they flee quickly out of his sight, and dare not appear again until he goes into his hole in the west.

He crawls along this hole till he comes to his narrow bed in the middle of the Earth. This is so small that it does not give him room to turn round, so when he wakes up next day he has to creep out to the east. Then his wife, the Moon, takes her rest.

Every month she grieves when he eats up some of the stars, and puts black over her gentle face to show her sorrow. This gradually wears off, till by the end of the month her face is bright again. The stars are happy with their mother, the Moon, and sing and dance as she moves among them. After a time other star children disappear, and she has once more to put on mourning; but she always cheers up again in due course.

HERCULES WITH HIS CLUB

THE celebrated hero Hercules, son of Jupiter, was, of course, bound to be enthroned among the gods in the skies, so the Greeks gave him a place of honour, and pictured him in a kneeling position, with his club in his right hand, an apple-branch in his left in memory of the apples of the Hesperides, and with a lyre near his feet.

The legend is that Hercules was fighting one day with stones, but had used them all up. Then Jupiter, seeing the danger of his son, rained down a shower of round stones. These Hercules bent down to pick up and throw at his enemies, and he thus was able to overcome them. This is why he is shown kneeling.

Many are the stories of his prowess and marvellous physical strength, but the most wonderful were his twelve labours, on the performance of which the Delphic oracle promised him immortality. These included slaying the Nemean lion, the Hydra, or water-snake, and the monster birds; capturing a stag with hoofs of brass and antlers of gold, the boar of Erymanthus, the mad Cretan bull, the horses of Diomedes, Geryon's oxen, and Cerberus, the dog of hell; securing Hippolyte's girdle; and fetching the golden apples from the Garden of the Hesperides in Africa.

By the wish of Hercules his body was burned on a pyre, and his spirit passed away in a cloud to Olympus, the home of the gods, where he married the goddess Hebe and became immortal.

A FAMILY GROUP

THERE are four constellations in the sky making quite a family group. Cassiopeia, the mother; Cepheus, the father; Andromeda, the daughter; and Perseus, the son-in-law, with, a little farther off, Pegasus, his winged horse. Cassiopeia foolishly declared herself to be more beautiful than the Nereides, and the angry nymphs, in revenge, persuaded Neptune to send a sea monster to trouble Ethiopia, where Cassiopeia lived, for she had married King Cepheus of that country. The story of Andromeda's exposure to the monster, and her rescue by Perseus, is told on page 4967 of this book.

Cassiopeia was pictured by the ancients in a southern constellation of thirteen stars, seated on her throne and holding a palm leaf in her hand. Cepheus is near her.

The constellation of Cassiopeia can be recognised very easily in the night sky; it takes the form of the letter M, or, as some see it, a W.

THE GREAT DOG

NEAR Orion, between the Hare and the Milky Way, as far south as we in the Northern Hemisphere can see, lies the Great Dog of Orion, containing one very brilliant star called Sirius. It used to be regarded as a warning by the Egyptians, just as a good watch-dog warns a house of coming danger. The dog in the sky could not bark, but its bright light let the Egyptians know of any harmful event about to happen.

When they saw the star in the early morning they knew the Nile would soon overflow. So one name they gave it was the Nile star. Of course they knew nothing of the real sources of the Nile, because no one had found them out in those days.

Sometimes they pictured Sirius as a man with a dog's head, a stew-pot in his arms, a feather under one arm, winged feet, and leading a duck and a tortoise.

The Greeks and Romans associated the Dog star with the heat of summer, and said that it burned up the fields and killed the bees. We still talk of the dog days in the hottest season.

THE PLEIADES

THESE seven stars were associated with seven beautiful sisters, daughters of Atlas, named Electra, Maia, Alcyone, Taygeta, Celaeno, Merope, and Sterope. They all married gods except Merope, whose light is less bright because she was wedded to a mortal, Sisyphus, King of Corinth. Electra's light also diminished through grief after the fall of Troy, which her son Dardanus had founded.

The word Pleiades comes from a Greek word meaning " to sail," and the constellation is thus named because it shines well in spring, at a good time for sailors to start on a voyage. Because, too, of their association with Ver, the spring, these stars are also called the Vergiliae. From the earliest times festivals and seasons were connected with the rising of the Pleiades, which took place in May.

The story runs that in Boeotia the giant Orion went in pursuit of the seven sisters, but they prayed to be saved from him, and were changed into doves. Now they are ever at a safe distance from him in the skies, at the back of the Bull and behind its protecting horns.

ORION, THE BELTED GIANT

ORION was a giant who wanted to marry Hero, or Merope, daughter of Oenopion, King of Chios; but this king, who took a dislike to the suitor because of his great height, thinking to rid himself of a troublesome person, consented to the marriage only on condition that Orion freed the island of Chios from the beasts that raged there. This he did, but King Oeno-

pion failed to keep his promise, and had him blinded. Then Orion was directed by a blacksmith, whom he carried on his back, to the best spot for facing the rising Sun, and through gazing at its brightness Orion recovered his sight.

According to one legend, Diana, through jealousy, slew him with her arrows; according to another, his death was due to the bite of a scorpion, which rose from the ground to punish him for boasting of his prowess as a hunter. He was carried to the heavens, and there shines as a constellation of brilliant stars, with a glittering belt round his body and his dog Sirius near him. He is found near the feet of the Bull, and is sometimes shown with a club or a sword in his hand and bearing a shield.

One of the stories about him is that he piled up a bank on the coast of Sicily to keep out the sea; another says that he was a worker in iron, and made an underground palace for Vulcan, the god of fire.

THE GREAT BEAR

LOOKING at this group of stars, so easily observed, for they never set in the Northern Hemisphere, people fancied they saw different objects represented by them. So the Greeks said: " It is a chariot; " the ancient Gauls called it Arthur's Chariot; the Americans, The Dipper; the English, Charles's Wain, or The Great Bear. There are two bears really, a Great Bear, or Ursa Major, and a Little Bear, or Ursa Minor. This is the legend of how they came to be there.

Jupiter and Callisto had a son named Arcas. Juno, who was jealous of Callisto, changed her into a bear, and her son, by mischance, was on the point of killing her, whereupon Jupiter, recognising the danger she would run from huntsmen, changed her into a constellation.

Arcas's kingdom was Arcadia, a happy land where people were taught by their king to till the ground and spin wool. One day while hunting he met a beautiful wood nymph in trouble because the tree over which she watched was in danger from a river in flood. Arcas saved the tree by turning aside the current; then he married the nymph, and when he died left his kingdom to his three sons. Jupiter at his death turned him into a bear like his mother, so that he has since kept her company as a constellation.

Nature's Wonderful Living Family in Earth and Air and Sea

The water spider takes a bubble of air to its home in a pool

LITTLE-MANY-LEGS

In the old days when those heroes of romance and chivalry of whom we read in history were still living, a doughty warrior, who had been on Crusade, had slain lions and Saracens, and braved every peril which he could understand, would have closed this volume of the Children's Encyclopedia with a bang and have crept trembling to bed.

For our present chat is about scorpions and spiders and some other things of ill-fame even in our own day, but of diabolical reputation in former times. Our forefathers, down to Shakespeare's time and far later, believed in dragons and fire-breathing basilisks, and thought that as scorpions ate venomous things to increase the power of their own venom, so these fabulous creatures lunched on scorpions to add to the intensity of their own evil poisons.

The Old Testament teems with references to scorpions, so our writers drew on their imagination for material with which to deck the creatures with terrifying attributes; scorpions which stung young girls to death on sight, which caused the lingering death of women, which ate men, which had feathers and flew afar to their mischief; scorpions which had such a hatred towards men that, screened off from access to his bed, they would mount

to his ceiling and hang, one from another, five or six deep, merely for the evil delight of inflicting a mortal wound.

The truth is that scorpions and spiders and their allies, while not exactly creatures to take to one's heart, are, for the most part, the victims of a libel. The one stings, the other bites, and both have an aching poison which may make a sensitive and nervous victim ill, or even kill in an exceptional case. But a shock, even a suggestion, may have that result in a rare instance, where neither scorpion nor spider is within a hundred miles.

Scorpions have their unpleasant aspect, undoubtedly, but it is wrong and foolish to overstate the case against them. They, like the spiders, are indispensable to us as snappers-up of countless multitudes of insects competing for food necessary to mankind.

If the order were nearly as fatal to human fortunes as these old beliefs represented, there ought to be no human family in existence, for, like the king crabs, their sea kindred, which we have already discussed, they are almost as old as the hills. They lived in the seas, breathing oxygen by means of gills; they came ashore and changed their gills into lungs such as mammals never had.

PREHISTORIC LIFE · MAMMALS · BIRDS · REPTILES · FISHES · INSECTS

The arrangement of these organs is suggested by their name—lung-books. They communicate with the atmosphere through narrow openings, and are composed of a number of thin projections, like the leaves of a book. The blood circulates through these, comes in contact with the air, and so is purified. By that strange improvement on the water-breathing gills the scorpion and its allies are able to live in the atmosphere as we are.

Like all the arachnids, to which they belong, scorpions have no neck. The head is really part of the thorax. Two pairs of appendages spring from the head—a small pincer on each side of the mouth, called the chelicera, and, behind these, a formidable pair of pincer claws, which serve to grasp prey and then act as jaws to tear and rend it in readiness for the mouth, which sucks the juices from the mangled fragments of a victim. Four pairs of clawed legs arise from the hinder part of the chest. Insects have only three such pairs.

A QUEER OLD BELIEF ABOUT THE DAINTY FORGET-ME-NOT

Whenever we look on the dainty forget-me-not, let us recall its old-time name in England—scorpion grass. If we used that, our amusing old counsellors told us, we should have no need to fear the bite of a scorpion. And truly they were right. We had no reason to fear scorpions in England, even if we did not call scorpion grass to our aid, for we never had scorpions in this country. They are fairly widely scattered about the Earth, and abound in southern Europe, but nowhere in a climate so irregularly warmed by the Sun as ours.

Temperature, rather than light, is the main requisite, for, though scorpions have three or four pairs of eyes, they see but dimly, and come out to hunt only at dusk. Touch and smell are their guiding instincts, and both faculties reside, apparently, in the great pincer-like claws which we call the pedipalps.

Nothing more than two or three inches away is visible to a scorpion, and experiment has shown that the creature will run partly over a cockroach without discovering it till its sensitive feelers touch it, when it will draw back and eat the unregarded booty.

The great lobster-like claws are carried in front of the head. They are not used for walking, nor do they have any share in the digging of the sandy home, for this is the work of the legs, with the tail to sweep away the accumulated débris.

The pedipalps, then, sense and grip objects. If the prey is small, the claws do the whole business of slaughter. A larger victim is, however, firmly grasped and held, while the tail is curved over the back and the sting brought down and introduced. After that there is no resistance; the little monster eats a paralysed meal.

THE TERRIBLE LITTLE CREATURE WHICH RUNS AWAY FROM LIGHT

Generally scorpions avoid human beings, and they run anywhere for seclusion from light. They delight to creep into beds, boots, and clothes, so that when we get into a bed, or put on our garments in the East, we trespass in the place which the scorpion has chosen as a sanctuary.

Then, if we are not frightened off by the threat of his angry pincers, he applies his poison-oozing sting, causing us violent pain and sickness. There are nervous weaklings who die at the bite of an adder, or a big spider. The same type of temperament may collapse under the shock of a scorpion bite, hence the melancholy indictment of which the poor scorpion can never prove himself guiltless.

The natural prey of the scorpion consists of beetles, crickets, spiders, many harmful insects, and, from time to time, small frogs and even tiny mice. Agile, elusive creatures all these, it will be noticed, for an assailant which does not readily detect prey at a distance. True, but the creatures caught by the scorpion are not all keener of sight than their captor. If fortune fails to smile, the scorpion must grin and bear it. He fasts habitually for five or six months of the winter season, though alive and alert as the wintering crayfish.

THE OLD NATURALIST WHO SPENT MONTHS IN WATCHING THE SCORPION

One item of diet has to be added. It is scorpion! The courting season always ends in that horrid tragedy. Before the wedding the males woo most ardently. The old French naturalist, Henri Fabre, devoted months to watching them, and we owe our knowledge in the main to his writings. The little male seizes a buxom female, greatly his superior in size and power. With upraised tails they exchange salutations; the tails entwined, and with

A LITTLE COMPANY OF SPIDERS

EUROPEAN TARANTULA

GARDEN SPIDER

WOLF SPIDER

A BIRD-EATING SPIDER IN SEARCH OF PREY

HOUSE SPIDER

RED SPIDER

A SOUTH AMERICAN TRAP-DOOR SPIDER

THE HOME OF THE
HOUSE SPIDER

COMMON HARVEST
SPIDER

THE NEST OF A SOUTH AFRICAN
TRAP-DOOR SPIDER

The pictures on these pages are by Mrs. M. H. Crawford, Messrs. Berridge, Collins, Johnson, Ward, and others

their hideous faces brought in contact, they exchange what a scorpion poet might dignify with the name of a kiss.

Then off they prance, the male grasping the female's claws, as a big man takes the tiny hand of a woman in his. He walks backwards, leading or gently dragging his mate after him. They may promenade for hours, even for days, in this way, till finally he induces her to approach a burrow which he has made.

THE CANNIBAL BRIDE WHO DINES ON HER BRIDEGROOM

With shrinking coyness she may decline or affect to decline the proffered hospitality, and he may insist, and, using his feet, set against the side of the home as levers, drag her in ; or he may turn testy and let her go. It is all very exciting and hazardous.

But the issue is never in doubt. Once the bashful lady accepts the home and fortune presented by the male, the end is in sight. She enters, settles down, and dines—on her bridegroom. But he is not stung to death—merely munched. Scorpion poison is not generally harmful to scorpion, although a big dose can be lethal. And it is possible that in conditions of excitement when scorpions wave their tails violently and accidentally sting themselves, the discharge of venom may be increased.

Eight inches is the greatest length to which scorpions are known to attain, three inches being the average of the European adult of the group, so the tales of their eating men and other victims of bulk are ridiculous. Even so, they have sufficient terrors for nervous folk who find them sharing their socks or pyjamas.

THE WONDERFUL SILK OF THE WORLD'S FIRST SPINNERS AND WEAVERS

What has the spider world to show in comparison with the petty villainies of the scorpions? Spiders have their poison, though not a sting; they are as voracious, in their way, as the scorpions in theirs, but though they come boldly into our daily lives, they do not inspire the fear among people in general which undying tradition has created in connection with their stinging cousins.

Really we ought to approach the spiders with more of marvelling than of repulsion. They were the world's first aeronauts, first builders, first aerial engineers, first spinners and weavers. How they origin-

ally succeeded in converting food into a natural glue, which, on entering the air, instantly becomes silk, we shall never be able to ascertain. Their silk glands are soft, and perish when the spiders die, so there is nothing in the fossil world to reveal how this wondrous gift first dawned in a creature new from the sea.

But there it is. A man of the wilds, faced by a wide, steep chasm, is defeated unless he can climb like a goat; and even goats cannot scale precipices. A spider is our master in the matter. He cocks up his spinnerets and squeezes out a number of tiny jets of material looking to the eye like a dark-coloured gum from a mistletoe berry. The jets unite as they emerge into one splendid strand of silk, stronger, in proportion to size and weight, than the finest steel ever compounded by the metallurgical wizards of Sheffield.

The strand grows and grows under the effort of the spider, floats off into the air, has its gummy end caught on a distant projection, and across this tightrope, this natural bridge, spun from its own substance, the spider proceeds in triumph to the conquest of a new world.

THE AGE-OLD MYSTERY OF THE BABY SPIDER'S LONG FAST

That is the magic of the adult; the baby spider has a feat at command not less astonishing. In some species the mother attends to her eggs and to her babies when they are born, and carries the little things about with her. They ride on her back, a vestment of life, guarded, transported, snugly housed, but fed—never! They reside on her body, fasting week after week for seven or eight months, without one particle of food, or one drop of moisture.

How do they sustain life, strength, and growth under such extraordinary hardship? The active sport and play in which they seem to indulge consume energy; their growth demands more, yet they take in no fuel to replenish their engines of life. But the time comes when their cycle of baby life is run. Their call comes to quit the mother. She lets them go without regret, as a hen beats away the chickens which she has cherished for a month or more. She would eat them if they tarried longer.

Their guardian angel now becomes as a consuming dragon to the little spiders, and they fly from her ; not actually, but in such a manner as to suggest the parallel. They climb to the nearest height, to the top of hedge or tree or wall; they spin out their little webs as the chasm-crosser spins his. The silk floats out fair and far from the unfed little bodies, and as the wind catches and hauls it into the air, the spiders securely attached to it, rise with it, soar, and float away, aviators without engines.

They cover our lawns and fields with their gossamer when they descend to Earth, the little webs gemmed with dew and gleaming like molten silver in the morning sunlight.

THE SPIDER-LIKE CREATURES LIVING IN THE OCEAN DEPTHS

That all spiders spin and all have poison is a safe rule, yet there are spider-like creatures in the deep seas, and in the shallow waters round British coasts, which, if they are poisonous, certainly do not spin. Silk web would be of no use in such turbulent wastes, it would seem. But are they spiders? The class which we are now considering are technically known as the Pycnogonida, and are not true spiders; they possess one pair of limbs in excess of the number proper to spiders. The extra pair is devoted, in the male, to the carrying of the eggs laid by the female.

This class ranges from our own coasts, through all seas and all depths, and various species are as variously coloured; some are scarlet; some match the corals; some are green in accordance with seaweeds; some transparent; some that live in the abysses are of a deep purplish red. Some have the gift of swimming, others merely crawl, down in the depths, where the weight of water is such as to crush man-made inventions flat, and to reduce vessels of glass to finest powder.

THE LITTLE SILKEN DOOR WHICH KEEPS THE SEA AT BAY

One sea spider, however, does spin. This is a member of the family of spiders which cover our country hedges with web; it is called Agalena labyrinthica. The sea species is the Agalena desis, a master builder of the ocean, which makes its home in crevices of rocks and coral reefs. At low tide it nips out into the open to feast on small crustacea, and, as some say, tiny fish. With the return of the tide it retreats to its fastness and walls itself up with silk, barricades out the sea with a doorway of massed gossamer. It can defy the sea whose advances mocked Canute, and when the

ocean ebbs afresh, it lowers its flimsy portcullis, and browses again in its little jungle on the rocks.

Another water spider may be searched out in any British pool. This one is the creator of the diving bell, whose like, in steel and iron, we used to employ for our submarine engineering. But air and silk are the only materials here. Anchoring itself by a strand of silk to a water plant, the spider marches down the stem, and spins a tent of silk beneath the surface.

Then it climbs up, turns the hinder end of its bristly little body into the air, collects a bubble of the atmosphere in it, dives with the bubble imprisoned between the bristles and its legs, and releases the life-giving supply in its tent. The little home swells, there is an atmosphere within it, and there the spider sleeps and lays her eggs, rears her babies, and lives the life of an enchanted princess in a fairy cave.

THE SPLENDID RAFT OF LEAVES BUILT BY A WATER SPIDER

Still keeping to the water, there is the famous raft spider, said to be rare in England, though common enough according to the writer's experience. It weaves a silken chain to bind together little leaves into a raft. On this it sails, to plunge every now and then into the water, or rather to walk on it. Water has a film on its surface; let those who doubt it watch a raft spider running over it, secure as a man on skis crossing a snowfield.

Let us turn again, however, to the spinners proper, and pause for a spell of delight before our great garden spider, whose orb web is not to be eclipsed by any wonder of the tropical spiders.

It is made in about an hour, but what an unrivalled hour of dazzling creative instinct it is! At the beginning of it the spider is a harmless little vagabond; at the end of it she has an estate hung up in the air, a home, a fortress, a snare for the unwary, all fabricated from her own small body. Of course she may not rush straight through her task, but may dawdle and dally and make it last over two or three occasions, but give her one open space, with suitable anchorage, and she can achieve a feat of natural magic.

The first requisite is to fix the beams of her chamber. She may either allow a strand to be blown so that its end shall catch a convenient point and form a line, or she may fix an end herself, then drop or crawl down, trailing out silk behind her, till she has reached the point she desires. Here she makes a little dab with the hinder end of the body, and so fixes the thread to where she would have it.

She makes, first, an upper and a lower beam in this way, and then doubly connects her parallels, and the scaffold of the circular net is there, a rough square.

THE LINES OF WEB WHICH ACT LIKE THE SPOKES OF A WHEEL

Next she has to form the radial lines which, all passing through the centre, are like the spokes of a wheel. She builds up the hub as she goes, for we can see her continually adding and strengthening there, putting in new silk and eating up the earlier deposit, or adding fresh material to that already in position.

As she builds she makes her structure her pathway. Having spun one thread, she walks along it to connect the next, and fastens each to the outer beams with a dab of silk. There may be 18, 20, or more of these, but they are all quite smooth, not sticky. These form the spiral, the great central section of the snare. The building of this is a splendid example of speed, method, and prudent care. She walks round and round the skeleton web, across the threads, producing web as she goes, and at each spoke, before attaching the new strand, she gives it a tug with a claw.

The little line stretches, and when it is at its extreme tension, she applies it to the spoke, and seems to seal it there with a touch of the spinnerets. Then she is off to the next spoke. The first two or three turns round the growing web simply furnish extra support for the structure, and they, too, are free from stickiness. Now, however, she pours out web which is decidedly sticky.

The substance is pulled out from the spinnerets, and it seems as though the exact amount necessary to reach from one spoke to the next is withdrawn each time, for there is always the same little pull for tightening, always an exact join when she applies the line to a spoke.

THE THOUSANDS OF GUMMY GLOBULES THAT COVER THE WEB OF A SPIDER

So she goes on, working from the circumference towards the centre, round and round, every spoke linked up till the web is complete. with hundreds of joinings. Yet it is all *one*, like so much rubber fabric

united when fluid. The work of this great hour is ended.

But, you will say, she still has to dot the web with those thousands and tens of thousands of gummy globules. No; she has really finished, and the globules are already symmetrically forming, without special application on her part.

The silk for the snare part of the web issues as a sticky stream. Although it apparently solidifies into silk, the surface does not dry, but retains a fluid adhesiveness. With the pull of the web this fluid ceases to be a uniform unbroken coating; it parts, as it were, running into little beads close together, but regularly grouped.

We see, then, that the spider produces different solutions—one for the framework which is not sticky, and one which is like a living gum, fitted to grip and hold any insect which may brush against it. She knows she has these different reservoirs of precious material, and she knows instinctively on which to draw.

The web is one of the most wonderful things in Nature. The spider works by instinct, but how marvellously she adapts her home to varying conditions, throwing out buttresses here to withstand an unexpected strain; adding a stout guy-rope there to pull the web out of the way of a descending drip of water; spinning a backstay where the sway of a shrub threatens to break down the fabric.

HOW THE GARDEN SPIDER MENDS HER BROKEN WEB

And how delightful it is to watch her when the wind has cast heavy plunging leaves into the web. She rushes to the breach, cuts the damaged web with her jaws, works frenziedly till the leaf is free, then drops it to the ground, and stitches up the rent like a little tailor.

To see a garden spider sprawling at her ease when her work is finished is to be present at one of the most satisfying things in natural life. Out of his own consciousness a poet or a composer weaves a symphony of words or music; out of her own body she has woven a symphony of silk.

Into it fly all manner of insects, midges by the score, flies, bluebottles, moths. At the least touch, she is alert. She does not see well. She picks up a strand in one of her talons and pulls on it. Vibrations travel along her line, and she races up or down the web as though wearing seven-league boots.

A WONDERFUL HOME MADE OF SILK

THE HOME OF THE GARDEN SPIDER

THE HEART OF THE SPIDER'S SILKEN WEB

If the victim be a fly, she gives it a fatal bite in the neck. She may then settle down to suck it dry, or if she is busy or sated, she spins a web all over it, and hangs it there, like a tiny ham on a farm ceiling, waiting till she has appetite.

In the case of a wasp or other stinging creature, she is wary in the extreme. She can kill the wasp, if she takes it at a disadvantage, but the wasp can kill her in fair fight. So she stands afar off and casts out her web like a little man with a tiny lasso. She nooses the wasp from a distance, runs round and round till she has bound it, head and limbs, body and sting. Then she creeps up, and it is she who makes the fatal wound.

Six spinnerets, fed from about 600 glands, equip the garden spider for her productive tasks, and one spider has been known to put forth a hundred yards of silk without a pause. There are many other great web spinners scattered about the Earth. The common house spider is no mean artist, much as tidy housekeepers detest it.

THE LITTLE PARLOUR INTO WHICH THE SPIDER INVITED THE FLY

There is a true parlour behind the sheet web, into which the fly was invited to walk, a far cleverer contrivance than ever fly has fashioned. It has a way in and another way out, to afford escape from danger, and, to crown all, it is weighted with grains of sand or other heavy particles to give it stability. The web of the house spider is a masterly work, but we must devote our space to the feats of the trap-door spiders.

These are numerous in species and methods. Some make their traps in trees, the majority in the ground. Here is a marvel of instinctive ingenuity. The spider digs a hole in the ground, to a depth of some inches, and lines the interior with silk. Then it covers the opening with a lid of silk, but bites this through all the way round, except at one spot. There the silk is left undisturbed and so forms a true hinge to the door.

Next the spider comes out and, with infinite industry, collects particles of earth and distributes these over the silken flap, then binds them in place with another layer of silk, adding more layers of earth and silk alternately until, in the builder's mind, safety is secured. After that the little master craftsman decorates the whole with moss and other tiny pieces of vegetation till it exactly matches its surroundings. When besieged in this little fortress by an enemy the spider clings to the under side of the door with its legs and pulls with all its strength to resist the attempt to open the fragile portal.

THE HAIRY GIANT AND THE BIRDS IT CATCHES IN ITS SNARE

These trap-door spiders belong to the same class as the dreaded bird-eating spiders. They are the giants of the order, huge, hairy brutes, six or seven inches across the legs.

They live in trees or in earth-burrows, and weave webs as thick as canvas. In these they catch birds and tiny mammals such as mice. Their bite is excessively poisonous, and when they have made the fatal bite, they suck the blood of bird or beast as our garden spider sucks the blood of a blue-bottle. They are altogether horrible, dangerous in their bite, and mischievous with their brittle hair, which causes intense irritation.

Another poisonous spider is the Tarantula, so named after a spider which, first found near Taranto in Italy, was supposed to produce dancing mania in its human victim. Tarantism was an age-long malady of the Middle Ages. In all likelihood it was an epidemic of emotional hysteria, a nervous affection of which we possibly see a variant in the so-called shell shock following our own World Wars. At any rate, people afflicted believed themselves to have been bitten by the Tarantula spider.

They danced with frenzy until they fell exhausted. Music was supposed to be a relief to their wrought-up feelings, so various melodies sprang into existence for the benefit of sufferers. From them we get the Tarantella of modern music.

THE DEADLY EFFECT OF THE BITE OF THE TARANTULA

How deadly the bite of the spider was we do not know, but it is certain that so-called Tarantula spiders in South America have bitten people and that people have died, but whether from fright, whether from auto-suggestion, or actually from the spiders' poison, cannot be determined. Fabre found that bees and wasps die at once from the bite, that a sparrow survives but three days, and that a healthy mole expires 36 hours after being bitten.

Our common wolf-spiders are of the

Tarantula group. These, though they trail a strand of web after them and make silken retreats in the earth, are active hunters in the open, and stalk their prey like cats, finally leaping on them with unerring accuracy. There are some 4000 species of these spiders, and none is better known than the active jumping species common to sunny walls and sandy banks in England. All these spiders carry their cocoons of eggs about with them.

Another interesting member is the field spider, which makes a small tubular nest in the crevices of a wall, or in the soil, and

in the open, is really a mite, but not to be confounded with the little red-haired mite whose six-legged larvae, called harvest bugs, attack our flesh and cause us intolerable itching and discomfort.

Mites are enormously numerous in numbers and species. Many species do not measure more than a hundredth of an inch, yet they are extremely harmful to ourselves, our animals, birds, and vegetation. They all bore and suck juice, whether it be sap or blood. They infest all kinds of life. They cause horrible diseases in man and animals, mange in dogs and horses; the

COMMON MILLIPEDE

A SCORPION OF CENTRAL AFRICA

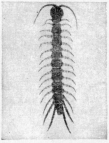
ENGLISH CENTIPEDE

A WEST INDIAN CENTIPEDE

DOMESTIC MITE

BULB MITES

BRITISH FALSE SCORPION

CURRANT BUD MITES

BROWN TICK

runs a labyrinth of strands to surrounding objects, to catch unwary passers-by, as we snare wild animals in a corral. More grotesque than any of these are the crab spiders, small but interesting because by their sidelong gait they imitate crabs.

There are a few so-called spiders which are not true spiders at all. There is, for instance, the harvestman—a good friend to us as a devourer of insects, but more nearly related to mites and ticks than to the spider. The so-called red spider, which bleeds strawberry leaves in the conservatory and many precious cultivated crops

larger ticks ruin our blackcurrant crops by causing "big bud," entering the young bud and causing it to swell so that it never turns to flower or fruit.

Other mites and ticks penetrate human hair and skin, and some cause great suffering to sheep. Ravenous as they are in the presence of food supplies, these mites and ticks can fast perhaps longer than any other known form of life.

To justify in full the title of our present chapter, we have yet to come to the true " many legs," though all that we have so far considered put to shame the relative poverty of the true insects in the matter of limbs. Now, however, we come to creatures in which Nature seems to have made a habit, when not otherwise engaged, of adding segments and legs, as if for experiment. The result is seen in the centipedes and the millipedes.

THE POISONOUS LITTLE CREATURES WITH MANY PAIRS OF LEGS

The centipedes are fierce flesh-eating creatures which lurk beneath stones, bark of trees, or other secret hiding places, and stir out only in the dark to hunt and slay. They vary in build, some having but 15 segments and as many pairs of legs; some having round about a hundred, though the number of paired legs is always an odd one. In the centipede with the maximum total, for example, the number would be 99 or 101, never 98 or 100.

They all have poison fangs; many of them, even in England, are phosphorescent. Wheeling a bicycle over a lawn one dewy night, the writer ran his front wheel over one of these creatures. The rubber tyre was marked with a strip of luminosity, which seemed actually to smoke.

The tropical centipede can paralyse a rabbit instantly by a touch of its poison. The thought is unpleasant, but so are most of the things with which the centipede grapples—for our good. The same Hand which gave the rose its thorn, the nettle its sting, the cactus its appalling defences, the snake and devil fish their venom, decreed this lethal fluid for the centipede, and enabled him to administer an anaesthetic to the victim on which he executes the will of destiny.

THE MILLIPEDE THAT EATS UP THE ROOTS OF THE CROPS

The millipede escapes all possible condemnation from human judgment in this matter, for he is innocent of poison. Long-bodied and oval, he has more legs than most of us would count, feeble, filament-like limbs, admirably adapted for the millipede's wriggles through the earth, where he gnaws the roots of our crops. His purpose in the scheme of the world's economy seems to be to destroy rubbish and decaying vegetation, and if we plant our vegetation in land which has been his family's from times before the advent of the mammal and reptile, then we tacitly invite him to appease his appetite on what must seem to him a gift of fortune.

It is curious that the poisonous centipede and the harmless millipede should arise from the same stock, but they do, and are still connected by a strange grim relic of the past in the sluggish slime-ejecting Peripatus. Some of them can twist and turn with a lithe activity which would do credit to an eel, but others, smaller and less powerful, have borrowed the habit of the trilobite, and, like the woodlouse and the hedgehog, can coil up into the semblance of a pill.

Creepy, crawly things are the heroes of this latest chapter of ours, things greatly dreaded by the fanciful and superstitious people who came before us in our green and pleasant land. They inherited their fears and their notions on which they were based. The ancients exalted the crab and the scorpion to the dignity of the stars, and there, in the Zodiac, they are today.

Can we wonder that men and women, who firmly believed that their lives were governed by specific stars, should look with apprehension on creatures whose form they thought they espied and named up in the gleaming heavens?

THE LITTLE MISS MUFFETS WHO ARE WISER THAN THE OLD ONE

We preserve the Zodiac with its portrait gallery, but no longer thrill with terror of the creatures in it. In that we are more enlightened than our ancestors. We know more of the nature of the creatures themselves than Shakespeare and Bacon knew. For that reason we have still a wholesome dread of scorpion and poisonous spider, but the dread is a rational one. It does not make us terrified that a scorpion will suddenly take wing and breathe down fire on us, or that a spider will turn from the devouring of snakes to devour us.

A spider, said our old wise men, is a worm of the air; and that, in the language of that day, meant a snake. Spiders are everywhere, and little Miss Muffet has successors in plenty, but, after all, we know that every spider in the world means the reduction, by great hosts, of the flies that would breed and carry disease. As for the mites and the ticks, we can think of no benefit that we derive from them, unless it is that their presence and their persecution of men and animals are a challenge to bright scientific minds, from whose investigations of the subject new realms of knowledge and wonder are for ever opening out to us.

PICTURE-STORY OF WATER POWER

From very early times man has utilised water power by means of mechanical contrivances, and the water-wheel driven by a running stream is thousands of years old. Here is a typical old water-wheel in Devonshire.

In China the water-wheel has been in use from time immemorial. Where materials for making substantial wheels were lacking, many devices have been used. This water-wheel in Indo-China is made of bamboo.

Norway, which has more available water power than any other country in Europe, now has modern power stations, but for centuries she has used water power in a primitive way. Here are saw-mills by a stream.

THE POWER OF MOVING WATER

Water power is sometimes used in mining where the metal-bearing gravel is at the surface. A powerful jet of water directed on the gravel washes it into a sluice, where it is dealt with in the ordinary way.

Nowhere more than in the United States of America, with its many great rivers, has the colossal power of moving water been put to such good use. Here is an aerial photograph of the dam at Bonneville, Oregon on the Columbia River, with its locks and great power-house.

THE MAN-MADE FALLS OF THE HOOVER DAM

The Hoover Dam across Boulder Canyon, main unit of one of the world's most ambitious water power schemes, supplies the south of California with about half of its power. Here the water that has turned the turbines is cateracting through the six outlet valves at the rate of about 30,000 gallons of water a second.

NIAGARA'S VAST SUPPLIES OF POWER

Niagara Falls have the largest resources of any water power site in Canada, and generate much of Ontario's electricity. Here, with Horseshoe Falls in the background, are the outlets of the Queenston-Chippawa Plant.

The Queenston-Chippawa Plant is the largest in Ontario, and produces 560,000 horse-power. This picture shows the penstocks, outgoing power-line towers, and penthouses of this great generating station.

INSIDE TWO GREAT GENERATING STATIONS

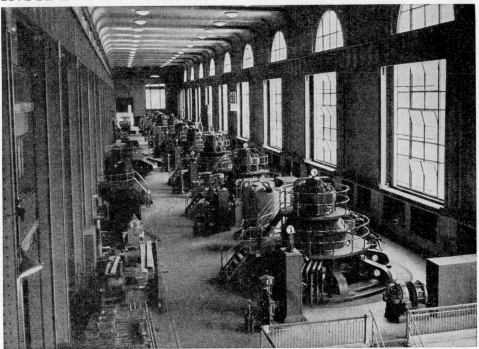

Canada stands second only to the U.S. in the production of water power. Hydro-electric installations generating nearly 15,000,000 h.p. provide energy equivalent to that of some 150,000,000 workers—ten times Canada's population. Here are the ten turbines of the Queenston-Chippawa generating station.

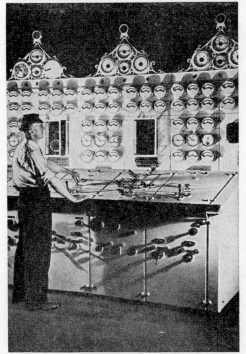

This picture shows an engineer watching the instruments on one of the panels in the control room of the Queenston-Chippawa generating station.

Here the gleaming shafts that connect turbines and generators in the power plant at the Hoover Dam are revolving at 180 r.p.m.

A RIVER IMPRISONED IN PIPES

When a river is harnessed it is imprisoned in pipes and brought to the turbines. Here are parallel pipe-lines at Kinlochleven, Argyllshire.

Sometimes a lake is harnessed, and here are pipe-lines carrying water to the power-station at Lake Coleridge, South Island, New Zealand.

The pipes that carry the water are of great strength and size, as can be seen here, and each pipe supplies a different turbine. The water can be regulated and directed away from the turbine if necessary.

A WONDERFUL PIPE-LINE MADE OF WOOD

In the great timber lands and the mining regions of British Columbia water power is in great demand, and river water is conveyed for miles in huge pipe-lines made of wood staves bound round with iron to prevent bursting. The pipe in the picture is four miles long and delivers the water to turbines at great pressure.

A GREAT CANADIAN WATER-POWER STATION

Canada now has nearly 30 million horse power available in its rivers at minimum flow, of which she has already developed half. Here are the power plant and dam on the St. Maurice River in Quebec.

This is an inside view of the great power house shown in the top photograph, and we see the many powerful generators that are worked by the turbines, driven by the force of the harnessed waters.

WATER POWER WORKING IN SCOTLAND

In Scotland the water power of lochs and rivers in the Grampians is harnessed for the generation of electric power. Here we see a power-house with a capacity of 66,000 horse power, and its transmission cables.

Water for the Grampian hydro-electric works comes from Loch Ericht, which was raised above its original level by this dam. Tunnels through the solid rock lead the water to the turbines in the power-house below.

HOW WATER IS TRANSFORMED INTO POWER

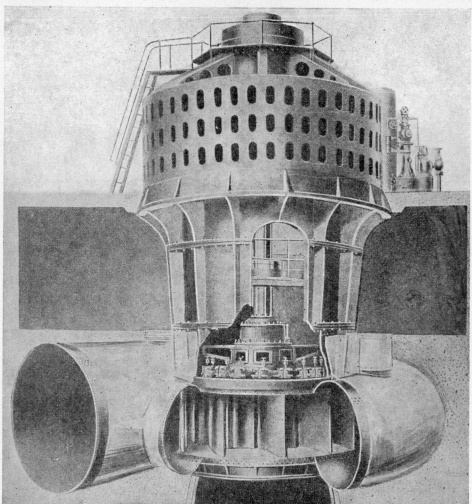

This section through a Westinghouse machine shows the turbine at the bottom and the electric generator at the top. Water rushes through the pipe against the blades of the wheel, which drives the generator.

When the electric power is generated it has to be rightly directed to the various places where it is required for use, and here we see the back of a big switchboard at a modern water power station.

A TURBINE TO CHANGE THE FACE OF AFRICA

Here is a giant turbine in Africa, where harnessed water power is helping to develop the continent

Pictures are by courtesy of the Governments of British Columbia and Canada, the C.P.R., and Balfour, Beatty & Company

HOW THE BOWLS ARE MADE

SAWING UP A LOG OF LIGNUM VITAE, THE HEAVY WOOD OF THE WEST INDIES FROM WHICH BOWLS ARE MADE

SHAPING THE BOWLS ON A LATHE FROM THE BLOCKS OF LIGNUM VITAE

AN EXPERT TESTING THE FINISHED BOWLS FOR THE BIAS, BY RELEASING THEM FROM AN AUTOMATIC CHUTE. See question on page 5615

Plain Answers to the Questions of the Children of the World

WHY DOES A POP-GUN GO POP?

THE pop of a pop-gun is, of course, a sound, and all sounds are waves of a particular kind produced in air. So the question really is: How does a pop-gun cause the kind of air-waves that we can hear? The answer is that air inside the gun is compressed and then suddenly released when the gun goes off. As it is released, it naturally expands or spreads itself out again to fill the space it filled before it was compressed. This means, of course, that as it expands it gives a quick push to the air on all sides of it, and so starts the wave of air, which spreads out in all directions from the point where it started, and reaches our ears. The kind of wave is one which we hear as a very short, sharp sound. It is short because the cause of it acts for only a very short time, and its sound is best represented by the word *pop*.

Pop is one of the many words which were invented in imitation of sounds. We use the word explosion to indicate the kind of sound that is made in a case like this, when a gas suddenly expands from a smaller to a larger space, and so causes a wave in the air. Now, if we notice what we do when we make the letters p and b, we shall find the reason why students of letters call these the explosive consonants. They are both produced by explosions, and if you say *both produced*, you will notice that the explosion is rather less for b and rather more for p; that is all the difference between them. But the present question is whether we are strictly right in calling p and b explosives, and the answer is Yes, for in making these consonants we actually do make little explosions; we do exactly the same as when we fire a pop-gun. We squeeze or compress the air in our mouths, and when we have done that we allow it to force itself through between our lips, which we began by closing. Try to say p or b with your mouth open!

Then the compressed air escapes explosively, as in the pop-gun when the cork flies out, and starts a wave in the air which we call p or b, according to the suddenness with which the air escaped. A p may be soft or a b loud, but that depends on what happens in the voice-box. The difference between the two, whether loud or soft, depends only on the suddenness of the explosion. So we learn that these consonants are called explosives not merely because they are like the sounds of little explosions, but because they are actually the sounds of little explosions caused by sudden expansion.

In a pop-gun, or in the case of the explosion that forms the letter p, the gas

FIRE · WIND · WATER · LIFE · MIND · SLEEP · HOW · WHY · WHERE

that is compressed and then allowed to expand is air which already exists as air. But there is no air or any other gas in a cartridge, and the question may be asked : Where does the gas come from that makes the noise and fires the bullet when a gun is fired ? What happens is that we suddenly burn a powder which, when burned, produces a large quantity of gas very suddenly. The gases produced are exceedingly hot, for they are heated by the burning which makes them, and a hot gas occupies a great deal of space, far more than a cold gas. When we fire a gun, therefore, we suddenly produce a great quantity of hot gas in a tiny space, which is not nearly sufficient to hold it. If this were done in a closed box it would burst the box, but in the case of the gun we have prepared a way out for it. We put a bullet in the way, and the gas, driving the bullet before it, starts the wave of sound which we call an explosion.

Why Does the Kettle Not Get Red-hot When It is Heated ?

The reason is that water will hold a very considerable amount of heat, and the water takes the heat from the kettle, and does not allow the bottom of the kettle ever to get hotter than the temperature of boiling water. That is hotter than our fingers can endure without being scalded, but it is much below the temperature at which iron becomes red-hot.

Who is Pierrot ?

The popular French song which says

Au clair de la lune, Mon ami Pierrot

has immortalised the name of Pierrot. Originally Pedrolino (a familiar diminutive for Pedro) was the name of a character on the Italian stage in the sixteenth century. Dressed all in white, and with his face chalked, he played the part of a buffoon-valet. In the seventeenth century the character passed into French comedy, and was generally represented as a young countryman with shrewd common sense. But the part of Pierrot is best known in pantomime. Here he wears an ample white frock with huge buttons and wide pantaloons; a black skull-cap fitting closely to his head throws into relief the dead whiteness of his face. Both cunning and simple, greedy and cowardly, Pierrot is also somewhat sentimental. He has a particular fondness for the Moon, and is not entirely insensible to the beauties of poetry. The thick chalk on his face, suppressing all the individual character of his features, helps him in all the plays of facial expression so important in these mute performances, so that Pierrot nearly always plays the chief part in pantomime.

What Was the First Stringed Instrument ?

Back through the ages we must go, centuries before the birth of Jesus, back to the very earliest records that exist of man's life on Earth, and there we find proof of the existence of instruments which must have taken more centuries still to reach that stage in development. In the wall paintings of the Egyptians, belonging to a period possibly 3000 B.C., we find pictures of harps shaped not unlike the instruments of today. They were handsome instruments, richly ornamented and standing more than six feet high, but differing from our modern harp in having no supporting pillar.

Nowadays by strings we mean the bowed instruments of the violin family; and in the lyre, which the ancient Greeks borrowed from the Egyptians, we have a forerunner of our fiddle. From the lyre we get the common name applied to all the members of the violin family; we also get the idea of a number of strings. But the principal parts, the sound box, finger board, and movable bridge, come from the monochord. This consisted of a single stretched string, and the Greeks in the time of Pythagoras could make the notes of the scale by cutting off portions of the string with a movable bridge.

Possessed of the lyre and the monochord, it was a small step to the production of an instrument conforming in its essentials to the fiddle, and we know that in the third century B.C. an instrument which was a combination of the lyre and monochord was in use among the Greeks.

The first bow that was used was probably the player's finger !

Is There Gold in the Sea ?

Gold is one of the things we should not expect to find in sea-water, but we do find it in a quite recognisable quantity. If we consider the enormous bulk of the sea the total quantity of gold in it must be considerable; yet it is not enough to repay the cost of getting it out, and so no one does so, except chemists, who do it for love of Nature and not for love of gold.

What Do We Mean By Crossing the Rubicon ?

The Rubicon is a small Italian river running into the Adriatic Sea sixty miles from the town of Rimini. At the time of Sulla, the famous Roman dictator, the short course of the Rubicon traced the frontier between the Roman province of Umbria and Cisalpine Gaul. Wishing to be guarded against renewed incursions, the Roman Senate had decreed that any-one crossing over the river with armed men would be regarded as a foe to the Republic. In 49 B.C., Julius Caesar happened to be in Cisalpine Gaul with some legions when he heard of the intrigues Pompey was brewing against him in Rome. Caesar made up his mind to revenge himself, and, gathering his legions, marched towards Rome. The Rubicon lay on his way. To pass beyond was to wage war against the Republic of Rome. Caesar stopped, hesitating for a few minutes on the bank of the river; but at last he shouted : *Alea jacta est!* (The die is cast) and ordered his troops to cross over. Since that day the expression " to cross the Rubicon " has been applied to all decisive, irrevocable resolves.

What Makes the Bowl Swerve ?

In the game of bowls, the balls do not roll in a straight line, but swerve round to one side or the other, and Shakespeare, who knew the game well, makes one of his Queens say (in Richard the Second):

'Twill make me think the world is full of rubs,
And that my fortune runs against the bias.

The curved course of the bowl is due to what is known as a bias, a word which really means two-faced, and that is what the bowl is. It is not a perfect sphere, although it may seem to be so; one side is a little rounder than the other. In other words, the difference is such that if it were greatly exaggerated the bowl would look like a pear or a peg-top. One side of the bowl is shaped like half an orange, and the other more or less like half a lemon, and the curvature of path is on the side marked by an ivory disc, the difference being almost too slight to be detected by sight or feel. At one time the bias was produced by inserting a piece of lead on one side of the bowl, but this practice is now generally discarded, and reliance is placed on the turning in the making. See pictures on page 5612.

Why is a Silver Spoon Blackened by Egg ?

A silver or silver-plated egg spoon is blackened by the egg because the sulphur in the proteins of the egg combines with the silver of the spoon to form silver sulphide, which is a black substance. It is the sulphur in the egg, which, when the egg gets stale and begins to decompose, combines with the hydrogen in the egg, and so forms sulphuretted hydrogen, the gas which gives to bad eggs their offensive odour. When spoons of nickel or pewter are used no blackening takes place.

What is Margarine ?

Margarine is a substitute for butter, made from animal or vegetable fats. The earliest margarine was made from animal fats, but now by far the greater part of the margarine that is consumed is manu-factured from vegetable oils, such as coconut oil. All the great firms of mar-garine manufacturers own extensive coco-nut plantations in tropical countries. The coconut oil is pressed out of copra, the commercial name for the dried kernel of the coconut, which is the part imported for use. Margarine was first made by a French chemist for use in the French navy in 1870, when, owing to the Franco-German War, butter was scarce. In nutritive value 102 pounds of margarine are equal to 100 pounds of butter. In its manufacture it is necessary to add Vitamin A, which is essential for the health.

What Makes the Colours of the Sunset ?

When the Sun is setting, its light does not come so straight down as when the Sun is high in the sky, but, in order to reach our eyes, it has to pass through a long layer of air. If you stick a needle straight into an orange it does not have to go far through the peel before it gets inside, but if you stick it sideways in the orange it has a long journey through the peel before it gets inside. So the light from the setting Sun passes through so much air, and through all the dust and smoke, and so on, that is in the air; and all these take something out of the white light, and throw out what they do not take. The things floating in the air are of all sizes, and so we get many different colours in sunset. So it comes about that sunsets are often finer when the air is not pure.

What is a Peppercorn Rent?

A peppercorn rent is the name given to a rent so small as to be merely nominal, intended not to bring profit to the owner, but simply to show the tenant's recognition of the fact that he is a tenant and not the owner. When peppercorn rents were first instituted, in the Middle Ages, they were by no means nominal, however, for spices, imported from afar, were expensive. A pound of pepper, paid every rent day, represented a substantial sum till about 200 years ago. Many other forms of these rents, such as a red rose, a horseshoe, a sugar loaf, are still in existence.

What is the Justinian Code?

Flavius Anicius Justinianus, the most famous of the Eastern Roman Emperors reigning at Constantinople, found Roman law in a hopelessly involved condition. Countless edicts had been issued by successive emperors, forming what we should call statute law, and not even the most learned could be sure which of their clauses had been superseded by later decrees and which remained in force. Similarly, the common law was embodied in an enormous number of treatises by hundreds of lawyers over hundreds of years, which no one man could possibly master.

Justinian in A.D. 527 appointed committees of lawyers to reduce this chaos to order. They worked for eight years, producing not what we should call a code now, but abridgments and consolidations of previous works, cutting out repetitions and contradictions. So that the Justinian was a code of Roman law, and it is used by students as a text-book today.

What Does Paying the Piper Mean?

" Be sure and pay the piper " means: be sure and pay your just debt, lest a judgment fall on you. According to the legend, which the poet Browning put into the poem beginning on page 6031, Hamelin, a town in Hanover, was infested with rats, and a stranger in many-coloured garb offered to charm the rats away with his piping in return for a certain sum. His offer fulfilled, the townsmen refused payment, whereupon the piper set up another tune and all the children of the town scampered after him and disappeared with him in a hole in the mountain, which closed behind them. Similar tales are told of magic fiddles in many places.

What is the Hall-Mark on Silver For?

The little marks found on real silver articles like cups, salvers, forks, spoons, watches, rings, and so on, are called hall-marks because they are stamped on under the direction of the Goldsmiths' Company, whose headquarters are the Goldsmiths' Hall in London. The hall-mark is an indication that the metal has been assayed and proved genuine, and it is divided into five separate compartments. The one with Britannia and a lion's head indicates the standard; another has the mark of the assay-town, as a crown for Sheffield, an anchor for Birmingham, and so on; a third has a mark denoting that the duty has been paid; a fourth has a date-mark consisting of a letter of the alphabet, a different letter being used for each year of the cycle; and a fifth compartment has the maker's mark, usually two or more initials. Sometimes a sixth compartment is added with the workman's mark.

How Does a Spirit Level Work?

A glass tube is nearly filled with spirit, and then sealed at both ends, so that when it is perfectly level—that is parallel with the horizon—the bubble of air left inside with the spirit is exactly under a line marked on the middle of the tube. The tube is fixed in a brass or wooden case very exactly made, so that when laid on a level surface the bubble is seen below the middle line. In this way the level of any surface, whether in carpentry or in building or in engineering, can be exactly tested. Sometimes pure alcohol is used, sometimes a mixture of ether and alcohol, and sometimes pure ether—ether without water—is used. The aim is to get a liquid so sensitive that the air bubble in it moves with the very slightest variation in the surface to be tested.

What is an Igloo?

The igloo is the Eskimo's winter hut, varying very much both in shape and the way it is constructed. In Alaska igloos are usually built of planks and covered with turf, while in Greenland the walls consist of stones and sods. Often it is built simply of snow. The entrance is by a narrow, half-underground passage, and though there is only one room, sometimes as many as forty people live in one house. Alaskan Eskimos have hearths in the centre of the room, but the Greenlanders rely for warmth on oil lamps.

Who Built the Cross on St. Paul's?

Contrary to what is generally supposed, it was not Christopher Wren who built the cross on the top of St. Paul's, although in his designs he provided for this. No doubt he would have completed his work, but George the First dismissed Wren from his position of surveyor-general solely for the purpose of putting in his place William Benson. This was in 1718, but so incompetent was Benson that he had to be dismissed after holding his office for only a year. The cross and ball were erected by Thomas Bird, an artist of no great reputation; but the cross and ball which now crown the cathedral are not those which Bird put there. The present ball and cross, designed by C. R. Cockerell, the Cathedral surveyor, were put up in 1821. It is interesting to know that in 1848 the Ordnance Surveyors erected a crow's nest on the top of

THE CROSS ABOVE ST. PAUL'S

the cross, as the best place from which a survey of London could be made. The ball is six feet in diameter and can hold ten or twelve people. It weighs 5600 pounds, and the cross, which is thirty feet high, weighs 3360 pounds. The top of the cross is 365 feet from the pavement of the nave.

Can We Make the Tides Work for Us?

For a very long time men have been trying to find some way of making use of the rising and falling of the sea in the daily tides. It is only possible to use the tides where the difference in the level at high and low water is very great, as is the case on the south-west coasts of England and the north-west coasts of France.

In the Severn Estuary, for instance, the difference between high and low water at the spring tides, when Sun and Moon are pulling together in the same direction, is 42 feet, and at the neap tides, when Sun and Moon are opposing one another, 21 feet. This was the spot suggested for the first experiment in the harnessing of the tides. A scheme for harnessing the power of the tides in the Severn Estuary included a great dam built across the mouth of the river, with a channel and locks for the passage of ships. Sluice-doors would admit the water when the tide was rising, and at the turn of the tide the doors would be closed to imprison the water above the dam. Then this would be let out gradually, working turbines as it ran away. When more power was being produced than was needed, this would be used to pump up water to a still higher level, where it would remain till more power was wanted than was being produced, and then this water would be let out to work additional turbines. In this way the great problem of storing power would be solved economically. The power produced by this harnessing of the tides in the Severn would, it is believed, be about equal to that obtained from some four million tons of coal a year.

What Was the Phoenix?

The phoenix, a fabulous bird of the ancient world, was especially known for its extraordinary beauty and for being the only living bird of its kind. It was said that when the phoenix felt death nearing it built a funeral pyre of branches, set it on fire, and lay on the bed waiting for the flames to consume its body. But another phoenix always rose out of the ashes. According to one account, of doubtful accuracy, the Egyptians made a divinity of the phoenix, which symbolised to them the immortality of the soul. In fact, they believed that directly after death a new being was formed, which they called the twin of the lost personality, and it was thought that it invisibly assumed the shape and features of the dead. This new being was supposed to inhabit the tomb, and the Egyptians put in the grave not only food, but familiar things without which the sleeper would be unhappy on waking.

Why Does a Potato Not Rot Under the Earth While it is Growing ?

If certain kinds of low vegetable life are present in the soil they may attack even the living potato and rot it; but usually the potato is protected by two things. One is its skin, which exists chiefly to keep out microbes and other things that would otherwise feed on it and rot it. The other thing is the life in the living cells which make the potato, especially those cells which lie on the outside of it and are the best part of its food-value. These cells, so long as they are alive, have the power of protecting themselves from most dangerous things, such as microbes or insects. When a potato rots it is because some other living things are using it as their food. The rotting of the bodies of animals and plants is not to be thought of as something bad or horrible. It is simply a chemical change produced by the life of other living creatures; their life benefits as the thing they feed on suffers.

Why Do We Rise to the Surface When We Dive ?

This is not a very easy question to answer. For one thing, it is possible to dive and not rise again. This may very easily happen when a man dives from a height into shallow water, and does not do the right thing when he gets under. He may then strike the mud at the bottom and stay there. That is the danger of diving from too great a height into shallow water. In such a case the diver's body would naturally go deeper than the water before it came up again. The secret of his success is that he turns his hands after he enters the water, and so changes his course. Apart from this, the reason why the diver comes up again is to be found partly in the action of his arms and legs under the influence of the powerful instinct to get to the air again, and partly in the elastic rebound of the water after he has struck it. We must also remember that the pressure of the water gets greater with every descending foot; and the diver's body, filled as his lungs are with air, is scarcely, if at all, heavier than the water itself. The case becomes different if he is injured, or if he is a drowning person unaccustomed to water, who breathes out the air of his lungs, and then breathes water in. That is as bad as letting water into the air-tight compartments of a boat.

How Many British Isles are There ?

Usually when we speak of the British Isles we mean the two large islands of Great Britain and Ireland, but if we take all the smaller islands and islets into consideration we come to the surprising fact that the British Isles number over 5000, most of them uninhabited. There are 500 Hebrides, of which about one-fifth are inhabited; the Orkneys and Shetlands have 190 islands between them, with 57 inhabited; and there are 140 Scilly Islands, though people live on only five. There are great numbers of small islands off the west coast of Ireland.

Why Do We Have Names ?

Plainly, we have names for the same reason that everything has a name. If we did not have names we should have to have numbers, like the numbers on motor-cars, which serve just the same purpose. Now, there are names which have meanings, and names which have none, and it is always well to know how much and how little a name means. There is something we call electricity, which means really that it has something to do with amber, for when you rub amber you get electricity, but people sometimes speak as if the name explained electricity, or as if it explained something else to say that it was electricity. That is because they do not know how little the name means.

Why Does the Moon Grow Brighter as the Sun Sets ?

If we watch the Moon as the Sun begins to set we shall see it grow brighter and brighter until, when the night has come, it is quite bright. Of course, it has really been shining all the time, but the Sun is sending so much light to our eyes, both directly and reflected from the air, that the light of the Moon seems pale, and not worth calling even *moonshine*. It is the same with all our opinions and feelings. One person in a room may shine so brightly by his talk that other people do not seem to shine at all; but when he goes we notice that they are shining, too. And if we have a headache and suddenly knock our shin hard against something, we shall not feel the headache until the stronger pain in our shin has passed away. The Sun *puts out* the Moon as it *puts out* the fire; it does not really do so, but it seems to our eyes to do so.

Why does a Bad Egg Float, Seeing that a Good Egg Sinks?

A fresh hen's egg consists of a mass of yolk, together with what we call the white of the egg, and this, being heavier than water, will cause the egg to sink when it is placed in water. But in an egg which has become rotten the yolk and white have split up into other things, and produce gases which cause the egg to be much lighter than it was before. Such an egg does not weigh as much as an equal bulk of water does, so that if placed in water it floats as an iron ship does and for precisely the same reason—that it is less heavy than the same bulk of water.

Why does my Voice seem Louder if I put my Hands Over my Ears?

We can help ourselves to answer this question if we consider the case of a sea-shell held over the ear. There is no sound made in the shell, but it picks up all the tiny sounds that are made in the room, and echoes them to the ear. Our hands held over our ears act in the same way.

But it is true that the special case where the voice is our own is rather different from others. Perhaps we are rather apt to think of sound as something that always flies "forward" from the place where it is made. But, just like the light of a candle, sound flies out equally in all directions, except in so far as special causes direct the waves or echo them.

So the sound made by our voices travels round beside our ears, and is caught and echoed into them by our hands. Not only do our voices sound louder, but they also sound very strange to us. This is because we usually hear our voices partly through the air waves coming against our ears, and partly by sound waves travelling through the head to the ears from the voice-box. Anything that alters the proportion of these two seems to change the voice.

Why do we Gild the Top of a Book?

We gild the top of a book partly for appearance and partly to present a smooth surface which will not so readily collect dust as the rough paper edges. The under surface of a book is naturally less seen when a book is in a bookcase and is less exposed to dust. In many cases the front of the book is also gilded, and sometimes the edges are gilded all round.

Why has a Flowerpot a Hole in the Bottom?

Like human beings, plants must have water to live, but stagnant water is almost as harmful to them as it is to us. If there were no hole at the bottom of the flower-pot any water that the plant did not drink would not be able to escape; the mould would become stagnant mud in which the plant would soon die.

Why Do the Beds of Rivers Change?

The Earth's crust is shrinking all the time as the interior cools and shrinks beneath it. This means that the lie of the land changes from age to age. and one consequence of this is that often the water of a river finds that its steepest and quickest course to the sea is different from what it used to be, and so the river-bed changes; the old one is deserted by the waters and a new one is formed.

But the water itself, as it flows, rubs and melts away the earth it flows over, and so grinds a deeper and ever deeper bed for itself. Thus it gets less and less likely to desert its old bed the longer it flows there. In many parts of the world we can see how water has hewn a path for itself even through solid rock. The railway engineer wishes to avoid carrying his trains uphill, just as the river water wishes to avoid travelling uphill; and so the engineer often bores a tunnel, rather than make the trains run out of their course. Sometimes the river makes a tunnel for itself, and we have a river running underground.

Are all Animals Born Blind?

It is not quite true that all animals are born blind, but it is true that most of the mammals, when they are newly born, do not at once begin to use their eyes. The eyes themselves are there, however, fully developed and ready to be used for seeing as soon as they have become accustomed to the strong light. The young of wild animals are born in a nest, selected by the mother, and this is generally placed in some dark and secluded place to which very little light gains access. They can open and shut their eyes, and when they begin to move and gradually come into light, the eyes also gradually become used to that light. So that really they are perfectly able to see at the time they require their sight.

What is the Red Cross?

The red cross on a white ground (the Swiss flag reversed) is the emblem of the Red Cross societies established in all civilised nations under the Geneva Convention of 1864 for the care of the wounded in war. By this Convention it was agreed that the hospitals, ambulances, and their attendants showing this badge should not be fired upon or otherwise molested in their work. Originally the badge was a Maltese, or eight-pointed cross (✖), similar to that worn by the knights of the Crusades, but now the plain Greek Cross (✚) is used.

What is the United Kingdom?

The United Kingdom of Great Britain and Ireland was the official title of the four countries; England, Wales, Scotland, and Ireland represented in the Imperial Parliament after the Act of Union adding Ireland came into force on January 1, 1801. Then, in 1922, Southern Ireland separated from the United Kingdom and became an independent country. But Northern Ireland, though it has its own local Parliament, still sends its representatives to Westminster, and so the title is now the United Kingdom of Great Britain and Northern Ireland.

What are the Rain-Tanks at Aden?

Aden in Arabia is one of the most barren and waterless places in the world, though 50,000 people live there. For water it depends on the distillation of sea-water, on an aqueduct, and on wells sunk from 120 to 190 feet in the solid rock; though part of the supply is still obtained from the ancient rain-tanks. These are a magnificent system of stone cisterns, built in the time of the city's medieval greatness to catch and store occasional showers of rain. Many of them are still serviceable, the water they collect being sold by auction.

Why are Official Notices Hung at Church Doors?

At one time everyone was supposed to attend public worship, so any notice placed on the door of the parish church was bound to be seen by practically all the parishioners. The Government have a very old right of using the doors of places of worship for hanging up notices, ar d that is why we see there notices about elections, rates, taxes, juries, and so on. Nowadays notices are usually fixed in the porch.

What Does Habeas Corpus Mean?

Habeas Corpus is Latin for *produce the body*. It is unlawful in British law for anyone to be held a prisoner except on a charge for which he has been or is about to be tried. If he is so held, an application may be made to the High Court of Justice for an order requiring him to be brought before the court for a decision as to the legality of his detention. This order which is addressed to whoever has him in custody, is called a writ of Habeas Corpus. This law, set out in Magna Carta, was actually in existence before that charter. It was ultimately embodied in a series of Acts of Parliament, the most important of which is that of 1679. In time of danger, as during World Wars, the Acts may be suspended by Parliament, but this is always unpopular, for they are felt to be our main safeguard against tyranny and illegality on the part of the Government.

Why Has a French Nail Grooves at the Top?

To enable the nail to grip firmly the wood into which it is driven. A nail smooth all the way down might hold tightly at first, but any vibration of strain, constantly repeated, would soon loosen it, as there would be little friction between the smooth nail and the wood in contact with it. It is friction that enables a nail to hold two pieces of wood together. The grooves give the nail something of the properties of a screw; but, of course, the screw's grooves are more pronounced.

What is a Beefeater?

Beefeater is the popular name for a member of the Yeomen of the Guard, a permanent body of veterans attendant on the British sovereign.

The oldest military corps in the world, they were founded by Henry VII in 1485. In those days their duty was to protect the king but now their function is ceremonial.

The corps, which still wear the original uniform of scarlet, black, and gold, consists of 100 yeomen, a captain, a lieutenant, an ensign, a clerk of the cheque, and four corporals called exons.

What is a Red-Letter Day?

A red-letter day is one that stands out in our life as a happy and delightful day. In almanacs special days and holidays used to be printed in red ink to mark them off from ordinary days.

The Story of the Beautiful Things in the Treasure-House of the World

Decorated arches in the
Alcazar at Seville

The Fountain of Lions in
the Alhambra

In the Court of the Fishpond
in the Alhambra

THE EASTERN BUILDERS

THE greatest architecture in the world may be called that which has overcome the greatest difficulties of building construction and at the same time attained perfect beauty of form.

The Greeks accomplished this; but we must remember that their constructional problems were few. With flat roofed buildings, of one storey only, the chief problem they had to meet was the placing of a sufficient number of columns in the exact position to support the roof.

The Romans overcame the next difficulty in historic building construction: the use of the arch and the throwing up of successive storeys. As for beauty of form, as we have seen, they used their Greek inheritance. What they had begun the successive powers of Europe developed.

In the meantime, in the Near East a new architecture was rising; it spread over Asia and also took root in Spain. This style has been called Mohammedan, Arabic, Moorish, Saracenic. The last is preferred by historians, as the architecture owed its birth to an event in the land of the Saracens. During the first few hundred years after Christ, some wandering tribes were living in the Arabian desert without any special home. As time went on they came to be known as Saracens or people of the East. To them, in the year 570, was

born a man called Mohammed, who shaped the religion—based on the writings of the Koran, which he put together—that bears his name. The tenets of Mohammed were accepted with great fervour by his people, and there grew up among them a passion to conquer the world and convert it.

These homeless desert people were not only natural fighters, but carried swords sharpened by their zeal. They overran Persia, Mesopotamia, Syria, Palestine, Egypt, North Africa, Spain; they threw an outpost of their dominion as far as northern India. Wherever they went they established an architecture which was different in every country and yet had a family likeness.

In more ways than one Saracenic architecture was a peculiar growth. As far as sacred buildings were concerned, it was not so much an architecture of temples as of houses of prayer. The Mohammedan places of worship lacked the very heart and core of an ancient temple—the shrine where the figure of the god was set. They were simply buildings where people gathered to pray, their faces turned toward Mecca. A little niche in the wall, called the Mihrab, indicated the direction of their holy city.

One of the laws of the Koran forbade any display, in sculpture or painting, of

PICTURES · STATUES · CARVINGS · BUILDINGS · IVORIES · CRAFTS

the human figure or animal forms. This restriction was the cause of the development of a brilliant geometric or fanciful ornament in flowing, fine lines, which still exists in architecture today under the name Arabesque. These religious buildings—mosques, they are called—were at first very plain erections; they might be described as square spaces roofed in where people could gather to worship. In their early history the roofs were flat; later the dome appeared, generally indicating the place of a tomb.

The most characteristic features of the finest Saracenic religious buildings are the pear-shaped, or pointed, domes, and the tall, strange minarets or towers where the priests mounted at appointed hours to summon the world to prayer. Their greatest beauty was restricted to the interiors, and in this they resembled those of Egypt, whose gaunt exteriors gave no hint of the grandeur of the hypostyle hall within.

THE ELABORATE ARCHES IN THE ARCHITECTURE OF THE SARACENS

The mosque walls were decorated in every possible space. Restraint, that keynote of great architecture, was unknown to the Saracens. They had a passion for arches, and the more ornate the happier they were. They used the pointed horseshoe, the ogee (like a round arch running up in a reverse curve to a narrow point), and others more elaborate. Arch after arch, rank on rank, as if they had been forest growths, rose up in their buildings. The richness of display, the illusion of countless lines and curves was helped by their peculiar formation which is described as stalactite vaulting. Their arches which vaulted the ceiling ran up from the supporting pillars in a series of small pointed shapes, or niches, rising up one above another like innumerable tiny arches, giving a honeycomb effect. This makes a peculiarly interesting feature of the Saracenic dome.

The architects presently had a great love for this honeycomb treatment of a surface, and used it freely as a decoration for capitals of columns, or to fill in spaces on exterior walls.

These builders were very ingenious in their method of what might be called architectural conquests. In each country they dominated they made use of existing styles and adapted them; so that we have Egyptian Saracenic, Spanish Saracenic, Indian Saracenic, and so on. There were two capitals, political and religious in one, of this strange, scattered dominion. One was at Baghdad in Persia, the other at Cordova in Spain.

THE LOVELY TOWERS WHICH MARKED THE GRANDEUR OF THE MOORS

The phrase, The Moors in Spain, denotes the period of Saracenic rule, from about 710 to 1492. These centuries were marked by the growth of a remarkable architecture. It cannot be called great, because more attention was paid to surface decoration than constructional beauty. But on the other hand this Saracenic spirit produced among other things the wonderful Giralda, at Seville, one of the most beautiful towers in the world.

Every now and then the Saracens built towers like this, for no use at all, it would appear, save to point a finger to the glory of the Mohammedan conquerors. Apart from their appreciation of the towers as symbols of their own grandeur, they must have had a love for them. The minarets of the east were never as beautiful as these separate towers which arose here and there, as in Morocco and Tunis.

When we look at the Giralda we have to forgive the meddling architects of the sixteenth century who were pleased to put a Renaissance belfry on the top of the Saracen tower. The two styles are not akin, and only the great beauty of the body of the tower saves the Giralda from thus being spoiled. We can see on the walls of the tower the rows of toy arches, and panels of honeycomb ornament, and we can appreciate the value of the unadorned spaces that support and frame the decoration.

THE WONDERFUL ALHAMBRA BUILT BY THE MOORS IN SPAIN

To Spain also belongs another very famous building, the best known of all erected by the Saracens, and that is the Alhambra, or Red Palace, at Granada. It was begun by one of the caliphs early in the fourteenth century and variously added to during the next two generations. The prince who planned it was a great architect and had already set up mosques in Palestine. Here he seemed to want to build something that should be the mirror of Saracen greatness and of his own glory.

Like the rest of the architecture of the Mohammedan people, the Alhambra was

THE BUILDINGS OF THE MOORS IN SPAIN

THE COURT OF THE LIONS IN THE ALHAMBRA AT GRANADA

WONDERFUL ARCHES IN THE GREAT MOSQUE
AT CORDOVA

A WINDOW IN THE HALL OF THE AMBASSADORS
IN THE ALHAMBRA

not built so much for permanence as for lavish display. Many of its pretty arches were shams, in that the weight which they should bear was already supported by lintels. The arches were merely set there to look nice. A greater sin against architectural laws could scarcely be imagined. And yet, although our reason is offended, we cannot but respond to the strange charm of the Moorish buildings. They cast a spell of their own across our present workaday life.

THE QUIET COURTS OF THE ALHAMBRA ENCLOSED IN THE RANKS OF ARCHES

Had the proud caliph of the west builded less proudly, and more wisely, we should not now be deploring the crumbling of his palace fabric, and the loss to the world of a singular beauty whose spirit can never, humanly speaking, be recaptured.

The Alhambra was more put together than planned. Its halls and apartments, among them the famous Hall of the Ambassadors in the Comares Tower, clustered about two large courts, which were set at right angles to each other and were enclosed in ranks of arches, single and double, their pretty honeycombed shapes rising from slender columns. One of these quadrangles was called the Court of the Lions and the other the Court of the Fishpond.

The love of the Saracens for parallel lines of opposing colours, for the interweaving of Arabic inscriptions in the ornament of a building, for wall decoration in gold and rich tints, is very clearly shown in their Red Palace at Granada. The huge mosque at Cordova shares the renown of the Alhambra in that it is the finest religious building set up by the Moors in Spain—perhaps the finest mosque outside Egypt.

THE ROMAN INFLUENCE IN THE MOORISH MOSQUE AT CORDOVA

None of the Spanish mosques was domed. The Cordova mosque is a remarkable building, only thirty feet high, and covering an immense area. It was built five hundred years earlier than the caliph's palace, and shows the Saracens' skill in adapting their building to architecture already existing in the countries they conquered. Roman columns and round arches and Roman capitals were used, along with those of Saracenic design, and Byzantine mosaics paved the mosque floor. The interior of the church is especially rich in colour, and was made radiant by numberless hanging lamps.

Of the mosques of varying importance, grandeur and style, which mark the passage of the Mohammedan conquest, the finest are in Cairo; of these, the Kait Bey mosque is generally considered the most beautiful. Others, whose fame is more historic and sentimental than architectural, are the Mosque-el-Aksah and the Dome of the Rock—the so-called Mosque of Omar—at Jerusalem, the Great Mosque, Mecca, the Great Mosque at Isfahan in Persia. Two fine mosques which bear the names of their founders, Suleiman and Ahmed, are at Istanbul, and are Byzantine in character, being planned in imitation of St. Sophia.

It is very interesting to note that during the Saracenic rule in Egypt some of the caliphs showed an inclination to adopt the idea of the Egyptian tomb-house. A few of them erected buildings in Cairo of an ornate style which were lightly used as pleasure houses and afterwards served as their tombs.

WHY THE SARACEN BUILDINGS WERE NOT MADE TO LAST

In India also this happened, as we shall presently see. But, generally speaking, the Mohammedans' absorption in the present was too strong to admit of any great interest in a future state. The Saracens were content to use flimsy materials which they knew could not withstand the wear of many generations. So did their fatalism, their constant " Allah's will be done," dominate the intelligence of a very gifted people.

One or two tombs proper still remain here and there in the lands the Saracen conquered, and to boys and girls of all ages the most important is that of the Lady Zobeide, wife of the Caliph of Baghdad, Haroun-al-Raschid. The tomb, an eight-sided erection with a queer, pyramidal roof, was set up when Baghdad was in her hey-day. Haroun only lived from 763 to 809, but he is immortal to time's end in the glamour of the Arabian Nights; and no one can forget Zobeide, whom he loved.

When the Saracens overran India, about the year 1000, they found for the first time in their conquests, an architecture for the most part more casual, more indifferent to constructional laws than their own—an array of temples of fantastic

EASTERN BUILDINGS IN SPAIN AND INDIA

THE RASHMANIE TEMPLE IN CALCUTTA

THE GIRALDA TOWER AT SEVILLE

A PORCH IN A COURT OF THE ALHAMBRA

A HALL IN THE ALHAMBRA

and grotesque appearance. The architecture of early India, like that of the Saracens, stands apart from the world's story. Nowhere does it mark the scale of progress from one stage of advancement to another, as in the case of Egyptian, Greek, and Roman work. It leads nowhere save into the blind alley of its own ideals. And yet we cannot pass this strange architecture, on which generation after generation expended its energy, without a thought for its qualities and an attempt to understand its workings.

THE GREAT MOUNDS THAT WERE SET UP FOR THE RELICS OF SAINTS

It was, as we may expect, an architecture of religion, and is best grouped under the headings of the different faiths that have been held in India in historic times.

Buddha preached his gospel in the fifth century before Christ. When, some three hundred years later, Buddhism became the religion of many of the races who peopled India, its architecture began to develop. Relic worship became a strong force and gave rise to the great mounds called Topes, built for receiving relics of saints. Some of these still exist, like the Sanchi Tope and others in Central India, huge round masses of brickwork raised on platforms with a processional path round them, and on the top of the mound the " tee " containing the saint's relics.

An elaborately carved rail, which looks like stone imitating wood, ran round the sacred enclosure, with huge gateways whereon is some of the earliest picture carving of the Indian artists. A model of a tope can be seen in the South Kensington Museum. Here and there carved and inscribed columns called Lats are set up. A fine one is at Allahabad. This early carving was of an individual nature, already foreshadowing the wealth of bizarre decoration that was to come.

THE MASSIVE TEMPLES OF BUDDHA CARVED OUT OF THE SOLID ROCK

The temples of Buddhism were carved out of the solid rock in the mountain face, and therefore have only one outer front. Through square openings and under great carved columns the worshippers passed into the gloom of the interior, in whose farthest depths was the sacred shrine. A great amount of work was spent on hewing out the roof and aisles of these gaunt places. The result was very impressive. Rows and rows of massive columns with carved capitals and surmounting sculptured forms flanked the shrine. The outer wall, where the entrance openings were hewed out, presented a strange aspect, with its long lines of carved shapes, the familiar seated Buddha-form being endlessly repeated. An enormous opening, horse-shoe shaped, was carved out above the level of the doors, to let light into the shrine, and this gave a curious top-heavy look to the temple front.

The finest of these rock temples are at Karli, Ajanta, Ellora, Elephanta, on the Western Ghats.

Jainism, which was contemporary with or earlier than Buddhism, provided a strikingly different temple architecture. Instead of being cumbrous, gloomy places carved out of the rock, they were radiant white marble piles flung up on the mountain side. In northern India this architecture was the strongest, and temple after temple arose in shining splendour to witness to the Jain faith.

THE FANTASTIC CARVINGS WHICH COVER THE WALLS OF JAIN TEMPLES

Mount Abu was holy ground to the Jains, and there they built a cluster of these temples. The two most famous of a great array are the Dilwarra temple, and that at Ranpur. On these interiors it seemed that architects and sculptors set themselves to work for their own delight and without any regard to unity or proportion. The instinct for grotesque decoration was forming which presently overgrew, like a fungus, the architecture of India.

Outwardly, and from a distance, the Jain temples were very fine, and had an air of semi-classic simplicity, with their great columned porticoes and mounting shapes. Close at hand it was seen how the wall spaces were endlessly carved. In the interiors—wonderful colonnaded aisles and shrines—it would seem that a host of sculptors had been turned loose, each a little mad, all dreaming, and in their dreams had carved and carved till not a square foot was without its fantasy.

This wealth of minute decoration was very pleasing to the Indian people, who cared nothing for proportion and construction, and only for the effect of the white, sculptured columns, domes, and walls. And the spirit of Jainism fostered this lavish display, as it was essential that each temple should contain a number of idol-cells wherein was sculptured the statue of the saint to whom it was dedicated. The more idol-cells in the fabric of the building, the better the saint was thought to be pleased. In some cases they numbered hundreds.

THE GREAT TEMPLES ON WHICH HUNDREDS OF MEN SPENT THEIR LIVES

Each of the twenty-four Jains, or saints, had an animal symbol which was always carved above the saint. Hence the profusion of animal forms and other mysterious symbols that filled the temples of this religion.

The rise of Brahminism in turn brought its changes, and the architecture generally known as Hindu arose. The great temple, Bhuvaneswar, on the eastern coast, is sometimes called the finest building of this class. A very famous one is close by, at Puri. All over India rose the Brahmin temples, each most profusely sculptured, each meaning the lifetime's work of many hundreds of men, by whose energies the deities, it was supposed, were well pleased. There were many styles among them, different shapes of entrances and different kinds of sanctuaries, roofs, columns. But over them all spread the phantasy of the sculptor—the most important element in the building.

In southern India rock-hewn temples arose, at a later date, of a different kind from those of the Buddhist Order, in that they are completely hewn out of the rock and stand as one solid, fantastic mass. This Dravidian architecture seems to summarise the Indian style of decoration. Around the walls which appeared to crouch and cling together, ran layer after layer of most finely wrought sculpture, some of it just curious symbolism, a great deal barbaric and rather revolting to the European matter-of-fact mind.

THE DECORATION OF THE SCULPTOR WHICH SPOILED THE WORK OF THE ARCHITECT

This decoration was always controlled by horizontal base lines. It is as if the sculptors began at the bottom, and when they had been all round the temple once, they incised a tremendous horizontal line and went on again, on the next layer, all round the temple walls; and on and on.

The horizontal effect thus obtained was very characteristic of a great part of Indian temples. The sculptors seemed to undo the architects' work. When walls and pyramidal roofs had been planned and

thrown up for a great height, this effect of height was immediately annulled by the insistence of the horizontal lines of the sculpture adorning them.

The Saracen invasion brought a certain purity into this land of exuberant art, a breath of clearer air, a style of expression that was at once nobler and more sane. When Delhi was made the capital of Mohammedan India a new architecture arose. Probably the most famous early building in this city which became so rich in lovely things was the Kutab Mosque, erected at the end of the twelfth century. It was built of white marble and red sandstone blended, with domes and colonnaded courts. Within the precincts rose a huge tower known as the Kutab Minar, one of the finest the Saracens erected. A model of it is in the South Kensington Museum. There we can see its delicate beauty and try to imagine what it looked like towering above the roofs of the ancient city.

HOW INDIAN ARCHITECTURE DEVELOPED IN THE SIXTEENTH CENTURY

The Kutab Mosque is only one of the number that marked the first centuries of Mohammedan rule. Later, in the sixteenth century, came the finest Indian Saracenic architecture, which was developing on simple and grand lines, leaving behind much of the casual prettiness of the Western buildings. Marble and decorative stone freely quarried in India inspired a more imposing and severe style of building, and as the Saracens' love of an exquisite finish in detail was strengthened by the influence of Hindu workmen, a very fine architecture was the result. Palaces, halls, mosques, and tombs arose all over India.

One of the Mogul rulers, Shah Jehan, was a great architect, and found time during his stirring reign to set up certain buildings which have carried his name and fame down over the tumultuous centuries of Indian history to our own day. He was founder of the modern Delhi which to the Mohammedan is still Shah Jehanabad—the city of Shah Jehan. There he built the Jama Masjid, a mosque of fine proportions, and at Agra the beautiful Pearl Mosque, in white marble.

Shah Jehan built at Delhi one of the greatest palaces, planned in the most royal manner, the world has ever known. Only fragments of it remain, overrun by English military buildings, and to the romantically minded this ruler's greatest work was the exquisite Taj Mahal, at Agra. This tomb house, erected in honour of the wife he so loved, was the finest flowering of Shah Jehan's rich imagination. It is built in perfect proportion, and shows most marvellous taste.

THE LOVELY TAJ MAHAL IN WHICH A LADY SLEEPS

The Taj Mahal stands on a platform 18 feet high and over 300 feet square, with a minaret at each corner of the platform. From the middle of the building rises the pear-shaped dome of the Saracens and four small domes cluster round it, like buds round a flower. The builder seemed to know that in raising this mausoleum he could not afford to deviate an inch from its symmetrical plan without losing something of its alluring charm. On the perfect shape of the white marble mass the Saracen artists laid their jewel work in many colours. Marble terraces and beautifully inlaid walks lead up to it; dark sentinel trees make an exquisite glow of its whiteness and light; the waters of Jumna River glide gently by, as if to soothe into eternal rest the human life and love that centred in the Taj Mahal.

The days of the Great Moguls in India were marked by architecture which within its own style was superb; buildings like the Mosque and Diwan-i-Kas at Fatehpur Sikri and the Sikandra Tomb, erected by Akbar, the grandfather of Shah Jehan. For some time the tradition of excellent building was kept, long after Shah Jehan followed his lovely wife to the grave. But, like all great movements, Mogul architecture, the finest expression of the Saracens in the East, topped its heights and then sank for ever.

THE CHINESE BUILDINGS WHICH SEEM TO BE NEARLY ALL ROOF

The architecture of China, changeless through many centuries, presents an aspect to the Western mind which can best be called quaint. The Chinese, like the Japanese, who modelled their buildings largely on the work of their neighbours, were artists in surface decoration rather than in building form. Had they not needed houses and temples they would never have built anything, whereas one feels with the Greeks and Normans that if they had not had the excuse of temples and halls and houses they would have found another reason for setting up lovely shapes in marble and stone.

The chief note of Chinese architecture is the roof treatment. When their builders wanted height, they laid on roof after roof, with their peculiar upward-curling, leaf-like corners, all elaborately decorated, till they had attained the size they desired. Their palaces, like that of the emperor at Peking, their temples, like the famous Confucian Temple of Heaven at Peking, their towers or pagodas, their pai-lous, or memorial gateways—all depend on upward-curling eaves for character. Chinese artists and architects seemed to be happy if they were given walls and shapes to decorate according to small, natural forms. They had the kind of vision that sees constant details, and is happiest when these details multiply on each other, like leaves on a tree. This vision makes excellent embroidery, perhaps, but does not produce architecture.

THE GREAT WALL WHICH STRETCHES ACROSS CHINA FOR 1400 MILES

Confucianism produced no great temples, as it was a scheme of moral laws, and had no priests. So that the tale architecture tells is silent during many centuries in China. And when Buddhism came in force in the first hundred years after Christ, the Chinese, having a tradition of no temples, probably could not see any reason for starting building them in great numbers. That they could construct when they wished we know from their bridges and from the Great Wall which, with its towers and remarkable masonry, runs up hill and down dale for some 1400 miles.

The pagoda is probably the most essentially Chinese in spirit of all the buildings of the Celestial land. The spirit of the Great Wall is Chaldean; but although the idea of the pagoda may have been borrowed from India, its treatment is the most Chinese thing in China.

The Japanese buildings—temples, pagodas, tombs, palaces—are of the same class, a little daintier, lighter, more flower-like, as one would expect from a people who are such artists in decoration based on natural forms. Although they endeavour to secure their buildings against earthquake shocks, they are never safe from destruction, as their history has told from time to time, and disasters that appal the world have occurred there even in our own century.

THE SPLENDID BUILDINGS LOOKING OUT ON THE COURT OF LIONS IN THE ALHAMBRA

·THE ENTRANCE TO THE KING'S SLEEPING APARTMENT IN THE ALCAZAR AT SEVILLE

COLUMNS AND ARCHES OF THE GREAT MOSQUE AT CORDOVA

THE HALL OF THE TWO SISTERS IN
THE ALHAMBRA

ARCHES LEADING TO THE COURT OF THE
LIONS IN THE ALHAMBRA

HALL OF THE AMBASSADORS IN THE ALCAZAR AT SEVILLE

THE KING'S SLEEPING APARTMENT IN
THE ALHAMBRA

A PORCH IN THE SUMMER PALACE OF THE
MOORISH KINGS AT GRANADA

THE FAMOUS MOSQUE OF OMAR AT JERUSALEM

ARCHES IN THE ENCLOSURE OF THE MOSQUE
OF OMAR

BEAUTIFUL MOSAICS ON THE MOSQUE
OF OMAR

THE COURT OF THE FISH-POND IN
THE ALHAMBRA

A COURTYARD IN PILATE'S HOUSE
AT SEVILLE

THE LOVELIEST BUILDING IN INDIA—TAJ MAHAL

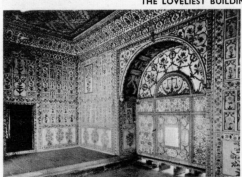

AN APARTMENT IN SHAH JEHAN'S PALACE
AT DELHI

SCREEN AROUND THE TOMBS IN
TAJ MAHAL

THE WEALTH OF CARVING INSIDE THE GREAT
MOSQUE AT CORDOVA

IN THE HALL OF THE AMBASSADORS IN THE
ALCAZAR AT SEVILLE

THE SPLENDID MOSQUE AT AKYAB IN BURMA

BUDDH-GAYA TEMPLE, NEAR
PATNA

A ROCK TEMPLE AT ELLORA
IN INDIA

CARVING ON THE KUTAB
MINAR AT DELHI

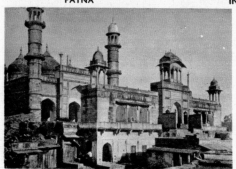

THE JAMA MASJID AT GWALIOR

THE SANCHI TOPE IN CENTRAL INDIA

A TRIPLE ARCH IN A TEMPLE AT PEKING

THE UMBRELLA PAGODA
AT PEKING

THE CARVED DOORWAY OF SHWEE
ZEEGONG TEMPLE IN BURMA

THE LOONG WAH PAGODA
NEAR SHANGHAI

THE MARBLE ARCHES AT THE MING TOMBS IN CHINA

THE TOMB OF ZENAB ALIYA AT LUCKNOW

THE ZENANA IN FORT AGRA   A RUINED INDIAN TEMPLE AT AHMEDABAD

The pictures in these pages are by Messrs. Anderson, Bourne & Shepherd, H. G. Ponting, and others

The Wonderful House We Live In, and Our Place in the World

THE DISTRIBUTION OF WEALTH

WHEN we looked at the production of wealth we saw that three things went to its making—Labour, Land, and Capital. Now we come to think how the wealth which is produced is shared between those who labour, those who own land, and those who own capital.

We may notice at once that in some cases a man who works for his living labours on his own land and uses only his own capital. There are many small farmers and land-workers in the world who are

Gleaming new coins from the Royal Mint, London.

in this position. Such a man derives his living from tilling a bit of land for himself, and his capital consists of his house or buildings, his stock of tools, machines, or seeds, and his animals. In such a case the worker is at one and the same time the owner of the land, a worker on it, and a capitalist who employs his own stock to make his labour more useful. As worker he not only labours, but supplies all the enterprise and managing ability which is put into the work done on the bit of land. Thus, as combined Worker, Landlord, and Capitalist, he takes for himself the whole produce of the undertaking.

There are other trades in which a single person may be at once worker, landlord, and capitalist. For example, a carpenter sometimes works for himself in a small workshop and uses his own tools and materials. He, too, enjoys the whole produce of his own work.

In modern work, however, it is common to find that those who work do not own either the land they work on or the capital

by which their work is made useful. Thus a factory may be built on land owned by a landlord, to whom rent is paid for the use of the land. The factory building and the machines in it may be owned by people to whom a part of the wealth produced by the factory is paid for the use of their capital. The persons actually working in the factory, from the manager to the boy in the office, may own neither the land nor any part of the factory, but draw payments for any work they do. In such a case as this a clear division can be made between the landlord, the capital, and the workers.

Usually, in modern business, a factory and the land on which it is built are owned by a company of people who have put together, or subscribed, the money needed to buy them; and the workers own little or none of the capital.

We give different names to the shares of the produce which are taken by the workers, the landlords, and the capitalists and they are as follows :

BODY, MIND, AND SOUL · CITIZENSHIP · ECONOMICS · GOVERNMENT

The share of the worker is called Salary or Wage; the share of the landlord is called Rent; the share of the capitalist is called Interest or Profit.

Let us deal first with the reward of labour. We saw in dealing with the production of wealth what a complicated thing labour is, including not merely hard work, which may or may not have a useful result, but the making of this hard work really fruitful by guiding it with intelligence, informing it with invention, and multiplying it by organisation. We cannot too often be reminded that it is necessary, not only to work, but to work in the best way, and that, while much work badly used may produce little wealth, a little work well used may produce much wealth.

In a manufacturing business, such as the making of textiles, or iron and steel, or engines, or ships, or chemicals, the workers may be divided into five classes.

1. *Organisers, or Captains of Industry.* These are the directors of the whole concern, who are responsible for the general management of its business in all its branches, and on whose enterprise and judgment depends its success or failure. They are paid sometimes by salary alone, but often by salary and a further payment which varies with the success of the business. Usually, too, they have shares in the business, and have therefore a further interest in making it profitable.

2. *Managers, Clerks, and Travellers.* The business side of the undertaking demands the employment of various orders of departmental managers, clerks to deal with books, orders, receipts and payments, and men usually called Commercial Travellers who are sent out to seek for orders. All are paid salaries, and often managers and travellers are paid additional sums (called bonuses or commissions) to encourage them to do more trade.

3. *Inventors, Scientists, and Artists.* These may either work inside or outside the business. A firm may use a patented invention and pay a certain sum to the inventor for each use of his invention, or it may buy the invention outright for a lump sum. So many inventions are no longer patented, because under our law a patent is only granted for a short term of years, that many firms work actually without paying anything to inventors. Some businesses employ a special staff of scientists to improve their productions. An

engineering firm, for example, has constantly to be working in this way. When a firm makes patterned cloths, or furniture, or earthenware, or other artistic things, it has to employ artists and designers to make its work beautiful.

4. *Skilled Workmen.* The workman who has learned how to use tools, or how to carry out the technical work of his craft, is called a skilled workman. Examples of this are bricklayers, carpenters, masons, plasterers, turners, fitters, and plumbers. Such men are indispensable in most manufacturing operations. They are usually paid weekly wages. In some trades payment is by Time—so much an hour, or day, or week. In other cases payment is by Results, that is to say, so much a job. Persons so paid are called Piece-workers.

5. *Unskilled Workmen.* In addition to skilled workers many businesses employ people to do simple tasks which call for no special training or knowledge. These are the unskilled workmen, and their wages are less than those paid to craftsmen. Thus, in the case of housebuilding, a bricklayer is paid more than the unskilled worker who carries the bricks and mortar for him to use.

The use of machinery has greatly multiplied the call for unskilled workers. With large-scale production, complicated processes can be broken down into a number of simple ones, which are easily taught. During the war, many unskilled workers were quickly trained to do jobs previously regarded as skilled. Nevertheless, highly skilled craftsmen are needed to make the machines before unskilled people can operate them.

We see, then, how complicated a thing is the reward of Labour, because work takes so many different forms. The other factors of wealth production, Land and Capital, also call for their payments, and we must now consider these.

Rent, the share of the landlord, is paid for the use of land or some other gift of Nature. In an old country like Britain, where every foot of land has been worked over, and little is left remaining in its natural condition, it is very difficult to distinguish gifts of Nature from the work of men. In common speech, therefore, we come to use the word Rent as applying to any payment made for the use of land and what is built on it. The true " rent," however, is not this total payment, but only that part of the payment which is made for the natural piece of land.

This distinction may seem unimportant, but it is not really so. Let us consider the rent of a London shop in Regent Street, and the rent of a building of similar size in, let us say, Basingstoke, or some other small town. Why is it that the building in Regent Street has a very heavy rent, while the building in Basingstoke has a very small rent? It is not through the building, because even if the building in Basingstoke cost more than the building in Regent Street, the Regent Street rent would still be much higher than the other. The real reason is that Regent Street is in such a *fine position*, and has so many more people passing through it than the street in the little country town, that a shopkeeper can sell more things in the same time in the London street than in the country street, and therefore it is worth while for the London shopkeeper to pay a higher rent. *Thus the real rent (the economic rent, as it is sometimes called) is the price of the natural advantage of the Regent Street site over the country site.*

HOW RENTS ARE AFFECTED BY NATURAL AND OTHER CONDITIONS

So it is in farming. If a farm has poor soil, or is badly situated, it yields less than a farm with a rich soil or a good situation, and therefore commands less rent.

So we see how some landlords may be able to obtain a high rent while others can get only a small one. In the case of farm land the rent depends on fertility and nearness to markets. In the case of building land it depends on the amount of business which can be done.

Sometimes, again, land may be specially valuable because there are minerals under the surface. If coal is discovered at a certain spot, coal mines and factories will be established. Houses and shops will arise, and so the land near the coal will become valuable and command a high rent.

Sometimes a railway will raise rents by bringing people together and creating a demand for houses in the neighbourhood. In the old days, when railways were first made, some landlords strongly objected to them, and prevented them from passing near their properties. When they did so they robbed themselves of rent without knowing it.

We come now to Interest and Profit, taken by the capitalist.

People who save up money and lend it for use in business receive a return which varies with the risk they take. When a person lends money to the Government of a great nation the risk he runs is comparatively small, and the payment he gets for the use of his money is small. Money lent on good security to an old-established business runs a greater risk, though it is still a comparatively small one. So it is with money lent on the pledge (or mortgage, as it is called) of good buildings, where the lender's security is in the fact that if he is not paid he may seize the buildings.

THE DIFFERENCE BETWEEN PROFIT ON CAPITAL AND INTEREST ON MONEY LENT

The payment for the use of money lent is called Interest, but when somebody lends money (or subscribes capital, as we call it) to set up a trading business, and there is no guarantee that the money will be repaid, a great risk has often to be taken, and the payment for such risk is called Profit.

So we see that the reward of capital consists of two distinct parts, the first being Interest (the payment for the use of money when it is almost certain the money will be safely repaid), and the second Profit (the payment for the risk taken in the matter).

If everyone who saved money wanted to keep it quite safe, there would be very little enterprise. It is just because some people are willing to take risk, on the chance of being paid for the risk, that capital comes to be invested in business enterprises. Enormous sums are sometimes lost by those who take such risks.

THE LAWS OF SUPPLY AND DEMAND AND THE DISTRIBUTION OF WEALTH

The distribution of wealth between Labour's share (wages and salaries), the Landlord's share (rent), and the Capitalist's share (interest and profit) is determined by the laws of demand and supply, which we have already studied. Here we are speaking of distribution, and not of production. Whether there is much production or not depends on how the labour, land, and capital are used.

Demand and supply affect rent as they affect prices. If a lot of people have to live in one place they all demand houses, and therefore there is a big call for land at one place. So the demand sends up the price of the land, or the rent paid for the use of it. Is it possible, in such a case, to increase the supply of land to the people who want houses? Curiously it is, because by making a good road or railway we could enable people to live farther away and get back quickly to the spot where business calls them together. So the homes of the people could be spread and, in effect, a larger supply of land could be made available for them, in which case the rent at the busy spot would fall.

With capital, too, demand and supply affect payments. For instance, if a new and successful trade springs up, big profits may at first be made in it. What happens, then, is that big profits induce more capitalists to put money into the new business, and so the supply of capital in that trade grows. The result of this bigger supply of capital is to bring down the profits. That is what has happened in the cinema trade, in which at first enormous profits were made. This led to much capital being provided to set up new picture-houses, and as a result the profits of the trade have fallen.

When we come to wages, we also find that demand and supply affect them as they affect the prices of goods.

THE DEMANDS FOR HIGH WAGES THAT ARE SOMETIMES BAD FOR TRADE

We saw in studying prices how the demand for goods really means the demand at a certain price. The demand for workers in practice means demand at a certain wage. The employer cannot pay more than a certain wage at any particular time if he is to employ at all. If more is asked, he cannot pay it, and he has to go out of business. It is useless for the employer to go on making goods which are too dear for people to buy; therefore, if labour demands a wage higher than can be borne by the goods out of the price at which they can be sold, the wage cannot be paid and the business must stop.

The supply of labour in a trade also governs the price of labour. For example, if the number of carpenters were suddenly doubled it would be very bad for the carpenters, because the amount of carpenter's work which people would be willing to pay for would not suddenly be doubled, and therefore the price of carpenter's work (wages) would fall. In practice, this does not happen, because

newcomers enter trades a few at a time, and the common experience of life prevents young people from entering trades which are not growing.

While, as we have seen, an employer cannot pay a worker more than the price of his goods allows, he may pay less if the worker is not able to protect himself. This arises from the fact we have already noticed, that so many people do not themselves own capital, and can, therefore, earn their living only by offering to work for people who do own capital. This gives the capitalist an advantage which can be modified only by good feeling and justice, or by the worker joining with his fellows to resist injustice if it occurs.

WHY GOOD TRADE UNIONS ARE A BENEFIT TO ALL

It was this weakness on the part of the worker in bargaining with the capitalist which led to the formation of Trade Unions. A Trade Union is a society of workers who are banded together to secure for themselves better conditions and the highest wages possible.

Let us clearly understand this. We saw that there is a certain wage beyond which the employer cannot go if he is to make a living for himself. He is entitled to that living, for his work is valuable to society and to the people he employs. He is a captain of industry, and, like the captain of a cricket club, he is indispensable. He is not entitled, however, to make undue profit by underpaying his workpeople. There is always the danger of his being a bad judge of his own case. The Trade Union, if it does its duty, will see that its members are not underpaid, and yet it will not be so foolish as to demand a wage higher than the trade will bear.

GOODWILL AND UNDERSTANDING WITHOUT WHICH WE CANNOT PROSPER

Sometimes, unfortunately, grave quarrels take place, and the capitalists and the unions cannot agree. Then we hear of labour troubles, which may take the form of a strike (which means that the workers refuse to go on with their work) or of a lockout (which means that the employers close their works and refuse to pay the wage demanded). Such misfortunes can be prevented only by goodwill and thorough understanding on both sides. That is why it is so important for everyone to understand these things about work of which we have been reading.

FLOWERS OF THE MOUNTAIN

1. FLAX-LEAVED GOLDILOCKS   2. THRIFT   3. TRAILING AZALEA   4. SPIGNEL   5. MOUNTAIN FORGET-
ME-NOT   6. MOUNTAIN BEDSTRAW   7. MOUNTAIN THYME   8 WILD MADDER   9. RED BEAR-BERRY

1. SWEET CICELY   2. WOOD VETCH   3. RED ALPINE CAMPION   4. GLOBE-FLOWER   5 CAT'S FOOT
5. VIVIPAROUS BISTORT   7. YELLOW PANSY   8. MOUNTAIN AVENS   9. ALPINE BARTSIA

FLOWERS OF THE SEASIDE

1. TREE MALLOW   2. SEA PURSLANE   3. SEA RADISH   4. HEMLOCK STORK'SBILL   5. SEASIDE SMOOTH
GROMWELL   6. COMMON TAMARISK   7. GOLDEN SAMPHIRE   8. MARSH MALLOW   9. PURPLE SEA
ROCKET   10. SMOOTH SEA HEATH   11. BLOODY CRANE'S BILL   12. COMMON FENNEL   13. HALBERD-
LEAVED ORACHE   14. SAND ROCKET   15. ENGLISH STONECROP   16. SEASIDE EVERLASTING PEA

1. YELLOW-HORNED POPPY   2. COMMON SEA LAVENDER   3. RED BARTSIA   4. BURNET ROSE
5. SEA WORMWOOD   6. SEAKALE   7. REST-HARROW   8. SEA CAMPION   9. DWARF TUFTED
CENTAURY   10. COMMON ALEXANDERS   11. SEA CONVOLVULUS   12. GREAT SEA STOCK
13. SEASIDE COTTONWEED   See page 5759 for the chapter on Flowers of the Seaside

The Story of the Peoples of All Nations and Their Homelands

The colossal Palace of Justice at Brussels

BELGIUM AND HER PEOPLE

THE small country of Belgium, slightly less than twice the size of York-shire—its area is 11,775 square miles—has always filled a very important place in European politics, trade, and industry; and there are two reasons for this. The first reason is that it lies at the crossroads of Western Europe, on the direct route between London and Berlin, and between Berlin and Paris. The second reason is that the country has valuable natural resources, and its people an indefatigable industry and tenacity.

Although Belgium is a small country, it is extremely varied in its natural character, and its inhabitants belong to two distinct races. The old Roman road which ran from Cologne, through Maastricht, Tongres, and Cambrai to Boulogne, follows at a short distance the course of the Meuse and the Sambre. By that route invading armies have marched into and across Belgium for centuries, and it is marked by many a battlefield, including the famous field of Waterloo, near Brussels.

Twice in this century has Belgium been overrun and occupied by the Germans, and twice has she taken up arms to defend herself against the invaders who violated her neutrality.

In the First World War the gallant resistance of King Albert and the rem-nants of his little army helped their British allies to hold the extreme western corner of the country through four bitter years of trench warfare. Ypres is an immortal name in Britain's story, and the great host of our men who fell in the defence of that Flemish city are remembered at the white arch of the Menin Gate, where the Last Post is sounded every evening.

It was at Mons that British troops first encountered the Germans in 1914, and they had fought their way back to Mons when the Armistice came in 1918. King Albert re-entered his liberated capital in triumph, but in 1934 he met a tragic death in a climbing accident, and his son Leopold came to the throne.

In 1940 when the Germans again crossed the frontier into Belgium the Belgians again resolved, without hesitation, to fight, but together with the British, French, and Dutch, they were swept away in the tide of " blitzkrieg," and after only eighteen days' campaign King Leopold ordered the cease fire and sur-rendered himself and his army to avoid further vain bloodshed.

Amidst all the confusion and bitterness of the time the king was widely re-proached. But whatever his motives may

THE FIVE CONTINENTS & 100 NATIONS & RACES THAT INHABIT THEM

have been, his actions became the subject of political controversy, and after the liberation of his country he remained in exile. In July 1951 he abdicated and his son Prince Baudouin became King.

In the old Roman days the Silva Carbonaria, the great forest of the Ardennes highlands, came down to their famous road, and a great part of the high land south-east of this line is still forest. In the forest-clad hills the Celtic population found refuge from Saxon and German invaders, and the Roman road which bounded the forest forms approximately the language line between the French-speaking Walloon population and the Flemish-speaking Teutonic races. If you draw on your map a line from Tongres to Courtrai, you have the northern limit of French as the language of the common people. The two races are very much mixed, and French pushes its way north of this line. Brussels, with less than a million people, is predominantly French, but the common tongue in the countryside is Flemish.

A DENSELY POPULATED LAND WITH SPLENDID COMMUNICATIONS

Belgium is the second most thickly populated State in Europe. A crowded little country with more than eleven million people, nearly 1000 to the square mile. This dense population is not congregated in large towns. In the Flemish districts great numbers of people live outside the towns in houses with gardens or plots of agricultural land, the produce of which helps to eke out their wages. The Flemish worker is more apt to crowd into the towns than his Walloon brother.

Belgium's communications are very highly developed, with 3200 miles of railways, and a similar mileage of light railways, the long-distance steam or electric tramways that link up the cities often running alongside main roads. There are 28,000 miles of roads and 1000 miles of canals and navigable rivers.

The hill country of the Ardennes is a continuation of the highlands of western Germany and Luxemburg. It is really a plateau, in the hills of which deep gorges have been cut by the Meuse and the Sambre and their tributaries. This is the delightful and romantic country where the Four Sons of Aymon hid from the vengeance of Charlemagne. Near Dinant they still show the traveller the

Roche Bayard, where the famous steed of Renaud or Rinaldo detached the great mass of rock from the mountain with a kick of its mighty hoof; and once a year, on the eve of St. John, the peasants say that Bayard can be heard whinnying in the forest. The limestone which is to be found thereabouts has been worn by the action of rushing streams into a thousand strange and fantastic shapes. Steep cliffs overhang the streams, and at Han is the famous labyrinth of grottoes through one series of which runs the River Lesse. In the neighbourhood of Dinant are great limestone cliffs, and many curious limestone caves with stalactites depending from the roof.

THE GREAT AREA IN WHICH COAL AND IRON ARE FOUND

To the north of the Meuse and the Sambre, in a line stretching for 115 miles from Liége to Namur, Charleroi, Mons, and St. Ghislain, are coalfields, with iron mines on each side of the rivers between Huy and Charleroi. The land of the Belgian black country lies about 150 to 600 feet above sea-level, and slopes gradually to the north-west, being drained by a number of rivers which run into the Schelde.

The rich soil of the plains of central Belgium is excellently suited for agriculture. Every inch of it is cultivated. The Belgian farmer generally owns his small-holding, and he and his family work very hard, in many cases producing two crops every year. The fertile belt stretches west into Flanders, and yields, under patient tillage, heavy crops of wheat, rye, sugar-beet, chicory, potatoes, and all sorts of vegetables, grown for export to France and England, as well as for the home market in Belgium. In the sheltered valleys of the Meuse the vine is grown.

HOW THE LOW-LYING LAND IS PROTECTED FROM THE SEA

The whole of Flanders is densely cultivated. Its two principal rivers are the Lys, famous for the retting of flax, and the Schelde, on which the great medieval free cities of Ghent and Antwerp grew up. To the north-west of the Lys lie the low hills made famous in the First World War, running in a line from Hazebrouck to Ypres. But the most curious district of Flanders is the strip of low-lying country, from five to ten miles broad, running

PALACE AND PARLIAMENT IN BRUSSELS

THE ROYAL PALACE IN THE BELGIAN CAPITAL

PALAIS DE LA NATION, IN WHICH THE SENATE AND THE CHAMBER OF DEPUTIES SIT

along the coast from Dunkirk on the other side of the French frontier to Antwerp.

This land is protected from the sea by a system of dunes a mile or more deep, and is drained by canals filled with fresh water. Between the canals lie the rich pastures known as polders. Near the French frontier the polders have to be kept dry by pumping. These districts were in the First World War flooded as a defence.

There are no natural harbours, but the mouths of the Yser at Nieuport, and of the canals at Ostend and Zeebrugge, have been made available for ships. All along the dunes watering-places with casinos and promenades have sprung up for people who want the sea bathing. Ostend is one of the gayest watering-places in Europe.

Low-lying country is the first glimpse the traveller sailing up to Antwerp gets of Belgium. Grass of a dazzling green, bordered here and there by a slip of shining sand between it and the water's edge, and tiny houses of a red brick as brilliant in tone as the grass; and, presently, the great cathedral tower and tall warehouses of Antwerp—just the same bright-coloured amphibious landscape as is characteristic of the Dutch coast. Large districts of Flanders have a very sandy soil. The long, straight roads are lined with trees, and the ditches with hedges which help to bind the sandy soil.

THE GREAT WEALTH NOW BEING WON FROM AN OLD TRACT OF BARREN LAND

Away to the north-east, north of a line drawn from Mechelen to the Dutch border near Maastricht, is a continuation of the coastal plain, a huge tract of barren sandy country which even Belgian industry had failed to render fertile. This is the Campine (or Kempenland), which stretches across the Dutch and German borders. Until not so long ago this was regarded as waste land fit for nothing but fir and larch. But it holds that most precious of gifts to an industrialised country, the " black diamonds " of coal. The coal is between 500 and 900 yards below the surface and makes good coking coal for the iron industry and for dealing with raw materials from the Belgian Congo—that wealthy colony of which we read in a later chapter (see Index).

The Belgian ironworks had formerly to buy coking coal from Germany; now they find they have seams which yield heavier returns than those of the old workings of the Meuse-Sambre coalfield. The development of the coal industry is changing the face of this desolate, barren country, and busy industrial centres have grown up like mushrooms. The sand, too, is excellent for glass, and all sorts of raw materials pour in through the port of Antwerp, which is close to the new field. New railway lines have been built and electrical methods have been adopted throughout this region.

WHY ANTWERP WAS LATE IN BECOMING A GREAT PORT

If we look at the map we see that Antwerp, the great port which is a rival to Rotterdam, is in a very strange position, for the south side of the broad estuary is Dutch as well as the islands. A small piece of what looks as if it must be Belgian mainland has remained Dutch.

It was because Holland held the entrance to the Schelde that Antwerp, more than fifty miles from the open sea, was prevented from becoming a great port until the last century. The Dutch did not want to allow so near a rival to Rotterdam. The navigation of the Schelde is under a joint commission of both Belgians and Dutch, but the Belgians are very conscious that the approach to their great river and their principal port is commanded by another nation. That was one of the reasons for the development of the new artificial port of Zeebrugge. The port of Zeebrugge is becoming an important harbour, its mole protecting the entrance of a ship-canal to Bruges, which is reviving again. There is a train-ferry service between Harwich and Zeebrugge, so that fragile goods can be shipped between England and Belgium without the cost and risk of lading and unlading at the ports.

THE DIFFERENCES BETWEEN THE PEOPLE OF HOLLAND AND BELGIUM

Although the Dutch and the Belgians have lived side by side for centuries, they have not always been good friends. The Dutch are, on the whole, rich and well educated; they are Protestants, and are of pure Teutonic race. They are a serious people. The Belgians, as we have seen, are crowded together; until recently their public educational system was left almost entirely to the individual commune; they are a mixed race, they profess the

WHAT THE TRAVELLER SEES IN BELGIUM

BRUSSELS MONUMENT TO GODFREY DE BOUILLON, HERO OF THE FIRST CRUSADE

THE STATUE OF RUBENS THE ARTIST, IN THE SQUARE AT ANTWERP

THE TOMB OF BELGIUM'S UNKNOWN WARRIOR IN THE CAPITAL

MODERN ASTRONOMICAL CLOCK IN A 14th CENTURY TOWER AT LIERRE

Catholic faith, and they have a keen, broad humour.

The most important Belgian heavy industries, the making of steel, mechanical construction (bridges, girders, steel frames for building, pumps, cranes, motors, engines, boilers, rail and tramway material), are naturally grouped on the coalfields, the chief centres being Liége and Charleroi, though there are also works at Brussels, Ghent, Mechelen (Malines), and Antwerp.

The making of sheet and plate glass, in which Belgium excels, is also mainly carried on on the coalfields. Zinc, with its by-product sulphuric acid, one of the most valuable of Belgium's natural resources, is found between Liége and Aachen (Aix-la-Chapelle), partly in the border territory of Moresnet, and is treated on the Sambre-Meuse coalfield and in the Campine. Pottery, paper, and works for the production of industrial chemicals, are scattered all over the country; cotton and linen mills are found at Ghent and elsewhere in east Flanders; woollen cloth factories in and around Verviers, Antwerp, and other places; tapestries and fabrics of mixed cotton silk and wool are made around Courtrai; carpets at Brussels and elsewhere; and there is the diamond industry of Antwerp, a trade which that city shares with Amsterdam.

THE GREAT WATERWAY, WHICH JOINS ANTWERP TO LIÉGE

A spectacular Belgian engineering achievement was the Albert Canal, which took nine years to plan and build, and was completed not long before the Second World War. It joins Antwerp to Liége, the centre of the iron and steel industries. Its purpose was not only to carry cargoes to the port, but to transport coal from the new Campine fields to Liége, where the seams are becoming exhausted.

Nearly 80 miles long, the Albert Canal has only six locks between the Meuse and sea level at Antwerp, and is navigable by barges of more than 2000 tons. The tragic irony of this great waterway is that, apart from its economic value, it was intended to be a strong military defence work. Indeed, with the bridges blown up, the sheer concrete banks and deep channel would have been a formidable obstacle to an invading army. But in 1940 the Germans seized bridges intact by a treacherous surprise attack, and their tanks streamed over the great water barrier as if it did not exist.

In spite of the country's development and in spite of the storms of war and revolution in the last 200 years, Belgium is, perhaps, the best country in Europe in which to study the medieval civic life and organisation of northern Europe. The monuments and the art of the prosperous centuries before Spain broke the Low Countries are still preserved.

THE ANCIENT CITY MEN USED TO CALL THE VENICE OF THE NORTH

Bruges is a fine example of the industrial city of those days. The houses and buildings of mellow red brick in her ancient streets and along the quiet canals made men call her the " Venice of the North."

In the thirteenth and fourteenth centuries, when the communes were freeing themselves from the feudal lords and building up the industry and trade which were to make the Flemish cities a marvel to later English travellers, the townspeople built the market hall with its belfry, often containing the marvellous carillon in which Belgian metal workers excelled. This hall was nearly always strongly built, and capable of defence. The tall belfry which ornaments so many Flemish cities, sometimes built as part of the Halles or markets, sometimes, as at Ghent and Tournai, a separate building, was a sign of the independence of the citizens; from the belfry the bell called the burghers to work and prayer, and the tocsin called them to arms to defend their liberties in case of emergency. Here and there, as at Ghent, the rival building, the fortified castle, still exists. There are many magnificent examples of this civic architecture in Belgium—the Cloth Hall of Ypres, destroyed in the First World War, but rebuilt; the Halles and Belfry of Bruges, of Ghent, and many another less famous town. The oldest of these belfries is at Tournai, for the building of which a charter was obtained from Philip Augustus of France in 1187. These are typical of old Belgium.

THE WONDERFUL SQUARE AT THE HEART OF BRUSSELS

Later, in the fifteenth and sixteenth centuries, when these same towns built their town halls, the architecture became highly ornate and decorative. The idea governing their flamboyant style was to display the splendour and riches of the town and its artistic genius; there was no longer any need of defence. Perhaps the most magnificent of the many fine town halls in Belgium is the Hotel de Ville on the Grand Place in Brussels.

The Grand Place is a wonderful square. Opposite the Hotel de Ville is the splendid Gothic Maison du Roi or Bread House (now a museum), and on the other sides stand the old houses of the merchant guilds, with their high serrated gables, their balconies, and their quaint sculptures. The town hall of Louvain,

of the Schelde and the Lys? Their art and their industry they owed in many cases to the monastic foundation. Most of the churches built in the days of Charlemagne and the following centuries in the Romanesque manner have perished, but parts of the church of St. Guy, at Anderlecht, of the minster church of Nivelles, and of some of the churches at Bruges, go back to this period.

But most of the great churches are built in the Belgian Gothic style; this was introduced in the cathedral at Tournai in the Twelfth century by French architects, but the builders of great Belgian churches

GENERAL VIEW OF THE CITY OF LUXEMBURG, CAPITAL OF THE GRAND DUCHY. See next page

which escaped when many buildings were destroyed in 1914, is a highly decorated example of Belgian civic art, but it has been much restored. Nowhere in Europe has civic architecture been more magnificent than in the Flemish cities. A nation of merchants, craftsmen, and manufacturers, subject for centuries to foreign rule, they found freedom and self-government in the city, and nothing was too good to express its greatness.

The old Belgians were also a deeply religious people. They venerated the saints as the founders of their loved cities. Had not St. Amand founded Ghent when he pitched his monastery at the junction

adapted it and made it national. The octagonal towers, the rounded turrets, and the width and spaciousness of the interiors give them their peculiar beauty.

The architects of Brabant were famous all over Europe. The cathedral of St. Rombaut at Mechelen, with its mighty square tower; of St. Bavon at Ghent; the church of Notre Dame du Sablon at Brussels, built for the Guild of Crossbowmen; the great church of St. Michel and St. Gudule at Brussels, with its two towers; and Antwerp Cathedral, of whose western towers only one was finished—these are only some of the wonderful Belgian Gothic churches.

Originally these churches were brilliant with colour, with mural paintings and with gold. Every kind of craftsmanship was lavished on them, in sculpture, in stone and wood, in brass, copper, and iron work, in tapestry, in stained glass, and in painting. Much of this treasure was destroyed by the Calvinists in the sixteenth century, and the churches again suffered in the Revolution in 1793, but much remains. The painters of each town in the fourteenth century formed themselves into a guild, like other tradesmen, but they did not confine themselves to easel work; many of them practised other crafts as well. Like the Greeks, the Belgians preferred their statues coloured. Jan van Eyck himself coloured some of them.

The Flemish cities, too, are rich in paintings of the great Flemish religious school. We may see great pictures by Roger van der Weyden, the brothers Van Eyck, Quentin Matsys, and the rest in our own National Gallery, but it is better to see them in the churches for which they were originally designed. In the old hospital of St. John, at Bruges, are the best works of Hans Memling. In the cathedral of St. Bavon, at Ghent, is Hubert and Jan van Eyck's Adoration of the Lamb. To Jan van Eyck is generally ascribed the discovery of the art of painting in oil; in any case the colours of this great series of pictures are still fresh after five hundred years. Antwerp Cathedral counts among its treasures Rubens' Elevation of the Cross and Descent from the Cross, and on the High Altar is the same painter's Assumption. Rubens painted many pictures for the Jesuit churches, some of them gay and full of the pleasure of life and far from devout, but the Jesuits did not hesitate to press secular art into the service of religion.

One other kind of architecture is peculiar to Belgium, that of the tranquil squares and gardens surrounded by low houses and adorned by a church. In the fourteenth century were devout men and women who took no religious vows, but found refuge from the world in these quiet places, working for their living with their hands, and giving their leisure to prayer. Some of these communities remain; they were for aristocrats, but most of them are now for simple working people.

These places have provided many poor men and women with a quiet home. Many were destroyed at the Revolution, and many have now been secularised. There is one at Bruges, on the bank of the Roya, and in Ghent there are two, so large as to be almost little villages by themselves.

Belgium is a highly modern industrial State, but the monuments of the pious craftsmen of the Middle Ages continue to be cherished as her greatest glory by the Belgians themselves and by those of us who, after crossing to Ostend or Antwerp, find ourselves suddenly seized with the enchantment of medieval Ghent and medieval Bruges. We turn back in imagination to the guildsmen—riotous, independent, and hard-working, but every one of them alive to beauty, and ceaselessly striving to embody it in art.

THE GRAND DUCHY OF LUXEMBURG

LUXEMBURG, adjoining France, Belgium, and Germany, is a Grand Duchy of 999 square miles, with a population of about 300,000, and a capital, Luxemburg, of 62,000 inhabitants. Its neutrality was guaranteed before the First World War, but the Germans disregarded the arrangement and the reigning Grand Duchess sympathised with them. After the German defeat the Grand Duchess abdicated, and her sister, the Grand Duchess Charlotte, succeeded her. This was confirmed by a national referendum.

Luxemburg was occupied by the Germans during the Second World War, and the Grand Duchess and her Government carried on in London.

The Constitution claims sovereign power for the nation. There is a chamber of deputies numbering 55. A Council of State of 15 members is chosen by the Sovereign. Luxemburg is rich in iron ore, and produces an amount of steel approaching two million tons in a normal year.

For many years Luxemburg has had economic union with Belgium, using her neighbour's currency and having no customs barriers against her. In association with Holland, these two countries have become known to the world as the Benelux countries, an outstanding example to bigger nations of what unity can achieve.

PICTURES OF BELGIUM

A FINE GROUP OF TOWERS IN GHENT

THE BELFRY AT BRUGES

THE TOWN HALL AT BRUGES

THE 13TH-CENTURY TOWN HALL
AT ALOST

RUE ST. MARTIN AND THE
CATHEDRAL AT TOURNAI

ST. ROMBAUT CATHEDRAL
AT MECHELEN

THE PUBLIC SQUARE AT DIXMUDE

THE TOWN AND CITADEL OF NAMUR ON THE RIVER MEUSE

THE COLUMN OF CONGRESS
IN BRUSSELS

THE CHURCH OF SAINT GUDULE
IN BRUSSELS

THE TOWN HALL OF
BRUSSELS

THE BEAUTIFUL GRAND PLACE IN THE BELGIAN CAPITAL

ANTWERP, THE SECOND CITY OF BELGIUM, SEEN FROM ACROSS THE SCHELDE

THE GREAT LION MONUMENT ON THE FIELD OF WATERLOO

DINANT ON THE MEUSE, WITH ITS CLIFFTOP FORTRESS

A CHARACTERISTIC LANDSCAPE IN FLANDERS

THE NEW CLOTH HALL TOWER AND THE CATHEDRAL AT YPRES

THE MENIN GATE, DEDICATED TO THE SOLDIERS OF THE BRITISH EMPIRE WHO FELL AT YPRES

THE HOUSE OF THE FRANC AT BRUGES

THE TOWN HALL OF LOUVAIN

A QUIET CORNER OF BRUGES

THE QUAI AUX HERBES AT GHENT

THE BROEL BRIDGE AT COURTRAI

THE TOWN HALL OF OUDENARDE

THE BOURSE, OR STOCK EXCHANGE,
IN BRUSSELS

MAGNIFICENT GUILD HOUSES IN THE
GRAND PLACE, BRUSSELS

BELGIUM'S BROADCASTING HOUSE IN THE CAPITAL

A STREET MARKET AND A FLOWER-SELLER IN BRUSSELS

For maps of Belgium see pages 5534 and 5535

One Thousand Poems of All Times and All Countries

THIS fine poem suggests something of the fierce spirit of the Vikings, those warriors of the sea whose home was in the part of Europe we call Scandinavia. When a Viking chief died his body was placed in a boat, and the boat, with full sail set and a fire lighted, was sent drifting out to sea. As the fire consumed the vessel and the body of the dead it was supposed that the chieftain thus made his last journey, entering into Valhalla, the home of the gods. In this stirring poem of King Balder's funeral voyage the tragic interest is the greater from the fact that the king is not dead when he sets sail for Valhalla but is voluntarily going forth to his fate. The king is named after one of the gods in the Norse mythology, and we are compelled to admire the indomitable spirit of these old pagans, whose stories of their imaginary gods are full of a beautiful bravery. This poem was written by Charles Mackay, a well-known poet and journalist,, who was born in 1814 and died in 1889.

THE SEA-KING'S BURIAL

M*Y strength is failing fast,*
  Said the sea-king to his men.
I shall never sail the seas
  Like a conqueror again,
But while a drop remains
Of the life-blood in my veins
Raise, oh, raise me from my bed,
Put the crown upon my head,
Put my good sword in my hand,
And so lead me to the strand,
  Where my ship at anchor rides
    Steadily :
If I cannot end my life
In the crimsoned battle-strife
  Let me die as I have lived,
    On the sea.

THEY have raised King Balder up,
  Put his crown upon his head ;
They have sheathed his limbs in mail
  And the purple o'er him spread;
And, amid the greeting rude
Of a gathering multitude,
Borne him slowly to the shore,
All the energy of yore
From his dim eyes flashing forth,
Old sea-lion of the North,
  As he looked upon his ship
    Riding free,
And on his forehead pale
Felt the cold, refreshing gale,
  And heard the welcome sound
    Of the sea.

THEY have borne him to the ship
  With a slow and solemn tread;
They have placed him on the deck
  With his crown upon his head,
Where he sat as on a throne;
And have left him there alone,
With his anchor ready weighed,
And his snowy sails displayed

To the favouring wind, once more
Blowing freshly from the shore,
  And have bidden him farewell
    Tenderly,
Saying: " King of mighty men,
We shall meet thee yet again
  In Valhalla, with the monarchs
    Of the sea."

UNDERNEATH him in the hold
  They had placed the lighted brand ;
And the fire was burning slow
  As the vessel from the land,
Like a stag-hound from the slips,
Darted forth from out the ships.
There was music in her sail
As it swelled before the gale,
And a dashing at her prow
As it cleft the waves below,
  And the good ship sped along,
    Scudding free;
As on many a battle morn
In her time she had been borne
  To struggle and to conquer
    On the sea.

AND the king with sudden strength
  Started up and paced the deck,
With his good sword for his staff,
  And his robe around his neck.
Once alone, he raised his hand
To the people on the land;
And with shout and joyous cry
Once again they made reply,
Till the loud, exulting cheer
Sounded faintly on his ear;
  For the gale was o'er him blowing
    Fresh and free;
And ere yet an hour had passed
He was driven before the blast,
  And a storm was on his path,
    On the sea.

POEMS · SONGS · BALLADS · VERSES AND RHYMES WITH MUSIC

" So blow, ye tempests, blow,
 And my spirit shall not quail;
I have fought with many a foe,
 I have weathered many a gale;
And in this hour of death,
Ere I yield my fleeting breath,
Ere the fire now burning slow
Shall come rushing from below,
And this worn and wasted frame
Be devoted to the flame,
 I will raise my voice in triumph,
 Singing free;
To the great All-Father's home
I am driving through the foam,
 I am sailing to Valhalla
 O'er the sea.

" So blow, ye stormy winds,
 And ye flames, ascend on high;
In easy, idle bed
 Let the slave and coward die!
But give me the driving keel,
Clang of shields and flashing steel,
Or my foot on foreign ground,
With my enemies around!
Happy, happy, thus I yield,
On the deck or in the field,
 My last breath, shouting On
 To victory.
But since this has been denied
They shall say that I have died
 Without flinching, like a monarch
 Of the sea."

And Balder spoke no more,
 And no sound escaped his lip;
And he looked, yet scarcely saw
 The destruction of his ship,
Nor the fleet sparks mounting high,
Nor the glare upon the sky;
Scarcely heard the billows dash,
Nor the burning timber crash;
Scarcely felt the scorching heat
That was gathering at his feet,
 Nor the fierce flames mounting o'er him
 Greedily,
But the life was in him yet,
And the courage to forget
 All his pain in his triumph
 On the sea.

Once alone, a cry arose,
 Half of anguish, half of pride,
As he sprang upon his feet,
 With the flames on every side.
" I am coming! " said the king,
" Where the swords and bucklers ring,
Where the warrior lives again,
Where the souls of mighty men

And the weary find repose,
And the red wine ever flows.
 I am coming, great All-Father,
 Unto thee !
Unto Odin, unto Thor,
And the strong, true hearts of yore:
 I am coming to Valhalla
 O'er the sea."

DIAMOND DUST

This fervent love song on a dewy morning is from the
pen of a popular English poet and novelist, John Oxenham.

My Lady walks on diamond dust,
 All meaner causeway scorning,
On diamond dust, on diamond dust,
Upon a sunny morning;
On diamond dust, because she must,
Since, all for her adorning,
Earth's crust becomes just diamond dust
Upon a sunny morning.

Ten thousand million gleaming eyes
Meet hers with merry twinkles,
And her quick feet with sparkles greet
And tiny rainbow-sprinkles.

And when she climbs the stile to cross
The shimmering, dew-drenched meadow,
Each blade of grass that sees her pass
To kiss her hem flings out a gem,
Which dies in her sweet shadow.

So jewels rare are everywhere
To welcome her sweet passing;
They are, I swear, beyond compare,
All earthly gems surpassing.
And so she walks on jewels fair,
All meaner causeway scorning,
On jewels rare beyond compare,
On every sunny morning.

A LAND DIRGE

This much-quoted and fanciful dirge is by John Webster,
who lived at the same time as Shakespeare, but was a little
younger. In it we can hear the ring of verse common to
that fine literary age. Webster also wrote for the stage.

Call for the robin-redbreast and the
 wren,
Since o'er shady groves they hover,
And with leaves and flowers do cover
The friendless bodies of unburied men.
Call unto his funeral dole
The ant, the field-mouse, and the mole,
To rear him hillocks that shall keep him
 warm,
And (when gay tombs are robbed) sustain
 no harm;
But keep the wolf far thence, that's foe
 to men,
For with his nails he'll dig them up again.

THE SLEEPING BEAUTY

This delightful poem is by Walter De La Mare, one of the most outstanding literary men of this century, and the greatest of all poets who have sung of childhood and its joys.

THE scent of bramble fills the air,
    Amid her folded sheets she lies,
The gold of evening in her hair,
    The blue of morn shut in her eyes.

How many a changing moon hath lit
    The unchanging roses of her face!
Her mirror ever broods on it
    In silver stillness of the days.

Oft flits the moth on filmy wings
    Into his solitary lair;
Shrill evensong the cricket sings
    From some still shadow in her hair.

In heat, in snow, in wind, in flood,
    She sleeps in lovely loneliness,
Half-folded like an April bud
    On winter-haunted trees.

CHIDE ME NOT

Ralph Waldo Emerson was one of the greatest essayists the world has known—the greatest of all American prose writers; he was also a poet who saw all life in Nature and man woven into one web.

CHIDE me not, laborious band,
    For the idle flowers I brought;
Every aster in my hand
    Goes home laden with a thought.

There was never mystery,
    But 'tis figured in the flowers;
Was never secret history
    But birds tell it in the bowers.

ADDRESS TO HIS NATIVE SOIL

This poem is by William Browne, who was born at Tavistock in 1591 and died about 1643. He is one of our lesser poets, and his verse, overloaded with detail and allegory, is little read today; but at its best his verse reflects a genuine love and understanding of the countryside.

HAIL thou, my native soil! thou blessed plot
Whose equal all the world affordeth not!
Show me who can? so many crystal rills,
Such sweet-clothed valleys, or aspiring hills,
Such wood-ground, pastures, quarries, wealthy mines,
Such rocks in whom the diamond fairly shines:
And if the earth can show the like again,
Yet will she fail in her sea-ruling men.
Time never can produce men to o'ertake
The fames of Grenville, Davis, Gilbert, Drake,
Or worthy Hawkins, or of thousands more,
That by their power made the Devonian shore
Mock the proud Tagus; for whose richest spoil
The boasting Spaniard left the Indian soil
Bankrupt of store, knowing it would quit cost
By winning this, though all the rest were lost.

JULIAN GRENFELL

This beautiful sonnet, honouring the valiant spirit of a young English poet who was killed in the First World War, was written by Maurice Baring (1874–1945). It is reproduced here by permission of the Hon. Maurice Baring's executrix, and Messrs. Heinemann, publishers of his Collected Poems.

BECAUSE of you we will be glad and gay;
    Remembering you, we will be brave and strong;
And hail the advent of each dangerous day,
And meet the last adventure with a song.
And, as you proudly gave your jewelled gift,
We'll give our lesser offering with a smile,
Nor falter on that path where, all too swift,
You led the way and leapt the golden stile.
Whether new paths, new heights to climb you find,
Or gallop through the unfooted asphodel,
We know you know we shall not lag behind,
Nor halt to waste a moment on a fear;
And you will speed us onward with a cheer
And wave beyond the stars that all is well.

BOATS AT NIGHT

This melodious sonnet is from the pen of Edward Shanks (1892–1953), who won wide fame as a poet, essayist, critic, and journalist. He was the first winner, in 1919, of the Hawthornden Prize for Imaginative Literature.

HOW lovely is the sound of oars at night
    And unknown voices, borne through windless air,
From shadowy vessels floating out of sight
Beyond the harbour lantern's broken glare
To those piled rocks that make on the dark wave
Only a darker stain. The splashing oars
Slide softly on as in an echoing cave
And with the whisper of the unseen shores
Mingle their music, till the bell of night
Murmurs reverberations low and deep
That droop towards the land in swooning flight
Like whispers from the lazy lips of sleep.
The oars grow faint. Below the cloud-dim hill
The shadows fade and now the bay is still.

HEART AND WILL

The theme of this poem is England's championship of freedom. The writer, William James Linton (1812–98), was not only a poet but a notable artist.

OUR England's heart is sound as oak;
  Our English will is firm;
And through our actions Freedom spoke,
  In History's proudest term;
When Blake was lord from shore to shore,
  And Cromwell ruled the land,
And Milton's words were shields of power
  To stay the oppressor's hand.

Our England's heart is yet as sound,
  As firm our English will;
And tyrants, be they cowled or crowned,
  Shall find us fearless still.
And though our Vane be in his tomb,
  Though Hampden's blood is cold,
Their spirits live to lead our doom
  As in the days of old.

Our England's heart is stout as oak;
  Our English will as brave
As when indignant Freedom spoke
  From Eliot's prison grave.
And closing yet again with Wrong,
  A world in arms shall see
Our England foremost of the Strong
  And first among the Free.

JOAN OF ARC

This sonnet in honour of France's great heroine is by Sir Harold Idris Bell, a distinguished authority on ancient manuscripts, who has made a deep study of Welsh literature, translating many poems into English verse.

ALONE she faced them, one unlettered
    girl,
Matched with their pride, their learning,
    and their skill;
Lawyer and churchman, noble, knight,
    and churl
Together leagued in one malignant will.
But what can malice against simple sooth?
She all alone, by gibe and scoff assailed,
Armed but with mother wit and native
    truth,
Over their learning and their arts pre-
    vailed.
What though, her voices mute, no helper
    nigh,
One bitter hour she stooped to mortal
    shame?
The moment passed, she put her weakness
    by
And went unfaltering to the final flame.
So like a beacon through the centuries
    dark,
For ever shines thy memory, Joan of Arc!

THE SKYLARK

One of the most musical and tender of the many songs addressed to the skylark, this carol came from the pen of a shepherd who in youth had scarcely any schooling—James Hogg (1770–1835), the Ettrick Shepherd, who became first a collector and then a writer of Scottish ballads.

BIRD of the wilderness,
  Blythesome and cumberless,
Sweet be thy matin o'er moorland and lea!
  Emblem of happiness,
  Blest is thy dwelling-place—
O to abide in the desert with thee!

Wild is thy lay and loud,
  Far in the downy cloud,
Love gives it energy, love gave it birth.
  Where, on thy dewy wing,
  Where art thou journeying?
Thy lay is in heaven, thy love is on earth.

O'er fell and fountain sheen,
  O'er moor and mountain green,
O'er the red streamer that heralds the day,
  Over the cloudlet dim,
  Over the rainbow's rim,
Musical cherub, soar, singing, away!

Then, when the gloaming comes,
  Low in the heather blooms,
Sweet will thy welcome and bed of love be!
  Emblem of happiness,
  Blest is thy dwelling-place—
O to abide in the desert with thee!

THE SHEPHERDESS

This charming picture of a soul serene and pure was written by the gifted poet and essayist Alice Meynell (1847–1922).

SHE walks—the lady of my delight—
  A shepherdess of sheep.
Her flocks are thoughts. She keeps them
    white;
She guards them from the steep.
She feeds them on the fragrant height,
And folds them in for sleep.

She roams maternal hills and bright,
Dark valleys safe and deep.
Into that tender breast at night
The chastest stars may peep.
She walks—the lady of my delight—
  A shepherdess of sheep.

She holds her little thoughts in sight,
Though gay they run and leap.
She is so circumspect and right;
She has her soul to keep.
She walks—the lady of my delight—
  A shepherdess of sheep.

LOVE NOT ME FOR COMELY GRACE

Here is a sample of the dainty love verses which abound in English literature, some of them, like this, by unknown writers. The idea in it is true as well as pretty, for we never know, wholly and exactly, why we love anybody.

Love not me for comely grace,
    For my pleasing eye or face,
Nor for any outward part,
No, nor for my constant heart:
    For those may fail or turn to ill,
        So thou and I shall sever;
Keep, therefore, a true woman's eye,
And love me still, but know not why:
    So hast thou the same reason still
        To doat upon me ever!

A SONG FOR THE NEW YEAR

This lovely peep into the heart of a wise man growing old is from the fine pen of Edmund Gosse. As life lengthens, the knowledge of what is best worth having should grow more clear. Alike in what is rejected as unsatisfactory and what is chosen as lastingly dear, Sir Edmund Gosse is a faithful guide, and his message is given in musical words.

What graven words shall mark as mine
    This milestone of a year?
What prayer shall be the worthy sign
    Of all I hope and fear?
        Not greed for gold—
        I'm growing old;
        Burdens I dare no more uphold;
Nor deem I meet for weary feet
The dust and struggle of the street.

Then shall I wish for utter peace?
    For light with calm around?
For all the stir of life to cease
    In apathy profound?
        Ah! no, too long
        I've warred with wrong,
        I've loved the clash of battle-song,
For me to drone in ease alone
Were heavier than a churchyard stone.

And fame? Alas! it comes too late,
    Or, coming, flies too soon;
It dawns as o'er the meadow-gate
    Peers up the yellow moon;
        It glows in power
        One feverish hour,
        Then passes like a perished flower;
Or sets, to rise in alien skies,
And cheat me of my lawful prize.

Why, then, my New Year's wish shall be
    For love—and love alone;
More hands to hold out joy to me,
    More hearts for me to own;
        And if the gain
        In part be pain,
Since time but gives to take again,
Yet more than gold a thousandfold
Is love that's neither bought nor sold.

ADDRESS TO AN EGYPTIAN MUMMY

Quite a number of the world's best-known poems were written by authors who only wrote one or two fine pieces. This poem is an example. Its author, Horace Smith (1779–1849), was a very active writer, but he produced nothing else as impressive as these fine, resounding verses, written when an Italian excavator named Belzoni brought mummies from Egypt to show in a museum of antiquities. Here we get the inquiring thoughts of Horace Smith as he looked at one of the embalmed figures. The poem rises at its close to a stately eloquence. A feature of it is the skill with which romantic and high-sounding names are woven into the lines, an art in which great poets of olden times excelled.

And thou hast walked about (how strange
        a story!)
In Thebes's streets three thousand years
        ago;
When the Memnonium was in all its glory,
    And time had not begun to overthrow
Those temples, palaces, and piles stupen-
        dous,
Of which the very ruins are tremendous?

Speak! for thou long enough has acted
        dummy;
    Thou hast a tongue; come, let us hear
        its tune;
Thou'rt standing on thy legs above ground,
        mummy!
    Revisiting the glimpses of the moon.
Not like thin ghosts or disembodied
        creatures,
But with thy bones and flesh and limbs
        and features.

Tell us for doubtless thou canst recollect,
    To whom should we assign the Sphinx's
        fame?
Was Cheops or Cephrenes architect
    Of either pyramid that bears his name?
Is Pompey's Pillar really a misnomer?
Had Thebes a hundred gates, as sung by
        Homer?

Perhaps thou wert a mason, and forbidden
    By oath to tell the secrets of thy trade;
Then say what secret melody was hidden
    In Memnon's statue, which at sunrise
        played?
Perhaps thou wert a priest—if so, my
        struggles
Are vain, for priestcraft never owns its
        juggles.

Perchance that very hand, now pinioned
        flat,
    Has hob-a-nobbed with Pharaoh, glass
        to glass;
Or dropped a halfpenny in Homer's hat;
    Or doffed thine own to let Queen Dido
        pass;
Or held, by Solomon's own invitation,
A torch at the great temple's dedication.

I need not ask thee if that hand, when
    armed,
    Has any Roman soldier mauled and
      knuckled,
For thou wert dead and buried and em-
    balmed
    Ere Romulus and Remus had been
      suckled;
Antiquity appears to have begun
Long after thy primeval race was run.

Thou could'st develop, if that withered
    tongue
    Might tell us what those sightless orbs
      have seen,
How the world looked when it was fresh
    and young,
    And the great deluge still had left it
      green;
Or was it then so old that history's pages
Contained no record of its early ages;

Still silent! incommunicative elf!
    Art sworn to secrecy? Then keep thy
      vows;
But prithee tell us something of thyself,
    Reveal the secrets of thy prison-house!
Since in the world of spirits thou hast
    slumbered,
What hast thou seen, what strange adven-
    tures numbered?

Since first thy form was in this box ex-
    tended,
    We have, above ground, seen some
      strange mutations;
The Roman Empire has begun and ended,
    New worlds have risen, we have lost old
      nations,
And countless kings have into dust been
    humbled,
    While not a fragment of thy flesh has
      crumbled.

Didst thou not hear the pother o'er thy
    head
    When the great Persian conqueror
      Cambyses
Marched armies o'er thy tomb with
    thundering tread,
    O'erthrew Osiris, Orus, Apis, Isis,
And shook the pyramids with fear and
    wonder,
When the gigantic Memnon fell asunder?

If the tomb's secrets may not be confessed,
    The nature of thy private life unfold;
A heart has throbbed beneath that leathern
    breast,
    And tears adown that dusty cheek have
    rolled.

Have children climbed those knees and
    kissed that face?
What was thy name and station, age and
    race?

Statue of flesh—immortal of the dead!
    Imperishable type of evanescence!
Posthumous man, who quitt'st thy narrow
    bed,
    And standest undecayed within our
      presence,
Thou wilt hear nothing till the Judgment
    morning,
When the great Trump shall thrill thee
    with its warning!

Why should this worthless tegument
    endure
    If its undying guest be lost for ever?
Oh, let us keep the soul embalmed and
    pure
    In living virtue: that, when both must
      sever,
Although corruption may our frame con-
    sume,
The immortal spirit in the skies may
    bloom!

WHERE LIES THE LAND?

It is our passage through life, and perhaps also the Earth's
voyage through Time, that Arthur Hugh Clough is here
hinting at. But, as he suggests, if we know not whence
or whither, in fair or foul weather, the voyage is a romance.

WHERE lies the land to which the ship
    would go?
Far, far ahead, is all her seamen know.
And where the land she travels from?
    Away,
Far, far behind, is all that they can say.

On sunny noons upon the deck's smooth
    face,
Linked arm in arm, how pleasant here to
    pace!
Or, o'er the stern reclining, watch below
The foaming wake far widening as we go.

On stormy nights when wild north-westers
    rave,
How proud a thing to fight with wind and
    wave !
The dripping sailor on the reeling mast,
Exults to bear, and scorns to wish it past.

Where lies the land to which the ship
    would go?
Far, far ahead, is all her seamen know.
And where the land she travels from?
    Away,
Far, far behind, is all that they can say.

ENGLAND, MY ENGLAND

This rapturous song to England, by William Ernest Henley, has been like the bugle call it commemorates. Its echoes have sounded in the poetry of Rudyard Kipling, Henley's successor as a patriot poet; and in its spirit millions of men offered their lives for their country in the two World Wars. Judged all in all, England has been worthy of this devotion.

WHAT have I done for you,
   England, my England?
What is there I would not do,
   England, my own?
With your glorious eyes austere,
As the Lord were walking near,
Whispering terrible things and dear
As the song on your bugles blown,
   England—
Round the world on your bugles blown!

Where shall the watchful sun,
   England, my England,
Match the master-work you've done,
   England, my own?
When shall he rejoice agen
Such a breed of mighty men
As come forward, one to ten,
To the song on your bugles blown,
   England—
Down the years on your bugles blown?

Ever the faith endures,
   England, my England!
Take and break us—we are yours,
   England, my own!
Life is good, and joy runs high
Between English earth and sky;
Death is death; but we shall die
To the song on your bugles blown,
   England—
To the stars on your bugles blown!

They call you proud and hard,
   England, my England:
You with worlds to watch and ward,
   England, my own!
You whose mailed hand keeps the keys
Of such teeming destinies,
You could know nor dread nor ease
Were the song on your bugles blown,
   England—
Round the Pit on your bugles blown!

Mother of Ships whose might,
   England, my England,
Is the fierce old sea's delight,
   England, my own,
Chosen daughter of the Lord,
Spouse-in-chief of the ancient sword,
There's the menace of the Word
In the song on your bugles blown,
   England—
Out of heaven on your bugles blown!

A BOY WAS BORN AT BETHLEHEM

We can never see Jesus as we ought to see Him unless we let our thoughts dwell on His life in imaginative sympathy. That is what Lord Kennet has done in this lovely poem. It is most human to think backward with tenderness of the place where our youth was passed, and, as Jesus was perfect in His humanity, it is not unallowable to suppose that dear memories of His earthly home may have been among the consolations that came in His final suffering.

A BOY was born at Bethlehem
   that knew the haunts of Galilee.
He wandered on Mount Lebanon,
   and learned to love each forest tree.

But I was born at Marlborough,
   and love the homely faces there;
And for all other men besides
   'tis little love I have to spare.

I should not mind to die for them,
   my own dear downs, my comrades true;
But that great heart of Bethlehem,
   He died for men He never knew.

And yet, I think, at Golgotha,
   as Jesus' eyes were closed in death,
They saw with love most passionate
   the village street at Nazareth.

DECEMBER'S SNOW

The shortening of life for each married pair by the passing of the years, but the failure of swift Time to weaken love that is true and deep, are here depicted with tenderest feeling and reassuring truth by Sir Arthur Conan Doyle.

THE bloom is on the may once more,
   The chestnut buds have burst anew;
But, darling, all our springs are o'er,
   'Tis winter still for me and you.
We plucked Life's blossoms long ago;
What's left is but December's snow.

But winter has its joys as fair,
   The gentler joys, aloof, apart;
The snow may lie upon our hair,
   But never, darling, in our heart.
Sweet were the springs of long ago,
But sweeter still December's snow.

Yes, long ago, and yet to me
   It seems a thing of yesterday:
The shade beneath the willow tree,
   The word you looked but feared to say.
Ah! when I learned to love you so
What recked we of December's snow?

But swift the ruthless seasons sped,
   And swifter still they speed away.
What though they bow the haughty head
   And fleck the raven hair with grey?
The boy and girl of long ago
Are laughing through the veil of snow.

A SONG FOR STOUT WORKERS

Here is a manly strain from the pen of that breezy Scotsman Professor Stuart Blackie. It is just the kind of inspiring appeal that would be expected by all who knew the vigour and outspokenness of the Professor, who was one of the most pronounced characters in the Edinburgh of his day. He lived between 1809 and 1895, was Professor of Greek and was very active in preserving the Gaelic language.

ONWARD, brave men, onward go;
　　Place is none for rest below.
He who laggeth faints and fails;
He who presses on prevails!

Monks may nurse their mouldy moods,
Caged in musty solitudes;
Men beneath the breezy sky
March to conquer or to die!

Work and live—this only charm
Warms the blood and nerves the arm,
As the stout pine stronger grows
By each gusty blast that blows.

On high throne or lowly sod,
Fellow-workers we with God;
Then most like to Him when we
March through toil to victory.

If there be who sob and sigh,
Let them sleep or let them die;
While we live we strain and strive,
Working most when most alive!

Where the fairest blossoms grew,
There the spade had most to do;
Hearts that bravely serve the Lord,
Like St. Paul, must wear the sword.

Onward, brothers, onward go!
Face to face to find the foe!
Words are weak and wishing fails,
But the well-aimed blow prevails!

THE SPRING IS COMING

In all lands the season of Spring is beautiful, and enlivens all living things. This description of some of its signs of approach in America is by the charming poet James Whitcomb Riley. The fifth verse refers to the preparations that are made for obtaining sugar from the maple tree.

WHEN country roads begin to thaw
　　In mottled spots of damp and dust,
And fences by the margin draw
　　Along the frosty crust
Their graphic silhouettes, I say
The Spring is coming round this way.

When morning-time is bright with sun
　　And keen with wind, and both confuse
The dancing, glancing eyes of one
　　With tears that ooze and ooze,
And nose-tips weep as well as they,
The Spring is coming round this way.

When suddenly some shadow-bird
　　Goes wavering beneath the gaze,
And through the hedge the moan is heard
　　Of kine that fain would graze
In grasses new, I smile, and say
The Spring is coming round this way.

When knotted horse-tails are untied,
　　And teamsters whistle here and there,
And clumsy mitts are laid aside,
　　And choppers' hands are bare,
And chips are thick where children play,
The Spring is coming round this way.

When through the twigs the farmer
　　tramps,
　　And troughs are chunked beneath the
　　trees,
And fragrant hints of sugar-camps
　　Astray in every breeze—
When early March seems middle May,
The Spring is coming round this way.

When coughs are changed to laughs, and
　　when
　　Our frowns melt into smiles of glee,
And all our blood thaws out again
　　In streams of ecstasy,
And poets wreak their roundelay,
The Spring is coming round this way.

NOVEMBER

This fine selection of the signs that November has come, and that winter is at hand, is from the pen of Hartley Coleridge, a true poet, though he did not attempt ambitious flights of song. Each little word picture in this poem shows close observation, and has a poetical glamour.

THE mellow year is hasting to its close;
　　The little birds have almost sung their
　　last,
Their small notes twitter in the dreary
　　blast—
That shrill-piped harbinger of early snows,
The patient beauty of the scentless rose,
Oft with the morn's hoar crystal quaintly
　　glassed,
Hangs, a pale mourner for the summer
　　past,
And makes a little summer where it grows:
In the chill sunbeam of the faint, brief
　　day
The dusky waters shudder as they shine,
The russet leaves obstruct the straggling
　　way
Of oozy brooks, which no deep banks
　　define,
And the gaunt woods, in ragged, scant
　　array,
Wrap their old limbs with sombre ivy
　　twine.

SOMETIMES

Are we the men we might have been ? That is a solemn question which all grown-ups may wisely ask. Here Thomas S. Jones (1882–1932), an American, asks it very daintily

Across the fields of yesterday
    He sometimes comes to me,
A little lad just back from play,
    The lad I used to be.

And yet he smiles so wistfully
    Once he has crept within;
I wonder if he hopes to see
    The man I might have been?

THE WARDEN OF THE CINQUE PORTS

When the Duke of Wellington died, though a very old man, he was Warden of the Cinque Ports, or five ports, that in ancient times guarded the coasts of Kent and Sussex. It was a period of some unrest, owing to the disturbing influence of Louis Napoleon in France, but the third and fourth verses of this poem exaggerate the watchfulness between country and country. Longfellow here tells how amid the sounds of war's watchfulness the veteran soldier died.

A mist was driving down the British
        Channel,
    The day was just begun,
And through the window-panes, on floor
        and panel,
    Streamed the red autumn sun.

It glanced on flowing flag and rippling
        pennon,
    And the white sails of ships;
And, from the frowning rampart, the
        black cannon
    Hailed it with feverish lips.

Sandwich and Romney, Hastings, Hythe,
        and Dover,
    Were all alert that day
To see the French war-steamers speeding
        over
    When the fog cleared away.

Sullen and silent, and like couchant lions,
    Their cannon, through the night,
Holding their breath, had watched, in
        grim defiance,
    The sea-coast opposite.

And now they roared at drum-beat from
        their stations
    On every citadel;
Each answering each, with morning salu-
        tations,
    That all was well.

And down the coast, all taking up the
        burden,
    Replied the distant forts,
As if to summon from his sleep the Warden
    And Lord of the Cinque Ports.

Him shall no sunshine from the fields of
        azure,
    No drum-beat from the wall,
No morning gun from the black fort's
        embrasure,
    Awaken with its call!

No more, surveying with an eye impartial
    The long line of the coast,
Shall the gaunt figure of the old Field-
        Marshal
    Be seen upon his post!

For in the night, unseen, a single warrior,
    In sombre harness mailed,
Dreaded of man, and surnamed the De-
        stroyer,
    The rampart wall had scaled.

He passed into the chamber of the sleeper,
    The dark and silent room,
And as he entered darker grew, and
        deeper,
    The silence and the gloom.

He did not pause to parley or dissemble,
    But smote the Warden hoar;
Ah, what a blow! that made all England
        tremble,
    And groan from shore to shore.

Meanwhile, without, the surly cannon
        waited,
    The sun rose bright o'erhead;
Nothing in Nature's aspect intimated
    That a great man was dead.

A LETTER

Here is a poet's pretty letter to a child; it was written to Lady Margaret Cavendish Holles-Harley, when she was quite young, by Matthew Prior, the early eighteenth-century poet. It was a time when children's first duty was to care for what their father and mother wished them to do. "My lord and lady" were Peggy's parents.

My noble, lovely little Peggy,
    Let this, my first epistle, beg ye,
At dawn of morn and close of even,
To lift your heart and hands to heaven.
In double duty say your prayer:
Our Father first, then *Notre Père.*

And, dearest child, along the day,
In every thing you do and say,
Obey and please my lord and lady,
So God shall love and angels aid ye.

If to these precepts you attend
No second letter need I send,
And so I rest your constant friend.

BABYLON

This poem is a most interesting instance of the free use of imagination in describing what was probably felt by people who took part in a historical movement long ago. The writer was John Buchan (1875–1940), Lord Tweedsmuir, one of the most versatile Scottish writers of this century.

WE are come back from Babylon,
　Out of the plains and the glare,
To the little hills of our own country,
　And the sting of our kindred air;
To the rickle of stones on the red rock's
　　edge
Which Kedron cleaves like a sword.
We will build the walls of Zion again
　To the glory of Zion's Lord.

Now is no more of dalliance
　By the reedy waters in spring,
When we sang of home and sighed and
　　dreamed,
　And wept in remembering.
Now we are back in our ancient hills,
　Out of the plains and the sun;
And before we make it our dwelling-place
　There's a wonderful lot to be done.

The walls are to build from West to East,
　From Gihon to Olivet,
Waters to lead and wells to clear
　And the garden furrows to set.
From the Sheep-gate to the Fish-gate
　Is a welter of mire and mess;
And southward over the common lands
　'Tis a dragon's wilderness.

The Courts of the Lord are a heap of dust
　Where the hill winds whistle and race,
And the noble pillars of God His house
　Stand in a ruined place.
In the Holy of Holies foxes lair,
　And owls and night-birds build;
There's a good deal to do ere we pitch it
　　anew
　As our father Solomon willed.

Now is the day of the ordered life
　And the law which all obey;
We toil by rote and speak by rote
　And never a soul dare stray.
Ever among us a lean old man
　Keepeth his watch and ward,
Crying " The Lord hath set you free,
　Prepare ye the way of the Lord."

A goodly task we are called unto,
　A task to dream on o' nights—
Work for Judah and Judah's God,
　Setting our land to rights;
Everything fair and all things square
　And straight as a plummet's string—
Is it mortal guile if once in a while
　Our thoughts go wandering?

We were not slaves in Babylon,
　For the gate of our soul lay free,
There in that vast and sunlit land,
　On the edges of mystery.
Daily we wrought and daily we thought,
　And we chafed not at rod and power,
For Sinim, Sabaea, and dusky Hind
　Talked to us hour by hour.

The man who lives in Babylon
　May poorly sup and fare,
But loves and lures from the ends of the
　　earth
Beckon him everywhere.
Next year he, too, may have sailed strange
　　seas,
　And conquered a diadem,
For kings are as common in Babylon
　As crows in Bethlehem.

Here we are bound to the common round,
　In a land which knows not change.
Nothing befalleth to stir the blood
　Or quicken the heart to range;
Never a hope that we cannot plumb
　Or a stranger visage in sight—
At the most a sleek Samaritan
　Or a ragged Amorite.

Here we are sober and staid of soul,
　Working beneath the law,
Settled amid our father's dust,
　Seeing the hills they saw.
All things fixed and determinate
　Chiselled and squared by rule—
Is it mortal guile once in a while
　To try and escape from school?

We will go back to Babylon,
　Silently one by one,
Out from the hills and the laggard brooks
　To the streams that brim in the sun.
Only a moment, Lord, we crave,
　To breathe and listen and see,
Then we start anew, with muscle and thew,
　To hammer trestles for Thee.

O WORLD, BE NOBLER

This appeal to live nobly so as to ease for tender hearts the burdens of the world is by Laurence Binyon (1869–1943), one of the great English poets of the twentieth century.

O WORLD, be nobler, for her sake!
　If she but knew thee what thou art,
What wrongs are borne, what deeds are
　　done
In thee, beneath thy daily sun,
　Knowest thou not that her tender heart
For pain and very shame would break?
O World, be nobler, for her sake!

SIMPLE SIMON MET A PIE-MAN

Simple Simon met a pie-man
  Going to the fair;
Said Simple Simon to the pie-man:
"Let me taste your ware."
Said the pie-man to Simple Simon:
"Show me first your penny!"
Said Simple Simon to the pie-man:
"Indeed, I have not any!"
He went to catch a dicky bird,
And thought he would not fail
Because he had a little salt
To put upon his tail.
He went to ride a spotted cow
That had a little calf;
She threw him down upon the ground,
Which made the people laugh.

Then Simple Simon went a-hunting
For to catch a hare,
He rode a goat about the street,
But could not find one there.
Simple Simon went to town
To buy a piece of meat:
He tied it to his horse's tail
To keep it clean and sweet.

Simple Simon went a-fishing
For to catch a whale,
And all the water he had got
Was in his mother's pail.

He went to take a bird's nest—
'Twas built upon a bough;
A branch gave way, and Simon fell
Into a dirty slough.
He went to shoot a wild duck,
But the wild duck flew away.
Says Simon: "I can't hit him
Because he will not stay."
Once Simon made a great snowball,
And brought it in to roast;
He laid it down upon the fire,
And soon the ball was lost.
He went to slide upon the ice
Before the ice would bear;
Then he plunged in above his knees,
Which made poor Simon stare.

Simple Simon went to look
If plums grew on a thistle;
He pricked his finger very much,
Which made poor Simon whistle.

He washed himself with blacking ball
Because he had no soap;
And then said to his mother:
"I'm a beauty now, I hope."

He went for water in a sieve,
But soon it all ran through.
And now poor Simple Simon
Bids you all adieu.

LITTLE VERSES FOR VERY LITTLE PEOPLE

LITTLE RAINDROPS

Oh, where do you come from,
    You little drops of rain,
Pitter-patter, pitter-patter,
    Down the window-pane?

They won't let me walk,
    They won't let me play,
And they won't let me go
    Out of doors at all today.

They put away my playthings
    Because I broke them all,
And then they locked up all my
      bricks,
    And took away my ball.

Tell me, little raindrops,
    Is that the way you play,
Pitter-patter, pitter-patter,
    All the rainy day?

They say I'm very naughty,
    But I've nothing else to do
But sit here at the window;
    I should like to play with you.

The little raindrops cannot speak,
    But pitter-patter pat
Means " We can play on *this* side:
    Why can't you play on *that* ? "

TOM THUMB'S ALPHABET

A was an Archer, who shot at a frog;
    B was a Butcher, who had a great
      dog;
C was a Captain, all covered with lace;
D was a Drunkard, and had a red face;
E was an Esquire, with pride on his brow;
F was a Farmer, and followed the plough;
G was a Gamester, who had but ill luck;
H was a hunter, who hunted a buck;
I was an Innkeeper, who dined on grouse;
J was a Joiner, who built up a house;
K was a King, so mighty and grand;
L was a Lady, who had a white hand;
M was a Miser, and hoarded his gold;
N was a Nobleman, gallant and bold;
O was an Oysterman, who went about
    town;
P was a Parson, and wore a black gown;
Q was a Quack, with a wonderful pill;
R was a Robber, who wanted to kill;
S was a Sailor, who spent all he got;
T was a Tinker, and mended a pot;
U was an Usurer, a miserable elf;
V was a Vintner, who drank all himself;
W was a Watchman, who guarded the door;
X was Expensive, and so became poor;
Y was a Youth, that did not love school;
Z was a Zany, a poor, harmless fool.

I HAD FOUR BROTHERS

I had four brothers over the sea,
    Perrie, Merrie, Dixie, Domine;
And each one sent a gift to me,
    Petrum, Partrum, Paradisi, Tempore,
    Perrie, Merrie, Dixie, Domine.

The first one sent a goose without a bone,
    Perrie, Merrie, Dixie, Domine.
The second sent a cherry without a stone,
    Petrum, Partrum, Paradisi, Tempore,
    Perrie, Merrie, Dixie, Domine.
The third sent a blanket without a thread,
    Perrie, Merrie, Dixie, Domine.
The fourth sent a book no man could read,
    Petrum, Partrum, Paradisi, Tempore,
    Perrie, Merrie, Dixie, Domine.

When cherry's in blossom there is no
    stone,
    Perrie, Merrie, Dixie, Domine.
When the goose is in the egg there is no
    bone,
    Petrum, Partrum, Paradisi, Tempore,
    Perrie, Merrie, Dixie, Domine.
When the wool's on the back there is no
    thread,
    Perrie, Merrie, Dixie, Domine.
When the book's in the press no man can
    read,
    Petrum, Partrum, Paradisi, Tempore,
    Perrie, Merrie, Dixie, Domine.

I HAD A LITTLE DOGGY

I had a little doggy that used to sit and
    beg;
But Doggy tumbled down the stairs and
    broke his little leg.
Oh, Doggy, I will nurse you, and try to
    make you well,
And you shall have a collar with a little
    silver bell.

Ah, Doggy, don't you think that you
    should very faithful be
For having such a loving friend to com-
    fort you as me?
And when your leg is better, and you can
    run and play,
We'll have a scamper in the fields and see
    them making hay.

But, Doggy, you must promise (and mind
    your word you keep)
Not once to tease the little lambs, or run
    among the sheep;
And then the little yellow chicks that
    play upon the grass,
You must not even wag your tail to scare
    them as you pass.

Imperishable Thoughts of Men Enshrined in the Books of the World

A portion of an ancient Egyptian Book of the Dead

THE LITERATURES OF THE EAST

THE literatures of the East are far older than those of Europe. They are almost equally extensive, and certainly have been the most influential in the history of the world.

On them are based all the great existing religions of mankind. The idea of Immortality has its origin in the literature of ancient Egypt. Tao-ism, Buddhism, Brahminism, the religion of the Parsees, Judaism, Christianity, and Mohammedanism each has a literature at its source, with some part of the East as its birthplace. Europe cannot make any such claim. Religions that may have grown with, or out of, its early literature have all passed away.

Where the literatures of Europe excel is in the variety of their subjects and treatments, and the world-wide range of their appeal. They penetrate everywhere because they embrace everything. The educated Hindu, Japanese, Chinese, or Negro reads the European literatures in proportion to his education; but with the single exception of the Hebrew literature, and in a small degree the Mohammedan Koran, which is an offshoot of Hebrew literature, the world does not read the literatures of the East.

They are studied by specialists for the light they throw on the growth, changes and spread of languages and ideas; for the information they give of the rise and modifications of religions; and for the glimpses they contain of remote history, early social life, and moral conceptions. They abound with poetry and with tales, for poetry and tales are natural to all mankind long before they have a written literature; and the poetry and tales, suiting the race which produces them, descend through succeeding generations to modern times. The poetry of religion, such as hymns and rules for moral guidance, have been specially transmitted by the priestly guardians of religion, and makes up a large part of the ancient literatures.

All these forms of literature are plentiful in the East, and attract all students who are engaged on a comparative survey of the mental and spiritual evolution of mankind through its many races. Yet Eastern literatures do not contain many of the great literary masterpieces which make a powerful appeal to all humanity, apart from the wonderful literature of the Hebrew race that has been collected from a thousand years and is now translated into nearly all languages under the general name of the Bible. In fact, the only Eastern writing that attracts widespread interest and is not Hebrew, and can be traced to a personal source, is the Koran.

ROMANCE · HISTORIES · DRAMAS · ESSAYS · WORLD CLASSICS

The other important writings that come to us from the East—important, that is, for the light they throw on early language and religion—are of unknown authorship and of great antiquity. They had been long preserved in men's memories before being recorded, and have been manipulated by priestly castes for centuries. They are mostly connected with the rites of religions that have entirely lost their hold on men's attention, outside of the communities that have inherited them as historical heirlooms.

THE FAITH OF THE EGYPTIANS THAT DEATH DOES NOT END LIFE

The literature of ancient Egypt, as illustrated in such writings as The Book of the Dead, is deeply interesting in so far as it shows that the men of the Nile Valley clearly did not hold the belief that death is the end of life, but expected the soul to journey on. Egypt is rich from the earliest times in the number of its simple tales, but their literary merits are small.

The empires of the Mesopotamian Plain, Babylonia and Assyria, possessed a culture. Their people, with an appreciation of the value of literary records, tried to summarise and preserve the knowledge that had come to them from the past. Many of the ideals of the Hebrew race were inherited from their Mesopotamian forefathers, or were acquired later by military or trading or exilic contact; but though there are copious fragments of early literature from the valleys of the Euphrates and Tigris, none of it reached as literature the customary standard of Hebrew writing as we have it in the Bible. Nor was this likely, for the Hebrews had not only the inspiration of a great idea, the idea of one God, but their writings were re-edited and revised for more than a thousand years later than the Babylonian records they knew.

THE ANCIENT SANSKRIT STORY TOLD IN EIGHTEEN BOOKS

The early Sanskrit literature of India consists largely of hymns of praise and prayer, with sacrificial formulas and incantations repeated by the priests and regarded as sacred. Later came the epic, the Mahabharata, or Great Tale, with many poems collected around it. It is divided into eighteen books, about eight times as long as Homer's Iliad and Odyssey and appears to contain some echoes from those immortal works. The poem was known to have existed in an early form some hundreds of years B.C., and underwent extensions and adaptations till about A.D. 200. It contains a considerable amount of miscellaneous poetry that admits it to rank as a classic, but without artistic form.

Another Indian epic in seven books, the Ramayana, has the appearance of being written chiefly by one author, and tradition gives his name as Valmiki. These Indian poems have the charms of a mild and tender spirit, and descriptive power in presenting natural beauty. India has an abundance of hymns and short, generally very short, lyrics, but its literature has not the force and concentration needed to secure world-wide attention. Though it fails to grip firmly the Western mind, it has had throughout the ages a strong influence on Indian religion.

A modern poet, Sir Rabindranath Tagore, writing in the Bengali tongue, won the Nobel Literature Prize in 1913, and in English translations he has a considerable circle of European readers.

A VAST ENCYCLOPEDIA WITH SIXTEEN HUNDRED VOLUMES

China has a stupendous literature, whether we think of its age, amount, or the completeness with which it covers all subjects. Nearly a thousand years ago it published an encyclopedia in a thousand sections, and a modern encyclopedia was issued in 1628 volumes.

Chinese literary history traces its earliest poetry back to 1800 B.C. Confucius, who was born in 551 B.C., found 3000 Odes in existence. He reduced them to 311 and made of them a classic. All Chinese poetry is in rhyme, and every literary Chinese is supposed to be a poet. As the writing of poetry has been going on for at least 3000 years, and it is a point of honour with an author's family that all his writings shall be published when he dies, the amount of Chinese poetry passes the bounds of imagination.

In every department of literature China has been profuse. Her legendary history begins at 2698 B.C., and in the eighth century B.C. the record becomes trustworthy. So vast had China's literature become in the third century B.C. that the emperor who reigned in 212 B.C. decreed that it should all be destroyed, and books should begin afresh with his reign. Vast quantities of books were burned, but many were concealed. No fewer than 460 learned men were put to death for hiding their books. All works on some subjects perished before the Emperor died and his successor set aside the decree of destruction. One effect was that men tried to re-write the lost books, and much doubt remains as to whether certain ancient books are the originals, or have been more or less replaced by later writers.

THE WIDE RANGE OF LIFE THAT IS COVERED IN CHINESE BOOKS

Chinese books cover the whole range of the national life, past and present, philosophy, economics, biography, travel, agriculture, astronomy, painting, fiction, and so on; but the habit, ingrained from an ancestry of thousands of years, of looking backward with admiration on the past, and following the customs of his race as the best that can ever be, have stereotyped the thoughts of the Chinese, and his literature has no freshness of outlook to offer men of other creeds. His literature is stagnant. We may read of his life to wonder curiously at his ways and habits of thought, but not for originality or stimulation. We must look far away into the past for books written by Chinese who once were original, and on whom the Chinese through all the ages have shaped their own lives unchangingly, if we are to find a Chinese literature that has force in it. We must look to the sage and historian Confucius, who lived from 551 B.C. to 479 B.C., or to Mencius, the disciple and explainer of Confucius, who lived from 372 B.C. to 289 B.C. It was their combined wisdom which too firmly moulded Chinese character, but has only reached the Western world in fragments, the best of them being, " What you do not like when it is done to yourself do not do to others."

During the twentieth century many attempts to break away from tradition have resulted in new forms of poetry, drama, and prose. It is possible that some modern writers will become outstanding.

WHEN THE JAPANESE MIND FREED ITSELF FROM THRALDOM

Japanese literature is an imitation and repetition of the Chinese up to the later half of the nineteenth century, when the Japanese mind almost suddenly freed itself from thraldom to the Chinese ideals, and began to take a share in the larger work of the whole world. Time has not yet allowed the emancipated Japanese

mind to express itself in the form of permanent literature, and its past is dead except as a fading sentimentality; but everyone hopes that a time will come when Japan will have something distinctive to say to the world through books.

Persia has a literature extending from a remote antiquity to the present through many great changes of her language. The earliest Persian tongue, as seen in the oldest part of the sacred books of the Zoroastrian religion, the Avesta, still the faith of the Parsees of Bombay, was closely akin to the earliest Sanskrit. That religion symbolises in the Sun a supreme Deity from whom emanates all good, and it finds expression in outbursts of poetic adoration. But Mohammedanism swept across the country, left the followers of Zoroaster only a remnant, and changed the language and the national thought, till Persian writings became little more than tales of romance and love lyrics, tinctured by a sad and almost cynical philosophy. The modern tendency of the language has been towards simplicity in construction and the colloquial in style, but Persia has not had the robustness of mind needed for the writing of great literature.

THE MELANCHOLY PERSIAN POEM IN A BEAUTIFUL ENGLISH DRESS

The Persian writers who have had vitality enough to appeal to the world outside the Persian plateau lived after the Arab-Mohammedan conquest. The most conspicuous are the epic poet Ferdowsi, whose History of the Persian Kings, a mine of romantic story, was published in A.D. 1011; Sa'adi, a writer of famous Odes, who died in 1292; and, greatest of all, Hafiz, the supreme lyrical writer of the Persian race, whose sweetness and melody have attracted notice from not a few poets of the West. Hafiz died in 1389. The poet best known to readers of English is Omar Khayyam, or the Tentmaker, whose pessimistic Rubaiyat was paraphrased in Victorian days by Edward Fitzgerald, with such musical melancholy that in its English dress it outcharmed the Persian original, and became an English classic.

The fact is that the Persian philosopher and astronomer is not typical of the Eastern spirit where the Mohammedan faith prevails; but he does strike the notes of doubt and revolt which have been sounded more loudly, but never so hauntingly, by certain modern pessimists living in the West.

The typical Mohammedan accepts unhesitatingly the ruling of an All-Merciful God, and bows to " whatever is " as the Divine Will, waiting the good time when that Will shall decree a different fate. He accepts the rules of his religion, and lives, in accordance with those rules, a temperate life that at times becomes abstinent to the point of austerity, and may even involve bodily suffering.

Omar Khayyam, whom everyone with any literary leanings now reads in translations as the one known Eastern poet outside the Bible and the Koran, did not hold these Eastern beliefs, or conform to these rules of living. He was the Eastern poet of revolt, preaching the unbeliever's pessimistic tenet, Let us eat and drink for tomorrow we die.

THE FAME OF OMAR KHAYYAM AS AN ASTRONOMER AND MATHEMATICIAN

It is not now supposed that Omar was ever really a tentmaker. Probably he inherited the classification from his father's trade; but he lived a life of thoughtful leisure, pensioned by his Sultan as the greatest astronomer and mathematician of his country and time. He lived with his own thoughts and studies and pleasures, and did not aspire to the official dignities and courtly occupations he might have had. His writings on mathematics, in Arabic, and his astronomical observations, gave him such fame that in 1079, when it was deemed advisable to reform the Calendar, and institute what is known as the Seljuk Era, the formidable task was assigned to him.

But Omar's studies were in the sad sort of astrology in which the stars evolved pitiless fates for men. He had no sustaining faith in noble destinies, and his sombre revolt against what is fixed and inexplicable in life was counterbalanced by a determination to enjoy whatever is immediately pleasant. To the good Mohammedan he was a daring atheist, and a wine-bibbing evil-liver untypical of the race of true believers. The freer thought of the West has seen in him a man who, long before our day, expressed, in his solemn quatrains, the melancholy hopelessness of the doubter who finds life a tantalising mystery. Here are two examples of Omar's pessimistic view of life as it finds expression in Fitzgerald's verses.

When You and I behind the Veil are past,
Oh, but the long, long while the World shall last,
  Which of our Coming and Departure heeds
As the Sea's self should heed a pebble cast.

    *   *   *   *

Earth could not answer; nor the Seas that mourn
In flowing Purple, of their Lord forlorn;
  Nor rolling Heaven, with all his Signs revealed
And hidden by the sleeve of Night and Morn.

THE WRONG IMPRESSION OF THE PERSIAN SPIRIT GIVEN BY OMAR KHAYYAM

Omar Khayyam is a memorable poet to that part of the world of the West that, like him, has never attained a faith in Divine governance for purposes inconceivably great and noble. To any Western reader he gives, in Fitzgerald's translation, a haunting musical setting to a dolorous mood; but men of his race and faith do not admit that he is a sufficiently representative poet of the Arab or the Persian spirit in religion.

The language in which, apart from the Hebrew, the East has spoken to the world (of course by translations) is the Arabic. There was a time, during the Dark Ages of Europe, when the best learning in the world was written in Arabic. The practice of medicine, for instance, was governed for 500 years by the writings of Avicenna, a Persian born at Bokhara in 980, who wrote all his books except one in Arabic; and the Spanish Moor, Averroes, born at Cordova in 1126, influenced greatly the thought of all the Christian world by re-introducing afresh to its notice Aristotle's system of philosophy. These are examples of literature once world-wide in its power, but now unknown except to the special student.

THE WONDERFUL COLLECTION OF STORIES KNOWN AS THE ARABIAN NIGHTS

An Arabic book that still has a wide circulation throughout the civilised world is The Thousand and One Nights. This treasury of romance, adventure, and wonders, which illustrates the Eastern custom of story-telling, is now pruned and altered so as to be an amusement for children, to whom it is most familiar as The Arabian Nights. Originally it was a revelation of the impurity of the Oriental mind, but has been cleansed of its foulness by editing and alteration, until it is one of the most innocent books in general circulation. It has no known author, but is a collection of tales from many sources in lands where the spoken story is the commonest form of amusement.

The book of books in Arabic throughout the whole of the Mohammedan world of over 200 million believers is the Koran. It may be questioned whether any book in the world is as well known by as many people as know the Koran. More probably know the Bible in some degree, but what they know of it is usually not known as well as Mohammedans know the Koran.

THE INFLUENCE OF THE JEWISH SCRIPTURES ON MOHAMMED

No other book claims to have a similar origin in as simple a manner. Mohammed was an epileptic poet with the intensest belief in his own inspiration. Whether he could read or write is doubtful. When he began his mission knowledge of Christianity and the Jewish Scriptures had been spreading in the East for over five and a half centuries. His knowledge of them was probably gained by hearsay, as was then customary in the East with all forms of knowledge and thought. The Arabs generally were superstitious idolaters. Mohammed was deeply impressed by the Jewish conception of One God, and he had heard of prophets who proclaimed with fervour that consummate idea. To a similar proclamation he devoted his life, believing he was inspired as other prophets had been.

He conceived the Almighty Creator as great and remote, but all-merciful and compassionate, and that an Angel came as an intermediary to tell him the Divine Will.

MOHAMMED AND THE MESSAGES HE CLAIMED TO HAVE FROM GOD

The message given in these angelic visitations he at once dictated, often just as he had emerged from an epileptic fit, to an attendant scribe, who wrote them down on any writing material he had at hand; and these messages, continued for years and covering many of the practical affairs of Arab life as well as religious exhortations, formed the Koran when they were finally collected. For this book, therefore, it is claimed that it is a direct revelation to a single prophet, and it is regarded by the devout Moslem as an all-sufficient guide; but its restrictions have been fatal to progress in all the countries where the religion of Mohammed has obtained influence over the people.

Viewed as a piece of literature produced in strange circumstances, often in the midst of dangers, by an ignorant but clever man, the Koran is unparalleled. It has lofty ideality, genuine poetry, and true eloquence, mixed with puerility, Eastern sensuality, and frequent contradictions, as the prophet forgot what he had said when he was speaking in differing circumstances. With all its faults it is, apart from the Bible, the great book of the East.

The Bible which, at a distance and through hearsay, prompted Mohammed to produce the Koran, is entirely different in character and origin. Instead of being one book, written by one author during a continuous period, it is a collection and compilation of many writings, widely separated in time and character. These writings have been frequently edited and combined. The thread on which they are strung, until the later parts of the New Testament are reached, is that of nationality—the story of the Hebrew race, and particularly its relation to the idea of One God, at first of a tribal character, but broadening out under the insight of the prophets until the final revelations of the New Testament are made.

THE WONDERFUL LITERATURE OF THE REMARKABLE HEBREW RACE

The remarkable Hebrew race has a very extensive literature of its own, apart from the selected writings which have been placed from time to time in the Biblical collection. Its religious expositions are expressed with keen controversy in the Talmud. The Apocrypha is one of the choicer illustrations, and there is a mass of Apocalyptic writings of which only one example, the Book of the Revelation, has been chosen for inclusion in the Bible. A historian of the more modern kind, Josephus, may also be mentioned, a Jew who won the confidence of the Roman authorities, though he never abated his zeal as a sympathiser with his race.

The Bible is so unique in its character, and has played such a wonderful part in the history of the world by its influence on humanity through the Christian faith, that it will be considered in a special article elsewhere. Here we would only add that its true effects on religion can never be traced, or its natural meanings be arrived at, till it has been studied as a piece—infinitely the most important piece—of the world's literatures, and each part of it illuminated by the historical surroundings which caused it to be written down.

It has been said that the blood of the martyrs is the seed of the Church, and very early in the history of the Christian Church did noble men and women like Stephen, the first of the martyrs, seal their testimony with their life, and by their heroic deaths prove the power of the faith that was in them.

The Story of the Most Beautiful Book in the World

The Life of Saint Paul

WE have followed the narrative of The Master's life. We have listened to his parables, we have heard his words, we have seen his acts. We know from his own lips why he came, and what it was that he revealed. He came to bring light, to reveal the Fatherhood of God and the Brotherhood of Man. Now we ask ourselves how this gentle teaching conquered the world, and the answer to this question brings us to the life of Paul. The disciples of Jesus formed a society to teach the good tidings of Jesus. They had no thought of destroying the Jewish religion ; they wanted to carry it forward with the spirit of their Master. They were a brotherhood, composed of all who followed the teaching of Jesus. This was the beginning of the Church. In the homes of believers the Apostles preached the gospel and the Church grew. How the mustard-seed was scattered abroad in the world, we read in the Life of Saint Paul, as Saul of Tarsus came to be named.

SAUL OF TARSUS

THE town of Tarsus was a busy place. It was the capital of a Roman province; its streets were full of merchants from many quarters of the world; ships were always loading and unloading at its wharves; besides this, the town was a seat of learning which attracted scholars from distant countries.

Two things we must notice in this beautiful town, which had the snow-capped Taurus range of mountains behind it, with the broad waters of the Cydnus flowing through it to the neighbouring sea, and a green and fertile valley all round, as delightful to the eye as it was prosperous to the husbandman. These two things are the wickedness of the people and the learning taught in its schools.

No words can exaggerate the depravity of the people of this pagan city. They had ceased to believe in their gods. They could not see in life anything serious or noble or beautiful. They believed that at their death all was over. And so they said to themselves: " As we must surely die, and death may come for us at any moment, let us eat, drink, and be merry." What did they understand by being merry? Their idea of merriment was living in sin. Love, self-sacrifice, charity, benevolence, and brotherliness were things they laughed at; the one thing for each man to do was to seek his own pleasure.

In such a wicked city, what was the learning taught by the professors? It was only the profitless learning of grammar books, silly disputes about the meaning of words. The professors, far from being good men of honourable and noble lives, were a quarrelsome, stupid, narrow-minded, and conceited set of coxcombs. This mighty seat of learning was nothing but a circus.

It is most important to make ourselves vividly conscious of this state of things in Tarsus at the beginning of our study of Paul's life. Let us have a distinct picture in our mind of this beautiful and busy place into which he was born, a place crowded by a population devoted to luxury, vice, folly, and an absurd and profitless learning.

In this city there was a number of Jews among the foreign element. Some of them, no doubt, were not unlike the rest of the population; but the great majority kept themselves aloof from the wickedness of their neighbours. Particularly was this the case with the Pharisees, the strict Jews devoted to the Law, who were even then looking for the Messiah.

We can imagine with what horror these good people would regard the depravity of the city. From the beginning of history we find the Jews spreading over the face of the Earth, living with other nations, wearing the dress and

GREAT FIGURES OF THE OLD TESTAMENT · THE LIFE OF JESUS

speaking the language of those with whom they live, but always maintaining their strict ideas about religion.

The Jews are a moral, clean, serious race. They cling to their morality in the face of terrible persecution. If ever a people deeply believed its religion, it is the Jewish people.

THE RELIGION OF THE JEWS, THE ONE CONTINUOUS FACT IN HISTORY

Nations have tried, time and again, to exterminate religion by exterminating the Jews; oppressors have sought to exterminate the Jews by exterminating their religion. But they have failed. Nothing is more persistent in human history than the Jew and his religion.

It was as the strictest of Jews that the little Saul grew up in Tarsus. He learned to speak Greek, because everyone spoke Greek; but he certainly did not study Greek literature. We can be quite certain he never read a page of Plato or Aristotle, and never listened to the music of Homer. He was taught Hebrew; he was trained carefully in everything to do with the Jewish religion; his chief literature, if not his only literature, was the Scripture.

But he had eyes, and he could see the horror of life in Tarsus, and could realise the inability of Greek learning to make people unselfish and good. The impression he received of this pagan city was to last him all his life, and to fill him with an energy against sin hardly equalled in the history of the world. He was also freed by this experience of his childhood from the delusion that pagan learning could make the world better.

SAUL'S EVERLASTING IMPRESSION OF LIFE IN A PAGAN CITY

Now there is a habit among the Jews, lasting to this day, which is very instructive and is founded on the wisdom of the ages. When a boy reaches his thirteenth year he is confirmed. This ceremony of Confirmation is in some ways not unlike the Christian service of Confirmation, but it has profound differences. The Jewish boy is told at his confirmation that hitherto his father has been responsible for his shortcomings, but that now he himself is responsible.

Responsibility educates. The Jewish boy is put on his honour to play the man. It is for him to know that goodness and evil are matters for his own decision. He can choose whether he will be good or bad: he is responsible. If he goes to ruin, he will have no one but himself to blame.

This service is accompanied by a public recital of part of the Sacred Law in the synagogue, so that the boy takes his place among his elders, feeling that he is no longer a child to be petted and indulged, but a responsible human being with a part to play in the world.

To Saul, who was marked out for the great honour of serving the Law of God as a Pharisee, and who was a boy with a natural morality and an instinctive hatred of what is base, this service must have come with tremendous meaning. The sights he had seen in the streets of Tarsus must have returned to his mind as he bowed himself before God, and felt the responsibility of life pressing on him. What could he do for the God of Israel?

SAUL GOES TO JERUSALEM TO STUDY UNDER A WISE TEACHER

He went to Jerusalem to study under the greatest doctor of that time, the Rabbi Gamaliel. Gamaliel was not like the Pharisees whom Jesus condemned. He was a good man; he had what we call a liberal mind—that is to say, he was not narrow and bitter—and he thought more of the Spirit of Scripture than of the letter of it. He was one of the best types of scholarly and learned Jews. Saul could hardly have had a better teacher.

But there was one thing that sorely troubled the ambitious brain of this pupil from Tarsus. According to the Jewish religion, God could only be served by obeying the Law. The Law was an immense number of rules and regulations. Men had to be careful about what they ate and drank, what they wore, and a thousand other things.

All day long, even by the most harmless and gracious action, they were reminded of some angry law. Saul felt that this was very hard. He wished he could serve God in some other way. Obedience to any law was not enough; he wanted to love the mighty Power who had made the universe, and had taught Israel the things of eternal life. However, it seemed that the only thing to do was to master the Law, and to obey it in every detail.

So Saul of Tarsus bent his great mind to the study of the Law, and before him he soon saw the straight road of a work for God along which he could travel.

In his native city he had seen Jews who mixed with pagans and degraded the House of Israel to the abominations of the heathen. These people he scorned and despised. He hated with a hatred almost ungovernable those Jews who were daring to set up new religions for themselves, who were actually making their own readings of the Law, and were departing from the authority of the Pharisees.

If there was one thing Saul of Tarsus knew above everything else it was that the Jewish religion had no rival in the world. He had seen what pagan religions did for their followers. He had seen what pagan learning did for its disciples. In all the world there was nothing that could approach in glory the ancient religion of Israel. This religion of Israel did keep men noble and women pure. It did make for happy homes, for kindness, for charity, and for responsibility to God.

THE GREAT MYSTERY OF THE EARLY LIFE OF SAUL

The Jews were not like the pagans. No; the Jews were the salt of the Earth. If the religion of Israel should be overthrown the human race would perish in sin. So Saul of Tarsus consecrated his life to overthrowing and bringing to punishment all those who were seeking to change the ancient religion or were setting up religions of their own. He felt that no higher work could come into his hands. We may fairly think of him at this period of his life as the Galahad of the Jews, a pure and noble man, arming himself for the glory of God and riding forth to punish the enemies of heaven. He went from Tarsus to Jerusalem, and in Jerusalem he lived among the Pharisees. He was with those very people most condemned by Jesus, the people whose whole energies at that time were bent on the destruction of Jesus. He himself hated intensely all who sought to alter Israel's ancient religion.

There are some who think it possible that Paul had been, even in the lifetime of Jesus, a very bitter propagandist for the ancient faith of his fathers. The Pharisees, it must be remembered, were ever passionately anxious to convert the world to their beliefs, so that it has been suggested by some critics that Paul was perhaps a sort of crusader in the days before the vision on the road to Damascus brought the great change in his life. In the first place, his nature was active, eager, impulsive; to sit still disputing about words would have irritated his nerves and filled him with restlessness. In the second place, he was dissatisfied with the Law in some ways, and it would be easier for him to forget that dissatisfaction in busy work than in sitting still.

If he stayed in Jerusalem disputing, his dissatisfaction would increase; but if he went abroad striking blows for goodness against evil, he would forget his troubles in the work of a life of action.

THE ABSENCE OF SAUL FROM THE SCENE OF THE WORLD'S GREAT TRAGEDY

So we think it is almost certain that, during the last months of the greatest tragedy in the world's history, Saul of Tarsus was not among the disputing Pharisees of Jerusalem, but was far away preaching the Law to those Jews in foreign lands who were beginning to forget God. If, in those distant scenes, any news reached him of the death of Jesus, he may have thought the matter of little importance. He did not return to take part in stamping out this new rebellion. It is not until four years after the Crucifixion that we meet with Saul as a fierce and bitter persecutor of the Christians.

But while this magnificent missionary of the Pharisees was championing the Law against paganism in foreign lands, a strange, wonderful, miraculous change was taking place in the Holy City. The death of Jesus, the shameful, ignominious death of the lowly Nazarene, far from silencing his humble and timorous followers—who had all forsaken him and fled—had suddenly endowed them with extraordinary courage and the most splendid eloquence.

THE MARVELLOUS CHANGE IN THE DISCIPLES AFTER THE CRUCIFIXION

The Pharisees, to their great vexation, saw that by destroying Jesus they had not destroyed the movement in his favour. The people of Jerusalem flocked to hear the preaching of Peter and John. So great was the power ascribed by the multitude to the chief of the Apostles that they would even stand to let the shadows of those good men pass across them. The chief priests sent for Peter and John, rebuked them, had them scourged, and sent them away hoping that the new sect would soon die out; but, instead of dying, it grew in numbers and in courage.

At last the priests were moved to take more definite action. Among the converts to the Galilean fishermen was a brilliant and able man named Stephen. This disciple, instead of preaching to the multitude, preached to cultured Jews in synagogues affected by the Greek spirit of learning.

STEPHEN'S VISION OF CHRISTIANITY AS THE GREAT WORLD RELIGION

The Apostles still thought that Jesus had intended to preach a new form of the Jewish religion. They had very little thought about the foreigners, whom they called Gentiles. All their efforts were made from within the Jewish Church. Stephen, on the other hand, was gifted with true vision. He looked away from the Jewish religion and from the narrow restrictions of a single race, and saw the secret of Jesus spreading among all nations and melting all religions into one. Such a man, so gifted, so brave, so eloquent, and so attractive, soon became marked down for death. He was dangerous. A scourging might do for so simple and rough a soul as Peter the fisherman, but this clever and daring man of the world must be treated with other means.

He was arrested and brought before the council. False witnesses came, who said: " This man ceaseth not to speak blasphemous words against this holy place and the Law; for we have heard him say that this Jesus of Nazareth shall destroy this place, and shall change the customs which Moses delivered us." And all that sat in the council, looking steadfastly on him, saw his face as it had been the face of an angel.

HOW STEPHEN DIED FOR THE FAITH AND BECAME THE FIRST MARTYR

Then Stephen, addressing them as " Men, brethren, and fathers," made a speech showing that the history of Israel was but a preparation for the coming of the Just One, whom they had murdered. At this the members of the council were filled with rage against him.

But he, being full of the Holy Ghost, looked up steadfastly into heaven, and saw the glory of God, and Jesus standing on the right hand of God; and said, Behold, I see the heavens opened, and the Son of Man standing on the right hand of God!

Then they cried out with a loud voice, and stopped their ears, and ran upon him with one accord, and cast him out of the city, and stoned him; and the witnesses laid down their clothes at a young man's feet, whose name was Saul.

And they stoned Stephen, calling upon God, and saying, Lord Jesus, receive my spirit. He kneeled down, and cried with a loud voice, Lord, lay not this sin to their charge. And when he had said this he fell asleep.

So died the first Christian martyr.

Now, in the terrible punishment of stoning to death, it was one of the laws that the witnesses themselves should inflict the punishment. In one sense this was a just enactment. It prevented, in some cases, the awful wickedness of false evidence. It is one thing to swear away a man's character; it is another thing to know that in swearing away his character you will have to stone the man to death.

But in this case the false witnesses were hounded on by religious zeal. Stephen was an enemy of their religion. They counted it as a righteous deed to stone him to death.

THE YOUNG MAN WHO STOOD BY WHILE THEY STONED STEPHEN

In order to do this work of stoning it was necessary to lay aside certain garments so that the arms might be free. The witnesses, in this case, laid their garments down at the feet of a young man whose name was Saul. He was evidently someone of position; the witnesses knew that no one would dare to lay hands upon their garments while Saul stood by.

It is one of the striking things in history that Saul of Tarsus, destined to become Paul the Apostle, should have witnessed the death of Stephen. For it was in the providence of God that Saul should be the very man to carry to a glorious and triumphant issue the idea of Stephen that Jesus came to save, not the Jews only, but all mankind. The beautiful spirit of Stephen, as it mounted from the bruised and bleeding body to heaven, may have seen his mantle descending on the shoulders of the young man at whose feet his enemies had laid their garments.

What, we ask ourselves, was the effect on Saul's mind of that cry: *Lord, lay not this sin to their charge ?* Did he feel he was hearing the first words of a gospel that would overspread the world and revolutionise the heart of man?

No; Saul of Tarsus, the devout Pharisee, heard the cry with contempt. All he gathered from it was that these Galileans were of a fanatical nature.

(Next chapter in this group, page 5807)

The Interests and Pleasures of Life for All Indoors and Out

MAKING A GARDEN POOL

A SMALL pool not only adds to the charm of a garden, but it also enables you to grow many beautiful and interesting aquatic or water-dwelling plants: and you can study the habits, and antics, of numerous kinds of fish that are quite at home under such conditions, from the fierce little native sticklebacks known to all schoolboys, to the gloriously-coloured goldfish of various remarkable breeds, like the Shubunkin and the Comet, whose Chinese ancestry dates back to long before the birth of Christianity.

Water has always been favoured for providing ornamental effects in gardens, and the earliest artificial pools were made by " puddling " them with clay worked into a plastic consistency. Nowadays it is much easier to make a pool of concrete, and surface this with cement to make it completely watertight.

The shape of the pond should conform, if possible, to its general surroundings. Thus, if the lay-out of the garden is on formal lines, with straight paths and symmetrical beds, and possibly a square or rectangular lawn, then the pool should be symmetrical in outline, too. If, however, the garden has been planned on more natural and informal lines, a pool of irregular shape

THE POOL PICTURED ABOVE IN THE MAKING

will look more attractive, with possibly a small bridge or stepping stones.

And you must choose the position for the pool very carefully. An open, sunny site is best : water lilies and most aquatic plants love the sun, and the leaves of these will provide the fishes with all the shade they need during the hot days of summer.

Water supply must be taken into account, although a continuous inflow of fresh water is not desirable. Once the pond has been filled and stocked with plants and fish, very little replenishment of the water will be necessary, and the plants themselves will help to keep it fresh and clean.

The simplest form of pool to construct is one that is saucer-shaped, with the sides gently sloping up to the soil level, but this is also the least satisfactory for plants and fish. A better plan is to make a rectangular pool with horizontal sides, surrounded by an underwater trough to hold soil in which the shallow-water aquatics can be planted.

For most of the smaller water lilies and aquatics suitable for ordinary pools, a depth of 12 to 18 inches is ample. The soil should be dug out to the overall measurements of the

CRAFTS · GAMES · NEEDLEWORK · PUZZLES · SCIENCE EXPERIMENTS

pool, not forgetting to allow for a four-inch thickness of concrete. If the bottom soil is soft, a layer of broken bricks or clinkers should be spread over it and rammed firm to provide a solid foundation for the concrete.

Now for mixing the concrete—for the bottom first. The best materials to use, and the correct proportions (by bulk), are one part of British Portland cement, two parts of coarse sand, and three parts of shingle. The sand should be measured out first and placed in a flat-topped heap, the cement being then spread on it and mixed thoroughly until no streaks of grey or brown show. The shingle is then spread over the heap, and the mixing repeated, turning the heap at least three times to get a complete blend, after which water is added, a little at a time, and mixing continued until the heap is a plastic, easily workable mass.

This is then spread in the bottom, at least four inches thick, and rammed down with a stout piece of wood to consolidate it. When it has set you can build the sides of the pool, but for these you will first of all need some rough wooden boards, nailed together to form a box, with crosspieces to hold the sides firmly in position. This formwork, as it is called, is built to rest on the floor of the pool, with a space all round of four inches between the boards and the earth sides, into which concrete is then shovelled, working round the pool in layers and pressing it down with the rammer as filling proceeds.

It is best to wait a week or so for the concrete to set before removing the formwork, after which, to make a really good job of the pool, the concrete can be surfaced with a fine cement mixture, one part (by bulk) of cement to three parts sand, applied in a thin layer with a wooden float or plasterer's trowel.

Having made the pool, you must not be in too great a hurry to put plants and fish in it; you must get rid of the impurities from the cement first. This can be done by filling the pool, then adding sufficient permanganate of potash crystals to the water to turn it the colour of claret. Leave it for a week or two, after which it can be emptied, washed down and refilled with fresh water.

The best time to plant the lovely water-lilies or nymphaeas is in May, just as they are beginning to grow. There are very many different kinds, but a few of the best for small pools are the white variety candida, reddish-yellow chrysantha, pink caroliniana, salmon-yellow flava, crimson Froebeli, wine-red Laydekeri purpurata, and cherry-red Marliacea ignea.

There are various ways of planting water lilies. You can set the roots in flower pots or wicker baskets of loam soil, and stand them on the bottom of the pool, or place them direct on the bottom in a small heap of loam soil enclosed by loose bricks.

There are, of course, many lovely moisture-loving plants that you can grow near the margins of your pool, or in the shallow under-water trough, like the pink and white-flowered water plantain (alisma), marsh marigold or caltha, flowering rush (butomus), some of the water and Japanese irises, the blue-flowered pickerel weed or pontederia, water musk (mimulus), and water forget-me-not (myosotis), not forgetting the moisture-loving ferns, ornamental rushes, cotton grasses, and sedges.

One of the loveliest of all water plants is the water hyacinth, which floats on the surface and needs no soil to sustain it, while if you propose to keep fish, water snails and other under-water animal life, you will need to stock your pond also with a few of the fascinating submerged oxygenating plants to keep the water pure, like the carnivorous bladderwort or utricularia, the translucent tape grass (vallisneria), the starwort (callitriche), and water milfoil (myriophyllum), all of which represent some of the most remarkable of all forms of plant life.

HOW TO MAKE A MAGIC KNOT

THIS is a trick which, once seen, can be performed by anybody. We ask one of our friends to take hold of a handkerchief by two of its opposite corners, and to tie a knot in it without leaving hold of the corners. This may seem not very easy — indeed, impossible ; but, like many tricks, it is only necessary "to know how" to be able to do it without difficulty. All that is required is that the person taking hold of the ends of the handkerchief should

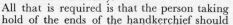
HOW THE HANDKERCHIEF IS HELD

fold his arms before doing so, as seen in the picture. Then, by simply unfolding the arms, the handkerchief is knotted as a matter of course. It is scarcely necessary to add that a handkerchief is not essential to the trick. A piece of string or tape will serve equally well. If string or tape be used, it should not be less than eighteen inches long. Too short a piece of string makes the trick much more difficult. Similarly, the handkerchief should be a large one.

HOW TO PLAY BADMINTON

That old favourite of children's games, battledore and shuttlecock, provided the foundation for Badminton, which has gained an international appeal since first played as a diversion for a country house party one wet afternoon in the 1870's.

The party was gathered at the Duke of Beaufort's seat in Gloucestershire. A cord was stretched across the hall, the children's battledore and shuttlecocks were pressed into service and the guests were highly entertained. As Badminton is the name of the Duke of Beaufort's country house, it was natural that the new game should take the same name. It was, of course, a very primitive form of the present game and did not win immediate popularity in England.

But in India badminton found more friends, and the first rules were drawn up at Karachi. Under these rules, the game returned to England and made such progress that a championship was inaugurated in 1899. International matches began four years later. The game has improved steadily and is under the efficient control of the International Badminton Federation. Some of the best players in the world are Danes.

Badminton is usually played indoors on a court measuring 44 feet by 20 feet. A net not more than two and a half feet deep is suspended midway across the court at a height of five feet.

At a distance of six and a half feet on each side of the net, and parallel with it, are the short service lines, while another line runs from the short service line to the back boundary line. Thus two courts are formed on each side of the net, as shown in the diagram. Two and a half feet inside each boundary line, and parallel with it, is another line, known as the long service line.

The racket is more slender than the one used for lawn tennis and has a longer handle. It varies in weight from five to eight ounces. The shuttle has a cord base, one to one and a half inches in diameter, to which are fixed 14 to 16 feathers, $2\frac{1}{2}$ to $2\frac{3}{4}$ inches in length. It weighs a quarter of an ounce.

Two players on each side is the usual personnel of the game and the first to score fifteen points wins.

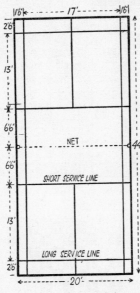

By winning the toss a side has the option of serving first or the choice of courts. If the winning side serves first, the opposing side has choice of courts. The first player on the serving side takes up his position in the right-hand court between the short and long service lines, and must hit the shuttle so that it goes over the net and into the court diagonally opposite to him. The player in that court must then return the shuttle before it touches the ground.

The shuttle must be kept in play across the net to any position within the outer bounds and by any player of either side. If one of the opposing side fails to return it an ace, or point, is scored by the serving side, and the next service is taken from the left-hand court.

The service must be delivered underhand; the shuttle must never be struck when it is at a higher level than the waist-line. Otherwise it is a fault, and the hand goes out. This means that the player's turn is finished for that innings, and the opposing side goes in. After the first innings, however, when a hand goes out the next player on his side serves, and not until both hands are out does the other side have its innings.

There are several faults which may mean a hand out if they are awarded against the serving side, or an ace for the serving side if they are awarded against their opponents. If the shuttle is sent out of the boundaries it is a fault; if, in serving, the shuttle fails to clear the net or falls short of the service line, or otherwise falls out of its proper court, it is also a fault. The shuttle must not touch any part of the players or their dress, neither may a player touch the net with his racket or any part of his body.

If, in serving, the shuttle hits the top of the net and continues its flight, it is known as a "let," and another service is allowed, as in lawn tennis; but, on the other hand, if the first service is otherwise at fault, no second attempt is allowed.

Should a shuttle fall on any line, it is regarded as having fallen in the court, but a foot on the line is considered out of court.

A TRICKY RETURN

THE PUZZLE OF THE PATCHWORK QUILT

An old man, who was dearly loved by all who knew him, had eleven relations who determined that they would give him a joint present on his eightieth birthday.

Each of them, even the smallest grandchild, was to contribute, and, as the old man wanted for nothing, it was considered best to give him something in the workmanship of which all the family could join. It was finally decided to make him a patchwork quilt.

Now, there were in this quilt, which was square, exactly 169 small square pieces of material of equal size, and it was arranged that each of the eleven relations should contribute a perfect square toward the quilt. These square sections, however, were not to be of the same size, for the older members of the family said it would be only fair if they gave larger squares than the younger.

There was some difficulty in arranging this, until one of the donors, who was good at geometry,

drew out a sketch of the quilt with its 169 small squares, and, after some thought, divided this into eleven squares of varying size, suggesting to each relation which square he or she should make. They all set to work, and then the finished pieces were joined together to make the quilt, which was presented to the old man, as shown in the accompanying picture.

He was delighted with his gift, and would amuse himself for hours trying, by examining the work and the patterns carefully, to find out the piece for which each relation had been responsible.

Take a piece of tracing or tissue paper and trace a copy of this quilt. Then see if with a pair of scissors you can divide it up into the eleven squares worked by the eleven relations.

The solution is given on page 5814.

ANSWER TO THE PUZZLE OF THE CHEQUERED SQUARE ON PAGE 5563.
The diagram on the left shows the route the soldiers marched.

DINING OUT—A GOOD GAME FOR A PARTY

Divide your guests into groups of five and seat them as far apart as possible. Then tell each party to send one member out of the room. He, you explain, is the waiter; those left in are the "diners out." You then tell each of them what he or she must order for a meal, reading from a prepared list of menus. These may vary as to the number of courses, but all should be quite ridiculous. This makes it more difficult for everyone to memorise the dishes, for no one is allowed to write anything down except yourself. You, naturally, must mark against each menu the name of the person to whom you have given

it, or you cannot keep a check on the game. When all have been told what they are expected to eat, you go outside and send the waiters in. Each goes first to his own table, and when he has taken all four orders, he comes out and repeats them to you. If they are right, he is sent on to the next table; if wrong, he must go back—again and again if necessary—until he can repeat all four correctly. So it often happens, that two or even three waiters are at one table together, which adds to the general fun. The one who first gets every single menu correct is the winner, and will deserve a small prize.

A SWING MADE OF MATCHES

A little model swing can be made from nine wooden safety matches, a piece of cotton, and a slip of cardboard.

We fasten the matches together with a little strong gum, in the way shown in the picture, and hang the cardboard seat from the top rail by two lengths of cotton. We then cut out a tiny figure of a boy or girl, using thin card such as postcards are made of. Having drawn and painted the face and clothes, we bend the figure into a sitting posture, and stick it with a dab of

gum on the centre of the seat to secure it. If we can stick something rather heavy, like a shot or two or a small leaden disc, to the underside of the seat, it will swing better. The loops by which the cotton lines holding the seat are fastened round the top rail of the framework should be fairly loose to allow easy movements backwards and forwards.

In making this model much scope is left for ingenuity and neatness. For instance, with a sharp penknife we can bevel the ends of the matches.

EASY GAMES WITH PLAYING-CARDS

There are a number of simple games that can be played with an ordinary pack of cards. Here are four of the best known among them.

SPADE THE GARDENER

SPADE the Gardener is a form of the game generally known as Happy Families. The number of players should be not fewer than three and not more than five. The cards taken from the pack and used for the game are the kings, queens, knaves, aces, and tens, so that twenty cards are used. These cards are given special names.

The king of spades is known as Spade the Gardener, from which the game gets its name. The queen of spades is called Spade the Gardener's wife, the knave of spades is Spade the Gardener's son, the ace of spades is Spade the Gardener's servant, and the ten of spades is Spade the Gardener's dog. The king of clubs is known as Club the Constable, the king of hearts is the Good-natured Man, and the king of diamonds is called Vicar Den.

Then these three each have a wife, a son, a servant, and a dog, just as Spade the Gardener has, these being the queen, knave, ace, and ten respectively. The cards are divided equally. The object of each player is to get possession of all the twenty cards. As in most card games, the player left of the dealer starts.

Suppose that he has the Good-natured Man's wife. He may ask any of the other players to give him the Good-natured Man. If he is lucky enough to have asked the right player, it is handed to him ; then he can ask for another of the family. If he should succeed in getting the whole family he can go on asking for cards to complete his other families.

The first time, however, that a player asks for a card from a person who does not have it, the privilege of asking passes to that player. A player is out of the game when he has given up all his cards.

After some time the families will all be completed, and will be in the hands of those players who are still in the game. Then the one who has the privilege of asking demands from one of the other players a complete family, such as the Club the Constable family, and if the player has that family, he must hand it over. Finally, all the families get into the hands of one player, who wins the game.

OLD MAID

ONE card is taken out of the pack and put aside. It is better if no one knows what card has been removed, although some people discard a queen. The pack, which now contains fifty-one cards, is dealt round one by one to all the players.

Each player looks at his cards. If he has two of one kind—such as two kings or two eights—he throws those two into the middle of the table face downward. When everyone has thrown away all the pairs he has, the player on the left of the dealer holds out the remainder of his cards, back upward, in the form of a fan, and the player on his left selects one from them without seeing what it is.

If this card pairs with one in his own hand, he throws the pair on the heap in the middle of the table ; but if the card is unlike any other in his hand, he must keep it. Then he holds out his cards and allows the player on his left to take one.

As pair after pair is thrown on the table, the cards in play become fewer and fewer. Every player who succeeds in pairing all his cards is out of the game, until at last one player is left with only one card. This will be of the same kind as the card originally withdrawn from the pack, and the player is called the old maid—or the old bachelor.

SNAP

THIS is rather a noisy card game, in which the players must be alert all the time. The more players the merrier is the party. The cards are dealt face downward, and no player looks at his cards. The player to begin turns over the top card of his heap, and places it face upward on the table some distance in front of him.

The next player does the same thing with the top card of his pile, and so on round the table, one player after another turning his top card face upward. While this is going on, if any player notices that a card turned up is the same kind of a card as the uppermost exposed card in front of himself, he calls out SNAP ! Whichever of the two players with similar cards calls out the word Snap first takes all the turned-up cards in front of the other player, and puts them beneath his un-turned heap. Then the game goes on again.

If a player calls Snap in error, the player whose card prompted him to call takes all his exposed cards. This prevents players from calling out Snap to every card that is turned over, in the hope that it may be like theirs. When a player loses all his cards, he is out, the winner of the game being the one who gains the complete pack.

SNIP-SNAP-SNORUM

THERE is more than one card game played under this name. This is the simplest of them.

Any number of persons may play, and each has in front of him five or six counters.

The cards are dealt out all round in the usual way. The player to start lays down a card, face upward. The next player puts down a card of the same face value if he can —that is to say, that he puts a queen upon a queen, or a seven upon a seven, and so on.

At the same time he cries *snip*. If he does so, the first player has to put one of his counters in the pool.

If the next player has a card of the same value, he plays it on the other two cards, and at the same time cries *snap*. Then the second player has to put two counters in the pool. If the fourth player can put another card of the same value upon the three that have been played, he does so and cries *snorum*, and the third player has to put three counters in the pool. As there are only four cards of each in the pack, it is impossible to go any farther than snorum.

Actually it seldom happens that four consecutive players have a card of the same value. If the second player has not a card of the same value as that played by the first player, he cannot play, and although another player may have such a card, he cannot play either. The play must be consecutive from the right to the left. The last player leads another card, and the player on his left tries to *snip* that card.

When a player has lost all his counters he retires from the game, which is won by the player whose counters last longest and who then takes the pool.

THE WANDERING HALFPENNY

FOR this trick we must get a pill-box of such size that a halfpenny lying flat inside will exactly cover the bottom. We line it inside at the bottom with paper cut the same size and pasted down smoothly, covering the inside of the lid in the same way. We must then take a halfpenny and cover one side of it with the same paper, trimming it neatly round the edges. The coin on one side will look like an ordinary halfpenny, but on the other like a disc of paper.

To work the trick, we borrow a halfpenny. After it has been given to us, we hand the box round for inspection. The general attention being taken up with this, we secretly exchange the borrowed coin for the prepared one, which we must have concealed beforehand in the right hand, holding it there by bending the fingers slightly against the lower joints of the second and third fingers.

We lay the prepared coin, papered side downward, on the table, where all can see it. The borrowed halfpenny we put secretly out of sight.

Having got so far, we take the open box in the left hand, and the prepared halfpenny between the forefinger and thumb of the right, keeping the uncovered side toward the company, and place it in the box, but in doing so we tilt it so that this side shall fall forward. It will therefore lie with the papered side uppermost.

We close the box, and shake it up and down, when the coin rattles, proving that it is still there. "Halfpenny Go!" we say. Again we shake the box, but this time from side to side, in which direction the coin has no room to move, and therefore cannot rattle. "It is gone!" we say, and opening the box, we allow anyone to look into it. Seeing the paper side of the coin, they take this to be the bottom of the box.

"Now," we say, "I will bring the half-penny back again." We close the box, saying, "Come!" Again we shake it, this time up and down. The coin is once more heard to rattle, having apparently returned from its wanderings. "It has come back, you see!" We open the box, and turn the halfpenny quickly out into our hand, into which it will fall with the papered side downward. It appears to be the borrowed halfpenny, for which we must again exchange it, gaining the chance to do so by inviting the spectators to examine the box once more.

This is a very good trick as it stands; but we can get a still greater effect by apparently conjuring away the halfpenny from the box altogether, and producing it somewhere else. One very good way is to bring forth the real borrowed halfpenny, marked to prove it is the same, from the middle of a ball of wool.

For this we need another little piece of apparatus, which we can make for ourselves. We take a piece of tin 3 inches long by 2¼ inches wide, and fold it down its longer edges to form a sort of flat tube, just large enough to let a halfpenny slip easily through it.

On one end of this tube we must wind some wool to form a ball, allowing the opposite end of the tube to stick out an inch or so, as in the picture. This ball, which should be about 3 inches in diameter, we put in one of our side-pockets.

THE TUBE IN THE BALL

When the box has been examined the second time, we put the right hand, containing the borrowed halfpenny, into the pocket or the bag or drawer in which we have concealed the ball, drop the halfpenny down the tube, and draw out the tube. As we do so we give the ball a squeeze to close up the hole. Then it may be freely handled.

We now order the halfpenny to pass into the ball of wool, which we finally hand to someone to wind off, say, round a book or a chair-back, or anything else that is handy.

The Story of the Boundless Universe and All Its Wondrous Worlds

THE WONDER OF LIGHT

THOUGH light has been studied for many ages, it is only within the last century or so that men probably learned enough to make them believe that it consisted of waves of energy; and we must learn that, though the wave theory of light is still generally believed to be true, there is another theory which supposes that light consists of a number of tiny units of radiation flying through space.

We know for certain that light moves, and yet this is a thing which we may naturally forget. Let us suppose we are out in the open air on a bright day, or that we are in a room lit by a steady light; or take the present moment and place as we are reading this page. It seems to us that there is something we call light illuminating this page, which simply stays where it is. But this is not at all what really happens.

All light everywhere is in movement, the most rapid movement in the universe. The light is pouring down from the sky, in at the window, or from the lamp, and up from the page to our eyes, as certainly as if it consisted of raindrops, but with vastly greater speed.

The first fact to learn is that there is something moving which makes light. This movement has been studied in various ways, and the rate of it has been found out. It is the same as the rate at which radiant heat and electric waves move, for light is a kind of electric wave. Light moves at a speed of 186,000 miles a second, or eight times round the world while the clock ticks once. So far as we know, this rate never changes.

Now, there are many kinds of movement, as we know, and this movement of light might be a movement of something that travelled from place to place, or it might be a wave movement which we could compare to the waves of water. When we throw a stone in a pond, the ripples run along the surface of the water, but it is not, of course, the surface of the water itself that runs.

When Sir Isaac Newton turned his incomparable mind to the study of light two theories held the field, one supposing that it travelled like waves of sound, others that the emanations were like those which produce the sense of smell.

Sir Isaac's reading of the emanation idea was that light consisted of very small particles of matter emitted by luminous bodies, always with the same velocity. This was Newton's corpuscular theory of light. It differs from the most modern theory because now it is supposed that the emanations are not particles of matter but of something like electricity.

ASTRONOMY · GEOLOGY · GEOGRAPHY · CHEMISTRY · PHYSICS · LIFE

The idea of light as an emanation set going like a wave by a luminous body began with Huygens, the Dutch contemporary of Newton. A century later Fresnel developed it in France; and Young in England invented the idea of the ether which was disturbed by the waves and was the carrier of them. Faraday completed the idea by showing that a ray of light could be deflected by an electro-magnet, and therefore was akin to electricity.

WHY THE WAVE THEORY OF LIGHT STILL HOLDS ITS GROUND

The reason why the wave theory still holds its ground is briefly this. If two sets of waves are going in the same direction, and if the crests of these waves come together, the combined crest will grow bigger. If the crest of one wave comes in the same place as the trough of the other, the crest will fill up the trough and the wave will be smoothed out and disappear. This will be true if the waves are waves of light. It is possible to arrange two beams of light so as to make their waves impinge on one another in this way. When this is done we get light when the waves combine with one another; darkness when they cancel one another. If wave motion is admitted, our minds naturally imagine something that is waving or being waved, and it was once found convenient to call that something the Ether, though this is now known not to exist.

Nevertheless the twentieth-century school of physicists, who are working at the structure of the atom and its electrical constitution, find very much to recommend some sort of theory of bits of light, or parcels of light, which are very, very small.

THE MODERN THEORY OF LIGHT WHICH IS NOT UNLIKE ISAAC NEWTON'S OLD IDEA

This is not so very unlike Newton's first rough idea of streams of corpuscles of light, or, as he would have called them if he had been born two centuries later, atoms of light.

These ideas have been coupled with the names of Professor Einstein and Professor Planck, who decided to disregard the ether, and they get a great deal of support from nearly all those who have been trying to make models of the atom, which would account for all the curious facts observed in the rays shot out from radium, or in the behaviour of X-rays when these are turned on to the atoms of other substances; or again in the appearance of the light coming from an incandescent gas when it is spread out to reveal itself in a rainbow band or spectrum. The workers in this field find it hard to abandon the wave theory. Sir Arthur Eddington declared that if the ether's existence could not be proved we should have to invent it. Sir William Bragg once observed that we used the wave theory on Mondays, Wednesdays, and Fridays, and the corpuscular theory on Tuesdays, Thursdays, and Saturdays.

Most of us are now familiar with the idea of the atom of matter as a solar system in which bits of electricity revolve at high speed round a nucleus, or sun.

There are several particulars in which the revolutions of these electrons differ from those of planets. The first is in their speed. When an electron is making its most jog-trot journey, it moves on an average 1400 miles a second, and as its orbit is very tiny it travels round its sun about 7000 billion times in a second.

THE MOVEMENT IN AN ATOM AND THE MOVEMENT IN A SOLAR SYSTEM

Secondly, in a solar system movement goes on continuously and equably, while in the atom there seem to be sudden jumps from one kind of motion to another; the electrons sometimes slowing down, then taking a sudden leap forward, moving, as one writer puts it, like fleas which crawl for a time and then hop.

Various explanations have been put forward to account for these hops and to link them up with the radiation of light from the atom. Planck's explanation was that when two electrons tangled up their paths and came into collision, the result was a release of energy taking the form of a bundle of bits of it; and it might be called a light quantum, the smallest possible packet of light.

The mathematicians got busy with the light quantum and found it would not do, and that the electrons in their paths would not produce it. Then Professor P. A. M. Dirac, of Cambridge, came forward with a new idea. The electron, or unit of negative electricity, is not the only planet in the atom's skies. There are positrons or units of positive electricity also. When electron and positron come into collision they strike out a photon. And the photon, with an energy of half a million volts, is the primary corpuscle.

(*Next chapter in this group, page 5815*)

The Story of Immortal Folk Whose Work Will Never Die

Sir Thomas Lawrence

Sir Henry Raeburn

George Romney   John Constable   Thomas Gainsborough   J. M. W. Turner

GREAT BRITISH PAINTERS

IF we who are interested in beautiful things in art had to name the most glorious century in our history, we should probably say at once the Eighteenth. During that hundred years there lived and worked the group of men who have lifted the name of Britain high and marked it with greatness—Constable, Reynolds, Gainsborough, Hogarth, Turner, Lawrence, Romney, Raeburn. Let us look at this immortal company of our British artists.

William Hogarth belongs more truly to London than any other English artist of great fame. He was born in November, 1697, in Bartholomew Close, in the City, near the fine old Norman church where he was baptised. The London of his times was a troubled, changing place, and the stamp of its history was seen within a stone's throw of his childhood's home. A few doors away, Milton had stayed in hiding during the Restoration of the Stuarts. In the same group of houses, a little later, young Benjamin Franklin lived while he was working for a printer who had set up his press in the Lady Chapel of St. Bartholomew's Church close at hand.

Hogarth's father was a man of varied pursuits, now schoolmaster, now printer's reader, now author. His changing work carried him here and there in London. William was taken from school early and apprenticed to a silver plate engraver near Leicester Square, known in those days as Leicester Fields.

From the first the boy's greatest diversion had been in watching people's faces. He would make sketches of features on any scrap of paper, and, when that failed, on his thumbnail. In his days—the days of pillories and old Newgate Gaol—there were plenty of unpleasant things to be seen in London. Hogarth was among the crowd who watched the heads of the traitors of the 1745 Jacobite rising stuck high on Temple Bar. Hogarth saw, in Leicester Fields, a man set up a telescope and point it at Temple Bar, plainly visible above the small houses; whereupon he was surrounded by a crowd who paid a halfpenny to peep at the revolting spectacle. Hogarth watched their faces.

When he was twenty-one his apprenticeship came to an end and he began to work on his own account, engraving on metal, later making engravings for booksellers. He took drawing lessons in the St. Martin's Lane Academy, whose head was Sir James Thornhill, the painter of some of the pictures on the dome of St. Paul's.

EXPLORERS · INVENTORS · WRITERS · ARTISTS · SCIENTISTS

Hogarth was an insignificant little figure, small, not very good-looking. But all men who had seen his sketches were interested in him. One of the writers in Hogarth's times tells us how two artists were walking through Cranbourne Alley, off Leicester Fields, when one exclaimed, " There! There's Hogarth ! " " What," exclaimed the other, " that little man in the sky-blue coat? " Off he ran, curious to see William more closely. When he turned the corner of the alley he saw him patting one of two quarrelling boys on the back, trying to persuade him to return to the fight.

HOGARTH'S ROMANTIC MARRIAGE WITH HIS MASTER'S DAUGHTER

In 1729 the world of art in London was startled by the news that Hogarth had made a runaway match with Jane, the only daughter of Sir James Thornhill. Sir James was furious. He shut his mouth tight, and his heart, and his purse. Presently he was reconciled. It was a pity he did not live long enough to see " that little Hogarth " famous.

In the meantime the artist's poor days were past. He had a fine house in Leicester Fields, with a sign that he had made for himself, of pieces of cork glued together and painted, fashioning " The Golden Head." And there was a brass plate on the door with the name of Hogarth on it.

William became as famous for his bitter tongue as for his satirical drawings. Horace Walpole went to see him one day about a history of painting. He cut the interview short by walking out of the house. " If I had stayed," Walpole afterwards remarked, " there remained nothing for him but to bite me."

THE MEETING OF ARTISTS WHICH GREW INTO THE ROYAL ACADEMY

If Hogarth had enemies he had also plenty of friends, including famous men like Dr. Johnson and Samuel Richardson. He had enough work during the day, when he was not visiting his friends or arguing, and at night people would see him taking his walk in Leicester Fields, a queer, strutting little figure in a scarlet cape and cocked hat.

In later life Hogarth became interested in the Foundling Hospital, Guildford Street. The institution had just moved there from its first home in Hatton Garden. Hogarth, one of the earliest guardians, summoned a number of fellow artists, and they began the work of decorating the walls of the new building free of charge.

The artists made a committee among themselves and arranged to meet every 5th day of November. This working committee meeting soon became a great annual dinner attended by artists and connoisseurs. Fashionable people used to visit the Foundling Hospital to see the pictures. Presently the artists arranged an annual exhibition of their work. From this grew the Society of English Artists, which developed into the Royal Academy.

In the meantime, Hogarth was growing old. He had a country house in Chiswick, as well as his town house. He would have been pleased—Hogarth never thought poorly of himself—had he known that one hundred and fifty years later people would look at his country home and go down Hogarth Lane, Chiswick. He died in October 1764, and was buried in Chiswick Churchyard.

Within a generation after Hogarth's death a boy was growing up in the country who was destined to bear as famous a title—young John Constable. John's father was a well-to-do miller and owner of land in the south border of Suffolk. His house was in the delightful village of East Bergholt, and there John was born in June 1776.

JOHN CONSTABLE AND HIS FRIEND THE VILLAGE PLUMBER

John was at school till he was seventeen. His best friend in those early years was the only one in Bergholt who really had any feeling for art, and that was the village plumber. He dabbled in landscape painting, and John worked with him.

The boy's father wished him to become a clergyman, but he gave way when he saw how averse to the idea John was, and he settled matters by taking him " into the business." John made a fine figure in his miller's coat—tall, handsome, and dark-eyed.

His spare time was spent with his friend the plumber, and in painting in a small room he had hired in the village. When he was nineteen, Mr. Constable allowed him to go to London to see if any luck lay in an artist's career. For some little time John's work was divided between East Bergholt and the capital.

When he was twenty-four he was admitted as a student of the Royal Academy.

THE VILLAGE PLUMBER HELPS YOUNG JOHN CONSTABLE TO PAINT A COUNTRY SCENE IN SUFFOLK

John's life in London was very much like that of any other artist who so far had not " arrived." He made pleasant friends, like Wilkie and Jackson, Stothard, and, later, Turner and Lawrence. He worked very hard, and tried his best to economise his resources. He was not extravagant, but he never had the knack of saying " No " to a borrower, and he never could resist a book he wanted. The result was that his money affairs were not satisfactory. Like Samuel Pepys, the diarist, he was always making little resolutions, and then forgetting them.

CONSTABLE DIES IN THE SPRINGTIME THAT HE LOVED SO WELL

Many years passed, their happiness chequered by periods of ill-health, by disappointment about his work, by the course of a true love affair which naturally did not run smooth. After five years of secret and difficult courtship, in 1816 John was able to marry the lady—Maria Bicknell, the granddaughter of the rector of East Bergholt.

Three years after his marriage John became Associate of the Royal Academy. Ten more years had to elapse before he became a member. They were filled with the ordinary incidents of a pleasant life and concentrated work, which seemed of little interest save to those concerned. The most important outward events were the exhibitions of Constable's work in France and the gold medal consequently given to the artist by the French king.

Constable died in 1837, in the midst of the English springtime he had always loved. During his life he had created something of a revolution in English art.

THE EARLY YEARS OF STRUGGLE OF A FAMOUS ARTIST OF SCOTLAND

One of the men who shares the honours of this period was a Scotsman, Henry Raeburn. He was the son of a manufacturer who, in turn, was descended from border folk. Henry was born at Stockbridge, then a pretty suburb divided by sunny braes from Edinburgh, on March 4, 1756. He and his brother William were left orphaned and poor in Henry's early childhood, and it appeared that a hard life lay before them. William, twelve years older, looked after Henry for some time. Then a good woman, Sarah Sandilands, sent him to Heriot's Hospital, or school, an honourable institution in Edinburgh where orphaned children were educated.

Sarah died long before the lad came to manhood. But her kindness and faith were justified, and it happened that her own granddaughter was one of those present when the " charity boy " was knighted at Edinburgh in 1822.

Henry was well educated at Heriot's in good manners as well as good scholarship. He left at the age of fifteen, in 1771, the year Sir Walter Scott was born, and was apprenticed to a goldsmith in Edinburgh. The boy had a certain amount of designing to do for his master, who was jeweller as well as goldsmith, and his taste in drawing was thus fostered. He contrived to have a few elementary lessons in " pencilling," and probably had his ambition roused by the sight of miniatures passing through his master's hands.

He was a boy of very fine intelligence that was waiting, it would seem, for the first outside gleam to set it aglow. In his spare time he began drawing, managed to buy some water-colours, and soon was painting miniatures himself. The years of his apprenticeship passed in close and steady industry. Before they were over his work as a goldsmith was receding into the background, and he was becoming known as a promising, self-taught artist.

YOUNG HENRY RAEBURN AND HIS LOVE OF THE OPEN AIR

A good friend now appeared in Henry's life, probably at the turning-point of it, and that was a portrait-painter called David Martin. Raeburn was introduced to the artist by his master the goldsmith, and dreams ran hazily in his head as he sat in Martin's studio and saw the pictures on the easels and about the walls. Henry copied a little of Martin's work, did portraits himself, and contrived to make a meagre living. Three years passed thus. Raeburn was now a striking figure, his border blood telling in him. He was well over six feet, and had the strong, striking face that generally marks the man who is self-made and has known what it is to fight. He did not spend all his time indoors. In spite of hard work he contrived to become an excellent archer and fisherman, and—strange as it sounds in thinking of those days—a good golfer. Everything interested him, from science and shipbuilding to architecture.

As his work in portraiture carried him into the houses of wealthy and cultured people, he became favoured in society,

THREE ARTISTS OF OUR GOLDEN AGE

SIR THOMAS LAWRENCE AS A BOY—FROM THE PAINTING BY MARGARET DICKSEE

HOGARTH'S PORTRAIT OF HIMSELF

GEORGE MORLAND AS HE WAS

liked for his simplicity, his lack of affectation, and his good manners.

In 1778 an idyll strayed into his life. The story is that Raeburn was sketching a landscape outside Edinburgh when a lovely lady walked into the scene. He put her into his drawing, " like a sunbeam in a shadowed dell." The lovely lady, who was the Countess Leslie, presently stood on his studio doorstep and asked to have her portrait painted. She was small, " plump but graceful, with soft, confiding eyes." The painter fell in love with her, and made an extremely good portrait. In two months the two were married. The idyll came home to stay.

It was a happy married life. There was money; children came; Raeburn, no longer troubled by poverty, went on with his work. After a few years he became dissatisfied with his technique, packed up and went to Rome. There he stayed for two years, working hard, studying the work of genius in another century.

SIR HENRY RAEBURN AS A CHRONICLER OF EDINBURGH'S HISTORY

When he returned he took a studio in George Street, and settled down to paint portraits again. Presently he found the studio inadequate, and, turning architect, he set up one himself. The building is now called Raeburn House, in York Place, Edinburgh. With a short interval in London, the artist worked here the rest of his uneventful life.

Before he laid down his brush he painted everybody of note in his generation; Sir Walter Scott several times. He thus became a chronicler of Edinburgh's intimate history. In 1814 he was made A.R.A., the next year R.A. A little later he was made a knight. The year after Raeburn was appointed the king's " limner and painter in Scotland, with all fees, profits, salaries, rights, privileges, and advantages thereto belonging." This quaint honour came too late for Raeburn to enjoy it. A few months later, in July 1823, he died and was buried in the graveyard of St. John's Church, Edinburgh.

As Raeburn alone would have made Scotland famous for his portraiture, so Gainsborough alone would have made England famous.

Thomas Gainsborough was born at Sudbury in May 1727, and the street where the house of his birth stood is now called Gainsborough Street in his honour. Thomas was the youngest of the nine children of John Gainsborough, a wool merchant. His uncle Humphrey was the master of Sudbury Grammar School, and there Tom, aged ten, went unwillingly to learn his lessons.

THE AMUSING STORY OF GAINSBOROUGH PAINTING HIS FIRST PORTRAIT

All his spare time, and a good many truant hours, were spent drawing trees and hedges in the lovely Sudbury district. His first portrait, while still a schoolboy, was that of a man who was contemplating the raid of a pear tree. Thomas was sketching the trees, and, looking up, saw this face above the fence staring longingly at the fruit. The boy-artist quietly drew the face, unseen by the would-be thief. It was what is called a " speaking likeness," and the sketch of Tom Peartree went down to posterity as the earliest portrait of the greatest portrait-painter of England.

When Thomas was fifteen his good father sent him to London to study art at the St. Martin's Lane Academy, where Hogarth had had lessons. The head was Francis Hayman, once a scene-painter, the friend of all the actors and musicians of London. Tom became one of the circle, and he kept that love for music and the stage to the end. He worked about a year at the academy, tried being a portrait-painter on his own account in Hatton Garden for a spell, then went home to Sudbury.

HOW TOM PEARTREE BROUGHT THOMAS GAINSBOROUGH NEW COMMISSIONS

Tom's next adventure was to get married in 1746 to beautiful Margaret Burr, the sister of one of his father's travellers. She had a little money and the two removed to Ipswich, then a charming, dreaming old town. Gainsborough took a nice house whose rent was six pounds a year, and he settled down very happily with his bride. He was twenty, Mrs. Gainsborough eighteen. They made a song and a jest of life, and Thomas also managed to find purchasers for some pictures.

Not very satisfied with his small notoriety, Gainsborough set up a copy of Tom Peartree just above his own fence, so that passers-by could see it and argue

THE EARLIEST KNOWN PORTRAIT SKETCH BY THOMAS GAINSBOROUGH WAS THAT OF A MAN HE
SAW ABOUT TO ROB A PEAR TREE IN AN ORCHARD

therefrom that a portrait-painter lived within. One of the passers-by happened to be Philip Thicknesse, the governor of Landguard Fort at the mouth of the Orwell. Thicknesse immediately gave the artist a commission, and became a very good friend of Gainsborough's until the two were separated almost thirty years later, by a sad quarrel.

After fourteen years in Ipswich, the Gainsboroughs and their two daughters removed to Bath, then a very gay, fashionable place. Here the artist's work prospered greatly. His price for a bust portrait was gradually raised from eight guineas to forty; for a full-length portrait it was a hundred.

The artist divided his time between music and painting. In a kind of frenzy of delight he took up first the violin, then the viol-de-gamba, and then the harp, then the lute, but was too impatient to become greatly skilled in any instrument. Gainsborough had more than his share of the artistic temperament and was also of a quick temper. It was largely owing to the very sweet disposition of his wife Peggy that his married life was a happy one. He was a strange mixture of a light-hearted gaiety that showed so happily in society, and a sombre dreaminess.

THE GREAT DAYS WHEN GAINSBOROUGH WAS SOUGHT OUT BY KINGS

In 1774 the artist and his family moved to London and lived in Schomberg House in Pall Mall. Gainsborough's rent for his rooms and studio was £300 a year. He had moved far from the little house at Ipswich ! He was now a great person, sought out by kings and princes. Not often does fortune come home to stay in the house of a genius in this manner. He had a happy old age, filled with " honour, love, obedience, troops of friends," and he died in August 1788, in a fine way, loving art to the close. Sir Joshua Reynolds came to see his great rival just before the end. " We are all going to heaven," said Gainsborough, " and Van Dyck is of the company." Visitors to Kew Gardens can easily find the tombstone marking the place where he was buried.

Sir Joshua Reynolds was a figure that stamped the art history of his generation. He was a Devonshire man, born at Plympton in July 1723, the seventh son of a clergyman who was master of the

Plympton Grammar School. Joshua went to school with the rest, and in 1740 was sent to London to study art. Hudson, the portrait-painter, was his master. Seven years later Joshua left London and settled at Devonport. There he became friendly with Commodore Keppel, and in 1749, when Keppel was in charge of a Mediterranean squadron, went abroad with him in his ship.

THE NEW FIGURE IN THE FASHIONABLE WORLD OF LONDON

Presently he arrived in Rome and stayed there three years, receiving his true art education. There also a sad misfortune befell him, a deafness, the result of a severe chill, of which he was never cured. He came home by way of Paris, settled in London, and began portrait painting. Presently the fashionable world of the capital became aware that a new power was among them, a smallish, roundish man, with red cheeks and blunt features, who painted portraits uncommonly well and gave the most indifferent face a distinction.

Before ten years passed he had become a very important person, and his studio at 47 Leicester Square was one of the chief centres of artistic and literary life of London. Reynolds never married. He had a great many friends, mostly writers and actors, and in 1764 he founded, with Dr. Johnson, the Literary Club—at the Turk's Head, Gerrard Street, in Soho. Its members were men who gave greatness to the century, men like Sheridan, Garrick, Burke, Boswell, Goldsmith.

Reynolds thoroughly appreciated his grandeur. He presently had a coach of his own with carved and gilded wheels, and panels painted with pictures of the four seasons. He was very earnest in his work and took any opposition seriously, so that " tiffs " with men like Walpole and his fellow artists chequered his career.

REYNOLDS BECOMES THE FIRST PRESIDENT OF THE ROYAL ACADEMY

Reynolds, however, was considered the most important artist in London, and it was natural that when the Royal Academy was founded in 1768 he should be its first president. It was also natural that the next year should see him knighted.

A few years later, in 1773, on a visit to Plympton, he was elected Mayor of his native town. By this time he was known as a man of literary attainments—his famous

A FAMOUS ARTIST'S FAMOUS FRIENDS

DR. JOHNSON VISITING SIR JOSHUA REYNOLDS IN THE ARTIST'S STUDIO

THE DYING GAINSBOROUGH SENDS FOR SIR JOSHUA REYNOLDS TO COMFORT HIM

The upper picture is by Francis Barraud; the lower picture is in the Mappin Art Gallery, Sheffield

Discourses on Art, delivered to the students of the Academy, are still read and quoted.

The year 1784 saw Reynolds still further honoured: he became painter to the king. But his work was coming to an end. A few seasons later his eyesight failed and he laid down his brushes. Serious and argumentative to the end, he carried on a quarrel with the Academy on the subject of principles in art and other, personal, affairs. But what he said was of little moment; his life's work of inestimable importance spoke for him. He died in February 1792, and was buried in St. Paul's Cathedral.

THE SMALL WOODEN FIGURES YOUNG GEORGE ROMNEY CARVED

Reynolds's greatest rivals were Gainsborough and Romney. At one time Romney, whose merit could not in any way touch that of Reynolds, caused Sir Joshua some anxious thoughts, as it seemed that Romney, who could flatter a sitter, was taking away his security.

George Romney was born at Beckside, Dalton-in-Furness, in December of 1734. He was the son of a joiner and cabinet-maker and, after a very short and inadequate schooling, was taken into his father's workshop. There was little money to spare in the family of nine sons and one daughter. George showed the first signs of his gifts in carving little wooden figures. While he was still only a youth he came across an illustrated edition of Leonardo da Vinci's Treatise on Painting. From that hour George's ambition was fired.

There was living in Kendal at the time a young artist called Steele, and when Romney was twenty-one he contrived to get himself articled to the painter. He was to work four years with Steele, and pay him twenty pounds a year.

THE HUMBLE BEGINNING OF ROMNEY'S ROAD TO FAME

But before the first year was well out Steele, an adventurer, had disappeared. The next year George married a pretty and sweet-natured girl called Mary Abbott, and set up as a painter in Kendal. He began humbly, painting signboards and taking any commission that came. But his distinct art in portraiture soon became known, and many people in Westmorland came to have their portraits painted.

All this time Romney, who was by nature a romantic, a wanderer, averse to any tie, had been dreaming of that paradise of provincial artists—London. As soon as he had enough money he left his wife and two children and went south. That was in 1762. Sweet Mary Abbott had need then of her good nature and her " stiff backbone," for she was deserted by her husband for thirty years.

During that time he lived in London, France, Italy, London again. He was hardworking to a degree, made enormous sums of money as he became more and more famous. Twice in the course of his prosperous years he visited his wife and children, but otherwise entirely neglected them. All his devotion was given to " the divine lady," as he called Emma Hart, who became Lady Hamilton.

When he was about sixty his health failed; he became a prey to melancholy, which presently threatened madness. Most of his friends were gone; a lonely old age lay before him. Broken in spirit, he returned home at last to Kendal and was nursed back to a semblance of health. But in a year or two he was dead.

THE POOR GENIUS WHO GALLOPED ALONG THE ROAD TO RUIN

A young man was living in London known to Romney, during the latter half of his life, whose pictures are very dear to the English public, George Morland. He was born in London in 1763, and very carefully brought up. His father was a crayonist, and trained his son himself.

The years of this artist's youth were strenuous. His father drove him hard, denied him pleasure, making him copy innumerable pictures, and afterwards selling the copies. The parental discipline was so strong that George only lived in order to be his own master some day. Romney offered to take him into his studio at a salary of £300, but the young painter determined not to be bound again in any way. As soon as he was free he fell headlong into a most disorderly and unfortunate way of life. While he was still young he became a confirmed drunkard. He was extremely eccentric, and given to the wildest freaks by way of amusement. At the same time his power of work was considerable, and after his marriage with Anne Ward he was soon able to maintain a household that was large, even if it was like a bear-garden.

As the years went on he became more and more spendthrift. The result was bankruptcy and a sorry tale of a wasted life. He did not walk to ruin ; he galloped there. His health, of course, was soon gone. It was a most lamentable end to a gifted life—a life that in spite of itself had been to some purpose, for during his last eight years Morland painted about 900 pictures and did over a thousand drawings. He died in unhappy circumstances in October 1804.

Even during Morland's lifetime reproductions of his work in plain or coloured mezzotint found a ready sale, and after his death his reputation as an artist steadily increased. The best of his stable scenes and pictures of country life are prized today for their artistic qualities, as well as for their value as faithful records of the England of the past, and the old mezzotints, if in good condition, usually command high prices.

Contemporary with poor George Morland was another painter of a very different character, Sir Thomas Law-

SIR JOSHUA REYNOLDS'S PORTRAIT OF HIMSELF AS A YOUNG MAN

rence, who lived from 1769 to 1830. He had a strange childhood. His father was a man who had descended from the level of a lawyer to that of innkeeper. Tom was born at the White Hart, Bristol. When he was a little boy his parents moved to the Black Bear, Devizes. He was an unusually clever child, with a trick of remembering poetry, and possessed of a natural art of recitation. When he was only five years old his father used to put him on the table and make him recite. Then Tommy was told to show how cleverly he could draw.

The innkeeper moved about here and there, and Tom went on drawing with his chalks. He became a kind of marvel, and people went to have their portraits done in pencil by this ten-year-old boy. He was a clever and handsome boy, studious, not at all conceited. This life of serious application, added to the painter's own gifts, naturally contributed to his success. Fortune also

J. M. W. TURNER, BY CHARLES TURNER
Reproduced by courtesy of Mr. C. M. W. Turner and The Studio

helped him. When he was twenty-one, and now in London, he painted the " picture of the year." From that time his career was assured. The great painters were dead —Gainsborough, Reynolds, Romney. On Lawrence the favours of the capital and the Court fell. When he was only twenty-four he became an Academician.

THE PUBLICAN'S SON AND THE BARBER'S SON WHO SLEEP IN ST. PAUL'S

This unusual success would have tried even the staunchest character. By degrees Lawrence got spoiled. He never ceased to work hard and to earn an excellent income, but his tastes changed. He wanted to go the pace, to be grand. He changed his smart rooms in Old Bond Street for a fine house in Piccadilly, overlooking the Green Park. Later he moved into Soho, then into Russell Square. He was still the most popular, most sought-out artist of his generation, flattered at home and abroad. He was knighted in 1815, and when he died in 1830, the innkeeper's son was buried in St. Paul's. Twenty-one years later a barber's son was buried there.

This was Joseph Mallord William Turner, by some said to have been born in Maiden Lane, Strand, by others, including Turner himself, at Barnstaple. Be that as it may, his childhood (he was born in 1775) was passed in the Maiden Lane house. The boy's father, like Lawrence's, was proud of the skill he soon showed in drawing, bought him paints and brushes and showed his work to his customers, saying delightedly, " William is going to be a painter."

William got no education save the barest rudiments, but he had a drawing in the Academy when he was fifteen. From boyhood's days onward he was a tireless worker. He coloured prints for an engraver, worked for an architect, exhibited year by year at the Academy, and presently made a public for himself.

THE GENIUS THAT LAY HID IN THE ODD LITTLE FIGURE OF TURNER

The story of Turner's life is a curious tale of character. It had no great outward happenings. Turner was Turner, and he worked. He had a most powerful ambition to excel; he had an inordinate desire to keep himself secret from the world. These two passions ruled his life. He never married. He was careful of money to the point of miserliness.

Nature had not been kind to him. He was short and stout, crooked-legged, red-faced, with the unmistakable eyes of the hoarder of wealth. A strange figure he must have made, tramping about Europe with a knapsack on his back, making at least one drawing a day. His associates in the Academy—he became a full member in 1802—looked strangely on this little man whose uncouth exterior concealed so much genius.

Had he married and had children his character might have broadened, softened. As it was he became more and more like a wonderful room with windows and doors kept continually bolted, a room illuminated only by his art. In his art he gave out the wealth that other people shed out in their lives, making the world beautiful with another kind of beauty.

Toward the end of his life Turner lived in Chelsea, near the river he loved, moving from lodging to lodging in order to keep his whereabouts hidden. When he was an old man, very wealthy, he changed his dwelling once more, finding cheap rooms that pleased him.

THE WONDERFUL COLLECTION OF PICTURES THAT TURNER LEFT TO THE NATION

When the landlady wanted a reference he showed her money. When she asked for his name he muttered a bit and then said, " What is *your* name? " " Mrs. Booth," said the landlady. " Then call me Mr. Booth," was Turner's reply. The neighbourhood, watching the funny little figure, presently dubbed him Admiral. Long before that time he had been called the Dutch Skipper.

But, however Turner might hide from the world, he could not secure himself from disease and death. He died in 1851, aged seventy-five. By an act of legacy, it would seem that he atoned for his miserliness. He left his fortune of some £140,000 to found a home for distressed artists. But, in ignorance, Turner did not word the will properly. It was contested in Chancery, and the money went to his cousins. His pictures and drawings he left to the nation on condition that they should be kept together in a " Turner " room. Thus he contrived that his name, hidden in his lifetime, should be for ever known after his death, remembered as not the least of that shining group that adds its lustre to the glory of our race.

The Great Stories of the World That Will Be Told for Ever

A scene from the Walt Disney film, Snow White and the Seven Dwarfs

SNOW WHITE AND THE DWARFS

ONE winter day, when the snow lay deep on the ground, a gentle queen sat by her window working. As she worked she pricked her finger, so that two little drops of blood fell from it.

The queen sighed and said: " How I wish that I might have a little daughter with cheeks as rosy as those drops of blood, with a skin as white as snow, and hair as black as the ebony window-frame!"

To her great delight the queen's wish was granted, and a little daughter came. She named her Snow White.

Soon after this the queen died, and Snow White's father, the king, married another lady, very beautiful, but very unkind and vain. She knew that she was the most beautiful lady in the land, because when she looked into her magic mirror and asked:

Say, glass that hangeth on the wall,
Who is the fairest of beauties all?

the glass would always answer:

Thou, Queen, art fairest of beauties all.

As the years passed, little Snow White grew into a very sweet and lovely girl, and one day when the vain queen asked the glass the old, old question, to her great surprise it replied:

Fair and lovely though the queen,
Snow White lovelier far, I ween.

This sent the jealous queen into such a frightful rage that she immediately called her servants and gave orders for Snow White to be killed. But the people in the castle loved Snow White, and, instead of killing her, one of them, a good, kind girl, took her into a wood and there left her, in the hope that somebody might see her and befriend her.

Left alone, poor Snow White wandered about in the wood until she came to a little cottage. She opened the door and went in. Inside she found seven little beds, seven little loaves, and seven little glasses of wine. She ate a good supper and then, being very tired, she lay down on one of the beds and fell fast asleep.

Now, the cottage belonged to seven dwarfs, and when it was quite dark they returned, lit their seven lamps, and entered. To their surprise they found a lovely maiden asleep.

" How beautiful she is !" they exclaimed, all together.

At this Snow White awoke and sat up in bed in alarm.

" Do not be afraid," said the dwarfs, " for you are among friends. But, tell us, how came you here? "

Snow White told her story, and the dwarfs, who were charmed with her beauty and sweetness, offered her a home.

" But," said they, " be careful to keep the door shut fast while we are away,

IMAGINATION · CHIVALRY · LEGENDS · GOLDEN DEEDS · FAIRY TALES

lest the jealous queen find you and do you harm."

Sure enough, the queen did find out where Snow White was, and, dressing up as an old woman, she set off for the cottage. Presently Snow White heard somebody calling: " Fine wares to sell! Fine wares to sell! "

She opened the window and leaned out, and indeed the ribbons and laces that she saw before her were so pretty that, forgetting all about the dwarfs' warning, she unbolted the door and ran out.

" I think I should like to buy some laces," said she.

" Let me fasten them into your dress for you," said the old woman, who at once set to work to tie them so tightly that Snow White fell down as if dead.

" There is an end to all your beauty," said the wicked queen.

Soon the dwarfs came home, and when they saw Snow White they guessed at once what had happened. Quick as lightning one of them drew out a knife and cut the cruel laces. In a few minutes Snow White revived and told her story. When they went away the next morning the dwarfs again warned Snow White to open the door to nobody until they returned.

Late in the afternoon Snow White looked out of her window and saw a strange old woman in a red shawl with a basket hanging on her arm.

" Fine wares to sell! Fine wares to sell! " she called.

" Oh, what beautiful combs those are! " cried Snow White.

" Try one in your hair," said the old woman, handing one in at the window.

Snow White took it in her hand, but the comb was poisoned, and when it touched her hair she fell down as if dead.

When the dwarfs returned home they saw the comb and drew it out, and immediately Snow White revived.

As soon as the wicked queen learned that Snow White had escaped a second time she painted her face, dressed herself as a peasant, and went again to the cottage. This time she took with her a beautiful apple, which she had filled on one side with poison.

" Would you like this rosy apple? " said she, holding it up to Snow White as she leaned out of the window.

But Snow White was wise now, and would not take it.

" Perhaps you think it is poisoned," said the old woman. " See, I will eat the green side and you shall have the red !"

The apple did look very tempting, and as the old woman had eaten one half it certainly could not be poisoned, thought Snow White. She took the apple and put it to her lips. But no sooner had she taken one mouthful than she dropped to the floor as if dead.

Then the queen returned to the palace, and, taking her magic mirror in her hand, asked once more:

Who is the fairest of beauties all?

This time the mirror answered:

Thou, Queen, art fairest of beauties all.

Then the queen knew that at last Snow White was dead.

At dusk the dwarfs returned to the cottage as usual, but this time all their efforts to restore Snow White were in vain. She was dead. Sorrowfully they dressed her in a beautiful robe, and placed her in a crystal box ornamented with gold, and set it on a hill for everyone to see.

One day a prince passed that way, and was so struck with Snow White's beauty that he paid the dwarfs a large sum of money to allow him to carry the box away. As it was lifted down one of the servants stumbled. The door of the crystal box flew open, the piece of poisoned apple fell out of Snow White's mouth, and she revived and sat up.

" Where am I ? " she asked.

The prince, who was overjoyed to find that the beautiful girl was still alive, came forward and helped her down. He had learned the story of the jealous queen's wickedness from the dwarfs, and so he was able to tell Snow White what had happened and how she came there.

" I love you better than anyone in the world," he said, when he had told her all. " Come with me and be my bride."

Snow White smiled and gave him her hand, and went away with the prince to his father's palace, where they married and lived happily together for the rest of their lives.

The queen was invited to the wedding; but she was so furious that the prince's love had brought Snow White to life again that she fell down in a fit, from which she never recovered.

THE LITTLE SPINNER AT THE WINDOW

Long ago, far away in the Shetland Islands, there once lived a little lame girl called Grete. Her home was built on the shore of a voe, or sea lake, that ran quite a distance inland. It was built of rough stones, and had only one window.

The roof was covered with green sods, with big white daisies and other flowers growing on it; wreathed, too, with ropes of seaweed, wound round stones, to prevent the sods from being blown off in high winds. There was no garden, but the ground was covered with fine white sand, full of shells, for the green waves curled at its edge only a little way off.

There was a fire of peat in the middle of its only room, and as there was no own lameness. For poor little Grete could not run about and join in games. Often for days she had to lie on her back, bearing a cruel pain that sometimes brought tears to her eyes.

One day when the sea roared and the spray struck against the small window, dimming it so that it was impossible to see out of it, Grete, whose leg ached badly, was lying on the bed by the window.

For once the girl's busy fingers were idle as she watched a big spider beginning to spin her web in the corner of the window. When she first noticed her she was running a line from one corner to the other, then she went back to the middle and made a line fast to another corner, and, after

A SHETLAND WOMAN KNITTING A SHAWL BY THE WAYSIDE

chimney the smoke had to find its own way out, so the walls looked black and dismal. Then a calf or some lambs, or even some little pigs, often shared the fireside in cold weather, and there was scarcely any furniture, for Grete and her mother were very poor. But they had a spinning-wheel and spun the sheep's wool into yarn, and knitted thick stockings and clothes for the fishermen.

On a sunny summer day the little island looked like fairyland, with other fairy islands shining in the distance; but Grete, who would sit at the window with her spinning-wheel and look out upon the island, knew it in winter storms as well, and was afraid then of the great sea which had caused her father's death and her making a sort of wheel with a lot of spokes all joining in the middle, she started off and began to work rounds.

How clever she was! She went round so fast that she made Grete feel giddy.

The spider somehow seemed to grow bigger and bigger, and her web covered more and more of the window and was getting as white as snow. Slowly she seemed to change, till she was no longer a spider, but a trow, a queer little man with a face like a rosy, dried-up apple. And the trow nodded his head at her, and said in a tiny voice: "Watch me, Grete, and you will know how to knit."

Yes, when she looked harder it was wool he was spinning, white and soft and fine; and the web—no, the knitting, of course—grew apace under his fingers. It was easy to see how such beautiful patterns could be made. Grete was learning how to do it fast, and the little trow turned every now and then, and smiled.

The door opened. So did Grete's eyes. And now there was only a real spider, with an everyday sort of web, and—it was very odd—she was no longer at work, but was all tucked up into a ball.

"Eh, Mother," she cried, "you have frightened away the trow just as I was getting on so grandly with learning the fine knitting."

"What has the wee wifie been dreaming about?" said her mother. "Oh, I am tired! It has been a weary day's work." And she sat down, not noticing, in her bewilderment, that Grete did not answer. The little girl could not explain just then, and felt she wanted to think it all over before she forgot the wonderful pattern she had learned so strangely.

She dreamed about it all night, and could scarcely eat any breakfast next morning, she was so excited; and her mother helped her to pick out all the whitest wool from the bundles, so that she might start carding and spinning it without delay.

It would not spin fine enough to please her the first day; no, nor the second day, but she persevered until she was satisfied, and as her wheel went whirring round she fancied she heard the trow's voice saying, "Try again, Grete. Try again."

She thought he was helping her all the time, for surely never had wool been spun of such fineness and evenness before. Then, too, the spider's web was there; and she had only to look at the window and the pattern seemed to stand out clearly again.

Before long the neighbours all came crowding in to see the wonderful shawl that looked like lace. The fame of it even reached the ears of a great lady in Lerwick, who sent a messenger in a boat to say she wished to see it.

Grete was sorry to part with her treasure, but her mother said it was a great honour for them, so it was borne away to Lerwick.

Then, one fine day, Grete saw a white sail making for the voe. Soon a lady was sitting beside her, and asking her about her work so kindly that she quite forgot to be frightened. And when the lady left she gave Grete a gold piece for the shawl, the first gold piece that had ever been seen on the island. Everybody wanted to learn how to get gold pieces, and Grete was delighted to teach them. So better days came, not only for Grete and her mother, not only for their own little island, but for all the islands near.

This is how the Shetlanders became so famous for their filmy, lace-like shawls, and how it is that they do them without rules or patterns or counting of stitches, in a way that cannot be imitated by people who live in other parts of the world, for no trow ever came to teach them, as Grete's friend taught her long ago.

THE CHILD TRUSTED WITH STATE SECRETS

WE look on Oliver Cromwell as a stern character, harsh to his opponents, and forbidding in his ways. Yet he could be very gentle to a little child; and for his little granddaughter he kept a warm place in his heart.

He liked to have the little girl often with him; and when she was only six years old would keep her by his knee as he sat at a Cabinet Council discussing affairs of State.

Some of his Ministers thought it unsafe to have even such a little girl listening while they talked about important matters concerning the country, and they let Cromwell know their fears.

"Why, there is no secret I would trust with any of you that I could not trust with that infant," was the reply.

Determined to prove to his Ministers that his trust in his little granddaughter was well merited, Cromwell one day whispered to her something in confidence, saying it was a secret, and she must not tell it. He then set her grandmother and mother to try to get the secret from her.

But no threats or bribes, or even a whipping, could make the little girl disloyal to the trust the grandfather put in his Puritan grandchild. At last they gave up the attempt to get the secret from her, unable to resist longer the plea that her grandfather had trusted her with a secret and she must keep it, though she did not wish to disobey her mother.

And so Cromwell's Ministers had no more fear that State secrets would be told when the loyal little girl knew them.

STORIES TOLD OF CHINESE BOYS

It is the ambition of every family in China to have at least one boy who shall distinguish himself in the examinations through which their public officials are chosen, and Chinese story-books are full of interesting tales of the cleverness and perseverance of studious boys.

THE BIG JAR OF WATER

A LITTLE boy named Kwang, who knew a great deal because he always paid attention to his lessons and tried to understand everything that came in his way, was playing with some other children when one of them fell into an earthenware jar full of water.

The vessel was a tall one, and none of the children could reach their comrade, who would certainly have been drowned had it not been for the wisdom of Kwang. Kwang took up a large stone lying on the ground, and, throwing it at the earthenware jar, broke the vessel. The water ran out, and the boy was saved.

THE BALL IN THE HOLLOW POST

IN a little village lived a boy named Yenfoh, who was very bright and clever and always knew what to do in difficult circumstances.

One day, while he was playing at ball with some companions, the ball struck the top of a hollow post and then fell to the bottom inside. All of them, with the exception of Yenfoh, thought the ball was lost. But Yenfoh knew what to do. He ran to the village well and drew a pail of water. Then, bringing this to the hollow post while the other children looked on in wonder, Yenfoh poured the water in, and the ball floated to the top, where it could be reached quite easily.

THE WEB OF CLOTH

MENCIUS was only three when he lost his father, but his mother worked hard so that her son might have the benefit of a good education.

She sent him to school, and at first Mencius liked going; but he soon slackened in his studies, and at last, throwing aside his books, he left the school and went home. He found his mother weaving a piece of cloth into which she had put a great deal of hard work, so that the cloth was worth a large sum of money. As soon as she saw Mencius walk into the house she took up a knife and cut the cloth from top to bottom.

" My son," she said, " you are not half as sorry to see me cut this cloth as I am to see you leaving your studies."

Mencius was so moved that he went back to school at once and studied hard.

THE SLEEPY STUDENT

IN the province of Tsu lived a boy who was very anxious to distinguish himself in the examinations, and thus to bring honour to his parents. But he found that after he had been studying for some hours he began to get very drowsy, and his head would nod till he fell fast asleep. This distressed him very much indeed.

At last he tied a cord to the end of his pigtail, and fastened this to a beam in the roof, so that when his head began to nod the pull of the pigtail roused him.

THE BOY WHO HAD NO PAPER

A LITTLE boy named Yang-see, who had lost his father when he was only four years old wanted to study for the examinations; but his mother lived in great poverty, and was unable to buy paper or pen and ink for him.

Little Yang-see was distressed at this, and for some time did not know what to do. But it was soon proved that where there is a will there is a way. The boy lived near the sea, and, going down to the shore, he took with him a stick, and with it worked out his problems on the sand.

THE HOLE IN THE WALL

A POOR boy named Kwang Hung was very fond of books, and loved to study. He worked for a magistrate, who, at Kwang Hung's own request, paid him in books instead of money. Yet the books were of little use, for the boy was too poor to buy oil for a lamp at night.

At last he thought of an idea. His next-door neighbour had lights, and so Kwang Hung made a little hole in the wall, and by holding his book in front of the hole he caught the light that came through.

THE BOY WHO FOUND LIGHT

IN the country parts of China the people are very poor—so poor that they are unable to have a light after dark.

A boy named Kang, who was studying for the examinations, found that if he was to succeed he could not waste all the hours of darkness. His family were too poor to buy oil, so what was he to do?

He remembered that glow-worms give a tiny light, and so he collected a large number, and by their light was able to continue his studies far into the night.

THE GIRL WHO SAW THE TSAR

A HUNDRED years ago a Russian officer offended the Tsar, and was banished, with a number of other exiles, to a dreary place in the north of Siberia.

The prisoners went through all manner of hardships, but this Russian officer was allowed to take with him his wife and little daughter, Prascovia, and so was saved the agony of separation.

Life to the exile in Siberia was a rough and hard one, and as the years went by it was very sad for the parents to watch their little daughter growing a big, untaught girl in such rough surroundings. Seeing her father so unhappy, Prascovia was unhappy too; and then one day, when she was nearly fifteen years old, the idea flashed into her mind that she ought to go to Petrogard and beg the Tsar to pardon her father.

Could she do it? To walk all those dreary hundreds and hundreds of miles to Russia! But her father only smiled.

Three years went by, and little Prascovia was growing helpful and womanly. She had never forgotten her cherished plan, and she put it before her father again. This time he listened to her, but begged her not to think of leaving them for such a dangerous venture. But Prascovia got another exile to write for a passport, and in six months that passport reached her.

Now that the way was open, Prascovia's father tried to dissuade her from starting. How could she, a penniless, unknown girl, get access to the Tsar even if she braved the dangers of the journey? But Prascovia put her trust in God, knelt to receive her parents' blessing, and with just one rouble in her pocket started on her long tramp.

On and on, through the miles of forests, over rough roads and across rivers, Prascovia plodded, sometimes losing her way, sometimes getting soaked with rain, often weak with hunger and spent with exhaustion. At times she met with kindness, was made welcome at a cottage, or got a lift in a cart; at other times she was ordered roughly away.

As winter came on and snow fell Prascovia's misery increased, and she was often hindered by the snow-drifts. When in a barge on the Volga she was pushed into the water by accident, and as a result fell ill; but some nuns nursed her.

At last Prascovia, much to her joy, reached Petrograd. A kind lady interested herself in the girl, and took care of her until an opportunity came to present her petition to the mother of the Tsar. This lady was touched with Prascovia's story, and promised to take her to the Tsar.

Now the way was clear, and two days later Prascovia was in the presence of the Tsar. To her relief, he received her kindly, promised inquiry into her father's trial, and gave her five thousand roubles.

And so Prascovia got the pardon for her father, and when the Tsar asked if there was anything she wanted for herself she begged for a like act of mercy for two friends of her father who were also exiles.

L'EMPEREUR ET LES FIGUES

This is a French translation of the story told in English on page 2634

UN empereur, voyant un vieillard planter un figuier, lui en demanda la raison. L'homme répondit que peut-être il vivrait pour goûter à ses fruits, mais que, même s'il ne vivait pas jusque là, son fils profiterait des figues.

"Eh bien," dit l'empereur, "si vous atteignez l'âge de pouvoir manger des fruits de cet arbre je vous prie de me le faire savoir."

L'homme promit, et sa vie se prolongea au point de voir l'arbre grandir et porter des fruits dont il put manger.

Ayant préparé quelques unes des plus belles figues dans un panier, il se rendit au palais, et, quand il expliqua sa présence, les gardes l'introduisirent auprès de l'empereur.

Le monarque, très content, accepta le cadeau de figues et donna des ordres pour que le panier du vieillard fût rempli d'or.

Cependant, près de la maison de ce vieillard, vivait une femme très envieuse, qui, voyant l'aubaine de son voisin, enveloppa des figues dans un panier à son tour et persuada son mari de les porter aussi à l'empereur avec l'espoir d'un panier d'or en retour.

Mais quand l'empereur apprit le message du paysan il ordonna à celui-ci de rester dans la cour et le fit cribler de figues. Quand l'homme rentra chez lui et raconta à sa femme tout ce qui s'était passé, elle le consola en disant : "Ah ! vous avez encore de la chance que ce fussent des figues et non de dures noix de cocos."

Nature's Wonderful Living Family in Earth and Air and Sea

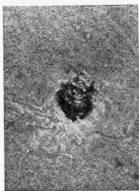  

The larva of an American cicada leaves its underground home and grows into a winged insect

THE MIGHTY INSECT

Linnaeus, the great naturalist, once made a statement which must often have caused young people to think him mad. "Three flies," he said, "consume the carcase of a horse as quickly as a lion could dispose of it."

We will ask not three flies, but one fly, to help us to a solution of this famous old enigma of Linnaeus.

A fly begins to lay eggs in the middle of April. Its eggs number, as a rule, about 120. These hatch in a fortnight, and ten days later the females of the new generation lay *their* eggs in turn.

Generation succeeds generation throughout the summer, and on into September, the great fly month of the season.

Now if all the descendants of the April fly live and produce eggs, the progeny of that first fly, after a lapse of the five warm months of the year, number the unthinkable total of about 5600 million insects.

That is the meaning, told in figures, of the saying of the immortal Linnaeus which must often have perplexed the little naturalists of his day.

It serves here to prepare us for the task of thinking in vast numbers, for all the Orders into whose stories we have so far probed are numerically but a handful compared with those of the insect world.

We know already some 250,000 species of insects, and believe that ten times as many remain to be named and described. Within those species the powers of multiplication have no parallel in the animal world, save among types in the water, and there we can count only the prodigious total of eggs produced by the mothers, not the young which grow up.

In the insect world the death rate is not so high, perhaps; there is greater seclusion and safety than in the open waters, and the result is that insects number incredibly more than all the other forms of life added together. They are tiny things—5000 big honey bees go to the pound; yet if we could mass all the great and small animals, birds, and reptiles, together in one huge scale, then put into the opposite scale the insects that people the Earth, the tiny things would be so colossal in total that they would far outweigh all the rest, though the elephants, rhinos, hippos, oxen, horses, and whales were of the company.

Their enormous numbers are accounted for in part by the fact that they reach full growth with extreme rapidity, and become parents almost at once; but there is also of course their great fertility to be considered. A queen bee lays as many as 80,000 eggs; while the queen of a white

PREHISTORIC LIFE · MAMMALS · BIRDS · REPTILES · FISHES · INSECTS

ant, or termite, colony produces her eggs, thousands and thousands of them, at the rate of one a second.

Naturally these hosts affect the fortunes of the human family. They are mingled bane and blessing. They are carriers and distributors of terrible diseases, agonising and fatal to man and beast. They can destroy our forests, and make a desert where a fruitful land was. They can eat up our vegetation and starve our cattle. They have from the dawn of human enlightenment been the agents which have defied and stricken us when we have sought to thrust out the bounds of civilisation in tropical and sub-tropical lands.

THE GREAT DEBT OF MANKIND
TO THE INSECT KINGDOM

On the other hand, we have humbly to confess ourselves unendingly in their debt. There is not a flower that grows merely for the delight of man, save where we ourselves have taken and improved wild species. The floral beauties, their scents and sweets, are there to crave the favour of insects.

Plant life needs fertilisation for the making of the seeds out of which its new generations will develop, and the insects are the beasts of burden which convey the vital pollen from one flower to another. To charm the senses of insects the flowers distil their honeyed nectar and breathe on the air their sweetest aroma, and light the way to their treasure house with all the colours that gladden sight.

Not all insect visitors are welcome; some are robbers who take without giving in return. But where the compact between insect and flower is authentic and of ancient standing, the modifications of the plant and of the insect are such as to beggar imagination.

The plant has its beautiful traps and adaptations, some of them noble little examples of engineering, some of them grimly comic snares; some, of course, as in the case of the insect-eating plants, treacherous paths to miserable death.

THE CUNNING WAYS IN WHICH THE
INSECTS ARE LURED TO THE FLOWERS

Those are exceptions; in general the special lure and reception chambers of the insect-wooing flower are dreams of lovely, gentle cunning. And the insects, on their part, are as marvellously furnished in order that they may co-operate with their hosts. There is a tropical flower with a

bell so deep that only a special type of moth proboscis, one of abnormal length, could penetrate its depths. Darwin predicted the existence of such a moth. It has been found, with precisely the length of sucking tube required.

Certain clovers grow only where the humble-bee exists to fertilise them, so that when we had given New Zealand her first clover, we had to supplement the gift with a load of humble-bee queens to make it grow and establish itself on the other side of the world, and to provide food for the domestic animals, which at the same time we were exporting to that lovely England of the Pacific. Also we sent queen bees to Japan to perform a like work for the fruit orchards of the Flowery Land.

Remote as their lives seem from ours, the insects have a very intimate association, for good and ill, with Man's existence and prosperity. Nature provides us with ladybirds to police the orange and lemon orchards where scale fatally abounds; the caterpillar of a moth spins silk to form one of the richest industries in the world.

HOW INSECTS HAVE HELPED ON
THE TRADE OF THE WORLD

The lac and cochineal insects have for ages been among the indispensables of commerce; a certain fly with a saw-like implement is responsible for the incomparable qualities of the Smyrna fig; a wood-boring beetle necessitated the presence in certain trees and vines of a bitter protective latex which, at long last, man found to be convertible into rubber.

On this depend the motor-car, the aeroplane, half the vessels of the surgery, and nearly all the insulating material for electricity, for the telegraph, telephone, wireless, trains, and trams.

Think, then, of the locust gnawing smiling farms down to wildernesses, of the dreadful warble fly torturing horses and cattle, of flies and mosquitoes which, in place of a man or woman taken now and then by a lion or a tiger, slay tens of thousands, even hundreds of thousands, of human beings. So, with good effect and evil recognised, we have the insects in their right perspective.

Insects never possess lung-books, but breathe by means of many tubes, or spiracles, opening on various parts of the body, to the outer air. Along these horny little tubes oxygen is conducted to the blood of the insect, and waste air is

ROUND THE YEAR WITH THE CORN-ROOT APHIS

1. Whole fields of maize are often ruined in America by a little insect called the corn-root aphis. In January, February, and March, if we uncover the nests of the small brown ant we shall see piles of tiny glossy black objects, oval in shape. These are the eggs of the corn-root aphis.

2. On warm days the ants bring the eggs up to the surface of the soil, as shown here, so that they may receive the air, and benefit by the warmth of the sun. On the other hand, in very cold weather they carry them farther down into the unfrozen earth for protection from the frost.

3. In April and May the aphis eggs hatch out, and the ants at once carry the young aphides to the roots of the smart-weed and foxtail grass. By the end of May the aphides begin to produce young, both winged and wingless varieties.

4. As soon as the maize plants are growing in June the brown ants carry the aphides to the roots, bringing to them even the winged insects that have flown about the field. All through the summer the aphides produce young.

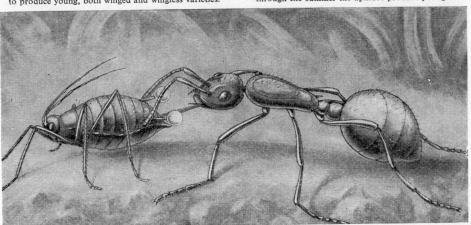

5. From June to September the ants attend the aphides, burrowing round the roots of the maize and carrying the pests from plant to plant. In return for this service the aphides supply the ants with sweet honey-dew, the ants stroking the insects with their antennae, thus milking them as cows are milked. All this time the aphides are multiplying, an aphis maturing and itself producing young eight days after it is born.

6. Each generation takes about 16 days, and there are 12 generations in a season. If all the progeny of an aphis lived, there would be next spring nine-and-a-half million million aphides, forming a line 7,850,000 miles long.

7. Aphides born in the summer are winged or wingless females, but at the end of September wingless forms are born which develop into ordinary males and females, and it is these females that lay the glossy eggs mentioned above.

expelled. As we watch a resting insect we may see it pant, the throbbing of its little body revealing the muscular effort which it exerts in pumping air in and out.

This system in bringing air in contact with the blood throughout the body has answered well, for insects are extraordinarily active for the most part, highly gifted in many ways—in locomotion, walking, climbing, running, leaping, flying; highly developed in sense, art, and courage.

THE INSECTS THAT TOOK THE WRONG TURNING AND LOST THE MASTERY

Yet, when we touch the question of insect blood, we pause in surprise and perplexity. Insects must at one time have been on the high road to the conquest of the Earth. They are ancient, they are numberless; they have inexhaustible supplies of food, for those that bite and gnaw, and for those that pierce and suck. They have such high mental faculties that some of them, notably the bees and ants, rank next to man as the creators of civilisations.

But in the reception of supreme gifts insects took a turning fatal to supremacy. It was open to them to receive warm red blood. The birds and the mammals gained the gift, and so reached the heights to which we have already traced them.

The insects remained content with cold blood, devoid of that sovereign property haemoglobin, the red colouring matter of blood. Cold-blooded they were, cold-blooded they continue, cold-blooded they must remain. They can never attain now to might of stature; they are committed for all eternity to small forms, and can never become mighty as individuals or species, save, of course, in numbers and in power to slay by their poisons.

THE GREAT TASK BEFORE NATURE IF THE MAMMALS SHOULD FAIL

That is what we mean when we say that should Man and the rest of the mammals fail, insects, incomparable in some directions, could never succeed to world mastery. Nature would have to start afresh from the very lowest forms and build up entirely new creatures on which to bestow the primacy of this fair Earth. It is a world-wide application of the parable of the Talents.

Many times during our readings together we have told how present-day life climbs its ancestral tree, repeats in the creation of an individual much of the life-story of the species. The insects afford an example of this more striking even than that furnished by the tadpoles of the amphibians, for here we may trace evolution from the egg to the grub, from the grub to the chrysalis, from the chrysalis to the perfect, full-grown insect.

This series of transformations is known as the *metamorphosis*. Any child who has reared butterflies from the eggs knows the process, yet there are millions of adults who cannot be brought to believe that these changes occur, and that the loathly, crawling grub will one day burst its melancholy prison house and become a radiant creature of the air.

Every rule has its exception, and the irregularity applies to the changes undergone by insects, for not all go through the complicated cycle. Many forms are born in the tiny image of their parents, and are compelled to moult and feed, feed and moult, untiringly, splitting off coat after coat, and growing on again till they attain full size and possess wings.

THE FIERCE LARVA OF THE DRAGON-FLY WHICH LIVES UNDER WATER

The grand dragon-fly serves as an example of the midway scheme, where there is a complete change of form and habit, but where the pupa or chrysalis stage is omitted. We find dragon-flies in the vicinity of water, but never see them enter it, swiftly though they swoop towards its surface in pursuit of insect prey. But they lay their eggs in that water, and from the eggs comes a strange, fierce larva, utterly unlike its parents.

Inertia is here an asset, it seems, for so terrifying a little monster, limited in speed, would never catch fast prey if it moved about. It clings to a water weed, hidden by its obscure colouration. But as it clings it can shoot out a horrid clawed limb, and grip like lightning a worm, snail, tadpole, even a dashing baby fish.

Methods differ with species of dragonflies, and it is interesting to observe that, while some of the larvae get along by waggling the tail like an oar, others employ the ancient plan of the octopus and secure movement by violently squirting out water from the body.

This career of underwater savagery lasts for a year, even more. At the end of that time the old maggot-like form is exchanged for one resembling a squat beetle. In this guise the creature at last climbs up a plant stem clear of the water, bursts off its last

SOME OF NATURE'S INSECT CHILDREN

1. Ringed club dragon-fly (Cordulegaster annulatus). 2. Giant stone-fly (Perla maxima). 3. Red nymph dragon-fly (Pyrrhosoma nymphula). 4. Flat book dragon-fly (Libellula depressa). 5. Bronze club dragon-fly (Cordulia aenea). 6. Beautiful maiden dragon-fly (Calopteryx virgo). 7. Common may-fly (Ephemera vulgata). 8. Giant dragon-fly (Aeschna grandis). 9. Robber dragon-fly (Lestes sponsa). 10. Golden osmylus (Osmylus chrysops). 11. Great green grasshopper (Tettigonia viridissima). 12. Small caddis-fly (Phryganea minor). 13. Leathery thrips (Phloeothrips coriacea).

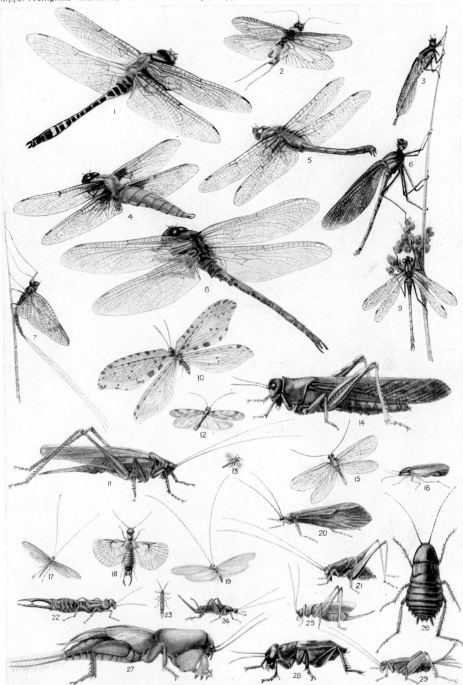

14. Migratory locust (Locusta migratoria). 15. Lacewing-fly (Chrysopa vulgaris). 16. German blatella (Blatella Germanica). 17. Two-colour triaenodes (Triaenodes bicolor). 18. Common earwig (Forficula auricularia). 19. Senile slender-horn (Leptocerus senilis). 20. Great caddis-fly (Phryganea grandis). 21. Grey scalywing (Pholidoptera griseoaptera). 22. River earwig (Labidura riparia). 23. Little earwig (Labia minor). 24. Wood nemobius (Nemobius sylvestris). 25. Sea-green grasshopper (Meconema thalassinum). 26. Domestic cockroach (Blatta orientalis). 27. Mole cricket (Gryllotalpa vulgaris). 28. Field cricket (Gryllus campestris). 29. House cricket (Gryllus domesticus). *See pages* 5709, 5835, 5959, *and* 6083.

DRAGON-FLIES, BEES, ANTS, AND FLIES

1. Meat-fly (Musca lardaria). 2. Ox-eyed astata (Astata boöps). 3. Drone-fly (Eristalis tenax). 4. Fiery-starred syrphus (Syrphus pyrastri). 5. Cow-dung fly (Scatophaga scybalaria). 6. Pale bishop's-mitre (Asopus luridus). 7. Crane-fly (Tipula longicornis). 8. Trogos ichneumon-fly (Trogos atropos). 9. Fiery ruby-tailed fly (Chrysis ignita). 10. Girdled tenthredo (T-thredo zonatus). 11. House-fly (Musca domestica). 12. Croesus saw-fly (Croesus septentrionalis). 13. Solid ichneumon-fly (Ichneumon crassorius). 14. Turnip saw-fly (Athalia spinarum). 15. Horse-fly (Hippobosca equina). 16. Broad tachina (Tachina grossa). 17. Field mellinus (Mellinus arvensis). 18. Feathered volucella (Volucella plumata). 19. Giant-tailed wasp (Sirex gigas). 20. Tawny digger (Pompilus fuscus). 21. Great gadfly or Cleg (Tabanus bovinus). 22. Sand cerceris (Cerceris arenaria). 23. Norwegian saw-fly (Sirex juvencus). 24. Scarlet hopper (Triepphora sanguinolenta).

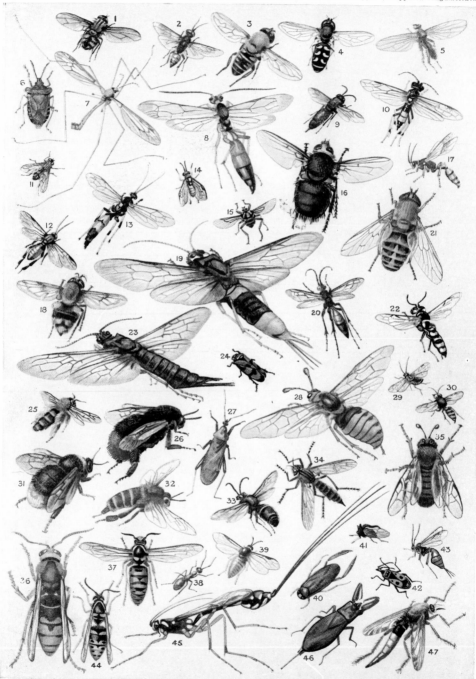

25. Hairy Dasypoda bee (Dasypoda hirtipes). 26. Stone humble-bee (Bombus lapidarius). 27. Fly-bug (Reduvius personatus). 28. Orange-coloured saw-fly (Cimbex lutea). 29. Garden saw-fly (Lyda hortensis). 30. Four-spot crabro (Crabro quadrimaculatus). 31. Apathus bee (Apathus vestalis). 32. Hive Bee (Apis mellifica). 33. Solitary ant (Mutilla Europoea). 34. German hornet-fly (Asilus Germanicus). 35. Hairy-bodied saw-fly (Trichiosoma lucorum). 36. Hornet (Vespa crabro). 37. Tree wasp (Vespa aborea). 38. Wood-ant (Formica rufa). 39. Rose saw-fly (Hylotoma rosa). 40. Water-boatman (Corixa Geoffroyi). 41. Eared hopper (Centrotus cornutus). 42. Scarlet bug (Pyrrhocoris apterus). 43. Ichneumon migrator (Spilocryptus migrator). 44. Common wasp (Vespa vulgaris). 45. Rhyssa ichneumon-fly (Rhyssa persuasoria). 46. Water-scorpion (Nepa cinerea). 47. Great hornet-fly (Asilus crabroniformis).

disguise, and emerges a dragon-fly. It is not yet perfect. The abdomen has to be straightened and lengthened, the wings also; but in an hour one of the most amazing of natural changes is completed, and we who watch know how true was the verse of Tennyson when he wrote:

Today I saw the dragon-fly
Come from the wells where he did lie.

An inner impulse rent the veil
Of his old husk; from head to tail
Came out clear plates of sapphire mail.

He dried his wings; like gauze they grew;
Through crofts and pastures, wet with dew
A living flash of light he flew.

THE BEAUTIFUL DRAGON-FLY WHICH FLIES ONLY IN THE SUNLIGHT

The dragon-fly is a giant among British insects, but, enormous as is his appetite for insects, which he catches on the wing, he is like the sundial, in that he is active only when the sun shines. Fortunately his aerial life extends over weeks and months, or we should too soon lose a precious ally. Very different is the fate of the may-flies.

When their three years' probation in the water, with all its varied methods of equipment and procedure for different species, has been completed, out they come to land, to divest themselves of their last disposable garment. Then away up in the air, the females to meet their lords, the males to dance with excited raptures among a thousand rivals for the favour of a lady who is a rare prize among so many courtiers.

Pond and stream and sluggish river seem to come to life as, day after day, the may-flies issue from them. Such hosts appear that again and again we hear rumours in country places of church spires and other buildings being on fire. The imaginary smoke is simply the multitude of air-dancing flies.

THE SHORT, GAY LIFE OF THE DANCING MAY-FLIES

Their dance is short. They may live for but an hour, they may live from sunrise to sundown; rarely do they last a couple of days. All the labour and marvels of change and growth which have taken place in the water go to this consummation, so swift, joyous, and dramatic. A chicken does not eat, or should not, for its first 36 hours of life. A mayfly never eats at all in its perfect form; but, while the baby bird is working up its first appetite, three generations of adult may-flies

have come into the air and passed out of life. Yet in that time tens of millions of eggs have been laid in the water to stock the stream with new hosts of larvae.

It may seem a great leap from these insects to the white ants, as the termites are called, but it is in this direction that affinity leads. The termites are not ants, much as some of their habits resemble the true ants. They pass from the larval to the adult condition by a series of gradual changes, but they go through no chrysalis state.

Among the most extraordinary of the social insects, they form vast colonies, either by tunnelling trees and throwing out huge barrel-shaped homes round the branches, by means of underground cities; or, more characteristic, cities which, with subterranean foundations, rise like massive hollow pillars twelve and more feet into the air.

Within these homes there are scenes of marvellous activity. The city is partitioned into compartments, cells, and walled divisions. In the centre are the king and queen, royal prisoners in this sense that the avenues leading to their apartments are made so narrow that the sovereigns cannot escape from them, while the workers can come and go at will.

THE WONDERFUL THING THAT HAPPENS INSIDE THE WHITE ANT'S CITY

All the queen has to do is to furnish eggs; the workers feed and clean her and her mate. She produces her eggs, thousands and thousands a day month after month. In the height of her season of productivity she is a mass of eggs, two or three inches long, and working like a machine, an egg a second, each carried away instantly by an anxious worker to the nursery.

When the grub hatches it is fed on chewed wood and saliva by its nurses, who, by varying the diet, can convert the ordinary worker into a warrior to fight for the general good, or into a royalty, or leave it to be a sexless toiler. The grub moults and grows, and if it is to be a prince or a queen obtains both eyes and wings; otherwise it may have neither, but join the community of workers sightless and with no organs of locomotion but legs.

Originally termites must have been valuable as devourers of decaying wood in a wild land. We have built out into their domain, and they cause us many a disaster.

They eat our telegraph poles; they mine beneath houses and eat the timber supports of the building; they tunnel furniture; they make meals of everything wooden.

That in itself is devastating, but the worst of it is that they never start on the visible surface. They tunnel invisibly, leaving a thin shell of material which suggests a solidity that does not exist.

THE TERRIBLE DESTRUCTION WROUGHT BY TERMITES IN THE TROPICS

If for nothing else our magnificent Natural History Museum would be worth a visit to see the effects of the termite attacks on lovely furniture eaten hollow by those creatures in the tropics.

A classic example of termite operations is this. They broke out one night from their underground city on which a human house had been built. They ate through the floor and came up beneath the foot of a table leg. Right up that leg they devoured their way, then through the top of the table, next down the leg to which they had by this time come, and so through the floor and home again. But they took on the way the late supper left on the table!

Nothing is safe from them—books, clothes, maps, handles of instruments, everything dear to the man pioneering far from the resources of civilisation. A seemingly sound house may crash about his ears, riddled by these insects, and with it will vanish the ruined treasures hoarded in library and oaken chest. We have no such problems as these at home, though some of ours are puzzling.

Following still the same path through this maze of classification, we are led next to a family of *Psocidae* which men call book-lice, winged in most species, wingless in others. Most of the family live out of doors, in moss and lichen, on trees and among fungus and plants, but one species comes into the house.

THE TINY CREATURE WHICH EATS ITS WAY THROUGH BOOKS

Although microscopic, it is active and voracious. It ruins our books if left long enough; it devours collections of dried plants, animals, and insects, and is the nightmare of the private museum. Bird-lice, which make poultry life unhappy, are cousins of the book-lice.

But our progress takes us now to things more to be dreaded than any of these,

the group which contains the locusts. First come the crickets, known to everybody who has lived in old houses or heard the monotonous chorus of the insects in bakehouses. Their home is in warm, dry places, commonly about the kitchen range, but they leap like pantaloons, and fly, when the mood possesses them, with great strength to a considerable height.

The power of their leap was once impressed on the writer when a cricket, taking an aerial leap, landed with a splash into a cup of tea held in the hand of the old lady to whom he was talking; and a nightmare recollection is of a swarm of crickets flying round and round the room one hot summer night, when fatal illness made the atmosphere seem wholly terrible to one childish mind.

But crickets are harmless enough, though intolerably noisy and destructive in a small way. Not only do they eat away the mortar of our walls; they have the audacity to gnaw holes in damp clothes which a careful housewife leaves on the horse to dry at night.

We have our field-crickets in Britain, and we have that wonder of the tribe, the mole-cricket, in which the two fore limbs are short, thick, and powerful with relatively enormous claws, outspread like the forepaws of a mole.

THE STRANGE THING THAT HAPPENS WHEN THE GRASSHOPPER TAKES A LEAP

With grasshoppers every child is familiar, creatures of the grass, the sunny bank, and the wood; but have we all noted that in leaping from danger they turn round in the air, so that on alighting they face in the opposite direction to that in which they started?

The common grasshopper is a hardy little fellow, but our two large British species are restricted to the warmer parts of the land, where, when we first see them, they are so huge and brilliant that we imagine them to be tropical imports.

As a rule, grasshoppers do little harm to us, but much good in that many of them add flies and other insects to their diet. In recent years Canada has had plagues of grasshoppers, which have caused havoc with the crops of south-western Manitoba, south Saskatchewan, and Alberta.

The habit grasshoppers have of eating other insects fortunately extends to the locusts, which, in time of famine, are as pronounced cannibals as anything that

THE LITTLE HOPPER ON THE LAWN

1. The little grasshopper on our lawns, known as the Green Grasshopper, of which several pictures are given on this page, is a harmless relation of the destructive locust of warm countries.

2. Though it has wings it is most often seen jumping, its long hind legs enabling it to take leaps of four feet or even more, which is equal to a boy jumping a distance of about fifty feet.

3. Sometimes the insect flies. It has two pairs of long wings, only the back ones being used for flight. During rest they are folded away delicately like a lady's fan under the narrow fore-wings.

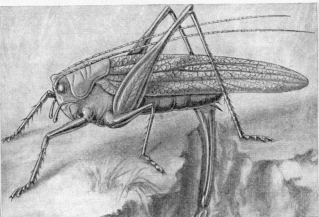

4. In the autumn the female burrows a hole in the ground with her ovipositor.

5. The ovipositor is in six parts, and the grasshopper alternately brings these parts together, pushing them into the earth, and spreads them apart to make the hole. At the bottom she lays from twenty to forty banana-shaped eggs, which are thus hidden from enemies till the spring. The mother then dies.

6. In spring the eggs hatch out into larvae like their parents, but wingless.

7. The little larva begins at once to feed and grow, but as its outside is hard and unyielding, it has to cast its skin about half a dozen times. In this picture we see the moulting process going on.

8. At each moult the wings become more fully developed, and this picture shows the final moult. At all stages the insect has powerful jaws, and eats not only leaves but insects, including its own kind.

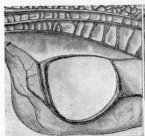
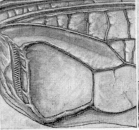

9. The whirring sound made by the male grasshopper comes from a kind of drum or tambourine on the right wing-case here,

10. On the left wing-cover is a grooved file-like vein, and this is drawn across the tambourine to make the familiar sound.

11. The whirring musical sound is the means employed by the male to attract the silent female, whose ears, as shown here, are on each side of the creature's front leg.

lives. To this fact we may owe the survival of agriculture in the hot lands over which these creatures sweep from time to time in their high-tide billions. If all lived and bred, vegetation would die before their remorseless advance.

They are many in species, and vary from a quarter of an inch in length to ten times that size. All have the common habit of drilling holes in the earth in which to lay their teeming eggs. From the eggs come little locusts, like their parents, but wing less until they have fed and moulted over a period which embraces half a dozen castings of skin.

Both then and when the wings have come the insects are fiercely voracious, and devour every green thing within reach and each other. When wings arrive, if the number of adults is too great to be accommodated by the land in which they feed, they rise and fly afar. The course of the winds undoubtedly influences their direction, for locusts which have emigrated do not fly back to the place whence they or their ancestors came.

A nucleus always remains at the original source, and today the old nursery exists in northern Africa from which were derived the frightful masses that constituted the locust plague of Egypt in the days of Moses and Aaron.

THE SWARM OF FLYING LOCUSTS WHICH STRETCHED FOR TWENTY-FIVE MILES

We have locusts in southern Europe and its islands, in Africa, in Asia, and America, and everywhere from time to time they swarm in their billions, as lemmings swarm in their tens of thousands. But lemmings only march slowly; the locusts fly with the speed of the wind, plus their own velocity, far and unweariedly, so that they can strike distant scenes of apparent safety as aircraft can now strike at what were formerly inaccessible islands.

Faintly to imagine their flying swarms we must recall the sum set by Linnaeus and the horse-devouring larvae of his three flies. One swarm is like another, save that some are greater than their fellows. One which scourged the land around Pretoria in modern times was estimated to be 25 miles in length, one and a half miles broad, and half a mile deep.

Johannesburg witnessed a flight in which the countless multitude made the white mountains brown, the sky dark as night, broke down the telegraph and tele-phone wires by their weight, stopped the railway service by making the lines impassable, and caused trams to run backwards downhill through their crushed bodies rendering the metals too slippery for the brakes to act.

An earlier swarm was said to cover 2000 square miles of land, so that when, providentially, a great wind arose and swept them into the sea, the tide cast up on the shore a solid bank of dead and putrid locust corpses four feet high and 50 miles in length.

THE HUNGRY HOST OF LOCUSTS WHICH BEGIN TO EAT EACH OTHER

All vegetation of field, forest, and plain disappears down the throats of the hosts, and is insufficient, so that locust eats locust. By their very numbers they automatically reduce their multitudes and so save great continental areas from virtual denudation.

War against locusts is waged today by the scientific experts of the United Nations Organisation.

Many of the grasshoppers are marvellously coloured to resemble vegetation, and prepare us to view the still greater marvels of their cousins, the stick and leaf insects, in which imitation attains perhaps its pinnacle of perfection. The stick insects have long cylindrical bodies which nothing but the movements of the creature reveal as not part of the tree or plant itself, while the leaf insects pass for foliage of the plant on which they rest, their limbs contributing to the deception by partaking of the guise of leaf and twig combined.

They are all insect eaters, and so are their kindred, the praying insects, to which the familiar praying mantis belongs. Here an extraordinary development of the two forelegs leads to an attitude of motionless rigidity in which the creature seems to be holding up its limbs in prayer till a possible victim hovers near, when out go the treacherous limbs like lightning, and the mantis's dinner is secured.

THE CUNNING COCKROACHES THAT CREEP INTO OUR HOUSES

It seems a big stride from these wonders to those horrors of our homes, the cockroaches, but such is the track of relationship. They fly when mature, which seems to be in their fifth year, but without their wings they are masters of action on the ground, fleet, elusive, cunning. We have three native species, but those which

A GROUP OF QUAINT INSECTS

A BRAZILIAN LANTERN-FLY

A BRITISH LANTERN-FLY

AN INDIAN LANTERN-FLY

BOOK-LOUSE

BEE-LOUSE

ROSE TREE APHIS
HIGHLY MAGNIFIED

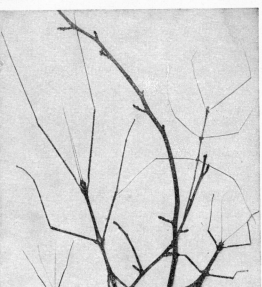

BRITISH WATER-
SCORPION

SHIELD-BUG

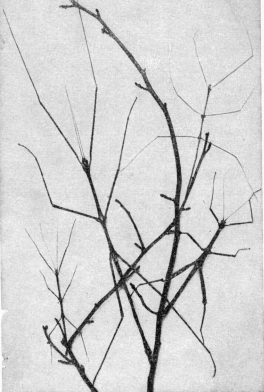

STICK INSECTS ON A TWIG

FROG-HOPPER

POND-SKATER

A TROPICAL WATER-BUG

LEAF INSECT

PRICKLY STICK INSECT

5719

infest our houses are importations from the tropics, and die if exposed to cold.

They are one of the minor plagues of life, crawling over food and corrupting it, sparing nothing from their foulness. On shipboard they are hated with reason, for at night they will nibble at the hair and at the quicks of sailors' nails, and it is believed that they do the same to the skin around the nails of the elephants' feet at the Zoo.

No such charges can be urged against their allies the earwigs, for though these come into the house, led by ivy and creepers to rooms whose light attracts, they keep in the main to the garden, where, while true to their natural role as devourers of garbage, they do serious damage to our flowers. Who does not know the enemy which has riddled the petals of his loveliest dahlias?

THE GREAT COMPANY OF TEN THOUSAND CURIOUS CREATURES

It would be well were all the bugs to treat us no worse, but of this gigantic company—perhaps ten thousand species are already known—several come into personal contact with us. The loathsome bed-bug, cause of misery, humiliation, and disease, to human beings, is one of the wingless ones which seems within recent time to have turned from plants to animals and man himself. Cleanliness and care could eradicate this pest from every human home in a year, but there is always the hopeless East to renew supplies.

There are winged bugs, big as bees, in tropical lands which, though not regular inmates of houses, fly at night into open bedrooms and drink human blood after the fashion of vampires and leeches— terrible wretches these. The enormous majority of bugs confine themselves to the open, and, with carnivorous exceptions, subsist on the juices of plants. Some of them are lovely in outline and colouration, and reveal Nature in her most artistic and ingenious mood in the fashioning of their eggs and nurseries.

Similarity in certain points as to structure has led to the grouping of enormous numbers of insects under the heading of bugs, which is a pity, for the name is repellent to the mind. So, however, it is, and we can but refer the student to such companies as the shield-bugs, the forest-bugs, the myriad plant bugs, and equally numerous flower-bugs, and note that our

merry pond-skaters and dashing but savage water boatmen, which fly as well as swim, are of the great bug group; as also are the so-called water scorpions, small in our ponds, but comparative giants in the tropics.

All these bugs are capable of emitting a highly unpleasant odour from fluid, a device for their protection against enemies.

THE SINGING CICADA WHICH IS KEPT LIKE A BIRD IN A CAGE

But we pass now to a related group, the *Homoptera*, in which this displeasing faculty is not present. First among them come the cicadas, in which the babies live to old age and the adults die young. That seems a paradox, but multiply the figures of the may-fly life and we have the solution of the puzzle.

A may-fly larva takes three years to grow up, and the perfect insect mates, lays its eggs, and is dead in a few hours. The larva of the cicada lives underground for *years*; then the complete insect comes out and runs its full course of adult life in a few days, or at most a few weeks. We have nearly a score of varieties in the warmer countries of Europe, where they are famous for their chirping song, produced by the males alone. "Happy are the cicadas," said a sour Greek sage, " for their wives are voiceless." The song of the male cicada is so cheery to some ears that the insects are kept in cages as are birds in temperate lands.

Development takes different periods with varying species. In America there is one species which requires 13 years, another takes 14, a third 15, and finally there is the famous 17-year cicada.

The eggs may be laid on the forest verge of a prairie, and there for 17 years the wingless larvae live in subterranean darkness, sucking the sap of roots and grass. Finally they emerge, winged, to find that a town has risen on their city, a house, shop, or factory on their nest.

THE STRANGE CICADA THAT LIVES IN THE DARKNESS FOR SEVENTEEN YEARS

After all this long preparation the adults make their honeymoon excursions, settle down on twigs to deposit perhaps 500 eggs for each robust female, then die at once. The eggs hatch into larvae, which forthwith burrow down into the soil and remain, the world forgetting, by the world forgotten, till the Earth and its family have grown 17 years older. This is the longest known period of youth outside the mammals, and there man and the elephant alone take longer to attain complete maturity.

It is strange that, while the cicadas so long avoid the light, their nearest kin, the gorgeous lantern-flies, so love the light that they carry lamps of their own creation and fill the night with gorgeous splendour.

The head is shaped like a lantern, and, while there are several species which are

flies; and close on their heels in the table come the plant-fleas, little winged creatures which use their pinions to help their leaping about the plants which they bore and suck. And then come the chief criminals of the rose garden, the aphides, or green-fly.

The cost of flowers and of food may be determined by these little villains. We find them on roses and other flowers, on fruit trees in the form of the woolly

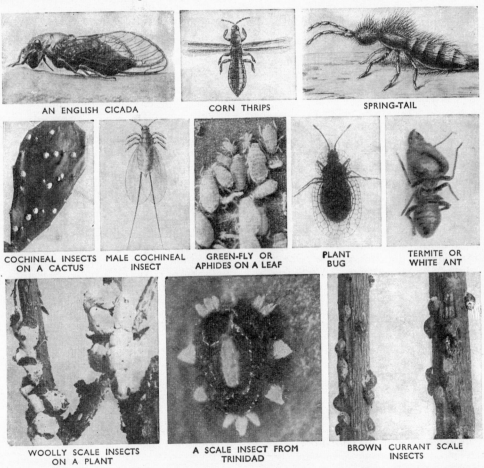

AN ENGLISH CICADA   CORN THRIPS   SPRING-TAIL

COCHINEAL INSECTS   MALE COCHINEAL   GREEN-FLY OR   PLANT   TERMITE OR
ON A CACTUS   INSECT   APHIDES ON A LEAF   BUG   WHITE ANT

WOOLLY SCALE INSECTS   A SCALE INSECT FROM   BROWN CURRANT SCALE
ON A PLANT   TRINIDAD   INSECTS

not known to give light, Sir G. H. Knibbs found that those which yield light have an enormous advantage over man-made illumination. Whereas our very best artificial light wastes all but four per cent of its energy in useless heat, the luminous lantern-fly has an efficiency of 99 per cent.

The frog-hopper or froth-fly, which punctures vegetation, turns the sap to frothy bubbles and lives in them as in a castle, is the closest relative of the lantern-

aphis, on vines as Phylloxera, on potatoes, cabbage, beans, hops, on important timber trees. Their life-story is marvellous, for the green-fly arises from eggs in spring, but is produced alive by its mother in summer. So terribly rapid is the rate of reproduction and so fertile the insects that, as Huxley has shown, if ten broods from one aphis came without hurt to perfection, that tenth brood would weigh more than 500 million stout men! They can drain the life out of the vegetation of an entire countryside.

Our chief natural defence against them are birds, lady-birds, and ichneumon flies; but these can be terribly insufficient, especially when the early months of the year are too cold for lady-birds to appear, but not for green-fly, which, unless early and effective steps are taken against them, multiply so rapidly as to deprive our gardens of roses. It has happened that pergolas, bushes, and standard trees have lacked foliage even in June, the month of roses.

THE LIVING SUCTION PUMP WHICH TAKES THE GOODNESS FROM THE GRAIN

One of the green-fly family, the grain aphis, attacks our growing corn, taking into its greedy stomach the vital fluid which should fill the ear with grain. But we must not attribute every shrivelled ear of corn to the aphis, for there are other enemies at work there, notably the corn-thrips, or *Thrips cerealium?* This is a tiny marauder belonging to the *Thysanoptera*, a little living suction pump, which drains the young grain and prevents it from developing. Others of the family attack the pollen of flowers and make the formation of seed impossible.

Somewhat resembling them are obscure little insects, the *Thysanura*, of which the spring-tails are perhaps the best known. They are the little people of stagnant waters, and damp, mossy places, warm or cold. Some give a thrust with their active, wonderful little tails and leap from the surface of the water into the air; others peep out at us when we raise a flower-pot. To others the under side of a small stone is all their world, while yet others, known as the glacier-fleas, are heroically at home where air is frosty and water is turned to ice, high up the Alps and other mountains.

THE LITTLE RED-JACKETS AT WAR IN THE ORCHARDS OF CALIFORNIA

They seem harmless enough, but a similar certificate cannot be awarded, save with exceptions, to the scale insects. These are little creatures in which the young and the females look like oval scales growing on plant life. In reality they are attached by their suction apparatus to the growth, draining away its life-juice.

Small, but enormously numerous, they infest orange, apricot, olive, peach, fig, and other fruit trees, as well as all manner of precious shrubs. Some years ago scale insects from Australia, harmless at home, were accidentally introduced into the great fruit orchards of California. They spread like a fire, and the whole fruit industry of the State seemed doomed to destruction.

Wise men, however, went to Australia to see why the scale insect did so little harm there. They found that it formed the food of various insects, notably of the lady-bird. So the enemy of the scale was carried to America and liberated in the orchards. The plan was entirely successful, and today the United States Government keeps millions of lady-birds as natural police, just as she keeps an army and navy.

There is some good in nearly every order, and we find it even among the scale insects. For the lac insect, from whose product we make sealing wax and the finest material in our varnishes for cars and carriages, is a scale insect, and so, too, is the cochineal insect. This was from time immemorial the source of a beautiful colouring matter.

HOW NATURE'S LITTLE SCAVENGERS HELP TO KEEP THE EARTH CLEAN

The cochineal insect is the parasite of certain cactus plants, on which it feeds exclusively, and was profitably farmed till coal-tar dyes came to give us cheaper material. Cochineal farming seems to be a ruined industry; but it must have been rather a tedious business collecting over 70,000 of the insects to form a pound weight of them.

So much, then, for a hasty opening glance at the insects. There are many of them that we have reason to fear, and we may wonder why they exist. Their role is plain. They are scavengers, they are harvesters, they are the agents down whose multitudinous throats is meant to disappear excess of vegetation in the world.

Without them the Earth would become rank with overcrowding in every phase of the botanical kingdom. We have appeared on their horizon, on their preserves, to share, to claim entirely for our own use the things they desire.

The one thing the Animal World never provided for was the civilisation of Man and his processes in taming the wilds. He and it have come; the older inhabitants, the insects, are still in possession where we pioneer and settle down. They continue as they began, so their war with mankind is inevitable.

PICTURE-STORY OF OUR FISHERIES

OFF TO THE FISHING GROUNDS

AT WORK IN THE NORTH SEA

The two principal methods of fishing are trawling and drifting. Trawling is used for catching fish lying at the bottom of the sea ; drifting for fish swimming near the surface. The smoky steam-driven drifters and trawlers are steadily being replaced by smart diesel vessels like this.

Herrings, pilchards, and mackerel are the chief catch of drift-nets round the British Isles. In this picture, taken on a drifter, the nets and floats are just going overboard, an operation which is known as shooting.

HAULING IN THE NETS BY DAY AND NIGHT

This picture shows the men of a drifter hauling in the nets with their catch. Drift-nets are supported in the water by cork-floats, and to keep them stretched out, lead weights are attached to their lower edges.

Fishing goes on by night as well as by day, and this picture shows the nets being hauled in at night full of silvery herrings. As many as 250,000 herrings may be netted in a night by one boat.

A BIG CATCH ON THE DOGGER BANK

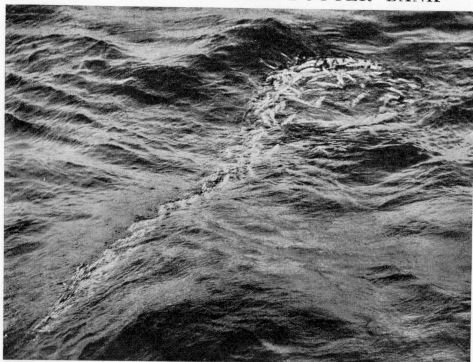

Here a net 65 yards long, containing over half-a-ton of fish, is being hauled to the boat's side on the Dogger Bank, where boats go in all weathers and remain fishing for several days.

The peaks of the annual herring harvest occur in October and November off East Anglia, where perhaps 350 or 400 million herrings will be caught. Here we see herrings being discharged from the hold of a drifter.

THE FISHING FLEET IS HOME

On the dockside all is bustle and activity when the fishing-boats have berthed and the catch is landed.

PICKLING A GREAT CATCH OF HERRINGS

The preparation of herrings for the markets is carried out mainly by Scottish fisher girls. They follow the herring catch down the East Coast and work for a week or two at a number of ports, coming as far south as Lowestoft and Yarmouth. Here we see Scottish fisher girls cleaning the herrings.

Huge quantities of herrings are pickled—that is, packed in brine—for export. In the picture on the left a girl is seen pouring brine into barrels; on the right the herrings are being packed into barrels.

The herring packing is one of the greatest industries of the east coast of England, and the enormous number of barrels used for the purpose may be gathered from this view taken at Yarmouth during the herring season.

CATCHING SPRATS, OYSTERS, AND MUSSELS

Sprats are caught in drift-nets, which fishermen are here letting out. The nets have pieces of cork along the top to keep them floating. One end is fastened to the boat, and the fish are caught in the meshes.

The most notable oyster-beds in England are those at Whitstable, in Kent, and here we see the oyster dredgers at work pulling up their catches from the sea bottom where the oysters live and breed.

Mussels are largely used as food in England and on the Continent, and here we see a big mussel bed in Holland exposed at low tide. These molluscs thrive between the high and low water lines on the coast.

OUT WITH THE DEEP-SEA TRAWLERS

 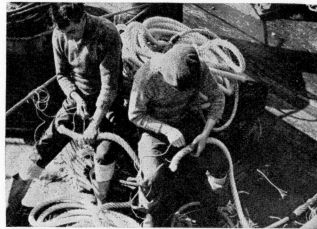

For deep-sea fishing the trawlers go many miles from their port and are away for about three weeks. While on the way to the fishing grounds the crew carry on with the preparation of nets, lines, and other equipment.

When fishing commences the crew don their sea-frocks, as seen on the left, before dropping the huge trawl overboard. The trawl is like a great stocking with a wide top, or mouth. The top part of the mouth is kept to the surface by aluminium " floats " while the lower part is held to the sea-bed by metal bobbins.

After about two hours' trawling the net is drawn in by powerful steam winches. The catch is brought to the surface in that part of the trawl called the " cod-end," as seen in the picture on the right.

THE CEASELESS ACTIVITY ON A TRAWLER

The cod-end, which is formed into a kind of bag by ropes, is swung aboard by a derrick. A member of the crew pulls on a slip-knot and the bag opens, the fish falling in a great cascade onto the deck.

As soon as the cod-end has been emptied it is made ready again and dropped overboard for the next catch, as seen here. Then the crew begin sorting and cleaning the fish on the deck before sending them down a chute to be packed in ice.

HOW THE EARTH'S CRUST IS FOLDED OVER

We often see in railway cuttings, cliffs, and elsewhere, stratified rocks which appear to be contorted and crumpled like this Carboniferous limestone gorge at Beau Parc, in County Meath, Ireland.

The rocky strata were laid down in water, and were horizontal, as this picture shows. As the crust of the Earth shrank, the pressure of other parts of the crust at the sides squeezed these rocks into folds.

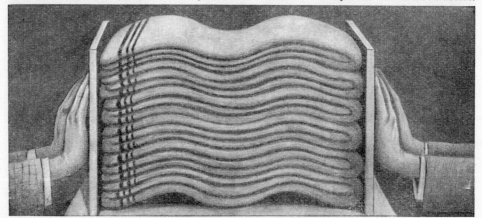

This picture explains by a simple experiment how the folding occurred. If several thick towels are arranged as shown, and then squeezed at the side, we get exactly the formation of the contorted limestone strata in the picture at the top of the page. See question on page 5735.

Plain Answers to the Questions of the Children of the World

CAN A FIRE LIGHT ITSELF?

ONE of the saddest disasters that can happen to a farmer is for a stack of new hay to catch fire and burn away to ashes. This is a thing that has happened ever since haystacks have been made, and until some years after Pasteur had made his wonderful discoveries about microbes it could never be understood.

Hay, and even partially dried grass, can be set on fire by the microbe which is responsible for hay fever. It is known as the bacillus subtilis, a little rod-shaped organism standing out from practically all other bacteria by its amazing powers of resistance to heat. We know how milk is boiled in order to kill the microbes it contains, which would otherwise turn it sour very quickly in hot or thundery weather; but we can boil the hay bacillus for ten or twenty minutes and it will come out of the ordeal as fresh as ever!

All microbes grow very rapidly in suitable conditions, and one will usually branch off into two in twenty seconds, two will become 16 in a minute, 16 will become 64,000 in five minutes, and so on. The bacillus subtilis, when growing rapidly in damp hay, produces a great amount of heat, and as this heat has no means of getting away in a closely packed haystack, such intense heat may be generated that the stack takes fire, and is destroyed.

Although the reason of these mysterious fires—vaguely put down to what is called spontaneous combustion—has only become known in our time as the result of our knowledge of bacteriology, farmers have always known how necessary it is to get their hay thoroughly dry before making it into stacks. They knew the result, but not the cause.

So the hay, when mown, is spread on the ground until it is thoroughly dry, and while it is drying the farmer is always anxious, because he knows that if rain falls, and the hay has to be stacked when slightly damp, there will always be danger of these fires. Dry heat kills the tiny spores of the hay microbe, and even the living microbe cannot grow if it has no moisture, so that the dry stack presents no danger from fire.

In order to keep a current of air blowing through the stack farmers often build their stacks round bunches of straw, pulling up the straw as the stack rises. In this way a series of passages or chimneys as they are called, are arranged in the stack through which the air is constantly blowing and drying the hay. Dry air is also pumped into stacks through pipes by means of small electric motors.

The hay microbe is undoubtedly the cause sometimes of starting heath fires,

FIRE · WIND · WATER · LIFE · MIND · SLEEP · HOW · WHY · WHERE

though in some recent fires of this kind the cause was thought to be the bottles left by picnic parties on the grass. The curved glass was believed to have acted like a burning-glass, and to have concentrated the sun's rays on the dry grass.

Of course, hay is not the only thing that can catch fire by itself, without being lighted by a match; we read on page 3040 how the same thing happens to coal.

Why Do We See a Black Spot in the Sky after Looking at the Sun?

The retina, or curtain, or sensitive plate, at the back of the eye never needs changing. You can see one picture after another, day after day, and year after year. But it is possible to work this screen too hard; for it is a living thing, and it is just because it is alive that it is able to recover itself for every new picture that we see with it. A photographic plate *sees*, as we may say, because certain chemical compounds that are upon it are changed by the light. The retina of the eye *sees* in the same way, but because it is alive it has the power of making afresh from moment to moment the particular kind of stuff the light acts on. But if you stare hard at any light so intense as the Sun itself, then, at that spot of the retina where the light falls, all the reserve supply of this sensitive stuff is used up; and now, if you turn your eyes somewhere else, that particular part is useless for the moment; it is blind, it sees nothing. But if it sees nothing, whereas all the retina round it sees light, that gives us the notion that we see a black spot—that is to say, a spot from which no light comes. But soon this wonderful living screen recovers, makes a fresh supply of the stuff light acts on, and the black spot disappears.

What is the Breeches Bible?

This curious name is often given to the English or Genevan Bible of 1560, which was translated principally by Puritans at Geneva. The word rendered aprons, in Genesis 3, verse 7, in the Authorised Version of 1611, is, in the Genevan Bible, translated breeches. Other versions of the English Bible have fancy names because of some mistake or curious translation. In what is known as the Printer's Bible, Psalm 119, verse 161, is misprinted "Printers have persecuted me without a cause," printers being substituted for princes. Tyndale's New Testament of 1538 is often called the Wife's Bible because 2 Corinthians 10, verse 11, is rendered "Think on his wife," intended for "think on this wise." The second edition of the Genevan Bible, 1562, later came to be called the Whig Bible, because in the Beatitudes we read "Blessed are the place makers" (peacemakers) and the opponents of the Whigs said they made lucrative posts for their friends. Another Bible is called the Servant Bible, because Genesis 3, verse 1, is misprinted, "Now the servant (instead of serpent) was more subtle than all the beasts of the field." In the Judas Bible, Matthew 26, verse 36, is given as "Then cometh Judas," instead of Jesus and his disciples. The Pagan Bible is an old version that contains a woodcut of Mount Olympus and the heathen gods. In the Vinegar Bible, printed at Geneva in 1717, the word Vinegar is substituted for Vineyard in the Parable in Luke 20. In the Bugges Bible, Psalm 91, verse 5 is rendered, "Be not afraid of any bugges by night." This is not a misprint. Bugges is simply the old English word for a bogey or bugbear. A somewhat similar instance occurs in the Treacle Bible, 1568, where the word treacle is substituted for balm in the verse "Is there no balm in Gilead," Jeremiah 8, verse 22. In the Douai version of 1609–10 this same word is translated rosin, and so that edition is called the Rosin Bible.

Why Does Boiling Water Feel Like Cold When We Put our Hands in it?

Though we can gain no knowledge except through our senses, we know that they are very apt to deceive us. The general rule about this is, that the senses deceive us least when they are concerned with something we are accustomed to; but they deceive us most when there is something unusual about the thing we are feeling or seeing. Another general rule is, that the senses are apt to deceive us. They work best with things they are accustomed to, and with things that excite them neither very little nor very much. In the skin of the hand there are special arrangements for feeling both hot and cold, and it is a very interesting fact that when the sensation of heat is extremely acute the brain is deceived for a moment or two, and makes us feel as if we were touching something cold. No one can explain how this mistake arises; but this question is well worth thinking about.

Who Is Uncle Sam ?

Uncle Sam is the name given by Americans to the Government and Administration of the United States in the widest sense—the human providence that watches over the welfare of the citizens. On the outbreak of the last war with Britain, in 1812, a contractor named Elbert Anderson went to Troy, on the Hudson River, in New York State, and there collected and packed stores for the American army. The stores were inspected on behalf of the Government by Ebenezer Wilson and his uncle, Samuel Wilson, whom the workmen knew as Uncle Sam. The barrels were marked E.A.—U.S., meaning *Elbert Anderson—United States*. But that name for their country was not yet very familiar to the workers, and one of them humorously suggested that the mysterious initials referred to Uncle Sam. The men took the joke with them into the army, and it soon became universal. Whether the original looked at all like the gentleman with the nanny-goat beard and starry waistcoat of the cartoonists we do not know.

How Does a Rock Become Folded ?

When we travel by train we must often see in railway cuttings stratified rocks which are bent out of the horizontal and appear to have been more or less folded over. This folding was caused by enormous pressure from the sides. We may prove this by a simple experiment. Let us arrange on a table a stack of neatly-folded thick towels. Now, if we take two boards and, placing them vertically at the sides, begin to press in, we shall find that the towels begin to fold together and to take the same form as the folded strata of rocks. This lateral pressure has been due to the contraction of the Earth's crust through cooling, and as any particular section of the crust shrinks it is squeezed into smaller space by the adjoining sections pressing against it, and it naturally folds up more or less in the process. See the pictures on page 5732.

Why Does Distance Make a Thing Invisible ?

A thing becomes visible because the waves of light it sends out, either from itself or reflected from itself, fall on the lens of the eye, as they might fall on a spectacle lens, and are then focused onto a part of the eye which sends them on to the brain. The brain then *sees*. The waves of light and the lens of the eye have by their joint action made a thing visible.

If, however, the object is too far away, or if, which is the same thing, the waves of light spread out from a very small area, they may be too few in number or may not be cast wide enough to be caught up by the narrow lens of the eye. If we had eyes which were eight feet in diameter instead of less than half an inch we should be able to gather far more of these travelling waves of light and consequently to see objects which we cannot now see. It is this purpose that the lenses of the great telescopes serve, for they gather up more light-waves than the unaided eye can do.

What Holds a Dewdrop in Its Place ?

Its stickiness. That is the simplest answer. We do not often think of water as sticky because there are so many other liquids, gums, oils, glycerine, for example, which are more so, but that water has a great deal of stickiness can be shown when an attempt is made to pour it out of a very fine tube. More scientifically we say that the surface of the dewdrop pulls hard against anything which tends to loosen its hold. If a small wineglass is filled with water, the water's surface will lie in a curve above the brim, the water kept from overflowing as if the surface were a skin. That is an example of surface-tension and the surface does, in fact, behave like a skin holding the water in place. Sometimes, as on a nasturtium leaf, this skin will keep the water in the shape of tiny globules. But if the ball-like shape of the waterdrop is broken by the unseen hairs or inequalities of a leaf or a blade of grass, the skin will still cling round the edges of the drop to the surface on which it finds itself.

Why are High Heels Bad for Us ?

Shoes with high heels are best avoided because they throw the body forward and transfer its weight from the natural arch of the foot, which is a beautiful and strong contrivance, on to the front bones and toes. These bones were not designed to bear this unjust share of the body's constant pressure on the ball, the sole, and the heel of the foot. The sinews of the ankle are also strained in the effort at accommodation. Nobody ever walks really well or gracefully in shoes with very high heels.

How is it That Asbestos Does Not Burn ?

Asbestos is already burned, and can be burned no more. It is also very difficult to melt, and will not melt with the heat of an ordinary flame; and so it can be used for many purposes—to line safes, for gas stoves, and so on. The word is taken from the Greek, and means unburnable. Of course, we cannot doubt that long ages ago such things were made by being burned or combined with oxygen when the Earth was a very different place. If we consider how much of the stuff in the crust of the Earth is already burned, that is to say, already combined with oxygen, if we consider that all water is already burned, and if we remember how much oxygen there still is in the air we shall understand how it is that about half of everything we know consists of oxygen.

Who Was Medusa ?

Medusa and her two sisters, Stheno and Euryale, were three divinities of ancient Greece known as Gorgons. Old coins of Corinth show us their horrible faces, which no human could peep at without being turned into stone. They had serpents for hair, boar's fangs for teeth, brass hands, and golden wings. Medusa was mortal, and this led the hero Perseus to think he could put an end to her evil works. Prompted by Minerva, he repaired to the ends of Earth, where the three monsters lay asleep. Then, careful not to look at them, his arm guided by the wise goddess, Perseus cut off Medusa's head, and secured it in a wallet. Her headless trunk gave birth to a winged horse, the famous Pegasus. The hero had to hurry away, pursued by the remaining Gorgons, and, had not an enchanted cap provided by Minerva made him invisible at last, Perseus would have been lost. He gave Medusa's head to Minerva, and this is why Greek statues represent Minerva's shield adorned with a grinning face entwined with serpents whose features express the smarting shame of defeat.

Which are the Most-Used Letters in the English Language ?

The relative frequency of the letters has been determined as follows: A 85, B 16, C 30, D 44, E 120, F 25, G 17, H 64, I 80, J 4, K 8, L 40, M 30, N 80, O 80, P 17, Q 5, R 62, S 80, T 90, U 34, V 12, W 20, X 4, Y 20, Z 2.

Why do we sometimes say " Gas " and sometimes " Vapour " ?

A vapour is really a gas, and a gas is a vapour. Only when a thing at ordinary temperatures is usually gaseous do we call it a gas. When we know a thing best as a liquid or a solid, such as water, we call its gaseous form a vapour. So a vapour is simply a gas, or the gaseous form of a thing that occurs in its most familiar form as a liquid or a solid.

Why Can We See Through Glass ?

Because the molecules of which glass is composed are so spaced and placed in the substance as to allow the rays of light to pass between them. In substances which are not transparent to light rays the molecules stop the rays and reflect them. Wood and leather are opaque to ordinary light rays; the molecules of these substances stand in the way. Yet if we employ an extraordinary kind of light, such as the X-rays, the waves of which are so small that the distances between them are smaller than the size of the molecules we speak of, then the X-rays find a way through. To ordinary light-rays most solid substances are opaque obstacles, and most liquids transparent. Glass is more like a frozen liquid than a solid.

How Did the French Flag Get Its Colours ?

Flags, the emblems round which soldiers used to rally in battle, bear different colours. In olden times each lord, who often lent his fighting men to the king, had a pennon of his own, and the monarch had a flag. In France the king's flag was blue. Under the reign of King Charles the Fifth, as a rebellion of the people threatened the throne, Etienne Marcel, the chief of the merchants, wishing to show that the power of the people equalled that of the King, had red added to the royal blue flag, for red was already the colour adopted by the revolutionaries. Later the French kings gave a place to white in memory of Joan of Arc, whose banner was a white one bearing golden fleurs-de-lys. It was only after the French Revolution of 1789 that, by La Fayette's inspiration, the three colours met for the first time on the national French flag. Napoleon kept it unaltered, but Louis the Eighteenth revived the white fleur-de-lys banner for some time, till King Louis Philippe restored the three-coloured flag.

Where is Angkor ?

Angkor, which was counted among the first towns of the world in the ninth century, is now a ruined town in Cambodia, an independent kingdom that was formerly part of French Indo-China.

The remains of Angkor give us the highest idea of the splendour of the Cambodians, for it was their capital for over a thousand years.

The city, surrounded with ditches 360 feet wide, offered admission through five huge doors guarded with towers. The best preserved of these doors leads directly to a magnificent temple.

In the centre of Angkor some remains are left of the king's palace, with ditches, terraces, elephants, giants, and monsters of all sorts, which represent supposed defenders of the castle. The area of the town, an exact square, with four corners corresponding to the four points of the compass—included three sacred enclosures. Angkor is a rare centre of archaeology.

What Do We Mean by Form in Music ?

If you have ever tried to compose a tune you will have found that to be satisfactory a tune must possess three things; a pleasing outline, good rhythm, and balance, or Form. Now balance is obtained by ensuring that the tune has a beginning, a middle, and an end.

That is expressing Form in a crude and elementary way, but if we compare the composing of a piece of music with the writing of a story we shall see that the explanation gives a broad idea of the meaning of Form.

To be a success a story must have definite characters, and must deal with the characters in proper order. As the story proceeds other characters are introduced, but the temptation to linger too long over the description of the district in which the characters live must be resisted, and the story, having begun well, and having had an interesting and intelligible *middle*, must proceed to an equally satisfactory *conclusion*.

As with the story, so with the musical composition. The characters of the story appear as melodies in music. They are called subjects, and the worth of the composition depends on the life in its subjects, as the story depends on the strength of its different characters.

So that when we speak of Form in music we mean the plan on which the music is based, and the way the plot is worked out. As in a book we can have a very simple story or a complicated one, so we can have in music something as simple as the tale of Jack and Jill, or a scheme as elaborate as that of, let us say, Goethe's Faust, or Handel's Messiah.

What is a Sonata ?

Accustomed to music which is unassociated with any particular story, emotion, or scene, it is difficult for us to realise what a wonderful step forward was made when men first began to compose music which was not set to words, and was neither an imitation nor a description. This sort of music was often called a *sound-piece* or a *sonata*, and it was in this sense that the word was first used.

A sonata is essentially a composition for an instrument, and nowadays we use the name only for works that have a certain plan. In the modern sense a sonata consists of *three or four movements of contrasting character*—grave and gay.

The first movement consists of a first theme which we can call A, joined by a bridge passage to a second subject, B, which is in a different key. This part is often rounded off by a tail-piece, or *coda*. Then comes a free development in which the composer often takes us through several keys, and does rather exciting things. This leads back once more to A, joined by a bridge passage to B, which is this time written in the same key as A; and finally a coda brings the movement to a conclusion.

Handel, Bach, Haydn, Mozart, and Beethoven all helped to develop Sonata Form, but Haydn had probably the greatest share in the work.

The best way to understand what is meant by Sonata Form is to play or listen to a first movement, and learn to recognise the subjects as they occur.

Why Do Chemists Have Coloured Bottles in Their Windows ?

These are a relic of the old days when apothecaries and alchemists used to have a number of retorts and jars in which they kept or prepared their mixtures. The chemist has dismissed the retorts from his shop, but retains the big jars in the shape of great glass bottles, full of coloured liquids.

Can a Man Have Two Shadows?

In a way a man can have as many shadows as there are sources of light to throw them. But a shadow can on some rare occasions leave a kind of shadow-photograph of itself, such as will last for a few moments on the surface where it is thrown. Such surfaces are said to occur on the crude oil pools of the oil-bearing districts of the American Middle West. These oil pools, especially when the Sun is shining on them, are perpetually throwing up millions of tiny bubbles, so small as to be invisible to the naked eye. A vessel containing sulphuric acid is always doing the same thing, as chemists know. But it is said that if a man interposes himself between the Sun and the pool, so that his shadow shuts off the heat, the gas bubbles cease temporarily on the shaded area, so that even when he moves away the place where his shadow fell remains outlined on the pool. Thus he might be said to cast more than one shadow at the same time.

What Does Perpetual Motion Mean?

Perpetual motion is motion which, once started, will not cease but will continue indefinitely and without regard to any surrounding circumstances which may tend to stop it. The chief of these circumstances in everyday conditions is friction, which, by converting some of the energy of motion into heat, gradually reduces the energy and so stops the motion. All perpetual clocks or other devices have failed because of this gradual whittling down of the original impetus of the motion, and perpetual motion of the kind imagined could only go on in a frictionless world where not even an atmosphere impeded motion. But even in empty, airless space there may be causes to exhaust motion.

Why Does a Lifeboat Not Sink?

A lifeboat has many contrivances to give buoyancy to it by making it lighter than the water on which it floats; but the contrivance which keeps it from sinking when the rushing waves lessen this buoyancy is the one-way valve. Valves of this kind resemble doors or flaps in a pipe so hinged that they will open downwards when a weight of water rests on them, but will not open upwards. Thus the valve will open to let wave water rush through the valve back to the sea, but the pressure of sea-water from below the valve will only close it more tightly.

What Does a Kitchen Midden Mean in the History Books?

The rubbish heaps which in all ages have stood beside houses in primitive countries, and on which the inhabitants have thrown such of their household goods as have become broken, damaged, or useless, are called middens. In the course of centuries the heaps have become covered up, but when the antiquarian digs down to them he finds in the broken potsherds, discarded bone implements, and other ancient rubbish, evidences of the ware the forgotten peoples used and the kind of lives they lived.

What Happens When We Blush?

The flow of blood to the skin is regulated through thousands of microscopic blood vessels which join arteries bringing blood from the heart to veins which take it back again. Each of these blood vessels has its own nerve to open or close it. Thus the nerve system controls the flow of blood to the surface of the skin, or to various areas of the skin's surface, just as it controls the flow of blood or oxygen to the muscles. When, therefore, the surface of the visible skin of the face becomes coloured with a blush, it is because some of the nerves have turned on the tap controlling the blood supply. The nerves may be disturbed by anger, fright, or shame, and turn on the tap involuntarily; for no one personally can control these flows of blood to or from the heart.

Who was Francis Xavier?

Francis Xavier, born of noble parentage in 1506, in his mother's castle of Xavero, south of the Pyrenees, is claimed to have been the greatest Christian missionary since the first century after Jesus. He was one of the seven first members of the Society of Jesus, the great Jesuit order founded by Ignatius de Loyola. His famous missionary wanderings were crowded into the last twelve years of his life. He visited the Portuguese colonies in India, Ceylon, and the Malay Archipelago, and finally Japan, and forbidden China, where, at San-chian, near Canton, he died of fever in 1552. He was buried in Goa. Francis Xavier is credited with the conversion of more than 700,000 people in less than ten years, and, though he shared the prevailing opinion of his time as to what should be done to heretics, he was kindly, humble, and deeply loving.

The Story of the Beautiful Things in the Treasure-House of the World

The Apse of St. Madeleine Church at Vézelay   The Basilica of St. Irene at Istanbul

ARCHITECTURE IN CHRISTIAN TIMES
THE THREE EARLIEST STYLES

THE term Christian architecture applies in reality to all the work of the Christian era, which may be said to date from the year the Cross triumphed in Rome. But it has been found necessary to make other classifications. Architecture is described as Romanesque, Gothic, Renaissance, Modern: but the term Early Christian is reserved for the work of some 500 years in Europe—from the time of Constantine, who, early in the fourth century, made Christianity the religion of the Empire, to the days of Charlemagne.

When the Christians in Rome found themselves in favour after the bitter years of persecution and were told they might have churches of their own instead of hiding in the catacombs, they were somewhat at a loss as to where to start and what to do. They were poor and not very numerous, and Roman by birth. It was both natural and expedient for them to continue the Roman tradition. They built their first churches on the model of the basilicas, and used any material that came handy. Like the Saracen mosques, these churches were meeting-houses only. There was no necessity to build a central shrine for the figure of the god, as in the case of pagan temples. Thus this Early Christian architecture is of the simplest

kind. Its interest is religious and historic rather than aesthetic. It was the cradle of a spiritual power unparalleled in history.

The basilican churches followed one general plan. They were long, rather low buildings, with flat timber roofs supported by rows of columns. Sometimes there were three aisles, sometimes five. Men sat on one side of the central aisle and women on the other. This aisle was wider and rose higher than the others, and in the clear stretch of wall were set window spaces, generally filled in with blocks of pierced marble.

At the end of the centre aisle stood what was known as the arch of triumph, leading from the rectangular body of the church to its rounded-out end, or apse. There was generally a dome roof to the apse, studded with mosaics and shining glass. The high altar, under a canopy supported by marble columns, stood in the space called the Sanctuary, between the arch of triumph and the apse.

Some of the basilicas must have presented a curious aspect in detail, as the beautiful marble columns were taken from discarded pagan temples or baths, cut down to the right length, and strung together in aisles, regardless of varying mouldings and carvings. But the general

PICTURES · STATUES · CARVINGS · BUILDINGS · IVORIES · CRAFTS

effect was of dignity, and the long vista of the central aisle gave an impression of length—an impression that was partly due to the unbroken lines of columns and partly due to the lowness of the roof.

THE CHURCHES SET UP FAR AND WIDE AS CHRISTIANITY SPREAD

A good number of basilican churches were set up in Italy as Christianity grew in power; in Rome there were thirty-one; several in Ravenna; they rose in Constantinople, Jerusalem, Bethlehem; in Asia Minor, Egypt, Africa. The largest is St. Paul-outside-the-Walls, Rome, built in the fourth century and reconstructed after the fire that almost destroyed it in 1823. Other well-known Roman basilican churches are St. Clemente, St. Maria Maggiore, St. Agnes-outside-the-Walls. The most famous of the basilican churches are the two dedicated to St. Apollinare, in Ravenna; their wall mosaics are among the most beautiful in the world.

The early Christian architects had a great love for mosaics. Their predecessors, the Romans, had formerly used them for floor decoration only. In the basilican churches they ornamented the walls wherever possible, and the apse domes shone down in a glory of blue and gold glass and lovely colours, full of light. The mosaics of the Ravenna churches were probably worked under Byzantine influence, of which we shall presently be thinking.

In the history of architecture two developments date from this period: the bell-tower or campanile, and the baptistery. From the Early Christian campanile grew the church towers of medieval Europe.

THE OLD PAGAN BUILDINGS USED BY THE CHRISTIANS FOR THEIR SERVICES

There was generally a baptistery—a separate building—attached to the principal church of a city, and at this time it was used for the purposes of the rite of baptism only. The baptistery was generally either circular or octagonal, and was based on the principle of the smaller Roman temples and tombs. A number of pagan buildings were taken over by the Early Christians for the purpose, and this adoption is one of the most interesting cases of grafting the new on the old that the tale of architecture supplies. It was necessary that the baptistery should be large, as not only had it to serve for several

churches, but the rite was only administered three times a year.

Very few baptisteries were built later than the eleventh century, and before that it became usual to place the baptismal font in the vestibule of the church. The three most important of the early days were at Rome, Nocera, and Ravenna.

The architecture called Byzantine is really of the Early Christian period and was built for Christian worshippers, but it is of a very different character indeed from the basilican churches of western Christendom. It dates from the time when Byzantium became the capital of the Roman Empire under the name of Constantinople. The Turks have named it Istanbul.

The port of Byzantium was already an old city, long peopled by Greeks, when Constantine made it the seat of his government. Upon the old town rose another that was the New Rome in more senses than one. It was against the instinct of any Roman emperor to take over a town and not impose on it at once something of Roman order, form, and grandeur.

THE WONDERFUL NEW ROME THAT AROSE IN THE EAST

The New Rome, as Constantinople was also called, was swept and garnished; aqueducts and great pillared water-cisterns built; magnificent erections set up to house the Emperor and his household and his army. Forums were laid out, six, one after the other, with a street that was the main artery of the town running through them. The most wonderful was naturally the Forum of Constantine. Thus was the old town transformed into a Roman city, the centre of a great commercial life, the pivot of a huge empire.

We remember from our chapter on Roman architecture that the forum was the heart of the town's life. This was true of the New Rome as of the old. But elsewhere there were changes. The Hippodrome, where chariot races were held, took the place of the Colosseum, with its gladiatorial fights, and Christian churches took the place of pagan temples.

The earliest were of the basilican type, like those in Rome. The oldest that now exists of the many erected in Constantine's day and after is St. John of the Studium. But the basilican churches of Western Christendom had been built by the Romans, with plenty of fine discarded temples and baths to serve as quarries. In

THE SPLENDID MOSQUE OF ST. SOPHIA

THE FAÇADE OF THE SECOND GALLERY

THE IMPERIAL BOX IN THE NAVE

THE MAGNIFICENT INTERIOR OF THE MOSQUE OF ST. SOPHIA IN CONSTANTINOPLE (NOW ISTANBUL)

THE WONDERFUL PILLARS AND ARCHES OF ST. SOPHIA

Constantinople, to begin with, the material to hand was poor—brick and concrete were all that could be relied on; marble and granite had to be imported. And the workmen and craftsmen were Greek. The spirit of old Byzantium, although its name was changed and Roman soldiers trod its streets, was nevertheless alive. Moreover, the East was always tapping at the door, so to speak. These two influences, Greek and Asiatic, presently became powerful.

HOW BYZANTINE ARCHITECTURE SLOWLY DEVELOPED FROM THE ROMAN

The change was gradual. It was not as if one day, or one year, a pure basilican church was set up, and the next a pure Byzantine. A little more of a feeling for many-domed roofs covering buildings on a square plan, a little less for rectangular aisles and flat roofs, a little more gorgeousness and a little less severity, and the change had come. Two hundred years after Constantine built his first church, St. Sophia arose.

This famous building, which has been a Turkish mosque since 1453, is the finest thing Byzantine architecture produced. St. Sophia marks the point of perfection which an art once may reach but never recapture. It stands isolated, unique, in the history of the world.

Byzantine architecture has never died out; it is the natural expression of the Greek branch of the Christian Church which is strongest in Russia and northern Europe. There are fine Byzantine churches in Kiev, Moscow, Leningrad; some in Yugoslavia and Greece; several in southern Italy, a good number in Asia Minor. From time to time churches are still built in the Byzantine manner; the Roman Catholic Cathedral, Westminster, is a modern example. But in no instance has the lofty beauty of St. Sophia been even distantly rivalled.

THE GLORIOUS DOMED ROOF OF THE MOSQUE OF SAINT SOPHIA

Greek architecture carried to perfection the principle of the square (trabeated) openings and pillar-supported roofs; Gothic architecture, as we shall presently see, developed to the highest genius the principle of the vaulted roof; in St. Sophia is the finest example of the domed roof which was the chief glory of Byzantine architecture.

The Emperor Justinian caused St. Sophia to be built toward the middle of the sixth century. Its architects were Anthemius of Tralles and Isodorus of Miletus, both Asiatic Greeks. The church is square in plan. Over its central space rises the great dome, 107 feet in diameter, and against its sides, so to speak, each leaning against each other and keeping each other up, are the half domes and quarter domes that roof in the rest of the stupendous building.

Inside, the general effect is of one enormous rounded shape that hangs over and cups in the mass of the interior which appears like one great oval nave. The eye runs along its lines and back, and is not arrested by ugly supporting masses. An ancient writer described the church of St. Sophia as being crowned by a canopy that rested in its place of its own accord, as if suspended by a chain from the skies.

Part of the great charm of contour that marks the interior of St. Sophia is due to the perfect judgment of its architects, who knew that a dome rising too high, so that the eye is wearied in following its lines, is false to the principle of beauty in dome construction. They therefore kept the dome shallow and covered it with gold, inset with mosaic pictures of apostles and saints.

THE BRILLIANT LIGHT THAT COMES THROUGH FORTY WINDOWS

Round the lower part of the great dome are forty small windows, twelve on the walls and others in the subsidiary domes, and through these openings the brilliant light of the East creeps in and adds a white radiance to the heavy richness of the interior. The walls and piers are lined with sheets of marble, white, green, blue, and black. Long rows of stately columns of many-coloured marble support the galleries that run round the church. Pattern mosaics cover the floor.

The Turks, changing the Christian church into a Mohammedan mosque, covered up or plastered over many of the mosaic pictures, in some cases hiding them under texts from the Koran. In the lovely apse, where the figure of Christ, brilliantly shaped in mosaics, once gleamed from the roof, they set their Mihrab, the niche that points to Mecca.

The Mohammedan invaders also added the four minarets that close in the outer buildings of St. Sophia, plastered over and washed the brickwork of the church in the horizontal bands of colour they so much liked, and destroyed the pillared entrance court that gave access to the arcaded porch of the church. Thus, from the outward appearance of St. Sophia, one would not guess the perfect beauty within.

In actual technique of construction, this famous church may be taken as an example of all Byzantine architecture. Each building was made of bricks and cement overlaid inside with marble and picture mosaic; in each the beautiful domed roof is the chief feature.

The earlier Byzantine architecture was generally more interesting in the interior than the exterior. The domes were built so as to be beautiful to the worshippers in the church. They were not too high. The result was that, seen from the outside, walls and roofs had a curiously compressed look, as if something had been flattened down. This is all the more evident to a European accustomed to the tall spire and towers of Gothic architecture. To an Eastern, bred in countries where buildings are flat-roofed, with long, blind walls pierced by small windows set high above the ground, this closed-in appearance is natural.

THE BYZANTINE BUILDINGS WHICH INSPIRED ST. MARK'S AT VENICE

There were many other Byzantine churches in Constantinople ; some have been converted to mosques, some destroyed by time and enemy hands. St. Irene is a beautiful church; another, called St. Saviour of the Chora, is known as the Mosaic Mosque because of the exceeding richness of its interior. It also has an interest in that its façade was copied when the Church of St. Mark was built in Venice. The real model of St. Mark's was a very fine Byzantine building called the Church of St. Saviour, in Constantinople.

St. Mark's, Venice, is one of the most famous churches of medieval Europe. It was built about the eleventh century on the site of a basilican church whose rectangular plan was changed, in the new building, for that of a Greek cross. The church has five domes, the chief one over the centre of the building and one on each arm of the cross. The mosaics of the interior are very wonderful. So cunningly is the church built, wall and pier sliding into dome, that the mosaics seem to run in unbroken contour round its walls. It would seem that the builders had

thought much less of the fabric of the church than of this gorgeous display.

The exterior, with its five portals facing the piazza of St. Mark, is one lovely mass of architecture and ornament of varying periods, of shining marble, alabaster, mosaic and gold bands. Many countries and generations gave of their treasures to St. Mark's, and the soft light of the sky and the sea's reflected radiance add an unparalleled beauty of their own.

THE PRIDE OF THE VENETIAN PEOPLE IN THEIR BEAUTIFUL CITY

Venice, a powerful republic in her great years, was in a position to take what she wanted, practically speaking, from anywhere. Her traders went near and far, east and west. The pride of the Venetians in their city was unbounded; no wealth was too great to spend on it. They were also an extremely independent people, and, though they borrowed the plan of St. Mark's from a pure Byzantine church, they refused to be bound by any laws of established taste. And here we ourselves can learn a lesson of judgment.

We have spoken of the logic and perfect taste of the Greeks. They developed a style of architecture and kept within the bounds imposed by the style. Thus they produced that master-work, the Parthenon. The Byzantine architects developed another style and kept, with equal logic and taste, within its limits. Thus they produced that other master-work, St. Sophia. The creators of these marvellous temples knew that in a great edifice one cannot play tricks. If a style is chosen it must be adhered to, and not a single inharmonious line added to the design.

MATERIAL FROM THREE CONTINENTS FOR THE MAKING OF ST. MARK'S

When the people of Venice built St. Mark's, it was suggested to them that having begun on a pure Byzantine model, the church should be finished so. But this seemed to the proud republicans to savour of a loss of liberty. They were not going to be dictated to by anyone; they would build their church as they wished. The ships of Venice swept the eastern seas and brought back from Alexandria and Asia Minor great columns of porphyry and alabaster, blocks of marble for facing. The bronze horses from Nero's arch in Rome came to decorate the front of St. Mark's. Presently " bonnets " were put on the domes. When the

Gothic spirit overtook Italy, arches, pinnacles, and niches were added to the pile. The result is that St. Mark's has a whimsical and alluring loveliness of its own, but can never rank among the great.

In spite of its beauty, there has always been something too luxurious and un-natural in Byzantine architecture. The gorgeousness of the mosaic-lined interiors may have stifled its life. Figures made of small cubes must needs be a convention, and in too many conventions Art cannot live. In any case, the pure Byzantine style is most suited to brilliant climates where large windows are unnecessary.

While this architecture was forming itself in the East, certain changes were taking place in Europe where the Christian church was growing in power, and the empire of Rome crumbling. The dawn of a new day of letters and art was ushered in by the founding of the Monastic orders. These presently became very powerful bodies, every generation or so needing new monasteries and churches. All that there was of learning and art in medieval Europe was implanted there by the monks. They were not only the schoolmasters of the continent, they were its architects.

THE STAMP OF OLD ROME ON THE FACE OF EUROPE

Rome had left her unmistakable stamp on all the European towns she had con-quered, and though the pagan empire was gone her work remained—monuments, bridges, buildings; for many centuries her roads were the chief highways of Europe. And although Eastern in-fluences, through traders and travellers, took root here and there, the finest thing in Europe was the handiwork of old Rome. So that when the new faith, ever increas-ing, groped for an expression in archi-tecture that would supersede the primitive basilican churches, it still seemed best to cling to that of the old pagan empire.

Basilican churches had been at their best a make-shift. They were chiefly unsatisfactory on account of their timber roofs which so easily exposed the whole building to danger of fire. In discarding them, architects were faced by a new difficulty. If they made flat stone roofs instead of wooden ones it meant the con-veyance of very large blocks of stone or marble for the purpose ; and this they could see might be done once or twice, but to make a general practice would be to kill all architecture except in districts that were rich in material.

These early builders found the solution of their difficulties in the simple vaulted roof carried by round arches, which could be made of small stones almost anywhere. As this style of roofing developed, the square-headed doorway or window was discarded for the round-headed opening. This feature, the round arch, formed the prevailing characteristic of the new archi-tecture, which presently became known as Romanesque. The influence of the old pagan style soon waned and died. Rome and Greece were forgotten, became ghosts that lay very still for several centuries.

THE ROMANESQUE CHURCHES BUILT ON THE PLAN OF A CROSS

Romanesque architecture grew in France, Italy, Germany; it came to Eng-land by way of the Norman Conquest, and is generally known there as Norman.

The plan of the Romanesque church was a development of the basilican, which was a rectangle with the apse thrust out at the eastern end. An arch of triumph, we remember, had divided the sanctuary or the place where the altar stood from the body of the building. In the Romanesque development the sanctuary was lengthened into the chancel or choir, and was divided from the rest of the church by a screen. In front of the chancel screen, on each side of the central aisle or nave, short arms were thrown out, making transepts. The plan thus became that of a long (Latin) cross, and we can see, in its de-velopment from the plan of the basilican church, the first of the changes that led to the more complicated plan of the Gothic church.

As the shape of the building altered in this way, the first of the spires and towers that are such features of our sacred architecture appeared—a development, we remember, from the campanile or bell-tower. They were thrown up from the body of the church either at the east or west end, or above the place where the transepts crossed the nave.

THE DEVELOPMENT OF THE APSE IN THE CHURCHES OF FRANCE

The many-apsed church appeared as Romanesque architecture developed. In-stead of the centre aisle being thrust out to form the apse, and the side aisles ending at a square wall, each aisle had its apse, and the transepts on the eastern face were rounded out too. The French developed the apse to an extraordinary extent. They had a strong feeling for the thrust-out shapes or bays from the eastward end of the church, and presently conceived the idea of throwing out a number of bays, like little apses, on the chief apse itself, so that in plan it looks like half an enormous rosette. This kind of treatment of the eastern end of a church was called chevet, and it continued long after Gothic supplanted Romanesque. The only complete chevet in England is formed by the little chapels that radiate from the apse of Westminster Abbey.

In some churches an aisle was run round the eastern end between the chancel enclosure and the apse wall, and was called the Ambulatory, where men could walk about and meditate. We can see this feature in many of our cathedrals and churches today. One, belonging to the Romanesque period, is that of St. Bartholomew, Smithfield.

This kind of arcaded walk brings us to the subject of cloisters—open spaces set with pillars of varying beauty, and cloistered buildings generally.

The great shapers of Europe, as we have said, were the monks. The monasteries and abbeys were the centres of interest and power in whatever province and country they arose, and some of their buildings were of very great dignity. We have produced more graceful, light, and beautiful buildings, but nothing so imposing as the monastic piles of medieval Europe.

The honours of architecture are generally accorded to the monks of the Cluniac Order, founded in 909. This great community of scholars and artists were among the first benefactors of Europe. Their huge and magnificent Abbey church at Cluny, near Lyons, was one of the most famous buildings in the world. It took forty years, about the end of the eleventh century, to build, and after giving joy and inspiration to men for seven hundred years, came down at Napoleon's order.

The church, as we can well understand, was the centre of any monastic establishment. On it the monkish artists spent their concentrated skill and in many cases very real genius. Around the church, like houses about a village green, clustered the rest of the buildings that were necessary for the life and maintenance of a large and enclosed and self-sufficing community.

The cloister court separated the church from the kitchens and dining halls, and this pillared space added a dignity of its own to the sacred building. In addition to the actual dwellings of the monks, which contained interesting apartments like those set apart for the brothers who were illuminating manuscripts, there were the guest houses, infirmary, prison or punishment cells, stables, granaries, bakehouse, mills, workshops. All these buildings were nobly set up, in accordance with the Romanesque style.

There are remains of monastic settlements like these at Fountains Abbey in Yorkshire, where one can walk through the ruined spaces and picture the busy, ordered life that flourished there from its founding in 1132 to its disruption in the sixteenth century.

These great masses of buildings had naturally a great effect on the architecture of the day. Cluny Abbey church is said to have served for a model of all Europe, and all over France memorable and sacred buildings arose, set up by the monks of various Orders. To go from one to the other is to follow a trail of beauty for whose creation the world has never been sufficiently thankful.

THE FINE OLD CHURCH AT ST. MARTIN DE BOSCHERVILLE NEAR ROUEN

Architecturally, the River Loire seemed to divide France in half. South of the river is the greater richness, where the Cluniac influence was strong, and also where Byzantine and pagan beauties still exerted a power. There were lovely capitals and columns to be had from discarded Roman buildings, fine masses of stone and marble. These churches of the south were consequently marked by most beautiful cloisters and very rich façades, or fronts. There were generally three doorways, each surmounted by not one rounded shape, but many; arch after arch falling into the thickness of the wall, each with its pillar and carved capital.

There is something in the shape of the pure Romanesque doorway that no successive architecture has achieved. It may be the exceeding charm of the low swing of the arch, from point to point of which the eye goes and comes, and is conscious of restfulness, of repose, of something returning upon itself, in Nature's inscrutable way. People who watch the sea find just the same kind of magic in noting the semi-circular, swinging trough between two wave crests.

WHY THE BUILDINGS OF NORTHERN FRANCE ARE SO SEVERE

In the north of France, where the thoughts of architects were not so much affected by the richness of an earlier empire, the buildings were sterner, more severe. There are very few anywhere whose fabric is not touched in some part by so-called improvers of a later era. North of the Loire the most important Romanesque buildings are the two Abbey Churches of Caen—the 'Abbaye aux Dames, founded by Matilda, wife of the Conqueror, and the Abbaye aux Hommes, also known as St. Etienne, begun by the Norman William himself.

Near Paris is the Abbey church of St. Denis, on which a fine early Gothic architect Abbé Suger, worked. St. Germain-des-Prés has managed to maintain its Romanesque look through many intervening centuries. South of the Loire are many wonderful piles like those of St. Madeleine at Vézelay, St. Gilles and St. Trophime at Arles, Notre Dame at Avignon, and Angoulême Cathedral.

In Italy the greatest triumph of the Romanesque period was the famous group at Pisa—the cathedral, the circular baptistery, and the campanile known as the Leaning Tower. In the south the fine cathedral of Monreale, near Palermo, shows a mixture of Early Christian, Byzantine, and Romanesque influence. St. Miniato in Florence, St. Michele in Pavia, St. Zeno Maggiore in Verona, and the Baptistery at Cremona, show respectively the varying appearance of Italian Romanesque architecture. Here the basilican influence lingered far longer than it did north of the Alps.

THE CHURCHES IN GERMANY BUILT ON EARLY CHRISTIAN LINES

A certain amount of Romanesque architecture appeared in Germany, principally in Saxony and the Rhineland. Charlemagne made it imperative for the Saxons to become Christian, and hence, in this province, a number of baptisteries were built on Early Christian lines. Circular churches arose with the sanctuary thrown out at the end.

Charlemagne had a strong feeling for architectural beauty, and he strove to awake in the German provinces something of the impulse for building fine churches that was so strong in southern Europe. Aix-la-Chapelle Cathedral rose at his orders, Charlemagne foreseeing that this building might presently serve as his tomb-house; and it would have been a fine record of Romanesque work if it had not been so much altered and improved in successive centuries. The original, quaint, polygonal body of the church remains, which was probably modelled on St. Vitale, Ravenna.

A PECULIAR FEATURE OF GERMAN ROMANESQUE ARCHITECTURE

One of the peculiarities of German Romanesque architecture is the double apsed church—that is to say, a church with an apse both at the east and the west end. Gernrode Abbey is the first built in this way. In other countries, apsidal features were reserved for the east end only, and thus the western end of the church could be devoted to the entrance façade. German architects placed their portals in the side of the church and richly ornamented them. And as they early showed their liking for round and octagonal turrets and many-sided domes, their buildings of this period are more picturesque than dignified.

The cathedrals of Trèves Worms, Spires, and Mayence are typical of the German feeling.

THREE GREAT STYLES OF BUILDING

THE IMPRESSIVE CATHEDRAL OF PISA AND THE LEANING TOWER

THE CATHEDRAL OF ST. MARK'S IN VENICE

28 1A8.

NOTRE DAME LA GRANDE, POITIERS | THE CATHEDRAL AT AVIGNON | ST. FREDIANO AT LUCCA

THE CLOISTERS OF THE BENEDICTINE MONASTERY AT MONREALE IN SICILY

THE INTERIOR OF MONREALE CATHEDRAL | THE APSE OF ANAGNI CATHEDRAL, ITALY | ORNAMENTED SHAFTS IN THE MONASTERY AT MONREALE

THE CHURCH OF ST. BASIL
AT MOSCOW

THE ROMANESQUE TOWER OF ST.
PORCHAIRE CHURCH, POITIERS

THE CATHEDRAL OF THE
RESURRECTION IN LENINGRAD

THE SPLENDID INTERIOR OF THE BASILICA OF ST. PAUL-OUTSIDE-THE-WALLS, ROME

ST. APOLLINARE NUOVO AT
RAVENNA

THE DOORWAY OF ST. MARK'S,
VENICE

THE CHURCH OF LA MARTORANA
AT PALERMO

THE CATHEDRAL AT SPIRES IN GERMANY

THE ABBEY AUX HOMMES AT CAEN
IN FRANCE

SAINT MADELEINE CHURCH AT VÉZELAY
IN FRANCE

THE CATHEDRAL OF WORMS IN GERMANY

CLOISTERS OF THE GREAT MOSQUE, DAMASCUS

THE CHURCH OF ST. SERNIN AT TOULOUSE

RUINS OF THE BASILICA AT KALAT SEMAN IN SYRIA

INTERIOR OF A BASILICA
IN RAVENNA

THE CHURCH OF THE NATIVITY
IN MOSCOW

A TWELFTH-CENTURY WINDOW
IN ST. MARK'S, VENICE

THE ABBEY AUX DAMES AT CAEN

THE CATHEDRAL OF MONREALE, PALERMO

THE SPLENDID CATHEDRAL AT PALERMO

A ROMANESQUE CAPITAL
AT MONREALE

THE INTERIOR OF
THE CATHEDRAL AT AVIGNON

A WINDOW OF ST. AGOSTINO
CHURCH, PALERMO

THE SOUTH SIDE OF AACHEN CATHEDRAL

CHURCH AND MONASTERY AT DAPHNE, GREECE

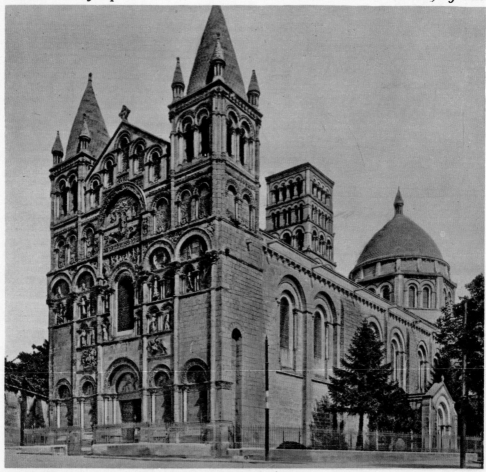

THE CATHEDRAL AT ANGOULÊME IN FRANCE

MAINZ CATHEDRAL AS IT
WAS RESTORED

CLOISTERS OF ST. TROPHIME
CATHEDRAL, ARLES

MAINZ CATHEDRAL BEFORE
ITS RESTORATION

The Wonderful House We Live In, and Our Place in the World

Regent Street, London, one of the greatest shopping centres in England

SPENDING AND SAVING

SPENDING is one of those things which do not seem to stand in need of much explanation, but which are found to be very puzzling when we come to think about them. The truth is that how we spend and whether we spend or save are very important things.

When we have money in our pockets it may seem that it really matters to ourselves more than to anyone else how we spend it. All sorts of shops invite us to come in and buy. We can turn our money into many different things according to our tastes. Does it matter what we choose to buy?

We must not be misled by the fact that goods of all sorts are in the shops waiting for us. Our purchase really affects more than the shopkeeper's stock.

When we spend, and thus become consumers of commodities, we do something to benefit a trade or trades. In effect, the spending amounts to a command for certain workers to be employed. Suppose that, having one shilling, we decide to buy with it a pot of jam. The spending of that shilling sets in train a long line of the most varied activities.

The shopkeeper, having sold the pot of jam, has one less in stock, and is by so much led to order more; whereas if people stopped buying jam he would not buy any more, and so all the trades which were concerned in making the pot of jam would feel the loss.

The jam itself is made out of fruit from English orchards, and sugar made from sugar cane grown in hot countries, or from sugar beet grown at home. It is boiled by apparatus made by engineers, and then put into jars made of glass. This glass is manufactured from sand and other materials, melted by coal gas. The jars bear paper labels, for making which trees have been cut down and turned into pulp. The labels are printed by machinery which uses various kinds of ink and colours. Another industry provides the metal cover for the jam jar, and ores have to be dug from the ground to make the metal.

All these processes cause people to be employed, in Canadian forests, on West Indian sugar plantations, in English glass works, as well as in the jam factory itself. Furthermore, all the various things concerned are transported by land and sea between all parts of the world, so that sailors, lorry drivers, and railwaymen all play their part.

How wonderful it is to think of our going into a shop with one shilling and

BODY, MIND, AND SOUL · CITIZENSHIP · ECONOMICS · GOVERNMENT

thus *commanding, in the buying of one pot of jam, a tiny fraction of the work of hundreds of people*. How plain it is, then, that the manner of our spending matters, not only to ourselves, but to all the world of work, that wise spending commands good work, while unwise spending commands unworthy work. *If we buy good things, we order good work to be done. If we buy useless things, we order people to do useless work.*

THE SCOFFERS WHO LAUGHED WHEN MARCONI BRIDGED THE OCEAN

The wants of civilised men are numerous, and are always increasing. The human mind is so wonderfully broad in its outlook that it is always discovering new things and longing to enjoy them. Not long before the First World War Marconi introduced wireless telegraphy, and when he announced that he had signalled the letter S across the Atlantic many people laughed and declared that he had deceived himself. Today we can sit in our own houses and listen to broadcasts from hundreds of wireless stations. Thus a new want has been created—a new object on which we can spend our money.

It is important to notice, however, that no human being needs more than a certain limited quantity of any particular thing, and that, as to spending generally, the more money we have to spend, the less satisfaction we get out of our increased power of spending.

A man can only eat a certain amount of food; it is useless to offer him more. The same thing is true of every particle of commerce. A boy wants a good cricket bat, but if he has one, he likes to stick to it until it is worn out, and he would not play cricket better if you gave him a hundred cricket bats.

Because of this, each pound added to a man's income yields a *diminishing satisfaction* as compared with the previous pound, because it will be spent on things he needs less urgently than the ones he already has.

RICH AND POOR FAMILIES AND THE TRADES OF LUXURY AND NECESSITY

If a man has only £100 a year, to add £10 to it means very much to him. If, however, he has £1000 a year, to add £10 matters less, while the addition of £10 to an income of £10,000 a year obviously matters very little.

Such considerations have much to do with the nature of spending. Suppose there are ten poor families each living on about £3 a week, and another family which has as much as the ten poor families possess between them. We can see at once how very differently the two incomes will be spent. The ten poor families will want a lot of bread, and bread will be one of the chief things bought with the £30 a week they have to spend. Because the one rich family has as much income as the ten poor families put together it will not want more bread; probably, indeed, it will eat less bread than the same number of people belonging to the poor families.

On the other hand the ten poor families will have to spend so much on the bare necessities of life—rent, food, clothes, lighting, coal, and household goods—that they will have very little left for luxuries. The rich family, after buying the necessities of life, will have a good deal left to spend on pleasures and luxuries. So we see that the spending of small incomes encourages the trades of necessity, while the spending of large incomes encourages the trades of luxury.

HOW CIVILISATION HAS CREATED A HOST OF NEW WANTS

It is desirable to abolish both poverty at one end of the scale and ostentatious luxury at the other. Happy is the country which has plenty of wise spenders and not too many reckless and wasteful ones.

It would be a mistake, however, to suppose that the desire to satisfy wants, or to spend money, is bad in itself. It is just because civilised men desire to satisfy a host of different wants which civilisation itself has created that they are encouraged to work for themselves and for their families. This striving leads to a greater production of wealth, and thus to the means of satisfying wants. It is true that sometimes the pursuit of wealth—the endeavour to get money to spend—leads to feverishness of mind and fretfulness of disposition; but as time goes on, and people learn that men can satisfy each other's needs and create a reasonable supply of goods and desirable things for all by co-operation, the discomforts and discords of modern life will gradually disappear from our midst.

Every year, just before the Budget is presented to Parliament, the Government publishes a small book, called the White

Paper, on National Income and Expenditure, which gives particulars of how much the British nation produced and consumed during previous years. These books of statistics are of great value to members of Parliament, to economists, and to all others who are interested in what is happening to the country's economic system. From them, we can find out how people spend their money.

Owing to the Government's control of both goods, and, indeed, money, in the years following the Second World War, together with the restrictive effect of a very high income tax, personal spending has undergone a great change. We shall talk, not of the money people *earned*, but of what they *spent* after paying their income tax.

HOW PEOPLE SPENT THEIR MONEY IN THE DAYS BEFORE THE WAR

In the year before the war, between a quarter and a third of the money that people spent went on food and drink. This included all kinds of food and non-alcoholic drinks, chocolates and ginger beer as well as bread and tea, food eaten in restaurants and milk bars as well as at home.

Next in demand was housing, and about an eighth of the money spent went on payment for house room, and on rates. This amounted to over ten pounds per head of the population. Almost as much again was spent on keeping the houses comfortable and fit to live in—lighting and heating; furniture for the rooms; hardware for the kitchen; and other household goods such as soap and matches.

Much money was also spent on clothing. When we add up expenditure on food, housing, and clothing, we find that it came to about two-thirds of all the money spent. The rest was spent on less essential things.

One interesting point is that more money was spent on alcohol and cigarettes than on clothing. How foolish this was ! Over nine pounds per head was going on drinking and smoking while many people needed better clothes and better houses. Houses and their furnishings make the homes of the people, and the character of these homes is very important for a nation's happiness. If well-fed, well-clothed people live in good houses, there will be a happier nation than if the money goes on alcohol and tobacco.

Two or three years after the war ended people spent more on every class of expenditure than they did in 1938, but as the prices of things had risen steeply during the war, this did not necessarily mean that they were getting more goods and services. It is interesting to see how *the way in which they laid out their money* had altered, to see how the proportion spent on different things had changed.

HOW THE WAR ALTERED THE WAY PEOPLE SPENT THEIR MONEY

Money spent on food and clothing did not quite make such a large proportion of the total as before, and the proportion spent on house room and household goods was much smaller. Just over half the money people spent went on food, housing, and clothes, instead of two-thirds. One big reason for this decrease was the shortage of supplies of these things after the war. Houses, for instance, were short because of wartime bombing, and because very few had been built for six years. Clothes were in short supply chiefly because workers in textile factories had been moved to other industries during the war, and it took time to get the clothing industry going again. Food was still rationed, because so much of it had to be imported. Therefore, it was impossible for people to spend as large a proportion of their money on these necessities as they normally used to.

It is fortunate for the well-being of society that there are some people who, instead of spending all their money, are careful to save a part of it. Let us try to understand what saving is.

THE LESSON MEN MIGHT LEARN FROM NATURE'S LITTLE CREATURES

If a man spends all he receives as he receives it he has nothing left to fall back on if he falls ill, or if trade becomes bad and he is unable to find work to do. Too many people are careless about saving. It is curious, in this respect, that human beings should be inferior in foresight to some of the animals. Not a few animals, like the squirrel, form stores to guard themselves against famine. If you give a squirrel a nut, and he is not hungry, he will go and bury it in a place from which he can recover it.

But man requires to save not only after the manner of the squirrel in " putting by for a rainy day," but for the purpose of increasing his powers of work.

The simplest form of such saving is when a man, who has tilled a piece of ground and grown and harvested a crop, takes care to save out of his harvest enough corn to sow as seed in the ensuing season. If he were foolish enough to eat all his corn, there would be no seed time, and no next harvest.

THE WAY IN WHICH A MAN CAN SAVE UP HIS LABOUR

Another simple illustration of saving may be given. Suppose that it takes a man a whole week to make a tool. In that case he gives up a whole week of his labour, and for what purpose? The answer is that he is *saving up his labour*, putting it into a tool, so that his future labour will be made all the more fruitful.

Simple as these illustrations are, they really cover the whole reason for saving. For, after all, the most complicated engine ever made is only a tool to help us to work better. By saving up money we can feed and support a number of men while they are not producing any food for themselves, so that their work can be directed to making an engine which, when made, will help us to produce far more food and other things than could be produced without it.

Take the wonderful modern agricultural machines with which harvest work is done. A single machine cuts the corn, threshes it, and deposits the grain into sacks ready for sale. With one of these machines a great field of corn, such as they have on the fertile lands of Canada or Argentina, is rapidly harvested with comparatively little work. There are other marvellous appliances to plough and harrow, drill and sow. Thus the raising of corn becomes a process so easily done that good wheaten bread can be eaten by hundreds of millions of people, who, if this machinery did not exist, would get very poor food indeed, as men did in the old days of perpetually recurring famines of which we read in our history books.

THE BENEFITS THAT THRIFT HAS CONFERRED ON THE WORLD

When, therefore, people are wise enough to save money to construct such machines, they really help the world to get plenty of good food. They do the same thing when they lend money to build railways to carry corn on land, and ships to carry corn across the seas to where it is needed; and

without careful saving these things could not be done.

It is the same with the mineral wealth of the Earth. Coal, and the ores which yield iron, copper, zinc, lead, tin, and other indispensable metals were just as much the possession of the world a thousand years ago as they are today, but they could only be used in tiny quantities because great machines did not exist to work them. Even a hundred years ago the amount of iron used was very small, because men had not discovered how to deal with it in big quantities. Even if all the machines now invented had been thought of, their invention would have been useless because there would not have been enough iron to make them with. And today, if people stopped saving, and did not by saving enable the great machines to be made, the world would speedily become as poor again as it was centuries ago, when so many people lived in grinding poverty.

WHY SAVING MAY BE CALLED THE HANDMAID OF INVENTION

Saving is thus seen to be the handmaid of invention. Invention, of course, is the main thing in wealth production. All the saving in the world would not avail much for the benefit of mankind unless science provided us with things in which to invest our savings worthily. But, having great inventions, it is our duty to devote work to carrying them out on a large scale, and that can only be done by saving the means to establish the necessary works.

All this is very important because our nation, like all the other nations, has not yet made sufficient use of the inventor's ideas. We want a better output of wealth, and that better output will never arrive until we make the best possible use of all the splendid inventions at our disposal. If our people would save more, and put their savings into good public and private enterprises, the condition of the nation would rapidly improve.

Wordsworth, in one of his best known sonnets, wrote that " getting and spending we lay waste our powers."

But the poet was anxious to contrast the peace of natural beauty with the feverish haste to be rich. Spending may be wise, though it is often foolish, and wise saving is as worthy of praise as miserly hoarding is deserving of blame.

The Story of the Marvellous Plants that Cover the Earth

Buck's-horn Plantain   Glasswort   Blue Fleabane

FLOWERS OF THE SEASIDE

LIKE the woodland, the meadow, and the heath, the seaside has its own flowers. Some of these are found growing only along the coasts and in salt marshes, while others, though not confined to the shore, are found there in larger numbers and in a more vigorous condition than elsewhere.

Of the many representatives of the great composite family perhaps the most striking is the golden samphire, a near relation of the elecampane and ploughman's spikenard, but not connected with the rock or sea samphire, which is a member of the parsley family.

The golden samphire is quite unlike any other British plant, its thick, smooth leaves being a curious yellowish green in colour, with the ends either blunt or divided into two or four points. These leaves are very numerous, and, like so many other shore plants that grow in mud flats or salt marshes, are very succulent.

By developing these thick, succulent leaves the plant tries to store up as much moisture as possible for its use, and so avoid the absorption of too much salt. Not only is the plant thick and leathery, but the outer skin, or cuticle, is thick, and the stomata, or breathing holes, are sunken. Further, as the leaves are long and narrow, there is less breathing out of moisture from their surfaces than in some other cases.

Though in appearance so unlike other British plants, the golden samphire is in structure typical of many seaside plants in that its flower-heads are not large. The reason for this is that the smaller the surface it presents to the prevailing winds, the less likely is the flower to be damaged or uprooted even in the severest gale. The flowers of the golden samphire are solitary, and the rays, as suggested by the name, are bright yellow. The plant is rarely more than a foot high, and the flowers open from late July to September. Occasionally the golden samphire is used as a substitute for the rock samphire, the leaves being pickled and eaten as a condiment, but they have not the same pleasing flavour as those of the rock samphire.

A much more common composite plant is the sea starwort, or sea aster, a stout, succulent plant growing sometimes two or three feet high, though it rarely reaches more than a foot. Here, again, the leaves are smooth, narrow, and succulent. The flowers grow in clusters, and are handsome, having the inner florets yellow, and the outer ones purple. Unfortunately, in low-lying situations the plant is often covered with mud, which gives it an unsightly appearance, but when it is found growing in higher and drier situations it is really very attractive.

BOTANY & ITS WONDERS · FLOWERS · TREES · HOW THINGS GROW

Quite different in kind, though of the same family, is the blue fleabane. Though found round our coasts it does not grow in mud flats or salt marshes, but in the pastures and on the banks a little farther removed from the sea. It is a much-branched, hairy plant about a foot high with lance-shaped leaves and clusters of flowers that have a pale yellow disc and pale purple rays or florets. The number and size of the flower-heads vary very much, and also the length of the florets. This plant, it must be understood, is not a near relation of the common fleabane, although that is also one of the composites. The blue fleabane is known to scientists as erigeron, from two Greek words meaning early and old, a reference to the early appearance of the grey seed-head. The common fleabane, on the other hand, is called scientifically pulicoria, from the Latin word for a flea, and the name is a reference to the strong smell of the plant, which is supposed to drive away fleas.

Ploughman's spikenard is a sister plant to the golden samphire. It is downy, has dull-green, lance-shaped leaves that are soft and cottony on the underside, and its dingy yellow flowers grow in clusters.

THE SEASIDE COTTONWEED WITH LEAVES COVERED WITH A SORT OF WOOL

The seaside cottonweed grows on sandy seashores, and its woody underground stem, or rootstock, runs deeply in the sand. The stems, which branch at the base, are hard and almost woody, and grow about a foot high. Both they and the toothed leaves are covered with a dense, white cottony wool, which almost hides the small, nearly globular heads of yellow florets in August and September.

The sea wormwood, another of the composites, is common in salt marshes and on moist cliffs. It closely resembles the common wormwood, but is smaller, and the stems rarely rise above 18 inches. The feather-like leaves, like the rest of the plant, are covered with white cottony down, and the flowers, which appear in August and September and grow in rather drooping racemes, are yellowish-brown in tint. This plant has the same properties as the common wormwood, though in a less marked degree. It is bitter, tonic, and aromatic, and has been used as a medicine in cases of fever. It has also been used to form a conserve, being beaten up with three times its weight of sugar. A popular idea that it was a valuable food for cattle arose because cattle feeding on salt marshes where the sea wormwood abounds have been observed to fatten very quickly. Cattle, however, do not generally eat the wormwood. Their progress must have been due to the richness of their pastures.

THE YELLOW-HORNED POPPY WITH THE SEEDS PACKED WITH OIL

Quite common on the sandy coasts of England and Ireland, though rarer in Scotland, is the yellow-horned poppy. This is a stout annual, with hard spreading branches, covered in all its parts with a bluish-green bloom. The thick, divided leaves are wavy and embrace the stem, and the large golden-yellow flowers are showy, but the petals fall off rapidly. The large seed-pods which then form are sometimes a foot long, and at first sight might easily be mistaken for stems bare of leaves. The seeds contain much oil. Altogether, the yellow-horned poppy is one of the most handsome of the seaside flowers.

The pink family is represented by the sea campion, a sister of the well-known bladder campion, or white bottle, which it somewhat resembles, though the flowers are larger and fewer than those of the bladder campion. The plant is in blossom almost the whole of the summer.

Belonging to the pink family is the sea purslane, a low, succulent, dark green plant, with a creeping rootstock and numerous thick and fleshy leaves. It forms tangled masses on sandy seashores, and is common from Portugal right up to the Arctic. Its flowers, which are small and few, grow in the forks of the stem. This must not be confounded with another plant, also called the sea purslane, a member of the goosefoot family, which is better known as the lesser shrubby orache.

THE PECULIAR PURPLE HIPS OF THE BURNET ROSE

In dry, sandy places near the sea the burnet, or Scotch rose, is easily identified. It is a small, bushy plant, growing rarely more than three feet high, and it is crowded with prickles, mostly straight and passing into mere bristles and hairs. The leaves are made up from seven to nine smooth leaflets with saw-like edges, and the solitary flowers are white. The fruit is in the form of globular hips which are dark purple, almost black in colour.

A pretty little plant found on pebbly seashores, though rather rare, is the

FLOWERS THAT BLOOM BY THE SEA

SMALL SCABIOUS

SPREADING SEA LAVENDER

SEA MILKWORT

PRICKLY SALTWORT

SAMPHIRE

SEA BLITE

NODDING THISTLE

ORACHE

PLOUGHMAN'S SPIKENARD

CARLINE THISTLE

SEA BUCKTHORN

SEA ASTER

SEA HOLLY

VERNAL SQUILL

seaside everlasting pea, which has purple flowers, variegated with crimson and fading to blue. Another member of the pea family common on sandy shores is the creeping rest-harrow, sometimes called the wild liquorice, a little shrubby plant with runners, oblong leaflets, and solitary flowers of a handsome bright pink. The plant has a strong odour, and its name of rest-harrow was given because of its very tough branches, which country people said could rest even under the harrow.

Members of the goosefoot family are most abundant in salt marshes and on the seashore, which is the chief reason the leaves are inclined to be fleshy. Many of the plants of this family are important articles of food for cattle, and even for human beings, and the sea beet, a succulent plant growing about two feet high, is believed to be the origin of the cultivated mangold-wurzel, the white or sugar beet, and the red beetroot.

THE MANY KINDS OF ORACHE FOUND GROWING ON THE SEASHORE

In the goosefoot family there are half a dozen kinds of orache, all found on the seashore, some very common. The spreading or common orache, a very variable plant, has flowers clustered in slender spikes, and the leaves all stalked ; the halberd-leaved orache, an equally common species, has dark green, mealy leaves and seeds of two sizes, the larger being brown and rough, and the smaller black and smooth ; the deltoid-leaved orache, also common, has nearly all its seeds small, black, and polished ; the less common grass-leaved orache has a stem striped with reddish, resinous lines ; and the rose-coloured orache, a common species, also has a stem striped with red. The most curious orache, however, is the frosted sea-orache, which is covered with silvery scales, giving the plant a whitish hue.

The shrubby sea blite, another of the goosefoots, is a smooth plant covered with a bloom that gives it a bluish-green tinge. Sometimes it is erect, and at other times low and spreading, but always shrubby at the base. The succulent leaves are very numerous, and almost cylindrical, and the flowers are green and inconspicuous. The annual sea blite is a low, straggling plant, bluish-green in summer and reddish in winter, and while its sister plant is found on sandy and shingly beaches, this is common on muddy shores.

The prickly saltwort, a shrubby annual, stiff and hairy, is a much-branched plant, and seldom grows a foot high. The leaves are awl-shaped and each ends in a sharp point, hence the name prickly saltwort.

The jointed glasswort is sometimes called saltwort, and also marsh samphire, though it has no relationship with the golden samphire, a composite, nor with the rock samphire, a parsley.

THE JOINTED GLASSWORT OF THE MUDDY SHORES, WITH ITS LEAFLESS STEMS

It is a curious plant, abundant on muddy seashores and on salt marshes. It generally grows about a span high, though it varies much in different districts and situations. The stems are succulent and jointed, quite leafless, but with two membranous attachments surrounding the base of each joint, within which, towards the extremities of the branches, are the tiny flowers, with only one or two stamens.

The young glasswort, gathered before the flowering season, is used as a substitute for rock samphire, but it is much inferior in flavour. It is pickled in the same way, being first steeped in a solution of salt and afterwards put in vinegar. It is much relished by cattle. The plant was formerly collected in large quantities from the muddy flats near the coast and burned for alkali, being first dried in the sun, and then made up into small heaps over holes which received the soda ash in a melted state as it ran from the burning mass. This alkali is still used in the manufacture of glass in countries by the Mediterranean.

The rock samphire is a member of the parsley family, and has a powerful aromatic odour. The fleshy leaves, gathered in May, make an excellent pickle. It is generally found growing in clefts of the rock close to the sea. The tiny flowers, arranged in many-rayed umbels, are white, and the seeds are contained in a short, smooth fruit-case.

THE SEA-HOLLY, WHICH GROWS WITHIN REACH OF THE SPRAY

Another member of the parsley family, the eryngo, or sea holly, grows generally on the loose sand within reach of the sea spray. The large, fleshy rootstocks, which were once eaten for their supposed restorative and stimulating properties, reach several feet into the sand. They are sweet and aromatic, and at one time were candied with sugar and sold in the shops as a sweetmeat. Falstaff refers to this practice when, in The Merry Wives of Windsor, he says, " Hail kissing-comfits and snow eringoes." The leaves of the sea holly are stiff, prickly on the margins, and, like the whole plant, covered with a mealy bloom that gives them a bluish-green tinge. The flowers are unlike those of most of the umbelliferous family in that they are arranged not in umbels, or flat clusters, but in compact heads, with several spiny leaves beneath. They are of a bluish hue, and open in July and August. The young shoots of the sea holly, when just emerging in the spring, are often gathered and eaten like asparagus.

TWO SEASIDE MEMBERS OF THE PARSLEY FAMILY, AND THEIR YELLOW FLOWERS

Two other members of the parsley family that grow by the seashore are the common Alexanders, a stout plant three or four feet high, with broad, bright green glossy leaves, greenish-yellow flowers, and dark brown, aromatic flowers ; and the common fennel, a well-known plant with leaves divided into hair-like segments and large umbels of yellow flowers.

The small scabious, a member of the teasel family, is often found growing in waste places near the sea. Its lilac blossoms are smaller and less handsome than those of the field scabious, and its leaves are divided and feather-like.

The primrose family is represented by the sea milkwort, which has no connection with the true milkworts. It is a small, smooth, fleshy plant, from four to six inches high, with a creeping rootstock, and tiny pink flowers. It flowers all the summer on the sands and in the muddy salt marshes where it thrives, and is found not only on the coasts of Europe, Asia, and America, but also by the inland seas of Asia.

The sea buckthorn, or sallow thorn, is the only member of its family growing wild in Britain, and the family is a small one, consisting of shrubs and trees, native to the northern hemisphere.

THE FRAGRANT BLUE FLOWERS OF THE DAINTY VERNAL SQUILL

The sea buckthorn is a willow-like shrub, from four to eight feet high, with branches ending in spines, and covered with a scaly scurf, very close and silvery on the underside of the leaves, and dense and rusty on the young shoots and flowers. The male flowers are small and greenish, and grow in clusters something like cat-kins, while the female flowers are solitary, but crowded in each axil. The fruit consists of small orange or brown berries, which are very juicy and acid. The fruits of several species of this, the oleaster family, are eaten in different parts of Europe.

The vernal squill, a member of the lily family, is a dainty and delicate little plant that is far less common than we should like it to be ; but it grows abundantly on some of the grassy slopes of the Cornish coast, and the clusters of fragrant, blue, star-like flowers are a joy to see. The plant has a small bulb, and lance-shaped leaves. Common on the east coast of Ireland, it studs the sandy pastures as thickly as daisies stud the English meadows. The autumnal squill, its sister plant, is about the same size, and has reddish-purple, pink, or violet-blue flowers.

Of the ever-present bindweeds a very beautiful plant is the sea convolvulus. The flowers, nearly as large as those of the great bindweed, are a delicate rose-colour striped with red or yellow, and the fleshy leaves are round or kidney-shaped, with broad lobes at the base. The rootstock is creeping, and the stems, which are short and not climbing, are usually buried almost completely in the sand.

MEMBERS OF THE CABBAGE FAMILY WHICH GROW BY THE SEA

Chief among the cabbage family is the well-known seakale, grown in gardens as a vegetable. The part eaten is the leaf stalk, which is blanched by being kept, like celery stems, from the action of light. The leaves are wavy, toothed, and fleshy, and the white flowers grow in clusters.

Purple sea rocket, another of the cabbage plants, is common on sandy shores, and in salt marshes. It has zig-zag branched stems, hard at the base and with loose, straggling branches a foot or more long. The few leaves are thick and fleshy, and the lilac flowers resemble those of the stock, but smaller. The most interesting feature about the purple sea rocket is its fruit. This consists of an oblong pod with no division or valve, but containing two seeds, and when ripe the upper part of the pod is mitre-shaped and erect, while the lower part, which has been described as shaped like the head of a pike, is hanging.

The sea radish, which some botanists regard as merely a variety of the common wild radish, or white charlock, is similar to that plant, but its leaves are more divided, the pods are longer, and the yellow flowers smaller. It is rare in England, though common enough round the Mediterranean.

Of the other members of the cabbage family, the great sea stock is a spreading plant, with purple flowers an inch across, which are very fragrant at night.

The common tamarisk, a handsome evergreen shrub that grows into a small tree, is common on the south and east coasts of England, but it has been planted, and is not truly indigenous to Britain. It has long, flexible branches, generally slightly drooping at the ends, and reddish in tint; the little pointed leaves are only about a twelfth of an inch long. The small pink or white flowers are crowded in spikes about an inch long, and appear in the early summer.

THE MANY USES THAT WE FIND FOR THE COMMON MARSH MALLOW

Two members of the mallow family flourish on the coasts, the common marsh mallow and the tree mallow. The marsh mallow grows two or three feet high with erect, unbranched stems bearing bunches of large, pale, rose-coloured flowers in the axils of the downy leaves. The starry down, by the way, is a very interesting and beautiful object for the microscope. The marsh mallow has a thick fleshy root like a parsnip, and the whole plant, especially the root, abounds in mucilage. It has long been used in the preparation of an ointment, is used with syrup for preparing a cough mixture, and a decoction from the leaves is sometimes used for fomentations.

The tree mallow is a tall, handsome plant, sometimes reaching a height of twelve feet, with a thick, woody stem. It is downy, and has many rose-coloured flowers with darker veins.

THE FOUR KINDS OF SEA LAVENDER GROWING ROUND THE BRITISH COASTS

A small member of the stonecrop family is found growing in rocky and sandy places near the sea, and is known as English stonecrop. It is only three or four inches high, has small leaves, pale green tinged with red, and the little white flowers are also often tinged with red. The plant is sometimes called English sedum, from its botanical name, which comes from the Latin word sedeo, I sit, and refers to the plant's habit of growing along the ground.

All four of the sea lavenders, members of the thrift family, grow on the British coasts, the spathulate sea lavender being not uncommon on rocky shores, while the common sea lavender is found on muddy coasts, and the matted sea lavender in the salt marshes of Lincoln, Norfolk, and Cambridge. The flowers are lilac-coloured and the flower stalks are leafless.

The sea plantain, easily distinguished from its sister plantains by its long, grooved, fleshy leaves, woolly at the base, is found on seashores as well as on the tops of mountains; and in Wales, where it abounds in the salt marshes and pastures near the coast, it is so greatly liked by the sheep that the Welsh call it sheep's herb. Buck's-horn plantain, common in gravelly places near the sea, is the only British species that has divided leaves. They are more or less downy, and the flowers are pale yellow. This plant was at one time regarded as a remedy for hydrophobia.

The common henbane is often found growing near the sea. Like the thorn apple, it is not a native of these islands, but has long been common as a wild plant, having escaped in days gone by from herb gardens where it was cultivated for its medicinal properties. It grows about three feet high, has large viscid leaves covered with soft down, and dingy yellow or cream coloured flowers with purple veins. The whole plant smells very disagreeably of mice, and it is strongly narcotic.

THE POISONOUS HENBANE AND THE WARNING GIVEN BY ITS SCENT

Accidental cases of poisoning by henbane are not very common as the unpleasant odour acts as a warning, but in one case a woman pulled up a quantity of henbane roots in a field and, supposing them to be parsnips, boiled them in a soup for her family. All those who took the soup were seized with giddiness, sleepiness, and indistinctness of vision, followed by delirium and convulsions. A case is on record, too, where the monks of a monastery ate the roots for supper, and were seized with frenzy that took strange forms. One rose at midnight and tolled the bell for matins, the rest attended, but could not read their books, while others read what was not in the books. Every part of the plant is poisonous, and in large quantities might easily cause death.

For medicinal purposes, however, the plant is exceedingly useful, but it should never be allowed to grow where cattle feed.

Two pages of coloured pictures of Flowers of the Seaside are given on 5643-44

The Story of the Peoples of all Nations and their Homelands

The Acropolis, on the heights above Athens, capital of Greece

GREECE AND ITS PEOPLE

No land has had such faithful friendship as Greece in modern times—friendship from those nations which understand how much is owed to the Greece of long ago, when the race nurtured in this little land produced the most vigorous thinkers who had appeared in the world.

Greece is the smallest country that has ever been great. Though for a few brief years she was great in warlike conquest—in the time of Alexander—her real influence in the past was exercised through her intellectual and artistic energy, and has survived in her language, thought, and art. But of Greece as a lasting force in history we read elsewhere. Here we glance at the country itself, and at its people and their ways of life, their troubles in the horrors of modern war, and their efforts in peace.

Almost exactly the same size as England, but with less than a fifth of England's population, Greece is composed of a much indented mainland and many islands. The mainland, running down to the Mediterranean, forms the southern part of the Balkan Peninsula. Albania, Yugoslavia, and Bulgaria lie to the north, the Aegean Sea and Turkey to the east, and the Ionian Sea, below the " foot " of Italy, to the west. Many of the Greek islands fringe the coasts, but the Cyclades and the Dodecanese groups lie scattered about the mouth of the lovely Aegean. There was great rejoicing when, in the early spring of 1948, the Dodecanese were restored by Italy, to whom they had been ceded by Turkey after the First World War. *Dodecanese*, in Greek, means " twelve islands," though there are actually 14 inhabited islands in the group.

Greece is a very mountainous country throughout, but there are fertile valleys and plains between the ranges, 7000 feet to 9000 feet, which run roughly from north to south. There are some rivers of moderate size in the north, but those in the south are little more than creeks; and no Greek river is navigable. Melting winter snows flood many of them, but big drainage schemes have been undertaken to lessen the damage due to this. There has also been much reclamation work in Greece's areas of lake and marsh land. Draining of Lake Copais alone made 50,000 acres available for farming.

For so small a country, the range of climate is extraordinary. In the northern and other mountainous districts, there is a long winter with frequent storms of snow and icy rain. But in the sea-lapped regions winter lasts barely three months, and March—sometimes even February—may bring sunny, balmy weather reminiscent

THE FIVE CONTINENTS & 100 NATIONS & RACES THAT INHABIT THEM

of a warm English midsummer day. Temperature may rise to over 100 degrees in the plains, but over the country generally summer is never unduly hot.

Skies are rarely cloudy, and the air is clear. On a spring day we can see, from the hills of Athens, the shining white sails of fishing boats rounding Aegina Island some twenty miles away. Spring brings sudden glory of flowers to soften the rocky, scrub-covered surface of such hills as are not covered by forests of pine, fir, and oak.

The people are intensely patriotic and will take up arms in defence of their country with single-minded purpose when confronted with a common danger. This was well shown in 1940, when Italy invaded from the north-west. In times of peace they are mainly farmers, intelligent and hard-working, and with a keen commercial sense. They are also a hardy people, in spite of malaria and other ills, which the Government have taken measures to fight.

Most of the people of the countryside live simple lives, and when work is done they still may fall to telling the old stories, singing the old songs, and tripping the old dance measures which link them with their romantic past. But in the towns, and particularly in Athens with its one-and-a-quarter million people, life is much the same as in many a more western European capital.

OLIVE GROVES AND VINEYARDS IN THE SHELTERED PLACES

Though more than half of the Greek peninsula is forest or barren rock, the people make the most of the pasture and ploughland left to them. In the more sheltered parts they grow olives, currants, raisins, grapes, and figs; but tobacco is the most important export. They sow their crops where they can. The Ministry of Agriculture gives valuable instruction in improved methods of crop production, and the use of machinery is encouraged through agricultural co-operative societies. Wheat production especially has made big strides. In some parts nomadic shepherds tend their sheep and goats, but the farmers rear cattle, pigs, and horses as well.

Though she is mainly an agricultural country, Greece has her industries as well, and the years after the Second World War found these expanding as the country recovered from her terrible devastation at the hands of the occupying Germans. She has no deposits of coal or oil, but she has rich iron ores, a valuable export, bauxite, nickel, and chromite, and also some manganese, lead, zinc, and emery. Her chief industries are smelting, textiles, cigarette-making, and ship-repairing.

THE SPLENDID WATERWAY WHICH LINKS EASTERN GREECE WITH WESTERN

Greece was ever a country famous for sailors, depending, like Britain, on her merchant fleets for her prosperity. Not only do her sea communications link her with the outside world; they also have to link different parts of Greece herself, since internal communication is so difficult. The Corinth Ship Canal, for instance, from the Aegean Sea to the Ionian, links eastern Greece with western.

The Greeks have reason to be proud of their achievement in reopening this canal for shipping as early as the spring of 1948. As the Germans retreated in 1944 they threw in 1200 tons of steel (the debris of two bridges), 105 railway wagons, four locomotives, 21 tons of railway track, and half a million cubic yards of rock and earth. This compelled ships to make a 400-mile detour.

Most Greeks occupied the post-war years in repairing destruction which, in proportion to her size, was probably heavier for Greece than for any other country in the world. The damage was estimated at £240,000,000, or two years' national income. But where there's a will there's a way, and the people set to and before long had rebuilt all of their main railway installations, more than 700 bridges, more than nine-tenths of their rolling-stock, and had laid more than 8000 miles of roads, of which a bare 300 miles had been left in good condition. By the use of new methods they were able to lay down fine asphalt roads, like so many ribbons, at the rate of five miles a day!

THE WORK OF RECONSTRUCTION AFTER THE RAVAGES OF WAR

One bridge they rebuilt is the famous Gorgopotamos Bridge which they had blown up to prevent Hitler from bringing down supplies to Piraeus, and from there to Rommel in North Africa. With new

OLD AND NEW CHURCHES OF ATHENS

THE CHURCH OF SAINT ELEUTHERIUS, THE EARLIEST KNOWN EXAMPLE OF BYZANTINE
ARCHITECTURE IN GREECE, BUILT EARLY IN THE NINTH CENTURY

THE NEW CATHEDRAL OF ATHENS

THE CHURCH OF SAINT THEODORE, REBUILT IN 1049

steel girders from America, the bridge was soon spanning its river again.

Then they had to rebuild Piraeus, the great port of Athens, at a cost of nearly £2,000,000, and also the ports of Thessaloniki (Salonika), Volos, Patras, and Alexandroupolis. As many as possible of 1300 razed villages and 250,000 buildings had to be rebuilt, and homes found for at least a sixth of the population.

The Athens airport at Ellenico was entirely modernised, as were the airfields at Jannina and Tripolis, while all-weather runways have been built at the airfields of Thessaloniki, Larissa, Kozani, and Kavalla.

HELP FOR GREECE TO WIN HER FREEDOM FROM TURKEY

All these works of reconstruction have resulted in an increase in the populations of the towns. Athens and Piraeus together have a population of nearly one-and-a-half million, and there are nearly a quarter-of-a-million in Thessaloniki.

A victim of the great Mohammedan invasion of eastern Europe, Greece, aided by Britain, France, and Russia, won her full freedom from Turkey in 1828. Thereafter, until 1924, Greece was a constitutional monarchy. In that year King George II was deposed, and a republic was proclaimed. In those days the country's most important figure was Eleutherios Venizelos, who had been Prime Minister during the greater part of the First World War and had secured for his country a vast extension of territory. Venizelos fell from power in 1933, and in 1935, after a plebiscite, King George came back. But the real ruler of Greece from 1936 until the outbreak of the Second World War was General Metaxas.

ONE OF THE MOST GLORIOUS EPISODES IN GREEK MILITARY HISTORY

General Metaxas was a dictator, and like all dictators he was diligent in the suppression of freedom. But it is now generally agreed that his administration was on the whole beneficial because it disciplined the country for the ordeal that followed.

In the late autumn of 1940 Italy attacked Greece, and this led to one of the most glorious episodes in Greek military history. This little country, united and inspired by patriotism, not only halted the advance of her powerful assailant

but turned it into a retreat and drove the invader from Greek soil and far into Albania beyond. But tragedy followed with the southward sweep of the German army, and for more than three years Greece was to suffer untold miseries under the heel of the Nazis. Hitler refused to import food—to a country almost entirely dependent on foreign countries for her physical subsistence—and famine and disease spread through the land.

King George and his ministers came to London, where they established a " Government in Exile." But the heads of the fighting services went to Cairo, where the Royal Hellenic Forces were reformed, later to give good service at Alamein—where the Allied fortunes turned—and in Tunisia. Britain and the United States more than replaced the very heavy Greek naval losses, and the merchant navy soon totalled more than a million tons of shipping.

YEARS OF TROUBLE FOR GREECE FOLLOWING THE SECOND WORLD WAR

By her own exertions, and by the help of the Allies, Greece was freed from the German yoke in October 1944. But her troubles were by no means over. Civil war broke out between Government forces and the Communist Guerrilla army, and the Communists tried to seize power. King George was recalled after a plebiscite in the autumn of 1946, but he came back to a turbulent country in which rival parties, with policies hopelessly opposed, strove to gain the mastery.

The king died in 1947, and was succeeded by his brother Paul. But guerrilla warfare continued, the rebels being helped by sympathisers in the neighbouring and unfriendly States. It went on, indeed, until September 1949, when the Greek Army wiped out the rebels. Then the Greeks were able to turn their energies to the rebuilding of their country.

Such is the story of Greece in our time. She has suffered as severely as any of Hitler's victims and has faced adversity with the courage that made her famous of old. Her hopes for the future are set in continued peace, and in friendship with her neighbours in the long-troubled Balkans. Token of this desire for friendship with her neighbours is in the Balkan Alliance between Greece, Yugoslavia, and Turkey, which was signed at Bled in August 1954.

PEOPLE A TRAVELLER MEETS IN GREECE

OLD AND NEW ON THE BATTLEFIELD OF PHARSALUS, WHERE CAESAR FOUGHT POMPEY

BOATMEN IN MYTILENE HARBOUR

RUMANIA AND ITS PEOPLE

RUMANIA has been compared to the Moon, for she has waxed and waned in size with the fortunes of history, and today is practically a Full Moon in shape, with an area of 91,671 square miles. The Soviet Union is her northern neighbour along the River Pruth. To the west is Hungary. In the south the Danube forms the frontier with Bulgaria and Yugoslavia, and to the east is the Black Sea. The Carpathians and the Transylvanian Alps, rising to over 7000 feet, form a ring running from the north through the centre of the country and then turning south-west.

There are deeply wooded areas, timber, indeed, being one of Rumania's most important natural resources. The rivers flowing through the Carpathians into the Danube and the Black Sea provide water power as well as vital service in irrigation and transport. Oil, methane gas, salt, coal, iron, copper, gold, and, silver are among her great resources, and more precious today, uranium, used in the production of atomic energy. Rumania's chief crops are maize and other cereals, sugar beet, potatoes, and vines ; in recent years, attempts have been made to cultivate rice and cotton. Livestock includes cattle, sheep, pigs, and oxen.

Historians are not all agreed about the origin of the Rumanian people. The name of the country is ample evidence of the Roman occupation and the language, too, developed from Latin, though it contains many Slav, Magyar, and Turkish words as well. Modern Rumanians are probably descended from the Vlachs, a mixture of the people who were living in Dacia when the Romans came, and the Slavs who later invaded the area, with the addition of Asiatic tribes like the Avars, Goths, and Petchenegs.

Rumanian history is the story of the three principalities of Wallachia, Moldavia, and Transylvania. The first two achieved independence under their separate rulers in the Middle Ages but were under the influence of the Turks by the middle of the 16th century. But the principalities never became part of the Ottoman Empire and this meant that the feudal structure of society was never destroyed, as it was in Bulgaria when she became a Turkish vassal. The Princes, or Voivodes, of Wallachia and Moldavia, and their nobles or boyars, owned enormous estates which were worked for them by poor peasants. Often the peasants revolted against their miserable conditions, but little improvement came until the redistribution of land in the reforms of 1920 and 1945.

During the period of Turkish domination the Rumanians made several efforts to gain their independence. Especially remembered in Rumania today are Stephen the Great of Moldavia and Michael the Brave of Wallachia. Michael, who lived at the end of the 16th century, actually managed to unite Moldavia and Wallachia for a few years.

In the 18th century the Turks allowed the Greek merchants of Constantinople to take over the administration of the principalities, but the Rumanians liked the Greeks no better than the Turks. Instead they looked to Russia, and in 1774, according to the Treaty of Kutchuk Kainardji, the Turks recognised Russia as the protector of Christians in the Ottoman Empire.

In 1821 Tudor Vladimirescu organised an insurrection in Wallachia aimed chiefly against the Greeks. Meanwhile many Rumanians, especially the Liberals, went to France to study and found their political ideals in the principles of liberté, egalité, and fraternité which had been proclaimed by the French Revolution in 1789.

The Rumanian democrats, led by Nicholas Balcescu, organised a revolt in Bucharest in 1848. Encouraged by the revolution in Paris the leaders demanded social reform, parliamentary government, and redistribution of the land in favour of the peasants. Unfortunately, Russian fears of Liberalism and the refusal of help from Kossuth and the Hungarian revolutionaries left the Rumanians without support. When the Turks and the Russians determined on joint efforts to stop the spread of revolutionary ideas the leaders fled to Paris.

After the Crimean War the Great Powers suggested the union of Moldavia and Wallachia, and this came at last in 1859, when one prince was elected to rule both principalities. The prince was Alexander Cuza, and he was followed by a German prince, Charles of Hohenzollern, in 1866. In 1881 Charles, or Carol as he was called in Rumanian, declared himself King of Rumania. Since 1918 Transylvania has also been part of Rumania, except for the period from 1940 to 1945 when Germany allowed the Hungarians to occupy it.

United Rumania has not had a long history nor a very happy one. None of the democratic parties was strong enough to prevent the country becoming more and more fascist in its organisation. Carol II, who became king in 1930, ruled as a dictator for ten years. In 1940 Rumania entered the Second World War on the side of Germany and Italy. When the armies of the Soviet Union entered Rumania in 1944, when Carol's son Michael had become king, the government declared war on Germany. But Rumania was long regarded as an ex-enemy State and not until 1955 was she allowed to join the United Nations.

Since 1945 the Rumanian Communist Party has gradually assumed control of the country, though the party merged with the Social Democrats in 1947 and is

HARVEST TIME AT A VILLAGE IN THE BRAILA DISTRICT OF RUMANIA

now known as the United Workers' Party. On December 30, 1947, King Michael abdicated and Rumania became a republic with a single chamber parliament known as the Grand National Assembly.

The country is now a member of the Warsaw Treaty, linked for defence with the Soviet Union and her other allies. She is also closely associated with these countries by economic treaties, and by similar organisation of her political and economic life.

There are over $17\frac{1}{2}$ million people in Rumania, nearly one-and-a-half million being in the capital, Bucharest, which is a cathedral and university city. Almost a tenth of the population are Hungarians,

and they mostly live in Transylvania, a self-governing region of western Rumania. These Hungarians are now guaranteed their rights by the constitution of 1952. They can make their own local laws ; they can educate their children in the Magyar language ; they have their own university, theatres, and newspapers. Other minorities in Rumania are Germans, Ukrainians, and Jews, and they also have schools and newspapers of their own.

Most Rumanians belong to the Greek Orthodox Church, though the Hungarian minority is Roman Catholic. Religious freedom is guaranteed by the constitution, but Church and State are separated, no religious instruction being allowed in schools and no religious parties in politics. Education is compulsory for children from seven to fourteen. There are many institutes of higher education as well as four universities.

Apart from Bucharest the chief towns are Jassy, a medieval university town in Moldavia ; Ploesti, the oil town ; Stalin, a growing industrial centre ; Cluj, also a university town ; and Constanza, a seaport and naval base on the Black Sea.

Industries include the old one of textiles, and new ones like engineering and chemicals. Like transport, they are all nationalised. Mining of coal and salt and the various precious metals also provides a great deal of work for the people as well as wealth for the country as a whole.

A new railway in the south links Bucharest and Ploesti and the main international line passes right across Rumania. The main industrial towns are linked by road and railway, but waterways form by far the most important means of transport. The Danube, for example, carries three-quarters of Rumania's exports, either down to the Black Sea or westward through the

Iron Gates. Many of the other rivers are also navigable, and their usefulness has been extended by canals, though the big Danube-Black Sea canal which was started in 1949 has never been completed. Rumania also has her own air transport as well as being served by foreign airlines. In the countryside, however, horses and ox-carts are still a familiar sight.

Although industry has grown rapidly since 1945 under the Three-Year and Five-Year Plans, agriculture still engages about three-quarters of the population. Ploughs are still often primitive though there are an increasing number of Machine Tractor Stations where peasants can hire tractors, combine harvesters, and other agricultural machinery. Most of the land is worked by small independent peasants. About one-fifth of the peasants, however, now work their land under the co-operative or collective system. In co-operatives the peasants join together to buy seed and stock, to hire machinery, and to sell their products. In collectives the peasants actually put their land into a common pool and co-operate in all activities, only keeping a small plot round their houses as private property. There are also a few farms owned by the State, but these are mostly experimental or research stations.

The Rumanians are well known for their folk art, and folk music and dancing are popular pastimes in Rumania. They have colourful embroidered costumes, knee boots, and jangling jewellery. Some peasants still live in huts, just as they have done for centuries, but there are other villages with new houses, electricity, and medical services. There is social insurance for all.

Life in Rumania today is a mixture of old and new, and much has still to be done to complete the modernisation of the country, educate her people, and fully develop all her great resources.

BULGARIA AND ITS STORY

BULGARIA takes its name from the Bulgars, an Asiatic tribe, who crossed the Danube near its eastern end and settled in the area to the south in the seventh century A.D. Modern Bulgarians, however, are Slavs and owe nothing to the Bulgars except their name.

Their country is in south-east Europe, on the east side of the Balkan Peninsula, the total area being 42,796 square miles. To the south lie Greece and Turkey, to the west is Yugoslavia, to the north is the Danube forming the frontier with Rumania, and to the east is the Black Sea. Along the Yugoslav border there are mountains which spread out from west to east across the centre and south of the country in two ranges, the Stara Planina and the Rhodope. Between these two lies the Maritza River basin. In the Rhodopes are the Rila Mountains (with Stalin Peak rising over 9500 feet) where the River Isker rises and then winds through many rocky gorges down to the Danube in the north. There are plains stretching back from the Danube and along the Black Sea coast in the east.

More than half of Bulgaria is mountainous, but the plains and valleys are fertile and grow maize, wheat, cotton, rice, tobacco, and sugar beet. There are vineyards and orchards in the hills and in the foothills of the Stara Planina Range are the rose gardens which produce attar of roses used in making perfume. Wild animals abound in the woods and forests, and sheep and goats are kept on the hills. Mineral resources include coal, iron, copper, lead, zinc, manganese, and uranium. In recent years oil has been found.

There are just over seven million people in Bulgaria, and nearly half-a-million of them live in the capital, Sofia, which is a cathedral and university city as well as an industrial centre. Other important and growing towns are Pleven and Trnovo in the north; Stalin (Varna) a port and shipbuilding centre on the Black Sea; and Plovdiv (formerly called Philippopolis after its founder, Philip of Macedon) which has become a leading industrial centre and the scene of an international trade fair.

The Bulgarians belong to the southern Slav race, and for this reason there have been many suggestions that they should form one nation with the Yugoslavs, whose name means south Slavs. Their language, very like Russian, is written in the same Cyrillic alphabet as that used by the Yugoslavs. Most of the Bulgarians belong to the Greek Orthodox Church, but there are also a few Moslems.

PEOPLE WE SEE IN RUMANIA AND BULGARIA

A RUMANIAN MUSICIAN
WITH HIS PAN PIPES

AT SCHOOL IN SOFIA,
CAPITAL OF BULGARIA

A GRAPE GATHERER OF
PRESLAV, BULGARIA

BREAKFAST TIME AT A HOSPITAL IN BUCHAREST, CAPITAL OF RUMANIA

SWING-TIME AT STALIN IN BULGARIA

YOUNG CHILDREN AT SCHOOL IN RUMANIA

When the warlike Bulgars arrived in south-east Europe they were soon absorbed by the more peaceful Slav population already living there. Their ruler, Boris, who lived in the ninth century, was converted to Christianity and joined the Eastern Church. It was during his reign that the two monks, Cyril and Methodius, set out from Constantinople to spread Christianity, first in Moravia and later in Bulgaria. They invented the Cyrillic alphabet and translated the liturgy and other religious works into Slavonic, or Old Bulgarian.

THE BULGARIAN EMPIRE FALLS TO THE TURKS

Another great Bulgarian ruler was Simeon, who lived at the beginning of the tenth century and made his court at Preslav, a centre of learning. Simeon extended the frontiers of Bulgaria and gave himself the title of Emperor and Autocrat of All the Bulgars and Greeks. A similar title was adopted by Ivan Asen in 1185 when he attempted to make Bulgaria as important as the Byzantine Empire which his people both envied and feared. But the real threat to Bulgarian independence came from the Turks and by the middle of the 14th century Bulgaria was a vassal state of the Ottoman Empire.

For five centuries Bulgaria remained under Turkish rule. It was a period of great tribulation for her, a period in which Christians were often persecuted and many of their churches destroyed.

THE LOVE OF FREEDOM WHICH LED TO HELP IN THE GREEK INDEPENDENCE MOVEMENT

Through this long period of Turkish domination it was the Bulgarian Orthodox Church which kept the spirit of freedom alive among the people. This love of freedom, still strong in the Bulgarians, led many of them to take an active part in the Greek Independence Movement.

Curiously enough, however, Bulgarian nationalism grew up as a protest against Greek domination as well as that of the Turks.

The first signs of Bulgarian nationalism appeared as a literary movement. In 1762 a monk called Paisi wrote a history of the Bulgarian people and he was followed by Bishop Sofroni, the first to have his works printed in Bulgarian. Then came other novelists and poets who described the exploits of early Bulgarian heroes and stressed the sufferings of the past five centuries. As a result there were many revolts against Turkish rule, culminating in the uprising of 1876 which was led by the poet Christo Botev. The Turks took steps to suppress the revolt and followed them up with wholesale massacres of the people. In our own House of Commons Mr. Gladstone drew attention to their dreadful plight.

In 1877 Russia declared war on Turkey and in March of the following year imposed her terms on a defeated enemy. These terms, unsatisfactory to other Great Powers in Europe, led to the Congress of Berlin—the famous " Peace with Honour " Congress—and as a result Bulgaria became an independent principality within the Ottoman Empire. The first ruler was Prince Alexander of Battenberg, and he was followed by Ferdinand of Coburg, who in 1908 proclaimed his country completely independent of Turkey and assumed the title of Tsar.

HOW THE WORLD WARS LED TO THE FALL OF THE MONARCHY

Then came two crippling wars in the Balkans, followed by further defeat as a result of Bulgaria's entry into the First World War on the side of Germany. In 1918 Ferdinand abdicated and was succeeded by his son Boris, who later showed strong leanings towards the Fascist countries. Gradually the Germans took control of Bulgaria's army and industry, and in 1941 she joined the Axis powers. But although she fought with Germany and Italy in the Second World War, she never declared war on Russia, and when Russia entered her territory in 1944 she sued for an armistice and soon had troops fighting with the Allies. A new government was set up which promised the restoration of a democratic constitution, the separation of Church and State, and free elections.

Since the 1945 elections the Communist Party has become more and more important, especially with the virtual disappearance of the Peasant Party and the linking of the Social Democrats with the Communists. On the 9th of September, 1946, the monarchy was abolished and a new constitution adopted. This is the official Bulgarian Liberation Day.

Bulgaria is now a republic with a parliament of one chamber, known as the Sobranye and elected from a single list of candidates. Church and State have been separated, and although there is freedom of worship no religious education is given in schools. There is compulsory free education for all children from seven to fourteen and many new schools have been built in the last few years. A health service has been developed and is gradually being extended into the rural areas.

Bulgaria, once wholly an agricultural country, is now fast becoming industrialised ; today two-thirds of her national production is from industry. Hydroelectric stations have been built on the Isker and Maritza, and there are new steel mills and chemical industries as well as the more traditional industries like textiles and leather goods.

The Danube provides a vital waterway, and the international railway running from Yugoslavia and through Sofia to Istanbul is a main artery. There is also a new railway running south of the Stara Planina range from Sofia to Burgas on the Black Sea, but rail and road transport generally are still greatly in need of development.

Industrialisation has not harmed agri-culture ; on the contrary, agriculture has benefited by the production of electric power and the provision of irrigation and machinery for the farms. Because the Turkish administration prevented the growth of large feudal estates, the Bulgarian peasants have never been downtrodden like the peasants of Hungary and Rumania. Even before the redistribution of land in 1945 there was a big group of independent peasants with a strong co-operative movement. Now some 77 per cent of them are in collective farms where the land is owned in common. The State hires out farm machinery and buys a certain proportion of the produce, the rest being sold on the free market.

A member of the United Nations and other international bodies, Bulgaria is allied to the Soviet Union and the other countries of eastern Europe in economic and military pacts. Linked with the Russians by similarity of language and religion, the Bulgarians also look upon them as liberators—from the Turks in 1878, and in more recent times from the Germans.

THE STORY OF ALBANIA

ALBANIA is a tiny country (about a third the size of Scotland) on the west coast of the Balkan peninsula in south-east Europe. Yugoslavia lies to the north and east, and Greece to the south-east. Across the Adriatic Sea in the west lies the " heel " of Italy, only 60 miles away at the Strait of Otranto.

Nearly all Albania is a rocky land of mountains, with the highest peak over 8000 feet. These mountains are cut by swift-flowing rivers which fall into the coastal plain and run down to the Adriatic Sea. Forests of oak, beech, fir, and chestnut cover wide areas; and as much of the lowland is marsh there is little land left for cultivation. Natural resources include asphalt, oil, copper, and chrome. Agricultural products are maize, wheat, tobacco, olives, wine, and citrus fruit. Goats, sheep, and donkeys are the most common domestic animals ; wolves, bears, and wild pigs still haunt the forests.

Like the country they live in, the Albanians are a rugged people. There are about 1,200,000 of them in Albania (other big Albanian communities live in Yugoslavia, southern Italy, and the U.S.A.) and they call themselves Shkypetare, Sons of the Eagle. They are descendants of people who lived in this part of Europe centuries ago, and invasions by Romans, Goths, Slavs, and Turks have done little to alter their language — an Indo-European language written in the Latin alphabet. Two thirds of the Albanians are Moslems ; just under a quarter belong to the Greek Orthodox Church ; and about one-twelfth are Roman Catholics.

The Ghegs, living north of the River Shkumbi, used to be organised in tribes, each tribe a law unto itself, with hunting rather than agriculture as their livelihood. Often they would " hunt " an enemy from a neighbouring tribe, for, according to the Law of Lek, an unwritten code which originated in the Middle Ages, one man's death was always answerable by that of another. In the south among the Tosks and on the coastal plain, a feudal society existed with the beys (a Turkish title) owning large estates cultivated by poor peasants. Both Ghegs and Tosks still have their own dialects.

The chief towns are Tirana, the capital, where modern buildings rise beside the minarets and old alleyways, Duresi (Durazzo), Vlone (Valona), Shkoder (Scutari), and Elbasan. These and other towns are all linked by road, but there is only one railway—from Duresi to Elbasan via Tirana. There are internal air routes, however, and international lines link Tirana with foreign cities. Although there is now a small factory at Duresi engaged in the manufacture of motors, horses and donkeys are a common sight, especially in rural areas.

Albanian history has been largely the story of a struggle against foreign domination. When the Turks arrived in the 14th century Albania had already been ruled not only by Rome and Byzantium, but also by the Serbs, Bulgarians, Sicilians, and Venetians.

Most famous of Albania's heroes is George Kariotas, or Skanderbeg as he came to be called from a corruption of his Turkish name and title, Iskander Bey. Born in 1403, he was educated in Constantinople and at first fought in the Turkish army. Then, inspired by the example of John Hunyadi of Hungary, he decided to raise the Albanians in revolt against Turkey and devoted the rest of his life to this cause. But Skanderbeg's efforts met with little success, for Albania remained under Turkish rule until the uprising of 1912 which led to independence in the following year.

But independence did not bring security. Greece, Yugoslavia, and Italy all eyed Albania greedily, and there was no political unity within the country. Bishop Fan Noli tried to introduce reforms, and so did Zog, who became successively prime minister, president, and, in 1928, king.

In 1939 Italy invaded Albania and after the collapse of Italy in 1943 the Germans took over. Meanwhile resistance groups formed. Some fought for the return of King Zog and others followed the Communists led by Enver Hoxha. The Communist partisans were so well organised that they were able to assume control at the end of the war, and their leader became Prime Minister.

The present government, guided by the Labour Party (the name taken by the Communists), is trying to modernise Albanian society. In December 1945 Albania was declared a republic and the constitution of 1950 gave her a president and a single chamber parliament elected by universal suffrage. Church and State were separated but religious freedom was guaranteed.

In 1938 over 88 per cent of the Albanians were illiterate but now education is compulsory for children from six to thirteen, and schools and technical colleges have been provided. A health service has been introduced and measures taken to combat malaria in the marshy areas. In 1946 came a land reform law which gave land to those who owned none, and some peasants began to co-operate with each other in working their land and selling their crops; but this system of agriculture is very limited as yet. Albania's industries now include sugar refining, textiles, and oil, but her considerable mineral wealth, especially of copper, is not yet fully exploited. On the other hand, shipyards (at Duresi), irrigation works, and an enormous hydroelectric station (at Tirana) are under construction.

Never a wealthy country, Albania now looks to the Soviet Union and the other countries of eastern Europe for help and advice in carrying out its plans for future prosperity.

PICTURESQUELY-DRESSED GIRLS OF ALBANIA'S SOUTHERN HIGHLANDS

PICTURES AND MAPS OF THE NEAR EAST

CORFU, FROM THE GARDEN OF THE ACHILLEION PALACE

THE WHITE TOWER OF
THESSALONIKI

A MOUNTAIN ROAD
IN CRETE

THE MONASTERY OF ST. BARLAAM
AT METEORA IN GREECE

THE 15TH-CENTURY CHAPTER HOUSE OF THE KNIGHTS OF ST. JOHN OF JERUSALEM AT RHODES

THE MODERN CITY OF ATHENS BUILT ROUND THE RUINS OF ANCIENT GREECE

PIRAEUS, THE PORT OF ATHENS

THE HARBOUR AND CITADEL, CORFU

THE SEAPORT OF CORFU

NAVARINO BAY IN THE ISLAND OF PYLOS

THE FORTRESS GUARDING THE CITY OF KAVALLA IN MACEDONIA

Some of the pictures in these pages are by courtesy of the Greek Information Bureau

GREAT EVENTS OF THE GREAT DAYS OF GREECE

Route of the Gauls, under Brennus, into Greece in 279 B.C.

At Philippi, in A.D. 53, Paul preached the Gospel in Europe for the first time. He was arrested, scourged, and imprisoned

The battle of Philippi in 42 B.C., in which Octavius (Augustus) and Mark Antony defeated Brutus and Cassius, settled the fate of the Roman Republic

Alexander the Great's route to India

TURKEY

ASIA MINOR

MYTILENE

ATARNEUS

Here is the supposed site of ancient Troy, which the Greeks captured about 1184 B.C. after a long siege

Many Goths perished in a naval engagement with the Romans near the Hellespont (Dardanelles) in A.D. 367

In 1822 the Turks massacred 40,000 Greeks, who had risen in insurrection in the Island of Chios

Alexander the Great was born at Pella in 356 B.C., and had Aristotle for his tutor

SALONIKA

Aristotle was born at Stagira in 384 B.C.

After Plato's death Aristotle retired to Atarneus and then to Mytilene, whence he was summoned in 343 B.C. to teach Alexander the Great

Edessa was the early capital of Macedonia before the Athenian Army at Samos, in 411 B.C., recalled the traitor Alcibiades to lead it against the Peloponnesians

Philip II, King of Macedon, who made himself master of the Greek World, except Sparta, was assassinated at Aegae in 336 B.C.

Here was Mount Olympus, the home of the Greek gods

At Thermopylae, in 480 B.C., 300 Spartans under Leonidas held the pass against the Persian hosts until they were beaten by treachery

CHAERONEIA

DELPHI

Pyrrhus, King of Epirus, one of the greatest generals of antiquity, sailed for Tarentum in Italy, in 280 B.C., with a big army and a number of elephants. These animals had never been seen by the Romans, who were terrified and defeated

Here at Dodona was situated the oldest Greek oracle, dedicated to Zeus

Epictetus, the Stoic philosopher, lived at Nicopolis after he and other philosophers were banished from Rome by Domitian

Here at Delphi was the Temple of Apollo, in which was the most famous oracle of ancient times. "KNOW THYSELF" was carved over the door

IONIAN ISLANDS

By the Congress of Vienna in 1815 the Ionian Islands, which had been ruled in turn by Venice and France, and had been a republic, were placed under the protection of England. They were finally ceded to Greece in 1864

At Actium, in 31 B.C., was fought the famous naval battle in which Augustus defeated Mark Antony and won the mastery of the world

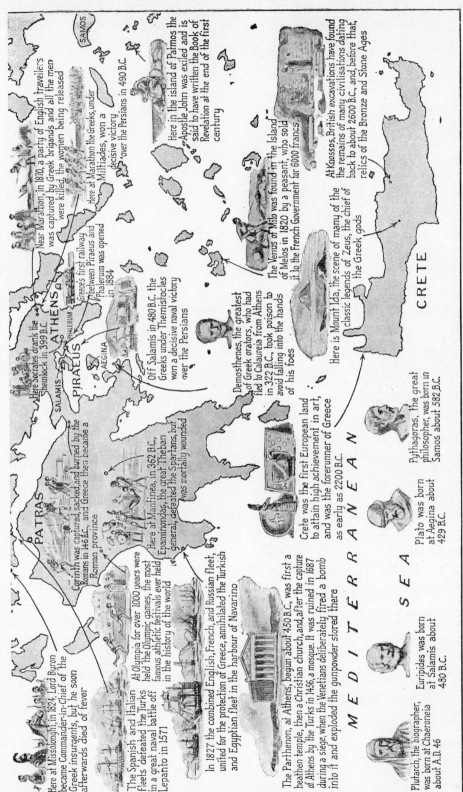

SAMOS

Near Marathon, in 1870, a party of English travellers was captured by Greek brigands and all the men were killed, the women being released

Here at Marathon the Greeks, under Miltiades, won a decisive victory over the Persians in 490 B.C.

Here in the island of Patmos the Apostle John was exiled and is said to have written the Book of Revelation at the end of the first century

Here Socrates drank the hemlock in 399 B.C.

Greece's first railway between Piraeus and Phalerum was opened in 1884

At Knossos, British excavations have found the remains of many civilisations dating back to about 2600 B.C., and, before that, relics of the Bronze and Stone Ages

The Venus of Milo was found in the Island of Melos in 1820 by a peasant, who sold it to the French government for 6000 francs

ATHENS

SALAMIS

PHALERUM

PIRAEUS

AEGINA

CRETE

Corinth was captured, sacked, and burned by the Romans in 146 B.C., and Greece then became a Roman province

Off Salamis in 480 B.C. the Greeks under Themistocles won a decisive naval victory over the Persians

Demosthenes, the greatest of Greek orators, who had fled to Calaureia from Athens in 322 B.C., took poison to avoid falling into the hands of his foes

Here is Mount Ida, the scene of many of the classic legends of Zeus, the chief of the Greek gods

PATRAS

Here at Mantinea, in 362 B.C., Epaminondas, the great Theban general, defeated the Spartans, but was mortally wounded

Here at Missolonghi, in 1824, Lord Byron became Commander-in-Chief of the Greek insurgents, but he soon afterwards died of fever

The Spanish and Italian fleets defeated the Turks in a great naval battle off Lepanto in 1571

At Olympia for over 1000 years were held the Olympic games, the most famous athletic festivals ever held in the history of the world

In 1827 the combined English, French, and Russian fleet, united for the protection of Greece, annihilated the Turkish and Egyptian fleet in the harbour of Navarino

Crete was the first European land to attain high achievement in art, and was the forerunner of Greece as early as 2200 B.C.

Pythagoras, the great philosopher, was born in Samos about 582 B.C.

Plato was born at Aegina about 429 B.C.

The Parthenon, at Athens, begun about 450 B.C., was first a heathen temple, then a Christian church, and, after the capture of Athens by the Turks in 1456, a mosque. It was ruined in 1687 during a siege, when the Venetians deliberately fired a bomb into it and exploded the gunpowder stored there

M E D I T E R R A N E A N   S E A

Euripides was born at Salamis about 480 B.C.

Plutarch, the biographer, was born at Chaeroneia about A.D. 46

NO COUNTRY HAS A MORE GLORIOUS PAST THAN GREECE, AND MANY OF THE MOST IMPORTANT EVENTS IN HER HISTORY ARE SHOWN HERE

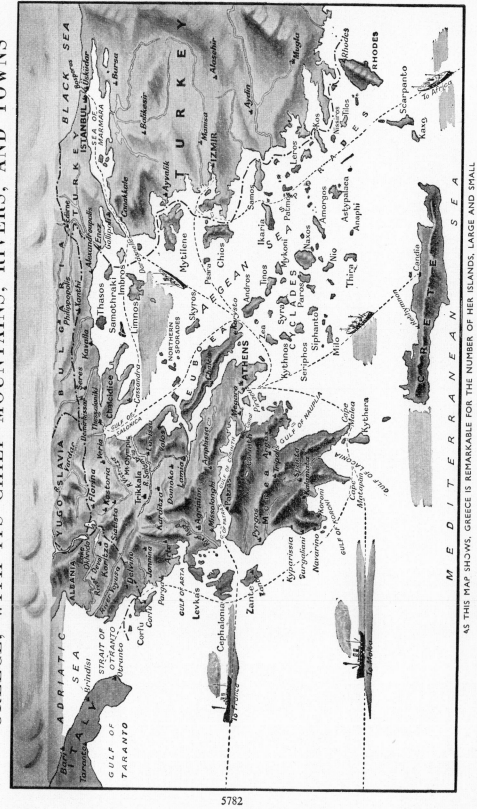

GREECE, WITH ITS CHIEF MOUNTAINS, RIVERS, AND TOWNS

AS THIS MAP SHOWS, GREECE IS REMARKABLE FOR THE NUMBER OF HER ISLANDS, LARGE AND SMALL

5782

GREECE AND HER GROWING INDUSTRIES

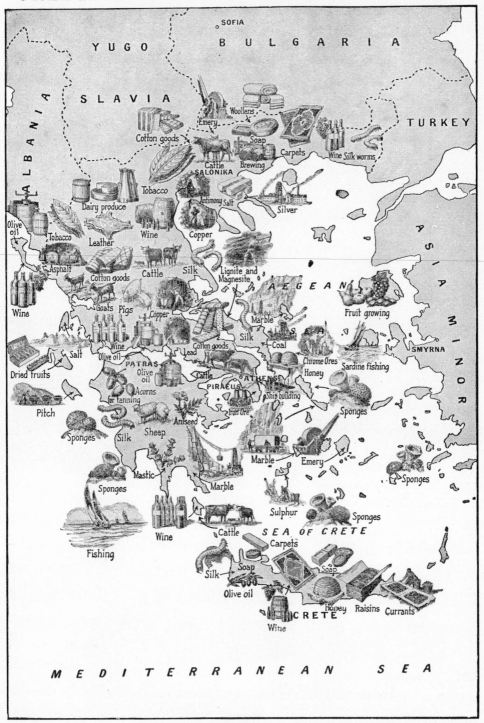

Greece, as can be seen by the pictures on this map, has many valuable industries. She needs only the blessings of peace and tranquillity to develop these, so that they may become of real importance not only to Greece herself, but also to the rest of Europe. Her trade in dried currants (small grapes) is very extensive.

HUGE GRAIN ELEVATORS IN THE TOWN OF BRAILA ON THE RIVER DANUBE

A FOREST OF DERRICKS IN THE OIL-PRODUCING REGION OF CAMPINA

THE PATRIARCHAL CATHEDRAL AT BUCHAREST, CAPITAL OF RUMANIA

A REST HOME FOR THE PEOPLE AT SINAIA, IN THE SOUTHERN CARPATHIANS

THE ATHENÉE, A FINE CONCERT HALL IN BUCHAREST

THE MODERN CATHEDRAL AT TIMISHOARA

THE CHURCH OF THE THREE SAINTS IN JASSY

THE COUNCIL BUILDING AT ORADEA, ON
THE RIVER CRISHUL REPEDE

ENGLISH PARK AT CRAIOVA, A TOWN IN
THE PROVINCE OF WALLACHIA

Many of our Rumania pictures are reproduced by courtesy of the Rumanian Legation in London

HOUSES SEEM TO RISE ONE ON TOP OF ANOTHER IN THE HILLSIDE TOWN OF TRNOVO,
ONCE CAPITAL OF BULGARIA

THE 19th-CENTURY ALEXANDER
NEVSKI CATHEDRAL IN SOFIA

THE TECHNICAL DEPARTMENT OF
SOFIA'S MODERN UNIVERSITY

THE RILA MONASTERY AT THE ENTRANCE TO THE DJUMAIA PASS IN THE BALKANS

SOFIA, CAPITAL OF BULGARIA, AS SEEN FROM THE BALCONY OF ITS UNIVERSITY

Many of our Bulgaria pictures are reproduced by courtesy of the Bulgarian Legation in London

BIRD'S-EYE VIEW OF RUMANIA AND BULGARIA

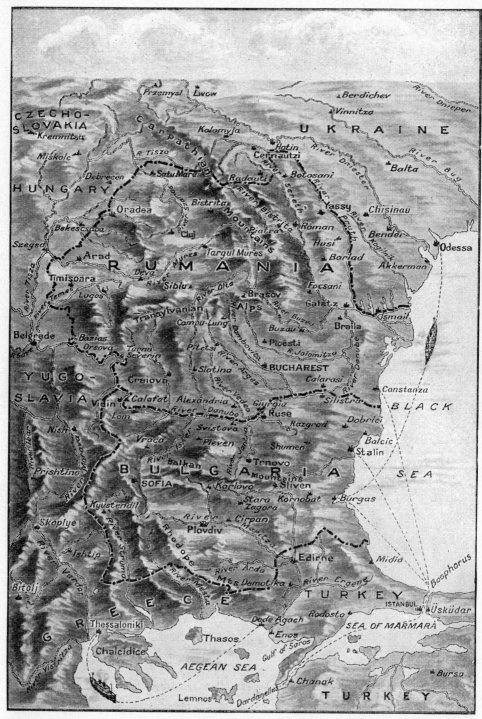

This map gives a relief picture of Rumania and Bulgaria. The principal rivers, mountains, cities, and towns are shown, and we see that both countries have a coastline only on the Black Sea, so that their vessels, before they can reach the high seas and main routes of the world's commerce, must pass through the Bosphorus, the Sea of Marmara, and the Dardanelles.

One Thousand Poems of All Times and All Countries

AHAB MOHAMMED

There are many beautiful stories in the history of the Arabian rulers, and most poets have at some time or other turned to the rich legends of the East for inspiring themes. Few of those stories are more attractive than that of Ahab Mohammed, which an American poet, James Matthew Legare (1823–59), set in this becoming dress of verse.

A PEASANT stood before a king, and
   said:
" My children starve, I come to thee for
   bread."
On cushions soft and silken sat enthroned
The king, and looked on him that prayed
   and moaned,
Who cried again: " For bread I come to
   thee! "
For grief, like wine, the tongue will render
   free.
Then said the prince with simple truth:
   " Behold,
I sit on cushions silken-soft, of gold
And wrought with skill the vessels which
   they bring
To fitly grace the banquet of a king,
But at my gate the Mede triumphant beats,
And die for food my people in the streets.
Yet no good father hears his child complain
And gives him stones for bread, for alms
   disdain.
Come, thou and I will sup together—
   come! "
The wondering courtiers saw—saw and
   were dumb!
Then followed with their eyes where Ahab
   led
With grace the humble guest, amazed, to
   share his bread.

Him, half-abashed, the royal host withdrew
Into a room, the curtained doorway
   through.
Silent behind the folds of purple closed,
In marble life the statues stood disposed;
From the high ceiling, perfume-breathing,
   hung
Lamps, rich, pomegranate-shaped, and
   golden-swung,
Gorgeous the board with massive metal
   shone,
Gorgeous with gems arose in front a throne:
These through the Orient lattice saw the
   sun.
If gold there was, of meat and bread was
   none
Save one small loaf; this stretched his
   hand and took
Ahab Mohammed, prayed to God, and
   broke:
One half his yearning nature bid him crave,
The other gladly to his guest he gave.
" I have no more to give," he cheerily
   said;
" With thee I share my only loaf of bread."
Humbly the stranger took the offered
   crumb,
Yet ate not of it, standing meek and dumb;
Then lifts his eyes. The wondering Ahab
   saw

POEMS · SONGS · BALLADS · VERSES AND RHYMES WITH MUSIC

His rags fall from him as the snow in thaw.
Resplendent, blue, those orbs upon him
    turned;
All Ahab's soul within him throbbed and
    burned.
"Ahab Mohammed," spoke the vision then,
" From this thou shalt be blessèd among
    men.
Go forth—thy gates the Mede bewildered
    flees,
And Allah thanks thy people on their knees.
He who gives somewhat does a worthy
    deed,
Of him the Recording Angel shall take
    heed.
But he that halves all that his house doth
    hold,
His deeds are more to God, yea, more than
    finest gold! "

TALKING IN THEIR SLEEP

Is this not a pretty poem? So simple and true! The hiding of life and its resurrection is one of the world's increasing wonders. The sympathy between outdoor things—trees, grass, and flowers—a sympathy limited and imperfect, is here daintily expressed by Edith M. Thomas (1854-1925).

You think I am dead,
    The apple tree said,
Because I have never a leaf to show—
    Because I stoop,
    And my branches droop,
And the dull grey mosses over me grow!
But I'm all alive in trunk and shoot;
    The buds of next May
    I fold away—
But I pity the withered grass at my root.

    You think I am dead,
    The quick grass said,
Because I have started with stem and blade!
    But under the ground
    I am safe and sound,
With the snow's thick blanket over me laid.
I'm all alive and ready to shoot
    Should the spring of the year
    Come dancing here—
But I pity the flower without branch or
    root.

    You think I am dead,
    A soft voice said,
Because not a branch or root I own!
    I never have died,
    But close I hide
In a plumy seed that the wind has sown.
Patient I wait through the long winter
    hours;
    You will see me again—
    I shall laugh at you then,
Out of the eyes of a hundred flowers.

THE APPLE WINDS

These charming verses, by Mr. Will H. Ogilvie, convey a lesson worth remembering, for in our care-free days of youth we are apt to welcome the winds that blow us good without thought of those to whom they may blow ill. The verses are printed with Mr. Ogilvie's permission.

I HAD no thought of stormy sky
    In days when I was small,
And all the world was bounded by
    Our ten-foot garden wall.
I never thought the storm-winds came
    From wrecks and ribboned sails;
I never knew them by their name
    Of equinoctial gales;
But sweeping round the orchard bends,
    Knee-deep in leaves of brown,
I only knew them as the friends
    That shook the apples down!

And I have travelled far and far
    And weary miles since then,
And battled where the storm-winds are
    That wreck the lives of men;
And back among the lime tree leaves,
    Grown gold before they fall,
I heard the song that autumn weaves
    When first the wild winds call;
And though their hand is chill and cold,
    Their face has winter's frown,
I know them for the friends of old
    That shook the apples down!

TO A BUTTERFLY

This little poem was composed by William Wordsworth at Grasmere on March 14, 1802, and it referred to the poet's childhood days spent in Cockermouth with his sister Dorothy, Emmeline being a fanciful name used by the poet instead of his sister's real name. It was true that Dorothy as a child used to enjoy chasing butterflies with her brother, and it was because she told him in later years that she had been afraid of brushing the dust off the insects' delicate wings that he wrote these verses.

STAY near me—do not take thy flight!
    A little longer stay in sight!
Much converse do I find in thee,
Historian of my infancy!
Float near me; do not yet depart!
    Dead times revive in thee:
Thou bring'st, gay creature as thou art,
A solemn image to my heart,
    My father's family!

Oh, pleasant, pleasant were the days,
The time when, in our childish plays,
My sister Emmeline and I
Together chased the butterfly!
A very hunter did I rush
    Upon the prey—with leaps and springs
I followed on from brake to bush,
But she, God love her, feared to brush
    The dust from off its wings.

MASSA'S IN DE COLD, COLD GROUND

The American Negro was conspicuous in the days of slavery for his loyalty to his master wherever he was treated with kindness. That feeling and the note of sentimental sadness which marks the race in certain moods are expressed in this famous lament, written by Stephen Collins Foster, who also composed the melodious wailing music to which it is sung. Foster died while the war of emancipation was in progress.

Round de meadows am a-ringing
  De darkeys' mournful song,
While de mocking-bird am singing
  Happy as the day am long.
Where de ivy am a-creeping
  O'er the grassy mound
Dere old massa am a-sleeping,
  Sleeping in de cold, cold ground.

      Down in de cornfield
        Hear dat mournful sound:
      All de darkeys am a-weeping—
        Massa's in de cold, cold ground.

When de autumn leaves were falling,
  When de days were cold,
'Twas hard to hear old massa calling
  'Cayse he was so weak and old.
Now de orange tree am blooming
  On de sandy shore,
Now de summer days am coming,
  Massa neber calls no more.

Massa make de darkeys love him
  'Cayse he was so kind;
Now dey sadly weep above him,
  Mourning 'cayse he leave dem behind.
I cannot work before tomorrow,
  'Cayse de tear-drop flow;
I try to drive away my sorrow
  Pickin' on de old banjo.

      Down in de cornfield
        Hear dat mournful sound:
      All de darkeys am a-weeping—
        Massa's in de cold, cold ground.

THE TWO ARMIES

Oliver Wendell Holmes teaches us here an old and familiar lesson. It is, perhaps, a poetic exaggeration to say the motto of valour's army is " Our glory is to slay." It is easy, too, to contrast the ruthless work of the fighters and the honour so readily awarded them with the merciful and often unnoticed ministration of the lovers of peace. But it is well that the poets who love the quiet ways of life should remind us of those who serve in the army of peace, as there are always too many ready to sing the praises of the fighters.

As Life's unending column pours
  Two marshalled hosts are seen,
Two armies on the trampled shores
  That death flows black between.

One marches to the drum-beat's roll,
  The wide-mouthed clarion's bray,
And bears upon a crimson scroll
  " Our glory is to slay."

One moves in silence by the stream,
  With sad yet watchful eyes,
Calm as the patient planet's gleam
  That walks the clouded skies.

Along its front no sabres shine,
  No blood-red pennons wave;
Its banner bears the single line
  " Our duty is to save."

For those no death-bed's lingering shade
  At Honour's trumpet-call,
With knitted brow and lifted blade,
  In Glory's arms they fall.

For these no clashing falchions bright,
  No stirring battle-cry;
The bloodless stabber calls by night—
  Each answers " Here am I ! "

For those the sculptor's laurelled bust,
  The builder's marble piles,
The anthems pealing o'er their dust
  Through long cathedral aisles.

For these the blossom-sprinkled turf
  That floods the lonely graves
When Spring rolls in her sea-green surf
  In flowery-foaming waves.

Two paths led upward from below,
  And angels wait above,
Who count each burning life-drop's flow,
  Each falling tear of Love.

Though from the hero's bleeding breast
  Her pulses Freedom drew,
Though the white lilies in her crest
  Sprang from that scarlet dew,

While Valour's haughty champions wait
  Till all their scars are shown,
Love walks unchallenged through the gate,
  To sit beside the throne!

A HEART TO KEEP

Over those who trust us in love we should watch with unfailing care, and think of them as of a beautiful marble cathedral, reserved sacred to pure, sweet thoughts. That is the idea expressed here, in smoothly chiselled lines, by Arthur O'Shaughnessy, a poet who died young in 1881.

If one should give me a heart to keep,
  With love for the golden key,
The giver might live at ease or sleep;
It should ne'er know pain, be weary, or weep,
  The heart watched over by me.

I would keep that heart as a temple fair,
  No heathen should look therein;
Its chaste marmoreal beauty rare
I only should know, and to enter there
  I must hold myself from sin.

THY WAY, NOT MINE, O LORD

Dr. Horatius Bonar, who was born in Edinburgh on December 19, 1808, and died on July 31, 1889, was a celebrated writer of hymns breathing the purest faith and hope. Other examples, besides the one which is here given, are " I heard the voice of Jesus say," and " A few more years shall roll."

THY way, not mine, O Lord,
    However dark it be;
Lead me by Thine own hand,
    Choose out the path for me.

Smooth let it be or rough,
    It will be still the best;
Winding or straight, it leads
    Right onward to Thy rest.

I dare not choose my lot;
    I would not if I might:
Choose Thou for me, my God,
    So shall I walk aright.

The kingdom that I seek
    Is Thine: so let the way
That leads to it be Thine,
    Else I must surely stray.

Take Thou my cup, and it
    With joy or sorrow fill,
As best to Thee may seem;
    Choose Thou my good and ill.

Choose Thou for me my friends,
    My sickness or my health;
Choose Thou my cares for me,
    My poverty or wealth.

Not mine, not mine the choice
    In things or great or small;
Be Thou my guide, my strength,
    My wisdom and my all.

THE IRISH HARPER

Thomas Campbell has in these favourite verses given us a pathetic and beautiful picture of the faithful friendship of a dog for its poor but kind master. It is no wonder that poets delight to praise the dog, whose friendship for its master is never affected by wealth or worldly position.

ON the green banks of Shannon, when
    Sheelah was nigh,
No blithe Irish lad was so happy as I;
No harp like my own could so cheerily
    play,
And wherever I went was my poor dog
    Tray.

When at last I was forced from my Sheelah
    to part
She said—while the sorrow was big at her
    heart:
" Oh, remember your Sheelah when far,
    far away,
And be kind, my dear Pat, to our poor
    dog Tray."

Poor dog, he was faithful and kind, to be
    sure,
And he constantly loved me although I
    was poor;
When the sour-looking folks sent me
    heartless away,
I had always a friend in my poor dog
    Tray.

When the road was so dark and the night
    was so cold,
And Pat and his dog were grown weary
    and old,
How snugly we slept in my old coat of
    grey,
And he licked me for kindness—my poor
    dog Tray.

Though my wallet was scant I remembered his case,
Nor refused my last crust to his pitiful
    face ;
But he died at my feet one cold winter's
    day,
And I played a sad lament for my poor
    dog Tray.

Where now shall I go, poor, forsaken, and
    blind ?
Can I find one to guide me so faithful and
    kind ?
To my sweet native village, so far, far
    away,
I can never more return with my poor dog
    Tray.

THE LAND OF NOD

No one ever remembered better than Robert Louis Stevenson the feelings and thoughts he had when he was a child. And he could put them into verse, too. When you are tired at night, suddenly you forget where you are, and you are in the Land of Nod. And there you remain till you wake up. When you are awake the Land of Nod disappears. Here the poet gives his recollections of these strange happenings.

FROM breakfast on all through the day
    At home among my friends I stay;
But every night I go abroad,
Afar into the land of Nod.

All by myself I have to go,
With none to tell me what to do—
All alone beside the streams
And up the mountain-sides of dreams.

The strangest things are there for me,
Both things to eat and things to see,
And many frightening sights abroad
Till morning in the land of Nod.

Try as I like to find the way,
I never can get back by day,
Nor can remember plain and clear
The curious music that I hear.

EVERY NIGHT I GO ABROAD, AFAR INTO THE LAND OF NOD.   See poem on page 5792.

FLEET STREET

In these lines the poet and novelist Sir Shane Leslie puts a wonderful thought that came to him in Fleet Street.

I NEVER see the newsboys run
  Amid the whirling street,
  With swift untiring feet,
To cry the latest venture done,
But I expect one day to hear
  Them cry the crack of doom
  And risings from the tomb,
With great Archangel Michael near,
And see them running from the Fleet
  As messengers of God,
  With Heaven's tidings shod
About their brave, unwearied feet.

TO THE MEMORY OF MY BELOVED MASTER, WILLIAM SHAKESPEARE

Here is a poem by Ben Jonson which disposes of all the ill-thinking people of later times who have declined to believe that Shakespeare could write the works that have always been known as his. Ben Jonson knew Shakespeare well. He was his friend and rival. Shakespeare died in 1616, and in 1623 his works were published by his theatrical friends. This is the introduction to the volume written by Jonson. No praise could be more unbounded. Ben Jonson, who had the privilege of knowing Shakespeare with personal intimacy, regarded him as the supremely great writer that the whole world has felt him to be through his books.

To draw no envy, Shakespeare, on thy
    name
Am I thus ample to thy book and fame;
While I confess thy writings to be such
As neither Man nor Muse can praise too
    much!
'Tis true, and all men's suffrage. But
    these ways
Were not the paths I meant unto thy
    praise!

    .   .   .   .   .

            Soul of the Age!
The applause, delight, the wonder of our
    stage!
My Shakespeare, rise! I will not lodge
    thee by
Chaucer, or Spenser, or bid Beaumont lie
A little further off to make thee room:
Thou art a monument, without a tomb,
And art alive still, while thy book doth
    live,
And we have wits to read, and praise to
    give.

    That I not mix thee so, my brain
    excuses;
I mean with great, but disproportioned
    Muses:
For, if I thought my judgment were of
    years,
I should commit thee surely with thy
    peers,

And tell how far thou didst our Lily
    outshine,
Or sporting Kyd, or Marlowe's mighty line.

    And though thou hadst small Latin
    and less Greek,
From thence, to honour thee, I would not
    seek
For names; but call forth thundering
    Aeschylus,
Euripides, and Sophocles to us,
Pacuvius, Accius, him of Cordova dead,
To life again, to hear thy buskin tread,
And shake a stage: or, when thy socks
    were on,
Leave thee alone, for the comparison
Of all that insolent Greece, or haughty
    Rome
Sent forth; or since did from their ashes
    come.

    Triumph, my Britain! Thou hast one
    to show,
To whom all scenes of Europe homage owe.
He was not of an age, but for all time!
And all the Muses still were in their prime
When, like Apollo, he came forth to warm
Our ears; or, like a Mercury, to charm.

    Nature herself was proud of his designs,
And joyed to wear the dressing of his lines!
Which were so richly spun, and woven so
    fit,
As, since, she will vouchsafe no other wit!
The merry Greek, tart Aristophanes,
Neat Terence, witty Plautus, now not
    please;
But antiquated and deserted lie,
As they were not of Nature's family.

    Yet must I not give Nature all: thy art,
My gentle Shakespeare, must enjoy a part.
For though the poet's matter Nature be,
His art doth give the fashion. And that he
Who casts to write a living line must sweat
(Such as thine are), and strike the second
    heat
Upon the Muse's anvil; turn the same
(And himself with it) that he thinks to
    frame;
Or for the laurel he may gain a scorn,
    For a good poet's made as well as born.

And such wert thou! Look how the
    father's face
Lives in his issue; even so the race
Of Shakespeare's mind and manners
    brightly shines
In his well-turnèd and true-filèd lines:

In each of which he seems to shake a lance!
As brandished at the eyes of Ignorance.

Sweet Swan of Avon!   What a sight it
were
To see thee in our waters yet appear,
And make those flights upon the banks of
Thames,
That so did take Eliza and our James.

But stay!   I see thee in the Hemisphere
Advanced, and made a Constellation
there!
Shine forth, thou Star of Poets, and with
rage,
Or influence, chide or cheer the drooping
stage:
Which, since thy flight from hence, hath
mourned like night,
And despairs day, but for thy volume's
light.

HARP OF THE MOUNTAIN LAND

Mrs. Hemans, whose poetry was very popular in the early
nineteenth century and is still widely quoted, lived in
Wales in her youth. She did well to write this enthusiastic
poem about the power of Welsh song, for it has always
persisted, and there is no more poetical race than the Welsh.
The Hirlas is a drinking horn.   Mona means Anglesey.

Harp of the mountain land! sound
forth again
As when the foaming Hirlas horn was
crowned,
And warrior hearts beat proudly to the
strain,
And the bright mead at Owain's feast
went round:
Wake with the spirit and the power of
yore!
Harp of the ancient hills! be heard once
more!

Thy tones are not to cease!   The Roman
came
O'er the blue waters with his thousand
oars:
Through Mona's oaks he sent the wasting
flame;
The Druid shrines lay prostrate on our
shores:
All gave their ashes to the wind and
sea—
Ring out, thou harp! he could not silence
thee.

Thy tones are not to cease!   The Saxon
passed,
His banners floated on Eryri's gales;
But thou wert heard above the trumpet's
blast,

E'en when his towers rose loftiest o'er
the vales!
Thine was the voice that cheered the
brave and free;
They had their hills, their chainless hearts,
and thee.

Those were dark years!   They saw the
valiant fall,
The rank weeds gathering round the
chieftain's board,
The hearth left lonely in the ruined hall;
Yet power was thine—a gift in every
chord!
Call back that spirit to the days of peace,
Thou noble harp! thy tones are not to
cease!

THE POET'S MISSION

The idea that the poet is the interpreter to other men of
Nature and of Man is here picturesquely expressed by Jean
Ingelow, the Victorian poet, who died in 1897.

Quoth the Cedar to the Reeds and
Rushes:
" Water grass, you know not what I do;
Know not of my storms and of my hushes;
And I know not you."

Quoth the Reeds and Rushes: "Wind,
O waken!
Breathe, O Wind, and set our answer
free;
For we have no voice, by you forsaken
For the Cedar Tree."

Quoth the Earth, at midnight, to the
Ocean:
" Wilderness of water lost to view,
Naught you are to me but sounds of
motion;
I am naught to you."

Quoth the Ocean: " Dawn, O Fairest,
Clearest,
Touch me with thy golden fingers bland;
For I have no smile, till thou appearest,
For the lovely land."

Quoth the Hero, dying, whelmed in glory:
" Many blame me; few have under-
stood;
Ah! my folk! to you I leave a story—
Make its meaning good."

Quoth the Folk: " Sing, poet; teach us;
prove us;
Surely we shall learn the meaning then.
Wound us with a pain divine, O move us
For this man of men."

JUDAS ISCARIOT

Robert Buchanan (1841–1901) was a poet, novelist, and dramatist, born in England of Scottish parentage. One of his finest poems is an imaginative picture in ballad form of Judas Iscariot after he had taken his own life in remorse for his treachery to Jesus. We give here the last half of the poem. The first half tells how the soul of Judas takes up his body and searches in all kinds of wild and lonely places for somewhere to bury it where it will never be seen. For months and years he wanders, carrying the body and finding no place that will serve as a grave. Then, at last, he sees a far-off light across the lonely waste, and, creeping towards it, he reaches it after more days of rain and more nights of rushing wind; and the description proceeds.

Twas the soul of Judas Iscariot,
   Strange, and sad, and tall,
Stood all alone at dead of night
   Before a lighted hall.

And the wold was white with snow,
   And his foot-marks black and damp,
And the ghost of the silvern moon arose,
   Holding her yellow lamp.

And the icicles were on the eaves,
   And the walls were deep with white,
And the shadows of the guests within
   Passed on the window light.

The shadows of the wedding guests
   Did strangely come and go,
And the body of Judas Iscariot
   Lay stretched along the snow.

The body of Judas Iscariot
   Lay stretched along the snow;
Twas the soul of Judas Iscariot
   Ran swiftly to and fro.

To and fro, and up and down,
   He ran so swiftly there,
As round and round the frozen Pole
   Glideth the lean white bear.

. . . Twas the Bridegroom sat at the table-
   head,
   And the lights burnt bright and clear:
" Oh, who is that," the Bridegroom said,
   " Whose weary feet I hear?"

Twas one looked from the lighted hall,
   And answered soft and slow,
" It is a wolf runs up and down
   With a black track in the snow."

The Bridegroom in his robe of white
   Sat at the table-head:
" Oh, who is that who moans without?"
   The blessèd Bridegroom said.

Twas one looked from the lighted hall,
   And answered fierce and low,
" 'Tis the soul of Judas Iscariot
   Gliding to and fro."

Twas the soul of Judas Iscariot
   Did hush itself and stand,
And saw the Bridegroom at the door,
   With a light in his hand.

The Bridegroom stood in the open door,
   And he was clad in white,
And far within the Lord's Supper
   Was spread so broad and bright.

The Bridegroom shaded his eyes and
   looked,
   And his face was bright to see:
" What dost thou here at the Lord's Supper
   With thy body's sins? " said he.

Twas the soul of Judas Iscariot
   Stood black, and sad, and bare:
" I have wandered many nights and days;
   There is no light elsewhere."

Twas the wedding guests cried out within,
   And their eyes were fierce and bright:
" Scourge the soul of Judas Iscariot
   Away into the night! "

The Bridegroom stood in the open door,
   And he waved hands still and slow,
And the third time that he waved his hands
   The air was thick with snow.

And of every flake of falling snow,
   Before it touched the ground,
There came a dove, and a thousand doves
   Made sweet sound.

Twas the body of Judas Iscariot
   Floated away full fleet,
And the wings of the doves that bare it off
   Were like its winding-sheet.

Twas the Bridegroom stood at the open
   door,
   And beckoned, smiling sweet;
Twas the soul of Judas Iscariot
   Stole in, and fell at his feet.

" The Holy Supper is spread within,
   And the many candles shine,
And I have waited long for thee
   Before I poured the wine! "

The supper wine is poured at last,
   The lights burn bright and fair,
Iscariot washes the Bridegroom's feet,
   And dries them with his hair.

PREPAREDNESS

This is a fine example of condensed philosophy from Edwin Markham (1852–1940), a gifted American poet.

For all your days prepare,
   And meet them ever alike:
When you are the anvil, bear;
   When you are the hammer, strike.

REQUIEM

Robert Louis Stevenson died on December 3, 1894, at
Vailima, on the island of Upolu, Samoa, and was buried
on the summit of the precipitous and wooded Mount Vaea.
A lifelong wanderer, he had already sent home this suggested
epitaph, which is inscribed on his hilltop grave.

UNDER the wide and starry sky
   Dig the grave and let me lie;
Glad did I live and gladly die,
   And I laid me down with a will.

This be the verse you grave for me:
   Here he lies where he longed to be;
Home is the sailor, home from sea,
   And the hunter home from the hill.

WHAT CAN A LITTLE CHAP DO?

The writer of this admirable poem for boys, John Oxenham,
put much stimulating thought and advice into his verse,
but he never succeeded better than in this fine, plain, and
truly helpful outline of the ideal boyhood.

WHAT can a little chap do
   For his country and for you?
What can a little chap do?

He can play a straight game all through:
   That's one good thing he can do.

He can fight like a Knight
For the Truth and the Right;
   That's another good thing he can do.

He can shun all that's mean,
He can keep himself clean,
Both without and within;
   That's a very fine thing he can do.

His soul he can brace
Against everything base,
And the trace will be seen
All his life in his face;
   That's an excellent thing he can do.

He can look to the Light,
He can keep his thought white,
He can fight the great fight,
He can do with his might
What is good in God's sight;
   Those are truly great things he can do.

Though his years be but few,
If he keep himself true
He can march in the queue
Of the Good and the Great,
Who battled with fate
And won through;
   That's a wonderful thing he can do.

And in each little thing
He can follow the King;
Yes, in each smallest thing
He can follow the King,
He can follow the Christ, the King.

GOD'S FOOL

Hate is the most repulsive thing in the world. It is hateful.
We ought to see it in all its ugliness. In this sonnet Elliot
Belestier, an American, pictures its deformity and folly.

I DREAMED one I had loved did me foul
   wrong,
   Till with relentless hate my soul was
     spent;
   When lo, the veil of mortal sight was
     rent
From all the universe, where weak and
   strong
Alike poured forth their voice in praiseful
   song,
   Save only one—a motley clown, age-
     bent,
   Vice-scarred, whose loathly, ghoulish
     look was lent
To his blank, idiot face by practice long.
A gaudy bauble in his hand he bore,
   And to belabour angels vainly tried;
Each stroke, rebounding, smote the
   striker sore.
   A homing angel passed; to him I cried:
   " What is yon fiend-faced clown, and
     what his state? "
" He is God's fool," he said; " his name is
   Hate! "

THE SEED SHOP

This poem, by Muriel Stuart, shows with dramatic power
how much poetry lies hidden in things that we, under the
influence of deadening custom, regard as commonplace.

HERE in a quiet and dusty room they lie,
   Faded as crumbled stone or shifting
     sand,
Forlorn as ashes, shrivelled, scentless, dry,
   Meadows and gardens running through
     my hand.

Dead that shall quicken at the call of
   Spring,
   Sleepers to stir beneath June's magic
     kiss,
Though birds pass over, unremembering,
   And no bee seek here roses that were his.

In this brown husk a dale of hawthorn
   dreams,
   A cedar in this narrow cell is thrust
That will drink deeply of a century's
   streams,
   These lilies shall make summer on my
     dust.

Here in their safe and simple house of
   death,
   Sealed in their shells a million roses leap;
Here I can blow a garden with my breath,
   And in my hand a forest lies asleep.

PICTURES IN THE FIRE

Many people have been attracted by the fancy of seeing pictures in the fire made by their own imagination. This poem gives an example of it by Adelaide Anne Procter, a daughter of the poet who wrote under the pen-name of Barry Cornwall. The pictures she feigns to see partly make up a kind of panorama of religions as they were conceived through the ages—dragons attacked by heroes, Pluto in the nether-world; the serpent of temptation; the Child that brought hope to the world—but they are mixed with other scenes, and the interpretation is not quite clear.

WHAT is it you ask me, darling?
　　All my stories, child, you know;
I have no strange dreams to tell you,
　　Pictures I have none to show.

Tell you glorious scenes of travel?
　　Nay, my child, that cannot be:
I have seen no foreign countries,
　　Marvels none on land or sea.

Yet strange sights in truth I witness,
　　And I gaze until I tire;
Wondrous pictures, changing ever,
　　As I look into the fire.

There, last night, I saw a cavern,
　　Black as pitch; within it lay,
Coiled in many folds, a dragon,
　　Glaring as if turned at bay.

And a knight in dismal armour
　　On a wingèd eagle came
To do battle with this dragon;
　　And his crest was all of flame.

As I gazed the dragon faded,
　　And, instead, sate Pluto crowned
By a lake of burning fire;
　　Spirits dark were crouching round.

That was gone, and lo! before me
　　A cathedral vast and grim;
I could almost hear the organ
　　Peal along the arches dim.

As I watched the wreathèd pillars
　　Groves of stately palms arose,
And a group of swarthy Indians
　　Stealing on some sleepy foes.

Stay; a cataract, glancing brightly,
　　Dashed and sparkled; and beside
Lay a broken marble monster,
　　Mouth and eyes were staring wide.

Then I saw a maiden wreathing
　　Starry flowers in garden sweet;
Did she see the fiery serpent
　　That was wrapped about her feet?

That fell crashing all and vanished;
　　And I saw two armies close—
I could almost hear the clarions,
　　And the shouting of the foes.

They were gone, and lo! bright angels,
　　On a barren mountain wild,
Raised appealing arms to Heaven,
　　Bearing up a little child.

And I gazed, and gazed, and slowly
　　Gathered in my eyes sad tears,
And the fiery pictures bore me
　　Back through distant dreams of years.

Once again I tasted sorrow,
　　With past joy was once more gay,
Till the shade had gathered round me,
　　And the fire had died away.

BEATI ILLI

John Addington Symonds, a brilliant man of letters and a poet who died in 1893, was very frail in health, but his writing always had a conspicuously manly strain that is well illustrated in the following verses. The meaning of the title is " Blessed are they," as in the Beatitudes.

BLEST is the man whose heart and hands
　　are pure!
He hath no sickness that he shall not cure,
No sorrow that he may not well endure:
His feet are steadfast and his hope is sure.

Oh, blest is he who ne'er hath sold his soul,
Whose will is perfect, and whose word is
　　whole,
Who hath not paid to common sense the toll
Of self-disgrace, nor owned the world's
　　control!

Through clouds and shadows of the
　　darkest night
He will not lose a glimmering of the light,
Nor, though the sun of day be shrouded
　　quite,
Swerve from the narrow path to left or
　　right.

HEY, NONNY!

In these tuneful verses Charles Kingsley, the famous poet, novelist, and preacher, gives us the helpful thought that we can make of each day a new beginning for our lives.

THE world goes up and the world goes
　　down,
　　And the sunshine follows the rain;
And yesterday's sneer and yesterday's
　　frown
　　　Can never come over again,
　　　　Sweet wife;
　　No, never come over again.

For woman is warm though man be cold,
　　And the night will hallow the day!
Till the heart which at even was weary
　　and old
　　　Can rise in the morning gay,
　　　　Sweet wife;
　　To its work in the morning gay.

THERE WERE THREE LITTLE KITTENS

There were three lit-tle kit-tens Put on their mit-tens, To eat some Christ-mas Pie.
Miaw wow! Miaw wow! Miaw! Miaw! Miaw!

These three little kittens
They lost their mittens,
And they began to cry:
Miaw! Miaw! Miaw! Miaw! Miaw!

Go, naughty kittens,
And find your mittens,
Or you shan't have any pie!
Miaw! Miaw! Miaw! Miaw! Miaw!

These three little kittens,
They found their mittens,
And joyfully did cry:
Miaw! Miaw! Miaw! Miaw! Miaw!

Oh, Granny dear,
Our mittens are here,
Make haste and cut up the pie!
Purr-rr! Purr-rr! Purr-rr-rr!

LITTLE VERSES FOR VERY LITTLE PEOPLE

BABY AT PLAY

Brow bender, Eye peeper,
    Nose smeller, Mouth eater,
Chin chopper,
Knock at the door: peep in,
Lift up the latch: walk in.

WEATHER WISDOM

Evening red and morning grey
    Set the traveller on his way.
Evening grey and morning red
Bring the rain upon his head.

WHEN GOOD KING ARTHUR RULED

When good King Arthur ruled this land
    He was a goodly king;
He stole three pecks of barley meal
    To make a bag-pudding.

A bag-pudding the queen did make,
    And stuffed it well with plums:
And in it put great lumps of fat,
    As big as my two thumbs.

The king and queen did eat thereof,
    And noblemen beside;
And what they could not eat that night
    The queen next morning fried.

LADYBIRD, FLY!

Ladybird, fly!
    Your father's hanging high;
Your mother's shut in Moscow Town,
Moscow Town is burning down.
    Ladybird, fly!

TWELVE HUNTSMEN

Twelve huntsmen, with horns and
    hounds,
Hunting over other men's grounds.
Eleven ships sailing o'er the main,
I wish them all safe home again.
Ten comets in the sky,
Some low and some high.
Nine peacocks in the air,
I wonder how they all come there.
Eight joiners in the hall
Working with the tools and all;
Seven lobsters in a dish
As fresh as any heart could wish.
Six beetles against the wall,
Close by a woman's apple-stall.
Five puppies of our dog Ball,
Who daily for their breakfast call.
Four horses stuck in a bog.
Three monkeys tied to a clog.
Two puddings would choke a dog,
With a gaping, wide-mouthed,
    waddling frog.

THE BOGIE MAN

A roguey, poguey Bogie Man goes
    dancing through our housey-pouse;
A roguey, poguey Bogie Man goes
    dancing through our house.
He takes himself and shakes himself till
    into bits he breaks himself!
A roguey, poguey Bogie Man goes
    dancing through our house.

A roguey, poguey Bogie Man goes roving
    through our housey-pouse;
A roguey, poguey Bogie Man goes
    roving through our house.
He bends himself and bends himself, and
    breaks himself and mends himself!
A roguey, poguey Bogie Man goes
    roving through our house.

THE BREAKFAST SONG

At five o'clock he milks the cow,
    The busy farmer's man.
At six o'clock he strains the milk,
    And pours it in the can.

At seven o'clock the milkman's horse
    Must go to town—" Get up! "
At eight o'clock Nurse Karen pours
    The milk in baby's cup.

At five o'clock the baby sleeps
    As sound as sound can be.
At six o'clock he laughs and shouts,
    So wide awake is he.

At seven o'clock he's in his bath,
    At eight o'clock he's dressed,
Just when the milk is ready, too,
    So you can guess the rest.

GRAMMAR IN RHYME

Three little words you often see
    Are articles A, An, and The.
A Noun is the name of anything,
As School or Garden, Hoop or Swing.
Adjectives tell the kind of Noun,
As Great, Small, Pretty, White, or Brown.
Instead of Nouns the Pronouns stand:
Her head, His face, Your arm, My hand.
Verbs tell of something being done:
To Read, Count, Laugh, Sing, Jump, or
    Run.
How things are done the Adverbs tell,
As Slowly, Quickly, Ill, or Well.
Conjunctions join the words together,
As men And women, wind And weather.
The Preposition stands before
A noun, as In or Through a door,
The Interjection shows surprise,
As Oh! how pretty! Ah! how wise!
The Whole are called nine parts of speech,
Which reading, writing, speaking, teach.

Imperishable Thoughts of Men Enshrined in the Books of the World
Chaucer's Canterbury Tales

WE have now glanced over the Literatures of the World, modern and ancient, and in the remaining chapters of this Group we shall look at some of the masterpieces of our English literature in greater detail. The first great English book, The Canterbury Tales, by the first great English poet, Geoffrey Chaucer, naturally has precedence. Chaucer ranks among our poets almost as high as the greatest, because he had a deep sense of humanity, a fine love of the beautiful in Nature, and a rare sense of humour. His best work was his Canterbury Tales, twenty-four in number, told by a band of pilgrims on their way to Canterbury, from the Tabard Inn in Southwark to the shrine of Thomas à Becket. Chaucer includes himself in the company. In an introduction he describes each of the pilgrims, who together make up a group of fourteenth century men and women typical of almost the whole range of English society. Here we retell six of the stories. The English language has changed much since Chaucer's time. Many syllables were pronounced at that time which now are silent, and the syllables were accented differently in words which were then newly brought into use from the French language. In our quotations accented syllables are marked. If Chaucer's lines are read aright they always flow smoothly, for he was a master of metre.

THE PATIENCE OF GRISELDA
The Tale Told by the Clerk

A CLERK in Chaucer's time meant a student, or any learned person. We still speak of a clergyman as a Clerk in Holy Orders. This is the story told by the student to his fellow-pilgrims.

A gifted but pleasure-loving nobleman named Walter, lord of the noble country of Saluces, in Italy, was asked by his subjects to marry, so that an heir might be left to them when he had gone. Near by his palace was a little village, which the marquis passed through whenever he went hunting.

Among the poor folk of this village dwelled a man called Janicula, who had a daughter, " the fairest under the sun." This humble maiden, whose name was Griselda, was as virtuous and dutiful and hard-working as she was beautiful. Often, when on his way to the chase, had the marquis's eye rested on Griselda, and, bearing in mind his people's wish, he determined that she should be his wife.

He had fixed a day for his wedding, as his people had desired, but the day came and still no one knew who was to be the bride.

All preparations were made for the ceremony. Costly dresses were made, gems prepared for his lady that was to be, and a gallant company invited to the feast. Then a brave procession, headed by the marquis, set out from the palace to escort the bride. The marquis led the way to the little village.

Here Griselda was busily engaged getting her household tasks done, so that she might afterwards stand at her father's door and see the wedding procession. As she was setting out to draw water at the well the marquis stopped the procession at her rude dwelling, and, calling her by name, asked for her father. Griselda answered that he was within, and then brought him forward to speak with the grand visitor.

After conferring with her father, the marquis asked Griselda if she would marry him, giving him all obedience. Griselda pleaded her unworthiness of so much honour, but replied that if it was her lord's will she would marry him and obey him in all things. Then the marquis, taking her hand, led her forth from the hut, and said to his people, " This is my wife. Honour and love her as you love me."

Griselda was straightway dressed in royal robes, and, looking more lovely than ever, was set on a beautiful horse, on which she rode to the castle, where the marriage was celebrated with much feasting and merriment.

ROMANCE · HISTORIES · DRAMAS · ESSAYS · WORLD CLASSICS

Walter and she then lived for a time in great happiness, Griselda winning all hearts. Then was Walter moved to try her obedience sorely. When a little daughter was born to them he told her that his people were displeased, and that she was the cause of the trouble. Obedient to her husband's wish, Griselda gave up her child, thinking she would never see it any more. When a son was born, him also she gave up. Then the marquis, chiding her with her lowly origin, though her conduct was such that one born and reared to fill a great position might have been proud of it, said that she must return to her father to make way for another whom he was to marry. In this, as in all other things, Griselda was submissive to her lord.

The people, who loved her, were angry at the marquis's cruelty. But when the new bride came in state with her brother from Bologna, and the people saw that she was fairer and younger than Griselda, they, with the fickle hearts of the crowd, thought that the marquis had done well.

Yet was Griselda to be further tried, for the marquis sent for her to greet the new arrivals, because she alone knew how such ceremony should be carried out. So in her humble attire Griselda went back to the castle to obey her cruel lord's behest. And all the guests wondered who this humble and beautiful lady was that knew such honour and such reverence. At last, when the feast was spread, the marquis called for Griselda, and, as if in jest, asked her how she liked his new wife.

" Right well, my lord," quoth she; " for in good fay,
A fairer saw I never none than she.
I pray to God give her prosperity;
And so hope I, that He will to you send

Pleasaunce enough unto your lifé's end.
One thing warn I you, and beseech also,
Hurté not ever with no tormenting
This tender maiden, as ye have done me;
For she is fostered in her nourishing,
More tenderly, and to my supposing
She coulde not adversity endure
As could a pooré fostered créature."

And when Walter saw her patience under this great trial his heart was at length touched.

" 'Tis enough, Griselda ! " he cried. " Be no more afraid. Now know I, dear wife, your steadfastness." He took her in his arms, and sought to comfort her, so overcome was she at what he said. He told her that it was her own daughter whom she had just received as his new bride, and that the boy was her son. He had sent the two to Bologna, where they had been fittingly cared for and brought up secretly. Griselda was then dressed in the royal robes; there was great rejoicing, and the rest of her life was full of happiness. Says the poet:

Full many a year in high prosperity
Lived these two in concord and in rest,
And richly his daughter married he
Unto a lord, one of the worthiest
Of all Italy; and then in peace and rest
His wife's father in his court he keepeth,
Till that the soul out of his body creepeth.
His son succeedeth in his heritage,
In rest and peace after his father's day;
And fortunate was eke in marriage,
Though he put not his wife in such a say.
This world is not so strong, no, by my fay,
As it hath been, in oldé timés yore,
And hearken what this author saith therefore.
This story is said, not for that wives should
Follow Griselda in her humility,
For this could not be borne, no, tho' they would ;
But for that every wight in his degree
Shouldé be constant in adversity
As was Griselda.

THE FOX REPAID IN HIS OWN COIN
The Tale Told by the Priest

THERE was once a poor widow, in the little yard attached to whose dwelling there lived a very fine cock. His name was Chanticleer.

One morning this bird awoke with terror, and told his mate, Pertelot, of a horrible dream which he had had, of a beast like a hound that threatened him. Dame Pertelot laughed her Chanticleer's

fears to scorn. It was, said she, the result of indigestion, for which she suggested that he should take certain remedies.

While Chanticleer was enumerating stories of dreams that had come true, he looked on Dame Pertelot's face, and, taking courage, begged that they should talk of cheerful things. By this time daylight had come, and, descending from his perch, Chanticleer strutted around as fierce as a lion, chuckling whenever he found a corn.

But one day, as he was proudly walking about the yard, crowing at the sun, he spied a fox that had crept in the night before and hidden in a bed of herbs. Then Chanticleer, reminded of his dream, would have fled, but the fox, addressing him, said:

"Gentle sir, alas! why would ye go? Be not afraid of me. I am your friend. I only came to hear you sing, for, truly, to you as sweet a voice is given as any angel hath that is in heaven. Your father and your mother both have been in my house. I never heard anyone except you sing so well as your father did. Let us hear, now, if you can imitate your father."

Chanticleer, much flattered by the remarks of the sly fox, stood high upon his toes, stretched his neck, made his eyes to close, and began to crow right loudly. Then Dan Russel the fox, jumping up, seized him by the throat, and fled with him towards his quiet home in the wood. Such an alarm was then raised by Dame Pertelot and the other hens that the widow and her daughters ran out of their dwelling and, seeing how matters stood, called the neighbours, who joined in the chase. Jack Straw and all his company never made such a to-do as was caused by the chase after the fox and Chanticleer. But as he was lying helpless in fear on the fox's back the cock thought of a plan.

"Dear sir," said he to his captor, "if I were you I would turn on yon proud fellows and tell them that, now I am near the wood, the cock shall here abide, and I will surely eat him, when I choose, whatever you may do."

"In faith," declared the fox, "it shall be done."

But as he spoke the cock slipped from his mouth and quickly flew high up on a tree out of reach. The fox then cried that he was sorry for frightening the cock. He did it, he said, with no base intent; and if Chanticleer would only come down again he would tell him why he had acted as he had done.

But Chanticleer replied that he had been deceived once and would not be deceived again. And so the fox was paid in his own coin—flattery.

THE STRANGE ADVENTURES OF A PRINCESS
The Tale Told by the Lawyer

CONSTANCE, the daughter of the Emperor of Rome, was of such goodness and beauty that, when travellers returned from that city, they could not sing her praises too highly.

The Sultan of Syria heard of her from his merchants, and was so affected by their reports that he sent word to her father offering to become Christian, with all his nobles, if only he might obtain the lady's hand in marriage.

The marriage took place; but the Sultan's mother, who was secretly opposed to the union, invited the bride and bridegroom, and all the Christian knights who accompanied them from Rome, to a great feast, at which she caused them to be treacherously murdered, all save Constance. Her she sent adrift to sea in a rudderless boat, with all the rich wedding gifts and a store of food and raiment.

In this frail bark Constance was driven far, and finally cast on the shores of Northumberland. Here she was found by the constable of a castle which stood near, and he and his wife Hermyngyld befriended her and became Christians.

A young knight of Northumberland, being refused by Constance, sought to bring her to a shameful death. He killed Hermyngyld secretly and accused Constance of the crime. She was tried before King Alla of Northumberland, whose gentle heart was touched with pity by her tears. A miracle occurred, which was thought to prove her innocence; so the false knight was put to death, and she became King Alla's wife.

But Alla had a mother, who was bitterly opposed to this marriage, and in her son's absence had Constance once more sent adrift with her baby boy. When King Alla discovered this, he killed his wicked mother with his own hand, and gave himself up to grief and lamentation. Meanwhile, Constance and her little son Maurice were rescued from a heathen land on which they had been cast, and eventually taken to Rome, where they were befriended by a kindly senator and his wife.

All this time Constance kept her pitiful story to herself, but her goodness caused her to be beloved by all.

Then King Alla, smitten with repentance for the death of his mother, journeyed on a pilgrimage to Rome, where he was received by the very senator who had befriended Constance; and, being invited to a feast by Alla, the senator took young Maurice with him.

Attracted by the child's face, Alla asked as to the boy's history. Musing on all that the senator could tell him, and full of thoughts of the wife he mourned as one that was dead, Alla afterwards went as a guest to the senator's house. Here Alla and Constance met, and knew one another immediately. Constance, who thought it was by Alla's orders she had been cast adrift, sank down in a swoon. Then the truth became known to her concerning the treachery of King Alla's mother; and, husband and wife being reconciled, Constance made herself known to her father, the Emperor; and so at last all were come to happiness.

Alla shortly after took his wife back to England. But only a little while in joy and pleasure lived Alla and his Constance before Alla died.

Constance then returned, for the last time, to Rome, where in course of years Maurice was made Emperor ; and the remainder of her days were passed in acts of virtue and charity, so that she died, as she had lived, beloved of all.

THE MEN WHO WENT TO KILL DEATH

The Tale Told by the Pardoner

IN those days there were men who were permitted to sell to others, in the name of the Pope, " pardons " for their sins. Such a pardon was known as a Papal indulgence. The men who sold these were called Pardoners. Here is the story told by the Pardoner whom Chaucer includes among his pilgrim group.

In Flanders lived a company of young revellers who practised all forms of folly and wickedness. Three of these ne'er-do-wells were one day seated in a tavern drinking, when a bell was heard tolling for a man who was dead. One thereupon called out to his servant to get for them the name of the dead man. The varlet replied that he had no need to go out to learn who it was that was dead.

" It was," said he, " told me two hours before you came here. The dead man was an old comrade of yours, and he was slain at night as he sat on his bench drinking by a silent thief men call Death, who hath killed a thousand of pestilence in this country."

The lad's story was confirmed by the taverner, who added that Death had that year slain men, women, and children, peasants and pages, within a great village a mile away.

At this one of the roysterers invited his fellows to join with him that they might seek out Death and slay him. And the three set out on their errand towards the village spoken of. On their way they met an old man, who besought their mercy.

" Nay, old churl," said they, " tell us where this same Death is that killeth all our friends, or thou shalt die."

" Now, sirs," replied the old man, " if ye be so eager to find Death turn up this crooked way, and you will find him in yonder grove beneath an oak tree, where I left him."

On learning this the three rowdies ran in the direction indicated, and, coming to the tree, found a great store of golden florins piled up. No longer did they think of their quest of Death, but forthwith sat down by the precious hoard.

" Fortune," said the youngest of the three, " has given us this treasure that we may live in mirth and jollity. It must be carried home to my house or to yours by night, because if men saw us with it in the daytime we should be hanged for carrying what is our own."

He proposed that they should draw lots to decide which of them should go to the town for food and wine, while the other two kept watch over the treasure. The lot fell on the speaker. When he had departed, one of the others said to his companion that it would be so much better if the gold were divided only between two of them for the shares would be larger.

" Two of us are stronger than one," said he, " and when our companion returns do you engage him, as it were, in a playful wrestling bout, when I will strike him with my dagger, and if you despatch him with yours, then all this gold shall be ours to gratify all our wishes and enable us to play at dice as much as we like." The second villain agreed to this dastardly plan.

But wicked thoughts entered also the mind of the youngest as he went towards the town, and, thinking how he could gain the gold for himself, he bethought him of the apothecary's, where, on the pretext that he wanted to kill rats, he bought some powerful poison.

Next he borrowed three bottles, into two of which he poured the poison. Filling then the bottles with wine, he returned to his companions, to whom he purposed giving the poisoned wine, drinking himself from the third and harmless bottle. When the other villains had killed him, as they had planned to do, they said, " Let us sit down and drink and make merry before we bury him." And one, taking up a bottle, one of those containing poison, drank from it and passed it to his companion, who also drank.

So the words of the old man who had told them that they would find Death under the oak tree were proved to be true.

THE ROMANCE OF THE LADY EMELYE

The Tale Told by the Knight

ONCE upon a time in ancient Greece there lived a great and powerful duke named Theseus.

No greater conqueror than he lived under the sun. He defeated the Amazons of Scythia, and married their Queen Hippolyta, whose fair young sister Emelye he took captive. On his way back to Athens he was met by weeping women, who besought his help, because the tyrant Creon had massacred their husbands and captured the throne of Thebes.

Sending Hippolyta and Emelye to Athens, Theseus turned aside, and with his army marched on Thebes. There he slew Creon by his own hand, and routed the tyrant's forces.

After the battle there were found, wounded and lying near where the fight had been fiercest, two handsome and richly-dressed young men, named Palamon and Arcite, cousins of the royal house of Thebes. Now, because of a vow he had made against Creon's house, Theseus ordered these young men to be kept in prison at Athens for life. When they had recovered from their wounds, Palamon and Arcite were thrown into a dungeon near the palace of Theseus.

It happened that the narrow window of their dungeon overlooked the royal garden, and here, one May morning, Emelye came forth to walk and gather flowers.

Her yellow hair was braided in a tress,
Behind her back a yardé long, I guess. . . .
And as an angel heavenly she sang.

Palamon himself awoke with the sun, heard the sweet song, and, peering through his prison bars upon the fair scene beneath, was stricken to the heart with love for the fair Emelye. His cry aroused Arcite.

" Cousin mine," exclaimed Arcite in alarm, " what aileth thee? Why criest thou? Take in all patience our imprisonment, for the stars ordained it when we were born."

" Cousin," replied Palamon, " you are wrong. It was not our imprisonment that caused me to cry out. The fairness of the lady that I see yonder in the garden is the cause of my woe. I know not if she be woman or goddess in human form."

Then went Arcite to the narrow window, and when he too saw Emelye his despair was even greater than Palamon's.

" If," he cried, " I cannot see her day by day, I shall be naught but a dead man." Then, for the first time in their lives, there sprang up enmity between the cousins.

This continued till one day a duke who knew Arcite, and who was an old and valued friend of Theseus, came to Athens, and, hearing of Arcite's captivity, begged Theseus to set the young Theban free. The request was granted on the condition that Arcite went his way, consenting never again to set foot on Athenian soil.

But at last Arcite could bear his pain no longer, and returned to Athens as a poor labourer. In this guise he obtained a humble post in the household of the duke, where his manners soon won him advancement. Then, one night, Palamon was enabled to drug his gaoler and to escape to a little wood near by, where he met Arcite, and the two fell to quarrelling afresh over the object of their mutual affection. At length Arcite said he would bring food and weapons, so that on the morrow they could fight for the lady.

They were engaged in this conflict when they were surprised by Theseus and his retinue. Theseus, learning from Palamon who they were, condemned both to death; but on the intercession of the ladies of the company he ordained that the two rivals should go away for fifty weeks, at the end of which period each should return with fifty knights, to attend a great tournament, the victor in which should have the fair Emelye's hand.

The time passed, and when the hour of the tournament arrived it was decreed by Theseus that life should not be wasted, but that should either of the leaders be taken prisoner or slain the tourney should cease. Palamon was struck down by the Indian King Emetreus in Arcite's company, and taken prisoner; but as Arcite was riding proudly to the spot where Emelye was sitting, his horse stumbled, and he was fatally injured by the fall. While lying at the point of death in the palace of Theseus in Athens, to which he had been carried, Arcite sent for Emelye and Palamon. To Emelye he spoke these last words of chivalrous devotion.

Farewell, my sweet! Farewell, mine Emelye!
And softly take me in your armés tweye (two)
For love of God, and hark to what I say.
I have here with my cousin Palamon
Had strife and rancour many a day i-gon (gone by),
For love of you, and eke (also) for jealousy.

But, he went on to say:

In this world right now I knowé none
So worthy to be loved as Palamon,
That serveth you, and will do all his life.
And if that ye shall ever be a wife,
Forget not Palamon, that gentle man.
And so a brave man died.

But when time had brought healing to the hearts of all concerned, Theseus sent for Palamon and Emelye, and, that of two sorrows might be made a perfect joy, the duke ordered that these two should take one another as husband and wife.

THE KNIGHT AND THE UGLY OLD WOMAN
The Tale Told by the Wife of Bath

A KNIGHT of King Arthur's Court, by an unworthy deed, had earned the penalty of death. But, the Queen and her ladies gaining the King's grace, the knight was handed over to the Queen, who promised him his life if, within a year and a day, he could tell her what it was that women most desired.

Time passed sorrowfully for the knight. No satisfying answer could he discover of anyone. Then, when the day on which he was once again to appear before the Queen drew near, and he was returning from his quest, he met an ugly old hag, who, addressing him, inquired what it was that he sought.

" Promise me," said the old woman, when he had told her his story, " that you will do the next thing that I require of thee, if it be in thy power, and I will tell thee the answer."

The knight gave her his word, and together they journeyed to the Queen's Court. Here, as instructed by the old woman, the knight declared that the thing most desired of women was power. This proved to be the correct answer to the difficult question, and he was accordingly adjudged to have saved his life.

Then up rose the old woman, and, telling the Queen of his promise, boldly asked his hand in marriage.

" Take all my goods and let me go rather ! " exclaimed the knight. But he was kept to his bond. When his newly wedded wife upbraided him for his treatment of her, he taunted her with her lowly birth, as well as her ugliness and poverty. To this she replied in words that have been full often repeated:

Look who that is most virtuous alway,
Open and secret, and most intendeth aye
To do the gentle deedés that he can,
And take him for the greatest gentleman.
Christ will we claim of Him our gentleness,
Not of our elders for their old richesse.
For tho' they give us all their heritage,
For which we claim to be of high peerage,
Yet may they not bequeathé, for no thing,
To none of us their virtuous living,
That made them gentlemanly calléd be,
And bade us follow them in such degree.

When the knight had repented him of his unknightly mood his wife asked him to choose which she should be—as she was, old and ugly, but devoted to him, or young and fair, but vain and fickle. In reply the knight put himself in his wife's " wise governance."

" Then," said she, " I have the mastery. And I will be to you both fair and true."

The knight, looking up, now saw, to his rapture, that what she said had come to pass. And the two lived to their lives' end in perfect happiness.

The Story of the Most Beautiful Book in the World

The Street called Straight

WHAT HAPPENED TO SAUL

WE may be sure that Saul of Tarsus was one of the most loyal and upright Jews alive in his day at Jerusalem. No man with a cleaner conscience or a more unwearying will ever laboured to keep the ancient religion of Israel pure and undefiled. When he saw how Stephen met his death he realised that the followers of Jesus were likely to prove the most dangerous enemies of the ancient faith.

But now he discovered, to his consternation and wrath, that here in Jerusalem, in the very citadel and stronghold of Israel, the faith of Israel was threatened by an enemy more dangerous than sin.

Imagine an Englishman going abroad to prevent his countrymen in Persia from becoming followers of Persia's gods; imagine him working in that foreign land with a passionate loyalty to the ancient religion of England, the religion which had made England so great and unique; imagine him reminding all his countrymen in that foreign land of the splendid history and the glorious spirit of England's religion, and bidding them, with the proud rebuke of patriotism, to be staunch, loyal, and true to their own religion. And then imagine this Englishman returning to England, only to find that in London itself a new religion was springing

up, threatening to overwhelm the old! What would be his feelings?

Such was the position of Saul. With all the burning energy of his extraordinary character, he immediately threw himself into the work of exterminating this new religion which presumed to set itself up against the ancient religion of Abraham, Isaac, and Jacob.

It is certain that Saul did not inquire what this new religion really taught. The followers of Jesus were called Nazarenes. Nazareth was a place on which the polished and educated Jews of Jerusalem looked down with contempt; to call a man a Nazarene was like calling him a boor or a rustic. Therefore it was enough for the scholarly Saul that this new sect came from Nazareth. These Nazarenes must be a set of ignorant fanatics. They actually dared to set aside the authority of the Sanhedrin.

Can we not see how Saul, with his lofty intellect and his impatient scorn of ignorance, would hate these Nazarenes? He went at once to the high priest, obtained authority to set about a vigorous persecution of the Nazarenes, and proceeded immediately to carry out this welcome mission.

News reached him that the heresy was springing up in Damascus, and the high

GREAT FIGURES OF THE OLD TESTAMENT · THE LIFE OF JESUS

priest " gave letters which authorised Saul to set up his court at Damascus, and to bring from thence in chains all whom he could find, both men and women, to await such mercy as Stephen's murder might lead them to hope for at the hands of the supreme tribunal."

When Saul started from Jerusalem on his long journey to Damascus, he thought he was setting out on an embassy of the highest importance. He did not realise that this journey was to become immortal, that so long as the world lasted men of all nations would look back on it, that it would remain written across the page of history for ever as the most momentous journey ever made by man.

In what form did he set out? It was with some splendour and display of authority. He was a Pharisee, a rabbi, the representative of the Sanhedrin, the viceroy of Israel's God. His cavalcade would consist of horses and mules handsomely caparisoned; his retinue would show him a courtier-like reverence and respect; he would travel with all dignity and comfort on a journey of 150 miles.

THE IMMORTAL JOURNEY THAT IS WRITTEN ACROSS THE PAGE OF HISTORY

The dignity was his natural right as an aristocrat of a proud race; it was essential to the great Pharisee setting forth to overawe and punish a dangerous rabble. How different the state and ceremony of this departure out of Jerusalem from that entry into it of the meek and lowly Saviour of the World, Jesus.

Saul, then, went with great state and ceremony; but in what kind of *spirit* did he go? One writer has supposed that a certain calm, as it were of weariness, fell upon the eager spirit of this unique man. His work in Jerusalem had been thorough and continuous; his body must have been tired, his mind exhausted. At least a week of travelling lay between him and his work of fresh persecution in Damascus. Would he not take the opportunity during these seven days to nurse his strength and restore his mental energies?

As the long journey drew to an end they left the desert and came into one of the most entrancing scenes on this beautiful earth—the view of Damascus, with its white domes, roofs, and walls shining in the sun, seen across a valley rich and fertile, watered by the two famous rivers of Damascus, and so full of colour and perfume and delight that the traveller feels himself in the fields of Paradise.

The sight of Damascus spurred the energies of Saul. There lay his work. Within those walls swarmed the infidels of Israel, who would make the proud race of Israel the laughing-stock of the world. It was his work to crush and stamp out this sect; it was his mission to destroy the enemies of Israel. On, with all haste! Jerusalem was delivered from the curse; Damascus now should feel the wrath of God.

THE VOICE THAT CAME TO SAUL AND THE VISION BY THE WAY

And so, in the glare and blinding heat of noon, this great man pressed on across the smiling valley to Damascus, breathing threats and slaughter against the disciples of the Lord.

Suddenly, in the silence of the noontide, " there lightened a great light. The whole valley vanished in a burst of flame. It seemed as though the whole atmosphere had caught fire, and they were suddenly wrapped in sheets of blinding splendour."

Saul and those that were with him flung themselves down upon the earth. In this natural instinct of man, confronted by some terrible exhibition of Nature's power, the servants were unconscious of reverence or superstition. Their first thoughts were surely those of self-preservation. But while they hid their eyes from the flame, fearing to look up, Saul was bowed to the dust, and in his soul were sounding the awful words, awful in revelation and awful in their divine pity: *Saul, Saul, why persecutest thou Me?* In the silence of his stricken soul Saul questioned: *Who art Thou, Lord?* And the voice answered: *I am Jesus of Nazareth, whom thou persecutest.*

THE BITTER REMORSE OF SAUL THAT FOLLOWED THE MARVELLOUS VISION

His dazzled eyes beheld the form of Him who uttered this reproach, and the form was that of Jesus, the Christ of the despised Nazarenes.

When Saul heard the voice and saw the form of that Jesus whom he had persecuted, his soul must have been so stricken with consternation and remorse that no actual thoughts passed through his mind. But afterwards, when his mortal brain had somewhat recovered from this impact of the supernatural, surely he must have reflected deeply and profoundly on the words: " I am Jesus of Nazareth."

One can feel that the soul of Saul must have reeled and staggered under the emotion of that moment.

Saul was bidden by this voice to rise, and go into the city, where it should be told him what to do. Whether he understood what had happened to him we do not know. Whether he realised what had befallen him we cannot tell. But when he rose from the dust, if he was not yet Paul the Apostle, he had ceased to be Saul the Persecutor. And his eyes were blinded.

HOW SAUL WAS LED THROUGH THE CITY GATE INTO DAMASCUS

Dean Farrar has described this moment with great force.

Saul rose, and all was dark. The dazzling vision had passed away, and with it also the glittering city, the fragrant gardens, the burning noon.

Amazed and startled, his attendants took him by the hand and led him to Damascus. He had meant to enter the city with all the importance of a Commissioner from the Sanhedrin, to be received with distinction as the representative of authority. He had meant to leave the city, perhaps, amid multitudes of his applauding countrymen, accompanied by a captive train of he knew not how many dejected Nazarenes. How different was his actual entrance!

He was led through the city gate, stricken, dejected, trembling, no longer breathing threats and slaughter, but longing only to be the learner and the suppliant of the lowest brother among those whom he had intended to destroy. He was ignominiously let out of the city, alone, in imminent peril of arrest or assassination, through a window, in a basket, down the wall.

SAUL ARRIVES AT THE HOUSE IN THE STREET CALLED STRAIGHT

There was living in Damascus a Jew named Ananias, one of the most earnest believers in Jesus of Nazareth. To this man there came a vision in the night, a dream wherein he heard the Voice of God speaking to his soul.

The Voice said to him:

Arise, and go into the street which is called Straight, and enquire in the house of Judas for one called Saul, of Tarsus; for, behold, he prayeth, and hath seen in a vision a man named Ananias coming in, and putting his hands on him, that he might receive his sight.

The words, " For behold, he prayeth," have gone to the ends of the world,

carrying hope and consolation to a multitude of souls. Saul was praying to God, praying to receive his sight—the true sight of his soul. And God's answer was to send human help. Prayer is not answered by supernatural magic: it is answered by God, but through human means. These words light up for us the darkness which enshrouds Saul's life for the first three days after his entrance into Damascus. Those three days were spent in prayer. He was blind; he was under the shock of his spiritual experience. In the house to which his people had guided him he lay in a silence that was like death, praying. He prayed to God for light.

In his dream, Ananias said to the Voice which had spoken to him: " Lord, I have heard by many of this man, how much evil he hath done to thy saints at Jerusalem; and here he hath authority from the chief priests to bind all that call on thy name." But the Voice answered: " Go thy way: for he is a chosen vessel unto me, to bear my name before the Gentiles, and kings, and the children of Israel: for I will shew him how great things he must suffer for my name's sake."

HOW SAUL PERISHED AND PAUL THE APOSTLE LIVED IN HIS PLACE

To disobey was no longer possible. Ananias, like the other faithful Nazarenes in Damascus, had been dreading the approach of this terrible envoy of the Sanhedrin; he had been expecting a summons to appear before Saul; perhaps he had anticipated scourging and death.

And now he was bidden to go to this persecutor, and was assured that Saul of Tarsus should carry the religion of Jesus to the foreign nations of the earth, should uphold it before kings, and should preach it even to the Jews.

And Ananias went his way (we read) and entered into the house; and, putting his hands on him said, Brother Saul, the Lord, that appeared unto thee in the way as thou camest, hath sent me, that thou mightest receive thy sight, and be filled with the Holy Spirit.

At these words it was as if suddenly scales dropped from before Saul's eyes. He received his sight, he rose up, and Ananias baptised him in the name of Jesus of Nazareth. Saul had perished. Paul the Apostle rose from his knees.

(Next chapter in this group, page 5925)

HOW TO SIGNAL WITH SEMAPHORE FLAGS

READY POSITION   ALPHABETICAL SIGN   NUMERICAL SIGN   CANCEL OR ERASE

C   O   M   E

A   S   H

O   R   E

These pictures show how to send messages to people beyond calling distance. In the top row the first picture shows the ready to start position ; the second sign shown is used after figures have been sent to indicate the return to letters and is called the alphabetical sign ; the third picture shows the numerical sign, which signifies that the letters following are to be read as numbers ; and the fourth means cancel the word being sent. The other pictures convey the message Come Ashore, but remember that although the pictures do not show it, the signaller would come to the ready position between words. Notice that dark flags are used against the very light background.

The Interests and Pleasures of Life for All Indoors and Out

SENDING MESSAGES IN SEMAPHORE

SEMAPHORE signalling is very easy to learn and to remember, and is an excellent way of exchanging messages with those who are far beyond shouting distance but still in sight.

The apparatus need only be of the simplest —a pair of semaphore flags, improvised in a few seconds from two white pocket-handkerchiefs. Usually though, signalling flags are one and a half to two feet square and are white with a blue stripe across the centre, or diagonal blue and white, or red and yellow. These are used against normal or dark backgrounds, while all blue flags show up better against very light backgrounds, such as chalk cliffs, as shown in the pictures on the facing page. Sometimes we may dispense with the flags and send the message with our arms only, but in that case we must be particularly careful to stand against a suitable background, so that the movement of our arms can be plainly seen.

Semaphore signalling should be performed with as much precision as military drill, and the only way to do this is by constant practice. Work on paper might alternate with practice out of doors across a lawn, until the letters come almost mechanically. Speed will follow naturally.

The semaphore alphabet is shown in the diagram on this page. The thick lines represent the body of the person who is signalling, and the thin lines stand for the flags held in the hands. The letter A is represented by holding the right-hand flag as if it were pointing midway between the VII and VIII of a clock-dial, assuming the feet of the signaller to be at VI and his head to be at XII. The angle between the arm and the body should be 45 degrees for such letters as A, and 90 degrees for other letters such as B.

It is good practice to put down the alphabet signals on paper, beginning by writing out the entire alphabet a few times. Then different letters may be set down at random, without consulting the alphabet, thereby testing the memory.

Another way which will help us to memorise the code, is to arrange the alphabet in circles as on the next page. Looking at circle No. 1, we see that the letters are signalled with only one flag, the other being held in front of the body as in the ready position. A, B, C, and D are sent with the right-hand flag, and E, F, and G with the left-hand flag. From circle No. 2 it will be seen that the letters H, I, K, L, M, and N are made by holding the right-hand flag in the position of A, and by moving the left-hand

THE SEMAPHORE ALPHABET AND SIGNS

A B C D E F G H I
J K L M N O P Q R
S T U V W X Y Z
ALPHABETICAL SIGN (LETTERS FOLLOW)   NUMERICAL SIGN (FIGURES FOLLOW)   CANCEL

CRAFTS · GAMES · NEEDLEWORK · PUZZLES · SCIENCE EXPERIMENTS

flag to the position placed opposite the letters. Then the third circle, which illustrates the letters O, P, Q, R, and S, shows the right-hand flag at the B position, and the left-hand flag moved round as indicated.

The fourth circle shows the letters T, U, Y, and the sign for Cancel, all of which are made by keeping the right-hand flag in the C position and changing only the position of the left-hand flag.

Circle No. 5 shows the right-hand flag in the D position, where it is held when indicating the numerical sign, and also for J, or the alphabetical sign, and for V, the position of only the left-hand flag being changed for these different signs.

Circle No. 6 shows that the letters W and X are indicated by holding the right-hand flag in the E position and changing the position of the left-hand flag only. Z is not shown here as it would need a diagram to itself, the right-hand flag being held at position F, with the left-hand at G, for this letter.

There are no special signals for the numerals, A standing for 1, B for 2, and so on, until we reach K, which represents nought. J is not used although it comes before K. When sending a message which includes figures, we proceed in the ordinary way until we reach the figures. Before sending these we should make the numerical sign, and this notifies those who are receiving that the next letters are to be read as figures. When the figures are finished we send the alphabetical sign and proceed as before.

The Erase or Cancel sign almost explains itself. It means that the word we are sending is to be cancelled, perhaps because we find that we have made a mistake in transmitting.

To send a message, we must stand in the position shown in the first picture on page 5810, with the two flags slightly crossed over one another, facing the direction in which the message is to be sent.

We must next send the calling-up sign, VE, and repeat this until we have attracted the attention of the persons to whom we wish to signal. They should acknowledge the calling-up sign with the general answer A, and when ready to receive our message send K, which means carry on.

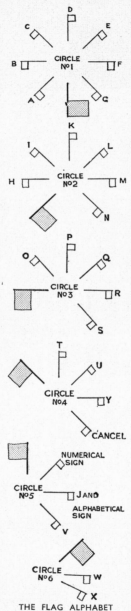

THE FLAG ALPHABET
SHOWN IN CIRCLES

As seen on page 5810, the letters of the semaphore alphabet are formed by the various angles at which the flags are held to the body. To send a message we must stretch out the arms to their full extent, and hold the flags in a straight line with the arms, never allowing them to droop from the hands and never inclining them to the rear. We should, however, turn on the hips when making a letter in which both flags have to be on the same side of the body, and be careful to observe the rule of keeping our arms at either 45 degrees or 90 degrees to the body. We must get smartness, style, and accuracy into our signalling action, for if the angles of the flags and arms are not exact, it will be impossible for the receiver to read our message correctly.

When sending a word the flags must be brought smoothly and without any hesitation from one position to the next. If it is necessary to repeat a letter, the arms should be brought in to the body and the sign for that letter made again. In between words the arms should be brought down to the ready position.

The correct way to take a semaphore message is to have two receivers, one to read the letters as they are sent and the other to write down the letters as the reader calls them out. When the sender brings his arms down to the ready position between words the reader calls out Group. This indicates the end of a word, and if the writer is satisfied that the word makes sense, he tells the reader, who is equipped with a pair of flags, to send the general answer, A. Then the sender carries on with the next word. If the general answer had not been made the sender would have repeated the word.

To save time when signalling, we should learn some of the abbreviations that are used. The most useful of these is the sign for a full stop, which is AAA. If it is necessary to send letters as capitals, we first send UK, the abbreviation for capitals, then the letters, and finally the alphabetical sign to denote return to ordinary letters. After every message we send AR. The writer, if satisfied, tells his reader to reply with R, received. Abbreviations should be answered by A.

HOW TO MAKE PAPER FLOWERS

To make paper flowers which look quite real needs patience and skill. But there are quick ways of getting a wonderfully effective show of paper flowers, and patterns for some of these are given here. For them we want coloured paper, and some wire.

ROSES

We will start with roses, for they are the most natural-looking of paper flowers. We take a strip of crêpe paper—red, pink, orange, or yellow—about 30 inches long and three inches wide. We fold it in half, so that it is 15 inches long when doubled. Again we fold it in half in the same direction, then in three equal parts, and once again into two parts.

We take a pencil and mark as shown by the line in the pattern for the rose-petal, taking care that the short tip of the line is on the folded side. We cut round this line with scissors and open out the paper, which will now show twelve petals.

But these petals are quite flat, while real rose-petals are curved. To get this effect, we take each petal between our fingers and thumbs and stretch gently.

Now we must curl the top edges of each petal. To do this, we hold the paper in the left hand, and with one blade of the scissors between the thumb and first finger of the right hand gently pass the petal under the thumb and over the blade, curling first the right side and then the left, but always curling in the same direction. Each petal should now be slightly hollow on the inside with its two tips curled outwards.

Next we make the stalk. We take a long strip of green crêpe paper, half an inch wide, and a piece of wire at least six inches in length. We cover the wire with the green, holding the paper in a slanting direction in the left hand and gradually turning the wire with the right hand until covered ; or we can leave the covering of the stalk until the finished flower has been fastened on. We

ROSE PETAL AND CALYX

A MIXED POSY MADE FROM THE INSTRUCTIONS GIVEN

double up one end of the stalk for about an eighth of an inch, and build up the flower around the other.

To do this, we gather the first four petals closely together to make the tight centre to the rose, fasten this centre securely to the wire and then gradually gather the rest of the petals round and round this. We fasten the whole flower-head firmly to its stalk by twisting wire or cotton around.

Next we must make the calyx of the rose—that is, the little green leaves forming a cup at the base of the flower head. We take a piece of green crêpe paper, three inches by two inches, fold it in half so that it is now one and a half inches by two, and then in the same direction into three equal parts. We cut as shown by the line in the pattern of the rose calyx. This makes six points when opened out. We cut off one, as we require only five; wrap the calyx round the outside rose-leaves and fasten with wire.

Sprays of leaves for the rose may be bought, or we can cut them from green crêpe paper, using a real rose leaf as a pattern. The leaves should be joined in along the stem by gathering each one at the base and wrapping nearly half an inch of this inside the stem covering as it is being wrapped around.

BIG DAISIES

Daisies are not quite so easy to make. We take a strip of yellow or white tissue or crêpe paper, ten inches long and two inches wide; fold it in half, so that it is five inches long, fold again in the same way, and still again.

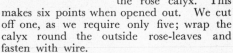

DAISY PETALS. CENTRE AND CALYX—ALL PATTERNS ARE HALF-SIZE

Now we draw three petals to the shape of the diagram, cut them out, then open the paper, which will now show 24 petals. To make the centre of the daisy, we must get some yellow crewel wool—about three yards will be sufficient. We wind this round three fingers of the left hand, and fasten a piece of wire round the centre of the loops, as shown in the illustration, leaving a long end to form the stalk. We bring the ends of the wool together and then cut the edges.

Next we take a piece of green paper, three inches long and one inch wide, to make the calyx of the flower; fold this in half, again fold in half, and cut out like the pattern.

Now we gather the strip of petals round the centre, if it is of tissue paper, first folding it in half. We arrange the petals carefully with the fingers, wrap the green calyx outside them, and fasten with wire; then cover the stalk.

DOUBLE DAFFODILS

To make a double daffodil, we cut a strip of yellow crêpe paper, 16 inches long and two inches wide, and fold it in half, making a double strip, eight inches by two; fold again three times in the same way, making 16 thicknesses. Then we mark the outline of the petal as shown in the diagram; cut it, open out the paper, and curl the edges of each petal slightly in the way described for the rose, but not making such a deep turn-back.

Now we take a strip of paler-coloured yellow paper, six inches long and two and a half

DAFFODIL
PETAL
AND
LEAF

inches deep, and fold into eight pieces—that is, by folding in half three times; mark and cut the petal in the same way as before.

We gather the first four petals of the 16-inch strip together, fasten the centre firmly to a wire stalk, and arrange the other petals round them; then take the paler-coloured piece and gather this round, fastening securely.

The daffodil has a brown leaf at the base of the flower. We make this from a small piece of light brown crêpe paper, one inch across and three inches deep; fold it in half, so that it is half an inch wide doubled, and cut as marked in the leaf diagram, starting from the outside edges. We open out the leaf and fasten it in as we cover the stalk. Leaves are made like this from green crêpe paper seven inches long and one inch wide.

CHRYSANTHEMUMS

For chrysanthemums, we must take a piece of yellow or white tissue paper 40 inches long and five inches wide ; fold it in half lengthways; cut a fringe one and a quarter inches deep along the folded edge; roll a little tightly to form a centre; fasten to a wire stalk; roll the rest of the fringe round this, and secure firmly.

THE PUZZLE OF THE BOOKS ON THE SHELVES

Harry pointed to the bookcase, where stood nine volumes of an encyclopedia that his father had given him for a birthday present that morning, and said, "Well, that's a funny thing !"

"What do you mean ?" asked his sister, Anne.

"Why," replied Harry, "just look ! I put the nine volumes on the shelves anyhow, intending directly after school to put them in their right order, and I was just going to do so when I made an odd discovery."

"I can't see anything particularly funny about the books," said Anne.

"Well," answered Harry, "look at the numbers of the volumes—6, 7, 2, and 9 are on the shelf at the top, and 1, 3, 4, 5, and 8 are at the bottom, and these taken as a fraction, $\frac{6729}{13458}$, are equal to one-half.

"So they are !" said his sister: "but that is just a chance. See if you can arrange them to make one-third."

"I reckon I can do that," answered

Harry, "and I will put them to represent $\frac{1}{4}$, $\frac{1}{5}$, $\frac{1}{6}$, $\frac{1}{7}$, $\frac{1}{8}$, and $\frac{1}{9}$, as well."

"I know you will never be able to do that," said Anne.

"Figures are funny things," replied Harry with a superior air, "and I'll very soon show you that I can do as I say."

First he arranged them so that the numbers taken as a fraction represented $\frac{1}{3}$. After thinking a moment or two he rearranged them to represent $\frac{1}{4}$, then $\frac{1}{5}$, then $\frac{1}{6}$, $\frac{1}{7}$, $\frac{1}{8}$, and $\frac{1}{9}$ in succession.

"There !" said he triumphantly.

"Bravo !" cried his sister. "I certainly would never have believed that you could do it. You will have to show me how it is done, and I will try it on the girls at school."

How did Harry arrange the volumes so that the two rows of figures formed fractions equal to $\frac{1}{3}$, $\frac{1}{4}$, $\frac{1}{5}$, $\frac{1}{6}$, $\frac{1}{7}$, $\frac{1}{8}$, and $\frac{1}{9}$?

The solution will be found on page 5933.

The solution of the problem of the Patchwork Quilt on page 5686.

This diagram shows how the quilt was made from the eleven squares.

The Story of the Boundless Universe and All Its Wondrous Worlds

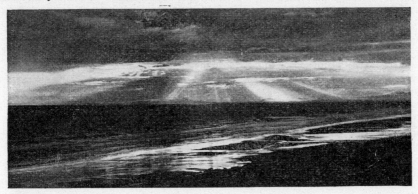

WHAT IS IT THAT MAKES LIGHT?

Scientists have made models of the atom to help us understand its structure and what goes on inside it. Let us imagine we are examining a few of these clever models. In some of them, the electrons (or bits of negative electricity) are pictured as flying about in the atom as motor-cars might run round a racing track, the chief differences being that the speeds of the electrons are enormously greater and the paths taken much more changeable.

It was supposed that when an electron hitherto in an outer path suddenly hopped into one nearer the centre of the atom, there would be some energy to spare in the atom's system because the path of one of its electrons had become shorter. This energy escaped from the atom, creating as it did so a splash spreading outward like a wave—a wave of light. Or if light were absorbed by the atom, and an electron made room for it by jumping to an outer orbit, the surplus energy might again be sent out.

The German physicist Max Planck showed mathematically that if hot bodies shed their heat gradually they would get colder faster. They must part with their heat in jumps. Light was the jump of an electron giving birth to a jump of energy. This was a light quantum, the smallest bit, or light quanta in packages of bits.

How small is a quantum? It must be small enough to enter an atom. It almost brings us back to Newton's theory of light as a curious mixture of corpuscular and wave theory. Sir Arthur Eddington coined for it the name of a wavicle : a package of quanta. If that commonly regarded as a wave partakes of the nature of a wave, may not that which we have commonly regarded as a particle partake also of the nature of a wave?

These explanations have not been entirely superseded by later suggested models of the atom, which include not merely a central nucleus of positive electricity, or proton, and electrons flying about this sun-like body, but other kinds of units.

Among them are the neutron, a particle without any electric charge, either positive or negative, and the positron, which is the opposite number of the negative electron and is a unit of positive electricity. One such supposition is that when a positron crashes into an electron the positron disappears, and the photon, the smallest possible unit of light, appears. We are warned to look out for wavicles in the electron.

For some time past the ether, which used to play a dominant part in physics, has been discredited. The ether was a

ASTRONOMY · GEOLOGY · GEOGRAPHY · CHEMISTRY · PHYSICS · LIFE

theoretical substance consisting of nothing material yet having the properties of an elastic solid. Elaborate tests and the theory of relativity have compelled modern scientists to give up the ether theory and declare quite candidly that light waves travel from their source in the sun, stars, and so on through empty space, without requiring any medium for their transmission.

Scientists cannot even experiment on how the waves behave on their journey through empty space, though they have definite theories on the subject. The value of theories, indeed, is to explain facts which can be fitted into them as clothes are packed into a wardrobe. The electron is spoken of, like the atom before it, as if it were a tiny hard lump, but no experimenter really means to assert that it is. It is spoken of as if it had a certain mass, but that is also more than we really see.

But, whatever it is that happens in the reactions between the atom, its components, and its surroundings, one of the results of collision is the production of *radiation pressure.*

HOW CLERK MAXWELL THOUGHT OUT WHAT TIME PROVED LONG AFTER

How interested Newton would have been to have learned about this pressure, which is true not only of light in the strict sense—that is to say, the waves that we can see—but is true of the other waves, rays, or radiations that we cannot see.

The famous James Clerk Maxwell, the original expounder of the theory of electric waves, declared long ago that light must have a pressure, and stated how much that pressure must be. This he did by means of sheer thinking-power, and because he had a real understanding of the nature of light waves. Within the present century students have independently proved that light has a pressure, and the force of it is just what Clerk Maxwell foretold.

When very careful and delicate experiments are made, and something that weighs very, very little is delicately hung by a slender thread made of quartz so that the tiniest touch will push it, we find that it is pushed when a ray of light is allowed to hit it; and the force of the push can be measured, and proves to be exactly what it ought to be to agree with the theory of light waves. It is wonderful to see this experiment and to see something pushed

as if a finger or a jet of water had struck it. We should remember the name of radiation pressure ; for it is certain that year by year we shall hear more about this subject.

HOLE IN A SHUTTER THAT REVEALED THE MYSTERY OF THE UNIVERSE

Light is one of the greatest facts in the Universe; and it is, therefore, one of the greatest facts of Nature that light, wherever it flies, has a pushing power. It is probable that the meaning and consequences of this pressure for the future of the Universe are all-important, and we cannot help wondering what the mind of the discoverer of gravitation would have found out if he had known about radiation pressure.

The most famous of all Newton's experiments was perfectly simple. All Newton did was to close his shutters, bore a hole that let a ray of light through into the darkened room, and then take a prism or three-sided piece of glass, and see what happened when the ray of light passed through it. He found that the ray of white sunlight was broken up into many colours. When, in place of a hole, he made a slit in his shutter, and let the light pass through the prism, he found that the white light was broken up into a band of colours, which were the colours of the rainbow. This band of colours is now called the *spectrum,* and by it many mysteries of the Universe have been revealed to scientists.

THE RAINDROPS THAT BREAK UP THE LIGHT AND MAKE THE RAINBOW

This experiment proved once and for all what could never have been guessed or believed—that the ordinary white light we know so well is a mixture of colours, and those colours are the colours of the rainbow. The rainbow itself is made out of white light, because the white sunlight is broken up into the colours that make it by being reflected from countless raindrops in the sky. These raindrops act as Newton's prism acted, and for the same reason.

This great discovery of the nature of white light marks the beginning of this part of science.

Newton, of course, went very carefully into the matter; he understood what happened, and why. He saw that when the light passes through the prism it is bent.

We know quite well how rays of light can be bent. As long as nothing bends them they travel in absolutely straight lines, but when they pass from air into water or water into air, or air into glass or glass into air, or in any other case, they are bent; so they come out from the prism at a different angle.

THE LITTLE BIT OF GLASS THAT SORTS OUT THE COLOURS IN THE SUNBEAM

If that were all, the consequence would simply be that the ray of white light, instead of striking the wall just opposite the hole, as it would have done if the prism were not there, would strike it somewhere else, because the prism had turned its course. But, just because the white light is not a single thing, but a mixture of all the colours of the rainbow, something else happens.

The rays of light making these different colours will differ from each other in the extent to which they are bent. The red rays, as Newton found, are the least bent, and the violet rays are the most bent. The consequence is that the light which went into the prism all mixed leaves it all sorted out, the red rays being least bent from the course they would have taken if the prism had not been there, the violet rays being the most bent, and the others taking their places in between.

Not only did Newton discover this, but he laid down the law quite rightly, showing that the colours of light are not the consequence of anything it strikes on or passes through, but are the natural properties of particular kinds of rays. If a thing is red, that is only because it throws back to our eyes red rays. As he said : " Some rays are disposed to exhibit a red colour and no other; some a yellow and no other; some a green and no other; and so of the rest." He saw, also, that there is an absolute law as to the bending of these rays, the same colour being always bent to the same degree, no matter where the light comes from.

THE GREAT MARVEL OF A LITTLE BAND OF COLOUR

This simple experiment of Newton's has led to such a vast number of consequences that it would take a book to describe the merest outlines of them. In various parts of the world there are great observatories which are devoted to repeating Newton's experiment with sunlight, but with elaborate instruments.

We already know that the band of colour obtained is called a spectrum, and everything seen in this spectrum has to be studied and noted and described and measured; we have to analyse the spectrum as we would analyse a mixture of chemicals in a glass vessel. This subject is known as *spectrum analysis*.

Spectrum analysis has to be applied not only to sunlight, but to the light from the planets; it has to be applied to the light from the stars and comets and nebulae. We can study even the invisible part of the spectrum, the rays beyond the violet and below the red, which can be photographed with special cameras.

In every part of the Sun's spectrum we find certain dark lines. Every one of these lines tells us something about the nature of the material in the Sun or any other star. The lines are dark because they are really due to *bright* lines of coloured light which are absorbed by the screen of glowing vapour surrounding the Sun. But when we burn a bit of metal in the laboratory at a much lower temperature, we see through the prism only the bright, coloured lines, and by measuring their exact position with a *spectrometer* we can discover the nature of the burning metal. By burning a tiny bit of an unknown substance in a suitable flame, the spectrometer will reveal the minutest trace of an element that may be too small to discover by chemical analysis.

HOW A PIECE OF GLASS CAN TELL US WHAT THE STARS ARE MADE OF

An analysis of the spectrum obtained by means of the prism teaches us of what elements the Sun and other heavenly bodies are composed.

It even enables us to tell whether stars are moving towards us or from us in the very line of our sight, and their speed.

It was not really until the nineteenth century that the wave theory of light found acceptance; and as we read all about sound in this book, it is worth knowing that it is the resemblance between sound and light which led the great Englishman, Dr Thomas Young, to ask whether light must not also consist of waves, as sound does. Young made the remarkable discovery that, under certain conditions, light added to light will produce darkness, because the waves of the one interfere with the waves of the other, as may happen with sound waves, and as we see when water waves are thrown back or reflected, from a breakwater, or in the backwash on the beach.

Now, here we have not only a fact supporting the wave theory, but also a very interesting explanation of a certain difference between light and sound.

If we let in a beam of light through a hole it certainly spreads out as it travels, but it does not at all behave as sound would. Sound would spread out equally in all directions, just as the light does from a candle standing in the middle of a room. But why does a ray of light remain narrow and not spread out sideways, so that the ray of light does not fill a whole room from side to side and from floor to ceiling as sound coming through a hole would fill it?

WHY A RAY OF LIGHT WILL NOT SPREAD OUT AND FILL A ROOM

The answer is that the waves going sideways from a ray of light almost entirely interfere with each other. A light wave does not move in the same way that a sound wave does, and a picturesque explanation of the difference is due to a famous mathematician, Bertrand Russell. Supposing, he says, a procession is marching to Hyde Park, and is now and again halted by the police at Piccadilly Circus. Whenever this happens the people behind will press up till they, too, have to halt and a wave of stoppage will travel down the procession as a similar wave does along the wagons of a luggage train when it stops. When the people in front move on they will thin out and this process of thinning out will also travel down the procession as the condensation due to stoppage did. These are what are called longitudinal waves, and sound waves are like that.

HOW LIGHT WAVES, UNLIKE SOUND WAVES, MOVE SIDEWAYS

But light waves are different. Suppose a mounted policeman rides along the right-hand edge of the procession. All the marchers will move away from his horse, as it passes, and this leftward movement will travel with the policeman along the procession. That is a transverse wave, though it moves with the procession, and light waves are like that.

We may think of all matter as made up of atoms surrounded on all sides by something which can be made to undulate by a

movement arising from the atom. Now think of a fish under water moving its tail. If we are watching we may see ripples, that is to say, waves made in the water by the movement of the fish's tail. And so if the atoms of matter are acting in the same manner as the fish does when it moves its tail they may set up a wave motion just as the fish does in the water; and that is exactly what happens whenever and wherever matter is luminous.

We are right to think of the matter in this case as made of atoms, and the atoms as being systems of electrons. It is the atomic systems themselves that are the source of light. A ball of iron might be set trembling or vibrating, and in this way might cause waves in the air which we should call sound; but no possible movement of the ball as a whole would cause light. If, however, we heat the ball without moving it at all something happens to the atoms of it or to the system of electric particles within the atoms, and they release pulses of energy which we call light. If the ball is only fairly hot the particular kind of waves in which these pulses of energy travel will be what we call red light; but if the ball becomes much hotter it is then what we call white hot, for now its atoms produce that mixture of waves which we are accustomed to call white light.

THE ATOMS THAT GIVE OFF THEIR OWN KINDS OF LIGHT

Now, if the iron ball is vaporised the throbbing atoms will send out particular waves which can be always recognised and are always the same, whether the vaporised iron is shining in a laboratory or in a star millions of miles away. This is true also of all elements.

It is a tremendous fact that every kind of atom known to chemists should be so specially different from all other kinds of atoms that it gives off light of a special kind. These different kinds of light are called the spectra of the various atoms or elements. Thus, there is a spectrum of iron, a spectrum of oxygen, and so on. In considering the nature of these we need not trouble for the present whether the wave theory of light, or the modern additions to it, be nearer the truth; it is sufficient for us here to speak as if the theory of wave motions were an exact law.

(*Next chapter in this group, page 5935*)

The Story of Immortal Folk Whose Work Will Never Die

Socrates about to die a martyr's death

THE IMMORTAL THREE
SOCRATES, PLATO, AND ARISTOTLE

IN the wonderful story of Human Adventure there are three names of such power over mankind that they seem to us eternal.

These are not the names of great conquerors, powerful kings, or bold discoverers of unknown lands, but the names of three Thinkers—Socrates, Plato, and Aristotle. These Greeks, who lived long before Jesus was born, are known in every nation of the world. Universities in all countries are still studying their works. Their immortality is part of the thinking life of the world.

But many know only their names. They have had no time to study their works. What did they teach? How is it that these names have an eminence beyond that of all other teachers? How is it that there is no thinking man alive who has not heard of these immortal three or does not owe them something? In what way is their immortality a part of our thinking life?

Let us see if it is possible to answer these questions with a simplicity which any intelligent person can understand.

One day, when the Greek army was in camp, a soldier who was popular with his comrades for cheerfulness and a joking courage, found himself suddenly rooted to the ground. He had fallen in a trance, and so he remained for twenty-four hours. When he came out of it, although he was still loved for his genial good nature, he was marvellously changed.

This soldier was a stonemason, and his name was Socrates. He was broad-shouldered, deep-chested, and strong-legged, with a face so funny in its ugliness and a head so huge for his body, that he was an object of friendly ridicule for other soldiers. They loved him; they admired him; they knew he was as brave and as strong as the best of them; but they could not help regarding him as an oddity.

He told men that the gods to whom they prayed were not worth a thought; that they had indeed been created by men like themselves; whereas there was something in the universe really deserving of man's adoration, something infinitely higher, grander, and more inspiring than anything on Earth, and that was God.

This divine being, said Socrates, was not, like the gods of the ancient world, of violent passions and brutal strength, always blustering, threatening, and interfering in human affairs. He was spirit. You might call Him Truth, or Beauty, or Goodness; but no name could explain

EXPLORERS · INVENTORS · WRITERS · ARTISTS · SCIENTISTS

Him. Perhaps the simplest way of thinking of Him was to know that He represented Perfection. We see beauty on the Earth but it is an imperfect beauty. God is the perfection of all beauty. We see goodness here, and truth, but they are imperfect. God is the perfection of all Truth and Goodness.

As this wonderful God is the creator of the universe, as it is His spirit which governs all things, the wise man, said Socrates, would see that there could be no happiness in life greater than communion with God. Hence the wise man must think about truth, beauty, and goodness. A wise man, in the idea of Socrates, will not try to make money, or dream of wearing fine clothes, or long to dwell in a big house; all those things will seem paltry and trivial in his eyes. What he will desire above and beyond everything else in human life is a sense of the presence of God in his soul. Therefore he will think about God. God will become the master-thought of his mind. His spirit will become familiar with God before it leaves the body to dwell with Him in the real world that lies beyond our world of shadows.

THE CLEVER TALK OF SOCRATES AS HE WALKED BAREFOOTED THROUGH ATHENS

Socrates did not preach. He did not even set up a school in which to teach his new ideas. He merely walked barefooted about Athens talking of these things to anyone who would discuss them. But his conversation was so witty and amusing, his character was so noble and lovable, that people of all classes flocked to him for knowledge. He was soon the greatest power in Athens. Then the priests frowned on him, and teachers of philosophy attacked him.

Thus Socrates was urged forward to another step in his revelation. It was a great thing to make men think of God as the invisible Perfection of the universe; it was a great thing to make them realise that to think about this Perfection was the chief end of human life; but something else remained to be done.

First there was the criticism of the priests. Who was this Socrates, telling them that the ancient gods were unworthy of worship? Who was this upstart to teach them what is truth? And there were the philosophers, who believed that they could guess how the world was made and explain to men the whole history of creation. These philosophers would have nothing to do with what Socrates called his revelations. They wanted to *know*. How was the world made? Why was it made? What is Nature? What is Life?

THE DIVINE RIGHT OF REASON IN THE THINGS OF THE SOUL

Socrates had a wonderful answer both for the priests and the philosophers. He claimed the sovereign right of *reason* to decide these matters. It was a tremendous claim; eventually it brought him to a martyr's death. He said that man could trust his reason; that the reason was divine; and that by the use of his reason man might approach God. If his reason told him certain gods were false, how could he worship them? What men believed in the past must not be allowed to bind men in the present. Reason must decide their beliefs.

But the philosophers, he said, were using their reason in a foolish fashion. There is a right way and a wrong way of reasoning. He said he could prove by reason that the reasoning of philosophers was false; and then he began to question the philosophers, and soon showed that they were talking nonsense. His questions are still the delight of the world. He could make the most eminent philosophers contradict themselves.

He made it clear that the mind can be deceived by the senses, and also by words. People allow their eyes to deceive them. They think they see all there is to be seen, but the invisible is greater than the visible, and what we see of the visible is not all there is to be seen even of that. As for words, men use them as if they were things; they get used to the word and fail to see the miracle of the thing the word stands for. Let them stop to think about words, and they will soon see how little they know.

THE QUESTIONS THAT MEN SHOULD ALWAYS BE ASKING THEMSELVES

Socrates told men that they must be honest. They must question themselves. They must develop conscience. They must always be asking themselves, Do I really believe this or that? and What does this word or that word really mean? Let them get into this habit of being honest with themselves, and they would soon find how little they knew, and how fitting it was that they should be modest before

SOCRATES SEES THE GREAT PEOPLE PASS BY

OFTEN SOCRATES MUST HAVE SAT LIKE THIS, WATCHING THE PROCESSION OF GREAT FOLK UP AND DOWN
THE ACROPOLIS IN ATHENS.

other men and humble in the presence of Eternal Wisdom.

In one of the most memorable pictures in literature we read how sublimely this noble spirit met a martyr's death when his enemies brought him to judgment. He might have escaped, but he preferred to die; and when one of his friends asked how he would like to be buried he replied, with a smile: " Just as you please, *if only you can catch me.*"

THE GREAT SCHOOL OF PHILOSOPHY PLATO FOUNDED IN ATHENS

Among those who listened to Socrates, and came to him, was a handsome and aristocratic youth named Plato. When Socrates was dead Plato took refuge in a town named Megara, where he met Euclid, and afterwards he went to Egypt and studied geometry, and to southern Italy, where he studied moral philosophy. He was forty when he returned to Athens and set up, in the groves of an ancient hero named Academus, a school of philosophy, from which we get our word Academy. He was a splendid figure, he had dignified and charming manners, and he was a passionate lover of wisdom.

Plato is one of the greatest men who ever lived. Some think he stands in solitary eminence high above all the sons of men. Undoubtedly he has exercised a tremendous influence on human life.

But it must be said of him that he lacked the moral splendour of Socrates. Not for him the coarse garment, the hermit's meal, the rigorous honesty of his master. What Socrates preached, Socrates practised. Sincerity was the very centre of his soul. He was something of a Puritan.

THE MAN WHO SOUGHT WISDOM AND LOVED BEAUTY WITH A PASSION

But Plato was of quite another disposition. He was above all else an artist. To him the whole beauty of life lay in *expression.* He wrote beautifully, and we can feel as we read him how he must have loved composing his books, leading quietly up from the simple words we use in conversation to such magnificent periods as seem to bring all heaven about our souls. It may be said that for Plato life itself was an art, and that he sought wisdom because of his passion to live beautifully.

It is chiefly from Plato that we learn what Socrates taught, for Socrates never wrote a line. But Plato developed the glorious simplicity of the ideas of Socrates, and wove them into a philosophy. Anyone can understand what Socrates taught, but it takes a philosopher to understand Plato. He preserves the simplicity of Socrates as his starting-point; but from that plain point he sets off on a journey which carries the simple mind beyond its understanding. Wonderful is the lofty genius of Plato, but when we have closed his works we may truly say that the soul of his philosophy is the simplicity of Socrates, which, in a few words, is this— that the visible is only a shadow of the Invisible, and that communion with God is the highest state of bliss possible to the human soul.

We can best understand the genius of Plato by finding out what were the opinions he sought to overthrow in Athens. What was the old idea he attacked in order to set up a new one? It was generally held that man is nothing more than a piece of mechanism which receives sensations. When it is hot we know by our sensations that it is hot; when it is cold we know by our sensations that it is cold; when we see a horse or a tree or a star it is by the sensations made on us by these things that we know them for horse, tree, or star. In other words, man is an animal.

THE BELIEFS THAT PLATO DESTROYED WITH HIS PITILESS LOGIC

Plato examined this doctrine and utterly destroyed it by his logic. He said that we do indeed receive impressions of things, as other animals do, but that we distinguish between them. All horses make the same impression on us, but we distinguish between a black horse and a white horse, between a beautiful and an ugly horse. When colour makes its impression on our senses we distinguish between green and yellow, blue and red.

But our sensations are only a part of our knowledge. The soul of our knowledge is the idea we form in our minds from the sensations. Suppose we hear a hideous noise. The sensation we receive is not hideous or sweet; it is simply a sensation of sound. The ear takes in waves of air, and we call it sound. But something within us is not content to call that sensation sound; it says: " This sound is hideous; it is discordant; it is wrong." And then other sounds enter the ear and this something within us says: " These sounds are beautiful; they are harmonious; they are right."

GREEKS WHOSE FAME WILL NEVER DIE

ARISTOTLE IN A THOUGHTFUL MOOD

AN ANCIENT SCULPTURE OF SOCRATES

A FINE BRONZE HEAD OF PLATO

Now, what would happen to us if we were robbed of this power to form ideas? We should simply receive impressions. We should know nothing of the various objects from which we received those impressions. We should have no *ideas*.

Plato suggested one particular idea, of which we are now only beginning to perceive the magnitude. He said that man's mind had invented the language of geometry, that geometry has nothing whatever to do with sensation, and that by means of geometrical reasoning man is able to explore the universe and discover its invisible laws. *Where did it come from, this marvellous idea of geometry?*

As Plato had been a disciple of Socrates, and developed his master's teaching, so

Aristotle believed many things which Plato believed, but he differed from his master in one all-important thing. Plato speculated about the mystery of the universe. Aristotle examined that mystery with eyes and hands.

He was the first naturalist, the first man of science. He felt that it was not enough to *think* about how the world was made, or how the mind gets its knowledge. He took the body of a dead animal and examined its structure. He set a hen on an egg and examined the egg as it turned into a chicken. He dissected fishes and birds. He collected plants and observed their growth. He consulted with hunters about the habits of animals, and with travellers about different countries and climates.

ARISTOTLE AND A PUPIL IN ATHENS

Aristotle was a disciple of Plato, and likewise developed his master's teaching. Aristotle came to Athens from Macedon, and lived for a little while the life of a young man of fashion; but, coming under the influence of Plato, he soon abandoned all trivial self-indulgence, became a passionate seeker after truth, married a woman he loved with all his heart, and lived one of the happiest domestic lives of which we have any record.

We know that he was a little man, with a thin feminine voice, and that he was so delicately constituted that while he was lecturing he had to walk about in order to exercise his body. We also know that he was gentle, modest, and kind. He was neither a hermit like Socrates, nor a man of luxury like Plato, but a domestic man of simple tastes and quiet dignity.

He bought all the old books he could find, and searched them for definite knowledge.

All this was something entirely new in Athens. Plato frowned on his brilliant student. It seemed to him the mark of an inferior mind to read books. Aristotle could not be an original genius if he had to read for ideas, instead of getting them out of his own mind. As for going down to quays to talk to fishermen, travellers, and hunters, surely it was a vulgar thing to do; and as for collecting birds, beasts, and insects, as for examining skeletons, surely this was turning knowledge to the basest of ends.

But Aristotle was a genius if ever a genius lived, and something told him that he was on a road which would lead mankind not only to true knowledge, but to great power.

PLATO AND ARISTOTLE AT THE SCHOOL OF ATHENS—PAINTED BY RAPHAEL ON THE VATICAN WALLS

In many of his conclusions Aristotle was wrong, but he did a work of infinite importance for mankind in bringing into existence the notion of a universal Law governing all things. He saw the order, the harmony, and the beauty of the universe as an expression of the Will of God. Human life was not at the sport of gods and demons. A man might stand upright and fearless on the Earth, knowing that the structure of the universe surrounding him was the work of a great Intelligence. Things did not happen by chance. There was no caprice in the universe. Law reigned everywhere. Let a man not cower beneath the heavens. Let him not dwell with fear in his soul. Let him seek out knowledge in the facts of the world, and trust to Truth.

To this very day the works of Aristotle are consulted by the chief scholars in Europe, and many hold that his was the greatest mind that has ever existed.

THE INVISIBLE WORLD OF THE ATOM WHICH SCIENCE IS NOW EXPLORING

But a new era has now dawned. Science, using the method of Aristotle, has found itself exploring an invisible world. Instead of watching with Darwin the habits of birds, beasts, fishes, insects, and plants, science is now exploring the invisible electric forces which compose the atom, and laying hands on the invisible and atomless stuff of the universe which we call the Ether. It is Aristotle's method, not Plato's; but the method of Aristotle has led even physical science into a region in which we feel the spirit of Plato moving forward. We follow Aristotle, and discover Plato once more.

So it comes about that we now look back with fresh interest and a new gratitude to the three greatest figures in the golden days of Athens, and marvel that so long ago they should have set us on the road which leads to a true understanding of the universe.

Socrates teaches us never to dogmatise, never to pretend, never to be false. He teaches us to be on our guard against self-deception. We must constantly examine our minds and our souls. Do we love goodness? Are we quite sure about that? How are we living? What are the things we like most? Do we truly long for truth and wisdom? Let us stop ourselves again and again, in our speech and in our actions, to be sure that words or things are not deceiving us. Do we long for wisdom? Then how are we living? There are only two things of which we can be perfectly sure—the existence of God and the existence of our own souls. Therefore let us care for our souls.

THE REAL WORLD OF THE SOUL IS THE WORLD OF IDEAS

Plato teaches us that every form of materialism is absurd. The material world is only a shadow, a dream-world, in relation to the soul. The real world of the soul is the world of ideas. We deceive ourselves when we think about things. It is not the things that are important, but the invisible idea behind them. God is not far off, or indifferent. He is everywhere. We dwell in Him. We are a part of Him. We can come into intimate communion with Him by desiring Perfection. " Trees and fields tell me nothing," said Plato; " men are my teachers." He makes us feel the glory of the human soul and the dignity of reason. Virtue is the law of our being.

Aristotle teaches us, above and beyond everything else, to *observe*. Trees and fields do indeed tell nothing to a man who looks at them superficially, but look at them with open eyes and understanding, seek to know how the grass grows and how the trees put forth fresh leaves in Spring, and trees will teach you the laws of God. It is not enough for us to sit with folded hands and closed eyes meditating on the thought of God. It is not enough for us to speculate on the divine mystery and say: Thus and thus have things come to pass. We must tear open the Earth to discover its secrets, we must wrest from Nature ever fresh power to extend our dominion; we must search and grope for additions to our knowledge; we must be content with nothing short of Truth.

THREE MEN OF THE OLD WORLD WHO INFLUENCE OUR LIVES TODAY

So it is that these three men enter into every part of our thinking life, and become in us one single influence making for the fulfilment of God's will upon Earth. To be worthy of this duty, which none of us can escape, we must follow where they lead us. We must be as honest as Socrates, as spiritual as Plato, as intellectual as Aristotle. We must do all that in us lies to develop that inner life, in an invisible realm, which is the only Reality in this world of shadows.

The Great Stories of the World That Will Be Told for Ever

A HEROINE OF THE SOUTHERN SEAS

FAR away in the Pacific Ocean are the Sandwich Isles, for the most part formed of coral, but with lofty volcanic mountains in their midst.

One of these is named Mauna Loa, and is one of the largest and most terrible volcanoes in the world. Its crater Kilauea contains a lake of liquid fire, from six to nine miles round, and the smoke of it rises like a cloud by day and night. The natives used to believe that amid the fire there dwelt a fierce goddess named Pe-le, whose bath was in the mighty crater, and whose hair was supposed to be the glassy threads that covered the hills. Everyone stood in awe of Pe-le, especially women.

The priests said that if a woman climbed the mountain, picked berries from the bushes and flung them into the lake of fire, the goddess would " shake with her thunders, and shatter her island."

But a hundred years ago Christian missionaries came to the island, and gradually the people gave up their faith in the fierce and savage deities they had worshipped, and began to serve the one true Maker of Heaven and Earth. Only the fear of Pe-le was still on them, and her mountain was the heathen stronghold.

Then a brave woman, strong in faith, resolved to defy the goddess in her fastness, and break the spell that bound the people.

Her name was Kapiolani, and she was the wife of Naihe, the public orator of Hawaii. This was in 1825.

One day she plucked a branch of the sacred berries, which it was sacrilege for a woman to touch, and started to climb the mountain. It was a toilsome and terrible ascent of two and a half miles; very dangerous, too, when she reached the slippery sheets of lava.

The enraged priests of Pe-le came out of their sanctuary among the crags, and tried to bar her way with threats, but she heeded them not. She pressed on to the summit, and then clambered down the side of the terrible crater till she stood on the brink of the boiling sea of fire.

Then she hurled into it the sacred berries, with the words:

" If I perish by the anger of Pe-le then dread is her power; but behold, I defy her wrath! I have broken her orders; I live and am safe, for Jehovah the Almighty is my God. His was the breath that kindled these flames; His is the hand which restrains their fury. Oh, ye people, behold how vain are the gods of Hawaii, and serve the Lord! "

Safely Kapiolani descended the mountain, having broken the power of superstition by her brave deed, and won her cause of faith and freedom.

IMAGINATION · CHIVALRY · LEGENDS · GOLDEN DEEDS · FAIRY TALES

THE BOY WHO SERVED HIS TRIBE

IN a wigwam in the woods of North America there once lived a very contented family of the Chippeway tribe.

Father and mother, brothers and sisters, all loved each other and the good things of the Earth. Yet in those days the Chippeways had no idea of growing grain, and lived only by hunting.

When Indian boys reach the age of fourteen they go into some lonely place to fast and meditate on the life before them. The eldest son of the family was now old enough to fulfil this custom. One day his father walked far into the woods with him, built a little wigwam, and told the boy he would bring food in a week's time.

Left alone, the boy spent his time in praying to the Great Spirit. It was not glory or fortune he desired, but only, in some way, to make life less hard for his fellows.

When the third day of his fast came the lad was weak, and could only lie in a kind of dream. All at once the curtains of the wigwam were parted, and a young Indian warrior entered. The plumes of his headdress, his mantle, his mocassins were all green. His voice was like the rush of breezes through boughs and reeds. He said: "The Great Spirit has heard your prayers. I have come to try your courage. Rise and wrestle with me."

The boy got to his feet, and a long, silent struggle began. At last the stranger said: "That is enough for today. I will return tomorrow."

The next evening they wrestled again, and now the lad seemed to gain strength from the touch of his adversary. The green-clad warrior praised him, and promised to come back.

Things fell out as before on the following evening, and the seventh day of the fast the warrior came once more. The lad was utterly exhausted by lack of food, but he pulled himself up the moment his visitor arrived, and directly they came to grips his strength returned. In fact, he threw his opponent.

The lad knelt by him, filled with horror to see that the warrior was dying. But the stranger smiled on him and said:

"Do not grieve. You shall see my green plumes again. But if you want me to live once more you must bury me, and keep my grave covered with clean, moist earth. When I have slept my fill I will break through it, and return to the sun."

So he breathed his last, and the boy obeyed his instructions with a heavy heart.

His father brought him food, and they returned together to the family. But the boy never forgot to tend his friend's grave. Only he kept the thing secret, fearing lest people should say it was a dream.

One day, after a week spent in hunting, the boy returned to the grave, and lo, it was covered in green plumes! When he drew near he saw they were broad leaves, but he had never seen the like, and he did not disturb their growth. The day came when golden tassels swung from them, and he brought his father to see.

The elder man looked and listened. "Son," he said, "this is a gift from the Great Spirit to the people."

And that, say the Chippeways, is how maize was given to the Indians.

LE BALAYEUR ET LA BANQUE D'ANGLETERRE

This is a French translation of the story told in English on page 2886

IL y a quelque temps un balayeur, qui entretenait la chaussée entre la Mansion House et la Banque d'Angleterre, et y passait toutes ses journées à attendre quelques sous, alla trouver un orfèvre et lui dit: "Combien pourrait valoir un bloc d'or aussi gros que ma tête?"

"Cher monsieur, je pars précisément déjeuner," répondit l'orfèvre. "Venez avec moi et nous discuterons l'affaire tout à l'heure."

Ils se rendirent au restaurant et firent un excellent déjeuner; puis, pendant que la balayeur fumait un cigare, l'orfèvre lui dit: "Eh bien, mon ami, montrez-moi à présent l'or en question."

"Mais je n'en n'ai pas," dit le balayeur.

"Comment!" reprit l'orfèvre furieux. "Cependant vous m'avez demandé d'acheter un bloc d'or aussi gros que votre tête!"

"Voyez-vous," répondit le balayeur, "je balaie la chaussée de la Banque d'Angleterre, et il m'est venu à l'esprit que peut-être quelqu'un pourrait y laisser tomber de l'or, et je voulais savoir combien je le vendrais."

"Sauvez-vous, espèce de vaurien!" s'écria l'orfèvre furieux.

"On dit que les rêves ne se réalisent jamais," pensa le balayeur en s'en retournant à son travail, "mais j'ai tout de même fait le bon repas rêvé."

THE HONEST SHEPHERD OF THE KING

This is the story they still tell in the Hungarian villages of the Honest Shepherd of King Matthias, who ruled four hundred years ago

KING MATTHIAS had a shepherd of whom he was very fond because he was so honest that he could not tell a lie.

One day the King of Prussia came to him on a visit, and as they sat at dinner Matthias began to praise his shepherd, saying how upright he was, how honest, not being able to say an untrue word though it should cost him his life.

" I don't believe it," said the King of Prussia.

" What will you wager that it is not so ? " asked Matthias.

" I'll wager anything in reason," said his guest.

" Very well, then," said King Matthias. " Let us settle it. If you can make my shepherd tell a lie I will give you half my kingdom; but if you fail you must give me half of yours."

The King of Prussia agreed, and his daughter, who had accompanied her father, made a note of the wager.

After that they ate and drank and made merry, and thought no more of the matter; but when the King of Prussia went to bed he suddenly remembered his wager, and not a wink of sleep did he get for thinking how he could set a trap for the shepherd so as to induce him to tell a lie. At last he hit on a plan.

He had heard that King Matthias had a golden lamb he was very fond of. If he could bribe the shepherd to give him the lamb the shepherd would have to invent a story to account for its disappearance; and so he would be caught in a lie. Next morning he dressed up as a peasant and went to the pasture where the shepherd was tending his sheep.

" Good morning, my boy," he said to the shepherd. " Do you know why I have come to see you ? "

" I shall know when you have told me," replied the shepherd.

" I want you to give me the golden lamb your master is so fond of. If you'll do that I'll give you enough gold to enable you to ride in a coach-and-six all your life."

" I cannot give you the lamb, your Majesty," replied the shepherd, who had recognised him. " What would my master say ? "

" You could tell him the wolves have eaten it."

" But that would be a lie. I have never told a lie, and I never will."

The King of Prussia saw that it was no good, and went home much discouraged. But hardly had he reached the house when a bright idea occurred to him. What if he were to send his daughter to persuade the shepherd ? Might she not succeed, perhaps, where he had failed ?

So the Princess, as beautiful as the day, went down to the pasture. She took with her a casket filled with as much gold as she could carry, and a bottle of strong wine.

" Good evening, shepherd," she said.

" Good evening, Princess. What brings you here so late ? "

" My great desire for the golden lamb which you would not give to my father. But you will give it to me, will you not ? "

" You know I cannot give it to you, Princess. It is not mine to give."

Then the Princess made him drink of the wine she had brought, and after that she tried again.

" Look," she said. " All this gold will I give you, and much more besides, if you will let me have the lamb."

But the shepherd, whom the wine had made unusually reckless and bold, shook his head.

" All the gold of all the world would not be enough to tempt me," he said; " but if you will give me one kiss you shall have the lamb. I swear it."

So the Princess gave him the kiss he asked for.

" And now," she said, " kill the lamb and skin it, for all I want is the fleece."

The shepherd killed the lamb and gave her the fleece.

The King of Prussia could hardly wait for the morning so that he could run to King Matthias and show him the golden fleece.

" Now we shall see," he said, " whether your shepherd will dare to tell the truth."

Meanwhile the shepherd had come to his senses, and realised what he had done. How was he to tell his master that the lamb was dead ? He would have him hanged, without doubt.

Sadly he started for the palace. As he walked across the fields he came to a hole in the ground, and, stopping before it, he stuck his crook into it so that it stood upright. Then he placed his hat on the top, and bent his knee as if he were standing before the King.

" Good morning, your Majesty," he said solemnly.

" Good morning, shepherd. What news? " he answered himself.

" Ill news, your Majesty. The golden lamb has run away."

" That is a lie, you rascal. If it had, the rest of the flock would have run with it."

Softly the shepherd pulled the stick out of the hole and went on.

" That lie was no good," he muttered.

He came to another hole, and as before he stuck his stick into it and placed his hat on the top, bending his knee.

" Good morning, your Majesty," he said again.

" Good morning. What news? "

" Ill news, your Majesty. The golden lamb has fallen into a well and been drowned."

" That is a lie, you rascal. If it had, the rest of the flock would have fallen in too."

" No good," muttered the shepherd, and, pulling out the stick, he went on.

For the third time he found a hole in the ground and stuck his stick into it.

" Good morning, your Majesty," he said, for the third time.

" Good morning. What news? "

" Very ill news, your Majesty. The golden lamb has been eaten by wolves."

" That is a lie, you rascal. If it had, the rest of the flock would have been eaten by the wolves too."

There was nothing for it; he would be obliged to tell the truth.

Then a sudden idea came to him so that he laughed out loud, and walked up to Buda Castle boldly.

King Matthias was sitting at the head of his table, with the King of Prussia on one side and the Princess on the other.

" God save your Majesties both," he said, " and also her Highness."

" Good morning, shepherd," said King Matthias. " What news? "

" The news I bring is none so ill, your Majesty. It is only this: I have given away your golden lamb for a black one which is much more beautiful."

" Indeed ? " said King Matthias. "And where is the black lamb that is so beautiful? Bring it at once."

" No need to bring it, your Majesty, for it is sitting at your own table," said the shepherd, pointing to the Princess.

King Matthias burst forth into a joyous laugh.

" Very well," he cried. " You have told the truth, and that is all I care about. You have helped me to win the half of a kingdom; it shall be yours."

The King of Prussia, as he had lost his wager, and not wishing to be behindhand in generosity, said he would cap the gift with the hand of his daughter.

" As you have got the kingdom you may as well have the Princess too," he said.

The Princess, who had liked the shepherd from the first, was glad to have him for her husband, so they sent for a priest then and there, and the marriage was solemnised that very same day with great splendour and festivity.

A TALE OF THE BARRIER REEF

ON a small island off Australia, inside the Great Barrier Reef, North Queensland, an Englishman was one day obliged to visit a distant town for supplies, leaving his wife and their baby in the care of their Chinese servant.

While he was away the servant came in great alarm, saying that the natives, who were very fierce and cruel, had come from the mainland, and were marching down the island toward their house. What could be done? There was no hiding-place on the little island, and the master had gone away in the only boat! The Chinaman hastily launched a huge copper vessel used for cooking, helped the woman and the child into it, and, taking a jug of water and a little food, paddled away to an uninhabited islet, three or four miles distant. From there they saw the natives arrive and destroy the little house.

As long as she lived the woman kept a diary of events, telling how the Chinaman made them as comfortable as possible, and how, after many days of self-denial, he went off by himself and hid in the bush, where later he was found, starved to death, wrapped in his old ragged quilt.

Alas! before help came the mother and her babe died too; and they were found with the diary that told the story.

THE SHEPHERDESS AND THE SWEEP

An old-fashioned oak cabinet, quite black with age and covered with fine old carving, once stood in a parlour. It was carved from top to bottom, roses, tulips, and little stags' heads with long, branching antlers, peering forth from amid the curious scrolls and foliage surrounding them. Moreover, in the centre panel of the cabinet was carved the full-length figure of a man. He was certainly not an ordinary man at all, but a most ridiculous charming! Close by her stood a little Chimney-sweep, likewise of porcelain. His face was as fresh and rosy as a girl's, which was certainly a mistake, for it ought to have been black. He and the little Shepherdess had been placed together from the first, and had long ago plighted their troth to one another.

Not far off stood a figure three times as large as the others; it was an old Chinese Mandarin, who could nod his

THEY REACHED THE TOP OF THE CHIMNEY, WHERE THEY SAT DOWN TO REST

figure; he had crooked legs, small horns on his forehead, and a long beard. The children of the house called him "the crooked-legged Field-Marshal-Major General-Corporal-Sergeant."

There he stood, his eyes always fixed upon the table under the pier-glass, for on this table stood a pretty little porcelain Shepherdess, her mantle gathered gracefully round her and fastened with a red rose; her shoes and hat were gilt, and in her hand she held a crook—oh, she was head; he declared that he was grandfather to the little Shepherdess, and when the crooked-legged Field-Marshal-Major-General-Corporal-Sergeant made proposals of marriage to the little Shepherdess he was delighted and nodded his head many times in token of his assent.

"Now you will have a husband," said the old Mandarin. "You will be the wife of a Field-Marshal-Major-General-Corporal-Sergeant, of a man who has a whole cabinet full of silver-plate besides

5831

a store of no one knows what hidden away in the secret drawers."

" I will not go into that dismal cabinet!" declared the little Shepherdess. " I have heard that eleven porcelain ladies are already imprisoned there."

" Then you shall be the twelfth, and you will be in good company," rejoined the Mandarin. " This very night, when the old cabinet creaks, your nuptials shall be celebrated as sure as I am a Chinese Mandarin." Whereupon he nodded his head and fell asleep.

But the little Shepherdess wept, and turned to the beloved of her heart, the porcelain Chimney-sweep.

" I believe I must ask you," said she, " to go out with me into the wide world, for here we cannot stay."

" I will do anything you wish," replied the little Chimney-sweep. " Let us go at once. I think I can manage to support you by my profession."

" If we could but get off the table! " sighed she.

He comforted her, and showed her how to set her little foot on the carved edges and delicate foliage twining round the leg of the table, and at last they reached the floor. But, turning to look at the old cabinet, they saw everything in a great commotion; the old Mandarin had awakened, and was rocking himself to and fro with rage.

" Oh, just see the old Mandarin! " cried the little Shepherdess; and down she fell on her knees in the greatest distress.

" Hast thou indeed the courage to go with me into the wide world? " asked the Chimney-sweep, taking her hand.

" I have," replied she.

The Chimney-sweep looked keenly at her, then led her to the stove.

" Oh, how black it looks! " sighed she. However, she went on with him, through the flues and the tunnel, where it was absolutely pitch-dark.

" Now we are in the chimney," said he; " and see what a lovely star there is shining above us! "

And there actually was a star in the sky, shining right down upon them, as if to show them the way. They crawled and crept till they reached the top of the chimney, where they sat down to rest. Heaven with all its stars was above them, and the town with all its roofs lay beneath them; the wide, wide world

surrounded them. The poor Shepherdess had never imagined all this; she leaned her little head on her Chimney-sweep's arm, and wept so that the gilding broke off from her waistband.

" This I cannot endure! " exclaimed she. " The world is much too large. Oh that I were once more upon the little table under the pier-glass! I shall never be happy till I am there again. I have followed thee out into the wide world, surely thou canst follow me home again if thou lovest me."

And the Chimney-sweep talked very sensibly to her, reminding her of the old Chinese Mandarin and the crooked-legged Field-Marshal - Major - General-Corporal-Sergeant; but she wept so bitterly, and kissed her little Chimney-sweep so fondly, that at last he could not but yield to her request. So with great difficulty they crawled down the chimney.

Everything was quite still. They peeped out. Alas! on the ground lay the old Chinese Mandarin; in attempting to follow the runaways he had fallen off the table, and had broken into three pieces.

" Oh, how shocking! " exclaimed the little Shepherdess. " Poor old grandfather is broken to pieces, and we are the cause of this dreadful accident."

" He can be put together again," replied the Chimney-sweep. " If they glue his back together and put a strong rivet in his neck he will be as good as new."

" Do you really think so? " asked she. And then they climbed up the table and settled down in their old places.

The Chinese Mandarin was put together; the family had his back glued and his neck riveted; he was as good as new, but he could no longer nod his head.

" You have certainly grown very proud since you broke in pieces," remarked the crooked-legged Field-Marshal-Major-General-Corporal-Sergeant, "but I must say, for my part, I do not see that there is anything to be proud of. Am I to have her or am I not? Just answer me that! "

The Chimney-sweep and the little Shepherdess looked anxiously at the old Mandarin; they were so afraid that he would nod his head. But nod he could not, and he was reluctant to tell a stranger that he had a rivet in his neck, so the young porcelain people always remained together. They blessed the grandfather's rivet, and loved each other all their lives.

MOTHER NATURE'S SPRING HELPERS

ONE beautiful morning in the Springtime Mother Nature met Father Time.

"Oh, Father Time," she said, "I am expecting company, and I must clean my house before they come. Do you know of anyone I could get to help me?"

Father Time smoothed his long, white whiskers. He shut his eyes and thought a minute. Then he opened them quickly.

"I have the very thing," he said. "I know just the boy for you. His name is Windy March. At times he is a little mischievous."

"Oh, I shall not mind that," said Mother Nature. "But can he sweep clean?"

"Clean as a whistle!" said Father Time. "I have known him sweep the hats off little girls' heads once in a while. He loves to play tricks on people."

"I KNOW THE BOY—HIS NAME IS WINDY MARCH."

"I will watch him well," replied Mother Nature. "Please tell him to come to my house. You don't happen to know of anyone I could get to do a little washing and scrubbing, do you?" she asked.

"Yes, indeed," said Father Time; "his sister, April Shower, cannot be beaten in that line. She leaves everything clean. My old friend, Madam Spring, says she could not do without her. She helps her every year. Her sister, Miss May, is a master-hand at laying carpets, and she is busy the year round weaving them. Her colours are wonderful and the water never hurts them. They will stand plenty of sun, too. She makes most of her carpets a rich green."

"Oh, Father Time," said Mother Nature, "thank you a thousand times! You do not know what a load you have taken from my mind. I will send word at once to Miss May for a new carpet —the most beautiful one she has. Good-bye. Give my love to Willie Winter; he is a good friend of mine," concluded Mother Nature. And off she went.

JACK FROST OPENS THE CHESTNUT BURRS

LITTLE Miss Chestnut and her two sisters lived up in a tree, in a prickly green house. The house was soft as velvet inside, but the sharp spikes on the outside kept away the squirrels.

But soon Jack Frost came along. Jack does not mind fences, so he knocked at the door of the Chestnut house.

"Little Miss Chestnut," he called, "are you ready to come out?"

But little Miss Chestnut replied :

"I am not quite ready yet, Mr. Jack."

So Jack went off to the house where Miss Hickory-Nut lived. She lived all alone in a round green cottage.

"Miss Hickory-Nut," he called, "are you ready to come out?"

But Miss Hickory-Nut replied :

"I am not quite ready yet, Mr. Jack."

So Jack went off to the low bush where Miss Hazel-Nut lived in a soft green tent. Miss Hazel-Nut was already peeping out.

"Miss Hazel-Nut," he called, "are you ready to come out?"

And little Miss Hazel-Nut replied :

"I am quite ready, Mr. Jack."

So she came down and waited below the bush while Jack went back to see if her neighbours were ready.

Jack knocked once more at the Chestnut house. Little Miss Chestnut opened the door so quickly that she and her sisters fell to the ground.

Then Jack knocked once more at the Hickory house. Miss Hickory-Nut opened the door so quickly that the house fell apart. And all the other houses opened too, and all the nuts came out of doors to see what the matter was.

The next day the children went for a walk. As they walked in the woods they spied the nuts. "See," they said, "the frost has opened the chestnut burrs."

WONDERFUL HOMES OF THE BEES AND WASPS

THE ROUND NEST OF
THE TREE WASP

THE LITTLE
GALL-WASP

A NEST BUILT BY A COMMON
WASP QUEEN

CELLS OF LEAF-CUTTER
BEE IN ROTTEN WOOD

THE LAYERS OF CELLS IN THE NEST
OF THE COMMON WASP

MUD WASP CELLS
ON A BRICK WALL

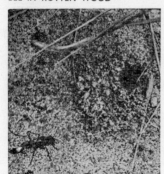

THE SPHEX WASP APPROACHES
ITS BURROW

A LARGE SWARM OF BEES ON
A FRUIT TREE

THE ENTRANCE TO A
HUMBLE-BEE'S NEST

TREE WASP'S NEST HIDDEN
AMONG THE FOLIAGE

COCOONS INSIDE THE NEST
OF A HUMBLE-BEE

A WASP'S NEST BUILT IN
A BANK

Nature's Wonderful Living Family in Earth and Air and Sea

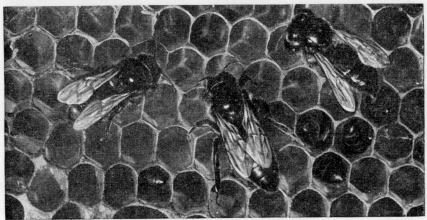

Bees making a comb ready for the queen

BEES AND WASPS

THE proudest and widest literature in the world, next to that of man and his affairs, is the literature of an insect. From the earliest days of learning down to now, poet, philosopher, scientist, and common observers have written of the life and labours of the bee. No other creature save Man himself has inspired so splendid a tribute to efficiency.

The reason is twofold. The economy of the hive is one of the abiding marvels of Nature, an extraordinary civilisation much more ancient than our own. Man has been compelled to observe it because he has dined in the bee's larder since days when he was a wild wanderer on the face of the Earth.

Bees were his sole fount of sweetness. Their honey was all he had to sugar his food and drink. Not until the seventeenth century was old did the product of the sugar-cane reach the poorer people of England. Even to the wealthy it was a luxury. For every drink that was sweetened, for every food whose acid sourness was to be subdued and rendered gracious to the palate, the bee was the source of sweetness, its golden honey the medium.

Honey was the forerunner of sugar. It is the standard of sweetness in the Bible,

where "sweeter also than honey and the honeycomb" are the judgments of the Lord. Every picture of earthly wellbeing in days when men walked near God, has honey as one of the principal sources of bodily contentment.

It was a delight of the table, a thing to sing songs about, a substance in which the Hebrews traded with their neighbours.

But if we desire further evidence as to the value set on honey, we may find it, surprisingly, in a text not of the Bible. It is written upon a tablet of sun-baked clay, left by an ancient Babylonian ruler, in the long long ago.

It is an epitaph, written by himself, by an old-time governor, Shamash-resh-usur, and we love him for the naive simplicity of his claims to the admiration and gratitude of posterity. He boasts of no military glory, of no territorial conquest. No, Shamash believes he is immortalised from the plain fact which he thus sets forth :

Bees, which collect honey, which no man had seen since the time of my fathers and forefathers, nor brought to the land of Sukhi, I brought down from the mountains of the Khabkha tribe, and I put them in the garden of Gabbari-ibni. They collect honey and wax. The preparation of honey and wax I understand, and the gardeners understand it.

PREHISTORIC LIFE · MAMMALS · BIRDS · REPTILES · FISHES · INSECTS

Shamash declared that posterity would ask with wondering reverence of his name and fame: " Is it true that Shamash-resh-usur, Governor of Sukhi, brought honey-bees into the land of Sukhi? "

A WEIRD SUPERSTITION ABOUT THE ORIGIN OF THE BEE

We cannot but fancy that Shamash, the pagan Babylonian, knew more of bees than did Samson, who was the first of men known to history to imagine that true bees issued from the body of a dead animal. Insects much resembling bees do still spring from such carrion, but not actual bees. Drone flies, which closely resemble bees, are thought to have deceived Samson as they deceived Virgil and many a more recent writer.

Indeed, the old literature of the bee teems with fantastic error concerning the life-story of these little insect benefactors of humanity.

Bees were thought not to be naturally born of parents, like other insects, but, if they did not proceed from the decaying body of a dead animal, to originate spontaneously on flowers, whence they were carried home as tiny babies by adult bees to the hives. Honey was a sort of dew from heaven, collected, not made by the insects.

We may laugh at such superstitions today, though the greatest scholars of antiquity and of the Middle Ages and later believed them. Indeed, it was not until Pasteur proved that life cannot arise without parent-life, that the fallacy was reluctantly abandoned by modern opinion.

THE CHILD OF TODAY WHO KNOWS MORE THAN VIRGIL KNEW

For 2000 years boys and girls were taught Virgil's story of the life of the bee, most beautiful in language, shrewdly observant of the truth in parts, fondly erroneous in others, enshrining all the old foolish notions which he had garnered from the legends of Egypt, and memorable for this lovely thought; that, as he says, bees are inspired with a portion of the soul of the universe:

Some have said that bees possess a share of the divine mind, and draw the breath of heaven; for they think that the deity moves through all lands and spaces of the sea and deep of heaven; that hence, flocks, herds, men, every kind of wild beasts, each one at birth, derive the delicate spirit of life; and so in course of things are restored to this fountain, and thither return again by dissolution; and there is no room for death,

but each flies up into the place of a star, and climbs the height of heaven.

Bees, to Virgil, as to his predecessors and followers for many a century, had no parents, we see, and all thought the hive to be governed by a king of more than natural powers. Today a child may know more of the facts of bee-life than was known by all the great minds which once concerned themselves with the problem.

And the charm of it all is that the reality is more wonderful than the myth and tradition woven by the imaginative old romancers. Now let unadorned Truth justify the saying.

Bee-keepers of today have improved on the natural home of the bee, by providing hives of timber in which are inserted trays bearing frames of wax ready for the bees to build their cells upon, so husbanding the insects' labours and making their yield of honey more prolific. But we will picture the scene within one of the old skep hives in the cottage garden, for the bees must do all the work themselves.

THE MASS OF WORKER BEES WHICH HANGS FROM THE ROOF OF A HIVE

See them placed in, or entering of their own free will, such a skep hive, the queen and her attendant swarm of workers. She is the mother of them all, it may be, and she is urgently impelled by Nature to add to her family. But within the hive all is bare, the interior of a dome of darkness, vast to the bees as the dome of St. Paul's or of St. Peter's in Rome to a human child.

A host of the workers begin at once to clean and garnish the chamber. The remainder hang themselves from the roof of the dome, clinging one to another, so that, as the molecules of a drop of water attached to a solid surface sustain the weight of the whole mass of fluid, so the bees at the top bear the pull of an entire curtain of bees hanging down from the roof almost to the floor.

Thus they hang, hour after hour, practically *thinking wax!* Beneath the edges of the segments of the body of a bee are glands which emit this wax. As it slowly makes its appearance it is collected by the legs of the bees and taken to the roof of the hive. Here a few master masons receive the material and model the foundations of the colony, which, like many birds' nests, is suspended, not raised from foundations below.

Soon a number of six-sided cells begin to appear, each joining others like itself. No sooner are a few cells ready than the queen throbs with anxiety to enter upon her duties. She must at once begin egg-laying. She produces her eggs in such haste that at first the workers cannot complete cells rapidly enough for her, and she will drop an egg into a half-finished cradle, but never two in one. So the house is built up, with thousands and thousands of cells. The work might be for eternity, so thorough, so systematic is it, so passionate the ardour with which the toiling bees exhaust their energies over their difficult task.

THE QUEEN BEE WHICH LAYS THREE THOUSAND EGGS IN A DAY

We marvel at the skill of poultry experts in evolving strains of fowls which lay upwards of 300 eggs a year; but this queen bee in her urgent ardour for the good of her race, lays over 3000 eggs a day! She is like a machine in her rapid production, yet unlike a machine in her deliberation.

She can lay eggs which will result in sexless workers, the humble beauties that we see about our flowers. She can lay eggs which will produce male bees, and eggs which will turn into queen bees. There are three kinds of cells—for the worker larvae, for the males, and for the royal children, and she has an egg ready for each. She can lay them with the regularity of a clock pendulum, she can determine their sex, she can cease laying if she chooses.

Throughout her activities she is attended by devoted and respectful maids of honour who follow her wherever she moves, never turning their backs on her. They feed her, they clean her, they caress her with seeming ecstasy. She is parent, sovereign, all in all to them.

Yet they do not really obey her. They are born to obedience, to observance of a law of which the queen-mother is only a living manifestation, and only two occasions can arise when their will is in conflict with hers.

HOW THE BEES HELP NATURE IN FERTILISING THE FLOWERS

Then the mastery is with the daughter slaves, not with the royal mother. We shall see presently how these crises come about.

While all this work is proceeding in the hive the workers whose mission it is to go out and forage, fly, day after day, from sunrise to sunset, visiting every flower within range which is not poisonous, and bears nectar and pollen. All in turn are beneficially plundered, but only one species at a time. There lies a vital value of the bee.

Flowers, to do well, need fertilising by the pollen of other flowers of their own kind. The bees, clad with many delicate bristles and hair-like processes, become covered with the mealy pollen of the flowers they visit, and, on entering flower after flower, leave fragments of that pollen wherever they penetrate. So the fertilisation is effected in the exact way that Nature designed.

The pollen, however, is far more abundant than the plants require. Great quantities of it are collected by the bees, and stored in little natural panniers or horny pouches on their hind legs. The insects bear off such burdens of the pollen for conversion into bee bread that sometimes they cannot reach the hive without resting by the way. As it is received it is placed in cells by other workers, covered with a little honey and sealed up, preserved for future use.

THE WONDERFUL VALVE THAT CONTROLS THE DISPOSAL OF THE NECTAR

The nectar is collected by the bee in two ways. The insect can lap up the fluid, where the supply is minute; but where plenty swells the nectaries of the bloom, the tongue can be fashioned into a pump, and the gracious drops sucked into the first of the bee's two stomachs.

None of the fables imagines a more complex wonder than actually exists here. The first stomach is simply a receiver into which the nectar is drawn from the flower. Should she wish, the bee can transfer some or all of it to the second stomach, access to which is given by means of a valve under her control; or the nectar can be returned direct to the mouth to be stored in the cells of the comb.

Thus, when she needs food, the bee permits some of the nectar and pollen to pass from the first to the second stomach, where the substances undergo digestive changes as does food when it passes into the stomach of a mammal.

Now, the nursing bees have to feed not only themselves but the larvae, which are as incapable of assimilating the untreated nectar as human babies are unable to digest the undiluted milk of a cow.

Therefore, the nurses pass the honey and pollen from the first to the second stomach, where, after it has been mixed with digestive juices, it is forced, by way of a special duct, back into the mouth, and is emitted, in a thick whitish fluid, called bee milk.

That is not the end of the natural mystery, for, according to need and nature, so is the food put forth by the bee. There is one food for the future neuter, there is a second for the male, and there is a third, the regal diet, for the grub which is to be a queen. In addition to all, the character of the food is changed by the nurse to suit each stage in the development of the larva.

The sole material out of which these vital diets are wrought are the juice and dust of flowers, but what a chemist there is to effect the changes necessary to enable them to juggle accurately with that minute speck of life which comes from the queen-mother's egg.

In this laboratory of life disciplined wonders are wrought to match these physical marvels. All is as perfectly ordered as in a man-made city, with separate duties for all. There are the queen's attendants, there are the nurses, the servants about the hive, who keep the place clean and healthy, carrying out débris like good sanitarians.

THE LITTLE LIVING FANS WHICH KEEP THE HIVE COOL

There are those who tend the weak, and those who collect the bodies of the dead and fly away with them from the hive. Not least astonishing are the ways of those who regulate the temperature of the hive. The busier the bees, the more the heat of their bodies rises, till the hive becomes unhealthily hot. Then the appointed corps of bees whose duty it is, fan for hours with their wings, to drive out the heated air and so restore the temperature to its proper level.

The workers have no joy beyond enthusiasm for labour. They have a mother but no children, no play, no recreation. They begin their toil as soon as they have the strength to stand; they work till their death which, in the summer, occurs in about six weeks. Those who last through the winter are of the latest broods of summer.

All the labour, all the refined organisation of the hive, is directed to the main-tenance of an adequate supply of live bees in the hive. The queen, when she takes her wedding flight, returns and never leaves the hive again till she has established an enormous colony of young bees in the cells. As these hatch out they take their turn as nurses in ministering to the wants of larvae still younger than themselves. At the end of a fortnight their probation is ended, and then, but not till then, they go forth to bring in food and wear and work themselves to death.

HOW THE BEE EATS ITS WAY INTO THE WORLD

Now let us peep into the cell in which an egg is deposited by the queen. In a few days it hatches and a grub floats in a bath of honey. As it grows its head reaches the top of the cell, and there it is fed by the working nurses. Two or three times in the course of its larval career the larva turns upside down, away from the nurses. Each time it does so it casts its skin, moults like a caterpillar.

Finally, like the caterpillar, it reaches a chrysalis stage, spins itself a silken cocoon, and rests entranced while Nature brings about the great change which transforms it from a grub into a bee. After three weeks the life in the cell is ended ; a new bee is about to enter the world. At the moment, however, it is sealed in its cradle.

Its cell is crowned with a mixture of pollen and wax. It must eat its way through. In so doing it feeds itself and gnaws a way to freedom. It comes forth at last, fully clad, but a weak and trembling bee, soft-winged, soft of limbs, incapable of sturdy action till the next day. Then, as soon as strength has come to it, it hastens to its nursemaid duties, and an older nursemaid is released to fly into the world and rifle flowers.

THE ANGRY QUEEN WHO TRIES TO KILL HER DAUGHTERS

Except that they are in larger cells and are differently fed, the development of the males and princesses is similar to that of the workers. But the drones are stingless, big but lazy, and have to be assisted to their meals. They do no work. They fly at the appointed time, to meet the young queens of other hives. It is their wedding day and their death day, for after their marriage flight they perish.

Should the drones be still alive at the end of the season the workers kill them

BEES, WASPS, AND SAW-FLIES

LEAF-CUTTER
BEE

THE QUEEN, WORKER, AND DRONE OF THE
COMMON HUMBLE-BEE

THE PALISADE
SAW FLY

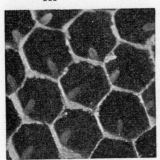

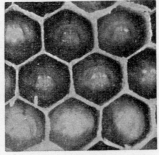

THREE STAGES IN THE LIFE OF A WASP—THE EGGS IN THE CELLS, THE LARVAE OR GRUBS, AND A YOUNG
WASP BREAKING OUT OF THE CELL

GIANT TAILED-
WASP, OR SIREX

ORANGE-COLOURED
SAW-FLY

A SOLITARY WASP

GOOSEBERRY SAW-FLY

COMMON WASP
DRONE

THE DRONE, QUEEN, AND
WORKER HORNET

COMMON WASP
WORKER

or expel them from the hive and leave them to die. No useless mouths find food in a winter city of the bees.

But now for the princesses, the potential queens who may found other families. Quite a different matter is here. The queen, their mother, is an ogress dire where they are concerned. She can brook no rival near her throne, not even her own daughters. As they grow up in the cell their voices come to them, and they raise the angry royal pipe. It infuriates their mother, and the fire of battle kindles in her angry heart. She makes towards their cells, intending to thrust in her barb and kill them. For the first time her slaves resist her. They will not let her play the murderess—yet.

Wiser than she, they gently but determinedly hustle her away from the royal cells. Now either she must go forth, leading a swarm with her, and leave the hive to a new queen from the cells, or tragedy must ensue. If the season be young the queen goes, and thousands of workers go with her.

NATURE'S MERCIFUL PROVISION FOR THE FUTURE OF THE RACE
Like the Israelites on quitting Egypt, they load themselves with treasure, though here it is their own, and consists only of food. So filled are they with good things that they are almost powerless to sting. Taking advantage of this fact, when we wish to take the honey, we blow smoke on the bees. This alarms them and makes them think of danger and journeys and load up with honey.

While the queen is waiting to swarm, and the young princesses are endeavouring to fight their way out of the cells, the prudent workers pile more and more wax on top of the cells to keep the young aristocrats in. Eventually they are permitted to come out, when the queen is gone. If more than one should emerge at the same time, two of them fight.

They know exactly where to plant their stings in order to administer a fatal thrust; but so powerful is the instinct for the preservation of the race, even at the cost of the individual, that if two queens in a death grapple are both so placed that each can kill the other, they draw apart and manoeuvre afresh, so that the lethal wound shall be inflicted by one only, permitting the other to survive and carry on the work of re-peopling the hive.

But not every queen can swarm in turn. The time comes when it is inexpedient for more bees to go forth to colonise. Then the workers allow the reigning mother to have her own way. She goes from cell to cell, and with a stab into each, slays all her royal daughters.

For three years she may rule her teeming children. Then her strength weakens, her flow of eggs begins to fail. In that case the workers either allow a younger queen to come out and put her to death, or they themselves turn in multitudes on her and quietly end her life so that perfect efficiency in reproduction may again reign in the home.

WHY THE BEES ARE AMONG MAN'S MOST VALUABLE ALLIES
In all else the neuters are the adoring slaves of the queen; but as we see, it is a principle that they worship, and she is the living symbol of that principle. So long as she is capable of producing eggs, day and night, throughout the summer, the rest wait on her like human slaves in attendance on an Oriental potentate. When she fails they turn on her and destroy her, or permit her destruction.

In any case the hive must be maintained at a high pitch of excellence. It is that supplies may feed not only the broods and workers, but the semi-hibernating family, throughout the winter, that bees work so hard. It is that which gives them such value to man. He takes their surplus honey, and they, in getting it, fertilise his flowers and fruit trees so thoroughly as to add a considerable amount yearly to the national wealth.

Such machine-like success attends the operations of the average hive that we might despair of human civilisation as hopelessly in the rear of this insect economy. But bees are as fallible as we are in our work for the common good.

THE TERRIBLE DISEASE WHICH KILLS THE BEES BY SUFFOCATION
They blunderingly admit parasites fatal to their lives and fortunes—such little horrors as the larvae of the oil beetle, which destroy the bee grub in its cell, death's head moths which steal the honey, and other obnoxious invaders. Moreover, their morality sometimes breaks down, with appalling results.

One of their deadliest foes is a mite which invades the breathing tubes of the bees, and sets up what is known as the

Isle of Wight disease. The bees are killed by suffocation. Nearly all the old English stock was exterminated in recent years by this malady. How came the contagion so widespread? Because from time to time bees forsake the paths of rectitude, and, instead of foraging on their own honest account, turn robbers and pillage the stores contained in weakly defended hives. In such hives lurked the disease, and the conquerors carried back the seeds of death with their spoils.

THE GREAT COMPANY OF INSECTS WITH 40,000 KNOWN SPECIES

Nothing is perfect, even in the civic system of the honey-bee, which is almost the highest yet, beneath that of man himself. Still, with these little flaws, it remains a scheme of wonder far excelling in ascertained fact, the misty miracles ascribed by all the old writers to these splendid little people.

But honey-bees are, of course, only one of innumerable sorts of bees. They belong, as a matter of fact, to a company of insects called the *Hymenoptera*, of which we know probably 40,000 species, while there are perhaps four times as many still to be discovered.

The wild bees are as interesting in their way as the citizens of the hives in theirs; but they are not social, they do not assemble in great colonies. Notable examples are the Andrena and Halictus, which tunnel little cells for their eggs in sandy soil, though the adults sleep on leaves, not resting, like fly or bird, on their legs, but holding on by their jaws. The mason-bee moulds grains of sand and saliva into a series of perfect cells, and sometimes not only takes possession of holes in our gates, posts, and doorways, but even blocks up our keyholes with these ingenious nurseries.

THE UNDERGROUND NEST OF THE FAMILIAR HUMBLE-BEE

The leaf-cutter bee is that artist which takes bites out of our foliage, leaving those crescent-shaped gaps which we see in laurel, rose, and other leaves. With the stolen parts it forms neat nests, rolling up the pieces of leaf, placing them in hollows or in special burrows and charging each cell with egg, pollen, and honey.

Still more industrious is the carpenter bee, which excavates chambers in the stems of plants or in trees, and makes its cradles in a series of these linked nurseries.

Most familiar of all the non-hive sorts are the humble-bees, of which we have several species. Some make their nests below ground, where one has obtained from a single home combs full of larvae filling a stable bucket. Others have their homes above ground, among coarse, close grass, and other herbage.

Fierce warriors as they may prove if molested, the humble-bees are good friends to us, for they are enormously industrious, perhaps the hardest workers of the entire bee family, and their value as fertilisers of clover alone is beyond all calculation.

Now we must turn to another vast company, the wasps, which, many in species and habit, may be grouped into two divisions, the hermit and the social kind. They make no honey, they perform no direct service for man, but they are indirectly valuable servants, inasmuch as they kill tremendous numbers of flies and other insects hurtful to us.

Let us at the outset get this matter into figures. It has been found that the inmate workers of a small wasps' nest brought home daily no fewer than 2000 flies, a number which might safely be multiplied by 10 or 12 as the season advanced and more flies appeared.

THE DREARY LIFE OF THE QUEEN WASP IN THE DARK WINTER MONTHS

Against this fact we have to remember that wasps do great injury to growing fruit, that they sting us very badly, that they sometimes run amok for unexplained reasons among horses and cattle, and drive them to madness and death with their virulent barbs.

In practice there is little to choose between the sting of bee and wasp. Both, inflicted on the tongue, may be fatal; both are highly painful and alarming to timid and susceptible people.

In a way, the home of the social wasp challenges a respect and admiration second only to that of the bee. We get nothing out of it but stings or a combful of grubs which fishermen use as bait. But the wonder is there, none the less.

It lacks the continuity of life proper to the hive, for there is no winter existence in the true sense of the term. The queen dozes away the dark, cold months, inert, comatose as a hibernating bat. All her family are dead, workers, drones, all save herself and rival queens.

In the early spring the queen makes a little hole in some secluded bank; she may even go back to a nest previously used. There she begins a comb, not of wax, but of a sort of paper, fashioned from woody fibres which she chews with her jaws into this substance. Here in the cells she lays her eggs, and hunts industriously to bring in food for the grubs as they hatch. When the neuter workers appear, they relieve her of her nursing and foraging duties.

THE PAPER NESTS HANGING IN THE BRANCHES OF THE TREES

They bring in food and tend the on-coming generations, and thousands on thousands of wasps appear in a single nest in the course of a hot summer. First come the sexless workers, then the males. They, like the drones of the hive, do no work, but fly forth to meet queens from other nests. The summer and autumn wane, and the combs, now raised tier on tier, are crowded with grubs not yet mature. But the time has come for all but the mother to die. The last act of the active workers is to kill all that remain unhatched.

The land is left once more to the queens. They alone survive to await the sleep of winter and the advent of a fresh spring.

The hornet is the largest of British wasps, an insect one inch in length and armed with a desperate sting. It nests in hollow trees, or beneath the eaves of out-houses, and its brood rarely consists of more than two hundred offspring in the most favourable seasons. Then there is a notable wall wasp with us which calmly digs away the mortar of our walls, forms a tube-shaped tunnel, and places its egg in it. Other wasps construct great paper nests attached to the branches of trees; some make their homes of mud, of clay, of sand mixed with saliva, and so forth.

The Sphex wasps catch grasshoppers and crickets, paralyse them, and store them, four to a chamber, in place of honey and pollen for their larvae.

THE TINY GRUB AND ITS BIG STORE OF FOOD

Practically all the wasps leave paralysed prey for the sustenance of their progeny, but the habit is not entirely to our advantage, for one member of the species captures honey-bees and serves them in the same way, five precious bees sacrificed to appease the appetite of each wasp grub.

Wasps undoubtedly possess intelligence, in some respects excelling that of the well-disciplined bee. A bee, enclosed in an un-corked bottle, whose base is extended toward the light, will beat its head raw trying to fly out of the bottom of the bottle; but the wasp will find its way to freedom through the open neck.

Watchers have noted with delight the extreme pains the wasp takes to learn the site of the place in which it has constructed its nest. It does not fly a mile away, and then back infallibly as the out-come of pure instinct. Before departing it flits from point to point, noting landmarks, here a leaf, there a stone and a blade of grass, farther away a whole bush or plant, till everything in the neighbourhood has been built up into a memory map. When it comes back from a long hunt, bearing a victim, it will drop its prey while it searches out its landmarks. No human airman is more careful in his observations of guide-posts than a wasp.

In addition to these greater wasps which we have been studying, there are innumerable related forms, which include one of the most important of groups, the thousands of species of ichneumon wasps, called generally ichneumon flies. They have the long apparatus at the tail which in the wasps and bees is a sting, but here is only a hollow drill serving to penetrate the body of a victim and thrust down an egg into the wound.

THE LITTLE WASP WHICH BURIES ITS EGG IN A CATERPILLAR

To these we owe unstinted gratitude, for the majority of them make caterpillars their living cradles. The idea is horrible, of course, but if it were not practised by these insects, caterpillars might devour the bulk of our vegetable crops.

Related to these are those master detectives, the parasitic gall-wasps, some of which pierce the tough nest of the mason-bee, and place an egg in the body of a hidden larva, while others, as the gouty-legged wasp, do the same to the larva of beetles living in water. Even more marvellous are the feats of the egg-wasps, which actually lay their eggs in the eggs of moths and butterflies, and so prevent these from hatching into caterpillars.

Another fascinating company are the true gall-wasps or Cynipidae. Not all the galls observed are produced by these minute wasps, but those on the oaks and the roses

A GROUP OF NATURE'S CLEVER CHILDREN

GIANT POMPILUS WASP

HAWTHORN SAW-FLY AND COCOON

RED-BANDED SAND WASP

HONEY BEE DRONE

HONEY BEE WORKER

HONEY BEE QUEEN

THE ICHNEUMON WASP, A PARASITIC FLY

A BRITISH SOLITARY WASP AND ITS NEST

POLISTES, A EUROPEAN SOCIAL WASP, AND ITS NEST

PSITHYRUS HUMBLE-BEES

THE MASON BEE AND ITS NEST

EUROPEAN CARPENTER BEES

The pictures on these pages are by Mrs. M. H. Crawford, Messrs. Collins, Hanley, Pike, Ward, and others

are. How the galls arise around the egg and developing larvae is still something of a mystery. It is fairly clear, however, that the gall is not injurious to the tree. As a matter of fact, we benefit, for the finest of the old inks was obtained from the gall nuts of the oak.

Closely related to these groups are the saw-flies, an important assemblage of insects of which foresters and tree lovers in general go in dread. Some infect the stems, some the leaves, and some the solid wood of trees and plants to the infinite hurt of the living growth.

WHY THE STEM SAW-FLY IS AN ENEMY OF MAN

The stem saw-flies are deposited by the parent in the stalks of rye and other grain, and the shoots of our pear and other trees. They live in the grub stage entirely on the substance of the host, and work terrible damage where their numbers are large. Hidden from human eyes, they eat the immature substance of a growth which should become food for Man.

Then there are the great tailed-wasps, the giant Sirex, and others, members of the *Siricidae*, which lay their eggs on pine trees, where their destructive larvae undergo so long a period of hungry infancy that often they do not complete their cycle of infant life till the tree has been felled, sawn up and built into the fabric or furniture of a house. Then out comes a booming Sirex, probably as startled at its unnatural surroundings as the lawful inmates of the abode at its unexpected and unwelcome appearance.

With the true saw-flies we are all more familiar, for they are among the worst pests we have in our beautiful pine woods. The eggs are laid on the leaves or needles of the trees in such numbers that when the larvae appear the tree seems alive with them; it is coloured by their swarming numbers, and its branches are bowed down with the weight of the crawling army of devourers.

HOW NATURE HELPS MAN BY KEEPING DOWN AN ENEMY

Any child in a garden has seen what havoc little green-fly can work with roses, killing old growth and preventing new, so we can all imagine the effect on pine trees of teeming swarms of lusty grubs of the saw-fly. They are indeed one of the greatest menaces to our timber. Here again we are aided by Nature, for it is known that no fewer than forty species of winged parasites infest the saw-fly larvae; while even the wicked little mice do us a good turn when winds and rains cast down the grubs, or when the larvae have turned into chrysalises and fallen to the ground.

It is the mission of entomologists to learn more and more of the ways of these beneficial parasites, and to encourage their multiplication, as lady-birds are protected and fostered for war with the insects which from time to time menace the fruit orchards of California and Australia. We badly need, for example, the perfect parasite for that little ruffian of the field and kitchen garden, the turnip saw-fly. A single female lays as many as 200 eggs on the leaves of the turnip, and all the summer the larvae slowly sap the juices which should be forming good turnips instead of more saw-flies.

Turnips have an unsuspected place in the history of the health and happiness of England. In those miscalled " good old days " we had no turnips, no root crops, no potatoes, and the rest. So our population was small and constantly exposed to the disease to which absence of fresh vegetables conduces.

THE BAD OLD DAYS FOR CATTLE BEFORE THE TURNIP CAME TO ENGLAND

There was no winter fodder for sheep or cattle, so all but a few poor animals had to be slaughtered in the autumn, and for the whole of the winter salted food, and not good at that, was the staple diet. When the turnip came, cattle and sheep might live through the winter and so afford fresh meat at need. The turnip gave them as good a hold on life as the laying up of stores in summer gave the wintering bee.

That is why we so begrudge the turnip saw-fly its freedom to maul and maim this indispensable food crop in Great Britain and elsewhere. But, turn where we may, we see a parasite for everything, we ourselves being the paramount parasite of all, levying toll everywhere on everything eatable and usable.

Men began with the bee and have written and sung its praises for thousands of years. When we have given a tithe of the attention to the things that live in the same lands with the bee, we shall no longer have need to fear the saw-flies and their ravenous allies. Till then our crops are not wholly our own, nor our woods and forests our indisputable property.

The Story of the Things We See About Us Every Day

The Penrhyn slate quarry in Wales

THE STONES OF OUR CITIES

IT took millions of years for Nature to form the rocks which make up the outer part of the Earth's crust, and in their making both fire and water were engaged. Now man is everywhere using these powers to break up the rocks and turn their fragments to his own use. In his search for the stones and marbles of his cities, man is for ever breaking up the surface of the Earth.

For untold ages the rocks stood apparently eternal and immovable, but no sooner did man appear than he began to cut away the everlasting hills. First of all he broke off loose fragments with which to make spearheads and arrow points and hammer heads to help him in his quest for food. He lived in caves until it occurred to him that it would be more convenient to carry away pieces of the rock and pile them up to form a hut.

So, from the rough Old Stone Age, when he had obtained more skill in the working of the stone and rock, man passed to the New Stone Age. He raised stone temples and monuments like Stonehenge, and from that time to this he has, with ever greater skill and power, been chipping away or splitting up and blasting the rock for the building of houses and temples, the raising of monuments, or the making of roads.

Yet so inexhaustible is the supply of material that after thousands of years of work there is scarcely any perceptible change of appearance in the bedrock itself. In the great Carrara quarries of the Apennines, for instance, worked for 2000 years, it is only when we stand in the quarries that we can see that any marble has been removed. At a distance the skyline is unchanged, the mountains look the same as ever. For while a great boulder blasted out of a cliff looks very big compared with a man, it appears as a speck against a mountain.

For coal, man must generally dig down below the surface, but for stone or marble he need not do that. The rocks in most cases lie within view, ready to be wrenched away. Every kind of stone for beauty or for use is to be had for the taking, though some kinds are not easily quarried.

Every year many millions of tons of rock of one kind and another are quarried from the Earth where they have rested for millions of years, and are sent away to distant places. In earlier ages men had to use the rock that lay nearest to their hand, but now, with the vast improvements in the means of transport, they can obtain rock from anywhere and take it to any part of the world.

INDUSTRIES · HOW THINGS ARE MADE · WHERE THEY COME FROM

PICTURE-STORY OF QUARRYING

Many kinds of stone are taken from the earth, but the methods of quarrying are much the same. Holes are drilled in the rock face and an explosive charge inserted. After the blasting the bigger lumps of rock are split by hand before being hoisted to the surface. Here is the scene at one of the most famous quarries in the world—on the Isle of Portland in Dorset.

Portland Stone is used for building in all parts of the world, and in this picture we see great blocks which have been prepared for export.

Here men are at the rock face deep in the quarry after blasting has removed great lumps of rock. Sometimes the lumps are huge—weighing seven or eight tons—and have to be split into smaller pieces by hand before being placed in chains and then hoisted to the surface by great cranes.

SAWING THE STONE INTO NEAT BLOCKS

To reduce the rough stone lumps into convenient blocks they are cut into varying sizes by saws. The cutting edge of a circular saw like this may contain more than 200 diamonds.

Here we see a series of saws which can cut a huge stone block into a number of slabs. The saws shown on this page can cut stone as easily as an ordinary saw will cut through timber.

SHAPING THE STONE FOR THE BUILDER

Here is a general view of a sawmill in which stone is cut to the required sizes. From the sawmill the roughly-cut stone goes to the stonemasons' shop.

The stonemasons are here seen at work, skilfully carving the rough stone blocks into neat shapes. When the stone leaves the shop it is ready for use.

IN A CORNISH GRANITE QUARRY

The scene after a big blast in the great Penryn granite quarry in Cornwall. Cornish granite is in great demand because of its strength and endurance. The power needed to crush it is 1171 tons to the square foot. This granite is generally used in the building of lighthouses in exposed positions.

QUARRYING SLATE IN NORTH WALES

This picture was taken in the largest slate quarries in the world, near Mount Snowdon in Wales. Here a pneumatic drill is being used to bore the rock face for blasting.

IN A WELSH SLATE QUARRY

Here is the scene in a slate quarry in Wales. Each loaded truck is hoisted by cableway to the top of the quarry and is taken to the " dressing sheds," where it is prepared for use.

In this picture we see loaded trucks arriving at a " dressing shed." Here the great slate blocks are sorted and cleaned, all waste being removed. The slate is then ready for the craftsman.

MAKING SLATES FOR THE BUILDER

The slates are split from the blocks by craftsmen using mallet and chisel. They are trimmed to the required size on a machine or by hand, as seen here, and are then ready for the builder.

HOW MARBLE LEAVES THE QUARRY

The great Carrara marble quarries in Italy are the most famous in the world. There are 400 quarries, and in a normal year at least half-a-million tons of marble are blasted from the mountainside.

After blasting operations the marble is split into small pieces, as seen in the picture on the left. Each piece is then made neat and clean by being cut on a wire saw or by hand. In the picture on the right we see trimmed blocks ready to be carried to the quarry workshops.

MARBLE READY FOR THE SCULPTOR

Here in this great yard the marble blocks are stacked ready for shipment anywhere in the world. From the workshops seen on the left of the picture, carved blocks are carried by cranes along the gantry to be loaded into railway trucks.

While in the yard each block is measured and valued, and it is ready for use. Sometimes, to meet a special need, the blocks have to be trimmed by hand, as seen in the picture on the right.

HOW THE EARTH PILLARS CAME THERE

Here we see a remarkable group of earth pillars in the Austrian Tirol, each with its umbrella rock on top. The different heights indicate that the earth pillars are at various stages in their formation, the tallest being the oldest.

This picture shows how the earth pillars seen above were formed. The rain sweeping down on the landscape washed away the soft bed of rock, but where large stones were embedded these acted as umbrellas, protecting the ground beneath. See question on page 5859.

Plain Answers to the Questions of the Children of the World

Sluicing for gold at a mine in New Zealand

WHAT BECOMES OF ALL THE GOLD?

SOME of it wears away, and so is lost, but most of it remains in the world in some visible form or other.

From the earliest times, long before what we call history began, gold was found in river sand. Its presence was detected by the gleaming grains of metal, which were separated from the soil by successive washings, and further search sometimes led to the discovery of nuggets of gold of various sizes. Primitive man used the precious metal to deck his body with ornaments made of beads strung together, and not until a later stage of his development did he learn how to work it into artistic forms and cast it into moulds.

Traces of gold decoration have been found even on flint knives of the Stone Age, and by the time of the First Dynasty in Egypt, more than 5000 years before the Christian Era, gold jewellery of exquisite fineness and artistic design was produced. Some of this remains to this day as a reminder that our boasted modern civilisation, in some ways at least, has much to learn from the story of the past.

The total amount of gold produced in ancient times is unknown, but that it was enormous may be judged by its lavish employment by David and his successor for the building of the Temple at Jerusalem.

Conquered nations were usually made to pay tribute in the form of gold, and enormous wealth thus passed from one owner to another. All the empires of the past amassed vast stocks of the precious metal by conquest, and even after the conqueror had carried off as much as could be found, there remained large amounts hoarded up or buried in the soil to evade detection. This practice of hoarding gold has been going on from time immemorial, especially in India and other Eastern countries.

The discovery of America gave a great impetus to gold production and the metal began to supplant silver as the chief medium of exchange, traders throughout the world agreeing to use it as an instrument for simplifying the exchange of one commodity for another. In 1816 England led the world by adopting a gold standard and fixing 85s as the price of an ounce of refined gold.

Gold production increased enormously, and so did that trade in which it formed the basis of all credit transactions. The annual production of 600,000 ounces in the beginning of the 19th century had risen to thirty times that quantity by its close, while in a recent year as many as 28 million ounces were produced. South

FIRE · WIND · WATER · LIFE · MIND · SLEEP · HOW · WHY · WHERE

Africa, whose mines round about Johannesburg were discovered toward the end of last century, produces nearly half of the world's annual supply, to which Canada and the United States are also big contributors. Russian mines now take third place to Canada, their production in a recent year reaching two million fine ounces.

Though before the First World War very much new gold was used in the arts and industry and one-fourth was coined, few coins are now minted, and all but about one-seventh is bought as bullion to be added to the reserves of the nations.

The total gold reserves held by the nations had reached over 770 million ounces at the outbreak of the Second World War, by far the greatest amount being held by America. In the critical months that have since passed the amounts held by other nations have fluctuated considerably, while the market price of gold has risen.

The gold currencies all the world over have been suspended, gold being mined and quickly buried again in national vaults where it is useless to the world at large. Whenever this has happened, gold is lost as much as the gold which lies in ships sunk at sea, or by the normal wear and tear from the handling of objects of art, and of gold coinage when gold was normal currency early in this century.

Why Do The Stars Twinkle?

No explanation yet offered has quite satisfied scientists as to why the stars twinkle. The theory that their light interferes with itself on its journey through space is not altogether satisfactory, and the suggestion that the thin pencil of light from a star is disturbed in our atmosphere, thereby giving a twinkling effect, is also inadequate. Another theory has been proposed by Professor Vegard, of Oslo University, Norway. He has declared that on the borders of the Earth's atmosphere is a layer made up of tiny crystals of nitrogen dust; that the Earth is enclosed in what has been described as a crystal globe; and that this layer of crystals high up in the atmosphere is responsible for some of the many strange things that happen.

It makes long-distance wireless possible by reflecting the waves and preventing them from being lost in space; it is the cause of the greenish colour of the Aurora Borealis; and to it is due the twinkling of the stars. The density of the dust-layer of nitrogen, the Professor explains, is very small and the average distance between the particles is comparatively large. If we drew a line through the dust atmosphere it might cut only a few particles, and this number might undergo considerable and rapid changes. When we look on a fixed star with the eye it is the average intensity through a cylinder, with a cross-section equal to the pupil of the eye, which determines the observed light intensity. Inside such a narrow cylinder the number of scattering particles may undergo considerable variations, and these variations may be seen as twinkling.

When Was Jesus Born?

Strange as it may seem, Jesus was born about 6 B.C.—that is, in the year 6 *Before Christ!* The exact year or month is not known, but the day was almost certainly not December 25, nor was the year that from which we date the Christian Era. This era was fixed by the Abbot Dionysius Exiguus in the sixth century, and places the birth of Jesus in the year of Rome 754. But Herod the Great died in the year of Rome 750, and we know that Jesus was already born when Herod was alive, though how long this event took place before the death of Herod we cannot say. Certainly it was not later than 5 B.C. and probably was between 6 and 7 B.C. These facts were found out in later times when, of course, it was impossible to alter the calendar. The month in which Jesus was born could hardly have been December, when nights are cold and shepherds do not remain in the open-air as they were doing at the Nativity. Shepherds began to camp out about the vernal equinox, March 25, so that almost certainly Jesus was born in the spring or summer.

How Long Does Money Take to Double Itself at Compound Interest?

The number of years an amount takes to double itself at any rate of compound interest not exceeding ten per cent per annum is approximately the number 70 divided by the rate per cent of the interest.

Thus £100 lent at compound interest at 5 per cent would become £200 in about $\frac{70}{5}$ years, or 14 years. The same sum lent at simple interest at the same rate would double itself in 20 years.

What is an Earth Pillar ?

Earth pillars are singular geological formations—clay capped by stones. They are found in the Austrian Tirol, and elsewhere, and consist of tall pillars of earth stuck full of stones and each surmounted by a large block of rock. At one time there was a bed of soft rock here, with many stones and rocks embedded in it. Then gradually heavy rains carried awa the soft material, but the larger stones and blocks of hard rock acted as umbrellas, protecting the soft ground immediately underneath. In the course of time a whole group of these pillars, each with its umbrella rock on top, was left standing like an army of giants in the valley or on the hillside. Earth pillars occur in Scotland and other parts of Great Britain, but it is in Tirol that they are seen at their best. The sculpturing of the taller examples began first; then came shorter ones, which only began to be cut out by the rains when they enjoyed the protection of their umbrella rock which lay farther down in the bed of soft material. On, or just above, the ground level we may see the beginning of the sculpturing of earth pillars. See pictures on page 5856.

What are Isotopes ?

Isotopes are " twin " atoms which behave exactly the same way chemically but are physically different. For example, water (H_2O) consists of two atoms of hydrogen and one of oxygen, but there are isotopes of hydrogen (*deuterium* and *tritium*) which have twice or three times the mass of ordinary hydrogen yet will chemically combine with oxygen atoms to make *heavy water*.

Uranium, from which atomic energy is released, is found in two natural forms—Uranium 238 and Uranium 235 ; and the second, which is the fissionable material needed for producing power, is present in natural ore only as one atom to every 140 of Uranium 238. But if the element Thorium is bombarded with the atomic particles, the neutrons, it is converted into yet another isotope of uranium—Uranium 233—which is also fissionable.

It is now possible to produce isotopes of any of the 92 natural elements. These are called " radioactive isotopes " because they emit rays of particles. As they behave chemically like ordinary elements, they can be made into chemical compounds, or absorbed into the living chemistry of plants, animals, or human beings ; and as they emit rays which instruments can detect, scientists can now use them as " tracers " and follow them. For example, they can trace radioactive iodine into the thyroid gland, or phosphorus into the bones ; they can trace iron into the blood cells.

In isotopes scientists now have a means of discovering things which they could never know before.

Do Our Brains Work While We Sleep ?

One part of our brain is working always, whether we are asleep or not. If this part stops working, then sleep must become death.

This is a part of the brain about which we never feel or know anything directly ourselves; it is the lowest part of all, and has nothing to do with thinking or consciousness; but it controls the beating of the heart, and gives the orders to the muscles by which we breathe. The highest part of the brain, which has to do with thinking, is probably never wholly asleep except, perhaps, in babies and very small children. But most of the brain should be asleep—which means at rest—when we are asleep. The deeper our sleep is, the more valuable it is, and the smaller the energy the wakeful part of our brain is giving out.

Dreams and nightmares prove that our brains work while we ourselves are sleeping. But, quite apart from them, we can prove in many ways that much, even of the higher part of the brain, works while we are asleep. Thus, for instance, a man may go to bed trying to solve some problem in science, or to complete a piece of poetry he is writing, or to invent a new combination of the pieces in chess, or to write a tune to the words of a song, or to do a thousand other things, and in the morning he may wake and find that during the night, while he was asleep, his brain has done everything he wanted. A poet once composed a poem in his sleep, and wrote it out the next morning.

Sometimes, when the brain has done its work, it will wake the man up, and if one is to be awakened at night, that is the pleasantest way in which it can happen. The French have a very good proverb which expresses this idea concisely in four simple words, It is, *La nuit porte conseil*, the night brings counsel.

What is an Oratorio ?

In 1533, Philip Neri, the son of wealthy people living in Florence, behaved in a most unusual way. He had been such a good lad—his nickname was " the good Pippo "—and now, instead of settling down to enjoy the good things of life, here was Pippo renouncing riches and insisting on going to live at Rome. For many years he lived there, ministering to the poor. Presently he became a priest, built a church, and then, in his desire to make religion attractive to the young, he began performances in which some of the sacred stories from the Bible were sung and acted in the oratory of his church. The young folk flocked to hear these performances, which, from the fact that they were given in Philip's oratory, were called oratorios. There had been similar performances before, but Philip's were a great advance on them.

In England at that time we had our splendid Mystery and Miracle plays, which, like the oratorios in Rome, were intended to teach those who could not read the wonderful stories of the Bible. The work of Philip Neri was followed up by others, and about 1600 a fine oratorio by Emilio del Cavaliere, called Soul and Body, was written. This work had scenery, acting, singing, and dancing; but it became customary to sing oratorios without stage setting, action, or dance, so that we may say that an oratorio consists of a sacred story set to music, but not acted.

Thus began the development of that form of musical work which has produced such masterpieces as the oratorios of Handel, Bach, Mendelssohn, and Elgar. These works are frequently performed by the great choral societies of Britain, and are perhaps the most universally popular of the great musical compositions.

Who Were Romulus and Remus ?

Romulus was the mythical founder of Rome and Remus was his twin brother. Their father was supposed to be the war god Mars, and their mother the daughter of a deposed king, whose usurping successor cast the twin babes adrift on the River Tiber in a trough. They floated ashore and were nursed by a she-wolf and fed by a woodpecker. When they grew up they formed a band of shepherds who restored their grandfather to his throne and slew the usurper. They then decided to build a city on the spot where their wolf foster-mother lived, but quarrelled as to which should be leader, and when Remus laughed at the walls his brother had begun to build Romulus slew him. When Rome was built—not in a day, as the proverb justly points out—Romulus found wives for his followers by carrying off the women of the Sabines, a mountain people living to the north-east of Rome, and then, making peace with the Sabines, reigned jointly with their chief as first king of the new city of Rome. After his death he was worshipped by the Romans as a god under the name Quirinus.

Which is the Biggest Animal ?

No creature, living or extinct, on land or sea, can compare in size with the whale. Specimens of the right whale have been found exceeding 60 feet long, and sperm whales of the same length have also been caught. But before the whale fishery was organised on modern lines, with many ships and modern guns in place of the old hand-thrown harpoons, whales no doubt had opportunities of living longer and growing bigger. One caught off the British Isles many years ago measured 95 feet and weighed 249 tons. A single whale will yield a ton and three-quarters of baleen or whalebone, and 280 barrels of oil.

Of land animals the largest living today is the African elephant, some specimens of which stand eleven feet high and weigh four tons. Their tusks alone have been found to weigh as much as 293 pounds the pair. The largest living species of rhinoceros is believed to weigh sometimes three or four tons. But the largest known land animal of all time is a monster rhinoceros which used to roam over Asia some three million years ago. A number of bones were found some years ago and pieced together, so that the animal could be reconstructed by scientists and an idea obtained of what it was really like. It stood at least 18 feet high, its shoulders alone reaching to 13 feet from the ground, and its weight must have been from 16 to 20 tons. It browsed on the tops of the trees very much as the tall, slender giraffe does today, and it was so big that the largest living rhinoceros could pass underneath its body and scarcely graze it. This giant animal has been named the baluchitherium, because its remains were first found in Baluchistan, on the western confines of India, in 1911.

MAKING LEAD SHOT IN A GREAT TOWER

These drawings show how lead shot is made. On the left is the inside of a shot tower, broken in the middle, as, of course, its whole length could not be shown. Lead is drawn to the top of the tower, where it is melted and poured from a ladle through a sieve. It forms into globules, which fall down the whole length of the tower into a tank of water,

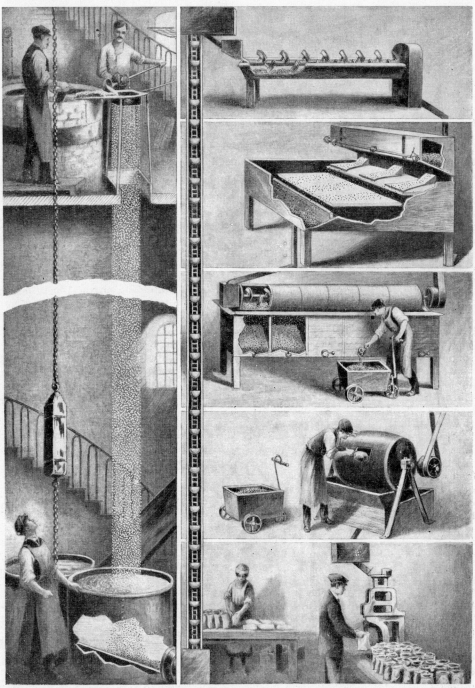

having cooled on the way. They then pass into a conveyer, which carries them to the factory. There they pass through a drying machine, then into a machine which automatically separates the perfect shot from the imperfect, and next into a cylinder which sizes them. From there they are passed into a revolving drum, which polishes them, and they are then weighed by an automatic scale into any quantities required, ready for packing.

Does a Seed Breathe ?

Seeds are no exception to the rule that every living thing must breathe. Nor are eggs. Perhaps you have never thought that an egg is alive? But if you varnish an egg, so that no air can get through the shell, it will die, and no chicken will come out of it. Now, the seed gets its air, or, rather, its oxygen from the air, as the worm does. So you must not plant the seed too deeply, or it will not get enough air, and then it will die. You may wonder that a seed should breathe, but that is because we always think of breathing as if the only kind of it were our breathing, with ribs and lungs. The air in the soil, which enables plants to grow from seeds and trees from acorns, and keeps alive worms and insects and many microbes, is known as *ground-air*, and as its warmth depends on the warmth of the soil, it is very different at different times of the year. That is one reason why certain illnesses attack us at certain times—because the warmth of the ground-air is just right for the growth of the microbes that cause those illnesses.

Could We Live Without Rain ?

If there were no rain there would be life only in the sea. In parts of the world where there is no rain there is no life. In our fortunate country we have no idea how rain is treasured and prayed for in other countries where there is not enough of it, or where it falls only at certain seasons of the year. We " do not know when we are well off " in this country: and especially the people who live in towns, on the food which is made in the country by the rain that falls there, do not know how good rain is, and how impossible our lives would be without it. We must think of rain, then, as something that cleans and washes the air, nourishes the vegetable life on which our own life depends, and ensures a supply of fresh water all the year round in every part of the world where sufficient rain falls.

What Does a Birthright Mean ?

In nearly every part of the world, at one time or another, alike among savages and among civilised people, the eldest son has special rights and privileges over the others. He often inherits most or all of his father's property, and has a special right to his father's title and position, whether as chief of a savage tribe or as a duke or king or as holding some other title or dignity.

This right of the first-born is called his birthright, and the Bible story of Esau and Jacob is sufficient to tell us how old this custom is. It has a special long name which we shall certainly meet sometimes, and which we must therefore learn. This right of the first-born is called the right of *primogeniture*. In some parts of the world this law of birthright has been abolished, and sons inherit equally, and have equal rights. France led the way in this respect, probably as a protest against the ancient custom of titles being transferred from father to eldest son.

What is an Internal Combustion Engine ?

In an ordinary steam-engine, whether the fuel be solid coal or liquid oil, the principle is to create steam outside the engine by means of the heat generated, and with this either to drive a piston backwards or forwards in a cylinder, or to let the steam act directly on thousands of tiny blades projecting from a shaft. In an internal combustion engine the principle is quite different. There the heat is applied to the working substance inside the cylinder. Engines fitted in most aeroplanes and motor-cars are of this type. Some stationary engines, utilising the same principles of operation, use coal gas instead of petrol. Another type of internal combustion engine is the compression-ignition, or Diesel, engine, which burns a fuel oil. Sprayed-in oil is ignited by the heat generated when the piston compresses the air in the cylinder. In petrol and gas engines the charge is fired by a spark.

What is the French Foreign Legion ?

Certain regiments of the French army, recruited from foreigners, chiefly officered by Frenchmen, and with headquarters in Algiers, are commonly known as the Foreign Legion. In peace time these troops supply garrisons for the French colonies, especially Algeria. The age and character of the recruits are not subject to a very strict inquiry, and some of the battalions are disciplinary units of conscripts. The Legion, which has a great reputation as a fighting force, underwent a number of changes after the First World War, its scope being much widened. Before 1919 it was composed of Alsatians and Lorrainers born under German rule as well as of men of others who had French sympathies or desired a life of adventure.

What is Marianne to the French?

Marianne is a French Christian name which the people gave to the guillotine during the Revolution of 1789. In memory of what the guillotine meant to them the French have kept the name of Marianne as a symbol of the Republic. She is represented as a robust woman wearing a white tunic, and with a Phrygian cap on her head. She stands for the primitive good sense of the people, fighting those who would endanger her rights of liberty, equality, and fraternity. Several secret societies were founded in France under the name of Marianne.

What Are Our Eyes Made Of?

If we could take an eye to pieces, and sort out all the things of which it is made, we should find that a great part of it is made of water, certainly not less than four-fifths of it. Besides water we should find the various elements that go to make up living matter, or protoplasm. In the eye we find many kinds of cells which consist of protoplasm, and others, such as the cells of the lens of the eye, which, though they were made by protoplasm, consist of something else quite peculiar to themselves. But in the curtain of the eye we should find the protoplasm mainly in the form of nerve-cells, and if we trace back the development of the eye, we find that the most important part of it—the part which really makes it an eye—has grown out from the brain, and is really a little part of the brain pushed forward. Part of the front of the eye is really skin that has been changed for the purposes of an eye, but the part that really makes the eye an eye is just as certainly part of the brain, when we come to know its history, as the rest of the eye is part of the skin.

Is the British Climate a Good One?

The climate of Great Britain is certainly one of the best in the whole world, though we are always complaining of it. For one thing, we have a splendid supply of air-cleansing and life-giving rain; we can scarcely guess what a famine of water means. And the rain does not come all at one time of year, interfering with everything when it comes, as in some parts of the world, and then requiring to be stored up very laboriously until the next rainy season; but it comes in fair quantities all the year round.

Are There More People Coming Into the World Than Going Out of it?

Certainly there are. There were never so many human beings in the world as there are today. All new knowledge about plants and animals, and the forces of Nature, mean, in the long run, that we are making the Earth a place capable of supporting more of us. Figures relating to India, which has the highest birth-rate in the world, show that about five million people are added to the population each year. In Europe the annual increase is much less, being under 200,000 for Great Britain.

This reckoning is not on the birth-rate, but on the difference between the birth-rate and the death-rate. In France the birth-rate and death-rate remain about equal. In the United States the population increases by about a million a year.

Which Are the Longest and Shortest Days?

The longest day is June 21, when the overhead Sun reaches its farthest north in the northern hemisphere. After June 21 the Sun appears to turn south till December 21, which is midwinter in the northern hemisphere, and then turns north again. December 21 is, therefore, the shortest day in the northern hemisphere.

Nevertheless the days immediately before and after the longest day and those before and after the shortest day are, reckoned in minutes, about the same length when the day is reckoned from the rising to the setting of the Sun. From year to year there are actually slight variations from these dates owing to the fact that the year is not exactly 365 days but 365 days five hours and 49 minutes; consequently the Earth is always lagging behind its true time. This lagging is made up by putting in a leap year every four years to bring solar time up to date.

Even so there are slight discrepancies and irregularities in the location of the longest and shortest days because they can never occur at exactly the same time and date every year, and a further irregularity is introduced by the influence of the planets on the Earth's motion. When, therefore, we say that the longest or shortest day is this or that date the assertion is approximate.

Why Has a Factory Chimney a Rim Round the Top ?

This is not merely to serve as an ornament, but to prevent the smoke blowing directly down to the ground, as it would do in certain conditions of weather were there no coping. When a very strong wind is blowing against the chimney steadily in one direction something like a vacuum is caused on the other side of the chimney, and if there were no coping the smoke, driven by the air above, would rush down to fill this vacuum. The rim, however, directs the smoke away from the chimney, beyond the area of the vacuum, and it is prevented from rushing down in a steady stream to the ground. The rim thus prevents the unhealthy smoke from reaching the ground.

How Did the White Line on the Road Begin ?

Safety on our roads is ensured to no small degree by the marking of their surface with a white or yellow line, or with a row of metal studs. This marking is most useful when it occurs at a bend. Realising that a white line along the middle of the road would help drivers to keep strictly to their half of the road the Automobile Association obtained the permission of the Brighton authorities to experiment at their own cost. Accordingly in 1924 the A.A. painted the first white lines on our highways at Preston on the London to Brighton road. It proved a great success, and in 1926 the Ministry of Transport recommended all local authorities to use the A.A. scheme.

What is a Blue Book ?

A Blue Book is a Government publication containing all the information, statistical and other, obtained concerning some given subject or subjects. It is published in a Blue paper cover, hence its name. A White Paper is also a Government publication, without the Blue cover; and is usually smaller in volume and content. Officially it is distinguished from a Blue Book because it is a Commons (or House of Commons) Paper, while the Blue Book is a " Command " publication.

Great Britain is the only country with the Blue cover. White is the cover mostly favoured. Chinese, Colombian, Norwegian, and Peruvian Government publications are White, and Egyptian White or Green ; the U.S.A. are Green or, if Diplomatic, Red ; and those of Soviet Russia's Supreme Court are also Red; Italian, Mexican, and Persian are Green ; Netherlands, Orange ; French, Yellow ; and Belgian, Grey.

Why is the Screw of a Mangle Loosened After Use ?

The usefulness of a mangle depends very largely on the tension of the spring that presses the top roller on to the under one. If the screw on the top of the mangle were not loosened, this spring would soon cease to work properly, and the rollers would not give to clothes of varying thickness passing through. Also, if the screw were kept tight, flat surfaces would form where the rollers touch.

Which is the Rainiest Place in the World ?

Cherrapunji, on the Khasi Hills of Assam, is generally regarded as the wettest spot on the Earth. In 1861 its rainfall reached 905 inches, as against London's average of 25 inches. Sometimes, however, it is much lower, as for example, in 1912, when it was only 376 inches. Its average is about 430 inches a year. On one occasion 150 inches fell in five days. Whether Cherrapunji is, after all, the wettest place on Earth is, however, now open to doubt, for records taken during recent years at Waialeale, on the island of Hawaii, give an average yearly rainfall of 518 inches. If this average is kept up over a long course of years then Waialeale will supersede Cherrapunji. The wettest place in England, Stye Head in Cumberland, has a yearly rainfall of 181 inches.

What is a Fiord ?

A fiord (or fjord) is a deep and narrow arm of the sea running far up into the land, with steep cliffs on each side. The chief examples of fiords are found on the coasts of Norway, Greenland, Alaska, and the southern part of New Zealand.

Fiords can only occur where a steep mountain range runs sharply down to the sea, and they are generally believed to be deep valleys that have been gouged out of the solid rock by glaciers that formerly slid down to the sea in these parts. Then, after the glaciers melted, the coast sank and let the sea into the very heart of the valleys. Fiords are usually shallower at the mouth and deeper inland.

The Story of the Beautiful Things in the Treasure-House of the World

Wells Cathedral

GOTHIC ARCHITECTURE IN ENGLAND

THE earliest buildings of any importance in England date from the Norman period, which really began before the Conquest, in the reign of Edward the Confessor. Prior to that are a few Saxon buildings of a simple style, naturally influenced by the remains of the Roman occupation. Of Roman work only ruins now exist: scraps of London Wall, Hadrian's Wall, mosaics, bath-chambers, and so on. But we know there were temples, basilicas, villas, in the Roman towns of Britain, as there were in other countries those great builders conquered. Saxon work of any obvious kind exists for us now in the form of a number of churches, like those at Worth, Sussex, at Escomb, Durham, St. Lawrence, Bradford-on-Avon, and Brixworth in Northamptonshire; and towers like Earls Barton, Northampton, and Barton-on-Humber. But there are many hidden Saxon remains in churches of a later style, and these are often not discovered until there is some reason for laying bare the old foundations.

The first important building of the English Romanesque or Norman style was a new church called the West Minster, dedicated to St. Peter, built by the Confessor. There is a tradition that the oldest church reared on this site was a

Saxon building set up about 616. In 960 St. Dunstan re-founded a Benedictine monastery there. A hundred years later the Confessor began the work of rebuilding and strengthening. He was buried in the church in 1066. We shall presently see how later rulers continued the work he began.

The Normans who settled in England after the conquest by William were, like the rest of their tribe, an intelligent, powerful people, capable of great mental elasticity, and with an innate feeling for artistic form. They were Christian, but none the less fighters; and from their combining a lofty motive with a soldier's skill sprang the chivalrous spirit of Norman England and France. And from their vigorous Christianity and desire to see some monument of their faith established, sprang the lovely churches of the period, built on the same lines as those of Normandy.

The English Channel was never a wide waterway, although we seem to consider it as a great barrier; and in the days when it divided Norman England from Norman France—the days of almost impassable roads and easy sailing—it was a little strait, continually being crossed. Thus into England filtered more and more of that European influence which had begun when Edward the Confessor, educated at the Norman Court, became king. Stone-masons

PICTURES · STATUES · CARVINGS · BUILDINGS · IVORIES · CRAFTS

and wood-carvers, craftsmen in metal and kindred workmen, came over in considerable numbers, and brought not only their tools, and presumably their families, but also their ways of thinking, and such education as the religious architecture of northern France had given them. The men who had planned the great Norman churches continued their work in England.

THE NEW STYLE OF ARCHITECTURE WHICH AROSE IN EUROPE

They loved unbroken masses and semi-circular shapes, as we can see from their walls and rounded arches, piers, and columns. They disliked a line broken up for a small and pretty reason. But before they had well established their new churches among the greenery, the rivers, and fens of England, before five successive Norman rulers had had time to consolidate their work, the spirit of architecture in Europe had changed. Romanesque had given place to Gothic, and the fever, spreading over the Continent, seized England.

But in the meantime a number of magnificent cathedrals and churches had been set up; and though almost all of them seemed destined merely to serve as the core of a later Gothic building, here and there we can see something of the work of the early shapers of England. In the cathedrals of Canterbury, Winchester, Rochester, Ely, Hereford, Norwich, St. Albans, Worcester, Oxford, Chichester, the touch of Norman builders is very plain, in choir, nave, or tower.

They reached their height in Durham Cathedral. This wonderful pile was of course added to later, but time has been kinder to Durham than to many of the cathedrals which rose in that wonderful hundred years following the settlement of the Normans in England. There is nowhere in England a more beautiful sight than the Norman nave of Durham Cathedral, with its fluted and spiraled columns.

THE WONDERFUL CHURCH FOUNDED BY A KING'S JESTER

Peterborough is another great cathedral which is Norman at heart, and the abbeys of Waltham and Tewkesbury point to the same inspiration.

In London there are two particularly fine specimens of these great masters' work, the White Tower with the little chapel of St. John, in the Tower of London, and St. Bartholomew the Great, Smithfield. This church is part of an Augustinian priory which, with the hospital near by, was founded in 1123 by Rahere, court jester in the reign of Henry the First.

Rahere was very ill in Rome. And he vowed a vow to God that, should his life be spared, he would build the finest priory in London next to that of the Benedictine monks at Westminster. Rahere's tomb is in the church (added some three hundred years later), and as we look at it we cannot help feeling glad that this witty courtier was spared to erect such a monument of gratitude as the priory of St. Bartholomew. He fulfilled his vow in a superb style, unstintingly, and the work that he left uncompleted his successor finished.

The church is all that is left of the priory, whose conventual buildings, lying on the south side—cloisters, refectory, chapter house, dormitory—have long been destroyed or served as foundations to other buildings. And that which is called the church is really only half of it.

THE CHANGES THAT HAVE COME OVER SAINT BARTHOLOMEW'S

We can get some idea of its original size if we remember that we enter at a modern doorway in a seventeenth-century tower which was built at the place where the transepts crossed the nave. Thus we walk straight into the choir itself, which is larger than many churches, and gives an impression of solemn grandeur, with its massive round columns and semi-circular arches. The place where the nave stood lies outside the present church wall, a bare stretch of stones reaching from the modern door to the pavement of Smithfield.

The long vista of nave and choir, with the lady chapel beyond the apse, ranked like a forest with those massive columns, must have been one of the finest things even in Norman times. And we are intensely thankful that part of this magnificent church remains. It has passed through more than usually troubled days. At one time the north transept was used as a blacksmith's forge. The lady chapel has been a printing works and, later, a factory. In 1896 it was rebuilt. Such of the conventual buildings as are not destroyed have been cleared of the superimposed buildings—one of them a stable—and this grand and unique pile, more than eight centuries old, is now able to tell a wonderful and historic tale.

There have been additions and alterations by successive centuries, but, merci-

THE SPLENDID CHURCHES OF ENGLAND

THE CRYPT OF CANTERBURY CATHEDRAL

THE GALILEE CHAPEL IN DURHAM CATHEDRAL

THE SOUTH PORCH AND WEST DOOR OF CANTERBURY CATHEDRAL

THE ENTRANCE TO THE
CHAPTER HOUSE AT BRISTOL

THE CRYPT OF WORCESTER
CATHEDRAL

THE NORTH AISLE OF
DURHAM CATHEDRAL

fully, not to any great extent. A Perpendicular clerestory rises above the Norman blind-story or triforium—the part of the wall that lies above the pillars of the aisle and below the aisle vaulting that supports the roof. A gallery sometimes runs behind the blind-story. It is called blind because this part of the wall is marked by rows of arches through which no light comes. And the blind-story is also called the triforium because inside the arches are usually set three other little arches (tri means three, and fores, openings). The clerestory and blind-story, or triforium, have been very important features of architecture ever since Norman or Romanesque times to the present day.

THE ROUND CHURCHES THE CRUSADERS INTRODUCED INTO ENGLAND

A most interesting little side development of Norman architecture was the round church. These builders loved circular lines in any case, hence their " wheel " windows, of which so few remain. But it is probable that the idea of the round church, which Romanesque workers on the Continent set up in imitation of the circular baptisteries, was introduced into England by travellers and Knights Crusaders who had seen the buildings of southern Europe, and particularly the church of the Holy Sepulchre at Jerusalem.

Very few of the circular churches are left ; there is St. Sepulchre, Cambridge, one at Northampton, another at Little Maplestead. The most famous is the Temple Church, London. Since early in the fifteenth century the Temple—a large area containing squares, gardens, and halls—has been one of the Inns of Court. Before that time it was the headquarters of the Knights Templars.

LONDON'S BEAUTIFUL ROUND CHURCH BUILT BY THE NORMANS

Like the Knights of St. John of Jerusalem, the Knights Templars were a military monastic order founded early in the twelfth century to protect Christian pilgrims to the Holy Land from the Saracens.

In London the Knights Templars settled on a site south of Fleet Street in 1161 and the round Temple Church is the one surviving part of the church built by them and dedicated in 1185. This was at a time when Romanesque was changing and the Gothic spirit growing, hence the architecture is called Norman transitional. The

original apse that carried the choir out from the circular nave has been replaced by a very fine early Gothic choir. The entrance porch and doorway and beautifully carved door are most delightful specimens of Norman skill, and under the gracious round curve we pass into the round church.

Though much restored in the 19th century, and again largely reconstructed after air-raid damage during the Second World War, it probably still looks today much as it did when pious hands first built it nearly eight centuries ago.

Bearing this in mind, it is impossible not to feel the mysterious power of beauty and history together as we stand in the Temple Church. This is particularly true for a visitor who happens to be there on that evening toward the end of the old year, when, by long custom, the choristers leave their stalls in the chancel and make a ring in the round church, and sing the oldest carols of the Christian faith. The finger-marks of history are plain in the Temple. Outside, in the garden, grew the white and the red roses wherefrom the quarrelling Yorkists and Lancastrians plucked their fate.

This brawl today,
Grown to this faction in the Temple garden,
Shall send between the red rose and the white
A thousand souls to death and deadly night.

THE SPIRIT OF THE CRUSADERS WHICH TEMPLE CHURCH RECALLS

But most of all we remember, as we return to the pure beauty of the actual shape of the Norman church, that spirit of noble adventuring, that mixture of soldiery and religion which was the stamp of Crusading times. Blake must have wandered much in and out of the Temple Church, and seen in dreams the steel-mailed Templars walk clanging across that beautiful tiled floor, and been aware of the spirit that has made England great when he wrote his lovely Jerusalem :

Bring me my Bow of burning gold !
Bring me my Arrows of desire !
Bring me my Spear ! O clouds, unfold !
Bring me my Chariot of fire !
I will not cease from Mental Fight,
Nor shall my Sword sleep in my hand,
Till we have built Jerusalem
In England's green and pleasant land.

This round church of many memories is among the last creations of any importance to bear the stamp of Norman work in England. Another architecture was growing whose beginnings are difficult to trace.

No one knows exactly why the term Gothic was given to the medieval architecture of Europe, which had nothing to do with the Goths. It is said that Raphael used the words in describing this " new " architecture that had appeared north of the Alps. In his mouth the term was scornful, for the word Goth was used to denote an uncultured person in contrast with a cultured Roman. However it may have been given, the term has clung, and in the passing centuries has lost its stigma.

HOW THE SEAT OF POWER MOVED STEADILY TO THE WEST

We can understand how distasteful the new architecture was to men whose ideas were bound to the old. Prejudice against an innovation is one of the most enduring traits of human nature. And as Europe owed all she knew of art to Greece and the East, there was something to be said for those who denounced a strange art which was abandoning classical tradition.

But these men, these worshippers of the old, did not, or would not, realise that the centre of the world's vitality was moving steadily westward. And as the seat of power changed, architecture changed.

Greece was the home of the rectangular, columned temple. The Romans copied it. The early Christians copied work of Romans and Greeks together in an inverted way, setting rows of columns inside a severe rectangular wall, whereas the Greeks had set rows of columns outside a severe rectangular wall. Thus, as one writer says, the basilican churches were Greek temples turned inside out.

Romanesque art was still derived from Greece and Rome, its chief characteristic the round-headed arch. But in the meantime the colonnade, the rows of columns that supported part of the roof, had changed to an arcade—rows of columns whence arches sprang that supported part of the roof.

THE LOFTY IDEALS OF THE BUILDERS OF THE THIRTEENTH CENTURY

So far the architecture of Europe is traceable to Greece. It was on the principle of the arch that the change came. The makers of new buildings, in that wonderful thirteenth century, were dissatisfied with what seemed to them the heavy, gloomy erections of the Romanesque type. The minds and souls of men were charged with lofty ideals, sacred aspirations, and a new love of beauty. They wanted to see buildings that would fling themselves heavenward in praise and joy, and be the outward and visible sign of an inward and spiritual grace. Thus they gradually discarded the massive round shapes of Romanesque arches and began throwing up the long, pointed arches that we call Gothic.

The love of this " aspiring " form became a fever. Upon these lighter, more airy buildings, towers and spires were set. And all over Europe an amazing architecture presently rose which had nothing of the repose of the old world's buildings, and stirred with a new vitality.

In the temples and churches of the East, windows had been almost unnecessary, because of the extreme clarity of the atmosphere. The colder and mistier light of our own countries made a certain amount of lighting imperative. The makers of the early cathedrals of northern Europe seized this chance of a new architectural feature with all the eagerness that marked the period. Windows presently became one of the most important parts of the fabric. The different periods of Gothic work may be determined by them.

THE FOUR GREAT FEATURES OF GOTHIC ARCHITECTURE

Thus we see three of the four characteristics of Gothic architecture: the pointed arch, the window, the tower or spire. The fourth, the buttress, is both an interesting development of Roman detail and an important point of Gothic construction.

The greatest problem in a large building is, as we can understand, the supporting of the roof. If it is supported in the Gothic way, by vaults that spring from arches, there is a great strain on the points of the walls where the arches press. An arch always tends to flatten itself; it thrusts out its ends against the wall or pier into which it is built. When many arches cross and combine to support a roof, the walls need very carefully treating. This is part of the problem of " strains " which bulks largely in an architect's work. If the thrust and strain of supporting arches are not properly met, the roof, or bridge or tunnel, or whatever the arches are carrying, will fall in.

When the Romans set a weight over one of their round arches they strengthened the part of the walls whereon the ends of the arch pressed by an extra thickness. It seemed to them advisable, in their adoration of Greek styles, to use a piece of an Order in this way. They made the column part of the wall, attaching it to the masonry at one side, and gave it a heavy base. This half column was called a pilaster, and formed a kind of prop against the thrust of the arch.

WHY THE BUTTRESS IS SO NECESSARY IN GOTHIC BUILDINGS

In Romanesque hands the pilaster became, so to speak, a flat piece of wall fastened on the other wall, sloping outward, for strength's sake, at the base. Presently, so that this greater basic weight should be acquired without making an unpleasant line, the ridge of the wall was shelved in three places. From this grew the buttress of Gothic architecture. The more arches there were, the more windows (set in arches, of course), the more necessity there was to strengthen the wall. Buttresses grew more and more important, heavier, more frequent. They ran the height of the building, working out very broadly as they descended. And as one of the necessities of architecture is that a line shall be properly stopped, they were presently surmounted by pinnacles. So we see that a constructional necessity was the cause of one of the chief features of Gothic architecture. People who have not had time to learn much about this subject are apt to think that buttresses were added, like towers, by way of ornament, and for no other reason.

As the centre aisles of the cathedrals were carried higher, and more and more windows set in the fabric, the arches of this highest part had to be outwardly supported by a flying buttress, which was in turn supported by the ordinary solid buttress. A wall which is nearly all windows has little strength, and, as strength must come in somewhere, the solid buttresses began to step out farther and farther, so to speak, from the building, and became like little towers in themselves. At the same time they were being narrowed so that all the available space between them should be given to windows.

THE GREAT ARTIST WHO PREFERRED THE CLASSICAL STYLE OF BUILDING

The architects of medieval cathedrals naturally became more and more engrossed in this most fascinating game of playing tricks with construction. No other architecture of any period or place has produced anything approaching the sheer cleverness, apart from beauty, of Gothic work. It was, as a writer has said, like a body that carried half its bones outside, and still lived. We can quite understand Raphael, loving the compact mass of classical architecture, with flat roofs and flawless contours, holding up his hands in horror at that architecture of Goths, yonder, north of the Alps.

The Romanesque builders had thought they were advanced men when they broke their long church or cathedral walls by a short nave, and threw out the chevet of the apse. No wonder the people of the Gothic period were proud of their achievement. Thousands of workmen laboured on those medieval cathedrals with tool and chisel. So that when all the sculpture and carving was done, all the numberless little saints set smiling and happy in their niches, the tale of Christ's life told in glass in the great windows, those medieval cathedrals must have seemed too beautiful to be real. It must have appeared a fantasy, this delicately balanced mass of lovely slender stones and sweeping lines and pointing spires, held together by fairy fingers.

THE THREE PERIODS OF GOTHIC ARCHITECTURE IN ENGLAND

By its very nature, true Gothic architecture could not last. It marks a period of development in the Christian era whose pure spirit can never be recaptured. So that the love we have for medieval buildings is the love of something which may easily be lost, and, once lost, is lost for ever.

For three hundred famous years cathedrals in France, Germany, and England were built in this style, which in itself was constantly changing or developing. In England Gothic architecture is divided roughly into three periods—that of the thirteenth century, called Early English; that of the fourteenth, called Decorated; that of the fifteenth, called Perpendicular. In a great many of our buildings these three styles meet, as one century made additions to the work of the century that went before it.

English Gothic architecture is marked by a sobriety and a strength that does not often appear in the French work of the same style. If a Gothic building has to be imposing it must excel in either length or height. The French attained a greater height, and the English a greater length. Although all this work was executed on the same principles, the effect of national character was inevitable; so that in time English Gothic became a distinctive architecture of its own.

In time, we say, for at the beginning of Gothic work there was very little difference. England and Normandy were still, practically speaking, one province, only divided by the Channel, and workmen still came and went as from one end of a kingdom to another. One of the most interesting cases of this exchange of labour was that of William of Sens—a little town south of Paris—being summoned to Canterbury in about 1170 to rebuild the cathedral on the lines of that he had set up in Sens. The French William built the choir and William the Englishman continued the work.

THE DOMINATING FEATURE OF THE EARLY ENGLISH GOTHIC

Early English Gothic was simple, of fine proportions, with lancet-shaped windows which were long and narrow, pointed at the head. This particular shape dominated not only the windows but the whole structure; arches, doorways, the lines of the roof vaulting, the clerestory and blind-story, all conformed to this delicate and beautiful shape. Londoners can see what Early English Gothic was in the choir and lady chapel of Southwark Cathedral (the nave has been restored), the chancel of the Temple Church, the chapel and crypt of Lambeth Palace, and certain parts of Westminster Abbey, of which we shall be thinking presently.

A great many of our provincial cathedrals happily retain something of the Early English spirit. We find it in the transepts of York Minster, the nave and chapter house of Lincoln Cathedral, the choir and transepts of Rochester Cathedral, the nave, transepts, and west front of Wells Cathedral, the choir, transepts, and the " Galilee Porch " of Ely Cathedral, and in parts of Southwell Minster, Worcester Cathedral, Beverley Minster, Glasgow Cathedral, Elgin Cathedral.

THE THREE SPIRES THAT TOWER ABOVE THE RIVER AT LICHFIELD

The finest and most complete evidence of what Early English Gothic was is shown at Salisbury and Lincoln.

The little cathedral of Lichfield—one of the smallest in England—also has a peculiar interest for students of this period. The main part is Early English, with an unusually fine west front. Lichfield is the only cathedral in England possessing three spires (added in the fourteenth century), two at the west front and one at the crossing of the nave and transepts. These three graceful points are known as the Ladies of the Vale.

The simple spire, without any parapet, surmounting a short tower at the crossing was a feature of Early English Gothic. In the later period towers became heavier, and sometimes stood alone, and sometimes were surmounted by spires. The French architects threw up their cathedrals to such an immense height that the structures could not support a heavy tower at the crossing. The central tower remains an English feature of Gothic architecture.

The most beautiful spire in England is that of Salisbury Cathedral. This building is one of our most precious possessions, a piece of the best Early English Gothic imaginable. Almost all the cathedral, as it stands, was built during the years 1220 to 1258. The spire, 404 feet high, the loftiest in the country, was added a hundred years later.

THE CATHEDRAL WITH A WINDOW FOR EVERY DAY IN THE YEAR

There is often a haphazard look about Gothic cathedrals, as if they grew rather than were planned. This is absent in Salisbury Cathedral. It is beautifully proportional and held together, shape falling upon shape, the spire rising triumphantly from their midst. By accident, or curious design, the cathedral is said to contain as many windows as there are days in the year, as many pillars as there are hours, as many doors as there are months.

The interior as well as the exterior is stamped with old English history. Monuments to some of the earliest bishops are here, and a great many nobles, some of artistic interest, some more memorable for the sake of the dead. Henry Fawcett, the blind Postmaster-General, has a memorial here.

Lincoln Cathedral tells another beautiful tale of old English genius. It rises on a hill above the town, washed by the clear East Country air, throwing bravely up its central tower as if proud that it is the highest central church tower in England. The measurement of this tower is 271 feet high. Eventually Lincoln will have to take second place in this matter, as the tower planned for the new Liverpool Cathedral by Sir Giles Gilbert Scott is to be 280 feet in height.

The earliest parts of Lincoln Cathedral, the choir and eastern transepts, were erected in about 1190 by an English architect, a Lincolnshire man. The building went on for over a hundred years, and at the end of that time, in about 1314, the " Angel Choir "—more in the Decorated style than the Early English—was built. The general plan is something like that of Canterbury, but the treatment, the solidity, the gravity, is very English, and owes less to foreign influence.

THE DECORATED SCREEN WALL ON THE FRONT OF LINCOLN CATHEDRAL

The west front of Lincoln Cathedral is of great interest, apart from the lovely work, in that it is a kind of decorated screen wall, and behind it rise the western towers. The screen wall is broken by very beautiful doorways, but this hardly atones for the way the towers seem to be cut in half, and have no base.

These towers, spires, and decorations at the western end of Gothic cathedrals grew out of the architects' desire to end the building in a comely manner, to hide the abrupt finish of the roofs of nave and aisles. If we look at our pictures of various cathedrals, we shall see what a wonderful development this is, always remembering that one of the chief points in architectural design is that line shall be properly stopped—the line in this case being the long length of the cathedral roof.

One of the most wonderful western fronts in Early English Gothic is that of Peterborough Cathedral. Here three immense arches run up the entire height of the building, with a gable on each arch, giving a grandeur and simplicity of line that has no equal. The façade is said to be the finest west front in the world. In this fine cathedral, therefore, is united most memorable work both of Norman and early Gothic period. Unfortunately, for all their solid, heavy masonry, the Norman builders made poor foundations. If Peterborough Cathedral had not been skilfully underpinned it would have been in ruin before our day.

THE WONDERFUL LANCET-SHAPED WINDOWS OF YORK MINSTER

Another trace of the genius of Early English Gothic is shown in the famous transepts of York Minster. Here, in the nothern transept, are The Five Sisters, five immensely long, lancet-shaped windows, side by side, fifty feet high and five feet wide. Some of the finest stained glass in England, made in the fourteenth century, is in this cathedral.

To the fourteenth century belong the west front and nave of York Minster, and here we can see the difference between the Early English and Decorated Gothic. The windows have become larger, and instead of being simple, lancet-shaped lights, are marked by elaborate stone traceries, which act like settings to the jewels of the coloured glass. This rich splendour and ornateness, spreading to all details of architecture in stone and wood alike, was the chief note of the Decorated period.

During this time a good many towers were set up on various cathedrals, and the " fancy " spire, rising from a tower base, sometimes many-sided, with parapets and lights and pinnacles appeared. Very fine chapter houses were built. Clerestories, set high in the walls, became more important, and blind-stories less important.

It is interesting to note, in passing, that Bristol Cathedral has neither clerestories nor blind-stories, the aisles being carried up almost the height of the nave. This cathedral, like those of Bangor, Llandaff, Ripon, St. Albans, Southwark, has been variously restored and added to.

THE FINE CHURCHES THAT WERE LOST IN THE FIRE OF LONDON

The interiors of Decorated Gothic buildings were marked by very elaborate roof vaulting, the ribs or surface ridges of the vaults making all kinds of geometric patterns. To this period belongs the star-shaped vaulting, where the ribs cross each other to make a star.

A fine specimen of Decorated Gothic architecture can be seen in the chapel of St. Etheldreda, in Ely Place, Holborn, originally the chapel of the Bishop of Ely's palace. Both east and west windows are excellent examples of the work of this period. The east cloisters of Westminster Abbey are also 14th-century work.

The builders of this period to which has been given, roughly, the limits of the fourteenth century, were employed in many ways in England, adding a chapel or a transept here and a tower there. There was no great demarcation between Early English and Decorated Gothic. Many churches were built which are lost to us through the Fire of London, and, of course, others perished in the great air attacks on the capital in the Second World War.

The Decorated period touched its height in certain parts of Exeter Cathedral, and the Lady Chapel, Ely. The carved work in stone and wood of Exeter Cathedral is among the finest in England. A great breadth and a wealth of stone tracery mark the windows; details like the minstrels' gallery are especially beautiful. One unique feature at Exeter is the carrying up of the north and south transepts into twin towers. It is interesting to note that in this cathedral is the heaviest peal of ringing bells in the world.

The genius of this wonderful fourteenth century in England did not restrict itself to the mere fabric of the building. Cathedrals and churches were frames, so to speak, wherein was set most lavish craft-work of all descriptions in wood and metal. The stone-workers, wood-carvers, and brass and iron-workers shared each other's zeal. When we think of the chancel screens or rood screens, the grilles, choir stalls, lecterns, bishops' " thrones," fonts, the most beautiful mellow glass that filled the richly traceried windows, the lovely illuminated psalters and missals that were used, we only think of details of that grandeur which the fourteenth century produced.

THE LOVELY LITTLE CHAPELS IN THE GREAT CATHEDRALS

During these generations most lovely tombs and monuments and shrines were set in the cathedrals. The story of these alone would make an entrancing book. They are a nation's portrait gallery, enabling us to see the kind of people our ancestors were; and in many cases they are exquisite works of art. Lovely little chantry chapels were set, generally in the bay of a cathedral aisle, screened from public view by magnificent carving and iron-work. Here, in the days before the Reformation, masses were said for the souls of the dead.

Piety and a love of beauty lay in the founding of these chantries, built by people rich enough to maintain them. As we think of them it is impossible not to remember the night watch of Henry the Fifth before Agincourt:

I Richard's body have interred anew,
And on it have bestowed more contrite tears
Than from it issued forced drops of blood. . . .
and I have built
Two chantries where the sad and solemn priests
Sing still for Richard's soul.

The Reformation and Puritan rebellion were the cause of the destruction of many of these fourteenth-century works of art. We can only be thankful that some are left, like that of Henry the Fifth himself in Westminster Abbey, Prince Arthur's Chantry in Worcester Cathedral, the Ramryge Chantry Chapel and St. Alban's shrine in the cathedral of St. Albans, the shrine of St. Thomas de Cantelupe in Hereford Cathedral, the tomb of Bishop Bridport in Salisbury Cathedral, the Percy Chapel in Beverley Minster.

THE CROSSES ON THE WAYSIDE FROM NOTTINGHAMSHIRE TO LONDON

A little of the romance of medieval England exists for us in the remnants of the Eleanor Crosses, set up at the order of Edward the First in memory of his beloved queen, Eleanor of Castile, who died at Harby in Nottinghamshire in 1290. The body was conveyed for burial in solemn procession, by slow stages, from Nottinghamshire to Westminster Abbey. Afterwards a cross was erected in each of the 12 places where the body reposed at the nightly halts.

The restoration of the cross at Waltham, near London, said to be finest of all, gives some idea of the richness of these memorials. One was erected at the village of Charing, the last halt before Westminster, hence the name, Charing Cross. It was taken down in the troubled seventeenth century, and a modern memorial in the station yard marks its site.

As the fourteenth century died away a slow change passed over its architecture, and with the next hundred years came the end of Gothic in the Perpendicular style. This, as its name suggests, was a fashion of Gothic wherein the lines were straight instead of curved. It may be noted in the upright lines of the window, the rectangular labels, and the panels that decorated walls, outside and in, in every available space.

THE MATCHLESS BEAUTY OF THE ROOF OF HENRY THE SEVENTH'S CHAPEL

Buildings were thrown to a great height, windows became enormous. Fan vaulting was the chief characteristic in the very elaborate roof work of the period. Its finest example is in the Henry the Seventh Chapel at Westminster, which is among the best architecture produced in fifteenth-century England.

The church of St. Margaret, Westminster, was built in this style and also the Savoy Chapel, Westminster Hall, St. George's Chapel, Windsor, and many of our finest church towers, notably in Norfolk, Somerset, and Gloucestershire.

The Perpendicular period left its stamp on Cathedrals like Winchester, Gloucester, Canterbury and Chester; on Beverley and Sherborne Minsters; and on the Beauchamp Chapel, Warwick. Manchester Cathedral was built during this time.

THE END OF THE GOTHIC SPIRIT IN ARCHITECTURE

No architecture surpassing the grace of that of the thirteenth or fourteenth century marked these generations. The Gothic spirit had spent itself. Constructionally, the work was becoming weaker, walls more and more like a patchwork of glass supported outwardly by enormous buttresses. Nothing more could be evolved from the style. Early in the sixteenth century it died out.

In Westminster Abbey more than any other cathedral the various styles of Gothic met. This great building has an especial place in hearts of the English-speaking peoples, for its roots and its associations lie deep in our history. At the hands of the early kings, from the Confessor onward, it passed through many stages and received the impress of the various styles.

The church which is now called Westminster Abbey was originally part of a great group of buildings, monastery and royal palace, the palace making way for the Houses of Parliament. The monastery was one of the largest Benedictine institutions in Europe, and round it presently gathered ordinary dwelling houses, like a village scattered about the monastery's feet. From this settlement grew the City of Westminster, an isolated town standing in the greenery and marshes of the Thames.

THE BUSY LIFE OF THE OLD MONASTERY OF WESTMINSTER

The monastery comprised the usual set of buildings, Abbey church, cloisters, refectory, dormitory, chapter house, mills, workshops, orchards. Its trout stream still flows, running under Great College Street to join the Thames. The monks' common court is now Dean's Yard. There was also an inner court which still exists as Little Dean's Yard. The abbot's house is now the Deanery, and this, with Jerusalem chamber and the dining hall, was rebuilt in the fourteenth century. Parts of the Confessor's Norman work still

exist—the chapel of the Pyx, and the undercroft close by.

To Henry the Third belong the honours of rebuilding very nobly a good part of the Abbey church, which, in general plan, resembles the Cathedral of Rheims. It is 511 feet long, and the nave has the highest Gothic vault in England. Henry moved the famous shrine of the Abbey's founder, Edward the Confessor, to its place in the chapel immediately behind the high altar, where the Coronation chair also stands.

For some seven hundred years this has been the greatest, the most venerated tomb in England. Sick people were brought there to be cured, and places were arranged at the side of the shrine where they might be placed. The monument of Purbeck marble was defaced at the Reformation; its richly jewelled decorations destroyed. Later, in the reign of Mary Tudor, a fine canopy carved in wood was set over the tomb. During the First World War this superstructure was removed for safety's sake, and afterwards restored.

THE NOBLE BUILDING WHICH BREATHES THE HISTORY OF ENGLAND

In the Confessor's Chapel five kings and six queens are buried. And in the various chapels that group themselves about the apse, forming the *chevet* we have mentioned earlier, a great many very illustrious tombs and shrines stand, foremost among them Henry the Fifth's chantry, the tomb of Henry the Third and his wife Elizabeth of York, the tomb of Edward the Third. Apart from the memory of the people immortalised, these tombs and monuments are examples of the art which was so rich in England during the Gothic ascendancy.

Such is the power of history in the Abbey, that we are apt to forget the very wonderful building, its details piling on each other to make the summed glory of our great years. Students of architecture go from door to door, from transept to transept, from nave to aisles, from chapter house to cloisters, tracing a century here and a generation there, in pillar and arch, vault and buttress. And they will probably end in Henry the Seventh's Chapel, that last soaring of our inspiration, which throws its flying buttresses outside into a work-a-day world, and inside, hoards its dear loveliness of wood and glass and stone.

NORMAN AND GOTHIC BUILDINGS

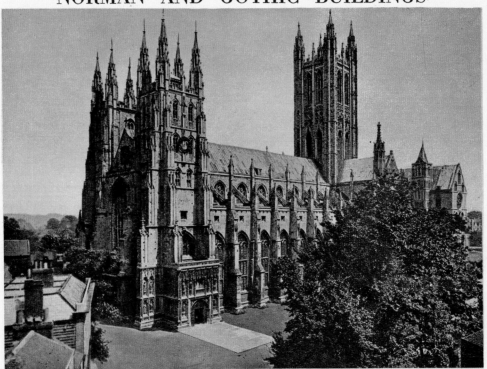

CANTERBURY CATHEDRAL SEEN FROM THE SOUTH-WEST

THE WEST FRONT OF YORK MINSTER, A BEAUTIFUL EXAMPLE OF THE PERPENDICULAR STYLE

ROMSEY ABBEY, IN HAMPSHIRE, AS SEEN FROM THE SOUTH-EAST

THE CHOIR OF ELY
CATHEDRAL

ST. ETHELDREDA'S SHRINE IN
ELY CATHEDRAL

THE NAVE OF WELLS
CATHEDRAL

THE NAVE OF THE CHURCH OF ST. CROSS,
NEAR WINCHESTER

HENRY THE SEVENTH'S CHAPEL IN
WESTMINSTER ABBEY

CHESTER CATHEDRAL AS SEEN FROM THE SOUTH-EAST

NORMAN DOORWAY
ROCHESTER CATHEDRAL

THE CHOIR OF CHRIST CHURCH
CATHEDRAL, OXFORD

THE SOUTH TRANSEPT DOOR
OF SOUTHWELL CATHEDRAL

THE ANGEL CHOIR IN LINCOLN CATHEDRAL

THE NAVE OF SALISBURY CATHEDRAL

HEREFORD CATHEDRAL AS SEEN FROM THE SOUTH-EAST

THE SOUTH PORCH OF GLOUCESTER
CATHEDRAL

ROCHESTER CATHEDRAL BEFORE THE
ADDITION OF ITS MODERN SPIRE

TEWKESBURY ABBEY AS SEEN FROM THE NORTH-EAST

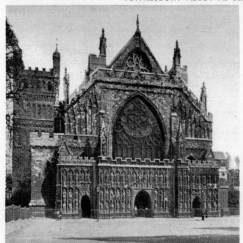

THE WEST FRONT OF EXETER CATHEDRAL

THE WEST FRONT OF PETERBOROUGH CATHEDRAL

DURHAM CATHEDRAL, TOWERING ABOVE THE ROOFS OF THE CITY

THE CENTRAL TOWER OF
DURHAM CATHEDRAL

THE TOWER AND SPIRE OF
NORWICH CATHEDRAL

THE TOWERS AND CLOISTERS
OF WESTMINSTER ABBEY

MANCHESTER CATHEDRAL FROM THE SOUTH

THE WEST FRONT OF ST. ALBAN'S CATHEDRAL

WORCESTER CATHEDRAL SEEN FROM THE NORTH-WEST

WEST FRONT OF LICHFIELD
CATHEDRAL

SOUTHWARK CATHEDRAL
IN LONDON

WEST FRONT OF LINCOLN
CATHEDRAL

YORK MINSTER SEEN FROM THE NORTH

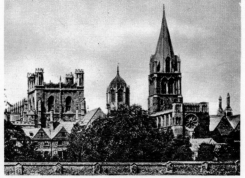

CHRIST CHURCH CATHEDRAL, OXFORD

GUILDFORD CATHEDRAL

THE WEST FRONT OF BRISTOL CATHEDRAL

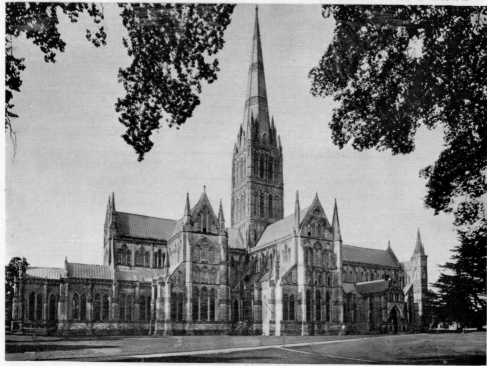

SALISBURY CATHEDRAL WITH ITS FAMOUS SPIRE

GLOUCESTER CATHEDRAL

THE WEST FRONT OF WINCHESTER CATHEDRAL

The Wonderful House We Live In, and Our Place in the World

The busy scene at a British coalmine

A NATION'S WEALTH

IN speaking of a nation's wealth it is important to see clearly that there does not exist anywhere in the world a great store of wealth into which we can, by some magic process or other, dip our hands and make ourselves rich.

Such will o' the wisps for long misguided the efforts of men and even of nations. It was a common belief in Europe for centuries that, somewhere or other, the world held gigantic stores of wealth, and many were the voyagers who set out to seek it. The illusion arose from the fact that men were apt to regard gold and silver and precious stones as the only real forms of wealth. Indeed, for a very long period the nations of Europe imagined that the whole object of external trade was to send out goods and get paid in gold, as though one could eat gold, or drink it, or put it to any but the most limited uses. This false idea about commerce did enormous harm to the nations which entertained it, but slowly men came to see that wealth lies in an abundance of useful commodities, and that gold is useful for a few ornamental purposes, and for measuring the value of other things.

The riches of the East are now known to be merely fables. All the Eastern countries were and are miserably poor, the average income of their inhabitants being a mere fraction of the incomes of the Western nations. Yet the wealth of the Indies was a phrase which kindled the imaginations of men for centuries.

The real source of wealth is not treasure-hunting, but *well-directed hard work*. There is no other means by which a nation can make itself prosperous. It is true that in ancient times one nation could make a raid on another, steal its possessions, and make slaves of its inhabitants. That was a not infrequent happening. Today such wholesale despoiling and enslavement could not lead to prosperity ; we live in a world in which the prosperity of any one nation is bound up with the prosperity of all the others. Two World Wars have shown how impossible it is for victor nations to collect huge indemnities from the nations they have vanquished.

Let us ask ourselves what it is that makes the wealth of Britain. Is this a wealthy country or a poor one ? If it is wealthy, can it be made wealthier ? If it is poor, can it be made wealthy ?

Of course, as we have seen, wealth is a relative thing, and it is still true to say that Britain is wealthy in comparison with most of the other nations of the world.

BODY, MIND, AND SOUL · CITIZENSHIP · ECONOMICS · GOVERNMENT

If, however, we measure up British wealth, we quickly find that, while there are a small number of people with much wealth, the majority of our people have very little, and that the nation as a whole does not possess a very great deal of wealth in proportion to population.

WHAT EACH OF US WOULD GET IF THE NATION'S WEALTH WERE DIVIDED UP

The accumulated wealth possessed by all the people of our country amounts to a sum which, if equally divided, would provide about £500 for each of us. Not £500 of gold or money, of course, but £500 worth of goods. This calculation takes account of cultivated farm lands; the growing trees in the woodlands; all the roads, hedges, ditches, and drains; the port, harbour, river, and canal works; the railways and mines, the warehouses, shops, and offices; the public buildings and the private houses; the factories, mills, and workshops; the ships and boats, and all the food and goods of every kind.

So we see at once that we cannot possibly describe our nation as wealthy. Even if we take the most common of all necessary things, a house to live in, we know that the greater number of the houses of our country are not very comfortable.

Why should this be ? Why is it that so little wealth has been accumulated ?

What we have clearly to realise is that Britain is not naturally a prosperous country, and that quite recently it was much poorer than it is now. If we go back for 200 years (or say six successive generations or lives) we find Britain a poor country whose chief occupation was farming, and not very good farming at that. The Britain of that day was a backward nation, with a tiny population, and apparently with little prospect of becoming anything better. The population of England, Wales, Scotland, and Ireland was little more than 10 million people, whereas today Greater London alone contains about 8 million.

THE DISCOVERY THAT MADE GREAT BRITAIN A WEALTHY NATION

How difficult it is to realise that, only 200 years ago, the whole of England and Wales contained fewer people than the Greater London of today !

The population remained almost stationary during a large part of the eighteenth century. That was not because many children were not born, but because so many children died through lack of good feeding and medical knowledge.

Then came the wonderful change which altered everything, and caused small, poor, and backward Britain to become the comparatively well-to-do country of the twentieth century. That change was due to the fact that a few clever and thoughtful men learned how to get coal in large quantities, and how, with it, to smelt iron, and to make goods on a big scale.

The old trouble about getting coal out of the ground was this. As soon as the coal was taken out, water accumulated and stopped further coal-getting. Then arose the great problem, how to pump water out of the coal-workings. Its solution showed how true is the saying that " Necessity is the Mother of Invention." The first successful steam engine was merely a coal-mine pumping machine, devised to get rid of the water which was the miner's chief trouble. Later, coal being heavy to carry, someone thought of putting down rails to help the coal-wagons, and thus necessity led to the invention we call the railway. The steam locomotive, again, was invented by colliery engineers.

THE TWO GREAT PERIODS IN THE HISTORY OF BRITISH INDUSTRY AND TRADE

It was found that by using coal for smelting, iron could be got from its ore, and we were able to make use of our fine stores of iron as never before. Then, with iron to make machines, and steam engines to drive them, all sorts of mechanical appliances were invented, and Britain became a manufacturing country. Stanley Jevons, a celebrated 19th-century economist, summed up these changes in words we shall do well to ponder :

The history of British industry and trade may be divided into two periods, backward from about the middle of the eighteenth century to the earliest times, and forward to the present and the future.

These two periods are contrary in character. In the earlier period Britain was a rude, half-cultivated country, abounding in corn, and wool, and meat, and timber, and exporting the rough but valuable materials of manufacture. Our people, though with no small share of poetic and philosophic genius, were unskilful and unhandy, better in the arts of war than those of peace; on the whole, learners rather than teachers.

But, as the second period grew upon us, many things changed. Instead of learners we became teachers; instead of exporters of raw materials, we became importers; instead of importers of manufactured articles we became exporters.

Now we can understand why the ten million English, Scottish, Welsh, and Irish of 1750 have grown into fifty million. Much more wealth came to be produced. Britain had no longer to depend on her own poor natural resources. She became the workshop of the world, and sold goods to merchants in every part of the globe. In exchange for these goods we received such large supplies of foreign and Colonial foods and materials that oversea commodities came to be found in every household. So there sprang up the great industries, some of which we examined in an earlier chapter of this series.

WHY WE SHOULD LOOK WITH HOPE-FULNESS TO THE FUTURE

We need not be surprised, then, that we are still actually poor in accumulated wealth, for only recently we were very poor indeed. We see that in six generations we have risen from what Professor Stanley Jevons called "a rude, half-cultivated country" to one of the wealthiest States of the world. Measured against many other nations, we are well-to-do; measured against such a standard of comfort as we could reasonably desire for all our people, we are poor. When we look to the future, we can find encouragement and ground for good hope in the fact that in two centuries we have made very considerable progress. While it is good to be dissatisfied with what has been so far achieved, it is good, also, by reminding ourselves of the conditions of the old bad times, to find ground for optimism.

We have seen how important it is to study organisation in the production of wealth. By organisation we take a clever idea, or good method of working, and cause many people to follow that clever idea or good method. When we do that, we in effect make all the organised people clever. We have certainly not yet done enough in the way of organisation.

HOW BRITAIN'S MANY RAILWAYS WERE BROUGHT UNDER ONE CONTROL

Take, for example, our railways. Until 1923 these railways were in the ownership of well over one hundred large and small companies, each of which owned and worked a certain section of line.

These companies were separately worked, and each had different ideas about management, about types of engines, coaches, and wagons, about signals, and about train times and connections. Consequently,

when we passed from the lines of one railway company to the lines of another, there were often great difficulties.

Then, by Act of Parliament, 120 British railway companies were organised into four big companies, and only a few small ones were left apart from these. In 1948 all the railways were brought into one organisation, known as British Railways. This made possible uniform methods of operation all over the country, and enabled economies to be made through this, and through standardising equipment and buying larger quantities at a time.

Since the early years of this century road transport increased greatly, because the internal combustion engine was rapidly developed for commercial use, and better roads were built to take the traffic. This resulted in great competition with the railways, and much of their passenger and freight traffic was carried by road instead. When the railways were nationalised, arrangements were made for the long-distance transport of goods by road to be nationalised too, so that one body of men can organise both road and rail transport. The canals were also brought into the scheme. Thus, there is now a unified system for the carriage of goods in this country.

WASTEFUL METHODS OF USING WEALTH WHICH CANNOT BE REPLACED

A far more important matter even than transport is the use of British coal to produce energy. The supply of coal is vital to our industries, but this country's coal will not last for ever. Millions of years ago, forests of trees died down and were turned into coal, and earth and rock was formed over them. The lump of coal which we burn in an hour took millions of years to form before men dug it from the ground, and we should be very careful how we use up wealth which we cannot replace.

Coal ought not to be burned as a crude fuel in hundreds of thousands of large and small furnaces and in millions of domestic grates and cooking stoves. It should be properly regarded as a raw material out of which to manufacture solid, liquid, and gaseous fuels, many chemical products, and electricity. The details of such transformations belong to the domain of science and industry, but here, in the study of economics, it is necessary for us to see that a nation can only grow in wealth by the proper and scientific application of labour to its resources.

One way of saving coal is to make full use of water power for generating electricity. This is already done on a large scale in countries which have many rivers coming down high mountains, as in Switzerland, Norway, and the United States. Scotland has much water power available in her mountains, and this is being developed for the generation of electricity.

THE CLEANLINESS THAT WOULD RESULT FROM THE USE OF ELECTRIC POWER

If we made full use of electricity all our work, public and private, manufacturing and domestic, would be assisted by the most convenient known form of energy. Our railways would all be electrical, so that travelling would be clean, quick, and comfortable. Our manufacturing towns would be bright and pleasant places. Our houses would be cleaner, because they would no longer be smothered with the dust produced by ordinary coal-burning.

The Electricity Commissioners were set up to work on this problem and they built a splendid network of electric cables, called the Grid, covering the entire country. This is rapidly increasing the use of electricity in industry, agriculture, and the home. In 1948 all electricity undertakings were nationalised, so that one body now organises the supply of electricity throughout the country.

In many other directions the principles of economic organisation need to be applied if we are to attain to a more advanced condition of wealth and comfort. We saw at an earlier stage of this story that there are many things which have no exchange value, such as fresh air and sunshine and physical and mental health. These things, although not strictly economic factors, are governed by good economy.

WHY OVERCROWDING IS A DANGER THAT SHOULD BE AVOIDED

If people crowd together stupidly, they thereby deprive each other of fresh air, sunshine, and physical and mental health. The well-planned use of land enables a big population to create economic wealth under conditions which conserve the first essentials of the health of the people. The meaning of a good wage must be

studied in the light of these things. It serves us nothing to speak of wage rates as being high or low, unless we create conditions under which a wage produces the means of a happy and comfortable life. If a town is badly constructed, with narrow streets and ill-ventilated, badly-lit houses, and if it has few open spaces and playgrounds, and poor places of amusement, and if the means of transport within it and around it are inadequate, no wage rate paid in it, however high, can afford the wage-earner a really good living. That is why Town Planning is so important. By making sure that factories are in the right places, that housing estates are properly laid out, and that transport services are well arranged, we can do much to make life better.

We have continually to apply our efforts not only to the production of commodities, but to the production of the right kind of commodities in the right place. The possibility of wealth for all emerges from such considerations. Most certainly everybody cannot be rich, because the state of being rich is the state of possessing advantages superior to those possessed by the majority. The state of wealth is another matter if we interpret wealth as well-being.

THE ORGANISATION THAT MULTIPLIES MAN'S POWERS A HUNDREDFOLD

There is no reason why, with the wonderful scientific devices now known to mankind, which are described and pictured in other pages of this book, modern men and women should not by their labour make each other healthy, happy, and comfortable. The quantity of wealth in its economic sense (commodities having value in exchange) necessary to serve the conditions of health and happiness is not so great that we may not hope to achieve its output. Every department of human productive endeavour is now furnished with working appliances which make the modern worker the equivalent of tens or even hundreds of his predecessors of a century ago. *Thus each man, given proper organisation, becomes a company of men, and each man's hands become a score, a hundred, or a thousand.*

It is true, then, that the nation can hope to grow wealthier, but not by any royal road. The only avenue to a better economic condition is that of hard work on well-organised and scientific lines.

The Story of the Marvellous Plants that Cover the Earth

A bogland scene in Scotland

FLOWERS OF THE BOGLAND

THE flowers of the bogland and marsh are largely those of the stream, but in addition to many stream flowers there are others which are confined to bogs and marshy land.

Perhaps the most interesting of these, though its flower is not the most beautiful or conspicuous, is the round-leaved sundew, whose curious habits have been illustrated on page 578. It feeds on insects, but a tiny piece of raw meat or a little of the boiled white of an egg placed on the leaves will cause the tentacles with which the leaves are fitted to close round the meal. A digestive fluid is then poured over the insect or meat, rendering the albuminous or proteid substances soluble, and the enriched digestive juice, or broth, is reabsorbed by the plant while the tentacles reopen and allow the undigested remains of the meal to fall off the leaf. It is a most interesting operation to watch, but much patience is needed to see it all through, for the sundew often spends many days over its meal, though gnats and such-like small insects are sometimes digested in two days.

The sundew is often not more than two inches high, though it may be as much as six inches. The reddish leaves all spring from the roots and, as explained on page 586, each sensitive and mobile tentacle

bears at its tip a drop of sticky fluid which holds any small insect alighting on the leaf in the belief that the fluid is honey. The small, pinkish-white flowers are borne on a slender, wiry stalk, rising from the tuft, or rosette, of leaves which, when not in action, lie pressed to the ground or with only a slight inclination upwards.

The sundew is extraordinarily clever in discerning those substances which are of use to it for food, and it rejects such as are useless. Thus, if, instead of placing meat, eggs, or an insect on the leaf, we use a piece of stone or glass or wood, the leaf remains practically motionless.

In olden times the sundew was regarded as an unfailing remedy for consumption. The juice of the leaves, though positively injurious to the skin, was also used as a cosmetic.

The common round-leaved sundew has a sister plant, the great sundew, also, though less frequently, found in spongy bogs and sometimes on damp heaths. It is a larger and stouter plant, the leaves being on larger stalks and these stalks being destitute of tentacles.

Another carnivorous plant found in the boglands of Britain, though belonging to a different family, is the common butterwort. Its form of growth is not unlike that of the

BOTANY & ITS WONDERS · FLOWERS · TREES · HOW THINGS GROW

sundew, for it has a rosette of broad leaves growing close to the ground, and the handsome violet flowers are on leafless stalks rising from the roots. The upper surfaces of the leaves, which are pale green in colour and have a frosted, parchment-like appearance, are covered with sticky glands, and the margins are rolled slightly inwards. When small insects alight on the leaves they are held by the sticky substance, and when rain washes them to the edges the leaves close over them. The glands of the leaves pour out a digestive ferment, and the leaf, after it has absorbed the broth thus formed, unrolls once more.

A WRONG IDEA ABOUT THE PLANTS THAT FEED ON INSECTS

Many farmers still have the mistaken idea that these carnivorous plants are among the chief causes of the baneful rot disease in sheep. The animals are supposed to eat the leaves, but they never do.

The crushed leaves of the butterwort have always been credited with medicinal properties, and country people often use them as a remedy for chapped skin. The leaves also have the property of curdling milk, the name butterwort being given because of the power the plant has of separating the cream from the milk. In Lapland the freshly-gathered leaves are placed on a strainer through which the milk of the reindeer is poured, or the milk is poured on the leaves and allowed to stand for a day or two, when it becomes coagulated. It is a favourite article of diet with the Laplanders and Norwegians.

Among several members of the parsley family found in the bogs and marshes is the wild angelica, the stalks of which, candied with sugar, form an attractive sweetmeat and are much used for garnishing cakes. The stalks, blanched like celery, also used to be eaten in salads. The root and fruit form an excellent tonic and an aromatic stimulant.

THE ANGELICA WHICH WAS ONCE REGARDED AS A PROTECTING ANGEL

Angelica is a tall and stout plant, sometimes reaching six feet, though more generally it does not exceed three or four feet. The whole plant is of a bright green, and the flowers, which are white tinged with pink, grow in large umbels. The stems are furrowed, slightly downy, and tinged with purple, and the large leaves have the foot-stalks much dilated at the base. The root, which is large and fleshy,

is exceedingly pungent. In Lapland the stalks are peeled and eaten raw. The name angelica was given to the plant in the old days because of its supposed power of averting pestilence; it was regarded as a ministering and protecting angel.

Another umbelliferous plant of the bogland is the marsh pennywort, or white-rot as it is sometimes called. This is very unlike other members of the parsley family, having round, smooth, shining leaves, an inch to an inch-and-a-half across, with hairy stalks, and a few tiny flowers hidden among the leaves.

Still another umbelliferous plant is the water hemlock, or cowbane, a tall, smooth plant with stout, hollow stems and divided leaves, with saw-like edges. The umbels of small white flowers are large and flat. The whole plant is exceedingly poisonous and its name of cowbane was given because it not infrequently destroys cattle when they eat the young leaves in the spring. Happily, it is not easily mistaken for any edible plant or there might be many sufferers among human beings. The plant was once much used for medicinal purposes and even now it is sometimes applied in poultices for rheumatism.

A RELATION OF THE ROSE WITH DINGY BROWN FLOWERS

The rose family is represented in the boglands and marshes by the marsh cinquefoil, a stout herbaceous plant, about a foot high, with a woody root-stock, reddish-brown leafy stems, feather-like leaves divided into five or seven leaflets, and a few large purplish-brown and rather dingy flowers.

Of the violet family we have the pretty little marsh violet, a sister plant of the sweet violet. It has the same heart or kidney-shaped leaves, although instead of being slightly hairy, like those of the sweet violet, they are perfectly smooth, and underneath they are often of a purplish shade. The flowers are a dainty blue or lilac with darker purplish veins, and are scentless. The plant is widely distributed over northern and central Europe, Asia, and America, and though it is often found in the south of England, it is much more common in the north and in Scotland. It flowers in the spring and early summer.

We have one of the lily family in the boglands—the bog asphodel, a rather dainty little plant, six or seven inches high, with tufts of narrow leaves that look almost like grass, and a spike of yellow, star-like flowers, which are succeeded by long, orange-coloured capsules. The botanical name of the plant is Narthecium ossifragum, the second word meaning bone-breaking. This description was given to the species because it was supposed that the bones of cattle feeding on the plant became soft. While animals sometimes suffer in this way in areas where the asphodel is found, the complaint is due not to the plant, but to the unhealthy nature of the boglands.

The handsome marsh marigold is a member of the buttercup family, and indeed its large golden flower is, in appear-

it was only after much suffering that they recovered. Hence the need for warning young children against putting any part of the plant in the mouth. The old practice of gathering the young buds and pickling them in the place of capers is certainly inadvisable, although no doubt the irritant properties are largely destroyed in the process. A yellow dye is obtained by boiling the petals with alum. Another buttercup of the boglands is the yellow meadow-rue, whose pale yellow flowers grow in crowded clusters.

Orchids are not generally flowers of the boglands and marshes, but one that may be found there occasionally is the summer lady's tresses, a plant that grows from six

LADY'S TRESSES   COTTON-GRASS   BUCK-BEAN

ance, much like a gigantic buttercup. The glossy, dark green leaves are kidney-shaped, and the stems, which are about a foot high, are very erect. The plant begins to blossom in March and often continues flowering till June. In some parts of England the children collect these handsome flowers to decorate the cottages on May Day. But, while attractive to the eye, the plant is very poisonous. It once happened that five people, who from poverty were compelled to resort to wild herbs for food, were poisoned by eating the marsh marigold. They were all seized with pain and violent sickness, followed by swellings over the whole body, and

to eighteen inches high, with leaves on the flowering stem and white flowers, larger and more loosely arranged than those of the autumn lady's tresses. They have a rather pleasant almond-like smell.

The beautiful little bog pimpernel, a sister of the scarlet pimpernel, is a member of the primrose family, and is quite a common plant on boggy ground and by the sides of streams. It is a slender creeping plant, a few inches long, with roundish leaves and elegant funnel-shaped flowers of pale pink, rather larger than those of the scarlet pimpernel. The plant is quite common all over the British Isles and western Europe.

The buck-bean, or bog-bean, is not a bean, but a member of the gentian family, and grows in wet bogs and shallow ponds where the short stem creeps or floats and scarcely rises above the water or wet ground. The creeping rootstock has thickly matted roots, and on the stem are dense tufts of leaves, each leaf consisting of a long stalk, sheathing at the base, and three roundish oval leaflets; hence the alternative name of the plant, the marsh trefoil. The flowers, which grow in a long stalked raceme, are very beautiful. When in bud they are pink, but as they open it is seen that the inner surfaces of the five fleshy petals are covered with a thick white fringe. The rootstock, which was frequently employed in former days as a tonic, is exceedingly bitter.

The marsh gentian, another member of the same family, has large bell-shaped flowers, deep blue in colour generally, but sometimes pink.

THE MEADOW CRANE'S-BILL WHICH IS THE LARGEST BRITISH GERANIUM

The meadow crane's-bill—a rather mis-named plant as it is found not in meadows generally but only in those which are very moist or by a river—is a geranium, the largest of all the British species. It often grows four or five feet high and its bluish-purple flowers are over an inch in diameter.

The composite family is well repre-sented in the bogs and marshes. Perhaps the most striking is the marsh plume-thistle, the tallest of all the British thistles. It is sometimes found growing as high as ten feet. The plant consists of one single, stout, hollow stem, which is branched near the top and armed all the way down with the spiny wings of the leaves, which run down the stem. The leaves themselves are narrow, wavy, and armed with short brownish spines. They are generally downy underneath. The flower-heads are small and more or less egg-shaped, and grow in clusters, the florets being deep crimson, purple, or sometimes white in colour. The plant flowers freely through-out the summer.

The marsh ragwort, another composite growing abundantly in wet places, is much like the common ragwort, though more slender, and it is not always easy to distinguish one from the other. The stem of the marsh ragwort, however, is not quite so tall as the other; it is more

branched and spreading, the conspicuous, bright yellow flower-heads are larger and fewer, and on larger stalks. The plant, too, is not so long-lived as its sister.

Another familiar composite is the com-mon fleabane, a plant about two feet high, which grows in masses and has large, flat, golden flower-heads. It has a woolly stem and the oblong leaves are soft, wavy, and downy, and clasp the stems. In eastern Europe the plant has been much used as a medicine for cases of dysentery, and a Russian army on an expedition to Persia, having been attacked by this com-plaint, is said to have been completely cured by using fleabane, which is very bitter and astringent.

THE BUR-MARIGOLD WHOSE BRISTLY SEEDS ARE DISTRIBUTED BY WOOLLY ANIMALS

The nodding bur-marigold, another of the composites, is a succulent plant, from one to two feet high, with spreading branches, and lance-shaped leaves with saw-like margins. The butter-like flower-heads, of brownish-yellow, droop and develop into oblong fruits terminating in three or four stiff bristles set with barbs, so that the fruits take a firm hold of the wool or hair of any animal coming in contact with them. In this way they are distributed and so the plant spreads from place to place. A sister plant, the trifid bur-marigold, is distinguished from the other species by having its leaves divided into three, its flowers smaller and more erect, and two more often than three bristles on its fruits.

Another composite, the marsh cudweed, is a small plant, four or five inches high, much branched, and cottony. The narrow leaves are downy, and the flower-heads, small and clustered together, grow within a tuft of long leaves at the ends of the branches. The flowers are yellowish-brown in colour.

THE BLUE MARSH VETCHLING BELONGING TO THE PEA FAMILY

The pea family has its representative in the blue marsh vetchling, though that plant is not very common. It is a climbing plant rather smaller than its sister, the narrow-leaved everlasting pea, though like it in general habit. The leaflets are narrow and acute, with from two to four pairs to each leaf. The flowers, which are not so broad as those of the everlasting pea, are bluish-purple, and there are from two to eight in each raceme, or bunch.

A GARLAND OF BOGLAND FLOWERS

MARSH PENNYWORT

GOLDEN SAXIFRAGE

MARSH ST. JOHN'S WORT

BOG ASPHODEL

COMMON BUTTERWORT

BIRD'S-EYE PRIMROSE

MARSH CINQUEFOIL

FALSE CYPERUS

ROUND-LEAVED SUNDEW

BOG MYRTLE

BOG PIMPERNEL

GRASS OF PARNASSUS

ANGELICA

The ivy-leaved bellflower, a dainty little plant, is often found growing in company with the bog pimpernel. It is a straggling plant with thread-like stems which rise four or five inches high; but if grass is near, the bellflower will climb to a height of a foot, or even more. The leaves, divided into five lobes, are of a delicate green, and the beautiful pale blue flowers grow singly on long, almost hair-like stalks. The flowers droop a little, and are found from July to September.

THE GOLDEN SAXIFRAGE WHICH GROWS ONLY AN INCH OR TWO HIGH

Several saxifrages are found in the marshes and damp, shady places, among them the common golden saxifrage, a little plant sometimes only two inches high and rarely exceeding six inches. It has a creeping stem and bright green roundish leaves, and the tiny yellowish-green flowers grow in terminal clusters. The grass of Parnassus, another member of the family, is a beautiful plant, well worthy of its poetic name. The flowers, an inch across, are ivory-white and beautifully veined; growing on flower-stalks eight or ten inches high, they stand up well above the oval leaves, and are very conspicuous.

The yellow marsh saxifrage is a handsome plant about six inches high, the flowering stem ending in a single large flower, yellow spotted with scarlet.

Several figworts grow in damp and marshy places. One is the marsh speedwell, or veronica, a weak and straggling plant with pale pink flowers and lance-shaped leaves, slightly toothed. It seldom grows more than six inches high, and is found all over Britain and throughout north and central Europe; also in Russian Asia and North America.

HOW THE MARSH RED-RATTLE OVERTOPS THE OTHER PLANTS

The marsh red-rattle is an erect plant, from six to eighteen inches high, with feather-like leaves and large crimson flowers. Sometimes in very damp places it thrives greatly, and overtops the other plants, its crimson flowers standing out conspicuously. A third figwort of the boglands is the knotted figwort, a coarse plant two or three feet high, with a disagreeable smell. It has a thick, fleshy, knotted rootstock, large pointed leaves, more or less heart-shaped and with saw-like margins, and dingy greenish-brown flowers. This plant is called by the French herbe du siège, because during the thirteen months' siege of La Rochelle by the army of Cardinal Richelieu, in 1628, the garrison for a long time lived on its tuberous roots. The taste and smell of these, however, is unpleasant, and they would only be resorted to for food in periods of extreme famine.

One of the heath family is found on peat-bogs, chiefly in the north. This is the marsh andromeda, sometimes called the marsh cistus and the wild rosemary, a small evergreen shrub with clusters of pretty, drooping pink flowers. It possesses narcotic properties, and is said to have killed sheep that cropped its leaves. Fortunately, sheep and cattle are not often able to approach the places where the plant grows.

The marsh St. John's wort, a shaggy plant with creeping stems, roundish downy leaves and pale yellow flowers, is found in spongy bogs, and the common marshmallow is found in marshes near the sea, growing two or three feet high, with bluish pink flowers.

THE TINY FLAX-SEED WHICH GROWS TOGETHER IN GREAT NUMBERS

A member of the flax family often found in these damp situations is the common flax-seed, a tiny plant only three or four inches high, with many tiny white flowers which would be overlooked did they not grow together in such large numbers. The small marsh valerian is an erect plant about a foot high, with pink flowers growing in clusters.

Among other plants of the bogs and marshes are the horse mint, a sweet-scented plant that grows in dense masses, with spikes of lilac flowers; its sister plant, the pennyroyal, a small plant with a pleasing scent and flavour, often cultivated in cottage gardens for making into a tea that is used as a remedy for colds; the lesser skull-cap, a slender plant, five or six inches high, with small pale pink flowers; the marsh willow-herb, a relation of the evening primroses, with a small pink flower; and two of the sedges, the false cyperus, with pretty tassel-like flower-spikes and sharp grass-like leaves, and the cotton-grass, a rush-like plant with tufts of cotton-wool sticking on the ends of its stems, which is sometimes used for stuffing pillows.

Two pages of coloured pictures of Flowers of the Bogland are given on 6127-28

The Story of the Peoples of All Nations and Their Homelands

Peter the Great at Deptford Dockyard, by Daniel Maclise, R.A.

RUSSIA THROUGH THE CENTURIES

FROM beyond a thousand years ago, when legend was beginning to merge into dim history, we first hear of Russia.

Then it was a land of mixed tribes badly governed, and feeling that it needed order first of all things. In those days the roving Northmen were the world's boldest men, and to them the Russian tribes living around Novgorod, within reach of the Baltic Sea, sent a message: " Our land is great and bountiful, but there is no order in it. Come and rule over us." Three bold Viking brothers responded to the invitation, crossed over from Scandinavia, and Rurik, the chief of the brothers, founded a line of kings.

Vladimir was the first Christian ruler, towards the end of the tenth century. He it was who chose to belong to the Eastern or Greek Church, and thereafter Russia was identified with that branch of Christianity. Often she held out a helping hand to smaller countries of Slavonic origin like herself, who were oppressed by their Mohammedan masters.

But civil war followed for centuries. The country was divided into rival principalities, and the more powerful among them, Novgorod, Kiev, and, later, Moscow, struggled for supremacy. This strife within the country was partly but not entirely checked by danger and disaster from the outside. Hordes of Mongols or Tartars, nomads from the deserts and steppes of Asia, descended on the country, and for more than 200 years Russia was obliged to treat them as conquerors, pay heavy taxes, and from time to time be plundered by fresh invaders. The most dreaded of these invasions, by what was called the Golden Horde, came from the valley of the Amur, in Eastern Siberia. Moscow was taken and burned by the Tartars more than once.

As time went on the Russians regained their independence. Ivan the Third, who reigned as Duke of Muscovy in the latter part of the fifteenth century, refused to do homage to the Tartar ruler, and founded the modern Russian State. He rebuilt Moscow. By this time the double-headed black eagle, used by the Greek Empire, was adopted as the arms of Russia.

Ivan the Fourth was called Ivan the Terrible because he was so insanely cruel, but he was also a man of great power. Born in 1530, he took the title of Tsar of all Russia, in 1547, after he had been a boy king from the age of three. He annexed many cities and States on the great Russian plain, till his dominions reached Astrakhan on the Caspian Sea, and stretched north-

THE FIVE CONTINENTS & 100 NATIONS & RACES THAT INHABIT THEM

ward as far as the White Sea and Siberia. He began to trade with England through Archangel, and he hoped to force a way to the Baltic Sea, but Poland and Sweden blocked his path westward. Ivan used the Cossacks to defend the eastern frontier of his realm, and it was a Cossack leader who conquered a large part of Siberia for him. In Central Russia Ivan stamped out all opposition with a relentless cruelty that

POOR PEASANTS HIDDEN FROM THE SIGHT OF THE EMPRESS CATHERINE AS SHE DROVE THROUGH THE VILLAGES OF RUSSIA

had the effect of weakening his country.

After Ivan died, in 1584, disorder followed. One consequence of his impoverishing wars was the reducing of the peasantry to a state of serfdom, which lasted for three hundred years. The labouring class was so lessened in numbers that the landowners competed for their services, and they were strictly forbidden to leave the estate on which they had been born. This

order left them in a condition approaching slavery. They had rights of tillage in the common land of the place, but they had to give their services for the cultivation of the estates of the landed proprietors, and they could not go elsewhere.

After about thirty years of disorder and war following the death of Ivan the Terrible, during which the Poles occupied Moscow and the Swedes Novgorod, the Russians rose in despair, drove out the invaders and called a National Assembly together, which elected Tsar Michael Romanoff, the first sovereign of a new dynasty. This was done in 1613, and the Romanoff family, chosen by the common consent of the people, continued to reign till 1917, when Tsar Nicholas the Second abdicated in favour of a Republic. During the Civil War that followed he and all his family were murdered by the Bolsheviks.

The most famous ruling member of the Romanoff family was Peter the Great, who began to reign personally when seventeen, and reigned from 1689 to 1725. Peter was determined to have his own way, and, happily, in some respects, it was a good way. As a child he was fond of boats and mechanical contrivances, and he perceived how backward his country was in these respects.

He went abroad to Holland and England, and later to other countries, and worked himself as a boat builder. Then he returned to Russia, and began to introduce some of the improvements he had observed in other lands, greatly to the disgust of many of his people. Living a remote life far away from other countries, and surrounded by races as simple and rough as themselves, the Russians were naturally very conservative and clung to their old customs. It was a national habit to grow a beard, and many simple-minded people thought it wrong to cut the beard or hair. But Peter made his chief officials shave as part of his plan for breaking up national habits, and giving fresh ideas a chance. He began by cutting off the beards of his principal officers himself. Afterwards a tax was put on beards.

It must not be supposed that Peter himself was much more civilised than his people. He was coarse, boisterous, and as tyrannical in spirit as most of the Russian rulers had been, but he saw that Russia needed certain things if she was to take her place among the foremost nations, and he tried to give her these things, even if he had to thrust them on her.

He tried to bring knowledge to the country through books, libraries and museums. He brought in foreigners to train Russian administrators. He extended the means of travel and of trade by making canals. He also gave Russia the beginnings of a navy, first on the White Sea and then on the Sea of Azov. His next dream of conquest was to make himself Emperor of the East, but Turkey blocked his way. Northward, however, after the death of Charles the Twelfth of Sweden, with whom he engaged in long wars with changeful success, he forced Sweden from the eastern shores of the Baltic and made that sea the chief Russian outlet to the west. He then built the city of St. Petersburg (afterwards Petrograd and then Leningrad) as his capital.

Peter the Great found Russia a half savage nation on the outskirts of Europe, and left it a nation that henceforward had to be reckoned with as a European Power almost in the first rank. The change was entirely due to his overmastering self-will and energy. As a man he was ruthless towards all who stood in his way. His power over the Russian people was shown by their acceptance, contrary to all their customs, of his second wife, Catherine, to reign after him as Empress, though she was of peasant birth; and in the

next seventy years, besides Catherine the First, three other women, Anne, Elizabeth, and Catherine the Second, held sovereign rule over Russia.

Catherine the Second, a German woman who is often called Catherine the Great, ruled for 34 years—till 1796. She usurped the throne after her husband, Peter the Third, was murdered, and held the position by sheer force of character and states-

THE METROPOLITAN PHILIP REFUSES TO GIVE HIS BLESSING TO IVAN THE TERRIBLE

manlike ability, though her private life was vicious. Catherine followed the plan of Peter the Great by bringing to her Court foreigners with helpful ideas. Her ambition could never be satisfied, and she made large additions to her empire, including the Crimea, taken from the Turks; the Black Sea region round Odessa; what is now the Lithuanian coast on the Baltic; and a large share of Poland.

In the reign of Catherine's son Paul, a sentimental weakling who was fascinated by Napoleon, and wished to join him in an attempt to divide the Turkish Empire between them, and then conquer India, another province was voluntarily surrendered by its prince to Russia. This was the ancient kingdom of Georgia beyond the Caucasian Mountains. The Emperor Paul was assassinated, and the accession of his son, Alexander the First, in 1801, opened the distinctly modern period of Russian history in which the country began to play a prominent part in the history of Europe as a whole.

At first Alexander was inclined to act in conjunction with Napoleon, if he could have his full share of influence throughout Europe; but presently he recognised that there was no room in Europe for two autocrats, and that Russia, next to England, was Napoleon's most persistent opponent. It was Russia's resistance to Napoleon's Moscow campaign, and her continuous pressure on his defeated army that led to the overthrow of the world's greatest adventurer. It was Alexander, prompted by Stein, the great Liberal statesman exiled from Prussia, who carried the Allies' pursuit through the gates of Paris.

THE HIGH IDEALS WITH WHICH A TSAR BEGAN HIS REIGN

Early in his reign Alexander had been alive to the need for an expansion of freedom in Russia, through improved education, more just government, possibly on constitutional lines, and the overthrow of the serf system. But when the armies of the European monarchies had crushed Napoleon, and placed France again under the blind tyranny of the Bourbon family, he reverted to the view that all nations, including Russia, would be happier under the government of rulers like himself than under any new-fangled ideas of liberty and self-control. But Russia had now come into the community of European nations, and many of her younger men knew the difference between Russian autocracy and the freedom of the West. The result was that disappointment showed itself in the underground form of secret societies plotting to bring about changes which could not be sought openly, and these societies were to trouble Russia for the next hundred years.

Alexander was succeeded in 1825 by his younger brother Nicholas, a hard, soldierly man who would stand no nonsense about liberty, and for thirty years he sternly discouraged all expressions of public opinion about the government. He equally disliked liberty in other countries, and helped the Emperor of Austria to crush rebellion among his Hungarian subjects. Nicholas did useful work in securing self-government for Wallachia and Moldavia (now the central parts of Rumania) and Serbia from the Turks, and the beginnings of freedom for Greece; but he pushed his opposition to Turkey so far that, finally, Great Britain and France supported Turkey against him in the unnecessary and badly managed but bravely fought Crimean War. During the reign of Nicholas the Russians completed the conquest of the brave Circassians.

THE HUMANE DECREE WHICH GAVE MILLIONS OF SERFS THEIR FREEDOM

The successor to Nicholas, Alexander the Second, was the only ruler Russia has ever had who tried sympathetically to reform her government and give her the institutions of a free country. In 1861 a decree was issued emancipating within two years all the serfs in the Empire. They numbered 23,000,000, and their joy at release from an irksome and unmanly thraldom was reflected round the world. Steps were also taken to establish a form of local government, and trial by jury was instituted. Attempts were made to develop the industries of the country. Tsar Alexander the Second was the popular national hero.

But disappointment followed. Prosperity did not come so swiftly as was expected. More reforms were asked for hastily, and were not granted. Secret societies again became active, and were repressed. Then murders of officials became common. Spying and counter-spying spread everywhere, and finally Alexander the Second, who had been hailed twenty years before as the saviour of his country, was murdered by a bomb thrown under his carriage as he rode through the streets of St. Petersburg.

HOW BRITAIN STOOD IN THE WAY OF RUSSIA'S ADVANCE TO THE EAST

During Alexander's reign, by the help of the Russian army, Bulgaria obtained freedom from the Turks, but the Russians were prevented from entering Constantinople by the threats of Great Britain and Austria, the British at that time being very

A TSAR LOOKS DOWN ON PARLIAMENT

PETER THE GREAT OF RUSSIA WATCHES THE PROCEEDINGS IN THE HOUSE OF LORDS

suspicious of Russia's widespread conquests in Central Asia and her approach towards India.

The successor of Alexander the Second, his son Alexander the Third, had no sympathy with what his father had done. He thought the extension of greater liberty to the Russian people a mistake, and he returned to the stern methods of government of the earlier Tsars.

THE TERRIBLE MAN WHO BANISHED THOUSANDS TO SIBERIA

His method of government was largely by his secret police. Opponents of his repressive ways were sent to imprisonment in Siberia by tens of thousands. This third Alexander's interference with his people extended to all their interests in life. Russians who believed in other religions than that of the Orthodox Greek Church were persecuted. The many nationalities that are contained in Russia were checked in the use of their own languages. The Russian language and Russian customs were enforced everywhere in all official doings. So discontent was spread throughout the land, and secret societies favouring revolution multiplied. Tsardom became a hated byword. Jealousy also sprang up between Russia and Germany, and this led to France and Russia drawing closer together in friendship till at last they were pledged allies. Meanwhile, Great Britain insisted that Russia should agree with her on a fixed boundary in Central Asia which Russia must not cross, as it was felt that India was being persistently threatened from the north.

This was the state of things when Alexander the Third died, and the last of the Romanoff rulers, Nicholas the Second, became Tsar in 1894. He was a very amiable but weak man, and he followed in the steps of his father. His sympathies were with the people, but his advisers recommended him to be strong and stern, and his wife, who had a great influence over him, sided with them. The secret revolutionary societies that used murder as a weapon revived.

THE LITTLE EASTERN NATION WHICH FLUNG BACK THE RUSSIAN GIANT

Meanwhile, Russian ambition had sent its armies to the Pacific coast across Siberia and had erected a great fortress there at Port Arthur, and the immense Chinese province of Manchuria, joined with European Russia by the Trans-Siberian railway, had fallen entirely under Russian influence, while Korea was threatened. The warlike Japanese were deeply stirred. They saw a giant power coming nearer and nearer, with what looked like irresistible force. Suddenly they declared war, and flung themselves on the outpost of the great Russian Empire.

The result astonished the world. On land and sea the Japanese were everywhere victorious. The Russian fleet was utterly destroyed. The great fortress was besieged, stormed, and taken. The Russian armies were flung back in great and terrible battles, and the Russian menace to the Far East was completely dispelled. The Japanese had fought as a united nation bent on freeing themselves from a great impending danger. The Russians, disunited at home, were half-hearted in the war and became discouraged and disorganised by failure. Russia at home was thrown into confusion. Government was at a standstill. Anything might happen. Then the cry for a real Parliament arose.

THE QUARREL WHICH WAS THE IMMEDIATE CAUSE OF THE FIRST WORLD WAR

A promise of a representative government was made by the Tsar at the same time that peace was signed with Japan (October, 1905), and the first Parliament met in April of the next year; but from that time onward the meetings showed that the tendency to mistake talking for business was particularly strong. The actual power of the Duma, as the Parliament was called, was very small, and its decisions might be ignored by the Tsar.

One cause of the First World War was the quarrel between Russia and Austria in the Near East; and when it broke out Russia found herself fighting with France and ourselves against Germany, Austria, and Turkey. We should be very ungrateful not to remember the help she gave in the first three years of the war.

Early in 1917 the Russians were exhausted. Threatened equally by mutinous soldiers and revolutionaries in Moscow and Petrograd (as Leningrad then was) the Government fell into confusion and lost control. The Tsar and Tsaritsa had fallen under the influence of a rascally priest, Rasputin, who led them to dismiss Ministers and Generals and interfere with the conduct of the war. He was seized and murdered by a group of officers, but by this time the mischief had been done.

In March, 1917, revolution broke out in Petrograd, the Tsar abdicated, and his Government collapsed. A Government of "moderate reformers" followed, which tried to continue the war, and again attacked the Germans with some success.

LENIN BECOMES THE NEW MASTER OF THE COUNTRY

This, however, only hastened the exhaustion of the army, and in the meantime the extreme revolutionaries (Bolsheviks, or "Men of the Majority") were hard at work undermining this moderate Government and laying plans for its destruction. At this moment the Germans played a crafty stroke by sending Lenin, a well-known revolutionary leader, in a sealed railway compartment from Switzerland into Russia, where he immediately took charge of the revolutionary movement.

For a few months the moderate Prime Minister, Kerensky, held his own, but in November, 1917, soldiers, sailors, and workmen stormed the Government buildings and compelled the Government to take flight. Lenin, under the title of President of the Council of People's Commissioners, became master of the country.

Lenin was an able, determined, and fanatical man, who believed that the war was the work of capitalists, and that if the Russian workers set the example of refusing to fight, all the other workers of the world would follow their example. In this he was greatly mistaken, and the Russians, having obtained an armistice, found themselves alone and helpless against Germany, which in March of the following year (1918) compelled them to accept the harsh Treaty of Brest-Litovsk, under which the Germans occupied the Ukraine, deprived Russia of her Baltic Provinces, and left Leningrad at the mercy of any invader from the borders of Finland and Estonia. The capital was now moved from Leningrad to Moscow.

ALL EXCEPT MANUAL WORKERS DEPRIVED OF THEIR RIGHTS AND PROPERTY

Government passed wholly into the hands of the Bolsheviks, a small but resolute body of Communists who proceeded at once to carry out their full policy of nationalising the banks and the land, placing workers in control of factories, disestablishing the Church, secularising schools, depriving almost everybody except manual workers of his rights and property.

The Bolsheviks called themselves the "dictatorship of the proletariat" (the common people), their idea being that the workers had won a great victory in the class war and were therefore entitled to as high a social status as other classes. To protect themselves they had powerful Red Guards formed from the remnants of the old army, and a secret police (the O.G.P.U.) which went all over Russia suppressing those who resisted.

Civil war with all its horrors was now let loose. On the night of July 16, 1918, the Tsar, his wife, son, and three daughters were executed in a house at Ekaterinburg (now Sverdlovsk) in which they had been held prisoners after the revolution. Scores of thousands more were shot, hanged, or died of frost and starvation in the next few months.

Terrible as these events were the Russians had better have been left alone to restore order and sanity, if they could, in their own way. But at the end of 1918 the French and British Governments, having their hands free, were tempted to lend their support to the White Russians (White as opposed to Red or Bolshevik Russians) who were preparing expeditions to march into Russia and destroy the Bolshevik regime.

FOREIGN INTERVENTION FAILS TO CHECK THE BOLSHEVIKS

All these expeditions failed, largely because the White Russians were as ruthless as the Red had been in their revolution; and the Russian peasants, caught between Red and White, preferred the Red, who promised to leave them in possession of the lands the Whites had come to recover.

Our own Government soon tired of helping, but the French persisted, and in 1920 encouraged the Poles to invade Russia. For a time they had some success and captured Kiev, but the Russians rallied and drove them back, and would probably have taken their capital, Warsaw, if the French had not come to their assistance.

There was much aimless fighting, and in October the Poles made peace with the Russians, and the Russians, having disposed of their other enemies, were now free to devote themselves to the establishment of their Communist State and to the furtherance of world revolution. For this purpose they created, in 1919, the Comintern, or Third International. They hoped that their Communist principles might gain a hold in those countries for which the German writer, Karl Marx, founder of international Communism, had designed them.

THE NEW ECONOMIC POLICY SET IN BEING BY LENIN

The establishment of their own Communist State proved a much more difficult business than they had expected. Russia had been exhausted by the war, and the revolution had destroyed a large part of the wealth that remained. It was, therefore, necessary to start all over again. Lenin began by trying what was called pure Communism, abolishing money, producing everything in common, and distributing what was produced by means of officials. But this speedily broke down; and, finding it impossible to feed, clothe, and supply the wants of a great population in this way, he gradually introduced something that he called the New Economic Policy by which private traders were allowed to sell goods for a profit (subject to heavy taxation) in the towns, while the peasants supported themselves out of what they grew on their farms and by selling to the towns what they did not require for their own use.

But in 1924 Lenin died and, after a sharp struggle, was succeeded by Stalin, who said that the idea of a nation of small farmer-owners was contrary to the principles of the Revolution, the principles laid down by Marx, whose book on Capital, published in 1867, is still the Communist bible.

STALIN COMPELS THE PEASANTS TO COME INTO COLLECTIVE STATE FARMS

True Socialism, said Stalin and the group of men who now came to power, could not permit the great majority of Russians to own property in land and work for their own private profit. The State must own the land, all must work for the State and be under the control of the State. So they changed the system under which the land was held, compelling many peasants to come into Collective Farms owned by the State and worked by the State, which took a certain part of the produce to feed the towns and left the rest to be divided among the peasants.

This scheme proved a great success, three-quarters of all the peasant holdings in the Ukraine being collective farms by 1934. In 1939 there were 242,000 collective farms, 4000 State farms and 1,300,000 peasant-owned farms, in the whole of Russia.

But Stalin and his men who now governed Russia were not content that she should be a nation of peasants. They wished to make her also a great manufacturing and industrial nation. Karl Marx had intended his principles chiefly for manual workers living in towns, and they could only be applied in Russia if new industries were established and large numbers of peasants set to work in them. So Stalin proposed a Five-Year Plan for establishing factories and power-stations all over Russia, and brought engineers, chemists, and workmen from America, Germany, England, and many other countries to help him.

Having abolished trade unions, and being in a position to compel people to do what they were told to do and accept the wages paid to them, the Bolsheviks had great advantages in carrying out their programme, and during the next three years they erected some of the largest factories and power-stations in the world.

BRITISH ENGINEERS PUT ON TRIAL FOR SABOTAGE AND CHARGED WITH SPYING

It was always rather difficult to work for them, for if things went wrong you were liable not merely to be dismissed but to be severely punished. When a machine broke down, it was frequently said that somebody had wilfully wrecked it, and many engineers and experts were sentenced to banishment or imprisonment for this offence. In 1933 a party of British engineers were convicted for supposed offences of this kind, and some of them sentenced to imprisonment, but the British Government insisted in their being released and allowed to leave the country.

Meantime Russia had been given a new title—The Union of Soviet Socialist Republics. Stalin was responsible for this, in 1923, the year after he became secretary of the Communist Party. The State was divided up solely according to nationality, and in each unit, even the smallest, the language of teaching was that of the racial group. There are now 16 of these Republics.

For many things they did the Bolsheviks undoubtedly deserve credit. They built large numbers of schools so that nearly all Russians can now read and write. They established crêches for young children, rest-houses for workmen, medical centres and convalescent hospitals in many parts of the country. They also provided music, theatres, and other entertainments free of cost. But they had great difficulty in keeping their people fed, clothed, and housed as they ought to be, and the life of the majority was a great struggle.

SACRIFICES OF THE PEOPLE BUOYED UP WITH PROMISES OF THE FUTURE

The young Communists regarded the new factories with great pride, and willingly went hungry and made all manner of sacrifices that more might be built; but the kind of factories built did not supply the needs of a great population, and the struggle with the peasants caused a great shortage of food. So the Russian people had to live, as we have lived in wartime, waiting in queues outside shops and stores to buy the amounts which the Government allowed them to buy; and some were in danger of having their rations stopped if they did not give satisfaction to the Government.

But the Communists were convinced that everything would come right if only they were given time, and they organised another Five-Year Plan to follow the first, and still another at the end of that. There have in fact been four Five-Year Plans. The third was interrupted by the Second World War, and the fourth began to operate early in 1946. In the meantime they called upon their fellow-citizens to " tighten their belts " and endure everything for the sake of the great example they were giving to the world and the great victory which awaited them.

Bolshevism was in their view a gospel for the whole world, and in those early days they had their agents and missionaries in foreign countries trying to spread the idea of Communism.

WHAT WESTERN CRITICS HAVE TO REMEMBER ABOUT RUSSIA

Those who believed in liberty, charity, and tolerance, and in rewarding men and women according to the work they did, naturally shrank from a system which appeared to extinguish all liberty and exalt one class above all other classes.

We have to remember, however, that the great mass of the Russian people were desperately poor and suffered grievous oppression and injustice under the Tsars and to think of their revolution as the violent explosion of long pent-up forces.

They were a people who had never known liberty, and it seemed much more natural to them than it does to us that, when the great change came, they should pass from one form of arbitrary government to another, from the dictatorship of the Tsars to a dictatorship of the proletariat.

To deal wisely with Russia has been one of the most difficult problems for the other Governments. For many years after her Revolution they refused to recognise her. For this they had some excuse, for many of the Russian leaders were never weary of proclaiming their intention to upset them, if they could; and large sums of money are said to have been spent in promoting Communist agitation in foreign countries.

In the years immediately preceding the Hitler War, Russia changed those tactics and tried to restore trade and enter into friendly relations with her neighbours. She entered the League of Nations, where her representatives gave the impression that their great country was sincerely anxious to keep the peace. Most of the other Governments met these advances half-way, and had not Germany, Italy, and Japan been so hostile to Russia, fearing her growing strength, it is possible that Russia's internal progress would have been all the world's gain.

STALIN'S PACT WITH GERMANY WHICH ASTOUNDED THE WORLD

Russia signed a pact of mutual assistance with Czechoslovakia and an even stronger military pact with France, so she regarded it as a distinct rebuff when she was not called in to take part in the Munich negotiations of 1938.

When in the following spring of 1939 Czechoslovakia was seized by Germany and a similar fate seemed in store for Poland and Rumania, Russia proposed a six-power conference, but our Government called it premature. So when a British mission endeavoured to win Russia's support for Poland against Germany Stalin astounded the world by signing a pact with Germany and marching into the east of Poland soon after Hitler's army had marched into the west.

It was not, however, certain what the real purpose of Stalin was, for at the same time he induced Lithuania, Latvia, and Estonia, at this time independent States, to yield him fortress posts on the Baltic, and waged a bitter war against Finland who declined to do so. Estonia, Latvia, and Lithuania were in no position to resist, and though Stalin gave clear pledges against interference in their internal affairs they were annexed in June, 1940, and completely Russianised, becoming the 14th, 15th, and 16th Soviet Republics.

A few weeks earlier the Russian Government, with a view to strengthening her southern frontier, demanded back from Rumania the Province of Bessarabia which had been taken from her in 1918. This, Rumania ceded, together with Northern Bukovina.

Hitler appeared to agree with these additions to the Soviet Union, but in reality he feared the growing power of his vast neighbour to the east.

TREACHEROUSLY ATTACKED BY HITLER, RUSSIA FIGHTS LIKE A TITAN

Having been worsted in the Battle of Britain, he feared that a further attack on our island would cost him dear, and that Russia might take advantage of his difficulties and attack Germany in the east. Accordingly he decided to overwhelm Russia before engaging in a final conflict with Britain. In June 1941, therefore, Hitler treacherously broke the treaty he had signed with Russia and attacked that country with all his forces. The same evening Mr. Churchill, in the British Parliament, proclaimed Britain the ally of Russia.

Hitler seems to have been surprised by the immense amount of tanks and other " armour " he found behind the Russian lines, and by the use the Russians made of the lessons in " defence in depth " learned from the campaign in France. Also, the Russian people answered as one man the call for the defence of the Fatherland. They remembered how they had thrown Napoleon back from Moscow, and they were determined that no invader should again set foot in their capital.

Every farm and every crossroad became a point of bitter resistance. Each night the Russians fought back to reduce the day's gains. At the same time, far behind the lines, the country's industry was reorganised, whole factories being transported to new and safer sites behind the Ural Mountains.

Nevertheless Hitler's Panzers drove forward relentlessly, in north and centre and south, across Stalin's " scorched earth." Leningrad endured a siege of more than five hundred days. Moscow was encircled and the city heard the thunder of the German guns on all sides. Then Stalin gave the word for a general counter-offensive in this area, and the Germans were rolled back from the city's gates.

HOW THE TIDE TURNED AND THE RUSSIAN ARMIES ROLLED WESTWARD

Next summer Hitler attacked again, on narrower fronts pointed to Stalingrad and the Caucasian oilfields. On both fronts it was touch and go for a long time, but at last the difficulties of ever-lengthening communications and ever-increasing loss of men and armour—the penalty of attack —proved too great, and the second and last thrust recoiled. From the spring of 1943 the issue was no longer in doubt. Westwards always the Russian armies rolled, until at last the Germans were driven back across the frontiers, and to Berlin, where they gave in.

This great victory was not won by the Russians alone. We must not forget how our own Navy, through storm and mine-field, fed Russia with munitions by way of her northern ports. We, and the Americans too, were attacking the Germans elsewhere, and so weakening their total forces. But full credit must be given to the new Russian Army that Stalin had trained.

When the war was over Russia found herself in possession of most of East Prussia and of Eastern Poland, while she took over a " zone " of Germany pending agreement on the future of the beaten country. This zone included Berlin, but the capital was left under the joint administration of Britain, Russia, America, and France. A little later, by treaty with Finland, Russia regained the province of Petsamo, previously ceded to Finland.

THE DISBANDING OF THE COMINTERN AND ITS REVIVAL AS THE COMINFORM

The Russians are still Communists. The Comintern was disbanded in 1943, but late in 1947 it was revived under the name of Cominform, as a " rallying point against imperialism " and as a means of getting Communists in other countries to work together for the spread of their creed.

Like all the other great Powers, Russia joined the United Nations Organisation after the war, and she took part in all its councils. Her participation was not at first happy; but with fuller understanding on all sides Russia should play a big part in ensuring that better world promised in the Atlantic Charter.

RUSSIA AND SIBERIA

THE TOWERS AND DOMES OF THE KREMLIN AT MOSCOW, SEAT OF GOVERNMENT IN THE SOVIET UNION

5903

THE SIXTEEN REPUBLICS FORMING THE VAST SOVIET UNION

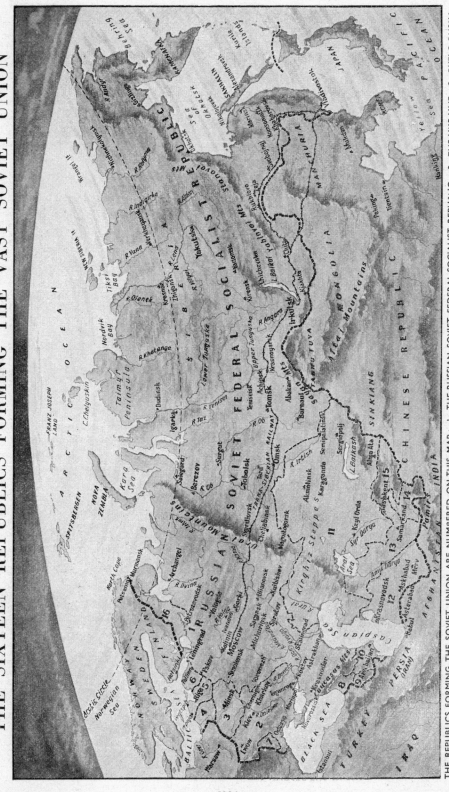

THE REPUBLICS FORMING THE SOVIET UNION ARE NUMBERED ON THIS MAP : 1, THE RUSSIAN SOVIET FEDERAL SOCIALIST REPUBLIC ; 2, THE UKRAINE ; 3, BYELO-RUSSIA ; 4, LITHUANIA ; 5, LATVIA ; 6, ESTONIA ; 7, MOLDAVIA ; 8, GEORGIA ; 9, ARMENIA ; 10, AZERBAIJAN ; 11, KAZAKHSTAN ; 12, TURKMENISTAN ; 13, UZBEKISTAN ; 14, TADZHIKISTAN ; 15, KIRGHIZIA ; 16, KARELIA.

SIBERIA, THE GREAT EASTERN TERRITORY OF THE U.S.S.R.

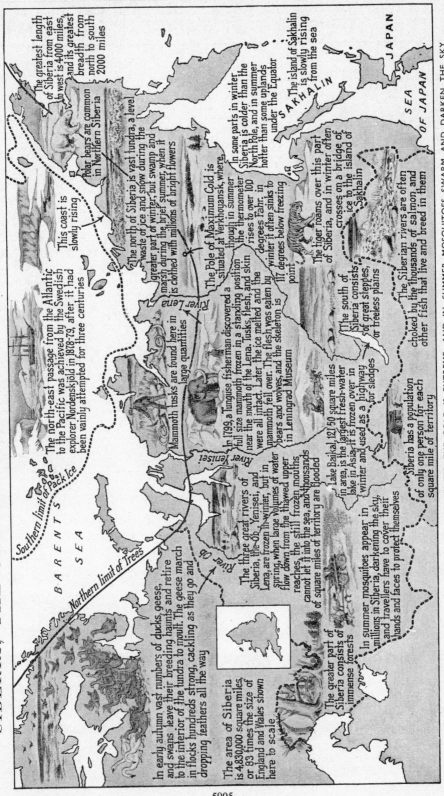

The greatest length of Siberia from east to west is 4000 miles, and its greatest breadth from north to south 2000 miles

Polar bears are common in Northern Siberia

This coast is slowly rising

The north-east passage from the Atlantic to the Pacific was achieved by the Swedish explorer Nordenskjöld in 1878-79, after it had been vainly attempted for three centuries

The north of Siberia is vast tundra, a level waste of ice and snow during the greater part of winter, but swamp and marsh during the brief summer, when it is clothed with millions of bright flowers

In some parts in winter, Siberia is colder than the North Pole, and in summer hotter than some uplands under the Equator

The island of Sakhalin is slowly rising from the sea

JAPAN

SAKHALIN

SEA OF JAPAN

The Pole of Maximum Cold is situated at Verkhoyansk, where, though in summer the thermometer rises to over 100 degrees Fahr., in winter it often sinks to 117 degrees below freezing point

The tiger roams over this part of Siberia, and in winter often crosses on a bridge of ice to the island of Sakhalin

In 1799, a Tunguse fisherman discovered a full size mammoth frozen in a standing position near the mouth of the Lena. Tusks, flesh, and skin were all intact. Later the ice melted and the mammoth fell over. The flesh was eaten by bears and wolves, and the skeleton is in Leningrad Museum

Mammoth tusks are found here in large quantities

River Lena

The south of Siberia consists of great steppes, or treeless plains

The Siberian rivers are often choked by the thousands of salmon and other fish that live and breed in them

River Yenisei

Southern limit of Pack Ice

BARENTS SEA

In early autumn vast numbers of ducks, geese, and swans leave their breeding haunts and retire to the interior of the tundra to moult. The geese march in flocks hundreds strong, cackling as they go and dropping feathers all the way

Northern limit of Trees

River Ob

The three great rivers of Siberia, the Ob, Yenisei, and Lena, are frozen in winter, but in spring, when large volumes of water flow down from the thawed upper reaches, the still frozen mouths cannot let it into the sea, and thousands of square miles of territory are flooded

Lake Baikal, 12,150 square miles in area, is the largest fresh-water lake in Asia; it is frozen over in winter and used as a highway for sledges

Siberia has a population of only one person for each square mile of territory

The area of Siberia is 4,830,000 square miles, or 83 times the size of England and Wales shown here to scale

The greater part of Siberia consists of immense forests

In summer mosquitoes appear in millions in Siberia, darkening the sky, and travellers have to cover their hands and faces to protect themselves

SIBERIA IS A LAND OF AMAZING CONTRASTS IN WINTER THE COLD IS EXTREME, AND IN SUMMER MOSQUITOES SWARM AND DARKEN THE SKY

THE ANIMAL AND PLANT LIFE OF SIBERIA

SIBERIA IS A VAST COUNTRY TEEMING WITH LIFE, AS CAN BE SEEN HERE. THE TIGER IS OFTEN
FOUND IN THE SOUTH

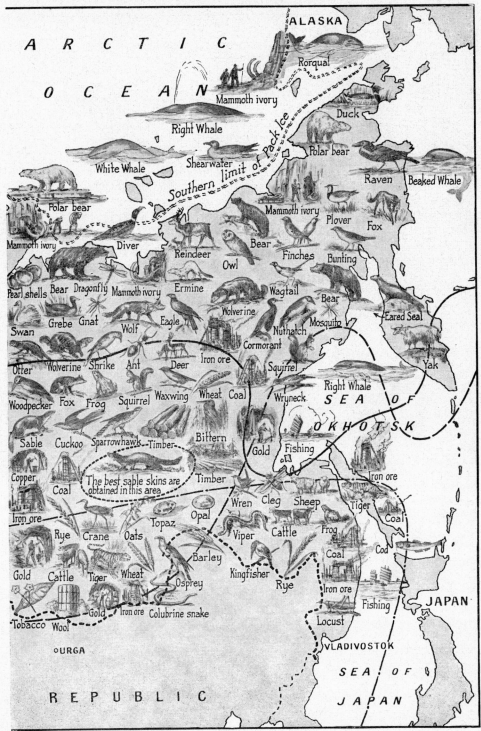

SIBERIA HAS MANY INFANT INDUSTRIES WHICH ARE BEING RAPIDLY DEVELOPED
UNDER EFFICIENT ORGANISATION

THE SOVIET REPUBLIC OF RUSSIA

A BIRD'S-EYE VIEW OF RUSSIA IN EUROPE AND OTHER SOVIET TERRITORIES

One Thousand Poems of All Times and All Countries

JOHN GILPIN

William Cowper, in this celebrated ballad, has made fun, in his own quiet way, of a worthy old linen-draper who used to have a shop in Paternoster Row, London, where he died in 1791 at ninety-eight. The story was told to the poet by a lady friend in order to entertain him, as he was inclined to melancholy, and, thanks to his genius, it has amused multitudes of readers, and will remain a favourite with the countrymen of the poet and the linen-draper.

John Gilpin was a citizen
    Of credit and renown,
A train-band captain eke was he
    Of famous London town.

John Gilpin's spouse said to her dear,
    ' Though wedded we have been
These twice ten tedious years, yet we
    No holiday have seen.

' Tomorrow is our wedding day,
    And we will then repair
Unto the Bell at Edmonton,
    All in a chaise and pair.

' My sister and my sister's child,
    Myself and children three,
Will fill the chaise, so you must ride
    On horseback after we.'

He soon replied, ' I do admire
    Of womankind but one,
And you are she, my dearest dear,
    Therefore it shall be done.

' I am a linen-draper bold,
    As all the world doth know,
And my good friend the calender
    Will lend his horse to go.'

Quoth Mrs. Gilpin, ' That's well said;
    And for that wine is dear,
We will be furnished with our own,
    Which is both bright and clear.'

John Gilpin kissed his loving wife;
    O'erjoyed was he to find
That though on pleasure she was bent
    She had a frugal mind.

The morning came, the chaise was brought
    But yet was not allowed
To drive up to the door, lest all
    Should say that she was proud.

So three doors off the chaise was stayed,
    Where they did all get in,
Six precious souls, and all agog
    To dash through thick and thin.

Smack went the whip, round went the
      wheels,
    Were never folk so glad.
The stones did rattle underneath
    As if Cheapside were mad.

John Gilpin at his horse's side
    Seized fast the flowing mane,
And up he got in haste to ride,
    But soon came down again.

For saddle-tree scarce reached had he,
    His journey to begin,
When, turning round his head, he saw
    Three customers come in.

So down he came; for loss of time,
    Although it grieved him sore,
Yet loss of pence, full well he knew,
    Would trouble him much more.

POEMS · SONGS · BALLADS · VERSES AND RHYMES WITH MUSIC

'Twas long before the customers
  Were suited to their mind,
When Betty screaming came downstairs:
  'The wine is left behind!'

'Good lack!' quoth he, 'yet bring it me,
  My leathern belt likewise,
In which I bear my trusty sword
  When I do exercise.'

Now, Mistress Gilpin, careful soul,
  Had two stone bottles found
To hold the liquor that she loved,
  And keep it safe and sound.

Each bottle had a curling ear,
  Through which the belt he drew,
And hung a bottle on each side,
  To make his balance true.

Then over all, that he might be
  Equipped from top to toe,
His long red cloak, well brushed and neat,
  He manfully did throw.

Now see him mounted once again
  Upon his nimble steed,
Full slowly pacing o'er the stones,
  With caution and good heed.

But finding soon a smoother road
  Beneath his well-shod feet,
The snorting beast began to trot,
  Which galled him in his seat.

So 'Fair and softly,' John he cried,
  But John he cried in vain;
That trot became a gallop soon,
  In spite of curb and rein.

So, stooping down, as needs he must
  Who cannot sit upright,
He grasped the mane with both his hands,
  And eke with all his might.

His horse, who never in that sort
  Had handled been before,
What thing upon his back had got
  Did wonder more and more.

Away went Gilpin, neck or nought,
  Away went hat and wig!
He little dreamt when he set out
  Of running such a rig!

The wind did blow, the cloak did fly,
  Like streamer long and gay,
Till, loop and button failing both,
  At last it flew away.

Then might all people well discern
  The bottles he had slung;
A bottle swinging at each side,
  As hath been said or sung.

The dogs did bark, the children screamed,
  Up flew the windows all;
And every soul cried out, Well done!
  As loud as he could bawl.

Away went Gilpin—who but he?
  His fame soon spread around:
He carries weight, he rides a race,
  'Tis for a thousand pound!

And still as fast as he drew near,
  'Twas wonderful to view
How in a trice the turnpike men
  Their gates wide open threw.

And now, as he went bowing down
  His reeking head full low,
The bottles twain behind his back
  Were shattered at a blow.

Down ran the wine into the road,
  Most piteous to be seen,
Which made his horse's flanks to smoke
  As they had basted been.

But still he seemed to carry weight,
  With leathern girdle braced,
For all might see the bottle necks
  Still dangling at his waist.

Thus all through merry Islington
  These gambols he did play,
Until he came unto the Wash
  Of Edmonton so gay;

And there he threw the wash about
  On both sides of the way,
Just like unto a trundling mop,
  Or a wild goose at play.

At Edmonton his loving wife
  From the balcony spied
Her tender husband, wondering much
  To see how he did ride.

'Stop, stop, John Gilpin! Here's the house!'
  They all at once did cry;
'The dinner waits and we are tired;'
  Said Gilpin, 'So am I!'

But yet his horse was not a whit
  Inclined to tarry there;
For why? His owner had a house
  Full ten miles off, at Ware.

So like an arrow swift he flew,
  Shot by an archer strong;
So did he fly—which brings me to
  The middle of my song.

Away went Gilpin, out of breath,
  And sore against his will,
Till at his friend the calender's
  His horse at last stood still.

The calender, amazed to see
  His neighbour in such trim,
Laid down his pipe, flew to the gate,
  And thus accosted him:

' What news? What news? Your tidings
    tell;
Tell me you must and shall;
Say why bare-headed you are come,
  Or why you come at all.'

Now, Gilpin had a pleasant wit,
  And loved a timely joke;
And thus unto the calender
  In merry guise he spoke:

' I came because your horse would come;
  And if I well forebode,
My hat and wig will soon be here;
  They are upon the road.'

The calender, right glad to find
  His friend in merry pin,
Returned him not a single word,
  But to the house went in.

Whence straight he came with hat and wig,
  A wig that flowed behind;
A hat not much the worse for wear,
  Each comely in its kind.

He held them up, and in his turn
  Thus showed his ready wit:
' My head is twice as big as yours,
  They therefore needs must fit.

' But let me scrape the dust away
  That hangs upon your face;
And stop and eat, for well you may
  Be in a hungry case.'

Said John: ' It is my wedding-day,
  And all the world would stare
If wife should dine at Edmonton
  And I should dine at Ware.'

So, turning to his horse, he said :
  ' I am in haste to dine;
'Twas for your pleasure you came here,
  You shall go back for mine.'

Ah, luckless speech and bootless boast!
  For which he paid full dear;
For while he spake a braying ass
  Did sing most loud and clear;

Whereat his horse did snort, as he
  Had heard a lion roar,
And galloped off with all his might,
  As he had done before.

Away went Gilpin, and away
  Went Gilpin's hat and wig;
He lost them sooner than at first,
  For why?—they were too big.

Now, Mistress Gilpin, when she saw
  Her husband posting down
Into the country far away,
  She pulled out half-a-crown.

And thus unto the youth she said
  That drove them to the Bell,
' This shall be yours when you bring back
  My husband safe and well.'

The youth did ride, and soon did meet
  John coming back amain;
Whom in a trice he tried to stop,
  By catching at his rein;

But not performing what he meant,
  And gladly would have done,
The frighted steed he frighted more,
  And made him faster run.

Away went Gilpin, and away
  Went postboy at his heels,
The postboy's horse right glad to miss
  The lumbering of the wheels.

Six gentlemen upon the road
  Thus seeing Gilpin fly,
With postboy scampering in the rear,
  They raised the hue and cry:

' Stop thief! Stop thief! A highway-
    man!'
Not one of them was mute;
And all and each that passed that way
  Did join in the pursuit.

And now the turnpike gates again
  Flew open in short space;
The toll-men thinking, as before,
  That Gilpin rode a race.

And so he did, and won it too,
  For he got first to town;
Nor stopped till where he had got up
  He did again get down.

Now let us sing, long live the king,
  And Gilpin, long live he;
And when he next doth ride abroad
  May I be there to see!

TWO RIVERS

Who wrote this grim warning of the comparative dangers
of the two borderland streams Tweed and Till nobody
knows, but there is a power in its fine simplicity which
almost makes one shudder as one reads it.

Says Tweed to Till:
    " What gars ye rin sae still? "
Says Till to Tweed:
" Though ye rin with speed
  And I rin slaw,
For ae man that ye droon
  I droon twa."

THE OLD HUNDREDTH

This version of the hundredth psalm was written in the latter part of the sixteenth century by William Kethe, a Scottish minister, who rhymed a number of the psalms. It was first printed at Geneva, then passed into the Scottish Psalter, and has been adopted in almost every hymn-book.

ALL people that on earth do dwell,
  Sing to the Lord with cheerful voice:
Him serve with fear, His praise forth tell;
  Come ye before Him and rejoice.

The Lord, ye know, is God indeed;
  Without our aid He did us make;
We are His flock, He doth us feed,
  And for His sheep He doth us take.

O, enter then His gates with praise,
  Approach with joy His courts unto;
Praise, laud, and bless His name always,
  For it is seemly so to do.

For why? the Lord our God is good,
  His mercy is for ever sure;
His truth at all times firmly stood,
  And shall from age to age endure.

THE ARAB'S FAREWELL TO HIS STEED

The Arab's devotion to his friend the horse is famous. But who, indeed, that is not a brute can fail to love his faithful horse, which serves him meekly and will always do its best for its master? The Hon. Mrs. Norton, one of the three lovely granddaughters of Richard Brinsley Sheridan, the dramatist, chose a fine subject in this poem, and she treated it with dramatic fitness as well as true feeling.

MY beautiful! my beautiful! that
  standest meekly by,
With thy proudly-arched and glossy neck,
  and dark and fiery eye!
Fret not to roam the desert now with all
  thy wingèd speed:
I may not mount on thee again—thou'rt
  sold, my Arab steed!

Fret not with that impatient hoof, snuff
  not the breezy wind,
The farther that thou fliest now so far am
  I behind.
The stranger hath thy bridle rein—thy
  master hath his gold;
Fleet-limbed and beautiful, farewell!—
  thou'rt sold, my steed, thou'rt sold.

Farewell! Those free, untired limbs full
  many a mile must roam
To reach the chill and wintry sky which
  clouds the stranger's home.
Some other hand, less fond, must now thy
  corn and bed prepare;
The silky mane I braided once must be
  another's care.

The morning sun shall dawn again, but
  never more with thee
Shall I gallop o'er the desert paths, where
  we were wont to be;
Evening shall darken on the earth, and o'er
  the sandy plain
Some other steed, with slower step, shall
  bear me home again.

Yes, thou must go! The wild, free breeze,
  the brilliant sun and sky,
Thy master's home—from all of these my
  exiled one must fly.
Thy proud dark eye will grow less proud,
  thy step become less fleet,
And vainly shalt thou arch thy neck thy
  master's hand to meet.

Only in sleep shall I behold that dark eye
  glancing bright;
Only in sleep shall hear again that step so
  firm and light;
And when I raise my dreaming arm to
  check or cheer thy speed,
Then must I, starting, wake to feel—thou'rt
  sold, my Arab steed.

Ah! rudely then, unseen by me, some
  cruel hand may chide
Till foam-wreaths lie, like crested waves,
  along thy panting side;
And the rich blood that's in thee swells in
  thy indignant pain
Till careless eyes which rest on thee may
  count each starting vein.

Will they ill-use thee? If I thought—but
  no, it cannot be,
Thou art so swift, yet easy curbed; so
  gentle, yet so free;
And yet, if haply, when thou'rt gone, my
  lonely heart should yearn,
Can the hand that casts thee from it now
  command thee to return?

Return!—alas, my Arab steed! what
  shall thy master do
When thou, who wast his all of joy, hast
  vanished from his view?
When the dim distance cheats mine eye,
  and through the gathering tears
Thy bright form, for a moment, like the
  false mirage appears?

Slow and unmounted shall I roam, with
  weary step alone,
Where with fleet step and joyous bound
  thou oft hast borne me on;
And, sitting down by that green well, I'll
  pause and sadly think,
" 'Twas here he bowed his glossy neck
  when last I saw him drink! "

When last I saw thee drink!—Away! The
  fevered dream is o'er!
I could not live a day and know that we
  should meet no more!
They tempted me, my beautiful! for
  hunger's power is strong,
They tempted me, my beautiful! but I
  have loved too long.

Who said that I had given thee up? Who
  said that thou wert sold?
'Tis false! 'tis false! my Arab steed! I
  fling them back their gold!
Thus, thus, I leap upon thy back and scour
  the distant plains!
Away! who overtakes us now may claim
  thee for his pains!

THE LAMENT OF THE IRISH EMIGRANT

This pathetic poem, describing an Irish emigrant's farewell
to his dead wife before he leaves his native land, was written
by Lady Dufferin, who died in 1867. The Dufferins are an
Irish noble family that has attained distinction in politics
and literature. The sadness of the poem is in keeping with
the feeling of the Irish people, who have been an emigrant
race, though their love of their country is unusually strong.

I'M sittin' on the stile, Mary,
    Where we sat side by side
On a bright May mornin' long ago,
    When first you were my bride;
The corn was springin' fresh and green,
    And the lark sang loud and high;
And the red was on your lip, Mary,
    And the love-light in your eye.

The place is little changed, Mary,
    The day is bright as then,
The lark's loud song is in my ear,
    And the corn is green again;
But I miss the soft clasp of your hand,
    And your breath warm on my cheek,
And I still keep list'ning for the words
    You never more will speak.

'Tis but a step down yonder lane,
    And the little church stands near,
The church where we were wed, Mary,
    I see the spire from here.
But the graveyard lies between, Mary,
    And my step might break your rest—
For I've laid you, darling! down to sleep,
    With your baby on your breast.

I'm very lonely now, Mary,
    For the poor make no new friends,
But, O, they love the better still
    The few our Father sends!
And you were all I had, Mary,
    My blessin' and my pride:
There's nothin' left to care for now,
    Since my poor Mary died.

Yours was the good, brave heart, Mary,
    That still kept hoping on,
When the trust in God had left my soul,
    And my arm's young strength was gone:
There was comfort ever on your lip,
    And the kind look on your brow—
I bless you, Mary, for that same,
    Though you cannot hear me now.

I thank you for the patient smile
    When your heart was fit to break,
When the hunger pain was gnawin' there,
    And you hid it, for my sake!
I bless you for the pleasant word,
    When your heart was sad and sore—
Oh, I'm thankful you are gone, Mary,
    Where grief can't reach you more!

I'm biddin' you a long farewell,
    My Mary—kind and true!
But I'll not forget you, darling!
    In the land I'm goin' to;
They say there's bread and work for all,
    And the sun shines always there—
But I'll not forget old Ireland,
    Were it fifty times as fair!

And often in those grand old woods
    I'll sit, and shut my eyes,
And my heart will travel back again
    To the place where Mary lies;
And I'll think I see the little stile
    Where we sat side by side:
And the springin' corn, and the bright
        May morn,
    When first you were my bride.

THE LAST WORD

This is Matthew Arnold's answer to the spirits of doubt and
disappointment that haunted him. He will not give in,
and he really believes in the victory of what is good.

CREEP into thy narrow bed,
    Creep, and let no more be said!
Vain thy onset! all stands fast;
Thou thyself must break at last.

Let the long contention cease!
Geese are swans, and swans are geese.
Let them have it how they will!
Thou art tired; best be still!

They out-talked thee, hissed thee, tore
    thee?
Better men fared thus before thee;
Fired their ringing shot and passed,
Hotly charged—and broke at last.

Charge once more, then, and be dumb!
Let the victors, when they come,
When the forts of folly fall,
Find thy body by the wall.

PACK, CLOUDS, AWAY!

Thomas Heywood, the author of this song, began writing when Shakespeare was reaching prosperity. Like Shakespeare, he was an actor as well as a dramatist. His plays were freely garnished with songs, of which the following is a joyous example. Stare means the starling.

PACK, clouds, away! and welcome, day!
    With night we banish sorrow.
Sweet air, blow soft; mount, lark, aloft
    To give my Love good-morrow!
Wings from the wind to please her mind,
    Notes from the lark I'll borrow;
Bird, prune thy wing! nightingale, sing!
    To give my Love good-morrow
Notes from them all I'll borrow.

Wake from thy nest, robin red-breast!
    Sing, birds, in every furrow!
And from each bill let music shrill
    Give my fair Love good-morrow!
Blackbird and thrush in every bush,
    Stare, linnet, and cock-sparrow,
You pretty elves, among yourselves
    Sing my fair Love good-morrow!
        To give my Love good-morrow!
        Sing, birds, in every furrow!

CHORUS FROM ATALANTA IN CALYDON

Algernon Charles Swinburne was 27 when, in 1864, he published Atalanta in Calydon, a drama on the Greek model, and was instantly hailed as a poet with exceptional lyrical qualities. It was this pagan chorus that particularly arrested attention. Undergraduates marched about mouthing it. Indeed, it has a wonderful swing, much poetical suggestion, and some truth: but it has no hope. Afterwards Swinburne continued to prove himself a great master of musical verbiage till his methods became dulled by use. In this poem he reached the summit of his life's performance.

BEFORE the beginning of years
    There came to the making of man
Time, with a gift of tears;
    Grief, with a glass that ran;
Pleasure, with pain for leaven;
    Summer, with flowers that fell;
Remembrance fallen from heaven,
    And madness risen from hell;
Strength without hands to smite;
    Love that endures for a breath;
Night, the shadow of light;
    And life, the shadow of death.

And the high gods took in hand
    Fire, and the falling of tears,
And a measure of sliding sand
    From under the feet of the years;
And froth and drift of the sea;
    And dust of the labouring earth;
And bodies of things to be
    In the houses of death and of birth;
And wrought with weeping and laughter,

And fashioned with loathing and love,
With life before and after
    And death beneath and above,
For a day and a night and a morrow,
    That his strength might endure for a
        span
With travail and heavy sorrow,
    The holy spirit of man.

From the winds of the north and the south
    They gathered as unto strife;
They breathed upon his mouth,
    They filled his body with life;
Eyesight and speech they wrought
    For the veils of the soul therein,
A time for labour and thought,
    A time to serve and to sin;
They gave him light in his ways,
    And love, and a space for delight,
And beauty, and length of days,
    And night, and sleep in the night.
His speech is a burning fire;
    With his lips he travaileth;
In his heart is a blind desire,
    In his eyes foreknowledge of death;

He weaves, and is clothed with derision;
    Sows, and he shall not reap;
His life is a watch or a vision
    Between a sleep and a sleep.

IT IS NOT DEATH

Thomas Hood is wronged when he is thought of chiefly as a humorous poet. His best work is serious. This fine poem on the forgetfulness brought by death would be enough, even if it stood alone, to safeguard the poet against that forgetfulness, which is his conception of death.

IT is not death that sometime in a
        sigh
This eloquent breath shall take its speech-
    less flight;
That sometime these bright stars, that
    now reply
In sunlight to the sun, shall set in night;
That this warm conscious flesh shall
    perish quite,
And all life's ruddy springs forget to
    flow;
That thoughts shall cease, and the im-
    mortal sprite
Be lapped in alien clay and laid below;
It is not death to know this—but to know
That pious thoughts, which visit at new
    graves
In tender pilgrimage, will cease to go
So duly and so oft; and when grass waves
Over the passed-away, there may be
    then
No resurrection in the minds of men.

THE LION AND THE UNICORN

THE LION AND THE UNICORN
WERE FIGHTING FOR THE CROWN ;

THE LION BEAT THE UNICORN
ALL ROUND THE TOWN.

SOME GAVE THEM WHITE BREAD.
SOME GAVE THEM BROWN.

SOME GAVE THEM PLUM CAKE
AND DRUMMED THEM FROM THE TOWN.

A IS FOR ALICE WHO WEARS A STRIPED FROCK

A is for ALICE
who wears a striped frock

B is for BOBBY
with only one sock

C is for CLARA
who's brushing her cat

D is for DAVID
he's broken his bat !

E is for EDGAR
who's swinging so high

F is for FANNY
who's rubbing her eye

G is for GEORGIE
at work on a sum

H naughty HETTIE
who's taking a plum !

I is for IVAN
who's spending a penny

J is for JANET
whose dolls are so many

K is for KEITH
with his big jolly laugh

L is for LAURA
who's knitting a scarf

a b c d e f g h i j k l m n o p q r s t u v w x y z
A B C D E F G H I J K L M N O P Q R S T U V W X Y Z

M is for MAX
who is building with bricks

N is for NETTIE
who's feeding the chicks

O is for OLIVER
proud of his boat

P is poor PHYLLIS
who's torn her new coat

Q is small QUEENIE
enjoying her bath

R is for REX
who is sweeping the path

S is for SUSAN
who is stringing her beads

T is for TED
busy planting some seeds

U is for UNA
just learning to ride

V is for VINCENT
who's off on a slide

W for WINIFRED
having a drink

X is for XIT
it's his pet name, I think

Here's Y and Z
who declare it a shame

To stay at the bottom
without any name

WHO COMES HERE?

5918

Imperishable Thoughts of Men Enshrined in the Books of the World

Stories From Spenser

IN allegory as used by Spenser the characters represent good or bad qualities. The Faerie Queene is a poetic allegory of the moral virtues, first printed in the year 1590. It takes us to Fairyland at the time of the annual festival, lasting twelve days, and on each of these days a brave knight has to go forth on some adventure to fight against evils. Gloriana, the Fairy Queen, stands for Glory ; Prince Arthur for the Spirit of Chivalry, St. George for Christianity, Sir Guyon for Temperance, Britomart for True Love, Sir Calidore for Courtesy, and so forth. The deeds of these and many other champions in overcoming the forces of evil are all told in the " Faerie Queene," which is the old way of spelling " Fairy Queen." Only six books of this great poem exist. The original plan of the work was probably not carried to completion, but, as it stands, it is an enduring monument.

UNA AND THE RED CROSS KNIGHT

ON the first day of the festival of the Fairy Queen there presented himself a tall, clownish young man, who, falling before Gloriana, desired a boon—as the custom then was—which, while the feast lasted, she might not refuse. This boon was that to him might befall an adventure during the festival. His prayer being granted, he seated himself on the floor, being thought unfitted by his rank to take a better place.

Soon after there entered a fair lady named Una, who was in mourning. She was riding on a white ass, with a dwarf behind her, leading a war-like steed that bore the arms of a knight. Falling before the Queen, this lady complained that her father and mother, an ancient King and Queen, had been shut up in a brazen castle by a huge dragon. Would the Queen, she prayed, send one of her knights to liberate her parents from the dragon?

Hearing her request, the tall, clownish young man begged that he might be entrusted with the adventure. All wondered at his temerity, and none more than the Fairy Queen and Una. But, the youth urging his suit, the lady said that unless the armour which she had brought could be worn by him, he could not succeed. Thereupon, the armour being put upon him, " he seemed the goodliest man in all that company." He was now given the rank of a knight, and,

mounting the strange horse which the lady had brought with her, he set forth with her as the Red Cross Knight, accompanied by the dwarf.

For a time the beauty of the country through which they passed drew their thoughts away from the perils that beset their enterprise. But ere long a great storm arose.

Enforced to seek some shelter nigh at hand,
A shady grove not far away they spied,
That promised aid the tempest to withstand;
Whose lofty trees, all clad in summer's pride,
Did spread so broad, that heaven's light did hide,
Not pierceable with power of any star;
And all within were paths and alleys wide,
With footing worn, and leading inward far;
Fair harbour that them seems, so soon they
    entered are.
And forth they pass, with pleasure forward led,
Joying to hear the birds' sweet harmony,
Which, therein shrouded from the tempest dread,
Seemed in their song to scorn the cruel sky.

Led on by delight, they did not notice, until the storm had passed and they wished to retrace their footsteps, that they had lost their way in Wandering Wood. Here was the den of Error, a fearsome monster, half woman, half snake, that dwelt in a darksome cave in the thickest part of the wood.

In no way daunted by the warnings of Una and her dwarf, the Red Cross Knight sought out this monster, which, after a terrible encounter, he killed. Then, proceeding on their journey, the travellers

ROMANCE · HISTORIES · DRAMAS · ESSAYS · WORLD CLASSICS

found their way out of the wood. Before long they met a venerable-looking old man dressed like a hermit who greeted them with fair words, bidding the Knight take rest with the westering sun. " So with that godly father to his home they went."

A little lowly Hermitage it was,
Down in a dale, hard by the forest's side,
Far from resort of people that did pass
In travel to and fro.

THE WICKED MAGICIAN MISLEADS THE RED CROSS KNIGHT

They passed the evening with fair discourse. Drooping night creeping on, their host showed them their sleeping-place. While they slept the seeming hermit, who was none other than the wicked magician Archimago, caused the Knight to dream that his lady Una was false. Believing his dream to be true, the Knight fared forth in anger from the Hermitage, leaving Una behind.

When Una arose she looked in vain for her Knight. She began to wail and weep; but

after him she rode, with so much speed
As her slow beast could make; but all in vain,
For him so far had borne his light-foot steed,
Pricked with wrath and fiery fierce disdain,
That him to follow was but fruitless pain;
Yet she her weary limbs would never rest,
But every hill and dale, each wood and plain,
Did search, sore grieved in her gentle breast,
He so ungently left her, whom she loved best.

One day, nigh weary of the irksome way, Una alighted from her slow beast. Resting in a secret shade, she was suddenly seen by a fierce lion. Eager for his prey, the king of the forest was rushing upon Una when he was stopped by the sight of her great beauty, and, instead of attacking her, kissed her wearied feet, licked her lily hands with fawning tongue, and became her devoted attendant and protector.

PRINCE ARTHUR KILLS THE GIANT AND THE TRAVELLERS MEET A NEW PERIL

After undergoing many hardships and dangers, Una at last met Prince Arthur and was safe.

When he left the enchanted Hermitage the Red Cross Knight again encountered deception in the form of Duessa, a daughter of Archimago. Duessa, who was disguised, led the Knight to the House of Pride and persuaded him to drink of the water of an enchanted spring, with the result that he fell an easy prey to the giant Orgoglio, who cast him into a dungeon. From this he was rescued by Prince Arthur, who killed the giant, exposed the falsity of Duessa, the giant's accomplice, and reunited the Red Cross Knight and Una.

Starting forth once more, these two came to the Cave of Despair, where a new kind of peril was met, to which the Knight all but yielded. Seeing all around the ruin wrought by Despair, the Knight threatened him with death; but so artfully did the villain speak in praise of death that, after trying to argue with him, the Knight yielded to his view, and, taking from his hand a dagger, was about to plunge it into his own breast, when Una snatched it from him and, casting it on the ground, said:

Fie, fie, faint-hearted Knight!
What meanest thou by this reproachful strife ?
Is this the battle which thou vauntest to fight
With that fire-mouthed Dragon, horrible and
    bright?
Come, come away, frail, feeble, fleshly wight,
Nor let vain words bewitch thy manly heart,
Nor evil thoughts dismay thy constant spright.
In heavenly mercies hast thou not a part?
Why shouldst thou then despair, that chosen
    art?

UNA TAKES THE KNIGHT TO THE HOUSE OF HOLINESS

Taking heart at these words the Knight rose up, and was taken by Una to the House of Holiness, where Faith, Hope, and Charity dwelt. Here he was taught repentance; here he saw a vision of the Holy City; and here he gained strength for his tremendous task.

Once more in Una's company the Knight set forth for the brazen tower wherein her parents were imprisoned for fear of the dragon. Encountering this fearful beast, the Knight fought with him for two days, and, coming again to the fight, gained the victory on the third day.

Then Una praised God, " and thanked her faithful Knight, that had achieved so great a conquest by his might."

Thus were the aged King and Queen liberated; and so it came to pass that with great rejoicing Una and the Red Cross Knight—who was none other than St. George—were united in happy wedlock.

Thrice happy man the knight himself did hold,
Possessed of his lady's heart and hand;
And ever, when his eye did her behold,
His heart did seem to melt in pleasures manifold.

SIR GUYON, CHAMPION OF TEMPERANCE

THE wicked magician Archimago, having learned that the Red Cross Knight had returned, as he was in duty bound, to the Court of the Fairy Queen, invented another scheme by which the hero might be brought to ruin. Accordingly, when he met Sir Guyon, the enchanter told a painful tale of how a beautiful lady, meaning Una, had been wronged by the Knight of the Red Cross.

Sir Guyon, the Champion of Temperance, set out to punish the recreant knight, but when they met Sir Guyon recognised his fellow adventurer; so the two champions exchanged courtesies and parted.

SIR GUYON VISITS THE CASTLE OF THE LADY MEDINA

Now, it was Sir Guyon's task to seek out and destroy the power of Acrasia, whose wiles had brought so much ruin to noble men. Pursuing his journey, he heard from a neighbouring thicket the voice of a woman crying. He alighted from his steed, and found Amavia dying by the side of her husband Sir Mordant, and with her little child on her knees. Sir Mordant was one 'of the victims of the cruel Acrasia.

After they had buried Sir Mordant and Amavia, Sir Guyon and the Palmer, a wandering pilgrim who accompanied him, found that Sir Guyon's steed and spear had been stolen by a boastful coward named Braggadocchio. Taking the infant with them, the two travellers made their way to the castle of the Lady Medina, or Golden Mean, who lived with her extravagantly-minded sisters Elissa (Too Little) and Perissa (Too Much).

The lovers of Elissa and Perissa were at enmity, and though both, when they saw Sir Guyon, went forth to attack him, before they could reach him they quarrelled together. Medina came out and succeeded in making peace, and all went into the Castle, where they sat down to a hospitable board, while Sir Guyon told of the adventure on which he was bound. Leaving the child to the care of Medina, Sir Guyon proceeded on his way on foot.

THE COWARDICE OF THE BOASTFUL BRAGGADOCCHIO

In the meantime, Braggadocchio, flourishing the stolen spear and mounted on Sir Guyon's steed, had by his show of false courage pressed a poor idler into his service. Thus armed and attended, he was met by Archimago, who, deceived as to Braggadocchio's character, accused Sir Guyon and the Red Cross Knight of slaying Sir Mordant.

Braggadocchio boasted of the punishment he would wreak on the heads of these knights. When advised that he had better be armed with a sword against such enemies, he declared that as he had killed seven knights with such a weapon, he had sworn never to bear a sword again, unless it should be the sword of the bravest of men.

Promising to secure for him the sword of Prince Arthur on the morrow, Archimago vanished so suddenly that the coward Braggadocchio and his equally alarmed attendant fled in haste into a thick forest. Here the shrill sound of a horn caused Braggadocchio to fall from his horse, and, like the coward that he was, he crept into a thicket. His attendant, Trompart, however, looking round, was amazed to see before him a beautiful huntress, Belphoebe, carrying in her hand a spear. While Belphoebe was asking of Trompart the course pursued by a hart she had wounded, she heard a noise in the thicket, and was advancing when Braggadocchio crawled from his hiding-place. He was telling her a lying story, but, undeceived, she threatened him and disappeared, whereupon he once more mounted his horse, and with Trompart went on his way.

THE ENCOUNTER WITH A MADMAN AND HIS UGLY MOTHER

While this incident was happening Sir Guyon and the Palmer encountered the madman Furor, with his ugly mother Occasion, whom the Knight overcame and bound, effecting at the same time the rescue of the youth Phedon, who, having been deceived by a false friend, had killed him, and then fallen into the hands of Furor.

The Palmer was telling Phedon of the folly of passion when there rushed out on them Atin, brandishing two darts. Atin sought to make Sir Guyon flee by telling him of his master Pyrochles, who was on his way thither, and against whom none could stand. Atin, who had been sent to find Occasion, taunted Sir Guyon with fighting against an old woman, and hurled against the knight one of his fearful darts. But this glanced harmlessly off his shield, and Sir Guyon escaped unhurt.

Pyrochles then appeared, and rushed at Sir Guyon, who, at length having him at his mercy, gave him his life, on condition that he rendered faithful service to his conqueror. Pyrochles then asked the Knight to let him release Occasion and Furor. This prayer having been granted, Occasion turned on both Sir Guyon and Pyrochles, and, while the tumult was proceeding, Atin hurried away to the bower of Acrasia to tell Pyrochles' brother Cymochles that his master was slain, and to urge him forth to vengeance.

Cymochles, spurring on his mission against Sir Guyon, came to the shores of Idle Lake, where he saw a little boat, in which sat a lady fresh and fair. By her sweet voice he was enticed aboard and taken to an enchanted isle.

Here he was lulled to sleep. Then the lady, whose name was Phaedria, a servant of Acrasia, betook herself to her boat again, and rowed to the other side of Idle Lake. Here she was seen by Sir Guyon, who asked her to ferry him over the water. Phaedria readily responded, but, when Sir Guyon stepped on board, she quickly shot the vessel away from land, so that the Palmer was left behind.

Arrived at the Island of Joy, Sir Guyon was attacked by the awakened Cymochles. Effecting a peace between the two, but unable to win Sir Guyon by her allurements, Phaedria took the Knight back to the other shore.

Resuming his journey, Sir Guyon came to the home of Mammon, the Money God, to whose temptations he might have succumbed but for the help of an angel. After three days of weary wandering in the underground realm of Mammon, Sir Guyon was found by the Palmer lying in a swoon. Sir Guyon was still lying helpless, when Pyrochles and Cymochles appeared and disarmed him. But at this juncture Prince Arthur came on the scene, and after a terrible encounter gained the victory and delivered Sir Guyon from his foes.

Having recovered strength in the House of Temperance, Sir Guyon resumed his quest. Setting sail on the sea, steered by the Palmer, he safely passed the Gulf of Greediness, the Rock of Vile Reproach, the Wandering Islands, the Quicksand of Unthriftihead, and the Whirlpool of Decay, till at last he reached the Bower of Bliss, Acrasia's home.

Here a new victim of the Queen of Base Pleasure was released by him, and, other victims who had been transformed by her into wild beasts having been restored to their natural forms, the temptress Acrasia was bound fast, and sent away captive to the Fairy Queen.

THE FACE IN MERLIN'S MIRROR

Britomart, the golden-haired daughter of King Ryence of Wales, looking one day into a glassy globe that Merlin the wizard had made, saw the image of Sir Artegall, a brave Cornish knight, and fell in love with him. Finding it impossible to make Britomart forget her vision, her old nurse took her to Merlin's cave, both assuming a disguise for the purpose.

The magician told them that it was Britomart's destiny to wed the noble Artegall, and to become the mother of a line of kings.

Donning the armour of Angela the Saxon Queen, and arming herself with a mighty spear, Britomart set forth with her nurse in search of Sir Artegall. They encountered Prince Arthur and Sir Guyon, who had met with many adventures since their overthrow of Acrasia and her champions. Seeing one whom he took to be a strange knight approaching, Sir Guyon rode forward against Britomart.

He was, however, quickly overthrown by the enchanted spear. Worse might have befallen him, but that wise counsels prevailed at the instance of the Palmer, who accompanied Sir Guyon, and the party rode on in good fellowship.

They had not travelled far before they saw the fair Florimell, rushing by on a milk-white palfrey, pursued by a grisly forester. Prince Arthur rode after Florimell, and Arthur's squire, Timias, went after the forester.

Britomart, finding her companions did not return, pursued her way with her own aged attendant. Leaving the wood in which they were, they came to a goodly castle, before which they saw a single knight withstanding the onslaught of six others, servants of Malecasta, the Lady of Delight, whose castle it was—Castle Joyous by name. The single knight was he of the Red Cross, St. George. He declared himself true to Una, whereas the others were championing Malecasta, whose object it was to make all strange knights enter her service or prove in combat that the lady they served was fairer than the Lady of Delight. Taking the side of the Red Cross Knight, Britomart overthrew four of his assailants. The other two submitting, all entered Castle Joyous.

Here, after passing through a chamber in which every pillar was of gold, embossed with pearls and precious stones, Britomart was escorted to an inner room of even greater magnificence, where sat the Lady of Delight, who, struck by the appearance of Britomart, and believing her to be a man, fell in love with her. In the end it was only by fighting that Britomart and the Red Cross Knight won their way from the dangerous castle.

Proceeding in company, the Knight told his companion of the prowess of Sir Artegall, and she in her turn told him her history. At length they came to a road where their ways parted, and they bade one another farewell. Coming to the sea, Britomart encountered Marinell, son of the sea-nymph Cymoent who, because of a prophecy that he should be dismayed or killed by "a virgin strange and brave," had fled from woman's love. Marinell, being laid low by Britomart, was carried by his mother to her home beneath the waves.

While Marinell was being tended by his mother, Florimell, who had been seeking him, was flying from Prince Arthur and Sir Guyon with as much fear as she had fled from the grisly forester. Prince Arthur, learning Florimell's story

PRINCESS BRITOMART, DISGUISED AS A KNIGHT, RESCUES THE LADY AMORET

from her squire, bethought him of his own faithful Timias; Timias, on his part, had come up with the forester at a ford, and had slain him and his two brothers.

Sorely wounded, he was found by Belphoebe, who, with her attendants, carried him to a fair pavilion in the forest, where she daily dressed his wounds and instilled into his mind a deeper devotion to beauty and purity.

Meanwhile Florimell had taken shelter in a humble cottage. Here lived a witch, whose wicked son so affrighted Florimell that she fled before the dawn. Pursued by a monster called up by the witch, Florimell came to the sea, and, seeing a boat in which an old fisherman was sleeping, leapt into this vessel, and with the oar pushed it out to sea and so escaped.

As the monster was wreaking vengeance on Florimell's defenceless palfrey it chanced that a knight, Sir Satyrane, came that way, and overthrew the monster, who, however, afterwards escaped to tell his tale to the witch. Then the witch made of snow a false Florimell, the real Florimell having been taken to the bottom of the sea by Proteus and, as she refused to wed her ugly suitor, cast into a dungeon. Now, all this time Amoret, the beloved of Sir Scudamore, had been imprisoned by the enchanter Busirane. After a series of adventures Britomart succeeded in liberating Amoret, with whom she fared forth to find Sir Scudamore, Amoret believing that her deliverer was a man. But Scudamore, deceived by lying tales, believed his Amoret to be false, and pursued his quest of her with a sorrowing heart.

On his way he met Sir Artegall, and, these two encountering Britomart, Sir Scudamore was unhorsed by the wonderful power of the enchanted spear. Sir Artegall went to Sir Scudamore's aid, the two fought long and valorously, when Britomart's helmet being struck aside, Sir Artegall was so overcome by her beauty that his arm fell powerless at his side, and he surrendered to her.

When Sir Artegall's helmet was removed and Princess Britomart saw his face, she recognised it as the one she had seen in Merlin's mirror.

Thus it was that the two were betrothed. But before the marriage could take place Sir Artegall had to depart on another adventure. Sir Scudamore bewailed his lost Amoret, who had been lost in a desert. Here she was captured by a monster. Saved first of all by Belphoebe, Amoret was finally rescued by Prince Arthur, and Marinell was wedded to Florimell in Cymoent's home under the sea.

THE QUEST OF THE BLATANT BEAST

SIR CALIDORE'S quest was the destruction of the Blatant Beast, Slander, which had attacked Sir Artegall. On his travels he fell in with a troop of shepherds, with whom he stayed for a time. Among their number was Pastorella. Pastorella was beloved of all the shepherds, but especially by Coridon.

Sir Calidore fell in love with the fair shepherdess, and sought by the exercise of knightly courtesy to win her regard. But she, unused as she was to the ways of courts, remained unmoved. Then the knight, doffing his armour, clad himself in shepherd's garb, and tended the sheep with her. Joining in the rural sports, he was challenged by the jealous Coridon to a wrestling bout. Coridon being defeated, Pastorella placed the oaken crown of victory on Sir Calidore's head, but he, " that did in courtesy excel," gave it to Coridon.

By such acts as these, Sir Calidore won his way among the shepherds and eventually in Pastorella's favour. One day, as he ranged over the fields, forgetful of his mission against the Blatant Beast, he came on " a place whose pleasance did appear to pass all others on the earth that were. . . . .

It was an hill, placed in an open plain,
That round about was bordered with a wood
Of matchless height, that seemed th' earth to
disdain;
In which all trees of honour stately stood,
And did all winter as in summer bud,
Spreading pavilions for the birds to bower,
Which in their lower branches sang aloud;
And in their tops the soaring hawk did tower,
Sitting like king of fowles in majesty and power.

And at the foot thereof a gentle flood
His silver waves did softly tumble down,
Unmarred with ragged moss or filthy mud;

Nor might wild beasts, nor might the ruder
clown,
Thereto approach; nor filth might therein drown;
But Nymphs and Fairies by the banks did sit
In the wood's shade which did the waters crown,
Keeping all noisome things away from it,
And to the water's fall tuning their accents fit.

In this beautiful spot Sir Calidore saw the Graces dance to the piping of poor Colin Clout. Going towards them, he was amazed to see them disappear. On another day, when Sir Calidore was with the hapless Coridon and Pastorella, a tiger rose out of the wood. Coridon ran to the rescue of his love, but, when he saw the beast fully, he was so alarmed that he fled. Sir Calidore slew the tiger with his shepherd's staff. Thus it was that the knight finally won the affection of Pastorella.

But his joy was turned to pain shortly after, for the maiden was stolen by brigands. Taking up the pursuit, Sir Calidore effected her rescue, and bore her to the Castle of Belgard. Here she was discovered to be the long-lost daughter of the good Sir Bellamoure and his Lady Claribell. Sir Calidore, leaving Pastorella in safety with her parents, set out again to seek the Blatant Beast. He was successful so far, at least, that he captured the monster, muzzled him with iron bands, and to the great joy of all, led him through all Fairyland. So muzzled did the beast long remain

Until that (whether wicked fate so framed
Or fault of men), he broke his iron chain,
And got into the world at liberty again.
Thenceforth more mischief and more scath he
wrought
To mortal men than he had done before.

Since that time none has succeeded in subduing him.

The Story of the Most Beautiful Book in the World

Paul preaching to the Men of Athens

THE CHANGE THAT CAME OVER PAUL

THE writer of the Acts of the Apostles says that after certain days spent with the disciples at Damascus, Paul " straight-way preached Christ in the synagogues, that He is the Son of God."

The writer of the Acts was a friend of Paul, and he composed this part of his chronicle from conversations he had with the great apostle in after years. His narrative does not profess to be an exact biographhy of Paul—the preachings and sufferings of the apostle were only part of the general narrative, which was an ac-count of Christ's Gospel after Christ's death. And so we find this statement that Paul straightway preached Christ in the synagogues corrected by Paul himself.

" I conferred not with flesh and blood," he said, " neither went I up to Jerusalem to them which were apostles before me; but I went away into Arabia."

Most men do not talk of their spiritual experiences; indeed, it is something more than a noble shrinking which prevents them. Human speech has no words for the profoundest of these convulsions of our nature. To the writer of the Acts of the Apostles Paul would not have *analysed* his feelings, nor have given any lengthy account of his thoughts and doings at that

crisis in his life. He would have drawn a veil over an experience so sacred. And so it comes about that the narrative makes an immediate preacher of Jesus, seeing that the space separating conversion from preaching was neither for the biographer nor the world, but for God.

However, a chance saying of Paul has told us something of that interlude between the hour when Ananias laid his hands upon him and the hour when he stood up in the synagogues, and, to the amazement of those who heard him, preached the Christ whom he had so resolutely persecuted.

Three years were to pass before the Jews in the synagogues were to exclaim: " Is not this he that destroyed them which called on this name in Jerusalem, and came hither for that intent, that he might bring them bound unto the chief priests ? "

It is of the first importance that we should convince ourselves of the full meaning of this truth. Three years is a long space of human life. Three years of in-cessant work and occupation is a long space, but three years of silent communing and silent adjustment of the character and brain to a new thought is like etern-ity. But for three years this fiery and

GREAT FIGURES OF THE OLD TESTAMENT · THE LIFE OF JESUS

impulsive scholar of the Sanhedrin gave himself up to a heart-searching examination, and to communion with Jesus of Nazareth. Following his conversion Paul spent three long, weary years in retirement from the world.

Before we follow the wonderful and adventurous life of Paul the Apostle, let us see that we understand the meaning of the word *conversion*. This noble word has been much abused and spoiled, but conversion, in its true sense, means simply *turning round*. A man's life is going in one direction; he turns round and goes in the opposite direction—that is conversion.

THE REVOLUTION IN A MAN'S CHARACTER THAT SCIENCE CANNOT ACCOUNT FOR

The conversion of Paul, the chief event in the history of the world next to the life of Jesus, was one of those total and complete revolutions in character before which science is dumb and all men reverent. It is not easy to change an opinion, but it is one of the hardest things in the world to stand up and say before everybody: *I was wrong*.

Paul had persecuted the Christians with fury and without pity. Now he had to acknowledge that he was wrong. What did this mean ? It meant, to his personal friends of the Sanhedrin he must say: *You are wrong;* and to the humble, trembling Nazarenes whom he had attacked and destroyed, he had to say: *You are right*. How angry those proud friends would be!

How suspicious would be the frightened Nazarenes! Imagine the wolf saying to his pack: " You are wrong to attack the sheepfold ; " and saying to the sheep : " Let me enter, for I wish to be like you." Can we see how difficult was the position of Paul at this trying time ? During his years of retirement he became aware of some physical affliction which he afterwards described as a thorn in the flesh.

THE DAYS IMMEDIATELY AFTER THE GREAT CHANGE IN PAUL'S LIFE

What this was we do not know. Some think it was a stammer, others a terrible sensitiveness which made public appearances an agony. Whatever it was, this thorn in the flesh made the apostle *self-conscious*. It would seem that he wished to be alone, to shrink from the world, to hide himself; but this was impossible. Christ had revealed the truth to his soul. Could he keep that truth

for himself ? No ; he must tell all the world of the vision. Not a man living on the earth, not a child to be born in all the generations of time for ever, but must hear of this vision. And yet there was this affliction which stood in his way. For if Paul, with his fiery and impetuous nature, had, on the very instant of his conversion, with all his impetuosity violently swung into an opposite direction, plunged into the work of preaching, what would have been the result ? The Jews would have said their Sanhedrist was mad ; the Nazarenes would have cried out that Christ had never revealed himself to the persecutor of Stephen. The apostle would have found himself utterly alone.

All the nations have proverbs which warn people against believing a man who cries " Hot " one minute and " Cold " the next. They are quite right. The conversion may be perfectly sincere, but its worth cannot be lasting or useful to the rest of the world when the man who has changed his mind *immediately* sets about denouncing those he has worked with, and blessing those he has cursed.

HOW PAUL WAS PREPARED IN THE WILDERNESS FOR HIS GREAT WORK

There can be no doubt that a man so impetuous as Paul would feel an overmastering desire to proclaim his change of mind to the world at once, on the instant, without reflection or repose. But Providence made him first blind, and afterwards led him into the wilderness, and there left him wounded with an infirmity which quieted him.

In those three years the soul of this great man was being slowly and mercifully prepared for the fortunes of a career unmatched in history.

What visions came to him, what whispers from the spirit world, we do not know. But at last the long vigil came to an end. Convinced that he must give his vision to the world, he left the wilderness, and came again to Damascus.

Let us see the position of the Nazarenes in Damascus. Ananias, who had baptised Paul, was accounted a just Jew. It is perfectly certain that he lived in the respect of Jews who would have killed themselves rather than own Jesus of Nazareth as the Christ of God. Therefore we see that Ananias was not a very advanced Christian, and that the Jews of Damascus were not very strict Hebrews.

PAUL WAS LET DOWN FROM THE CITY WALL IN A BASKET BY NIGHT

In fact, the very reason of Saul's mission to this distant city was to put an end to a spirit of tolerance. He wanted not only to destroy the Nazarenes, but to awaken the easy-going Jews to an unbending sternness in their religion. Damascus was one of those dangerous places where Jews were not very strict, and boasted of being openminded and tolerant. A Jew who felt that Jesus of Nazareth had brought a message from God, and who even accepted Him as the long-promised Messiah, was not molested ; on the contrary, so long as he held these opinions quietly and decently, he provided the strict Jews with an interesting subject for conversation.

It is remarkable that this, too, was the position of affairs in Jerusalem before Saul arrived from Tarsus with his burning indignation and his flaming loyalty to the Law. The Nazarenes, indeed, were treated with an amused contempt. They were tolerated. The Sanhedrin considered that by destroying Jesus they had done all that was required of them; the ignorant fishermen who still proclaimed him as the Christ were too obscure for notice.

PAUL TEACHES THAT A NEW AGE HAD DAWNED UPON THE WORLD

It was Saul of Tarsus who had caused the change of attitude which resulted in the scourgings and martyrdoms of the Christians in Jerusalem; and it was Paul the Apostle who changed the whole spirit of Damascus. Later it was Paul who changed the attitude of the whole world.

But let us return to the entrance into Damascus of this wonderful man. He was received with some natural misgiving, which deepened into alarm when he appeared in the synagogue and disputed with the Jews concerning Jesus. He not only angered the loyal Jews, he annoyed the Nazarenes as well. He was too much in earnest.

Paul argued with an energy which challenged the learned doctors to give a decided answer. He was not merely disputing on an interesting subject of conversation. He was showing men that God had fulfilled prophecy, that Christ had come, that the old order was finished, that a new age had dawned upon the world. Either this was false or true. If false, let them refute him. If true, let them bow down and worship.

So relentless was Paul that at last the Jews woke up to their danger. This man would disturb the quiet peace in which they lived, and it was quite clear they must endeavour to get rid of him.

The gates of the city were watched to prevent him from escaping, and Paul learned that his doom was decreed. What! At the very beginning of his career, before he had spoken to any of the Apostles who had seen and known Jesus, before he had preached to the foreign nations, before he had told all the world of his wonderful vision—no, this was impossible! He was told by some people who were favourable to him how he might escape from the city.

PAUL'S ESCAPE BY A WINDOW WHILE HIS ENEMIES WATCH THE GATES

He was led to a house built over and into the city wall, which had a window opening on the country outside. When night had fallen, and the patrol had passed beneath the window, Paul was placed in a big basket, and was lowered safely to the ground.

It was the beginning of a life full of strange adventures. From the wall of the city which would not have him, the lonely man turned away, and through the darkness of the night he set his face towards Jerusalem.

There is an appropriateness in this romantic escape as the start for what was perhaps the most " strange eventful story " of any preacher's career. Late in his life the apostle gave a condensed account of what he had done and suffered. In all the annals of heroic travel there is nothing to excel, perhaps not even to approach, his record of perils dared, pains endured, opposition faced from fanatic mobs, from unfaithful friends, from stern, indifferent rulers; dangers by land and sea, shipwreck and weary travel.

THE VISION OF GREAT EVENTS THAT MAY HAVE COME TO PAUL

Did any vision of the long, hard way ahead come to him as he tramped in the night southward out of the Syrian capital? Had he any glimpse of the distant scenes of his life's great drama, when he would face in Athens, without a moment's shrinking, the questioning contempt of the world's intellectual capital, nay, would carry his message to imperial Rome itself ?

If any of these premonitions did cross his mind that night we may be sure that they would have an exultant welcome.

(Next chapter in this group, page 6053)

The Interests and Pleasures of Life for All, Indoors or Out

On the William IV penny on the left, the rose, the thistle, and the shamrock appear.   On the second coin, a Queen Victoria penny, are the lighthouse and ship, which are absent from the Edward VII penny on the right.

MAKING A COLLECTION OF COINS

THERE are few museums of a general character without a collection of coins among their most prized exhibits. Often these are British coins only, but in many cases, especially if the museum is a large and important one, there will be hundreds of pieces of foreign money belonging to all countries and to all times.

A collection of coins is really an object-lesson in history. Let anyone, for instance, who has a shillingsworth of coppers look at his pennies and halfpennies, and he will possibly find five different heads upon them. There may be coins bearing the portrait of Queen Victoria; others with the heads of Edward VII, George V, George VI, and, of course, Queen Elizabeth II.

Coins with Edward VII's portrait will not be found earlier than 1901, and here, then, we learn at once that he was the first sovereign to begin a reign in Britain in the 20th century.

Round the recent bronze coins appears the Latin inscription DEI GRATIA REGINA : F.D. The first two words mean by the Grace of God, and regina means queen. The initials F.D. (short for Fidei Defensor—Defender of the Faith) take us back to the days of Henry VIII, when he championed the Pope against Martin Luther. But the early coins of Queen Elizabeth's reign have a longer inscription : DEI. GRA. BRITT : OMN : REGINA : F.D.

The three words BRITT: OMN: REGINA: denote Queen of all the Britons. The phrase therefore meant that in addition to Britain at home there are other Britains, or lands, dominions, and colonies associated with Britain, in distant parts. But from 1954, to meet the new conception of the Commonwealth, the words BRITT: OMN: have been dropped. Until 1949, bronze coins and threepenny pieces bore, after the letters F : D :, the words IND : IMP :, meaning Emperor of India.

On the other side of a modern penny we find Britannia ruling over the waves, with a shield that bears the design of the Union Jack, and a lighthouse; and here again we have suggested to us Britain's splendid naval history, and the story of the union of England, Scotland, and Ireland under one flag, the Union Jack.

The groats, or four-penny pieces, of William IV and Queen Victoria

On the earlier coins of Queen Victoria we find on either side of the figure of Britannia the Eddystone Lighthouse and a ship in full sail.

Now, though a collection of coins may be worth thousands of pounds, and some rich men spend a fortune in obtaining all kinds of rare coins for their private museums, there is not the slightest reason why every boy and girl should not begin at once to make a collection of coins.

Of course, we shall not be able to obtain rare coins of gold and silver, but we can

CRAFTS · GAMES · NEEDLEWORK · PUZZLES · SCIENCE EXPERIMENTS

begin with the copper coinage that is in circulation today. We can, from our pocket-money, put aside a penny, a half-penny, and a farthing of each of the kinds we have mentioned—that is, coins from the reign of Queen Victoria to that of Queen Elizabeth. We should get the best preserved coins that are obtainable, and if later we come across a newer and better specimen, we can always put it in the place of the one which we already have in our collection.

This penny of Henry III is very valuable. It is of gold, and both sides are shown.

Having put aside the bronze coins, that we wrongly call coppers, which are now in general circulation, we must be on the look-out for older coins. Perhaps we may come across coins of William IV, George IV, and even George III. Although no longer in circulation they are sometimes kept by relatives and friends, and it may be possible to get one or two of the coins. The earliest farthings of Queen Victoria, too, should be looked out for. They were of copper instead of bronze,

Not often have British coins borne both the king's and the queen's heads. The left-hand picture is a William and Mary halfpenny, and the right-hand coin is a Mary I and Philip shilling.

and the coins were rather larger and thicker than those now in use. We should tell our friends that we are making a collection of coins, and ask them, if they come across any of that older money, to keep it by, and exchange it with us for more modern coins.

Now and again we can purchase old coins on stalls in London and provincial market - places. Among all kinds of odds and ends, metal teapots, pieces of necklaces, and the like, the stall-keeper sometimes has a pile of coins, and for a few pence it is often possible to buy a copper, or even a small silver, coin of an earlier reign. If coin-collecting

On the left is a King Alfred penny 1000 years old, and on the right an Oliver Cromwell farthing.

becomes our favourite hobby there are, of course, dealers whose business it is to sell coins of all kinds to collectors, and we can consult their catalogues and make a selection suitable to the dimensions of our pocket-money.

On the copper coinage of William IV, the king is given his Latin name of Gulielmus

IIII, and underneath the figure of Britannia on the reverse side will be seen the rose, thistle, and shamrock. In the coinage of George the Fourth he had his Latin name of Georgius, and while on the pennies and half-pennies the four is given as IV, on the farthings it is IIII. The pennies and halfpennies have on the reverse side, in the earliest coinage of the reign, an Irish harp crowned, but the farthings have Britannia with a lion lying at her feet. The later coinage of the reign has Britannia in all three cases, but without the lion at her feet.

In the reign of George the Third the copper coinage included a very large twopenny-piece that looks something like a two-ounce weight, for it has, in common with the penny of this reign, a broad, raised rim all round. Special copper coins were struck for the Isle of Man. Farther back than this, of course, the coins become rarer, and, if purchased, will be more expensive. An interesting thing we shall notice in comparing the portrait side of the coins of different reigns is that the direction in which the face looks is changed with each new ruler—that is, Queen Victoria looks to the left, Edward VII looks to the right, George V to the left, and so on.

But both George V and VI face the same way because Edward VIII followed George V, although no coins bearing his head were issued. Of course, we have only spoken of bronze and copper coins, but we may be able to afford to collect silver ones, too. A very interesting coin to have is a groat, or fourpenny-piece. That of Queen Victoria has a portrait on one side, and on the other side Britannia seated.

All this may seem a small beginning for a collection of coins, but some of the most valuable collections were started in this way. Patience and constant watchfulness for new specimens is the secret.

HOW TO PLAY NETBALL

BASKET BALL, brought to Britain from the United States in 1891, was the foundation on which modern Netball was laid. The British variation of the older game has won wide popularity, particularly among schoolgirls. Very little equipment is required.

The ball is an Association football, 27 to 28 inches in circumference. Each goal consists of an upright pole 10 feet high, with an iron ring 15 inches in diameter at the top. This projects horizontally and attached to it is a net, open at both ends. The ball has to pass through the net from top to bottom in order to score a goal. The ground is laid out rather like a hockey field, as shown in the accompanying diagram.

Seven players form a regulation team. They are known as (1) goal-shooter; (2) attack; (3) attacking centre ; (4) centre; (5) defending centre; (6) defence; (7) goalkeeper. The pitch, as shown in the diagram on the next page, is divided into three equal areas, but the only players permitted to operate in all three are the attacking centre, centre, and defending centre, though none of these may enter the shooting circles. Defence and goalkeeper are restricted to their own court (including the shooting circle) and the centre court. Attack and goal-shooter may use only the attacking and centre courts. Anyone straying outside her particular courts is classed as offside, and the penalty is a free pass to the opposition.

The captains toss for choice of ends or first centre pass. The centre pass, taken by alternate centres, opens the game at the start of each half and after every goal scored. The game starts with the two centres standing facing each other from either end of the 9-foot centre line and with the goals they are attacking to their respective left hand sides. The umpire bounces the ball between them, and the centre of the team who has won the privilege of receiving the centre pass, collects it. All the other players may move immediately the whistle signals the opening of the game.

No player may run or walk with the ball and neither must she hold it for more than three seconds. Therefore, the centre makes an immediate pass to a colleague, who also passes it on with the object of making swift progress to the opponents' goal. Naturally, the opponents seek to intercept and institute an attack on their own account.

The ball is passed on until it comes into the possession of an attacking player in the shooting circle. You will recall, however, that the only two players who may operate there are the attack and the goal-shooter. The player with the ball now attempts to score a goal in the manner already described. There must be no interception from the opposition while the shot is taken, but the defenders stand prepared to collect the ball should the shot fail.

As in other team games, there are penalties for the infringement of rules. A free pass is awarded to your opponents if you hold the ball longer than three seconds when in play; if you throw it up and catch it again, except in shooting at goal; if you kick it or strike it with your fist, or if you walk or run with it. You may turn round or move one foot in any direction while holding the ball, but you must not take a complete step from the spot where you received it. You may bounce it once to gain possession, but once possessed, it must not be bounced again. You are not allowed to roll it along the ground. All passes should be made with sufficient space between yourself and your comrade for a third person to pass through. You must not move into an offside position.

The free pass penalising the above offences must be taken from the spot where the breach occurred, and no player must stand within nine feet. The pass may not be taken directly at goal, and can be intercepted in the normal way. For more serious offences the penalty is a free throw for goal.

The free throw is awarded to the opposition when a player removes the ball from the possession of another; when she charges, pushes, holds, or otherwise obstructs. If any such fouls occur within the shooting circle, the attacker fouled may decide to take a free throw at goal from the spot where the

TAKING A SHOT AT GOAL

offence was committed. If she does not exercise this option, the captain can name another player to take the throw, but in this case it must be taken from any point outside the shooting circle. The thrower's feet must be clear of the circle line; the throw must be directed at goal and not to another player. If the throw fails to score, the thrower may not score with a second try unless the ball has been touched by another player after the first attempt. Any breach of these rules means an award of a free pass to the defending side.

If the ball goes out of the ground by passing over the side or goal lines, it should be thrown in by a player of the side opposing the player who last touched it. It may be thrown in any direction, but both feet must be behind the line when the throw is taken. No player must stand within nine feet of the thrower. If the throw-in is taken from a part of the

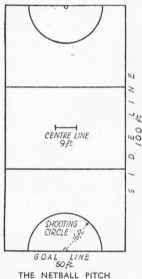

CENTRE LINE
9 ft.

SIDE LINE 100 ft

SHOOTING
CIRCLE 16 ft.

GOAL LINE
50 ft.

THE NETBALL PITCH

goal line bounding the shooting circle, it must not be taken by a player not allowed in the circle in the normal course of play. Any breach of the throw-in rules is penalised by the throw being awarded to the opposition.

If the ball goes out of play after being touched simultaneously by opposing players, the umpire must bounce it near the spot where it crossed the line to restart the game. A bounce is also taken when two opponents find themselves in possession of the ball at the same moment. When the bounce is taken, the players concerned must stand nine feet apart, facing each other and with their backs to the side lines. The umpire must stand nine feet from both, so that the three form a triangle.

The usual duration of a game is fifteen minutes each way and the issue is decided by the goals scored. Ends are changed at half-time.

FUN WITH A FLEET OF LITTLE BOATS

WE can spend happy hours playing with little boats in a tub or bath of water, and there are many things in the garden or the home from which nimble fingers can soon build a fleet of varied craft.

There is, for instance, the half of a walnut-shell. We divide the walnut carefully with a knife, taking pains not to crack the shell, remove the nut, and scrape the inside of the shell clean. As this is suitable for a sailing-boat, we get a piece of stiff white paper, gum one side round a piece of match-stick, and with a little sealing wax secure the mast to the bottom of the boat. The picture shows what it looks like when finished.

A WALNUT-SHELL BOAT

We can make another boat out of half a lemon cut lengthways. We remove the pulp, trim the edges with scissors, and put the coracle-shaped boat in the oven to dry and harden. Strips of card should be inserted for seats on which little wooden dolls to represent ancient Britons can be seated, and the oars can be cut from wooden spills.

If we get a large piece of cork or a small block of wood, we can shape it into a modern liner, an oil tanker, or a destroyer.

A REED-GRASS RAFT

Some shells make very good boats, and float well. The long-shaped razor-shell answers for a canoe. Paper can be pasted over the two ends, and an uncovered space left in the middle where the " crew " may sit.

Mussel-shells also make good boats; and small, black, closed ones will suggest not only dangerous torpedoes, but porpoises floating on the surface of the water.

An acorn in a cup can serve the purpose of a buoy, if we secure a thread to the

A RAZOR-SHELL CANOE

stalk and a weight to the other end of the thread, which must, of course, be long enough to reach the bottom of our sea. Acorns can also be cut lengthways, the nuts removed, and each half of the shell used for a small boat, the flat end forming the stern, and the pointed end the bow.

As shipwrecks do sometimes occur, it is just as well to have a lifeboat or a raft on our miniature sea. A raft might be made of match-sticks, or pieces of reed-grass roped together with coarse white cotton, as shown here. Small strips cut lengthways from a bottle cork will answer the purpose of a raft, and will refuse to sink.

THE MYSTERIOUS PENNY

THIS is a penny through which a tiny hole not larger than the thickness of a pin has been bored, close to the edge. With this the young conjurer needs a long hair. A piece of fine pink silk will answer the same purpose, and is in some respects more manageable. A few inches of the hair, or silk, are passed through the hole in the coin, and the ends tied together to form a loop.

This loop must be big enough that, when passed over the forefinger as far as it will go, the coin hangs down over the lowest joint of the middle finger, as shown in the accompanying picture.

Then the performer must practise making the coin disappear and reappear; or, in other words, transferring it to the back of the hand, where it will naturally be invisible, and bringing it again to the front. The disappearance may be effected in two ways.

HOW THE PENNY SHOULD HANG

The first is by a quick backward turn of the wrist, the coin swinging over by its own weight. The second is to tip it back with the end of the thumb. All these movements must be covered by a slight sweep of the arm backward, to cover the disappearance of the coin, and forward for its reappearance.

But a clever conjurer is not content with merely causing the disappearance of anything. He makes the vanished object reappear in unexpected places. Here is a simple example of this. With the prepared coin hung concealed in the right hand, the performer borrows a penny, which he takes in the left hand, letting it lie on the joints of the second and third fingers. Making a half-turn of the body from left to right, he apparently places it in the right hand, in reality keeping it still in the fingers by slightly bending them, and showing in the right hand the trick coin, as if that were the one just lent to him. The other hand is drawn away, palm downward, as if empty.

Showing the trick coin lying flat on the hand, the performer then asks someone to spread a handkerchief over it. " Go! " he says. He lifts the handkerchief gently by the centre, but the coin has disappeared, having been tipped over by the thumb to the back. Again he has the palm covered and brings the coin, by tilting the hand as he removes the handkerchief, mysteriously back again. At this point there will probably be a cry of " Up his sleeve," the sleeve having from time immemorial had the credit of half a conjurer's deeds.

To disprove this, he quickly pulls up his sleeve, and with the arm bare vanishes the coin once more, but at the moment of saying " Go! " thrusts forward the closed fist of the left hand, and hands back the borrowed coin to its rightful owner.

TRICKS WITH MATCHES AND MATCHBOXES

FOR the first of these tricks we need an ordinary box of safety matches. We open the box slightly and then, pressing the opening down tightly on the loose skin of the back of the hand, we close the box, pinching in a small portion of the skin.

When the hand is held out flat the box remains horizontal as if it were simply lying on the back of the hand; but if we bend the hand by closing the fist loosely the box rises perpendicularly, drawn up by the skin.

Then we remove the box and take out one match. This we balance on our thumb. Holding out the right thumb slightly bent, we place the match in the fleshy crease of the knuckle, then straighten up the thumb and the match will be held upright in the crease, yet seems to be balanced on the surface.

The next trick needs a little preparation. On the table we have three matchboxes, and we announce that one only contains matches, though actually they are all empty, a box about half full of matches being previously concealed up one of our sleeves. It does not matter which sleeve as long as we remember where we put it.

To prove our statement, we pick up the boxes one by one and shake them. One of them—it can be whichever we like—we shake in such a way as to rattle the matches in the concealed box, which naturally misleads the onlookers. The other two we either pick up with the other hand, or we take care not to rattle the invisible box. Then we put the three boxes on the table, quickly switch them around, and offer a small prize—say a sweet—to anyone who, at the first try, finds the box containing matches.

SOLUTION OF THE PUZZLE OF THE BOOKS ON THE SHELVES

On page 5814 is a problem of nine books on two shelves. Harry undertakes to place the books so that the two rows of figures shall form certain fractions. This is how he did it:

$$\frac{6729}{13458} = \frac{1}{2}, \quad \frac{5832}{17496} = \frac{1}{3}, \quad \frac{4392}{17568} = \frac{1}{4}, \quad \frac{2769}{13845} = \frac{1}{5},$$

$$\frac{2943}{17658} = \frac{1}{6}, \quad \frac{2394}{16758} = \frac{1}{7}, \quad \frac{3187}{25496} = \frac{1}{8}, \quad \frac{6381}{57429} = \frac{1}{9}.$$

THE GAME OF WHAT-ANIMALS-ARE-THESE?

HERE are some puzzle questions which deal with some of the animals that are described in the Nature section of this book. The answers are given on page 6058.

A LITTLE CREATURE CLEVERER THAN MAN

1. In our garden there is a beautifully-made little creature which can do things no human being can do. It makes out of its own body a rope strong enough for it to walk on, but so thin that one hundred of its strands make only the thickness of a hair; so strong that it serves as a net to entrap prey; and it can withstand rain, wind, frost, and heat. See, here is one of our little friends up in the loft. It has four pairs of legs, a body in two pieces, and eight little eyes, so no wonder it can see all about it. What is its name?

THE ARMOUR-PLATED OLD MAN OF THE GARDEN

2. We find a very different animal hidden away under the lettuces. He has had one hundred and fifty birthdays and may have many more yet, for he takes life easily. He always carries his house with him. It is made of hard bony plates and a flat breast-plate underneath, having a space in front for his head and two legs to peep out, and another at the back for his two short hind legs. If we hurt his feelings, he draws back his head within his house. Let us tempt him with a juicy bit of lettuce. He takes a bite and the piece is gone; but he may not eat again for weeks, and he goes to sleep all the winter in as cosy a corner as he can find. When he does move about he goes very slowly indeed, and many a more tiny creature could easily race him. He has a cousin who lives in a river, and another who basks on the sea-coast and who may one day be made into soup for dinner. When he himself dies his bony armour may be made into little boxes and combs. What do we call him?

THE MOST AWKWARD ANIMAL ON THE EARTH

3. In the forests of Africa is an animal which in the course of ages has changed to suit its home. It liked to eat the leaves on the tall acacia, so it grew a long neck to reach them. Thorns of prickly plants, the leaves of which it wanted, pierced its lip, so it grew a hard skin to keep it from pricks. To protect its nose from thorns and sand blown by the wind, it learned to close its nostrils tightly. To get away from animals that attacked it, rather than fight, it lengthened its legs, so that it could outrun other animals. It is usually gentle, but can be very dangerous when it gets angry. Its coat is covered with large spots. Each of the four feet has two toes, and the strong hoofs are used in fighting. Being so tall, it finds drink-ing very awkward, and has to straddle its legs almost like the legs of a camera. How should we like to stoop nineteen feet to drink out of a pond? Fortunately it rarely gets thirsty. What is the name of the animal?

THE JELLY THAT WRAPS ITSELF ROUND THE FOOD IT EATS

4. Living in a drop of water is a curious little creature, so simple that it is a mere speck of jelly. It has no real limbs, but it puts out " false feet " whenever it likes, and these it wraps round its food—a tiny living plant—without troubling at all about having no mouth. Its jelly-like mass thickens round the outside to form a kind of protecting wall. One peculiar thing this little creature can do is to divide itself into two new ones, each with a little dark part near its centre called the nucleus. So now it need not play about alone, for the two can float away in the water and seek their own adventures. Some of their relatives are dangerous and cause disease, another is kind and kills these when they get into our blood. What is its name?

A BEAST THAT FLIES WITH ITS HANDS

5. To fly with hands! That is what we do in dreams, but there is a curious little animal that really uses its hands as wings, for it has made by the aid of its limbs a kind of para-chute with which to fly. It suspends itself to the branch of a tree by hooks at the ends of its thumbs when it wants a rest, or decides to go to sleep during the winter. It likes to flit about in the twilight, and seems as though it would dash its little body against trees and houses. But no, it swerves aside, for though it has small eyes it has large ears and a delicate sense of touch, so that it knows when danger lies ahead. It is very quick indeed in its movements in the air. It does good in our country by eating insects that are harmful. It is the only mammal that can fly like a bird. Can we tell its name?

THE ROMPING SCHOOL ON THE SURFACE OF THE SEA

6. Out at sea big, dark creatures suddenly appear on the surface of the water, all tumbling about and rolling over and over. Look at the white on their under-sides. Now there is a baby one, and the whole family joins in a fine romp. A moment more, and they are all under water, diving for mackerel or herrings. They do not swim close in shore, but if we could see one near we should find it has a very small ear, one nostril on the top of the head, and many sharp teeth in its jaws. On its back fin are little horny lumps, which remind us of the armour its ancestors used to wear. Its body contains much oil. We may have seen these creatures from a steamer round our coast. What are they called?